ACCOUNTING INFORMATION SYSTEMS

Concepts
and Practice
for Effective
Decision Making

ACCOUNTING INFORMATION SYSTEMS

Concepts
and Practice
for Effective
Decision Making

FOURTH EDITION

Stephen A. Moscove, Ph.D.

Professor,
Department of Accounting
and Computer Information Systems
University of Nevada, Reno

Mark G. Simkin, Ph.D.

Professor,
Department of Accounting
and Computer Information Systems
University of Nevada, Reno

Nancy A. Bagranoff, DBA, CPA

Assistant Professor
Department of Accounting
The American University

John Wiley & Sons

New York
Chichester
Brisbane
Toronto
Singapore

Cover photography by Ken Karp

Library of Congress Cataloging in Publication Data
Moscove, Stephen A.
    Accounting information systems concepts and practice for
effective decision making / Stephen A Moscove, Mark G. Simkin,
Nancy A. Bagranoff.--4th ed.

Bibliography
    1. Accounting--Data processing   2. Information storage and
retrieval systems--Accounting.   I. Simkin, Mark G. II. Bagranoff,
Nancy A.   III. Title

HF56979.M62   1190   657'.028'5--dc20   89-70583

ISBN 0-471-50449-1

Printed in the United States of America

Printed and bound by Malloy Lithographing, Inc.

10 9 8 7 6 5 4

To my children, Justin, Jodi, and Sarah Moscove

To my parents, Edward and Selma Simkin, and my grandmother, Edna Cohen

To my husband, Larry, and our children, Amanda, Scott, Stacia, and Kara

About the Authors

Stephen A. Moscove earned his B.S. degree in accounting (June 1965) and his M.S. degree in accounting (June 1966) from the University of Illinois. Dr. Moscove received his Ph.D. degree in business administration (majoring in accounting) from Oklahoma State University (July 1971). He is a member of Beta Gamma Sigma (the honorary business administration society) and Beta Alpha Psi (the honorary accounting society).

Dr. Moscove worked as an auditor for Price Waterhouse & Company during 1966 and 1967. From 1970 to 1980 he was a member of the faculty of the Department of Accounting at the University of Hawaii. During this period, Dr. Moscove was a visiting professor at the University of Miami (Coral Gables, Florida), in 1973, and a visiting professor, in 1974, at the University of New Orleans. In September 1980, Dr. Moscove was named chairman of the Department of Accounting and Computer Information Systems at the University of Nevada, Reno. He is currently on the faculty of the University of Nevada, Reno. During the summer of 1988, Dr. Moscove was a visiting professor at Northeastern University in Boston, Massachusetts.

Dr. Moscove has published numerous articles in professional journals. One of his articles ("Accountants' Legal Liability," *Management Accounting,* May 1977) won a national award from the National Association of Accountants.

Mark G. Simkin received his A.B. degree from Brandeis University (1965) and his MBA (1968) and Ph.D. degrees (1972) from the Graduate

School of Business at the University of California, Berkeley. Before assuming his present position of professor in the Department of Accounting and Information Systems, University of Nevada, Reno, in 1980, Professor Simkin taught in the Department of Decision Sciences at the University of Hawaii. He has also taught at California State University, Hayward, and the Japan America Institute of Decision Sciences, Honolulu; worked as a research analyst at the Institute of Business and Economic Research at the University of California, Berkeley; programmed computers at IBM's Industrial Development–Finance Headquarters in White Plains, New York; and acted as a computer consultant to business companies in California, Hawaii, and Nevada.

Dr. Simkin is the author of more than 50 articles that have been published in such journals as *Decision Sciences, JASA,* the *Journal of Accountancy,* the *Communications of the ACM, Interfaces,* the *Review of Business and Economic Research,* and the *Journal of Bank Research.*

Nancy A. Bagranoff received her A.A. degree from Briarcliff College (1970), B.S. degree from the Ohio State University (1973), and M.S. degree in accounting from Syracuse University (1978). Her DBA degree was conferred by the George Washington University in 1986 (accounting major and information systems minor). Dr. Bagranoff was awarded a university scholarship at Syracuse University and a School of Government and Business Administration fellowship at the George Washington University. She is a member of Beta Gamma Sigma, the National Association of Accountants, and the American Accounting Association.

Before her appointment as Assistant Professor of Accounting at the American University, Professor Bagranoff taught at George Mason University. She also taught at Syracuse University, Virginia Commonwealth University, and the George Washington University, prior to receiving her doctorate degree. From 1973 to 1976, she was employed by General Electric in Syracuse, New York, where she completed the company's Financial Management Training Program. Dr. Bagranoff is a certified public accountant, licensed in the District of Columbia since 1982.

Professor Bagranoff has published several papers in regional proceedings of the American Accounting Association and has published articles in the *Journal of Accountancy* and the *Journal of Accounting and EDP.* She is currently working on several research projects in the area of accounting information systems. She is a co-founder of the Washington Accounting Research Society, and has presented papers at their meetings. During the summer of 1989 she facilitated a session on "Using the Computer in the Accounting Information Systems Course" at the second annual conference on Computers in Accounting Education at Loyola College in Baltimore, Maryland.

Preface

The introduction of a computer into a company's business system greatly alters the accountant's organizational duties. Automating the accounting information system means the accountant no longer has to perform time-consuming functions such as recording journal entries, posting these entries to ledger accounts, and preparing trial balances. Instead, the computer is able to handle these data processing activities on a routine basis. As a result, accountants are becoming involved in the more dynamic functions of their organizations, such as aiding in management decision making and designing more effective business information systems.

The purpose of this book is to analyze the role of accounting information systems within companies' operating environments. In our current era of technology, it is difficult to discuss modern accounting information systems without emphasizing computers. Therefore, the computer's effects on these systems will be stressed throughout. Our intent is not to make accounting students computer programmers or electronics experts. However, today's accounting graduate must be able to understand the capabilities, as well as the limitations, of computers in order to interact effectively with a company's computerized data processing system.

Especially for the student, a reasonable question to ask of any book is "What's in it for me?" This book concentrates on modern computer equipment and modern procedures for processing accounting data. Thus, throughout the various chapters we provide extensive discussions of microcomputers, integrated accounting packages, and real-time processing systems.

The writing style is simple and clear. There are many figures and photographs to aid in learning. Examples are provided to make the reading more interesting and to demonstrate the application of concepts to real-world situations.

Each chapter begins with an outline and a list of important questions that aid studying and alert students to the important concepts of the chapter. The chapters end with a summary and list of key terms discussed in the chapter material.

A wide variety of end-of-chapter exercises include discussion questions, problems, and cases. Many new cases have been incorporated in the fourth edition. The variety of exercises, questions, problems, and cases enables students to examine many different aspects of each chapter's subject matter and also enables instructors to vary the exercises assigned each semester. A number of exercises are adapted from the Certified Public Accountant (CPA) and Certificate in Management Accounting (CMA) examinations. A few cases are also adapted from the Canadian Chartered Accountant (CA) examination. These will help students prepare for professional examinations and provide them with an understanding of professional-oriented problems.

The arrangement of the chapters permits *flexibility* in the instructor's subject matter coverage. Certain chapters may be omitted if students have covered specific topics in prior courses. In writing the text, we have assumed that all students will have completed a basic financial accounting course and a basic managerial accounting course. The text is designed principally for a one-semester course covering accounting information systems.

Recognizing that present and future students are more computer-literate than past students, we have made a significant change in the coverage of computer hardware and software topics in the fourth edition. Previous editions of this book provided an in-depth coverage of topics that are usually dealt with in data processing or management information systems courses. Since students are now likely to have had some exposure to these subjects, either in college, on the job, or even in high school, we have changed our approach to this material. Chapter 4 provides an overview of these topics, with an emphasis on *new* technology and developments, particularly relevant to *accounting* information systems. The fourth edition of this text is now organized as follows.

Part One (Chapters 1–4) introduces the vital role that accounting information systems play in today's business world. Because managers are major users of accounting information, Part One examines various management concepts of importance to accountants and discusses how these concepts affect the design and operation of accounting information systems. Budgets are important managerial planning and controlling tools. Because accountants play an active role in their organizations' budgetary activities, Chapter 3 stresses the *informational* aspects of budget systems and also examines the computer's functions in the budgetary process. A major section on electronic spreadsheets is included. This provides instructors with the opportunity to teach students to use spreadsheet software to solve accounting problems. Most students will have been exposed to the detailed procedural aspects of budget preparation in prior accounting courses. Therefore, the detailed procedural work in preparing budgets is minimized in Chapter 3. The subject of budgeting is approached from the standpoint of its importance to an organization's *planning* and *controlling* activities. For those schools with a separate budgeting course, it is possible to exclude this material or just cover the sections that analyze the computer's role in budgeting. Chapter 4 is designed to provide students with a fundamental knowledge of the role of technology in accounting information systems. The chapter focuses on computer hardware technology, and covers the important subject of data communications. Accounting systems often include networks and data communications, so this topic is particularly important. Again, in schools where this subject has been covered in-depth in a prerequisite course, this chapter may be skipped, or the section on data communications may be covered exclusively.

Part Two (Chapters 5–8) emphasizes the accounting information system's functions of collecting, recording, and storing business data. In this edition, we have expanded this material, adding coverage of source documents and reports associated with common accounting information systems, and adding a chapter that deals exclusively with documenting an accounting information system. Chapter 5 discusses transaction processing; the focus is on inputs or source documents and outputs or reports in accounting systems. This discussion includes the subject of coding transactions. Chapter 6 is the new chapter on system documentation. Material on document and system flowcharting from previous editions of this text is retained in this chapter. In addition, the chapter describes data flow diagrams and some other documentation tools. Since documenting a system is crucial to internal control, this chapter is an important one. Chapter 7 emphasizes the types of data processing that can be achieved when performing accounting functions if a company implements a computerized *data base* system. Chapter 8 brings together many of the concepts discussed in Part Two by providing an extensive illustration of both a manual and a computerized data processing system (emphasizing the computerized system) for handling a company's "accounts receivable" transactions.

An important function of accountants working within organizations' accounting information systems is to develop efficient and effective internal control systems. The subject of internal control (in both manual and automated systems) is discussed throughout the book and is emphasized in Part Three (Chapters 9–12). A unique chapter in Part Three is Chapter 11, which focuses on computer crime and computer security. This chapter discusses and analyzes some of the more important real-world computer

crimes. This allows students to examine the consequences of inadequate control and security. This chapter has been updated to cover some of the latest issues in this area, such as computer viruses. To conclude Part Three, Chapter 12 covers the important topic of *auditing* computerized accounting information systems. This chapter makes a good EDP supplement for the auditing course.

Accountants often participate in systems studies of companies' data processing problems, leading to the development of better (and more internal control conscious) accounting information systems. Part Four (Chapters 13–15) examines systems studies through an in-depth coverage of performing a systems study for an organization. The topics in Part Four are illustrated by a prototype example—the conversion of a company's manual accounting information system to a computerized system, and the accountant's role in this conversion process. Many of the computer and accounting concepts developed in previous chapters are integrated in Part Four's discussion of systems study.

Part Five of this book looks at some special topics related to accounting information systems. Chapter 16 has been added to the fourth edition to address emerging accounting decision support and expert systems. Accounting information systems encompass much more than transaction processing today. This chapter discusses in depth the higher levels of information and knowledge processing. Three important types of organizations (the small business organization, the service organization, and the not-for-profit organization) are directly examined in Chapters 17 and 18. Accounting information systems for small business firms are explored in Chapter 17, whereas accounting information systems for service and not-for-profit organizations are examined in Chapter 18. The subject of microcomputers within a business firm's system is stressed in Chapter 17. Since service and not-for-profit organizations are becoming an increasingly important part of our economy, the discussion of these organizations in Chapter 18 should be of particular interest to students.

This accounting text provides a wide variety of exercises at the end of each chapter. In most chapters there are three types of exercises, discussion questions, problems, and cases. The discussion questions rely heavily on the material presented in the chapters, although some require the use of prerequisite accounting knowledge for complete answers. Problems are largely computational and provide alternative illustrations of the chapters' analyses. The end-of-chapter cases are shorter than those provided at the end of the text, under the heading, "Comprehensive Cases." However, they still require considerable thought to arrive at logical answers. Accounting students will find these cases very different from the structured accounting problems they are used to encountering in financial and managerial accounting courses. This is helpful to instructors in broadening the education of these students and acquainting them with more real-world unstructured scenarios.

An issue frequently raised in accounting classes is the extent to which topics involving quantitative methods should be covered. As previously mentioned, this book assumes only an introductory background in financial and managerial accounting. But at a few points within the discussion, quantitative techniques such as linear programming become relevant. Because quantitative topics are covered extensively in other business courses, we have chosen to minimize quantitative methodology, relegating essential mechanics to Appendix A. Individual

chapters are thus written in such a way that the quantitative methods may be omitted without detracting from an understanding of the chapter material. At the discretion of the instructor or the interest of the student, however, the quantitative examples in Appendix A may be included as part of the reading materials to expand the scope of a particular chapter.

In 1987, the American Accounting Association released the *Report of the AAA Committee on Contemporary Approaches to Teaching Accounting Information Systems*. In this report, the special committee identified nine content areas for accounting information systems (and prerequisite) courses. In this text, we have addressed all of these content areas. Although many of these content areas are discussed throughout the book, the table that follows identifies the chapters that provide the major coverage of each topic.

ACCOUNTING INFORMATION SYSTEMS COURSE
CONTENT AREA COVERAGE

Content Area	Chapter(s)
Database Concepts	7
Internal Control	9, 10, 11
Technology of Information Systems	4
Use of Systems Technology	8, 16, 17
Accounting Information System Applications	5, 16, 18
Management Use of Information	13, 16
Management of Information Systems	2, 3
Systems Analysis and Design	13, 14, 15
Auditing of Accounting Information Systems	12

Acknowledgments

We thank the many people who struggled with us during the writing, editing, and production of this book and without whose help this endeavor would not have been possible. First on our list of acknowledgments are the loved ones who stuck by us, sacrificed for us, and supported us while the midnight oil burned dimmer and dimmer. Few but these people know the trials and tribulations of textbook writing. For their patience and understanding, we are deeply indebted.

A large number of our colleagues and professional acquaintances were also extremely helpful. In this regard, we owe a special tribute to the memory of the late John Crain, our initial Wiley editor. John inspired, encouraged, and supported us, and gave this effort the head start that enabled us to push to completion. We also gratefully acknowledge the work of our past editor, Lucille Sutton, our present editor, Karen Hawkins, and our copyediting supervisor, Gilda Stahl. In addition, we wish to thank the various reviewers who spent many hours of their valuable time reading and evaluating the earlier drafts of our work. They include Jerome V. Bennett, Ronald R. Bottin, John W. Buckley, Deane M. Carter, Richard Chen, Owen Cherrington, Thomas Gibbs, Leonard W. Hein, Richard W. Lott, Robert L. Paretta, George Potter, Martin B. Roberts, Marshall Romney, Mike Ruble, Avi Rushinek, E. Burton Swanson, and John H. Wragge.

Other individuals who contributed insightful comments or suggestions include Jim Cavaco, Ronald Copeland, Chuck Deliot, Patricia Edge, Linda Golding, N. Lane Kelley, Frank Logan, William Newman, Terry Nunley, Peter Shannon, John Sherman, Hugh Watson, Glenda Wilson, Reginald G. Worthley, Anne Riley, Philip Jacoby, and Shirley Corteill.

Two professional accounting groups we especially thank are the American Institute of Certified Public Accountants and the Certified Management Accountants of the National Association of Accountants. The AICPA permitted us to use problem materials from past CPA examinations, and the Certified Management Accountants permitted us to use problem materials from past CMA examinations.

The last group of people we wish to thank are also the foundation of our work—our students. Many semesters' worth of accounting information systems classes, plus several summer school classes, struggled with us through earlier drafts of our manuscript and served as "guinea pigs" for ambiguous test questions, unclear exercises, and overdemanding cases. We collectively thank these students for their patience and understanding. In addition, several students were particularly helpful to us in the development of this textbook. They are Carla Chock, Chi-Duk Choi, Kathryn Chung, Kevin Dooley, Tom Hamby, Sandra Iwamoto, Kalfred Kam, Lo-sai Rose Kwan, Gary Nakayama, Richard Zon Owen, William Pape, Norma Jean Puerner, Donna Rhodes, Harry Siegelberg, and Terry E. Trout.

September 1989
Stephen A. Moscove
Mark G. Simkin
Nancy A. Bagranoff

Contents

Contents

PART THREE
Internal Controls Within Accounting Information Systems / 297

9
Preventive and Feedback Controls for Accounting Information Systems / 299

10
Controls for Computerized Accounting Information Systems / 332

11
Accounting Information Systems and Computer Crime / 380

12
Auditing Computerized Accounting Information Systems / 412

PART FOUR
Systems Studies for Effective Accounting Information Systems / 459

13
Systems Study: Planning and Analysis / 461

PART FIVE
Special Topics Related to Accounting Information Systems / 627

PART SIX
Comprehensive Cases / 723

CASE 1
Vancouver Recreational Products / 724

CASE 2
Aqua Spray / 730

PART ONE

An Introduction to Accounting Information Systems and Their Role in Management Decision Making

Part One will examine the accounting function in today's complex business world. Since accounting's principal goal is to communicate relevant information to individuals and organizations, Chapter 1 will look at the process by which accounting achieves this goal within the business environment.

A major user of the information provided by accounting is the *management* of business organizations. Accounting information is often essential to managers for decision making. Consequently, for accountants to contribute efficiently and effectively to managerial decision making, they must have a good understanding of management concepts (such as **planning** and **controlling**) and how these concepts affect the design and operation of accounting information systems. Chapters 2 and 3 will therefore examine those management concepts relevant to accountants working within an accounting information system. Chapter 2 will define and analyze various managerial concepts, stressing their relationship to accounting information systems. Budgets are important managerial planning and controlling tools. Since accountants in most companies have a major role in the budgetary processes, Chapter 3 will emphasize the important contributions that accountants, working within organizational accounting information systems, make to budget planning and controlling. This chapter will stress the informational aspects of budget systems and devote minimal attention to budget preparation. The role of computers in budget systems will be examined in considerable detail within Chapter 3.

The final chapter in Part One describes the technological environment of the accounting information system. While students are likely to have been exposed to hardware and software technology in a previous course, Chapter 4 will review these concepts briefly and explain their effect on accounting information systems.

1

Accounting Information Systems and the Accountant

Among the important questions that you should be able to answer after reading this chapter are:

1. What is an accounting information system and how does it differ from a management information system?
2. In what ways should accounting and electronic data-processing employees interact within a business system?
3. Why is an accounting "audit trail" important to an efficiently operated business system?
4. What contribution does the accountant make to an organization's planning and controlling activities?
5. Why should today's accountant have an understanding of behavioral analysis, quantitative methods, and computerized systems?

INTRODUCTION

The accounting function has an important role in the successful operation of today's businesses. This function is to provide individuals and groups both within and outside of a company with relevant information for decision making. This chapter will first analyze the definition of a system to give the reader a basic understanding of business information systems. Then it will examine the various contributions of an accounting information system to modern business systems.

Many accounting information systems consist of two major components: financial and managerial accounting. Their information-providing functions will be discussed here. An important objective of financial accounting is to process efficiently a company's business transactions so that informative financial statements (e.g., the income statement and the balance sheet) can be prepared. Therefore, in a supplement at the end of this chapter, we will review the **accounting cy-** **cle,** which enables organizations to process their business transactions. The types of information that result from the processing of transactions within the accounting cycle will be stressed in our supplement to Chapter 1. Managerial accounting typically encompasses three major areas: (1) cost accounting, (2) budgeting, and (3) systems study. Each one of these components will be discussed in turn.

The computer's current popularity in handling firms' data processing has significantly affected accountants' functions. This chapter briefly analyzes some of the important ways that the accounting and the computer function should interact in computerized data processing. Later chapters will stress the operational aspects of computerized accounting information systems. In addition to computers, two areas that have influenced accounting are behavioral analysis and quantitative methods. The effects of each of these on the accounting function will be briefly discussed.

DEFINITION OF SYSTEM

A **system** is an entity consisting of interacting parts (subsystems) that attempts to achieve a multiplicity of goals. An "entity" is a separate unit of accountability. In this book, the **business entity** will be emphasized. For a system to function efficiently and effectively, its subsystems must interact. This interaction is achieved principally through the communication of relevant information between the subsystems. Figure 1-1 reflects the business entity called the Alan Company and its interacting parts. The Alan Company manufactures and sells sporting goods equipment such as baseballs, basketballs, and footballs. (Note to students: In many of our examples throughout the book, we will use the Alan Company to illustrate aspects of accounting information systems.)

The large circle in Figure 1-1 is the total business organization system. The company's top management will establish broad future goals for the entire system. Included within the Alan Company's multiplicity of goals could be such objectives as a satisfactory level of income, a high-quality production product, and a program of minimum environmental pollution. As will be emphasized later in our book, we assume that most business organizations attempt to achieve a long-run satisfactory profit performance rather than a long-run maximizing profit performance (which economists often discuss). The former represents a lower level of income earning than the latter. The Alan Company's internal environment includes all its subsystems (also called "departments") that will attempt to contribute to achieving the system's broad goals. Each subsystem establishes its own specific operational goals based on the broad goals of the total system. An effectively functioning system exists when each subsystem achieves its operational goals, which in turn contribute to the company's broad goals. To accomplish this, the subsystems must continually interact so that every subsystem

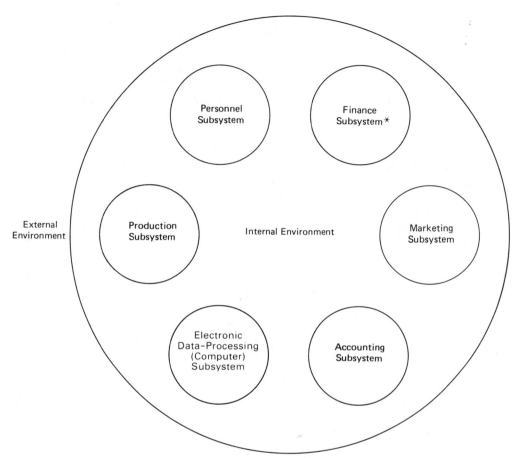

FIGURE 1-1 The Alan Company system. [*This subsystem's major responsibility is to obtain asset resources for the company at a reasonable cost (e.g., borrowing money from a bank and having to pay 10% interest on this borrowed money) and then monitor the efficient use of those resources by the other subsystems.]

is aware of its internal and external environments. In fact, the external environment represents a large element that affects the internal operations of a system.

The interaction of subsystems with the internal and external environments occurs through communication of relevant information for decision making within the system. Toward this end, the Alan Company has an electronic data processing (EDP) subsystem. This subsystem acquires a large quantity of data from the system's internal and external environments. The data must then be sorted, processed, and communicated through reports to the other subsystems. Data that have meaning to the recipient (e.g., a production manager) are called **information.** The word **data** refers to facts or figures that have little, if any, meaning and therefore are not useful to the recipients' business decision making. **Information,** on the other hand, refers to meaningful facts or figures that can be used in making business decisions. An important function of any modern business system is to efficiently convert the massive amount of available internal and external data into relevant information. Based on the types of information needed for decision making by subsystem managers to achieve their operational goals, a communication network of information that flows to the subsystems is established.

To illustrate the inefficiencies that can occur from a lack of information communication among subsystems, assume that the Alan Company's production subsystem has as one of its 1990 goals the monthly production of 10,000 cartons of golf balls. However, based on demand forecasts by the marketing subsystem, it appears that 1990 sales will be only about 6000 cartons a month. In each of the first six months of 1990 the production subsystem achieves its goal of producing 10,000 cartons of golf balls. Actual monthly sales are between 5500 and 6500 cartons from January through June.

This example illustrates system **suboptimization,** commonly caused by poor communication among subsystems. Suboptimization results from an individual subsystem achieving its own goal (or goals) but not contributing to the total system's goal (or goals). The production subsystem achieved its production goal of 10,000 cartons of golf balls each month. However, because the original projected demand as well as the actual monthly sales were far short of 10,000 cartons, a large stockpile of golf balls occurred during January through June. The extra dollars tied up in this inventory asset are nonproductive to the total system (i.e., the Alan Company). This excessive investment in inventory could possibly have been put into some other endeavor of the Alan Company where it would earn a positive rate of return. Thus, the high monthly activity level of the production subsystem contributed *negatively* to the total system operation.

The Alan Company's suboptimization problem could have been avoided through effective communication between production and marketing. The information obtained by the marketing subsystem from the external environment regarding sales demand for golf balls should have been communicated to the production sub-

system. This, in turn would have caused the production subsystem to reduce the number of golf balls manufactured during January through June. The result would have been a smaller dollar investment in the golf ball inventory. Following the decision to curtail the monthly production level of golf balls, perhaps part of the unused plant facilities could have been used for the increased monthly production of another product line (based on demand forecasts by the marketing subsystem). In addition, the Alan Company's management may have decided to invest some of the extra dollars in marketing research for the eventual development of a new product line.

This example emphasizes the extreme importance of communication between an organization's subsystems. When one subsystem is aware of activities and decisions occurring in other subsystems of the organization, it is better able to make effective decisions within its own subsystem that contribute positively to the organization's goals.

Prior to defining and analyzing an accounting information system is a brief discussion comparing a manual data processing system to a computerized data processing system.

Comparison of Manual and Computerized Data Processing Systems

A computer is basically a tool for use in processing data. There are three major stages in the performance of data processing. These three stages (which exist in both manual and computerized data processing systems) are input, processing, and output. An organization's data processing function encompasses the activities of *collecting* data from both within and outside of its system (this relates to the **input** stage of data processing), *transforming* the data into information (this relates to the **processing** stage of data processing), and *disseminating* the information to individuals, such as subsystem managers, to aid their decision-making functions (this relates to the **output** stage of data processing).

Everyone processes data on a daily basis whether at a job, at school, or at home. Figure 1-2 shows a simplified picture of a manual data processing system.

In a company's **manual data processing system,** such items as a desk, a person, a filing cabinet, and a tray are used. The tray accumulates incoming and outgoing documents. For example, a purchase invoice received from a supplier for payment would initially go into the incoming documents tray.

Before relating the items in Figure 1-2 to the three stages of data processing mentioned earlier, each of these items can be renamed based on its function. The person is in the center of all data processing work for a company and can therefore be referred to as the **central processor.** The filing cabinet shown in Figure 1-2 provides **permanent storage** for the data that are collected within the company. The desk top provides **temporary storage** for data that are currently being processed. It holds less data than a filing cabinet; however, the desk top is obviously easier and faster to work from than a filing cabinet. Finally, the sections of the tray can be divided into **input devices** and **output devices,** depending on whether they are utilized for organizing incoming or outgoing documents.

Input devices are used to collect data for a data processing system, whereas output devices are used to disseminate information to individuals.

We can now modify Figure 1-2 to reflect the functional relationships among the items in our manual data processing system. These functional relationships are shown in Figure 1-3.

With a manual data processing system similar to the one shown in Figure 1-3, there could be as many input devices and output devices as are necessary. Furthermore, our manual system could have additional filing cabinets for permanent storage, additional desks and their tops being used for temporary storage, and additional people working as central processors. By having a person processing data that are input into the manual system, these data should be converted to useful output information for decision-making purposes.

When using a computerized data processing system, we would find electronic components performing quite similar functions to those performed in a manual data processing system. These electronic components are called **hardware.** Figure 1-4 provides an overview of a **computerized data processing system** and its functional relationships. (The various components shown in Figure 1-4 will be discussed extensively in later chapters.)

A convenient way to examine computer hardware is to relate each component to its counterpart in a manual data processing system. Input devices such as a computer terminal are data collectors, which are used to enter data into the computer. A person will be involved in preparing the data that enter a company's computer. The central processing unit (CPU) of a computerized system is equivalent to the person of a manual system performing the role of central processor.

Sometimes people get confused when attempting to understand the difference between temporary storage (sometimes called primary storage) and permanent storage (sometimes called secondary storage) in a computerized data processing system. However, this confusion should be eliminated if we relate the re-

FIGURE 1-2   A manual data processing system.

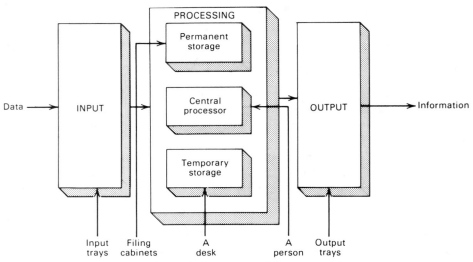

FIGURE 1-3   Functional relationships in a manual data processing system.

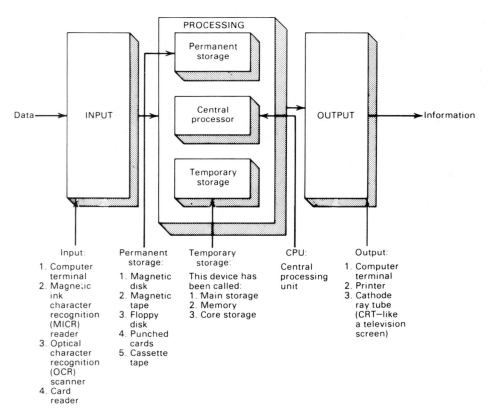

FIGURE 1-4   Functional relationships in a computerized data processing system.

lationships developed in Figures 1-2 and 1-3 for a manual data processing system to the computerized data processing system in Figure 1-4. When using a manual system, one can obtain data from a filing cabinet (which can be thought of as permanent storage) and then place the data on the desk top (which can be thought of as temporary storage) in order for a person to perform processing work on these data. Under a computerized system, data contained on a permanent storage device (such as magnetic disk or magnetic tape) are entered into the computer's temporary storage device (often called main storage, memory, or core storage) for processing work to be performed on the data by the CPU.

The output from a manual system would be processed by a person. On the other hand, the output from a computerized system is processed by the computer's CPU and possibly printed out on a printer output device or displayed on a CRT output device. Finally, as with a manual system, the processing of data that are input into a computerized system should result in these data being converted to useful output information for decision-making purposes.

AN ACCOUNTING INFORMATION SYSTEM DEFINED AND ANALYZED

Each subsystem within the Alan Company (see Figure 1-1) could be analyzed in considerable depth to understand its contribution to the company's operating performance. Because this text is accounting oriented, however, we will direct our attention to the accounting subsystem's role in a business information system. The accounting subsystem of an organization performs the *service function* of transforming financial data into useful *information* that aids management, creditors, current and potential investors, and others in making decisions. The accounting subsystem is, therefore, often referred to in this book as the "accounting information system." We specifically define an accounting information system as

> an organizational component which accumulates, classifies, processes, analyzes, and communicates relevant financial-oriented, decision-making information to a company's external parties (such as current and potential investors, federal and state tax agencies, and creditors) and internal parties (principally management).

The accounting information system is actually one major component of a management information system. The difference between them is in the scope of coverage. Whereas an accounting information system accumulates, classifies, processes, analyzes, and communicates relevant **financial information,** a management information system performs these functions for *all* types of information affecting a company's operations.

For example, the Alan Company's EDP subsystem may perform an analysis of customer product preferences based on input data accumulated by the marketing subsystem. The resultant information from this analysis should aid the marketing subsystem in planning its future sales promotion. This market report represents processed information from the Alan Company's management information system, but is beyond the scope of the accounting information system.

The following illustrations emphasize the types of data provided by a company's accounting information system.

1. The Stanley Schmidt Swimming Suit Manufacturing Company (which produces and sells beach apparel) has experienced significant increases in demand for its products. The limited manufacturing capacity of its current production plant has resulted in the loss of considerable sales because the company cannot maintain adequate merchandise inventory in stock. Stanley Schmidt, president of the company since its inception 10 years ago, wants to expand operations but is unsure which of two directions to pursue: (a) to expand the present manufacturing capacity of his company's 10-year-old plant

facility or (b) to construct an additional plant facility 20 miles from town, where Stanley owns 15 acres of land. To reach the best decision, Stanley should request his company accountants to estimate the expected costs and benefits from each alternative. Based on this information, Stanley will be in a better position to plan his company's best course of action.

2. Archibald Archer, a recent college graduate with a degree in architecture, has been operating his own construction design business for the past few months. Business has been proceeding quite well, except for one problem: Archie has found it difficult to maintain an adequate cash balance to meet day-to-day operating expenditures. Most of Archie's creditors sell supplies to his company with cash discount terms of 2/10, n/30. However, the company's inadequate cash balance has often resulted in Archie's being unable to pay an invoice within the 10-day discount period, thereby losing the 2% cash discount. Archie says that it is impossible for him to know what level of cash the company should maintain since he is never sure what expenditures are necessary each business day. To help solve this problem, the company's accounting information system for accounts payable disbursements needs some modifications. Perhaps the accounts payable invoices should be filed according to specific payment dates (i.e., for each invoice, the final date on which it can be paid in order to receive the allowed cash discount). Also, Archie's accountant should do some cash budgeting of the company's weekly projected cash inflows and projected cash outflows. These weekly cash planning projections from the accounting information system will enable Archie to control his company's cash flow more efficiently.

3. The Brian Burger Bargain Basement Bonanza is a retail clothing store that sells low-quality apparel at discount prices. The store has its own credit card system with which customers, once approved, can charge their purchases. Because of the large volume of credit sales, the company's management has decided to com-

puterize its manual system for processing accounts receivable. Computer specialists within the store's EDP subsystem are uncertain what data should be maintained in the computer file of customer receivables. They are also uncertain about the data content of weekly and monthly printout reports to management reflecting accounts receivable transactions. The store's accountants should be able to enlighten the computer specialists about the collection and processing of accounts receivable data. Information concerning each credit customer (such as name and address, account number, credit terms, and credit limit) should be stored within the computer system. A weekly printout of an accounts receivable aging analysis should be provided to management along with a report disclosing the names and balances owed of those customers whose account balances are over 90 days past due. The individual accounts that are over 90 days past due can be immediately turned over to the store's credit and collection department for investigation, and these customers should be denied any further credit until their accounts are cleared up. A monthly printout of each customer's statement should also be provided by the computer. The accounts receivable transactions statements will serve as bills for mailing to the individual customers.

These examples demonstrate some of the informational needs of companies that can be satisfied by their accounting information systems. Example 3 illustrates an important relationship that is stressed throughout this text—the interaction between the accounting information system and the EDP subsystem. Under a manual data processing system (i.e., a system in which most of the data processing is performed without the aid of machines), the clothing store's accountants would accumulate credit card sales data for each customer on a sales invoice source document, classify the data on the sales invoice according to type of product sold and customer account number, and process the sales transaction through the company's sales journal and ledgers (both general and subsidiary ledgers). Finally, the accountants would communicate the relevant credit sales information needed by a department manager (e.g., the credit and collection department manager) through manually prepared reports, such as an accounts receivable aging analysis and customer billing statements. The analysis of the communicated accounting report information would then be performed by the manager (or managers) within the specific department receiving the report.

An EDP subsystem takes over the detailed and time-consuming processing activities formerly performed by accountants. Before a company's computer can process financial data, however, the accounting information system must still accumulate and classify the transaction data (in our example, credit sales) to be processed by the computer. To achieve this requires close coordination of accounting subsystem employees and EDP subsystem employees. The accountants must understand the capabilities and limitations of their company's computer in order to accumulate and classify the accounting data in a suitable form for computer processing. On the other hand, EDP employees must understand the processing needs of the accountants so that they can design adequate computer files for storing the accounting data and write suitable computer programs to prepare information reports containing the relevant accounting data for decision making.

Upon completion of the computerized processing of an accounts receivable aging analysis report, for example, the accountants obtain this report and deliver it to credit and collection department managers for their analysis. Under a manual data processing system, the accountants normally spend so much time in processing data that they often cannot participate in the analysis of their report data. A computerized data processing system, however, relieves them of many time-consuming activities (such as recording and posting journal entries, determining general ledger account balances, and preparing trial balances), and they can typically become

directly involved in the analysis of accounting report data. Thus, in our example, the accountants would likely contribute to the analysis of the computerized accounts receivable aging schedule by discussing its contents with credit and collection department managers. If these department managers were, for example, dissatisfied with the number and dollar amounts of credit customers having balances over 90 days past due, they might want to consider tightening the company's credit-granting policies. Before adopting stricter credit policies, however, the accountants should analyze what effects these changed policies would likely have on the company's future earnings and future cash flows. Upon receiving these projections from accounting, credit and collection department managers should have an improved basis for deciding whether or not to change credit-granting policies. Of course, to provide the managers with information regarding future earnings and future cash flows, the accountants need to accumulate the relevant data, which is then processed by the computer.

With the establishment of an EDP subsystem, the accounting information system normally becomes the center of data communications in the company. Often, a report request comes into the accounting subsystem from another subsystem. The accountants then accumulate the necessary data for this report and send them to the EDP subsystem for report preparation. The processed report is transmitted to the accountants who deliver it to the specific subsystem that requested the report. Figure 1-5 illustrates the communication network of possible report requests by some of the Alan Company's subsystems and the subsequent preparation and distribution of these reports.

The Alan Company's marketing subsystem, for example, is considering the introduction of several new product lines into the company's sales mix. As reflected in Figure 1-5, the marketing subsystem requests an analysis of expected profit margins from the proposed new product lines. The accountants project the ex-

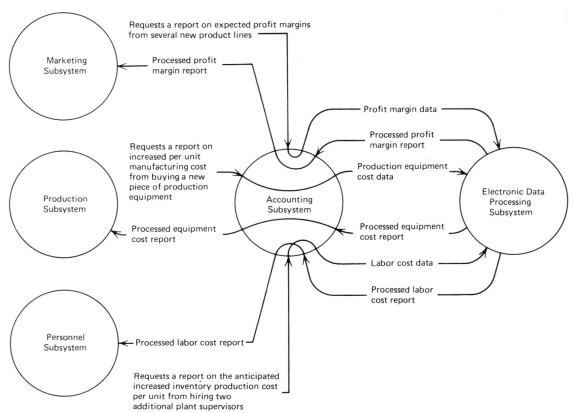

FIGURE 1-5 Examples of the Alan Company's communication network for processing and distribution of subsystem report requests.

pected cost and revenue data associated with each proposed product line. These data are submitted to the EDP subsystem, where a report is prepared. The finished report goes to the accounting subsystem, which passes it on to the marketing subsystem managers. Of course, the accountants will likely meet with marketing managers to discuss the report's contents.

It should also be noted that additional communications beyond those indicated in Figure 1-5 will be required. For example, before the accountants can perform their analysis of expected costs and revenues from the new product lines, both marketing and accounting employees must talk with production managers regarding the plant's capacity to handle the manufacture of the new product lines. Furthermore, if the present factory labor force is not sufficient to handle the increased manufacturing, production managers and accountants will have to communicate with personnel managers concerning the hiring of additional labor. The data relating to increased labor costs will be used in the analysis of the proposed new product lines' profit margins.

This discussion has emphasized two relevant aspects of modern business systems: (1) the importance of communication between a company's subsystems prior to reaching a specific decision and (2) the vital role played by the accounting subsystem in generating information to aid other subsystems in decision making.

Within the accounting subsystems of many or-

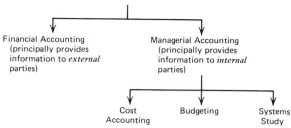

FIGURE 1-6 An accounting subsystem. (The financial and managerial accounting components are not mutually exclusive; that is, information from the financial accounting component is used within the managerial accounting component, and vice versa.)

ganizations there are two major informational components: financial and managerial accounting. Figure 1-6 illustrates these two components. The financial and managerial accounting areas are each *sub-subsystems* of the accounting subsystem. These two accounting information system components are now analyzed further.

Financial Accounting

The major objective of financial accounting is to provide relevant information to individuals and groups outside an organization's boundaries. (Of course, individuals within a company, such as managers, also use financial information in their decision making.) As previously mentioned,

these external parties include current and potential investors, federal and state tax agencies, and creditors. Financial accounting's objective is achieved principally through the preparation of periodic financial statements (income statement, balance sheet, retained earnings statement, statement of cash flows, etc.).

The basic inputs to the financial accounting structure are transactions measured in monetary terms. An **audit trail** of accounting transactions is maintained within a company's system, which enables one to follow the flow of data through the system. The Alan Company's financial accounting audit trail is reflected in Figure 1-7. Relevant data from source documents are input into the financial accounting structure and are filed for possible later use, such as verifying the dollar amount recorded in a particular journal entry. The processing-of-transactions function encompasses *recording* journal entries from the source documents, *posting* these entries to general and subsidiary ledger accounts, and *preparing* a trial balance from the general ledger account balances. The Alan Company has an EDP subsystem, which handles the processing function. Thus, the journal entries and the ledger account balances information are maintained on computer storage devices (magnetic tape, magnetic disk, or some other medium). With the use of computer programs, the company's financial statements are printed out periodically, as are

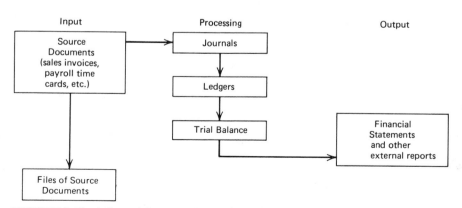

FIGURE 1-7 A financial accounting audit trail.

any other desired output reports. A good audit trail within the Alan Company's financial accounting information system permits a manager to follow any source document data from the initial input stage through the processing stage and to the data's location on an output report. In an effectively developed audit trail, data can be followed through a system because people within the system thoroughly understand the methods and procedures for accumulating and processing the data. As a result, one can reconstruct how data were handled by the system.

Later chapters will analyze various audit trail problems that can occur when a company uses computerized rather than manual data processing. For example, before the Alan Company acquired a computer, its accounting transactions were recorded manually and posted to the general ledger. Following a specific transaction's processing, a manager who wanted to check the recording of the transaction could obtain the manually prepared journal, locate the page where the transaction was recorded, compare the transaction with the original source document (e.g., compare the dollar amount of a recorded sale with the filed copy of the invoice), and also check the mathematical accuracy of those general ledger account balances affected by the posting of the transaction. Thus, because all of the accounting work could easily be seen, the manager would have no difficulty following a transaction's audit trail through the accounting information system. When the Alan Company obtained a computer to handle its accounting transaction processing, however, the activities associated with a business transaction were no longer visible. The work of recording a journal entry, posting the entry, and determining updated general ledger account balances was all done within the company's computer. The manager would therefore have a more difficult job tracing the audit trail of a specific accounting transaction. Many fraudulent acts have been committed as a result of the difficulty of following organizations' audit trails. Later chapters will analyze how companies utilizing computers for data processing can solve their audit-trail problems.

Through the "processing of transactions," a financial accounting information system generates a large amount of information for both external and internal parties. Transaction processing is a major part of an organization's **accounting cycle.** The information-generating attributes of the accounting cycle and the role of transaction processing within this cycle are examined in the supplement at the end of our chapter.

Managerial Accounting

The managerial accounting sub-system has as its principal objective providing relevant information to the company's management (the internal parties). The three components within the Alan Company's managerial accounting sub-subsystem are cost accounting, budgeting, and systems study (see Figure 1-6). In comparing managerial accounting to financial accounting, eight important differences can be identified, as follows.[1]

1. Managerial accounting focuses on providing financial data for internal (management) uses.
2. Management information needs, satisfied in part by managerial accounting, are relatively more oriented to the *future* than to the past.
3. Managerial accounting is *not* governed by generally accepted accounting principles.
4. Managerial accounting emphasizes relevance and flexibility of data, in contrast to financial accounting.
5. Relatively more emphasis is placed on non-monetary data in managerial accounting, often at the expense of financial precision.
6. Managerial accounting focuses more on organizational divisions (segments) than on the entity as a whole.
7. Managerial accounting draws heavily from other disciplines (economics, quantitative methods, etc.).
8. Managerial accounting is not mandatory.

[1] Ray H. Garrison, *Managerial Accounting,* 5th edition (Homewood, Illinois: BPI, Irwin, 1988), p. 15.

Two major managerial functions in a modern organization are **planning** and **controlling.** Each of these important functions will be analyzed thoroughly in later chapters. At this point, it should be emphasized that *planning* involves establishing goals and objectives for the future performance of a company, whereas *controlling* is a monitoring procedure to enable the company's management to ascertain whether the planned goals and objectives are being achieved. When actual performance deviates significantly from the plan, management attempts to determine the causes for this deviation and then institutes corrective action.

For example, the Alan Company estimates that 5000 basketballs will be sold during February 1990. This estimation reflects the company's *planned* basketball sales for February. At month-end, a comparison is made of actual basketball sales with the planned sales. This comparison represents the *control* mechanism. Assume that actual February sales are only 2400 basketballs. Management will then investigate the causes for the actual sales being 2600 basketballs below the planned estimate (5000 estimate – 2400 actual) and attempt to institute corrective action so that future months' actual basketball sales will increase. (It should be noted, however, that a possible cause of this unfavorable variation could be inaccuracies in the February sales estimate.)

The managerial accountant makes an important contribution to the planning and controlling functions of a company's management through cost accounting, budgeting, and systems study. These three components of managerial accounting are now briefly discussed.

Cost Accounting

A cost accounting system aids management in planning and controlling its various acquisitions, processing, distribution, and selling activities. In the broadest sense, the focus is on the *value added* by an organization to its goods or services, and this focus remains the same whether the organization is a manufacturing firm, a bank, a hospital, or a police department. For example, a plumber who repairs a customer's leaking water pipe performs a value-added function because the repair increases the efficiency of the customer's plumbing system.

For an organization producing a physical product, there are typically three major cost elements incurred in manufacturing the product: direct raw materials, direct labor, and production overhead (the indirect production costs). A valuable planning and controlling technique used by many production companies is *standard costs.* These costs are determined before the production process begins and represent estimates of what the manufacturing costs should be under conditions of efficient production. The accountant helps management determine the standard costs for direct raw materials, direct labor, and production overhead. Because the standard costs are determined in advance of production, they are an important managerial planning tool. The control aspect of standard costs comes into play when actual production occurs. Timely reports that compare actual with standard production costs enable management to ascertain areas of production inefficiency that require correction.

For the control aspect of a standard cost accounting system to function effectively, the timely production performance reports to management must also disclose who was responsible for any unfavorable performance. To be timely the information should be received within a relatively short period following the performance. This enables management to institute corrective action before too many inefficiencies occur. If, for example, the Alan Company's management receives monthly performance reports comparing actual with standard production costs, any inefficiencies within the system will continue throughout a particular month. Management is unable to investigate immediately any ineffective performance because it is not aware of the inefficiencies until month-end. If weekly production reports are provided to management, however, corrective action can be taken before too many inefficiencies occur. The *speed* of computerized data processing systems used by many companies today has contributed to the timely reporting of production information to management.

Upon receiving a timely production report, the Alan Company's managers can take corrective action on unfavorable performance only if the information system enables them to determine who is responsible for the inadequate performance. Many organizations utilize a **responsibility accounting system** to help their managements trace unfavorable performance to the individual (or individuals) that caused the inefficiencies. Under a responsibility accounting structure, each subsystem within an organization is held accountable only for those financial items over which its employees have control. Controllable items are those that the subsystem's employees can cause to increase or decrease. Thus, when a particular cost expenditure exceeds its standard cost, managers can trace this inefficiency to the responsible employee (or employees) and institute immediate corrective action.

For example, the Alan Company's purchasing department (a component of the company's production subsystem) is responsible for acquiring the necessary raw materials to manufacture basketballs. From an analysis of the quality of raw materials desired in the basketballs and the suppliers' market prices for these materials, the standard raw materials costs are established. Weekly reports from electronic data processing are provided to management, disclosing any significant variations between the actual and standard raw materials purchase costs as well as any significant variations between the actual and standard raw materials used in production. Management can immediately investigate these variances to determine their causes and decide on necessary corrective action. An unfavorable raw materials purchase cost variance, for example, may be caused by the purchasing department ordering better-quality materials (which cost more) than the production standards specify.

The foregoing brief illustration demonstrates a responsibility accounting system with timely performance reports. Because the purchasing department is responsible for raw materials ac-

quisitions, any purchase cost variation from standard can be traced to this department. (Similarly, a raw materials usage variance can be traced to the specific production department that used the raw materials.) Also, the weekly computerized reports allow management to analyze variances and initiate corrective action within a relatively short time period.

Budgeting

A **budget** is a financial projection for the future and thus is a valuable managerial *planning* aid. The Alan Company develops both short- and long-range budget projections. The former represent detailed financial plans for the coming 12-month period, whereas the latter reflect less-detailed financial projections for 5 to 10 years into the future.

A good budgetary system is also a useful managerial *control* mechanism. Because budgets indicate future financial expectations, the Alan Company's management is concerned about the causes of any significant variations between *actual* and *budget* results during the budget year. Through timely performance reports comparing actual operating results with the preestablished budgets, the company's management can investigate the reasons for significant budget variations. Management should correct unfavorable variations and reward favorable variations (e.g., a salary increase). A favorable budget variation may direct management to specific activities that can benefit the company's future operating performance. For example, assume that the Alan Company's actual sales of footballs in June 1990 significantly exceed the original budget projection. This may be the result of the footballs having wider public appeal than marketing anticipated. To take advantage of the situation, the Alan Company's marketing managers may increase their future advertising expenditures for promoting football sales and thereby obtain an even larger share of the market.

A budgetary system affects all subsystems within an organization. Budget preparation therefore requires good communication between all the organization's subsystems. Because of the strong financial emphasis in budgets, the Alan Company's managerial accounting component has major responsibility for the organization's budget system. This component coordinates the preparation of the other subsystems' budgets and then monitors each subsystem's actual performance. The computerized processing of the Alan Company's budgetary and actual operating data by its EDP subsystem enables management to obtain timely feedback reports comparing actual with budget results. This allows the management to take corrective action on unfavorable budget performance more quickly following the inefficient performance.

The budgeting area of managerial accounting will be analyzed further in later chapters (especially Chapter 3).

Systems Study

An organization having a problem with its current information system (e.g., production performance reports may be taking too long to prepare following actual manufacturing activities) may hire outside consultants (also called systems analysts) to recommend changes or, as in the Alan Company, utilize company employees to help solve information systems problems. The managerial accountants' abilities to understand internal financial systems have qualified them to perform systems studies for organizations. Many certified public accounting firms (e.g., Arthur Andersen and Company) have separate management advisory services departments that perform systems studies as well as other consultation for their clients. Of course, accountants are not the only professional group doing systems work. Because all the subsystems (marketing, electronic data processing, production, personnel, accounting, etc.) within a business system must interact effectively, a systems study of an organization's problems requires expertise in business areas beyond accounting. In fact, many business consulting firms utilize a **team approach** when performing a systems study. This team of consultants might include ac-

countants, marketing specialists, computer experts, production managers, engineers, and industrial psychologists.

The essential steps in performing a systems study are as follows.

1. **Planning.** This entails organizing the systems study team and formulating the strategic plans for the information system.
2. **Analysis.** This involves a thorough review of the company's current system so that the system's strengths and weaknesses can be ascertained.
3. **Design.** Based on analysis of the company and its system, changes are suggested that will eliminate the weaknesses and maintain the strengths. By eliminating the weaknesses, the new design will hopefully solve the company's systems problems.
4. **Implementation and Follow-up.** Based on the design recommendations, the necessary changes are incorporated into the company's system. The revised system will then replace the old system in handling daily operating activities. After the revised system has been operating for a certain time period (four months, for example), a follow-up evaluation of the new system takes place to determine if it has solved management's problems and is thereby contributing to the company's goals and objectives. If areas of weakness are still found in the new system, further recommendations can be made and implemented.

The preceding discussion was very broad in order to briefly introduce the subject of systems study. Later chapters will analyze each of these four essential steps in greater detail.

MAJOR INFLUENCES ON ACCOUNTING INFORMATION SYSTEMS

The growth and sophistication of modern organizational systems have made accountants' information-providing functions more difficult.

To meet the challenges of complex systems, accountants have expanded their knowledge beyond traditional accounting subject matter. We will briefly discuss three areas that have greatly affected accounting information systems: behavioral analysis, quantitative methods, and computers.

Behavioral Analysis

Whether involved with a cost accounting system, a budgetary system, or a systems study change, the accountant must recognize that *people* work in the system. The best system "on paper" will not be effective upon implementation unless the needs of an organization's people are considered when designing the system. Accountants do not have to be psychologists. But they should understand how people are motivated toward positive organizational performance.

When, for example, accountants are designing some changes in a company's current information system, they should recognize that some employees might resent the suggested changes even if these modifications contribute positively to the company's goals. A systems change ordinarily will require certain individuals to perform their jobs differently from the past. A change from the normal routine can be frustrating. To reduce this frustration and thereby foster positive employee attitudes toward a systems change, the accountants should encourage the employees to *participate* in the systems study. This participation includes not only keeping the employees well informed regarding the reasons for change, but also encouraging them to make suggestions in areas where they feel changes are needed. The employees should be motivated to accept a new system if they contributed to its development.

Since the job of accountants is to communicate relevant information to people, they must have an understanding of how people *perceive* information and then reach decisions from it. Basically, perception is the specific meaning that an individual attaches to a communicated message. Identical information may be perceived differently by two people partly because of their dissimilar backgrounds. Thus, accountants should be familiar with the basic psychological characteristics of the decision makers to whom they will communicate, so that their messages can be designed and communicated to allow the best possible organizational decisions.

A production supervisor, for example, typically thinks in terms of physical manufactured units rather than dollar production costs. Thus, if the actual raw materials used in manufacturing a product exceed the standard quantity during a specific week, the accountant should communicate this unfavorable variance to the supervisor in terms of the excess raw materials used rather than merely report the excess dollar cost of the raw materials entering production. The supervisor should have a better understanding of the production inefficiency if physical units rather than dollars are emphasized. As a result, the supervisor will likely be motivated to correct the production inefficiency.

Quantitative Methods

The **operations research** field includes various quantitative techniques to aid management decision making. Some of these techniques are statistical analysis, linear programming, PERT (program evaluation and review technique) analysis, waiting-line theory, simulation, and regression analysis.

Accountants use quantitative tools to increase the effectiveness of the information they provide to management. For example, due to increased sales of sporting goods equipment and the resultant need for additional productive capacity to meet these sales, the Alan Company's accountants could be asked to help management to decide whether to build a new production plant across town or expand the current plant. The accountants would attempt to project the future costs and benefits associated with both alternatives and then make a recommendation. Because the future involves *uncertainty* and the accountants are trying to forecast the future operating results from two alternative actions, their analysis might be made more meaningful by using statistical probability theory.

As another example of accountants' use of quantitative techniques, assume that the Alan Company's management is attemptng to determine the optimal sales mix of its sporting goods products to maximize the company's total contribution margin (sales revenue *minus* controllable expenses, which are normally the variable expenses). The company's accountants can aid management's decision by preparing a linear programming analysis of the various sales mix combinations.

Let us assume that the analysis and design steps of a systems study have just been completed for the Alan Company and the recommended changes are ready for implementation. To aid this process, the accountant who partcipated in the systems study can develop a quantitative PERT network diagram of the specific activities required (and their expected time estimates) for implementing the new system.

A few of the quantitative techniques that accountants can employ to perform their organizational functions more effectively have been briefly described here. A couple of specific quantitative examples will be presented in Appendix A (which should be studied when the subjects in Chapters 3 and 15 are discussed) to illustrate the accountant's use of quantitative techniques in business situations involving decisions that affect the future.

Computers

Electronic data processing has significantly changed accountants' functions in an organization. Prior to computerized business information systems, accountants often spent a large amount of their workday manually processing data (e.g., recording journal entries, posting these entries to ledger accounts, preparing trial balances, and preparing the financial statements). In many firms, the computer has taken over the bulk of these data processing tasks

and thereby allowed accountants to become more involved in decision making in their organizations. The computer's ability to handle an organization's routine bookkeeping has been a major cause for the growth of managerial accounting. Accountants are now concentrating on the design of systems, the development of budgets, and the recommendation of future managerial actions in a wide variety of operational areas.

The accounting subsystem must continually interact with the EDP subsystem. A large quantity of the input data to the computer must be provided by accounting. Accountants should understand the capabilities as well as the limitations of a computer so they can perform their jobs effectively. In fact, the computer's ability to execute complex mathematical calculations in a short time period has been an important stimulus for accountants' increased use of operations research quantitative techniques when providing information to management.

SUMMARY

The subsystems included in an organization's management information system must communicate with one another so that each subsystem contributes positively to the total system's goals. The accounting subsystem of most organizations includes two major components: financial accounting and managerial accounting. The former's major function is to provide relevant information to external parties, whereas the latter's major function is to provide relevant information to internal parties (i.e., management).

The accounting information system is a major component of an organization's management information system. A company's external and internal parties rely heavily on the financially-oriented information that accounting provides for their decision making. Because a large amount of accounting information is generated through the periodic performance of the accounting cycle, this chapter's supplement will analyze each of the nine cycle steps typically performed within an organization's financial accounting information system. The "heart" of the accounting cycle is the processing of business transactions. Therefore, in discussing the accounting cycle steps, *transaction processing* will be emphasized.

The significant areas where managerial accountants perform an important role in an organization's information system include the development of cost accounting systems, the planning and controlling of budgetary systems, and the performance of systems studies to improve the organization's information system.

Today's accountants must be familiar with computerized information systems and be able to interact with an organization's EDP subsystem. A brief comparison of a manual data processing system to a computerized data processing system was provided in this chapter. When working in a business system, the accountants must understand the motivations of people and their decision-making processes. Furthermore, the accountants can contribute more positively to a system's effectiveness by using operations research techniques in many of their analyses for management.

Key Terms You Should Know

accounting cycle
accounting information system
audit trail
budgeting
central processing unit
computerized data processing system
controlling
cost accounting
data
financial accounting
information
input devices
management information system

managerial accounting
manual data processing system
operations research
output devices
perception
permanent storage
planning
source documents
suboptimization
system
systems study
temporary storage

OVERVIEW OF REMAINING TEXT MATERIALS

The current chapter examined the role of accounting information systems in today's business world. For accountants to contribute to the development of efficient and effective business systems, they must have a good understanding of management concepts (principally *planning* and *controlling*) and how these concepts affect the design and operation of accounting information systems. Continuing Part One of this text, Chapters 2 and 3 emphasize those management concepts of importance to accountants working within an accounting information system. Chapter 2 defines and analyzes various managerial

concepts, stressing their relationship to accounting information systems. Chapter 3 describes the important contributions of budget systems to managerial planning and controlling activities. Various ways a computer can be used in a company's budgetary information system (such as with electronic spreadsheet programs) will also be examined in this chapter.

The final chapter in Part One, Chapter 4, provides an overview of computer concepts. Because modern business systems often have computerized processing of accounting data, accounting employees must be familiar with the capabilities and limitations of computers and be able to communicate with EDP employees. Many of the subsequent chapters in this book assume the student has some prior knowledge of the hardware and software concepts associated with electronic data processing. The purpose of Chapter 4 is to show how that prior knowledge relates to the study of accounting information systems.

A vital role of an accounting information system within an efficient and effective organizational system is to aid the collecting, recording, and storing of financial data as well as converting these data into useful managerial decision-making information. Thus, Part Two (Chapters 5–8) examines several data processing approaches used by companies to enable relevant information to be provided to their managements. The emphasis throughout these four chapters will be on data collecting, recording, and storing within a computerized accounting information systems environment. The coding of accounting data and processing of accounting transactions are stressed in Chapter 5. Since a system must be appropriately described in order to be understood, the major subject of Chapter 6 is documentation for the accounting information system. Chapter 7 explains the use of *files* and *data bases* within accounting information systems. To complete Part Two of the text, Chapter 8 provides a detailed illustration of both a manual and a computerized accounting information system for processing an organization's accounts receivable transactions.

To reduce the risk of errors and irregularities in an accounting information system's functions of collecting, recording, and storing business data, a system of *internal controls* is essential. Part Three (Chapters 9–12) analyzes in depth the topic of internal control within both manual and computerized data processing systems. Chapter 9 introduces the reader to the internal control concept, whereas Chapter 10 examines the development of good internal controls in companies using computers for processing their accounting data. Because frauds of significant dollar amounts have sometimes been committed in firms using computers for processing accounting data, Chapter 11 investigates the important and interesting subject of computer crime and computer

security. As a means of both preventing and detecting fraud within companies' computerized data processing systems, the performance of good *audit* procedures is extremely important. Therefore, to complete Part Three, Chapter 12 will look at accountants' audit control procedures in those organizations with computerized accounting information systems.

Part Four ties together many of the previous chapters by discussing the activities involved in developing efficient and effective information systems (Chapters 13–15). Accountants often participate in systems studies to help a company solve its problems associated with a lack of good information flow for managerial decision making. Part Four examines the activities that are essential when performing a study of a company's information systems problems, emphasizing accountants' functions in systems study work. The systems study consists of four major phases and Chapters 13–15 describe the steps and procedures associated with each of these phases. The major emphasis throughout Part Four will be on a systems study to convert an organization's manual accounting information system to a computerized system (although a systems study may involve conversion of one automated system to a different automated system as well).

Chapters 16, 17, and 18 (Part Five) cover some special topics important for accounting information systems. While the majority of this book focuses on *transaction processing,* Chapter 16 describes higher levels of processing which require decision support systems and expert systems. Chapter 17 looks at the information needs and problems facing a small company (emphasizing the role of minicomputers and microcomputers in small companies' systems) in today's competitive business world, stressing the accounting information system's functions within small companies. Chapter 18 analyzes the unique aspects of accounting information systems in service organizations (such as a restaurant or accounting firm) and not-for-profit organizations (such as a state university or a city police department).

In addition, two other features are provided. Part Six, following Chapter 18, includes several comprehensive real-life cases for analysis. These cases require the student to apply many of the concepts presented within the textbook. Finally, the appendices will cover some specific quantitative analysis problems that are referred to in various chapters as well as several other peripheral topics.

Discussion Questions

1-1. Discuss the relationships, if any, between an organization's operational goals and its broad goals.

1-2. This chapter illustrated suboptimization within the Alan Company's production subsystem. Try to think of additional suboptimization situations that could occur in an organization's system.

1-3. Discuss some of the possible behavioral problems that managerial accountants may face when they attempt to communicate relevant information about an organization's system to internal parties.

1-4. Many people have a stereotyped image of an accountant as a person with ice water in his or her veins, who sits at a desk all day recording debits and credits and considers balancing the books to the penny the number-one priority. If a high school senior (trying to decide what major to study in college) asked you what accounting is and what types of functions the accountant performs in an organization, what would you tell this student?

1-5. Because financial accounting and managerial accounting perform different functions for an organization, do you see any possible conflicts between these two accounting components?

1-6. Two major functions of an organization's management are planning and controlling. Discuss some of the ways that an accountant contributes to these managerial functions.

1-7. Discuss some of the important characteristics of a good organizational system.

1-8. Assume that you are the chief accountant of the Bogle Bright Corporation, a household furniture manufacturer and retailer. Your company is having some problems with its information system. For example, the marketing subsystem manager claims that the production subsystem supervisor often ignores (for several months) the requests for increased production

of specific types of furniture. These production requests are the result of actual furniture orders by customers. The excessive delays within the production subsystem concerning the manufacture of the furniture have frequently caused dissatisfied customers to take their future business to competitors. The Bogle Bright Corporation's president has assigned you the job of hiring an accountant systems analyst consultant to come into the company and help solve its problems.

Questions

A. What major characteristics would you look for in the accountant to be hired as your company's consultant?

B. Assume for a moment that you are the outside consultant hired by the Bogle Bright Corporation. What approach might you use to solve the company's current problems between its marketing and production subsystems?

1-9. This chapter has briefly discussed the impact of computers on organizational information systems. Just for fun, project yourself 10 years into the future. Describe what you think the computer's functions in a modern organization will be at that time.

1-10. What purpose is served by an organization's periodic performance of the accounting cycle steps?

1-11. Differentiate between an accounting information system and a management information system.

1-12. Why do many organizations bother to classify their business transactions into a few broad categories? Discuss some of the categories of business transactions that would likely exist for a professional baseball team.

1-13. Discuss the following statement. With the availability in many companies today of computers for performing data processing activities, the accountant's organizational role has declined significantly.

1-14. Discuss some of the communicative interactions that should take place between a company's accounting employees and its EDP employees.

1-15. What is meant by the phrase "financial accounting audit trail"? In which type of accounting information system, manual or computerized, would you expect to find a "clearer" audit trail? Explain your answer by providing an audit trail example under both a manual data processing system and a computerized data processing system.

1-16. Based upon the discussion in this chapter, compare a manual data processing system to a computerized data processing system.

CASE ANALYSES

1-17. *The Parable of the Spindle**

Once upon a time the president of a large chain of short-order restaurants attended a lecture on "Human Relations in Business and Industry." He attended the lecture in hope he would learn something useful. His years of experience had led him to believe that if human relations problems ever plagued any business, then they certainly plagued the restaurant business.

The speaker discussed the many pressures which create human relations problems. He spoke of psychological pressures, sociological pressures, conflicts in values, conflicts in power structure, and so on. The president did not understand all that was said, but he did go home with one idea. If there were so many different sources of pressure, maybe it was expecting too much of his managers to think they would see them all, let alone cope with them all. The thought occurred to him that maybe he should bring in a team of consultants from several different academic disciplines and have each contribute his part to the solution of the human relations problems.

And so it came to pass that the president of the restaurant chain and his top-management staff met one morning with a sociologist, a psychologist, and an anthropologist. The president outlined the problem to the men of science and spoke of his hope that they might come up with an interdisciplinary answer to the human relations problems. The personnel manager presented exit-interview findings which he interpreted as indicating that most people quit their restaurant jobs because of too much sense of pressure caused by the inefficiencies and ill tempers of coworkers.

This was the mission which the scientists were assigned: find out why the waitresses break down in tears; find out why the cooks walk off the job; find out why the managers get so upset that they summarily fire employees on the spot. Find out the cause of the problems, and find out what to do about them.

Later, in one of the plush conference rooms, the scientists sat down to plan their attack. It soon became clear that they might just as well be three blind men, and the problem might as well be the proverbial ele-

phant. Their training and experience had taught them to look at events in different ways. They decided that inasmuch as they couldn't speak each other's languages, they might as well pursue their tasks separately. Each went to a different city and began his observations in his own way.

First to return was the sociologist. In his report to top management he said:

"I think I have discovered something that is pretty fundamental. In one sense it is so obvious that it has probably been completely overlooked before. It is during the rush hours that your human relations problems arise. That is when the waitresses break out in tears. That is when the cooks grow temperamental and walk off the job. That is when your managers lose their tempers and dismiss employees summarily."

After elaborating on this theme and showing several charts with sloping lines and bar graphs to back up his assertions, he came to his diagnosis of the situation. "In brief, gentlemen," he stated, "you have a sociological problem on your hands." He walked to the blackboard and began to write. As he wrote, he spoke:

"You have a stress pattern during the rush hours. There is stress between the customer and the waitress. . . .

"There is stress between the waitress and the cook. . . .

"And up here is the manager. There is stress between the waitress and the manager. . . .

"And between the manager and the cook. . . .

"And the manager is buffeted by complaints from the customer.

"We can see one thing which, sociologically speaking, doesn't seem right. The manager has the highest status in the restaurant. The cook has the next highest status. The waitresses, however, are always 'local hire' and have the lowest status. Of course, they have higher status than bus boys and dish washers, but certainly lower status than the cook, and yet they give orders to the cook.

"It doesn't seem right for a lower status person to give orders to a higher status person. We've got to find a way to break up the face-to-face relationship between the waitresses and the cook. We've got to fix it so that they don't have to talk with one another. Now my idea is to put a 'spindle' on the order counter. The 'spindle,' as I choose to call it, is a wheel on a shaft. The wheel has clips on it so the girls can simply put their orders on the wheel rather than calling out orders to the cook."

When the sociologist left the meeting, the president and his staff talked of what had been said. It made some sense. However, they decided to wait to hear from the other scientists before taking any action.

Next to return from his studies was the psychologist. He reported to top management:

"I think I have discovered something that is pretty fundamental. In once sense it is so obvious that it has probably been completely overlooked before. It is during the rush hours that your human relations problems arise. That is when the waitresses break out in tears. That is when the cooks grow temperamental and walk off the job. That is when your managers lose their tempers and dismiss employees summarily."

Then the psychologist sketched on the blackboard the identical pattern of stress between customer, waitress, cook, and management. But his interpretation was somewhat different.

"Psychologically speaking," he said, "we can see that the manager is the father figure, the cook is the son, and the waitress is the daughter. Now we know that in our culture you can't have daughters giving orders to the sons. It louses up their ego structure.

"What we've got to do is find a way to break up the face-to-face relationship between them. Now one idea I've thought up is to put what I call a 'spindle' on the order counter. It's kind of a wheel on a shaft with little clips on it so that the waitresses can put their orders on it rather than calling out orders to the cook."

What the psychologist said made sense, too, in a way. Some of the staff favored the status-conflict interpretation while others thought the sex-conflict interpretation to be the right one; the president kept his own counsel.

The next scientist to report was the anthropoligist. He reported:

"I think I have discovered something that is pretty fundamental. In one sense it is so obvious that it has probably been completely overlooked before. It is during the rush hours that your human relations problems arise. That is when the waitresses break out in tears. That is when the cooks grow temperamental and walk off the job. That is when the managers lose their tempers and dismiss employees summarily."

After elaborating for a few moments he came to his diagnosis of the situation. "In brief, gentlemen," he stated, "you have an anthropological problem on your hands." He walked to the blackboard and began to sketch. One again there appeared the stress pattern. between customer, waitress, cook, and management.

"We anthropologists know that man behaves according to his value systems. Now, the manager holds as a central value the continued growth and development of the restaurant organization. The cooks tend to share this central value system, for as the organization prospers, so do they. But the waitresses are a different story. The only reason most of them are working is to help supplement the family income. They couldn't care less whether the organization thrives or not as long as it's a decent place to work. Now, you can't have a noncentral value system giving orders to a central value system.

"What we've got to do is find some way of breaking up the face-to-face contact between the waitresses and the cook. One way that has occurred to me is to place on the order counter an adaptation of the old-fashioned spindle. By having a wheel at the top of the shaft and putting clips every few inches apart, the waitresses can put their orders on the wheel and not have to call out orders to the cook. Here is a model of what I mean."

When the anthropologist had left, there was much discussion of which scientist was right. The president finally spoke. "Gentlemen, it's clear that these men don't agree on the reason for conflict, but all have come up with the same basic idea about the spindle. Let's take a chance and try it out."

And it came to pass that the spindle was introduced throughout the chain of restaurants. It did more to reduce the human relations problems in the restaurant industry than any other innovation of which the restaurant people knew. Soon it was copied. Like wildfire the spindle spread from coast to coast and from border to border.

Questions

1. In your opinion, which of the three scientists offered the most plausible explanation of the restaurant's problems? Explain.
2. In recommending the spindle, the scientists are tacitly admitting that the restaurant is a form of system. Name the kind of system they are thinking of and show how the restaurant meets the requirements of a system.
3. All the three scientists have recommended the use of a spindle to solve the restaurant's problems. Can you think of any new problems the spindle system might cause?

1-18. *A Need for Control**

Standard Building Service Company of St. Louis is a 15-year-old company that provides janitorial services for office buildings and industrial plants. Standard was purchased five years ago by Leslie Waller, and at the time of purchase, annual sales were approximately $500,000. In three years he was able to double the sales volume to the present level of $1,000,000, but for the past two years, sales volume has remained relatively constant. Waller attributes the lack of growth of the past two years to his being unable to call on new accounts because the business has grown to such an extent that his full energies and time are required in solving the myriad of problems that arise each day. He recognizes that the few new accounts he does obtain do no more than offset the normal turnover of accounts lost each month.

Janitorial services are usually performed after the tenants have left the building for the day; consequently, very few of Standard's employees start work before 6 P.M. Waller has found from experience that in order to keep employees, he must offer them at least 20 hours of work a week. On the other hand, very few people seem willing to work more than 25 hours a week. As a result, the work force of approximately 275 men and women are part-time employees. Waller also found that by hiring persons presently employed he is assured of stable, motivated employees. However, since his employees are working full-time elsewhere, there is considerable resistance when supervisors expect an above-average amount of work from them.

A recent analysis of the 121 accounts serviced by the company shows that 40 customers require the services of only 1 person working a maximum of 25 hours a week. Thirty-five accounts require 2 people with a total man hours ranging from 35 to 50 hours a week. Fifteen accounts require an average of 100 man-hours a week, thus utilizing the services of up to 4 employees. There is one large indusrial plant that requires 500 hours of service each week and approximately 20 workers. The remaining 30 accounts range between 100 and 400 man-hours each week, and require between 4 and 16 employees.

Mr. Waller is not sure which size job yields the most profit. Jobs are priced on a rule-of-thumb basis and

depend upon the type of floor surfaces, the amount of building traffic, number and types of offices, and other similar factors. Mr. Waller and one of this two full-time supervisors estimate the manpower requirements for each new job. An analysis of company records shows that for the past five years, variable costs—direct labor and materials (waxes, detergents, etc.)—average about 80 to 85 percent of total revenue.

The full-time organization consists of Mr. Waller, two supervisors, a secretary, an accountant, and a supply man who also maintains some of the larger pieces of cleaning equipment such as the floor polishers. In addition, there are five part-time supervisors, each of whom supervises 40 to 50 workers in a given geographic area of the city. Most of their time and energy is spent in delivering supplies and materials to the various buildings within a given geographic area of the city. They also reassign personnel as the need arises and collect the weekly time cards. The two full-time supervisors have no specific duties assigned to them nor is either one responsible for the work of any particular part-time supervisor.

At the present time Mr. Waller has only two sources of information to guide him in the operation of his business. One of these is customer complaints, which serve as a check on the quality of the work. The other source is the weekly payroll, which is prepared by a local bank. Each week time cards are submitted to the bank and from these records payroll checks are prepared. The bank also maintains the necessary social security and income tax records. In addition, a summary is prepared showing the total man-hours per week for each job. At present, no consistent use is made of this information. However, on the occasions when he has examined these weekly reports, Mr. Waller has found that the total hours per week run as much as 400 hours in excess of the number of hours used in computing the price of the services. There is no record of the use of supplies for each job.

Questions

1. Is there a need for control in this company? Why?
2. If controls are needed, which areas of the business are most in need of control?
3. What type of standards are now being used? What kind would you recommend?
4. How can the organization be modified to improve the control function?

---

* Used with the permission of Henry I. Sisk, *Management and Organization* (Cincinnati: Southwestern Publishing Com pany, 1977).

1-19. *The Board of Directors*

The Board of Directors of a corporation must recognize its responsibilities from both an external and internal perspective. The external perspective is necessary in its responsibility to represent the stockholders, and the internal perspective is essential in the understanding of internal financial and operating data and problems. One description of the responsibilities the Board of Directors must accept is the following:

* Plan for and evaluate corporate economic or strategic performance.
* Evaluate managerial performance and plan for management succession.
* Ensure that the company is socially responsible and complies with relevant laws and regulations.
* Ensure the integrity of the company's externally disseminated financial statements and reports.

To handle these responsibilities effectively and efficiently, corporate boards establish committees for selected areas. The Board committees most frequently found for the Fortune 500 corporations are: audit, compensation, nominating, executive, and finance.

Questions
1. Identify and discuss the type and nature of financial information that should be provided to a corporate Board so it can properly discharge the specific responsibilities listed above.
2. Discuss the types of activities for which each of the committees of the Board identified above would likely be responsible.

CHAPTER 1 SUPPLEMENT

The Accounting Cycle and Transaction Processing

The processing of business transactions that occurs in the performance of an organization's accounting cycle will be discussed in this supplement. We will stress the various types of information that are provided to external and internal parties as a result of executing effectively the accounting cycle steps.

Figure 1-8 illustrates the typical accounting cycle steps utilized by most organizations for processing their business transactions.

Financial statements provide useful information to current and potential investors, creditors, management, and so on, regarding the periodic operating success of a company (reflected by the **income statement**), the financial condition of a company as of a specific data (reflected by the **balance sheet**), and the periodic inflows and outflows of cash (reflected by the **statement of cash flows**). In order to obtain the monetary amounts for their financial statements, organizations must maintain a record-keeping system on a day-to-day basis. This system, in effect, transforms *data* that are generated by a company's day-to-day business transactions (e.g., selling merchandise, purchasing inventory, and paying liabilities) into meaningful *information* for communication to external parties (as well as the company's management). This data-transformation process is called the **accounting cycle.**

We will now examine each of the nine accounting cycle steps illustrated in Figure 1-8. The discussions will stress their information-providing aspects. Thus, by analyzing the accounting cycle steps, we will give examples of the types of information that are provided by a company's accounting information system.

Step 1: Preparing Transaction Source Documents
An accounting "business transaction" results from any monetary event that causes a change in an asset, liability, owners' equity, revenue, or expense account. Remember, separate accounts are maintained in an organization for every monetary item so that information is available regarding the dollar balances of these individual financial items—the dollar balance of *cash,* the dollar balance of *accounts receivable,* the dollar balance of *notes payable,* and so on. Transactions can occur from business activities between a company and either some external party (e.g., when the Alan Company sells sporting goods to a customer) or an internal party (e.g., when the Alan Company pays its employees their salaries).

Accounting Cycle Steps

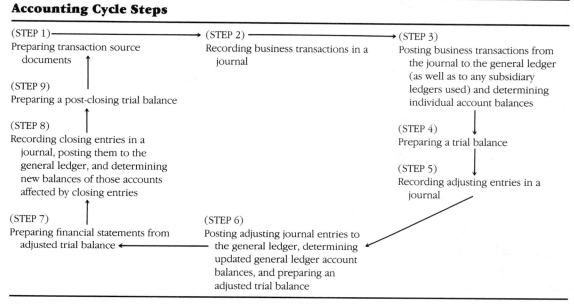

(STEP 1)
Preparing transaction source documents

(STEP 9)
Preparing a post-closing trial balance

(STEP 8)
Recording closing entries in a journal, posting them to the general ledger, and determining new balances of those accounts affected by closing entries

(STEP 7)
Preparing financial statements from adjusted trial balance

(STEP 2)
Recording business transactions in a journal

(STEP 6)
Posting adjusting journal entries to the general ledger, determining updated general ledger account balances, and preparing an adjusted trial balance

(STEP 3)
Posting business transactions from the journal to the general ledger (as well as to any subsidiary ledgers used) and determining individual account balances

(STEP 4)
Preparing a trial balance

(STEP 5)
Recording adjusting entries in a journal

FIGURE 1-8 Accounting cycle steps.

For a business transaction to enter an organization's accounting information system, it must be quantitative and also be measurable in monetary terms.

Business transactions result in the creation of **source documents.** To illustrate, assume that a customer of the Alan Company purchases several footballs. This sale will trigger the preparation of a sales invoice by an Alan Company sales clerk. The sales invoice represents a transaction *source document* (also called an **original record**), which is the basis for entering the football sales transaction into the Alan Company's accounting information system. As shown in Figure 1-7, a sales invoice source document is used as "input" for the financial accounting audit trail.

Source documents represent visual evidence regarding the occurrence of business transactions. In many companies today a financial transaction is not subject to entry into their accounting information systems until proper source documents are prepared and approved. The types of source documents used by businesses will vary depending on each firm's special operating characteristics. A few of the more common source documents used by busi-

ness organizations, in addition to the previously discussed *sales invoice,* are as follows.

Purchase invoices	Reflect the bills received from another company for the quantity and cost of inventory items or other assets purchased from that company.
Receiving reports	Reflect the actual quantity of inventory items or other assets delivered to a company from another company.
Bills of lading	Reflect the freight charges on physical goods shipped to a company.
Employee time cards	Reflect the number of hours worked by a company's employees during a specific pay period (the time card is the basis for comput-

Voucher checks   ing an employee's salary)

Reflect the payees (i.e., individuals to whom cash is paid) and amounts paid for various goods and services.

By utilizing source documents, a company can collect (or accumulate) its transaction data for subsequent entry into the accounting information system. Furthermore, the transaction source documents represent the starting point in a company's **audit trail** through its information system's accounting cycle. The efficient collection of accounting data in a format in which they can be properly reflected within an accounting information system will be analyzed in Chapter 5.

Step 2: Recording Business Transactions in a Journal

After accounting data are collected on a source document, they are recorded in a company's journal. A journal is kept within an accounting information system to provide an organization with a chronological record of the economic activities (measured in monetary terms) that occur throughout its life. If, for example, a managerial executive needs information regarding specific economic activities that took place on June 12, 1991, the executive can turn to the page (or pages) of the company's journal used on that date. It should be noted that if a company processes accounting data with a computer, the journal might be maintained on a storage medium such as magnetic tape. In this case, a computer printout of that day's journal entries would have to be prepared.

In many organizations a large volume of monetary transactions occur during accounting periods, but normally these transactions can be classified within a few broad categories (discussed below). The classification of transactions by categories permits the firms' accounting information systems to process efficiently the hun-

dreds or thousands of monetary events that take place. Furthermore, the enormous volume of transactions is one of the major factors causing many organizations to replace their manual accounting information systems with computerized accounting information systems. Some of the more common categories of business transactions are (1) the purchase of economic resources (i.e., assets), (2) the incurrence of operating expenses, (3) the sale of products and services, and (4) the receipt and payment of cash. A very important category of business transactions (not listed above) commonly found in a manufacturing firm relates to the accumulation of production costs (i.e., the direct raw materials, the direct labor, and the production overhead) associated with the firm's "work in process inventory" and "finished goods inventory" accounts. To review the processing of business transactions and to emphasize the relevant information that is generated from business transaction processing, we will discuss each one of the four broad categories of transactions just described.

1. Purchase of Economic Resources In a merchandising firm, two major types of asset resources acquired are (1) inventory (a current asset) and (2) equipment such as cash registers and display racks (long-term assets). The basic journal entries to reflect the acquisitions of these types of asset resources are as follows:

(1) *Acquisition of Inventory*
Merchandise inventory*	X	
Accounts payable		X

(2) *Acquisition of Equipment*
Equipment	X	
Due to equipment suppliers†		X

---

* This *debit* assumes the use of a perpetual inventory system. If a periodic inventory system were employed, the "purchases" account rather than the "merchandise inventory" account would be *debited*.

† Because many companies use their "accounts payable" liability account only to reflect credit purchases of inventory, a special liability account "due to equipment suppliers" is therefore *credited* here.

If cash is paid immediately for the acquisition of inventory or equipment, the transaction would be classified under category 4—the receipt and payment of cash. Examining journal entry (1), the "merchandise inventory" account is a general ledger asset account that accumulates the total costs of all inventory items acquired for eventual sale to customers. In those companies that sell several products, a subsidiary inventory ledger would likely be maintained. This subsidiary ledger would contain a separate account for each inventory item. The use of individual inventory accounts within the subsidiary ledger enables a company's managers to know the quantity and cost balance of every inventory item. This information, which is not provided by the general ledger inventory account, is essential to management in planning the acquisitions of additional inventory product items (for those products whose subsidiary ledger balances have reached their economic reorder points) and in analyzing slow-moving inventory items (products whose subsidiary ledger balances have little or no reductions from sales transactions). If a company has a larger number of suppliers from whom it purchases inventory on credit, detailed managerial information regarding the dollar amounts owed to each creditor is essential so that future cash disbursements can be planned. In addition, for those creditors offering cash discount terms such as 2/10, n/30, the company needs information about the specific cash discount terms of each creditor so that the various creditors can be paid within the allowed discount periods. The accounting information system can provide management with data concerning accounts payable liabilities through the utilization of an accounts payable subsidiary ledger. [Note that the *credit* part of journal entry (1) is to the accounts payable general ledger account.] Within this subsidiary ledger, a separate account is maintained for each creditor, indicating such things as the dollar balance due and the cash discount terms available.

In journal entry (2), the general ledger "equipment" account is *debited* for long-term asset acquisitions. To provide management with

detailed information about each piece of equipment (such as its cost, estimated useful life, and estimated salvage value for computing the annual depreciation), an equipment subsidiary ledger containing a separate account for each equipment item can be used.

2. Incurrence of Operating Expenses The basic journal entry to recognize a company's operating expenses is shown below (this entry is merely a generalized summary to illustrate operating expenses that may occur in an organization).

Operating Expenses

Wages expense	X	
Payroll taxes expense	X	
Rent expense	X	
Advertising expense	X	
Utilities expense	X	
Wages payable		X
Taxes payable on wages		
(separate accounts would		
be used for FICA taxes,		
withholding taxes, etc.)		X
Rent payable		X
Advertising payable		X
Utilities payable		X

Note that this journal entry is illustrative of only some of the more common business operating expenses. Individual companies are likely to have many other operating expenses. Also, an expense transaction in which cash is immediately paid would be classified under category 4—the receipt and payment of cash.

To determine the operating expenses for "wages expense" and "payroll taxes expense" as well as the liabilities for "wages payable" and "taxes payable on wages," detailed payroll data would have to be maintained within a company's accounting information system. A payroll subsidiary ledger containing a separate account for each employee would likely be used. The accounting information system must accumulate within this subsidiary ledger specific payroll data about every employee (such as social security number, exemptions claimed, gross earnings, deductions for FICA and withholding taxes, and net pay) for both tax and financial statement reporting purposes. In a manufacturing firm, the accounting information system must be designed to distinguish between production wages and nonproduction wages. Regarding production wages, a further distinction is necessary between the wages of direct laborers (which are debited to the inventory manufacturing accounts) and indirect laborers (which are debited to the production overhead accounts). The wages earned by nonproduction employees (salespersons, administrative employees, etc.), on the other hand, are recognized as operating expenses of the period in which they are incurred. Because of the large volume of computations often required in payroll, computerized payroll processing is a tremendous time saver.

The expenses recorded for rent, advertising, and utilities are reflective of typical operating efforts in carrying out a company's business activities. The month-end dollar balance of the advertising expense account, for example, would likely be of interest to a company's marketing manager. By relating the balance of this account to the company's month-end sales account balance, the marketing manager has a basis for evaluating the effectiveness of various advertising endeavors (e.g., commercials on radio and television, display ads in newspapers, etc.).

3. Sale of Products and Services A merchandising firm (such as a hardware or clothing store) sells a *tangible* product to its customers, whereas a service organization (such as a law firm or medical clinic) sells an *intangible* product. Presented here are the basic journal entries to reflect the revenue-earning functions of (1) a merchandising firm and (2) a service organization (in our example, a law firm).

(1) *Merchandising Firm*
Accounts receivable	X	
Product sales revenue		X
Cost of merchandise sold	X	
Merchandise inventory		X

(2) *Service Organization*
Accounts receivable	X	
Legal services revenue		X

If cash is received immediately at the time merchandising firms or service organizations perform their revenue-earning functions, the revenue recognition transactions would be classified under category 4—the receipt and payment of cash. Several detailed records supporting a merchandising firm's journal entries that reflect its product sales are maintained within the firm's accounting information system. To provide credit and collection department managers with information regarding the dollar balance owed to the firm by each credit customer, an accounts receivable subsidiary ledger could be used. The total of the individual customer account balances within the subsidiary ledger should equal the total of the general ledger accounts receivable account. Many companies that have a large volume of credit sales transactions use computers to maintain their accounts receivable subsidiary ledgers. Once a week, for example, credit-sales transactions of a company together with customer payments can be recorded by the EDP subsystem's computer to update the accounts receivable subsidiary ledger. In addition, the computer can be programmed to prepare a weekly accounts receivable aging analysis (which provides valuable information to credit and collection department managers concerning the effectiveness of their firm's credit-granting policies) and customers' monthly billing statements.

The merchandising firm can also maintain a product sales subsidiary ledger to support the various *credits* to its general ledger product sales revenue account. This subsidiary ledger might include such detailed information as sales by product lines, sales by individual salespersons, and sales by regions of the country. These types of sales information would be extremely vital to the firm's marketing managers in evaluating prior periods' sales activities and in forecasting future sales.

The second journal entry illustrated for the merchandising firm assumes the use of a *perpetual* inventory system, whereby the cost of merchandise sold expense account and the merchandise inventory asset account are updated at the time of each sales transaction. Separate detailed subsidiary ledgers can be maintained within the accounting information system to support the cost of merchandise sold and the merchandise inventory general ledger accounts. The cost of merchandise sold subsidiary ledger would include detailed cost information about each product item sold. This information, as well as information from the product sales subsidiary ledger, enables accounting employees to analyze the profit margins of the firm's various product lines. With the foregoing information available, the firm's marketing managers can better plan their company's future sales mix of specific products by emphasizing those product lines having the largest profit margins. As discussed previously, a subsidiary inventory ledger provides important information for planning the acquisitions of additional inventory product items and for analyzing slow-moving inventory product items.

Since a law firm does not sell a tangible product, its journal entry to reflect earned revenue would include only a *debit* to the accounts receivable account (or if cash is immediately received, a *debit* to the cash account) and a *credit* to the legal services revenue account. For those service organizations that bill customers for work performed, the use of accounts receivable subsidiary ledgers would provide them with important information regarding the dollar balance owed by each customer. In a service organization that provides a variety of services, a subsidiary ledger to support the organization's general ledger revenue account can provide useful information for managers. For example, the law firm's subsidiary ledger relating to its legal services revenue general ledger account would contain specific information about the firm's earned revenues from each of its many legal services (such as revenues from divorce cases, revenues from felony cases, and revenues from estate and trust cases). By examining this subsidiary ledger, the partners of the law firm are able to analyze the types of legal services that are earning the greatest revenues.

4. Receipt and Payment of Cash Many businesses (both merchandising and service organizations) have cash receipts from two major types of transactions: (1) cash sales and (2) collections of accounts receivable from previous credit sales. The basic journal entry to reflect cash receipts from these two types of business transactions is as follows.

Cash Receipts

Cash	X	
Product sales revenue*		X
Accounts receivable		X

*For a service organization, the account title *service sales revenue* could be used.

As discussed previously, subsidiary ledgers can be maintained for each of the general ledger accounts (i.e., product sales revenue and accounts receivable) *credited* in the preceding journal entry.

It is quite common for most companies to make cash payments based on previously incurred liabilities. Therefore, the following journal entry is representative of an organization's cash payment activities.

Cash Payments

Accounts payable	X	
Due to equipment suppliers	X	
Taxes payable on wages (separate		
accounts would be used for		
FICA taxes paid, withholding		
taxes paid, etc.)	X	
Rent payable	X	
Advertising payable	X	
Utilities payable	X	
Cash		X

Each of the *debits* is to a liability account, indicating a reduction in the liability as a result of making a cash payment. For any of the liability accounts in which there is a large volume of transactions (such as accounts payable), a subsidiary ledger providing detailed information about the individual transactions affecting the account can be maintained.

Current information regarding a company's cash account balance is very important to management (especially to the financial executives within the finance subsystem). In those organizations having a finance subsystem separate from accounting, the finance managers are responsible for their company's cash planning. Cash planning involves a projection of the future *sources* of cash (e.g., cash sales, collections of accounts receivable, and sales of stocks and bonds) and the future *uses* of cash (e.g., operating expense payments, interest payments to bondholders and short-term creditors, and dividend payments to stockholders). Following a company's cash planning activities, the cash account should be monitored quite closely by the finance managers. This monitoring of cash enables the finance managers to ascertain whether the actual cash activities (reflected by the cash account) are in line with the original cash planning projections.

If, for example, the cash account balance is becoming too large, the finance managers should examine possible investment opportunities for this excessive cash. Because the buildup of cash within an organization's checking account does not contribute to a positive rate of return on assets, the finance managers may want to consider investing excessive cash in more productive assets such as marketable securities. On the other hand, should the cash account balance become too small, a company may find it difficult to meet some of its liabilities that are coming due. Consequently, the finance managers will have to investigate possible sources of cash (such as borrowing money from the bank) to avoid being delinquent in paying any liabilities. If an unanticipated capital acquisition becomes necessary (e.g., a major piece of manufacturing equipment requires replacement), a heavy drain on a company's cash balance can result. To obtain the needed cash for the purchase of an expensive piece of equipment or other long-term asset, the finance managers may want to consider issuing bonds or selling additional stock.

Step 3: Posting Business Transactions from the Journal to the General Ledger and Determining Individual Account Balances

Within an accounting information system, a *general ledger* is a "book" containing detailed monetary information about an organization's various assets, liabilities, owners' equity, revenues, and expenses. A separate account (often called a T account) is established for each type of monetary item in a business firm. Without information available to both external and internal parties regarding the dollar balances of the firm's many assets, liabilites, and so on, successful business performance would be difficult because effective organizational decisions by external parties (e.g., potential investors and creditors) as well as internal parties (e.g., management) are often based on specific account-balance information. If the Alan Company's personnel manager, for example, wants accounting information concerning the total wages paid to employees after the first quarter of the year, he or she can refer to the page in the general ledger where the T account for wages expense is located.

Step 2 of our accounting cycle involved the recording of business transactions in a journal. As was emphasized during the step 2 discussion, the journal provides a chronological record of all monetary events occurring in a company and indicates the accounts and amounts of the *debits* and *credits* for every business transaction. However, this journal fails to provide information regarding the individual dollar balances of the various financial items in a company. For example, if an organization's managers wished to know the monetary balance of their company's accounts receivable asset, they would find this information in the specific T account maintained for accounts receivable in the general ledger. The journal, on the other hand, would *not* provide information regarding the actual dollar balance of accounts receivable. Rather, it would include only the various *debits* and *credits* that were recorded to the accounts receivable account during a specific time period (e.g., one month). Therefore, to provide management with information concerning the accounts receivable dollar balance, the specific debits and credits recorded in the journal for accounts receivable must be transferred to the T account for accounts receivable in the general ledger through a process called *posting*. (The *debits* and *credits* to accounts receivable would also be posted to the specific customers' accounts within the accounts receivable subsidiary ledger.) After the posting process is completed, the dollar balance of each general ledger account is determined.

For a company to have an effective accounting information system, both a journal and a general ledger are necessary. The major benefit of a journal is that it provides a complete chronological listing of an organization's monetary transactions. The journal tells the "complete story" of each business transaction, because the debit and credit parts of the transaction are shown together with a short explanation. However, without a general ledger, it would be rather difficult to determine the monetary balances of the individual accounts. The general ledger takes over where the journal leaves off by providing information regarding the dollar balances of an organization's accounts. On the other hand, the general ledger does not disclose in one location the complete picture of an economic transaction. For example, the *debit* part of a transaction may be recorded in account number 200 of the general ledger, whereas the *credit* part of this same transaction may be recorded in account number 380. Functioning together in a company's accounting information system, the journal and the general ledger provide relevant information about the monetary transactions that have occurred. The posting process provides a cross-reference between the two.

Step 4: Preparing a Trial Balance

The time period over which companies prepare financial statements (e.g., monthly, quarterly, semiannually, yearly) is determined by individual company policy. Because income taxes, both federal and state, must be paid to the government each year, a firm must prepare financial statements at least once a year as a basis for computing its tax liability.

When a company wants to prepare an income statement and a balance sheet (i.e., its financial statements), all of the posting work must be finished so that the dollar balances of the various general ledger accounts, which are used in preparing the financial statements, can be determined. Assume that the Alan Company prepares monthly financial statements. Therefore, by the end of every month, all of the company's posting from its journal to the specific general ledger accounts should be completed. Upon completion of this posting work, each general ledger account balance is determined so that the company will know the dollar amounts of its individual accounts.

After these account balances are computed, a financial schedule called a **trial balance** is prepared. A trial balance lists all the general ledger accounts together with their end-of-period dollar balances. The trial balance facilitates (1) the determination of whether the *total debit* and *total credit* account balances are *equal* and (2) the preparation of a company's financial statements. The trial balance is just what its name implies, a "trial run" to ascertain the monetary equality of an organization's accounts with *debit* and *credit* balances before the organization's financial statements are formally prepared.

Step 5: Recording Adjusting Entries in a Journal

After finishing step 4 of the accounting cycle, a company's general ledger accounts have dollar balances within them which represent the account balances at the end of a specific time period (e.g., a month or a year). Before preparing the company's financial statements, however, certain **adjustments** (adjusting journal entries) may be necessary in the accounts. The need for adjusting journal entries within an accounting information system is based on two accounting principles: (1) the **periodicity** principle and (2) the **matching** principle.

The *periodicity* principle is derived from the word *periodic*, which means "occurring at regular intervals." In accounting, we assume that after a specific time period (a month, six months, a year, etc.), a company can accurately determine the dollar balances of its general ledger accounts and then prepare its financial statements. This process is commonly called adjusting and closing the books. (The **books** are an organization's accounting records: the journal, the general ledger, etc.) At the end of a month, for example, when a business firm wants to prepare its income statement and balance sheet, the *periodicity* principle assumes that the firm is at a specific "cutoff point" in its operating activities and can therefore provide relevant financial information to interested parties such as potential investors, creditors, and management. These parties do not want to wait until the end of a firm's life to acquire financial information. They want it at specific times throughout the organization's operating life. The periodicity principle enables a company to provide financial statements at specific time intervals prior to the company's termination. Furthermore, an organization *should* attempt periodically to present to its financial statement users the most accurate income statement and balance sheet possible. This will give them reliable information for financial decision making regarding the organization.

The objective of the *matching* principle is the accurate computation of a company's net income (or net loss) as well as the accurate determination of dollar amounts for balance sheet accounts each time the company's financial statements are prepared. An organization should recognize "revenues" when they have been *earned,* either by selling products or providing services to customers (even though cash has not yet been received), and "expenses" should be recognized upon receiving a *service* from someone or something (even though cash has not yet been paid). The matching principle attempts to relate accurately a company's *revenues earned* (i.e., the *accomplishments*) to the *expenses incurred* (i.e., the *efforts put forth*) in earning those revenues prior to the preparation of the financial statements.

Basically, there are four major types of adjusting entries possible at the end of a company's accounting period, as described in the following list.

1. Adjusting entries for *accrued liabilities* (commonly referred to as *unrecorded expenses*).
   Example:

Wages expense	X	
Accrued wages payable		X

2. Adjusting entries for *accrued assets* (commonly referred to as *unrecorded revenues*).
   Example:

Accrued rent receivable	X	
Rent revenue		X

3. Adjusting entries for *prepaid assets* (commonly referred to as *deferred expenses* or *prepaid expenses*).
   Example:

Insurance expense	X	
Prepaid insurance		X

4. Adjusting entries for *advanced payments by customers* (commonly referred to as *deferred revenues*).
   Example:

Advanced payment for services*	X	
Services revenue		X

*This account is a liability account which would be initially *credited* when the advanced payment is received. Having provided the customer with some product or service, the company records the above adjusting entry at period end.

These four examples of adjusting entries do not represent all the types of adjustments necessary for a business firm at the end of its accounting period. However, they do illustrate the adjusting-entry concept. At the end of an accounting period, when a company wants to prepare financial statements, it should strive for accuracy within the financial data. To achieve this accuracy, all the monetary activities during the accounting period should be examined and a determination made if anything has happened that is not presently recognized in the accounting records. If unrecorded economic events exist, adjusting entries are required. After all adjusting entries are recorded, an organization's financial data have been updated. The resulting financial statements reflect a more accurate picture of the organization's business activities for the accounting period, thereby providing better information for decision making to the statements' users.

Step 6: Posting Adjusting Journal Entries to the General Ledger, Determining Updated General Ledger Account Balances, and Preparing an Adjusted Trial Balance

After a firm's adjusting entries are recorded in the journal, the debits and credits of these entries are *posted* to the correct general ledger accounts in the same manner as the regular business transactions recorded during the accounting period. Upon completion of the posting work, the updated monetary balances of those accounts affected by the adjusting journal entries are determined. Once this is done, a company's financial data are current for the preparation of its financial statements. Preceding the preparation of the income statement and balance sheet, however, is an **adjusted trial balance.** Because a trial balance is prepared after all business transactions during an accounting period are recorded and posted and each general ledger account balance is determined, the equality of total debits and total credits within the accounts is ascertained before the adjusting journal entries are recorded and posted. The purpose of preparing this second trial balance (called the adjusted trial balance) is to determine if the equality of debit and credit account balances still exists following the adjusting entry process.

Step 7: Preparing Financial Statements from Adjusted Trial Balance

When the adjusted trial balance is finished and thus reflects the updated financial data, the financial statements (principally the income statement and the balance sheet) can be prepared. The adjusted trial balance contains all the information needed for the preparation of the financial statements. Figure 1-9 illustrates a computerized printout of the Alan Company's income statement and balance sheet.

Step 8: Recording Closing Entries in a Journal, Posting Them to the General Ledger, and Determining New Balances of Those Accounts Affected by Closing Entries

An organization's revenue and expense accounts are *subdivisions* of the owners' equity accounts. The major reason for utilizing separate revenue and expense accounts is to provide better information about a company's operating activities to management and other interested parties. Remember, however, that a business firm's net income or loss belongs to its owner (or owners). Therefore, at the end of an accounting period, a company records and posts **closing entries** to eliminate its individual revenue and expense account balances and transfer the net income (or net loss) into the owner's (or owners') equity account (or accounts). Because revenue and expense accounts are subdivisions of the owners' equity accounts, whose balances are closed at the end of an accounting period, revenue and expense accounts are often called **temporary accounts** or **nominal accounts** (since they are "temporarily" established each accounting period in order to accumulate the monetary information regarding the period's operating activities). On the other hand, balance sheet accounts (the asset, liability, and owners' equity accounts) are not subdivisions of any other business accounts whose balances are closed at period-end, and are thus often called **permanent accounts** or **real accounts.**

It is important for a company to prepare financial statements as soon as possible after the close of its accounting period so that the information contained in the financial statements is available for analysis by groups such as management, potential and current investors, and creditors. The owners' equity accounts on the company's balance sheet include the net income (or net loss) for the particular period. Before the recording and posting of the closing journal entries, however, the owners' general ledger accounts do not include the net income (or net loss) for the accounting period. To update the owners' capital accounts and thereby have them agree with the

Alan Company

Income Statement
For the Month Ended January 31, 1991

Sporting goods sales		$50,000
Less: Sales returns and allowances	$ 1,000	
Sales discounts	800	1,800
Net sales		$48,200
Less: Cost of sporting goods merchandise sold		18,000
Gross profit on sales		$30,200
Operating expenses		
Administrative expenses	$15,000	
Selling expenses	10,000	
Total operating expenses		25,000
Income from operations		$ 5,200
Less: Nonoperating items		500
Interest expense		
Net income		$ 4,700

Balance Sheet
January 31, 1991

Assets

Current assets:			
Cash		$ 5,000	
Accounts receivable (net)		8,000	
Raw materials inventory	$ 1,500		
Production in process inventory	5,000		
Finished goods inventory	15,000	21,500	
Office supplies		650	
Prepaid expenses		500	
Total current assets			$35,650
Long-term assets:			
Machinery and equipment		$200,000	
Less: Accumulated depreciation		50,000	150,000
Total assets			$185,650

Equities

Current liabilities:			
Accounts payable	$18,000		
Wages payable	2,000		
Total current liabilities		$ 20,000	
Long-term liabilities:			
Notes payable (due in 3 years)		30,000	
Total liabilities			$ 50,000
Stockholders' equity:			
Common stock, $20 par value (6,000 shares			
authorized, 5,000 shares issued)		$100,000	
Retained earnings		35,650	
Total stockholders' equity			135,650
Total equities			$185,650

FIGURE 1-9

owners' equity shown on the balance sheet, closing journal entries are recorded and posted (and the new balances determined for those accounts affected by the closing entries) upon completion of the financial statements.

Step 9: Preparing a Post-Closing Trial Balance

After a company's closing entries are journalized and posted, all the revenue and expense accounts have *zero* dollar balances and the owners' equity capital accounts include the current period's net income (or net loss). A **post-closing trial balance** is then prepared to ascertain if the accounts with debit balances equal those with credit balances. (Remember, the last time we prepared a trial balance in our accounting cycle was in step 6, the *adjusted trial balance*.) The preparation of the post-closing trial balance is the final accounting cycle step. The "equality" of debit and credit account balances provides a company some assurance that no errors were made in its accounting records during the period. The company is then ready to repeat the accounting cycle for the next period.

Summarizing Comments on the Accounting Cycle

Since the major objective of the nine accounting cycle steps is to enable a business to prepare its financial statements as well as update the dollar balances of its general ledger accounts, the length of the cycle is determined by how often these statements are prepared. If monthly financial statements are desired, for example, the accounting cycle is repeated every month. There are, however, exceptions to this rule that specific firms incorporate into their accounting information systems. For example, certain organizations may prepare monthly financial statements without going through the formal process of recording and posting their closing journal entries each month. Rather, they wait until year-end to journalize and post the closing entries. The monthly performance of the accounting cycle would thus involve only steps 1 through 7. Then, at the end of the year, steps 8 and 9 (involving the closing entry process and the post-closing trial balance) would be performed along with steps 1 through 7.

 **2**

Management Concepts and Their Effects on Accounting Information Systems

Among the important questions that you should be able to answer after reading this chapter are:

1. Why don't most organizations attempt to maximize their long-run profits?
2. How can an organization's accounting information system help control environmental pollution?
3. How do the accounting and electronic data processing subsystems interact in developing and implementing a responsibility accounting system with a management-by-exception reporting structure?
4. Why is knowledge of a company's organizational structure important in the design of the accounting information system?
5. How can an organization integrate centralization and decentralization into its structural design?
6. Is it preferable to locate an organization's data processing function within the accounting subsystem or as a separate subsystem?

INTRODUCTION

Today's accountant is an important contributor to management decision making. To operate a business efficiently and effectively, management requires information for both short-range decisions (affecting the current 12-month period) and long-range decisions (affecting several years into the future). For accountants to provide management with this short-range and long-range information, they must understand the organization's structural design. Knowledge of the organizational structure will make accountants aware of the specific types of information required for decision making at the various managerial levels (top management, operating management, etc.). The accountants can then communicate the relevant information to man-

agers so they can make effective organizational decisions. This chapter discusses some important management concepts that underlie an organization's structural design. Those management concepts that are essential for accountants to understand in order to perform their information communication function effectively are emphasized. Additional management concepts of importance to accountants when performing systems studies will be analyzed in later chapters. As discussed in Chapter 1, a company's accounting subsystem performs a service function of converting financially-oriented data into useful information. Consequently, the accounting subsystem can be referred to as the accounting information system. In this chapter, as well as later ones, the term *accounting information system* will therefore be used as a synonym for the accounting subsystem.

ESTABLISHING ORGANIZATIONAL GOALS (A PLANNING FUNCTION)

Accountants must thoroughly understand their organization's goals in order to make a positive contribution to their accomplishment. A **goal** basically represents what one is attempting to achieve. Most people, as well as organizations, have several goals. Ideally, the multiplicity of goals that employees and their organizations have should be in harmony with each other. The harmony among employees' goals and organizational goals is called **goal congruence.** This means that in the process of achieving personal goals, the individual employee also contributes toward accomplishing organizational goals. On the other hand, frustration can result when the positive achievement of one goal conflicts with other goals, which is called **goal incongruence.** This type of frustration occurs in both individuals and organizations.

Organization theory suggests that an individual usually joins a company for personal gain but, in the course of time, gradually learns to accept, and work toward, the company's goals.

Both large and small businesses encourage such learning and acceptance of organizational goals by permitting employees to participate in developing these goals; by creating profit-sharing and employee professional improvement programs; by organizing social activities such as bowling leagues, picnics, and the like, which create the feeling of a working "family"; and, in general, by making employees feel that it is their company. Nevertheless, discord between personal goals and organizational goals still can occur. One example would be the individual's desire for promotion to an area for which he or she is not fully qualified. You might also recognize the above example as the "Peter principle"—a person is promoted to his or her level of incompetency. In such situations, the individual's goal of personal achievement conflicts with the organization's goal of increased operating efficiency. Other examples of conflict include personal location preferences versus organizational needs, and personal desires for more subordinates versus organizational policy on maximum supervision (called span of control).

For an organization's multiplicity of goals to be in harmony, the organization should consider its employees' needs when establishing these goals. The accounting information system plays a major role in providing relevant information to an organization's management regarding the establishment and eventual achievement of its specific goals. An important way to resolve conflict is by providing information about organizational operations. The accounting information system attempts to provide this relevant information to each organizational subsystem (as well as to top management) so that the subsystems and top management can contribute positively to the company's goals, thereby avoiding goal conflict.

The two major organizational goal categories are (1) nonoperational goals (normally long-range, broadly stated goals of top management) and (2) operational goals (normally short-range goals established by each subsystem to contribute positively toward accomplishing the nonoperational goals). We will now discuss each of these categories.

Determining Nonoperational Goals (Typically a Long-Range Planning Function)

As discussed in Chapter 1, two important managerial functions are planning and controlling. Most organizations perform both long-range and short-range planning. The former is normally the function of an organization's top management and is sometimes also called **strategic planning.** Through its long-range strategic planning, the organization develops a "plan of attack" for the future. The strategies established by top management are usually expressed in broad, nonoperational terms. For example, the long-range nonoperational goals developed by the Alan Company's top management are the attainment of:

1. A satisfactory level of net income.
2. A high quality of manufactured sporting goods.
3. A responsive and motivated group of employees.
4. A contribution to a clean environment through pollution control.

These goals are nonoperational because they are stated very broadly and reflect the long-range accomplishments desired by the Alan Company's top management.

Chapter 1 pointed out that most organizations do not attempt to maximize their long-run incomes (or profits). Rather, they more commonly set a satisfactory profit performance as one of their goals. It is difficult to attach a quantitative number to this satisfactory level of income. Basically, a satisfactory income is below a maximizing income, which *satisfies* the various persons (the stockholders, the board of directors, etc.) associated with the specific organization. If management's profit performance fails to satisfy its stockholders, for example, many of the top managers may find themselves looking for other jobs.

Arguments Against Long-Run Profit Maximization Goal

There are three major reasons why most organizations strive for a satisfactory, rather than a maximizing, level of long-run net income. First, and probably most important, is the fact that a nonoperational goal of profit maximization would probably conflict with an organization's other nonoperational goals. Maximizing profits would require each of the specific nonoperational goals to also be directed toward profit. In many organizations, this does not occur. Often, one or more of an organization's nonoperational goals actually run counter to increasing profits. For example, some of the employee benefit programs that the Alan Company institutes (which will be reflected as additional operating expenses on the company's income statement) to achieve its nonoperational goal of a responsive and motivated work force may actually decrease the company's annual net income. Also, the additional expenditures incurred by the Alan Company in contributing to a clean environment will likely reduce profits. Thus, when an organization has a multiplicity of goals that are not all directed at increased profitability, considerable goal conflict could result if profit maximization were a goal. A satisfactory profit performance goal, however, should be in harmony with other organizational goals.

A second argument against profit maximization relates to an organization's difficulty in ascertaining its profit-maximizing performance level. Economists tell us that profit maximization occurs when an organization operates at the point where marginal revenue equals marginal cost. This theory sounds nice, but actually deriving the marginal revenue and marginal cost data for a specific company can be quite difficult, if not impossible.

Third, if an organization attempted to develop a current-year budget that incorporated a profit maximization goal, certain decisions may be made that actually harm long-run organizational performance. For example, within the Alan Company's marketing subsystem is a research and development component. Its function is to develop new and innovative products as well as improve the quality of current product lines. Because research and development costs represent operating expenses in the year of their incurrence, the Alan Company's managment could increase its 1991 income performance by reducing the current year's expenditures for research and development. However, this decision could lead to reduced profits in future years if the company's competitors continue to develop new and improved products. The long run effects of the Alan Company's attempt to maximize its short-run profits in 1991 might cause the company to obtain a smaller share of the future sporting goods sales market because of its competitors' superior products. This would obviously lead to a reduction of profits for the Alan Company in the long run.

Determining Operational Goals (Typically a Short-Range Planning Function)

Employees within the Alan Company's individual subsystems (accounting, production, marketing, finance, personnel, and electronic data processing) must thoroughly understand their company's long-range goals and attempt to contribute

positively to these goals. Each subsystem is responsible for developing operational goals that will help accomplish the company's nonoperational goals. To achieve these nonoperational goals, employees from the various subsystems should communicate with one another so that their goals are in harmony, rather than in conflict. We will now examine the role played by the Alan Company's accounting information system in achieving the company's operational goals.

Accounting Information System's Role in Achieving Operational Goals

The accounting information system's major contribution to the Alan Company's top-management nonoperational goals is the development of long-range as well as short-range operational budgets. Because budgets affect all organizational subsystems, the accountants must communicate with each subsystem's employees and seek their participation in planning, implementing, and controlling the budgetary system. Budgeting (both long-range and short-range budgets) will be covered extensively in Chapter 3. The purpose of briefly analyzing budgeting at this point is to show the accounting information system's major contribution to its organization's planning and controlling functions, which lead to the accomplishment of the organization's multiplicity of goals.

In its short-range planning, assume that the Alan Company wishes to prepare the 1991 operating budget. The company's budget committee, including representatives from top management and each of the company's subsystems, meets in September of 1990. Because of accountants' training as financial experts, and because the budget is a financial projection, the company's managerial accountants on the budget committee are appointed as committee coordinators. In the process of developing the 1991 budget, the committee's job is to make operational the previously stated nonoperational goals of top management. Each subsystem's operational budget should contribute positively to these goals.

We will now discuss the accounting information system's specific role in aiding the accomplishment of the Alan Company's four nonoperational goals (mentioned earlier).

Accounting Information System's Contribution to Nonoperational Goal of Satisfactory Net Income Performance

The previously discussed arguments against profit maximization should be understood by the accountants when they perform their functions as budget coordinators. Accountants on the budget committee must develop projected financial statements for 1991 that will guide the Alan Company toward satisfactory income performance.

For example, in accumulating the data for the company's 1991 projected income statement budget, the accountants must develop the revenue and expense estimations with an understanding of top management's goal to achieve satisfactory rather than maximizing profits. One of the major expenses on a manufacturing firm's income statement is its "cost of goods sold" resulting from sales of manufactured inventory items. When the accountants aid the production subsystem in developing its standard manufacturing costs for raw materials, direct labor, and production overhead, they should be aware of the company's goal of achieving satisfactory operating performance. Therefore, these standard manufacturing costs (determined in advance of production activity) should be based on a reasonably efficient level of performance rather than a maximizing performance output. Once determined, the company's standard manufacturing costs for its various types of sporting goods inventory items would represent useful information to aid the development of the production subsystem's 1991 operating budget.

In attempting to develop a satisfactory level of sales revenue for the 1991 income statement budget, the Alan Company's marketing subsystem must estimate the expected sales of the many sporting goods equipment product lines. Some techniques of forecasting sales demand will be discussed in Chapter 3. It should be emphasized here, however, that an important marketing subsystem function is to determine a satisfactory sales mix of product lines for the company's projected budget of sales items. A sales mix represents the quantity combination of the many products an organization hopes to sell. To aid the marketing subsystem in determining this sales mix, the Alan Company's accounting information system can provide marketing with relevant information regarding the manufacturing costs associated with the various sporting goods product items.

Accounting Information System's Contribution to Nonoperational Goal of High-Quality Manufactured Goods

The production subsystem has the primary responsibility for achieving this top-management goal. Production managers may hire quality control experts who inspect the manufactured sporting goods to make sure they meet the designated quality standards.

The accounting information system's major role concerning quality production would be to financially justify the level of quality sporting goods desired by top management. To execute this function, the accountants would perform a cost/benefit analysis for the Alan Company's individual sporting goods products. Ideally, the benefits expected from each product line (i.e., the revenues that eventually will result from selling the specific product) should exceed the company's costs in manufacturing it. At a minimum, each product line should make a positive **contribution margin** (excess of selling price over variable manufacturing, selling, and administrative expenses) toward covering those fixed costs associated with the product.

One of the important variable costs that affects the quality level of a company's manufactured product is the purchase price of the raw materials used in production. The accountant's analysis of the raw materials costs that would be necessary to achieve top management's desired production quality level may indicate that the high-quality materials needed for production are too costly, resulting in a negative product line contribution margin (total variable costs exceed selling price). With this information, the accountant may recommend that top management decrease the quality level for the specific product line. This would enable the production subsystem to purchase a lower-cost raw material. By slightly altering the finished product's quality level, the company may be able to convert a negative product line contribution margin to a positive one.

Once an agreement is reached regarding the quality level of raw materials for each manufactured product line, the accountant can further contribute to top management's quality product goal through timely performance reports disclosing any significant variations between the actual quality level of raw materials purchased and the quality level of raw materials that should have been purchased (based on the established quality standard). The subject of timely performance reports will be emphasized later in this chapter.

Accounting Information System's Contribution to Nonoperational Goal of Responsive and Motivated Employees

The personnel subsystem has the primary responsibility for achieving this goal. As a result of effective personnel selection procedures, adequate compensation, efficiently operating training programs, and the involvement of employees in challenging activities, the Alan Company's labor force should have positive attitudes toward their work environments.

The accountants, in performing their cost accounting, budgetary, and systems study functions, must consider the human element within a company. Rather than just informing the employees what their budget allowances will be or unilaterally introducing a systems change, for instance, the accountants should seek the employees' participation in making these decisions (*participative* management). Employees should be more responsive and positively motivated to achieve their company's goals if they participate in various decisions affecting their work environments.

Consider, for example, the process involved in developing the standard number of labor hours· in manufacturing the Alan Company's

many sporting goods product lines by the production subsystem. The accountants within the accounting information system would have a major role in developing these labor standards and subsequently reporting to management any significant variations between actual and standard labor hours. If the standards for employee performance are too high (**strict** standards), most production employees will be unable to attain them, causing management to evaluate the employees unfavorably. Obviously, this situation can lead to employee frustration. If, however, the accountants allow the production employees to participate in the development of the standards with the objective of setting the labor standards at a level that the "average" employee can achieve (**attainable** standards), the employees should feel that the standards are fairer. As a result, the employees should be more responsive and thus motivated to operate effectively under the standard cost system. Timely performance reports that compare actual with standard labor hours should motivate employees to perform favorably in relation to these "attainable" established standards. Further motivation can result from monetary and promotional benefits to those employees who perform favorably.

Another behavioral aspect of the accountants' organizational duties concerns the design of subsystem managers performance reports that fairly reflect each manager's contribution to top management's nonoperational goals. If a subsystem manager is evaluated on the basis of operating items over which he or she has no control, the individual may become frustrated. As will be emphasized later, the accountants can contribute to employee motivation by designing subsystem performance reports that evaluate each subsystem manager only on the manager's controllable operating activities. This is called a **responsibility accounting system.**

Accounting Information System's Contribution to Nonoperational Goal of a Clean Environment Through Pollution Control

The Alan Company's production subsystem makes an important contribution to this goal by utilizing efficient machinery and equipment in its manufacturing process, thereby minimizing environmental pollution.

The accounting information system's role in achieving adequate pollution control would be directed toward helping management decide which of the many possible pollution-reducing approaches is economically most efficient. For example, assume that the Alan Company's present manufacturing equipment is causing a level of environmental pollution in excess of minimum government pollution standards. The accountants could perform an analysis of the expected costs versus the expected benefits to the company of either making its current manufacturing equipment more efficient (possibly by adding pollution control devices to the equipment and replacing some of the motors, etc., on the older equipment) or completely modernizing the production plant (by disposing of this equipment and purchasing new equipment). The benefits that the accountants would attempt to measure from each alternative include such things as reduced pollution, improved quality of manufactured products (from using more efficient production equipment) which would likely lead to increased sales of the company's sporting goods, and the estimated increase in sporting goods sales resulting from the favorable public image created by the company's environmental pollution program. The accountants would recommend that pollution control alternative offering the greatest benefits in relation to its costs.

Once management has reached a decision regarding which pollution program to undertake (based on discussions between manufacturing department managers and top management) and has established its standard level of acceptable pollution, the accounting information system would provide pollution control *variance* reports. These reports would compare the actual levels of pollution from the new program with the predetermined standard pollution levels, thereby informing manufacturing department managers and top management whether or not their pollution control program is operating effectively. The accounting information system's role in environment control is only part of an important area in the accounting profession called **social reporting.** Under this type of reporting, accountants attempt to measure the impact on society of various organizational activities, such as energy conservation and fair employment practices (e.g., hiring a sufficient number of women and minorities).

EVALUATING THE ACHIEVEMENT OF ORGANIZATIONAL GOALS (A CONTROLLING FUNCTION)

Upon establishing each subsystem's operational goals (a planning function) that will contribute to top management's nonoperational goals, a reporting structure is needed to ascertain whether or not the subsystems' planned operational goals are being achieved. Through the controlling function of timely reports comparing each subsystem's actual performance with its budgeted performance, those organizational areas that are operating inefficiently can be determined and necessary corrective action taken. This controlling function is extremely crucial because without such evaluation reports, top management as well as operating management (i.e., the subsystem managers) would be unaware of a specific subsystem's contribution to the nonoperational goals. Figure 2-1 reflects the important relationship between organizational planning and controlling.

After an organization's plans are established, the controlling function takes over and monitors the success or failure of these plans. As Figure 2-1 illustrates, the controlling function can lead back to further planning where revisions are made to correct specific inefficient operating performance. Obviously, however, if actual performance is progressing according to original plans, revised planning will be unnecessary.

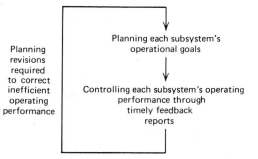

FIGURE 2-1   The planning and controlling relationship.

The Accounting Information System's Role in Performance Reporting

The principal function of managerial accounting is to communicate relevant information to internal parties. These internal parties include an organization's top management as well as the operational managers within each subsystem. Certain organizational communications are oral; however, a large amount of a company's communications takes place through written reports. An extremely important type of written report is the **performance report,** which evaluates a subsystem's success or failure in accomplishing its operational goals. One of the major criteria for assessing a subsystem's achievement of its operational goals is the subsystem's actual performance compared with its predetermined budget. Because accountants are usually the coordinators of their organization's budgetary system, they have the important function of designing and communicating the organization's performance reports.

For these reports to fulfill their control objectives, they must have two characteristics. First, the reports should be *timely* so that a minimum period elapses between an activity and the feedback reflecting its actual performance. Second, the reports should provide *relevant information* to their recipients so that they can take the necessary action to accomplish the organization's goals.

To achieve these two characteristics in performance reports, the accountants work closely with EDP employees. The speed of a computer in processing data has enabled faster feedback of performance information to individual subsystems and top management. This allows a subsystem's managers to correct inefficiencies in a shorter time following their occurrence. However, the computer's ability to process data quickly is unproductive to a company's decision making unless the data provided to the computer are relevant.

The data input stage is the principal link between the accounting information system and EDP. The accountants must understand the information needs of each manager (subsystem managers and top management) in their organization in order to accumulate for computer processing the relevant data needed for effective decision making.

An important organizational concept is the delegation of authority by top management to the managers within each subsystem. In small organizations, this is often minimal because the owner (or owners) is (are) aware of everything that occurs in the organization and can make all the necessary decisions. However, in large organizations, it is impossible for one or a few top managers to keep abreast of all organizational activities and make timely decisions within the various subsystems. Size and complexity have been the major factor causing top management to delegate decision-making authority to lower-level managers so that these organizations will function more efficiently. When a subsystem manager is given the authority to perform certain activities, this manager should also be held responsible for his or her actions. However, in the final analysis, top management remains responsible for the actions of its subsystem managers in achieving the organization's goals. Responsibility cannot be delegated from one individual to another. For example, if a specific subsystem fails to accomplish its operational goals, the organization's stockholders will hold top management responsible for this inefficiency.

The accountants should be aware of the authority and responsibility relationships within their organization because each subsystem's performance report must be "tailor-made" to measure the success or failure of the subsystem to execute those functions over which it has authority and responsibility.

Responsibility Accounting System for Performance Reporting

In designing performance reports that provide relevant information regarding the positive or negative contribution of each subsystem toward achieving the organization's nonoperational goals, the accountants should utilize a responsibility accounting system. Under this type of reporting system, they must first analyze the authority and responsibility structure of their organization. Then, a reporting system is developed whereby each subsystem is evaluated only on those activities over which it has *control*. A controllable item is one that the subsystem can cause to change. By evaluating a subsystem's performance on the basis of activities that it can control, a fairer and truer picture of its operating performance is obtained. Only those operating items over which the subsystem has control and for which it is therefore responsible should be included in its budget. The subsequent evaluation of a particular subsystem's performance would include a comparison of the subsystem's actual controllable items with its budgeted controllable items. Any significant variations between actual results and budget projections would be the responsibility of that subsystem.

A control system is normally not effective unless one can trace who is responsible for an inefficiency. Through a responsibility accounting system, inefficiencies within an organization can be traced to the specific subsystem (or subsystems) that caused them, and corrective action can then be planned.

Another important advantage of a responsibility accounting system is from a *behavioral point of view*. If a responsibility accounting system is not used, subsystems will often be evaluated on the basis of activities outside of their control. This can cause frustration to a subsystem's management. In many organizations, the accountants' performance report is the major criterion used by top management to evaluate a particular subsystem manager's effectiveness. Think of yourself for a minute as the Alan Company's manager of the basketball manufacturing department. Figure 2-2 illustrates two possible performance reports to evaluate your department during January 1991. Version 1 is based on a responsibility accounting system, whereas version 2 includes cost items over which you have no control (i.e., a nonresponsibility accounting system). Which of these two performance reports would you consider to be a truer picture of your effectiveness as basketball manufacturing department manager?

Figure 2-2 assumes that the basketball manufacturing department has authority and responsibility for the dollar expenditures on raw materials, direct labor, and variable overhead utilized in production (which may not be true in all organizations). Because the department's actual controllable costs were $500 below the January budget, you as the manager would likely receive a favorable evaluation on the basis of the version 1 report, which evaluates this department's performance based on the monetary items it can control.

The version 2 performance report could make you somewhat frustrated. Here, monetary items over which you have no control (the fixed overhead, the allocated selling and administrative expenses, and the allocated research and development expenses) are being charged to your budget and used to evaluate your subsequent performance. The end result is that your department's actual costs are $900 over the January budget, causing top management to look unfavorably at your department. The major factors causing the unfavorable performance were the three monetary items for which you had no authority and responsibility. For example, the $800

The Alan Company

Basketball Manufacturing Department Performance Report for the Month of January 1991

Version 1

Costs	Budget	Actual	Variation— Favorable (Unfavorable)
Raw materials for production	$ 6,000	$ 5,800	$200
Direct labor for production	10,000	10,100	(100)
Variable overhead	8,000	7,600	400
Totals	$24,000	$23,500	$500

The Alan Company

Basketball Manufacturing Department Performance Report for the Month of January 1991

Version 2

Costs	Budget	Actual	Variation— Favorable (Unfavorable)
Raw materials for production	$ 6,000	$ 5,800	$200
Direct labor for production	10,000	10,100	(100)
Variable overhead	8,000	7,600	400
Fixed overhead	7,000	7,200	(200)
Allocated selling and administrative expenses	3,000	3,800	(800)
Allocated research and development expenses	2,000	2,400	(400)
Totals	$36,000	$36,900	($900)

FIGURE 2-2

excess of allocated selling and administrative expenses over the budget may have been the result of overtime wages paid to administrative personnel. This overtime may have been necessary because of careless and inefficient performances by some administrative employees.

Naturally, if the Alan Company's top management executives received the version 2 report in Figure 2-2 and examined each line closely, they would see that your department performed successfully on its controllable financial items. But, as is sometimes true, top management may look only at the bottom line, indicating a $900 net unfavorable operating performance. Because top management now considers your department inefficient during January, your morale and motivation may drop considerably due to the unfair basis of evaluation.

Management-by-Exception for Performance Reporting

A common problem faced by many organizations having computerized management information systems is the massive quantity of data printed out by their computers. A company may intentionally create additional unnecessary reports just to feel it is obtaining full value from its expensive computer equipment. Another factor causing "excessive data reporting" is the status attached by many business managers to receiving internally generated reports. The more reports a manager receives, the greater importance the manager may attach to his or her role in an organization.

Whatever the causes of excessive reports may be, the result can often lead to inefficient decision making. If a subsystem manager is faced with a situation in which a quick decision is needed, the relevant information for this decision may be buried in the mass of reports on the manager's desk. Consequently, the manager may reach a decision based on some irrelevant criteria. If the needed information had been readily available, the manager's final decision may have made a more positive contribution to achieving the company's goals.

Along with designing a responsibility accounting system, the accountants can help reduce the massive number of reports flowing through a company's system by incorporating a management-by-exception reporting structure into their company. The underlying assumption of management-by-exception is that if a specific operating activity is progressing according to plan, there is no reason to report this information to management. Only when a particular activity deviates significantly from the original plan (an *exception*) should the information be immediately reported to the responsible manager (or managers) so that necessary action can be taken.

A management-by-exception reporting structure offers several advantages to a company. First, it reduces the length and number of reports generated by the company's information system because reports are prepared only when significant operating deviations exist and include only information about these significant deviations. This advantage results in important cost savings because processing a report and communicating it through the system can be costly. Second, management-by-exception reporting reduces the amount of time that highly paid managers must spend reading reports. They will therefore have additional time to perform more productive functions. Third, and perhaps most important, the managers will receive reports only when it is essential for them to take action on some aspect of their specific subsystem's performance. A subsystem exception report will thus direct a manager to actual operating functions that require immediate attention rather than to each of the subsystem's many activities, whether they need corrective adjustments or not.

What constitutes a significant variation from plan and should therefore be reported to management often involves subjective judgment. Accountants, with their understanding of an organization's financial operating activities, should have a valuable input to these decisions.

To demonstrate the advantages of a management-by-exception reporting system, assume that a weekly computerized report goes to the Alan Company's marketing managers comparing this subsystem's actual sales with its budgeted sales. The input for the report comes from each salesperson's actual orders as well as from the budget projections that the accounting information system helped develop. The format of this weekly report was designed by the company's accountants. Figure 2-3 illustrates the Alan Company's sales report for the third week of January 1991.

Imagine yourself as a manager in the Alan Company's marketing subsystem who reads this detailed sales report each week (together with many other market reports). You may become frustrated and begin skimming the large volume of reports that cross your desk. This could cause you to overlook some relevant information that requires your immediate attention. If a management-by-exception reporting structure had been designed by the accountants, the weekly computer printout would not include all the data in Figure 2-3, but only those budget variations that were considered significant. For example, examining the total budget and total actual sales of golf balls, the 70 cartons under budget may not be considered significant. After a closer look at the individual causes of this variation, however, two significant facts are revealed. Mr. Baker's golf ball sales in region F were 250 cartons under budget, whereas Ms. Worthley's sales in region S were 100 cartons over budget. Under management-by-exception reporting, this information about Baker and Worthley's golf ball sales would be provided to marketing management. Information regarding any one of the Alan Company's other product-line regional sales whose budget variations were considered significant would also be included.

Assume that accounting and marketing managers have agreed as to what constitutes a significant budget variation for each product line in the various sales regions. Figure 2-4 reflects the Alan Company's sales *exception report* for the third week of January 1991.

By comparing Figure 2-4 with Figure 2-3, it is obvious that the exception report will permit more efficient and effective decision making by the marketing managers. This exception report can be read faster than the complete sales data in Figure 2-3, and, more important, it immediately discloses those budget variations that are significant.

It is important to note that management-by-exception reports include both favorable and unfavorable budget variations. This reporting method can thus be a useful motivational device for recognizing superior employee performance. For example, Ms. Worthley's 100 golf ball sales cartons over budget in region S would be fully recognized by her superiors. On the other hand, Mr. Baker's 250 golf ball sales cartons be-

low budget in region F would be discussed with him and plans made for trying to increase this region's future golf ball sales.

The Computer's Role in Management-by-Exception Reporting

Through communications among managers of the accounting information system, marketing, and EDP, decisions can be reached for each product line as to what constitutes a significant budget variation and therefore a reportable exception. Because budgets reflect future projections, it is quite unlikely that actual operating results will be identical with budget projections. Some budget variation should be expected solely because of random chance.

Let's assume that the Alan Company's marketing managers and its accountants believe that a budget variation of ± 12 cartons of golf balls per week is acceptable in sales region A. Because the budget during the third week of January was 80 cartons in region A (see Figure 2-3), this particular week's acceptable range of sales for the region would have been from 68 to 92 cartons (80 ± 12). The Alan Company's EDP employees would have programmed their computer for this acceptable range of golf ball sales in region A. The budget data for each week's regional golf ball sales (as well as the sales of other sporting goods items) would be contained on a computer storage medium. We will assume that the Alan Company uses magnetic tape for storing its budget data. Then, every week when the transaction tape of actual sporting goods sales is processed with the master tape containing the budget data, the computer program will check whether the actual sales of each product item fall within the acceptable limits. For golf balls, this would mean that as long as region A's actual third week's sales in January are within 68 to 92 cartons, no exception report on golf balls is generated. Only for those sporting goods items where the actual sales are outside the acceptable limits would an exception report be printed out for management's attention.

The Alan Company

**Report of Budget to Actual Sales Quantities
Third Week of January 1991**

| | Baker Sales Regions[a] | | | | | | Barnes Sales Regions[a] | | | | | | Myers Sales Regions[a] | | |
| | A | | F | | | | C | | R | | | | B | | |
Product Description	B[b]	A	V	B	A	V	B[b]	A	V	B	A	V	B[b]	A	V
Baseball bats	75	80	5	40	70	30	70	35	(35)	90	92	2	80	77	(3)
Baseball gloves	48	50	2	38	37	(1)	50	47	(3)	35	38	3	60	65	5
Baseball shoes	25	28	3	32	31	(1)	30	31	1	31	21	(10)	40	38	(2)
Baseballs	110	100	(10)	90	94	4	80	85	5	100	95	(5)	85	87	2
Basketball shoes	40	38	(2)	40	57	17	35	32	(3)	25	24	(1)	50	53	3
Basketballs	100	98	(2)	90	93	3	110	108	(2)	100	98	(2)	80	84	4
Bowling balls	60	63	3	50	51	1	70	67	(3)	40	42	2	50	52	2
Bowling shoes	10	11	1	8	10	2	15	13	(2)	18	19	1	8	9	1
Footballs	80	84	4	90	91	1	100	104	4	60	62	2	90	87	(3)
Golf bags	30	31	1	18	16	(2)	10	11	1	23	15	(8)	20	19	(1)
Golf balls	80	90	10	300	50	(250)	70	95	25	100	105	5	160	175	15
Golf carts	5	6	1	10	6	(4)	10	12	2	9	7	(2)	15	18	3
Tennis balls	100	110	10	90	91	1	100	98	(2)	80	83	3	110	114	4
Tennis rackets	50	51	1	80	83	3	70	69	(1)	90	92	2	40	44	4
Tennis shoes	35	38	3	30	31	1	40	37	(3)	20	23	3	15	14	(1)

[a] These letters (A, F, C, R, etc.) represent codes for the different geographical areas that each salesperson is assigned.

[b] B represents budget projection of sales quantity. A represents actual sales quantity, and V represents variation from budget (parentheses indicate below budget).

FIGURE 2-3

The type of reporting structure discussed here increases the computer's usefulness to a company's information system. The speed capability of the computer permits a timely analysis of budget versus actual sales for the individual sales personnel in their assigned regions. And, by incorporating a management-by-exception reporting structure into the company's system, the computer will print out only those significant budget variations that require management's immediate attention. Naturally, this reporting structure can be utilized for analyzing operational performance in areas other than sales (e.g., comparing actual with standard manufacturing costs within the Alan Company's production subsystem).

CENTRALIZED AND DECENTRALIZED ORGANIZATIONAL STRUCTURES

Knowledge of an organization's structure (that is, the relationship of various job activities and responsibilities) is important for the accountant in designing and evaluating the accounting information system. Designers of accounting information systems must concern themselves with organizational structure for three major reasons. First, each position within the organizational structure requires decision making. It is the objective of an

																Totals	
Myers (cont.)			**Williams**						**Worthley**								
Sales Regions[a]			**Sales Regions**[a]						**Sales Regions**[a]								
T			**G**			**I**			**S**			**C**				Totals	
B[b]	**A**	**V**	**B**[b]	**A**	**V**	**B**[b]	**A**	**V**	**B**[b]	**A**	**V**	**B**	**A**	**V**	**B**[b]	**A**	**V**
50	54	4	80	83	3	70	68	(2)	20	35	15	40	41	1	615	635	20
70	64	(6)	45	49	4	50	48	(2)	40	43	3	25	21	(4)	461	462	1
44	47	3	30	34	4	28	30	2	30	32	2	40	37	(3)	330	329	(1)
110	115	5	90	88	(2)	85	88	3	90	92	2	100	104	4	940	948	8
40	42	2	40	25	(15)	40	42	2	35	33	(2)	40	42	2	385	388	3
90	86	(4)	80	76	(4)	90	88	(2)	75	78	3	85	84	(1)	900	893	(7)
60	58	(2)	30	33	3	25	28	3	40	39	(1)	55	53	(2)	480	486	6
10	13	3	11	14	3	5	4	(1)	10	11	1	20	22	2	115	126	11
60	61	1	100	101	1	95	97	2	80	78	(2)	90	94	4	845	859	14
8	10	2	20	23	3	30	29	(1)	11	14	3	15	17	2	185	185	0
100	90	(10)	500	525	25	160	175	15	300	400	100	100	95	(5)	1870	1800	(70)
15	17	2	10	9	(1)	3	7	4	20	18	(2)	24	26	2	121	126	5
90	92	2	100	98	(2)	80	83	3	90	92	2	110	114	4	950	975	25
70	73	3	60	61	1	20	18	(2)	10	11	1	30	27	(3)	520	529	9
20	22	2	10	8	(2)	40	41	1	30	28	(2)	40	42	2	280	284	4

FIGURE 2-3　(Continued)

accounting information system to help provide the information for that decision. Therefore, an understanding of each job and its decision requirements is necessary. It is especially important to be able to distinguish between **line** and **staff positions** in this organizational structure for this purpose. Line positions are those where the job responsibilities relate directly to the goal of the organization. For instance, in a manufacturing organization, line positions would likely be those jobs related to the production of the product. Staff positions, on the other hand, are not directly related to accomplishing organizational goals but, rather, support line positions in this effort. Examples are jobs in the accounting function and the data processing function.

A second reason that designers of accounting information systems must understand an organization's structure is to enable them to understand **information flow** in an organization. This is important in order to accomplish such tasks as developing a chart of accounts. Typically, organizations are structured in a hierarchy. The top level of the hierarchy represents top management and the bottom level represents operational employees—those who are responsible at the lowest level for accomplishing organizational goals. Accounting information may flow in several directions in this type of structure. Some information may flow from the bottom up. Since the lowest level is concerned with daily operations, employees at this level have access to certain kinds of information first. They may send this information upward to top management. Other information may flow from the top down. The top level of management is responsible for

The Alan Company

Exception Report of Budget to Actual Sales Quantities
Third Week of January 1991

Product Description	Baker — Sales Region F			Barnes — Sales Region C			Barnes — Sales Region R			Myers — Sales Region T			Williams — Sales Region G			Williams — Sales Region I			Worthley — Sales Region S		
	B^b	A	V	B^b	A	V	B	A	V	B^b	A	V	B^b	A	V	B	A	V	B^b	A	V
Baseball bats	40	70	30	70	35	(35)													20	35	15
Baseball shoes							31	21	(10)												
Basketball shoes	40	57	17										40	25	(15)						
Bowling shoes										10	13	3	11	14	3						
Golf bags							23	15	(8)												
Golf balls	300	50	(250)	70	95	25													300	400	100
Golf carts	10	6	(4)													3	7	4			

[a] These letters (F, C, R, T, etc.) represent codes for the different geographical areas that each salesperson is assigned.

[b] B represents budget projection of sales quantity. A represents actual sales quantity, and V represents variation from budget (parentheses indicate below budget).

FIGURE 2-4

formulating the strategic plans and goals of the organization. These goals must be communicated to lower levels of management. Finally, information may flow in a horizontal direction. An employee at a particular level may need to communicate with others, in different functional ares or associated with other products or divisions, at the same level in the organizational hierarchy. A study of a company's organizational structure will reveal valuable information about these flows. It may also demonstrate that the company could benefit from a reorganization in terms of more efficient communication of information.

The third reason why accountants need to understand organizational structure is to enable them to evaluate an accounting information system. Knowledge of the organization's structure helps in determining whether or not informational needs are being met. It also helps in deter-mining whether the company is organized in a manner consistent with good internal control. A good system of internal control requires clear lines of authority and responsibility. In addition, it calls for appropriate segregation of duties, which will be discussed in Chapters 9 and 10. Basically, segregation of duties is important so that no individual controls a transaction from its initiation to its appearance in financial statements.

The role of the accounting subsystem (as well as the other subsystems) within an organization's operating environment is greatly influenced by top management's philosophy of organizational structure. The two major structural types are centralized and decentralized systems. When comparing centralized and decentralized organizational structures, two relevant functions should be considered: **decision making** and **information processing.**

Centralized versus Decentralized Decision Making

In an organization where decision making is centralized, top management makes the major strategic and policy decisions for the entire organization. Line managers execute the decisions. One way of organizing for this type of centralized decision making is with a functional organizational structure. Figure 2-5 illustrates this type of structure. The President will work with the Vice Presidents representing each function, to determine policy and goals for the firm. The Vice Presidents have centralized decision-making authority over their entire functional areas. For example, although a firm makes several products, the Vice President of Marketing will determine general promotional policy for all product lines. This is in contrast to a decentralized organization where each product line is represented by a Marketing Manager who has authority to determine promotional policy for a specific line. Figure 2-6 shows this type of decentralized organizational structure.

Management must choose the type of decision-making organizational structure best for its particular firm. This involves consideration of some behavioral factors. For instance, managers may be more motivated if decision making is decentralized as this allows decisions to be made at lower levels, thereby encouraging greater participation by lower-level managers in the decision-making process. Another factor to be considered is size of the organization. A very large organization which uses a centralized organization structure is likely to have problems with control. A large organization in which top management desires centralized decision-making powers may choose a hybrid organizational structure, centralizing some decisions (e.g., decisions about major capital investments) while decentralizing others (e.g., choice of advertising medium and amount of promotional expenditures for each product).

Regardless of the decision making organization structure chosen, care must be taken to ensure that the measures used for performance evaluation reflect it. If decision making is cen-

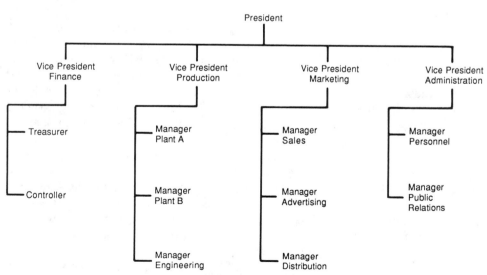

FIGURE 2-5 Centralized organizational structure (by function).

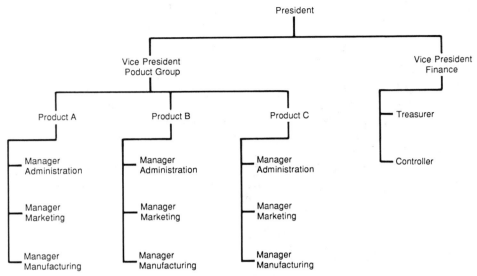

FIGURE 2-6   Decentralized organizational structure (by product line).

tralized, managers cannot be evaluated for decisions over which they have no control. This relates to the topic of responsibility accounting discussed earlier in the chapter. Responsibility accounting is one way in which the choice of structure for decision making affects the accounting information system.

Centralized versus Decentralized Information Processing

The choice of centralized versus decentralized information processing can be made independent of the structure of organizational decision making. The implementation of a computer into a company may centralize the information processing functions within the electronic data processing subsystem. This is the case where a centralized data processing subsystem exists, although a company may choose to utilize **distributed data processing** instead. With distributed data processing, each subsystem processes its own data much as in a manual system. Where the data processing function is cen-

tralized, decentralized decision-making functions can become centralized under top management.

For those organizations having computerized data processing systems, the "ideal" organizational structure may be a mix of centralization and decentralization. The information processing functions would be primarily centralized within the EDP subsystem (some distributed processing may be used where appropriate). The advantages of this are to increase vastly the speed of the organization's data processing activities and to permit more challenging work for the other subsystem's employees. The computer, in effect, takes over the often time-consuming and noncreative "busywork" of processing organizational data. For example, before a computerized data processing system existed in the Alan Company, its accountants spent large amounts of time performing bookkeeping-type tasks. With the computer taking over many of these bookkeeping activities, the accountants were able to get involved in more dynamic functions such as advising top management on financial decisions and designing more efficient and effective operating systems.

The major point is that centralizing data processing does not automatically require centralizing decision making. On the contrary, centralized information processing by the EDP subsystem will allow employees more opportunities for creative activities by eliminating busywork from their jobs. Therefore, through computer processing of timely reports which are communicated to the specific subsystem (or subsystems) managers requiring the report information, decentralized decision making can continue within an organization. The behavioral advantages resulting from participation by subsystem managers in decision making will also continue.

ORGANIZATIONAL LOCATION OF ELECTRONIC DATA PROCESSING FUNCTION

The computer's placement within an organization is very important from a structural point of view because its location tends to dictate the types of data processing performed. In discussing the Alan Company's system, the computer facility has been treated as a separate subsystem. However, because some organizations use their computers primarily for processing financial data, EDP responsibilities may be located within the accounting subsystem. A possible negative consequence of having the EDP function as part of the accounting subsystem is that the accountants will exercise too much control over data processing functions and incorporate their personal biases into the company's information system (e.g., overemphasis on monetary compared with nonmonetary quantitative data).

When computers first became popular, they were used principally for processing financial data. This factor justified the location of the computer facility within the accounting subsystem.

However, the computer's increased popularity in business, together with the better understanding of its capabilities, has caused a large number of organizations to use their computers for nonfinancial processing activities. Marketing, for example, may use the computer for forecasting future market demand for specific product lines. Production managers can use the computer to help plan optimal inventory manufacturing schedules as well as to determine economic reorder points and reorder quantities for the efficient purchase of raw materials needed in the manufacturing process. Because of these varying specialized demands for computerized data processing, many organizations today prefer to perform their EDP functions in separate subsystems.

When the EDP function is located outside the accounting subsystem, it can either be centralized under a Vice President of Information or a Chief Information Officer, or the company may choose a distributed data processing approach. With a distributed data processing approach, components of the computerized information system are located throughout the organization. This works particularly well when the decision making of an organization is also decentralized. In that case, each division, product line, or geographical region will maintain its own computer and perform its own data processing functions. Where decision making is centralized but distributed data processing is desirable, each functional area, such as marketing, personnel, finance, and production may have a separate EDP facility. It is probable, however, in this case, that all of these facilities would be integrated to some degree. Distributed data processing may take place, but a Chief Information Officer or Vice President of Information may be appointed to coordinate the data processing activities of the organization as a whole.

Whether data processing is centralized or decentralized, it provides a service to those who receive its output. There is a cost attached to this service and users should be charged for it in some manner. The absence of a charge for information ignores the fact that information is a resource with cost attached to it. If users don't have to pay for information they receive, they may be tempted to request unnecessary information and reports. This contributes to **information overload,** where decision makers are provided with too much information to absorb and use effectively. In addition, costs for the data processing function may be very high in providing this much output. Alternatively, if the charge for information output from the data processing function is too high, users will be discouraged from requesting information and reports that might allow them to make better decisions. In setting a price for data processing services (called a *transfer price*), a company should consider the effect on users as well as how the set price allows management to evaluate the performance of the data processing function. Note that these problems and trade-offs are similar to those experienced with any transfer pricing system. Management must try to set a price for an internally produced product, in this case, information, which encourages other organizational units to purchase the most efficient quantities of it.

SUMMARY

This chapter has discussed some of the important management concepts that affect an organization's accounting information system.

After top management plans its long-range, nonoperational goals, each organizational subsystem must develop operational goals that contribute positively to these nonoperational goals. The accounting information system's major contribution to accomplishing top management's nonoperational goals is the development of long-range as well as short-range operational budgets that will achieve a satisfactory long-run net income for its organization. Several arguments were presented in the chapter as to why most organizations do not attempt to maximize their long-run profits. Because of the strong financial

emphasis in budgets, managerial accountants are normally the coordinators of their organization's budgetary system. An organization's accounting information system also makes important contributions to top management's other nonoperational goals, such as a high quality of manufactured inventory, a responsive and motivated group of employees, and a program of environmental pollution control.

Following an organization's budget planning process, the accounting information system has a major role in monitoring the success or failure of these plans. The accountants, being familiar with each subsystem's delegated decision-making authority and its responsibility for decisions, must interact with the EDP subsystem to prepare timely performance reports that analyze each subsystem's contribution to the organization's nonoperational goals. To evaluate fairly each subsystem's performance, the accountants should design a responsibility accounting system, which compares the subsystem's actual results with its preestablished budget on only those activities that are controllable by employees of the subsystem.

To emphasize the variations from budget that require management's immediate attention, the accountants will often incorporate a management-by-exception structure into their responsibility performance reports. The computer programs for processing the organization's operating data can be written to recognize significant budget variations and immediately print out the managerial exception reports.

The use of a computer ordinarily causes centralization of an organization's information processing functions within the EDP subsystem. Through timely computerized performance reports to the responsible subsystem managers, however, decentralized decision making can be maintained within each subsystem. As a result of top management continuing to delegate decision-making authority to subsystem managers, these managers should be positively motivated to achieve their organization's nonoperational goals.

Key Terms You Should Know

centralized organizational structure
contribution margin
controlling
decentralized organizational structure
decision making
goal
goal congruence
goal incongruence
information flow
information overload
information processing
line positions

management-by-exception
nonoperational goals
operational goals
performance report
planning
profit maximization
responsibility accounting system
satisfactory level of net income
social reporting
staff positions
strategic planning

Discussion Questions

2-1. Why is it important for today's accountant to have an understanding of management concepts?

2-2. Discuss how frustration can enter into an organization's multiplicity of goals.

2-3. What do you think is the rationale in most organizations for having strategic planning performed by top management rather than subsystem managers?

2-4. Why is it essential for an organization's planning and controlling functions to be highly interrelated?

2-5. Because budgets represent future financial projections and an organization's accountants are considered the financial experts, wouldn't the most expedient and efficient budgetary development approach be to have the accounting information system take complete charge for determining each subsystem's future budget? Explain.

2-6. Do you agree or disagree with the arguments given in this chapter that most organizations do not attempt to maximize their long-run profits? Discuss.

2-7. You have learned in a prior accounting course that many organizations incorporate standards for raw materials, direct labor, and production overhead into their cost accounting systems. Then, for each of these three manufacturing costs, variances are computed by comparing the actual costs with the predetermined standard costs. Let's look closer at only the raw materials manufacturing cost. Rather than computing just one total raw materials variance by comparing the actual costs with the standard costs, normally the accountant

will analyze two components of the total raw materials variance: the price variance and the usage variance. What do you feel are the advantages, if any, of determining a separate price and usage variance for raw materials over computing just one total raw materials variance?

2-8. You are an accountant within the accounting information system of the Dumbo and Dang Land Development Company. Through computerized processing methods, the company's EDP subsystem handles all the financial data affecting each subsystem's operating performance. Most of the subsystems financial data are processed weekly. Assume that you are given the job of implementing either a responsibility accounting system or a management-by-exception system into the company (you definitely cannot implement both systems). Which of these two systems would you choose? Explain.

2-9. A major function of a management-by-exception reporting system is to disclose inefficient operating performance so that management can initiate corrective action. Why is it common for a management-by-exception reporting structure also to reflect favorable operating performance for which no corrective action would be necessary?

2-10. What are some of the important ways that employees from the accounting information system and from the EDP subsystem interact in designing, implementing, and controlling a management-by-exception reporting system?

2-11. What are the major differences between a centralized organizational structure and a decentralized organizational structure? How does each of these two structures affect the role of the accounting information system in an organization?

2-12. For an organization's controlling function to be effective, why is it essential to prepare timely performance evaluation reports?

2-13. Comment on the following statement: Because an organization's computer facility will handle the processing of timely performance reports about each subsystem's operating activities, the accounting information system need no longer concern itself with the organization's performance reporting system.

2-14. Why is it important for accountants to understand the decision-making authority and responsibility of each subsystem manager in their organization?

2-15. Because top management can delegate decision-making authority to subsystem managers, doesn't it seem logical that top management should also delegate to them the responsibility for their decisions? Discuss.

2-16. What are the advantages, if any, to an organization of utilizing a responsibility accounting system?

2-17. The Palmer Company has a manual data processing system and the Pocket Company has a computerized data processing system. Both companies are approximately the same size in terms of business volume and number of employees. For which of these two companies do you think a management-by-exception performance reporting system would be more beneficial? Explain.

2-18. As a subsystem manager, which type of organizational structure (centralized or decentralized) would you prefer to work under? Why?

2-19. Assume that you are responsible for pricing EDP services in a centralized organization where a central data processing function exists. What factors would you consider in determining an appropriate amount to charge for services?

2-20. Think of some specific organizational situations in which centralized decision making would likely be preferable to decentralized decision making.

2-21. Because accountants are not trained to be either environmental experts or psychologists, is it fair to expect them to contribute to achieving top management's nonoperational goals of pollution control and highly-motivated employees? Explain.

2-22. The Big Bright Bagel Company began business February 15, 1991, and has established the following subsystems: accounting, electronic data processing, production of bagels, marketing and sales of bagels,

and personnel. The company's top management is currently analyzing several of the important decision-making activities within its system and attempting to decide which of these decision functions should be centralized and which decentralized. The following are the activities being considered.

1. Capital expenditures for production equipment.
2. Capital expenditures for the pollution control program.
3. Establishing selling prices for the different types of bagels that are manufactured.
4. Scheduling the production of bagels.
5. Granting credit to bagel customers.
6. Allowing sales discounts to bagel customers.
7. Salary increases and promotions for subsystem managers.

Requirement

Assume that you are hired as a consultant to help the Big Bright Bagel Company decide which of these seven decision-making functions should be centralized and which decentralized. With the limited information provided in this question, make a recommendation to the company's top management for each of these functions. Give good arguments for every recommendation.

2-23. You are a member of the Bribe Bargain Basement Company's top management. Your company currently has the following subsystems: accounting, production, marketing, and personnel. Due to the rapid growth in the past few years, the company's present manual data processing system (under the accounting subsystem's coordination) has been unable to keep up with the increased information demands by the various subsystems. Therefore, your company has decided to replace its manual data processing system with a computerized data processing system. As a top management executive, you are given the responsibility for deciding whether to establish the new computer facility as a separate subsystem or to integrate it within the accounting subsystem. What are some of the key factors you should consider in reaching your decision?

Problems

2-24. The Big Juicy Hamburger Corporation operates a chain of restaurants throughout the United States. The top management at corporate headquarters exercises control over each restaurant's following functions: the construction of each restaurant's building facility and the depreciation method selected for the building, the number of managers hired at each restaurant as well as their annual salaries, and all expenditures associated with promotional efforts and advertising at each restaurant.

The managers of the individual restaurants have decision-making authority and responsibility for all the many other operating activities associated with their specific restaurant. Presented in the following table is the monthly budget performance cost report for the Big Juicy Hamburger Corporation's restaurant (located in Springfield, Illinois) for June 1991.

Cost Item	Budget	Actual
Salaries of clerical workers at the Springfield restaurant	$ 5,000	$ 5,200
Salaries of cooks, waitresses, and dishwashers at the Springfield restaurant	7,000	7,400
Salaries of supervisory managers at the Springfield restaurant	12,000	12,500
Depreciation of Springfield restaurant's cooking equipment, dishes and silverware, tables and chairs. and cash registers	4,500	4,300
Depreciation of Springfield restaurant's building	3,000	3,400
Electricity, water, and telephone expense	300	375
Cost of food used in cooking meals	25,000	24,500
Cost of cooks' and waitresses' uniforms	400	420
Cost of napkins, dish towels, and cleaning soap	175	190
Advertising and promotional expense	1,000	1,400
Totals	$58,375	$59,685

Requirement

The Big Juicy Hamburger Corporation's top management has decided that a responsibility accounting system would be an effective means for evaluating each restaurant's monthly operating cost performance. Prepare the June 1991 performance report for the Springfield, Illinois restaurant under the corporation's responsibility accounting system.

2-25. The Best Sellers Book Company is a publisher of college textbooks. The company's operating data are centrally processed by its EDP subsystem. Each subsystem (production, marketing, accounting, finance, and personnel) receives computerized performance reports and has decision-making authority delegated from top management.

In the past few months, the managers of most subsystems have been complaining about the criteria used by top management for evaluating their operating performances. The major complaint has been the number of noncontrollable items included within an individual subsystem's performance report.

You are one of the accountants working in the company's accounting information system and have been asked by top management to design and implement a responsibility accounting system for evaluating each subsystem's monthly operating performance. You suggest to top management that a further improvement could be made in the company's performance reporting system if a management-by-exception structure were also incorporated into the new system. The top management executives agree with the suggestion, and you are given the approval to design and implement the new reporting system.

You are currently analyzing the marketing subsystem's March 1991 budget projection data compared with its actual cost performance during March under the company's old reporting system. The March 1991 performance report computer printout appeared as shown below.

After familiarizing yourself with the delegated authority given the marketing subsystem managers by top management, you accumulate the following information.

1. The marketing subsystem managers make their own decisions regarding the number of salespeople and clerical people to hire as well as how much to pay these employees.
2. The marketing subsystem occupies the entire second floor of the company's building and has a separate electric utilities meter on this floor.
3. The marketing subsystem managers have complete decision-making authority for all advertising expenditures associated with promoting textbook sales.

Your next major task is to determine the variations from budget that should be considered significant.

Through discussions with marketing subsystem personnel and top management, the following budget variability schedule is developed.

Budgeted Dollar Cost Range	Acceptable Budget Variation
$ 1–$ 500	±$ 50
$ 501–$1000	±$ 100
$1001–$3000	±$ 300
$3001–$5000	±$ 500
$5001–$7000	±$ 700
$7001–$9000	±$ 900
Over $9000	±$1200

You then talk to computer specialists within the company's EDP subsystem about the required revisions in marketing's monthly performance report. Based on the information you provided these computer specialists, they make the necessary computer program changes to accomplish your new responsibility accounting system with a management-by-exception reporting structure.

Requirement

Prepare the computer printout of the marketing subsystem's March 1991 performance report as it would actually appear under your newly designed system.

Cost Item	Budget	Actual	Variation—Favorable (Unfavorable)
Allocated depreciation of company building	$ 1,000	$ 1,100	($ 100)
Salaries of salespeople	8,000	9,000	(1,000)
Promotional textbook materials sent to college professors	2,000	2,600	(600)
Allocated portion of administrative expenses	1,000	1,600	(600)
Textbook advertising in professional journals	800	825	(25)
Utilities expense	300	375	(75)
Salaries of clerical employees in marketing subsystem	5,000	4,900	100
Totals	$18,100	$20,400	($2,300)

CASE ANALYSES

2-26. Decentralization—Fact or Fiction?*

Dynamic Industries, a diversified manufacturer of automotive replacement parts, is a company that is growing rapidly as the result of an aggressive policy of acquisition. Board chairman John Rafferty believes that the growth of his company is sound and that the main reason for the extremely rapid growth is due to the operation of the company on a highly decentralized basis. Since growth is the result of acquiring companies that are going concerns, Rafferty encourages the managements of the subsidiary companies to carry on

as they had prior to joining Dynamic Industries. At present, discussions regarding merger are being held with Central Electronics, a company that manufactures a broad line of electronic components, many of which have applications in the defense and space industries. Central Electronics is interested in Dynamic Industries because Dynamic could supply the much-needed capital to complete the final stages of the development of a high-performance transformer and the building of a plant in which to manufacture the new product. However, George Owens, the founder and president of Central, realizes the potential dangers of merging with another company in that he might lose control of his own firm and be placed in the position of being an employee for a larger corporation.

But Rafferty continually assures Owens that Dynamic Industries operates on a highly decentralized basis and describes their concept of decentralization as follows:

---

* Used with the permission of Henry I. Sisk, *Management and Organization* (Cincinnati: Southwestern Publishing Company, 1977).

We expect you, as the president of a subsidiary company, to manage as you have in the past. You are successful with your own company and there is no reason why you shouldn't continue to be a success operating as a part of Dynamic. The major functions of sales, manufacturing, engineering, and product development are all yours to do with as you see fit. In a sense we are sort of the banker; that is, we supply the money that you need for capital improvements and expansion. Even though the profits of each subsidiary company go into the corporate till, it is still like having your own company because your pay for the year is a combination of a guaranteed salary and a percentage of the net profits of your company.

Thus assured, Owens decided to merge with Dynamic Industries.

During the first six months all went well and Owens saw very little of anyone from corporate headquarters. At the beginning of the seventh month, the corporate controller paid Owens a visit and explained to him in detail the company's requirements for profit planning and requested that Owens develop a profit plan, a detailed forecast of Central's revenues and operating expenses for the coming year. Though very pleasant, the controller made it quite plain that should the performance of the company deviate significantly from the forecast, a team of cost accountants and industrial engineers would arrive from headquarters to determine the cause of the deviation and to recommend necessary changes.

Shortly after this experience with the controller, the industrial relations vice-president of Dynamic Industries called on Owens and informed him that a member of the corporate industrial relations staff would be on hand to conduct the coming negotiations with the union representing Central's employees. Owens protested, saying that he had been negotiating his own labor contracts for years; however, it was explained to him that because of company-wide employee benefit plans, such as pensions and insurance, and to prevent the unions from pitting one subsidiary company against another in the area of wages, centralized control over negotiations was very necessary. At the time of this visit, the provisions of the company's salary plan were outlined to Owens and arrangements were made for the installation of the corporate clerical and supervisory salary plans by a member of the headquarters industrial relations staff.

The following month Owens called Rafferty and asked what steps should be taken to secure capital for the new building intended for the manufacture of the high-performance transformer. Rafferty answered by saying, "I'll have someone from the treasurer's office call on you and show you how to fill out the forms used in requesting funds for capital expansion. It's quite a process, but remember you are only one of 15 subsidiaries and they all seem to want money at the same time. Whether or not you get it this year depends not only upon your needs but also upon the needs of the other 14 companies."

Questions

1. Has Dynamic Industries decentralized its operations as much as possible? Explain.
2. As George Owens, president of Central Electronics, would you regard the management policies of the parent corporation as primarily centralized or decentralized? Explain.
3. Is Dynamic Industries exerting too much control over Central Electronics? Why or why not?
4. Recommend the optimum degree of decentralization for the situation described in this case.

2-27. *Dual Standards at Harden*

Harden Company has experienced increased production costs. The primary area of concern identified by management is direct labor. The company is considering adopting a standard cost system to help control labor and other costs. Useful historical data are not available because detailed production records have not been maintained.

Harden Company has retained Finch & Associates, an engineering consulting firm, to establish labor standards. After a complete study of the work process, the engineers recommended a labor standard of 1 unit of production every 30 minutes or 16 units per day for each worker. Finch further advised that Harden's wage rates were below the prevailing rate of $7 per hour.

Harden's production vice-president thought this labor standard was too tight and the employees would be unable to attain it. From his experience with the labor force, he believed a labor standard of 40 minutes per unit or 12 units per day for each worker would be more reasonable.

The president of Harden Company believed the standard should be set at a high level to motivate the

	January	February	March	April	May	June
Production (units)	5100	5000	4700	4500	4300	4400
Direct labor hours	3000	2900	2900	3000	3000	3100
Variance from labor standard	$1350 U	$1200 U	$1650 U	$2250 U	$2250 U	$2700 U
Variance from cost standard	$1200 F	$1300 F	$ 700 F	$ 0	$ 400 U	$ 500 U

workers, but he also recognized that the standard should be set at a level to provide adequate information for control and reasonable cost comparisons. After much discussion, management decided to use a dual standard. The labor standard recommended by the engineering firm of one unit every 30 minutes would be employed in the plant as a motivation device, and a cost standard of 40 minutes per unit would be used in reporting. Management also concluded that the workers would not be informed of the cost standard used for reporting purposes. The production vice-president conducted several sessions prior to implementation in the plant, informing the workers of the new standard cost system and answering questions. The new standards were not related to incentive pay but were introduced at the time wages were increased to $7 per hour.

The new standard cost system was implemented on January 1, 1991. At the end of six months of operation, the above statistics on labor performance were presented to top management (U designates an unfavorable variance; F, a favorable variance).

Raw materials quality, labor mix, and plant facilities and conditions have not changed to any great extent during the 6-month period.

Questions

1. Discuss the impact of different types of standards on motivation, and specifically discuss the effect on motivation in Harden Company's plant of adopting the labor standard recommended by the engineering firm.
2. Evaluate Harden Company's decision to employ dual standards in its standard cost system.

(CMA Adapted)

2-28. WRT Inc.

Denny Daniels is production manager of the Alumalloy Division of WRT Inc. Alumalloy has limited contact with outside customers and has no sales staff. Most of its customers are other divisions of WRT. All sales and purchases with outside customers are handled by other corporate divisions.

Daniels perceives the accounting department as a historical number-generating process that provides little useful information for conducting his job. Consequently, the entire accounting process is perceived as a negative motivational device that does not reflect how hard or how effectively he works as a production manager. Daniels tried to discuss these perceptions and concerns with John Scott, the controller for the Alumalloy Division. Daniels told Scott, "I think the cost report is misleading. I know I've had better production over a number of operating periods, but the cost report still says I have excessive costs. Look, I'm not an accountant, I'm a production manager. I know how to get a good quality product out. Over a number of years, I've even cut the raw materials used to do it. But the cost report doesn't show any of this. Basically, it's always negative, no matter what I do. There's no way you can win with accounting or the people at corporate who use those reports."

Scott gave Daniels little consolation. Scott stated that the accounting system and the cost reports generated by headquarters are just part of the corporate game and almost impossible for an individual to change. "Although these accounting reports are pretty much the basis for evaluating the efficiency of your division and the means corporate uses to determine whether you have done the job they want, you shouldn't worry too much. You haven't been fired yet! Besides, these cost reports have been used by WRT for the last 25 years."

Daniels perceived from talking to the production manager of the Zinc Division that most of what Scott said was probably true. However, some minor cost-reporting changes for Zinc had been agreed to by corporate headquarters. He also knew from the trade grapevine that the turnover of production managers was considered high at WRT, even though relatively few were fired. Most seemed to end up quitting, usually in disgust, because of beliefs that they were not being evaluated fairly. Typical comments of production managers who have left WRT are:

- "Corporate headquarters doesn't really listen to us. All they consider are those misleading cost reports. They don't want them changed and they don't want any supplemental information."
- "The accountants may be quick with numbers but they don't know anything about production. As it was, I either had to ignore the cost reports entirely or pretend they are important even though they didn't tell how good a job I had done. No matter what they say about not firing people, negative reports mean negative evaluations. I'm better off working for another company."

A recent copy of the cost report prepared by corporate headquarters for the Alumalloy Division is shown below. Daniels does not like this report because he believes it fails to reflect the division's operations properly, thereby resulting in an unfair evaluation of performance.

ALUMALLOY DIVISION
Cost Report
for the Month of April 1991
($000 omitted)

	Master Budget	Actual Cost	Excess Cost
Aluminum	$ 400	$ 437	$ 37
Labor	560	540	(20)
Overhead	100	134	34
Total	$1060	$1111	$ 51

Questions

1. Comment on Denny Daniels' perception of

   a. John Scott, the controller.
   b. Corporate headquarters.
   c. The cost report.
   d. Himself as a production manager.

   Then discuss how his perception affects his behavior and probable performance as a production manager and employee of WRT.

2. Identify and explain three changes that could be made in the cost information presented to the pro-

duction managers that would make the information more meaningful and less threatening to them.

(CMA Adapted)

2-29. The Kristy Company

The Kristy Company has grown from a small operation of 50 people in 1974 to 200 employees in 1991. Kristy designs, manufacturers, and sells environmental support equipment. In the early years every item of equipment had to be designed and manufactured to meet each customer's requirements. The work was challenging and interesting for the employees as innovative techniques were often needed in the production process to complete an order according to customers' requirements. In recent years the company has been able to develop several components and a few complete units which can be used to meet the requirements of several customers.

The early special design and manufacture work has given the Kristy Company a leadership position in its segment of the pollution control market. Kristy takes great pride in the superior quality of its products and this quality has contributed to its dominant role in this market segment. To help ensure high-quality performance, Kristy hires the most highly skilled personnel available and pays them above the industry average. This policy has resulted in a labor force that is very efficient, stable, and positively motivated toward company objectives.

The recent increase in government regulations requiring private companies to comply with specific environmental standards has made this market very profitable. Consequently, several competitors have entered the market segment once controlled by Kristy. While Kristy still maintains a dominant position in its market, it has lost several contracts to competitors that offer similar equipment to customers at a lower price.

The Kristy manufacturing process is very labor intensive. The production employees played an important role in the early success of the company. As a result, management gave employees a great deal of freedom to schedule and manufacture customers' orders. For instance, when the company increased the number of orders accepted, more employees were hired rather than current employees being pressured to produce at a faster rate. In management's view, the intricacy of work involved required employees to have ample time to ensure the work was done right.

	J	F	M	A	M	J	J	A	S	O	N
							1991				
Absenteeism rates	1%	1%	1%	1%	.5%	1%	2%	4%	6%	8%	11%
Turnover rates	.2%	.5%	.5%	.5%	.3%	.8%	.7%	1.4%	1.9%	2.5%	2.9%
Direct labor efficiency variance (unfavorable)	—	—	—	—	—	$(10,000)	$(11,500)	$(14,000)	$(17,000)	$(20,500)	$(25,000)
Direct materials usage variance (unfavorable)	—	—	—	—	—	$(4,000)	$(5,000)	$(6,500)	$(8,200)	$(11,000)	$(14,000)

Management introduced a standard cost system that they believed would be beneficial to the company. They thought it would assist in identifying the most economical way to manufacture much of the equipment, would give management a more accurate picture of the costs of the equipment, and would be used in evaluating actual costs for cost control. Consequently, the company should become more price competitive. Although the introduction of standards would likely lead to some employee discontent, management was of the opinion that the overall result would be beneficial. The standards were introduced on June 1, 1991.

During December, the production manager reported to the president that the new standards were creating problems in the plant. The employees had developed bad attitudes, absenteeism and turnover rates had increased, and standards were not being met. In the production manager's judgment, employee dissatisfaction has outweighed any benefits management thought would be achieved by the standard cost system. The production manager supported this contention with the data presented above for 1991, during which monthly production was at normal volume levels.

Questions

1. Explain the general features and characteristics associated with the introduction and operation of a standard cost system that make it an effective cost control tool.
2. Discuss the apparent impact of Kristy Company's cost system on
   a. Cost control.
   b. Employee motivation.

3. Discuss the probable causes for employee dissatisfaction with the new cost system.

(CMA Adapted)

2-30. *Quality Footwear*

Ned Gabler has been in the shoe business for 23 years and operates Quality Footwear, a 15-store chain in New York, New Jersey, and eastern Pennsylvania. Quality Footwear has grown steadily from the first store in Manhattan to the current level. Conservative styles, quality shoes, moderate pricing, and attentiveness to customer needs have characterized the operation of Quality Footwear from the beginning.

Gabler's operations manager, Chuck Staub, keeps in touch with each of the 15 stores in the chain in order to respond to any needs or emergencies that arise and to be sure each has enough inventory on hand. There is relatively little problem in maintaining the proper assortment of shoes in stock, because each store stocks the same limited assortment of shoe styles and colors. The demands on store managers are relatively few and each manager is given latitude in running the store as long as the firm's basic policy of quality service to customers is followed. Staub's job is made easier as well by the standardization among stores in terms of limited offerings and stability in the customer base.

Quality Footwear is structured around five equal general manager levels as shown by the organizational chart in Figure 2-7. The staff is well established except for the position of general manager-facilities, which Gabler has intended to fill for the past year. Unfortunately, the acquisition of the 22 stores that make up the Twentieth Century Shoes (TCS) chain has occupied most of his time. The purchase recently was final-

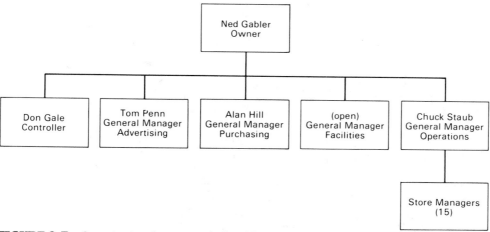

FIGURE 2-7 Organizational structure before TCS acquisition.

ized and has expanded Gabler's geographic sales area along the Atlantic coast into the South and Southeast.

Prior to concluding an acquisition agreement, Gabler had carefully surveyed the entire organization of TCS and visited every store in the chain. The prior owners had more than doubled the number of outlets in the last three years, and Gabler believed that the haste showed by the way the stores were being operated. There were inconsistencies among stores in terms of customer service, cleanliness and neatness, and the adequacy of the shoe styles in stock. Store management seemed to vary widely from very courteous and efficient to indifferent and lackadaisical. Each store manager enjoyed a great deal of autonomy. The TCS general manager was strained to keep up with operations.

TCS serves a larger area with more stores but has lost money in two of the last three years. In addition, TCS serves a slightly different market. TCS's customers are 5 to 10 years younger and tend to be more fashion conscious; thus, the TCS market segment is more competitive and will require more promotion. TCS also carries a range of accessories that includes socks, shoelaces, polish, and some novelty items, none of which are found in the Quality stores. However, Gabler believed that the increased market area and the attractive acquisition price made up for the losses and other problems. Gabler intends to retain his conservative product line as the core of his new stores and supplement it with the best-selling lines and accessories of the TCS units in all 37 stores.

Gabler asked Staub to prepare an organizational chart that would integrate the two chains and bring the total organization to a level of profitability that Quality Footwear has experienced. Staub submitted the chart that appears in Figure 2-8.

District managers will assume responsibilities similar to those previously covered by Staub, and store managers would have the same responsibilities that had been carried by the managers of the original Quality stores. In addition, each store manager would be responsible for stocking accessories and advising central purchasing of the stock and recommending shoe lines to meet regional differences in style and demand.

Questions

1. Compare and contrast the organizational responsibilities and reporting relationships under the original and proposed organizational structures for each of the following persons/positions.

   a. Chuck Staub.
   b. Alan Hill, general manager-purchasing.
   c. Don Gale, controller.
   d. District managers.

2. Discuss whether each of the following functions are either more centralized or more decentralized under the proposed organizational structure.

   a. Quality Footwear store managers.
   b. TCS store managers.
   c. Purchasing function.

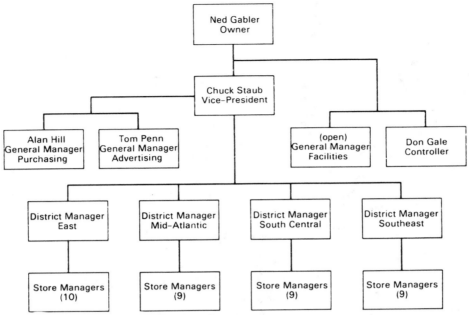

FIGURE 2-8   Proposed organizational structure.

3. Review the proposed organizational structure that Chuck Staub has prepared.

   a. Discuss the strengths of the proposed organizational structure.
   b. Identify the weaknesses of the proposed organizational structure and explain how you would change the proposed structure to eliminate each identified weakness.

   (CMA Adapted)

2-31. *Universal Concrete Products*

Jack Merritt is the controller for Universal Concrete Products, a manufacturing company with headquarters in Columbus, Ohio. There are seven concrete product plants throughout the country. The company has recently changed its organizational structure and is now decentralized. Each plant is headed by a general manager, who has responsibility for operating the plant like a separate company.

Jack has asked one of his accountants, Scott McDermott, to organize a small group to be in charge of performance analysis. This group is to prepare monthly reports on performance for each of the seven manufacturing plants. These reports consist of budgeted and actual income statements. Variances are to be accompanied by written explanations and appraisals. Each member of Scott's group has been assigned to one specific plant and is encouraged to interact with management and staff in that plant, in order to become familiar with operations.

After a few months, the controller began receiving complaints from the general managers at several of the plants. The gist of these complaints is that Scott's staff members are interfering with operations and in general "getting in the way." In addition, the managers complain that they feel as though someone is constantly "looking over their shoulder" to see if they are operating in line with their budget. Two managers pointed out that the work the performance analysis staff is trying to do should be done by them (i.e., explanation of variances).

The president of Universal, Hector Xavier, has also complained about the new system for performance evaluation reporting. He claims that he is unable to "wade through" the seven detailed income statements, variances, and narrative explanations of all variances each month. As he put it, "I don't have time for this and

I think much of the information I am receiving is irrelevant!"

Questions

1. Do you think it is a good idea to have a special staff in charge of performance evaluation and analysis?
2. In a decentralized organization such as this one, what would seem to be the best approach to performance evaluation?
3. Explain how management-by-exception reporting can be used in this situation.

2-32. Accunav Company

Accunav Company was started in 1985 by Margo Muray and John Carter. Muray and Carter developed Accunav's first product which applies microchip technology to the LORAN-based navigation system. Accunav's product enables LORAN, previously used to navigate only ships, to be used in aircraft. As a consequence, Accunav is a pioneer in the new market, and the company is growing rapidly.

Muray and Carter are electrical engineers; however, they also share the administrative duties of Accunav. Muray is the President of the company and Carter holds the position of Vice-President of Finance. Accunav follows a simple staffing pattern; when the company's growth overwhelms a position, another person is hired to assume some of the responsibilities. In this manner, Accunav has created the positions of Vice-President of Marketing and Vice-President of Manufacturing.

Until recently, Carter has been reluctant to relinquish control over some key positions and currently has ten people reporting directly to him. Now, in order to free some of his time for research and development activities that interest him, Carter is proposing the creation of two new positions, Treasurer and Controller. The ten people reporting to him would maintain their present duties and responsibilities but would report to the Controller and Treasurer as shown in the proposed reorganization of Accunav's financial department that is presented in the next column.

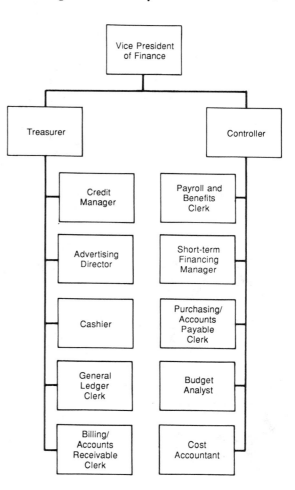

Questions

1. Discuss why Accunav Company's present Finance Department should be reorganized.
2. Discuss the strengths of John Carter's reorganization proposal for the Finance Department.
3. Describe the functional and structural weaknesses of John Carter's reorganization proposal for the Finance Department.
4. Accunav is considering setting up an EDP subsystem in conjunction with automating their entire information system. Describe how you would determine the organizational location of the EDP subsystem.

(CMA Adapted)

3 Budgetary Accounting Information Systems

Among the important questions that you should be able to answer after reading this chapter are:

1. What are the three major principles for effective budgeting?
2. What are the essential items that should be included in a subsystem's long-range budgetary program proposal?
3. What is a cost/benefit analysis and what are some of the difficulties involved in preparing one?
4. Does "zero-based budgeting" mean that a company is so unsure about its future that no budgetary planning exists?
5. What are responsibility centers and how do they contribute to an efficient and effective budgetary information system?
6. What role does the electronic data-processing subsystem play in the planning and controlling functions of an organization's budgetary system?
7. What is an electronic spreadsheet computer program and how can one be used within an accounting information system?

Case Analyses

Roletter Company

Forecasting Automobile Demand

The ATCO Company

Kelly Petroleum Company

Merriman Company

Ferguson & Son Mfg. Company

Family Resorts Inc.

INTRODUCTION

Today's business world is characterized by rapid technological change, strong competition among companies in many industries, and large organizations with sophisticated computerized information systems. Under these conditions, it is essential for organizations to operate efficiently and effectively to obtain the most value from their limited financial resources (monetary items) and nonfinancial resources (people, scarce commodities such as electricity and gasoline, etc.). To survive and prosper, an organization should plan and control its future course of action. Without formal planning, the organization would function on a day-to-day basis with little or no thought about future challenges and opportunities. Consequently, the organization's management may find itself at an operating disadvantage relative to those competitors who are planning their short-range and long-range futures.

As discussed in Chapter 2, both long- and short-range budgets are important to an organization's planning and controlling functions. Through a formal budgetary system, the organization attempts to quantity its long- and short-range plans so that each subsystem contributes positively to top management's goals (such as satisfactory long-run profit performance and high-quality inventory items for sale to the consuming public).

Periodic performance reports comparing budget allowances with actual results inform management whether or not its goals are being achieved.

Chapter 2 emphasized that managerial accountants working within a company's accounting information system are the coordinators of their organization's budgetary system. Because no extensive discussion of budgetary systems was provided in Chapter 2, and because of the importance of the role played by accountants in planning and controlling a budgetary information system, this topic is examined in this chapter. Most students should already know the procedural aspects of budgeting. Therefore, our discussion of budgetary systems will concentrate more on the valuable contribution the budget process makes to an organization's information system than on specific budget procedures.

A complete budgetary information system includes long-range budgets (which project operating activities, for example, 5, 10, or 15 years into the future) and short-range budgets (which project operating activities for the upcoming 1-year period). This chapter's objectives are threefold: (1) to examine the essential principles of a good budgetary information system, (2) to analyze the accounting information system's role in long- and short-range budgetary activities, and (3) to discuss computerized budgetary information systems.

IMPORTANT PRINCIPLES FOR EFFECTIVE BUDGETING

Whether discussing long- or short-range budgeting, there are three major principles that should be followed when planning and operating a budgetary system: communication, participation, and flexibility. Each of these principles will now be briefly analyzed.

Communication Within Budgetary System

To develop realistic budgets for the future, an organization must have information concerning its internal and external environment. The internal environment encompasses all the subsystems within the organization. Because budgetary planning covers the entire organization, each internal subsystem (accounting, marketing, production, electronic data processing, etc.) will be affected by the budgetary process. As discussed in Chapter 1, the external environment is a major element that affects the organization's current and future operating activities. It includes the state of the economy (inflation, war, unemployment, etc.), the degree of competition from other companies in the same industry, and the like.

The development of an effective budgetary system requires that complete information be available about each organizational subsystem. After all, how can you plan for the future without information about those subsystems that will play a role in it? In order to acquire complete information so that meaningful budgets can be developed, a communication network among the organizational subsystems must be instituted by the budget planners.

This communication network cuts across all subsystems' boundaries and permits the accumulation of relevant information needed in the budget process. For example, when the Alan Company's marketing subsystem is developing the detailed product-line budget of sales for 1991, it must obtain information about such things as total market demand for sporting goods equipment and competitors' share of this market. After developing its tentative sales plan, marketing must communicate with production to ascertain whether manufacturing capacity is adequate to produce the quantity of sporting goods expected to be sold.

Participation Within Budgetary System

An organization's employees often have a negative attitude toward budgets. This is caused by the confining or restrictive nature of a budget. For example, once budgets are established, employees are expected to operate within their budget allotments. Thus, for many people, budgets represent limitations that are imposed on them and also a means by which others "watch over" and control their performance. Consequently, there are two major reasons for having an organi-

zation's employees participate in the development of the budgetary system: (1) to foster a positive attitude to company budgets and (2) to achieve more realistic budgets, thereby contributing to the company's operating performance.

Motivation of Employees

If only accountants are involved in preparing budgets, many employees working within the other subsystems may be unresponsive to their organization's budgetary system. One of the most effective means of motivating these people to react favorably to budgets is employee participation in the budgetary process. Because all employees will be affected in some manner by the budgets, the organization should, within reasonable limitations, attempt to involve as many employees as possible in the budgetary planning process. A company often forms a budget committee, which is responsible for planning and controlling the company's budgets. Representatives from top management and each subsystem are included on this committee, and managerial accountants serve as committee coordinators. The committee may also include members from the company's union to represent employee interests in such matters as equitable budget allocations for salaries and fringe benefits.

Each subsystem's employees will participate in developing their departmental budget. The resulting budget then goes to the budgetary committee, which reviews the departmental requests and either accepts or rejects them. A rejection should be accompanied by an explanation of the reasons for not approving the budget. The subsystem's employees can then go back and make the necessary changes in their original proposal. The budget committee can also make specific suggestions concerning a subsystem's dollar allotment. Once the subsystem's budget is approved by this committee and actual operating performance under the budget begins, the subsystem employees should be more positively motivated to achieve the budget because they had a voice in determining it. Thus, through budget participation by all organizational sub-systems, the budgets can be a positive, rather than a negative, planning tool.

Realistic Budgets

When developing an organization's budgets, two dangers should be avoided: (1) making the budgets **too strict** and (2) making them **too loose.**

Budgets that are "too strict" require such a high level of performance that very few employees are able to meet them. Because employees' operating performance will be evaluated by their subsystem managers (and, in turn, the subsystem managers by top management) on the basis of actual results against budget projections (the control function of a budgeting system), unduly strict budgets will likely give the "appearance" of unfavorable performance. Many of the subsystems may actually be operating quite efficiently; however, with strict budgets based on the expectation of unrealistically high performance levels, they appear inefficient. This situation can cause negative employee attitudes toward the budgetary process.

Budgets that are "too loose" (which therefore have **slack** in them) can also be harmful to an efficiently operated organizational system. Loose budgets are set at such a low level of performance that most employees can function inefficiently and still meet operating targets. The inefficiencies in operating performance will not be disclosed because each subsystem will appear to be performing successfully when actual results are compared with the budget performance levels. These easily attainable budgets can cause employee laziness. Loose budgets can even be counterproductive because they do not challenge the participants and thus have the potential to make an employee feel that his or her work "does not matter."

The "ideal" budgetary system falls somewhere in between those that are too strict and those that are too loose. These budgets are often called • **realistic** (or **attainable**) budgets because they reflect a reasonable level of performance that is neither too difficult nor too easy to achieve. In actual practice, realistic budgets are difficult to develop. On the one hand, operating employees (and even subsystem managers) will be pushing for loose budgets. At the same time, top management may be arguing for strict budgets. Consequently, for an efficient and effective budgetary system to emerge, some compromise is necessary.

One of the best techniques for achieving this compromise and the resultant realistic budgets is through subsystem employees' participation in developing the budgetary plans. For example, a subsystem may initially prepare a budget projection that is too loose. When this budget is subsequently reviewed by the budget committee, however, the committee should spot the budget's looseness and make it known to the subsystem. The subsystem's management will then have to revise the budget projection to eliminate the operational slack and make it acceptable to the committee. Thus, the participation between the subsystem's management and the budget committee in developing the budget should eventually lead to a realistic subsystem budget.

Although an accounting information system cannot solve the budgetary dilemma of subsystems' employees (which includes managers of the subsystems) and top management, an organization's accounting information system *can* provide a basis for compromise. This compromise is achieved largely through periodic performance reports identifying the causes of significant budget variations. For example, it is difficult for a union to argue that the budgets are too strict if the record shows that unfavorable budget performance was caused by high worker absenteeism and turnover. (Of course, the union's counterargument may be that this employee absenteeism and turnover was the result of the employees' frustrations from being unable to work within the strict budgets.) Similarly, it is difficult for top management to argue that the prior budgets were either attainable or too loose if performance reports show that a considerable amount of overtime work from experienced employees was required to meet them. This is just common sense, yet it is equally obvious that the relevant information *must be available* if objective decisions are to be made regarding fair and attainable performance levels within the operating budgets. An accounting information system should provide the valuable budgetary information.

The participation leading to the establishment of each subsystem's budget should be a positive motivator for budget acceptance by all the subsystems. The resultant motivation should cause the subsystems' employees to have favorable attitudes about achieving their realistic budgets. If this occurs, each subsystem will then be making a positive contribution to its organization's operating performance.

Flexibility Within Budgetary System

When budgets are prepared, they should reflect the best expectations of an organization's future operating activities. As the future unfolds, however, conditions may change from what was originally projected in the budgetary system. For example, a new sporting goods manufacturer may appear on the market during 1991 and greatly affect the Alan Company's original expectations of 1991 sales demand for sporting goods. When the company's budget committee was coordinating the 1991 budgets back in September 1990, it may not have been aware of this new competitor.

To achieve flexibility within a budgetary system once an organization's budgets have been prepared and actual operations commence, the budgets should be monitored to ascertain whether the many assumptions on which these budgets were based are still valid. If internal or external environmental factors change and make the original budget projections invalid, the budgets should be revised. This revision would take into consideration the new information about the organization's operating environment, and should provide improved information to guide the organization's operating activities.

The opposite of flexible budgets are **static (or fixed) budgets.** Once developed, static budgets are never revised, regardless of the subsequent knowledge obtained about the internal and external environment. Static budgets can result in an organization's budgetary system contributing *negatively* to its operations. Because additional knowledge about the organization's operating enviornment would not be included in its budgets under a static budgetary system, comparisons of actual operating results (based on current operations) with budget projections (based on inaccurate expectations about the current operations) could lead to improper management decision making. For example, an actual operating activity may appear favorable when compared with an outdated, static budget. However, by comparing the performance of the activity with an updated, flexible budget, managerial conclusions about the activity's success may be completely different.

Flexible budgets are an important part of an organization's *control* system because internal and external environmental changes are immediately recognized through revised budgets. For example, a weekly computerized report comparing an organization's actual sales with its budget of sales for a newly introduced product line can provide marketing managers with timely feedback regarding consumers' reactions to this new product line. If actual weekly sales are continually below budgetary expectations, this unfavorable situation may be due to quality deficiencies in the product line. This information will permit production managers to modify the product line's manufacturing specifications with the hope that consumer demand will subsequently increase. Based on new expectations for the revised product line, adjustments to the original sales projections will then be necessary. Because of the manufacturing specification changes, the accountants will have to provide revised cost data for the production budgetary projections associated with this product line.

LONG-RANGE BUDGETARY SYSTEMS

Chapter 2 defined strategic planning as a long-range planning approach whereby top management establishes broad, nonoperational goals. These goals reflect the organization's "plan of attack" (or strategies) for long-run success. Nonoperational goals represent the framework within which each organizational subsystem develops operational goals that help to achieve these long-range goals.

In addition to their short-range operational goals for the coming year, many subsystems will be involved in long-range projects that extend beyond a one-year period. The long-range projects, that are either currently in progress or being considered for future implementation, form the framework of an organization's long-range budgetary system. Because an organization's long-range budgeting consists of various projects (or programs) that cover a period longer than one year, another term commonly used for this type of budgeting is **programming.**

The relevant aspects of long-range budgeting will now be analyzed. Included in our discussion will be an example of long-range budget programs for the Alan Company.

The essential features of an organization's long-range budgetary system are as follows.

1. A systematic method for generating program proposals by each subsystem.
2. A systematic method for evaluating program proposals, and objective criteria by which to select programs for implementation.
3. A systematic method for periodic zero-based review of ongoing programs and new program proposals.

Generating Program Proposals

Most long-range budget programs involve a major monetary expenditure that will commit an organization to a specific course of action for several years. Therefore, each subsystem that wishes to undertake a long-range project should be required to prepare a formal proposal for the budget committee describing the project's goals, estimated costs, and estimated benefits. The process involved when performing a cost-benefit analysis will be illustrated later in this chapter. It should be emphasized here, however, that normally a project will not be approved by the budget committee unless its expected benefits exceed its expected costs.

The fact that a significant long-term asset investment is associated with most program proposals makes it imperative for an organization's top management to review the proposals and either accept or reject them. The degree of top management involvement in reviewing program proposals depends on the individual company. This chapter assumes that the type of budget committee previously discussed (i.e., a committee with representatives from top management as well as each organizational subsystem and the union) will also be responsible for reviewing long-range program proposals and deciding whether or not to implement them.

Even though qualitative factors can influence the acceptance or rejection of a program proposal, each proposal should contain as much quantifiable data as possible. These quantifiable data should be expressed in terms of the expected dollar cash costs compared with the dollar cash benefits expected from the proposal's implementation. This provides the budget committee with a common denominator (i.e., *dollars*) for comparing one project proposal with another, although the individual projects that are proposed may be quite dissimilar. Regardless of which subsystem is submitting a program proposal, the requirements for monetary quantification normally results in the accounting information system aiding the subsystem in gathering the monetary data. Figure 3-1 illustrates the program proposals submitted to the Alan Company's budget committee by its subsystems during September 1990 for possible implementation as of January 1, 1991.

When the four program proposals in Figure 3-1 are submitted to the company's budget committee for review, the committee will be better

Alan Company Program Proposals

September 1990

Subsystems	Program Proposal	Estimated Years of Value from Program	Program Goals
Production	Replace some of the current sporting goods manufacturing equipment with new equipment.	5 years	To increase the efficiency of the sporting goods manufacturing process and also to increase the quality of manufactured sporting goods.
Marketing	Advertising promotion campaign on the national television networks.	6 years	To broaden the market for sporting goods equipment and thereby increase current and future years' sales.
Personnel	Educational program to allow managerial employees the opportunity of returning to college for their master's degrees.	20 years	To increase the supervisory skills of managers so that they can be more efficient and effective employees.
Accounting and Electronic Data Processing	Convert the inventory recordkeeping system for sporting goods from batch processing to on-line, real-time processing.[a]	5 years	To provide more timely reports to management on sporting goods inventory activities and thereby increase the effectiveness of management's decision-making functions relating to the inventory system.

[a] Under the Alan Company's present batch-processing system, day-to-day inventory transactions are accumulated (i.e., batched) at week's-end and then processed by the computer in order to update the various inventory accounts. With an on line, real-time processing system, however, each inventory transaction would be immediately processed through the accounts at the time the transaction occurs, thus providing management with continuous updated inventory account balance information.

FIGURE 3-1   Four long-range proposals for the Alan Company.

able to compare one program with another if each program's expected monetary costs and monetary benefits are available.

Evaluating Program Proposals and Selecting Programs for Implementation

Because most organizations have only so much money annually to allocate-to long-range programs, and because the total dollar cost of pro-

gram proposals may exceed the maximum allocated budget expenditures, the evaluation of program proposals often results in the rejection of some projects.

The **cost/benefit analysis** for each program proposal submitted to the budget committee for review should contain a comparison of the expected cash outflows (costs) with the expected cash inflows (benefits) during the estimated number of future years that the program will be of value to the organization. The benefits from a program will also include any cash outflow reductions (called cash savings) that are anticipated. For example, computerizing a company's bookkeeping procedures may cause a reduced cash outlay for clerical salaries. This expected cash savings would be one of the benefits from the proposed computer system.

The various program proposals submitted by an organization's subsystems involve *future* cash outflows and *future* cash inflows. In addition, each program's future cash flows often cover a different expected time period from those of the other program proposals. (See the estimated years of value from the Alan Company's four program proposals in Figure 3-1.) To facilitate comparison of the costs and benefits of the program proposals having different years of future value, each proposal's annual net cash flow should be converted to its **present value.** Since the Alan Company's budget committee, for example, is *presently* attempting to compare one project proposal with another, all project proposals should be based on the present values of their net cash flows. This will provide the committee with a comparative basis for selecting and rejecting projects.

Present Value Analysis for Ranking Program Proposals

Present value analysis is founded on the "time value of money." For example, $1 received today has more value than $1 received a year from today. In the former case, you have the opportunity of immediately using the dollar acquired today for some productive purpose, or, at least, putting it in a bank and collecting interest. If you must wait a full year to receive this dollar, you lose the opportunity to use it in the following 12 months.

Basically, the longer you must wait to receive a dollar, the less valuable that dollar is today. The largest rate of return that could be earned on a dollar by having it in your possession today is called the *opportunity cost.* For example, if you could earn 12% annually on a $1 investment, but

had to wait a year to acquire the dollar, you sacrifice the *opportunity* to obtain the 12% return this year. Assuming you can always earn a positive return on your available cash, dollars received in the future are less valuable today.

The present value tables (Figures B-1 and B-2) shown in Appendix B have been mathematically derived, based on the compounding of interest. (Those readers not previously exposed to present value analysis and the mathematical logic of Figures B-1 and B-2 should read the section of Appendix B entitled "Present Value Computational Examples.") It should be noted that both tables are based on the present value of $1. Once you know the present value of $1 for some future number of years at some opportunity cost (the various interest percentages in the columns of the present value tables), you can convert this $1 present value result to any other present value quantity desired.

Assume, for example, that your grandfather's will specifies that you shall receive a lump-sum payment of $5000 two years from today. If you currently had this $5000 in your possession, you estimate that an 8% return could be earned. Using the present value table in Figure B-1 of Appendix B (which determines the present value of a future lump-sum payment based on your opportunity cost), this $5000 has a present value of $4285 [the present value of $1 to be received in two years at an 8% interest rate (the opportunity cost) = .857; .857 × $5000 = $4285]. Since the present value of $1 two years hence at an opportunity cost of 8% is $0.857, multiplying this $1 present value amount by $5000 gives you the desired answer. The present value table for a future lump-sum payment *assumes* that this payment does not occur until year's end (rather than during some month prior to the end of the year). If a lump-sum payment is actually to be received at a specific time other than the end of the year, such as November 15, the present value mathematical difference (from continuing to use the assumption of the present value table in Figure B-1) would normally be minimal.

To illustrate the use of the present value table

in Figure B-2 of Appendix B, assume that you own a small apartment building. You estimate that the net cash flow from this building will be $7000 per year for the next 10 years, computed as follows.

Cash receipts per year from rental leases		$25,000
Less: Cash disbursements per year for building expenses. . .		
Maintenance	$12,000	
Utilities, taxes, and insurance	4,000	
Repairs on building	2,000	18,000
Net cash flow per year		$ 7,000

Whenever a series of equal cash flows is anticipated for several years into the future (called an *annuity*) and you wish to determine the present value of these future cash flows, use the present value table of Figure B-2. This table *assumes* that each year's cash flow does not occur until the end of the year (which obviously is not always the case; however, the mathematical difference from this assumption compared with the assumption of uniform cash flows throughout the year is normally minimal). If your opportunity cost is estimated to be 12%, the 10-year, $7000 annual net cash flow from your apartment building has a present value of $39,550 (the present value of $1 to be received annually for the next 10 years at a 12% opportunity cost = 5.650; 5.650 × $7000 = $39,550). Because the present value of $1 annually for the next 10 years at an opportunity cost of 12% is $5.65, multiplying this $1 present value amount by a $7000 annual net cash flow gives you the desired answer.

Selecting Programs for Implementation

It is essential for a company's budget committee to know the present value of each program

proposal's anticipated costs and benefits in order to review and compare adequately all the subsystems' proposals. The actual computation of a program's present value is performed at the time the proposal is being prepared by an organizational subsystem. Because of the accountants' knowledge of financial data, they will usually participate in a subsystem's cost/benefit analysis as well as the conversion of the results to present value. Thus, when a subsystem (with the aid of accountants) submits its program proposal for budget committee review, a present value analysis has already been performed on the proposal.

After reviewing all the program proposals, the budget committee may rank each proposal based on the proposal's **excess present value index** (the ratio of the program's total present value of the anticipated net cash flow to the present value of the total expected cash investment required for the program). For example, the Alan Company's four program proposals submitted in September 1990 (Figure 3-1) would be ranked from 1 through 4 by the budget committee. The proposal with the largest excess present value index would be ranked first, the one with the next largest excess present value index second, and so on. It should be pointed out, however, that there are other methods besides the excess present value index method for ranking program proposals (e.g., the internal rate of return method, the payback method, etc.). Because these methods are emphasized in other accounting courses, they will not be discussed here.

Figure 3-2 illstrates the ranking procedure for project proposals under the excess present value index method for the Alan Company's four subsystem program proposals submitted in September 1990 (the dollar figures are assumed). As Figure 3-2 discloses, the key factor that determines a program proposal's ranking is the program's excess present value index. The numerator of this index reflects the total present value of the program proposal's cash benefits over its cash costs. The denominator, being the present value of the total cash asset investment, reflects the fact that for most long-range programs, dollar

Alan Company's Ranking of Program Proposals

September 1990

Ranking	Subsystem's Program Description	Total Cash Asset Investment Required	Total Present Value of Program's Projected Annual Net Cash Flow During its Estimated Years of Value (Alan Company's Opportunity Cost is assumed to be 10%)	Excess Present Value Index
1	Converting the sporting goods inventory record-keeping system from batch processing to on-line, real-time processing.	$28,000[a]	$36,680	1.31, or 131% $\left(\dfrac{\$36,680}{\$28,000}\right)$
2	Acquiring new sporting goods manufacturing equipment (this equipment's expected salvage value at the end of five years will be zero) to replace some of the old equipment.	$35,000	$44,800	1.28, or 128% $\left(\dfrac{\$44,800}{\$35,000}\right)$
3	Increasing the sporting goods sales market through a national television promotional campaign.	$ 6,000[b]	$ 7,500	1.25, or 125% $\left(\dfrac{\$7,500}{\$6,000}\right)$
4	Allowing managerial employees to increase their educational levels by returning to college for master's degrees.	$ 2,000[c]	$ 2,300	1.15, or 115% $\left(\dfrac{\$2,300}{\$2,000}\right)$

[a] Included within this $28,000 investment would be the costs of computer equipment (the specific equipment required for this conversion will be leased rather than purchased from the computer manufacturer) and computer programming changes, the costs of transferring the inventory data from a batch processing storage medium (for example, magnetic tape) to a storage medium better suited to on line, real-time processing (e.g., magnetic disk), etc.

[b] Included within this $6,000 investment would be the costs of market research that determine the best advertising strategy to use, the costs of negotiating a marketing contract with an advertising agency, etc.

[c] Included within this $2,000 investment would be the costs of personnel subsystem managers' travel, food, and lodging to enable them to visit several college campuses and then determine which one offered the best graduate program to meet the company's needs, the costs of administering aptitude tests to the company's managerial employees as a basis for selecting those managers who will initially enter the master's degree program, etc.

FIGURE 3-2 The four program proposals of Figure 3-1, ranked according to their excess present value indexes.

investments in assets are required. If a program's total cash asset investment is paid over several years, this investment must also be converted to its present value using present value tables. The cash asset investments for the program proposals in Figure 3-2 are already at their present values because it is assumed that the cash outlays necessary for those programs selected would be made immediately.

If the budget committee only used each proposal's net cash flow present value as the criterion for approving or rejecting programs, and ignored its present value asset investment, misleading program rankings could result. For example, Figure 3-2 indicates that the Alan Company's program proposal for converting its inventory system to on-line, real-time processing has the number one ranking. Even though the new manufacturing equipment program proposal has a greater present value for its projected annual net cash flows ($44,800) than this proposal ($36,680), the former is less attractive because the present value of the asset investment required for the equipment ($35,000) is larger than the present value of the asset investment necessary to convert the company's inventory system to on-line, real-time processing (only $28,000).

The use of an excess present value index for ranking program proposals results in the highest rankings for those proposals expected to contribute most productively to the efficient use of an organization's limited asset resources. By comparing the number one and the number two ranked program proposals in Figure 3-2, it can be seen that the total present value of the annual net cash flow from the inventory system proposal is 1.31 times greater than this proposal's present value asset investment, whereas the total present value of the annual net cash flow from the manufacturing equipment proposal is only 1.28 times greater than the program's present value asset investment. Therefore, more efficient asset utilization is expected from the inventory system program proposal.

We should point out that whenever a program proposal's excess present value index is greater than 1, the program would be expected to earn a larger rate of return than its opportunity cost. On the other hand, if the excess present value index is less than 1, the program is expected to earn a smaller rate of return than its opportunity cost. Finally, should the excess present value index be exactly equal to 1, the program would be expected to earn the same rate of return as its opportunity cost.

Assuming that the Alan Company is able to allocate a maximum of $64,000 in 1991 for implementing long-range programs, the proposals ranked 1 and 2 in Figure 3-2 (a total asset investment of $63,000) would be approved. The program proposals ranked 3 and 4 would have to be rejected based on the $64,000 maximum budget allocation for long-range projects. Implementing the national television promotional campaign program (ranked number 3) would cause the 1991 cost of programs (totaling $69,000) to exceed the $64,000 maximum.

The process of estimating the annual cash costs and the annual cash benefits from programs can be extremely difficult. The present values of the annual cash flows for the Alan Company's four programs were assumed to emphasize the process involved in a long-range budgetary system rather than emphasizing the detailed procedural computations required to determine each program's annual cost/benefit relationship. Chapter 14, which covers systems design, presents an analysis of how a program's annual cash costs and annual cash benefits are estimated.

Two further comments are warranted regarding the data in Figure 3-2 and the budget committee's acceptance or rejection of specific program proposals. First, the *risk* factor associated with each program proposal was ignored. Risk refers to the possibility of the expected outcome from a proposed program not occurring. The greater the uncertainty associated with an expected outcome, the greater the risk factor. Some companies attempt to compensate for this risk factor by increasing their opportunity cost percentage (thereby giving a lower present value result) on those program proposals with higher uncertainty of expected outcomes. For program proposals with less uncertainty, the opportunity cost percentage can be decreased (thereby giving a higher present value result). Incorporating risk factors into program proposal analyses can have a significant effect on program rankings. However, it is difficult to determine how much to increase or decrease a company's opportunity cost percentage to include risk factors in long-range budgeting.

Second, the Alan Company accepted for implementation only those program proposals ranked 1 and 2 in Figure 3-2 because of the $64,000 maximum budget allotment in 1991 for long-range programs. Assume that the $64,000 maximum was established because this dollar amount represents the maximum cash the Alan Company can generate internally in 1991 for long-range programs. Rather than immediately reject the programs ranked 3 and 4, however, the Alan Company could investigate outside sources of cash (e.g., selling additional shares of stock, issuing bonds, etc.) to enable otherwise rejected programs to be accepted. As long as the anticipated rate of return from a program exceeds the **cost of capital** (e.g., the after-tax interest expense on bonds and the dividend payments on stock) associated with external financing, raising additional cash from outside sources can be good financial strategy. The subject of outside cash sources for financing long-range programs can become quite complex; therefore, it was ignored in our analysis of the Alan Company's four program proposals.

The point should also be made here that when the estimated years of value from program proposals differ widely, it may be necessary (for purposes of computing the total present value of each program proposal's net cash flow) to establish a life span that is common to all the investments being considered for implementation. To illustrate, one possible approach is to use as the time period for analysis that program proposal having the *shortest* estimated years of value. Program proposals with longer estimated years of value would be treated as if they were terminated early (i.e., when the program proposal with the shortest estimated years of value is terminated). The expected salvage values on the early termination date of these proposals are used to measure the proposals' *values* as of this termination date. In the analysis of program proposals in our text, however, we will not concern ourselves with making adjustments to individual program proposals because of differing estimated years of value for various long-range project proposals.

Periodic Zero-based Program Review

A company's budget committee approves specific program proposals for implementation in the coming budget year because it feels that these programs will make the greatest contributions to the organization's strategic plans. By attempting to quantify monetarily program proposals' annual cash costs and annual cash benefits, converting these costs and benefits to present values, and then comparing each program proposal's total present value of its net cash flow with the present value of the proposal's total asset investment, the budget committee has a reasonable basis for approving or rejecting specific programs.

Periodic program review should be part of an organization's budgetary planning and controlling system. Before beginning a new budget year, all current long-range programs should be reviewed by the budget committee. Consideration should be given to dropping those programs that are not accomplishing their anticipated goals and replacing them with other, more productive long-range projects.

The process of periodically reviewing both new program proposals and ongoing programs before they are approved for the subsequent year is called **zero-based budgeting.** In a nutshell, zero-based budgeting prevents a company from "wasting more dollars in the future." To illustrate, assume that in 1991 the Alan Company purchased only $8000 worth of the total $35,000 of new manufacturing equipment approved in the production subsystem's program. When the budget committee evaluates this program's achievements during the latter months of 1991 to decide whether to continue the program into 1992 (and acquire additional manufacturing equipment), the committee may believe that the increased quality level of manufactured sporting goods (one of the program's goals shown in Figure 3-1) is not being accomplished. Rather than continue this program into 1992, thereby spending more dollars for new equipment, the budget committee may decide to drop the program and not replace the present manufacturing equipment. The new equipment already acquired during 1991 would continue to be used in the manufacturing process.

In zero-based budgeting, existing programs have no priority over new program proposals. They must compete on an equal footing (in other words, at a *zero-base*) for the following year's asset resources devoted to long-range programs. A cost-benefit analysis must again be performed on each existing program to justify it. By also performing cost-benefit analyses on all the new program proposals, priorities are reestablished through a ranking hierarchy of both the existing programs and the new proposals based on their excess present value indexes, as previously discussed. The result may be that certain programs will emerge with higher excess present value indexes than some existing programs, causing the budget committee to phase out certain old programs and replace them with the new, more efficient ones.

A zero-based budget review is expensive because each ongoing program has to be re-evaluated in depth. Also, the evaluation process can have adverse behavioral effects on the particular subsystems' managers whose programs are being reevaluated because no manager likes to have an ongoing program dropped. For these reasons, the zero-based review is often performed once every few years rather than annually. The hope of the budget committee is that no specific ongoing program will have a significant negative effect on the organization's strategic goals during the intervening years (perhaps three or four) between zero-based reviews.

SHORT-RANGE BUDGETARY SYSTEMS

In addition to program budgets that reflect long-range plans, an organization must also prepare short-range operational budgets for the coming year. Each organizational subsystem's short-range budget should reflect that subsystem's operational goals. Successful performances (favorable actual results compared with the budget projections) by the subsystems will result in their positive contributions to the goals of the total system.

Both short-range and long-range budgets are important planning and controlling devices. Long-range program budgets reflect an organization's plan of attack for current and future success. These budgets normally are prepared prior to the 12-month, short-term budgets. However, when planning the detailed short-term budgets, the monetary consequences of long-range approved programs must be considered.

For example, the operation of the Alan Company's long-range program that converts its inventory system from batch processing to on-line real-time processing will begin in January, 1991, and is expected to have a five-year life (see Figure 3-1). During each of these five years from 1991 through 1995, when the Alan Company's short-range budgets are planned, the costs of operating the new inventory system must be incorporated into the annual budgets. In effect, the short-range budgetary process takes the organization's long-range programs as given and attempts to ascertain annually the monetary costs and benefits of the approved programs.

Short-range budgets are often prepared according to the functional areas of an organization. Thus, the Alan Company's annual budgetary planning system might include budgets for the sales function (by product lines), the inventory and manufacturing functions (also by product lines), the marketing function, the personnel function, the EDP function, and so on. An alternative to this functional approach is the **responsibility center** approach. This approach to budgeting is based on the concept of a **responsibility accounting system,** discussed in both Chapters 1 and 2. Under this budgetary method, each subsystem's annual budget includes only those cost and/or revenue items over which the subsystem has control (and therefore responsibility for the monetary amounts of these items).

The concept of a responsibility center is illustrated in Figure 3-3. This schematic diagram of a responsibility center is a broad representation and can be applied to most types of organizations (manufacturing, service, or not-for-profit). In a manufacturing firm, various quantities of direct raw materials, direct labor, and production overhead (indirect manufacturing items such as insurance on the factory, depreciation on the factory building and equipment, taxes associated with the factory, salaries of supervisors, etc.) reflect the efforts (or inputs) put forth to create salable products (the accomplishments or outputs). The specific manufacturing process represents the conversion work performed to achieve the desired outputs.

A service organization (such as a medical clinic) also uses combinations of inputs to obtain one or more outputs. For example, the principal input of a medical clinic is the *hours* of professional skill exercised by its doctors in treating patients. These hours (the conversion work) should produce an intangible service product, the improvement of patients' health services. Both service organizations' and not-for-profit organizations' (such as a university) information systems will be examined intensively in Chapter 18.

When using a responsibility center approach in developing an organization's short-range budgetary system, the various inputs (quantities of raw materials, labor-hours, etc.) must be combined somehow to arrive at a total budget allowance for the specific responsibility center involved. It is not possible, for example, to add directly 1000 units of raw materials to 400 labor-hours and arrive at any sort of common denominator to reflect the responsibility center's total short-run budgeted inputs. To develop a common measuring unit of a center's short-range budgeted inputs, the accounting information system will convert all of the responsibility center's dissimilar inputs to dollars. The resultant total costs become a reflection of the center's resources used to achieve its specific goal (or goals).

Ideally, the outputs of a responsibility center can also be measured in dollars. For a profit-oriented organization such as a manufacturing firm or a medical clinic, the output measurement is dollars of revenue earned from providing a product or service to the clientele. The revenue function may not always represent a complete measure of output, especially in the short run. It may be difficult, for example, to measure the short-run additional dollars of sales revenue resulting from an advertising promotional campaign.

The preceding has been a general discussion of responsibility centers. The major reason for using a responsibility center approach within an organization's budgetary system is to provide better managerial information regarding the planning and controlling of the annual budgets. Through a responsibility budgetary approach,

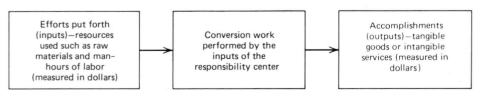

FIGURE 3-3   A schematic diagram of a responsibility center.

each responsibility center is held accountable for only those inputs and/or outputs it can actually cause to increase or decrease. Therefore, when actual performance varies significantly from the budget, management is able to trace this budgetary variation to the specific responsibility center accountable for the variation, and planning revisions can then begin.

Since the operating characteristics of organizations (as well as the individual subsystems within the same organization) often vary widely, there are several different types of responsibility centers that may be established. The four major ones are cost (or expense), revenue, profit, and investment centers. Based on a company's organizational design and the types of budgetary information desired, more than one of these types of responsibility centers may be incorporated into the company's system.

We will now briefly discuss each of these four approaches to establishing responsibility centers. In addition, we will examine the use of **divisionalized** structures within profit and investment responsibility centers.

Cost (or Expense) Centers

Cost centers are responsibility centers in which only *inputs* are measured monetarily. No attempt is made to measure a cost center's output in monetary terms. The two major types of cost centers are the engineered cost center and the discretionary cost center.

In an *engineered cost center,* budgetary planning and controlling are normally based on a standard cost accounting system. Utilizing financial data accumulated by an accounting information system, standard costs are determined in advance. These standards represent what the center's costs should be under conditions of operating efficiency. For example, each of the Alan Company's manufacturing components (such as basketball manufacturing, baseball manufacturing, and football manufacturing) within its production subsystem would likely be a separate engineered cost center for budgetary purposes.

Following the budgetary planning of each center's standard costs, the accounting information system performs budgetary control by accumulating the individual center's actual incurred costs and preparing management-by-exception reports covering significant budget variations. In the case of the Alan Company, which has an EDP subsystem, the accountants will provide actual and standard cost data for each cost center to the computer facility. The company's computer then prepares these management-by-exception reports.

Predetermined standards of efficiency cannot be developed for a *discretionary cost center.* By definition, discretionary costs involve the *subjective judgment* of management. It is extremely difficult, if not impossible, to determine an "efficient" amount of these costs for a responsibility center. Therefore, comparing actual costs with budget costs does not measure efficiency within a discretionary cost center. A good example of a discretionary cost center is the research and development component found in many organizations. This operating component is often part of a company's marketing subsystem. It is difficult, if not impossible, to establish a standard, efficient number of dollars for research projects. Most research projects are long term, thereby making a determination of their success or failure in any 12-month time frame very difficult. Also, even though a specific research project may appear unsuccessful, some of its findings may eventually lead to other, fruitful research endeavors.

Revenue Centers

Revenue centers for budgetary planning and controlling are often found within the sales component of an organization's marketing subsystem. These are responsibility centers in which *outputs* are measured monetarily; however, no formal procedure is established for relating revenue centers' monetary outputs to their monetary inputs (costs).

Revenue center budgets measure the performance of the sales component of a company's marketing subsystem in selling products to customers. A separate revenue responsibility center should likely be maintained for each of the Alan Company's product lines sold by the marketing subsystem. The revenue responsibility centers' budgets for the individual product lines are based on each product's forecasted sales (sales forecasting will be discussed later in this chapter) during the coming 12-month period. As the budget year unfolds, the Alan Company's accounting information system will accumulate the sales data for management-by-exception computer reports of actual product-line sales to budget product-line sales for every revenue center. These reports will reveal favorable and unfavorable performances by the individual revenue responsibility centers.

Even though specific managers of each revenue center are held "responsible" for meeting their budgets, the revenue budget has limited usefulness as a tool for evaluating a center's operating efficiency. For example, the revenue center budget of the basketball sales component within the Alan Company's marketing subsystem is derived by multiplying expected sales quantities of basketballs by the expected unit selling price. However, many of the relevant variables (such as marketing efforts by competitors and unemployment in the economy) that affect the product line's actual sales quantity and actual selling price are beyond the control of the sales managers. It is therefore difficult to hold these basketball sales managers completely responsible for significant variations between actual and budgeted sales of their product line. If the company's budget committee uses the responsibility budgets for the revenue centers as its basis for evaluating specific sales managers' operating performances, the committee should be aware of the many uncontrollable variables that affect the revenue centers' activities. Otherwise, the budgetary information reporting system can lead to unfair evaluations of these centers' positive or negative contributions to the Alan Company's goals.

#3 Profit Centers

Under a **profit center** organizational structure, a specific responsibility center is accountable for "both sides of the ledger": inputs (costs or expenses) and outputs (revenues). Where feasible and practical within an organization, the use of profit centers for budgetary planning and controlling has several important advantages over the use of cost centers or revenue centers. Neither cost centers nor revenue centers by themselves measure the totality of an organizational component's performance. Cost centers are responsible only for monetary inputs, with no attempt made to relate these inputs to monetary outputs. At the other extreme, revenue centers are responsible for monetary outputs, but no attempt is made to relate these outputs to monetary inputs.

For a specific organization to earn a satisfactory net income, the efforts put forth (inputs or expenses) must result in a greater amount of accomplishments (outputs or revenues). You should recognize this basic relationship between revenues and expenses as the accountant's income statement. When an organization's revenues exceed its expenses, we call the resultant difference *net income*. Thus, the profit center approach makes each organizational center responsible for a specified level of income performance that will contribute positively to the company's goals.

Another important advantage of profit centers is that the centers' managers are typically delegated more authority and responsibility for decision making. This increases decentralization within the organization. Because the measure of performance in a profit center is broadened to include both inputs and outputs, the profit center's managers should have decision-making authority and responsibility for their *controllable* inputs and outputs. To emphasize only the controllable monetary activities of a profit center when evaluating its performance, many organizations utilize a *contribution margin profit mea-*

sure (profit center's revenues minus profit center's controllable expenses, which are typically the variable expenses) for planning each center's budget. A positive contribution margin (excess of revenues over controllable expenses) indicates that the profit center is "contributing" toward its noncontrollable expenses (typically the fixed expenses). Any excess of the contribution margin over the noncontrollable expenses reflects a profit, or income, for the center. The profit center's operating efficiency is determined by comparing its actual contribution margin with its budgeted contribution margin.

#4

Investment Centers

In those organizations for which a significant investment is necessary to generate income, an **investment center** approach may be better than the profit center approach. Both of these organizational configurations commonly use the actual contribution margin compared with the budgeted contribution margin of each responsibility center as the key criterion in evaluating operating performance. With a profit center structure, however, no direct consideration is given to the dollar investment of assets that was used. Under an investment center structure, a specific responsibility center's contribution margin is directly related to the assets used while earning this contribution margin income. Because the efficient use of assets is important to all organizations, failure to relate a responsibility center's income to its investment in assets can cause misleading evaluations of the center's operating performance.

For example, assume that the home appliances department of a major manufacturer had contribution margin income of $20,000 in 1990 and $30,000 in 1991. At first glance, it may appear that the department had a significant improvement in operating performance during this two-year period. Suppose, however, that on further investigation, it was determined that an $80,000 asset investment existed in the home appliances

department during 1990. At the beginning of 1991, however, this department acquired $70,000 worth of additional manufacturing equipment, making its total asset investment $150,000. As a result of this increased asset investment, the home appliances department's return-on-capital (contribution margin income/asset investment) actually decreased from 25% in 1990 ($20,000 contribution margin income/$80,000 asset investment) to 20% in 1991 ($30,000 contribution margin income/$150,000 asset investment). The use of the investment center approach in evaluating the home appliances department's performance thus reveals a decline in the efficient use of assets in 1991 compared with 1990.

This illustration is oversimplified (e.g., no consideration was given to the depreciation relating to the home appliances department's assets), but it serves to demonstrate the more accurate information that can be provided about a department's performance using the investment center approach. Increased contribution margin income by a department from one year to the next does not automatically reflect improved operating performance if this income growth is the result of an increased asset investment.

When an investment center's annual budget is developed, the projected contribution margin earnings of the center should be related to its budgeted asset investment. In most cases, this would result in a budgeted asset investment increase being accompanied by a budgeted contribution margin income increase. By then relating the budgeted income to the budgeted asset investment, a projected return-on-capital criterion can be preestablished for the investment center. The budget committee's evaluation would then compare the center's actual return-on-capital with its budgeted return-on-capital.

Divisionalization of Profit and Investment Centers

Profit centers as well as investment centers are commonly used in large organizations having a structural configuration called *divisionalization.* Under this structural arrangement, each center is entirely responsible for the manufacturing and marketing functions relating to its product line (or lines). General Motors Corporation is a good example of a divisionalized organizational structure. Each of the corporation's automobile divisions is treated as a separate investment center, individually responsible for the manufacturing and marketing functions associated with its specific automobile models.

Divisionalization has both advantages and disadvantages. On the advantage side, the large degree of decision-making authority and responsibility held by the divisions' managers should motivate them to achieve their organization's goals. Also, with top management personnel at company headquarters delegating this decision-making authority and responsibility to the divisions, these higher-level managers will be relieved of the time-consuming, day-to-day operational decisions necessary at each division. Top management will thus be able to spend additional time on such important activities as strategic planning for the company's long-range future.

A disadvantage that can result from divisionalization is too much competition and friction among division managers. Because every division is, in effect, a separate organizational unit, it is possible for the divisions to lose sight of the fact that they are all part of one big organization. Top management at company headquarters places strong emphasis on each division's profit performance as a measure of divisional efficiency. Therefore, a division's managers may become so involved in their own profitability that some of their activities actually harm other divisions' performances. This can cause overall lower accomplishments for the total organization, resulting in **suboptimization.** For example, Division A of a company may have the opportunity to obtain a major manufacturing order from a customer. However, the division does not currently have machine time available within its plant to manufacture the order within the speci-

fied deadline date. Another division (Division B) of the same company may be aware of this manufacturing capacity shortage but still might not allow Division A the temporary use of some of its idle machinery. Division A therefore loses the order, causing the division's profitability and the entire company's profitability to be less than it could have been.

To avoid a problem of this nature, the company's top management personnel must encourage cooperation among the division managers. One possible approach to achieving cooperation among divisions is for top management to give verbal praise to a specific division that aids another division's operating performance. Also, top management should encourage a "team spirit" among all its division managers and emphasize to these managers that even though certain of their activities may not directly benefit their own divisions, the activities' execution contribute positively to the organization's total goals.

COMPUTERIZED BUDGET SYSTEMS

The next several sections of this chapter look at the role played by a company's EDP subsystem in the budget process. In doing so, we will discuss some ways that the computer can be used within a budgetary information system, analyze the role of quantitative methods and the computer in budget planning, explain the meaning of electronic spreadsheet computer programs, and briefly discuss how spreadsheet models can be utilized in an accounting information system.

Computer's Use Within a Budgetary Information System

Up to this point, we have discussed only briefly the computer's role in the budget process. For example, in the execution of budgetary control, the computer's data processing speed enables it to process on a timely basis management-by-exception performance reports reflecting significant budget variations. Management can thus immediately investigate these variations and initiate corrective action.

A common reaction from people with no practical experience in budgetary planning is, "Big deal! Estimating a company's future sales, planning its inventory levels to satisfy sales demands, hiring sufficient employees to handle the company's expected operating requirements, etc., all appear to be rather straightforward." Actually, quite the contrary is true. Both long- and short-range budgetary planning tend to become very complex. This complexity is caused by the many variables that must be considered when planning an organization's budgets. The following descriptions of some of the variables that the Alan Company's budget committee must consider in performing its budgetary functions are illustrative.

1. **Historical company performance.** Past historical results cannot be ignored when planning the company's future course of action because historical data often provide good insights into probable future outcomes.
2. **Internal and external variables affecting sales.** When forecasting future sales demand for the Alan Company's many sporting goods product lines, several key questions must be answered. For example, if an additional $20,000 is budgeted this year for advertising efforts associated with the company's product lines (an *internal* variable), what will be the expected increase in the current year's sporting goods sales? Or, what are the adverse effects, if any, on this year's sporting goods sales as a result of increased unemployment and inflation in the economy (*external* variables)?
3. **Asset resources of company and their allocation.** The Alan Company has only so many dollars' worth of asset resources such as cash and production equipment. Budget decisions must be made regarding the most efficient use of these asset resources. For example, the manufacturing capacity of the company's present production equipment

may be insufficient to produce the various quantities of sporting goods that the sales forecasts reveal can be sold in the coming year. A long-range decision must then be made by the budget committee either to purchase additional equipment that will enable increased sporting goods production or to maintain the present level of manufacturing equipment, with the result that the production output to meet the projected sales forecasts will be impossible. If the latter decision is made, the budget committee must determine the optimal production mix feasible based on the plant's available manufacturing capacity. This will likely result in the reduced production and the resultant lost sales of those product lines having the smallest *contribution margins*.

The preceding examples identify a few types of variables that must be considered in a company's budgetary planning activities. Proper consideration of these variables will normally require complex analyses of large volumes of data. Using a manual system to analyze budget variables would require considerable time and likely slow down the budget-planning process. However, the availability of a computer could greatly facilitate the analyses of many complex variables that are expected to affect a company's future financial projections.

For example, in planning the Alan Company's short-range budgets for 1991, historical financial data (such as cash and credit sales by product lines, cost of merchandise sold by product lines, and income statement ratios) for the past three years should be available on a computer storage medium such as magnetic tape. Assume that the accountants on the budget committee are currently preparing projected cash flow budgets (i.e., budgets showing estimated cash inflows *minus* estimated cash outflows) for each month in 1991. Important projections required for the monthly cash budgets are estimations of the average time interval to collect the accounts receivable from credit sales. To help the accountants in projecting these cash collections, they could request a computer report reflecting the company's collectibility experience during the past three years. The report may reveal that on the average, for the last three years, approximately 30% of each month's credit sales is collected in the actual month of sale, another 50% in the subsequent month, 17% in the second month following the actual sales, and the remaining 3% is written off as uncollectable.

Obtaining this information would likely be quite time-consuming under a manual data processing system. With the use of the company's computer, however, it can be acquired rather quickly by the accountants. The credit and collection department's managers and the accountants will then discuss the historical collectibility percentages and determine whether these percentages are reflective of the future and should thus be used in preparing the 1991 monthly cash budgets. Assuming that the decision is made to use the average collectibility percentages of the prior three years in the 1991 cash flow budgets, monthly estimations of credit sale cash collections could then be determined from multiplying the monthly projections of product-line credit sales (based on sales forecasts) by the collectibility percentages. These calculations would, of course, be performed by the computer, and the resultant computerized cash collections schedule would be available for subsequent use in the cash budgets. Figure 3-4 reflects the Alan Company's computer printout budget projections of monthly cash collections from credit sales. (Because this projection schedule is only for illustrative purposes, the dollar amounts are assumed.)

One of the major uses of computers in budget planning and controlling is to answer "what if" questions. For example, assume that the cash collections from credit sales data in Figure 3-4 are incorporated into the Alan Company's monthly cash flow budgets for 1991. Following three months of operations (the end of March 1991), a management-by-exception performance report covering the sales of baseballs reveals that

Alan Company
Budget Projections of Monthly Cash Collections in 1991 from Credit Sales

Cash from Credit Sales	Jan.	Feb.	March	April	May	June	July	Aug.	Sept.	Oct.	Nov.	Dec.
30% of total credit sales for the month	$ 6,000	$ 4,500	$ 5,400	$ 4,800	$ 5,100	$ 5,700	$ 7,200	$ 6,900	$ 6,000	$ 6,300	$ 4,800	$ 8,500
50% of previous month's credit sales	12,000	10,000	7,500	9,000	8,000	8,500	9,500	12,000	11,500	10,000	10,500	8,000
17% of second previous month's credit sales	4,000	4,080	3,400	2,550	3,060	2,720	2,890	3,230	4,080	3,910	3,400	3,570
Total monthly cash collections	$22,000	$18,580	$16,300	$16,350	$16,160	$16,920	$19,590	$22,130	$21,580	$20,210	$18,700	$20,070

FIGURE 3-4

actual quantity sales are far in excess of budget. Unless baseball production is increased, adequate inventories of this product line will not be available to meet future baseball sales for the remaining months of 1991. The extra demand over budget for baseballs is analyzed by the marketing managers as a short-range condition; therefore, action to acquire additional manufacturing equipment (a long-range budget decison) that will increase the plant's manufacturing capacity is rejected by the budget committee. Because the plant is currently operating at full capacity, an increase in baseball production will necessitate a reduction in the manufacture of one or more of the company's other sporting goods product lines. In reaching a budget revision decision, the budget committee will want to answer "what if" questions such as the following.

1. WHAT IF, for the remaining months in 1991, we increased the production of baseballs by 4000 units each month, decreased the monthly production of footballs by 1000 units, and decreased the monthly production of basketballs by 2000 units? WHAT effect would this change have on future months' cash flows?
2. WHAT IF we initiated the same budget revisions as in (1)? WHAT effect would this change have on future months' operating incomes?

To perform **"what if" analysis** and answer questions such as these will require considerable data processing work. For example, in answering question 2, regarding future months' operating incomes, revised budgets for sales and revised budgets for cost of merchandise sold during each of the remaining months in 1991 will have to be prepared. Furthermore, to prepare the revised budgets for cost of merchandise sold will necessitate revised budgets for production (which reflect the monthly quantities of each product line to be manufactured) and revised cost budgets for raw materials, direct labor, and production overhead.

Through the budget committee's use of the company's computer, however, those revised budgets that reveal the operating income performance changes from production-mix changes can be quickly prepared by the EDP subsystem. With the revised budget data in hand, the budget committee can determine whether or not to institute the inventory production revisions.

Thus, to answer "what if" questions (which occur frequently within many organizations' budget systems), the speed capability of a computer makes it a valuable tool for providing the budget committee with timely financial information for decisions concerning budget changes. If the financial effects from anticipated budget revisions have to be determined manually, the time interval required to provide the financial information to the budget committee will likely be so long that the committee will be unable to take immediate action on the proposed revisions. The consequences will often be reduced operating efficiency by the company due to the time delays in initiating budget revisions.

To explore further the computer's role in a budgetary information system, we will now look briefly at a few quantitative methods and their use within a computerized system for budget planning.

Quantitative Methods and the Computer: Aids to Budget Planning

In analyzing the role of quantitative methods and the computer in budgeting, we will examine two major phases of the budgetary planning process: (1) the sales forecasting phase and (2) the allocation-of-resources phase. An important analytical trait common to both of these budgetary planning phases is the ability to abstract their important characteristics in a mathematical model. Such models attempt to represent "real-world" behavior through the construction of mathematical relationships. When it is possible to construct these relationships, recognized quantitative methods may be applied to generate solutions to the forecasting and the allocation-of-resources problems at hand. At the outset, however, the temptation to oversimplify real-world complexities as a means of "fitting" known mathematical techniques to difficult problems must be avoided. The use of a sophisticated model does not necessarily guarantee "good" answers if the model has been misapplied in the first place.

The Sales Forecasting Phase

The major difficulty in forecasting short-range as well as long-range sales demand lies in the potentially large number of variables (such as the unemployment rate and the level of inflation in our economy, the actions of competitors, etc.) and their degree of influence on future demand. Inaccurate judgment regarding any of the variables' influence on sales demand can lead to inaccurate forecasts.

Ideally, all the relevant variables influencing a company's sales demand should be quantified. Then, it is desirable to measure the *separate* effects of each variable on sales demand in order to forecast future demand levels (both short- and long-range) for the company. One of the most widely recognized analytical tools utilized for this purpose is the **multivariate forecasting model,** in which the *dependent* variable, sales, is presumed to be a linear function of a set of *independent* (causal) variables.

The multivariate model, as well as other types of forecasting models, tends to provide "point" estimates of future demand (i.e., a single value of future demand) based on "point" estimates of each of the model's independent variables. Because expectations concerning the future are uncertain (especially for such causal variables as the unemployment rate or competitors' selling prices), however, the levels of the independent variables are more likely to be predictable within some potential range of future operating activity.

Fortunately, the computer can play a major role in the sales forecasting process even when only imprecise estimates of the independent variables are known. This involves the use of *simulation*. If the computer is programmed with the sales forecasting model (regardless of the model's degree of complexity) and various assumptions about the magnitude and causality of key variables are input (by a repetitive process), a company's computer can provide as many different sales forecast outcomes (based on the differing assumptions about the independent variables) as the company desires. These various outcomes can then be reviewed by the budget committee and a determination made of which sales forecast estimate appears most realistic.

The Allocation-of-Resources Phase

Following the sales forecasting process, any *constraints* (limitations) relating to production must be considered in finalizing a company's budgets for sales. Allocating a company's limited asset resources to various activities as part of budgetary planning can be very difficult if there are several possible resource allocation alternatives. A quantitative modeling method for solving business optimizing problems is **linear programming.** This mathematical approach to solving problems can be used when the following conditions exist.

1. The optimizing desired objective can be quantified in linear form.
2. The resource constraints can also be mathematically quantified in linear relationships.
3. The decision variables exhibit constant returns to scale.

Quantitative analysis example 1 (see Appendix A) provides a simple illustration of the graphic method of linear programming in solving a company's optimal resource allocation problem. Normally, the accountants' major role in helping to solve a linear programming problem is to provide the relevant cost data that are incorporated into the mathematical relationships. This information can then be used to analyze, for example, product lines' individual contribution margins in a production mix decision-making situation. Additional information, such as the estimated time it takes to manufacture each product line, must also be provided to the budget planners in establishing their linear programming model. These time estimates will come from the production subsystem.

The linear programming example discussed in Appendix A does not involve a large number of variables and can thus be solved with "pencil and paper." However, in many budgetary planning situations where linear programming is used, the number of variables is much greater, making a manual calculation impossible. In these complex situations, it is possible to use a computer software package for linear programming such as Lindo or MPSS to solve the problem. The quantifiable decision-making data can then be input into the computerized linear programming model and the optimal solution to the problem can be printed out. There are many statistical software packages available, which include linear programming models.

ELECTRONIC SPREADSHEETS

A number of computer software developments have occurred in the past few years to aid companies in performing such accounting functions as short-range budgeting, financial statement analysis, portfolio management, and financial forecasting. Some of these tasks are now performed with **fourth-generation programming languages (4GLs)**—for example, IFPS (Interactive Financial Planning System). A key aspect of these languages is that they are *nonprocedural,* meaning that they focus less on the steps or procedures necessary to accomplish a specific task and more on the problem and/or output required by the user.

By far the most popular budgetary planning tool available to the accountant is the **electronic spreadsheet**—software that first became available on microcomputers but that is now also commonly available on minicomputers and mainframe computers. The earliest versions of spreadsheet software for microcomputers (e.g., VisiCalc) provided simple grids of rows and columns, enabling managers to prepare large budgets that were easily revised by changing some of the spreadsheet values. Advanced versions of these spreadsheets (e.g., Lotus 1-2-3, Excel, Quattro, and VP Planner Plus) have much greater capabilities, including expanded row and column dimensions, graphic capabilities, word processing, automatic file linking (allows a change in one worksheet to affect other worksheets), sideways printing, presentation graphics, and special recalculation abilities.

An electronic spreadsheet is similar to the worksheet of a manual system except that entries are input into a grid created by a computer. This computerized worksheet (see Figure 3-5 for an example of an income statement projection for Alex Company) is organized as a grid of columns and rows, thereby defining a large quantity of individual cells. Each cell is uniquely identified by its column and row coordinates—for example, B5 using Lotus 1-2-3 (as shown in Figure 3-5) or R2C5 (for row 2, column 5) using Multiplan. The exact number of columns and rows in an electronic spreadsheet will vary from software package to software package, but will usually equal or exceed 64 rows by 64 columns.

Electronic spreadsheet programs combine the convenience and familiarity of a pocket calculator with the powerful memory and computational capabilities of a computer. The number of cells in an electronic spreadsheet is usually too large to be entirely displayed on a computer video screen. Thus, the user's video screen becomes a "window" through which a portion of a much larger spreadsheet can be seen. An individual working with the electronic spreadsheet system can move, or "scroll," this window in any one of four directions in order to look at any part of the worksheet while it is being prepared. Furthermore, with some electronic spreadsheet programs, the user can split the computer screen into two windows in order to see any two parts of the worksheet at the same time.

```
              A              B         C           D        E
 1   ALEX COMPANY
 2   DIVISION 1
 3   Income Statement for Year             ---------
 4   Ending December 31, 1991          |   NOTES
 5   (All figures in thousands)        |   ---------
 6                                     |
 7   Sales                   $2,000    |  Constant
 8     Less: Cost of Goods Sold 1,200  |  Constant
 9                           -------    |
10   Gross Margin             $800     |  Formula:   +B7-B8
11                           -------    |
12   Selling and Admin. Expenses       |
13     Sales Commissions @ 5%  $100    |  Formula:   +B7*.05
14     Sales Salaries @ 10%     200    |  Formula:   +B7*.10
15     Shipping Expenses @ 8%   160    |  Formula:   +B7*.08
16     Admin. Expenses @ 3%      60    |  Formula:   +B7*.03
17                           -------    |
18   Total Expenses           $520     |  Formula:   @SUM(B13..B16)
19                           -------    |
20   Net Income               $280     |  Formula:   +B10-B18
21                           =======
```

FIGURE 3-5 A simple income statement projection implemented on an electronic spreadsheet. Constants and cell formulas are shown in the notes. INFORMATION TO STUDENT: The function @SUM(B13. . .B16) means the same thing as B13+B14+B15+B16.

Financial Analysis Using Spreadsheets

Each cell of an electronic spreadsheet program is capable of storing an alphabetic title, a number, or a formula. Usually, a formula will be defined as a function of other cells. For example, as illustrated in Figure 3-5, a worksheet for preparing an income statement would define the contents of its "net income" cell as a function of the cells containing gross margin and total expenses. In addition, since net income is defined as a function of revenues *minus* expenses, any change in either gross margin or total expenses will automatically change the net income figure (see Figure 3-6). Therefore, when a company's budget committee is performing its budgetary planning and analyzing "what if" questions in regard to future income performance, possible changes in various revenues and expenses can be examined to ascertain their effects on net income.

Although an income statement can be arranged as a single column of data, a firm's budget committee, such as Alex Company's, might want to project each revenue and expense line five years into the future (see Figure 3-7). With an electronic spreadsheet, the columns of the spreadsheet reflect the years of the income statement forecast and the rows of the spreadsheet would represent the individual revenue and expense items. The cells in the years' columns 1991, 1992, 1993, 1994, and 1995 would be defined as percentage growth formulas of cells to their immediate left. Thus, once the initial data have been entered for 1991 (column B), the computer can automatically perform the projection computations required. This five-year budgetary projection illustrated in Figure 3-7 can be altered (see Figure 3-8) to examine alternative assumptions—for example, a different rate of growth in sales revenues.

Capital Budgeting on Spreadsheets

In addition to using electronic spreadsheets for short-term budgeting and long-term financial planning as previously discussed, an electronic spreadsheet can also be used to perform capital budgeting analysis (which is a type of long-term financial planning). To illustrate, consider the following problem. The Merit Company has decided to obtain an additional computer, which it plans to install on January 1, 1991. It can either purchase a machine or lease one. The following data are provided about these two options.

```
            A              B        C      D      E
 1  ALEX COMPANY
 2  DIVISION 1
 3  Income Statement for Year          ---------
 4  Ending December 31, 1991         |   NOTE
 5  (All figures in thousands)       | ---------
 6                                   |
 7  Sales                   $1,950   | The $1,950 sales figure was
 8  Less: Cost of Goods Sold  1,200  | altered manually. All other
 9                           ------- | amounts were recalculated
10  Gross Margin              $750   | by the spreadsheet program.
11                           -------
12  Selling and Admin. Expenses
13  Sales Commissions @ 5%     $98
14  Sales Salaries @ 10%       195
15  Shipping Expenses @ 8%     156
16  Admin. Expenses @ 3%        59
17                           -------
18  Total Expenses            $507
19                           -------
20  Net Income                $243
21                           =======
```

FIGURE 3-6 The income statement of Figure 3-5, in which an important "constant"—sales revenues—has been altered to examine what effect it will have on net income.

1. The purchase price of the computer is $230,000. Maintenance, property taxes, and insurance will be $20,000 per year. If the computer is leased, the annual rent will be $85,000 plus 5% of annual billings. The lease price includes maintenance.

2. Due to competitive conditions, the company feels it will be necessary to replace the computer at the end of three years with one that is larger and more advanced. It is estimated that the computer will have a resale value of $110,000 at the end of the three years. The computer will be depreciated on a straight-line basis for both financial reporting and income tax purposes. (*Note:* Ignore the Accelerated Cost Recovery System under the Economic Recovery Tax Act of 1981 when analyzing depreciation in this problem.)

3. The income tax rate is 48%.

4. The estimated annual billing for the services of the new computer will be $220,000 during the first year and $260,000 during each of the

```
            A                     B       C       D       E       F
 1  ALEX COMPANY - DIVISION 1           Projected
 2  Income Statements for Years         Growth at
 3  Ending December 31
 4  (All figures in thousands)             9.00%
 5
 6
 7                             1991    1992    1993    1994    1995
 8  Sales                     $2,000  $2,180  $2,376  $2,590  $2,823
 9  Less Cost of Goods Sold    1,200   1,308   1,426   1,554   1,694
10  Gross Margin              ------  ------  ------  ------  ------
11                            $800    $872    $950   $1,036  $1,129
12  Selling and Admin. Expenses ------  ------  ------  ------  ------
13  Sales Commissions @5%     $100    $109    $119    $130    $141
14  Sales Salaries @ 10%       200     218     238     259     282
15  Shipping Expenses @ 8%     160     174     190     207     226
16  Admin. Expenses @ 3%        60      65      71      78      85
17  Total Expenses            ------  ------  ------  ------  ------
                              $520    $567    $618    $673    $734
18                            ------  ------  ------  ------  ------
19  Net Income                $280    $305    $333    $363    $395
20                            ======  ======  ======  ======  ======
```

FIGURE 3-7 A five-year budget projection using an electronic spreadsheet.

	A	B	C	D	E	F
1	ALEX COMPANY - DIVISION 1		Projected	-----------------------		
2	Income Statements for Years		Growth at	|Note: This growth rate|		
3	Ending December 31		10.00%	|altered from 9.00% |		
4	(All figures in thousands)			-----------------------		
5		1991	1992	1993	1994	1995
6						
7	Sales	$2,000	$2,200	$2,420	$2,662	$2,928
8	Less: Cost of Goods Sold	1,200	$1,320	$1,452	$1,597	$1,757
9		------	------	------	------	------
10	Gross Margin	$800	$880	$968	$1,065	$1,171
11		------	------	------	------	------
12	Selling and Admin. Expenses					
13	Sales Commissions @ 5%	$100	$110	$121	$133	$146
14	Sales Salaries @ 10%	200	220	242	266	293
15	Shipping Expenses @ 8%	160	176	194	213	234
16	Admin. Expenses @ 3%	60	66	73	80	88
17		------	------	------	------	------
18	Total Expenses	$520	$572	$629	$692	$761
19		------	------	------	------	------
20	Net Income	$280	$308	$339	$373	$410
21		======	======	======	======	======

FIGURE 3-8 The spreadsheet budget of Figure 3-7, in which an alternate growth rate of 10%, instead of 9%, is used to investigate the net income effects on the Alex Company.

second and third years. The estimated annual expense of operating the computer is $80,000. An additional $10,000 of start-up expenses will be incurred during the first year.

5. If it decides to purchase the computer, the company will pay cash. If the computer is leased, the $230,000 can be otherwise invested at a 15% rate of return.

6. If the computer is purchased, the amount of the investment recovered during each of the three years can be reinvested immediately at a 15% rate of return. Each year's recovery of investment in the computer will have been reinvested for an average of six months by the end of the year.

Figure 3-9 illustrates an electronic spreadsheet (in this case, using Lotus 1-2-3) that might help the managers of the Merit Company decide which of these two options is best. Certain values, such as estimated sales and individual expenses, are entered as constants in the spreadsheet, whereas other values, such as total expenses, taxes, and the net cash flows, are computed with formulas. Perhaps the most unusual element in this spreadsheet is the use of the predefined @NPV function to compute the present value figures observed in rows 21 and 22 of the spreadsheet. In Lotus 1-2-3, this is expressed as

@NPV (r, data range) where r represents the interest rate and data range represents the set of cells containing the net cash flows to be discounted. Other spreadsheets have similar predefined financial functions, although they are often expressed slightly differently.

For the problem at hand, the net present value computations suggest that the lease plan should be preferred to the purchase plan, since $76,000 is greater than $54,000. However, the company managers might wish to change some of the assumed constants in order to examine alternate assumptions. For example, if the assumed interest rate is changed to 9% from the present 15%, the net present values will change to $90,000 for purchasing and $85,000 for leasing, thus switching our priorities. This alternate analysis would take time if performed manually but is easily achieved by changing just a single value in the spreadsheet. (It took the authors less than five seconds!)

The Power of Electronic Spreadsheets

Electronic spreadsheets are an important tool for accounting information systems because they lend themselves to the types of computational analyses performed by accounting pro-

	A	B	C	D	E	F	G
1	MERIT COMPANY						
2	CAPITAL BUDGETING PROBLEM	Int. Rate		15%			
3	Prepared by John Helms						
4		--------Purchase Plan--------			--------Lease Plan--------		
5		Year 1	Year 2	Year 3	Year 1	Year 2	Year 3
6	Sales	220	260	260	220	260	260
7	Expenses						
8	Maint., Taxes, Insurance	20	20	20	0	0	0
9	Operating Expenses	90	80	80	90	80	80
10	Depreciation	40	40	40	0	0	0
11	Rent	0	0	0	96	98	98
12	Total Expenses	150	140	140	186	178	178
13							
14	Income Before Taxes	70	120	120	34	82	82
15	Federal Taxes @ 48%	34	58	58	16	39	39
16	Net Income	36	62	62	18	43	43
17	Salvage Value	0	0	110	0	0	0
18							
19	Cash Flow (=net income + de-	76	102	212	18	43	43
20	preciation + salvage value)						
21	Present Value of Cash Flows	284			76		
22	Less Initial Investment	230			0		
23							
24	Net Present Value:	54			76		
25							
26							

FIGURE 3-9 An electronic spreadsheet model to help the Merit Company make a capital budgeting decision. All amounts are in thousands of dollars. NOTE: The amounts for "Present Value of Cash Flows" (e.g., 284) were computed with a predefined net present value (NPV) function explained in the text.

fessionals. The previous examples have demonstrated the power of electronic spreadsheets to facilitate data entry and perform required computations quickly. Other advantages of electronic spreadsheets are as follows.

Formatting

Sometimes, how a financial analysis appears is just as important as what the analysis says. Electronic spreadsheets enable their users to create financial reports and projections that are both mathematically accurate and "letter perfect." Pleasing outputs are achieved by the ability of most electronic spreadsheets to align text and numbers, present figures in a variety of numerical formats (e.g., percent, integer, rounded, or dollars), create titles and headings for each of several pages, and print only selected portions of large analyses. Some of the most recently announced spreadsheets also have advanced word-processing capabilities, thereby enabling users to create both reports and financial analyses with the same software.

Altering Data

Electronic spreadsheets are able to remember the constants and formulas entered into them. When alterations must be made, users will change only the relevant portions of the spreadsheets; all other values that are dependent upon these altered constants or formulas will automatically be recomputed. This recalculation capability makes electronic spreadsheets powerful budgetary tools, since mistakes and omissions are easy to correct or modify.

Performing "What If" Analysis

Beyond changing data for mechanical reasons, managers often wish to alter data for analytical reasons. **"What if" analysis** (discussed earlier in our chapter) refers to changing model parameters (important constants that reflect different potential values) in order to examine the effects of such things as alternate interest rates, revenue projections, cost projections, or hiring policies. This computational ability is a powerful planning tool, since managers must usually decide *today* how best to control projects and investments that will extend years into the future. "What if " analysis enables these managers to explore a large number of alternate "scenarios" and to choose courses of action that limit exposure to risk.

Linking Spreadsheets

It often happens that the outputs (results) from one spreadsheet analysis are the inputs for a second analysis. For example, the sales projections in Figure 3-7 might have been determined by earlier work that also used a grid of numbers. Another powerful feature of most spreadsheets is the ability to link spreadsheets together so that important values are communicated. This makes it possible for changes in one spreadsheet to be automatically reflected in "chained" spreadsheets that depend upon the one spreadsheet for input data.

Creating Graphics

The term **graphics** refers to figures, line drawings, and charts that depict data relationships in a visually stimulating way. Most advanced electronic spreadsheet packages have a graphics capability that enables users to create x-y graphs, line charts, bar charts, stacked-bar charts, and pie charts using spreadsheet data. Figure 3-10, for example, illustrates a stacked-bar chart depicting the selling and administrative expenses of Figure 3-7 for the years 1991–1995. Figure 3-11 shows a pie chart of selling and administrative expenses for 1991 based on Figure 3-7, and Figure 3-12 depicts a line chart of net income for the five-year period 1991–1995 using the data from Figure 3-7. Spreadsheets make such graphs remarkably easy to draw. Newer versions of these spreadsheets enable users to create even fancier graphs such as 3-D graphs, graphs that use icons instead of bars, and high-low close graphs. Many spreadsheets can also create data files that can serve as *input* to professional graphics software.

Interfacing with Other Software

As noted, it is often convenient to use spreadsheets in conjunction with other software

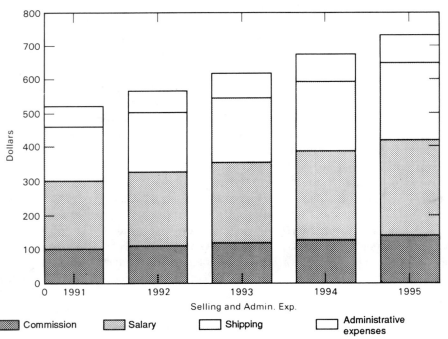

FIGURE 3-10   Stacked-bar chart of selling and administrative expenses.

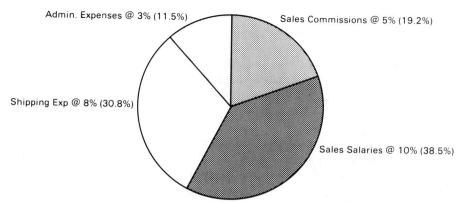

FIGURE 3-11   Pie chart of selling and administrative expenses for 1991.

packages. For example, spreadsheets can be used to create the records for data base management systems or to perform worksheet analyses on data records that are in a data base already. Similarly, it may also be convenient for managers working with spreadsheets on microcomputers to **download data** from corporate mainframe computers or minicomputers into the micros spreadsheets. Electronic spreadsheets facilitate this software interfacing, thereby allowing users to "mix and match" their software usage as needs dictate.

SUMMARY

Budgetary systems are the focal point of many organizations' entire management information

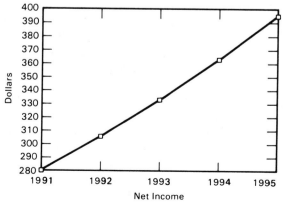

FIGURE 3-12   Line chart of net income.

systems. Through an efficient and effective budget system, which includes both long-range and short-range budgets, an organization plans its future. Any significant deviations from the "planned route" will be reported to the organization's management for investigation and subsequent action.

Thus, budgeting systems allow "management by logical planning and controlling." Without budgetary information systems, the consequences may be "management by crises."

The strong financial emphasis within budgets means that accountants have an important role in the development, implementation, and control of their organization's budgetary system. An efficient and effective budget system requires good communications among all the organizational subsystems, participation by employees from all the subsystems in the budgetary planning process, and flexibility built into the budgetary system so that environmental changes during the budget year can be reflected through revised budgets.

A firm's long-range budgetary system includes various subsystem programs that extend for several years into the future. Each subsystem program proposal for budget committee review should include the anticipated goal (or goals) of the program and the estimated life of the program. To enable the budget committee's comparison and subsequent ranking of all the subsystems' proposals, every program proposal should include a cost/benefit analysis of the proposal's anticipated cash costs and anticipated cash benefits. The costs and benefits relating to programs concern long-range future financial events. Therefore, to provide the budget committee with better information when evaluating the proposals, all anticipated costs and benefits of each program should be converted to their present values (based on the company's opportunity cost). By then relating each program proposal's total present value of the projected net cash flow to the present value of the total expected cash investment required for the program, an excess present value index can be determined for every program proposal. Ranking all the program proposals based on these indexes will provide the budget committee with a reasonable criterion for approving or rejecting specific programs.

The four principal responsibility center configurations for short-range budgetary purposes are cost or expense centers (only *inputs* are measured monetarily), revenue centers (*outputs* are measured monetarily with no attempt to relate the monetary inputs to the monetary outputs), profit centers (both *inputs* and *outputs* are measured monetarily and related to one another to enable a measurement of these centers' income performances), and investment centers (same as profit centers except that a center's income performance is related to its required investment in assets to generate earned income). Large organizations having a divisionalized structure often use either a profit center or an investment center responsibility arrangement for budget planning and controlling purposes. In those divisionalized organizations where major asset investments are necessary for the individual centers to earn an income (as in an automobile manufacturing firm), the investment responsibility center approach will typically provide a better measure of the centers' operating performances than the profit responsibility center approach.

A computer's speed capability in processing data makes it an important tool to aid a company's budgetary planning and controlling activities. For example, when budget revisions are contemplated, a considerable amount of computational work is normally required to analyze the effects of the proposed revisions on the company's future operating performance. With a computerized data processing system, proposed budget revisions and their effects on future company financial performance can be processed quickly. A computer's processing speed thus provides timely budget revision reports to the budget committee for evaluating proposed budget changes.

Budget planning includes two major phases: the sales forecasting phase and the allocation-of-resources phase. In both, mathematical models can be developed to aid the budget committee's planning functions. The degree of sophistication that characterizes many mathematical planning models makes a computer an indispensable tool of the budgetary planners. Using sales forecasting models and linear programming models for budget planning offers the potential for significantly increasing the efficiency and effectiveness of an organization's budgetary planning process.

The final part of this chapter discussed electronic spreadsheets. These software programs are commonly used by individuals with microcomputers to create customized financial planning models such as short-term income-forecasting models, long-term planning models, or capital budgeting models. An electronic spreadsheet enables a manager (1) to perform a wide range of data analyses in a convenient and systematic manner, (2) to change values for data in order to correct errors or to perform "what if" analysis, (3) to format text and numbers in a large variety of professional-looking ways, (4) to link separate spreadsheets together so that the output from one spreadsheet becomes the input to another, (5) to create graphical displays, and (6) to interface with a variety of other computer software.

Key Terms You Should Know

budget committee
communcation within budgetary system
cost/benefit analysis
cost (or expense) centers
divisionalization
download data
electronic spreadsheets
excess present value index method
flexibility within budgetary system
fourth-generation programming languages (4GLs)
graphics
investment centers
linear programming
long-range budgeting
Lotus 1-2-3
microcomputers

multivariate forecasting model
opportunity cost
participation within budgetary system
present value analysis
profit centers
programming
realistic budgets
responsibility center approach to budgeting
revenue centers
short-range budgeting
static (or fixed) budgets
too loose budgets
too strict budgets
"what if" analysis
zero-based budgeting

Discussion Questions

3-1. Discuss the advantages, if any, of having a computerized information system for processing budget performance reports.

3-2. Discuss some of the important items that should be included in a subsystem long-range budget program proposal. For each of these named items, indicate *why* you think it is important.

3-3. The Novelty Toy Company has a manual data processing system. Increased sales volume in the past few years has led to a significant increase in its accounts receivable transactions from credit sales, a significant increase in its inventory of various toys to meet sales demand, and a significant increase in new employees. The toy company's top management is currently reviewing an accounting subsystem long-range budget program proposal that recommends the conversion of the accounts receivable, sales, inventory, and payroll processing functions from the present manual system to a computerized data processing system (using batch processing).

In the cost/benefit analysis accompanying this program proposal, what do you think would be some of the quantitative monetary benefits?

3-4. This chapter discussed three important principles of good budgeting: communication, participation, and flexibility. If you were limited to including

only one of these principles in your organization's budgetary system, which of the three would you choose? Why?

3-5. In developing the long-range and short-range budgets for a retail store that sells stereo equipment, records, television sets, and radios, what types of information would you need about the store's internal and external environment? Be specific.

3-6. Give some specific examples of *constraints* that may prevent a company that manufactures automobile tires from selling a specified number of tires during the year.

3-7. Why should an organization attempt to analyze its long-range future outlook before making a major capital expenditure?

3-8. This chapter emphasized that one effective way of motivating people to have a positive attitude toward their organization's budgetary system is through participation. Can you think of additional ways that might motivate people to respond favorably to a budgetary system? Discuss.

3-9. Why is it important to have realistic budgets within an organization's budgetary system?

3-10. Give arguments for either agreeing or disagreeing with the following statement: "Flexibility of budgets allows an organizational subsystem to change its original budget projection whenever actual operating results vary significantly from the subsystem's predetermined budget. As a result, the subsystem's actual performance will always appear fairly close to its budget."

3-11. One of your best friends (who possesses very little knowledge of accounting) has recently been promoted to a top management position at an advertising agency. An important function that this person will now perform is reviewing long-range budget program proposals for various promotional campaigns to benefit the agency's client's. How would you (as a knowledgeable accountant) explain in simple terms to your friend the importance of using "excess present value indexes" when evaluating various program proposals?

3-12. Periodic program review should be part of an organization's long-range budgetary system. Would you consider this review process a *planning* function or a *controlling* function? Explain.

3-13. What do you feel are some of the inefficiencies, if any, that could occur within an organization's long-range budgetary system if "zero-based budgeting" did not exist?

3-14. The Gutter Ball Bowling Company manufactures all types of bowling equipment (balls, shoes, etc.). For the first time in the company's 10-year operating history, its management has decided to incorporate a budgetary system for planning and controlling. The company's treasurer believes that the detailed short-range budgets for the coming year should be prepared prior to the 5-year, long-range budget projections because the former are easier to plan than the latter. Do you agree with the treasurer? Why?

3-15. Discuss some of the important similarities and differences between short-range and long-range budgeting.

3-16. What is the *responsibility center* approach to short-range budgeting? Discuss the similarities and differences among the four major types of budgetary responsibility centers analyzed in this chapter.

3-17. Steve Miller, marketing manager of the Priced Right Pill Company, recently made the following comments to the company treasurer: "With our company's recent policy of cost efficiency, it seems to me that we could save a great deal of money by eliminating the budget committee. The subsystem managers on this committee spend hours working on the budgets and they never seem to agree on anything! Meanwhile, these managers are continuing to receive their large salaries while they waste time sitting around talking about the coming year's budgets. I feel that our company's budgetary planning for each year would be

much more effective as well as less costly if every subsystem submitted its own budget directly to you for approval."

What are your reactions to Steve Miller's comments?

3-18. Traditional short-range budgeting is based on functional areas of a company, whereas a more modern approach to short-range budgeting is to structure the annual budgets according to responsibility centers. If you were the coordinator of your company's budget system, which of these structural configurations for the company's short-range budgetary system would you favor? Why?

3-19. Because earned revenues are one of the key variables that affect the annual profit of an organization, is there any difference between the revenue center budgetary approach and the profit center budgetary approach to establishing an organization's responsibility centers? Explain.

3-20. Discuss some of the advantages and disadvantages of a *divisionalized* organizational structure. Try to think of some real-life organizations (other than the one discussed in this chapter) that probably would have a divisionalized structure.

3-21. What are the differences, if any, between an engineered cost center and a discretionary cost center? Is it possible to have both of these cost center structures within the same organizational subsystem? If your answer to the previous question was yes, try to think of an example where both engineered and discretionary cost centers might exist within a specific subsystem.

3-22. The Portwood Brian Power Company is a management consulting firm with offices in several major cities. The managers of each office have been complaining continually to top management about their limited decision-making authority and responsibility under the company's present revenue center budgetary organizational structure. After considerable thought, top management has finally agreed to change the responsibility center arrangement of the individual offices so that each one will have decision-making authority and responsibility for both its controllable inputs and its controllable outputs.

Assuming that you are a member of the company's top management staff, what type of responsibility center structure would you recommend for the consulting firm's individual offices? Justify your recommendation.

3-23. The Sink-Free Ship Building Corporation manufactures and sells recreational boats as well as all types of boating supplies (maps, compasses, CB radios, etc.). In the past few years, the corporation's boat sales have increased at a higher percentage than those of its competitors.

The corporation's planners are currently accumulating the relevant data for the long- and short-range budgets. Discuss some of the key variables that should be considered in developing the Sink-Free Ship Building Corporation's long- and short-range budgetary systems. Also include in this discussion the complexities that would affect your analysis of each of these key variables.

3-24. What advantages might the investment center approach offer over the profit center approach in establishing an organization's responsibility center budgetary system?

3-25. The Kurtiss Kandy Kompany (more popularly known as the 3 Ks) recently installed a computer facility to process timely reports needed by its accounting, marketing, and production subsystems. The company's management has elected to establish its computer facility as a cost center for budgetary planning and controlling purposes. Each month the computer facility is allocated a fixed number of dollars with which to operate. At month-end, a performance report is prepared that analyzes the actual costs compared with the budgeted costs of the computer facility.

The budget committee is confused regarding the causes of a recurring problem that arises during the latter part of every month. Beginning in either the third or fourth week of the month, complaints start coming in from the subsystems' managers about the refusal of the computer facility to process certain reports. Typically, these complaints do not occur in either the first or second week of the month.

As a member of the company's budget committee, what do you think is the cause (or causes) of this problem between the computer facility and other subsystems? What recommendations would you make to solve the problem?

3-26. Which type of budgetary responsibility center (a cost center, a revenue center, a profit center, or an investment center) do you feel should be used for a company's EDP subsystem? Why?

3-27. During its consideration of budget revisions, a company's budget committee will often want answers to "what if" questions. Describe (with some specific examples) what is meant by "what if" questions and discuss how an organization's computer can help to answer these questions.

3-28. The Modern Clothing Store manufactures and sells evening apparel for women. Its management recently installed a batch processing computerized data processing system. This mechanized system enables the company to acquire more current information about clothing inventory balances and to increase the timeliness of the billing function (a majority of the company's clothing sales result from customers using their credit cards), thereby speeding up the cash collection process from credit sales.

The clothing store's computer facility was established as a profit center, whereby a transfer price was charged to each subsystem that requested a computerized report. Linda Moss, president of the Modern Clothing Store, felt that one of the major advantages of establishing the company's computer facility as a profit center would be the increased monthly income that the store would earn as a result of the computer facility earning an income on its data processing services to other subsystems. By adding the computer subsystem's monthly income to the income from clothing sales, she logically concluded that the company's profits would be higher.

As a knowledgeable accountant, how would you explain to Linda the fallacy in her thinking?

3-29. What is meant by "the allocation-of-resources phase" of budgetary planning? Are there any similarities between the sales forecasting phase and the allocation-of-resources phase of budgetary planning? Discuss.

3-30. Discuss some of the possible ways that an organization's computer facility can aid the budgetary planning process.

3-31. The Big Bun Hamburger is a fast-food restaurant chain located throughout the East. The company's budget committee is currently attempting to put together the 1991 budget of sales for the entire chain of restaurants.

Each of the individual restaurants is established as a profit center. The only cost responsibility that is excluded from each restaurant's profit budget is the marketing function. Marketing activities for all the restaurants are centralized at the Big Bun Hamburger's main office in Chicago.

Assume that you are an employee of the company's marketing subsystem and are responsible for developing a forecast of 1991 anticipated sales for the total chain. Your forecast will be turned over to the budget committee for review and either acceptance or rejection. Discuss some of the variables that you would consider when developing the 1991 sales forecast. Indicate how a change in each of these variables could have either a positive or a negative effect on sales. (*Note:* Make any reasonable assumptions that you think are necessary regarding the external and internal environmental factors that affect the Big Bun Hamburger restaurant chain.)

3-32. Discuss the role that an electronic spreadsheet and Lotus 1-2-3 can play in a firm's accounting information system.

3-33. Elwood Bank is a large municipal bank with several branch offices. The bank has a computer department that handles all data processing for the bank's operations. In addition, the bank acts as a service bureau by selling its expertise in systems development and its excess machine time to several small business firms.

The computer department currently is treated as an expense center of the bank. The manager of the computer department prepares an expense budget annually for approval by senior bank officials. Monthly operating reports compare actual and budgeted expenses. Revenues from the department's service bureau activities are treated as "other income" by the bank and are not reflected on the computer department's operating reports. The costs of serving these clients are included in departmental reports, however.

The manager of the computer department has proposed that the bank management convert the computer department to a profit or investment center.

Requirements

A. Describe the characteristics that differentiate (1) an expense center, (2) a profit center, and (3) an investment center from each other.

B. Would the manager of the computer department be likely to conduct the operations of the department differently if the department were classified as a profit center or an investment center rather than an expense center? Explain your answer.

(CMA Adapted)

Problems

3-34. The Buffalo Blades (a professional baseball team) has experienced a serious reduction in ticket sales during the past few seasons. As a result of this decline in attendance, top management is currently considering several long-range budget program proposals that it hopes will lead to increased future ticket sales.

Presented here are the program proposals that have been submitted for top-management review. Any approved programs will be implemented January 1, 1991. Assume that the time period during which these proposals are being reviewed is September 1990.

Proposal 1. Acquire Harvey Goldman (last year's top home run hitter in professional baseball) from the Detroit Devils. An $80,000 cash payment would have to be made immediately to Detroit for Goldman's contract. Goldman would then be signed to a five-year contract with the Buffalo Blades at an annual salary of $150,000. By having a top star of Goldman's caliber playing baseball with Buffalo, management estimates that ticket sales will be approximately $175,000 greater next year, and will decrease by $10,000 a year over the following four years. Harvey is expected to retire at the close of the 1995 baseball season.

Proposal 2. Institute a three-year marketing campaign in Buffalo and surrounding cities within 100 miles of Buffalo. This promotional campaign will include advertising announcements on television, radio, and newspapers to stimulate public interest in attending Buffalo baseball games. The initial cash investment necessary to begin this promotional campaign will be $30,000. The annual cash operating costs of the advertising program are estimated to be $40,000 for each of the program's three years (1991, 1992, and 1993). Also, the increase in ticket sales resulting from the promotional program is anticipated to be as follows during the next three years.

1991	$50,000
1992	$60,000
1993	$64,000

Proposal 3. Construct a modern restaurant within the baseball stadium grounds. This restaurant would be situated so that people could enjoy a meal while watching the action on the baseball field. A $100,000 initial cash investment would be required to purchase the necessary equipment associated with the restaurant. As a public gesture to help the baseball franchise survive, a local Buffalo construction company has offered to build the restaurant structure at no cost to the

mflm

Blades. It is anticipated that the restaurant's equipment will have a six-year useful life and a $10,000 salvage value at the end of this time period. The annual depreciation on the equipment will be $15,000. Also, the annual net cash flow (excess of annual cash receipts over annual cash disbursements) expected from the restaurant's operations during the six years from 1991-1996 is $16,000. Management believes that the added attraction of a modern restaurant at the baseball stadium will result in approximately $9000 additional ticket sales in each of the next 6 years.

$9000 ea yrs
for 6 yrs

Requirements

Assume that a maximum of $135,000 is allocated for long-range project expenditures during 1991 and that the Buffalo Blades' opportunity cost is 10%. Ignoring income tax considerations, perform the necessary analyses on the three program proposals to enable top management's determination of which projects to approve and which to reject in 1991. Based on your analyses, which program proposal (or proposals), if any, should be implemented by top management?

3-35. The EDP subsystem of the Williams Mattress Corporation was initially established January 1, 1991 as a profit center for budgetary planning and controlling purposes. The total asset investment necessary to begin operations within the corporation's computer facility was $400,000. Presented below is this subsystem's summarized budget and actual results for the calendar year 1991.

	Budget	**Actual**
Transfer price revenues		
earned	$300,000	$315,000
Expenses:		
Controllable		
fixed and variable		
expenses	180,000	175,000
Noncontrollable		
fixed and variable		
expenses	70,000	73,000

At the beginning of 1992, the Williams Mattress Corporation purchased $100,000 worth of additional hardware equipment for its computer facility. As of December 31, 1992, the corporation's summarized budget and actual operating data appear as follows.

	Budget	**Actual**
Transfer price revenues		
earned	$370,000	$415,000
Expenses:		
Controllable		
fixed and variable		
expenses	240,000	250,000
Noncontrollable		
fixed and variable		
expenses	80,000	82,000

In evaluating the operating performance of the computer facility during 1991 and 1992, management used a contribution margin profit measure. Discussions are currently taking place within the corporation's budget committee to change the responsibility structure of the EDP subsystem from a profit center to an investment center. Should this change be approved, the income measure used to evaluate the performance of the computer facility will continue to be the subsystem's contribution margin.

Requirements

A. Under the present responsibility center structure of the computer facility, evaluate quantitatively the subsystem's operating performance during 1991 and during 1992. Do you feel that the EDP subsystem's operating performance improved in 1992 over 1991? Explain quantitatively.

B. Assuming that the computer facility had originally been established as an investment center rather than a profit center on January 1, 1991, repeat the same quantitative analysis as in (A). In performing your analysis here, further assume that the $400,000 capital expenditure in 1991 and the $100,000 capital expenditure in 1992 were the actual amounts budgeted for these expenditures in each of the two years.

C. If you were a member of the Williams Mattress Corporation's budget committee, would you recommend the continuance of the profit center structure for the computer facility or the conversion of this subsystem's organizational structure to an investment center? Explain.

Note: *When analyzing each problem requirement, ignore the depreciation associated with the assets of the computer facility.*

3-36. NOTE TO INSTRUCTOR: This problem should be assigned only if quantitative analysis example 1 on linear programming (see Appendix A) is covered in the course.

The Spotless Carpet Company manufactures and sells two types of vacuum cleaners, upright and canister. The company's budget committee is currently involved in evaluating the marketing and production subsystems' short-range budget projections for the calendar year beginning January 1, 1992.

The sales forecasts from the marketing subsystem show that the maximum number of upright vacuum cleaners and canister vacuum cleaners that can be sold during 1992 is approximately 100,000 and 200,000, respectively. These demand estimates are based on a $150 selling price for each upright vacuum cleaner and a $100 selling price for each canister vacuum cleaner.

The production subsystem manager reports that the capacity of the plant for manufacturing vacuum cleaners during 1992 is 120,000 hours. The manager of this subsystem also indicates that the standard production time for an upright vacuum cleaner is 1 hour and the standard production time for a canister vacuum cleaner is 30 minutes.

The company's managerial accountant, after studying the production process for vacuum cleaners, estimates the standard variable manufacturing costs to be $120 for each upright and $75 for each canister. The total standard fixed costs for operating the production plant during 1992 are estimated to be $150,000.

Requirement

Using linear programming (the graphic approach), determine the optimal mix of upright and canister vacuum cleaners that should be manufactured by the Spotless Carpet Company's production subsystem during the 1992 budget year.

3-37. NOTE TO INSTRUCTOR: This problem should be assigned only if quantitative analysis example 1 on linear programming (see Appendix A) is covered in the course.

Excelsion Corporation manufacturers and sells two kinds of containers—paperboard and plastic. The company produced and sold 100,000 paperboard containers and 75,000 plastic containers during the month of April. A total of 4000 and 6000 direct labor hours were used in producing the paperboard and plastic containers, respectively.

The company has not been able to maintain an inventory of either product, due to the high demand.

This situation is expected to continue in the future. Workers can be shifted from the production of paperboard to plastic containers and vice versa, but additional labor is not available in the community. In addition, there will be a shortage of plastic material used in the manufacture of the plastic container in the coming months because of a labor strike at the facilities of a key supplier. Management has estimated there will be only enough raw material to produce 60,000 plastic containers during June.

The income statement for Excelsion Corporation for the month of April is shown in the following table. The costs presented in the statement are representative of prior periods and are expected to continue at the same rates (or levels) in the future.

Excelsion Corporation
Income Statement
For the Month Ended April 30, 1992

	Paperboard Containers	Plastic Containers
Sales	$220,800	$222,900
Less: Returns and allowances	$ 6,360	$ 7,200
Discounts	2,440	3,450
	$ 8,800	$ 10,650
Net sales	$212,000	$212,250
Cost of sales		
Raw material cost	$123,000	$120,750
Direct labor	26,000	28,500
Indirect labor (variable with direct labor hours)	4,000	4,500
Depreciation— machinery	14,000	12,250
Depreciation—building	10,000	10,000
Cost of sales	$177,000	$176,000
Gross profit	$ 35,000	$ 36,250
Selling and general expenses		
General expenses— variable	$ 8,000	$ 7,500
General expenses— fixed	1,000	1,000
Commissions	11,000	15,750
Total operating expenses	$ 20,000	$ 24,250
Income before tax	$ 15,000	$ 12,000
Income taxes (40%)	6,000	4,800
Net income	$ 9,000	$ 7,200

Requirements

A. The management of Excelsion Corporation plans to use linear programming to determine the optimal mix of paperboard and plastic containers for the month of June to achieve maximum profits. Using data presented in the April income statement, formulate and label the

    1. Objective function.
    2. Constraint functions.

B. Identify the underlying assumptions of linear programming.

C. What contribution would the management accountant normally make to a team established to develop the linear programming model and apply it to a decision problem?

                                 (CMA Adapted)

3-38. NOTE TO INSTRUCTOR: This problem should be assigned only if quantitative analysis example 1 on linear programming (see Appendix A) is covered in the course.

Girth, Inc. makes two kinds of men's suede leather belts. Belt A is a high-quality belt, and belt B is of somewhat lower quality. The company earns $7 for each unit of belt A that is sold, and $2 for each unit sold of belt B. Each unit (belt) of type A requires twice as much manufacturing time as a unit of type B. Further, if only belt B is made, Girth has the capacity to manufacture 1000 units per day. Suede leather is purchased by Girth under a long-term contract that makes available to Girth enough leather to make 800 belts per day (A and B combined). Belt A requires a fancy buckle, of which only 400 per day are available. Belt B requires a different (plain) buckle, of which 700 per day are available. The demand for the suede leather belts (A or B) is such that Girth can sell all that it produces.

The accompanying graph displays the constraint functions based on these facts.

Requirements

A. Using the graph, determine how many units of belt A and belt B should be produced to maximize daily profits.

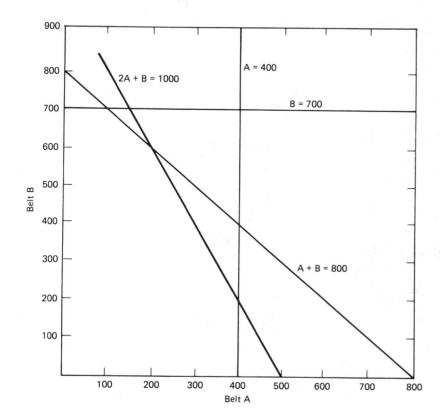

B. Assume the same facts as above except that the sole supplier of buckles for belt A informs Girth, Inc. that it will be unable to supply more than 100 fancy buckles per day. How many units of each of the two belts should be produced each day to maximize profits?

C. Assume the same facts as in B except that Texas Buckles, Inc. could supply Girth, Inc. with the additional fancy buckles it needs. The price would be $3.50 more than Girth, Inc. is paying for such buckles. How many, if any, fancy buckles should Girth, Inc. buy from Texas Buckles, Inc.? Explain how you determined your answer.

(CMA Adapted)

3-39. NOTE TO INSTRUCTOR: This problem should be assigned only if quantitative analysis example 1 on linear programming (see Appendix A) is covered in the course.

Part A

The Witchell Corporation manufactures and sells three grades (A, B, and C) of a single wood product. Each grade must be processed through three phases—cutting, fitting, and finishing—before it is sold.

The following unit information is provided.

	A	B	C
Selling price	$10.00	$15.00	$20.00
Direct labor	5.00	6.00	9.00
Direct materials	.70	.70	1.00
Variable overhead	1.00	1.20	1.80
Fixed overhead	.60	.72	1.08
Materials requirements in board feet	7	7	10
Labor requirements in hours			
Cutting	3/6	3/6	4/6
Fitting	1/6	1/6	2/6
Finishing	1/6	2/6	3/6

Only 5000 board feet per week can be obtained. The cutting department has 180 hours of labor available each week. The fitting and finishing departments each have 120 hours of labor available every week. No overtime is allowed.

Contract commitments require the company to make 50 units of A per week. In addition, company policy is to produce at least 50 additional units of A, 50 units of B, and 50 units of C each week to actively remain in each of the three markets. Because of competition only 130 units of C can be sold every week.

Required

Formulate and label the linear objective function and the constraint functions necessary to maximize the contribution margin.

Part B

The graph provided on the next page presents the constraint functions for a chair manufacturing company whose production problem can be solved by linear programming. The company earns $8 for each kitchen chair sold and $5 for each office chair sold.

Required

A. What is the profit maximizing production schedule?

B. How did you select this production schedule?

(CMA Adapted)

3-40. Create an electronic spreadsheet model similar to the one illustrated in Figure 3-5 for all four divisions of the Alex Company. NOTE TO STUDENTS: The only constants in this model are the sales figure and the cost of goods sold (CGS). All other values are computed from these numbers.

Additional Requirements

A. Use the same model to compute the net income for each of the following divisions of the Alex Company (all figures in thousands).

	Division 1	Division 2	Division 3	Division 4
Sales	2,000	1,250	5,221	250
CGS	1,200	988	3,670	284

B. Perform a similar analysis assuming that each division increases its sales by 10% and its CGS by 5%.

C. Perform a similar analysis assuming that each division loses 7% of its sales but its CGS only decreases by 3%.

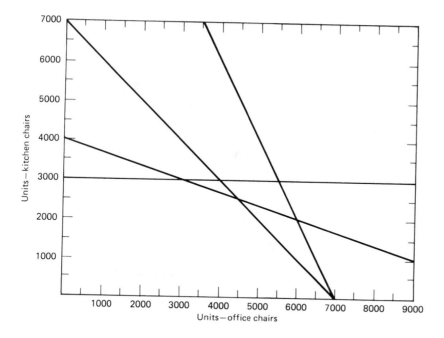

3-41. Create an electronic spreadsheet model similar to the one illustrated in Figure 3-5 for the Gary Company (see "note to students" in Problem 3-40). Use the following relationships.

Sales:	$2,550,000
CGS:	1,255,000
Sales Commissions:	6% of sales
Sales Salaries:	15% of sales
Shipping Expenses:	12% of CGS
Admin. Expenses:	5% of sales
Interest on Loans:	$12,000/month

3-42. Observe the electronic spreadsheet model illustrated in Figure 3-7. Create a similar model and perform the following analyses.

A. Recreate the initial model shown.
B. Assume a growth rate of 6%. What happens to the division's net income figures for each of the next five years as a result?
C. By how much must sales grow in order for the division to reach a target net income figure of $500,000 in 1995?
D. What will happen to the division's net income figures if shipping expenses increase to 10% from their current 8%?

3-43. Refer back to Problems 3-40 and 3-42. Assume a growth rate of 10% to perform the following analyses.

A. Answer parts A, B, C, and D in Problem 3-42 for Division 2 of the company.
B. Answer parts A, B, C, and D in Problem 3-42 for Division 3 of the company.
C. Answer parts A, B, C, and D in Problems 3-42 for Division 4 of the company.

3-44. Refer to Figure 3-9. Recreate this spreadsheet using an interest rate of 15%.

A. Which plan do you recommend at an interest rate of 12%?
B. At what interest rate (to the nearest tenth of a percent) will the company be indifferent between the two plans?
C. Which plan do you recommend if the interest rate is 15% but the expected salvage value of the computer under the purchase plan is only $80,000?

3-45. The manager of the Cooke Manufacturing Company has asked you to prepare a flexible budget for October for its line of Redskin seat cushions. The following data are available for actual operations in a recent typical month:

Seats produced and sold	9,000
Direct materials cost	$45,000
Direct labor cost	$36,000
Fixed manufacturing costs	$32,000
Average selling price/seat	$20
Fixed selling and administrative expenses	$14,000

It is expected that a 10% increase in the selling price will take effect in October. The only variable selling expense is a 10% commission for manufacturer's representatives expenses. The only variable overhead cost is $2 per seat for a patent royalty. Salary increases effective in October are $6000 annually for the production manager and $9000 per year for the sales manager. Direct material prices are expected to rise 10% in October. No other cost changes are anticipated.

Required

Use electronic spreadsheet software to prepare a flexible budget for October, showing expected net income in a contribution margin income statement format, at each of three levels of volume: 8000 units, 10,000 units, and 12,000 units.

CASE ANALYSES

3-46. *Roletter Company*

Roletter Company makes and sells artistic frames for pictures of weddings, graduations, christenings, and other special events. Bob Anderson, Controller, is responsible for preparing Roletter's master budget and has accumulated the information below for 1990.

Labor related costs include pension contributions of $0.25 per hour, workers' compensation insurance of $0.10 per hour, employee medical insurance of $0.40 per hour, and social security taxes. Assume that as of January 1, 1990, the base figure for computing social security taxes is $37,800 and that the rates are 7 percent

for employers and 7 percent for employees. The cost of employee benefits paid by Roletter on its employees is treated as a direct labor cost.

Roletter has a labor contract that calls for a wage increase to $9.00 per hour on April 1, 1990. New labor saving machinery has been installed and will be fully operational by March 1, 1990.

Roletter expects to have 16,000 frames on hand at December 31, 1989, and has a policy of carrying an end-of-month inventory of 100 percent of the following month's sales plus 50 percent of the second following month's sales.

Questions

1. Using an electronic spreadsheet program, prepare a production budget and a direct labor budget for Roletter Company by month and for the first quarter of 1990. Both budgets may be combined in one schedule. The direct labor budget should include direct labor hours and show the detail for each direct labor cost category.

2. For each item used in Roletter's production budget and its direct labor budget, identify the other component(s) of the master budget (budget package) that would also use these data. (Hint: You may want to consult a cost accounting textbook in preparing your solution.)

(CMA Adapted)

3-47. *Forecasting Automobile Demand*

Mr. Ted Salsberg is a marketing vice-president with the National Vehicles Corporation. He has served with the company for 17 years, beginning his career as an assembly line supervisor, and then gradually working his way up through the company ranks in marketing, production, and corporate finance. For the last 3 years, Mr. Salsberg had been assigned the task of forecasting

1990

	January	February	March	April	May
Estimated unit sales	10,000	12,000	8,000	9,000	9,000
Sales price per unit	$50.00	$47.50	$47.50	$47.50	$47.50
Direct labor hours per unit	2.0	2.0	1.5	1.5	1.5
Wage per direct labor hour	$8.00	$8.00	$8.00	$9.00	$9.00

future private automobile sales for the purpose of making detailed marketing and production decisions. No task had ever given him more headaches. Projections of the future were inevitably risky and consumers had been especially erratic of late in the purchase of what was becoming a very expensive durable good.

The history of automotive production in the last few years had been very unusual. More and more safety items such as seat belts and shock-absorbing bumper equipment were required by law, and emission control standards also required the production of increasingly sophisticated smog-control devices. These requirements also resulted in raising the production cost of the average automobile, and had been responsible for National's three biggest price increases in the last five years. Because consumers' reactions to higher prices varied from year to year, however, the effects of tighter safety standards and more stringent emission controls on future automotive sales were difficult to predict.

Other factors besides production costs tended to affect the consumer price of the typical automobile. For example, of late, the company had experimented with a rebate program in which new owners were given certificates by the dealers. These certificates were redeemable from the manufacturer for $250, $300, $400, or $500, depending on the particular car the consumer had purchased. Results of the program were mixed. In some areas of the country, the rebate program had spurred large increases in automotive purchases; in others, the increases had been negligible.

Since automobiles were "big ticket" items, Mr. Salsberg knew that consumer income also played an important role in the decision to purchase a new vehicle. At the present time, the national economy was in a moderate upswing and consumer personal disposable income had been climbing slightly over the previous year. Last week, the president of the United States appeared on television to report an optimistic view of the nation's economic future. However, Mr. Salsberg didn't trust politicians very much, especially in the year before an election, as it was. He did take note of the president's promise for a tax cut for the current calendar year. Mr. Salsberg especially pondered the effect of the tax cut on personal disposable income, the likelihood of such a tax proposal passing the Congress in the face of the nation's current budget deficit, and the influence the tax cut would be likely to

have on consumer durable-goods spending, should this tax cut pass the legislature.

Credit was also an important consideration. Interest rates had fluctuated widely in the last few years, and these fluctuations were also known to have an important bearing on automobile purchases. Sometimes, for example, an extra 2%, 1%, or even 1/2 of 1% in installment loan interest rates made the difference between a family qualifying for a car loan or being rejected. Financing was considered so important in the car purchase decision, in fact, that National Vehicles was seriously considering the formulation of a new subsidiary, tentatively called N. V. Finance, to provide stable financing to those customers who otherwise might not qualify for an automobile installment loan.

Other factors also weighed on Mr. Salsberg's mind, although he did not have a clear idea of how important any of them were. One consideration was the price of gasoline. Since 1973, the retail price of gasoline had more than doubled, and there was good reason to believe that even higher prices could be expected in the near future. What effect this would have on automobile purchases was speculative. It appeared that some families bought compact cars expressly to save on gasoline expenditures. Other purchasers seemed to consider the automobile a status symbol and bought luxury cars despite their relatively poorer fuel economies and greater maintenance costs.

A second consideration was depreciation on cars purchased for business use. In many instances, depreciation was the most important "expense" that the typical business car owner incurred, although no out-of-pocket cash was spent for this expense. How fast the newer cars could be depreciated was an interesting point for Mr. Salsberg, especially because he knew that the new-car market broke down into two major groups: first-time purchasers and replacement purchasers.

As he pondered this second consideration, Mr. Salsberg also realized that he had neglected to consider the fleet owners. Included in such businesses were rent-a-car companies, leasing companies, and taxicab companies, all of which acquired new vehicles yearly. Mr. Salsberg wondered how important their business was.

Questions

1. Evaluate the factors Mr. Salsberg has considered in his analysis of the purchase of a new automobile.

Which factors would you consider important and which would you consider unimportant?
2. What additional factors would you consider if you were asked to construct a three-month forecast of automobile sales demand for Mr. Salsberg?
3. What variables would you wish to *quantify* in your automobile sales demand analysis and where would you get the information?
4. What qualitative factors would influence your automobile sales forecast? How would you incorporate such factors into a quantitative prediction of future automobile sales?

3-48. The ATCO Company

The ATCO Company purchased the Dexter Company three years ago. Prior to the acquisition Dexter manufactured and sold plastic products to a wide variety of customers. Dexter has since become a division of ATCO and now only manufactures plastic components for products made by ATCO's Macon Division. Macon sells its products to hardware wholesalers.

ATCO's corporate management gives the Dexter Division management a considerable amount of authority in running the division's operations. However, corporate management retains authority for decisions regarding capital investments, price setting of all products, and the quantity of each product to be produced by the Dexter Division.

ATCO has a formal performance evaluation program for the management of all its divisions. The performance evaluation program relies heavily on each division's return on investment. The income statement of Dexter Division, presented here, provides the basis for the evaluation of Dexter's divisional management.

The financial statements for the divisions are prepared by the corporate accounting staff. The corporate general services costs are allocated on the basis of sales dollars, and the computer department's actual costs are apportioned among the divisions on the basis of use. The net division investment includes division fixed assets at net book value (cost less accumulated depreciation), division inventory, and corporate working capital apportioned to the divisions on the basis of sales dollars.

Questions

1. Discuss the financial reporting and performance evaluation program of ATCO Company as it relates to the responsibilities of the Dexter Division.

2. Based on your response to question 1, recommend appropriate revisions of the financial information and reports used to evaluate the performance of Dexter's divisional management. If revisions are not necessary, explain why.

(CMA Adapted)

Dexter Division of ATCO Company
Income Statement For the Year Ended
October 31, 1991 ($000 omitted)

Sales		$4000
Costs and expenses		
Product costs		
Direct materials	$ 500	
Direct labor	1100	
Factory overhead	1300	
Total	$2900	
Less: Increase in inventory	350	$2550
Engineering and research		120
Shipping and receiving		240
Division administration		
Manager's office	$ 210	
Cost accounting	40	
Personnel	82	332
Corporate costs		
Computer	$ 48	
General services	230	278
Total costs and expenses		$3520
Divisional operating income		$ 480
Net plant investment		$1600
Return on investment		30%

3-49. Kelly Petroleum Company

Kelly Petroleum Company has a large oil and natural gas project in Oklahoma. The project has been organized into two production centers (Petroleum Production and Natural Gas Production) and one service center (Maintenance).

Maintenance Center Activities and Scheduling

Don Pepper, Maintenance Center manager, has organized his maintenance workers into work crews that serve the two production centers. The maintenance crews perform preventive maintenance and repair equipment both in the field and in the central maintenance shop.

Pepper is responsible for scheduling all maintenance work in the field and at the central shop. Preventive maintenance is performed according to a set schedule established by Pepper and approved by the production center managers. Breakdowns are given immediate priority in scheduling so that downtime is minimized. Thus, preventive maintenance occasionally must be postponed, but every attempt is made to reschedule it within three weeks.

Preventive maintenance work is the responsibility of Pepper. However, if a significant problem is discovered during preventive maintenance, the appropriate production center supervisor authorizes and supervises the repair after checking with Pepper.

When a breakdown in the field occurs, the production centers contact Pepper to initiate the repairs. The repair work is supervised by the production center supervisor. Machinery and equipment sometimes need to be replaced while the original equipment is repaired in the central shop. This procedure is followed only when the time to make the repair in the field would result in an extended interruption of operations. Replacement of equipment is recommended by the maintenance work crew supervisor and approved by a production center supervisor.

Routine preventive maintenance and breakdowns of automotive and mobile equipment used in the field are completed in the central shop. All repairs and maintenance activities taking place in the central shop are under the direction of Pepper.

Maintenance Center Accounting Actitivies

Pepper has records identifying the work crews assigned to each job in the field, the number of hours spent on the job, and parts and supplies used on the job. In addition, records for the central shop (jobs, labor hours, parts, and supplies) have been maintained. However, this detailed maintenance information is not incorporated into Kelly's accounting system.

Pepper develops the annual budget for the Maintenance Center by planning the preventive maintenance that will be needed during the year, estimating the number and seriousness of breakdowns, and estimating the shop activities. He then bases the labor, part, and supply costs on his plans and estimates and develops the budget amounts by line item. Because the timing of the breakdowns is impossible to plan, Pepper divides the annual budget by 12 to derive the monthly budget.

All costs incurred by work crews in the field and in the central shop are accumulated monthly and then allocated to the two production cost centers based upon the field hours worked in each production center. This method of cost allocation has been used on

Oklahoma Project
Maintenance Center Cost Report
For the Month of November 1991
(in thousands of dollars)

	Budget	Actual	Petroleum Production	Natural Gas Production
Shop hours	2,000	1,800	—	—
Field hours	8,000	10,000	6,000	4,000
Labor—electrical	$ 25.0	$ 24.0	$ 14.4	$ 9.6
Labor—mechanical	30.0	35.0	21.0	14.0
Labor—instrumentation	18.0	22.5	13.5	9.0
Labor—automotive	3.5	2.8	1.7	1.1
Labor—heavy equipment	9.6	12.3	7.4	4.9
Labor—equipment operation	28.8	35.4	21.2	14.2
Labor—general	15.4	15.9	9.6	6.3
Parts	60.0	86.2	51.7	34.5
Supplies	15.3	12.2	7.3	4.9
Lubricants and fuels	3.4	3.0	1.8	1.2
Tools	2.5	3.2	1.9	1.3
Accounting and data processing	1.5	1.5	.9	.6
Total	$213.0	$254.0	$152.4	$101.6

Pepper's recommendation because he believed that it was easy to implement and understand. Furthermore, he believed that a better allocation system was impossible to incorporate into the monthly report due to the wide range of salaries paid to maintenance workers and the fast turnover of materials and parts.

The November cost report for the Maintenance Center that is provided by the accounting department is shown on the previous page.

Production Center Managers' Concerns

Both production center managers have been upset with the method of cost allocation. Furthermore, they believe the report is virtually useless as a cost control device. Actual costs always seem to deviate from the monthly budget and the proportion charged to each production center varies significantly from month to month. Maintenance costs have increased substantially since 1989, and the production managers believe that they have no way to judge whether such an increase is reasonable.

The two production managers, Pepper, and representatives of corporate accounting have met to discuss these concerns. They concluded that a responsibility accounting system could be developed to replace the current system. In their opinion, a responsibility accounting system would alleviate the production managers' concerns and accurately reflect the activity of the Maintenance Center.

Questions

1. Explain the purposes of a responsibility accounting system, and discuss how such a system could resolve the concerns of the production center managers of Kelly Petroleum Company.
2. Describe the behavioral advantages generally attributed to responsibility accounting systems that the management of Kelly Petroleum Company should expect if the system were effectively introduced for the Maintenance Center.
3. Describe a report format for the Maintenance Center that would be based upon an effective responsibility accounting system, and explain which, if any, of the Maintenance Center's costs should be charged to the two production centers.

(CMA Adapted)

3-50. *Merriman Company*

Thomas Dauton is manager of reports in the office of senior vice-president Frank Lee of the Merriman Company. Until 5 months ago Lee was a regional vice-president in charge of manufacturing operations for Region 8 of the company, and Dauton was his assistant. At that time Lee was promoted to the newly created position, senior vice-president, and given the responsibility for all of Merriman's manufacturing operations. Twelve regional manufacturing vice-presidents report to him.

Lee has visited each region since taking over his new job and Dauton has accompanied him on most of these trips. Relations with each regional vice-president, as Dauton observes them, range from fairly cool to enthusiastically cooperative. Lee's replacement in Region 8 had been one of Lee's stronger assistants; each of the other 11 regional vice-presidents had been in his job for at least 6 months (and as long as 10 years) before Lee's promotion. The least enthusiastic greeting came from the regional vice-president who was the other most likely candidate for senior vice-president. Dauton also noted that one other regional vice-president appeared uninterested in the visit and did not seem enthusiastic about the new organizational arrangement; this regional vice-president has been in his present position for 8 years and is due to retire within the next 18 months.

Each regional manufacturing vice-president is required to file a monthly report that contains detailed comparisons of budgeted and actual costs of production for the previous month and an explanation of the differences from budget. Prior to Lee's appointment as senior vice-president of manufacturing, these reports have been sent by the tenth of the following month to the executive vice-president for operations, a member of the three-man president's office of the corporation. The reports are still due in the president's office by the tenth of the following month, but Lee now receives the reports first. The 12 regional reports are then submitted by Lee, along with his own summary and narrative, to the president's office.

This new reporting arrangement was Lee's idea and he insists that the summary be carefully prepared before it is submitted to the president's office. The company policy guide, as yet unchanged, requires the regional vice-presidents to submit their reports by the tenth day. Lee has asked the regional vice-presidents to submit the reports by the seventh of the month. This will allow Dauton adequate time to prepare the analysis for Lee's review before it is submitted to the president's office. The request is not unreasonable, as the company recently installed an efficient computer-based information system that can get the necessary information to the regional vice-presidents by the fourth day.

The regional vice-presidents have acknowledged the request and have agreed to try to meet the schedule established by Lee. Two regions, however, have not met the schedule for the past three months even though Dauton is sure they could with a little effort. He believes one region is not cooperating because its vice-president is still irked at not being promoted to the senior vice-president position. The office for this region has called each of the last three months on the seventh day to say the report was not ready but would be ready on the tenth day. The other report, from the region headed by the near-retirement vice-president, has arrived on the tenth day each month but no notice or explanation of the delay has been given.

This past month Lee made it clear to Dauton that he wanted the report he would submit to the president's office ready for his review by noon on the ninth day, rather than late on the tenth day. The reports from all but the two regions mentioned arrived early on the seventh day. Dauton waited until the eighth day before drafting the report with the hope that the two recalcitrant division reports would arrive. When the reports did not arrive, Dauton called his counterparts in the divisions to get what information he could so that he could complete his draft of the report. From these informal sources plus the regular reports of the other divisions he was able to complete the draft on time. The final report, more carefully prepared than in prior months, was ready for the president's office by noon on the tenth day. The details that had been acquired by phone for the two divisions were verified when their reports were received. The report was delivered by mid-afternoon to the president's office.

Questions

1. Identify and discuss the organizational and behavioral factors that cause the difficulties Frank Lee and Thomas Dauton are experiencing in preparing a complete and timely monthly summary report for the president's office.
2. How should Frank Lee and Thomas Dauton proceed to improve the reporting process? Be sure

your answer includes recognition of organizational structure, authority and responsibility, and communication and motivation factors.

(CMA Adapted)

3-51. Ferguson & Son Mfg. Company

Tom Emory and Jim Morris strolled back to their plant from the administrative offices of Ferguson & Son Mfg. Company. Tom was manager of the machine shop in the company's factory; Jim was manager of the equipment maintenance department.

The men has just attended the monthly performance evaluation meeting for plant department heads. These meetings had been held on the third Tuesday of each month since Robert Ferguson, Jr., the president's son, had become plant manager a year earlier.

As they were walking Tom Emory spoke. "Boy, I hate those meetings! I never know whether my department's accounting reports will show good or bad performance. I'm beginning to expect the worst. If the accountants say I saved the company a dollar, I'm called 'Sir,' but if I spend even a little too much—boy, do I get in trouble. I don't know if I can hold on until I retire."

Tom had just received the worst evaluation he had ever received in his long career with Ferguson & Son. He was the most respected of the experienced machinists in the company. He had been with Ferguson & Son for many years and was promoted to supervisor of the machine shop when the company expanded and moved to its present location. The president (Robert Ferguson, Sr.) had often stated that the company's success was due to the high quality of the work of machinists like Emory. As supervisor, Tom stressed the importance of craftsmanship and told his workers that he wanted no sloppy work coming from his department.

When Robert Ferguson, Jr. became the plant manager, he directed that monthly performance comparisons be made between actual and budgeted costs for each department. The departmental budgets were intended to encourage the supervisors to reduce inefficiencies and to seek cost reductions. The company controller was instructed to have his staff "tighten" the budget slightly whenever a department attained its budget in a given month; this was done to reinforce the plant supervisor's desire to reduce costs. The young plant manager often stressed the importance of continued progress toward attaining the budget; he also made it known that he kept a file of these performance reports for future reference when he succeeded his father.

Tom Emory's conversation with Jim Morris continued as follows.

Emory: I really don't understand. We've worked so hard to get up to budget and the minute we make it, they tighten the budget on us. We can't work any faster and still maintain quality. I think my men are ready to quit trying. Besides, those reports don't tell the whole story. We always seem to be interrupting the big jobs for all those small rush orders. All that setup and machine adjustment time is killing us. And quite frankly, Jim, you were no help. When our hydraulic press broke down last month, your people were nowhere to be found. We had to take it apart ourselves and got stuck with all that idle time.

Morris: I'm sorry about that, Tom, but you know my department has had trouble making budget, too. We were running well beyond budget at the time of that problem, and if we'd spent a day on that old machine, we would never have made it up. Instead we made the scheduled inspections of the forklift trucks because we knew we could do those in less than the budgeted time.

Emory: Well, Jim, at least you have some options. I'm locked into what the scheduling department assigns to me and you know they're being harassed by sales for those special orders. Incidentally, why didn't your report show all the supplies you guys wasted last month when you were working in Bill's department?

Morris: We're not out of the woods on that deal yet. We charged the maximum we could to our other work and haven't even reported some of it yet.

Emory: Well, I'm glad you have a way of getting out of the pressure. The accountants seem to know everything that's happening in my department, sometimes even before I do. I thought all that budget and accounting

stuff was supposed to help, but it just gets me into trouble. It's all a big pain. I'm trying to put out quality work; they're trying to save pennies.

Tom Emory's performance report for the month in question is reproduced in the following table. Actual production volume for the month was at the budgeted level.

Machine Shop—October 1991
T. Emory, Supervisor

	Budget	Actual	Variances
Direct labor	$ 39,600	$ 39,850	$ 250U
Direct materials	231,000	231,075	75U
Depreciation— equipment	3,000	3,000	0
Depreciation— buildings	6,000	6,000	0
Power	900	860	40F
Maintenance	400	410	10U
Supervision	1,500	1,500	0
Idle time	0	1,800	1,800U
Setup labor	680	2,432	1,752U
Miscellaneous	2,900	3,300	400U
	$285,980	$290,227	$4247U

Questions

1. Identify the problems that appear to exist in Ferguson & Son Mfg. Company's budgetary control system and explain how the problems are likely to reduce the effectiveness of the system.
2. Explain how Ferguson & Son Mfg. Company's budgetary control system could be revised to improve its effectiveness.

(CMA Adapted)

3-52. Family Resorts Inc.

Family Resorts Inc. is a holding company for several vacation hotels in the northeast and mid-Atlantic states. The firm originally purchased several old inns, restored the buildings, and upgraded the recreational facilities. The inns have been well received by vacationing families as many services are provided that accommodate children and afford parents time for themselves. Since the completion of the restorations ten years ago, the company has been profitable.

Family Resorts Inc.

Responsibility Summary ($000 omitted)

Reporting Unit: Family Resorts
Responsible Person: President

Mid-Atlantic Region	$605
New England Region	365
Unallocated costs	(160)
Income before taxes	**$810**

Reporting Unit: New England Region
Responsible Person: Regional Manager

Vermont	$200
New Hampshire	140
Maine	105
Unallocated costs	(80)
Total contribution	**$365**

Reporting Unit: Maine District
Responsible Person: District Manager

Harbor Inn	$ 80
Camden Country Inn	60
Unallocated costs	(35)
Total contribution	**$105**

Reporting Unit: Harbor Inn
Responsible Person: Innkeeper

Revenue	$600
Controllable costs	(455)
Allocated costs	(65)
Total contribution	**$ 80**

Family Resorts has just concluded its annual meeting of regional and district managers. This meeting is held each November to review the results of the previous season and to help the managers prepare for the upcoming year. Prior to the meeting, the managers have submitted proposed budgets for their districts or regions as appropriate. These budgets have been reviewed and consolidated into an annual operating budget for the entire company. The 1990 budget has been presented at the meeting and was accepted by the managers.

To evaluate the performance of its managers, Family Resorts uses responsibility accounting. Therefore, the preparation of the budget is given close attention at headquarters. If major changes need to be made to the budgets submitted by the managers, all affected parties are consulted before the changes are incorporated. Presented in the column to the left is a page from the budget booklet that all managers received at the meeting.

Questions

1. Responsibility accounting has been used effectively by many companies, both large and small.
   a. Define responsibility accounting.
   b. Discuss the benefits that accrue to a company using responsibility accounting.
   c. Describe the advantages of responsibility accounting for the managers of a firm.
2. Family Resorts Inc.'s budget was accepted by the regional and district managers. Based on the facts presented, evaluate the budget process employed by Family Resorts by addressing the following.
   a. What features of the budget preparation are likely to result in the managers adopting and supporting the budget process?
   b. What features of the budget presentation shown above are likely to make the budget attractive to managers?
   c. What recommendations, if any, could be made to the budget preparers to improve the budget process? Explain your answer.

(CMA Adapted)

The Technology
of Accounting
Information Systems

Among the important questions that you should be able to answer after reading this chapter are:

1. What are the major components of a central processing unit, and in general, what functions do each perform?
2. What is data transcription and how desirable is this to accounting information systems?
3. What types of input and output devices are commonly used by accounting information systems?
4. What are the common application areas for POS terminals, MICR media, and OCR media?
5. How do magnetic tapes, magnetic disks, floppy disks, and laser disks each store data and why is such storage important?
6. What is data communications and what equipment is used to transmit data to and from remote sites?
7. What advantages are there to creating local area networks?

INTRODUCTION

Although many efficient accounting information systems are manual, many more are computerized. Five important components of a computerized accounting information system are: (1) hardware, (2) software, (3) personnel, (4) data, and (5) procedures. *Computer hardware* refers to the computer machinery and related data processing devices in the system. The purpose of this chapter is to discuss some of this equipment in detail.

We begin by examining the heart of any computer system—the central processing unit or CPU. This section of the chapter discusses how CPUs store data in their memories, manipulate data in microprocessors, and transport data internally. Because microcomputers have become so important to accountants and accounting information systems, this section emphasizes these devices in the discussions.

A central processing unit must input the data it will process from other, external devices, and output processed information in forms that are convenient to end users. The second section of the chapter discusses selected input and output devices that perform these functions. Again, microcomputer devices are stressed.

The primary memories of most CPUs are too limited and too volatile to store the vast amounts of file data required by most accounting applications. This is the job of secondary storage devices such as magnetic tapes and disks. Secondary storage devices are discussed in the third section of the chapter.

Many accounting applications work best when users can access centralized information and processing power from remote locations. Computer communications equipment makes this possible. Microcomputers are especially important pieces of communications equipment when they act as remote terminals or connect to each other in local area networks. The subject of data communications is discussed in the fourth and final section of the chapter.

Since most students in accounting information systems courses have already taken a survey computer class, the discussions here are necessarily brief. The major focus is on those devices that are most important in accounting applications. Thus, this chapter is useful both as a review of computer hardware and as a study of such hardware in *accounting* applications.

CENTRAL PROCESSING UNITS

Figures 4-1 and 4-2 suggest that most computer hardware surrounds a **central processing unit** or **CPU.** The processing power of these units varies considerably, ranging in capabilities from the most limited types of computers—**microcomputers**—and increasing through **minicomputers, mainframe computers,** and **supercomputers.** Advancing technology has blurred the boundaries that separate these devices, but Figure 4-3 compares the capabilities of representative ones. Because CPUs are so important to all other hardware operations, most complete computer systems are named after them.

Thus, for all intents and purposes, the CPU *is* the computer and, in industry, the terms "CPU" and "computer" are used interchangeably.

As illustrated in Figure 4-4, a CPU consists of three major components: (1) **primary memory,** (2) an **arithmetic-logic unit** (ALU), and (3) a **control unit.** All of these components are physically contained within the mainframe of the CPU itself, although their functions are quite different.

Primary Memory

The **primary memory** of a CPU is very similar to the memory of a home calculator—except that a home calculator has only one or two memories,

FIGURE 4-1 Typical computer hardware include a CPU (foreground), printers (right), tape drive (top), and disk drives (top left).

whereas a larger computer typically has many millions. Primary memory is also called main memory, mainframe memory, or primary storage. Primary memory is used to store such items as data, operating system instructions, or application-program instructions. Because the memory capacity of a CPU often determines how much "work" it can do, primary memory is often used as a measure of a computer's processing capabilities.

Although the very first computers were analog devices that used vacuum tubes, almost all computers today are **digital computers.** The fundamental unit of storage in these devices is a **binary digit** or **bit.** As its name suggests, a bit has only two states, represented by 0 or 1. Figure 4-5 illustrates some ways of creating binary digits. Most manufacturers today use very large scale integration (VLSI) to create thousands of integrated circuits on a single silicon memory chip.

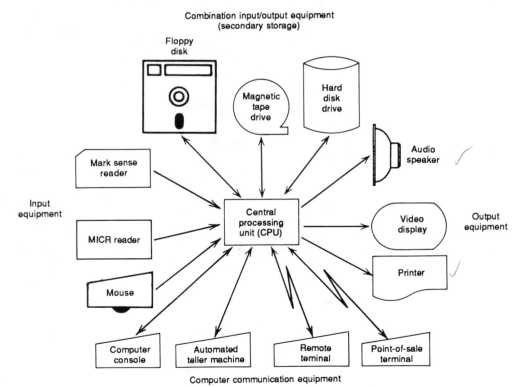

FIGURE 4-2 A schematic drawing of on-line computer hardware.

Type of Computer	Speed (Number) of Instructions/Second	Typical Storage (Bytes)	Maximal Number of Peripherals
Microcomputer	250000	1–10 Mb	less than 10
Minicomputer	millions	10–100 Mb	less than 50
Mainframe	hundreds of millions	over 100 Mb	hundreds
Supercomputer	about 1.5 bilion	over 100 Mb	hundreds

FIGURE 4-3 Characteristics of typical computer types.

The computer industry typically combines bits into bit codes such as **ASCII** (American Standard Code for Information Interchange) to represent our familiar letters, decimal numbers, and punctuation marks. By far the most common bit grouping is the 8-bit **byte.** Thus, the primary memory capacities of most computers are typically measured in bytes—**kilobytes** (kB or k) or **megabytes** (MB or M). Although kilo means "one thousand" in the metric system, k usually represents 2^{10} or 1024. Thus, 1 kilobyte of computer storage is exactly 1024 storage locations. Similarly, a megabyte of computer storage is 2^{20} (=1,048,576)—that is, approximately 1 million storage locations. At the time this book was written, the memory capacities of the smallest microcomputers were 640K or less, whereas the memory capacities of the largest supercomputers were 1000 megabytes (a **gigabyte**) or more.

Each byte of primary memory is unique, and is therefore assigned a unique address. This address is much like the number on the door of a hotel room, and is used in much the same fashion. When a guest is to be located at a hotel, the individual's room number is first determined and then called. Similarly, when a single data value is required from the memory of the central processing unit, the address of the data is determined first and then used to access the byte of computer storage where it resides. Some manufacturers (e.g., CDC) do not use byte architecture for computer storage. These companies typically use other bit groupings (e.g., 60 bits) called **words.** In such instances, each computer word is assigned a unique address for identifica-

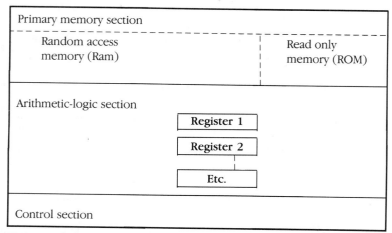

FIGURE 4-4 The components of the central processing unit (CPU) of a computer system.

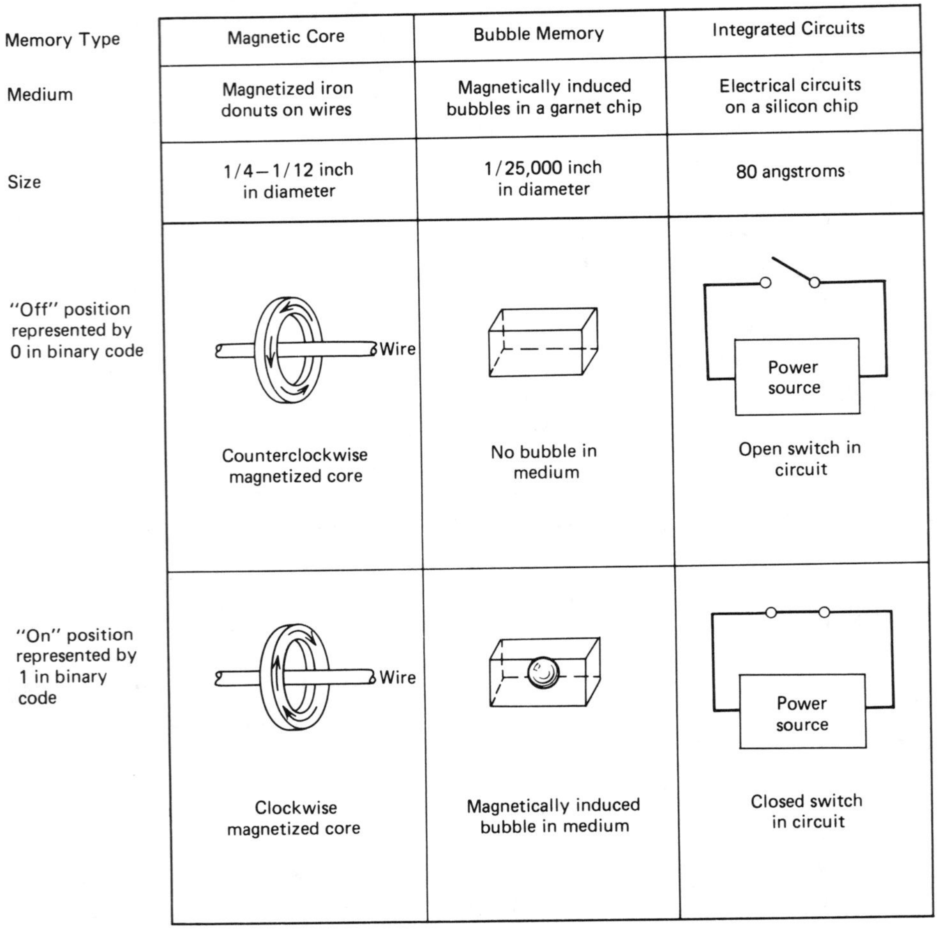

Memory Type	Magnetic Core	Bubble Memory	Integrated Circuits
Medium	Magnetized iron donuts on wires	Magnetically induced bubbles in a garnet chip	Electrical circuits on a silicon chip
Size	1/4—1/12 inch in diameter	1/25,000 inch in diameter	80 angstroms
"Off" position represented by 0 in binary code	Counterclockwise magnetized core	No bubble in medium	Open switch in circuit
"On" position represented by 1 in binary code	Clockwise magnetized core	Magnetically induced bubble in medium	Closed switch in circuit

FIGURE 4-5   Three methods of creating the binary digits, or bits, used in digital computers.

tion. The idea of data addressability, however, is the same.

In microcomputers, the memory available to users for storing data or instructions is called **random-access memory** or **RAM.** Some microcomputers also contain additional memory that has been permanently encoded with instructions and that can only be read. This is **read-only memory** or **ROM.** The terms ROM and RAM are misleading in that both types of memory can be accessed randomly (i.e., in any order) and both contain addressable storage. The distinguishing feature of RAM is the user's ability to *alter* the data stored in it—a characteristic not possible with ROM.

Arithmetic-Logic Units

Most central processing units cannot manipulate data directly in computer memory. Rather, such tasks as addition, subtraction, multiplication, division, and comparison must be performed in the **arithmetic-logic unit** or **ALU.** The typical ALU performs these tasks with specially-designed storage locations called **registers.** The very smallest microcomputers have relatively few such registers, whereas the very largest computers may have several sets of them. These registers are important because the memory locations in primary storage do not have the circuitry for performing data computations.

To understand how the arithmetic-logic unit of a CPU works, suppose we wanted a CPU to add two numbers together. We must first write a computer program to store these numbers in separate storage locations of CPU memory. The computer program would then transfer one of these numbers to a specific register, then access the second number from memory and add it to the first, and, finally, store the results by transferring the answer to a third memory location of the CPU storage. If we want to see the result, yet additional instructions would be required to print the answer on a printer.

Admittedly, the steps by which a computer performs simple arithmetic functions appear unnecessarily cumbersome. However, a modern computer's "cycle speed" (its ability to execute a single instruction such as an addition or data transfer), is very fast and getting faster all the time. For example, second-generation computers measured their cycle speeds in **microseconds** (millionths of a second), third-generation computers measured their cycle speeds in **nanoseconds** (billionths of a second), and current, fourth-generation computers measure their cycle speeds in **picoseconds** (trillionths of a second). Future computer equipment will measure cycle speeds in **gigaseconds** (quadrillionths of a second). Although accounting information systems rarely require such speeds, the excellent processing capabilities of modern CPUs are important to those accounting applications performing volume work (e.g., centralized banking networks).

The computer design, or architecture, of a CPU determines how registers perform their data manipulating tasks. In most computers, these tasks are performed sequentially—that is, one addition or subtraction at a time. In certain larger computers, and also in those microcomputers

with **coprocessors,** many of these manipulations can be performed in parallel. This latter approach is a way of achieving **multiprocessing**—that is, processing more than one set of data at the same time.

Control Units

The third and last component of the CPU is the **control unit.** As its name suggests, a control unit acts like the supervisor on a loading platform, overseeing operations and making sure that things are done in an orderly fashion. Among its other responsibilities, the control unit determines the sequence in which computer-program instructions are executed, and coordinates the activities of the computer's peripheral equipment as they perform the input, output, and storage tasks dictated by the computer programs stored in the CPU. If this section of the CPU strikes you as a kind of boss of operations for the computer system as a whole, you have the right idea.

Most arithmetic-logic units are combined with control units and manufactured on silicon chips called **microprocessor chips** (Figure 4-6). Advancing technology and production improvements have significantly reduced the costs of manufacturing such chips, thus making them usable in home appliances, automobiles, and office equipment as well as modern computers. Figure 4-7 summarizes the capabilities of the Intel line of microprocessors—those microprocessors used in IBM-compatible microcomputers.

INPUT AND OUTPUT DEVICES

A central processing unit must work closely with external, **peripheral equipment** to perform data processing tasks. In most accounting applications, for example, a CPU must input data from external devices as well as output processed information in forms and formats that are conve-

FIGURE 4-6 A microprocessor chip held between fingers.
(Photo courtesy of IBM.)

IBM Model	Intel Chip	Date Announced	Size of Data Register	Maximum Address Capability	Clock Speed (Megahertz)	Bus Size
none	4004	1969	4 bits	4k	2	4 bits
PC	8080	1974	8 bits	64k	2	8 bits
PC	8088	1979	16 bits	640k	4.77	8 bits
XT	8086	1978	16 bits	1 Mb	8	16 bits
AT	80286	1982	16 bits	16 Mb	12	16 bits
PS/2	80386	1985	32 bits	4 Gb	25	32 bits
NA	80386sx	1988	32 bits	4 Gb	16	16 bits
NA	80486	1989	32 bits	4 Gb	33	32 bits

FIGURE 4-7 Performance characteristics of various Intel microprocessor chips.

nient to end users. Input and output equipment are therefore vital hardware components of complete computer systems.

Input Devices

Some accounting information systems depend on volume transaction and file-record inputs for gathering and maintaining financial data. But even where the amount of input data is small, most systems require input methods and procedures that ensure the complete, accurate, and cost-effective input of accounting data. Usually, there are several ways of capturing and inputting financial data. In these instances, system designers must pick those input procedures and devices that best meet the input objectives of accuracy, completeness, and cost-effectiveness. Sometimes, this means starting with manually-prepared documents and transcribing them into machine-readable formats. At other times, it may be possible to capture data that is already in convenient, machine-readable form. Both of these possibilities are explored in greater depth in the paragraphs that follow.

Source Documents and Data Transcription

The starting point for collecting data in many accounting information systems is a **source document.** Examples include time cards, job application forms, packing slips, survey results, production logs, employee application forms, patient intake forms, cash disbursement vouchers, and travel reimbursement forms.

Typically, source documents are prepared manually. This makes them convenient to complete on-site by individuals with no computer background or training. If the information obtained from these source documents is used to create or update a computer file, a second use of source documents is as backup in the event the file is damaged or destroyed. A third advantage of a manually-prepared source document is that it often serves as evidence of authenticity. For ex-

ample, the existence of a cash disbursement voucher proves that a cash disbursement was made and the money was not pilfered from a cash fund.

A final advantage of manually-prepared source documents is to help establish an audit trail. As discussed in Chapter 1, accountants require audit trails to help them trace data through accounting information systems. Because we cannot observe how data are manipulated in a computerized system as easily as in a manual system, an effective audit trail that allows users to reconstruct intermediate data and operations is essential. Source documents are often the starting point of this audit trail.

The greatest disadvantage of manually-prepared source documents is that they are not machine readable. Thus, in order to process source-document data electronically, it is necessary to transcribe the initial, source-document data into machine-readable media. This activity is called **data transcription.** Typically, this is performed on **key-entry devices** such as computer terminals, microcomputers, or offline key-to-disk devices. Most of these devices: (1) have video screens that simultaneously display information as it is keyed; (2) can run *edit software* that checks input data for accuracy, completeness, reasonableness, and consistency; (3) permit users to correct errors when (and if) they are detected; and (4) utilize software programs with help screens and other online documentation to help users input data accurately.

The most important drawback of key entry devices is that they are part of the inefficient process of data transcription—a labor-intensive activity that is often costly, time-consuming, and nonproductive. Data transcription also has the potential to bottleneck data at the transcription site, embed more errors in machine-readable data than it detects, and provide opportunities for fraud, embezzlement, or sabotage. Is it any wonder, then, that most system designers prefer data-capturing methods that capture data in immediate, machine-readable formats? A few of these possibilities are described next.

POS Devices

Since an estimated 75% of the information required by retailers can be captured at the point of sale, retail businesses now commonly use automated **point-of-sale (POS) terminals**—in effect, "smart cash registers"—to record pertinent data electronically at the time a sale is made. This allows the direct recording of sales information, and also allows retailers to centralize price information in online computers. Changing prices thus becomes a matter of altering a single value in a computer file.

POS systems are especially useful for data entry. With them, the sales data obtained at the checkout-station are transmitted directly to a computer where they can be checked for accuracy, reasonableness, or completeness, and also stored for later uses—for example, preparing sales reports. One obvious advantage of POS data-gathering is that it eliminates intermediary data media—for example, sales tickets that must be transcribed before processing. Other advantages of POS data collection systems are listed in Figure 4-8.

Tag and Bar Code Readers

Tag and bar code readers perform data capture functions automatically. Older devices called tag readers used punched card with circular holes punched through stiff paper. By inserting the tag between the "jaws" of the reader and momentarily shutting them, the tag was read and the sales data automatically entered into the register terminal at the sales counter.

A variation of this technique are the **optical bar code readers** that use optical techniques to decipher the vertical lines of a bar code (Figure 4-9). Although bar codes were first used by railroads in 1967 to help identify the location of railroad cars, the most popular use of optical bar codes today has been in supermarkets and discount stores. Here, over 85% of products sold use the **universal product code (UPC)**, in which several pairs of vertical bars identify the manufacturer as well as the item itself.

1. Clerical errors, such as a salesperson's incorrect reading of a price tag, are detectable, and even potentially correctable, automatically.
2. Such standard procedures as the computation of a sales tax, the multiplication of prices times quantities sold, or the calculation of a discount can be performed using the register-terminal as a calculator.
3. Processing errors caused by illegible sales slips can be reduced.
4. Credit checks and answers to questions about customers' account balances are routinely handled by using the cash register as an inquiry terminal.
5. The inventory-disbursements data required for inventory control are collected as a natural part of the sales transaction.
6. A breakdown listing by the computer of sales by type of inventory item, dollar volume, sales clerk, or store location is possible because the data required for such reports are collected automatically with the sales transaction and may be stored for such use.
7. Sales and inventory personnel levels can be reduced because the manual data processing functions required of such personnel have largely been eliminated.

FIGURE 4-8   Advantages of point-of-sale (POS) input devices.

Most optical bar codes are read by either passing the merchandise code over an optical reader, or by passing a hand-held wand over the retail price tag or label. The readers or wands, in turn, are connected to computers that interpret the bar codes, record the information, prepare a sales

FIGURE 4-9   An example of the universal product code (UPC), which is often preprinted on the labels of retail products for merchandise identification and computerized checkout.

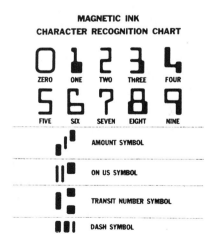

FIGURE 4-10 The MICR code of the American Banking Association.

slip for the customer, and record the sales information in separate computer files for marketing and inventory control purposes. Thus, optical bar codes enable retailers to store retail prices directly in computer memory, thereby eliminating the need to price each item separately. Like POS systems, this facilitates price changing (since only the price information stored in the computer must be altered) as well as the collection of customer charges at the checkout counter itself.

MAGNETIC INK CHARACTER RECOGNITION CHART

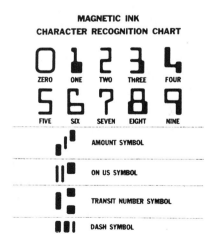

| 0 | 1 | 2 | 3 | 4 |
| ZERO | ONE | TWO | THREE | FOUR |

| 5 | 6 | 7 | 8 | 9 |
| FIVE | SIX | SEVEN | EIGHT | NINE |

AMOUNT SYMBOL

ON US SYMBOL

TRANSIT NUMBER SYMBOL

DASH SYMBOL

FIGURE 4-11 The American Banking Association MICR chart.

Magnetic Ink Character Recognition

The banking industry has pioneered the development of magnetically encoded paper commonly called **magnetic ink character recognition, or MICR.** If you have a checking or savings account, you are probably already familiar with this system if you tried to read the odd-looking numbers (Figure 4-10) printed at the bottom of your check. This type font (i.e., the set of machine-readable letters and numbers used in the code) has been standardized for the entire country (Figure 4-11). Thus, a check you write anywhere in the United States or Canada is machine-processable by any bank.

Many nonbanking applications now make use of MICR coding—for example: (1) utility companies (for preparing machine-readable customer bills), (2) mortgage companies (for payment coupons), (3) colleges and universities (for preparing advanced registration forms), and (4) CPA firms (for preparing customer confirmation slips). Note that many of these applications use MICR media as **turnaround documents**—that is, documents that are initially prepared by a company, then sent to individuals, and finally returned to the company for further data processing.

MICR coding enjoys a number of advantages. For one thing, MICR documents can be used for direct computer input since they are, already, machine readable. MICR coding is also quite flexible: documents of varying sizes, thicknesses, or widths may be used without hampering the processing capability of the reading/sorting equipment. A third advantage is that standard MICR code is readable by humans (although perhaps just barely!). This is a rare exception to the general rule that an item is either machine readable or human readable, but not both.

A final advantage of MICR encoding is that, in many applications, it eliminates the need for further encoding—the important account number and other information are already inked on the paper. This ensures uniformity in the coding process and expedites data processing. The chief disadvantage of MICR is that the magnetic strength (called the magnetic flux) of the inked characters diminishes over time, thus making the documents unreliable as an input medium when they must be used in several different applications. For this reason, most banks save check information on microfilm rather than the checks themselves.

Optical Character Recognition

Optical character recognition (OCR) uses optical, rather than magnetic, reading devices to interpret the data found on source documents. Typical OCR devices, therefore, use light-sensing mechanisms and laser technology to perform the character-recognition function required to interpret recorded data.

The essence of OCR is pattern recognition—the ability of a machine to identify a recorded symbol as a familiar form. For this reason, the simpler the character font (set), the cheaper and more efficient the OCR system. **Mark-sense media** (such as the type used in computerized exams) form "characters" of simple rectangles or ovals that are blackened with a pencil and are perhaps the most elementary form of OCR.

More sophisticated versions of OCR use com-plete character sets of numbers and letters, and therefore achieve a more versatile recording system. A common use of OCR data collection is the billing operations of a public utility company. For example, a meter reader may use an ordinary pencil to record the water or gas usage at your home simply by marking the appropriate columns of a special meter form. Such forms are then collected later at the utility company's processing office where your bill can be prepared (see Figure 4-12).

Machine-printed characters, such as the type font of the American National Standards Institute may be used to encode bills, invoices, tickets, and other source documents that are ultimately interpreted with optical scanning devices. For example, the attendant at the gasoline service station often makes use of an inexpensive OCR imprinting device (Figure 4-13) to make a credit-card sale. This enhances both the human-readability and the machine-readability of the input.

Like magnetic ink character recognition, the chief advantage of OCR is the ability to input source-document data directly into a computer, thereby avoiding data transcription. The most critical problem of OCR is reliability. Some authors also suggest that OCR requires a more rigid format than other systems—an argument that is true for human-generated formats using handwritten input but not applicable when using the standardized font of the American National Standards Institute. Finally, optical character readers tend to be expensive in comparison with other input devices.

Plastic Cards with Magnetic Strips

Many plastic cards have a magnetic strip affixed to one side of them that resembles a piece of magnetic recording tape. Credit cards are one example (Figure 4-14). Other examples include magnetically-encoded badges that are used for identification purposes and plastic door keys that are used for security purposes.

Typically, the magnetic strip affixed to these cards are used to maintain information about the

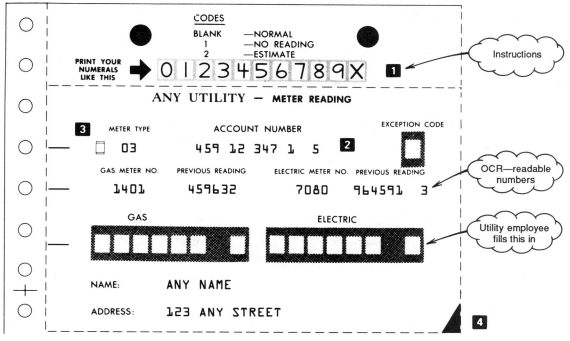

FIGURE 4-12   A form to collect utility-meter data using OCR. (Form courtesy of IBM.)

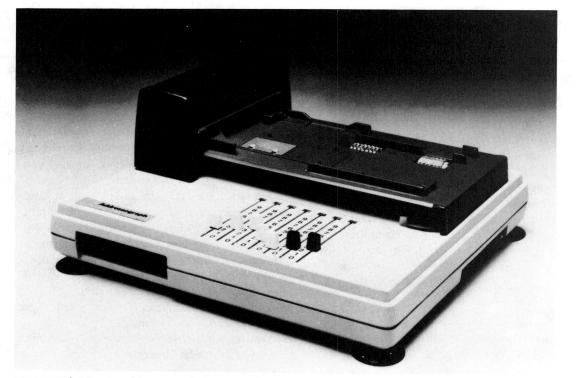

FIGURE 4-13   An addressograph data recorder for imprinting an OCR credit-card sales slip. (Photo courtesy AM International.)

FIGURE 4-14   The back of a standard credit card has a magnetic strip on which credit information is coded.

user—for example, the user's checking account number, savings account number, credit-card number, and expiration date. In the United States, the magnetic strip of the plastic card has been divided into distinct physical areas and, by agreement, each major industry using these cards has been assigned its own space. Thus, for example, the International Airline Transport Association (IATA), the American Banking Association (ABA), and the savings and loan industry each use a separate portion of the card's magnetic strip. This enables each industry to code information pertinent to its own needs on the card without fear that, by accident, the card will be misused in another application.

Accounting information systems use mag-strip cards to capture data at the time these cards are used. For example, credit cards can be encoded with credit limits directly on the card, and this information can be acquired immediately every time the card is used. Similarly, data gathering is facilitated because the information is obtained by highly sensitive, but reliable, electronic equipment that is not prone to human transcription error. Thus, a 13-digit credit card number, which is time consuming to communicate vocally, is accurately transmitted in much less time electronically.

Audio Input

Audio input means communicating with a computer through audio (sound) devices. For exam-

ple, a few microcomputer devices currently enable users to dictate input directly into a microphone, but both their reliability and their vocabularies are limited. The more common applications today use touch-tone telephones to "dial" credit-card numbers, account numbers, and menu selections directly into computers. These uses are particularly important to those accounting applications requiring input data from end users at remote sites.

Output Devices

Computerized accounting data is worthless if it cannot be output in forms that are useful and convenient to end users. Printed output is one possibility, but video (displayed) output, audio output, and file output are other possibilities that we can explore in this and the following sections of the chapter.

Printers

Accounting information systems produce many types of printed outputs—for example, (1) detail reports, (2) summary reports, (3) exception reports, (4) demand reports, (5) custom reports, (6) spreadsheets, (7) word processing documents, and (8) graphs and charts. Printers are thus especially important to accounting information systems because printed output is human-readable and often forms the basis of managerial action. Printed output is also called **hard-copy output** to distinguish it from such alternatives as screen displays or audio output.

Printers are usually classified by the way they print characters on a print page. Some printers use percussion mechanisms (**impact printers**) while others do not (**nonimpact printers**). Printers can also be described as character-at-a-time (**serial**) printers, line-at-a-time (**line**) printers, or page-at-a-time (**page**) printers. Several examples of these different types of printers are discussed in the paragraphs that follow.

Dot-matrix printers (Figure 4-15) are serial impact printers that form characters from dots on

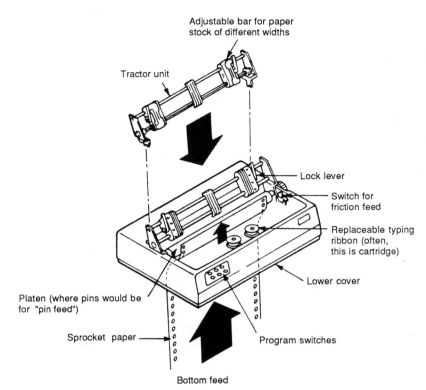

Adjustable bar for paper
stock of different widths

Tractor unit

Lock lever

Switch for
friction feed

Replaceable typing
ribbon (often,
this is cartridge)

Lower cover

Platen (where pins would be
for "pin feed")

Sprocket paper

Program switches

Bottom feed

FIGURE 4-15   The components of a typical dot-matrix printer. "Tractor-feed" printers use a detachable "tractor" unit to feed continuous-form paper through the printer, whereas "pin-feed" printers have pins permanently mounted on their platens. Many of these printers also have friction-feed capabilities by adjusting a switch near the carriage. *Source:* From Mark G. Simkin, *Introduction to Computer Information Systems for Business* (Dubuque: William C. Brown, Publishers, 1987). Reproduced by permission.

a print page. For example, 45 dots arranged in a 5-by-9 matrix might be used to form print characters (Figure 4-16). Larger matrices that use as many as 24 pins in a double-column print head are also possible. Dot-matrix printers are popular with microcomputers because they are inexpensive but are highly flexible tools. Figure 4-17 describes some of the most important features of dot-matrix printers.

Thermal printers are nonimpact serial printers that closely resemble dot-matrix printers in looks, speeds, and capabilities. These printers use heated wires that burn tiny dots in heat-sensitized paper. Although inexpensive, the slow speeds of thermal printers and the somewhat "greasy" feel of the special paper they sometimes use makes them a poor choice for most professional accounting applications.

Daisywheel printers are also serial impact printers that use a removable typing element to form characters on a print page (Figure 4-18).

Daisywheel printing has a professional (*letter*) quality to it because each print character is solid (not dots) and the print resolution is therefore high. But the print speeds of even the fastest daisywheel are slow compared to those of dot-

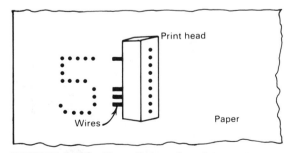

Print head

Wires

Paper

FIGURE 4-16   Many dot-matrix printers use a single "column" of wires that move quickly in a horizontal direction to create matrix of dots. (The inked ribbon that normally is threaded between the print head and the paper is not shown here.)

Bidirectional printing—the ability of the print head to print in both forward and backward passes, thereby speeding printing by avoiding "returns" to the left margin (like typewriters).

Compressed printing—the ability to squeeze letters together (e.g., to print 132 characters in the space normally allotted for 80 characters).

Foreign language characters—the ability to print the special non-English characters of such foreign languages as Greek, French, or Russian.

Friction feed—the printer's ability to grip regular stock paper like a typewriter.

Multiple-form paper—the ability to use multipart paper or forms requiring carbons.

Overstriking—the ability to strike the same letters twice to create boldface printing.

Printing oversized letters—the ability to print characters at double, triple, and even quadruple height.

Programmability—the ability to define your own print characters and print-control characters—e.g., to create special output graphics.

Serial and parallel data transmission—the ability to accept data from a computer either as a stream of sequential bits (serial data transmission) or as a set of nine bits at once (parallel data transmission).

Sheet feeders—the ability to add a device that automatically feeds single pages into the printer one at a time (like a photocopy machine).

Size of carriage—the ability to feed sheets of paper into the printer that are wider than 8 1/2 inches.

Size of buffer—the ability to store output data in a temporary memory, thereby temporarily freeing the microcomputer for other uses.

Speed of printing—the ability to print output quickly in either draft or NLQ mode. Usually measured in characters per second (cps).

Subscripting and superscripting—the ability to raise or lower the print page slightly, or otherwise create superscripts and subscripts.

Tractor feed or pin feed—the ability to mount continuous-form paper on the printer through either a separate "tractor" mechanism or pins mounted directly on the carriage ("pin feed").

Variable line density—the ability to vary the number of lines per vertical inch on the print page.

Variable type fonts—the ability to type in various type styles—e.g., block letters, italics, or script. A physical selector switch on the printer that allows you to pick from draft mode, near-letter-quality (NLQ) mode, or other fonts is particularly handy.

Adapted from Mark G. Simkin, *Discovering Computers* (Dubuque, Iowa: William C. Brown, Publishers, 1990).

FIGURE 4-17   Important features of dot-matrix printers

FIGURE 4-18   A daisywheel printer and a closeup of a daisywheel typing element.

matrix, draft-quality printing, and downright laborious compared to those of line or page printers. Thus, only small-volume accounting applications use them.

Ink-jet printers are serial nonimpact printers that create characters by spraying tiny jets of ink onto printer pages. Print resolution tends to be high; speed low. Some ink-jet printers can print in multiple colors, using multiple nozzles and ink reservoirs.

Chain printers are line impact printers that utilize multiple sets of teletype characters (like those on typewriters) embossed on a chain (like a bicycle chain). To create a line of output (Figure 4-19), each hammer in the printer waits until the proper print character is aligned between itself and the print page, and then strikes. **Band printers** are very similar except that they use a metal band instead of a print chain. Because several characters will usually be in proper alignment at any given instant, several hammers typically strike concurrently and the print line is assembled quickly. This enables line printers to print between 300 and 3000 lines per minute—an important speed advantage in high-volume accounting applications.

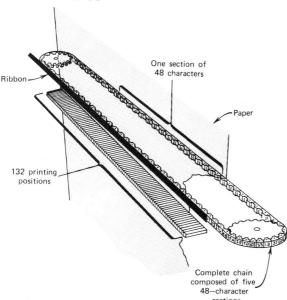

FIGURE 4-19 A print chain. (Photo courtesy of IBM.)

Ribbon

One section of 48 characters

Paper

132 printing positions

Complete chain composed of five 48—character sections

Laser printers are page nonimpact printers that create printed output in much the same way as duplicating machines: a laser sensitizes the printed portions of a page, which then attracts toner. The costs of microcomputer-based laser-printer models tend to be high compared to dot-matrix or daisywheel printers, but so is output resolution and print quality. Larger models can cost over $300,000, but output speeds are much higher than smaller models. Laser printers have become especially important in **desktop publishing** applications requiring proportional and micro spacing, multiple print columns and type fonts, graphics and icons embedded in the printing, and text that wraps-around figures.

As should be obvious from the preceding discussions, two of the most important considerations in choosing printers for computerized accounting applications are print quality and print speeds. Print speeds are important because many accounting applications require large volumes of printed output. For example, a payroll processing task may require payroll checks for thousands of employees. Similarly, in an accounts receivable application, a separate bill must be prepared for each customer. Because for both of these applications, several lines must be printed for each employee or customer, the total number of printed lines for the processing runs can be very large. Situations requiring hundreds of thousands or even millions of lines are common in business applications today. To avoid slowdowns caused by these large processing volumes, high-speed printing with nonimpact printers may be essential.

Video Output

Many accounting applications are online, real-time systems that permit users to access file data and perform accounting tasks as soon as data are entered into a computer. An example would be a modern accounts receivable system. In these instances, hard-copy output that clutters offices with paper and that takes time to print may be less desirable than fast, **soft-copy** video screen displays.

There are four major types of display-screen

technologies. Cathode ray tubes (CRTs) use electron guns to create video output in much the same way as televisions. But today's computerized CRT screens are actually digital devices (*monitors*) that bit-map computer output to individual dots or **picture elements (pixels** or **pels)** onscreen. The displayed characters or graphics output is created out of grids or blocks of these pixels. IBMs three video standards for microcomputers—CGA, EGA, and VGA—are described in Figure 4-20, although there are non-IBM graphics standards as well.

Three other types of display screens are lighting-emitting diode (LED) displays, liquid crystal displays (LCDs), and gas plasma displays. These three work roughly the same way—by using very small electrical currents to excite the liquids or gases in tiny enclosures embedded in the glass of the display screen. These types of screens work especially well in laptop and portable microcomputers because they are flat, reliable, and do not require vacuum enclosures.

Monochrome monitors use a single color (e.g., green) against a single background (e.g., black) to display video images. These often suffice in many accounting applications. Color **(RGB) monitors** are usually more visually appealing, but they cost more and require special video cards and color-creating software to work properly.

The standard size of most display screens—80 columns wide by 25 rows high—is usually inadequate to display an entire accounting document, report, or spreadsheet. Some screens can display a few more rows or columns of data, but these devices cost more and some accounting software packages may not be compatible with them. In those accounting applications requiring long hours of screen input, the availability of good screen contrast, sufficient ambient lighting, and comfortable working conditions are often more crucial than screen size or coloring abilities. Some states have recently passed laws establishing minimum standards for these items in work settings.

SECONDARY STORAGE DEVICES

The memory of a central processing unit is too expensive and too limited to serve the entire storage needs of a typical organization. Thus, most accounting information systems also use secondary storage such as magnetic tape or disk to store accounting data. Common to most **secondary storage devices** is the ability to store information on a removable storage medium such as a reel of magnetic tape or a disk pack, thereby greatly increasing the amount of infor-

Feature:	CGA (Color Graphics Adapter) Standard	EGA (Enhanced Graphics Adapter) Standard	VGA (Video Graphics Adapter) Standard
Year first announced	1981	1984	1987
IBM product	IBM PC	IBM AT	IBM PS/2 models 50 and up
pixel elements (rows × columns)	200 × 640	350 × 640	480 × 640
Pixels per character (rows × columns)	8 × 8	14 × 8	16 × 9
Maximal number of colors in one display	4	16	256

FIGURE 4-20 Three IBM graphics standards.

mation that can be made available to a CPU through a single machine device.

Since well over 90% of all present accounting data processing uses magnetic tape or disk storage, we shall examine these two types of storage media in detail. Magnetic drums and mass storage systems (MSSs) are two other types of secondary storage devices. However, these devices are usually not as important in typical accounting applications and are therefore not examined here.

Magnetic Tape

The **magnetic tape** used by computers is about 1/2 inch in width and is very similar to the standard recording tape used on home tape recorders. One side of the tape is coated with magnetic oxide and is used for recording; the other shiny side serves as backing. All reading and writing is done by a **tape drive** (Figure 4-21).

Magnetic recording tape is wound on reels that usually have metallic cores and plastic sides. A standard reel measures 10 1/2 inches in diameter and contains 2400 feet of magnetic tape. Half-reels of 1200 feet and "hypertape" lengths of 3600 feet are also available. A visible silver rectangle on the tape called a load marker separates the leader or take-up portion of the magnetic tape from the data recording portion, and a similar end of reel marker performs the same function for the anchoring portion of the magnetic tape.

Magnetic Tape Encoding

Magnetic tape can be recorded at different speeds, thus varying the density of the information on this medium. Common tape densities are 1600 and 6250 characters per inch (cpi), although newer drives can record more than 38,000 characters per inch. Compared with floppy disks, the advantages of magnetic tape at these higher densities should be obvious: A standard, 7-pound reel of tape can store the equivalent of over 500 floppy disks worth of data! This is important to accounting information systems requiring mass storage for archiving or backup.

As illustrated in Figure 4-22, the recording

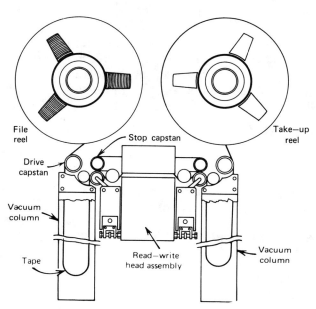

FIGURE 4-21 A schematic of the tape reels, drive capstans, and read/write head assembly. (Schematic courtesy of IBM.)

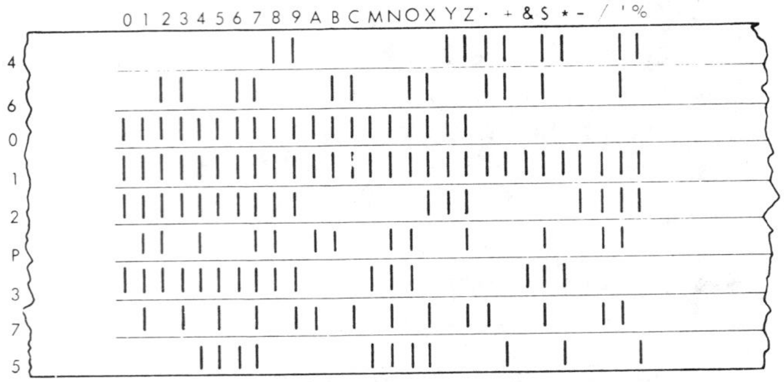

0 1 2 3 4 5 6 7 8 9 A B C M N O X Y Z · + & S * - / ' %

FIGURE 4-22   Nine-channel (track) magnetic tape coding.

surface of magnetic tape is divided into channels or **tracks,** and one vertical column of bits (at the same position on each track) is used to represent a single character. Most tapes today use a nine-track format that enables them to use a standard 8-bit byte to represent each character.

As you may have guessed already, the **parity** channel (track P) of the tape does not encode information, but serves as a check on the other bits comprising the character on the tape. Every time a data transfer is performed, computer hardware tests each character for proper parity. This is called a *parity check.* When a parity error is encountered, either certain error routines are automatically executed by the computer or the computer operator is called. Thus, no bits can be "dropped" accidentally in the encoding or reading process and go undetected by the system.

On most secondary storage media, bits are grouped together to form individual data items stored in *data fields,* which in turn are grouped together to form computer **records** (Figure 4-23). Typically, a logical computer record will contain the information about one file entity— for example, one employee, customer account, or inventory item. If fixed-length records are used, the same amount of space is reserved for each record. Variable-length records, which only utilize as much room as actually needed for each data field or record, obviously conserve space at the expense of consistency.

On magnetic tape, **interrecord gaps (IRGs)** of about 3/4-inch separate one record from another (Figure 4-24). Where file records are small, however, several individual ("logical") records can be blocked together to eliminate several IRGs and therefore conserve space. The information between two IRGs in this instance is called a *physical record.*

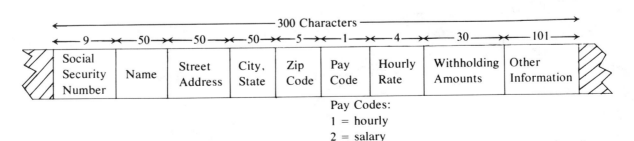

FIGURE 4-23   An employee record on magnetic tape.

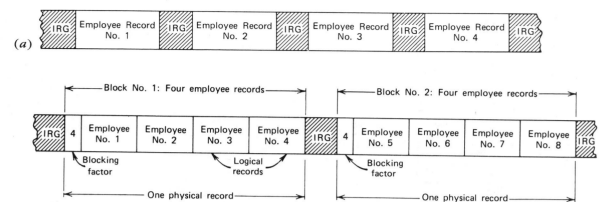

FIGURE 4-24　(*a*) Employee records separated by interrecord gaps (IRGs). (*b*) Eight employee records (logical records) blocked into two physical records.

Advantages and Disadvantages of Magnetic Tape

The most important advantage of magnetic tape is its cost—less than $25 a reel or one cent per megabyte. This is why tape is commonly used to create backup files—even if the originals are stored on disks. Magnetic tape is also faster to read than such other media as OCR or MICR documents, and can also store data more compactly than these media.

One disadvantage of magnetic tape is that it stores data sequentially, and thus cannot be used for direct-access files (or therefore real-time accounting applications). Another problem is that tape reading and writing is slow compared to disks. This makes tape less convenient to use in large-volume applications involving thousands of file records—that is, the type of processing typical of many accounting information systems.

Magnetic Disks

As illustrated in Figure 4-25, a single **magnetic disk** closely resembles a stereo record—that is, a platter about 20 inches in diameter. Recording takes place on both sides of the platter, whose surfaces are smooth and coated with an oxide similar to that of magnetic tape. Also, as with magnetic tape, this coating can be magnetized to form the "on" and "off" bits of a binary code.

To read the information on a disk, the entire pack is mounted on a disk drive, which spins the pack very quickly on its spindle. Actual reading or writing on the disk is performed through special read/write heads attached to the drive. There is a separate head for each recording surface of the disk pack, but (for most disk drives) all the read/write heads are attached to a common arm. These are called "moveable head disk drives" because the arm moves all read/write heads simultaneously to position any one of them for encoding or deciphering.

The storage capacities of magnetic disks vary considerably. The smallest ("hard") disks used in microcomputers hold as little as 20 megabytes, whereas large commercial devices store in excess of 1.5 gigabytes (billion bytes) of data. Although these larger storage capacities seem excessive, such important accounting applications as the billing operations of public utility companies require them.

Magnetic Disk Encoding

The recording surface of a disk is divided into concentric (not spiraling) circles, or tracks, each of which is just wide enough to encode one bit of

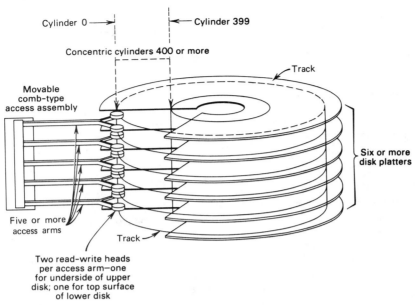

FIGURE 4-25   Magnetic disks on a common spindle (spindle not shown). (Photo courtesy of IBM.)

information. Encoding an entire character therefore takes place in sequential groups of bits along the circumference of the track. Like magnetic tape, magnetic disks also employ parity bits for data transmission and control.

The physical characteristics of disk systems make it possible to directly place, or find, a record on a disk pack. This is because each record is placed at a unique storage location with an address that completely identifies its position on the pack. Thus, disk systems are **direct-access storage devices (DASDs).** The fact that each record on a disk is locatable through a unique record address means that all records stored on the pack are immediately accessible to the user (through the computer). Hence the term **random access** and the reason why most real-time accounting information systems use disks for file storage.

Advantages and Disadvantages of Magnetic Disks

One advantage of disk storage over tape storage is the direct-access (random-access) capability of

the disk system. This makes disk files particularly useful for such online applications as airline reservations or police records, in which immediate access to specific records is required. Similarly, updating disk records is generally much easier than updating magnetic tape records. For example, if a company maintained a magnetic tape file of employee records organized by social security number, then the hiring of only one additional employee would necessitate recopying the entire tape file in order to insert the new record in its appropriate position in the file. In contrast, a disk record can be added to a direct-access file at any time; it is not necessary to recopy the entire file for this purpose.

As suggested by Figure 4-26, magnetic disks have faster data transfer rates than tape systems, again making disks more popular when response time is important. An important application of this property is to use disk storage as **virtual memory**—i.e., to augment the primary memory of a central processing unit. Data is swapped back and forth between the two units as though they were a single large memory. The result is to make

Media	Device	Input	Output	Unit of measurement	Typical Rates of Speed		
					low	medium	high
Input and Output Devices							
Punched cards	Card reader	X		Cards/minute	100	600	2,000
	Card punch		X	Cards/minute	100	300	500
Paper tape	Tape reader	X		Characters/second	100	350	2,000
	Tape punch		X	Characters/second	20	100	300
Magnetic ink	Reader	X		Documents/minute	750	1,200	2,500
Paper	Optical scanner	X		Documents/minute	100	300	1,500
	Printer		X	Lines/minute	300	600	18,000
	Terminal	X	X	Characters/second	30	120	960
Cathode ray tube	Display		X	Characters/second	250	1,000	10,000
Microfilm	COM		X	Thousand characters/second	30	60	500

Media	Device	Storage Capacity	Range of Transfer Rates, Thousands of Characters per Second		
			Low	Medium	High
Secondary Storage Devices					
Magnetic tape	Tape drive	million characters per tape	15	200	1,250
Magnetic disk	Disk drive	Over 1 billion characters per pack	250	885	3,000
Floppy disk	Floppy disk drive	21 million characters on 3 1/2-inch diskette	30	100	150
Magnetic drum	Drum storage unit	4 million characters per highspeed drum	275	800	1,200
Mass storage	Mass storage device	Up to 472 billion characters	806	806	885
Video disk	Video disk drive	Over 2 billion characters per disk	150	250	500

FIGURE 4-26 A comparison of input/output speeds for selected media.

the memory of the CPU appear to be much bigger than it actually is, thereby enabling users to execute programs too large for primary memory.

Disks also have their drawbacks. One problem is cost: A single disk pack may cost up to 200 times as much as a single full reel of magnetic tape. Another drawback is the bulkiness of disk packs, which are difficult to store. (In contrast, the physical width of the recording tape reel is less than an inch.)

Floppy Disks

As illustrated in Figure 4-27, **floppy disks** (also called diskettes) come in three sizes: 8 inch, 5 1/4 inch, and 3 or 3 1/2 inch. Some word processing systems continue to use the earlier, 8-inch floppy disks because these are the largest and at one time had the greatest capacities. Most standard (personal) microcomputers use the middle, 5 1/4-inch floppies, whereas most lap-top microcomputers and the newer desktop microcomputers use the smallest, 3-inch size.

A schematic of the most popular, 5 1/4-inch floppy disk is illustrated in Figure 4-28. The floppy disk itself is a round, oxide-coated diskette permanently encased in a paper or plastic sleeve. This diskette is rotated within the sleeve by its floppy disk drive for reading or writing purposes.

FIGURE 4-27   Three sizes of floppy disk drives.

Only the portion of the floppy disk that can be accessed through the read/write slot or "window" is used for recording purposes. In Figure 4-28, also note the write-protect slot. On 5 1/4-inch diskettes, this is left uncovered for writing purposes, but is covered with tape by the user to protect information and place the diskette in "read-only" mode.

Floppy Disk Encoding

Like the surfaces of hard disks, floppy disks are divided into 40 or more concentric tracks, each just wide enough to encode a single bit. Single sided (SS) diskettes use just one side for recording, whereas double-sided (DD) diskettes use both sides. Single-density (SD) diskettes record data at 3200 bits per inch, whereas double-density (DD) diskette formats double this. Quad-density (QD) diskettes record data at 12,800 bits per inch, thereby enabling the floppy diskettes of all sizes to hold more than 1 megabyte of data.

Most floppy disks are formatted with operating systems that divide each track into subunits called **sectors.** For example, MS-DOS 2.3 creates sectors of 512 bytes each. Each sector is assigned a unique address, enabling the floppy disk drive to access any record, once its sector location is known. The floppy disk's *file allocation table (FAT)* maintains a complete listing of files, assigned sector locations, and bad (unusable) sectors.

Advantages and Disadvantages of Floppy Disks

The addressability of records on floppy disks enables users to create both direct-access and sequential files. This makes floppy disks an important media for accounting information systems that are implemented on microcomputers—a common use in both large and small businesses. The compact size of floppy disks is another advantage for such purposes as desk storage, mailing, or software distribution.

Storing data on floppy disks is not particularly cheap—as much as $1 per megabyte. However

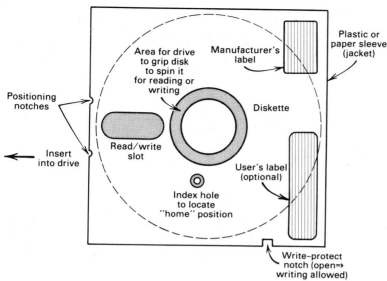

FIGURE 4-28   The anatomy of a 5¼-inch diskette (floppy disk).

since floppy disks are reusable, they are useful for key-entry tasks as discussed earlier. Thus, although floppy disks are commonly associated with microcomputers, many accounting information systems that have been implemented on minicomputers and mainframe computers also use them for data preparation, input, output, and off-line storage purposes.

Laser Disks

An emerging technology that is expected to become increasingly important in creating secondary storage is **laser disk** technology. As illustrated in Figure 4-29, the basis of this storage is a laser, or video, disk, which closely resembles a large, compact disk (CD) platter. The laser disk is mounted on a laser disk reader in much the same fashion as a stereo record is mounted on a stereo turntable. The laser disk drive then reads information from the platter using a focused laser beam as illustrated in Figure 4-30.

Like compact disks (CDs), laser disks consist of plastic bases that are first treated with light-sensitive coating. The disks are encoded with lasers that permanently "burn" tiny nodules or

raised bubbles into spiraling tracks on their inner surfaces. The presence or absence of these nodules is used to represent the zeros and ones of our familiar binary codes.

One of the most important advantages of laser disks is their incredible storage capabilities. Because lasers can be focused very precisely, a video laser disk can hold more than 2 billion bytes of data on each of its two sides. This is the equivalent of more than 5000 floppy diskettes, and sufficient to store 1 million pages of average-size text.

Laser disks suffer from two principal drawbacks. One is that, until recently, they are not reusable. This is because the "etched" nodules

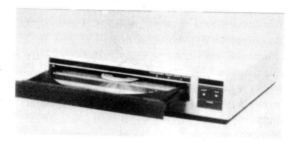

FIGURE 4-29   A laser disk reader.

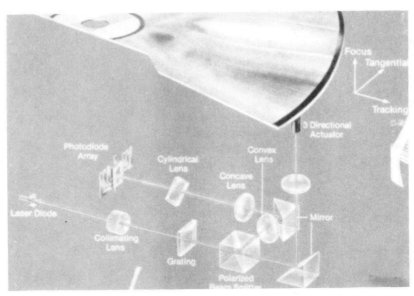

FIGURE 4-30 How a laser disk is read.

on the disk created by the laser beams are perma-nent. This characteristic is unacceptable to businesses that wish to maintain changeable file information, although it doesn't diminish the usefulness of laser disks for storing computer programs or archiving data. The other problem is that, at present, the cost of laser disk readers remains high, making them less appealing to ini-tial purchasers. Thus, as stated earlier, laser disks are still an emerging technology rather than an established one.

✳ DATA COMMUNICATIONS

Although central processing units transfer data internally (e.g., from primary memory to arithmetic-logic units), the term **data commu-nications** commonly refers to the transport of data to and from remote locations. Many ac-counting information systems use data commu-nications to transfer data to and from centralized offices—for example, savings-and-loan systems (for centralizing customer-activity information) and stock brokerage houses (for distributing

stock-market data). Another common application is to connect microcomputers and related de-vices in local area networks. Accountants should know about data communications because (1) so many accounting information systems use them, (2) this will help them plan and install client networks, and (3) CPA auditors may need to eval-uate the capabilities of a network for safe-guarding transmitted information and ensuring data integrity.

Remote Data Communications

Digital computers transmit data digitally—in discrete, electrical pulses. The presence of a pulse represents a "1" and the absence of a pulse represents a "O." Pulses sent in sequence (down a single wire) are known as **serial data trans-mission,** whereas pulses sent in parallel (down several wires in a cable) are known as **parallel data transmission.** Most microcomputers use serial data transmission (that use RS232 cable connectors) for computer mice and keyboards; parallel data transmission (that use Centronics cable connectors) for printers.

Communications Channels

The path that data takes in remote data communications is called a **communications channel.** Examples of such channels are (1) twisted-pair wire, (2) coaxial cables, (3) optical fibers, (4) microwaves, and (5) radio (satellite) waves. To use these channels, it is usually necessary to convert the electrical pulses of digital data transmission into a more convenient, more reliable form. For example, the electrical pulses of a computer are converted to light pulses for optical fibers.

The popularity of twisted-pair data communications is due to the widespread availability of phone service. When using telephone lines or **telecommunications, modems** ("modulators-demodulators") are required to translate the digital pulses and rests of "normal" computer communications into audio frequencies that can be transmitted over voice-grade phone lines. The data path is thus from sending computer (in digital or pulse format), through a modem (that translates the data into analog format), over the communications channel (i.e., the phone line), into another modem (that translates the analog format back into a digital one), and finally to the receiving station (say, mainframe computer) for use.

Data transmission speeds over phone lines are commonly measured in **baud.** Technically, baud measures "frequency changes per second." But at low transmission speeds, baud is equivalent to "bits per second." For example, a baud rate of 2400 means 2400 bits per second. Common baud rates over phone lines are 1200, 2400, and 9600 baud. If one start bit and the one stop bit are used for each eight-bit character, 2400 baud also translates to 240 characters per second because each character requires 10 bits. The data transmission rates of coaxial cables or fiber optics often exceed 1 million bits per second.

Communications Protocols

In all data communications applications, the sending and receiving stations must use compatible data transmission formats. These formats are called **communications protocols.** Examples of such protocols are the transmission speed, the type of duplex ("half" or "full"—required for transmission checking), the error testing procedures used, the transmission type (synchronous versus asynchronous), and the parity type (odd versus even). Although these topics are beyond the scope of this book, it is important for accountants to understand that communications protocols vary and that there is no universal transmission standard. This often leads to great inconvenience for data communications users. It is one reason (among many) why most long-distance networks must be custom designed and built by communications experts.

Terminals

A common device used in data communications is a **remote terminal** (or a microcomputer, acting as a remote terminal). Many terminals are also called **visual display terminals (VDTs),** to distinguish those devices containing video screens from printing terminals. VDTs can also be classified as "dumb" or "smart." **Dumb terminals"** can do little more than transmit data. **Smart terminals** (Figure 4-31) support such

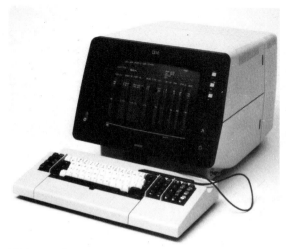

FIGURE 4-31 An example of a computer terminal.

items as onscreen editing, buffer memories, programmable function keys, and printers. The exact capabilities of a smart terminal vary with the model and (usually) its price. Since smart terminals typically cost under $500 whereas fully-configured microcomputers can cost over $5000, it is not surprising that many accounting applications use terminals rather than microcomputers for data operations.

Local Area Networks

One particularly important type of data communications is **local area networks (LANs)**—see Figure 4-32. LANs are collections of computer devices such as microcomputers, printers, hard disks, and terminals that are connected together for communications purposes.

Why Use a LAN?

Accounting information systems commonly use LANs to provide several users access to the same hardware, software, computer files, or to each other. Briefly, the general advantages of local area networks include the ability to:

1. Share computer equipment. For example, two microcomputers can share a hard disk or printer, thus saving equipment costs.
2. Share computer files. The users of word processing centers and accounts receivable systems often require access to the same file information—a need satisfied with a LAN.
3. Save software costs. A single copy of a software package can be made available to all users on the network, thus saving the expenses of separate software for each workstation.
4. Enable unlike other computer equipment to communicate with each other. Not all computers use the same operating system—for example, microcomputer DOSs versus minicomputer operating systems. But these devices can still communicate with each other through a common LAN.
5. Facilitate communications. Electronic mail messages can be sent back and forth, thus enabling users to avoid walks down long cor-

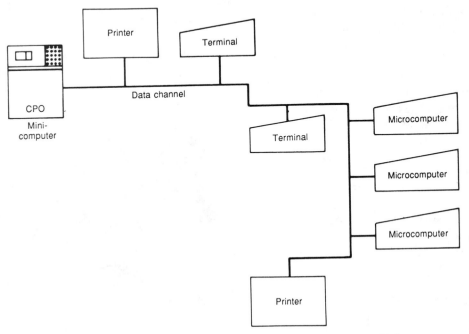

FIGURE 4-32   A local area network with representative devices attached.

ridors and staircases, or playing "telephone tag."

Some Applications

LANs enable users to feed data into common files, or to extract information from such files when necessary. It is for this reason that the central or host computer in a LAN is often called a **file server.** Examples of accounting applications that rely upon local, but centralized, file information include accounts receivable systems, accounts payable systems, inventory control systems, point-of-sale systems, and order entry systems.

Local area networks can also provide access (called **gateways**) to **wide area networks** spanning regional or national areas. This enables all the employees of an organization (such as retail store chains) to share data locally among the several branch offices of the same metropolitan area, and also nationally. This capability of providing computer "power" at local levels is called **distributed data processing.**

Another important use of local area networks is **electronic mail.** Here, messages are transmitted directly from the sender and stored in a computer "mail-box" file of the recipient. This latter individual then retrieves messages at his or her convenience. Electronic mail helps users (1) maintain many messages in an orderly, paperless fashion, (2) communicate directly with each other by avoiding message-taking secretaries, (3) send the same message to multiple recipients simultaneously (by maintaining mailing lists in word processing software files), and (4) overcome the time-shift problems of recipients in distant time zones.

SUMMARY

A computerized accounting information system includes hardware, software, people, data, and procedures. Similarly, the hardware of such systems includes central processing units and devices for input, output, secondary storage, and data communications.

The capabilities of central processing units determine the type of computer system: microcomputer, minicomputer, mainframe computer, or supercomputer. All CPUs contain primary memory for temporarily storing data or program instructions, arithmetic-logic units for manipulating this data, and control units for interpreting program instructions and supervising computer operations. All digital computers store and manipulate data in discrete bits, which are typically combined into eight-bit bytes.

Although some accounting information systems initially gather data on source documents that require data transcription, it is usually better if input data are captured in machine-readable formats. Devices that assist in this are POS terminals, automatic tag readers, optical bar code readers, MICR readers, OCR readers, and magnetic strip readers. The use of audio input, which enables users to speak into microphones or use telephones, is expected to increase in the future.

The outputs of an accounting information system often determine the entire system's usefulness or convenience. Printers produce hard-copy output by character, line, or page. The most common serial printers are dot-matrix, thermal, daisywheel, or ink-jet. Line printers include chain printers and band printers, whereas laser printers are page printers. Another popular type of output is soft-copy or displayed output—either in monochrome or RBG (color). Most microcomputer and VDT monitors use cathode ray tubes, although LED displays, LCD displays, and gas plasma displays are also common. In many accounting systems, the ability of a display screen to produce graphics using screen pixels is important.

Accounting information systems require permanent mass storage for maintaining accounting files, data bases, and computer programs. Magnetic tape is a sequential-storage medium that is often used for inexpensive back-up or archival purposes. Magnetic disks are more expensive than tapes, but also have direct-access capabilities and are therefore commonly used for online, real-time accounting applications. Floppy disks also have direct-addressing capabilities, but their limited storage capacities make them more useful for data transfer than permanent data storage. Finally, laser disks can store billions of bytes of data on a single optical disk, and are therefore expected to become increasingly important in future accounting applications.

Accounting information systems use data communications to transfer file information, support file inquiries, or transmit computerized data or programs over long distances. The technology of data communications is complex and requires communications protocols or standards for transmission accuracy. Data communications also helps users create local area networks for such purposes as sharing computer equipment or files, saving software costs, connecting disimilar computer equipment, or supporting electronic mail.

Key Terms You Should Know

arithmetic-logic unit (ALU)
ASCII
audio input
band printer
baud
binary digit (bit)
byte
central processing unit (CPU)
chain printer
communications channel
communications protocol
control unit
coprocessor
daisywheel printer
data communications
data transcription
desktop publishing
digital computers
direct-access storage device (DASD)
distributed data processing
dot-matrix printer
dumb terminal
electronic mail
file server
floppy disk
gateways (local area networks)
gigabyte (G)
gigasecond
hard-copy output
impact printer
ink-jet printer
interrecord gap (IRG)
key-entry device
kilobyte (k)
laser disk
laser printer

line printer
local area network (LAN)
magnetic disk
magnetic ink character recognition (MICR)
magnetic tape
mainframe computer
mark-sense media
megabyte (M)
microcomputer
microprocessor chip
microsecond
minicomputer
modem
monochrome monitor
multiprocessing
nanosecond
nonimpact printer
optical bar code
optical character recognition (OCR)
page printer
parallel data transmission
parity
peripheral equipment
picosecond
pixel
point-of-sale (POS) system
primary memory
random access
random-access memory (RAM)
read-only memory (ROM)
record
register (ALU)
remote terminal
secondary storage devices
sector (floppy disk)
serial data transmission

serial printer
smart terminal
soft-copy output
supercomputer
tape drive
telecommunications
thermal printer

track (tape and disk)
turnaround document
universal product code (UPC)
virtual memory
visual display terminal (VDT)
wide area network
word (in primary memory)

Discussion Questions

4-1. Why is an understanding of computer hardware important to accountants?

4-2. What is the difference between computer hardware and computer software?

4-3. Is a central processing unit really "central"? Why or why not?

4-4. Name the three sections of the central processing unit and describe the functions of each.

4-5. What is the difference between on-line and off-line computer equipment? Give several examples of each type of equipment.

4-6. Why is the central processing unit sometimes called the "heart" of the computer center?

4-7. Describe the concept of location addresses in the CPU. How are these addresses similar to street addresses? How are they different?

4-8. Decide the following argument between Mr. McAllister and Mr. Thacker.

McALLISTER: The trend in computers these days is toward bigger, more sophisticated machinery. Why, nowadays the larger CPU can do the work of hundreds of smaller machines and still have time to twiddle its thumbs. The cost of processing has been reduced substantially, too, in these larger models. Like every other form of big business, there are economies of scale.

THACKER: Wrong! You can buy a hundred microcomputers for the price of one minicomputer, each almost as capable.

4-9. Explain the function of the source document in accounting information systems. Why are they often manually prepared?

4-10. What is meant by the term *data transcription?* Why is data transcription important to accounting information systems?

4-11. What advantages does a POS system have over a manual, sales-tag system? Many of the largest, most sophisticated firms are adopting POS systems despite the fact that a POS cash register is much more expensive than a nonautomated cash register. What does this tell you about the analysis that went into the decision to purchase such systems?

4-12. Discuss the use of optical bar codes. How is this code beneficial to accounting information systems?

4-13. The use of the universal product code to identify products in supermarkets has met with some consumer resistance. Do you think such resistance is reasonable? Why or why not? Discuss supermarkets in your area that use such a system.

4-14. Indicate why you would agree or disagree with the following statement. "Mark-sense cards would be much more efficient than employee time cards for gathering data about employee working hours."

4-15. What types of output are there besides printed output? Name several possibilities, and describe a possible accounting use for each output type you mention.

4-16. What is the difference between an impact printer and a nonimpact printer? What is a serial printer, a parallel printer, a line printer, and a page printer?

4-17. How do dot-matrix printers, thermal printers, daisywheel printers, ink-jet printers, chain printers, band printers, and laser printers differ in the way they create print characters? How do these different methods affect print quality and print speed? Why are different print speeds and qualities important to different types of accounting information systems?

4-18. Identify the meaning of each of the following terms:

a. Hard-Copy output
b. Soft-Copy output
c. Pixel
d. Monochrome
e. RGB monitor

4-19. Why use secondary storage at all? Why not just keep everything in the memory section of the central processing unit, where it will be immediately available?

4-20. Magnetic tape may be likened to home recording tape, home movie projection film, and floppy disks. In what ways are these analogies accurate? In what ways are they inaccurate?

4-21. Explain why magnetic tape is called a sequential file medium.

4-22. Why is magnetic tape usually nine-track magnetic tape? What are the advantages of nine-track tape over seven-track tape?

4-23. What factors should be considered in order to compute the space requirements of a collection of magnetic tape records on a reel of tape?

4-24. A file of magnetic tape records is too large to fit on a single reel of tape. What can be done? What implication does this have for the external label information on the magnetic tape reel?

4-25. "Show me a floppy disk and I'll show you a file that is better recorded as a magnetic tape file." Comment.

4-26. In what ways are the tracks of a disk similar to the tracks of magnetic tape? In what ways are they different?

4-27. Describe the address system of a disk pack. Why is it important? How is it used?

4-28. Magnetic disks are faster, more flexible, and have greater storage capacity than magnetic tapes. Why do firms ever bother with tape if this is so?

4-29. The Horwitz and McBride Company is a retail clothing store that sells apparel for men and women. The company's accounts receivable subsidiary ledger is maintained on magnetic tape. Every Friday, the week's credit sales to customers as well as the cash collections from credit customers are input into the computer to update the accounts receivable tape file. On the last working day of each month, the computer prints out individual customer statements, which are then mailed to the credit customers.

The clothing store's management is considering the use of floppy-disk storage rather than magnetic tape storage for its accounts receivable subsidiary ledger data. Discuss some of the possible arguments against making this computer storage media change.

4-30. Explain the following terms with respect to magnetic disks.

a. Disk pack
b. Disk drive

c. Disk address
d. Track
e. Virtual memory

4-31. Are the following devices sequential-access devices or direct-access devices?

a. Laser disk
b. Magnetic tape
c. Magnetic disk
d. Floppy disk

4-32. The Tim Lochary Company uses magnetic disk, floppy disk, and magnetic tape storage. Why do you think the company feels it is desirable to use all three types of storage media?

4-33. Would a magnetic tape file system or direct-access magnetic disk system more likely be used in the following applications? Why?

a. Hospital billing system
b. Airline reservations
c. FBI file of missing persons
d. Sporting goods store inventory control

4-34. What is data communications? Why does data communications often involve remote sites? Why should accountants know about data communications?" How do accounting information systems use data communications?

4-35. What is serial data transmission? What is parallel data transmission? What is a communications channel?

4-36. Explain the meaning of each of the following terms:

a. Telecommunications
b. Baud
c. Communications protocol
d. Smart terminal
e. Dumb terminal

4-37. What is a local area network? Why are they created?

4-38. What are some of the general advantages of local area networks? How are LANs used to help create accounting information systems?

4-39. What is a network gateway? What is a LAN file server? How can LAN gateways and file servers be used in accounting information systems?

Problems

4-40. Are the following input equipment, output equipment, or combination input/output equipment?

a. Card punch
b. Card reader
c. CRT screen
d. Printer
e. Disk drive
f. Keyboard terminal
g. Magnetic drum
h. Magnetic tape drive
i. Mass storage device
j. Paper tape reader
k. Paper tape punch

4-41. Which component of the central processing unit performs each of the following functions?

a. Determines the order in which instructions are executed.
b. Multiplies two numbers together.
c. Coordinates peripheral equipment to perform input, output, and storage tasks.
d. Stores data in unique locations.
e. Compares two data values to decide which is larger.
f. Provides a transient "rest-place" for data being transferred from one computer medium to another (e.g., disk to magnetic tape).
g. Signals the computer operator that a processing function has been completed.

4-42. How many different bit combinations can be represented with each of the following sets of bits?

a. BCD (6 bits)
b. ASCII-7 (7 bits)
c. EBCDIC (8 bits)

4-43. All the following terms may be found in everyday language but have special meaning to the computer-oriented accountant. Provide both a common definition and a more technical definition for each.

a. Card
b. Field
c. Tape
d. Information
e. Data
f. Punch
g. Column
h. Character
i. Smart
j. Channel

4-44. Data processing is replete with special terms, phrases, and other language unique to the industry. Following is a set of *acronyms*—special words composed of the first letter, or first few letters, of a set of words. Identify each.

a. POS
b. I/O
c. MICR
d. EDP
e. OCR
f. UPC
g. CPU
h. ABA

4-45. Figure 4-33 is an inventory report from the Perry Products Company. Suppose that the report were generated from a stack of issuance-and-receipt ("transaction") source documents that were filled out

PERRY PRODUCTS WEEKLY INVENTORY TRANSACTIONS Week of: January 3-10, 1991						
Date of Transaction	Stock Number	Supplier Code	Unit Cost	Units Received	Units Issued	Net Value of Transaction
1-3-88	152349	51-978	$21.50	100		$2,150.00
	245637	52-888	.59		200	118.00–
1-4-88	567883	80-875	1.68	100		168.00
	23567	11-677	22.98	1		22.98
	876665	14-987	98.00		2	196.00–
	.	.	.			.
	.	.	.			.
	.	.	.			.

FIGURE 4-33 An inventory report from the Perry Products Company.

by the warehouse personnel. What information would be required on the documents to generate such a report?

4-46. The Bill J. Keenan Company keeps its employee records on a magnetic tape file. The file has been written at a tape density of 800 characters per inch, each fixed-length unblocked record being of size 300. Assume that standard interrecord gaps of 3/4 inch are used, and the company has 15,000 employees.

a. What is the length of each logical record? Each physical record?
b. How long is the entire tape file?
c. Is the company using this file system as efficiently as possible? Why or why not? Do you think the company should change this system? If so, how?

4-47. Suppose, in Problem 4-46, the Keenan Company decides to use a blocking factor of 4.

a. How long is each logical record now? Each physical record?
b. How much space on the tape would be saved by using this blocking factor?

4-46. Given the following information, compute the amount of tape needed to create a complete magnetic tape file.

a. Record format: 400 characters each; fixed length.
b. Blocking factor: none
c. Recording density: 1600 cpi.
d. Number of records: 20,000.

4-49. How would your answer change in Problem 4-48 if there were a blocking factor of 4?

4-50. Arrange the following list of devices in ascending order by input/output speed (using highest speeds).

a. Card reader
b. Card punch
c. Paper tape reader
d. Paper tape punch
e. Magnetic tape
f. Magnetic disk
g. CRT
h. Magnetic drum
i. COM

4-51. The Worthley National Bank has 100,000 checking accounts at its National City office. These accounts are maintained as a master file of 1200 characters each.

Required

a. Suppose the bank were to store the records on magnetic tape. How many *feet* of tape would be required, using an unblocked record format and a tape density of 800 characters per inch?
b. Answer part A if the records were blocked, using a blocking factor of 8 and a tape density of 800 characters per inch.

4-52. The Salsberg Hospital Supply Company has approximately 15,000 inventory items that it maintains on a tape file. Each record has a fixed length of 400 characters.

Required

a. Suppose that to create a new master file record, the information must first be keyed onto floppy disks. How many floppy disks would be required to recreate the entire file of 15,000 records.
b. How many feet of magnetic tape would be required to store the entire file of inventory records? Assume a blocking factor of 10 and a tape density of 800 characters per inch.

4-53. The Kritchman Sales Service maintains a mailing list of addresses of 200,000 "upper-income" residents in the New York metropolitan area. Each name and address is stored as an unblocked, variable-length record on magnetic tape using a tape density of 800 characters per inch. The smallest record is only 100 characters in length. The largest is 300 characters. An average requirements length would be 160 characters.

a. Approximately how many feet of tape would be required for this file if a magnetic tape file were used?
b. What would be an upper limit to the amount of magnetic tape, in feet, required for this file?

4-54. The Nebrasco Oil Company operates its own charge-card division, enabling holders of the company's credit card to charge all service station bills to their account as needed. Each time a charge is made, the pertinent information is recorded and ultimately encoded in a computer record. Design and draw an efficient record layout similar to Figure 4-23 for the Nebrasco Company based on the following information.

a. Customer account number (10 digits)
b. Station number (5 digits)
c. Entry date
d. Date of transaction
e. Amount of gasoline purchased (always less than $100)
f. Amount of oil, fluids, etc., purchased (always less than $75)
g. Amount of parts and automotive supplies (always less than $4000)
h. Amount of labor charges (always less than $1000)
i. Amount of taxes charged on transaction (always less than $600)

4-55. Design and draw the record layout for the Gilbert Company's accounts receivable cash collections system, as dictated by the following informational needs. Remember that a compact format is important.

a. Date of entry
b. Invoice reference number (5 digits)
c. Amount paid (maximum is $999.99)
d. Discount (percent)
e. Name of company making payment (allow 25 characters)
f. Number of check (5 digits)
g. Date of check

4-56. Puerner Products manufactures a variety of machine tools and parts used primarily in industrial tasks. To control production, the company requires the information listed below. Design an efficient record format for Puerner Products.

a. Order number (4 digits)
b. Part number to be manufactured (5 digits)
c. Part description (10 characters)
d. Manufacturing department (3 digits)
e. Number of pieces started (always less than 10,000)
f. Number of pieces finished
g. Machine number (2 digits)
h. Date work started
i. Hour work started (use 24-hour system)
j. Date work completed
k. Hour work completed
l. Work standard per hour (3 digits)
m. Worker number (5 digits)
n. Foreman number (5 digits)

4-57. Some of the following terms are acronyms while others are not. For those terms that are acronyms, state the full meaning:

a. RS232
b. baud
c. bit
d. VDT
e. LAN
f. DASD
g. pixel
h. DS,DD

CASE ANALYSES

4.58. *The Fritz Grupe Company*

The Fritz Grupe Company uses its computer to help it process mail orders. A separate computer record on a floppy disk is prepared for each item required in each order. The direct costs for the data-transcription portion of this operation include:

a. Monthly rental of offline key-entry workstations: $200 each
b. Monthly salary of key-entry operators: $1,200 each
c. Cost of diskettes (not reused): $1.00 each

The company gets about 500 orders per week. Each order is different, of course, but on average requires 5 items. Also, on average, each item requires 50 keystrokes. The error rate is approximately 5 percent.

A. Assume for simplicity that all errors are corrected the first time they are changed, that there are exactly four weeks in a month, and that the operator keystroke rate averages 2,000 strokes per hour. How many workstations does the company need to keep up with its input volume?
B. Compute the monthly cost for this data-entry operation, using your answer in part A.
C. What does your answer in part B tell you about the benefits of some type of automated, machine-readable data capture for this application?

4.59. *Town and Country Building Supply*

Town and Country Building Supply was founded in 1899 by Chung Ali Kai, who immigrated from China at the age of 15. Beginning with $60,000 in starting capital, the company thrived for almost a year before burning to the ground in an accidental fire. After the disaster, the young Chinese entrepreneur was faced with a $25,000 liability because the business had not been insured. Determined to rebuild, he began afresh, managing to survive a panic in 1907, a second catastrophic fire in 1919, the Great Depression of 1930–1933, and the ravages of World War II.

Town and Country had begun as a wholesale and retail supplier of home building materials, an interior decorator, and a wholesale supplier of rice. In 1920, the interior-decorating segment and rice-supply segment of the business were abandoned, and the firm began to devote its entire attention to hardware, plumbing, and building supplies. In 1950, a brand-new $200,000 facility was constructed on 5 acres of land purchased on Highway 52—close enough to town to permit easy access for downtown shoppers but far enough away to permit the construction of a 50-car parking lot.

Today, after over 90 years in business, the firm continues to prosper; Town and Country is one of the busiest building supply companies in the area. In part, this success is due to the firm's popular chief executive and son of the founder, David Kai, who is well known for his many charitable activities, and also due to the company's purposeful response to the retail growth of the industry. The firm now operates four stores, some of which have as many as 20 merchandising departments. A special House-Planning Department has also been created to provide consultation and information services to the contracting trade and also to private homeowners. Other new programs include a full-service garden center and (in the main store) a complete kitchen and bath improvement center.

The company has also concentrated on the wholesale side of its business. Almost all of the area's building contractors are personal acquaintances of David Kai, and the company does a substantial amount of wholesale business, most of which is conducted on credit. As in the retail side of the business, Town and Country's wholesale policy has been to develop a one-stop shopping center for all home-improvement needs.

One recent proposal placed on Mr. Kai's desk is to use point-of-sale terminals instead of the company's standard cash registers. These would be connected to a new computer system. It has been suggested that automating the company's sales activities would be of great value in both the retail and wholesale segments of the business. Mr. Kai is not familiar with computer equipment but is forward thinking and realizes that other businesses have been installing such equipment. Certainly he is anxious to do anything that would be cost-effective for the business, to make things easier for his customers, and to increase the efficiency of his operations. Your task is to assist Mr. Kai by evaluating the proposal and making a recommendation.

4.60. *Wingard National Bank*

Wingard National Bank's credit-card department issues a special credit card that permits credit-card holders to withdraw funds from the bank's automated teller windows at any time of the day or night. These windows are actually "smart" terminals connected to the bank's central computer. To use them, a bank customer inserts the magnetically encoded card in the automated teller's slot and types in a unique passcode on the teller keyboard. If the passcode matches the authorized code, the customer goes on to indicate (1) whether a withdrawal from a savings account or a withdrawal from a checking account is desired and (2) the amount of the withdrawal (in multiples of $10). The teller-terminal communicates this information to the bank's central computer and then gives the customer the desired cash. In addition, the automated terminal prints out a hard copy of the transaction and provides this information to the customer together with the cash.

To guard against irregularities in the automated cash transaction described, the credit-card department has imposed certain restrictions on the use of the credit cards when customers make cash withdrawals at automated teller windows.

1. The correct passcode must be keyed into the teller keyboard before the cash withdrawal is processed.
2. The credit card must be one issued by Wingard

National Bank. For this purpose a special bank code has been encoded as part of the magnetic-strip information.

3. The credit card must be current. If the expiration date on the card has already passed at the time the card is used, the card is rejected.
4. The credit card must not be a stolen one. The bank keeps a computerized list of these stolen cards and requires that this list be checked electronically before the withdrawal transaction can proceed.
5. For the purposes of making withdrawals, each credit card can only be used twice on any given day. This restriction is intended to hold no matter what branch bank(s) are visited by the customer.
6. The amount of the withdrawal must not exceed the customer's account balance.

Questions

1. What information must be encoded on the magnetic-card strip on each Wingard National Bank credit card in order to permit the computerized testing of the policy restrictions?
2. What tests of these restrictions could be performed at the teller window by a "smart terminal" and which tests would have to be performed by the bank's central processing unit and other equipment?
3. Prepare a program flowchart indicating the ordered processing logic that would have to be followed in order to enforce the credit-card limitations identified earlier.

4.61. Wallace Manufacturing Company

Production control at Wallace Manufacturing Company operates as follows. Every Wednesday, the production-control manager, the manufacturing-operations foreman, and the vice-president of production meet to plan the production for the coming week. A list of products and quantities to produce is prepared, typed by the vice-president's secretary, and then keyed directly into a computer terminal in the production-control manager's office. As the products are keyed in, the computer automatically checks the company's inventory file to make sure that the finished product

desired is not already overstocked and also checks to make sure that enough raw materials are available to produce the amount of finished product desired. If all is in order, the planned-production requirements are logged onto a production-request file on computer disk, and a hard-copy document is printed for each member of the planning team and delivered on Thursday of each week.

Each Friday, the production-request file is merged with an open production orders file, which contains all production orders not completed to date. At the same time, the computer prepares a card deck of operations cards and a job-step listing. Each punched card represents one processing step or operations step in the manufacturing sequence for the production of finished product. A computer listing is also prepared that summarizes these job steps for all products scheduled for production in the coming week.

The punched cards slip into special envelopes affixed to the sides of work bins that roll from job-step site to job-step site and are color-coded by major operation type. As each job step is completed, the associated card is pulled from its envelope and sent directly to data processing. Here the cards are batched and processed on a daily basis. Initially, the cards are simply rewritten on magnetic tape. Next, they are sorted by production batch number and coordinated with the open production orders file to update this file. At the same time, the computer prints an operations summary report listing those operations that have been completed, by product number, and also listing those production orders still pending.

Questions

1. Describe in some detail the types of inventory files that the Wallace Company must have in order to provide the preceding information.
2. Is the open production order file likely to be a sequential file or a direct-access file? Why?
3. What information is likely to be found on the job-step cards? Why are such cards placed on the *outside* of the work bins in special envelopes?
4. What additional information might be collected from the job-step sites through the use of these cards?
5. Suggest at least one improvement for this information system.

REFERENCES AND RECOMMENDED READINGS FOR PART ONE

Ackoff, Russell L. "Towards a System of Systems Concepts." *Management Science* 17 (July 1971), pp. 661–671.

Allen, Robert J. "Electronic Spreadsheets: A Next Step." *Modern Office Technology* (December 1984), pp. 56–64.

American Accounting Association. "Report of the Committee on Accounting and Information Systems." In *Committee Reports: Supplement to vol. XLVI of the Accounting Review.* Evanston, IL: 1971, pp. 287–350.

Anderson, Anker V. *Budgeting for Data Processing.* New York: National Association of Accountants, 1983.

Anderson, Anker V. *Graphing Financial Information: How Accountants Can Use Graphs to Communicate.* New York: National Association of Accountants, 1983.

Antle, Rick, and Demski, Joel S. "The Controllability Principle in Responsibility Accounting." *Accounting Review* 63 (October 1988), pp. 700–718.

Berdine, W. H. "Strategic Planning and Attributes of External Information." *Managerial Planning* 24 (January–February 1976), pp. 17–21.

Bodenstab, Charles J. "Exception Reports for Management Action." *Financial Executive* 37 (Nov. 1969), pp. 58–67.

Buchanan, Jack R., and Linowes, Richard G. "Understanding Distributed Data Processing," *Harvard Business Review* 58 (July–August 1980), pp. 65–75.

Butterworth, John E. "The Accounting System as an Information Function." *Journal of Accounting Research* 10 (Spring 1972), pp. 1–27.

Carr, Arthur. "Accounting Information for Managerial Decisions." *Financial Executive* 45 (August 1977), pp. 40–44.

Carruth, Paul J., and McClendon, Thurrell O. "How Supervisors React to 'Meeting the Budget' Pressure." *Management Accounting* 65 (November 1984), pp. 50–54.

Cerullo, Michael J. "Data Communications: Opportunities for Accountants." *The CPA Journal* 54 (April 1984), pp. 40–47.

Chenhall, Robert H. "Authoritarianism and Participative Budgeting: A Dyadic Analysis." *Accounting Review* 61 (April 1986), pp. 263–272.

Clancy, Donald K. "The Management Control Problems of Responsibility Accounting." *Management Accounting* 59 (March 1978), pp. 35–39.

Clark, Richard S. "Four Sure Steps to Strategic Planning." *CA Magazine* (March 1986), pp. 24–30.

Cohen, Jeffrey B. "Ethics & Budgeting; Standards of Ethical Conduct for Management Accountants." *Management Accounting* 70 (August 1988), pp. 28–31.

Cushing, Barry E. "Pricing Internal Computer Services: The Basic Issues." *Management Accounting* 54 (April 1976), pp. 47–50.

Cushing, Barry E., and Rommey, Marshall B. *Accounting Information Systems and Business Organization,* 4th ed. Reading, MA: Addison-Wesley, 1987.

Davis, Gordon B. "Computer Curriculum for Accounting and Auditors—Present and Prospective." in *Education for Expanding Computer Curriculums,* Daniel L. Sweeney, ed. New York: American Institute of Certified Public Accountants, 1976, pp. 12–21.

Davis, Gordon B., and Olsen, M. *Management Information Systems: Conceptual Foundations, Structure, and Development,* 2nd ed. New York: McGraw-Hill, 1985.

Dearden, John. "Will the Computer Change the Job of Top Management?" *Sloan Management Review* 25 (Fall 1983), pp. 57–60.

Diebold, John. "Information Resource Management—The New Challenge," *Infosystems* 24 (June 1979), pp. 50–53.

Dietz, Devon D., and Keane, John D. "Integrating Distributed Processing within a Central Environment." *Management Accounting* 62 (November 1980), pp. 43–47.

Edwards, Morris, "Understanding Data Communication's Basics." *Infosystems* 25 (July 1978), pp. 48–54.

"Evaluating the Pros and Cons of Different Accounting Systems." *Management Accounting (UK)* 65 (Nov. 1987), pp. 10–11.

Galbraith, Jay R. *Organizational Design: An Information Processing View.* Reading, MA: Addison-Wesley, 1973.

Gordon, Lawrence A., and Miller, Danny. "A Contingency Framework for the Design of Accounting Information Systems." *Accounting, Organizations and Society* 1, 1 (1976), pp. 59–69.

Hasz, Thomas W., and Boockholdt, J. L. "How Houston Lighting & Power Applied DDP." *Management Accounting* 65 (March 1983), pp. 56–59.

Hay, Leon E. "What Is an Information System? The Legal, Conventional, and Logical Constraints." *Business Horizons* 14 (Feb. 1971), pp. 65–72.

Hessinger, Paul R. "Distributed Systems and Data Management." *Datamation* 27 (November 1981), pp. 179–182.

Hopwood, Anthony G. "Towards an Organizational Perspective for the Study of Accounting and Information Systems." *Accounting, Organizations and Society* 3, 1 (1978), pp. 3–13.

Joseph, Gilbert W. "Why Study Accounting Information Systems?" *Journal of Systems Management* 38 (September 1987), pp. 24–26.

Leitch, Robert A., and Davis, K. Roscoe. *Accounting Information Systems.* Englewood Cliffs, NJ: Prentice-Hall, 1983.

Lord, R. J. "Probabilistic Budgeting". *Cost and Management* 52, 3 (May–June 1978), pp. 14–19.

Marra, Michele L., and Radig, William J. "Audit, Compilation or Review: Closing the Expectation Gap." *National Public Accountant* 32 (April 1987), pp. 30–32.

McCauley, Herbert N. "Developing a Corporate Private Network." *MIS Quarterly* 7 (December 1983), pp. 19–33.

McGinnis, Edward C., and Maglione, Lawrence G. "Taking VisiCalc to the Limit." *Management Accounting* 65 (January 1984), pp. 41–45.

McLaughlin, Michael J., and Katz, Michael S. "Distributed Processing: Second Generation." *Infosystems* 26 (February 1979), pp. 38–42.

Mills, William B. "Drawing Up a Budgeting System for an Ad Agency." *Management Accounting* 65 (December 1983), pp. 46–51.

Mitchell, William G., and Wilkinson, Joseph W. "POS Systems Revolutionize Retailing." *Journal of Systems Management* 27 (April 1976), pp. 34–41.

Moscove, Stephen A. "Computerized Budgetary Systems." *Cost and Management* 57, 6 (May–June 1983), pp. 14–19.

Moscove, Stephen A. "A Model to Evaluate Managerial Operating Performance." *Cost and Management* 2 (March–April 1984), pp. 28–34.

Paddock, Harold E. "Voice Input a Reality." *Internal Auditor* 60 (December 1983), pp. 23–26.

Pasewark, William R., and McCabe, Kelly S. "Preparing and Maintaining a Budget Manual." *Management Accounting* 69 (May 1988), pp. 33–35.

Rath, Sudhansu S. "Systems Approach to Accounting." *Journal of Systems Management* 28 (June 1977), pp. 36–38.

Redman, Louis N. "The Planning Process." *Managerial Planning* 31, 6 (May–June 1983), pp. 24–40.

Rommey, Marshall B., and Krogstad, Jack L. "Management Accountants—in the Middle of the Computer Muddle." *Cost and Management* 52, 3 (May–June 1978), pp. 4–9.

Rushinek, Avi, and Rushinek, Sara. "Distributed Processing: Implications and Applications for Business." *Journal of Systems Management* 35 (July 1984), pp. 21–27.

Schoderbek, Peter P., Kefalas, Asterios G., and Schoderbek, Charles G. *Management Systems: Conceptual Considerations,* rev. ed. Dallas: Business Publications, 1980.

Simkin, Mark. "Decision Trees on Electronic Spreadsheets." *Encyclopedia of Microcomputers.* New York: Marcel Decker, 1987.

Sobol, Michael L. "Data Communications Primer for Auditors." *EDPACS* 11 (March 1984), pp. 179–186.

Stallings, William, "Beyond Local Networks." *Datamation* 29 (August 1983), pp. 167–176.

Ullrich, Robert A., and Wieland, George F. *Organization Theory and Design.* Homewood, IL: Richard D. Irwin, 1980.

University of Kansas. *Perspectives on the Accounting Profession: The Present and the Future.* September 5, 1985.

Vanecek. Michael T., Zant, Robert F., and Guynes, Carl S. "Distributed Data Processing: A New 'Tool' for Accountants." *The Journal of Accountancy* 48 (October 1980), pp. 75–83.

Walker, Charles W. "Profitability and Responsibility Accounting."*Management Accounting* 53 (December 1971), pp. 23–30.

Wallace, Robert E. "Why Strategic Planning." *Journal of Information Systems Management* 3,2 (Spring 1986), pp. 49–51.

Walsh, Myles E. "What is a Data Center?" *Journal of Systems Management* 35 (January 1984), pp. 20–29.

Wheelock, Alton R., "Service or Profit Center?" *Datamation* 28 (May 1982), pp. 167–176.

Winski, Donald T. "Distributed Systems: Is Your Organization Ready?" *Infosystems* 25 (September 1978), pp. 38–42.

Wise, David. "Better Budgeting for Better Results: The Role of Zero-Base Budgets." *Management Accounting (UK)* 66 (May 1988), pp. 35–36.

Zald, Mayer N. and Johnson, H. Thomas. The Sociology of Enterprise, Accounting and Budget Rules: Implications for Organizational Theory/Accounting, Organizations and Rules: Toward a Sociology of Price—A Comment on Zald." *Accounting, Organizations & Society (UK)* 11 (April–May 1986), pp. 327–343.

PART TWO

Accounting Information Systems for Collecting, Recording, and Storing Business Data

A major role of an accounting information system is to aid the collecting, recording, and storing of financially-oriented data, as well as converting these data into meaningful information for management decision-making. The four chapters in Part Two discuss various data processing and data management approaches that provide relevant information to management. The emphasis throughout these chapters will be on computerized accounting information system environments.

Chapter 5 discusses the inputs and outputs associated with transaction processing. The discussion includes descriptions of the specific source documents and reports associated with the major transaction processing systems of an accounting information system. The supplement to this chapter examines the collecting and recording of accounting journal entry data by a manufacturing firm that uses a manual data processing system.

The documentation of an accounting information system is important in that it allows management, auditors, users, and systems analysts to understand the basic processes and functions of the system. Chapter 6 describes various techniques that can be used to document the system. These techniques include flowcharts and data flow diagrams.

155

The capabilities of an accounting information system are determined, in part, by how the system stores accounting data. In computerized environments, this leads to the study of computer files, methods of file organization, and the concepts of data bases. The purpose of Chapter 7 is to discuss these subjects in detail and to illustrate how accounting functions can be performed more efficiently and effectively with computerized data base systems. This includes analyzing the trade-offs associated with various kinds of file and data base structures. To emphasize the value of data bases to accounting information systems, several common accounting processes (e.g., preparing financial statements, planning and controlling budgets, and purchasing inventory on credit) are examined in the supplement using traditional manual data processing systems as well as computerized data base systems.

Finally, to conclude Part Two, Chapter 8 provides an in-depth illustration of a manual and two computerized accounting information systems for processing *accounts receivable*. This chapter will integrate many of the concepts surrounding the collection, recording, and storage of accounting data in one of the most important accounting applications of the typical organization.

5 Processing Accounting Transactions

Among the important questions you should be able to answer after reading this chapter are:

1. Why does the management of accounting data in an accounting information system begin with the design of output reports?
2. What are the elements of good forms design and how are source document forms used to collect data for accounting information systems?
3. Why are codes used in accounting information systems and what different types of codes are available?
4. What is a company **chart of accounts** and why are block codes often used for them?
5. What are the inputs and outputs associated with the major accounting transaction subsystems?
6. What are just-in-time and materials requirements planning systems?

INTRODUCTION

Accounting information systems depend heavily on the flow of data through various organizational subsystems, and it is important that this data flow be managed, controlled, and expedited. There are three characteristics of "good" data: (1) accuracy, (2) completeness, and (3) timeliness. These characteristics should be viewed as goals or objectives toward which an accounting information system strives. The more successful an accounting information system is in accomplishing these goals, the more effective the system will be.

As accounting data flow through organizational channels, there is the possibility that data will be lost, inaccurately copied, delayed, or misinterpreted. This chapter focuses on means of collecting data accurately and ways of avoiding misinterpretation. It also highlights specific accounting applications and the data that is collected for each of these.

Managing the flow of data in an accounting information system begins with the design of output reports. This is because output reports are the end products of an accounting information system and therefore part of an organization's information goals. We want these reports to serve managerial needs and thus define informational requirements first. The topic of designing output reports is discussed first in the chapter.

The information on output records dictates the types of data that must be collected in order to generate these reports. Basically, system designers work backward from the reports to determine the right data to collect (this process is discussed later in this book in the chapters about system development). The term *right data* implies two things: (1) collecting the proper accounting facts and statistics that will serve the objectives of the system and (2) *not* collecting data that do not serve a useful purpose. The use of source documents in the collection of useful accounting information is discussed next in the chapter.

The collection of accounting data usually involves the design of input forms, sales slips, personnel applications, and related source documents that serve initially to record accounting data in an efficient format. Good forms design is therefore critical, since the remainder of the data flow depends on it. This topic is also discussed in the second section of the chapter.

To assist in the collection and processing of accounting data, data are often *coded*. For example, a number code is often used in addition to a prose description in sales catalogs in order to identify a product uniquely. The topic of coding accounting data is discussed in detail in the third section of this chapter.

The types of source documents and reports that serve as inputs and outputs in an accounting information system may be related to specific accounting applications. These applications or modules are the *building blocks* of an integrated accounting information system. The final section of this chapter examines the major transaction processing applications that comprise an accounting information system. These are general ledger, accounts receivable, accounts payable, inventory, and payroll applications. These applications are discussed throughout the book. The focus in this chapter is on the inputs and outputs of these applications in terms of source documents and reports.

REPORT DESIGN: A PREREQUISITE TO EFFECTIVE DATA COLLECTION

The design of effective accounting information systems usually begins by considering the outputs from the system. These outputs are informational objectives for an accounting information system and are therefore goals toward which the system should strive. Thus, outputs are designed first.

Among the outputs of an accounting information system are (1) reports to management, (2) reports to investors and creditors, (3) files that retain transaction data, and (4) files that retain current information about accounts (e.g., inventory records). From the perspective of managerial decision-making, perhaps the most important of these outputs are the reports to management. This is because these reports are the tools the manager uses to take action. Further, the majority of accounting data collected by an organization ultimately appears on some type of internal and/or external report. Therefore, managerial reports are also important because they are a prerequisite to establishing the organization's data collection processes.

An Example of Report Design: The Statement of Cash Flows

To illustrate the concept of report design, consider the major financial reports of the S. C. Scott Company. One report prepared for the S. C. Scott Company's management, stockholders, and creditors is the **Statement of Cash Flows.** Accountants within the S. C. Scott Company's accounting subsystem have determined the basic design for this report, illustrated in Figure 5-1. (Note that the indirect method for determining cash from operating activities has been selected.)

After establishing the format of this report, the company can implement data-collection procedures to accumulate the necessary data for the

Statement of Cash Flows. For instance, assume the S. C. Scott Company sells a piece of its production equipment on September 7, 1990, at a cash price of $5000. Assume that this equipment had originally cost $8000 when purchased, and as of September 7 the accumulated depreciation on the equipment is $4000 after the adjusting entry below was recorded. The data collected surrounding this September 7 transaction would result in the following journal entries.

Depreciation expense	50	
Accumulated depreciation-production equipment		50
(To update the depreciation on the sold equipment)*		
Cash	5000	
Accumulated depreciation— production equipment	4000	
Production equipment		8000
Gain on disposal of long-term assets		1000
(To recognize the sale of the equipment)		

*This adjusting entry updates the depreciation on the production equipment since the last time (September 1) depreciation was recorded on the equipment. We are assuming that the S. C. Scott Company records monthly adjusting entries for an item such as depreciation.

The data collected regarding the $50 depreciation expense, the $1000 gain, and the $5000 cash proceeds from the sale would appear within the S. C. Scott Company's general ledger accounts after these entries are posted. The design format of the company's Statement of Cash Flows necessitates the inclusion of the $50 depreciation expense (added to the cash provided from operating activities), the $1000 gain (deducted from the cash provided from operating activities), and the $5000 cash proceeds (added to the cash provided from investing activities). This means the accountants must make sure they have properly collected (in journal entries and then posted to correct general ledger accounts) the $50, $1000, and $5000 amounts for ultimate inclusion in the

S. C. Scott Company

**Statement of Cash Flows
For the Year Ended December 31, 1990**

Cash Flows from Operating Activities

Net Income	$X	
Add (Deduct) items to convert net income to cash basis:		
Increase in accounts receivable	(X)	
Increase in inventory	(X)	
Increase in prepaid expenses	(X)	
Gain on sale of fixed asset	(X)	
Increase in accounts payable	X	
Increased in accrued payables	X	
Depreciation	X	
Loss on sale of fixed asset	X	
Net Cash flow from operating activities		$X

Cash Flows from Investing Activities

Purchase of fixed assets	(X)	
Proceeds from sale of fixed assets	X	
Net Cash flow from investing activities		X

Cash Flows from Financing Activities

Proceeds from issuing common stock	X	
Proceeds from incurring long-term debt	X	
Issuance of cash dividend	X	
Net Cash flow from financing activities		X
Net increase in cash		$X

FIGURE 5-1 The design format for the S. C. Scott Company's Statement of Cash Flows.

Statement of Cash Flows. It should further be noted that both the $50 depreciation expense and the $1000 gain will appear in the S. C. Scott Company's income statement, and the $5000 cash proceeds will appear in the company's balance sheet as part of its "cash" asset.

The preceding example has been somewhat oversimplified. But it illustrates the point that, for data collection to be performed effectively, the types and contents of reports must first be known. Otherwise, either the data required for certain reports may not be properly collected or data that are unnecessary may be collected. Both

of these situations will cause inefficiencies in a company's data collection process.

Considerations in Report Design

Good output reports tend to have similar characteristics. Among them are the following traits.

Usefulness

A report must serve some managerial purpose. For the preceding example, the preparation of the statement of cash flows enables the company to provide information regarding changes in its cash balance and to express these changes in a convenient format. Often, a convenient format not only serves internal managerial purposes but also helps such financial statement readers as stockholders, creditors, and potential investors.

Computerized accounting information systems are especially guilty of generating more reports, and also including more data in reports, than managers can use. The term **information overload** describes this problem, although the term is actually a misnomer. By definition, *information* is useful and therefore should not overload an individual. (A better term would be *data overload*.) In any event, management reports should only be prepared if they will be useful, not because someone thinks they are a good idea.

Wherever possible, managerial reports should contain summary information, be concise and efficient, and, most important, be *action oriented*. Summarizing information enables the manager to avoid unnecessary details and to concentrate on what is important. Brevity and succinctness contribute to these goals. Finally, **action-oriented reports** support managerial decision making and therefore allow the manager to correct problems or change plans.

Convenient Format

It should go without saying that output reports should be legible and clear, but sometimes this fundamental rule is violated. Beyond this, good managerial reports should be well formatted and easy to read.

Convenient formats must be determined on a case-by-case basis. For example, summary reports should contain financial totals, comparative reports should list like numbers (e.g., budget versus actual figures) in adjacent columns, and descriptive reports (e.g., marketing reports) should present results in a systematic fashion. Finally, numbers should be expressed in the units (dollars, dozens, and so forth) most useful to the recipients.

Identification

Good managerial reports always contain fundamental identification, including headings (company name, organizational division or department, etc.), and page numbers. The reports of accounting information systems are usually time oriented and therefore should also include dates. Balance sheets and similar reports should indicate the date "as of" a specific point in time. Income statements and similar reports should indicate a span of dates for the reporting period (e.g., for the month ended June 30, 1990). Also, as a general rule of thumb, it is helpful to include the frequency of the report in the heading (e.g., "Quarterly Marketing Summary").

Since most accounting reports are prepared periodically, it is also a good idea to assign an identification to the report *form* as well as the report. Usually, this number is recorded in the documentation of the accounting information system as well as printed in the heading of the report. When preprinted forms are used, identification numbers are also necessary, for example, when ordering new supplies.

Consistency

The reports of an accounting information system should be consistent in at least three ways: (1) over time, (2) across departmental or divisional levels, and (3) with general accounting practice. Accounting reports should be consistent over time so that the information will be easy to understand and so that the information from one period can be compared with that of another.

Reports should be consistent across departmental levels so that supervisors may compare departmental performance and create standards for the company. Where the need for reporting consistency conflicts with the informational needs of individual departmental managers, either several types of reports can be created or compromises in the format of specific reports can be reached.

Finally, report formats should be consistent

with general accounting practice. This makes reports intelligible to external readers and also more understandable to managers internally.

SOURCE DOCUMENTS: COLLECTING THE DATA FOR OUTPUT REPORTS

From the standpoint of an accounting information system, the chief concerns in the data collection process are accuracy, timeliness, and cost-effectiveness. (From an accounting viewpoint, an activity or process is considered to be *cost-effective* if its anticipated benefits are expected to

exceed the anticipated costs.) The purchase order in Figure 5-2 is a case in point. This **source document** represents a purchase order by Sneaks and Cleats, a retail sporting goods shop, for 15 sets of golf clubs and 20 basketballs from the Alan Company. Although this purchase order must be completed manually, the fact that the order blank has been preprinted ensures legibility of the name and address of the purchasing company and completeness in the ordering data. If Sneaks and Cleats (the purchasing company) were a large organization, additional copies of the purchase order, each on a different colored paper, would likely be prepared for internal use. For example, one copy would be retained by the purchasing department to document the order and to serve as a reference for future inqui-

---

PURCHASE ORDER

ORDER NO. 36551

SNEAKS AND CLEATS
Route 59
Nanuet, New York, 10955

DATE: *OCT. 5, 1991*

To: *ALAN COMPANY*

125 KING STREET

HONOLULU, HAWAII 96822

SHIPPING INSTRUCTIONS:

DO (DO NOT) INSURE

SHIP VIA:

SMITH SHIPPING

We wish to order the following:

CATALOG NO.	QNTY	DESCRIPTION	PRICE	TOTAL
A356024	15	"SWEATY PALMS" GOLF CLUBS	$60.00	$900.00
A135757	20	MITEEDUNK BASKETBALLS	3.50	70.00
		TOTAL		$970.00

Signed: *F. Winnett*

SNEAKS AND CLEATS

FIGURE 5-2 A serially numbered purchase order.

ries. Copies would also be sent to the accounting and receiving departments. The use of carbon sheets to prepare these duplicate copies would be cost-effective inasmuch as the preparation of the original copy would automatically create the additional, departmental sheets. We also note that the purchase orders bear a serial number, 36551. When purchase orders are numbered sequentially, each such form is uniquely identified. This both enhances later referencing and serves as an important means of internal control.

To accommodate the purchase order of the Sneaks and Cleats Company, the Alan Company will ship the desired merchandise and send, under separate cover, a sales invoice. The sales invoice document is illustrated in Figure 5-3. Note that much of the information on the original purchase order is duplicated on the invoice. New information includes the terms of the sale, "2/10, n/30" (2% discount allowed if bill paid within 10 days, full amount due within 30 days otherwise), the date of the purchase order (reference date),

the date the order was shipped, and the (pre-printed) sales invoice number. The Alan Company would prepare at least six copies of the invoice. Two (or more) copies would serve as a bill for the customer. A third copy would be retained by the shipping department as a record that the order had been filled. A fourth copy would be sent to the accounting department to be used in the processing of accounts receivable. A fifth copy would be kept by the sales department for future reference. Finally, a sixth copy would be sent to the inventory department for updating its records on the specific inventory items sold.

Source documents of the types reviewed here help manage the flow of accounting data in several ways. First, they dictate the kind of data to be collected and help ensure *legibility, consistency,* and *accuracy* in the recording of this data. Second, they encourage the *completeness* of accounting data because the information required is clearly enumerated on these forms. Third, they

SALES INVOICE

ALAN COMPANY
125 King Street
Honolulu, Hawaii 96822

INVOICE NO.
18977

To: Sneaks and Cleats

Route 59

Nanuet, N.Y., 10955

Terms: 2/10, n/30

Purchase Order No.: 36551

Reference Date: Oct. 5, 1991

Date Shipped: Oct. 14, 1991

Shipped Via: Smith Shipping

CATALOG NO.	QNTY	DESCRIPTION	PRICE	TOTAL
A356024	15	"Sweaty Palms" Golf Clubs	$60.00	$900.00
A135757	20	Miteedunk Basketballs	3.50	70.00
				$970.00
				48.50
			Sales Tax at 5%	
			Total Due	$1,018.50

FIGURE 5-3   The sales invoice used for the purchase order of Figure 5-2.

serve as *distributors of information* because multiple copies of the same form can be sent to those individuals or departments that need the information. Finally, source documents help to establish the *authenticity* of accounting data. This is useful for such purposes as establishing an audit trail, testing for authorization of payments or inventory disbursements, or establishing accountability for the collection or distribution of money.

Both manual and computerized accounting information systems use source documents extensively. Later in this chapter we discuss the source documents associated with various accounting information system applications. Also, the supplement to this chapter provides an example of how source documents are used to collect and record accounting data for a manual application. Here, we turn our attention directly to ways in which data are collected, recorded, and stored within computerized accounting information systems.

CODING

Accounting information systems depend heavily on the use of codes to record, classify, store, and retrieve financial data. For example, it is possible in a manual system to use simple alphabetic descriptions when preparing summary journal entries. In contrast, computerized systems more often use **alphanumeric codes** (i.e., codes that use numbers and letters) to record accounting transactions. In a production application, for example, the manual journal entry

(1) Direct raw materials inventory   X
        Indirect raw materials
            inventory   X
                Accounts payable   X

would more likely be recorded as

(1) Direct raw materials inventory
        12345   X

    Indirect raw materials
        inventory 13456   X
            Accounts payable 45678   X

Here, the numbers 12345 and 13456 are codes for the raw materials inventory accounts, and the number 45678 is the code for the accounts payable general ledger account. (We shall look more closely at codes for such accounts shortly.)

Codes are used for a number of reasons, including the representation of inventory accounts, payroll accounts, and plant and equipment accounts. But these are not the only uses of codes. Other applications will now be described.

Purposes of Codes

Codes serve many purposes in accounting information system, including the following.

1. **Uniquely Identify Accounting Data.** Accounting information systems find it necessary to uniquely identify such things as individual accounts or specific transactions. For example, more than one person may have the same name. Thus, payroll files or bank account files use a social security number or a privately assigned bank account number, rather than individuals' names, to identify each account uniquely. Similarly, to guard against mix-ups in the recording of sales transactions, the typical firm will use a unique invoice number to distinguish among its many different credit sales. The assignment of a unique identification code fits directly with the concept of the record key (described in Chapters 5 and 20). Thus, codes not only facilitate identification but also aid information retrieval.

2. **Compress Data.** In general, written descriptions waste space. For example, airlines use the code "F" to designate "first class" and "Y" to designate "coach" because these codes are simpler to use and do not require as much space. Similarly, most accounting information systems will code a date such as March 24, 1988, as 03/24/88 because this code says the same thing in less space.

3. **Classify Accounts or Transactions.** Usually, it is important for accounting information systems to classify accounts by type (e.g., bank checking account, savings account, or time deposit account) or to classify transactions by type (e.g., credit sale versus cash sale), by date, or perhaps by geographic location. Codes facilitate this classification. For example, a bank might use a two-digit prefix before an account number to indicate the type of account. Similarly, the Alan Company might have a one-digit code on its sales invoices to indicate whether a sales transaction was for cash or credit.

4. **Identify Items to Appear on Reports.** Many microcomputer accounting applications require their users to code their accounts in such a way that the code also identifies whether or not it appears on a financial report—for example, an income statement or balance sheet. This enables users to prepare managerial reports in accord with generally accepted accounting principles as well as business needs.

5. **Convey Special Meanings.** It is sometimes necessary to convey data in such a way that it is meaningless to most but conveys information to those "in the know." A department store, for example, might announce "Code 9" over the loudspeaker, which may be a call to a security officer. Examples of such codes used in accounting information systems include credit ratings (which might be embedded in a credit card number), passwords (which enable a user to gain access to computerized accounting data), or catalog item numbers (which actually convey the price of the item).

There are several types of accounting codes typically used in accounting information systems. Among these are (1) mnemonic codes, (2) sequence codes, (3) block codes, and (4) group codes.

Mnemonic Codes

Mnemonic codes help the user remember what they represent. For example, on an em-

ployee job application form, a company might ask the respondent to code "M" for male and "F" for female. These codes are easy to remember, yet are more convenient than using the words *male* and *female* to describe the sex of the applicant. Similarly, the U.S. Post Office uses a two-digit code (such as NV or CA) to represent the individual states (Nevada or California in these examples).

Typically, mnemonic codes consist of alphabetic characters because they are acronyms (i.e., codes made up of the first letter or first few letters of a term or phrase). An advantage of alphabetic codes is that there are 26 different symbols for each digit of the code. Thus, there are 26 possibilities for a one-digit alphabetic code, 26 times 26, or 676 different possibilities for a two-digit alphabetic code, 26 times 26 times 26, or 17,576 possibilities for a three-digit alphabetic code, and so forth.

Alphabetic codes enable the user to represent a large number of different possibilities with relatively few code digits or positions. If the code is mnemonic, however, this space efficiency is usually lost. For example, a catalog sales company might wish to assign an alphabetic code for the color of a particular product. Thus, yellow would be coded "Y," green would be coded "G," and so forth. However, even if there were only 10 colors, a single-letter code might be insufficient if two of the colors were blue and black (each starting with the letter *b*). For this reason, the company (like most retail stores today) would have to use a two- or even three-digit code to represent the color or, alternatively, use a numeric code.

The fact that mnemonic codes have a large number of possible combinations is also a disadvantage. This is because there is the potential to make a mistake and create a set of letters that has no meaning. Such a problem would be considerable, for example, for the airline traveler who wanted luggage sent to JFK (i.e., John F. Kennedy Airport in New York City), but whose luggage was mislabeled "FKJ," for which there is no airport.

A final disadvantage with alphabetic codes is that, in general, it is easier for humans to sort items by number than to alphabetize them. Thus, if a set of accounting transactions is to be processed manually, numeric codes are often more efficient. However, this is not a problem in computerized applications.

Sequence Codes

As the name implies, a **sequence code** is merely a sequential set of numbers that are used to identify customer accounts, employee payroll checks, customer sales invoices, and so forth. When a sequence code is also used for accountability—as in the coding of movie ticket numbers or the numbering of payroll checks—the sequence counts by ones for control purposes. On the other hand, if the code is primarily used for identification or the ordering of data—as a social security number for employee records—this is not necessary.

Sequence codes are easy to understand, and because they are used so often in many personal applications (e.g., check numbers), they have intuitive appeal. Sequence codes also facilitate record retrieval in sequential files because the code naturally orders the accounting data in a meaningful way.

Sequence codes can also act as an important accounting control—for example, to identify missing sales invoices or payroll checks by gaps in prenumbered sets of these items. As noted earlier, this characteristic can also be used for ensuring accountability where valuable accounting records are concerned.

Sequence codes also have disadvantages. Where accounting file records are numbered sequentially by units (i.e., 1, 2, 3, etc.), additions to the file can only be made at the end of the file. Even when sequential files have gaps (as, for example, in our payroll example), sequential files require complete file rewrites in order to insert a record in its logical place. Furthermore, sequential file searches are inefficient because a potentially large number of records must be searched in turn before the specific record desired is located.

An additional disadvantage of sequence codes is that they usually do not convey meaning. Thus, for example, assigning credit customers sequential account numbers would not indicate what type of credit risk the customer is, what geographical area the customer was from, the customer's ability to pay bills, and so forth.

Block Codes

Block codes are sequential codes in which specific blocks of numbers are reserved for particular uses. In a typical application, the lead digit or two lead digits in the sequence code act as the block designator and the subsequent digits are identifiers. A common use of block codes is in constructing product codes. For example, a catalog sales company might use a six-digit product code as follows.

Product	Product Type
1XXXXX	Clothing
2XXXXX	Hardware
3XXXXX	Housewares
4XXXXX	Toys
5XXXXX	Jewelry

A block code is often used to create a chart of accounts. A **chart of accounts** is a list that describes all the accounts used by a business for its income statement and balance sheet. Figure 5-4 illustrates the use of a block code to create a chart of accounts.

In Figure 5-4, the blocks of the code are reserved for the major categories of accounts used by an organization. Thus, for example, the block of numbers from 100 to 199 are used for current assets, the block of numbers from 200 to 299 are used for noncurrent assets, and so forth.

As illustrated in Figure 5-4, each major block of the coding system includes many different types of accounts within the account category. The lead number in the block (e.g., 1xx for current assets in Figure 5-4) is used to describe the types of accounts within the block.

Major Accounts

100–199	Current assets
200–299	Noncurrent assets
300–399	Current liabilities
400–499	Long-term liabilities
500–599	Owners' equity
600–699	Revenue
700–799	Cost of goods sold
800–899	Selling and administrative expenses
900–999	Nonoperating income and expenses

Detailed Listing of Current Assets

100	Current assets control account
110	Cash
120	Marketable securities
121	Common stock
122	Preferred stock
123	U.S. government bonds
124	Corporate bonds
125	Money market certificates
126	Bank certificates
130	Accounts receivable
140	Prepaid expenses
150	Raw materials inventory
160	Goods-in-process inventory
170	Finished goods inventory
180	Notes receivable

FIGURE 5-4   A block code used for a company's chart of accounts.

Block codes enjoy most of the same advantages as sequential codes—that is, a natural ordering, a systematic procedure for classifying accounting transactions, and the ability to identify accounts uniquely. In addition, block codes usually reserve extra space within each major block for new accounts. This preserves the usefulness of the block coding system since the sequential codes themselves do not have to be repartitioned when new accounts are added. A final advantage of block codes is that their systematic organization enhances understanding of the accounting system and facilitates the processing of accounting transactions. As a result, fewer procedural errors are made and the entering of accounting data is more cost-effective.

A disadvantage of block codes is that they are not mnemonic and are thus meaningless without a table to interpret them. Furthermore, although block codes typically have gaps in them, this feature is not unique to block codes—any sequential file (for example, a payroll file organized by employee social security number) can also have gaps. Thus, there is no special reason to organize an accounting file with block codes if all the user needs is gaps between certain records. Finally, by their very nature, block codes will eventually require reorganization when the positions assigned to a category are exhausted by the specific accounts within that account category. Since it is often not clear at the outset which account categories will require the most numbers, planning the number of positions within categories is difficult.

Group Codes

A **group code** is made up of two or more subcodes that have been combined. Each subcode is called a *field* of the group code, and thus it is equally accurate to consider a group code as a set of fields, each of which describes separate accounting data. To illustrate, imagine a bank that has substantially fewer than 100,000 customers at each of its branch offices. The bank can assign a five-digit customer number to each account as follows.

XXXXX = customer account number

Then, to indicate which branch the customers are from, the bank can assign a two-digit prefix.

BB XXXXX = branch account number
where
BB = branch number, and
XXXXX = customer account number.

Finally, when bank customers make deposits and withdrawals, the bank can create a unique transaction code by adding a two-digit field to represent the transaction type.

BB XXXXX TT = transaction code
where
BB = branch number,
XXXXX = customer account number, and
TT = transaction type: 01 = deposit; 02 = withdrawal; 03 = service charge; 04 = interest payment; etc.

Examples of group codes abound. For example, the J. C. Penney Company uses a relatively long group code to identify the products in its sales catalogs. The group code is

CC MMI NNND V = product code
where
CC = catalog identifier (identifies the catalog from which the customer is ordering),
MM = merchandise reporting subdivision (i.e., the number of the department responsible for the item),
I = item code,
NNN = stock number,
D = check digit (see Chapter 10 for an explanation), and
V = code for amount of variable information that must be added to complete the order for this item: A = no variable information; B = one-digit variable item (e.g., size S, M, L); C = two-digit variable item (e.g., two-digit color code); D = three-digit variable item (e.g., size and color code); etc.

Thus, an item with the code YY-738-3656-C (a set of draperies), is interpreted as catalog YY, stocked by department 73, item type 8 (draperies), stock number 365, check digit 6, and variable code C (two-digit color code required with order).

Some companies choose to use a group code to organize their chart of accounts. The fields within the code are used to identify such items as division, major category of the general ledger account, subsidiary ledger account, and so on. For example, a company might use the following group code.

XXX YYY F SSS T = account code
where
XXX = primary account category (e.g., current assets),
YYY = subaccount category (e.g., furniture, stationery, etc.),
F = financial statement code (B = balance sheet, I = income statement),
SSS = sequence number on financial statement (orders the appearance of the account on the statement), and
T = type code (used to indicate whether the account also affects such statements as the statement of changes in financial position or the cash flow statement).

Group codes have a number of advantages. Among them are the following.

1. Group codes are extremely flexible because they can incorporate mnemonic codes, sequence codes, and block codes within them. A good illustration of this combination of codes in a group code is the course-numbering system for a university. At the University of Nevada, Reno, for example, the code is

AAAA CNN = course number
where
AAAA = alphabetic descriptor (mnemonic),
C = recommended class level (1 = freshman, 2 = sophomore, 3

= junior, 4 = senior, 5 =
entry level graduate, 6 = first-
year graduate, 7 = non-first-
year graduate), and

NN = course number (block numbers
are assigned within
departments).

2. Group codes can summarize a great deal of information in a fairly limited space. This is especially important when a company wishes to record transaction data in an efficient format. The bank account example discussed previously provides an illustration.

3. Group codes can be constructed to denote a hierarchy of data. For example, the date March 24, 1991, which is typically coded as 03/24/91, could also be coded 910324 because this sequence of numbers captures the hierarchy of year, month, and day of chronological events. This code could then be used for sorting transactions by day of occurrence.

4. Group codes enable the user to classify and reclassify financial data according to the fields of the code. For example, the J. C. Penney Company product code enables the company to prepare a sales report either (1) by catalog (using the lead digit of the product code), (2) by stocking department (using the second field), (3) by major item type (using the third field), or (4) by particular product (using the fourth field).

Group codes also have some disadvantages. Among these are the following.

1. Group codes can become overly complex. The longer a code becomes, the greater the chance for data transcription error and the less convenient the codes are to use. Long credit card numbers such as VISA numbers or MasterCard numbers suffer from this problem.

2. Group codes may not serve the purposes for which they are intended. If a group code is used merely to identify a particular account or type of transaction, for example, a sequence code may work just as well.

3. Group codes may tie information together when there is no need for this. For example, just because it is possible to link an account number with a date code in order to form a transaction code does not mean that it is a good idea. The choice of fields in a group code is a function of the purpose(s) for which the code will be used.

Design Considerations in Coding

Accountants are often asked to aid in the design of efficient accounting codes. Discussed below are several design criteria that may be useful in performing this task.

Usefulness. The most important requirement of an accounting code is that it serve some useful purpose. The introductory remarks of this section described some of these purposes in depth. For example, if a product code in a manufacturing firm is intended to aid in a responsibility accounting system, it is necessary that at least one portion of the code contain a production department code in order to trace the responsibility for the manufactured items. In short, it is important that an accounting code serve its intended use.

Consistency. Wherever possible, accounting codes should be consistent with those codes already in use. For example, if a retailer primarily does business with one supplier, and this supplier already has a product code, it does not make sense for the retailer to make up a new one. Likewise, if an organization must construct an employee file, it is often advisable to use existing social security numbers rather than assign new employee numbers for identification purposes.

Efficiency. An accounting code should be as succinct as possible. The fewer the digits in the code, the less space is required to enumerate the code, the less chance there is for data transcription errors, and the more useful the code becomes. This is the "KIS" approach—keep it simple!

Allowance for Growth. In most accounting applications, managers must plan for possible future expansion. For example, the codes in a company's chart of accounts should allow for the creation of extra accounts.

Standardization. Accounting codes should be standardized throughout all levels of an organization and also between different divisions or departments of the same organization. Insisting on standard codes increases organizational communication and promotes consistency in an organization's accounting activities.

ACCOUNTING INFORMATION SYSTEMS APPLICATIONS

An accounting information system consists of one or more applications that group related transactions and provide reports on that application's activities. While the nature and types of applications will vary depending on the information needs of a particular organization, some of these are common to most accounting information systems. These include general ledger, accounts receivable, accounts payable, inventory, and payroll transaction applications. These are discussed throughout this text as examples of various accounting information systems concepts. In the following section, we continue our discussion of reports and source documents by describing the particular reports and source documents associated with each of these major accounting system applications.

General Ledger

The **general ledger** application is common for all types of accounting entities. It encompasses the accounting cycle described in the Supplement to Chapter 1. Basically, transaction information is collected from source documents and transcribed into a journal entry format. Journal entries are then processed, either manually or by a computer, and entered in ledger accounts. General ledger information is used to develop trial balances and financial statements, the primary outputs of a financial accounting information system.

A general ledger system is based on the **chart of accounts.** As mentioned earlier in this chapter, a chart of accounts is usually classified with a block code, each code block representing a specific category of accounts. Transaction information is gathered from various source documents and then coded with the accounts to be debited and/or credited. Almost any type of source document may provide data affecting accounts in the general ledger subsystem. For example, a **remittance advice** is a source document that accompanies a customer's payment on account. The remittance advice signals an accounting clerk to make a journal entry to debit the cash account and credit accounts receivable. Note that this particular journal entry affects another accounting module—the accounts receivable subsystem. Since the general ledger contains all accounts, transactions affecting other accounting information system applications will also impact the general ledger subsystem. In this way, we say that an accounting information system is integrated, with relationships existing among various applications. An example of this integration is the relationship between the accounts receivable application and general ledger. The general ledger contains a control account for accounts receivable and the accounts receivable module maintains data about each individual customer's accounts receivable.

In addition to generating trial balance and financial statement reports, the general ledger application may produce other output reports. These include reports on performance against budgeted financial statements, lists of transactions for each account, and a list of journal entries that are out of balance (i.e., debits do not equal credits). **Performance reports** can be designed to show any variances from budget, or they may be designed as exception reports, showing only those variances outside predefined parameters. For example, a report could be generated which only lists expense accounts in excess of 10% over budgeted amounts. **Transaction listings** are useful in analyzing the activity for a specific account. Remember that journal entries are chronological listings of transactions. They do not easily reveal activity related to a particular account. Finally, reports that show journal entries or groups (batches) of journal entires that are out of balance provide a necessary audit trail in tracking down causes for trial balances that do not balance. When a computer is used to process transactions, out of balance amounts for groups of journal entries may be placed in a special account called a **suspense account.** A listing of activity in the suspense account is then generated by the computer system so that processing is not interrupted and discrepancies can be resolved when time allows.

Accounts Receivable

Accounts receivable (A/R) applications have as their objective the timely control of customer accounts. In order to accomplish this purpose, several types of reports are generated from data collected on source documents related to customers and sales. The nature of the source documents and reports for an accounts receivable subsystem are discussed below. Manual and computerized processing of accounts receivable is described in detail in Chapter 8.

A **sales order** is issued at the time a customer places an order with a company. This order is used by an accounts receivable clerk to prepare a **sales invoice** (one was shown in Figure 5-3). The sales invoice reflects the product or products purchased, cost, and the terms of payment. When the customer makes a payment, the payment is accompanied by a **remittance advice.** As noted in the section on general ledger subsystems, the remittance advice is used to make a journal entry recording the payment on account. Another source document that affects accounts receivable is the **debit/credit memorandum.** These memoranda are issued when there is a discrepancy about the amount owed or when goods are returned. For example, Customer A may have

returned $500 in merchandise to the Martin Company because it was damaged. Since the customer has not yet paid the bill for the goods, a credit memorandum is issued to reduce the customer's accounts receivable balance. A debit memorandum would be issued if the customer was originally charged too little for goods sold. Debit and credit memoranda are also used in connection with the accounts payable subsystem.

Several types of output are issued from accounts receivable processing. One of these is the **customer billing statement,** which summarizes all of the outstanding sales invoices for a particular customer and shows the amount currently owed. Other reports generated by the accounts receivable subsystem include the aging report, the bad debt report, and the cash receipts forecast. The **aging report** shows each accounts receivable balance categorized by time outstanding. For instance, if terms of sale are net 30, the aging report might show current accounts receivable, those accounts 1 to 30 days overdue, those accounts 30 to 60 days overdue, those accounts 60 to 90 days overdue, and those accounts that are more then 90 days past due. As you can see, it is important to consider what information is most important for a particular organization when designing report formats. The **bad debt report** contains information about collection follow-up procedures for overdue customer accounts. This allows management to see if collection efforts are being made, and whether or not they are effective. In the event that a customer's account is determined to be uncollectible, the account will be written off to an allowance account for bad debts. A detailed listing of this account may be another output of accounts receivable applications.

All of the data gathered from source documents by an accounts receivable application can be used as input to a **cash receipts forecast.** Data such as sales amounts, terms of sale, prior payment experience for selected customers, and information from aging analysis and collection reports are all inputs to this forecast (see for example, Figure 3-4 in Chapter 3).

Accounts Payable

Accounts payable processing is closely related to accounts receivable in that it is just the flip side of the picture. In the case of accounts receivable we are keeping track of an asset that reflects amounts owed *to us*. An accounts payable application tracks the amounts owed *by us* to vendors. The major objective of accounts payable processing is to ensure that vendors are paid at the optimal time. The purpose is to take advantage of cash discounts offered, and/or to avoid finance charges for late payments.

An important part of accounts payable is its list of vendors. This list reflects those merchants with whom the company has been authorized (by the purchasing department) to do business. It therefore serves as a control against making payments to vendors who do not exist. Before a payment is made to a vendor, the accounts payable clerk will match together several source documents: the purchase order, a receiving report, and a purchase invoice. These documents are matched and packaged together as a **voucher** that supports the payment itself. The purpose of this procedure is to maintain the best possible control over cash payments to vendors. The **purchase order** is a source document issued by the purchasing department. When someone in the organization requests an item (e.g. supplies, raw materials, or equipment), a requisition is issued to the purchasing department. The purchasing department is then responsible for procuring the item. At that point, the purchase order is issued.

An example of a purchase order is presented in Figure 5-2. One copy of the purchase order may be sent to the receiving department to serve as a **receiving report** or to prompt the receiving department to issue a separate receiving report. This copy of the purchase order should be specially coded (or colored) to distinguish it from other copies of the purchase order if a separate receiving report is not issued. The receiving report copy may leave blank the quantities ordered that are listed on the purchase order. This is done

for control purposes, so that workers receiving the goods are encouraged to perform their own counts, rather than haphazardly approve the amounts shown on the purchase order.

Another source document, a **shipping notice,** accompanies the goods sent. The shipping notice contains information about the date shipped, the point of delivery (either shipping point or destination), the carrier, the route, and the mode of shipment (e.g., rail). A copy of the shipping notice may be sent to the customer with the **purchase invoice.** This is important to an accounts payable application as accounts payable accruals include liability for goods shipped FOB shipping point, which have left the vendor but have not yet been received by the customer.

Typical outputs of accounts payable processing are the vendor checks and accompanying check register, discrepancy reports, and a cash requirements forecast. The **check register** lists all checks paid for a particular period. Checks are typically processed in batches and the check register is produced as a by-product of this processing step. **Discrepancy reports** are necessary to note any differences between quantities or amounts on the purchase order, receiving report, and purchase invoice. For example, a receiving report may indicate that only 12 units of product were received, the purchase order shows that 20 were ordered, and the purchase invoice bills us for 20. This would be noted on a discrepancy report that would trigger an investigation. It is likely in this instance that two shipments of merchandise were made, and one shipment has yet to be received. In that event, this discrepancy will be cleared from the next report upon receipt of the second shipment.

A **cash requirements forecast** can be produced by an accounts payable application in the same manner as a cash receipts forecast is made in accounts receivable processing. By looking at source documents such as outstanding purchase orders, unbilled receiving reports, and sales invoices, a prediction of future payments and payment dates can be made. Naturally, this forecast is easier to make with a computerized accounts payable system than with a manual system. In either processing environment, however, accounts payable clerks must be careful to include all amounts for which the company is liable. Together, the cash receipts forecast and the cash requirements forecast will serve as the foundation for the cash budget.

Inventory

Processing inventory transactions is a very important accounting information system in a merchandising or manufacturing firm. Not only is inventory likely to be one of an organization's major balance sheet assets, but it also impacts the income statement's expense for the cost of goods sold. The primary objective of inventory transaction processing is to ensure that inventory transactions are processed so that the inventory and cost of goods sold accounts are correctly stated. This includes maintaining control over inventory.

The types of inventory accounts that a company includes on its balance sheet vary with the type of organization. A merchandising organization's raw materials are also its finished goods since finished goods are bought and sold. A manufacturing organization, on the other hand, must account for raw materials inventory, work in process inventory, and finished goods inventory. An accounting information system for a manufacturing organization may include a job cost application as well as an inventory application. Service organizations would be unlikely to have an inventory processing application since their only inventory is supplies, but they may use a job costing subsystem to track time and billing for each job. Since inventory processing is most complex in a manufacturing firm, we will focus on this type of organization in the following discussion of source documents and reports. The process is similar for a merchandising firm. The difference is that the procedure for raw materials applies to the finished goods that are purchased from suppliers.

When raw materials are needed on the pro-

duction floor, a **materials requisition form** is issued to acquire more material from stores where the raw material is kept. If the level of inventory in stores falls below a certain predetermined level, the inventory control clerk issues a **purchase requisition** to the purchasing department. The purchasing department uses the purchase requisition to create a **purchase order.** Sometimes the purchase of materials is triggered automatically, as when a computerized **economic order quantity (EOQ)** model system is used. After materials are ordered, they are shipped by vendors. The shipment is accompanied by a **packing slip,** releasing the goods for packaging and shipment (a copy of the shipping notice discussed in accounts payable processing may serve as a packing slip). Other source documents associated with inventory purchases are the **bill of lading,** which reflects the freight charges on goods shipped. The bill of lading is documented evidence of the contractual agreement between the shipper and the carrier. When merchandise inventory is received at its destination, a clerk will complete the receiving report. A copy of this source document is kept in receiving, with other copies sent to accounts payable and purchasing.

Reports that are output by an inventory processing application include price lists, periodic usage reports, inventory reconciliation reports, and a detailed inventory status report. The price list is maintained to show prices paid for goods. This helps the purchasing department decide which supplier to order from. These price lists are also necessary for determining the standard costs to be used in budgeting. **Periodic usage reports** can provide information about how much material is being used in various production departments. Managers use the reports to detect waste by comparing usage to output or units of finished goods produced. An **inventory reconciliation report** is issued for a company that uses a perpetual inventory system. When a physical inventory is taken, results are compared with book balances, and discrepancies are noted on this reconciliation report. A **detailed inven-**

tory status report should be issued periodically so that purchasing and production can keep an eye on inventory levels.

The cost of ordering inventory, running out of inventory, and ordering inventory must all be considered in determining optimal levels. Two special types of computerized inventory processing systems can be useful in maintaining these optimal levels. These are just-in-time (JIT) systems and material requirements planning (MRP) systems.

Just-In-Time Systems[1]

A **just-in-time (JIT) system** is based on a philosophy that may be applied to all aspects of a firm, including production, purchasing of materials needed for production, and delivery. At the heart of the JIT philosophy is the view that all inventories (direct materials, work in process, and finished goods) are undesirable and should be eliminated or at least minimized. A JIT system is driven by final product demand, so that the right product is manufactured at the right time in the right quantities. A JIT inventory technique relates all manufacturing activities to the physical process of production. The ideal goal of JIT is to acquire direct materials "just in time" to be used in production work and to produce and deliver finished goods inventory "just in time" to be sold, thereby resulting in no or minimal inventories on hand.

JIT purchasing of materials needed for manufacturing is the basic requirement for successful JIT production of a finished product. Reliability of suppliers and dependability of material supplies with zero defects are the basic conditions for implementing any JIT purchasing system. Historically, manufacturers have selected suppliers for each production season on the basis of the lowest bids or highest quality or they have dis-

tributed their purchasing requirements for materials among a number of suppliers to avoid over-dependency or emergency shortages. Under JIT purchasing, a few reliable suppliers, with a total commitment to quality control, are selected for longer periods. The acquisition of materials for production is based on the teamwork concept. The basis is trust, confidence, cooperation, and joint commitment. These characteristics are achieved, it is hoped, by close coordination between manufacturers and suppliers, with the result that the manufacturers receive quality materials from their suppliers at the correct time and in the correct quantities.

The implementation of JIT purchasing represents a major step toward eliminating (or, at least minimizing) direct materials inventory. Quality control is another key element of a JIT system. To help in achieving the goals of a JIT production system, each department (or work station) along an assembly line performs its part of the manufacturing work on a product immediately so that there are no delays in transferring work in process to the next department (or work station) along the assembly line. Thus, the assembly line functions on a *demand-pull basis,* with authorized production activity at each work station based on the demand of subsequent (or down-stream) work stations. The emphasis is on minimizing the production lead time of each finished unit or product. The production lead time is the interval between the first stage of production and the time the finished product comes off the assembly line. In a well-functioning JIT production system, stoppage of work along the assembly line (for such things as unavailable direct materials or defective work from a previous work station) will be minimized.

Material Requirements Planning Systems

In order for a just-in-time system to work, a **material requirements planning (MRP) system** must be in place. An MRP system is a planning system that focuses initially on the amount

---

[1] Portions of ths section on just-in-time systems and the next section of material requirements planning systems are reprinted with permission from Stephen A. Moscove and Arnold Wright, *Cost Accounting with Managerial Applications* (6th edition, Houghton Mifflin Company), 1990.

and timing of finished goods demanded, then determines the derived demand at each of the prior stages of production for direct materials that need to be purchased and for product components that are manufacturing internally. Working backward, each finished product is sequentially separated into its necessary direct materials and components. Included within an MRP system are the following:

1. A master production schedule that indicates both the quantity and the timing of each product item to be manufactured.
2. A bill of materials file that reflects the direct materials and components required for each completed product. Note that under an MRP system, it is necessary to differentiate external purchases of direct materials from components derived from previous steps in the production process.
3. An inventory report for each direct material and component. Each of these items is reported in a separate computer record that includes details on the number of items on hand and the arrival times and quantities of items scheduled to be received.
4. The expected time interval between the initiation of each purchase of direct materials and the receipt of these materials in the factory storeroom (the lead time for material acquisitions).
5. The expected construction time for each component produced internally.

A computer is an essential tool in processing the data on a timely basis for the effective operation of both material requirements planning and just-in-time systems. If changes in external conditions occur, the computerized data processing system can quickly analyze the effects of these changes on manufacturing activities. For example, if a specific customer asks that an order for a substantial quantity of the firm's manufactured product be deferred for six weeks, the automated data processing system can immediately readjust the quantities of direct materials to be purchased and the production schedules.

Payroll

The major purpose of payroll processing is to pay employees. Payroll processing also involves maintaining employee earnings records (a payroll history), complying with various government tax and reporting requirements, reporting on various deduction categories (e.g., pension funds or group insurance), and maintaining a relationship with the personnel department.

Source documents used in conjunction with processing payroll are personnel action forms, time sheets, payroll deduction authorizations, and tax withholding forms. **Personnel action forms** are sent to payroll from the personnel department. They are used to document the hiring of new employees or changes in employee status. For example, a personnel action form is sent to payroll when an employee receives a salary increase (Figure 5-5). These documents are very important for control purposes.

Time sheets are used to keep track of hours worked. In some companies, a time clock is used and employees must "punch in" when they arrive for work. In other companies, or for certain types of employees, the employee records hours worked on a time sheet, such as the one in Figure 5-6. However time is recorded, hours worked should be authorized by an employee's supervisor and a payroll clerk should look for the appropriate authorization prior to processing. If a job cost system is used, time sheets for employees can be cross-referenced with time recorded on jobs.

Payroll deduction authorizations are filled out by employees to authorize a payroll system to deduct amounts for items such as parking, insurance, retirement, and union dues from gross pay. An authorization form should exist for each deduction. Withholding forms must also be completed for each employee so that gross pay is reduced by the appropriate withholding tax. The W-4 form is filled out by employees to help calculate the correct withholding for federal income taxes.

Outputs of payroll processing include pay-

Salary Increase Recommendation

Based on the attached appraisal form, the following recommendation is made for:

Name: Jane Doe
Position: Accounting Clerk
Social Security Number: 111-22-3333

Current Salary: 13,520.00
Current Bonus Level: 00%
Last Increase Date: 08/22/88
Next Increase Date: 08/22/89

Current Performance Rating:
(from attached appraisal)   _____

Salary Increase Guidelines:

Outstanding:	6–9%	9–12 months
Superior:	4–6%	12 months
Good:	3–4%	12–15 months
Provisional:	0%	Review again in 90 days.

In view of the Current Performance and the Salary Increase Guidelines, I recommend the following salary treatment:

Percentage Increase: _____ %
New Salary: $_____
Effective Date: ____/ ____/ ____

Promotions:
In the case of a promotion, a standard 5% increase for the promotion, and a pro-rated merit increase (based on time since last merit increase) is appropriate. The next increase will be considered from the date of promotion.

Other Considerations:
In some situations it is possible to advance a salary beyond the above guidelines as an exception, with the President's approval. Some typical situations are, but not limited to, equity adjustment, job reevaluation, etc. If such is the case here please provide justification below:

_____

Approvals: _____ Supervisor
               _____ Supervisor's Supervisor
               _____ Director of Personnel

Exception approval if needed: _____ President

FIGURE 5-5 Personnel action form for salary increase. (Courtesy of Vie de France Corporation).

VIE DE FRANCE CORPORATION
TIME REPORT

NAME_____

DEPARTMENT_____

PAY PERIOD ENDING_____

SOCIAL SECURITY NO._____

Type of Hours	WEEK 1							WK 1	WEEK 2							WK 2	WEEK 1 + WEEK 2
	SUN	MON	TUE	WED	THU	FRI	SAT	Subtotal Hrs Worked	SUN	MON	TUE	WED	THU	FRI	SAT	Subtotal Hrs Worked	Totals
Hours Worked																	
Hours Sick								/////								/////	
Holiday Hours								/////								/////	
Vacation Hours								/////								/////	
Other*								/////								/////	

* Brief explanation of hours worked over 40 and other absences:

_____

_____

_____

I certify that the above is a correct record of hours worked by me.

_____
Employee Signature

Payment is approved:

_____
Supervisor Signature

FIGURE 5-6 Time report to be filled in by employee. (Courtesy of Vie de France Corporation).

checks, check registers, deduction reports, tax reports, and payroll summaries. As you can imagine, the processing of **paychecks** should be subject to very strict internal control procedures (discussed in Chapters 9 and 10). **Check registers** accompany the printing of paychecks and list gross pay, net pay, and deductions. Information from these reports can be used to make journal entries for salary, labor, and payroll-tax expenses. **Deduction reports** contain summaries of deductions for employees as a group. **Tax reports** are reports required by the government for income tax, social security tax, and unemployment tax information. Some of these taxes are paid entirely by the employee, but others are shared by the employer. In addition, many different types of **payroll summaries** may be issued, depending on the nature of the organization. An example would be a summary report on overtime hours worked in each department.

Payroll processing can be both tedious and repetitive. For this reason, the payroll function was one of the first accounting activities to be computerized. Today, many companies find that it is not worth their while to perform their own payroll processing. These companies use service bureaus to do their processing of paychecks and payroll reports. Service bureaus are discussed in Chapter 14.

SUMMARY

This chapter has discussed the management of accounting data as it flows through an accounting information system. When planning a new system, an accountant usually starts by designing the outputs from the system. These outputs, and especially managerial reports, become the goals of the accounting information system and therefore provide a focus for the prerequisite tasks of data collection and data processing.

The fundamental instrument for collecting data in the typical accounting information system is the source document. These forms should be designed so that they are easy to read, easy to understand, serve both to collect and distribute information and/or to establish authenticity or authorization.

Accounting data are often coded. Accounting codes can be used to identify accounting information uniquely, to compress data, to classify accounts or transactions, or to convey special meanings. Four types of codes were discussed in this chapter: (1) mnemonic codes, (2) sequence codes, (3) block codes, and (4) group codes. The choices among these codes and the way these codes are constructed are determined by (1) the code's use, (2) the need for consistency, (3) considerations of design efficiency, (4) an allowance for growth, and (5) the desire to use standard codes throughout a company.

The accounting information system in an organization is likely to consist of more than one transaction processing application. The make-up and number of applications will vary with the information needs of the organization. Some applications, however, are common to many different types of organizations and were thus included in our chapter discussion. The general ledger processing system is the most common, since it results in the financial statements that show the performance of the organization. General ledger processing is discussed in this chapter in terms of its output reports and source documents. Other applications that commonly form an organization's accounting information system are accounts receivable, accounts payable, inventory, and payroll. Many of the source documents and reports that are inputs and outputs of these applications are described in this chapter.

Key Terms You Should Know

action-oriented report
aging report
alphanumeric codes
bad debt report
bill of lading
block codes
cash receipts forecast
cash requirements forecast
chart of accounts
check registers
customer billing statement
debit/credit memorandum
deduction reports
detailed inventory status report
discrepancy reports
economic order quantity (EOQ)
general ledger
group code
information overload
inventory reconciliation report
just-in-time (JIT) system
material requirements planning (MRP) system
materials requisition form
mnemonic code

packing slip
paychecks
payroll deduction authorization
payroll summaries
performance reports
periodic usage reports
personnel action forms
purchase invoice
purchase order
purchase requisition
receiving report
remittance advice
sales invoice
sales order
sequence code
shipping notice
source document
statement of cash flows
suspense account
tax reports
time sheets
transaction listings
voucher

Discussion Questions

5-1. What are the characteristics of "good" accounting data? Why is the collection of good data a goal of an accounting information system?

5-2. What are some of the typical outputs of an accounting information system? Why do system analysts concentrate on managerial reports when they start to design an effective accounting information system. Why not start with the inputs to the system instead?

5-3. What are some of the criteria that should be considered when designing managerial reports for an accounting information system? Can you think of any others beyond those described in the chapter? If so, what are they?

5-4. In the text, it was stated that external reports should be consistent with general accounting practice. What do you think is meant by this statement? Be as specific as you can.

5-5. Describe the role of source documents in an

accounting information system. What functions do they serve besides that of data collection?

5-6. There are many automated methods of collecting accounting data (e.g., point-of-sale terminals). Common to many of these methods is the ability to avoid the manual recording of data. Hence, many of these methods do not generate a source document as do manual systems. What are the implications of this observation to accounting information systems?

5-7. For a financial statement such as the statement of cash flows, why is it important for an accountant to establish a design format before collecting the data that go into the statement?

5-8. Provide some examples of typical source documents utilized in a manufacturing firm's accounting information system. For each source document example you give, discuss its purpose or purposes.

5-9. The chapter supplement discusses nine journal entries in the Alan Company's process cost system. Select any three of these entries and discuss the source document or documents that must be prepared prior to recording each journal entry.

5-10. What are the purposes of accounting codes? Why are they used?

5-11. Consider the following: "Accounting codes obscure more than they reveal. Thus, codes are much better suited to espionage work than accounting work." Do you agree or disagree? Why?

5-12. Explain the relationship between an alphabetic code and a mnemonic code. How are they similar? How are they different?

5-13. What is a sequence code? What are the advantages of sequence codes? What are their disadvantages?

5-14. What are block codes? What are the advantages of block codes? What are their disadvantages?

5-15. What is a chart of accounts? How are block codes used to create a chart of accounts?

5-16. What is a group code? What are the advantages of group codes? What are their disadvantages? How are group codes related to the chart of accounts?

5-17. In the text, it was stated that group codes can be used to designate a hierarchy of data. An example of arranging the figures in a date was given to illustrate this ability. In computerized accounting information systems, however, it is necessary that the data values be expressed in a specific sequence (such as year, month, and day) to express this hierarchical relationship? Explain how this is possible.

5-18. Describe some considerations that are useful in the design of accounting codes. For each consideration named, provide an example other than those presented in the textbook to illustrate your point.

5-19. Some of the major subsystems of an accounting information system were discussed in this chapter. What are some of the other transaction processing applications that an organization might have?

5-20. The general ledger application is fundamental to an accounting information system. How do the other applications discussed in this chapter interact with it?

5-21. What are the inputs (source documents) and outputs (reports) associated with accounts receivable? What are the functions or objectives of processing accounts receivable?

5-22. How is processing accounts payable different from accounts receivable processing? How are these applications "mirror images" of each other?

5-23. Are the inputs and outputs of an inventory processing application likely to be different for a restaurant versus a car manufacturer? In what way?

5-24. What do you see as some advantages and disadvantages associated with a just-in-time system? How would a just-in-time system and materials requirements planning system be related?

5-25. Why is payroll transaction processing so repetitive in nature? Why do some companies choose to have payroll processed outside instead of in-house?

Problems

5-26. Your telephone number is a good example of a code. Identify what type of code your telephone number is and also identify the various components within this code.

5-27. Listed below are several types of accounting data that might be coded. For each data item, recommend a type of code (mnemonic, sequence, block, or group) and give reasons for your choices.

a. Employee identification number on a computer file.
b. Product number for a sales catalog.
c. Inventory number for the products of a wholesale drug company.
d. Inventory part number for a bicycle manufacturing company.
e. Identification numbers on the forms waiters and waitresses use to take orders.
f. Identification numbers on airline ticket stubs.
g. Automobile registration numbers.
h. Automobile engine block numbers.
i. Shirt sizes for men's shirts.
j. Color code for house paint.
k. Identification numbers on payroll check forms.
l. Listener identification for a radio station.
m. Numbers on lottery tickets.
n. Identification numbers on a credit card.
o. Identification numbers on dollar bills.
p. Passwords used to gain access to a computer.
q. Zip codes.
r. A chart of accounts for a department store.
s. A chart of accounts for a flooring subcontractor.
t. Shoe sizes.
u. Identification number on a student examination.
v. Identification number on an insurance policy.

5-28. The Yvonne Gold Company is the manufacturer of well-known women's cosmetics. The company has been identifying its products with sequential numbers, but it has become clear that this system is no longer efficient. You have been brought in as a consultant to create a more useful product code. The following information is made available to you.

a. The company has 11 major types of products (e.g., eye makeup, face creams, etc.), which it markets in four different product lines ("Ms. Makeup," "Billie," "Avant Garde," and "Tonight").

b. Within each major product category, there are as many as 185 different products.

c. A very important attribute of women's cosmetics is color. Some products have only 1 shade whereas others have as many as 53 shades.

d. Some products are manufactured by the company whereas others are manufactured for it. There are currently a total of 82 outside suppliers or subcontractors.

e. The company would like to include a "unit" indicator as part of its product code. This portion of the code tells whether the product is sold in individual units, sets, dozens, or some other unit number.

Design an efficient group code for the Yvonne Gold Company. Make sure that you indicate how many digit positions you will set aside for each portion of your code and also indicate the meaning of each portion of the code.

5-29. Ghymn Gadgets is a marketer of inexpensive toys and novelties that it sells to retail stores, specialty stores and catalog companies. As an accountant working for the company, you have been asked to design a product code for the company's merchandise. In analyzing this problem, you have discovered the following.

a. The company has three major product lines: (a) toys and games, (b) party and magic tricks, and (c) inexpensive gifts. There are major subproducts within each of these product lines, and the number of these categories is 25, 18, and 113, respectively.

b. The company has divided its selling efforts into five geographic areas: (1) the United States, (2) the Far East, (3) Europe and Africa, (4) South America, and (5) International (a catchall area). Each major geographic area has several sales districts (never more than 99 per area). Between 1 and 20 salespeople are assigned to each district.

c. As noted earlier, there are three major categories of customers, and certain customers can also purchase goods on credit. There are five different classes of

credit customers and each rating indicates the maximum amount of credit the customer can have.

Design a group code that Ghymn Gadgets could use to prepare sales analysis reports. Be sure to identify each digit or position in your code in terms of both use and meaning.

5-30. Fritzche Junior College uses the following coding system to designate classes.

AAAA NCCC T = class code

where

$\quad$ AAAA = alphabetic descriptor (e.g., MATH; 20 currently),
$\quad\quad\quad$ N = class level (1 = freshman, 2 = sophomore),
$\quad\quad$ CCC = class number, and
$\quad\quad\quad$ T = term code (F = fall, S = sprng, U = summer, V = varies).

a. How many different class codes are there currently, assuming the class number can be any three-digit number?

b. How many different class codes are there, assuming that the alphabetic descriptor could be any four letters?

c. How many different class codes are there, assuming that each "A" was any letter, each "N" was any number, each "C" was any number, and each "T" was any letter?

5-31. The EBCDIC code is a binary code that uses 8 bits. Each bit is either a zero or a one. How many different combinations of bits are possible in the EBCDIC code?

5-32. The Sierra Valley Utility Company uses the following code to identify its customers.

AA T NNNN B = customer account number.

where

$\quad\quad$ AA = area (12 possible),
$\quad\quad\quad$ T = customer type (5 possible),
$\quad$ NNNN = customer number (4 numeric digits), and
$\quad\quad\quad$ B = billing cycle (9 possible).

How many different combinations of codes are there for the coding system?

5-33. Recall the group code banking example provided earlier in the chapter. Assuming a bank has five branches and five customers with the following corresponding codes, develop group codes for the transactions given.

Branch	Code
1	01
2	02
3	03
4	04
5	05

Customer	Code
1	18763
2	00847
3	01324
4	14423
5	00075

CC
01 = men's dept.
02 = women's dept.
03 = sports dept.
04 = baby dept.

T
S = small
M = medium
L = large
X = X-large

II
10 = vendor 1
15 = vendor 2
20 = vendor 3
25 = in house

SS
14 = Mary
07 = Jim
15 = Sally
24 = Judy

Transactions

a. Customer 5 withdraws $75 from branch 3.

b. Customer 2 deposits $133 at branch 1.

c. Customer 4 incurs a service charge of $1.72 at branch 2.

d. Customer 3 receives an interest payment of $43.25 from branch 5.

5-34. The ABC Co. uses account codes for all of its accounting procedures. Given the following account codes, prepare the journal entries for the transactions given.

Account	Code
Material A inventory	42
Material B inventory	32
Material C inventory	27
Vendor 1	48
Vendor 2	57

Transactions

a. Purchased $370 of material A on credit from vendor 1.

b. Purchased $400 of material B for cash from vendor 2.

c. Returned $250 of defective material C to vendor 1 that had been purchased on credit (assume full refund).

5-35. The Bloomerdales Department Store uses a group code to record sales. This code is composed as follows.

CC T II SS = sales code

where

  CC = department code,

   T = clothing size,

   II = item brand code, and

  SS = salesperson code.

Given the following individual codes, interpret the group codes given.

Group Codes

a. 04-M-25-24

b. 01-X-20-14

c. 03-S-10-15

d. 02-S-15-15

CASE ANALYSES

5-36. S. Dilley & Co.

Ollie Mace has recently been appointed controller of a family-owned manufacturing enterprise. The firm, S. Dilley & Co., was founded by Mr. Dilley about 20 years ago, is 78% owned by Mr. Dilley, and has served the major automotive companies as a parts supplier. The firm's major operating divisions are heat treating, extruding, small parts stamping, and specialized machining. Sales last year from the several divisions ranged from $150,000 to over $3 million. The divisions are physically and managerially independent except for Mr. Dilley's constant surveillance. The accounting system for each division has evolved according to the division's own needs and the abilities of individual accountants or bookkeepers. Mr. Mace is the first controller in the firm's history to have responsibility for overall financial management. Mr. Dilley expects to retire within six years and has hired Mr. Mace to improve the firm's financial system.

Mr. Mace soon decides that he will need to design a new financial reporting system that will do the following.

1. Give managers uniform, timely, and accurate reports on business activity. Monthly divisional reports should be uniform and available by the 10th of the following month. Company-wide financial reports also should be prepared by the 10th.

2. Provide a basis for measuring return on investment by division. Divisional reports should show assets assigned each division and revenue and expense measurement in each division.
3. Generate meaningful budget data for planning and decision making. The accounting system should provide for the preparation of budgets that recognize managerial responsibility, controllability of costs and major product groups.
4. Allow for a uniform basis of evaluating performance and quick access to underlying data. Cost center variances should be measured and reported for operating and nonoperating units including headquarters. Also, questions about levels of specific cost factors or product costs should be answerable quickly.

A new chart of accounts, as it appears to Mr. Mace, is essential to getting started on other critical financial problems. The present account codes used by divisions are not standard.

Mr. Mace sees a need to divide asset accounts into six major categories (i.e., current assets, plant and equipment, etc.). Within each of these categories, he sees a need for no more than 10 control accounts. Based on his observations to date, 100 subsidiary accounts are more than adequate for each control account.

No division now has more than five major product groups. The maximum number of cost centers Mr. Mace forsees within any product group is six, including operating and nonoperating groups. He views general divisional costs as a nonrevenue-producing product group. Altogether, Mr. Mace estimates that about 44 natural expense accounts plus about 12 specific variance accounts would be adequate.

Mr. Mace is planning to implement the new chart of accounts in an environment that at present includes manual records systems and one division which is using an EDP system. Mr. Mace expects that in the near future most accounting and reporting for all units will be automated. Therefore, the chart of accounts should facilitate the processing of transactions manually or by machine. Efforts should be made, he believes, to restrict the length of the code for economy in processing and convenience in use.

Requirement

A. Design a chart of accounts coding system that will meet Mr. Mace's requirements. Your answer should begin with a digital layout of the coding system. You should explain the coding method you have chosen and the reason for the size of your code elements. Explain your code as it would apply to **asset** and **expense** accounts.

B. Use your chart-of-accounts coding system to illustrate the code needed for the following data.

1. In the small-parts stamping division, $100 was spent by foreman Bill Shaw in the polishing department of the Door Lever Group on cleaning supplies. Code the expense item using the code you developed.
2. A new motorized sweeper has been purchased for the maintenance department of the extruding division for $3450. Code this asset item using the code you developed.

(CMA Adapted)

5-37. *Brasher Car Manufacturing Company**

The Brasher Car Manufacturing Company has implemented a program whereby its customers can call a district representative toll-free to lodge any complaints, or dissatisfactions, which they feel were not adequately handled by their dealer. The district representative then attempts to aid the customer by coordination with the dealer, the manufacturer, or both. Phase I of this program was launched by a national advertising campaign. The major objectives of Phase I were to fortify the company's image in the area of customer service, and to increase customer confidence in the reliability of the company's product.

The objective of Phase II has been formulated, but the detailed modifications to the original program have not been firmed up. The basic goal of Phase II is to create feedback from the customers to the manufacturer. The data flowing through the feedback loop would be stored in a data base, where it would be available to various functional areas within the corporation. Two obvious users would be the design engineers and quality control people. It is apparent that information from the field would be valuable in quickly replacing defective parts and improving the design of parts and components. The corporation executives see the network of district representatives as a

---

* Used with the permission of John G. Burch, Jr., and Felix R. Strater, Jr., *Information Systems: Theory and Practice* (New York: Wiley, 1986).

skeletal framework which could be expanded to handle the demands of Phase II.

Additional Background Information

In addition to handling customer complaints, the district representative also serves as a watchdog on the dealers in his zone. In this role, he must ascertain that the individual dealers, franchised by the company, are complying with the service standards imposed by the corporation. The office staff and facilities of the representatives are presently limited to those needed in the performance of Phase I duties.

Two coding structures utilized by the corporation may be useful in this problem. The first is the serial number affixed to each auto. A sample serial number and its interpretation is given on the next page.

2G 29 R 4 G 106113 = auto serial number

2 G	Brand name (major manufacturers produce several brands)
2 9	Body style (station wagon, sedan, etc.)
R	Engine (code representing engine model)
4	Year (last digit of year)
G	Factory (factory where produced)
106113	Car's serial number (unique code depicting one particular car)

A second code structure is used for identifying parts. Each individual part of an automobile is coded with a nonintelligent, seven-digit number. (A nonintelligent number is one used only for identification and has no coded meaning.) To facilitate the retrieval of part numbers, all the part numbers are structured within a directory code. The directory code is composed of five digits. The first two run from 00 to 15 and identify the major subsystems; i.e., 01 represents engine cooling, oiling, and ventilating systems. The last three digits are a serial code representing the individual parts incorporated in the major subsystem. An example may provide clarity. Let us assume that we're trying to locate the part number for the oil pump cover gasket for a 1989 six-cylinder Bassethound. The Bassethound is one of the brands produced by the major manufacturer, Dogs, Inc. Searching the directory we find that 01.724 is the directory number for oil pump cover gaskets. This number is the general part number for all oil pump cover gaskets produced by Dogs, Inc. Looking in the parts manual under 01.724 we find the

specific part numbers for this particular gasket for the individual years and models. Searching this list we find that the gasket for a 1989 Bassethound six-cylinder has a part number of 3789970. This number identifies the exact part.

In concluding the background information, one point should be emphasized. Under the present system, the district representative only receives information concerned with customer complaints. The details and financial arrangements of warranty service performed by the dealer in a satisfactory manner are communicated directly between manufacturer and dealer, bypassing the district representative. You may desire to alter this information flow in your solution.

Questions

Bearing in mind the extensive resources available to a major automobile producer, present your ideas about the following aspects of the proposed Phase II system.

1. Specific description of the data that should be collected.
2. How the data should be collected, and by whom.
3. How the data should be transmitted to the manufacturer.
4. How the data should be stored at the corporation's main office in order to facilitate retrieval by numerous users.

5-38. Universal Floor Covering

Universal Floor Covering is a manufacturer and distributor of carpet and vinyl floor coverings. The home office is located in Charlotte, North Carolina. Carpet mills are located in Dalton, Georgia, and Greenville, South Carolina; a floor-covering manufacturing plant is in High Point, North Carolina. Total sales last year were just over $250 million.

The company manufactures over 200 different varieties of carpet. The carpet is classified as being for commercial or residential purposes and is sold under five brand names with up to five lines under each brand. The lines indicate the different grades of quality; grades are measured by type of tuft and number of tufts per square inch. Each line of carpet can have up to 15 different color styles.

Just under 200 varieties of vinyl floor covering are manufactured. The floor covering is also classified as being for commercial or residential use. There are four separate brand names (largely distinguished by the type of finish), up to eight different patterns for each brand, and up to eight color styles for each pattern.

Ten different grades of padding are manufactured. The padding is usually differentiated by intended use (commercial or residential) in addition to thickness and composition of materials.

Universal serves over 2000 regular wholesale customers. Retail showrooms are the primary customers. Many major corporations are direct buyers of Universal's products. Large construction companies have contracts with Universal to purchase carpet and floor covering at reduced rates for use in newly constructed homes and commercial buildings. In addition, Universal produces a line of residential carpet for a large national retail chain. Sales to these customers range from $10,000 to $1,000,000 annually.

There is a company-owned retail outlet at each plant. The outlets carry overruns, seconds, and discontinued items. This is Universal's only retail sales function.

The company has divided the sales market into seven territories, with the majority of concentration on the East Coast. The market segments are New England, New York, Mid-Atlantic, Carolinas, South, Midwest, and West. Each sales territory is divided into 5 to 10 districts with a salesperson assigned to each district.

The current accounting system has been adequate for monitoring the sales by product. However, there are limitations to the system because specific information is sometimes not available. A detailed analysis of operations is necessary for planning and control purposes and would be valuable for decision-making purposes. The accounting systems department has been asked to design a sales analysis code. The code should permit Universal to prepare a sales analysis that would reflect the characteristics of the company's business.

Questions

1. Account coding systems are based upon various coding concepts. Briefly define and give an example of the following coding concepts.

   a. Sequence coding.
   b. Block coding.
   c. Group coding.

2. Identify and describe factors that must be considered before a coding system can be designed and implemented for an organization.

3. Develop a coding system for Universal Floor Cover-

ing that would assign sales analysis codes to sales transactions. For each portion of the code:

a. Explain the meaning and purpose of the position.

b. Identify and justify the number of digits required.

(CMA Adapted)

5-39. *Margro Corporation*

Margro Corporation is an automotive supplier that uses automatic screw machines to manufacture precision parts from steel bars. Margro's inventory of raw steel averages $600,000 with a turnover rate of four times per year.

John Oates, President of Margro, is concerned about the costs of carrying inventory. He is considering the adoption of a "just-in-time" inventory control system in order to eliminate the need to carry any raw steel inventory. Oates has asked Helen Gorman, Margro's Controller, to evaluate the feasibility of "just-in-time" for the corporation. Gorman identified the following effects of adopting "just-in-time."

- Without scheduling any overtime, lost sales due to stockouts would increase by 35,000 units per year. However, by incurring overtime premiums of $40,000 per year, the increase in lost sales could be reduced to 20,000 units. This would be the maximum amount of overtime that would be feasible for Margro.
- Two warehouses presently used for steel bar storage would no longer be needed. Margro rents one warehouse from another company at an annual cost of $60,000. The other warehouse is owned by Margro and contains 12,000 square feet. Three-fourths of the space in the owned warehouse could be rented for $1.50 per square foot per year.
- Insurance and property tax costs totaling $14,000 per year would be eliminated.

Margro's projected operating results for the current fiscal year are presented in the next column. Long-term capital investments by Margro are expected to produce a rate of return of 12 percent after income taxes. Margro is subject to an effective income tax rate of 40 percent.

Margro Corporation
Pro Forma Income Statement
For the Year Ending December 31, 19XX
($000 omitted)

Sales		$10,800
(900,000 units)		
Cost of goods sold		
Variable	$4,050	
Fixed	1,450	5,500
Gross profit		$ 5,300
Selling and		
administrative		
expenses		
Variable	$ 900	
Fixed	1,500	2,400
Income before		
interest and		
income taxes		$ 2,900
Interest		900
Income before		
income taxes		$ 2,000
Income taxes		800
Net income		$ 1,200

Questions

1. Calculate the estimated dollar savings (loss) for Margro Corporation that would result next year from the adoption of the "just-in-time" inventory control method.
2. Identify and explain the conditions that should exist in order for a company to successfully install "just-in-time" (include the need for and a description of a material requirements planning system in your answer).

(CMA Adapted)

CHAPTER 5 SUPPLEMENT

Manually Collecting and Recording Accounting Data: An Example for a Manufacturing Firm

To examine the collection of accounting data in a manual system, consider the journal entries for recording the business transactions of a typical manufacturing company. The Alan Company sells its sporting goods on both a wholesale and retail basis to buyers around the country. Let us assume that the company uses a *process cost system* to collect the accounting data associated with the manufacture of baseball bats. The journal entires, in summary form, that would reflect the production and sale of these baseball bats are as follows.

(1) Direct raw materials inventory	X	
Indirect raw materials		
inventory	X	
Accounts payable		X
(2) Production in process		
inventory—baseball bats	X	
Baseball bat production		
overhead	X	
Direct raw materials		
inventory		X
Indirect raw materials		
inventory		X
(3) Baseball bat production		
payroll	X	
Cash		X
(4) Production in process		
inventory—baseball bats	X	
Baseball bat production		
overhead	X	
Baseball bat production		
payroll		X
(5) Baseball bat production		
overhead[1]	X	
Cash		X
Accumulated		
depreciation—		
production equipment		X
(6) Production in process		
inventory—baseball bats	X	
Baseball bat production		
overhead		X
(7) Finished sporting goods		
inventory—baseball bats	X	
Production in process		
inventory—baseball		
bats		X

[1] This *debit* includes the allocated rent, utilities, and depreciation associated with baseball bat production activities.

(8) Cash	X	
Sporting goods sales		X
(9) Cost of sporting goods sold	X	
Finished sporting goods inventory—baseball bats		X

For each one of these nine journal entries, some type of source document (or documents) would be needed to collect the required data for the accounting entry. To study this problem in more detail, let us examine each of these entries in order.

(1) Direct raw materials inventory	X	
Indirect raw materials inventory	X	
Accounts payable		X

This entry reflects the purchase on credit of both direct and indirect raw materials needed for baseball bat production. Separate subsidiary ledgers would be maintained for each of these two categories of raw materials (also, an "accounts payable" subsidiary ledger would likely be used) so that production subsystem managers will have information available regarding the physical quantity and cost balance of every raw materials item. The detailed data within the subsidiary ledgers for direct and indirect raw materials inventory and accounts payable would be maintained for both reference and late use. For example, a listing of each inventory item's balance within the direct raw materials inventory subsidiary ledger would help management identify low inventory levels, and thus replenish stocks in a timely fashion. Journal entry (1) is based on the following three source documents: the *purchase invoice* (i.e., the *bill*) mailed to the Alan Company by its supplier, the *purchase order* prepared by the Alan Company for the acquisition of inventory, and the *receiving report* prepared at the time the raw materials arrive at the Alan Company.

(2) Production in process inventory—baseball bats	X	

Baseball bat production overhead	X	
Direct raw materials inventory		X
Indirect raw materials inventory		X

This entry reflects the requisition of both direct raw materials (the cost of which is *debited* to the "production in process inventory—baseball bats" account) and indirect raw materials (the cost of which is *debited* to the "baseball bat production overhead" account). A source document called a *raw materials requisition* would be prepared by the baseball bat production supervisor at the time additional raw materials were needed for manufacturing activities. This source document is delivered to the production materials storeroom, where a clerk would issue the quantity and type of raw materials listed on the requisition form. The raw materials requisition source document would then be used by the accounting department for recording the journal entry.

(3) Baseball bat production payroll	X	
Cash		X

This entry reflects the total wages earned by those employees involved in baseball bat production. To simplify, payroll taxes and withholdings have been ignored. For accounting purposes, a payroll subsidiary ledger with information about each employee's earnings would be maintained. Entries to this subsidiary ledger would be initiated by the individual employee time cards, reflecting the number of hours worked during the specific pay period.

(4) Production in process inventory—baseball bats	X	
Baseball bat production overhead	X	
Baseball bat production payroll		X

This entry allocates the period's total wages for direct labor and indirect labor. The cost of direct labor is debited to the "production in process inventory—baseball bats" account, and the cost of indirect labor is debited to the "baseball bat production overhead" account. To make this labor allocation, each production employee would be classified as either a direct or indirect laborer. For hourly employees, information recorded directly on their time cards would make this distinction. Almost all supervisory employees would be classified as indirect labor.

(5) Baseball bat production
        overhead   X
            Cash   X
            Accumulated
                depreciation—
                production equipment   X

This entry reflects additional overhead costs associated with baseball bat production. The Alan Company's total period costs for such items as rent, utilities, and depreciation on manufacturing equipment would be ascertained from the following source documents: the *lease agreement* for the period's rent; the *utilities bill* (or *bills*) received through the mail for the period's electricity, water, and so on; and the *fixed-asset ledger* (which contains detailed information about each long-term asset such as original cost, estimated salvage value, estimated useful life, and depreciation method used) for the period's depreciation. Concerning the fixed-asset ledger, the actual source documents are the *purchase invoices,* which disclose the original costs of each long-term asset. Because all of the long-term asset cost data would be recorded within the fixed-asset ledger, however, we treat this ledger itself as the source document. By using conventional allocation methods, a portion of these rent, utilities, and depreciation costs incurred by the Alan Company would be charged to the manufacturing activities associated with baseball bat production. For example, depreciation on specific production equipment could be allocated to

baseball bat production based on the percentage of the equipment's total production machine-hours used in manufacturing baseball bats.

(6) Production in process
        inventory—baseball bats   X
            Baseball bat production
                overhead   X

This entry reflects the application of production overhead costs to the period's manufacturing work performed on baseball bats. Following conventional accounting procedure, overhead costs are applied to production work on the basis of a "predetermined overhead rate." For example, let us assume that the Alan Company uses a predetermined overhead rate based on direct labor hours. Therefore, the source document serving as a basis for ths journal entry would be time cards of "direct labor" employees. By adding all the actual labor hours reported on these time cards, the total number of direct labor hours would be computed. This figure would then be multiplied by the predetermined overhead rate, and the resultant dollar amount recorded in the journal.

(7) Finished sporting goods
        inventory—baseball bats   X
            Production in process
                inventory—baseball
                bats   X

This entry reflects the completion of some baseball bat inventory and the transfer of the inventory from the production department to the finished goods storeroom. Throughout our illustration, we have assumed that individual general ledger accounts were maintained specifically for baseball bat production overhead, baseball bat production in process inventory, and baseball bat finished sporting goods inventory. If, however, the Alan Company used a single production overhead account, production in process inventory account, and finished sporting goods inventory account to accumulate the various costs of manufacturing *all* of its sporting goods items, then separate subsidiary ledgers would be necessary to support each of these three general ledger accounts.

In a process cost accounting system, the focal point for collecting the costs associated with each type of manufactured product is the *departmental cost report*. This report (a separate one is prepared, for example, each week for every manufactured product) discloses the direct raw materials, direct labor, and applied overhead costs of both finished and in process inventory work. Thus, the data within the departmental cost report relating to baseball bat production would, in effect, be the source document for determining the dollar cost of finished baseball bat production.

(8) Cash   X
        Sporting goods sales   X

This entry reflects the actual sale of finished baseball bats for cash. To provide information to company management regarding the sales of each of the many sporting goods products, a "sporting goods sales" subsidiary ledger would likely be maintained. Included within the subsidiary ledger would be a separate account, indicating both physical quantities and dollars of sales, for every sporting goods product sold by the Alan Company. A *sales invoice* source document would be the basis for recording journal entry (8).

(9) Cost of sporting goods sold   X
            Finished sporting goods
                inventory—baseball
                bats   X

This final entry, which is recorded only under a perpetual inventory system, reflects the expense and inventory reduction to the Alan Company for specific quantities of merchandise sold. In terms of reference, the sales invoice mentioned previously for journal entry (8) would also be the source document for this entry. However, the dollar amount of the debit and the credit for entry (9) would be determined by using the company's inventory records and applying an inventory costing method (such as FIFO or LIFO) to the physical quantity of baseball bats sold.

The assumption throughout this example was that the Alan Company's data collection and recording activities were performed under a manual data processing system. In a firm having a large volume of accounting transactions, the major drawback of a manual system for data collection and recording is its slowness in handling various accounting functions. As a consequence, timely output reports reflecting the company's accounting transactions are not provided to management.

For example, under the Alan Company's manual data processing system, there may be a considerable delay before accountants are able to provide a departmental cost report to the baseball bat production supervisor. The supervisor could thus be unaware of inefficiencies in the production of baseball bats. The use of a computerized system for processing accounting data would enable a manager to receive timely reports and thus take action quickly to correct inefficient performance.

Documenting Accounting Information Systems

Among the important questions that you should be able to answer after reading this chapter are:

1. Why is documenting an accounting information system important?
2. What are *document flowcharts* and how are they used to help manage the flow of data in accounting information systems?
3. What do the symbols for a document and system flowchart mean?
4. How is a *data flow diagram* different from a flowchart?
5. What does a data flow diagram look like and how can it be used to document an accounting information system?
6. What kind of "data about data" are recorded in a data dictionary and how is a data dictionary used to augment a data flow diagram?
7. How are program flowcharts, decision tables, and structured English used as documentation tools?

INTRODUCTION

Documentation is a vital part of accounting information systems. The logical and physical flows of accounting data and information cannot be understood without appropriate documentation. In this chapter, we examine the reasons why an accountant needs to understand these flows. In addition, several documentation tools are described.

Flowcharts are often used to describe the flow of accounting data through a system. These tools are valuable because they can pictorially represent data flows that would take many pages of narrative description. In this sense, flowcharts reinforce the old adage, "a picture is worth a thousand words." Two types of flowcharts are *document flowcharts* and *system flowcharts*. Actually, a document flowchart is a special type of system flowchart. Document flowcharts are discussed first in the chapter because they are easier to understand than the general system flowcharts.

While flowcharts provide documentation for the accounting information system in terms of a physical description, other tools are more useful for describing the logical flow of data. A documentation tool frequently used for this purpose is the *data flow diagram*. Data flow diagrams show logical flows of data and the processes that transform the data. Data flow diagrams are accompanied by a *data dictionary,* which describes all the characteristics of the data in the diagram.

Other documentation tools are used to describe more detailed levels of processing within the accounting information system. These include program flowcharts, decision tables, and pseudocode. While an accountant does not need to be a computer programmer in order to understand the processing that occurs in a particular application, it is necessary to be somewhat familiar with documentation describing the processing that takes place in the program. Therefore an understanding of program flowcharts, decision tables, and pseudocode will enable an accountant to follow the data flows and data processing in a particular application program.

WHY DOCUMENTATION IS IMPORTANT

Documentation includes all the flowcharts, narratives, and other written communications that outline the inputs, processing, and outputs in the information system. It is, in effect, a description of the system. This description may be of logical flows of data and data processes in a proposed system, or it may be a physical representation of an existing system. Documentation can take many forms, such as written narrative, flowcharts, data flow diagrams, or tables. It may even consist of answers to a questionnaire.

There are at least three reasons why documentation is important. First, it explains how a system works. For example, just observing an information system at work would be impractical, and it would be difficult to detect all information flows and processing that takes place in this

way. Reading through a written description of the inputs, processes, and outputs associated with the information system, on the other hand, would be an easier way to learn about the system. A still easier way might be to look at a "picture" of the system in the form of a flowchart. Pictures are often said to be "worth a thousand words" and this is generally true for flowcharts.

Another reason that documentation is important is that it helps those involved with designing new accounting information systems to develop their ideas for a new system and communicate those ideas to others. Documentation tools are useful for this in provviding a structure that facilitates the communication process. For example, a narrative description may vary significantly, depending on who has written it. The individual reading the narrative may interpret it differently from the way it was intended. Other individuals may interpret it in still other ways. But a system flowchart or data flow diagram that uses a standard set of symbols is more likely to be interpreted the same way by all parties viewing it.

A third reason for documenting an accounting information system is that it provides valuable information to auditors. In performing an audit of an organization, the auditors first evaluate the internal control system. Examining the system documentation allows them to determine where the strengths and weaknesses are with respect to internal control. The relative strength or weakness of the internal control system will largely determine the scope of the audit. After the internal control system is evaluated, the auditors must trace sample outputs of an information system back to the original transactions that created them (e.g., tracing inventory assets back to original purchases). Information system documentation also helps them with this, as they need to know how the information system works in order to do this tracing. The documentation describing the system serves as an audit trail for the accounting transactions.

DOCUMENT FLOWCHARTS

A useful tool for pictorially representing the physical flow of documents through the various departments of an organization is called a **document flowchart.** A document flowchart is a special kind of **system flowchart** (discussed in the next section of this chapter) that is especially useful in the analysis of accounting information systems.

The term "document" is used here in a broad sense to include all types of written communications in an organization (e.g., memos from one manager to another, performance reports, purchase orders, and sales invoices). When constructing a document flowchart, some accountants and analysts will also include, where applicable, any movement of physical goods (e.g., the movement of inventory from the receiving department to the inventory storeroom in a purchase transaction) and any information flows

not involving documents (e.g., a sales clerk telephoning the credit and collection department to check a customer's outstanding accounts receivable balance prior to approving a credit sale).

Document flowcharts make use of special symbols, as illustrated in Figure 6-1. Some of these symbols (e.g., the process symbol) are similar to those of common computer system flowcharts, whereas others (e.g, the physical goods symbol) are unique to document flowcharts. Unlike the symbols for system and program flowcharts, the symbols for document flowcharts are not standardized.

Constructing a document flowchart begins with identifying the different departments or groups involved with the information system. One of these departments might be the point where documents originate, and another might be where copies of documents are filed. These departments are listed across the top of the flowchart as headings (Figure 6-2). A document's flow is traced from the department where it originates until its final disposition. There may be multiple copies of a document.

When designing a document flowchart, there are two guidelines to observe. The first is to carefully align the documents and activities of each department under their corresponding departmental headings. Another guideline is to identify each copy of an accounting document with a number and be sure to account for the distribution of each copy in the flowchart.

A Simple Example

To illustrate how document flowcharts are created, consider the hiring of a new employee at the Alan Company (see again Figure 6-2). This process begins when a particular department develops a vacancy. A "Job Vacancy" form is then completed by this department and forwarded to the personnel department. The personnel department then advertises for the position and, with the help of the requesting department, interviews applicants.

When someone is found to fill the vacancy, the personnel department prepares a "Position Hir-

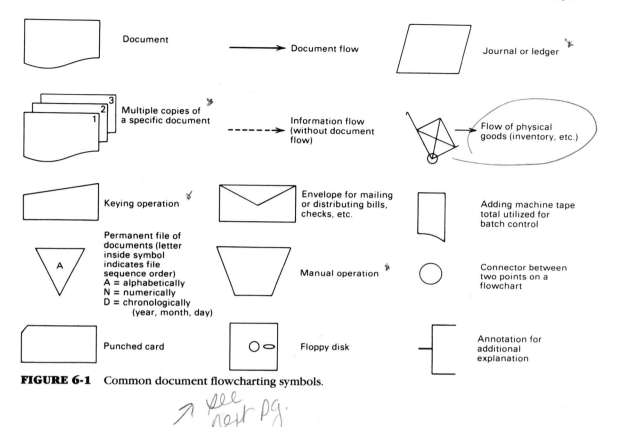

FIGURE 6-1 Common document flowcharting symbols.

ing" form in triplicate. The first copy is filed in the personnel department's manual file, which is organized by employee social security number. The third copy is stapled to the job vacancy form and returned to the requesting department where it is filed alphabetically by employee last name.

The second copy of the Position Hiring form is forwarded to the payroll department. Here, the form is used as an authorization document to create a payroll record for the new employee. Thus, the information on the form is keyed directly into the department's computer system using an online terminal located in the payroll office. The Position Hiring form is then filed for reference and also as evidence that the employee's form has been processed.

Figure 6-2 illustrates a document flowchart depicting this data flow. Although document-flowchart drawing is more an art than a science,

there are certain steps that can be followed to draw them. These will now be discussed.

The first step is to identify the participants. For this particular case, there are three of them: (1) the department that wishes to fill a job vacancy (called the "requesting department" in Figure 6-2), (2) the personnel department, and (3) the payroll department. Each of these departments is identified along the top of the document flowchart.

The next step is to identify the source documents involved. Here, there are two major ones: (1) the Job Vacancy form, which we presume is prepared as a single copy, and (2) the Position Hiring form, which we are told is prepared in triplicate. In practice, multiple-copy forms are usually color coded. However, in document flowcharts, these are usually just numbered and a separate page is attached to explain the color-number equivalencies.

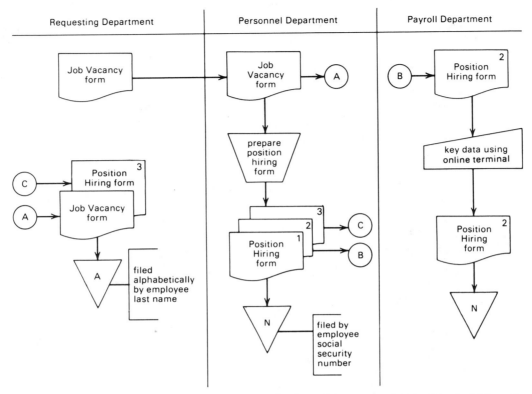

FIGURE 6-2   A document flowchart illustrating the flow of documents involved in the hiring of a new employee. (See text for a description of this process and the steps for creating this document flowchart.)

The third step in drawing a document flowchart is to depict how the documents are created, processed, and used. This is probably the most complex task, and the designer must often use considerable latitude and ingenuity to represent data flows and processing activities accurately. A document's first appearance should be under the department in which it was created. The physical flow of forms (i.e., when forms are actually sent from one place to another) is represented by solid arrows. The transmitted document should then be redrawn to indicate its "arrival" in the receiving department (see the document flow of the Job Vacancy form as an example).

Where there are a large number of document transmittals, connector circles are used to avoid complicated flow lines. Each circle is given a unique symbol (e.g., a letter or Roman numeral) for identification purposes. These symbols can

also be used to reference other pages if necessary. In Figure 6-2 several circle connectors have been used (with letters A, B, and C) to avoid cluttering the drawing.

The last step in the creation of a document flowchart is to add annotations (if necessary) to explain activities or symbols. These annotations are little notes to the reader that are used for clarification. Although this step is largely optional, it is much better to "overdocument" a complicated process than to "underdocument" it, so annotation should be used when in doubt.

A More Complex Example

To illustrate a more complex example of a document flowchart, consider the Beccan Company, a discount tire dealer that operates 25 retail stores in a metropolitan area. The company operates a centralized purchasing and warehousing facility and employs a perpetual inventory system. All purchases of tires and related supplies are placed through the company's central purchasing department to take advantage of the quantity discounts offered by its suppliers.

The tires and supplies are received at the central warehouse and distributed to the retail stores as needed. The perpetual inventory system at the central facility maintains current inventory records, which include designated reorder points, optimum order quantities, and balance-on-hand information for each type of tire or related supply.

The participants involved in Beccan's inventory control system include (1) retail stores, (2) inventory control, (3) the warehouse, (4) purchasing, (5) accounts payable, and (6) outside vendors. The inventory control department is responsible for the maintenance of the perpetual inventory records for each item carried in inventory. The warehouse department maintains the physical inventory of all items carried by the company's retail stores. All deliveries of tires and related supplies from vendors are received by receiving clerks in this department and all distributions to retail stores are filled by shipping clerks in this department. The purchasing department places every order for items needed by the company. The accounts payable department maintains the subsidiary ledger with vendors and other creditors. All payments are processed by this department.

Figure 6-3 illustrates the document flowchart for the Beccan Company's inventory control system. This figure has been constructed using the following descriptions of the documents. In real-life applications, this descriptive information is obtained first, and the flowchart drawn afterward. However, for the purposes of study, it may be constructive to examine Figure 6-3 concurrently with a reading of the narrative.

Retail Store Requisition (Form RSR)

This document is submitted by the retail stores to the central warehouse whenever tires or supplies are needed at the stores. The shipping clerks in the warehouse department fill the orders from inventory and have them delivered to the stores. Three copies of the document are prepared. Two copies are sent to the warehouse. The third copy is filed for reference.

Purchase Requisition (Form PR)

An inventory control clerk in the inventory control department prepares this document when the quantity on hand for an item falls below the designated reorder point. Two copies of the document are prepared. One copy is forwarded to the purchasing department and the other is filed.

Purchase Order (Form PO)

The purchasing department prepares this document based on information found in the purchase requisition. Five copies of the purchase order are prepared. The disposition of these copies is as follows: copy 1 to vendor, copy 2 to accounts payable department, copy 3 to inventory control department, copy 4 to warehouse, and copy 5 is filed for reference.

Receiving Report (Form RR)

The warehouse department prepares this document when ordered items are received from vendors. A receiving clerk completes the document by indicating the vendor's name, the date the shipment is received, and the quantity of each item received. Four copies of the report are prepared. Copy 1 is sent to the accounts payable department. Copy 2 is sent to the purchasing department. Copy 3 is sent to the inventory control department. Copy 4 is retained by the warehouse department, compared with the purchase order form in its files, and filed together with this purchase order form for future reference.

Invoices

Invoices received from vendors are bills for payment. Several copies of each invoice are prepared by the vendor, but only two copies are of

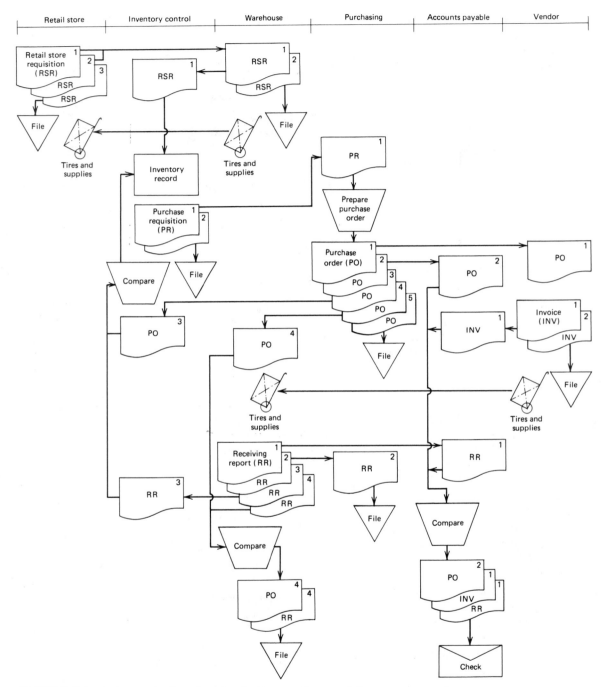

FIGURE 6-3 A document flowchart for the Beccan Company's inventory control system.

concern to the Beccan Company: the copy that is received by the company's accounts payable department and the copy that is retained by the vendor for reference. The accounts payable department compares the vendor invoice with its file copy of the original purchase order and its file copy of the warehouse receiving report. Based on this information, adjustments to the bill amount on the invoice are made (e.g., for damaged goods, for trade discounts, or for cash discounts), a check is prepared, and the payment is mailed to the vendor.

Figure 6-3 depicts the flow of data for this inventory application in a document flowchart. As before, note that the flowchart is divided into columns. The number of columns is determined by the number of participants in the accounting function. For the illustration at hand, there are six participants: (1) the retail stores, (2) the inventory control department, (3) the warehouse department, (4) the purchasing department, (5) the accounts payable department, and (6) the vendors.

Some analysts draw columnar lines in the document flowchart to separate the departmental activities as in Figure 6-2. Where the flow of data back and forth between departments is considerable, extra lines unnecessarily complicate the picture and should be avoided. However, vertical alignment of the symbols for the documents and activities under each department heading is important to clearly identify document and data processing responsibilities.

SYSTEM FLOWCHARTS

Document flowcharts are a special kind of system flowchart. They are *document oriented,* whereas other system flowcharts are process oriented. This means that the document flowchart focuses on *documents* (inputs and outputs) and the system flowchart includes more information about the *processes* that take place. Most of the symbols used in system flowcharts are industry conventions standardized by the National Bureau of Standards (Standard x3.5), although some companies use flowchart conventions of their own. Figure 6-4 illustrates common system flowcharting symbols.

Some system flowcharts are very general in nature, providing an overview of the system. These are called **high-level system flowcharts.** An example of a high-level flowchart is given in Figure 6-5. Notice that the inputs and outputs of the system are specified by the general input and output symbol, a parallelogram. In more detailed level system flowcharts, the specific form of these inputs and outputs would be indicated by symbols such as those for magnetic tape, documents, disk, and so on. Processes are also explained only in general terms in a high-level flowchart. Figure 6-5 refers to only one process, the payroll program. A more detailed or **intermediate-level system flowchart** would describe all the processes performed by the payroll program, and the specific inputs and outputs of each process. (An intermediate-level system flowchart for payroll processing is shown later in Figure 6-7.) A low-level flowchart would be a program flowchart, describing the steps of a particular application program.

Flowcharting Guidelines

Flowcharting is an art, not a science. This causes problems for some auditors and accountatns because they are used to dealing with more precision than that present in the flexible craft of flowcharting. Although there are no strict rules to indicate exactly how to construct a system flowchart for a given application, there are some guidelines that, when followed, will produce "better" flowcharts. These guidelines are as follows:

1. A process symbol should always be found between an input and an output symbol. This is referred to as the "**sandwich rule**" for obvious reasons.
2. Flowcharts should read from top to bottom and from left to right. In drawing or reading a

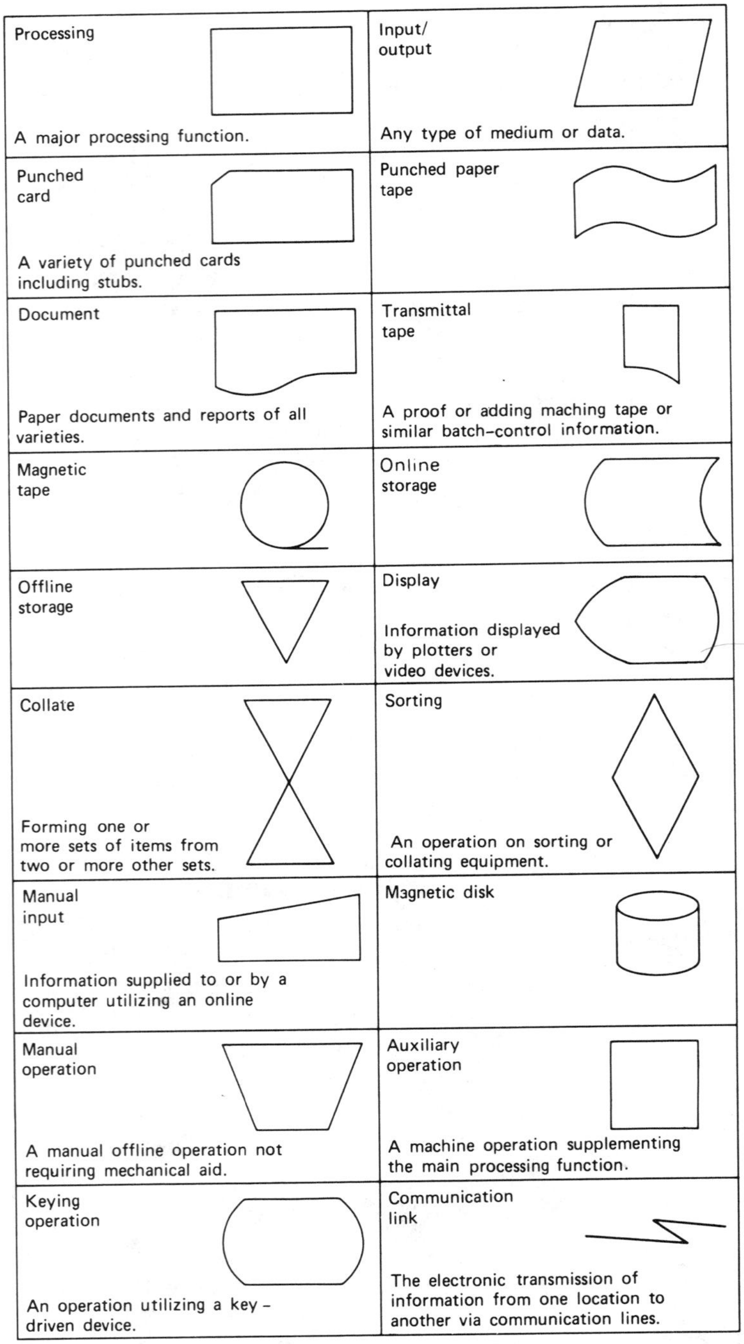

Processing A major processing function.	**Input/ output** Any type of medium or data.
Punched card A variety of punched cards including stubs.	**Punched paper tape**
Document Paper documents and reports of all varieties.	**Transmittal tape** A proof or adding maching tape or similar batch-control information.
Magnetic tape 	**Online storage**
Offline storage 	**Display** Information displayed by plotters or video devices.
Collate Forming one or more sets of items from two or more other sets.	**Sorting** An operation on sorting or collating equipment.
Manual input Information supplied to or by a computer utilizing an online device.	**Magnetic disk**
Manual operation A manual offline operation not requiring mechanical aid.	**Auxiliary operation** A machine operation supplementing the main processing function.
Keying operation An operation utilizing a key-driven device.	**Communication link** The electronic transmission of information from one location to another via communication lines.

Information displayed from the terminal (handwritten annotation)

FIGURE 6-4   System flowcharting symbols. (Courtesy of IBM Corp.)

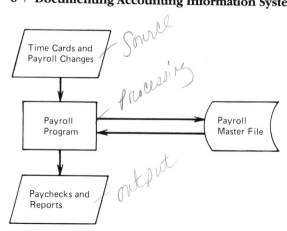

FIGURE 6-5 High-level system flowchart for payroll processing.

flowchart, you should begin in the upper left-hand corner.

3. Appropriate symbols should be used, depending on the type of flowchart. Some flowchart symbols are reserved for program flowcharts (e.g., the decision symbol) and some are used in document flowcharts (e.g., the online storage symbol).

4. Avoid "clutter" in a flowchart by avoiding crossed lines. Connector symbols should be used when crossing lines is unavoidable. It is wise to draw at least one sketch of a flowchart before designing the final draft.

5. Descriptions and comments should be used on the flowcharts for clarification. These may be contained in an annotation symbol (refer to Figure 6-1), attached to a process or file symbol, or within a symbol itself. Striping is another method of including explanation in a flowchart. An example is drawing a line horizontally through a file symbol and placing a letter below the line to indicate whether data or records are stored alphabetically, numerically, or chronologically within the file. A narrative may be included with the flowchart for further description.

A Simple Example

It is probably easiest to understand system flowcharts by studying their use in a simple application. Figure 6-6 illustrates a system flowchart for a magazine distributor—that is, a system flowchart for a computer system used to maintain a file of magazine subscribers and, ultimately, create mailing labels.

The flowchart begins with source documents that are prepared by the magazine subscribers and mailed to the company. These address-change forms indicate the subscriber's old address, new address, and subscription number (found on an old mailing label). This information is then keyed into an online terminal. This terminal provides access to an online computer that temporarily stores these data as a file of address-change requests. This keying activity will be performed continuously, so we may characterize this processing as "daily processing."

Once a week, the change request records are used to update the subscriber master file. (The concept of a master file is discussed more fully in the next chapter.) This means that information about new subscribers will be added to the file and the addresses of existing subscribers will be changed. A "Master File Processing Report" is also prepared by this program to document the additions and modifications made to the file. This completes the "weekly processing."

Once a month, postal labels must be prepared for the magazine's monthly mailing. The subscriber master file serves as the chief input for this program and the two major outputs are the labels themselves and a Processing Report documenting these activities. This is "monthly processing."

A system flowchart helps accountants trace the flow of accounting data through a computerized system. Thus, it can be used to identify sources of data, places where data are temporarily stored, and outputs on which processed data appear. Indirectly, the system flowchart also indicates processing cycles (daily, weekly, or monthly),

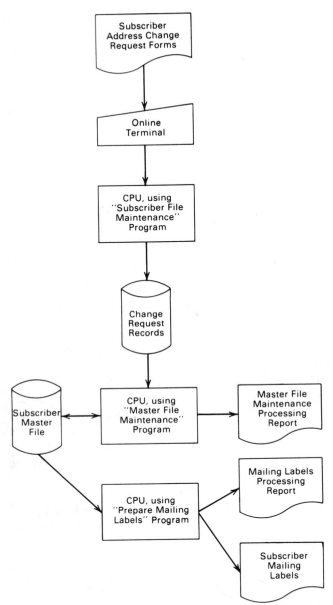

FIGURE 6-6 A system flowchart illustrating the computer steps involved in maintaining a subscriber master file and creating monthly mailing labels.

hardware needs (e.g., disk drives and printers), and potential bottlenecks in processing (e.g., manual keying). For these reasons, system flowcharts are a valuable documentation tool for computerized accounting information systems.

A More Complex Example

A classic example of computerized data processing is a company's payroll processing. Although such systems tend to be complex, a simplified version is provided in Figure 6-7.

Suppose that the Alan Company prepares a weekly payroll for those employees working at one of its production facilities. The basic employee information is maintained on a *payroll master file* stored on magnetic disk. There is one record on the magnetic disk file for each employee at the facility, and each record contains such basic information as employee social security number, name, address, and deduction codes. Those employees who work on an hourly basis have hourly pay rate information stored in their payroll records. Those employees who are on salary have weekly salary information stored

in their payroll records. The payroll file is organized in ascending sequence according to employee social security number.

During the course of the week, any changes to the payroll master file are keyed directly onto a disk through a terminal located in the personnel office. Such changes reflect (1) modification of pay rates for employees given raises or promotions, (2) increases or decreases in the number of income tax exemptions, (3) individual revisions to payroll savings plans, (4) employee changes of name or address, and so forth. At the end of each week, all the changes requested by

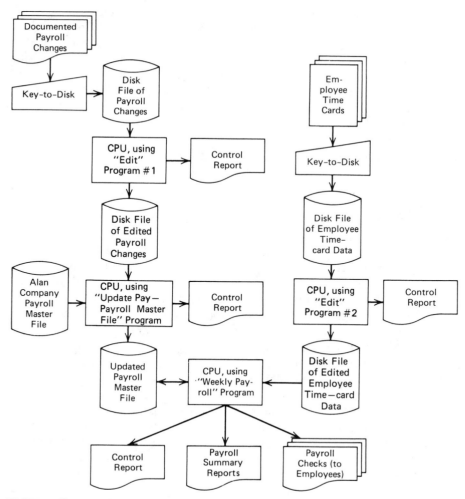

FIGURE 6-7　System flowchart for computerized processing of the Alan Company payroll.

the Alan Company's personnel office are taken from the temporary disk file and *edited*. This means that the file change requests are checked for accuracy, reasonableness, and meaning. (The specific types of tests performed are reviewed at length in Chapter 10.) The computer program that performs this editing is called an **edit program,** and the output from it is a set of edited payroll change records, sorted in ascending employee social security number sequence. The resulting sorted disk file of payroll changes is then input together with the payroll master file to alter the master file payroll records as desired.

Once the modifications to the payroll master file have been made, the Alan Company can prepare the weekly payroll. At the end of each week, time cards from the various departments within the company facility are collected and brought to the computer center. At first, the information found on the time cards is simply transferred onto a magnetic disk file. Here, the time card information is edited in a fashion similar to the editing of file change data described above. After this editing has taken place, the actual payroll checks can be prepared in a separate processing phase.

Payroll processing is a major data processing task. Inputs to this processing include the payroll master file and the (edited) time card data file. Outputs include an updated payroll master file (reflecting new year-to-date payment and deduction amounts), a control report (indicating computer control total data and the like), a payroll summary (including who was paid what and with which check), and of course the payroll checks themselves.

Figure 6-7 documents this payroll narrative in a system flowchart. The flow of information on the upper left-hand side of the figure begins with the payroll change requests made by the personnel department. The keying operation that transfers the change requests directly to the disk is called an **online job entry system.** This keying operation, the editing of these change requests on a weekly basis, and the use of these change requests to update the employee master file are depicted in sequence reading down the left-hand portion of the system flowchart.

The upper right-hand side of the figure traces the time card data through the payroll system. Employee time card data are keyed onto a disk file and eventually sorted into social security number sequence. Finally, in the lower portion of the figure, the updated payroll master file and the edited disk file of employee time card data are ready for use in preparing the weekly payroll.

Each time a file is sorted or updated, a separate computer processing step using the central processing unit is required. (The computer programs used to perform this processing are discussed in general terms later in this chapter.) Thus, the change requests made by the personnel department update the payroll master file in one processing phase, the time card data are edited in a second processing phase, and the payroll checks are prepared in yet a third processing phase. Generally speaking, this is the way data processing proceeds in almost all accounting information system applications: one step at a time.

A second thing to notice about the system flowchart is that each processing phase of the payroll usually involves the preparation of one or more **control reports.** These reports provide processing-control information and help the Alan Company staff correct errors as they are detected by the processing system.

A final thing to notice about the system flowchart is that it represents a flow or **job stream** of accounting data through the various processing phases of the accounting system. The acquisition of accounting data on a timely, accurate, cost-effective basis and the processing of these data into useful information are the objectives of this job stream.

This example has been simplified to introduce the fundamentals of system flowcharting on an elementary level. System flowcharts are very important to accounting information systems because they document the flow of information through the computerized portion of the accounting subsystem's data processing and therefore trace the audit trail. Accountants use these flowcharts to familiarize themselves with new accounting applications, to help them identify an accounting information system's strengths and weaknesses, and to assist them in their roles as auditors and management consultants. In recognition of this, both the American Institute of Certified Public Accountants and the National Association of Accountants have consistently included test questions in their professional examinations that require a working knowledge of system flowcharts.

DATA FLOW DIAGRAMS

Data flow diagrams represent a logical view of an accounting information system. They are primarily used in the systems development process, either as a tool for analyzing an existing system, or as a tool for planning the new system. The logical description does not include detail about physical features of a system such as the specification of input and output devices. Rather, it depicts the logical processes and flows of data through the information system.

The basic symbols used in data flow diagrams are presented in Figure 6-8. Data flow diagrams employ much fewer symbols than do flowcharts since the emphasis is not on specific devices or documents. The square is used to represent a **data source** or **data destination.** For example, a source of data might be a customer. To show this, a data flow diagram would include the word customer inside the square symbol. The circle (sometimes referred to as a "bubble") symbol is used to indicate a process. These processes are ones which change or transform data. Processes are described with a label inside the circle. The label includes a verb, describing the data transformation. **Data flows** or **data streams** are shown on a data flow diagram by a line and arrow. The arrow indicates the direction of the flow. The fourth symbol is an open-ended rectangle, representing a data store or repository of data. The data store is often a file of some sort.

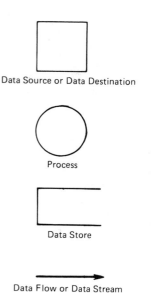

Data Source or Data Destination

Process

Data Store

Data Flow or Data Stream

FIGURE 6-8 Symbols for data flow diagrams.

As with system flowcharts, data flow diagrams have levels that depict various amounts of detail. A high-level data flow diagram is first prepared to provide an overall picture of an application or system. This general overview diagram is referred to as a context diagram (Figure 6-9). It shows the net inputs and outputs of the systems application as well as the data sources and destinations external to the application. The context diagram is then *decomposed* or broken down into successively lower levels of detailed diagrams. These will show more detailed processes and the inputs and outputs associated with each. In this way a set of data flow diagrams is linked together to form a hierarchy. A data flow diagram for a payroll processing application is shown in Figure 6-10. The procedure "process payroll reports" would be broken down into several processes (e.g., process withholding reports, process miscellaneous deduction reports, process payment register) in a lower level diagram.

A data flow diagram is composed of both **data elements** and **data structures.** A data element is the lowest level of a data flow. It is data that

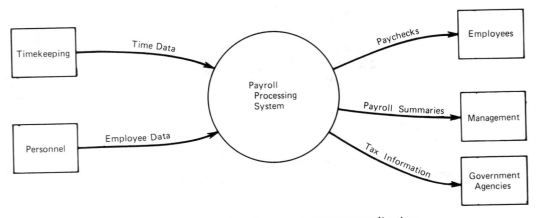

FIGURE 6-9 A context diagram for a payroll processing system application.

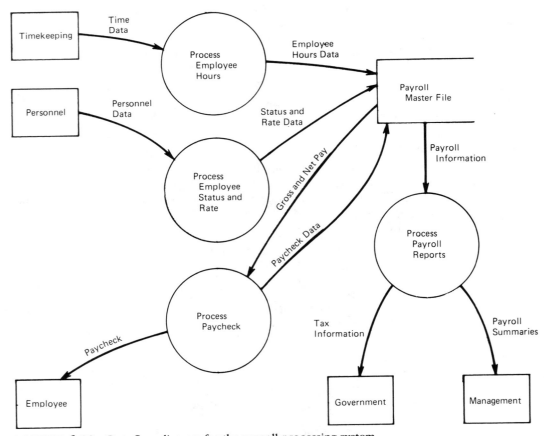

FIGURE 6-10 Data flow diagram for the payroll processing system.

cannot be broken down into smaller pieces. Data elements are linked together with other pieces. An example of a data structure would be "name-address" where a customer name is linked to the customer's address. Both customer name and customer address are data elements. A **data dictionary** accompanies data flow diagrams and contains "data about data" or descriptions of all the data elements and data structures used in the data flow diagram. An entry in the data dictionary includes the name of the data structure, the type of data structure (either a data element, data flow, or data store), the content of the data structure in terms of data elements and their relationships, and comments. For a complex system, data dictionaries can be difficult to create and maintain. Because of this, some software packages are available that can create computerized data dictionaries.

OTHER DOCUMENTATION TOOLS

There are many other tools for documenting an accounting information system besides flowcharts and data flow diagrams. Some of these tools are used to describe specific application programs or processes within the system. Three of these tools are: (1) program flowcharts, (2) decision tables and, (3) pseudocode. Since these are tools that are generally used by programmers and system analysts rather than by accountants, they are described only briefly. Accountants should have some familiarity with these tools, however, since they will want to examine them when auditing an information system or reviewing the design for a system.

Other tools are also available for documenting an accounting information system. A few of these are described later in this textbook as part of the discussion of the system development process. The documentation tools and techniques discussed in this chapter can be used in the systems development process, as well as for other purposes of understanding the system.

Program Flowcharts

A **program flowchart** (Figure 6-11) outlines the logic sequence for a particular computer program and diagrams the order in which data processing takes place. Once such a flowchart has been designed, it is usually shown to a supervisor for approval. Upon approval, the program flowchart is then used as a "blueprint" for coding the computer program itself. After the program has been completed, it is advisable to check it against the flowchart to make sure it is in order.

As a documentation aid, it is important that the program flowchart uses recognizable processing symbols. These symbols include most system flowchart symbols plus a few others that are reserved for program flowcharts. Examples of specific programming flowchart symbols are the diamond (indicates a decision) and the oval (indicates a termination point such as stop or start). Special templates with the standard symbols for program flowcharting may be purchased and are often used by programmers and system analysts. These templates are relatively inexpensive and their conformance to industry standards ensures accuracy in documentation. Their use also speeds the documentation effort.

Like system flowcharts and data flow diagrams, program flowcharts may be designed at different levels of detail. The highest level program flowchart is referred to as a **macro program flowchart** and provides an overview of the data processing logic. A lower-level program flowchart would indicate the detailed programming logic necessary to carry out a processing task. A detailed program flowchart for a sales-report application is presented in Figure 6-11.

Decision Tables

Where a data processing task involves a large number of conditions and subsequent courses of action, program flowcharts tend to be long and complex. For example, in a payroll application, the computation of federal withholding tax depends on the employee's gross salary, number of

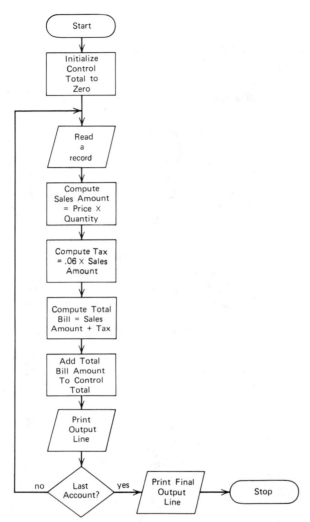

FIGURE 6-11 A detailed program flowchart for a Sales Report Application.

dependents, marital status, and so forth. Because a separate decision point (diamond symbol) must be used to test for each of these conditions in a program flowchart, the flowchart becomes complicated.

Decision tables outline the set of conditions a given data processing task might encounter and indicate the appropriate action to be taken (i.e., the data processing task that should be performed) for each separate possibility. Some-

times, decision tables are used as an alternative to program flowcharts. More commonly, they are used in addition to these flowcharts.

To illustrate, imagine a credit union that pays interest to its depositors at the rate of 7% per annum. Accounts of less than $5 are not paid interest. Accounts of $1000 or more that have been with the union for more than one year get paid the normal 7% plus a bonus of .5%. Figure 6-12 illustrates a decision table to help the credit union decide how much interest to pay each account.

Note that the decision table consists of four parts: (1) the **condition stub,** which outlines the potential conditions of the application; (2) the **action stub,** which outlines the potential actions to be taken in the application; (3) the **condition entries,** which depict all of the possible combinations likely to occur; and (4) the **action entries,** which outline the action to be taken for each combination of conditions. The *rules* at the top of the decision table set forth the combination of conditions that may occur and what action is to be taken for each.

For the illustration at hand, there are three conditions that affect the data processing of each account: (1) account balance less than $5, (2) account balance less than $1000, and (3) account one year old or less. As defined, each of these conditions can now be answered "yes" or "no." Since there are two answers for each of three conditions, there are 2 times 2 times 2, or 2^3 = 8 conditions. This computation determines how many rules there will be in the decision table. Thus, in general, if there are n conditions, there will be 2^n rules.

In Figure 6-12 Y stands for yes and N stands for no. Thus, the combination of Ys and Ns in the condition entry portion of the table illustrates each possible condition the data processing task might encounter. Further, using Xs, the decision table also shows what course of action should be taken for each condition (i.e., how much interest should be paid to each account). A blank used as an action entry indicates that a particular action is not taken.

		Rules								
		1	2	3	4	5	6	7	8	
	Conditions									
	Account balance less the $5	Y	Y	Y	Y	N	N	N	N	
Condition	Account balance less than $1000	Y	Y	N	N	Y	Y	N	N	Condition
stub	Account 1 year old or less	Y	N	Y	N	Y	N	Y	N	entries
	Actions									
	Pay no interest	X	X	X	X					
Action	Pay 7% interest					X	X	X		Action
stub	Pay 71/2% interest								X	entries

FIGURE 6-12 A decision to help a credit union decide how much interest to pay each account. (The apparent errors in rules 3 and 4 are explained in the text.)

Using Ys and Ns to define the set of all possible conditions in a decision table sometimes results in conflicting possibilities. This has happened here because it is impossible for an account balance to be less than $5 and simultaneously greater than $1000 (rule 3 in Figure 6-12). Further, it sometimes happens that one particular data characteristic overrides any other considerations and dictates a single course of action. An example of this is also found in the illustration: if an account balance is less than $5, no interest is paid regardless of the amount of time the depositor's money has been with the credit union (rules 1, 2, 3, 4).

Where condition conflicts or data redundancies as just described develop, it is desirable to reformulate the decision table in a more consistent, compact format. Figure 6-13 illustrates the revised decision table. Note that the resultant table now contains only 4 rules, not 8. However, all the important conditions of the data processing task are presented along with their appropriate courses of action.

The major advantage of decision tables is that they summarize the data processing tasks to be performed for a large number of data conditions in a compact, easily understood format. This increases program understanding, resulting in fewer programmer errors and also fewer omissions of important processing possibilities. An increase in computer programmer productivity is therefore also gained. Finally, the decision table serves as an important documentation aid when new data processing conditions arise or changes in organizational policy result in new courses of action for existing conditions.

This last advantage of decision tables is particularly important to accounting information systems because of the accountant's concern for accuracy and completeness in the processing of financial data. The decision table documents the logic of the computer program and therefore permits the auditor to review this logic in a convenient form.

The principal drawback of decision tables is that they do not show the order in which data

	Rules			
	1	2	3	4
Conditions				
Account balance less than $5	Y	N	N	N
Account balance less than $1000	*	Y	N	N
Account 1 year old or less	*	*	Y	N
Actions				
Pay no interest	X			
Pay 7% interest		X	X	
Pay 71/2% interest				X

FIGURE 6-13 The decision table of Figure 20-7, revised. An asterisk (*) means that the condition does not affect the course of action.

conditions are tested and/or processing actions are taken. This is a major deficiency because the order in which data is tested or data processing is performed is often at least as important as the data tests or processing tasks themselves.

A second drawback of decision tables is that they require an understanding of documentation techniques beyond flowcharting. A third drawback is that decision tables require extra work to prepare, and this work may not be productive if program flowcharts must be prepared anyway. A final drawback is that the preparation of a decision table does not guarantee the accuracy or completeness of a data processing task; it is merely a tool that has the potential to improve program design.

Pseudocode

Pseudocode uses certain words of the English language in a structured format to describe programming logic. For this reason, a form of psuedocode is sometimes referred to as structured English. Pseudocode means "imitation code." It is not a real programming code since it is not written in a programming language that a computer would understand. Pseudocode can be used to describe the logic in a system as well as in a program.

The terms used in pseudocode are a limited set of verbs (e.g., ADD, SUBTRACT, DO) and condition terms such as IF, THEN, and ELSE. These terms can be used to describe logic indicated in a decision table or program flowchart. There are some conventions for pseudocode that include rules about indenting sentences or terms to show sequences of relationships.

Pseudocode, decision tables, and program flowcharts all can be used to facilitate **structured programming.** Structured programming is used to build computer programs that are organized carefully in a top-down, modular fashion. Structured programming enables system analysts to develop programs more quickly because programmer responsibilities can be assigned on a module-by-module (i.e., portion-by-portion) basis, and also because the programs can be tested, corrected, and documented on a module-by-module basis. This structuring is also important to accounting information systems because processing controls become more identifiable in structured programs and because the documentation for structured programs has the potential to be more easily understood. Further, structured programming techniques are important to accounting information systems because they usually increase development productivity and impose standards in the analysis and design of computerized accounting systems.

SUMMARY

Three reasons for documenting an accounting information system are: (1) to promote an understanding of how the system works, (2) to help those involved with designing new accounting information systems to develop their ideas and communicate them to others, and (3) to provide information to auditors about the internal control system.

Although a written narrative can be used to document an accounting information system, several tools are available that are more efficient. One of these tools is a flowchart. Several types of flowcharts were described in this chapter. Document flowcharts were explained first as they tend to be the easiest to understand and follow. Other types of flowcharts include system flowcharts, program flowcharts, and data flow diagrams.

System and program flowcharts provide good physical descriptions of an accounting information system. A documentation tool that provides a logical view of a system is the data flow diagram. The view is logical because it is more concerned with processes and the flow and transformation of data than with the physical devices that might be used for input, processing, and output. Data flow diagrams, together with a data dictionary, form a powerful documentation tool for describing a system. They are often used in system development, as well as by accountants who are trying to understand a system.

Other documentation tools discussed in this chapter are decision tables and pseudocode. These, together with program flowcharts, are useful for developing structured programs. Although accountants do not need to be programmers in order to evaluate or design an accounting information system, being able to understand the logic of an application program is important. Familiarity with these documentation tools promotes this understanding.

Key Terms You Should Know

action entries
action stub
condition entries
condition stub
context diagram
control reports
data dictionary
data elements (in data flow diagram)
data flow diagrams
data flows
data streams
data structures (in data flow diagram)
decision tables

document flowchart
edit program
high-level system flowcharts
intermediate-level system flowcharts
job stream
online job entry system
macro program flowchart
program flowchart
pseudocode
sandwich rule (flowcharting)
structured programming
system flowchart

Discussion Questions

6-1. Why do you think it is so important to adequately document an accounting information system?

6-2. In what ways would an auditor be interested in accounting information systems documentation?

6-3. Can you think of any reasons, apart from the three reasons given in the chapter, why documentation is important?

6-4. Distinguish between system flowcharts, program flowcharts, and document flowcharts. How are they similar? How are they different?

6-5. What are the purposes of document flowcharts? How does a document flowchart assist each of the following individuals: (1) a systems analyst, (2) a system designer, (3) a computer programmer, (4) an auditor, (5) an expert in the fields of data security and internal controls?

6-6. What is the difference between a high-level system flowchart and an intermediate-level system flowchart?

6-7. A program flowchart can be thought of as a low-level system flowchart. What distinguishes it from other system flowcharts?

6-8. Although flowcharting is an art rather than a science, there are some guidelines that can be used to make "better" flowcharts. What are these guidelines for system and document flowcharts?

6-9. How are data flow diagrams different from flowcharts?

6-10. What are the four symbols used in data flow diagrams? What does each mean?

6-11. What is the relationship between a data flow diagram and a data dictionary? Describe the types of entries that would be made in a data dictionary.

6-12. What is the purpose of a decision table? How might a decision table be useful to an accountant?

6-13. Discuss the following statement. "Decision tables are more compact; program flowcharts show more processing logic."

6-14. What is structured English and what do we mean by "pseudocode"?

6-15. How do program flowcharts, decision tables, and pseudocodes facilitate structured programming? Do you think that it is advantageous to use structured programming? Why?

Problems

6-16. Draw a document flowchart to depict each of the following situations.

a. An individual from the marketing department of a wholesale company prepares five copies of a sales invoice, and each copy is sent to a different department.
b. The individual invoices from credit sales must temporarily be stored until they can be matched against customer payments at a later date.
c. A batch control tape is prepared along with a set of transactions to ensure completeness of the data.
d. The source document data found on employee application forms are used as input to create new employee records on a computer master file.
e. Delinquent credit customers are sent as many as four different inquiry letters before their accounts are turned over to a collection agency.
f. Physical goods are shipped back to the supplier if they are found to be damaged upon arrival at the receiving warehouse.
g. The data found on employee time cards are keyed onto hard disk before they are entered into a computer for processing.
h. The data found on employee time cards are first keyed onto a floppy disk before they are entered into a computer job stream for processing.
i. A document flowchart is becoming difficult to understand because too many lines cross one another. (Describe a solution).
j. Three people, all in different departments, look at the same document before it is eventually filed in a fourth department.
k. Certain data from a source document are copied into a ledger before the document itself is filed in another department.

6-17. Develop a document flowchart for the following information flow.

Individual stores in the Pit-Stop convenience chain prepare two copies of a goods requisition form (GRF) when they need to order merchandise from the central

warehouse. After these forms are completed, one copy is filed in the store's records and the other copy is sent to the central warehouse. The warehouse staff fills the order and files its copy of the GRF form in its records. When the warehouse needs to restock an item, three copies of a purchase order form (POF) are filled out. One copy is stored in the warehouse files, one copy goes to the vendor, and the third copy goes to the accounts payable department.

6-18. The XYZ Co. is a producer of industrial goods. The company receives purchase orders from its customers and ships goods accordingly. Assuming that the following conditions apply, develop a document flowchart for the XYZ Co.

a. The company receives two copies of every purchase order from its customers.
b. Upon receipt of the purchase orders, the XYZ Co. ships the goods ordered. One copy of the purchase order is returned to the customer with the order and the other copy goes into the company's purchase order file.
c. The XYZ Co. prepares three copies of a shipping bill. One copy stays in the company's shipping file and the other two are sent to the customer.

6-19. The data entry department of a small midwestern manufacturing company has the responsibility of converting all of the company's shipping and receiving information to computer records. Because accuracy in this conversion is essential, the firm employs a strict verification process. Prepare a document flowchart for the following information flow.

a. The shipping department sends a copy of all shipping orders to the data entry department.
b. A keypunch operator keys the information of the shipping order onto a floppy disk.
c. A supervisor checks every record with the original shipping order. If no errors are detected, the floppy disks are sent to the computer operations staff and the original shipping order is filed.

6-20. Identify the conventional use of each of the system flowcharting symbols shown at the top of page 211.

6-21. Suttor Industries is a maker of women's apparel and sportswear. To get some idea of how many accounts are currently being paid by the company's accounts payable processing system, the firm's chief

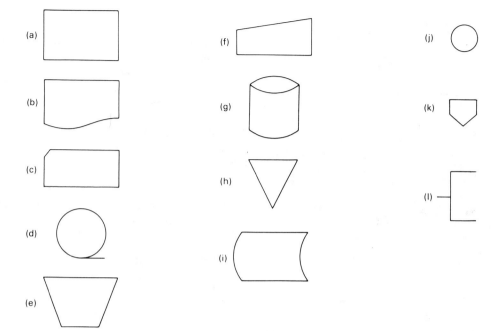

executive officer, Lucille Suttor, has asked the company's programmer, Joanne Trucko, to design a computer program. Joanne is given the documentation describing the company's disk file of accounts payable records, which stores all the accounts payable for the present month. "Joanne," said Lucille Suttor, "I'd like to know how many accounts we pay and what the average payment is for each account."

Reading the documentation describing the accounts payable file, Joanne discovers that the disk file contains one record for each account and that each record contains the total amount owed to the account. Further, because the number of accounts varies somewhat from one month to the next, the total number of records on the file is not available in the documentation.

Design a system flowchart describing the computer processing necessary to ascertain the information required by Lucille Suttor.

6-22. The order-writing department at the James Dueberry Company is managed by Frank Fox. The department keeps two types of computer files: (1) a customer file of authorized credit customers and (2) a product file of items currently sold by the company. Both of these files are direct-access files stored on

magnetic disks. Customer orders are handwritten on order forms with the James Dueberry name at the top and "item lines" for quantity, item number, and total amount desired for each product ordered by the customer below the name.

When customer orders are received, Frank Fox directs someone to input the information at one of the department's computer terminals. After the information has been input, the computer program immediately adds the information to a computerized "order" file and prepares five copies of the customer order. The first copy is sent back to Frank's department, the others are sent elsewhere.

Design a system flowchart that documents the accounting data processing described here. Also, draw a data flow diagram showing a logical view of the system.

6-23. The Gary Welter Company uses a computerized general ledger accounting system to prepare its monthly trial balance. On a weekly basis, the company uses its accounts receivable disk file, its accounts payable disk file, its payroll disk file, its assets and depreciation schedule disk file, and its cash transactions file to update its general ledger disk file. The output from its weekly processing includes a General Ledger Listing Report, a General Ledger Processing

Report, and an updated general ledger disk file. The updated general ledger file is then copied so that a backup file is available should need for one arise.

At the end of each month, the most recent copy of the general ledger disk file is used to prepare a trial balance. The general ledger file is used in a monthly closing processing run to prepare a trial balance and a Monthly Closing Processing Report. The new general ledger disk file output from this data processing is used the next week as the entire processing sequence is repeated.

Figure 6-14 outlines this processing cycle in a system flowchart. However, the descriptions for each symbol have been omitted from all but one symbol in the flowchart. Using the description of the Gary Welter

Company's general ledger accounting system, complete the flowchart by writing a description in each symbol.

6-24.   Figure 6-15 is a system flowchart for processing the sales transactions and sales remittances of the Berger Corporation. The analyst who prepared the flowchart was able to draw the appropriate symbols, but was called away before she could finish putting labels in their proper places. Fill in the missing description for each symbol. Don't forget to identify the processing runs.

6-25.   The City of Bettem is contemplating legalizing off-track betting on horse races, and has hired a systems analyst to design a real-time computer system that might perform the data gathering, recording, and data

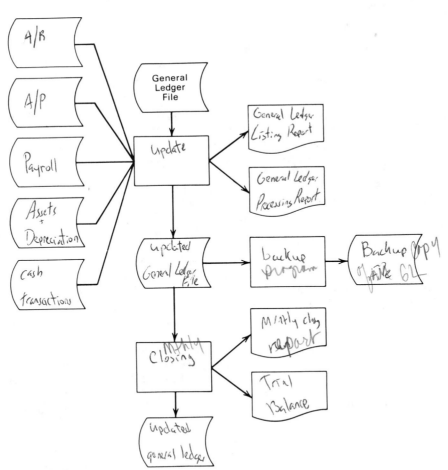

FIGURE 6-14   The computerized general ledger system of the Gary Welter Company.

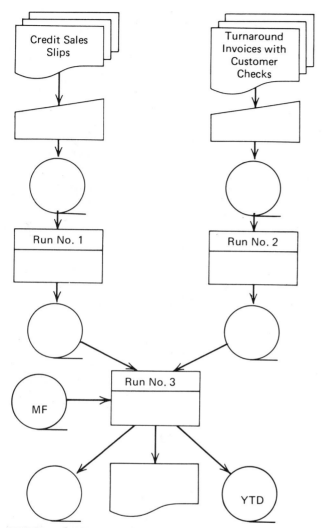

FIGURE 6-15 System flowchart for processing the sales transactions of the Berger Corporation.

processing for it. The systems analyst drew the systems flowchart in Figure 6-16 just before mobsters from the syndicate "rubbed him out." In your own words, describe how the system would work based on this flowchart. Assume that your description would be presented to the city council, so try not to be too technical.

6-26. The Kathryn Wilson Publishing Company maintains an online data base of subscriber records which it uses for preparing magazine labels, billing renewals, and so forth. New subscription orders and subscription renewals are keyed on terminals. The entry data is checked for accuracy and written on a master file. A similar process is performed for change-of-address requests. Processing summaries from both runs provide listings of master file changes.

Once a month, and just prior to mailing, the company prepares mailing labels that it forwards to its production department for affixing to magazines. At the same time, notices to new subscribers and renewal subscribers are prepared. These notices acknowledge receipt of payment and are mailed to the subscribers.

The company systems analyst, Brent Bowman, prepared the system flowchart in Figure 6-17 shortly before he left the company. As you can see, the flowchart

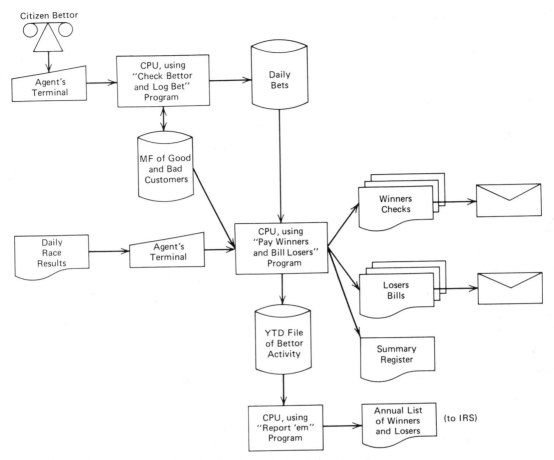

FIGURE 6-16   System flowchart for the city of Bettem's horse-racing system.

is incomplete. Using your knowledge of this and related chapters, finish the flowchart by labeling each flowcharting symbol. Don't forget also to label the processing runs labeled "CPU."

CASE ANALYSES

6-28. *Croyden, Inc.*

The factory payroll system at Croyden, Inc., works as follows. The personnel department is responsible for hiring employees and maintaining a current payroll file of workers authorized to receive payroll checks. Three copies of employee application forms are maintained. The first is forwarded to the payroll department. The remaining two are filed.

At the beginning of each workweek, payroll clerk 1 reviews the payroll file to determine the employment status of factory employees, prepares time cards, and distributes them to factory workers as they arrive for work. The employees use these time cards to punch a time clock each day they report for work.

The factory foreman prepares a clock card of authorized hours. At the end of each week, the employees' time cards are submitted to the foreman. The foreman reviews them, initials them for authorization of payment, and, with the use of the clock card, prepares a summary of regular and overtime hours. This summary is filed in the foreman's office. The employee

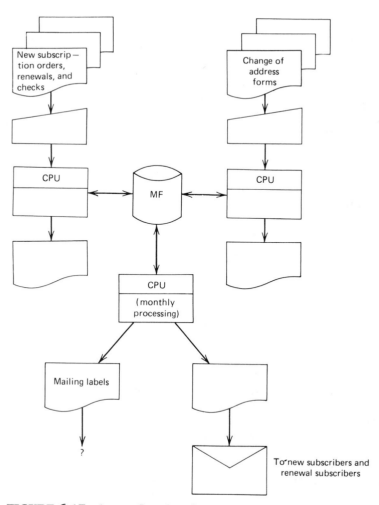

FIGURE 6-17 System flowchart for processing the subscription orders and changes for the Kathryn Wilson Publishing Company.

time cards are forwarded to clerk 2 in the payroll department.

Clerk 2 also computes regular and overtime hours for each employee and then consults the payroll master file for authorized employee status. Payroll checks for all authorized employees are prepared, as well as two copies of a payroll register. The first copy of the payroll register is filed in the payroll office. The second copy is forwarded to the bookkeeping department.

Clerk 2 turns the actual payroll checks over to clerk 1. Clerk 1, who is also responsible for the custody of the signature stamp machine, verifies the identity of

each employee before delivering signed checks to the foreman for distribution to factory workers.

The bookkeeping department verifies the accuracy of the payroll register (e.g., by cross-footing totals) and also uses this register to prepare sequentially numbered payroll checks. The check forms are forwarded to payroll clerk 2. The payroll register is then filed.

Questions

Prepare a document flowchart for the Croyden Company's payroll system. The headings for the document flowchart should include (1) factory employees,

(2) factory foreman, (3) personnel department, (4) payroll department (payroll clerk 1), (5) payroll department (payroll clerk 2), and (6) bookkeeping department.

(AICPA Adapted)

6-29. *Valpaige Company*

The Valpaige Company is an industrial machinery and equipment manufacturer with several production departments. The company employs automated and heavy equipment in its production departments. Consequently, Valpaige has a large repair and maintenance department (R & M) for servicing this equipment.

The operating efficiency of the R & M department has deteriorated over the past two years. Further, repair and maintenance costs seem to be climbing more rapidly than other department costs. The assistant controller has reviewed the operations of the R & M department and has concluded that the administrative procedures used since the early days of the department are outmoded due in part to the growth of the company. The two major causes for the deterioration, in the opinion of the assistant controller, are an antiquated scheduling system for repair and maintenance work and the actual cost system to distribute the R & M department's cost to the production departments. The actual costs of the R & M department are allocated monthly to the production departments on the basis of the number of service calls made during each month.

The assistant controller has proposed that a formal work order system be implemented for the R & M department. The production departments would submit a service request to the R & M department for the repairs and/or maintenance to be completed, including a suggested time for having the work done. The supervisor of the R & M department would prepare a cost estimate on the service request for the work required (labor and materials) and indicate a suggested time for completing the work on the service request. The R & M supervisor would return the request to the production department which initiated the request. Once the production department approved the work by returning a copy of the service request, the R & M supervisor would prepare a repair and maintenance work order and schedule the job. This work order provides the repair worker with the details of the work to be done and is used to record the actual repair and maintenance hours worked and the materials and supplies used.

Producing departments would be charged for actual labor hours worked at a predetermined standard rate for the type of work required. The parts and supplies used would be charged to the production departments at cost.

The assistant controller believes that only two documents would be required in this new system—a *Repair/Maintenance Service Request* initiated by the production departments and the *Repair/Maintenance Work Order* initiated by the R & M department.

Questions

1. For the *Repair/Maintenance Work Order* document:

   a. Identify the data items that would be important to the repair and maintenance department and the production departments that should be incorporated into the *work order*.
   b. Indicate how many copies of the *work order* would be required and explain how each copy would be distributed.

2. Prepare a document flowchart to show how the *Repair/Maintenance Service Request* and the *Repair/Maintenance Work Order* should be coordinated and used among the departments of Valpaige Co. to request and complete the repair and maintenance work, to provide the basis for charging the production departments for the cost of the completed work, and to evaluate the performance of the repair and maintenance department. Provide explanations in the flowchart as appropriate.

(CMA Adapted)

6-30. *Decision Tables for Accounts Receivable Processing*

One application of decision table analysis is for processing accounts receivable. For example, imagine that the Kenneth Garmon Company, an office products distributor, must decide what to do with delinquent credit-sales accounts. Mr. Barton Orange, the credit manager, has divided up the accounts into the following categories: (1) accounts not past due, (2) accounts 30 days or less past due, (3) accounts 31 to 60 days past due, (4) accounts 61 to 90 days past due, and (5) accounts over 90 days past due. For simplicity, assume that all transactions for each account fall neatly into the same category.

Mr. Orange decides what to do about these customer accounts based on the history of the account in general, and also the activity that has transpired during the account's delinquency period. Sometimes, for example, the customer will not communicate at all. At other times, however, the customer will either write to state that a check is forthcoming or make a partial payment. Mr. Orange has tended to be most understanding of the customers who make partial payments because he considers such payments to be acts of good faith. Mr. Orange has tended to be less understanding of the customers who only promise to pay or those who simply do not respond to follow-up bills from the company.

Mr. Orange has four potential actions to take in the case of credit delinquency. First, he can simply wait (i.e., do nothing). Second, he can send an initial letter to the customer, inquiring about the problem in bill payment and requesting written notification of a payment schedule if payment has not already been made. Third, he can send a follow-up letter of inquiry, indicating that a collection agency will be given the account if immediate payment is not forthcoming. Fourth, he can turn the account over to a collection agency. Of course, Mr. Orange prefers to use one of the first three actions rather than turn the account over to a collection agency because his company only receives half of the total bill if the collection agency becomes involved.

Questions

1. Design an efficient decision table for the Kenneth Garmon Company and provide a set of reasonable decision rules for Mr. Orange to follow. For the present, ignore the influence of a customer's credit history.
2. Expand the decision analysis you have prepared in Question 1 to include the credit history of the customer accounts. You are free to make any assumptions you wish about how this history might be evaluated by Mr. Orange.

6-31. *The Springsteen Company*

The Springsteen Company is a medium-size manufacturer of musical equipment. The accounts payable department is located at company headquarters in Asbury Field, New Jersey. The accounts payable department consists of two full time clerks and one supervisor. They are responsible for processing and paying approximately 800 checks each month.

The accounts payable process generally begins with receipt of a purchase order from the purchasing department. The purchase order is held until a receiving report and the vendor's invoice have been forwarded to accounts payable. At that time, the purchase order, receiving report, and invoice are matched together by an accounts payable clerk and payment and journal entry information are input to the computer. Payment dates are designated in the input and these are based on vendor payment terms. Company policy is to take advantage of any cash discounts offered. If there are any discrepancies among the purchase order, receiving report, or invoice, they are given to the supervisor for resolution. After resolving the discrepancies, the supervisor returns the documents to the appropriate clerk for processing. Once documents are matched and payment information is input, the documents are stapled together and filed in a tickler file by payment date until checks are issued.

When checks are issued, a copy of the check is used as a voucher cover and is affixed to the supporting documentation from the tickler file. The entire voucher is then defaced to avoid duplicate payments. In addition to the check and check copy, other outputs of the computerized accounts payable system are a check register, vendor master list, accrual of open invoices, and a weekly cash requirements forecast.

Question

Draw a context diagram and high-level data flow diagram similar to those in Figures 6-9 and 6-10 for the Springsteen Company's accounts payable process. Use the symbols shown in Figure 6-8.

7

Computer Files and Data Bases for Accounting Information Systems

Among the important questions you should be able to answer after reading this chapter are:

1. What is the difference between batch and real-time data processing?
2. What is meant by the term *accounting data base* and how does this data base differ from any other set of computer files?
3. What are the major differences between sequential computer files and direct-access computer files, and what data processing operating characteristics make some accounting applications better suited to one of these file systems rather than the other?
4. What is meant by "chaining," and how is it used to speed the access of information in the computerized accounting information system data base?
5. How are accounting data bases used in practice? For example, how are the data required for their creation, maintenance, and use organized, stored, and processed in order to provide meaningful information for management?
6. What are the advantages and disadvantages of accounting data bases?

INTRODUCTION

Chapter 5 discussed the data collection process for accounting information systems. Chapter 6 suggested some ideas for managing the flow of accounting data in terms of documenting that flow. In this chapter the flow of data through an accounting information system is traced by examining data management, storage, and retrieval in detail. Here, we are not concerned with how the data are collected. The focus is on the organization and storage of data for retrieval and use.

Two primary ways to handle data are file structures and data base structures. In this chapter, each of these will be examined in detail. Within either a file or data base structure, the data may be organized or retrieved in a certain manner. Thus, the choice of file versus data base structures leads to still more choices. There are trade-offs associated with all of these choices. These trade-offs are important to accountants in designing and using accounting information systems. Understanding them helps accountants to handle data in an optimal fashion.

We begin by reviewing the concept of a computer file and discussing how it is updated in both batch and real-time processing environments. Secondly, data bases are discussed. Although it is possible to provide data bases manually, usually the data processing volume of a business organization is large enough to make a computerized data base approach cost-effective. Thus, we concentrate on computerized data bases. The final section of the chapter examines some applications of accounting data bases through the study of system flowcharts and brief descriptions of familiar accounting data processing applications. For comparative purposes, the accounting data processing applications discussed are also flowcharted and analyzed in a manual data processing environment.

COMPUTER FILES

Storing computerized accounting data involves organizing the data into a hierarchy. At the lowest level of the data hierarchy is a character. The character may be alphabetic, numeric, or alphanumeric. Characters are grouped together to convey meaning in the next higher level of the data hierarchy, a **field.** An example of a field is a customer name or account number. Fields are grouped to form a **record.** A computer record stores information about one employee, one invoice, one customer, and so forth. At the highest level of the data hierarchy is a **file.** A **master file** is a perpetual file on which status information is stored. Examples of master files are the Alan Company's status file of inventory records (*inventory master file*) and its status file of employees (*employee master file*).

Figure 7-1 illustrates the Alan Company's computer record for an inventory application. Here, we recognize such basic information as the inventory item number, the unit price, and, of course, the balance on hand. These data fields represent the basic, "status" data of the file record and are critical to the decision-making efficiency of the Alan Company's managerial staff. In addition, we observe some less familiar information such as vendor code and pointer addresses. These will be discussed at length in the later section on data bases.

Inventory item number	Assembly code	Vendor code	Assembly pointer address	Vendor pointer address	Balance on hand	Order quantity	Purchase price	Standard price	Standard quantity	Item description	Other information and codes
2120	38	100	C	D	260	2000	4.57	3.89	500	wood stock	. . .

FIGURE 7-1   The Alan Company's inventory master file record.

Record Keys

The data item in each computer record that distinguishes one record from another on the computer file is called the **record key.** This key identifies the record on the file and is used when information retrieval requires that a specific employee, inventory item, or credit account be accessed. Consequently, the record key must also be unique. Thus, an employee file often uses an individual's social security number, an inventory file often uses a special part or raw materials number, and an accounts receivable file often uses a special account number. In each case, the data item will be unique to the individual master file record and therefore useful for record-identification purposes.

In practice, it is sometimes convenient to combine two or more record fields to serve as the record key for a single computer record. For example, an inventory file might combine the part number with a warehouse or location code to identify a record uniquely or a bank might combine its branch code with a customer account number to serve as the record key. The advantage of this approach is that the record key serves double duty. On the one hand, the combined number serves to identify the computer record uniquely. On the other hand, the separate numbers in the record key have informational content in their own right, although individually they may not be unique to the record in which they are stored. Thus, for example, two checking accounts might have the same account number but could be distinguished from each other by their different branch codes.

Where the information on a computer file serves multiple users, it is also possible for a computer record to have more than one record key. For example, the inventory manager of the Alan Company might wish to access inventory records by item number and therefore require that the inventory item number field in the inventory record be used as a record key. Alternatively, the accounts payable department might wish to access the inventory file by supplier, and therefore require that the vendor code be used as a record key. In such instances, *both* data fields in the computer record will be used as record keys. The record key given the highest priority, and the record key that must be unique, is called the **primary record key,** or just the *primary key.* For the example at hand, this would be the inventory item number.

The data fields in the computer record that are given lower priority are called **secondary record keys.** For the inventory example here, a secondary record key would be the vendor code. Secondary record keys are not necessarily unique. However, secondary record keys enable multiple users to access information from the same file and therefore lessen the number of computer files a company must maintain in order to perform its accounting operations. This concept is discussed in detail in the "Data Base" section of this chapter.

Batch versus Real-Time Data Processing

The status of the information on a master file must be updated continuously to reflect business activity. People write checks, raw materials get requisitioned from inventory, and customers buy merchandise on credit. In each case, it is necessary to update the status information on the computer file. Customarily, the activity requiring master file updating is called *transaction activity,* and the information reflecting this activity is recorded on special computer records called **transaction records.** For control and audit purposes, transaction records are almost always recorded on a file of their own. Thus, the typical company is likely to have at least two principal files for each accounting application: a master file, which maintains the account status, and a **transaction file,** which maintains the activity information described earlier.

To update an accounting master file, the transaction data are processed in one of two ways: *batch* or in *real-time* data processing. Each technique has both advantages and disadvantages but both have the same fundamental purpose: to update the status information of the master file with the data of the transaction file in a cost-effective manner.

Batch Data Processing

With **batch data processing,** transaction items are collected, grouped, and processed together, that is, in a batch. Where transaction activity is low, the transaction data are collected over time and processed only when there are enough data to make a master file update efficient—for example, once a week or even on a demand basis. However, banks that may process as many as 100,000 checks per day often choose to process check-cashing activity in batch because of certain financial control procedures available in batch processing environments. (Controls are discussed in Part Three.)

Just because transaction data are processed in batch does not mean that these data must be collected entirely with manual methods. Figure 7-2, for example, illustrates a system flowchart for **online processing,** in which the data-collection process has been partially automated.

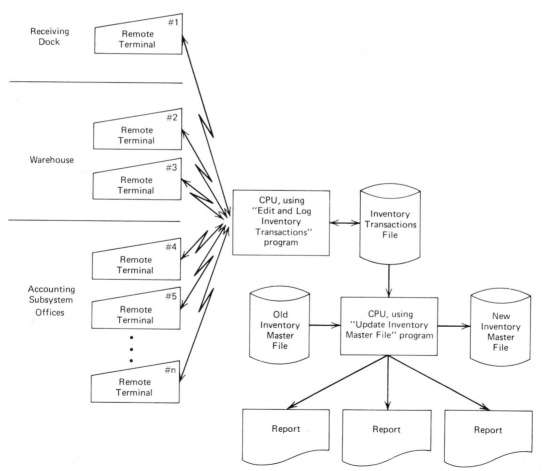

FIGURE 7-2 A system flowchart for the collection, storage, and use of inventory transaction data for the Alan Company's batch processing operations. This is a remote job entry (RJE) system.

In the figure we observe that computer terminals have been installed at the Alan Company's receiving dock, in its warehouse, and in its accounting subsystem offices. These terminals are online or in direct communication with the Alan Company's central computer, where the central processing unit can route incoming data directly to a waiting transactions file. In the flowchart, this file is stored on a magnetic disk. When a shipment of raw materials is received at the receiving dock, a receiving clerk will enter the receipts data directly into the computer via the remote terminal. These data will be checked for accuracy and then written directly on the special online transactions file, to await batch processing.

A similar description applies to the warehouse. As raw materials are disbursed from the warehouse, and also as finished goods flow back to the warehouse for temporary storage, the appropriate information is logged into the computer by means of the on-site computer terminal. Like the raw materials receipts data, the warehouse data may be checked for input accuracy and transferred to the transactions file to await batch processing.

The terminals in the accounting subsystem are used primarily for inventory file maintenance. When authorization is obtained to buy raw materials from a new supplier, for example, it will be necessary to create new inventory records to reflect the new inventory items. Similarly, when suppliers go out of business, when business with an existing supplier is terminated, or when certain raw materials are no longer purchased by the company, it may be necessary to delete specific computer records from the inventory master file. Finally, with the passage of time, it will probably become necessary to update certain other data fields in the computer record, for example, the inventory item's purchase price. In all these instances, the accounting subsystem's staff will perform the required file maintenance by inputting the transaction information to the computer through their terminals.

In a batch processing environment, transaction data are stored on a transactions file until a master file update is executed. At that time, the status of the master file records are changed to reflect the transaction activity, and the process of collecting transaction data begins anew. The transaction file containing the "old" transaction data would no longer be of immediate use and could conceivably be erased or its disk storage used for some other purpose. More commonly, however, this information will be retained as a history of activity and for certain other functions not pertinent to our immediate discussion of batch processing.

Real-Time Data Processing

Were the inventory records of the Alan Company to be processed using **real-time data processing,** the intermediate steps of maintaining the transaction data temporarily on a transactions file would not be required. In real-time processing, each transaction would cause an update of the appropriate master file at the time the transaction is entered into the system. Thus, inventory-receipts data would immediately increase the inventory balances of the affected items, inventory-requisition data would immediately decrease these inventory balances, and any file-maintenance data would immediately change the file as dictated by the type of change requested. The inventory file would therefore constantly be updated as transaction data were input—hence the term "real-time data processing."

It should be noted that in actual practice, real-time processing of accounting data is a matter of degree, depending on the particular accounting application involved. For instance, a company may be using real-time data processing to update both its inventory and cash receipts files. However, there could be a longer time lag between the occurrence of a transaction and the updating of the files for cash receipts transactions compared with inventory transactions.

Real-time data processing has the potential to maintain a more current master file. Moreover, because the master file record is accessed at the time the input transaction is processed, real-time data processing can result in a much more thorough editing job. For example, when the Alan Company's warehouse clerk inputs an inventory account number in preparation for increasing the balance field, the computer system can find the record and output the item description on the terminal screen to help the clerk verify that the desired master file record has, in fact, been found. Similarly, if the clerk inputs a master file number for which no inventory record exists, this condition can also be determined immediately and the clerk notified. Corrections of inaccurate transaction data are thus greatly enhanced with real-time data processing because faster feedback from the computer system is possible.

Real-time data processing systems also have drawbacks. For one thing, they are more expensive than batch processing systems because they must use direct-access devices such as disks instead of cheaper magnetic tape. Also, to guard against unwarranted access to the computer system and also to guard against costly human error, a much more elaborate set of controls and backup procedures must be implemented. Typically, such controls are costly to develop, costly to maintain, and almost never 100% foolproof. Thus, a real-time computer system has the potential to be much more vulnerable than a batch processing system to both intentional and unintentional input error. These problems of internal control are discussed more fully in Part Three.

A final difficulty with real-time computer systems is that they are harder to audit. This problem arises from the technicalities involved in updating direct-access records in place (discussed shortly). This difficulty also tends to add to the expense of developing, running, and documenting real-time computer systems and makes such systems less desirable.

Despite their shortcomings, real-time computer systems are gaining in popularity and now, often are replacing batch systems. One reason for this is that computer hardware costs have been decreased rapidly, and thus, it is now easier for a

company to afford a real-time data processing system. A more telling argument, however, is that companies now appear to be more willing to pay the price to obtain the advantages of immediate updating and therefore the currentness and timeliness offered by real-time computer systems.

Sequential Files

The method by which accounting data are organized in accounting files has an important bearing on how the data can be updated, retrieved, and maintained. Although there are many file structures that might conceivably be used to maintain accounting data on a computer file, we shall concentrate on only two of these: sequential files and direct-access files. These are two of the most common forms of file organization, and a knowledge of the way these structures work—their advantages and their disadvantages—is important in understanding how accounting files are used to support the various accounting activities of a business organization.

As their name implies, **sequential files** are typically organized in ascending, record-key sequence. The records on an ascending sequential file can be organized numerically, alphabetically, or chronologically. Such file records can also be arranged in some type of *descending* sequence.

Magnetic tape is the most obvious computer storage medium for sequential files, although such direct-access devices as hard disks and floppy disks can also be used to store sequential files. Sometimes, for example, a disk will be used to store a sequential file on a temporary basis, as when two sequential files are being merged (to form a single file of records organized sequentially). At other times it is more convenient to store a permanent sequential file on disk because disks have faster data transmission rates than magnetic tapes, and thus faster data processing results. Finally, for those computer systems without any magnetic tape storage, all sequential files will be stored on direct-access media by default.

Why Organize Computer Files Sequentially?

Sequential files are easy to conceptualize and therefore have intuitive appeal. This appeal is strengthened by the fact that most manual accounting systems maintain accounting data in similar, ascending sequential order (e.g., according to invoice date, employee social security number, or bank account number). Perhaps less obvious is that when sequential files are computerized, they also tend to make efficient use of computer storage. This results from the fact that, by definition, a sequential file is written on contiguous storage locations of a magnetic tape or disk, thus completely filling the computerized storage areas assigned to the file. This characteristic is not always true of direct-access storage files (as will be explained shortly).

There are many reasons why an accounting information system might choose to organize at least some of its files on a sequential basis. When chronological order is important (as, for instance, in assessing the delinquency status of credit customer accounts), a sequential ordering of credit sales records by activity date would be useful in determining which accounts receivable were overdue. This organization, by the way, would also serve as an internal control of data processing: the sequential order of the records on the file guarantees that all delinquent records will be identified because they would follow all the nondelinquent records on the file. A similar sequential ordering of purchase invoices, inventory receipts, or payment vouchers would make sense for those files that require processing in chronological order.

A sequentially-ordered file of accounting records may also be an efficient method of file organization when a large number of transaction records are involved in updating a master file at any one time. In such instances, a substantial proportion of the master file records will have to be accessed and changed no matter how the file is organized. A sequential file may be even faster than a direct-access file to perform this data

processing if both the master file and the transactions file are already in sequential order. Thus, sequential files are particularly well suited to batch processing systems in which the time between processing updates is sufficient to guarantee the high volume of transactions required to make the sequential-update process cost-effective. In such situations, a direct-access file approach may not be as efficient.

In commercial accounting applications, there are many times when every record on an accounting file must be processed. Sequential files are convenient for storing accounting records for such times and, in addition, ensure that this data processing is complete. When a company prepares billing statements for its customers, for example, it will have to access every credit record on its accounts receivable file to make sure that all customers are sent billing statements. Similarly, a bank will want to send account balance statements to all its active accounts, and an inventory control manager may want the computer to scan the balance field of every inventory record on the company's inventory master file in order to identify stock items requiring replenishment.

A final argument in favor of the sequential file is found when the processing involved in a given computer processing task requires little more than printing selected information from each record on the file. For example, it may be necessary to print a listing of accounts payable invoices or employee payroll checks. In these circumstances, computer files organized sequentially by invoice number or employee social security number would probably be as effective as any method of file organization for maintaining the necessary file information.

The reason a sequential master file is not normally used in real-time processing is because the master file must be searched from the beginning of the file, record by record, every time an update transaction is to be processed. On the average, therefore, half the master file will have to be passed (i.e., read) before the required master file record is encountered—if, in fact, it is encountered at all. With a sequential file of any reasonable length, this search time would be exorbitant. A further argument against the use of a sequential master file for real-time data processing is that such a system virtually precludes the insertion of new records or the deletion of old records on the master file. To accomplish these tasks, it would be necessary to recopy the entire file every time such a request for an addition or deletion were made. Clearly, unless the master file was tiny or these requests were very infrequent, this constant recopying of the master file would be impractical. Thus, for real-time processing it is better to use direct-access files.

Direct-Access Files

Direct-access files are commonly stored on magnetic disks or floppy disks, where each record on the file can be located directly once its physical address on the storage medium is known. This addressability characteristic of direct-access files makes them ideal for inquiry applications in which a user wants to know the up-to-the-minute status of a particular accounting record. Thus, for example, airline reservation systems, perpetual inventory systems, and point-of-sale recording systems all make use of online direct-access files.

Normally, only master files are maintained as direct-access files. This is because only master file records need be accessed repeatedly for updating and other file-maintenance purposes. Transaction files, which maintain activity data, can also be used more than once, but with these files, the system will rarely need to access a *specific* record. Thus, transaction files are usually maintained sequentially in either chronological or account number order.

Direct-Access by Indexing

Direct-access files may be organized in any number of ways, but in order to achieve the access by address, one of two methods is generally used: (1) an indexing approach or (2) a randomizing approach. With an **indexing approach,** direct-access file records are stored in any available storage locations of a magnetic disk (or other direct access storage device), and a computer program creates an index table of record keys and associated storage locations (addresses). The table is kept in either primary memory of the CPU or stored as a separate computer file. Figure 7-3 illustrates such an index.

In Figure 7-3, the index record-key entries are in ascending numeric sequence, and the letters in the figure represent physical addresses on the disk. In actual practice, of course, these letters would be numbers specifying the exact location on the disk where the corresponding master file record can be found (e.g., track and sector number). The master file records identified in this portion of the index are illustrated in Figure 7-1, and they are described in greater detail shortly.

Accessing a master file record using an index approach is much like finding a book in a library. At the library, the user first goes to the card catalog, finds the physical location of the book from the card catalog entry, and then proceeds to the shelf stacks to locate the book. In similar fashion, when a computer master file record is to be accessed, the user first has the computer program search the (sequentially ordered) index entries, and, finding the appropriate record key

Record Key	Disk Address[a]
⋮	⋮
2120	A
2121	B
2135	C
3436	D
4009	E
4668	F
⋮	⋮

FIGURE 7-3 An index of disk addresses for the Alan Company's inventory file. ([a] Letters are used symbolically here. Each letter represents a different disk address consisting of cylinder number, track number, and record count.)

listing, proceeds to the physical address of the disk dictated by the associated index entry.

Although the index lists record keys in ascending sequence, the records themselves can be scattered throughout the file in any order. The physical organization of records does not necessarily dictate the way records are accessed. After all, as long as we have the address of a desired master record, its physical position on the disk should not matter. Sometimes, however, it is convenient to order these master records sequentially on a direct-access device but still maintain an index for search and retrieval purposes. In these cases, the master file is said to be an **indexed sequential file.** An indexed sequential file is a direct-access file because the index is used to access records directly. Because the records themselves are ordered on the file, however, the master file is also sequential.

Direct-Access by Randomizing

A problem associated with direct-access by indexing is that in order to accomplish direct-access, two activities must take place. The first is the access and search of the index, to locate the address of the record. The second is accessing the record itself. A direct-access method which avoids this is called the **randomizing approach.** With a randomizing approach, the record key is converted directly to a physical address on the direct-access file and the record subsequently stored in the location thus computed. Later, when the same file record must be accessed, the computer program performs the same algorithmic (i.e., step-by-step) computation as when the master file record was first stored on the file. This should compute the same physical location address as before, and the computer system can then proceed directly to the computed address on the disk to access the record desired.

To illustrate, suppose that 575 employee records are to be stored as a direct-access disk file using a randomizing approach. Each employee is assigned a seven-digit employee number when hired, and this number is also used as a record key. One possible "prime-number division method" or "hashing scheme" of creating a direct-access file with these records would be to take a prime number that is larger than 575, such as 599 (to leave space for new hires), and set aside 599 disk locations for these records, numbered 0–598.

The hashing computation scheme for this problem would be to *divide* the employee number (for example, employee 7654321) by the prime number (599). The quotient from this calculation would be ignored but the remainder (= 299) would be used initially to store, and later to access the employee record with record key 7654321.

An important characteristic of direct-access files using a hashing algorithm for record storage and retrieval is that file records tend to be scattered randomly throughout the file, giving rise to the name **random-access file.** The greatest advantage of such an approach is that it enables a computer system to avoid a sequential search through an index before storing or accessing a particular file record.

Against this advantage is the problem that not every physical location available for use on the file will necessarily have an actual record stored in it. Thus, the method potentially wastes space. Another problem is that conflicts for the same storage location can develop since more than one record (e.g., records 7654321 and 7640544) can hash to the same location (i.e., location 299). Although several solutions to this problem are possible (for example, by creating an *overflow area* for records with the same address), they tend to complicate the procedure and inhibit processing efficiency.

Updating Direct-Access Files

Direct-access files can be updated with either batched transactions or transactions taken one at a time on a real-time basis. In either case, the updating process is roughly the same. The process begins by taking a single transaction and determining which master file record requires updating. This will identify a unique record key.

The master file record desired can then be accessed directly using either the index approach or the hashing approach discussed here.

Once the required master file record has been accessed, the actual data processing can take place. The master file record stored on the direct-access file is read and copied into the memory of the central processor. Here, the record key may be verified again to make sure this is the master file record desired, and then the record can be updated as necessary—for example, by decreasing the balance field by the quantity of an inventory–reduction transaction. Once updating has been completed, the "new" master file record is written back on the direct-access file in exactly the same location at which it was found. This completes the update process for a single transaction. If transactions are processed in batch, subsequent operations repeatedly perform these steps in analogous fashion until all the transactions have been processed.

A common question asked when reviewing the update process of direct-access files is, "What happens to the information of the 'old' master file record after an updated master file record has been written in its place on the file?" The answer to this question is simple: the information is lost. From an accounting standpoint, therefore, direct-access files have a very undesirable feature— updating in place has the potential to lose the audit trail. If a company were 100% certain that all of its transactions were recorded accurately, the audit trail problem might not be too serious. There is little likelihood, however, that all transactions are accurate. Consequently, the problem remains of how the system can recover when one or more incorrect transactions have "contaminated" the file. Furthermore, a similar problem is posed when the physical device itself fails (e.g., when the disk device suffers a "head crash" and the read/write head scars the writing surface of a disk), thus rendering the file unreadable. In both instances, the user must take precautionary measures.

The most common solution to these problems is a process called the **false update.** In effect, two copies of the master file are used at the start of each processing period—for example, at the beginning of each day. The first file is stored away as a backup copy, and the second is placed online for processing purposes. Updating is "false" in the sense that all accounting transactions processed into the master file are considered temporary until the processing day is over. At this time, the transactions stored on yet a third file may be "proofed" or checked to make sure they are legitimate by using a variety of techniques (discussed in Part Three under "Internal Control"). Only when there appears to be assurance that the day's processing has in fact been executed properly will the updated master be accepted as current. At this point, the new file is copied and another day's "false-update" processing can commence.

DATA BASES

The proliferation of computerized accounting applications in recent years has been marked by a parallel growth in the number of computer files needed to support the various data-processing functions of a business organization. Typically, companies have computerized their operations "piecemeal," that is, by computerizing first one and then another, of its manual accounting tasks until all operations are automated. Under such circumstances, the computer files needed to support such applications are developed independently of each other, and the coordination of the information stored on these files is often minimal. The result is **data redundancy,** in which many of the computer files of an organization contain duplicate information. For example, in the top portion of Figure 7-4, three files of the Alan Company are depicted in which the computer record of each file contains at least one data field common to the other two.

Although the maintenance of separate file information for each accounting application is not a bad solution, it does have several drawbacks. The maintenance of each file will require separate computer processing, for example, and the

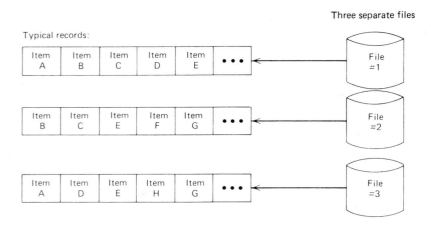

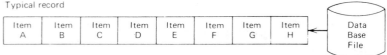

FIGURE 7-4   A data base approach to accounting files minimizes data redundancy.

practice of preparing two backup copies of each file for security purposes leads to the retention of nine files for our three-file illustration. Thus, where feasible, it often makes sense to pool the data from separate accounting applications into a common body of information called a computer **data base.** This leads us to the definition: a computer data base is a set of one or more computer files that minimizes data redundancy and is accessed by one or more application programs for the purposes of data processing.

An example of a data base approach for our three-file illustration is provided in the bottom portion of Figure 7-4. In this case, all three files have been combined into one, and most, if not all, of the data redundancy has been eliminated. Now all three application programs can utilize the same computer file, computer operations have been simplified, and fewer backup files need be maintained for security purposes.

It is uncommon to use sequential organization for accounting data bases. This is because, by definition, sequentially-ordered data are accessed in some predetermined order. Usually, it is unlikely that any particular sequential ordering is ideal for more than one organizational subsystem sharing a common computer data base. With multiple use of the data, therefore, the data must be sorted into a different logical sequence for each accounting application. This is both inefficient and time-consuming. Thus, sequential organization is rarely used to organize the data bases in accounting information systems.

The data base approach has several different advantages. One obvious advantage is that the data base makes efficient use of computerized storage space while continuing to serve the informational needs of the previously separate files' users. Moreover, when separate subsystems within an organization pool their data, a second advantage is that each subsystem has access to the other's information. For example, pooling of manufacturing and marketing data will have the added capability of providing distributional sales data, which may be of assistance to the production subsystem in planning manufacturing levels.

Where subsystems are each gathering their own data, the data base approach also has the important advantage of relieving some of the users from their data-gathering responsibilities. Of course, this is not always the case. Sometimes the data required by one subsystem can be acquired only by that subsystem's users. However, even partial relief from the burdens of data collection and storage can sometimes save a company thousands of dollars yearly in terms of labor hours and computer data processing time.

Physical Versus Logical Data Structures

Data bases are typically stored on direct access storage devices such as magnetic disks. The term **physical data structure** refers to where the computer records physically reside on the disk and how these disk records are accessed. For a sequentially ordered file, records are physically located next to each other in sequence. For example, customer records on a customer master file would be stored sequentially by customer identification number. With data bases, records need not be grouped together in any particular physical order. In fact, data base records may be dispersed throughout the storage medium. This means that a customer record might physically reside next to a vendor record or an inventory record. The data base is a pool of data elements, therefore, physical location is not so important as in a file system.

What does matter is the **logical data structure.** An application program has a logical order in which it expects to find records. A data base can satisfy this record-ordering requirement by linking records together. For example, a customer record that is stored physically next to an inventory record can be logically linked to other

customer records when data are accessed by an accounts receivable application program. In this way, the logical data structure is independent of the physical ordering of data in the data base.

To provide the logical ordering of data records, the physical data records are *chained together* with **pointer fields.** These pointer fields indicate the locations of other, similar records. Sometimes the pointer fields are embedded in the data base records, other times they may be contained separately in an index. For example, a pointer field in a customer record might contain an address for the next customer record (see again Figure 7-1). Alternatively, an index file can be maintained that lists customer identification record keys and the associated address for the next customer record.

The distinction between physical data structures and logical data structures is important to accounting information systems because it differentiates between the *maintenance* and *upkeep* of records on the one hand (i.e., the steps needed to keep records current), and the *uses* of these records (e.g., the presentation of the information on a managerial report) on the other. Data bases must have some sort of physical structure. But if the data in a data base can be accessed in logical ways that are different from physical structure, greater use can be made of the data. This is another way of saying that data bases can increase processing flexibility by enabling the accounting information system to produce managerial reports independent of the way the data are stored on the storage media.

Schemas and Subschemas

The logical structure of a data base and the interrelationships among data elements are described in the data base **schema.** This schema is part of the data base management system (to be discussed shortly) and may be thought of as a *map* of the data base. Any particular user or application program will normally be interested in only part of the data base. This view is contained in a **subschema.** Whereas the schema can be pictured as a map of an entire *city*, the subschema would be a picture of specific *neighborhoods*. The schema and subschema provide links between the physical and logical structures in the data base.

Data Dictionaries

From the standpoint of the accountant, the basic unit of information in computerized accounting information systems is the data item. Examples of data items include an employee name, a bank account number, a payroll withholding year-to-date balance, and so forth. These data items are initially collected in separate fields on source documents, stored in separate fields of one or more computer records, altered by other data items on transaction or activity records, and output in separate fields of managerial reports.

A **data dictionary** is a computer file that maintains descriptive information about the data items of an accounting information system. Thus, a data dictionary is a data file about data. Each computer record of the data dictionary contains information about a single data item used in the accounting information system. This item information may include:

1. Classification information about the item's length, data type (alphabetic, numeric, alphanumeric, etc.), range (e.g., from 1 to 5 if the item were a type of employee code), and so forth.
2. The identity of the source document(s) used to create the data item.
3. The names of the accounting programs that modify the data item (e.g., the programs that perform maintenance).
4. The names of the accounting programs that update the data item.
5. The identity of the computer programs or individuals permitted to access the data item for the purpose of record inquiry.
6. The identity of the computer programs or individuals *not* permitted to access the data item for the purpose of record inquiry.

As new data items are added to an accounting data base, they are also used to create new computer records in the data dictionary. Similarly, when old data items are deleted from the data base, their corresponding records may be dropped from the data dictionary. Finally, when new computer programs are added to the set of accounting information system programs that access data items in the system, the data dictionary is updated to reflect the fact that these new programs now use certain items to perform data processing tasks.

Data dictionaries have a variety of uses. One is as a documentation aid to programmers and systems analysts who study, correct, or enhance either the computerized data base or the computer programs that access it. As suggested in points 5 and 6 in the preceding list, the data dictionary is also used for data base security—for example, to prohibit certain employees from gaining access to sensitive payroll data.

Accountants can also make good use of a data dictionary. For example, a data dictionary can help establish an audit trail because it identifies the input sources of data items, the potential computer programs that use or modify particular data items, and the managerial reports on which the data items are output. When an accountant is assisting in the design of a new computer system, a data dictionary can serve as an important documentation tool in establishing data paths for the new system. Finally, a data dictionary can serve as an important aid when investigating or documenting internal control procedures because the basis for edit tests, methods of data security, and so forth may be stored as part of the dictionary's file information.

An accounting information system need not maintain a centralized data base of accounting information to make good use of a data dictionary. Even a manual accounting system or a partially automated system can use a data dictionary to advantage. Conversely, it is possible to implement a very effective data base without simultaneously maintaining a data dictionary. However, given the wide variety of uses that can be made of a data dictionary, taking an inventory of data items and maintaining this information as a computerized data dictionary is often one of the first tasks to be performed when implementing a data base system. Given the preceding discussion, the accountant's role in the creation, maintenance and use of this dictionary should be obvious.

DATA BASE STRUCTURES

There are a number of ways that data bases can be structured. Data base structures are important to accounting information systems because, as should be clear from the preceding examples, the way in which accounting records are organized has an important bearing on how the information can be used to produce accounting reports. Since a data base is merely a computer file that minimizes data redundancy and is accessed by one or more users, conceivably any type of physical file organization could be used in a data base. However, three types of data structures are typically used in accounting information systems: (1) hierarchical data structures, (2) network data structures, and (3) relational data structures. Each of these will now be described briefly.

Hierarchical Structures

Accounting data are often organized in a hierarchy. For example, a company can have several sales offices, each sales office can have several salespeople, each salesperson can have several customers, each customer can make several purchases, and each purchase can include several items. As illustrated in Figure 7-5, the data generated by the sales office have a natural hierarchical structure: the line items of a single purchase make up a sales invoice, the invoices can be grouped together by customer, the customers can be classified by salesperson, and salespeople can be grouped together by sales office. Thus, in Figure 7-5, the data in such an accounting application fan out in successively smaller branches like a tree. For this reason,

hierarchical data base structures are also known as **tree structures.**

Typically, hierarchical data structures have a genealogy that naturally organizes the data by

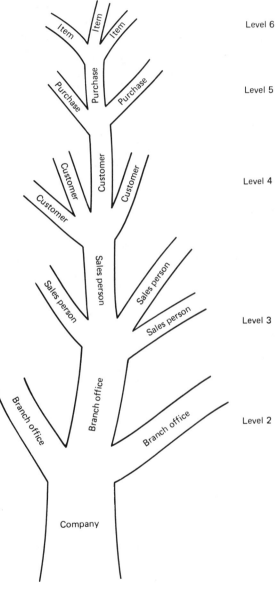

FIGURE 7-5 The hierarchy of marketing data for a sales company. This kind of data organization is called a tree data structure.

levels. This means that some data items must first exist before successive data levels can be created. In our sales illustration, for example, salespeople must exist before there are customers, customers must exist before there are sales, and sales must exist before there are line items on a particular invoice. For any two adjacent record levels, the "elder," or higher-level, record is sometimes called the **parent record,** and the "younger," or lower-level, record is called the **child record.** Similarly, two child records belonging to the same parent record are called **sibling records.**

The hierarchy of data in a tree structure is preserved by storing the information in the data base using the parent-child relationships that organize it. Thus, the line items of the same sales invoice are stored together, the sales invoices of the same customers are stored together, the customer records for a single salesperson are stored together, and all the data records for the same sales office are stored together. Here, the term *stored together* could mean that like items are *physically* stored next to one another on the same storage medium, or that like items are *logically* linked to one another with chain addresses on a magnetic disk. Each parent record acts as a natural control break for the group of records, and the aggregation of sales data for each data level is straightforward with this type of structure.

Network Structures

Not all accounting data can be organized in a natural hierarchy. Often, data items within accounting records are interrelated in several ways, and a single hierarchical data structure cannot adequately capture data relationships in a simple manner. For example, the inventory records of the Alan Company are related by type of inventory item (e.g., finished goods versus raw materials), by vendor, by usage in manufacture (i.e., assembly code), by storage location in a warehouse, and so forth. Thus, the data in the inventory records are related to one another in several ways and no simple physical ordering of the records can reflect these multiple relationships.

Accounting records that have multiple relationships with one another can be linked together in logical **network data bases** with the use of record chains. Pointer address fields can be embedded in the data records to link similar inventory records together in record chains. As noted earlier, the result is that the data base maintains data relationships that the computer system can then use to produce output reports.

Relational Structures

The types of data base structures just discussed require that they be planned in advance. This means that if accounting data of one type (e.g., raw materials inventory records) are to be used in conjunction with accounting data of another type (e.g., finished goods inventory records), the data base must be constructed to accommodate this linkage. Many relationships can exist among accounting data items, and it is extremely difficult to anticipate all of them at the time an accounting data base is first constructed. Thus, while the creation and use of an accounting data base is typically a vast improvement over a simple file, a hierarchical data structure or a network data structure affords little *additional* processing flexibility once further data processing needs are encountered.

The problem of accommodating data relationships after a data base is created can be partially solved with the use of a **relational data base.** Like other types of data structures, the relational data base is typically stored on magnetic disk—for example, as a direct-access file. In addition to the file records, however, a relational data base also includes several indexes or **inverted lists** to assist the computer system in accessing accounting records.

To illustrate, consider the data relationships of the raw materials inventory records of the Alan Company. One way to organize these data would be by vendor. Another way would be to organize these data by assembly. Yet a third way would be to organize them numerically by inventory item number. A fourth way to organize this data would be by standard order quantity.

To permit an accounting information system to access the data from the inventory data base in all these different ways, a relational data base uses a set of indexes, as illustrated in Figure 7-6. When a listing of inventory items by vendor is required, the computer system can use the vendor index to access raw material inventory records in order of supplier. Similarly, when a listing of inventory items by number is required, the computer system can use the raw materials index to access raw material inventory records in order of inventory number.

The two major advantages of relational data bases are that (1) they enable the computer system to accommodate a variety of inquiries in an efficient manner, and (2) additional indexes can be constructed at a later point in time as new data processing requirements dictate. In terms of the cost-effective use of accounting data, these advantages are very important.

The three major disadvantages of relational data bases are that (1) the index portion of the data base must be created and maintained along with the data base records themselves, (2) the index itself requires disk storage and in some cases, may be very large, and (3) the file index must be searched sequentially before the actual records are obtained. Despite these drawbacks, relational data bases are a very popular way of structuring data in accounting information system data bases.

DATA BASE MANAGEMENT SYSTEMS

As the name implies, **data base management systems** are special computer programs that maintain, manipulate, and retrieve the basic data within the data base and provide tools for creating useful reports to organizational management. Thus, for example, a typical data base management system would be capable of adding, deleting, or modifying accounting records in an accounting information system data base, sorting or indexing these records into a predetermined sequence according to any identifiable data field within the records, modifying pointers, and printing specific records according to some specified selection criterion.

In typical accounting applications, data base management systems act as an interface between computerized accounting programs and the accounting data. This relationship is illustrated in Figure 7-7 for a simplified payroll application. In the figure, various types of payroll programs are listed on the left-hand side and the accounting data base is depicted as a file symbol on the right-hand side. In between is the data base man-

Vendor		Assembly		Raw Materials		Standard Quantity	
Value	Disk Address[a]	Value	Disk Address[a]	Value	Disk Address[a]	Value	Disk Address[a]
100	A	38	A	2000s	A	100	B
	D		C		B		E
	F		D		C	250	D
228	B	40	B	3000s	D	400	F
	C		E	4000s	E	500	A
402	F		F		F		C

[a] Letters refer to physical disk addresses.

FIGURE 7-6   Indexes for the records in a relational data base.

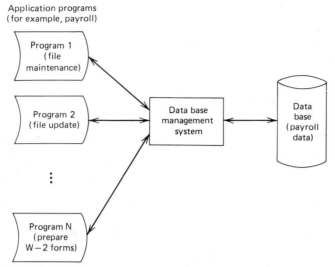

Application programs
(for example, payroll)

FIGURE 7-7 A data base management system acts as an interface betweeen the computer programs of an accounting application and the data base of accounting data required.

agement system that supports the following types of data processing.

1. Direct access to the accounting information system data base for data inquiries.
2. Maintenance such as changing employee address information or altering the number of dependents claimed for federal income tax withholding.
3. Updating, such as updating year-to-date totals when new paychecks are distributed to employees.
4. Reporting, such as issuing federal W-2 statements of wages earned.
5. Sorting, such as listing payroll records alphabetically by employee last name instead of sequentially by employee social security number.

Inasmuch as data base management systems involve sophisticated computer programming, most organizations acquire DBMSs from commercial sources. DBMS software packages are available for many different types of computers, including microcomputers. Figure 7-8 lists exam-

ples of data base management systems, along with names of the commercial vendor for each system. Prices for these systems are as little as $50 for microcomputer based DBMSs and in excess of $100,000 for large systems. As you might expect, the larger and more expensive the DBMS, the more flexible and versatile it is likely to be.

Data Definition Languages (DDLs) and Data Manipulation Languages (DMLs)

As noted earlier, data base management systems perform a large number of data-related tasks. Usually, these tasks are performed with the help of special programming languages called **data definition languages (DDLs)** and **data manipulation languages (DMLs).** For example, data bases must first be initialized with data. Usually, this is performed with a data definition language. Data definition languages have commands for specifying such data characteristics as record formats, record keys, record sizes, and data structures.

Data Base Management System	Software Vendor (hardware system)
Microcomputers*	
Condor 3	Condor Computer Corp.
Cornerstone	Infocom Inc.
DataEase	Software Solutions Inc.
dBASE III Plus, dBASE IV	Ashton-Tate
DDQuery	Venet-Ulyiams Inc.
Enrich	Migent Software Inc.
Formula IV	Dynamic Microprocessor Associates Inc.
Foxbase Plus 2.1, Foxbase Plus 386 2.1	Fox Software
Paradox OS/2	Borland Int'l
Power-base	Compuware Corp.
R:base 5000, R:base OS/2	Microrim Inc.
Minicomputers, Mainframe Computers**	
ADABAS	Software AG (IBM computers)
BASIS	Batelle Columbus Laboratories
DATABASIC	Consumer Systems
DATACOM/DB	Applied Data Research, Inc. (IBM computers)
DBMS-10, DBMS-20	Digital Equipment Corp. (Dec-system -10 and -20)
DB2	IBM (MVS Systems)
DG/SQL	Data General Corp., (AOSNS)
Focus	Information Builders, Inc. (VM, MVS, Wang VS)
IDM/R	Cullinet Software
IDS/II	Honeywell Information Systems (Honeywell DM-IV)
IMAGE	Hewlett Packard
INQUIRE	Infodata Systems, Inc.
IMS/VS	IBM (IBM computers)
MODEL 204	Computer Corp. of America
RAMSIS II	Mathematica Products Group, Inc.
SEED	International Data Base Systems, Inc.
SYSTEM 1022	Software House (DEC systems)

Data Base Management System	Software Vendor (hardware system)
SYSTEM 2000/80	Intel Corp.
TOTAL	Cincom Systems, Inc.

* All systems are relational data bases for IBM microcomputers and compatibles.

** Systems without hardware modifiers are not hardware dependent.

FIGURE 7-8 Examples of commercially available data base management systems (DBMSs). Computer hardware on which these software systems run is listed in parentheses.

A data manipulation language enables users to access data base records, update data base records, replace data base records, delete data base records, and protect data base records from unauthorized access. In short, therefore, DMLs permit users to manipulate the data stored in the data base. Unlike other types of high-level programming languages, however, DDLs and DMLs usually perform specific data functions as part of the software of the data base management system. In this sense, they are not general-purpose programming languages, but perform specific tasks.

Advantages and Disadvantages of Data Base Management Systems

Data base management systems are important to accounting information systems because they free the user from the mechanical aspects of data inquiries, record maintenance, updating, and reporting, and permit the user to concentrate on the *uses* of accounting data. This is not to say that data base management systems eliminate these functions but rather that they *facilitate* such functions and make them easier to perform. Thus, users can spend less time on these functions and more time on the managerial uses of accounting data.

In a wider context, perhaps the most important aspect of a data base management system is the formal recognition that many different types of accounting applications (or other information processing applications) can use the same type of data base system, and that the development of a good, flexible, maintenance-and retrieval system is not application dependent. The result is that software developers have been able to write very sophisticated DBMSs that greatly expand the user's capacity to store accounting data, greatly accelerate the user's ability to retrieve data, and greatly improve the user's flexibility in changing, processing, or reporting accounting data. These advances have led accounting information systems specialists to think not in terms of specific accounting applications, but in terms of the general data-manipulating requirements of the applications.

There are also some important disadvantages of data bases. Perhaps the most important is that DBMSs can be expensive to lease, purchase, or develop. It is not uncommon, for example, for a mainframe system to cost in excess of $100,000, and some systems can only be leased, not purchased.

Another disadvantage is that data base management systems can be inefficient to run. The addition of a DBMS to a computer system means that additional software must be executed before file records are accessed. This additional computer time can add to the total time it takes to execute a data processing task.

A final disadvantage is that many data base management systems are *machine dependent,* meaning they can only run on certain types of computers. Figure 7-8 provides some idea of this dependency by listing the computer systems on which the various software packages work. Machine dependency can pose a problem to an organization that might want to switch to different computer hardware in the future. Despite these shortcomings, the use of data base management systems is growing.

ACCOUNTING APPLICATIONS USING DATA BASES

To conclude this chapter, we present illustrations of how the computerized data base concept can efficiently contribute to the processing of accounting transactions and the preparation of financial reports. These illustrations will center on the following accounting processes.

1. The accounting cycle steps leading to the preparation of a company's income statement and balance sheet.
2. The preparation of budget projections, the comparison of actual operating results with these projections, and the completion of budget performance reports.
3. The processing of cash disbursements for credit purchases (emphasizing the credit purchase of inventory).

These three processes will first be discussed using manual data processing methods. Then, to emphasize the data processing effectiveness of computerized data base systems, we will examine them again with a data base approach. It should be emphasized, however, that because every company's system is somewhat different, the specific data processing procedures will vary from one company to another.

Manual Data Processing Systems

Under a manual data processing system, much of the work associated with each one of the three accounting processes described earlier would have to be performed independently. As business transactions occur, they would be processed through a company's accounting cycle steps (discussed in Chapter 1) for ultimate appearance within financial reports—principally, the income statement and the balance sheet.

Subsequently (perhaps monthly), various transaction data recorded within the company's general and subsidiary ledgers (e.g., the total sales reflected in the general ledger account and the sales product line reflected in the sales subsidiary ledger) would then be used to prepare budget performance reports. Under the supervision of the company's budget committee, the long-range and short-range budgets would have been prepared prior to the beginning of the particular year's operating activities. At the close of each month the accountants would take the budget projection financial data, compare these data with the actual financial results contained within the ledgers, and prepare management-by-exception performance reports of significant budget variations. Figure 7-9 summarizes this

data processing for the accounting-cycle activities and for budgetary analysis.

We will now turn our attention to the manual data processing activities associated with inventory credit purchases and the issuance of cash disbursement checks for these inventory purchases. These activities are summarized in Figure 7-10. As various inventory items (such as raw materials needed for sporting goods production) reach their reorder points, a company's inventory storeroom clerks would initiate purchase order requisitions for each inventory item's reorder quantity.

When the inventory items arrive at the receiving platform, the receiving managers check their

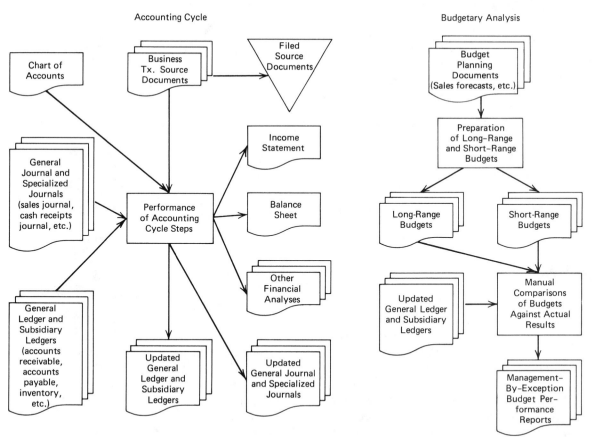

FIGURE 7-9 The manual process associated with accounting cycle and budgetary analysis work.

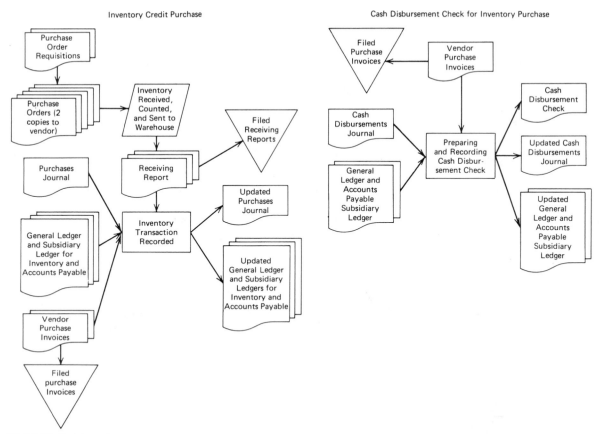

FIGURE 7-10 The manual processes associated with an inventory credit purchase and a cash disbursement check for that purchase.

purchase-order files to ascertain that this inventory delivery was actually ordered by the company. The inventory items are then counted, and this count is recorded on a receiving report. When the receiving report arrives in the accounting subsystem, the accountants compare the receiving report data with their copies of the purchase order and the purchase invoice bill from the vendor. The accountants then record the inventory purchase transaction in the *purchases journal* (assuming a periodic inventory system, the journal entry would be *debit* the *purchases* account and *credit* the *accounts payable* account). This transaction is eventually posted to both the general ledger and the subsidiary

ledgers for inventory and accounts payable. In order to take advantage of cash discounts offered (e.g., terms of 2/10, n/30), the purchase invoice would be filed (together with the receiving report copy) according to cash discount payment date so that it can be paid within the discount time period.

When the payment date of the invoice arrives, a cash disbursement check is authorized, prepared, and recorded in the cash disbursements journal, posted to the general ledger and the accounts payable subsidiary ledger, and mailed to the vendor together with one copy of the purchase invoice. (The journal entry recorded would be *debit* the *accounts payable* account and *credit* the *cash* account.) The second copy of the purchase invoice is kept on file within the accounting subsystem in a *paid invoices file*. Figure 7-10 summarizes in broad terms these accounting processes for an inventory credit purchase and for the issuance of a cash disbursement check relating to this inventory purchase.

Computerized Data Processing Systems

As emphasized in the preceding section, each accounting process in a manual data processing system (such as performing the accounting-cycle steps, analyzing budget variations, and processing inventory purchase and cash disbursement transactions) is performed independently. With the use of a computerized data base system, however, a company's computer is able to integrate the performance of accounting processes, thereby contributing to data processing efficiency.

To illustrate, Figure 7-11 reflects in broad terms the accounting processes associated with financial statement preparation and budgetary planning and controlling activities. A company's journal entries during an accounting period and

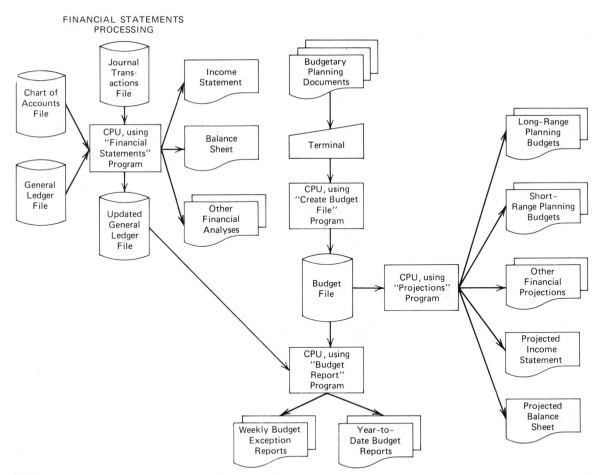

FIGURE 7-11 System flowchart of the computerized data base processes associated with financial statement preparation and budgetary planning and controlling.

its period-end adjusting entries are accumulated on a magnetic disk file called the *journal transactions file.* Using this file together with the *chart of accounts file* and the *general ledger file,* and utilizing the *financial statements program,* the computer then performs the necessary accounting cycle steps for the preparation of the company's financial statements. (Additional computer runs would be necessary to update the accounts receivable subsidiary ledger, the accounts payable subsidiary ledger, the inventory subsidiary ledger, etc.) An income statement, a balance sheet, and other financial analyses (such as a retained earnings statement) are printed out by the computer and an updated file for the general ledger is created.

Figure 7-11 also discloses the budgetary planning and controlling activities within the company. The *budget file* in Figure 7-11 includes long- and short-range budget projection data. This file results from the execution of the *create budget file program.* By using the *projections program,* the computer can print out the company's long- and short-range budgets as well as the projected financial statements. The heart of the integration between the accounting cycle activities and the budget activities is in the *budget report program.* The data inputs to this program are the *budget file* and the actual operating results contained within the *updated general ledger file.* Through the *budget report program* using these files, weekly budget exception reports and year-to-date budget reports are printed out by the computer.

An examination of the system flowchart for the credit purchases of inventory and the authorization of accounts payable cash payments for these purchases (see Figure 7-12) reveals further integration of accounting processes. Using the *edit and purchase order log program* with purchase order requisitions as input, an *unsorted purchase orders file* is prepared. Using a sort utility program, a *sorted file of purchase orders* by vendors is created. The *vendor master file* (which contains information about each inventory vendor such as name, address, etc.) and the *purchase*

orders sorted by vendors file are then used as input to the *purchase order program.* This program creates five purchase order copies, a summary log by vendors of purchase orders processed, and a *pending purchase orders file* (i.e., purchase orders mailed to vendors for which the inventory items have not yet been received).

The heart of the integration of the accounting processes for inventory purchases and cash payment authorizations associated with these purchases is the *match pending purchase orders to purchase invoices program.* The set of input data for this program will be the file of pending purchase orders and the purchase invoice receipts file. The latter file is created as follows. When a vendor purchase invoice is mailed to the company, the invoice is manually compared to the receiving report relating to the particular inventory purchase. If the two source documents are in agreement (that is, the quantity of inventory items shown on the receiving report agrees with the quantity reflected on the purchase invoice), the data from the "confirmed vendor purchase invoice" such as inventory description, inventory quantity, and total cost, are keyed into the terminal to create the *purchase invoice receipts file.*

Regarding those pending purchase order file items for which a match is obtained between a purchase order and a purchase invoice (from the "purchase invoice receipts file"), the purchase invoice data will be printed out on a *matched purchase invoice report.* The *match pending purchase orders to purchase invoices program* will also update the company's inventory accounts (i.e., the updated inventory master file created from the old *inventory master file;* see Figure 7-12) and prepare the *inventory authorized payments file.* This file will be used in other computer runs to process cash disbursement checks for creditors (see Figure 7-13) and to update the general ledger and accounts payable subsidiary ledger.

Figure 7-13 illustrates the system flowchart associated with issuing cash disbursement checks to creditors. Determining which liabilities are due

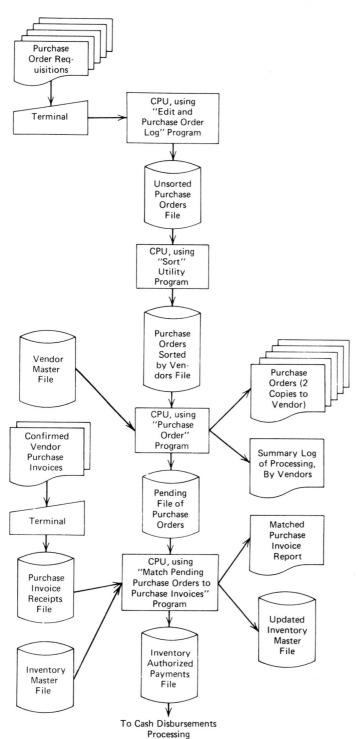

FIGURE 7-12 The computerized data base processes associated with credit purchases of inventory and cash payment authorizations.

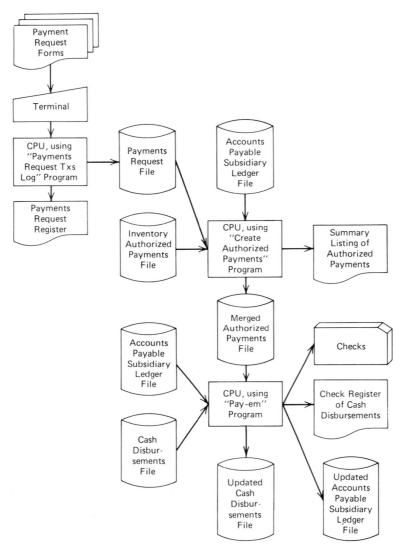

FIGURE 7-13 System flowchart of the computerized data base processes associated with issuing cash disbursement checks to creditors.

for payment in order to take advantage of any cash discounts offered as well as to avoid delinquent vendor payments is handled by the *create authorized payments program.* The inputs to this program are the *accounts payable subsidiary ledger file,* the *inventory authorized payments file* (created in the system flowchart of Figure 7-12), and the *payments request file.* The payments request file reflects liabilities other than

for the credit purchase of inventory. Both this file and the *payments request register* are created by using the *payments request transaction log program,* whose input consists of various payment request forms (such as requests for insurance premium payments, for monthly utility bill payments, and for monthly rent payments).

The *merged authorized payments file* and a *summary listing of authorized payments* are prepared using the *create authorized payments program.* Included on the *merged authorized payments file* are data (such as name, address, and amount owed) regarding each creditor that should be issued a cash disbursement check.

Through the execution of the *pay-em program,* which uses as input the *merged authorized payments file,* the *accounts payable subsidiary ledger file,* and the *cash disbursements file* (containing the date, check number, payee, amount, etc., for each cash disbursement check issued), individual cash disbursement checks for issuance to creditors are prepared. In addition, this program updates the accounts payable subsidiary ledger file and the cash disbursements file and also creates a *check register of cash disbursements. The updated cash disbursement file* will be used as input in a subsequent computer run (not described here) to prepare the company's bank reconciliation statement.

Concluding Comments on Accounting Applications

The purpose of illustrating the preceding accounting applications under both a manual data processing system and a computerized data base processing system was to emphasize the data processing effectiveness that can result from the latter system. A computerized data base system can integrate the performance of many accounting processes, thereby contributing to data processing efficiency. This integration is normally difficult to achieve under a manual data processing system. It should be noted, however, that establishing a computerized data base system in a company will require a significant expenditure. Unless the anticipated benefits from the data base system are expected to exceed the system's costs, some alternative data processing system should be considered.

AIS at Work—NAARS: An Accounting Data Base

While many companies maintain their own data bases for internal applications, there are also external data bases. External data bases are sometimes referred to as public data bases since they are available to anyone who elects to subscribe to them.

An example of a public data base that is available for online access is the National Automated Accounting Research System (NAARS). NAARS is provided through the joint efforts of the American Institute of Certified Public Accountants and Mead Data Central, Inc., and made available through the LEXIS® search and retrieval system. NAARS is a computerized data base containing information from thousands of annual reports. The information included in the data base consists of financial statements, footnotes, and auditor reports from annual reports of thousands of companies whose stocks are listed on an exchange or traded over-the-counter. In addition to annual report information, the NAARS data base contains Generally Accepted Accounting Principles information such as Accounting Research Bulletins, Accounting Principles Board Opinions, Auditing Standards, and Financial Accounting Standards Board Statements and Interpretations.

As you can imagine, the NAARS data base is an extremely useful tool for those interested in conducting accounting research. Public accounting firms use NAARS in many different research applications. For example, the data base can be used to determine how companies are accounting for certain events, to investigate disclosures related to special accounting standards, and to identify trends in reporting. The data base is used by accounting researchers at universities, industry management, authoritative accounting bodies such as the FASB, and government agencies.

Access to NAARS is typically obtained through a personal computer and a modem. A subscriber can search the data base to retrieve data which meets a specific requirement. For example, annual reports can be searched for footnotes that describe special leasing arrangements. Search terms are defined by the user (subscriber). NAARS reveals the number of documents in the data base which meet the search specifications. It can provide the full text of those documents or partial text, as requested. The search terms can be modified if the results are not satisfactory. As you might expect, the successful use of this data base is dependent on the skill of the user in developing a search strategy and specifying the correct terms. Familiarity with the system improves the efficiency of use.

Two examples of how searches can be made with NAARS illustrate the actual use of the system. For example number one, suppose an audit client is interested in finding examples of how other companies disclose decisions to amortize patents. The search instructions to the computer might be phrased as follows: I/S (AMORTIZ!) AND FTNT (AMORTIZ! W/SEG (PATENT W/10 AMORTIZ!)). This tells the computer to look for reports where the income statement contains the word "amortize" in any form (e.g., amortization, amortized) and also a footnote about amortization that includes the word patent within ten words of the word "amortize." W/SEG stipulates that the words "patent" and "amortization" should occur within the same segment in order to meet the search specifications. In this case, the segment is the footnote segment. Within seconds, the user is advised of how many reports for specified fiscal years meet the search criteria stated.

A simpler search example involves a researcher interested in obtaining examples of qualified opinions in auditors' reports. The search terms REPRT (SUBJECT TO) are sufficient for this search. This would cause the data base to search auditor reports for "subject to" opinions. In the event that the researcher is interested in examples of "subject to" opinions that have been qualified due to some specific condition, the search can be narrowed by using terms that describe the condition (e.g., uncertainty over the outcome of pending litigation).

SUMMARY

This chapter has discussed the concept of computerized data bases and has illustrated how such data bases are used in accounting information systems. In such systems, the principal means by which accounting data are stored and referenced is through the use of individual records which are collectively organized into computer files.

Typically, the master file in an accounting application is maintained and updated by transactions that reflect business activity. These transactions may be used to update the master file in at least one of two ways: (1) in batch data processing and (2) in real-time data processing. Using a batch approach, transaction records are collected on a separate computer file for a period of time and then used to update the master file in periodic data processing cycles. Using a real-time approach, the master file is updated as soon as the transaction record is input to the computer. Both magnetic tape files and magnetic disk files are suitable computer storage media for batch processing. However, only magnetic disk files are normally used in real-time data processing situations because of the need for immediate access to master file records.

There are two principal types of file organization: sequential and direct access. Normally, sequential files store computer records in ascending record-key sequence, although the use of some other data field in addition to the record key is sometimes used for this purpose. Sequential files have a natural organizational logic, use file space efficiently, and are often as effective as any method of file organization when a large proportion of a master file must be accessed in a data processing task. Direct-access files, on the other hand, exploit the addressability characteristic of their storage media and permit their users to locate file records on a more immediate basis. This chapter has discussed two major techniques for accessing file records on direct-access files: (1) an indexing approach and (2) a randomizing approach. Although fundamentally different in concept, both of these approaches permit the direct access of a computer record on a direct-access file without the need to search through a master file on a record-by-record basis.

Accounting data bases are typically implemented as direct-access using magnetic disks. Data bases minimize the data redundancy that results when different accounting applications maintain duplicate information in their files, and data bases are also an efficient means of integrating the accounting information that is collected, processed, and used by different subsystems within an organization. Thus, we have defined an accounting information system data base as a set of one or more computer files that minimizes data redundancy and is accessed by one or more application programs for the purposes of data processing.

To produce reports from information stored in a data base, it is usually necessary to access computer records in a specific order. A common means of accomplishing this data access is through the use of pointer addresses, in which each computer record in the logical sequence stores the disk address of the next record in one of its data fields.

The last section of this chapter illustrated three accounting applications that might be performed either manually or with a computerized data base: (1) the preparation of a company's financial statements, (2) the preparation of budget reports, and (3) the processing of cash disbursements for credit purchases, emphasizing the credit purchase of inventory. The manual processing involved in each of these accounting applications was reviewed, and both system flowcharts and brief descriptions were used to illustrate how these tasks might be computerized. Under manual processing, each processing task is performed independently. With a computerized data base approach, however, the execution of these accounting processes can lead to a high degree of integration. This integration increases the effectiveness of the accounting information system.

Key Terms You Should Know

batch data processing
child record
data base
data base management system (DBMS)
data definition language (DDL)
data dictionary
data manipulation language (DML)
data redundancy
direct-access file
false update
field (in a record)
file
hierarchical data base
indexed sequential file
indexing approach
inverted list
logical data structure
master file
network data base

online processing
parent record
physical data structure
pointer field
primary record key
random-access file
randomizing approach
real-time data processing
record
record key
relational data base
schema
secondary record key
sequential file
sibling record
subschema
transaction file
transaction records
tree structure

Discussion Questions

7-1. Why is the storage of accounting data important to an accounting information system? How does the method of data storage affect the way in which the accounting data are *used*?

7-2. Describe the function of the *record key* in the typical accounting file. Are such keys simple or complicated? Name four files that might commonly be found in an accounting information system environment and, for each file, identify a data field that could conceivably be used as a record key.

7-3. Describe the relationship between an accounting master file and an accounting transactions file. Are both of these files created about the same number of times? Explain.

7-4. Provide some reasons why a company might want to keep a permanent copy of its transaction records. Why aren't these records thrown out after they have been used?

7-5. What is the difference between batch and real-time data processing systems? Give some advantages of each approach.

7-6. A common difficulty encountered in data processing updating of a master file is the "no-master-file-record-found" condition. Explain this condition in detail. When would such a condition be likely to occur? What can be done about this condition in both batch and real-time data processing environments?

7-7. What problems do real-time data processing systems pose for auditing functions? How are these problems avoided with batch processing systems? What steps are commonly taken in accounting practice to overcome the real-time data processing problems you have described?

7-8. What is an *accounting data base*? What distinguishes an accounting data base from a typical, "garden-store-variety" accounting file of computer records?

7-9. Mr. John Langtree has been an auditor with an old, reliable CPA firm for many years. He had seen the first computers installed in his clients' offices and the computer's use expand rapidly over the past 30 years. When asked why he had never learned computer methodology, Mr. Langtree responded: "No need. The computer does nothing more than what it is told and, further, mostly does only what manual accounting systems have been doing for more years that I care to remember." Comment.

7-10. Describe the relationship, if any, between (1) computer technology and (2) the manner in which accounting records are logically ordered on a computer file. Consider in your discussion such factors as data processing speeds, type of secondary-storage devices, and remote-terminal access to the central processing unit.

7-11. Name some advantages of sequential computer files. What are the disadvantages of this method of file organization?

7-12. Why are sequential files not normally used in real-time data processing applications? Is such an approach impossible or simply impractical? Explain.

7-13. Direct-access files, by definition, must have an "addressability" characteristic. What is this characteristic, and why is it important for direct-access files?

7-14. In direct-access files, either an "index approach" or a "randomizing approach" is used to organize records. Describe each approach in detail. What are the advantages and disadvantages of each? Which of these two approaches do you prefer? Explain.

7-15. How is a direct-access file updated? How does this updating differ from updating sequential master files? How would you respond to the following common question regarding direct-access file updating: What happens to the old record?

7-16. What is meant by the term *false update*? What is "false" about it? If it is false, why is it used?

7-17. With data bases, it is often convenient to differentiate between physical and logical data structures. What is the meaning of each of these terms and why is this distinction important to accounting information systems?

7-18. What is a data dictionary? What types of information are maintained in a data dictionary? What uses can be made of a data dictionary?

7-19. A student taking a class in accounting information systems was introduced to the concept of a data dictionary and commented: "Professor, it seems to me that data dictionaries are useful in computerized accounting information systems but would serve little purpose in a manual system." Comment.

7-20. This chapter of the textbook has reviewed three types of data base structures. Identify each type and explain each in enough detail to distinguish one type of structure from another. Are these data structures *physical* structures, *logical* structures, or some combination?

7-21. What is meant by the terms *parent record,*

child record, and *sibling record?* What type of data structure uses these types of records? How are these records used?

7-22. Provide an example of an accounting application that might make use of a hierarchical data structure for records other than the sales example illustrated in the chapter. In your example, discuss how the characteristic tree structure of the data base would result from your grouping of file records.

7-23. Explain how the concept of *network data structure* is related to the concept of *record chaining.* Is it possible to create a network data structure without record chaining?

7-24. What advantages does a relational data base offer over other types of data structures? What disadvantages does it suffer? Can you think of any additional advantages or disadvantages beyond those cited in the text? If so, what are they?

7-25. What are data base management systems? Are they the same as data bases? Why are DBMSs classified as software and not hardware?

7-26. What are data manipulation languages and data definition languages? How are these languages related to data base management systems? How are these languages related to data bases?

7-27. Professor Errorprone had read just enough about data bases to be dangerous. During the course of one of his lectures, the professor stated, "Data bases are a wonderful invention, but are only cost-effective for large computerized accounting applications. They are ill-advised for small accounting systems, and, of course, cannot be implemented in manual systems." Comment.

7-28. Discuss both the advantages and the disadvantages of using a computerized data base system rather than a manual system for executing accounting processes. In this discussion, provide some specific accounting application examples that illustrate your previously mentioned advantages and disadvantages.

7-29. Refer back to Figure 7-11. Discuss the advantages of a computerized data base system compared with a manual system for executing the accounting functions associated with "financial statement preparation" and "budgetary planning and controlling."

7-30. Refer back to Figure 7-12. Discuss the advantages of a computerized data base system compared with a manual system for executing the accounting functions associated with "credit purchases of inventory" and "cash payment authorizations."

7-31. Refer back to Figure 7-13. Discuss the advantages of a computerized data base system compared with a manual system for executing the accounting function associated with issuing cash disbursement checks to creditors.

7-32. Discuss the overall purpose(s) of computerized data bases as they relate to accounting information systems. How do such data bases make the accountant's job easier? How do such data bases make the accountant's job more difficult?

7-33. Progress in the design and development of computer-based management information systems has been impressive in the last two decades. Traditionally, computer-based data processing systems were arranged by departments and applications. Computers were applied to single, large-volume applications such as inventory control or customer billing. Other applications were added once the first applications were operating smoothly.

As more applications were added, problems in data management developed. Businesses looked for ways to integrate the data processing systems to make them more comprehensive and to have shorter response times. As a consequence, the data base system composed of the data base itself, the data base management system, and the individual application programs was developed.

Requirement

A. Explain the basic differences between the traditional approach to data processing and the use of the data base system in terms of
  1. File structure.
  2. Processing of data.
B. Many practitioners have asserted that security in a data base system is of greater importance than in traditional systems.
  1. Explain the importance of security and the problems that may arise in implementing security in a data base system.
  2. Identify special control features a company should consider in its data base system.
C. Identify and discuss the favorable and unfavorable issues, other than security, that a company should consider before implementing a data base company.

(CMA Adapted)

Problems

7-34. Will Grant is the head accountant for the John Wallace Construction Company. This company manufactures hardwood cabinets and counters used in the construction of single-family homes and multiple-family condominiums. The cabinets and counters are prefabricated in the factory and then shipped, ready-made, to the construction site for installation. One day, Will Grant was given the data listed in the following table describing the prices and quantities of various raw materials that the company had just used in the manufacture of 200 kitchen counters, company catalog number 1098-E (Koa wood finish). Using the data provided, prepare a raw materials variance report for the Wallace Company.

Item	Actual Quantity Used	Standard Quantity	Actual Cost per Unit	Standard Cost per Unit
7664	100	100	$ 3.98	$ 3.50
7990	240	200	4.50	4.75
8777	310	300	25.85	25.50
8832	290	300	8.77	8.77

7-35. The Ekroth Company is currently involved in the conversion of its manual data processing system to a computerized data processing system for handling its accounting functions. One of the major accounting processes that will be handled by the new computer system is the company payroll. As the company began to analyze its needs, it became clear that the payroll file would be used by several departments within the company. For example, the personnel department would need to access the file in order to prepare the initial employee records and make pay-rate changes. The accounting department would also need access in order to disburse paychecks. Even the company credit bureau would need to access the file to credit employees with contributions.

Making any assumptions you consider reasonable, draw a set of system flowcharts indicating how the various users of payroll information might utilize a payroll file: (1) using manual methods and (2) using a new, computerized data base approach.

7-36. Refer to Problem 7-35. Assume that the Ekroth Company will also be computerizing the information describing its plant and equipment. Again, making any

reasonable assumptions you wish, draw system flowcharts of (1) how the company's plant and equipment data might be processed under a manual system and (2) how the company's new computerized system might handle this same accounting function using a data base.

7-37. Annette Sproule and Associates has just computerized its accounts receivable file and wishes to age its credit-sales transactions. Each record on the file represents a separate sales transaction that is yet to be paid, and the file is organized as follows. All sales transactions for the same credit customer have been stored together on the file in ascending order of transaction date. Each set of all such transaction records is blocked as a variable-length physical record. The record blocks are arranged in ascending account-number order.

Requirement

A. Draw a diagram illustrating how the transaction records will be stored on the accounts receivable file.

B. Develop a system flowchart for the computer processing required for this aging task, assuming the accounts receivable transaction file is stored on magnetic disk. The output from this processing is the aging report.

Item	Payroll	Personnel
1	Employee name	Social security number
2	Employee 1st line address	Employee number
3	City	Employee name
4	State	Employee 1st line of address
5	Zip Code	City and state
6	Telephone area code	Zip Code
7	Telephone number	Date of hire
8	Department code	Department code
9	Pay rate (regular)	In-house phone extension
10	Pay rate (overtime)	Home telephone area code
11	Social security no.	Telephone number
12	Number of federal tax deductions	Date of last raise

7-38. The Earl Wilson Manufacturing Company is nationally known for its fine golfing products, including clubs, bags, and related equipment. The company's payroll department is redesigning its computer records so that they can also serve the personnel department in a consolidated data base. The table on page 248 lists several data items required by each department. Note that these items are not in any consistent order. Recommend a data base record format for these records and, for each data item, recommend a field length (i.e., a maximal number of characters). Hint: see Figure 7-1.

7-39. The Kim Boal Company wishes to create a small employee file of 478 records as a direct-access file. Assume that locations 000–499 are available on a disk and that employee social security numbers are used as record keys. The system designers decide to use the hashing technique described in the text, using the low-order seven digits of the employee social security numbers. Given this decision, indicate the disk location of each of the following employee records:

a. 078-34-5566
b. 575-32-8766
c. 575-78-4442
d. 129-67-6612
e. 322-38-3939

7-40. A catalog sales company creates invoice records using customer telephone numbers as record keys. These are then stored as a direct-access file using a hashing technique to store individual records. The algorithm is as follows: (1) Divide the telephone number by 16,383. (2) Use the digits in the remainder to determine a disk location for storage. For example, telephone number 323-1966 would have a remainder of 4515. The record would therefore be assigned disk location 4515. Perform a similar computation for each of the following telephone numbers.

a. 788-4554
b. 344-6789
c. 323-1877
d. 388-5633
e. 988-6931

CASE ANALYSES

7-41. Kensler Company

The controller of Kensler Company has been working with the data processing department to revise part of the company's financial reporting system. A study is

under way on how to develop and implement a data-entry and data-retention system for key computer files used by various departments responsible to the controller. The departments involved and details on their data processing-related activities are as follows.

General Accounting

- Daily processing of journal entries submitted by various departments.
- Weekly updating of file balances with subsystem data from areas such as payroll, accounts receivable, and accounts payable.
- Sporadic requests for account balances during the month with increased activity at month-end.

Accounts Receivable

- Daily processing of receipts for payments on account.
- Daily processing of sales to customers.
- Daily checks to be sure that credit limit of $200,000 maximum per customer is not exceeded and identification of orders in excess of $20,000 per customer.
- Daily requests for customer credit status regarding payments and account balances.
- Weekly reporting to general accounting file.

Accounts Payable

- Processing of payments to vendors three times a week.
- Weekly expense distribution reporting to general accounting file.

Budget Planning and Control

- Updating of flexible budgets on a monthly basis.
- Quarterly rebudgeting based on sales forecast and production schedule changes.
- Monthly inquiry requests for budget balances.

The Kensler Company's manager of data processing has indicated to the controller that batch processing is the least expensive processing technique and that a rough estimate of the cost of each of the other techniques would be as follows.

Technique	Cost in Relation to Batch Processing
Online processing	1.5 times
Real-time processing	2.5 times
Online inquiry	1.5 times

Questions

1. Define and discuss the major differences between the input and options of the following processing techniques.

    a. Batch processing.
    b. Online processing.
    c. Real-time processing.

2. Identify and explain (a) the type of input technique and (b) the type of file inquiry that probably should be employed by Kensler Company for each of the four departments responsible to the controller. Assume that the volume of transactions is not a key variable in the decision.

    a. General accounting.
    b. Accounts receivable.
    c. Accounts payable.
    d. Budget planning and control.

(CMA Adapted)

7-42. Paper, Inc.*

A systems-analysis study has been completed in a large company (called Paper, Inc.) that manufactures and markets various types of paper for the printing industry. This study initially was intended to identify the informational requirements related to the purchasing function, but was subsequently expanded to include the accounts payable function as well. The justification for expanding the study was based on the similarity of the data required in the data base to support each function.

The study identified the need for purchasing to maintain three files: (1) a vendor master file containing name, address, purchasing terms, and miscellaneous descriptive data, (2) an open purchase order file containing all of the data related to purchase orders placed but not yet completed, and (3) a history file of purchases made in a two-year period, by product, within vendor. At the time of the study, these files were maintained in a manual system.

The accounts payable department on the other hand required the following files: (1) a vendor master file that contains the descriptive data necessary to produce and mail a check for purchases received, (2) a file of invoices from vendors received but not yet paid, and (3) a one-year history file of paid vendor invoices. Currently, accounts payable maintains a manual vendor master and open invoice file. A tab system was used to create checks to vendors and to maintain paid invoice history.

The company leases a minicomputer with both magnetic tape and disk storage available in a batch processing mode. Approximately 20% of all purchases are considered rebuys from an existing vendor. At any point in time there are 3000 active vendors, 5000 open purchase orders, 1500 open invoices, and annually the company places 40,000 purchase orders.

Questions

1. How many data files are necessary in the required data base?
2. What data fields will be required in each data file? (Prepare a table or matrix that illustrates the relationship of data fields among files.)
3. What storage medium should be used for each data file?
4. How should each file be updated, and which department is responsible for keeping each file current?

7-42. Santa's Toys*

A large manufacturer of children's toys (called Santa's Toys) is considering the implementation of a marketing information system to assist its sales force. There are approximately 300 salespeople working out of 15 branch offices throughout the continental U.S. and Canada. The goal of the system will be to have customer sales history files online at central headquarters that can be accessed by remote terminals at each branch office during normal business hours. New customer orders and shipments that are received from each branch office nightly will update the sales history file that same night.

There are approximately 30,000 customers on the file at any one time. Approximately 50 customers are added, and 20 customers deleted, daily. History will be maintained for 13 months by product for each customer. Each customer is expected to have a master record with descriptive data equal to 100 characters.

---

* Used with the permission of John G. Burch, Jr., and Felix R. Strater, Jr., *Information Systems: Theory and Practice* (New York: Wiley, 1986).

* Used with permission of John G. Burch, Jr., and Felix R. Strater, Jr., *Information Systems: Theory and Practice* (New York: Wiley, 1986).

The average number of product records per customer is expected to be 20, each with 70 characters of information. Finally, projections indicate that the volume of order and shipment records for updating the history file will be 3000 nightly.

Questions

1. How many files would you recommend for this data base?
2. Would you recommend that these files (this file) be placed on tape, disk, or some other medium? Explain.
3. Roughly, how much room would be required to store 30,000 customer records on your recommended file(s)? How much room would be required to store 13 months' worth of product history records on your recommended file(s)?

7-44. The Huron Company

Huron Co. manufacturers and sells eight major product lines with 15 to 25 items in each product line. All sales are on credit, and orders are received by mail or telephone. Huron Co. has a computer-based system that employs magnetic tape as a file medium.

All sales orders received during regular working hours are typed on Huron's own sales order form immediately. This typed form is the source document for the keypunching of a shipment or back-order card for each item ordered. These cards are employed in the after-hours processing at night to complete all necessary record keeping for the current day and to facilitate the shipment of goods the following day. In summary, an order received one day is processed that day and shipped the next day.

The daily processing, which has to be accomplished at night, includes the following activities.

1. Preparing the invoice to be sent to the customer at the time of shipment.
2. Updating accounts receivable file.
3. Updating finished goods inventory.
4. Listing all items back-ordered and short.

Each month the sales department would like to have a sales summary and analysis. At the end of each month, the monthly statements should be prepared and mailed to customers. Management also wants an aging of accounts receivable each month.

Questions

1. Identify the master file that Huron Co. should maintain in this system to provide for the daily processing. Indicate the data content that should be included in each file and the order in which each file should be maintained.
2. Employing the system flowcharting symbols used in the chapter, prepare a system flowchart of the daily processing required to update the finished goods inventory records and to provide the necessary inventory reports (assume that the necessary magnetic tape devices are available). Use the annotation symbol (Figure 4-5) to describe or explain any facts that cannot be detailed in the other flowcharting symbols.
3. Describe (a) the terms that should appear in the monthly sales analysis report(s) the sales department should have and (b) the input data and master files that would have to be maintained to prepare these reports.

(CMA Adapted)

7-45. Mariposa Products

Mariposa Products, a textile and apparel manufacturer, acquired its own computer in 1978. The first application to be developed and implemented was production and inventory control. Other applications that were added in succession were payroll, accounts receivable, and accounts payable.

The applications were not integrated due to the piecemeal manner in which they were developed and implemented. Nevertheless, the system proved satisfactory for several years. Generally, reports were prepared on time, and information was readily accessible.

Mariposa operates in a very competitive industry. A combination of increased operating costs and the competitive nature of the industry have had an adverse effect on profit margins and operating profits. Ed Wilde, Mariposa's President, suggested that some special analyses be prepared in an attempt to provide information that would help management improve operations. Unfortunately, some of the data were not consistent among the reports. In addition, there were no data by product line or by department. These problems were attributable to the fact that Mariposa's applications were developed piecemeal and, as a consequence, duplicate data that were not necessarily consistent existed on Mariposa's computer system.

Wilde was concerned that Mariposa's computer system was not able to generate the information his managers needed to make decisions. He called a meeting of his top management and certain data processing personnel to discuss potential solutions to Mariposa's problems. The concensus of the meeting was that a new information system that would integrate Mariposa's applications was needed.

Mariposa's controller suggested that the company consider a data base system that all departments would use. As a first step, the controller proposed hiring a Data Base Administrator on a consulting basis to determine the feasibility of converting to a data base system.

Questions

1. Identify the components that comprise a data base system.
2. Discuss the advantages and disadvantages of a data base system for Mariposa Products.
3. List the factors that Mariposa Products should consider before converting to a data base system.

(CMA Adapted)

8

A Manual and Two Computerized Accounting Information Systems

Among the important questions you should be able to answer after reading this chapter are:

1. In what ways can the maintenance of a manual accounts receivable system be boring and error-prone?
2. In what ways can the maintenance of a computerized accounts receivable system be boring and error-prone?
3. What does an automated accounts receivable processing system use to replace the subsidiary ledger of the manual accounts receivable processing system?
4. Why does a computerized accounts receivable processing system break down the processing into a number of runs? In particular, why can't all the data processing be done at once?
5. A computerized accounts receivable processing system is accurate, reliable, and cost-effective when a large number of accounts are to be maintained. Why would anyone argue in favor of a manual system?

**Supplement: Manual Versus
Computerized Accounts Receivable
Systems**

**References and Recommended Readings
for Part Two**

INTRODUCTION

Up to this point, we have discussed accounting information systems piecemeal. This was necessitated by the large amount of computer concepts and systems background to be understood. Here, we illustrate a typical accounting information system that integrates these various application concepts in a unified data-collecting, data processing, and information-dissemination system. Thus, the purpose of this chapter is to tie together our preceding discussions by examining a practical accounting application. To accomplish this purpose, we have chosen an accounts receivable system for illustration. It should be noted that this is an arbitrary choice since such alternate applications as payroll, inventory control, or accounts payable would be equally appropriate.

To set the stage, the following section discusses accounts receivable functions in general terms and describes how these functions would be performed in a manual system. In the next section of the chapter, we turn our attention to a batch-computerized version and examine what must be done to implement such a system in a business environment.

Many businesses are now using online accounting information systems. In the third section of this chapter, we examine yet another version of an accounts receivable (A/R) system, a real-time system, and explore what benefits such a system might offer to a business that already has a manual or batch-computerized system.

As businesses become familiar with their accounts receivable systems, they become more aware of the need to *control* their accounts as well as maintain and process data *in* their systems. This important topic of managerial decision making with accounts receivable is the subject of the fourth and final part of this chapter.

A MANUAL ACCOUNTS RECEIVABLE INFORMATION SYSTEM

The purpose of an **accounts receivable system** is to accommodate the individual or firm desiring to defer payment and to provide orderly procedures for recording, processing, and reporting of the acquisitions of, and payments for, goods purchased on credit. For illustration, let us assume that the Alan Company sells sporting goods equipment to department stores, sporting goods shops, and other retail outlets on a credit basis. Marketing account representatives write up the bulk of the company's business on sales invoices that are then forwarded to the accounting subsystem for processing. When a new customer wishes to make purchases on credit, pertinent credit information would be requested and sent to the credit manager for appraisal. If the credit application is approved, a credit limit would be imposed representing a maximum dollar amount of purchases that could be made without cash payment. The new customer would then be informed of the credit decision and advised of company approval to buy sporting goods equipment up to the limit of the credit allowance.

In a manual accounts receivable system, the dollar total of each credit sale would be recorded in a specialized **sales journal,** as illustrated in Figure 8-1. One copy of the sales invoice serves as the source document for each entry, and the invoice number as well as the transaction amount are recorded. Sales discount terms have been omitted from the entries in the figure under the assumption that all credit sales are 2/10, n/30 (2% discount if payment is made within 10 days of the invoice date, and full amount due within 30 days if discount not taken). If the Alan Company allowed for variable credit terms, an additional column of the journal would be required to record this information as well. The sales journal is used only for recording credit sales. Cash sales transactions would be recorded in a separate cash receipts journal. Periodically (e.g., weekly or monthly), the totals entered in the sales journal would be posted to the proper general ledger

Alan Company Sales Journal				Page 1
Date	Account Debited	Invoice Number	Subsidiary Ledger Posting	Amount
1991				
Nov. 2	Cuff Links Golf Shop	152–325	✓	653.00
2	Laynor's Department Store[a]	152–326	✓	4,622.18
2	Laynor's Department Store[a]	152–327	✓	264.37
2	Blacky's Beer and Sports	152–328	✓	58.25
4	Roxanne's Resort	152–329	✓	612.00
30	Jump and Gyp	152–388	✓	752.15
				25,652.81

[a] It is assumed that two separate credit sales were made to Laynor's Department Store on November 2; thus, two separate sales invoices were prepared.

FIGURE 8-1   The recording of credit-sales information in the Alan Company sales journal (posting references have been excluded).

accounts: a debit to accounts receivable and a credit to sales.

The sales journal provides a running tally of the company's credit sales transactions but is insufficient to provide the information required to compute the account balances of individual customers—for example, to permit monthly customer billing or to check on an individual customer's current account balance before approving an additional credit sale. The detailed information required for these functions is maintained in the accounts receivable **subsidiary ledger,** which contains an account for each credit customer of the company. Each time a credit sale is made, the total invoice amount is recorded in the sales journal and posted to the customer's subsidiary ledger account, as illustrated in Figure 8-2. The check marks in the Subsidiary Ledger Posting column of Figure 8-1 as well as Figure 8-2 indicate that this posting has been performed. Figure 8-2 also illustrates the posting of the totals from the sales journal to the

two general ledger accounts: accounts receivable and sales.

Customer payments are recorded in the specialized **cash receipts journal** illustrated in Figure 8-3. When a payment is received, the date is carefully scrutinized to determine the customer's eligibility for a discount. For those payments that do not qualify for a discount, the payment is simply entered in the specialized cash receipts journal as a debit to the cash account and a credit to the accounts receivable account. For those payments that do qualify for a discount, a portion of the total amount of the original sale is treated as a debit to the sales discounts account. Naturally, many cash receipt items will be entered in the cash receipts journal, but we have principally illustrated the transactions affecting accounts receivable in order to focus on the accounts receivable accounting application.

In addition to posting the credit payments in the specialized cash receipts journal, credit entries are made to the individual customer ac-

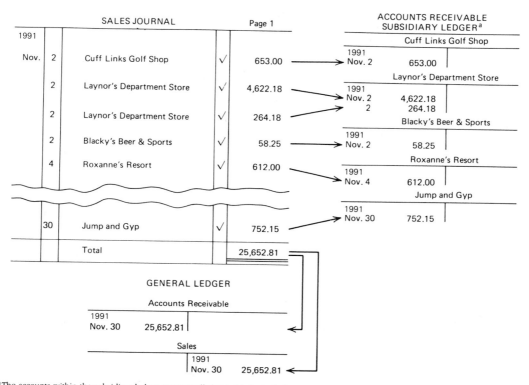

aThe accounts within the subsidiary ledger are normally kept alphabetically by customer name. For illustrative purposes here, however, we have not maintained this alphabetical sequence.

FIGURE 8-2   The posting of information from the sales journal to (1) the subsidiary ledger, (2) the Accounts Receivable account of the general ledger, and (3) the Sales account of the general ledger. Posting reference numbers have been excluded from the subsidiary ledger as well as the general ledger accounts for Accounts Receivable and Sales.

counts within the subsidiary ledger. The posting of the cash receipts transactions from the cash receipts journal to the general ledger as well as to the accounts receivable subsidiary ledger follows the same logic as was previously discussed for sales invoices recorded in the sales journal, and thus has not been illustrated here. When a payment is made by a customer, however, it is treated as a credit to the customer's account and entered in a straightforward manner in the accounts receivable subsidiary ledger.

In the area of accounts receivable, a problem may arise when customer payments do not correspond to individual line-item invoice entries within their subsidiary ledger accounts. This could happen, for example, when a partial payment is made by a customer. If a company were to use a **balance-forward system,** this would not cause any particular difficulty because under a balance-forward system, only the net total balance owed by the customer is maintained. However, if an **open system,** in which customer payments were matched with particular invoices, were used, this could pose some problems. For the sake of simplicity, it is easiest to assume that when a partial payment is made, it reduces the balance(s) of the customer's oldest invoice(s) due in the accounts receivable subsidiary ledger. The distinction between an open accounts receivable system and a balance-forward accounts

Alan Company Specialized Cash Receipts Journal								
Date	Payment Description	Subsidiary Ledger Posting	Sales Discounts Debits		Cash Debits		Accounts Receivable Credits		Misc. Credits		Acct. No.
1991											
Nov. 6	Blacky's Beer & Sports	✓	1	17	57	08	58	25			
6	Rental Income	✓			250	00			250	00	
9	Cuff Links Golf Shop	✓	13	60	639	40	653	00			
10	Jack's Jungle Shop	✓	6	44	315	56	322	00			
12	Blue Pearls	✓			48	00	48	00			
12	Roxanne's Resort	✓			84	32	84	32			
29	Don's Desert Digs	✓	1	93	94	55	96	48			
30	Haugerud's Hoops	✓			29	99	29	99			
			33	87	4,000	00	3,783	87	250	00	

FIGURE 8-3 The entry of payments to the cash receipts journal (posting reference numbers have been excluded).

receivable system is especially important to the computerized version of this accounting system.

Once a month, billing statements are prepared for those customers owing money to the Alan Company. To perform this function, the information from each accounts receivable subsidiary ledger account must be examined, and a billing statement prepared for those customers having outstanding balances. Obviously, for those accounts with a large number of credit purchases and payments during the month, it is easiest to prepare a single-line statement indicating the total amount due. Because of the potential for misunderstanding, a detailed statement showing all transactions with accompanying sales invoice information, as illustrated in Figure 8-4, is desirable. Inasmuch as the customer who generates a large number of transactions is also likely to be considered a "good customer" (in terms of

sales volume and therefore profitability), the need for detailed communication is important. However, this itemization process also involves a lot of work. For example, detailed customer billing statements require the recording of sales invoice numbers in the subsidiary ledger every time a credit sales transaction takes place. In addition, there would be the time and effort expended in preparing the detailed billing statements.

Beyond the preparation of monthly customer billing statements, it is desirable for the Alan Company's credit manager to review customer accounts on a periodic basis. One reason for this review is to make sure that individual accounts have not exceeded their credit limits. Another reason is to determine which customer transactions, if any, to write off as bad debts. A third reason is to assess credit policy—for example, to

ALAN COMPANY   CUSTOMER STATEMENT

125 King Street
Honolulu, Hawaii
96822
(808) 257-3286

11960099
CUSTOMER
NUMBER

SHIP TO:
Laynor's Department Store
9980 Fifth Ave
Los Altos, CA. 95230

BILL TO:
Laynor's Department Store
9980 Fifth Ave
Los Altos, CA. 95230

8/31/91
DATE

LOCATION (IF OTHER THAN ABOVE)
11960001 WORLDWIDE "STORE 1"

DATE	TRANSACTION	INVOICE	AMOUNT
6/16/91	INVOICE	115151	273.06
7/20/91	INVOICE	116293	586.84
7/23/91	INVOICE	116784	363.33
7/28/91	PAYMENT	116784	363.33−
8/02/91	INVOICE	117430	50.69
8/07/91	INVOICE	117945	720.80
8/12/91	ADJMENT	117945	108.44−
8/15/91	INVOICE	118302	1043.40
8/23/91	INVOICE	118303	256.59
8/30/91	INVOICE	119187	546.09
8/31/91	ADJMENT	999999	4.10
8/31/91	ADJMENT	999999	12.96

ACCUMULATED PRIOR LATE CHARGES   4.10
CHARGE ON AMOUNT OVERDUE   12.96
DEFERRED CHARGES   256.59

.00	273.06		
90 & OVER	OVER 60		
590.94	2265.50	PLEASE PAY▶	3129.50
OVER 30	CURRENT		

FIGURE 8-4 An example of a manual billing statement. Note the aging analysis in the lower left-hand corner, which is unusual for manual systems.

examine the possibility of extending additional credit if the Christmas season is near or to increase the credit limits of those accounts that appear to merit higher risks. Yet a fourth reason is to use this credit information in the evaluation of related activities—for example, a policy to offer cash discounts to those customers ordering slow-moving merchandise or a policy to discontinue the acceptance of credit cards other than those of the company itself. A final reason is to utilize the credit-sales data as a means of evaluating the marketing staff.

Each of these uses of the company's credit information would necessitate a slightly different analysis of the accounts receivable data. For example, in assessing bad debts, a common approach is to perform an aging analysis in which each customer's account balance is classified into categories of (1) portion not past due, (2) portion from 1 to 30 days past due, (3) portion from 31 to 60 days past due, (4) portion from 61 to 90 days past due, and (5) portion over 90 days past due. Figure 8-5 provides an example of such an analysis. The greater the proportion of a customer's account balance that is past due, the more likely it is that the credit customer will default. Thus, as the majority of a customer's credit purchases fall further and further in arrears (i.e., become listed in the right-most columns of the aging analysis report), the greater the potential that the customer's account balance will have to be written off as a bad debt.

The relative percentages at the bottom of the analysis are also useful to the manager. For example, large percentages in the intermediate ranges of the past-due categories (columns 3 and 4 of Figure 8-5) may signal a lack of adequate cash incentives for prompt payment or slow pursuit of delinquent accounts. An investigation of the possible reasons for delinquent accounts may lead to appropriate managerial action such as tightening credit-granting policies. It should also be noted that a large dollar figure at the bottom of the last column, indicating a nonpayment from the accounts past due over 90 days, is not necessarily a poor reflection on the credit manager. As in any business decision-making situation, there must be some allowance for acceptable risks. Thus, the absence of any accounts over 90 days past due may actually signal too stringent a credit policy.

Further uses of this credit information would require alternative data analyses, very few of which could be performed easily using manual methods with a large volume of credit sales transactions. For example, if the Alan Company sold to 5000 retailers on credit, then a time-consuming customer-by-customer examination of all 5000 accounts would be necessary to determine those customers who had exceeded their credit limits. Similarly, calculating information concerning credit sales by region of the country, product line, or marketing representative would be quite

Alan Company

Analysis of Accounts Receivable By Age
December 31, 1991

Customer	Total	(1) Not Yet Due	(2) 1–30 Days Past Due	(3) 31–60 Days Past Due	(4) 61–90 Days Past Due	(5) Over 90 Days Past Due
G. M. Schley	$ 500					$ 500
D. Jenness, Inc.	500		$ 150	$ 350		
Peterson's	800		200	380	$ 220	
Kramer Corp.	2,000	$ 800	450	750		
Bogle Shop	550	500	50			
Others	38,650	18,150	11,650	3,770	2,780	1,300
Totals:	$43,000	$19,450	$12,500	$5,250	$3,000	$2,800
Percentage:	100	45	29	12	7	7

FIGURE 8-5   An aging analysis for the Alan Company's accounts receivable.

time-consuming. Thus, both considerations of data volume and the need for specific types of managerial reports that are not cost-effective to prepare under a manual system lead to the consideration of a computerized system.

COMPUTERIZED ACCOUNTS RECEIVABLE INFORMATION SYSTEM #1: A BATCH SYSTEM

As an alternative to a manual accounts receivable system, a business might consider a **batch-computerized accounts receivable processing system.** These systems closely resemble the manual accounts receivable system in concept, although not in appearance or procedure. Computer files on magnetic tape or disk replace the sales journal, the cash receipts journal, the general ledger, and the accounts receivable subsidiary ledger of the manual system. In addition, the posting functions are automated. Ultimately, however, computerized accounts receivable systems perform the same principal functions as the manual system: the collection, processing, and reporting of transactions involving credit sales.

Computer Files

The basis of automated accounts receivable systems is the **accounts receivable master file,** which, for the purposes of illustration, will first be assumed to be a file of magnetic tape records. Not counting the header and trailer labels on this file (which contain file-control information), the tape will contain two basic types of records: **master records,** as illustrated in Figure 8-6 and **transaction (tx) records,** as illustrated in Figure 8-7. The *master record* contains the customer's account number, which serves as the file's record key, a special record code to distinguish master records from the transaction records, the customer's name and address, balance due (as of the beginning of the month), credit limit, and certain other information such as assigned salesperson's code, a flag (one-digit code) to indicate if the account is past due, a shipping code, and a special code for sales discounts. This master record is permanent on the file and is removed only when business with the associated customer is terminated.

The *transaction records,* or **detail records,** represent customer activity on the file. There will be one such record for each credit sale or cash payment transaction by the customer in a given time period. Like the master record, the detail record will contain the customer's account number to serve as a record key, a record-type code to identify the record as a transaction record, an additional transaction code to indicate a payment or credit sale, a reference sales invoice number, an "amount" field to indicate the dollar value of the transaction, a product-type code, a sales-terms field, a salesperson code in the event that more than one sales representative can make a

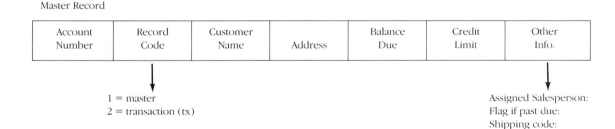

FIGURE 8-6 The master record for an accounts receivable file.

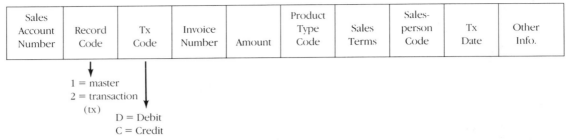

FIGURE 8-7 The transaction (detail) record for an accounts receivable file.

sale to the same customer, a transaction date, and perhaps additional information not shown in Figure 8-7.

Records on the accounts receivable tape file are maintained in strict numerical sequence according to each record's account number. Master records are followed by transaction records, if any, as illustrated in Figure 8-8. For sorting purposes, the record-type code (1 = master record, 2 = transaction record) is combined with the account number to maintain this order.

If transaction records were first keyed onto floppy disks and then periodically transferred onto magnetic tape, it would be desirable that these records be *blocked* (see Chapter 5). The reason is that each detail record would require less than 80 characters of tape length and unblocked records of this type on the file would waste too much magnetic tape with interrecord gaps. Blocked records would eliminate this problem.

In effect, the accounts receivable file represents a merging of the sales journal, the cash-collections-from-credit-sales portion of the cash receipts journal, and the accounts receivable subsidiary ledger (which are all from the manual accounts receivable system). When the accounts receivable file is created (e.g., in transition from a manual system), only the master records would be placed on the file in order to initialize it with customer account data. (Transaction records can be added later through normal processing once the file has become operational.) For example, the master-record information could be encoded first on floppy disks with a key entry device.

As an alternative to using a magnetic tape file, the accounts receivable master file can be maintained as a direct-access file stored on one or more magnetic disks. Using this approach, the sequential ordering of accounts receivable master records on the file would no longer be necessary; these records could be scattered randomly throughout the file. To find any particular record on the magnetic disk file, one or more of the direct-access techniques discussed in the previous chapter could be used.

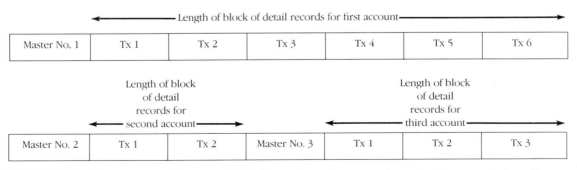

FIGURE 8-8 The sequence of master and detail records on the accounts receivable magnetic tape file.

Like master records, accounts receivable transaction records could also be scattered throughout the file in random order. To link master records and transaction records together, however, the transaction records pertaining to each master record would be chained. With this approach, therefore, a pointer field in each record would be used to store the disk address of the next transaction record in the sequence. Thus, for each account, the entire sequence of master record "followed" by transaction records (which would have to be maintained in a strict *physical* sense if the file were stored on magnetic tape) would be maintained only in a *logical* sense if the accounts receivable file were stored on magnetic disk.

Daily Processing Runs

The daily processing for the accounts receivable system, as might be implemented using a random-access master file, is illustrated in Figure 8-9. Here, we are assuming that the Alan Company would use remote terminals located in regional offices to input credit sales data on a daily basis. Thus, credit sales invoices, adjustment slips (e.g., a credit memorandum for returned merchandise), and cash receipts slips would provide the source document data to be keyed into the terminals for computer processing. This type of input system is conventionally called **remote job entry (RJE)** because the data necessary for the computer processing are collected and input to the computer from locations other than the immediate computer site.

Inputting Data to the System

For the illustration at hand, it is assumed that the Alan Company's marketing subsystem will be responsible for the input of credit sales data, that the Alan Company's accounting subsystem will be responsible for the input of cash receipts data, and that both subsystems can make adjustments. This assumption reflects the primary responsibilities of these respective subsystems (i.e., market-

ing and accounting) to generate source data for an accounts receivable accounting information system. When later processing takes place, each subsystem can check the resulting reports using their own source data and make corrections as needed. (The type of control information required for such checks is discussed in Chapter 10). However, as long as the data were input to the computer on a remote basis, no material changes in the flowchart of Figure 8-9 (top) would be necessary if different input responsibilities were assigned to the two subsystems.

As the sales and cash receipts data are entered by the marketing and accounting subsystems through remote terminals, these data would be edited by the Alan Company's computer to check for accuracy and completeness using the company's "Edit and Transaction Log" program. Those transactions that pass the screening tests of this program would be logged onto a **transactions file** stored on magnetic disk to await further processing. Those transactions that fail one or more of these tests would be rejected. In this latter case, the computer would relay an error message to the sending remote terminal, indicating the reason(s) for the transaction's rejection. The program would then direct the computer to await new instructions from the user—for example, an indication that a corrected version of the rejected transaction data is to be input or a request for information regarding the customer account in question. Thus, with the Alan Company's accounts receivable system, the user is able to interact with the computer system in a kind of question-and-answer format. In such instances, the user is said to **dialogue** with the computer because the user inputs data, the computer responds, and so forth, as in a conversation. This type of processing environment is quite efficient because errors may be corrected immediately at their input source and very little training is necessary for those assigned the task of inputting the data.

At the computer center, the daily use of the Edit and Transaction Log program will produce two principal types of output. The first output is

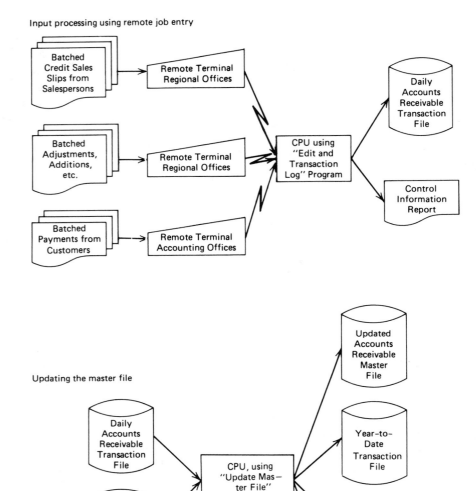

FIGURE 8-9 Accounts receivable daily processing.

the disk transaction file, which stores the transactions from the day's processing, as previously discussed. The second output is the Control Information Report, which contains descriptive information concerning the day's data processing. At a minimum, for example, this report would identify (1) each remote terminal accessing the system and using this accounts receivable processing routine, (2) how many transactions of each type (credit sales, adjustments, cash receipts, etc.) were logged onto the transaction file, and (3) the time(s) of day when this input took place. Normally, the report would also compute certain control totals such as the dollar total of credit sales and the dollar total of cash receipts. The Control Information Report would be reviewed by responsible employees to confirm the completion of the day's processing and would also serve as a control mechanism should the batch totals maintained by the regional offices fail to match the batch-control totals computed by the processing run itself.

Updating the Master File

Once the data have been logged onto the transactions file, it is possible to use this file to update the accounts receivable master file. Thus, in the accounts receivable update run, new transactions would be added to the file and the various informational fields of each master record would be modified as needed to reflect the current status of each account. This update run is shown in the bottom portion of Figure 8-9, reflecting the assumption that the master file would be updated daily. If the Alan Company so desired, however, it could also collect these transactions on its transactions file until, say, the end of the week and update the master file on a weekly basis. The decision regarding the frequency of updating the master file would depend on the volume of processing involved, how current the Alan Company wanted its accounts receivable file to be at any point in time, and the willingness of the company to incur the costs of running its master file update processing five times a week instead of only once a week.

As illustrated in Figure 8-9, the outputs from the master file update run include a **year-to-date transactions file,** an updated accounts receivable master file, an Exceptions Report of Unprocessed Items, and an Accounts Receivable Daily Processing Report. The year-to-date transaction file contains all the transactions that have affected the accounts receivable master file since the beginning of the (calendar or fiscal) year. If necessary, the year-to-date transactions file can be used with a backup copy of the accounts receivable master file (containing information about credit customers' accounts up to the end of the last calendar or fiscal year) to recreate the present accounts receivable file should the present copy be lost, stolen, or vandalized. However, it is more convenient to save an extra copy of yesterday's current master file and the corresponding day's transactions file for recreating a current master file. This is because fewer transaction records are involved in a single day's activity than in several months' worth of activities, and thus less data processing would have to be performed.

The second output from the daily accounts receivable processing run is the updated accounts receivable master file. As a result of this processing run, those accounts receivable transactions reflecting the day's receivables activities will be added to the file, defunct master file records will be dropped, and new accounts receivable master records (representing new customers) will be added. In addition, for selected master file records, certain field information such as the customer's address or credit limit will be changed to reflect the current informational status of customer accounts.

The third output from the daily processing run is the Exceptions Report of Unprocessed Items. There are many reasons why transactions cannot be processed: the use of an account number in a transaction record for which no associated master record can be found, the presence of an unrecognizable transaction code (i.e., a code that does not represent a cash receipt, a credit sale, or other typical transaction associated with accounts receivable), the indication of a credit sale at discount terms for which the customer does not normally qualify, and so forth. All such unprocessable items are listed in this exceptions report and must be handled on an item-by-item basis. In the case of edit rejections, for example, the sales invoice or other source document supporting the transaction record is referenced and the appropriate corrections are made. In more extreme cases, the salesperson, customer, or both must be contacted to correct the difficulty.

Perhaps the most immediately useful output from the daily processing run is the Accounts Receivable Daily Processing Report. This **hardcopy document** (i.e., printed report) contains all the transactions and other corrections that were accepted by the processing program and used to update the accounts receivable master file. A sample portion of this report is illustrated in Figure 8-10. For a company with thousands of credit customers, this document could be quite bulky. Yet, it is much less bulky than the corre-

			Additions		Deductions				Balance
Customer	Date	Invoice Number	Amount Billed	Misc.	Payment Received	Discount Allowed	Returns & Allowances	Misc.	
	Nov.								
63421									0 —
	2	152–325	653 00						
	2	152–325			639 40	13 60			0 —
63422									200 —
	2	152–328	58 25						
	2	152–328			57 08	1 17			200 —
63423									215 34
	2	152–326	4,622 18						
	2	152–327	264 37						5,101 89

Alan Company Accounts Receivable Daily Processing Report
Date: Nov. 2, 1991

FIGURE 8-10   A portion of the Accounts Receivable Daily Processing Report. (See Figures 8-1 and 8-3. The Cuff Links Golf Shop is account 63421. Blacky's Beer and Sports is account 63422, and Laynor's Department Store is account 63423. Also, for the purposes of illustration, customer payments have been accelerated to the date of the credit sales so that they might appear on the same daily report.)

sponding storage required for the subsidiary ledger journals of the manual accounts receivable system. The Daily Processing Report is printed on a customer-by-customer basis. Obviously, the Daily Processing Report is an important reference for employees helping customers who desire information about their accounts, for managers who desire information about the credit status of selected customers, and for data processing personnel or others who require an **audit trail** of the processing runs. In addition, the Daily Processing Report of customer activity contains important control information that may be used to test the accuracy of the data processing work. For example, the cash receipts total from this report *plus* the cash receipts total from the exceptions report should equal the total cash receipts.

Weekly Processing Runs

Weekly, the Alan Company will want to produce summary reports analyzing credit sales and selected types of customer payment activity. Two such reports that might be produced weekly are a Weekly Sales Report by Region and a Status Report of Delinquent Accounts. These reports would be produced using a current copy of the accounts receivable master file as illustrated in Figure 8-11.

The Weekly Sales Report by Region summarizes the company's credit sales (ignoring cash sales) on a region-by-region basis. Individual customers would not be shown on the report,

but within each region a breakdown by product type would be made showing credit sales on a product-by-product basis. Using this report, marketing and production managers would be able, for example, to adjust sales and production activities to changing credit-sales conditions. To produce such a report, the Weekly Processing computer program would scan the accounts receivable master file on an account-by-account basis looking for those credit-sales transactions that have taken place during the past week. Current sales transactions would be used to prepare the report. Other transaction records or master file records would be ignored.

Scanning the entire contents of the accounts receivable master file will take time even if the file is stored on a very fast magnetic disk. If sales volume were low, therefore, a company might choose to produce this type of report monthly instead of weekly. As an alternative, however, it would also be possible to store each week's transactions on a separate week-to-date transactions file. At the end of each week, the necessary transaction records—and only these records—required for the preparation of the weekly sales report would be stored on the week-to-date transactions file. The convenience of this approach, however, would have to be weighed against the inconvenience of maintaining a separate computer file for this purpose.

The second report to be produced each week is the Status Report of Delinquent Accounts. This report would list the names, account numbers, and balances of those customers who were seriously in arrears in their payments. The question of how far behind a customer must be before the account would be considered "seriously in arrears" is not easy to answer. Interestingly enough, most retail stores who buy on credit do not suddenly stop making payments when their businesses turn sour. At first, only a few payments are missed, and thus some of the retail store's credit purchase transactions become past due, whereas others are current. With the passage of time, however, the store in trouble will begin to send payments for current transactions only, tak-

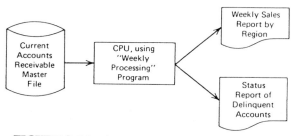

FIGURE 8-11   Accounts receivable weekly processing.

ing advantage of the cash discounts offered for speedy payments on these purchases, and allow its older credit purchase transactions to fall further and further in arrears. Thus, the question of when an account is seriously delinquent is a policy question that must be answered by the company credit manager, the financial vice-president of the company, or perhaps a policy committee that deals with issues concerning credit and collection activities.

The Status Report of Delinquent Accounts would also help the credit decision maker decide when to cut off further credit to a customer and when to write off a particular account as a bad debt. Thus, the delinquency report is a perfect example of the management-by-exception reporting principle in which attention of the manager is focused only on those items of interest.

Monthly Processing Runs

To assist it in managing its credit information, the Alan Company might consider two monthly processing runs: (1) a complete aging analysis and (2) a billing to customers. Each of these will now be discussed.

Aging Analysis

To study the delinquency of accounts receivable in greater detail, it is advisable to perform a complete aging analysis on a monthly basis. Because a complete aging analysis would require a search through the entire master file, it is not necessary, or even desirable, that this function be performed weekly; once a month is generally sufficient. Note that the computer run time for such processing when several thousand accounts must be examined would be considerably less than what would be required in staff time for the preparation of a complete aging analysis under a manual data processing system.

Some accounts receivable systems maintain the aging status of the transactions of each customer account as an integral part of the customer's master file record. Thus, in addition to

the fields of the master record, as illustrated in Figure 8-6, balance fields for the total amount of credit purchases not yet due, the total amount of purchases 1 to 30 days past due, and so forth, would be included in each master record of the file. Every day, these fields would be updated by the daily processing run using the date-field information of all transaction records on the accounts receivable master file to perform this function. The chief advantage of such a system is that the information required for the aging analysis is immediately available at the time a report or bill is prepared (see the lower left-hand corner of Figure 8-4). The chief disadvantage is that the aging information is stored in potentially thousands of master records, thus utilizing extra file storage space.

At the same time the master file is processed to produce the aging analysis (top half of Figure 8-12), it is also possible to produce a Salesperson Activity Report. Because there is a salesperson code in each sales transaction record of the file, and because at the end of a month there will be approximately four weeks of such sales records on the file, all the information required to produce the salesperson's report would be at hand. The report would indicate the credit sales of each salesperson, possibly broken down into subcategories such as customer type, quantity, and dollar sales value of specific inventory items sold, or some other classification deemed important to the company and for which the required data are available on the file. The information contained in this report would be useful for setting sales quotas, for evaluating performance by comparing actual sales with budget projections, and perhaps for making other related personnel decisions (e.g., promotion decisions).

Customer Billing

The other processing run performed on a monthly basis would be the billing statement routine (bottom half of Figure 8-12). Again, the accounts receivable master file serves as a primary input. The output includes the billing

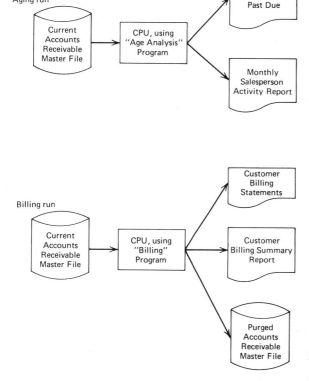

FIGURE 8-12 Accounts receivable monthly processing.

there would be little reason to maintain the past month's transaction records on the file (under a balance-forward accounts receivable system). Thus, these records could be purged from the file by the monthly processing program, and the processing run can output a new file of master records only. Each master file record would, however, contain an updated "balance" field to reflect the account's current amount owed.

If the company processed its accounts receivables using an open system, a slightly different approach would be required. In particular, only those credit-sales transactions for which there were matching customer payments could be dropped from the file. All credit-sales transactions for which there were no corresponding payment transaction would have to be maintained on the file until a credit payment to the company was received or the customer account was written off as a bad debt. With the open-system approach, therefore, a fairly large number of transaction records are kept on the file for certain customer accounts, and in addition, extra processing effort to match customer payments with corresponding credit-sales transactions is required. However, the open system would also be more precise in maintaining customer account activity information.

Summary of Computerized Accounts Receivable System #1

Figure 8-13 summarizes the entire information flow of the computerized accounts receivable accounting information system with a comprehensive system flowchart. Note that daily, weekly, and monthly accounting system processing runs have been included on the same flowchart to provide the necessary summary information. A chronological distinction between these runs may be made, however, by observing the titles of the programs within the CPU processing symbols and observing the titles of the output reports.

It should also be noted that the summary flowchart does not fully reveal the additional ac-

statements to be sent to each customer and a Customer Billing Summary Report (for processing control). Note that all the information required for the customer statements is immediately available from the master records of the file or from the associated transaction records. Of course, the billing statement output would be printed on preprinted forms so that only the variable information pertinent to each customer's account would be printed. Heading information such as company logo and field-identification information would be preprinted on the forms. (The less work required of the printer, the faster the entire operation.)

Once the billing process has been completed,

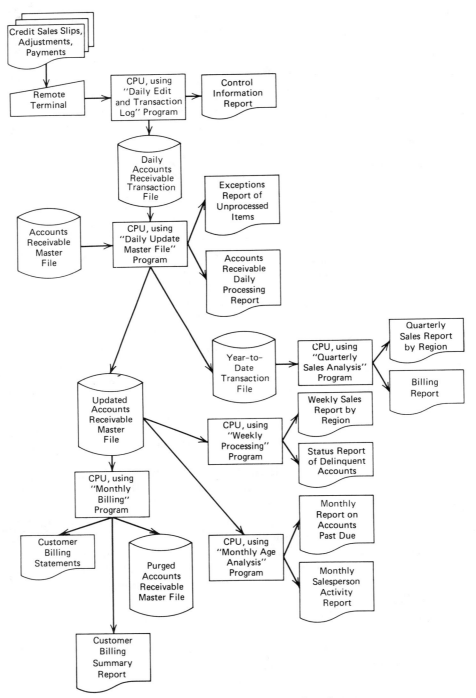

FIGURE 8-13 Accounts receivable summary system flowchart.

counting and computer processing tasks normally required to support the accounts receivable system. For example, the computation and maintenance of control-total information at the Alan Company's regional offices, the preparation and physical movement of backup computer files, and the actual distribution of copies of the various reports to the users have been omitted. These are vital activities in the normal, everyday functioning of such an accounting information system, and their importance should not be overlooked.

A final point concerning the accounts receivable accounting information system is that it does not exist in isolation. The same sales information captured by the Alan Company's regional sales offices, for example, might also be used in a computerized point-of-sale inventory system to update inventory account balances. Similarly, information about the cash received in the payments portion of the accounts receivable application would be used when reconciling the bank checking account. Finally, it should be clear that accounts receivable business activity has an important bearing on the company's balance sheet and income statement. Thus, in effect, the accounts receivable accounting information system is part of an even larger accounting information system.

COMPUTERIZED ACCOUNTS RECEIVABLE INFORMATION SYSTEM #2: A REAL-TIME SYSTEM

Batch processing systems are convenient because they perform processing runs at scheduled times and consolidate data to conform to these times. However, businesses often prefer **real-time accounts receivable processing systems** to batch systems—for example, because real-time systems perform important processing tasks on a "demand" (as-needed) basis. Real-time systems are online systems in which users are in direct communication with the computer.

Most real-time accounts receivable systems are **menu-driven systems,** meaning that users are provided a selection of on-screen choices, or "menus," from which to choose processing tasks. Figure 8-14 illustrates the "main," or "opening," menu for such a system. Note that there are several possibilities and, as we shall soon see, secondary menus with yet additional choices for each "main" choice. Let us look at each possibility separately below.

Entering Sales Data and Preparing Invoices

Figure 8-14 shows that the user has selected choice A, "Invoice Routines." Figure 8-15 illustrates the secondary menu resulting from this selection. Here, we see yet further processing choices, from which the user has picked A1, "Enter Invoice Transactions." This option enables the user to input the data for new sales orders directly to the system.

The top portion of Figure 8-16 illustrates how data entry is performed for this system. Using online terminals, data-entry clerks key the information from either sales documents or spontaneous telephone orders directly into the system. Note that at the time the data are entered, the system maintains three online master files: (1) a customer master file similar to the one described previously, (2) a product master file that contains detailed information about each product for sale, and (3) an invoice transaction file that is created as a result of this input process and that contains ordering, but not payment, information.

Online master files offer several advantages for the order-entry function of an accounts receivable application. One advantage is that many keystrokes are saved because most customer data (such as full name, shipping address, and billing address) and product data (such as product de-

```
ACCOUNTS RECEIVABLE:   MAIN MENU

        A    INVOICE ROUTINES
        B    MASTER FILE MAINTENANCE ROUTINES
        C    CASH RECEIPTS ROUTINES
        D    ANALYSIS AND CONSOLIDATION ROUTINES
        X    EXIT FROM A/R SYSTEM

        INPUT A CHOICE:   A
```

FIGURE 8-14   Most real-time accounts receivable systems are "menu-driven." This is an example of the opening, or "main," menu for an accounts receivable online system.

```
ACCOUNTS RECEIVABLE:   INVOICING ROUTINES

        A1     ENTER INVOICE TRANSACTIONS
        A2     UPDATE/CHANGE INVOICE TRANSACTIONS
        A3     DISPLAY CUSTOMER ACCOUNTS
        A4     DISPLAY INVOICE TRANSACTIONS
        A5     SORT INVOICES BY CUSTOMER NUMBER

        A10    PRINT INVOICE REGISTER
        A11    PRINT CUSTOMER INVOICES
        A12    PRINT BACK-ORDER REPORT
        A13    PRINT INVOICE A/R SUMMARY REPORT
        A14    PRINT EDITED INVOICES ONLY

        X      EXIT FROM THIS MENU

        INPUT A CHOICE:   A1
```

FIGURE 8-15   The invoicing routines of an online accounts receivable system are shown in this second menu.

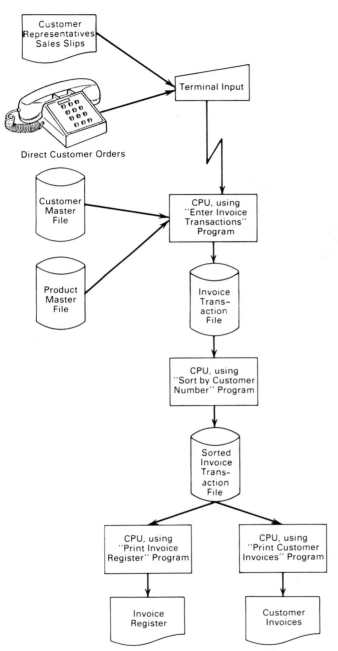

FIGURE 8-16   A system flowchart for the invoicing portion of a real-time accounts receivable system.

scription and current sales price) are already stored in the customer and product master files. Thus, only variable information such as the customer's purchase order number, the product numbers, and the product quantities must be keyed into the system.

Another advantage of online master files is that clerks are able to verify immediately that the customer's account number and other ordering information (such as billing address) are accurate. If they are in error, clerks can correct this information using other processing routines. Furthermore, clerks can ask the product file questions about the availability of a certain product. Finally, if a customer is seriously in arrears on his or her account balance, the system can be programmed to inhibit the entry of further sales data until the customer's delinquent account is cleared.

Periodically—usually daily—the online invoice transaction file can be sorted by customer number (bottom portion of Figure 8-16) and an invoice register (containing summary information that describes invoice sales) can be printed, visually inspected, and approved. This is achieved by choosing choices A5 and A10 from the menu of Figure 8-15. After making these choices, actual customer invoices can be prepared using choice A11 from this same menu. (Packing slips are often prepared simultaneously with these invoices.)

The ability to create invoices at the time a sale is made, rather than at month-end processing, is an important distinction between real-time systems such as this one and the batch-processing system described previously. For one thing, the real-time system provides greater control since the business, not the system, determines when invoices are printed. Of equal importance is the fact that orders are filled quickly, thus speeding the customer's receipt—and therefore payment—of invoices. This latter fact means that a business can expect better cash flows and have less of its assets tied up in receivables.

Master File Maintenance Routines

Figure 8-17 illustrates some of the options typically required in the creation and maintenance of master file records. These maintenance routines are necessary because records for new customers or products must be added to their respective files, business addresses must be changed, and current, hard-copy reports of these files must be prepared for manual reference—for example, in case the computer system "goes down."

In Figure 8-17, the user has chosen option B2, "Alter Product Master File Record." In this option, the computer system will enable the user to alter one or more of the data fields in a specific product master file record. This would be necessary, for example, if the product description, price, or quantity-on-hand fields were in error or if the product itself was being discontinued and the associated record dropped from its master file. A similar rationale applies to altering the records of the customer master file.

Cash Receipts Processing

In many real-time systems, the cash receipts function is separated from the order-entry function both as a convenience and as a control. Figure 8-18 illustrates a cash receipts data processing menu and suggests some of the processing possibilities involved. In this particular example, the user has selected C1, "Enter Cash Receipts Transactions," which enables the user to post cash payments to individual accounts.

Figure 8-19 illustrates the computer files and processing involved in this posting process. As customer payments are keyed into online terminals, the system uses the online customer master file and invoice transaction file to verify the customer's account number, the invoice number(s) to be paid, and other input data. For example, an incorrectly keyed customer account number can be detected since it will either result in a no-

```
ACCOUNTS RECEIVABLE:   MASTER FILE MAINTENANCE
                       ROUTINES

    B1    ALTER CUSTOMER MASTER FILE RECORD
    B2    ALTER PRODUCT MASTER FILE RECORD
    B3    DISPLAY CUSTOMER MASTER FILE RECORDS
    B4    DISPLAY PRODUCT MASTER FILE RECORDS
    B5    SORT CUSTOMER MASTER FILE
    B6    SORT PRODUCT MASTER FILE

    B10   PRINT CUSTOMER MASTER REGISTER
    B11   PRINT PRODUCT MASTER REGISTER
    B12   PRINT CUSTOMER CHANGE REPORT
    B13   PRINT PRODUCT CHANGE REPORT

    X     EXIT FROM THIS MENU

    INPUT A CHOICE:   B2
```

FIGURE 8-17   The master file maintenance routines menu of an online accounts receivable system.

```
ACCOUNTS RECEIVABLE:   CASH RECEIPTS ROUTINES

    C1    ENTER CASH RECEIPTS TRANSACTIONS
    C2    UPDATE/CHANGE CASH RECEIPTS TRANSACTIONS
    C3    DISPLAY CUSTOMER ACCOUNTS
    C4    DISPLAY CASH RECEIPTS TRANSACTIONS

    C10   PRINT CASH RECEIPTS REGISTER
    C11   PRINT EDITED CASH RECEIPTS  TRANSACTIONS  ONLY
    C12   PRINT BANK DEPOSIT REGISTER

    X     EXIT FROM THIS MENU

    INPUT A CHOICE:   C1
```

FIGURE 8-18   The cash receipts processing menu of an online accounts receivable system.

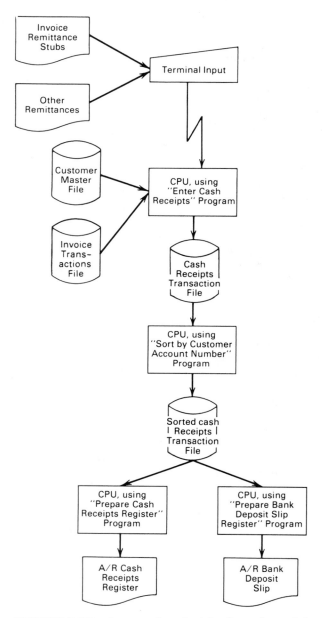

FIGURE 8-19 A system flowchart for the cash receipts processing portion of a real-time accounts receivable system.

master-record-found condition or will display the wrong customer name if a matching record is found. It should be noted that many accounts receivable systems use detachable, machine-readable remittance stubs with their invoices. In these circumstances, the data-input task associated with cash receipts is automated and the aforementioned input tasks will either be limited or eliminated entirely.

As illustrated in Figure 8-19, the invoice transaction file discussed previously is also online in this processing application, thereby enabling the system to match payments with invoice transactions. To check on the accuracy of payments, the system can compare the payment amounts with those stored in the invoice records.

The real-time accounts receivable system can also test for the appropriateness of cash discounts. To do so, it will use the cash payments date and the sales invoice date already stored in the invoice records to determine the number of days that have passed since a sale was made. This cash payments date is compared to the date of the original sales transaction, and the system then determines the eligibility of any particular payment for a cash discount. If the cash discount is allowed, the system can determine the accuracy of the balance due by adding the cash payment to the cash discount and comparing this figure to the invoice amount. If a difference is found, the system can alert the user to this problem with an error message and allow the operator to take whatever actions are required.

Another important component of cash receipts processing is the preparation of a "cash receipts register." This report lists customer names and numbers, customer check dates and numbers, and similar information. It is created by choosing choice C10 from the cash receipts menu of Figure 8-18 and is almost always created daily. As illustrated in the lower part of Figure 8-19, it is usually convenient first to sort cash receipts transactions into either invoice-number sequence, remittance-number sequence, or customer-number sequence in order to produce a logical report. Some systems permit all three sequences as different report options.

The cash receipts register can also serve as a bank deposit slip since customer check numbers, cash amounts, and cash totals are also printed on the register. However, since the cash receipts register also contains a large amount of additional information about customer payments, it is more likely that a separate, simplified "bank deposit register" report will be created for making bank deposits. This second report is created

as a user option by selecting choice C12 from the cash receipts menu.

Some businesses prefer a **lock-box cash receipts system** in which customers mail their payments directly to a bank. The bank then deposits the payments in the company's account and merely forwards the invoice stubs and a summary deposit register to the company for processing. This approach enables a company to avoid the problems of handling cash receipts or preparing daily bank deposit slips.

Analysis and Consolidation Routines

Figure 8-20 illustrates the menu for the analysis and consolidation routines of the online real-time accounts receivable system. Note that two of the choices in this menu are sorting options (D2 and D4), enabling users to resequence the accounts receivable master file or the invoice file by account names, account numbers, or important dates.

Another interesting option in the menu of Figure 8-20 is D5, "Adjust Small-Balance Totals." Interactive processing using online systems are especially useful in selectively viewing and making adjustments to master file records of interest. A recurrent condition for the master file records of an accounts receivable accounting information system is the **small-balance problem,** in which small credit or debit balances remain in customer accounts after all invoices have been paid. If choice D5 is chosen, the system might respond:

→ WHAT SMALL-BALANCE AMOUNT DO
   YOU WISH TO EXAMINE? $XX.XX
→ WHAT ACCOUNTS ARE TO BE
   EXAMINED (ENTER A FOR ALL)?

These questions enable users to examine master file accounts selectively and to eliminate all master file balances less than a cutoff amount—for example, less than $1.00—thus bringing the small balances to zero.

Another important task of any computerized accounts receivable system is to delete invoices

```
ACCOUNTS RECEIVABLE:   ANALYSIS AND CONSOLIDATION
                                   ROUTINES

    D1    DISPLAY A/R MASTER FILE RECORD(S)
    D2    SORT A/R MASTER FILE RECORDS
    D3    DISPLAY INVOICE MASTER FILE RECORD(S)
    D4    SORT INVOICE MASTER FILE RECORDS
    D5    ADJUST SMALL-BALANCE TOTALS (A/R MASTER FILE)
    D6    DELETE PAID-IN-FULL INVOICES

    D10   PRINT DELETED INVOICE REPORT
    D11   PRINT ADJUSTED SMALL-BALANCES REPORT
    D12   PRINT AGING SCHEDULE
    D13   PRINT A/R STATUS REPORT

    X     EXIT FROM THIS MENU

    INPUT A CHOICE:   D6
```

FIGURE 8-20   The analysis and consolidation menu of an online accounts receivable system.

that have been paid in full. This is a task of choice D6 of the Analysis and Consolidation menu. Figure 8-21 is a system flowchart that illustrates this process in detail. During the run, the system uses the current invoice transaction file and the current customer master file as inputs. The outputs include a "purged" invoice file, an updated customer master file, and a year-to-date invoice transaction file. This enables a business to delete paid invoices from the current invoice transaction file and to create an audit trail for these invoices using option D10: "Print Deleted Invoice Report."

MANAGERIAL DECISION MAKING WITH ACCOUNTS RECEIVABLE

There are many reasons why business managers should carefully control their accounts receivable. One is that the collection of accounts receivable by a company reflects business policy towards its credit customers. Thus, collection procedures must be both strong enough to assure a reasonably high percentage of payments and delicate enough to assure the continued goodwill of customers.

Another reason for the importance of accounts receivable control is that receivables have an important effect on the cash flow of a company. During downturns in the economy, businesses often experience a marked slowing of customer payments. This can have adverse effects upon the general cash flows of a business and thus emphasizes the need to control accounts receivable functions.

Yet a third reason for the importance of accounts receivable control concerns sales. Since a high percentage of the total sales of many companies are credit sales, the statistics generated from accounts receivable data are often useful managerial tools for controlling related business activities—for example, back-ordering pro-

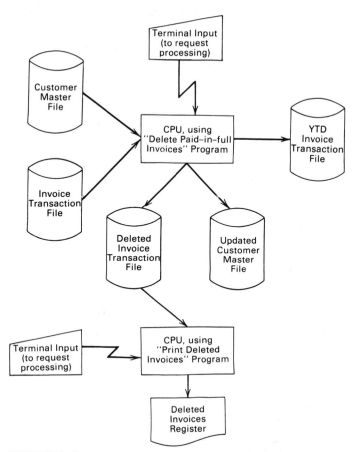

FIGURE 8-21   A system flowchart for deciding paid-in-full invoices processing.

cedures, inventory stocking, or production policies.

Finally, it should be noted that even though accounts receivables are listed as assets on a company's balance sheet, receivables are *only* legitimate assets if they can be collected. Uncollectible receivables are worthless.

Figure 8-22 provides a list of useful ratios that a business might wish to compute with its computerized system using accounts receivable data. Also included in this list are comments that indicate how these ratios might be helpful to a business. In general, it is difficult to imagine how a manual system could generate such ratios on a timely basis.

Of special importance in the list of Figure 8-22 is the computation of the **average collection period.** This ratio is important since the dollars tied up in receivables may have to be financed by short-term borrowing at high interest rates and thus may be a considerable expense to a business. Furthermore, after the average collection period has been computed, it can be compared to industry ratios as a measure of operating performance for a particular business.

Once the means to calculate an average collection period have been established, this figure can be recomputed over time to determine a trend. In general, decreasing values for average collection periods are preferred to increasing values,

Statistic	Formula	Comments
(1) Average invoice dollar total	$= \dfrac{\text{Gross dollar total of outstanding invoices}}{\text{Number of outstanding invoices}}$	The larger the number, the more business per sale.
(2) Average invoice line item dollar total	$= \dfrac{\text{Gross dollar total of all outstanding invoices}}{\text{Total number of invoice line items}}$	The larger this number, the more business per line item. This value can also be compared to the *cost* of A/R's per line item.
(3) Percentage of back orders	$= \dfrac{\text{Number of line items back-ordered}}{\text{Total number of invoice line items}}$	A large percentage figure, or a figure that is increasing, may signal poor inventory control.
(4) Percentage of orders cancelled	$= \dfrac{\text{Number of line items cancelled}}{\text{Total number of invoice line items}}$	If ordered items are cancelled instead of back-ordered, this statistic is also a measure of inventory control.
(5) Total number of customers	$=$ Count of customers on customer master file	A measure of credit business, can be viewed as a check by multiplying this figure by (1) above.
(6) Ratio of credit sales to cash sales	$= \dfrac{\text{Gross dollar total of all credit invoices in a month}}{\text{Gross dollar total of all cash sales in a month}}$	If cash sales (c) can be estimated reliably, this ratio (r) can be used to predict credit sales (A) using the formula: $A = r \times c$.
(7) Average collection period (in days)	$= \dfrac{\text{Average accounts receivable in dollars}}{\text{Sales}}$	This figure can be compared to industry averages to measure credit control. Also, the longer this period, the more costly the A/R function to the company.

FIGURE 8-22   Various performance ratios that can be computed for controlling accounts receivable.

since decreasing values mean shorter collection periods and therefore more effective operations for the company. When short-term interest costs are high, businesses have been willing to spend large amounts on automated accounts receivable systems in order to speed the preparation of invoices and reduce average collection periods. One firm, for example, spent approximately $200,000 on a computerized system, reduced its collection period by 18 days, and reduced its average outstanding receivables by $850,000! We have also noted that most computerized accounts receivable systems create a year-to-date invoice transaction file containing credit sales and payment data. This file is a "gold mine" of raw data awaiting evaluation. If, for example, the account numbers had been coded so that the first few digits represented the geographical location of customers, then this file could be used to prepare a marketing report of credit sales by regions of the country. Similarly, because each sales transaction contains the total amount billed the customer, a **histogram of sales invoices** (i.e., a table indicating the number of sales invoices less than \$100, the number of sales invoices between \$100 and \$250, etc.) could be constructed from the data. Such a report might be useful in deciding the amount of trade discounts offered to customers doing business with the company, in evaluating changes to salespersons' commission rates, and so forth. Finally, **cross-tabulation reports** could be generated in which salesperson versus regional credit sales, customer types versus credit sales terms, or credit sales terms versus dollar business categories could be prepared. As you can probably tell from these suggestions, the possible combinations are endless.

It is unlikely that such reports would be prepared on a weekly, or even monthly, basis. At best, quarterly or semiannual runs to produce these reports would be made because compiling such information would take time even on the computer, and such things as seasonal fluctuation in sales and changes in company policies would likely make analyses of the information on less than a quarterly basis meaningless. Unlike the weekly or monthly operational reports discussed earlier, however, the usefulness of this type of data processing is not diminished by the fact that these reports are processed less often. The major point is that the year-to-date transaction file can serve as a valuable data base for many different management informational needs, and these needs can be adequately met through the proper exploitation of the information contained on the file. Also, with a computerized accounts receivable processing system, it is now cost-effective to generate these reports.

The supplement to this chapter compares manual and computerized accounts receivable systems. A number of factors that help a company decide which of these two types of systems is better to use are discussed in it.

SUMMARY

The purpose of an organization's accounts receivable accounting information system is to provide orderly procedures for recording, processing, and reporting credit activity. In this chapter, we have examined three systems for performing this function: a manual accounts receivable system and two computerized accounts receivable systems. Each system attempts to satisfy certain basic informational needs associated with the accounts receivable processing operations, although how these needs are met differs considerably between the two systems.

In the manual accounts receivable system, the data surrounding credit sales are recorded in the sales journal, the cash receipts journal, the general ledger, and the accounts receivable subsidiary ledger. The mechanics of recording customer credit purchases and payments were reviewed, and it was noted that a large volume of credit customers in a company would substantially limit the efficient generation of manually prepared customer billing statements as well as many of the specialized informational reports desired by management.

The basis of a batch computerized accounts receivable system is an accounts receivable master file, which for the purposes of illustration was assumed to be a magnetic disk file. This file maintained two types of records: (1) master records, containing such information as customer account number, customer name and address, and balance due, and (2) transaction or detail records, containing such activity data as credit sales amount, cash receipts amount, or field changes (such as credit limits). In the batch accounts receivable information system, the master records are created initially from information obtained in commercial customers' credit applications. Transaction records for the computerized accounts receivable system are created initially from such source documents as sales invoices and cash receipts slips. The information on these transaction source documents is keyed onto a temporary transactions file from remote company terminals. At the end of each day, these transactions are coordinated with the accounts receivable master file. The output from this daily processing includes an updated accounts receivable master file, a year-to-date transaction file, an Exceptions Report of Unprocessed Items, and an Accounts Receivable Daily Processing Report.

The processing needs of a company also include weekly, monthly, and quarterly reports. A weekly processing routine would provide, for example, a Weekly Sales Report by Region and a Status Report of Delinquent Accounts. Monthly processing provides a Monthly Aging Analysis Report, a Monthly Salesperson Activity Report, customer billing statements, and a Customer Billing Summary Report. Also, once a month, a company may purge all of the accounts receivable transaction records from its master file (if the company used a *balance-forward* accounting system) or its payment-matched transaction records (if the company used an *open* accounting system).

As an alternate to a batch processing system, a business might wish to consider a real-time accounts receivable information system. The data processing tasks in this system were divided into four major parts: (1) entering sales data and preparing invoices, (2) master file maintenance, (3) cash receipts processing, and (4) analysis and consolidation functions. Most of these functions can be performed "on demand," thereby enabling a business to dictate its processing requirements to its system instead of the other way around.

A final section of this chapter explored the need for managerial decision making with accounts receivable. This section stressed the importance of managerial control—for example, in order to reduce the average collection period for receivables. This topic therefore transcends the idea of *processing* accounts receivable data and emphasizes the need for managerial *control and direction*. Thus, the discussions pointed out some important accounts receivable ratios and noted how yet further important analyses might be made using the year-to-date invoice transaction file as a data base.

Key Terms You Should Know

accounts receivable system
average collection period
balance-forward accounts receivable system
batch-computerized accounts receivable processing system
cash receipts journal
cross-tabulation report
detail record
dialogue
hard-copy document
histogram of sales invoices
lock-box cash receipts system

master file
master records
menu-driven system
open accounts receivable system
real-time accounts receivable processing systems
remote job entry (RJE)
sales journal
small-balance problem
subsidiary ledger
transactions file
transaction records
year-to-date transaction file

Discussion Questions

8-1. Describe the procedure(s) by which a bookkeeper would enter a credit sales transaction and a cash receipts transaction into a manual accounts receivable system.

8-2. Describe the procedure(s) by which a credit-sales transaction and a cash receipts transaction would be entered into a computerized accounts receivable system.

8-3. The Barry Render Sport Shop purchases sporting goods equipment from the Alan Company on a credit basis. On March 5, the shop made a purchase of $400 with cash discount terms of 2/10, n/30. When the shop received its monthly statement from the Alan Company on April 2, this $400 purchase was still shown as outstanding even though the shop was sure the bill had been paid on March 12. How would an accountant working for the Alan Company go about checking this discrepancy:

1. Under a manual accounts receivable system?
2. Under an automated accounts receivable system of the types described in this chapter?

8-4. An automated accounts receivable operation often uses a preprinted billing statement form, as illustrated in Figure 8-4. How would a large-scale purchase of equipment by a company making more purchases than could be listed on this form be handled with a computerized billing system?

8-5. Discusss the meaning of the following terms as they are used in the chapter: (a) dialogue, (b) remote job entry, (c) year-to-date, (d) manual override.

8-6. In what sense does the computerized accounts receivable system "put distance" between a company and its credit customers?

8-7. What types of decision-making information are provided to a company's management in an aging analysis of accounts receivable? If a company has no credit customers whose account balances are over 90 days past due, is this situation always a good sign of operating efficiency? Explain.

8-8. What advantages does a batch-processing accounts receivable processing system have over a manual system?

8-9. What advantages does a manual accounts receivable processing system have over an automated system? (Hint: see the chapter supplement.)

8-10. The William Remus Mattress Company manufactures and distributes mattresses, box springs, and headboards to companies thoughout the Southwest. It sells to about 300 companies in total, and extends credit to approximately 150 of its customers. Most of these credit sales are to small retail outlets owned by personal friends of William Remus Mattress Company president, John Downs. Up to this point, Mr. Downs has used a manual accounts receivable system to maintain the credit information about his customers. Recently, a Mr. Kirkland Fasttrack has approached Mr. Downs to suggest that he automate his system, using a new small computer system sold by Mr. Fasttrack's company. Mr. Fasttrack has pointed out the many advantages of his computerized system, including the automated billing operation.

1. Superficially, would you recommend that Mr. Downs upgrade his accounts receivable operation to an automated one? Why or why not?
2. What information would you need to evaluate the proposal more thoroughly?

8-11. Mr. Paul Berry is the treasurer of a small aerospace manufacturing company in southern California. His company buys much of its equipment on credit from parts manufacturers throughout the country including the Tippy Wing Rivet Company. Mr. Berry believes that his company should pay its bills promptly—within 10 days of purchase (typical cash discount terms offered are 2/10, n/30) in order to maintain good credit relations with its creditors and also to take advantage of the 2% cash discount made available to the company for prompt payment. The Tippy Wing Rivet Company uses an automated accounts receivable system. On August 15, Berry's company purchased $2150 worth of equipment from Tippy Wing. However, on the company's billing statement received at the end of the month, neither the purchase nor the payment (which was made August 24) appeared. What could have happened? If the transaction does eventually show up on the September bill, do you believe that Berry's company is still entitled to the 2% cash discount? Explain.

8-12. This chapter began discussing an automated accounts receivable system as it might be implemented with a sequential tape file of master records. Later in the chapter, the analysis assumed a random-access disk file. What differences are there in the use of the tape file and the disk file? (For example, could both of these files be updated the same way?) Do both require the same kinds of processing runs? Be as specific as possible.

8-13. At the end of the chapter, it was suggested that the accounts receivable year-to-date transaction file was a very rich source of information and could be used as a data base for the generation of further decision-oriented reports. What reports might these be? What decisions might be based on these reports? Are these decisions limited to the accounting aspects of accounts receivable? Discuss.

8-14. How far in arrears must a delinquent account be before it should be written off as a bad debt? As a general credit manager, what policy would you install at the Alan Company for a situation in which a good customer has paid its bills regularly but claims payment for a bill that, according to company records, is six months past due?

8-15. What is the difference between a balance-forward accounts receivable system and an open accounts receivable system? What are the implications of these differences to computerized accounts receivable systems?

8-16. How does a real-time accounts receivable system differ from a batch accounts receivable system? Explain at least three differences.

8-17. What is meant by the term *menu-driven system?* What is the opposite of menu-driven? Why are online accounts receivable systems often menu-driven?

8-18. What is meant by "master file maintenance" using an online accounts receivable system? What master files are maintained? Who maintains them? How are they maintained?

8-19. When master files are accessed using a real-time accounts receivable system, the system is said to "verify" the correct account. What does this mean? How is account verification handled in a batch system or a manual system?

8-20. What is a "lock-box cash receipts system"? How does it work? What advantages does such a system have over more conventional ways of handling customer cash payments? Is a lock-box system confined to real-time accounts receivable systems or can other types of systems use it?

8-21. What is the "small-balance problem" associated with accounts receivables? Why is it a problem? What can be done about it?

8-22. Identify several performance ratios or statistics that might be computed from accounts receivable data and that might be used to help control accounts receivable. For each ratio or statistic you mention, indicate *how* it might help control accounts receivable.

8-23. Explain why each of the following might be an important advantage of a real-time accounts receivable system over either a manual system or a batch system.

1. Immediate editing of transactions as they are entered into the system.
2. Shortens the time between taking orders and the shipment of merchandise.
3. Shortens the time between receipt of cash and eliminates associated outstanding invoice(s).
4. Avoids transporting data physically.
5. Immediate customer billing by invoice.
6. Ability to prepare demand reports.

Problems

8-24. In the text, it was suggested that some accounts receivable applications use a computerized master file record that includes an aging analysis for each account. Redesign the master file record of Figure 8-6 to include aging information. When would this information be updated?

8-25. One of the weekly reports suggested for the accounts receivable processing system is a Weekly Sales Report by Region. This report was described but not illustrated. Design such a report, indicating precisely what information would be contained in it.

8-26. Refer to Problem 8-25. Prepare a detailed program flowchart that would enable a programmer to write a computer program for the preparation of the Weekly Sales Report by Region. Note that regional sales information is not explicitly found in any transaction records. Yet, this information might be extractable from other data fields of the transaction records. Explicitly state what assumptions you have made regarding regional sales information.

8-27. Refer to Figure 8-9, which illustrates the updating of an accounts receivable master file with a daily accounts receivable transaction file. For this update run, design a detailed program flowchart that would illustrate the computer processing logic for this data-processing task.

8-28. Figure 8-12 illustrates the aging run for the Alan Company's accounts receivable monthly processing. Design a detailed program flowchart that illustrates the computer processing logic for this data-processing task.

8-29. Figure 8-12 illustrates the billing run for the Alan Company's accounts receivable monthly processing. Design a detailed program flowchart that illustrates the computer processing logic for this data processing task.

8-30. Figure 8-23 is a system flowchart for P. Miesing and Company's purchase order data processing. Prepare a narrative to accompany the flowchart describing this purchase order function. Include in your narrative (1) what source documents are involved, (2) what computerized data processing takes place, (3) what data inputs are used to prepare purchase orders, and (4) what outputs are prepared from this processing function.

8-31. Consider the following narrative which describes the data processing involved with the receipt of

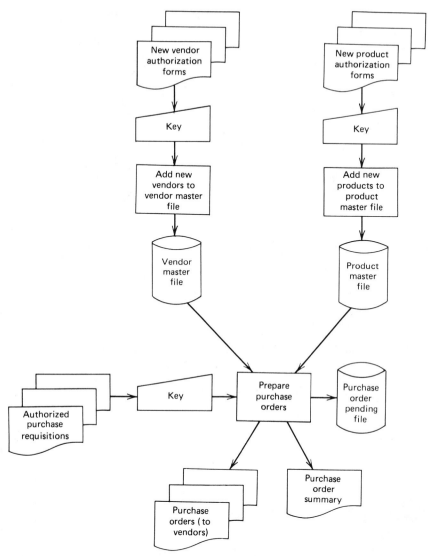

FIGURE 8-23 System flowchart illustrating the preparation of purchase orders for P. Miesing and Company.

merchandise at P. Miesing and Company (this continues Problem 8-30).

Once P. Miesing and Company recieves goods at its warehouse, receiving personnel prepare material receipts forms indicating the date, the vendor, and the amount of each product received. These forms are delivered to the company's computer center, where key entry personnel use the information of these source documents to create a new material receipts file. The new material receipts file is used to print several copies of a receiving report (which are sent to management) and also to prepare stock tickets (which are sent to the warehouse). Further, on a daily basis, the new materials receipt file, along with the vendor master file, the product master file, and the purchase orders pending file, is used to update the accounts payable file. The output from this update run is a revised accounts payable file (reflecting updated accounts payable records) and a processing summary.

Use good system flowcharting technique to draw the data processing described in the narrative.

8-32. Bagranoff and Sons uses an online computer system to perform its cash receipts data processing. In

Figure 8-24 are two display screens and a system flowchart that help document this data processing. Write a narrative to explain this system in detail. Include in your description an indication of what computer files are involved in the process and how the user interacts with the screen formats illustrated to perform the data processing.

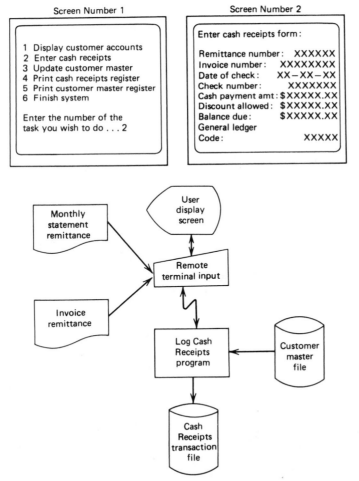

On line Screens

Screen Number 1

```
1 Display customer accounts
2 Enter cash receipts
3 Update customer master
4 Print cash receipts register
5 Print customer master register
6 Finish system

Enter the number of the
task you wish to do . . . 2
```

Screen Number 2

```
Enter cash receipts form:

Remittance number:  XXXXXX
Invoice number:   XXXXXXXX
Date of check:      XX – XX – XX
Check number:       XXXXXXX
Cash payment amt: $XXXXX.XX
Discount allowed: $XXXXX.XX
Balance due:      $XXXXX.XX
General ledger
Code:               XXXXX
```

FIGURE 8-24   The online display screens and system flowchart for the cash receipts data processing of Bagranoff and Sons.

CASE ANALYSES

8-33. *Jacobs Manufacturing Company*

Jacobs Manufacturing Company maintains an accounts payable system using magnetic tape files. The master file contains information about the major vendors supplying materials and other services to the company. The transaction file contains expense detail records, which contain pertinent information about company purchases, and payment detail records, which contain pertinent information about supplier reimbursements. The formats of the master file record, the expense detail record, and the payment detail record are shown in Figure 8-25.

A purchase is initiated with the manual preparation of a purchase order, a signed copy of which is for-warded to the supplier. Upon receipt of the merchandise, this voucher information is coordinated with the invoice information of the shipment itself, and the complete set of data is forwarded to the EDP center for keypunching to floppy disks. This creates the expense detail record as illustrated.

Once a month, the following processing is performed.

A. Cash disbursements by check number.
B. Preparation of purchase journal reports arranged by (a) account charged and (b) vendor.
C. Listing of outstanding payables.

Questions

1. Explain when and how the expense detail transaction record and the payment detail transaction record would be created on the file.

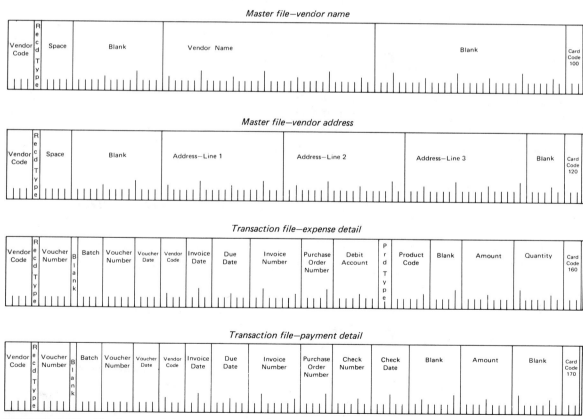

FIGURE 8-25 The format of the accounts payable master file record, the expense detail record, and the payment detail record of the Jacobs Manufacturing Company.

2. Draw a set of system flowcharts that document the data processing runs outlined.
3. What information would likely be found on the reports listed in the run(s) listed previously? What information on the files would be required to generate these reports?

(AICPA Adapted)

8-34. *Wekender Corporation*

Wekender Corporation owns and operates 15 large departmentalized retail hardware stores in major metropolitan areas of the southwest United States. The stores carry a wide variety of merchandise, but the major thrust is toward the weekend "do-it-yourselfer." The company has been successful in this field, and the number of stores in the chain has almost doubled since 1978.

Each retail store acquires its merchandise from the company's centrally located warehouse. Consequently, the warehouse must maintain an up-to-date and well-stocked inventory ready to meet the demands of the individual stores.

The company wishes to hold its competitive position with similar type stores of other companies in its marketing area. Therefore, Wekender Corporation must improve its purchasing and inventory procedures. The company's stores must have the proper goods to meet customer demand, and the warehouse in turn must have the goods available. The number of company stores, the number of inventory items carried, and the volume of business all provide pressures to change from basically manual routines to mechanized data processing procedures. Recently, the company has been investigating three different approaches to mechanization—punched card system, computer with batch processing, and computer with real-time processing. No decision has been reached on the approach to be followed.

Top management has determined that the following items should have high priority in the new system procedures.

1. Rapid ordering to replenish warehouse inventory stocks with as little delay as possible.
2. Quick filling of orders and shipping of merchandise to the stores (this involves determining if sufficient stock exists).

3. Some indication of inventory activity.
4. Perpetual records to determine quickly inventory level by item number.

A description of the current warehousing and purchasing procedures is given below.

Warehouse Procedures

Stock is stored in bins and is located by inventory numbers. The numbers generally are listed sequentially on the bins to facilitate locating items for shipment. Frequently this system is not followed and, as a result, some items are difficult to locate.

Whenever a retail store needs merchandise, a three-part merchandise request form is completed—one copy is kept by the store and two copies are mailed to the warehouse the next day. If the merchandise requested is on hand, the goods are delivered to the store accompanied by the third copy of the request. The second copy is filed at the warehouse.

If quantity of goods on hand is not sufficient to fill the order, the warehouse sends the quantity available and notes the quantity shipped on the request form. Then a purchase memorandum for the shortage is prepared by the warehouse. At the end of each day, all the memos are sent to the purchasing department.

When ordered goods are received, they are checked at the receiving area, and a receiving report is prepared. One copy of the receiving report is retained at the receiving area, one is forwarded to accounts payable, and one is filed at the warehouse with the purchase memorandum.

Purchasing Department Procedures

When the purchase memoranda are received from the warehouse, purchase orders are prepared. Vendor catalogs are used to select the best source for the requested goods, and the purchase order is prepared and mailed. Copies of the order are sent to accounts payable and the receiving area, one copy is retained in the purchasing department.

When the receiving report arrives in the purchasing department, it is compared with the purchase order on file. The receiving report is also checked against the purchase invoice before the invoice is forwarded to accounts payable for payment.

The purchasing department strives periodically to evaluate the vendors for financial soundness, reliability, and trade relationships. However, because the volume of requests received from the warehouse is so great, this activity currently does not have a high priority.

Each week a report of the open purchase orders is prepared to determine if any action should be taken on overdue deliveries. This report is prepared manually from scanning the file of outstanding purchase orders.

Questions

1. Wekender Corporation is considering three possible automated data processing systems: punched card system, batch processing system, real-time computer system.

   a. Which of these three systems would best meet the needs of Wekender Corporation? Explain your answer.
   b. Briefly describe the basic equipment components that Wekender would need for the system recommended.

2. Regardless of the type of system selected by Wekender Corporation, data files will have to be established.

   a. Identify the data files that would be necessary.
   b. Briefly indicate the type of information that would be contained in each file.

(CMA Adapted)

8-35. *Deake Corporation*

Deake Corporation is a medium-sized, diversified manufacturing company. Fred Richards has been promoted recently to manager, property accounting section. Richards has had difficulty in responding to some of the requests from individuals in other departments of Deake for information about the company's fixed assets. Some of the requests and problems Richards has had to cope with are as follows:

1. The controller has requested schedules of individual fixed assets to support the balances in the general ledger. Richards has furnished the necessary information, but he has always been late. The manner in which the records are organized makes it difficult to obtain information easily.
2. The maintenance manager wished to verify the existence of a punch press that he thinks was repaired twice. He has asked Richards to confirm the asset number and location of the press.

3. The insurance department wants data on the cost and book values of assets to include in its review of current insurance coverage.
4. The tax department has requested data that can be used to determine whether Deake should switch depreciation methods for tax purposes.
5. The company's internal auditors have spent a significant amount of time in the property accounting section recently, attempting to confirm the annual depreciation expense.

The property account records that are at Richards's disposal consist of a set of manual books. These records show the date the asset was acquired, the account number to which the asset applies, the dollar amount capitalized, and the estimated useful life of the asset for depreciation purposes.

After many frustrations, Richards realized that his records are inadequate and he cannot supply the data easily when they are requested. He decided that he should discuss his problems with the controller, Jim Castle.

Richards: "Jim, something has got to give. My people are working overtime and can't keep up. You worked in property accounting before you became controller. You know I can't tell the tax, insurance, and maintenance people everything they need to know from my records. Also, that internal auditing team is living in my area and that slows down the work pace. The requests of these people are reasonable, and we should be able to answer these questions and provide the needed data. I think we need an automated property accounting system. I would like to talk to the information systems people to see if they can help me."

Castle: "Fred, I think you have a good idea, but be sure you are personally involved in the design of any system so that you get all the information you need."

Questions

1. Identify and justify four major objectives Deake Corporation's automated property accounting system should posses in order to provide the data that are necessary to respond to requests for information from company or auditor personnel.

2. Identify the data that should be included in the computer record for each asset of the property account.

(CMA Adapted)

8-36. *Value Clothing*

Value Clothing is a large distributor of all types of clothing acquired from buy-outs, overstocks, and factory seconds. All sales are on account with terms of net 30 days from date of monthly statement. The number of delinquent accounts and uncollectible accounts has increased significantly during the last 12 months. Management has determined that the information generated from the present accounts receivable system is inadequate and untimely. In addition, customers frequently complain of errors in their accounts.

The current accounts receivable system has not been changed since Value Clothing started its operations. A new computer was acquired 18 months ago, but no attempt has been made to revise the accounts receivable application because other applications were considered more important. The work schedule in the systems department has slackened slightly, enabling the staff to design a new accounts receivable system. Top management has requested that the new system satisfy the following objectives.

1. Produce current and timely reports regarding customers that provide useful information to:
   a. Aid in controlling bad debts.
   b. Notify the sales department of customer accounts that are delinquent (accounts that should lose charge privileges).
   c. Notify the sales department of customers whose accounts are considered uncollectible (accounts that should be closed and written off).
2. Produce timely notices to customers regarding:
   a. Amounts owed to Value Clothing.
   b. A change of status of their accounts (loss of charge privileges, account closed).
3. Incorporate the necessary procedures and controls to minimize the chance for errors in customers' accounts.

Input data for the system would be taken from four source documents—credit applications, sales invoices, cash payment remittances, and credit memoranda. The accounts receivable master file will be a machine-readable file organized by customer account number. The preliminary design of the new accounts receivable system has been completed by the systems department. A brief description of the proposed reports and other output generated by the system follow.

1. **Accounts Receivable Register**—a daily alphabetical listing of all customers' accounts that shows balance as of the last statement, activity since the last statement, and account balance.
2. **Customer Statements**—monthly statements for each customer showing activity since the last statement and account balance; the top portion of the statement is returned with the payment and serves as the cash payment remittance.
3. **Aging Schedule, All Customers**—a monthly schedule of all customers with outstanding balances displaying the total amount owed with the total classified into age groups—0–30 days, 30–60 days, 60–90 days, over 90 days; the schedule includes totals and percentages for each age category.
4. **Aging Schedule, Past-Due Customers**—a schedule prepared monthly that includes only those customers whose accounts are past due (i.e., over 30 days outstanding, classified by age). The credit manager uses this schedule to decide which customers will receive delinquent notices, temporary suspension of charge privileges, or have their accounts closed.
5. **Activity Reports**—monthly reports that show:
   a. Customers who have not purchased any merchandise for 90 days.
   b. Customers whose account balance exceeds their credit limit.
   c. Customers whose accounts are delinquent, yet have current sales on account.
6. **Delinquency and Write-off Register**—a monthly alphabetical listing of customers' accounts that are:
   a. Delinquent.
   b. Closed.
   These listings show name, account number, and balance. Related notices are prepared and sent to these customers.
7. **Summary Journal Entries**—entries are prepared monthly to record write-offs to the accounts receivable file.

Questions

1. Identify the data that sould be captured and stored in an accounts receivable master file record for each customer.

2. Review the proposed reports to be generated by the new accounts receivable system.
   a. Discuss whether the proposed reports should be adequate to satisfy the objectives enumerated.
   b. Recommend changes, if any, that should be made in the proposed reporting structure generated by the new accounts receivable system.

(CMA Adapted)

8-37. *Ranco Wholesale*

Ranco is a small manufacturing firm that sells only to distributors. All sales are made on credit with terms of n/15. Dave Leemon, the Controller, has asked Barbara Tracey, the Credit Manager, to design a cash receipts projection model. He wants to know whether cash collections can be projected accurately by week from current accounts receivable. Tracey is to consider only credit sales already made.

Customer	Average Days from Invoice to Payment
Morse Chemical	42
Farrel Industries	35
Rhodes Discount	33
Yale Union	31
TechCo	25
All other customers	17
Average for all customers in total	34

Tracey asked Jim Hurd, the Supervisor of Data Processing, to analyze accounts receivable for the last six months and determine the average days that elapse between the invoice date and the date payment is received. Hurd gave her the report shown here.

Hurd indicated that the accounts receivable records show that over 90 percent of all credit sales are with the five companies detailed while the other 20 distributors account for the remainder. He also indicated that the only uncollectible accounts occurred in the "all other customers" category and averaged two percent of billings. Hurd gave Tracey the age analysis of the accounts receivable file as of November 30, 1990, as presented below.

Questions

1. Prepare a projection of cash collections by customer by week for the first three weeks of December 1990 using the age analysis of the accounts receivable file that is presented and the average collection period of each individual customer.
2. Explain why Barbara Tracey should use the average collection period of each individual customer rather than using the overall average collection period of 34 days.
3. The projection of cash collections by week was only prepared for a three-week period.
   a. Identify the maximum period of weeks for which the projection can be prepared before it becomes inaccurate.

RANCO
Accounts Receivable Age Analysis
November 30, 1990

Customer	0–7	8–14	15–21	22–28	29–35	36–42	Total
Morse Chemical	$ 13,000	$40,000	$ 90,000	$ 22,000	$25,000	$30,000	$220,000
Farrel Industries	5,000	10,000	5,500	12,000	20,000	7,500	60,000
Rhodes Discount	235,000	15,000	20,000	25,000	15,000	—	310,000
Yale Union	27,500	1,000	—	35,000	16,500	—	80,000
TechCo	2,500	4,000	18,500	15,000	—	7,000	47,000
All other customers	18,000	13,000	17,000	3,000	1,500	500	53,000
Total	$301,000	$83,000	$151,000	$112,000	$78,000	$45,000	$770,000

Days from Invoice Date

(CMA Adapted)

b. Explain why the projection becomes inaccurate if it is extended beyond this point.

c. Barbara Tracey would like to develop a computer model to generate this projection of cash collections by week. Describe a computer model that would produce this projection of cash collections.

4. Can the data Jim Hurd produced be used by Ranco for any purposes other than cash management? Explain your answer.

CHAPTER 8 SUPPLEMENT

Manual Versus Computerized Accounts Receivable Systems

There are considerable differences between the manual and the computerized accounts receivable applications as they have been described in Chapter 8. Care must be taken to avoid saying one system is better than the other—this conclusion is not obvious despite the heavy emphasis of our text on the advantages of computerized data processing. As the following paragraphs should make clear, which system is better depends on a number of factors.

One clear distinction between the two accounts receivable data processing systems is the different amounts of machinery and other special equipment they require. Under the manual system, only a few bookkeepers and some accounting journals and ledgers are required, whereas with the automated version a complete computer system must be in place. If only the accounts receivable area were to be automated in a business organization, there might be a processing cost advantage in utilizing the manual system. The decision would require a comparison of the expected costs and benefits of the manual system versus the computerized system (i.e., a cost/benefit analysis). If the computer hardware required for the accounts receivable processing were also used for such other tasks as payroll preparation or inventory file maintenance, however, then only the incremental costs of utilizing the computer system for the accounts

receivable processing function should be used in the evaluation. Whether or not this incremental cost would be less than the processing costs of the manual system is speculative.

Yet another consideration would be processing speed. To perform the accounts receivable function effectively, the processing of the data and the preparation of the required reports must be executed on a timely basis. Where the processing environment involves large volumes of data and limited staff, the automated accounts receivable systems appear to have an advantage. Many thousands of transaction records can be processed in a short period of time using computerized equipment, and high-speed printers can output reports at the rate of 20,000 lines a minute.

For all the speed of the automated accounts receivable system, however, surprising lags in batch processing still can occur. For example, where transactions are batched at the end of the week, any sale that is made late Friday might not be keyed into the computer until Friday of the following week—a lag of 7 days! In addition, if a transcription error is made in this sales transaction but not detected until the update routine of the weekly processing run, the transaction would not be recorded for another week, resulting in a 14-day lag. Finally, if this processing lag extended just past the monthly billing run, the customer might not be billed for nearly 6 weeks past the purchase date! This is one reason that batch systems are inferior to real-time processing systems for such accounting functions as accounts receivable, where timely processing and a current master file are important.

A manual system for processing accounts receivables might be more responsive. Even if errors were made in the recording, posting, or billing operations, it would be reasonable to expect the manual system to handle these problems on an exceptions basis, and prepare a special customer statement by hand, if necessary. In any event, there would be no compelling reason to wait an entire month. This is not to say that the automated version of the system would make no provision for *manual overrides* (i.e., processing customer accounts as an exception to normal processing) or other special ways of handling problems on an individual basis. In practice, however, the fact that the computer is "supposed to handle" the accounts receivable operation often compels employees to process as many transactions as possible through normal channels.

There is also the question of processing errors. As far as the automated versions of the accounts receivable system are concerned and barring hardware failures, the computer will never make a processing error. Moreover, both hardware and software controls usually are adequate to ensure processing accuracy even with unrepresentative data situations. Because a manual system depends on error-prone humans to perform the brunt of the processing, there is clearly a greater potential for *processing errors* in the manual system.

Processing errors are not the only kind of errors that can be made. There are also transcription errors, and here, the manual system may have an advantage. This is because, as the two versions of the systems have been designed, the manual accounts receivable system works directly with the sales invoices and other source documents of the system, whereas the computerized accounts receivable operation works principally with a *transcribed* version of these documents on magnetic disk. Because the bookkeeper in the manual system avoids the computer-version task of transcribing the data from the invoice or other activity item to the disk, there is less chance for transcription errors. In addition, the bookkeeper is likely to have more direct contact with the marketing staff and steady customers of the firm, and is therefore better able to resolve data questions quickly.

As discussed in Chapter 1, following an *audit trail* of transactions through an organization is often more difficult in a computerized data processing system than in a manual system. Establishing a good audit trail in a company is an important part of developing an efficient and effective internal control system. Because of their significance, internal controls within accounting

information systems will be extensively examined in Part Three (Chapters 9–12).

The matter of individual judgment may also be considered in our comparative analysis. In general, for processing applications in which the overwhelming proportion of the work is *algorithmic* (i.e., predefined and step by step) and in which large volumes of similar transaction items must be processed, a computerized accounts receivable version is the better alternative. On the other hand, where transaction items are largely dissimilar and a high degree of individual judgment is required, the accounts receivable manual version may prove superior. Just how judgmental the accounts receivable system is for the particular firm would determine the desirability of one version over the other.

Finally, there is the psychological aspect of the automation itself. By and large, customers do not like to be treated as impersonal numbers. But in computerized accounts receivable systems, customers can become just that—numbers. Furthermore, the computerized accounts receivable application puts distance between the credit customer and the company (which is making the credit sales to individual customers). For example, the purchaser no longer actually pays his or her creditor, but rather a mechanical intermediary that neither recognizes individuality nor appreciates the customer's business.

REFERENCES AND RECOMMENDED READINGS FOR PART TWO

Accounts Payable and Purchase Control System. Sunnyvale, Ca: Data Design Associates, 1982.

Anderson, Earl H., and Techavichit, Joseph V. "Database Systems and the Controller." *The Internal Auditor* 39 (February 1982), pp. 46–49.

Appleton, Daniel S. "Law of the Data Jungle." *Datamation* 29 (October 1983), pp. 225–230.

Ashton, Robert H. "Behavior Implications of Information Overload in Managerial Accounting Reports." *Cost and Management* 48 (July–August 1974), pp. 37–42.

Bainey, Kenneth R. "The Data Foundation." *Journal of*

Systems Management 34 (December 1983), pp. 30–38.

Balbus, Peter G., and Healey, Joseph L. "Out of the Labs and Into the Streets." *Datamation* 30 (September 1, 1984), pp. 96–106.

Baylin, Edward N. "System Diagramming Methods: Which Works Best?" *Journal of Information Systems Management* 4 (Summer 1987), pp. 29–39.

Bhaskar, Krish. *Building Financial Models: A Simulation Approach.* London: Associated Business Programmes, 1978.

Blanning, Robert W. "Model-Based and Data-Based Planning Systems." *Omega* 9, 2 (1981), pp. 163–167.

Burch, John G. Jr., and Grudnitski, Gary. *Information Systems: Theory and Practice,* 4th ed. New York: Wiley, 1986.

Caniano, Steven. "All TP1s Are Not Created Equal." *Datamation* 34 (August 15, 1988), pp. 51–53.

Carey, Jane M., and McLeod, Raymond Jr. "Use of System Development Methodology and Tools." *Journal of Systems Management* 39 (March 1988), pp. 30–35.

Carlis, J. V., March, S. T., and Dickson, G. W. "Physical Database Design: A DSS Approach." *Information and Management* 6 (August 1984), pp. 211–224.

Caruso, Robert L. "Paying Bills the Electronic Way." *Management Accounting* 65 (April 1984), pp. 24–27.

Cerullo, Michael J. "The Data Base Concept." *Management Accounting* 59 (November 1977), pp. 43–47.

CODASYL (Conference on Data Systems and Languages). "Data Base Task Group Report, 1971." New York: Association for Computing Machinery, April 1971.

Cohen, Leo. *Data Base Management Systems.* Wellesley, Ma: Q.E.D. Information Sciences, 1976.

Coleman, Raymond J., and Riley, M. J. "The Organization Impact of MIS." *Journal of Systems Management* 23 (March 1972), pp. 13–19.

Curtice, Robert M. "Getting the Database Right." *Datamation* 32 (October 1986), pp. 99–100.

Curtice, Robert M., and Jones, Paul E., Jr. "Database: The Bedrock of Business." *Datamation* 30 (June 15, 1984), pp. 163–166.

Date, C. J. "Relational Data Base Concepts." *Datamation* 22 (April 1976), pp. 50–53.

Davis, Richard K. "New Tools and Techniques to Make Data Base Professionals More Productive." *Journal of Systems Management* 35 (June 1984), pp. 20–25.

Dick, James B., Heister, Michael, and Lowman, Brad. *Micro Manual: BASIC, Word Processing, Spreadsheet, and Data Base.* Boston: PWS Publishers, 1986.

Dwyer, Terence J. "TUXEDO Transaction Processing System for 3B Computers." *AT&T Technology* 3, 1 (1988), pp. 40–45.

Eilon, Samuel. "What Is a Decision?" *Management Science* 16 (December 1969), pp. B172–B189.

Eliason, Alan I. *Business Information Processing: Technology, Applications. Management.* Palo Alto, Ca: Science Research Associates, Inc., 1980.

Enrick, Norbert L. "Be Mean About Management Reporting." *Computer Decisions* 2 (September 1970), pp. 28–31.

Farin Jeff, and Nazario, Amor. "DBMS Basics." *Infosystems* 33 (June 1986), pp. 42–47.

Finneran, Thomas R., and Henry, Shirley J. "Structured Analysis for Data Base Design." *Datamation* 23 (November 1977), pp. 99–113.

French, Robert L. "Making Decisions Faster with Data Base Management Systems." *Business Horizons* 23 (October 1980), pp. 33–46.

Gore, Martin, and Stubble, John W. *Elements of Systems Analysis,* 4th ed. Dubuque, Iowa: William C. Brown, 1988.

Greenwood, Frank, and Greenwood, Mary M. "Principles of Office Automation." *Journal of Systems Management* 35 (February 1984), pp. 13–17.

Hamel, Bob. "Colonial Penn Ties by Tandem." *Network World* 4 (January 26, 1987), pp. 17–18.

Holland, Robert H. "DBMS: Developing User Views." *Datamation* 26 (February 1980), pp. 141–144.

Holmes, Kenneth E. "Office Automation—Five Years Old and Growing." *Journal of Systems Management* 35 (September 1984), pp. 8–11.

Howe, D. R. *Data Analysis for Data Base Design.* London: Edward Arnold Publishers, 1983.

Hubbert, J. "Data Base Concepts." *The EDP Auditor* (Spring 1980), pp. 25–32.

Introducing General Ledger, Accounts Payable, Payroll, and Data Collection System Support for IBM Systems/34 2nd ed. Atlanta, GA: International Business Machines Corporation, 1978.

Joplin, Bruce, and Pattillo, James W. *Effective Accounting Reports,* Englewood Cliffs, NJ: Prentice-Hall, 1969.

Kalogeras, Gus. "Data Base—the Technical Heart of an Information Center." *Journal of Systems Management* 35 (November 1984), pp. 36–37.

Kindred, Alton R. *Introduction to Computers,* 2nd ed. Englewood Cliffs, NJ: Prentice-Hall, 1982.

Kneer, Dan C., and Wilkinson, Joseph W. "DBMS: Do You Know Enough to Choose?" *Management Accounting* 66 (September 1984), pp. 30–38.

Kroenke, David M. *Database Processing.* Chicago: Science Research Associates, 1977.

Kroenke, David M. *Business Computer Systems: An Introduction.* 2nd ed. Santa Cruz, CA: Mitchell Publishing, 1985.

Lin, W. Thomas, and Harper, William K. "A Decision-Oriented Management Accounting Information System." *Cost and Management* 55 (November–December 1981), pp. 32–36.

Lowenthal, Eugene. "Database Systems for Local Networks." *Datamation* 28 (August 1982), pp. 97–106.

Martin, Merle P. "Making the Management Report Useful." *Journal of Systems Management* 24 (May 1977), pp. 30–37.

Mayer, James A. "MIS at International Paper: An Integrated Teleprocessing Network." *Management Accounting* 61 (April 1979), pp. 24–27.

McKenney, James L., and McFarlan, F. Warren. "The Information Archipelago-Maps and Bridges." *Harvard Business Review* 60 (September–October 1982), pp. 109–119.

Mintzberg, Henry, *Impediments to the Use of Management Information.* New York: National Association of Accountants, 1975.

Moscove, Stephen A. "A Model to Evaluate Managerial Operating Performance." *Cost and Management* 58, 2 (March–April 1984), pp. 28–34.

MSA General Ledger Accounting System. Atlanta, GA: Management Science America, Inc., 1983.

National Association of Accountants. *Classification and Coding Techniques to Facilitate Accounting Operations.* Research Report 34. New York: National Association of Accountants, 1959.

Nolan, Richard L. "Orders of Office Automation." In *Managing the Data Resource Function,* 2nd ed.

Richard L. Nolan, ed. New York: West, 1982, Chapter 8.

Nusbaum, Edward E., Bailey, Andrew D., Jr., and Whinston, Andrew B. "Data Base Management. Accounting, and Accountants." *Management Accounting* 58 (May 1978), pp. 35–38.

O'Malley, Christopher "Maximizing the Power in DataBase Programs" *Personal Computing* (November 1987), pp. 147–155.

Page, John R., and Hooper, H. Paul. *Accounting and Information Systems,* 2nd ed. Reston, VA: Reston Publishing Co., 1982.

Pakrul, Herbert A. "A Decision Maker's Perspective on How the Accounting System Can Meet User Needs." *Cost and Management* 51 (September–October 1977), pp. 12–19.

Perry, William E. "Facilitating the Systems Audit Through Preparing a Flowchart." *Journal of Accounting & EDP* 4 (Spring 1988), pp. 51–52.

Poor, Alfred. "Database Power Puts On An Easy Interface." *PC Magazine* 6 (January 27, 1987), pp. 109–117.

Radford, K. J., "Information Systems and Managerial Decision Making." *Omega* 2, 2 (1974), pp. 235–242.

Robinson, Leonard A., Davis James R., and Alderman, C. Wayne. *Accounting Information Systems.* 2nd ed. New York: Harper and Row, 1986.

Rockart, J. F., and Scott-Morton, M. S. "Implications of Changes in Information Technology for Corporate Strategy." *Interfaces* 14 (January–February 1984), pp. 84–95.

Scott, George M. "A Data Base for Your Company?" *California Management Review* 19 (Fall 1976), pp. 68–78.

Simkin, Mark G. *Computer Information Systems for Business.* Dubuque, Iowa: William C. Brown, 1987.

Smith, James F., and Mufti, Amer. "Using the Relational Database." *Management Accounting* 4 (October 1985), pp. 43–54.

Smith, Lloyd, and Madsen, Kent. "Nonstop Transaction Processing." *Datamation* 29 (March 1983), pp. 167–179.

Snoball, Doug. "Information Load and Accounting Reports: Too Much, Too Little or Just Right?" *Cost and Management* 53 (May–June 1979), pp. 22–28.

Stallings, William, "The Integrated Services Digital Network." *Datamation* 30 (December 1, 1984), pp. 68–80.

Sweet, Frank. "What, If Anything, Is a Relational Database?" *Datamation* 30 (July 15, 1984), pp. 118–124.

Summers, Edward Lee. *Accounting Information Systems* Boston: Houghton Miffin Company, 1989.

Tsichritzis, D. C., and Lochovsky, F. H. "Designing the Data Base." *Datamation* 24 (August 1978), pp. 147–151.

Tyson, Thomas, and Sadhwani, Arjan T. "Bar Codes—Speed Factory Floor Reporting." *Management Accounting* 69 (April 1988), pp. 41–48.

Van Rensselaer, Carl. "Centralize? Decentralize? Distribute?" *Datamation* 25 (April 1979), pp. 88–97.

Walsh, Myles E. "The Fictional Demise of Batch Processing." *Infosystems* 27 (March 1981), pp. 64–68.

Wilkinson, Joseph W. "Designing a Common Data Base." *Cost and Management* 50 (March–April 1976), pp. 25–29.

Wolfe, Christopher, and Yoder, Steven E. "Designing Databases for Accounting." *Journal of Accountancy* 164 (October 1986), pp. 138–143.

PART THREE

Internal Controls Within Accounting Information Systems

Part Three intensively analyzes the topic of **internal control** within both manual and computerized data processing systems, emphasizing the latter. Internal control structures are stressed in this text because, in most organizations, the managerial accountants have the major responsibility for developing, implementing, and monitoring effective internal control systems. These systems can reduce the risk of errors and irregularities going undetected in an accounting information system.

Chapter 9 introduces the basic concept of internal control by analyzing the various characteristics of an effective internal control system. Many organizations have encountered difficulties with their internal control systems upon acquiring a computer to handle their accounting data processing functions. Chapter 10 therefore examines the types of internal controls that are commonly used within computerized accounting information systems.

Over the past several years, a number of fraudulent acts (such as the embezzlement of assets) have been committed by employees working in a computerized accounting information system. Often, the opportunities for employees to commit these acts have been attributable to failures in the accountants' internal control systems. Chapter 11 examines the important and interesting topic of computer crime (several actual computer crimes will be discussed and analyzed) and looks at its effects on the design and operation of internal control systems. One useful way of both preventing and detecting fraud within computerized data processing systems is by performing thorough and comprehensive *audit* procedures. Therefore, to conclude Part Three of this book. Chapter 12 analyzes the auditing activities associated with computerized accounting information systems.

Preventive and Feedback Controls for Accounting Information Systems

Among the important questions that you should be able to answer after reading this chapter are:

1. Why would a retail department store be willing to let customers shoplift some of its merchandise inventory?
2. Does a "hash total" represent your food bill at a student cafeteria?
3. Why has the introduction of an electronic data processing subsystem into an organization sometimes led to employee embezzlement of asset resources?
4. If your company gave you the responsibility for handling as well as recording the cash receipts, how might you commit a successful embezzlement of this cash?
5. Is the only purpose of an internal control system to enable management to detect employee fraud?

INTRODUCTION

Accounting information systems involve aspects of an organization's financial resources and thus the control of these resources leads directly to the need for controls *within* accounting information systems. One reason for controls is that employee crime is on the rise and safeguards are needed to thwart embezzlement, fraud, and theft. Another reason is to establish and maintain accountability over a company's financial assets. A third reason is because controls must be *designed* into systems, and thus require the help of managerial accountants, financial planners, and auditors in designing, implementing, and monitoring a system of controls. Finally, accounting information systems require controls to reduce the risk of introducing undetected errors, improper data, or unwarranted processing into an accounting information system.

This chapter is the first of four chapters on internal control (i.e., controls established *within* an organization's system). The current chapter examines the essential characteristics of a good internal control system and gives some real-life examples of the types of irregularities that can occur without good controls.

THE INTERNAL CONTROL CONCEPT

The American Institute of Certified Public Accountants (AICPA), a major accounting professional body that has as one of its functions the clarification of accounting terminology, defines **internal control** as

> the plan of organization, and all of the coordinate methods and measures adopted within a business, to safeguard its assets, check the accuracy and reliability of its accounting data, promote operational efficiency, and encourage adherence to prescribed managerial policies."[1]

There are four major functions involved in this definition of internal control: (1) safeguarding of assets, (2) checking the accuracy and reliability of accounting data, (3) promoting operational efficiency, and (4) encouraging adherence to prescribed managerial policies. Internal control is basically concerned with establishing controls *within* a company's business system to achieve these four functions.

Those controls that are established with the intent of safeguarding assets and checking the accuracy and reliability of accounting data are called **preventive** or **accounting controls** (or "before the fact" controls). In other words, they are established to *prevent* some inefficiency from occurring. For example, a company's management may establish as one of its preventive controls that the accountants responsible for recording cash receipts transactions should not have access to the cash itself. Employees who have no record-keeping functions regarding cash receipts transactions would be given responsibility for such activities as counting cash receipts and making daily bank deposits for these receipts.

This preventive control is designed to safeguard the company's cash asset as well as to check the accuracy and reliability of the accounting data recorded in the company's records. By separating the related organizational functions associated with cash (that is, the recording of cash receipts transactions and the actual handling of cash), one employee's work activities serve as a check on the work activities of the other employee. The amount of cash receipts recorded by the accountant, for instance, should equal the actual amount of cash counted and deposited in the bank by a different employee. Furthermore, if the employee handling cash attempts to steal some of the cash receipts, he or she would have a difficult time concealing this

---

[1]The Auditor's Study and Evaluation of Internal Control," *Codification of Statements on Auditing Standards* (New York: American Institute of Certified Public Accountants, 1985), AU Section 320.08.

theft, since the employee would not have access to the accounting records to cover up the shortage of actual cash deposited. If, on the other hand, there was not good separation of related organizational functions surrounding these cash activities and the same employee performed both the cash-record-keeping and the cash-handling functions, this employee would have a greater likelihood of being successful in stealing cash. Upon "pocketing" some cash receipts, the employee could then attempt to conceal his or her theft by falsifying the accounting records. The "separation of related organizational functions" preventive control will be discussed more extensively later in this chapter.

The controls that specifically promote operational efficiency and encourage adherence to prescribed managerial policies take over where the preventive controls end. This group of controls is often called **feedback** or **administrative controls** (or "after the fact" controls). For example, a company's EDP subsystem processes timely responsibility accounting performance reports for management (discussed in Chapter 2) that disclose significant variations of actual production costs from the standard production costs. As a result, the company's management is provided after-the-fact feedback regarding any inefficient manufacturing performance. Corrective action can then be initiated.

The AICPA provides thorough definitions of *administrative control* and *accounting control* that emphasize the importance of business transactions to an efficient and effective internal control system. The definition of internal control by the AICPA encompasses both administrative control and accounting control as follows:

> **Administrative control** includes, but is not limited to, the plan of organization and the procedures and records that are concerned with the decision processes leading to management's authorization of transactions. Such authorization is a management function directly associated with the responsibility for achieving the objectives of the organization and is the starting point for establishing accounting control of transactions.

> **Accounting control** comprises the plan of organization and the procedures and records that are concerned with the safeguarding of assets and the reliability of financial records and consequently are designed to provide reasonable assurance that:
>
> a. Transactions are executed in accordance with management's general or specific authorization.
> b. Transactions are recorded as necessary (1) to permit preparation of financial statements in conformity with generally accepted accounting principles or any other criteria applicable to such statements and (2) to maintain accountability for assets.
> c. Access to assets is permitted only in accordance with management's authorization.
> d. The recorded accountability for assets is compared with the existing assets at reasonable intervals and appropriate action is taken with respect to any differences.[2]

A major function of an accounting information system is to process business transactions. Since these definitions of both administrative and accounting controls emphasize the important role of business transaction execution and processing within an internal control system, the internal control area is thus an integral part of an accounting information system. The point is further made by the AICPA that for an effective internal control system to exist in a company, the administrative controls and the accounting controls cannot be treated as mutually exclusive but rather should be interrelated.

To illustrate the important interrelationship of accounting and administrative controls, assume that every Friday afternoon the Martin Beverage Company's sales departments (soft drink sales department, snack food sales department, etc.) of its marketing subsystem send their week's batch of sales invoices to the EDP subsystem for processing. A preventive, or accounting, control that may be established within the sales departments is the addition of the sales invoice numbers before these invoices are sent to the EDP

---

[2]Ibid., AU Sections 320.26 and 320.27.

subsystem. This "control total" of invoice numbers is called a **hash total**—that is, a number that is meaningless to the information system and is used only for control.

The computer is also programmed to add the sales invoice numbers and print out the result after all the week's invoices have been batch processed. The hash total of invoice numbers reported in the computer printout (the feedback, or administrative, control) is then compared with the sales departments' hash total. Ideally, the two numbers should agree, thereby providing reliable information that all the sales invoices sent to the EDP subsystem were actually processed. If the two hash numbers disagree, management is informed that something went wrong; for example, one or more sales invoices may have been lost "in transit" to the EDP subsystem. (This would result in the company never billing a customer for a credit sale.) The hash total control will also reveal any sales invoices that may have been accidentally processed twice.

It should be noted that a control such as the hash total control, which checks the accuracy and reliability of accounting data flowing through a firm's information system, is often referred to as an **internal check control.** Internal check is basically a verification function relating to companies' accounting data that are processed by organizational information systems. Use of the double-entry system in accounting, whereby the total debits must equal the total credits for each recorded business transaction, is an additional means of executing the internal check control. For example, in a manufacturing firm's journal entry for its weekly payroll, debits to various inventory accounts and various expense accounts are typically recorded. Credits are recorded to liability accounts for such items as taxes on employees' earnings, union dues, insurance, and net earnings owed to employees. At the conclusion of this often complex operation of processing the payroll, the resultant comparison of total debits to total credits in the payroll journal entry provides a very useful check on the accuracy of the payroll process. An error that is make in the

payroll processing activities will likely cause a discrepancy in total debits equaling total credits. Action should then be initiated to discover and correct the error.

The preceding internal control example of the hash total illustrates two important characteristics of an internal control system: (1) both the preventive (accounting) and the feedback (administrative) aspect of an internal control must exist and be interrelated for the control to be effective, and (2) preventive and feedback controls are not designed solely to discourage fraud and embezzlement by company employees.

In the example of the Martin Beverage Company's hash total control, the feedback control (a computer printout showing the hash total summation of the sales invoice numbers) would not be effective without the initial preventive control (the sales departments' accumulation of a hash total of sales invoice numbers before the invoices are sent to the EDP subsystem). A printout disclosing the total of the sales invoice numbers is meaningless unless there is a previously determined number for comparison. On the other hand, the preventive control established by the sales departments would be useless without the feedback control from the company's EDP subsystem. What good is a hash total if there is no subsequent control number to compare it with? Figure 9-1 illustrates this important interrelationship between the Martin Beverage Company's preventive control and feedback control for the movement of sales invoices into the EDP subsystem. (For the remainder of this text, the terms *preventive* and *feedback controls* will typically be used rather than the terms *accounting* and *administrative controls*.)

When the Martin Beverage Company's weekly sales report is received by the marketing manager, the manager should immediately compare the sales invoice number hash total printed on the computer report with the sales invoice number hash total accumulated by the sales departments before the invoices were delivered to the EDP subsystem. EDP's sales invoice hash total of 2377 shown in Figure 9-1 provides good evi-

---

Martin Beverage Company's Internal Control for Sending Sales Invoices to the EDP Subsystem

Preventive Control (established by the sales departments of the marketing subsystem)—hash total of week's sales invoice numbers	**Feedback Control** (established by the EDP subsystem as part of processing the week's batch of sales invoices)—hash total printout on sales report of the invoice numbers processed

Invoice Numbers[a]

    472
    473
    476
    477
    479

Total 2377 (hash total)   2377 (hash total)

Hash Total Numbers Agree

[a] In actual practice, the number of sales invoices transferred to the EDP subsystem would be much greater than the number assumed in this illustration. Also, the illustration further assumes that invoice numbers 474, 475, and 478 were *voided* during the week.

FIGURE 9-1

dence to the marketing manager that all the week's sales invoices were actually processed by the computer. Should the hash total numbers of the EDP subsystem and the sales departments disagree, the marketing manager (or some other designated employee) must then attempt to determine the cause of this discrepancy.

The Martin Beverage Company's control structure for sales invoices sent to the EDP subsystem also demonstrates that a system of internal control is established for reasons other than just discouraging employee fraud and embezzlement. A major purpose for establishing good internal controls is to detect "human errors." For example, a discrepancy between the hash total maintained by the Martin Beverage Company's sales departments and the hash total printed by the computer would more likely be caused by human error rather than an outright attempt by some employee to falsify the week's sales data. A hash total discrepancy could have been caused by the data-entry operator accidentally misplacing one of the sales invoice source documents before its contents were input on a magnetic

tape. This human error should be detected as a result of the Martin Beverage Company's internal controls for sales invoice processing. Although incidents of fraud and embezzlement by employees against their companies get more publicity from the mass media, the majority of errors and other inefficiencies in an organization are the result of human mistakes. (After all, what newspaper would print a story about a data-entry operator accidentally failing to process a sales invoice?)

Feedforward Control Systems

As discussed previously, feedback controls are established in a company to disclose, for example, significant deviations of actual production costs from standard production costs. However, some companies' accountants feel that a possible problem related to feedback controls is that they do not "signal" a variation from planned performance until the variation has become significant. As a consequence, costly deviations from originally established plans may persist or even worsen before corrective action is initiated.

In an attempt to solve this type of problem, some organizations have supplemented their feedback control systems with what is often called **feedforward control systems.** The major goal of a feedforward control system in a company is the *prediction* of potential variations from plans so that adjustments can be made to prevent problems before they occur and become significant.

A good example of an area where a feedforward control system could be effective is in performing a firm's cash-planning activities. An important goal in a company's cash-planning system is to maintain the company's cash balance at some predetermined level. All organizational activities and decisions that affect the level of cash would be included in the feedforward control system for cash planning. Among the important variables that should be monitored in a feedforward control cash-planning system are the amounts of sales (both cash sales and credit sales), the collections of accounts receivables from credit sales, the purchases of inventory (both cash purchases and purchases on account), the payments on accounts payables for inventory acquisitions as well as for other items previously acquired on credit, the payments for expenses such as salaries, selling, and administrative, and the payments for capital expenditures, taxes, and dividends.

An individual (or individuals) in the company (e.g., the treasurer or the financial vice-president) would be responsible for the cash-planning system and the resultant monitoring of the above mentioned types of variables. The *control standard* on which the monitoring takes place for the cash-planning area would likely be "a desired range within which the balance of cash should fall." This desired range may, in turn, be based on a predetermined relationship between the cash balance and the balances of current liability accounts as well as the balances of other current asset accounts.

The company's accounting information system will perform the functions within the feedforward control system of measuring actual cash flows and of predicting future cash flows and cash balances through use of the budgetary process. Of course, the company's computer can aid the accounting information system in processing the relevant data accumulated. As a result of the close monitoring of all variables affecting the company's cash flows, the feedforward control system will be able to provide timely information to predict any expected deviation of the actual cash balance from the planned cash balance before the deviation actually occurs and becomes significant. If, for example, the actual cash balance is predicted to drop below the predetermined level, a managerial decision may immediately be made to delay certain noncritical cash expenditures in order to avoid the borrowing of money from a bank with the resultant interest cost. On the other hand, if the actual cash balance is predicted to exceed the predetermined level, management may immediately make a decision to invest the excess cash in interest-bearing securities that are highly liquid.

In conclusion, a feedforward control system attempts to make predictions about future deviations from plans before the deviations actually occur. Under a feedback control system, these predictions are not made. Thus, feedforward controls enable management to take immediate action before significant deviations from plans occur. An electronic spreadsheet is often used as a tool to aid the efficient and effective functioning of an organization's feedforward control system.

Cost of Ideal Controls

In deciding what types of internal controls to incorporate in its system, a company should attempt to estimate the operating costs of a proposed control and then relate these costs to anticipated benefits. Only those controls whose expected benefits exceed their expected costs should be implemented.

For example, the Justin & Jodi Self-Service Company is a large discount store selling home appliances, clothing, and many other merchandise items. The company's management is currently worried about the large amount of shoplifting that has taken place in the past several months. As a result, management is considering some possible controls that would reduce this shoplifting problem. If no controls are implemented, management estimates the total annual loss to the company from shoplifting would be approximately $100,000. Two alternative preventive controls are being considered as a means of solving the shoplifting problem.

1. Hire 12 plain-clothed security guards to patrol each of the store's 12 aisles. At an approximate annual salary of $14,000 for each security guard, this control would cost the company an estimated $168,000 per year.
2. Hire three plain-clothed security guards to patrol the aisles and also install several cameras and mirrors throughout the store to enable management to observe any shoplifters. The estimated annual cost of this control would be $45,000.

With the objective of reducing shoplifting, alternative 1 (hiring 12 security guards) would appear to be the *ideal* control. Assuming the guards are properly trained and perform their jobs efficiently, the discount store's shoplifting should be reduced to almost zero. Even if shoplifting were completely eliminated, however, alternative 1 should not be implemented because the control's anticipated costs ($168,000 per year) exceed the control's anticipated benefits ($100,000 per year—the approximate annual shoplifting loss that would be eliminated).

With alternative 2 (hiring three security guards plus installing cameras and mirrors), the store's management estimates that the total annual loss from shoplifting can be reduced from $100,000 to $30,000, the net benefits therefore being $70,000. Since the second alternative's expected benefits ($70,000 per year reduction of shoplifting) exceed its expected costs ($45,000 per year), management should select the alterna-

tive 2 control for implementation into its system rather than the alternative 1 control.

The point of the preceding example is that in many cases, the introduction of ideal controls (which would reduce the risk to practically zero for any undetected errors and irregularities) into an organization's system is impractical. If a control's expected costs exceed its expected benefits, the effect of implementing the control will be to decrease operating efficiency for the entire organizational system. From a cost/benefit viewpoint, therefore, a company's management will often install controls that are less than ideal. Management must learn to live with the fact that a certain degree of risk (caused by undetected errors and irregularities) is inherent in its preventive control system.

To emphasize the important role of a company's management in developing and maintaining an internal control system, the following statement was issued by the U.S. Senate Committee on Banking, Housing, and Urban Affairs.

The establishment and maintenance of a system of internal control and accurate books and records are fundamental responsibilities of management. The expected benefits to be derived from the conscientious discharge of these responsibilities are of basic importance to investors and the maintenance of the integrity of our capital market system. The committee recognizes, however, that management must exercise judgment in determining the steps to be taken, and the cost incurred, in giving assurance that the objectives expressed will be achieved. Here, standards of reasonableness must apply. In this regard, the term "accurately" does not mean exact precision as measured by some abstract principle. Rather, it means that a company's records should reflect transactions in conformity with generally accepted accounting principles or other applicable criteria. While management should observe every reasonable prudence in satisfying these objectives, the committee recognizes that management must necessarily estimate and evaluate the cost/benefit relationships of the steps to be taken in fulfillment of its responsibilities under this paragraph. The accounting profession will be expected to use their professional judgment in evaluating the systems maintained by companies. The size of the business, diversity of operations, degree of centralization of financial and operating management, amount of contact by top management with day-to-day operations, and numerous other circumstances are factors which management must consider in establishing and maintaining an internal control system.[3]

The ideas expressed in the preceding statement eventually were incorporated into the **Foreign Corrupt Practices Act of 1977.** This act was passed by Congress and signed into law in December 1977. The act grew out of a desire to prohibit bribes to foreign officials by publicly held companies. To accomplish this, it contained several provisions regarding internal control. The requirement that companies implement effective internal control systems is intended to reduce the risk of questionnable or illegal foreign payments.

Specifically, with respect to internal control, the act provides that publicly held companies (those subject to the Securities Exchange Act of 1934) have a system of internal accounting controls that is *sufficient* to provide *reasonable assurances* regarding certain handling of transactions and assets. The language of the act (*sufficient* and *reasonable assurances*) is purposely somewhat vague about the internal control requirements. As demonstrated earlier, maintaining an ideal set of controls is not generally cost effective. So, companies need to balance the amount of controls with the cost of such controls. For this reason, the Foreign Corrupt Practices Act cannot require companies to maintain a *perfect* set of internal controls.

Unfortunately, the vague language in the act, while necessary, makes it difficult for companies to be sure of compliance. Management is responsible for compliance with the Foreign Corrupt Practices Act, not a company's external auditors. But management may not be clear about whether

simply having an external audit is adequate for compliance. In reality, the external auditor surveys the internal control system only to determine the amount of substantive testing (the scope of the audit) necessary in the audit engagement. This means that the external auditor does not evaluate the adequacy of an internal accounting control system with respect to the Foreign Corrupt Practices Act. Because of this management responsibility, managers are advised to consider general guidelines for compliance set forth in the 1979 AICPA publication, "Report of the Special Advisory Committee on Internal Accounting Control." This publication is directed at managers and it provides help in evaluating the internal accounting control system.

Since the passage of the Foreign Corrupt Practices Act, there has been some controversy about the need for a management report on internal control. In 1979 the SEC proposed some rules for this. These rules would have called for a management report explaining compliance with the Foreign Corrupt Practices Act. In 1980, however, the proposed rules were withdrawn. The SEC has since encouraged management to provide such a report on a voluntary basis.

Internal Audit Subsystem's Control Function

Many organizations, especially the larger ones, have within their systems a separate subsystem called **internal auditing**. (The audit function will be discussed extensively in Chapter 12.) The internal audit area is a service subsystem whose major function is to help design and implement preventive controls within the other organizational subsystems and, through the use of feedback controls, to review periodically the performance of each subsystem. The important role played by internal auditors in reviewing their organization's internal control system is indicated by the American Institute of Certified Public Accountants as follows:

> When an entity has an internal audit department, management may delegate to it some of its

[3]Report of the Senate Committee on Banking, Housing, and Urban Affairs, May 2, 1977 (Report No. 95-114).

supervisory functions, especially with respect to the review of internal control. This particular internal audit function constitutes a separate component of internal control undertaken by specially assigned staff within the entity with the objective of determining whether other internal controls are well designed and properly operated.[4]

The internal audit staff usually consists of accountants who, because of their education and training, have the ability to design effective controls to safeguard an organization's assets and to evaluate the operating performance of individual subsystems. In those companies with no separate internal audit staff, the managerial accountants within the accounting subsystem normally play a major role in establishing the preventive controls and overseeing the performance of the feedback controls.

The principal advantage of having a separate internal audit subsystem is that it is completely independent of all the other subsystems within an organization and can therefore be objective when reviewing the operating performances of each subsystem (which also encompasses a review of the accounting subsystem's operational activities). If the internal audit function were assigned to the accounting subsystem, complete objectivity would be more difficult, if not impossible, to achieve because the accountants would be evaluating their own subsystem's activities. Due to the importance of objectivity, good organizational design requires the internal audit subsystem's auditors to report directly to top management, which ensures their complete independence from the subsystems whose work is evaluated.

The valuable service function performed by internal auditors in establishing and monitoring an organization's control system is also recognized by the external auditors working for public accounting firms. When the external auditors come into a company to evaluate the fair presentation of its financial statements, these auditors may rely on much of the internal audit subsystem's previous work in establishing and monitoring controls (provided that certain characteristics of the internal auditors with respect to independence are evident). The existence of an effective internal audit subsystem will often enable the external auditors to perform less testing of an organization's financial transactions and therefore save the organization time and money.

To understand thoroughly the importance of good internal control within an organization's information system, the major components necessary for an effective preventive control system and an effective feedback control system to exist are discussed in the following two sections.

EFFECTIVE PREVENTIVE CONTROLS

The components that are essential to an organization's preventive control system are (1) a good audit trail, (2) competent employees, (3) separation of related organizational functions, and (4) physical protection of assets. Each of these preventive control components will now be analyzed.

Good Audit Trail

A good **audit trail** means that a manager (or any other employee) is able to follow the path of accounting transactions from the initial source documents to their final disposition on a report. The audit trail is probably the most important preventive control because it enables management "to know what is happening" throughout all the phases of accounting data processing. As a result, a company should be able to detect and correct any errors and irregularities occurring within its accounting information system. Without a good audit trail, it would be quite easy for errors and irregularities in the processing of accounting data to go undetected.

[4]"Using the Work of an Internal Auditor," *Codification of Statements on Auditing Standards* (New York: American Institute of Certified Public Accountants, 1985), AU Section 8010.02.

When establishing its audit trail, an organization should prepare a policies and procedures manual that includes such things as (1) a chart of accounts describing the purpose of each general ledger account (as well as the accounts within the subsidiary ledgers) so that the debits and credits from accounting transactions are recorded in the correct accounts, (2) a complete description of the types of documents (e.g., sales invoices, shipping reports, payroll time cards, and purchase orders) that will be used as the basis for recording financial activities, and the correct procedures for preparing and approving the data included on these documents, and (3) a complete description of the authority and responsibility delegated to individual employees for such functions as recording specific types of accounting transactions (e.g., cash receipts and disbursements transactions) and making specific organizational decisions (e.g., when to write off a customer's account as uncollectible).

Defining the accounts within the chart of accounts, describing the documents to be used, and indicating which employees have been delegated authority and responsibility for specific activities greatly enhances an organization's audit trail. If, for example, one of the Martin Beverage Company's sales managers has a question about the processing of last week's sale of 100 cases of soft drinks to a specific customer, this manager can examine the policies and procedures manual and immediately ascertain in which accounts the transaction should have been recorded, what source document (or documents) should have been prepared for the transaction, and which employee (or employees) had the authority and responsibility for handling the transaction (e.g., approving the customer's credit and establishing cash discount terms). After acquiring this information, the sales manager should be able to follow easily the audit trail for the sale of soft drinks. Any error or irregularity in handling the sales transaction (e.g., the shipping report disclosing that 110 cases were sent to the customer, whereas the sales invoice indicates that the customer was billed for 100 cases) should be detected by the manager when tracing this transaction along the audit trail.

Some companies use document flowcharts (previously discussed in Chapter 6) to help them follow the flow of transactions through their accounting information systems. For control purposes, the preparation of a document flowchart can enable a company's accountant (perhaps an internal auditor) to identify important control points. A **control point** is an information system attribute or procedure relating to a control objective. It is a location in an information system where an organizational or procedural practice is required to prevent inaccurate data (e.g., erroneous data) from entering the information system, to detect unusual as well as missing transactions, or to ensure that all necessary corrections are made.

To illustrate the use of a document flowchart in identifying control points, assume the following facts about the purchasing activities of the GoodLumber Company.

> GoodLumber Company is a large regional dealer of building materials that requires an elaborate system of internal controls. The document flowchart of the purchasing activities is presented in Figure 9-2. It should be noted that the format of this document flowchart is somewhat different from the document flowcharts illustrated in Chapter 6. (The reference numbers appearing to the left of the document flowchart symbols are included for convenience—they would not normally be part of the flowchart.)
>
> The activities in the purchasing department start with the receipt of an approved copy of the purchase requisition (PR) from the budget department. After reviewing the purchase requisition, a prenumbered purchase order (PO) is issued in multiple copies. Two copies are sent to a vendor, one retained in the purchasing department, and the remainder distributed to other departments of GoodLumber. The second copy of the purchase order is to be returned by the vendor to confirm the receipt of the order. This copy is filed according to PO number in the PO file.
>
> A receiving report (RR) is completed in the receiving department when shipments of materials

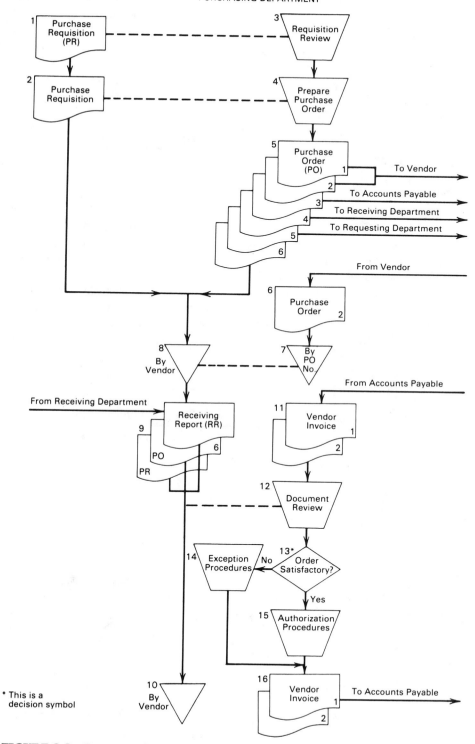

PURCHASING DEPARTMENT

FIGURE 9-2 Document flowchart of purchasing activities.

arrive from vendors. A copy of the receiving report is sent to the purchasing department and attached to the purchase order and purchase requisition in the vendor's file.

The accounts payable department normally receives two copies of a vendor's invoice. These two copies are forwarded to the purchasing department for review with various documents related to the order. Purchasing will either institute authorization procedures for the payment of the invoice or recommend exception procedures.

Based on the document flowchart of Good-Lumber Company's purchasing activities in Figure 9-2, we can now identify the control points. This is done in Figure 9-3. The first column of Figure 9-3 identifies the control points by using the reference numbers appearing to the left of the document flowchart symbols. The second column describes the nature of the control activity required for every control point identified.

Finally, the third column of Figure 9-3 explains the purpose of, or justification for, each control activity.

A document flowchart can also be a useful tool when performing the analysis phase of a systems study. The document flowchart's important role in systems analysis work will be discussed in the section of this book (Part 4) describing systems study.

Computer's Effect on Audit Trail

The introduction of a computer into an organization's data processing system can create problems regarding the audit trail. In a manual data processing system, following the audit trail of an accounting transaction is normally not difficult. In a computerized system, however, the transaction processing is performed within the computer. As a result, the audit trail becomes more

Control Points

Reference Numbers[a]	Control Activity	Control Purpose or Justification
4	Purchase orders are prepared from purchase requisitions.	Documentation is created for both issue and comparison.
5	Purchase orders are issued in multiple copies.	Multiple copies facilitate both the segregation of duties and subsequent control points in the system.
7,8	The copies of purchase orders retained in the purchasing department are compared to the copies returned by vendors.	This comparison facilitates the control of open purchase orders.
9	Copies of receiving reports are matched with, and attached to, the purchase requisitions and purchase orders in the file.	This matching determines whether the items received are the items ordered.
12,13	Invoice, receiving report, purchase order, and purchase requisition are compared and procedures are determined.	This comparison determines whether the vendor invoice is accurate (i.e., whether it covers the items requisitioned, ordered, and received in good condition, and whether prices and credit terms are correct). If there is a problem, exception procedures are followed to resolve the problem.
14,15	Authorization of payment.	Authorization by the purchasing department prevents improper payment by accounts payable.

[a] See Figure 9-2.

FIGURE 9-3   Identification and evaluation of control points.

difficult to follow. Figure 9-4 reflects the data processing sequence for the Alan Company's financial transactions in a manual accounting information system compared to a computerized accounting information system.

Under a manual system, all four stages through the audit trail involve people working with pencil and paper. The procedural activities as well as the output from each data processing stage are visible to the human eye, which makes it quite easy for a manager to follow the audit trail of specific accounting transactions. With a computerized system, however, the only stage of data processing clearly observable to the human eye is the preparation of transactions' source documents. (In fact, with some highly sophisticated online computer systems, hard-copy source documents for transactions are not prepared.) Stages 2, 3, and 4 of the manual system are performed internally by computer equipment, thereby obscuring the audit trail. Furthermore,

some financial data processed internally by the computer may never by seen by an organization's management. For example, performance reports of the Alan Company's sporting goods manufacturing activities are based on the management-by-exception principle. Thus, only significant variations of actual production costs from standard production costs are printed out by the company's computer for analysis. This means that the large quantity of production cost data that does not deviate significantly from the standard costs never appears in hard-copy management-by-exception performance reports.

When computers first became popular in business, internal auditors (as well as external auditors working for public accounting firms) tended to ignore the existence of these computers within their companies' information systems. When an internal auditor wanted to trace the audit trail of specific accounting transactions, he or she would audit "around the computer." Un-

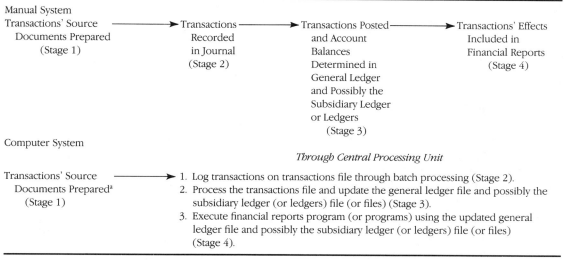

FIGURE 9-4 **Manual compared with computerized data processing of the Alan Company's financial transactions.**

der this approach, the auditor acquires computer printouts of financial data and then traces specific items from these printouts back to the various source documents. The auditor also performs tracing from the source documents to the computer printouts. Basically, he or she ignores the entire processing functions within the computer.

The number of computer frauds and errors that have taken place over the last several years has caused most internal auditors (as well as external auditors) to audit "through the computer." Using this approach, the internal auditor becomes familiar with the company's hardware and software, helps establish the preventive control system for the computer center, and also periodically reviews the control system to make sure it is functioning properly. Thus, a through-the-computer audit allows a company's internal auditor to understand better what is happening inside the computer, thereby making the data processing audit trail easier to follow. Both "auditing around the computer" and "auditing through the computer" are discussed in greater detail in Chapter 12. Specific controls over processing in a computerized environment are discussed in Chapter 10. The components of good internal control described throughout the remainder of this chapter apply to both manual and computerized processing systems.

Competent Employees

Another important preventive control that should exist in an organization is **competent employees**. Because a company's personnel will be working continually with organizational assets (e.g., handling cash, acquiring and disbursing inventory, and operating production equipment), incompetent employees can cause inefficient use of the company's asset resources, thereby thwarting management's prescribed policies and goals.

Personnel Subsystem's Function in Obtaining Competent Employees

The personnel subsystem has a major role in the successful implementation of this preventive control. Personnel managers are often responsible for the initial interviews of prospective employees. It is important that when interviewing potential employees, these managers thoroughly understand the level of human qualifications necessary for specific jobs. Otherwise, an individual hired for a job may be either overqualified or underqualified, both of which are undesirable situations from the operational efficiency viewpoint.

When employees are overqualified, their salaries may be too high (based on the types of organizational functions performed) and they may be bored with their work. Excessive salaries in relation to the level of work being performed for a company typically lead to operational inefficiency. In effect, the company is paying too much for the employees' service benefits received. Also, if we think of employees as a human-resource asset, the placement of individuals in job functions for which they are overqualified is an inefficient use of asset resources. Employees' boredom is also a cause of operational inefficiency. In fact, some bored employees, in an attempt to make their jobs more challenging and exciting, have initiated techniques for embezzling assets from their companies.

When employees are underqualified, they may become frustrated and possibly resent their company. Inability of the employees to fulfill their job responsibilities will adversely affect operational efficiency. Furthermore, negative feelings of employees toward their employer can lead to additional inefficiency within a company. To "get back" at the company for the frustrating nature of their jobs, the employees may intentionally violate company policies and procedures.

To avoid the negative aspects of hiring either overqualified or underqualified employees, a major function of personnel managers is to obtain the best possible matching of job qualifications to people qualifications. Even though a prospective employee's educational background and prior work experience may not qualify him or her for a specific job, this situation can hopefully be alleviated through adequately planned training programs to increase the skills of employees and thus make them more productive human resources.

The personnel subsystem should also establish equitable policy guidelines for employees' salary increases and promotions. Ideally, the criteria for these two reward mechanisms should be fairly uniform within all of an organization's subsystems so that each employee feels that he or she is being treated fairly in relation to the other workers. Equitable company-wide policies established by the personnel subsystem for salary and promotion rewards should contribute toward employees' loyalty and operational efficiency.

Bonding of Employees

People working within a company's accounting subsystem are often given responsibilities for handling assets susceptible to theft (e.g., liquid assets such as cash and marketable securities). These employees should be both competent and honest. One approach used by many organizations to reduce the risk of loss from employee theft is to acquire **fidelity bond coverage** on those employees having direct access to assets subject to misappropriation. The fidelity bond can be obtained from an insurance company. The insurance company will investigate the backgrounds of all employees that an organization desires to have bonded. In issuing this fidelity bond, the insurance company assumes liability (up to a specified limit) for the individual employees who are named in the bond. Should some of these employees later embezzle assets from their organization, the insurance company is monetarily responsible to the organization for the resultant loss.

Separation of Related Organizational Functions

The **separation of related organizational functions** means that those employees who are given responsibility for the physical custody of specific organizational assets should not also be given responsibility for the record-keeping functions relating to the assets. Otherwise, an employee could misappropriate company assets and then attempt to conceal this fraud by falsifying the accounting records.

Separation of Related Functions: An Example

Assume that Jerome Stein, one of the Acne Company's accountants, is responsible for preparing the daily bank deposit from accounts receivable check payments mailed in by credit sales customers. Jerome accumulates the day's cash receipts checks (the physical-custody function), endorses the checks, fills out the bank deposit, and prepares a listing of each customer's payment (these last three functions are the record-keeping functions). This list of customers' payments is then sent to the computer center for the end-of-the-week update of the accounts receivable subsidiary ledger. Since separation of duties among employees does not exist for the cash receipts functions, Jerome could steal some of the customers' payment checks and then exclude them from the daily bank deposit and from the listing that goes to the computer center.

Let us further assume that one check today, for $300 from Mary Kelley, is "pocketed" by the accountant. Thus, Mary's cash payment is not recorded anywhere within the company's accounting information system—and Jerome Stein is $300 richer! For Jerome successfully to commit this fraud, however, he must eventually reflect on his cash receipts list sent to the computer center a $300 credit to Miss Kelley's account. (Otherwise, when she is mailed her monthly statement, we would expect her to complain about not receiving credit for the $300 payment.) Therefore, to cover his tracks, Stein must make sure that before Mary Kelley's monthly bill is sent, the $300 fraud has been transferred from her account to some other customer's account.

For this example, assume that the Acne Company bills its customers monthly under a **cycle**

method. (On the first of each month, all customers whose last names begin with A–F are billed; on the tenth of each month, all customers whose last names begin with G–O are billed; and on the twentieth of each month, all customers whose last names begin with P–Z are billed.) Thus, by the tenth of the month, when Mary Kelley's bill is mailed, Jerome Stein must eliminate the $300 fraud from her account.

He easily solves this problem by using a $400 cash payment check received on the seventh of the month from another credit customer, Jack Taussig. Since Taussig's statement will not be mailed until the twentieth of the month, Jerome endorses the $400 check, includes the $400 within the daily bank deposit, and on the cash receipts list sent to the computer center he shows a $300 credit to Mary Kelley's account and only a $100 credit to Jack Taussig's account. Jerome has thus shifted his $300 embezzlement from Kelley's account to Taussig's account, and Mary Kelley's balance owed the company will be correct when her monthly statement is mailed.

Before the twentieth of the month, when Jack Taussig's bill is sent, his account balance will also have to be "corrected" in this same manner (i.e., by using other customers' cash payment checks as the basis for crediting his account a total of $300). In actual practice, the Acne Company's accountant would probably be embezzling many cash receipts checks each month and attempting to "cover his tracks" for all these embezzled checks.

The preceding example illustrates the type of fraud that employees can execute on their company's cash asset. The technical term used for embezzling cash payments from credit sales in this manner is called the **lapping of accounts receivable.** Our example emphasizes what can happen without a "separation of related organizational functions" preventive control. One possible preventive control measure that the Acne Company could use to avoid this type of cash fraud is to make one employee (Harvey Hunt) responsible for taking the day's cash receipts

checks and preparing an adding machine tape of the total dollar amount of checks (let's assume that Wednesday's cash receipts checks total $5000). Then the checks are turned over to a second employee (the accountant, Jerome Stein), who endorses the checks, makes out the bank deposit, and prepares the detailed listing that is sent to the computer center.

The computer center, when processing the customers' payments at week's end, can obtain a separate printout total of each day's cash receipts checks from customers. For Wednesday of this week, the total of the customers' cash receipts processed by the computer should be $5000. The actual dollar figure printed out by the computer should then be compared with the adding machine tape control total accumulated by Harvey Hunt. These two monetary totals should agree. Any discrepancy would be immediately investigated by management, and the irregularity causing the difference should be detected.

This control would prevent the employee (Jerome Stein) who is responsible for all the detailed record-keeping activities (endorsing checks, preparing the bank deposit, and listing each customer's cash payment) from embezzling any specific checks. Theft of any checks would cause the computer printout of a specific day's total cash receipts checks to be less than the control total accumulated by Harvey Hunt on the adding machine tape.

When accountants participate in designing a company's information system (discussed in Part Four), they have a major responsibility to design the system in such a way that no single employee has too many related functions, thereby reducing the risk of asset embezzlement. It should be emphasized here, however, that no separation of related functions preventive control completely eliminates the possibility of employee embezzlement. Through **collusive efforts** (in which two or more employees work together), the separation of related organizational functions preventive control for safeguarding a company's assets can be circumvented. Good separation of duties merely reduces the risk of fraud because two or more people must now join forces to execute a fraudulent activity successfully.

For example, the Acne Company's Hunt and Stein could steal check payments by working together. Harvey Hunt could omit specific checks from the daily adding machine tape control total. These same checks would also be excluded from Jerome Stein's daily bank deposit and his daily cash receipts listing sent to the computer center. Stein would then falsify the endorsements on the embezzled checks and split the proceeds with Hunt. Thus, the computer printout of a specific day's total cash receipts checks would still agree with Hunt's adding machine tape total and the embezzlement would therefore not be detected. A control method for detecting this fraudulent activity is now discussed.

Role of Internal Audit Subsystem

A company's internal audit staff would have a major role in designing effective separation of duties among organizational employees (which is the *preventive* part of the control), and also in monitoring the efficient performance of this control (which is the *feedback* part of the control). For example, on a surprise basis, one of the Acne Company's internal auditors can take possession of the day's endorsed cash receipts checks, the day's bank deposit, and the day's detailed cash receipts listing for the computer center as soon as the accountant, Jerome Stein, has finished these three record-keeping activities.

The auditor first ascertains whether the total bank deposit dollar amount agrees with the total dollar amount on the listing prepared for the computer center. Next, the auditor traces each customer's check to the cash receipts list prepared by Stein. If any discrepancies arise between specific customers' checks and what is actually shown on Jerome Stein's cash receipts list, the possibility exists of accounts receivable lapping. The key to the internal auditor's verification work is the element of surprise. If, for

example, Jerome Stein and Harvey Hunt knew in advance about this surprise audit procedure, they would obviously refrain from any fraudulent activities on the specific day the internal auditor planned to do the verification work.

Physical Protection of Assets

The purpose of the **physical protection of assets** is to maintain a company's assets in a safe physical location, thus reducing the risk of employee misappropriation. For example, an organization's inventory of merchandise should be kept in a storage area that is accessible only to those employees given the custodial responsibility for this asset, thus preventing unauthorized employees from stealing merchandise. Inventory items coming into the storage area (possibly a separate warehouse in those organizations having large quantities of inventory) should be counted by the inventory clerk (or clerks). The clerk should then sign a receiving document, which formally establishes this employee's responsibility for the delivered items. After the inventory is moved into the storage area, any authorized employees requesting some of the inventory should sign the inventory clerk's issuance report, thereby relieving the clerk of further responsibility for these requisitioned inventory items. Periodically, the organization's internal audit staff should supervise a physical count of the actual inventory items on hand in the storage area. The quantities of specific inventory items counted should then be compared with the quantities of these items shown in the detailed inventory records. (To achieve good separation of related organizational functions, the detailed inventory records should be maintained by employees of the accounting subsystem rather than by the inventory clerk.) Any discrepancies between the physical count and the inventory records should be investigated by the internal auditors in order to determine the cause (or causes) of these discrepancies.

An organization's important documents (such

as the corporate charter, all major contracts with other companies, and registration statements required by the Securities and Exchange Commission) should be accessible only to authorized management personnel. Many organizations keep their important documents in fireproof safes on their own premises or in rented storage vaults at banks.

Physical Protection of Cash Asset

The susceptibility of cash to theft by employees as well as the risk of human error in handling cash (due to the large volume of cash receipts and disbursements transactions that many organizations have) makes it essential for an organization to institute physical protection safeguards for its cash asset. In addition to acquiring fidelity bond coverage on those employees handling cash, the following two controls for cash should also be used: (1) the majority of cash disbursements for authorized expenditures should be made by check and (2) the daily cash receipts (received either in the mail from credit customers or through over-the-counter sales) should be deposited intact at the bank. Each of these two physical protection control areas are now briefly discussed.

Cash Disbursements by Check

A good audit trail of cash disbursements is essential to avoid the occurrence of undetected errors and irregularities in the handling of cash. To this end, most organizations use prenumbered checks (to maintain accountability for both issued and unissued checks) for making authorized cash disbursements.

An additional preventive control that may be incorporated into a company's cash payments system is a **voucher system** for its disbursements. As you may remember, a *voucher* is a document that thoroughly describes an accounting transaction requiring an eventual cash outlay (e.g., the purchase of office equipment on credit). A voucher can be approved for payment by an authorized employee (or employees) only after all the supporting documents relating to the payment have been attached to the voucher and reviewed by this employee. For example, assume that the voucher in Figure 9-5 was prepared by one of the Alan Company's accountants (Harry Price) on June 15, 1991 for the purchase of an office typewriter from Swann Machine Company. Before this voucher is approved for payment by the Alan Company's treasurer, George Bone, the following supporting documents would be attached to the voucher and reviewed by Bone.

1. A copy of the *purchase order* prepared at the time the typewriter acquisition was approved. The purchase order indicates the Alan Company's intent to buy the electric typewriter from the Swann Machine Company at a specified cost ($900).
2. A copy of the *receiving report* prepared by the Alan Company's receiving department when the typewriter was delivered. The receiving report indicates that the Alan Company actually received the typewriter asset that will eventually be paid for by a cash disbursement check.
3. A copy of the *purchase invoice* from the Swann Machine Company indicating the dollar amount owed. The purchase invoice should be compared with the purchase order and the receiving report before George Bone signs the $900 check. (At that time, the Date Voucher Paid and Check Number part of the Figure 9-5 voucher would be completed.)

Upon issuance of a cash disbursement check to pay a voucher, the specific supporting documents should all be stamped "PAID" to prevent their being presented at some future time for a second payment. As a further precaution, many organizations require two different authorized employees to approve vouchers and sign cash disbursement checks for all expenditures over a specified dollar amount (e.g., over $500). Thus, when a voucher system and prenumbered checks for cash disbursement transactions are used, the audit trail of cash outlays can easily be traced.

The prenumbered voucher document and the prenumbered check document (rather than coins and currency for cash disbursements) are both physical items that reduce the risk of employees' misappropriation of cash. Once a month, a company's bank reconciliation statement (analyzing the causes of discrepancies between the company's checking account records and what the bank's records indicate) should be prepared by an employee who has no cash-related responsibilities—e.g., an internal auditor.

Making cash disbursements by check is an effective preventive control. However, a company may have various small cash expenditures to make during an accounting period. It is more efficient to pay cash for these expenditures than to follow the formal company procedure of using checks. For good operating efficiency, the Alan Company should use a **petty cash fund** for its small, miscellaneous expenditures. To exercise control over this fund, one employee called the *petty cash custodian* should be given the responsibility for handling petty cash transactions. If the Alan Company establishes its petty cash fund at $100, this money should be kept under the custodian's control in a locked box, and the custodian should be the only individual with access to the fund.

Alan Company
VOUCHER

Cash disbursement to be made to: Swann Machine Company

8913 Southwest Avenue

New Orleans, Louisiana 70122

Voucher No. 185

Date   June 15, 1991

Accounts	Account Numbers	Debit	Credit	
Office equipment	230	900		
Vouchers payable	320		900	

Explanation: Purchase of an electric typewriter from Swann Machine Company on purchase order number 74.

Voucher Prepared by:	Voucher Approved by:	Date Voucher Paid:	Check Number:
Harry Price (Accountant)	*George Bone* (Treasurer)		

FIGURE 9-5   Alan Company voucher for the purchase of an office typewriter.

Cash Receipts Deposited Intact

The importance of having physical protection safeguards for an organization's cash expenditure activities also holds true for its cash receipts activities. Each day's accumulation of cash receipts should be "deposited intact" at a bank. In the typical retail organization, the total cash receipts for any specific working day will come from two major sources: checks arriving by mail from credit-sales customers and currency and checks received from over-the-counter cash sales. Daily intact deposits of cash receipts means that none of these cash inflows should be used by company employees to make cash disbursements. Rather, every penny collected should go directly to the bank and a separate checking account used for cash disbursements. The intact deposit of cash receipts enables the audit trail of cash inflows to be easily traced to the bank deposit slip and the monthly bank statement. On the other hand, if employees of a company were permitted to use some of the day's receipts for cash disbursements, the audit trail for cash could become quite confusing, thereby increasing the risk of irregularities.

The physical protective device that should be used for the cash receipts from over-the-counter sales is a cash register. The specific type of cash register employed will be determined by the company's needs. For a small grocery store, a cash register that simply rings up a sale would probably be adequate. For a major retailer with large daily volumes of over-the-counter sales, however, a point-of-sale recorder (which can integrate such functions of the company as credit evaluation, sales, inventory, and billing) would probably be more beneficial.

A good internal control system for the cash register's efficient use is to give each employee operator a specific amount of currency (in order to make change) for which the operator is accountable at the beginning of his or her shift. The internal tape within the cash register that records the amount of every sale should not be accessible to the operator. (The employee's supervisor should have the key that unlocks the section of the cash register where the internal tape is stored.) This prevents the operator from manipulating the tape contents to cover up a fraudulent act.

At the end of the employee's shift, the supervisor should examine the internally stored tape to ascertain the total cash sales that were recorded. The supervisor then counts the cash within the register (subtracting the specific quantity of money provided the operator at the beginning of his or her shift), and this amount should be equal to the total of the internal tape. In many organizations, the cash register operator is made responsible for any discrepancy between the internal tape amount of cash sales and the actual cash in the register.

A cash register's display window (showing the actual amount rung up by the operator each time a sale is made) should be visible to the customer. This preventive control, in effect, brings the customer into the control system. The customer is able to detect either an accidental or intentional error by the cash register operator in recording a sale. An obvious intentional error would occur when the operator rings up an actual $10 sale for only $5 and pockets the difference. A company may have signs located near its cash registers asking customers to tell the manager about any purchases that are recorded incorrectly on these registers. As proof of the discrepancies, the customers can take their ejected cash register tape receipts directly to the store manager. The manager may even reward the customers with free gifts!

EFFECTIVE FEEDBACK CONTROLS

As discussed at the beginning of this chapter, feedback controls are established within an organization to encourage operating efficiency and adherence to managerial policies. Essential components to a company's feedback control system are

1. Efficient preventive controls.
2. A responsibility accounting system.
3. Timely performance reports.

Since component 1 has already been analyzed in this chapter and components 2 and 3 were discussed in Chapter 2, on management concepts, the discussion here will be directed toward these components' roles in a feedback control system.

Efficient Preventive Controls

For a feedback control system to achieve its objectives, some type of standards or criteria for the various organizational functions must already exist. This allows the feedback control system to measure whether actual operating performance is efficient or inefficient based on the preestablished standards or criteria.

The predetermined standards or criteria are an organization's **preventive controls**. A standard cost accounting system, a budgetary system, or criteria such as competent employees and physical protection of assets can all be considered preventive controls designed to safeguard an organization's asset resources from inefficient use. The preventive controls represent guidelines for efficient operating performance. Without these efficiency guidelines, it is very difficult for management "to evaluate positive or negative performances" (the feedback control area) within specific subsystems. For example, if the Alan Company did not have predetermined standard costs for the sporting goods manufacturing processes, it would be difficult for management to evaluate whether the actual production costs were too high or too low.

A Responsibility Accounting System

As discussed in Chapter 2, a **responsibility accounting system** means that each organizational subsystem's performance is evaluated on the basis of only those operating items or activities over which it has control. For feedback controls to achieve the objective of encouraging operating efficiency, these controls must be designed to differentiate between each subsystem's controllable and noncontrollable items (or activities). The production subsystem managers' noncontrollable items (such as the dollar amount of building depreciation allocated to the production subsystem), for example, should not be included within the feedback control criteria used to evaluate their operating efficiency, because the managers are unable to influence changes in these noncontrollable items. On the other hand, the production managers should be held accountable for those items that they can control, such as excessive direct labor costs incurred in manufacturing the inventory.

Because a responsibility accounting system makes a distinction between a subsystem's controllable and noncontrollable items and then evaluates the subsystem's operating efficiency only on its controllable items, the establishment of an effective responsibility accounting structure is essential to an organization's feedback control system. To illustrate, a *responsibility accounting system* for the Alan Company's sporting goods manufacturing process is developed by ascertaining which of the production costs are controllable by each manufacturing component (such as the basketball manufacturing component) and which are noncontrollable. If the Alan Company's production managers were permitted to determine their controllable and noncontrollable costs, they might tend to categorize certain controllable items as noncontrollable, thereby eliminating their responsibilities for these cost items. Management's subsequent feedback control evaluation of operating efficiency (by comparing standard to actual production costs) would give misleading results because those controllable costs that should have been included in the evaluation were excluded.

To prevent this situation from occurring, the Alan Company's internal auditors (who should have an objective, unbiased attitude toward the production subsystem) could participate in the decision-making function of determining each production manager's controllable and noncontrollable cost items. This effectively established responsibility accounting system should lead to an effective feedback control system.

Timely Performance Reports

Once an organization has implemented various preventive controls and a responsibility accounting structure, the "heart" of its feedback control system, which is **timely performance reports,** can become operative. The purpose of timely performance reports is to provide a company's management with relevant information about how efficiently the implemented preventive controls are functioning. The use of a management-by-exception system in preparing these performance reports will give management feedback information regarding those preventive control areas that deviate significantly from their preestablished criteria. However, for management to determine specifically which employee (or employees) caused a deviation so that corrective action can be implemented, the performance reports should include only those functional activities that individual employees can control. Thus, performance reports that provide information to management about the operating efficiency of preventive controls should be based on the organization's responsibility accounting structure. For example, having implemented the Alan Company's standard cost accounting system for each manufacturing component of the production subsystem, and having determined which costs are controllable and noncontrollable by the individual managers of the manufacturing components, timely performance reports can then be prepared for each manufacturing area, disclosing the significant deviations of actual from standard controllable costs.

As emphasized in previous chapters, an organization's electronic data processing subsystem can play a major role in increasing the timeliness of performance reports. The computer's speed in processing data enables management to receive feedback performance reports of exceptions much sooner after they have occurred than would be possible with a manual system. Quicker after-the-fact performance reports should lead to increased operating efficiency because management's attention is directed to significant preventive control deviations requiring corrective action before these deviations get too far "out of hand."

Some accountants consider performance reports as only reflecting analyses of monetary items (e.g., comparing actual production costs with standard production costs). However, if an organization's performance reports are to function as true feedback controls that signal the need for corrective action, the term *performance reports* should be used in a broad sense to also include nonmonetary evaluations of preventive controls. For example, one of a company's important preventive controls is that the functions of cash handling and cash record keeping are performed by different employees (the separation of related organizational functions preventive control). On paper, the above preventive control sounds great.

When the internal audit staff periodically observes the cash-handling and cash-record-keeping functions, however, they may find that this preventive control is being ignored. (The employee responsible for handling cash receipts checks is also participating in the record-keeping functions relating to these checks.) Upon discovering this deviation from the predetermined preventive control, the internal auditors should issue an immediate performance report memo to top management or the accounting subsystem's management, or both (depending on the company's report communication structure), describing what is actually happening in the cash receipts functions. Corrective action can then be initiated.

Whenever a company's internal auditors (or other organizational employees) evaluate the operational efficiency of preventive controls, the feedback control system is operational. Thus, all the major preventive control components discussed earlier in this chapter (a good audit trail, competent employees, separation of related organizational functions, and physical protection of assets) should be evaluated periodically by a company's feedback control system to ascertain whether these preventive controls are functioning properly. For any significant deviations reported, management should initiate immediate corrective action to enable its business system to function effectively.

SUMMARY

This chapter has analyzed the importance of good internal controls to an efficiently operated accounting information system. Before an organization introduces a specific control procedure into its system, the control's estimated annual operating costs should be compared with its estimated annual benefits. This cost/benefit analysis typically causes the organization to implement a less than ideal control because the perfect control's (one that reduces the risk to almost zero of any undetected errors and irregularities) costs would be likely to exceed its benefits.

An effective internal control system includes both preventive controls (also called before-the-fact or accounting controls) and feedback controls (also called after-the-fact or administrative controls). The preventive controls are designed to safeguard an organization's assets and to check the accuracy and reliability of accounting data. The important components of a preventive control system include a good audit trail, competent employees, separation of related organizational functions, and physical protection of assets. Using the computer for processing accounting transactions has often made a company's audit trail difficult to follow, thereby increasing the risk of misappropriation of assets by employees.

Upon implementing the preventive controls into a company's system, the feedback controls begin functioning by evaluating the operational efficiency of these preventive controls. This eval-uation is accomplished through timely performance reports, which disclose any significant variations of actual operating performance from the standards or criteria established for the preventive controls. To enable management to determine which subsystem employee (or employees) caused the variations, the performance reports should be based on the company's responsibility accounting structure. If management knows which specific organizational area (or areas) caused the operating inefficiencies, it can then initiate corrective action on these inefficiencies. Use of the computer in processing and printing out performance report data has enabled management to receive feedback reports about inefficient preventive controls requiring corrective action much sooner than in a manual data processing system. In addition to feedback controls within their systems, some companies utilize feedforward control systems. A feedforward system's major goal is to predict potential variations from a company's predetermined plans in order to prevent problems before they actually occur and become significant. Upon predicting areas of potential problems, adjustments can be made immediately.

Employees of the internal audit subsystem (in those organizations having this service subsystem) play a major role in a company's internal control system. Because internal auditors are independent of the other organizational subsystems (and consequently objective and unbiased toward these subsystems), they should participate in designing and implementing each subsystem's preventive controls, and also participate in evaluating the efficiency or inefficiency of these implemented preventive controls. Periodic internal audit reviews of the preventive control system to ascertain whether the implemented controls are achieving their intended goals enable the audit staff to make an important contribution to organizational operating efficiency. By receiving timely internal audit feedback reports, management can initiate necessary corrective adjustments to those preventive controls that are not functioning effectively.

Key Terms You Should Know

accounting controls
administrative controls
after-the-fact controls
audit trail
before-the-fact controls
collusive efforts
control point
cycle method
feedback controls
feedforward control systems
fidelity bond coverage
Foreign Corrupt Practices Act of 1977
hash total
internal auditing

internal check control
internal control
lapping of accounts receivable
performance reports
petty cash fund
physical protection of assets
preventive controls
purchase invoice
purchase order
receiving report
responsibility accounting system
separation of related organizational functions
voucher system

Discussion Questions

9-1. Why are accountants so concerned about their organization having an efficient and effective internal control system?

9-2. Discuss any similarities and differences between preventive controls and feedback controls. Which of these two categories of controls do you feel is more important to an organization's effectively operated accounting information system? Explain.

9-3. An example was provided in this chapter of a hash total control for processing sales invoices. Try to think of some other situations in which a hash total could be an effective control within an organization's accounting information system.

9-4. Judy Williams recently earned her master's degree in accounting from a major university. Her first job after college was as a managerial accountant for the Pretzel Pastry Company. The company is currently in the process of converting its manual data processing system to a computerized data processing system. Judy was asked by the chief systems consultant (Harvey Hyatt) to make some suggestions regarding the types of preventive controls that should be implemented into the company's new computerized information system.

After thinking about possible preventive controls for several days, Judy returned to Harvey with the following comments: "Harv, in my opinion, our new computer is the only preventive control we need. Since the computer is not capable of committing an embezzlement or making a computational error, my feeling is that all the types of preventive controls that I have studied in textbooks are unimportant to our company."

If you were Harvey Hyatt, would you agree or disagree with Judy Williams' observations? Explain.

9-5. What role does cost/benefit analysis play in an organization's internal control system?

9-6. Besides the separation of related functions approach illustrated in this chapter, can you think of any other procedures that an organization could use to help prevent lapping of its accounts receivable? Discuss.

9-7. The Mary Popkin Umbrella Manufacturing Company maintains an inventory of miscellaneous supplies (e.g., pens, pencils, typing paper, typewriter ribbons, and envelopes) for use by its clerical workers. These supplies are stored on shelves at the back of the office facility, easily accessible to all company employees.

The company's accountant, Percey Malcumson, is very much concerned about the poor internal control over the company's office supplies. He has estimated that the monthly loss due to theft of supplies by company employees averages about $150. To reduce this monthly loss, Percey has recommended to management that a separate room be set aside to store these supplies, and that a company employee be given full-time responsibility for supervising the issuance of the supplies to those employees with a properly approved requisition. By implementing these controls, Percey believes that the loss of supplies from employee misappropriation can be reduced to practically zero.

If you were the Mary Popkin Umbrella Manufacturing Company manager responsible for either accepting or rejecting Percey Malcumson's preventive control recommendations, what would your decision be? Explain. Try to think of some additional preventive control measures that the company might implement to reduce the monthly loss from theft of office supplies by employees.

9-8. Evaluate the following statement: "Because an internal audit subsystem does not directly contribute to an organization's revenue-earning functions, and, in fact, often interferes with the other subsystems' operating activities (e.g., by entering a subsystem's work area and taking the time to evaluate the operating efficiency of its specific preventive controls), the organization would probably increase its overall profitability by completely eliminating the internal audit staff."

9-9. The following are descriptions of systems of internal control for companies engaged in the manufacturing business.

1. When Mr. Clark orders materials for his machine-rebuilding plant, he sends a duplicate purchase order to the receiving department. During a delivery of materials, Mr. Smith, the receiving clerk, records the receipt of shipment on this purchase order. After recording, Mr. Smith sends the purchase order to the accounting department where it is used to record materials purchased and accounts payable. The materials are transported to the storage area by forklifts. The additional purchased quantities are recorded on storage records.

2. Every day hundreds of employees clock in using time cards at Generous Motors Corporation. The timekeepers collect these cards once a week and deliver them to the tabulating machine department. There the data on these time cards are transferred to punched cards. The punched cards are used in the preparation of the labor cost distribution records, the payroll journal, and the payroll checks. The treasurer, Mrs. Webber, compares the payroll journal with the payroll checks, signs the checks, and returns the payroll checks to Mr. Strode, the supervisor of the tabulating department. The payroll checks are distributed to the employees by Mr. Strode.

3. The smallest branch of Connor Cosmetics in South Bend employs Mary Cooper, the branch manager,

and her sales assistant, Janet Hendrix. The branch uses a bank account in South Bend to pay expenses. The account is kept in the name of "Connor Cosmetics—Special Account." To pay expenses, checks must be signed by Mary Cooper or by the treasurer of Connor Cosmetics, John Winters. Ms. Cooper receives the canceled checks and bank statements. She reconciles the branch account herself and files canceled checks and bank statements in her records. She also periodically prepares reports of disbursements and sends them to the home office.

Requirements

A. List the weaknesses in internal control for each of the preceding three systems.
B. For each weakness in these three systems, state the type of error(s) likely to result. Be as specific as possible.
C. How would you improve each of the three systems?
(AICPA Adapted)

9-10. Since an organization's internal audit staff consists of accountants, shouldn't the internal auditors be a component of the organization's accounting subsystem? Explain.

9-11. Why is an organization's accountant so concerned about a good audit trail through the accounting information system? Discuss some of the specific items that should be included in an organization's audit trail.

9-12. Lane Nelson, the recently hired managerial accountant of the Wintergreen Sugar Company, made the following comments to his supervisor: "Our internal auditors waste a great deal of time and money auditing through the computer system. I strongly believe that the internal auditors could adequately perform their organizational functions by obtaining computer printout reports and tracing the report data back to the original source documents. There is no reason for the internal auditors to concern themselves with the sophisticated hardware and software of the computer system which created the output reports." Do you agree or disagree with Lane Nelson's comments? Explain.

9-13. Why are *competent employees* an important component of an organization's preventive control system? Discuss some of the personnel subsystem's important responsibilities in obtaining competent employees for its organization.

9-14. Clyde Pocket is currently working his first day as a ticket seller and cashier at the First Run Movie Theater. When a customer walks up to the ticket booth, Clyde collects the required admission charge and issues the movie patron a ticket. To be admitted into the theater, the customer then presents his or her ticket to the theater manager, who is stationed at the entrance. The manager tears the ticket in half, keeping one half for himself and giving the other half to the customer.

While Clyde was sitting in the ticket booth waiting for additional customers, he had a "brilliant" idea for stealing some of the cash from ticket sales. He reasoned that if he merely pocketed some of the cash collections from the sale of tickets, no one would ever know. Because approximately 300 customers attend each performance, Clyde believed that it would be difficult for the theater manager to keep a running count of the actual customers entering the theater. To further support Clyde's reasoning, he noticed that the manager often has lengthy conversations with patrons at the door and appears to make no attempt to count the actual number of people going into the movie house.

Do you think that Clyde Pocket will be able to steal cash receipts from the First Run Movie Theater with his method and not be caught? Explain why you think Clyde's theft will not be detected or, if you believe that he will be caught, explain how his stealing activity will be discovered.

9-15. How can the separation of related organizational functions among employees prevent undetected errors and irregularities regarding a company's asset resources?

9-16. Why is a company's internal control system strengthened by having daily, intact deposits of cash receipts at a bank rather than using some of these cash receipts for making cash disbursements?

9-17. As a recently hired internal auditor for the Dagwood Discount Department Store (which has approximately 500 employees on its payroll), you are currently reviewing the store's procedures for preparing and distributing the weekly payroll. These procedures are as follows.

Each Monday morning, the managers of the various departments (e.g., the women's clothing department, the toy department, and the home appliances department) turn in their employees' time cards for the previous week to the accountant (Morris Manning). Morris then accumulates the total hours worked by each employee and submits this information to the store's computer center to process the weekly payroll. The computer center prepares a transaction tape of employees' hours worked and then processes this tape with the employees' payroll master tape file (containing such things as each employee's social security number, exemptions claimed, hourly wage rate, year-to-date gross wages, FICA taxes withheld, and union dues deduction). The computer prints out a payroll register indicating each employee's gross wages, deductions, and net pay for the payroll period.

The payroll register is then turned over to Morris, who, with help from the secretaries, places the correct amount of currency in each employee's pay envelope. The pay envelopes are provided to the department managers for distribution to their employees on Monday afternoon.

To date, you have been unsuccessful in persuading the store's management to use checks rather than currency for paying the employees. Most managers that you have talked with argue that the employees prefer to receive currency in their weekly pay envelopes so that they do not have to bother going to the bank to cash their checks.

Assuming the Dagwood Discount Department Store's management refuses to change its present system of paying the employees with cash, suggest some internal control procedures that could strengthen the store's present payroll preparation and distribution system.

9-18. You have been engaged by the management of Alden, Inc., to review its internal control over the purchase, receipt, storage, and issuance of raw materials. You have prepared the following comments, which describe Alden's procedures.

- Raw materials, which consist mainly of high-cost electronic components, are kept in a locked storeroom. Storeroom personnel include a supervisor and four clerks. All are well trained, competent, and adequately bonded. Raw materials are removed from the storeroom only upon written or oral authorization of one of the production foremen.

- There are no perpetual inventory records; hence, the storeroom clerks do not keep records of goods received or issued. To compensate for the lack of perpetual records, a physical inventory count is taken monthly by the storeroom clerks, who are well supervised. Appropriate procedures are followed in making the inventory count.

- After the physical count, the storeroom supervisor matches quantities counted against a predetermined reorder level. If the count for a given part is below the reorder level, the supervisor enters the part number on a materials requisition list and sends this list to the accounts payable clerk. The accounts payable clerk prepares a purchase order for a predetermined reorder quantity for each part and mails the purchase order to the vendor from whom the part was last purchased.
- When ordered materials arrive at Alden, they are received by the storeroom clerks. The clerks count the merchandise and see that the counts agree with the shipper's bill of lading. All vendors' bills of lading are initialed, dated, and filed in the storeroom to serve as receiving reports.

Required

Describe the internal control weaknesses and recommend improvements in Alden's procedures for the purchase, receipt, storage, and issuance of raw materials. Organize your answers as follows.

Weaknesses	Recommended Improvements

(AICPA Adapted)

9-19. Discuss some of the internal control advantages to an organization by using a voucher system and prenumbered checks for its cash disbursement transactions. Are there any circumstances under which a voucher system with prenumbered cash disbursement checks would not be efficient to use by an organization? Explain.

9-20. The customer billing and collection functions of the Robinson Company, a small paint manufacturer, are attended to by a receptionist, an accounts receivable clerk, and a cashier who also serves as a secretary. The company's paint products are sold to wholesalers and retail stores.

The following describes *all* of the procedures performed by the employees of the Robinson Company pertaining to customer billings and collections.

1. The mail is opened by the receptionist, who gives the customers' purchase orders to the accounts receivable clerk. Fifteen to 20 orders are received each day. Under instructions to expedite the shipment of orders, the accounts receivable clerk at once prepares a five-copy sales invoice form that is distributed as follows.

   a. Copy 1 is the customer billing copy and is held by the accounts receivable clerk until notice of shipment is received.
   b. Copy 2 is the accounts receivable department copy and is held for ultimate posting of the accounts receivable records.
   c. Copies 3 and 4 are sent to the shipping department.
   d. Copy 5 is sent to the storeroom as authority for release of the goods to the shipping department.

2. After the paint ordered has been moved from the storeroom to the shipping department, the shipping department prepares the bills of lading and labels the cartons. Sales invoice copy 4 is inserted in a carton as a packing slip. After the trucker has picked up the shipment, the customer's copy of the bill of lading and copy 3, on which are noted any undershipments, are returned to the accounts receivable clerk. The company does not "back-order" in the event of undershipments; customers are expected to reorder the merchandise. The Robinson Company's copy of the bill of lading is filed by the shipping department.

3. When copy 3 and the customer's copy of the bill of lading are received by the accounts receivable clerk, copies 1 and 2 are completed by numbering them and inserting quantities shipped, unit prices, extensions, discounts, and totals. The accounts receivable clerk then mails copy 1 and the copy of the bill of lading to the customer. Copies 2 and 3 are stapled together.

4. The individual accounts receivable ledger cards are posted by the accounts receivable clerk by a bookkeeping machine procedure whereby the sales register is prepared as a carbon copy of the postings. Postings are made from copy 2, which is then filed, along with the attached copy 3, in numerical order. Monthly, the general ledger clerk summarizes the sales register for posting to the general ledger accounts.

5. Since the Robinson Company is short of cash, the deposit of receipts is also expedited. The reception-

ist turns over all mail receipts and related correspondence to the accounts receivable clerk, who examines the checks and determines that the accompanying vouchers or correspondence contains enough detail to permit posting of the accounts. The accounts receivable clerk then endorses the checks and gives them to the cashier, who prepares the daily deposit. No currency is received in the mail and no paint is sold over the counter at the factory.

6. The accounts receivable clerk uses the vouchers or correspondence that accompanied the checks to post the accounts receivable ledger cards. The bookkeeping machine prepares a cash receipts register as a carbon copy of the postings. Monthly, the general ledger clerk summarizes the cash receipts register for posting to the general ledger accounts. The accounts receivable clerk also corresponds with customers about unauthorized deductions for discounts, freight or advertising allowances, returns, etc., and prepares the appropriate credit memos. Disputed items of large amount are turned over to the sales manager for settlement. Each month the accounts receivable clerk prepares a trail balance of the open accounts receivable and compares the resultant total with the general ledger control account for accounts receivable.

Requirement

Discuss the internal control weaknesses in the Robinson Company's procedures related to customer billings and remittances and the accounting for these transactions. In your discussion, in addition to identifying the weaknesses, explain what could happen as a result of each weakness.

(AICPA Adapted)

9-21. The Kowal Manufacturing Company employs approximately 50 production workers and has the following payroll procedures.

The factory foreman interviews applicants and, on the basis of these interviews, either hires or rejects them. When an applicant is hired, he or she prepares a W-4 form (Employee's Withholding Exemption Certificate) and gives it to the foreman. The foreman writes the hourly rate of pay for the new employee in the corner of the W-4 form and then gives the form to a payroll clerk as notice that the worker has been employed. The foreman verbally advises the payroll department of rate adjustments.

A supply of blank time cards is kept in a box near the entrance to the factory. Each worker takes a time card on Monday morning, fills in his name, and notes in pencil on the time card his daily arrival and departure times. At the end of the week the workers drop the time cards in a box near the door to the factory.

The completed time cards are taken from the box on Monday morning by a payroll clerk. Two payroll clerks divide the cards alphabetically between them, one taking the A-to-L section of the payroll and the other taking the M-to-Z section. Each clerk is fully responsible for her section of the payroll. She computes the gross pay, deductions, and net pay, posts the details to the employees' earnings records, and prepares and numbers the payroll checks. Employees are automatically removed from the payroll when they fail to turn in their time cards.

The payroll checks are manually signed by the chief accountant and given to the foreman. The foreman distributes the checks to the workers in the factory and arranges for the delivery of the checks to the workers who are absent. The payroll bank account is reconciled by the chief accountant, who also prepares the various quarterly and annual payroll tax reports.

Requirement

List your suggestions for improving the Kowal Manufacturing Company's system of internal control for the factory hiring practices and payroll procedures.

(AICPA Adapted)

9-22. Jane Dough is a cash register operator at the Fresh Food Grocery Store. She has been working at this job for the past five years. Recently, Jane has been buying many luxury items for her own personal use (e.g., last week she purchased a brand-new 25-inch color television set as well as a new stereo system). Some of Jane's fellow workers have been curious about how she can afford these expensive items on the small salary paid to a cash register operator.

The gossip regarding Jane's expensive buying habits was accidentally overheard in the lunchroom today by the store's accountant, Carl Bogle. After lunch, Carl walked over to the grocery store location where Jane worked. Without Jane being aware of Carl's presence, he observed her operating functions on the cash register. During this 15-minute observation period, Carl noticed several instances when Jane rang up a smaller monetary amount on her cash register than the actual selling price of an item. For example, a 2-pound carton of cottage cheese sells for $1.45; however, Jane recorded this item on her cash register at only $.50 when a customer purchased a carton of cottage cheese.

Assume that the only internal control currently existing in the Fresh Food Grocery Store for its cash register operators is that the store manager provides each operator a specific amount of coins and currency with which to make change at the beginning of his or her shift. Suggest some good internal controls (both preventive and feedback controls) that would make it difficult, if not impossible, for Jane Dough to execute successfully her fraudulent activity.

9-23. Why are efficiently operated preventive controls essential to an organization's feedback control system?

9-24. Is it possible for a company to have an effectively operated feedback control system without also having a responsibility accounting system? Discuss.

9-25. What aspect of an organization's budgetary system would represent *preventive controls* and what aspect would represent *feedback controls?*

9-26. In recent years distribution expenses of the Avey Company have increased more than other expenditures. For more effective control, the company plans to provide each local manager with an income statement for his or her territory showing monthly and year-to-date amounts for the current and the previous year. Each sales office is supervised by a local manager; sales orders are forwarded to the main office and filled from a central warehouse; billing and collections are also centrally processed. Expenses are first classified by function and then allocated to each territory in the following ways.

Function	Basis
Sales salaries	Actual
Other selling expenses	Relative sales dollars
Warehousing	Relative sales dollars
Packing and shipping	Weight of package
Billing and collections	Number of billings
General administration	Equally

Requirements

A. Explain responsibility accounting and the classification of revenues and expenses under this concept.
B. What are the objectives of profit analysis by sales territories in income statements?
C. Discuss the effectiveness of Avey Company's comparative income statements by sales territories as a tool for planning and control. Include in your answer additional factors that should be considered and changes that might be desirable for effective planning by management and evaluation of the local sales managers.
D. Compare the degree of control that can be achieved over production costs and distribution costs and explain why the degree of control differs.
E. Criticize Avey Company's allocation process for each of the following expense items: (1) other selling expenses, (2) warehousing expense, and (3) general administration expense.

(AICPA Adapted)

9-27. Why are timely performance reports considered to be the heart of an organization's feedback control system?

9-28. Each week, the inventory manager of the Easy Make Hardware Store receives a 10-page computer printout containing every merchandise inventory item's current quantity on hand. The manager, after analyzing this inventory listing, decides which inventory items have reached a sufficiently low quantity level to require reordering. The manager then sends the descriptions of these inventory items to the purchasing agent, who places the orders for additional inventory from the designated suppliers.

Try to think of a more efficient inventory reporting system that could be used in the Easy Make Hardware Store.

9-29. The Mass Media Company, which publishes a weekly news magazine, prides itself on having highly competent employees performing the various organizational functions. The company's personnel subsystem supervises training programs for all new employees hired by the company. These training sessions are designed to make the employees more productive once they begin executing their assigned company duties.

As an internal auditor working for the Mass Media Company, how would you go about evaluating the actual competency of the employees? *Note:* In answering this question, feel free to relate your discussion to specific types of jobs you would expect to find in a news publishing company (e.g., typists, editors, sports writers, and accountants).

9-30. Discuss how a feedforward control system differs from a feedback control system.

9-31. The cashier of the Easy Company intercepted Customer A's check payable to the company in the amount of $500 and deposited it in a bank account that was part of the company petty cash fund, of which he was custodian. He then drew a $500 check on the petty cash fund bank account payable to himself, signed it, and cashed it. At the end of the month, while processing the monthly statements to customers, he was able to change the statement of Customer A to show that A had received credit for the $500 check that had been intercepted. Ten days later he made an entry in the cash-received book that purported to record receipt of a remittance of $500 from Customer A, thus restoring A's account to its proper balance, but overstating the cash in the bank. He covered the overstatement by omitting from the list of outstanding checks in the bank reconcilement two checks, the aggregate amount of which was $500.

List what you regard as five important deficiencies in the system of internal control in this situation, and state the proper remedy for each deficiency.

(AICPA Adapted)

9-32. Discuss the meaning of the "internal check" control.

9-33. Discuss what is meant by the term *control point*.

CASE ANALYSES

9-34. Noble Company*

Several years ago, the Noble Company installed electronic data processing equipment. Applications include inventory processing, accounts receivable and payable processing, production scheduling, and payroll preparation. Problems have occurred with the accounts payable system and the internal audit staff has been called in to evaluate proposed changes.

*Used with the permission of Roy E. Baker, *Cases in Auditing with Supplemental Readings.* (Englewood Cliffs, N.J.: Prentice Hall, Inc., 1979).

Current Procedures

The accounts payable section of the accounting department prepares the input to the computer system for all vendors invoices, which includes information about each vendor's name and address, invoice number, amount due, and either an expense account identification or inventory updating data including stock number, units received, units back-ordered, and so forth. On a weekly basis, the data are used to prepare an invoice register with appropriate distributions of dollar amounts to either inventory or various expense classifications.

Twice a month the data processing subsystem also prepares checks and a check register for the accumulated invoices. The common discount terms for Noble are 10 days after the end of the month. In order to take advantage of the discounts on the second monthly processing run, check preparation is usually scheduled for either the eighth or ninth of the month, with the result that a large batch of checks is delivered to the accounting department on the ninth or tenth.

When the checks are received, the accounting department matches them with supporting data and forwards both checks and supporting data to two authorized check signers. The supporting documents are reviewed, initialed, and the checks signed manually. Each check is countersigned by the treasurer. Under this system, checks are often not mailed until the twelfth or thirteenth and some discounts are disallowed as a result.

Proposed Changes

To alleviate the problem, the company proposes to have all checks for amounts of $250 or less reviewed by two other clerks, who will be authorized to sign with facsimile plates. No further review would be required. The company presents the following points to support its belief that there are adequate controls.

1. Typical check distributions by amounts are:

Amount	Percent of Checks	Percent of Total Disbursements
Under $50	36	2
$50–$250	44	5
Over $250	20	93

2. The clerks will review supporting documents. If there seems to be any irregularity, the checks will not be signed by facsimile, but will be forwarded to the regular check-signing channels.
3. The signing devices will have counters. The number of checks signed will be reconciled to the number of checks prepared by the data processing center.
4. Bank accounts are reconciled independently of the accounts payable section.
5. The clerks will have no duties involving data preparation or matching of checks to supporting documents.
6. Checks signed with the facsimile plate will be imprinted "Void for amounts greater than $250."

Questions

1. Do the proposed changes include adequate controls?
2. If these proposed changes do not include adequate controls, what further suggestions would you make?

9-35. Old New England Leather*

Old New England Leather is a large manufacturer and marketer of quality leather goods. The product line ranges from wallets to saddles. Because of the prevailing management philosophy at Old New England Leather, the company will accept orders for almost any leather product to be custom-made on demand. This is possible since the leather craftsmen employed by the company perform a job in its entirety (i.e., the company does not utilize production-line techniques). Each leather craftsman is responsible for the complete manufacturing of a given product. Currently, the company employs about 150 leather craftsmen and has been growing at an annual rate of 20% each of the last 3 years. However, management does not anticipate this growth rate in the future, but instead sees a steady annual growth rate of 5% over each of the next 10 years.

Old New England Leather markets a proprietary line of leather goods worldwide. However, these stock products compose only 50% of the output from the craftsmen. The remaining products are produced to

---

special order. When a custom order is received, the specifications for the order are posted along with an expected shipping date. Each craftsman is then eligible to bid on the order or a part of it. Once the bids are evaluated, the company's management determines which individual has agreed upon the date, and accepts the lowest bid for production. It is this custom part of the business which has shown the greatest growth in recent years. During the last 12 months, there has been an average of 600 orders in process at any one time.

Along with growth, Old New England Leather's management has incurred many problems related to providing consistent, on-time delivery. It appears that the skilled craftsmen often fail to report on a timely basis when a job is complete. In addition, management has never had a satisfactory control for ensuring that orders are worked on in a priority sequence. Other problems, such as a craftsman overcommitting himself in a given time period or simply losing an order, are also becoming serious.

The company leases a medium-size computer for processing payroll, inventory, accounts receivable, accounts payable, and so forth. This computer has capabilities for online processing with as many as 20 terminals. Currently, there are 10 terminals in operation throughout the plant.

Question

Propose a system for controlling the production of orders that will benefit the craftsmen, management, and the company's customers.

9-36. Newton Hardware, Inc.

The flowchart in Figure 9-6 depicts the activities relating to the sales, shipping, billing, and collecting processes used by Newton Hardware, Inc.

Question

Identify the weaknesses in the system of internal accounting control relating to the activities of a) the warehouse clerk, b) bookkeeper A, and c) the collection clerk. Do not identify weaknesses relating to the sales clerk or bookkeepers B and C. Do not discuss recommendations concerning the correction of these weaknesses.

(AICPA Adapted)

* Used with permission of John G. Burch, Jr., and Felix R. Strater Jr., *Information Systems: Theory and Practice* (New York: Wiley, 1986).

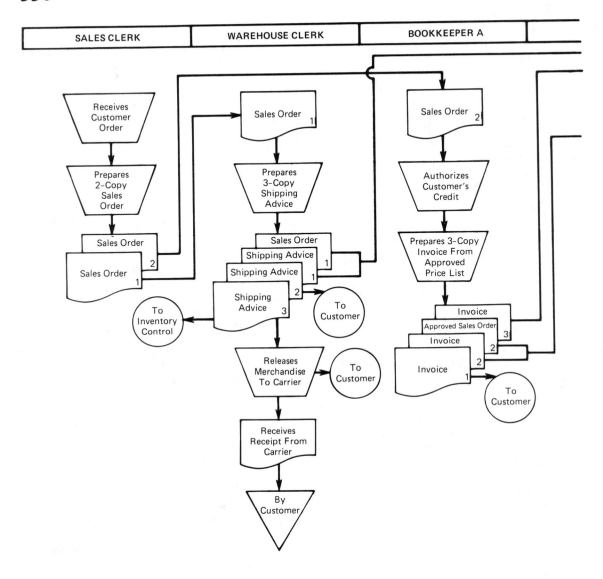

SALES CLERK	WAREHOUSE CLERK	BOOKKEEPER A

FIGURE 9-6 Flowchart for Newton Hardware, Inc.

BOOKKEEPER B	BOOKKEEPER C	COLLECTION CLERK

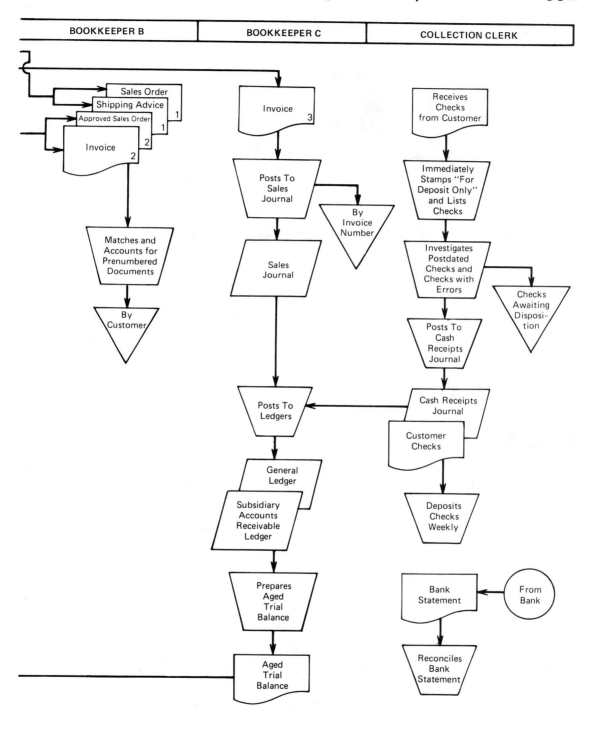

10

Controls for Computerized Accounting Information Systems

Among the important questions that you should be able to answer after reading this chapter are:

1. What is the meaning and purpose of application controls?
2. What controls are used to ensure the accurate observation, recording, and transcription of accounting data into machine-readable media?
3. What ensures the accuracy of a computer in performing standard computational procedures such as additions and subtractions, and standard logical operations such as deciding which of two numbers is larger?
4. What controls would prevent a programmer from instructing a computer to transfer a large sum of money to his or her bank account from a dormant account?
5. What is the grandfather-father-son method of file security and why is it important to accounting information systems?

Olympia Manufacturing Company
Simmons Corporation
VBR Company
OBrien Corporation
Ajax Inc.

Supplement: An Example of Controls: The MSB Company Payroll

INTRODUCTION

In many ways, controls are even more important for a computerized accounting information system than for a manual one. One reason for this is that the automated accounting information system is likely to process more data than the manual one, thereby making the number of potential errors that much greater. Another reason is that the automated accounting information system tends to gather, process, and store activity data in forms that are not human-readable. Hence, although human supervision once served to ensure data accuracy and integrity, this is no longer possible with computerized systems. Finally, the automated accounting system has blurred the audit trail, making it more difficult to follow.

The purpose of this chapter is to discuss the objectives and functions of controls for the automated accounting information system and to indicate how both automated and manual controls are integrated in the overall system configuration. Understanding these controls is essential to auditing "through" the company's computer system, and also auditor testing of these controls to see if they are operating correctly. Obviously, a thorough grasp of automated controls is also crucial in the prevention of computer crime, fraud, and embezzlement.

A few examples make clear the wide scope of problems that have plagued automated accounting information systems in the past.

- A man from Milwaukee, Wisconsin, received a letter from the Social Security Administration informing him of his death and notifying him that they were cutting off his monthly benefits. It took him three weeks to convince the local office that he was alive but his wife had died.
- The computer of a western business refused to acknowledge a woman's credit until she paid her previous bill of $0.00. When she finally gave up writing letters and wrote out a check for

$0.00, the computer accepted her "payment" but charged her a late fee.
- Youth Corps workers in New York programmed their computer to issue over $2,750,000 in bogus paychecks before they were caught.
- A business located in Palo Alto, California, found that it was losing sales because it did not have a particular computer program to use in conjunction with its engineering work. One of the company's programmers was able to plug into the computer memory of a rival firm and print out a copy of the program, which was valued at $300,000.
- A hotel in Chicago had a policy of sending thank-you letters to all its paid-up guests, thanking them for their patronage. A mix-up in mailing lists caused the letters to go out to the wrong people. As a result, hundreds of Chicago women received letters thanking their husbands for their business.

In the pages that follow, we shall attempt to outline a number of controls that are useful in computerized accounting information systems. For the sake of organization, we will begin with a general discussion of the meaning and purpose of such controls. This discussion provides a framework for the review of three specific types of controls: (1) input controls, (2) processing controls, and (3) output controls.

Some controls are general and do not neatly fit into a single input, processing, or output category. A separate section of the chapter provides examples of general controls and discusses their special uses in computerized accounting information systems.

To illustrate the use of both manual and automated accounting controls in an operational setting, the supplement at the end of this chapter discusses payroll controls for the MSB Company. In the supplement, some controls are not mentioned, reminding us that controls should be used only when they promise benefits in excess of their costs.

INTERNAL CONTROL IN A COMPUTERIZED DATA PROCESSING ENVIRONMENT

Statement on Auditing Standards No. 48 issued by the American Institute of Certified Public Accountants (AICPA) discusses the major characteristics that differentiate a computerized data processing system from a manual system and reviews how these differences affect internal control procedures. Excerpts from this statement are presented in Figure 10-1. Statement on Auditing Standards No. 48 goes on to state:

> Where computer processing is used in significant accounting applications, internal accounting control procedures are sometimes defined by classifying control procedures into two types: general and application control procedures. Whether the control procedures are classified by the auditor into general and application controls, the objective of the system of internal accounting control remains the same: to provide reasonable, but not absolute, assurance that assets are safeguarded from unauthorized use or disposition and that financial records are reliable to permit the preparation of financial statements.[1]

General controls relate to many of a company's computerized accounting activities. They often include control over the development, modification, and maintenance of computer programs as well as control over the use of, and changes to, data maintained on computer files. **Application controls** relate to individual computerized accounting applications, for example, edit tests (discussed later in this chapter) that verify customers' account numbers and credit limits.

The major purposes of application controls are to ensure the accurate and complete processing of accounting data and to see that processed data are distributed only to the proper recipients. A vast number of policies, methods, and procedures potentially contribute to this goal, and it is therefore constructive to identify those characteristics of controls that make them useful to accounting information systems. Considerations in the design of good accounting controls include:

1. Authorization.
2. Data accuracy and completeness.
3. Processing accuracy and completeness.
4. Timeliness of inputs, processing, and outputs.
5. Security of inputs, outputs, and computer files.
6. Security of the computer system.
7. Cost-effectiveness.

These are the operational objectives of application controls. Specific examples of controls that help to achieve these objectives are discussed in later sections of this chapter.

Application controls are often preventive rather than feedback-type controls, and many of them are designed merely to detect errors that would otherwise go unnoticed. This is important in a computerized environment where the intuitive judgmental ability of human processing (e.g., knowing that a figure of 400 for weekly hours worked by an employee would be unreasonable) is lacking.

A final point to understand about application controls is that not all the controls discussed in this chapter would be likely to exist in any one accounting information system. Each organizational system is somewhat different, and a specific control that might be useful for one system may be of little or no value for another. Furthermore, if a specific company actually implemented all the computerized controls discussed in the following pages, there is a strong likelihood that the annual operating costs of maintaining this control system would greatly exceed the annual benefits obtained from the control system. Thus, when a company is setting up its accounting information system, it is important for management to select conscientiously only those controls that appear to be *cost-effective*—that is,

---

[1]"The Effects of Computer Processing on the Examination of Financial Statements," *Codification of Statements on Auditing Standards* (New York: American Institute of Certified Public Accountants, 1985), AU Section 1030.05.

a. Transaction trails. Some computer systems are designed so that a complete transaction trail that is useful for audit purposes might exist for only a short period of time or only in computer-readable form. (A transaction trail is a chain of evidence provided through coding, cross references, and documentation connecting account balances and other summary results with original transactions and calculations.)

b. Uniform processing of transactions. Computers process similar transactions with the same processing instructions. Consequently, computer processing virtually eliminates the occurrence of clerical error normally associated with manual processing. Conversely, programming errors (or other similar systematic errors in either the computer hardware or software) will result in all like transactions being processed incorrectly when those transactions are processed under the same conditions.

c. Segregation of functions. Many internal accounting control procedures once performed by separate individuals in manual systems may be concentrated in systems that use computer processing. Therefore, an individual who has access to the computer may be in a position to perform incompatible functions. As a result, other control procedures may be necessary in computer systems to achieve the control objectives ordinarily accomplished by segregation of functions in manual systems. Other controls may include, for example, adequate segregation of incompatible functions within the computer processing activities, establishment of a control group to prevent or detect processing errors or irregularities, or use of password control procedures to prevent incompatible functions from being performed by individuals who have access to assets and records through an online terminal.

d. Potential for errors and irregularities. The potential for individuals, including those performing control procedures, to gain unauthorized access to data or alter data without visible evidence, as well as to gain access (direct or indirect) to assets, may be greater in computerized accounting systems than in manual systems. Decreased human involvement in handling transactions processed by computers can reduce the potential for observing errors and irregularities. Errors or irregularities occurring during the design or changing of application programs can remain undetected for long periods of time.

e. Potential for increased management supervision. Computer systems offer management a wide variety of analytical tools that may be used to review and supervise the operations of the company. The availability of these additional controls may serve to enhance the entire system of internal accounting control on which the auditor may wish to place reliance. For example, traditional comparisons of actual operating ratios with those budgeted, as well as reconciliations of accounts, are frequently available for management review on a more timely basis if such information is computerized. Additionally, some programmed applications provide statistics regarding computer operations that may be used to monitor the actual processing of transactions.

f. Initiation of subsequent execution of transactions by computer. Certain transactions may be automatically initiated or certain procedures required to execute a transaction may be automatically performed by a computer system. The authorization of these transactions or procedures may not be documented in the same way as those initiated in a manual accounting system, and management's authorization of those transactions may be implicit in its acceptance of the design of the computer system.

g. Dependence of other controls on controls over computer processing. Computer processing may produce reports and other output that are used in performing manual control procedures. The effectiveness of these manual control procedures can be dependent on the effectiveness of controls over the completeness and accuracy of computer processing. For example, the effectiveness of a control procedure that includes a manual review of a computer-produced exception listing is dependent on the controls over the production of the listing.*

---

* The Effects of Computer Processing on the Examination of Financial Statements, *Codification of Statements on Auditing Standards* (New York: American Institute of Certified Public Accountants, 1985). AU Section 1030.05.

FIGURE 10-1 Characteristics that distinguish computer processing from manual processing.

those controls that promise benefits in excess of their costs. For purposes of discussing application controls in the following sections of this chapter, we will categorize these controls as input controls, processing controls, and output controls.

INPUT CONTROLS

Input controls attempt to ensure the validity, accuracy, and completeness of the data fed into an accounting information system. It is desirable to test input data for the attributes of validity, authenticity, accuracy, and completeness as early as possible in the job stream. There are at least five reasons for this.

1. Data that are rejected at the time they are input can be more easily corrected—for example, by reference to a readily available source document.
2. Data that have been transcribed accurately are not necessarily good data, merely data that have been copied correctly. Further data testing is useful.
3. It is not cost-effective to screen accounting data continuously throughout the processing cycles of the accounting information system. Past some point in the job stream, all data are considered valid and error free.
4. It is vital that an accounting information system not use inaccurate data in later data processing operations. This protects master files and safeguards computer processing in later stages of the job stream.
5. An accounting information system cannot provide good information if it does not start with good data. The alternative is **GIGO—garbage in, garbage out.**

For the purposes of discussion, it is convenient to divide the general topic of input controls into five categories: (1) data observation, (2) data recording, (3) data transcription, (4) edit tests, and (5) access to the computer. Each of these will now be discussed in greater detail.

Data Observation

Recording the activities of individuals, groups, businesses, and institutions forms the bulk of the data entering an accounting information system. An organization often finds it useful to install one or more observational controls to assist in the data-collection process.

As noted in Chapter 9, one such control is the introduction of a *feedback mechanism*. A primary example in the data-collection process would be the use of **confirmation slips** in the preparation of sales orders. With such a mechanism, a salesperson might write up a sales order and present the completed document to the customer for approval. The customer confirms the order with a signature, thereby attesting to the accuracy and completeness of the data contained therein. Other examples of confirmation controls include the use of (1) **turnaround documents,** in which errors may be corrected directly on the data medium, and (2) any other communication device—for example, a telephone—in which one party may validate the data gathered by another. In each of these cases, the probability of accuracy in the initial observation of the data is increased because a validating procedure is at hand.

In some cases, such as those involving long-distance transactions, inexpensive feedback may not be possible. As an alternative to feedback control (or perhaps in addition to such controls), the recording process can also make use of **dual observation.** Here, the accuracy of the data-recording function is enhanced because more than one person performs it. In the medical profession, the examination of X-rays by more than one physician provides an illustration. In commercial applications, the dual-observation control is often *supervisory*. Here, the observer's supervisor is required to confirm the accuracy of the data gathered by the subordinate. Such a procedure also serves to control fraud because it is difficult to record inaccurate data intentionally when the observation process itself is supervised.

Data Recording

Once observed, the data must be recorded. When recording is performed manually, the recording sheet becomes the source document, which then serves as the primary input to the manual as well as to the computerized accounting information system. Data collection is an area in which a great deal of automation has taken place. For example, the use of *magnetic-striped credit cards or point-of-sale (POS) recording devices* to encode data has been found to lessen substantially the error rate in the recording process as well as to eliminate the expense involved in the transcription of the data to machine-readable formats.

In some instances, automated data recording is not feasible and an initial source document must be prepared manually. To encourage recording accuracy, several controls are possible. One is to use **preprinted recording forms** such as the inventory receipts slip illustrated in Figure 10-2. Such forms ensure that all the information required for processing has been recorded and also enhance accuracy in the recording process. For example, the exact number of spaces required for such field items as the inventory part number or date is clear because a box has been provided for each numerical digit, thus guarding against a loss or addition of digits in these fields.

Recording forms have other advantages. For example, the preprinted numbers at the top of each form serve as a transaction identification for reference purposes, and the fact that these numbers are preprinted also guarantees that this reference is unique. In terms of recording accuracy, the preprinted form is useful in that it imposes uniformity in the data-recording process. Referencing and cross-checking are thereby enhanced.

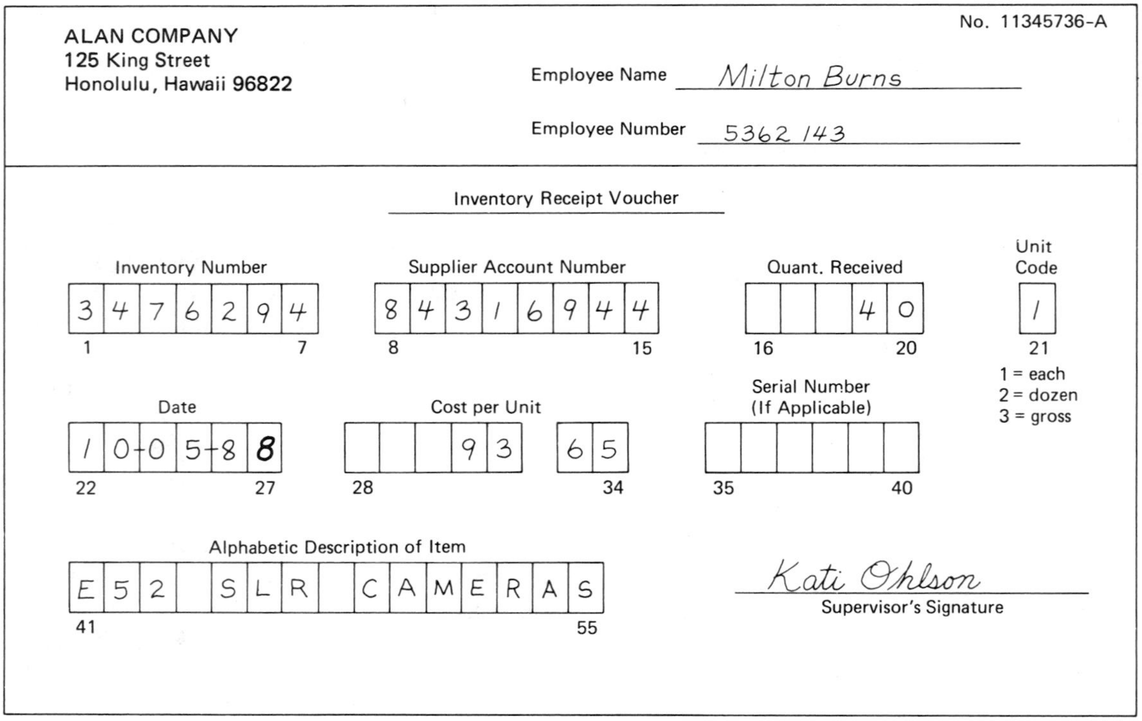
ALAN COMPANY
125 King Street
Honolulu, Hawaii 96822

No. 11345736-A

Employee Name Milton Burns

Employee Number 5362 143

Inventory Receipt Voucher

Inventory Number: 3 4 7 6 2 9 4 (1–7)

Supplier Account Number: 8 4 3 1 6 9 4 4 (8–15)

Quant. Received: 4 0 (16–20)

Unit Code: 1 (21)
1 = each
2 = dozen
3 = gross

Date: 1 0 0 5 8 8 (22–27)

Cost per Unit: 9 3 6 5 (28–34)

Serial Number (If Applicable): (35–40)

Alphabetic Description of Item: E 5 2 S L R C A M E R A S (41–55)

Kati Ohlson
Supervisor's Signature

FIGURE 10-2 A preprinted recording form for inventory receipts.

Dual observation or supervisory control can also be used in conjunction with the preprinted data-collection form to improve data-recording accuracy. In some instances, the signature of the approving officer for each document is warranted and a space on the form, as illustrated in Figure 10-2, may be designed in the format. Alternatively, if only special situations require approval—for example, the approval of a credit sale in excess of $500—the situations triggering such action may be preprinted on the document.

Data Transcription

Data transcription refers to the preparation of data for computerized processing. If the data in the accounting information system were to be processed manually, the transcription step would not be necessary because no computer would be used. The avoidance of a transcription step is one obvious advantage of the manual system over the automated one.

In computerized accounting information systems, information should be organized on the source document in such a way as to facilitate the transcription process. Thus, well-designed, preprinted forms are an important control because they encourage adherence to this general principle of source-document/computer-input compatibility.

As suggested by Figure 10-3, computerized accounting information systems can use a number of alternate media for data transcription, including floppy disks, online hard disks, or (rarely) punched cards. Here, we shall concentrate on systems that use either floppy disks or online hard disks since these systems are common and both can provide an interactive computing environment for input tasks.

In data-transcription environments, the user typically sits at a workstation consisting of a keyboard and a CRT terminal screen. One important input control is the use of **preformatted screens** to assist in the transcription process. This preformatted screen is much the same as the preprinted recording form discussed earlier, except that it is flashed on the cathode ray tube (CRT) of the terminal instead of printed on paper. When the format of the information is outlined on the CRT, the user follows this format to

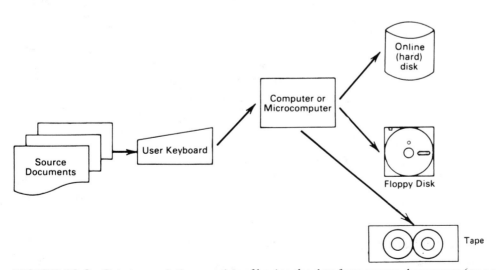

FIGURE 10-3 Data transcription consists of keying the data from source documents (or perhaps telephone conversations) into machine-readable media in preparation for subsequent computerized data processing.

input the required data. Thus, for example, to input a six-digit inventory code number, the user might utilize the screen format shown below. As the user inputs the inventory account number, the spaces over the underlines would fill with data. When all the data have been input, therefore, the full six-digit inventory number will be clear.

A special type of preformatted screen makes use of a **mask** to accomplish the same purpose as the underlines mentioned earlier. For input purposes, a mask is a set of blinking boxes on the screen with each box the size of a single input character. As the user inputs data, the boxes on the screen are replaced with the input characters. Upon completing the input for a particular data field, the user should find that the mask has been replaced with the completed input. If the data input is incomplete, however, a portion of the mask will still remain and the user is alerted to this fact because the unfilled boxes of the mask continue to blink.

Edit Tests

Both computers and programmable key entry devices can be programmed to perform **edit tests.** The purpose of edit tests is to examine selected fields of input data and to reject those transactions (or other types of data input) whose data fields do not meet the preestablished standards of data quality. Any number of edit tests are possible. Among them are:

1. **Tests of numeric field content,** which make sure that such data fields as social secu-

rity number, invoice number, or date contain only numbers.
2. **Tests of alphabetic field content,** which make sure such fields as customer name contain only alphabetic letters.
3. **Tests of alphanumeric field content,** which make sure that fields such as inventory parts descriptions contain letters or numbers, but no special characters.
4. **Tests for valid codes** (e.g., M = male, F = female).
5. **Tests of reasonableness** (e.g., regular hours worked by an employee less than or equal to 40).
6. **Tests of algebraic sign** (e.g., account numbers always positive).
7. **Tests of completeness** (no blanks in fields requiring entries).
8. **Tests of sequence,** which make sure that successive input data are in some prescribed order (e.g., ascending, descending, chronological, or alphabetical).
9. **Tests of consistency** (e.g., that all transactions for the same sales office have the same office code number).

Editing tests can also be coordinated in what is called a **redundant data check** to ensure data accuracy. The idea is to encode repetitious data on a file or transaction record, thereby enabling a later processing test to compare the two data items for compatibility. For example, a candy company could use both an inventory code number and an alphabetic code designator to represent the same inventory item. A master list of numeric and alphabetic designators would be maintained by the computer program performing the inventory processing. If the inventory number 75642 (representing chocolate caramels) was encoded incorrectly in a transaction with the alphabetic designator "VC" (standing for vanilla caramels), the transaction would be rejected because the two different designators for supposedly the same item failed to match.

To illustrate the use of edit tests, consider Figure 10-4, which shows the video display screen

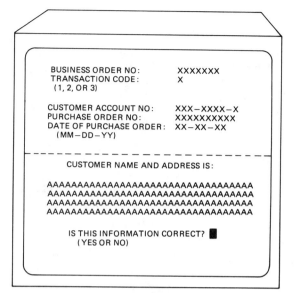

FIGURE 10-4 The split-screen display for entering customer order information into an online system. The box in the lower right-hand portion of the screen indicates the position of the input cursor.

for entering customer order information with an online system. This is a customer order entry application that businesses use to enter customer orders for goods directly into computer files.

Once the basic order data are input, the system can translate the information into instructions for filling the order from inventory, thereby improving delivery time to the customer. The data identification listed on the left-hand side of the screen (e.g., business order number, transaction code, etc.) is displayed by the computer system when the user indicates that the order entry function is desired. (The user would indicate this choice on another display screen not show.) The X's on the right-hand side of the display screen represent data supplied by the user.

As the user inputs data, each of the fields would be tested for such attributes as field length, numeric content, and so forth. Figure 10-5 lists examples of edit tests that might be performed on each data item entered. (Assume that the customer account number is a group code using a three-digit region prefix, a four-digit customer number, and a one-letter credit rating suffix.)

If the user makes a mistake that can be detected by these edit tests, the display screen will flash an error message. For example, if an individual inputs an eight-digit business order number when the maximum number of digits permitted is seven digits, the system might display the error message on the next page.

Data Item	Edit Test
Business order number	Numeric test on each digit
	Test of completeness—all 7 digits
Transaction code	Valid code test (1, 2, or 3 only)
Customer account number	Valid region code—first 3 digits
	Each digit numeric—middle 4 digits
	Valid credit code—last digit
	Test of completeness—all 8 digits
Purchase order number	Each digit numeric—all digits
	Test of completeness—all 10 digits
Date of purchase	Test of completeness—all 6 digits
	Each digit numeric—all 6 digits
	Month digits—only integers 1–12
	Day digits—only integers 1–31
	Year digits—only this year or last year

FIGURE 10-5 Edit tests that might potentially be used for the data fields of Figure 10-4.

```
┌─────────────────────────────────────┐
│  ┌──────────────────────────────┐   │
│  │                              │   │
│  │  TOO MANY DIGITS ENTERED     │   │
│  │                              │   │
│  │  DATA RECEIVABLE WAS:        │   │
│  │  12345678                    │   │
│  │                              │   │
│  │  MAXIMUM NUMBER OF DIGITS    │   │
│  │  PERMITTED FOR BUSINESS      │   │
│  │  ORDER NUMBER IS 7.          │   │
│  │                              │   │
│  │  PLEASE REENTER BUSINESS     │   │
│  │  ORDER NUMBER                │   │
│  └──────────────────────────────┘   │
└─────────────────────────────────────┘
```

The screen format illustrated in Figure 10-4 is called a **split-screen display** because part of the screen is provided for user input (in this case the top half) while the remainder of the screen displays the computer's response. If all of the input data passes the edit tests outlined earlier, the computer system will use the customer account number to access the appropriate customer record from the online customer account master file. The customer name and address information will be taken from this record and displayed on the screen for verification (these are the A's on the bottom of the screen).

If the customer name and address match the customer name on the source document purchase order, the user would answer "YES" to the question "IS THIS INFORMATION CORRECT?" If any of the information keyed on the screen is wrong (including the business order number, the transaction code, etc.), the user can answer "NO." The system will then permit the user to correct any mistakes on the screen, for example, by moving the cursor to the incorrect field and retyping the correct data.

The computer programs that perform the type of editing tests described previously are sometimes called **user-friendly software**. What makes software user friendly is the ability to provide **prompts** (i.e., explicit input identification) for terminal data inputs, to output explicit error messages identifying the type of problem encountered, and (usually) to permit the user to reenter corrected data rather than aborting a procedure. The term *user friendly* has no technical

meaning and is often used more as an advertising tool than an input control.

Check Digits

It is possible for a data field to pass all of the edit tests described earlier and still be invalid. For example, a bank might use the incorrect account number 537627 when preparing a transaction instead of the proper account number 537621. When the incorrect number is keyed into a remote terminal and submitted to the logical tests described earlier, it would (1) pass a test of numeric field content ensuring that all digits were numeric, (2) pass a test of reasonableness ensuring that the account number itself fell within a valid range of values (e.g., account number greater than 100,000 and less than 800,000), (3) pass a test of sign (account number positive), and (4) pass a test of completeness (no blanks). Thus, it is apparent that additional controls are required for this error to be detected.

One control is to incorporate an **unfound-record test** in the data processing routine used to update the master file of bank records. With this approach, any transaction for which there is no corresponding master file record would be recognized as invalid and rejected from the transaction sequence (it would be returned for correction). But what if a master file record did exist for account 537627—the incorrect account number? This would indeed be unfortunate because our "unfound-record" control would not work and, what is even worse, the legitimate master file record with account number 537627 would be updated with the data generated by another customer.

An alternative to the unfound-record test is to expand the six-digit data field of the account number to seven digits with a **check digit.** Normally, the check digit is computed as a mathematical function of the other digits in a numeric field, and its sole purpose is to test the validity of the associated data.

To illustrate, consider the original (correct) account number 537621. The sum of these six digits is $5 + 3 + 7 + 6 + 2 + 1 = 24$. One type of check digit would append the low order digit of this sum (4) to the account number. The seven-digit value 5376214 would be used instead of the six-digit series 537621 to represent the account. The computer program would duplicate this computational procedure at the time of data access, and therefore validate the accuracy of the data before the transaction was used to update a master file record. Thus, had bank personnel input the incorrect account number 5376274 for processing, this number would be detected immediately as erroneous data: the check digit computed from the first six digits (which is 0 for this account number since $5 + 3 + 7 + 6 + 2 + 7 = 30$) would not correspond to the attached check digit ($= 4$).

Check digits are tedious to compute manually. For this reason, most accounting information systems prepare lists of valid account numbers (complete with check digits) for customer assignment. The generation of a precomputed list of valid account numbers is itself a control since it guards against the manual computation of an erroneous check digit.

It should be observed that the use of a check digit is not an automatic guarantee of data validity. For example, the check-digit procedure described here would be unable to distinguish between the correct account number 5376214, and the transposed number 5736214, because the transposition of digits does not affect their sum. (See Problems 10-30, 10-31, and 10-32 at the end of the chapter for check-digit techniques that do include order in the construction of check-digit values.) Moreover, check digits cannot detect fraudulent data. An embezzler who is clever enough to create a fictitious account number will certainly also be clever enough to code the correct check digit for the account number. Finally, most check-digit systems, no matter how complicated, cannot guard against the rare event in which two mistakes cancel each other out in terms of the check-digit calculation. Thus, for example, the check-digit control *alone* would not catch the mistaken coding of account number

5826214 for the (correct) account number 5736214—the check digits are both correct at 4.

One final drawback of check digits is that they require the encoding, processing, and storage of a number that is redundant information—that is, a number easily computed from the other values of an account number and therefore serving no informational purpose. In this sense, a check digit is a waste of time and space.

Access to the Computer

An important type of input control not related to data accuracy involves access to the computer itself. Here, we are not referring to physical access, which is discussed in greater detail later in this chapter, but rather to "logical access" or usage—for example, via a remote terminal. Such logical access would permit the user to call for printouts of sensitive corporate data (e.g., sales projections or executive salaries), or permit access to expensive programs acquired by the company's computer personnel. Thus, regulating who is permitted logical access to the computer is an important control in terms of safeguarding the physical assets, software, or sensitive information of the organization.

Since remote terminals may be placed anywhere in the country and hooked up to the computer by means of ordinary telephone lines (some facilities have a normal telephone number for this purpose), it is difficult to safeguard logical computer access with direct physical surveillance of terminals. Therefore, most computer centers use **password codes** to restrict access. Such codes vary in length and type of password information required, but all have the same intent: to limit logical access to the computer only to those authorized to have it.

Passwords are not a foolproof safeguard because passwords can be lost, given away, or stolen. Their effectiveness can be improved by certain precautions, such as changing passwords on a frequent basis. However, even the most elaborate security system can be broken easily if the computer thief has obtained the important information necessary for computer access. Not long ago, for example, a security expert working as a management consultant bet an EDP manager $100 that he could gain access to the company's new million-dollar processing system in one hour. The manager quickly took the bet, thinking that here was an easy $100. The company had just installed a new, elaborate password-control system to safeguard computer access and new passwords were used each day. The bet was on!

The security expert calmly made two ordinary phone calls. The first was to a supervisor's home to inquire which computer operators were on duty that night. The expert was informed that "Steve" was one of them. The other phone call was to the computer room itself. The consultant told Steve that he had misplaced his password, that he had an important computer program to run, that he had just talked to Steve's supervisor, and that it would be all right for Steve to give him the code over the phone. Steve was hesitant but the security analyst persisted. Finally, Steve looked up the password in the security control log and gave it to the consultant. The consultant now had all the information needed to "rip off" the computer at leisure. The whole process took less than 15 minutes!

This horror story is unusual only in that it involved a wager between two friends and ultimately did not result in any loss to the company. In most other instances, the thefts are real, and therefore so are the losses. Thus, most computer experts point out that the security system of the computer facility is only as good as the people who run it. Statistics reveal, in fact, that a surprisingly high percentage of computer fraud is performed by the very people who are supposed to be guarding the computer system. We shall return to this point in Chapter 11.

PROCESSING CONTROLS

Processing controls are concerned with the manipulation of accounting data after such data are input to the CPU. As you know, once data

enter the computer, they disappear from human observation. However, good computer processing controls can go underground together with the data.

It is convenient to divide our discussion of processing controls into two parts: (1) those controls related to processing at the time of data access and (2) those controls that primarily involve data manipulation at a later phase in the processing cycle.

Data Access

Suppose you were the data processing manager at a bank. The transactions each day consist of a large number of checks written by the bank's 100,000 customers. These checks are magnetically encoded pieces of paper of varying length and width. The account number and bank number are precoded magnetically on the checks, and the amount of each check itself is later encoded by one of the bank's clerical staff after the check has been presented to the bank for payment. The problem: how to make sure that all these checks are correctly processed by the computer.

Control Totals

One common processing control is to batch the checks in bundles of 100, 150, or 200 checks each, and prepare a special **batch control document** (Figure 10-6) to serve as a control on the contents of the bundle. The information on this document might include the bundle number, today's date, and the total dollar amount for the checks themselves. When computer processing commences, the special information on the lead, control record is accessed first and the control total is stored in CPU memory. As the checks are accessed individually, their amounts are also accumulated in computer memory. Once all the checks in the batch have been read, the accumulated total is compared with the figure in the control total. A match signals acceptable processing. A nonmatch signals an error, which may then

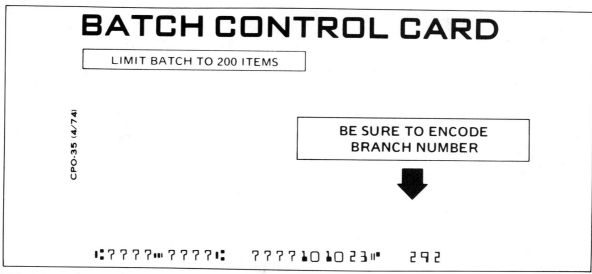

FIGURE 10-6   A batch control check for a bank. (Courtesy of Bank of Hawaii.)

be traced either to an error in the batch total or to some difficulty in the processing itself (e.g., the inability of the MICR reader to understand the information on one or more checks). When data problems such as this arise, it becomes clear why more than 200 checks are rarely used in the batching process. How would you like to find the input error in a batch of, say, 500 checks?

A **control total** such as the one illustrated in the previous example involves a dollar amount and is therefore called a *financial control total.* Other examples of financial control totals include the sum of credit sales in an accounts receivable application, the sum of cash disbursements in an accounts payable application, or the sum of net pay in a payroll application. Accounting information systems also use *nonfinancial control totals,* which compute nondollar sums, for example, the sum of the total number of hours worked, the total number of boxes shipped, or the total number of discount coupons processed. Financial control totals and nonfinancial control totals are easy to compute and have obvious meaning. For these reasons, such controls are widely used in business and are

an extremely important type of control in accounting information systems.

As we have already observed in Chapter 9, control totals do not have to make sense in order to be useful. For example, when bank checks are being processed, the sum of the account numbers in a batch of transactions might be computed to form a *hash total.* The actual figure is meaningless, but the fact that it has been computed is useful as a check against an "internal" tally of this same hash total by the computer at the time of data access.

Another type of control total often used by data processing facilities because of its simplicity is the **record count.** With this control, the number of transaction items are counted twice: once when preparing transactions in a batch and again when actually performing the data processing. For example, if magnetic tape is used as an input medium, record counts of both the number of logical records and the number of physical records on the file may be made. This information is stored in the trailer record (i.e., the last **control record**) of the file or, if the file is very large, on special control records placed at strategic portions of the file. Thus, for example, every time a computer program uses a magnetic tape file, the number of logical records and the number of physical records are counted and compared with the existing counts in the trailer records, or control records, to ensure completeness in the processing function.

Record counts are not as efficient as other types of control totals because the record count serves only as a check on the *number* of items accessed, whereas the batch-control total (e.g., dollar sums) provides a test on the *information contained within the batched transactions* as well. However, there is nothing to prevent data processing personnel from using both types of controls.

Other Data-Access Controls

A number of other processing controls can be used at the time data are accessed. When the data stored on magnetic tapes or disks are accessed, for example, selected fields of each tape or disk record can be edited upon input to the CPU using editing methods discussed earlier to ensure data accuracy. Check digits can be computed where necessary to validate codes.

Internal consistency in the file can also be examined using specialized programming routines. For example, it is a simple matter to check a magnetic tape file of accounts receivable records for account number sequence, or a magnetic disk file of payroll records for duplicate entries. Such routines are sometimes called **embedded auditing routines** because, in effect, they audit the data stored on computer files in much the same fashion as an internal or external auditor might if such files were maintained manually.

Standard **file-label processing routines** programmed into the operating system of the computer center may also be used to advantage (see page 355). These routines can be programmed to check file names to make sure that the correct file is being processed and to count the number of logical and physical records that were processed on a sequential accounting file.

The file-label processing routine will compare these control totals with those record counts stored in the file's trailer label in order to check for processing completeness.

Processing controls invisible to the accountant (and even the computer operator or programmer) often run parallel to the logical tests just discussed. Hardware **parity tests,** for example, are performed during data transmission to make sure that no communication errors occur during the data-access process. A parity test involves adding an extra *on* bit to characters as needed so that all characters contain an even (or odd, depending on the system) number of *on* bits. **Error recovery procedures** are also built into computer operating systems so that, for example, tape-cleaning activity for a particular tape drive (a mechanical activity performed by the tape drive itself) can be initiated automatically in the event that a portion of a magnetic tape cannot be deciphered. Such procedures can be programmed into the computer software if desired, so that a computer operator is notified only when such recovery procedures fail.

Data Manipulation

Once the data have been validated by earlier portions of data processing, they usually must be manipulated in some way to produce useful output. In the data-manipulation phase, the data can be *accidentally manipulated* by error or *intentionally manipulated* for personal gain. In this section, we discuss controls that guard against accidental data manipulation errors. Since the control of intentional errors is really the control of personnel, we shall defer a discussion of this topic to the later section on personnel controls.

One of the most obvious protections against accidental processing errors is to ensure the proper functioning of the central processing unit. This is clearly a hardware consideration, and is normally performed through the careful testing and maintenance of the CPU. Usually, testing is performed on a periodic, scheduled basis—for example, once a week—and is accomplished with special hardware-checking, machine-language programs called **maintenance programs.** At busy computer centers, such testing takes time—time that might otherwise be used for processing files, testing programs, and so forth. In contrast, microcomputers self-test themselves when they power up.

Several data-manipulation controls are available to ensure processing accuracy between hardware servicing. One is **dual computation,** in which the arithmetic-logic unit of the central processing unit is required to perform the same calculation twice, using different registers each time. The results are then compared to see if the answer is the same in each case. Another control is *CPU parity testing*, in which the parity bit of each byte of data is checked whenever a data movement is initiated within the memory of the central processing unit. A third processing control tests for **overflow** (which happens when you attempt to store too large a number in CPU memory) and **underflow** (which happens when you attempt to store too small a number in CPU memory). A fourth control involves the specialized use of **read-only memory (ROM),** in which portions of the CPU's internal storage are set aside for instructions or special data values related to program processing (e.g., the maintenance of record counts or hash totals), and which cannot be erased by the application programs in the CPU. A fifth control often used in multiprogramming (i.e., in time-sharing computer systems when more than one computer program uses the CPU at the same time) divides the memory portion of the central processing unit into user *workspaces*. The **workspace control** involves limiting each user to his or her designated workspace and, in some circumstances, making sure that one user cannot copy the data of another into the original user's work area.

Although most of these hardware controls are performed automatically, it is also possible for the programmer to code special processing routines, called *error routines*, which enable a computer program to recover from such problems as overflow or parity checks without halting data processing. Sometimes, for example, it may be possible for a particular calculation to be ignored without losing the overall effectiveness of the processing program. At other times, it may be more desirable for the program to output an error message than to abort the entire program because of one technical error. Thus, through programmed error routines, the user can maintain control of the data processing when processing irregularities arise. Since it is usually inconvenient, and sometimes even very costly, to rerun an entire file-processing program, error routines are potentially very effective processing controls.

Another processing control is to make sure that the processing program is complete and thorough in its data manipulation. Ordinarily, this is accomplished by examining **software documentation.** System flowcharts, program flowcharts, data flow diagrams, and decision tables can also act as controls in this regard because they help systems analysts do a thorough job in planning the data processing.

Once computer programs have been coded, they are translated into machine language by an error-testing **compiler.** The compiler controls the possibility that a computer program contains programming language errors. A computer program can also be tested with specially designed test data that expose the program to all the exception conditions likely to occur during actual programming use. The function of test data, is examined in greater detail in Chapter 12.

Whereas test data is used to examine the processing capabilities of a single computer program, **system testing** is used to test the interaction of several computer programs in a job stream. In accounting information systems, the output from one computer program is often the input to another. Thus, system testing is an important processing control for accounting information systems because it tests not only the processing capabilities of individual programs but also the linkages between these programs. Techniques for system testing are beyond the scope of this text and will not be reviewed here.

Because most computer programs go through

many minor modifications after they have been implemented, it is also wise to perform **periodic data tests** to ensure continued processing accuracy. This latter precaution is often overlooked. One data analyst stated, "Over the course of the last few years, we've made so many alterations to our programs that we're no longer sure of what we have in them. We can't keep up with the program change requests, much less the documentation changes. Any resemblance these programs have to the original flowcharts is purely coincidental." Here is a situation in which another round of tests using test data would be highly desirable.

OUTPUT CONTROLS

Once data have been processed internally by a computer system, they are usually transferred to some form of output medium for storage or, in the case of printed output, prepared as a report. However, the presence of computerized output does not, in and of itself, assure the output's accuracy, completeness, authenticity, or timeliness. For this, additional **output controls** are needed. The three major types of controls we shall examine here are controls for (1) validating processing results, (2) tape and disk output, and (3) regulating the distribution and use of printed output.

Validating Processing Results

A company can establish the authenticity of processing results by using preprinted corporate paper for important reports or by viewing information directly from terminals that are currently online to the company's computer system. Many companies assign identification numbers to specific report forms and these numbers can also be used for validation purposes if they are printed in the heading of each report page.

Although the timeliness of output is largely dependent on the timeliness of earlier input and processing, time-dependent controls are still possible at the output phase. Assigning accountability for the prompt and efficient delivery of important output to a single employee—for example, a person from a specially-formed control group—increases output control since these tasks then become a measure of personal work performance. Also, printing dates (or ranges of dates) in report headings controls against mix-ups—for example, the use of last year's figures for this week's decisions.

In some accounting information systems, the accuracy of computerized output can be established through the preparation of **activity listings** or **proof listings** that document processing activity. These listings provide complete, detailed information about all changes to master files and thus contribute to a good audit trail. In small accounting applications, organizational employees can use such activity listings to trace file changes back to the events or documents that triggered them and therefore verify current file information or printed information as accurate output.

In large, computerized accounting applications, the use of complete proof listings to ensure the accuracy and completeness of output may be impractical because of the volume of transactions and file records involved in the data processing or the disbursed nature of the users (e.g., a large inventory application with several, geographically-separate warehouses). In such instances, the use of exception reports or summary reports that pinpoint *material changes* may be more cost-effective.

The accuracy and completeness of computerized output can also be validated by using several control totals such as those on the report illustrated in Figure 10-7. As noted earlier, control totals provide important evidence concerning both the number of records processed as well as the financial and nonfinancial content of the file records used in this processing. Although these totals are actually computed during processing, the fact that they are not seen until the output is prepared perhaps justifies their classification as an output control.

```
┌──────────────────────────────────────────────────────────────────────────────────────────┐
│                          DOHR COMPANY POSTING LEDGER                                       │
│                          FOR THE WEEK 1-5-91 TO 1-10-91                                     │
│                                                                                            │
│   PARIS PLANT                                                                              │
├──────────────────────────────────────────────────────────────────────────────────────────┤
```

ACCT. NO.	CENTER	TRANS. CODE	SOURCE CODE	TRANS DATE	DEBITS	CREDITS	ACCOUNT BALANCE	DESCRIPTION
1102							83,235.67	BEGINNING BAL
	0104	10	30230232	1-5-91	387.60			ASSEMBLY 8765
	0231	10	34763766	1-5-91	100.00			ASSEMBLY 2366
	6720	50	38733610	1-7-91		50.00	82,798.07	ORDER 73653
1103							13,487.67	BEGINNING BAL
	0104	10	37836353	1-5-91	224.78			ASSEMBLY 2876
	0104	48	26353439	1-6-91		653.67		VOUCHER 265-7
	7298	50	47837498	1-8-91		123.78	14,040.34	FINISHED GOODS

GRAND TOTALS	23,476.87	67,578.22
TOTAL ASSETS	8937,836.98	195,856.56

TOTAL RECORDS IN FILE (START):	2978
TOTAL RECORDS READ:	2978
TOTAL RECORDS ADDED: 000	
TOTAL RECORDS DELETED: 000	
TOTAL ERROR RECORDS: 000	
TOTAL RECORDS (END):	2978

FIGURE 10-7   A proof listing showing control totals.

Tape and Disk Output Controls

Since computer output to tapes and disks is not normally verified by direct human observation, as is the case with manually printed output, special care must be taken to ensure accuracy in the encoding of information on these output media. Hardware controls such as parity-bit checking, and software controls such as check digits, can be carried along with the informational output during output transmission to make sure that no digits are lost in the communication process. These controls were discussed earlier.

One interesting feature of output controls for disk drives and tape drives that does not have an input counterpart is the presence of a built-in *dual recording mode* to enable these machines to check on recording accuracy. It works as fol-

lows. First, the tape or disk is encoded with the desired information, such as an accounts receivable record or a bank savings account record. Next, this information is read again using the reading mechanism of the tape or disk drive. Finally, a comparison is made to verify the original output. In most instances, the comparison of the initial output data with the newly recorded data will result in a confirmation of identical information, and the tape or disk system is then able to signal the CPU that the required writing operation has been successful. This is called an **echo check.** An unfavorable comparison implies that a hardware failure has occurred. In such instances, either a second write attempt can be initiated or the computer operator can be notified for alternative action.

When tape and disk files are involved in the

output function, **file-label processing** assumes an important role in output control. Among other things, this file-label processing requires the updating of information in the trailer record to reflect the new status of the file. Thus, for example, the number of logical and physical records residing in an updated file must be recorded in the trailer record, since this information will be used as a processing control when the file is later used for input. Similarly, the file expiration date should be carefully checked by the computer program and updated, if necessary, to indicate a longer retention cycle if one is deemed necessary.

The recording of output control totals other than the aforementioned record counts also serves a useful purpose in data processing. Examples include the recording of dollar balances in an accounts payable file, the recording of hash totals for an inventory-parts file, and the recording of item summaries in a transactions file of credit-customer activity.

Printed Output Controls

One of the more compelling aspects of output control deals with the matter of **forms control.** Perhaps the most interesting situations involve computerized check-writing applications, in which MICR forms or perforated printer forms become the encoding media for the preparation of company checks. Usually, these forms are preprinted with the company's name, address, bank account number, and sometimes even the authorized signature of the company treasurer. (For obvious reasons, it is preferable that the authorized signature be put on later.) Thus, control over these forms is vital.

The most common type of control utilized with computer-generated check-writing procedures is the coordination of a *preprinted check number* on the printer form with a computer-generated number that is inked on the same form at print time. The numbers on these **prenumbered forms** advance sequentially and are prepared by the form's supplier according to

the specifications of the organization. The computer-generated numbers also run sequentially and are initialized by adding 1 to the check sequence number stored from the last processing run. These numbers should match during normal processing. Discrepancies should be examined carefully and the causes fully resolved.

Cash-disbursement checks are not the only type of printer form using preprinted numbering as a control mechanism. Almost any type of printer form that can be burst (i.e., separated) into pages can be prenumbered and therefore controlled. In fact, even common computer paper (measuring 11 by 16 inches) is usually prenumbered as a matter of convenience to users. Other types of forms that enjoy a special control advantage when prenumbered include (1) reports containing sensitive corporate information, (2) computer-generated lottery tickets, athletic event tickets, or cultural event tickets, and (3) utility and telephone bills. For example, by recording the numbers of the athletic events tickets assigned to district sales outlets, the central box office's accountant can make a complete analysis of which tickets were sold and which were returned.

Another dimension of output control concerns the distribution of reports. Computer reports often contain sensitive information and it is important that such information be restricted. Thus, for example, the payroll register indicating who was paid during a given pay period, and how much they were paid, would be the type of report whose distribution should be restricted.

The most common form of distributional control is through an **authorized distribution list.** For each output report, the computer facility keeps a list of authorized users and prepares only enough copies of the report to satisfy the number of users on this list. Where data processing activities are centralized, it is sometimes possible to have representatives from each user group physically visit the computer center to pick up their copy of a sensitive report. In these instances, a notebook, or *log*, of pickups can be maintained and the pickup employee asked to sign the book.

The employee's identification number is recorded for security purposes at the time the report is taken. Where this is not possible, bonded employees can be authorized to deliver reports to users, and random checks on the distribution of these reports can be made by their supervisors to verify distribution.

After sensitive reports have been used, it is important to destroy them properly. Most companies have **paper shredders** for this purpose. Shredding reports is more desirable than throwing them away because discarded reports can be retrieved from trash bins.

GENERAL CONTROLS

Application controls are often called **transaction controls** because they concentrate on the input, processing, and output of accounting data that typically result from business transactions. However, a number of additional controls that are not strictly associated with the processing of accounting transactions should also be considered for computerized accounting information systems. These additional controls are called **general controls.** Five categories of general controls that we shall discuss here are: (1) personnel controls, (2) file security controls, (3) control groups, (4) auditing controls, and (5) computer facility controls.

Personnel Controls

An accounting information system depends heavily on people for the initial creation of the system, the input of data into the system, the supervision of data processing during computer operations, the distribution of processed data to authorized recipients, and the use of approved controls to ensure that the aforementioned tasks are performed properly. General controls that affect personnel include: (1) separation of related organizational functions, (2) insistence on the two-week vacation rule, (3) use of computer accounts, and (4) an informal knowledge of employees.

Separation of Related Organizational Functions

Chapter 9 has discussed the importance of separating organizational responsibilities in manual systems. In computerized accounting information systems, duties that are normally distinct have a tendency to become integrated. The gathering of **incompatible functions** within an automated environment is explained in *Statement on Auditing Standards No. 48*, which reads in part:

> Incompatible functions for accounting control purposes are those that place any person in a position to both perpetrate and conceal errors or irregularities in the normal course of his duties. Anyone who records transactions or has access to assets ordinarily is in a position to perpetrate errors or irregularities. Accordingly, accounting control necessarily depends largely on the elimination of opportunities for concealment. For example, anyone who records disbursements could omit the recording of a check, either unintentionally or intentionally. If the same person also reconciles the bank account, the failure to record the check could be concealed through an improper reconciliation. In an accounting system using a computer to print checks and record disbursements, the computer may also generate information used to reconcile the account balance. If the same person entering information into the computer to execute the payment process also receives the output for the reconciliation process, a similar failure could be concealed. These examples illustrate the concept that procedures designed to detect errors and irregularities should be performed by persons other than those who are in a position to perpetrate them: that is, these procedures should be performed by persons having no incompatible functions.[2]

Statement on Auditing Standards No. 48 makes some additional comments regarding incompatible functions when an organization has a computerized accounting system:

> In a computerized accounting system, functions that would be incompatible in a manual system

---

[2]*Ibid.,* AU Section 1030.05.

are often performed by computer. Individuals who have access to computer operations may then be in a position to perpetrate or conceal errors or irregularities. This need not be a weakness if there are control procedures that prevent such an individual from performing incompatible functions within the accounting system. These control procedures might include (*a*) adequate segregation of incompatible functions within the data processing department, (*b*) segregation between data processing and user department personnel performing review procedures, and (*c*) adequate control over access to data and computer programs.[3]

An important control used to limit the potential dangers of incompatible functions is to define clearly the organizational responsibilities of the account subsystem and the EDP subsystem, and to make sure that these responsibilities do not overlap. Authorization for the payment of payroll checks or vendor (accounts payable) checks, for example, should be initiated by personnel in the accounting subsystem, not by EDP personnel. Similarly, all changes to the master files or transaction files of the accounting information system should be authorized by individuals in the user (accounting) subsystem, not by individuals working directly within the computer subsystem.

The use of **authorization forms** helps to implement these controls. Here, we are referring to one or more manually prepared forms that document the source of the file change request, the type of data processing required, and the date of the request. A supervisory signature can also be included on the form. The use of an online system may mitigate against the use of authorization forms. Here, the appropriate control would be the preparation of a *hard-copy log of file request changes* (or other data processing requests) listed according to date and user identification (e.g., employee number or password access code).

If transactions are batched for data input, it is the user department's responsibility to prepare manual batch-control totals and to maintain these batch-control total figures for later review. However, it is the responsibility of the computer subsystem to use internally maintained control totals (e.g., record counts in the trailer labels of sequential files) to verify actual data processing accuracy and completeness.

It is also important to separate organizational responsibilities within the computer department itself. Here, the separation is between the individuals involved in the development and maintenance of computer systems on the one hand and those individuals involved in the day-to-day operations of the computerized data processing on the other. The former group is composed chiefly of programmers and systems analysts, that is, individuals who understand the details of the computerized data processing. The latter group is composed of computer operators, data entry personnel, and forms clerks, that is, individuals whose knowledge of computerized data processing should be limited. Keeping the functions of these individuals separate controls the possibility of a programmer entering fictitious data for personal gain or of a data entry clerk programming the computer to cover the theft of organizational assets. The *physical* separation of these two organizational subunits in distinct work areas, as well as the *logical* separation of these responsibilities, helps to enforce this control.

Separation of organizational responsibilities can also be applied in the development of large scale computer systems. One preventive control is to make sure that no individual programmer or systems analyst is responsible for the development of a complete accounting information system at the time the system is designed. When individuals do not have complete control over the design of processing routines, they are less capable of building unwarranted subroutines into the computer coding. Furthermore, they must work harder to keep any of their own self-created processing routines from being discovered by others.

If the computerized software package of an accounting information system is developed internally by organizational personnel, separation of duties during the development and test-

---

[3]*Ibid.*, AU Section 1030.05.

ing of the computer program also helps to ensure processing security. Similarly, when design changes are incorporated into the system at a later stage of the system's life cycle, close scrutiny of these modifications and perhaps retesting the entire system with live (i.e., real) data are essential.

An alternative to developing software internally is to contrast out some, if not all, of the important processing portions of the accounting information system. This approach shifts accountability from the shoulders of the company's internal staff and onto the shoulders of the contractor. Because there is usually less incentive for an "arms-length" contractor to create fraudulent processing programs, a company may anticipate a high likelihood of honest work. If it so desires, the purchasing company can insist that the contractor company be bonded so that there is provision for recovery of damages in the event of problems. (Of course, it is also possible for a company to bond its own computer employees.)

The Two-Week Vacation Rule

Fraudulent schemes such as the lapping of accounts receivable or the manipulation of dormant bank accounts depend on the constant attention of the perpetrator for success. For example, the lapping of accounts receivable requires that the perpetrator continually apply the most recent payments of some accounts to cover the monies already stolen from other accounts. A safeguard against such schemes, therefore, is to insist that employees take vacations in blocks of time—for example, two weeks. This **two-week vacation rule** denies the individual the vital time necessary to cover a fraud and avoid detection. As an historical matter, it is interesting to note cases in which the absence of this simple control was a factor in huge computer thefts.

Use of Computer Accounts

Most computer centers maintain a system of separate **computer accounts** that are assigned to users on either an individual or group basis. Usually, each account is assigned a unique password. When the user logs onto the computer, the computer checks the password against a master list of accounts. Only users with current accounts are permitted access to further computer resources. The account numbers assigned to users are also used for accumulating computer charges. This control is important when computer resources are scarce or there is some fear that computer time may be used for "outside" contract programming.

When a user is trying to gain access to the computer system from a remote terminal, a **call-back procedure** may be used. After the password is entered by the user, the connection is broken. An automatic dial-back device is used by the computer to call back the authorized phone number for the terminal which has logged on. Failure to reconnect indicates that someone has attempted access from an unauthorized terminal.

A further use of computer accounts is to limit user access to particular computer files or programs. This protects certain files or programs from unauthorized use. In addition, it is possible to place resource limitations on account numbers—for example, limiting the user to so much connect time, so much disk space, so much CPU time, and so forth. This controls against such accidental errors as when a programmer accidentally throws the computer into an endless loop or mistakenly exceeds the space limitations of the disk library.

Production-oriented computer systems are often configured in the following manner to protect data and programs. An area is set up for each programmer to serve as a developmental testing area. Here, programs are either created or modified once they have been loaded from a master account of source language programs. The programmer is the only one with the passwords or other keys (account information) to the individually assigned area. Similarly, the programmer is the only one able to place the source language programs in the development area after validation has occurred. This is illustrated in Figure 10-8.

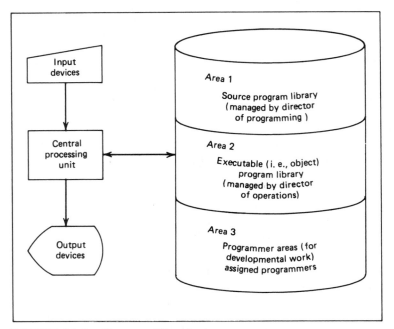

FIGURE 10-8   The use of libraries in a computer system.

When a computer program has been successfully tested and readied for use, the source-language version is transferred to the source library and the compiled version (machine language code) is transferred to the operational (i.e., production) account by the operations manager. This machine-code version is no longer modifiable and can be executed only by the operations staff. Thus, it is protected from unauthorized tampering.

Informal Knowledge of Employees

An **informal knowledge of employees** and their activities can be an important clue in the detection of fraudulent activity. Consider the following examples.

• The manager of a midwestern company became suspicious when he found out that one of his employees took expensive vacations in Acapulco, Mexico, every year. An investigation revealed that the employee had been embezzling thousands of dollars from the company.

• The branch manager of an East Coast bank appeared to be a very conscientious employee, almost never taking a vacation and always personally attending to customer inquiries about discrepancies in their bank balances. Little did his employers know that this man *had* to stay at his post every day—he had stolen more than a million dollars from the bank's depositors and came in daily to cover up his fraud.

• The janitor's questions about the bank's new computer system were attributed to the enthusiasm the bank was trying to foster in all its employees. Imagine the manager's surprise when it was discovered that the answers to the janitor's questions enabled him to log on a terminal after hours and credit his account with $2500!

The problem of controlling employees within the environment of computerized accounting information systems is discussed in Chapter 11. Suffice it to say here that an informal knowledge of employee interests and behavior may play an important role in both preventing and detecting intentional error.

File Security Controls

It is essential that a computerized accounting information system safeguard its magnetic tape and disk files from both accidental and intentional error. Among the reasons for these safeguards are:

1. The computer files are not human-readable. Controls must be installed to ensure that these files *can* be read when necessary.
2. The typical computer file contains a vast amount of data. In general, it is not possible to reconstruct such files from the memories of employees.
3. The information contained on magnetic tapes and disks is in a very compact format. The destruction of as little as 1 inch of recording medium may mean the loss of thousands of characters of data.
4. The data stored on computer files are permanent only to the extent that tiny bits have been magnetized on the recording tracks. Power disruptions, power surges, and even accidentally dropping the tape reel or disk pack may cause damage.
5. The data stored on computer files may be confidential. Information such as advertising expenditure schedules, competitive bidding plans, payroll figures, and innovative software programs must be protected from unwarranted use.
6. The reconstruction of file data is costly no matter how extensive the company's recovery procedures. It is usually more cost-effective to protect against file abuse than to depend on backup procedures for file protection.
7. File information itself should be considered an asset of the company. As such, it deserves the same protection accorded other organizational assets.

The purpose of file security is to protect computer files from either accidental or intentional abuse. This requires procedures to make sure that computer programs use the correct files for data processing and procedures to create backup copies of critical files in the event that original copies of a file are lost, stolen, damaged, or vandalized. The following paragraphs discuss various controls to accomplish these ends.

An *external file label* is a small, gummed-paper label affixed to the outside plastic cover of a tape reel, disk pack, or floppy disk envelope. This label identifies the file—usually with a large, group-coded number. Embedded in this code may be an indication of what applications access this file or where the file is stored in the tape and disk library. Other information typically found on the external file label includes the cycle time of the file (e.g., how often the file is used), the last time the file was accessed, the expiration date of the file, and the record format of the file.

In addition to external labels, most computer files also use *internal file labels*. An internal file label is a special computer record created for control purposes. Almost all computer files have at least one internal file label containing, at a minimum, the same type of identification information found on the external file label.

With sequential files, the first record stored on the file is the internal file label called the *file header label*. Nonsequential files also have internal labels, although the location of these labels will vary with the method of file organization used. Most computer companies have standard file-label processing routines that first access the file's header label and then validate the file name, file number, and so forth, of the tape or disk file. This type of control ensures that the computer program is processing the correct files and that the files themselves are in proper order. If desired, special secret passwords can also be required of file users to make sure that only authorized computer programs or users access sensitive file information.

Sequential files also maintain an internal control label called the *file trailer label*. As we have already noted, the purpose of the file trailer label is to signal the end of the file and to maintain control-total information useful in testing the completeness of the file processing.

To make sure that a magnetic tape input file is not used as an output file or accidentally written on, the magnetic tape reel's **file-protect ring** can be removed, thus placing the reel in a "read-only" processing mode (see Figure 10-9). For microcomputers that use cassettes, little plastic flanges on the back of the cassette casing can be broken off to obtain the same result. There is no counterpart of this control for hard disks, although floppy disks can be file-protected by covering notches in their envelopes.

Finally, file controls also include the preparation of duplicate copies of current files for security purposes and the storage of such file copies in secure locations away from the computer center. This control is important in the event of fire, theft, or vandalism, and should be part of the standard operating procedure of the company. A common method of file control is the so-called **grandfather-father-son method of file security,** in which three generations of a master file, together with the transactions files used to update them, are secured for this purpose.

Figure 10-10 illustrates the idea for a master file that is updated at the end of each business day. Monday's master file and Monday's transactions file are used to prepare the master file for Tuesday morning. Similarly, Tuesday's master file plus Tuesday's transactions file are used to prepare the current master file for Wednesday. Thus, at Wednesday noon, Monday's master file would be the grandfather file, Tuesday's master file would be the father file, and Wednesday's master file would be the current, or son, file. Thus, the Monday and Tuesday files would be stored at secure locations away from the computer center. In the event that Wednesday's master file is rendered inoperative, the company can recover simply by preparing another copy of it from the Tuesday (father) files. Even if both the Wednesday master file and the Tuesday master

FIGURE 10-9 The file-protect ring of a magnetic tape reel. When this plastic ring is removed, the reel is placed in read-only mode.

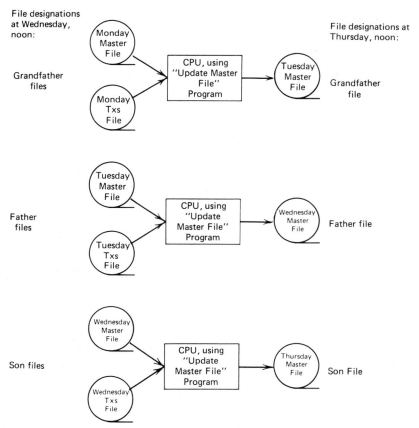

File designations at Wednesday, noon:

Grandfather files

File designations at Thursday, noon:

Grandfather file

Father files

Father file

Son files

Son File

FIGURE 10-10 The designation of three sets of master files, using grandfather-father-son file entry.

file are no good, there is still the Monday master file.

On Wednesday night, the process moves forward. As soon as the master file for Thursday is prepared, there is a shift of file ranking. Tuesday's master file becomes the grandfather file, Wednesday's master file becomes the father file, and the now-current Thursday file becomes the son file. Monday's file is no longer needed and can therefore be erased. Thus, the process continues in chronological sequence. Of course, all this need not occur on a daily or even weekly basis. Many master files are not updated every day. Thus, in alternative accounting applications, the periodicity of the work will differ, although the steps necessary to maintain the computer file's security will not.

When disk files are used, the problem of maintaining backup copies of the disk pack is compounded by the fact that disk files can be updated in place. This means that the disk file is modified by accessing an old record, changing certain information, and then writing over the old record on the disk pack, thereby erasing what was there before. Thus, whereas it is a simple matter to relabel an old tape reel as a father or grandfather file, it is necessary to physically copy the entire disk file to maintain a backup copy. Because disk packs are both bulky and expensive, this copying is normally done onto tape reels. Occasionally, even source documents and printed output are used for backup purposes, but these, of course, are not machine-readable. Thus, the tape or disk copy of a disk file has a distinct advantage over either source documents or printed output when used for backup.

Control Groups

A **control group** is a set of one or more individuals responsible for the creation, enforcement, and use of application controls in an organization. The size and composition of a control group vary. Small organizations may use a single individual to perform the tasks of the control group whereas large organizations may have a separate control group of several individuals for each of its major subsystem.

The following are among the tasks commonly performed by control groups:

1. Create control policies and procedures governing the collection, input, processing, and distribution of computerized data.
2. Draft formal procedures for the submittal of input data.
3. Maintain registers of computer access codes.
4. Maintain control totals for master files and transaction files.
5. Help supervise the acquisition of new accounting software or the enhancement of existing accounting software.
6. Review software documentation, especially technical documentation dealing with application controls, authorized programming changes, and supervised testing.
7. Coordinate security controls with subsystem users and specific computer personnel such as the data base administrator or the file librarian.
8. Enforce established control procedures—for example, make sure that the computer subsystem does not unilaterally alter batch-control totals when subtotals do not match processing totals.

Not every control group is likely to perform all of these functions, and some companies may feel that a control group is not needed. Given the wide variety of potential tasks a control group might perform, however, the use of a control group is itself an important control for an accounting information system.

Auditing Controls

The general topic of auditing accounting information systems is discussed in Chapter 12. An audit of an accounting information system, however, is itself an important type of control.

Many of the controls in an accounting information system are procedural, that is, they depend on the execution of procedures to work. One of the most important tasks of an auditor, therefore, is to verify that these control procedures are being followed. For example, an audit permits the examiners to observe (1) how carefully related organizational responsibilities are separated, (2) how carefully batch-control totals are computed and reconciled to computer processing totals, (3) how closely backup procedures are followed for the protection of computer files, and (4) whether or not fallback procedures are adequate (explained in greater detail shortly).

The findings of an audit help planners identify system strengths and weaknesses. Quite often, system weaknesses include either the absence of application controls or a failure to follow the application controls already (supposedly) implemented. Thus, another use of the audit is to recommend policies and procedures that further control the accounting information system.

Audits can either be *planned* or *surprise*. **Planned audits** are scheduled and specific dates are set aside for them. **Surprise audits** are not announced in advance. Both types of audits are discussed in greater detail in Chapter 12. However, the potential of either a planned audit or a surprise audit is itself a control that may serve as a deterrent to dishonesty. In this sense, audits may be considered both a preventive and a feedback control.

Computer Facility Controls

Like any other investment, the physical assets of the computer center—the CPU, the peripheral devices, the tape and disk files of the computer library, and so forth—deserve protection. Destruction of, or damage to, these assets represents both a real danger and an important area of computer-systems control. Physical loss can happen in only one of two ways: through accident or intent. Thus, current effort in the area of physical security is devoted to **computer facility controls** that prevent both unintentional and intentional harm.

Locate the Computer Center in a Safe Place

Several years ago, a disgruntled taxpayer decided to teach the Internal Revenue Service a lesson. First, the taxpayer walked to the outside of the IRS building where his tax forms had been processed. The unhappy man then proceeded to shoot at the agency's central processing unit through an open window with his 12-gauge shotgun! Although some might argue that the major lesson to be learned from this story is that taxes are too high, there is also the suggestion that the computer center of the typical organization should not be placed in a location that has easy public access. Thus, for most business data processors, the ground-floor showroom—once the desired location for many computer operations—has given way to basements, separate buildings, and other sites away from passageways that are easily accessible to employees or the public. Locations guarded by armed personnel are obviously the most preferred, but any placement that has a limited number of secured entrances is desirable.

The location of the computer center should also guard against natural disasters such as fire, flood, or earthquake. Although it is impossible to protect a computer completely from such hazards, advanced planning can minimize exposure to them. For example, protection from fire can be increased by locating computer facilities away from boiler rooms, heating furnaces, or fuel storage areas. Similarly, protection from floods is possible by locating computer facilities on high ground or the upper stories of office buildings. Finally, earthquake damage can be controlled by locating computer facilities in single-story buildings or in heavily reinforced ones.

Limit Employee Access

Very few people have reason to be *inside* the computer machine room. Once the computer software has been fully developed, implementation can proceed smoothly through the computer operator's use of documentation manuals. Therefore, executives, data entry operators, and even company programmers have very little reason to enter a machine room.

To discourage potential mischief makers, several facility safeguards are possible. One is to require all company personnel in the vicinity to wear *color-coded identification badges* with full-face pictures. Only people authorized to enter the machine room would be assigned an identification badge of a particular color. A second precaution is to place a guard (sometimes even a secretary will do) at the entrance to the machine room; the door to the room is self-locking and can be "buzzed" open only by the control person, who permits only authorized personnel to enter. Finally, there is the strict control of access to the center through the issuance of keys, dial-lock combinations, or other door-controls which limit access only to authorized employees. With regard to this last safeguard, it is also a good idea to change locks or lock combinations often and to use keys that cannot easily be duplicated.

Having listed all these safeguards, it must now be stated that the record of intentional vandalism as documented in the next chapter indicates that the overwhelming majority of vandalism has been performed by embittered former employees, corporate executives, and other vindictive personnel. These people are likely to have a thorough understanding of the computer center's security systems and thus are likely to know how to get around them. If there is any lesson to be learned from the historical record, it is that an unhappy employee, or former employee, who has (or had) access to the computer center is a potential walking time bomb. Thus, there is special reason to make sure that there are no personnel problems in this area of corporate operations. The general rule is to hire slowly and fire quickly.

Outline Fallback Procedures

Several years ago, an angry employee programmed his company's computer to erase a few tape records from an accounts receivable file every time the accounts receivable program was run. It was not until several runs later that the mischief was discovered and the company found itself in a real bind. It contacted customers to request the information that would enable it to reconstruct records and, in desperation, even took out full-page advertisements in newspapers begging customers to come forward with their billing information. Few did, and the company eventually went bankrupt.

This story points out that the preparation and maintenance of backup copies of important tape and disk files is an imperative part of more general **fallback procedures.** Normally, the important tape reels and disk packs containing current information about the firm's activities are maintained by an EDP librarian in a secured file library. Access to such files is usually limited to authorized personnel. It is also clear, however, that such a control is insufficient to guard against the type of problem described here.

We have already discussed the grandfather-father-son control feature used to safeguard computer files. No matter how backup copies of the files are obtained, it is conventional practice to store the grandfather and father files in areas away from the current, or son, file. This prevents the possibility of losing both the current file and both backup copies should physical disaster strike a common storage location. Some companies rent bank vaults for this purpose whereas others use their own fireproof safes. One small company we know stores backup copies of its most current files in the garage of its EDP manager (which is fine provided you can trust the EDP manager!).

In addition to physical problems with its processing files, a company can also experience operational difficulty with its central processor. Just as with any other piece of hardware that is in constant use, there is a normal amount of wear

and tear on the machine. Occasionally, something happens and the CPU "goes down." At such times, it is obvious that a fallback plan for emergency processing is required. What is needed is processing time on another computer.

Not just any computer will do, however. Most accounting information systems are geared to the operating system and processing characteristics of the specific company's installation and, thus, another computer configuration exactly like the inoperative one is required. Several possibilities exist. One alternative is to arrange for the rental of computer time from a service bureau organization or a time-sharing organization. (Both of these types of organizations are discussed in later chapters.) A second approach is to reach a reciprocal agreement with a nearby company that has the same computer model. Common to both of these possibilities is the forward planning necessary to reach such agreements and the forethought for contingencies.

Finally, it is desirable for an organization to prepare for a major disaster such as a fire, earthquake, flood, hurricane, and so on. This is called a **disaster recovery plan** and its purpose is to enable the organization to process data while computer equipment is being replaced and computer files are being reconstructed. Elements in the disaster recovery plan include alternative methods of data collection, the use of alternative computer equipment, the acquisition and use of backup computer files, and temporary methods of information distribution. There are companies that specialize in assisting organizations in these matters. Their facilities include storage vaults for computer files, perhaps several different types of computer equipment and related peripheral devices, and even trained EDP personnel to perform emergency data processing.

Buy Insurance

Although the purchase of insurance is the first activity that occurs to many persons when computer safeguards are discussed, it is actually the protection of last resort. The reason is that insurance does not actually protect the purchaser from loss—it merely compensates for such losses when they occur. Thus, it is not a preventive control but serves only "after the fact."

Insurance policies for computer damages are usually limited in coverage and may not reimburse policyholders for such occurrences as civil disorder, acts of God, or employee larceny. Furthermore, compensation usually is restricted to the actual damages suffered by the firm. As you may imagine, a fair estimate of what these losses entail is not an easy matter. Of special difficulty is placing dollar values for second- or third-generation computer equipment that has long since lost any real market value, yet performs vital data processing services for the computer center. Partially damaged equipment is yet another problem. The list goes on and on, but you get the idea: there is little advantage to relying solely on insurance for the protection of the computer facility.

SUMMARY

This chapter has focused on controls for computerized versions of the accounting information system. Controls for automated accounting systems are important for a number of reasons: (1) computerized systems tend to involve large volumes of data that are more efficiently processed, and therefore controlled, by automated (as opposed to manual) methods, (2) much of the processing involves data media that are not in human-readable form and hence must be controlled through mechanized methods, (3) the audit trail has become more difficult to follow (especially in online computerized systems) and therefore must be traced with automated methodology, and (4) computer crime has become an important consideration that requires that computerized systems have stringent supervision and sophisticated controls for adequate protection and detection. However, computer controls are not necessarily oriented toward catching, or frustrating, computer crooks. Any number

of accidental mistakes in data observation, collection, transcription, processing, or output can occur. Computerized controls are as much involved in catching these types of errors as in catching criminals.

The controls for computerized accounting information systems are often called *application controls.* These controls are designed to provide reasonable assurance that the recording, processing, and reporting of accounting data are performed accurately and completely. For convenience, this chapter discussed three major categories of application controls: input controls, processing controls, and output controls.

Input controls attempt to ensure the validity, accuracy, and completeness of data fed into an accounting information system. Input controls include (1) methods that encourage the accurate observation and recording of accounting data, (2) methods that assist in the accurate transcription of accounting data into machine-readable media such as MICR forms, floppy disks, or online input files, (3) the use of edit tests, (4) the use of check digits, and (5) methods that restrict logical access to computers and computerized data from remote terminals.

Processing controls are used to ensure data processing accuracy while accounting data are being processed by a computer. Processing controls include the use of control totals, standard file-label processing routines, hardware parity tests, error recovery procedures, CPU maintenance and testing programs, dual computation, various types of CPU hardware controls, read-only memories (ROMs), user-assigned workspace controls, software documentation, error-testing compilers, system testing, and periodic data testing.

Output controls ensure the accuracy, completeness, and proper distribution of data from the computer. Output controls include various controls for writing data on tape or disk files, file-label processing routines, data transmission controls, and the use of paper shredders. Output controls also include the need to validate the accuracy, authenticity, timeliness, and completeness of computer output through such means as control totals and proof listings.

General controls are nonapplication controls that do not conveniently fit in the categories of input, processing, or output controls. Personnel controls, for example, include the separation of related organizational functions, the use of the two-week-vacation rule, the use of computer ac-

counts, and an informal knowledge of employees. File security controls include the use of external and internal file labels, the use of file-protect rings and flanges, and the grandfather-father-son method of file security. The use of control groups, planned audits, surprise audits, and various types of computer facility controls are additional general controls.

Key Terms You Should Know

activity listings
application controls
authorization forms
authorized distribution list
batch-control document
callback procedure
check digit
compiler
computer accounts
computer facility controls
confirmation slips
control group
control record
control total
data transcription
disaster recovery plan
dual computation control
dual observation control
echo check
edit tests
embedded auditing routine
error recovery procedures
fallback procedures
file-label processing routines
file-protect ring
forms control
general controls
GIGO (garbage in, garbage out)
grandfather-father-son file security
incompatible functions
informal knowledge of employees

input controls
maintenance programs
mask (terminal input)
output controls
overflow (CPU)
paper shredders
parity testing
password code
periodic data test
planned audit
preformatted input screen
prenumbered forms
preprinted recording forms
processing controls
prompts (input screen)
proof listings
read-only memory (ROM)
record count
redundant data check
separation of related organizational functions
software documentation
split-screen display
surprise audit
system testing
transaction controls
turnaround document
two-week vacation rule
underflow
unfound-record test
user-friendly software
workspace control

Discussion Questions

10-1. The introduction to this chapter stated that "in many ways, controls for a computerized accounting information system are even more important

than they are for a manual one." In what ways is this statement justified? In what ways is it *not* justified?

10-2. What is the meaning and purpose of "application controls"? Are application controls useful only to computerized versions of accounting information systems?

10-3. Within the chapter, it was stated that not all the controls discussed would be advantageous for a particular accounting information system. The general rule is that a specific control should be used only if its benefits exceed its costs. Discuss in greater detail what kinds of benefits these would be.

10-4. "Supervision doesn't always guarantee a control; sometimes it just guarantees a conspirator." Discuss.

10-5. Enumerate the advantages of preprinted source documents, and indicate why each advantage is useful as a control for an accounting information system. Can you think of any disadvantages? Discuss.

10-6. For years, color-coded forms have served as one of the most effective means of differentiating data documents in information systems. To what extent has this control been exploited in automated accounting information systems?

10-7. Jean & Joan Cosmetics has a complete line of beauty products for women and maintains a computerized inventory system. Inventory items are identified by an eight-digit product number, of which the first four digits classify the beauty product by major category (hair, face, skin, eyes, etc.) and the last four digits identify the product itself. Enumerate as many controls as you can that the company might use to ensure accuracy in this eight-digit number when updating its inventory-balance file.

10-8. The sales manager of an insurance office called a sales personnel meeting to discuss the problems he had been having with his salespeople filling out the insurance forms. "Ladies and gentlemen," he explained, "you all know how hard our Ms. Wiskovski works around here, and she is too busy with her other chores to correct your mistakes on our intake forms. So from now on, I will dock each person $5 for every mistake we catch on the form." Comment.

10-9. Discuss the method(s) by which greater accuracy can be obtained in transcribed data. What problems can you foresee in these so-called controls?

10-10. Explain how each of the following can be used to control the input, processing, or output of accounting data: (a) preformatted screens, (b) edit tests, (c) terminal screen masks, (d) check digits, (e) passwords, (f) activity or proof listings, (g) control totals.

10-11. The security of an accounting information system is only as good as the honesty of the people that run it." Comment.

10-12. What is the difference between logical access to the computer and physical access to the computer? Why is the security of both important?

10-13. Why has it been said that in some circumstances the implementation of a computerized accounting information system has actually helped, rather than hindered, the would-be company embezzler?

10-14. Discuss the following statement: "The separation of related organizational functions is very difficult in computerized accounting information systems because computers often integrate such functions to perform data processing tasks. Therefore, such a control is not advisable for those organizations using computers to perform their accounting functions."

10-15. Discuss the role of the control total in accounting information systems. Why are control totals insufficient to guard against data inaccuracies?

10-16. Donna MacAdam was a computer operator working for the Third National Bank of Fat City. At one point she complained to her friend that she hated her job. "It's a dead-end situation," she said. "Half of the time I'm working night shifts and all the time I just push buttons. I know I'm supposed to type 'YC6' every time I get an 'ENTER' instruction on the console, but I don't know why I do it. I think I'll quit and become an accountant!" Comment.

10-17. E. Wilson and Associates hired a consulting team from Meat, Hardwick, and Thistle to discuss application controls for the company's accounting data processing. In one of the workshops, the seminar leader stated, "We can classify all errors in processing accounting data as either accidental or intentional. Controls such as edit tests are primarily aimed at the former type whereas controls such as personnel controls are primarily aimed at the latter type." Comment.

10-18. "Because a human cannot read what is written on a tape or disk, there is no way to be sure that what is being written is correct." Do you agree? Why or why not?

10-19. Automated data collection techniques enable the accounting information system to avoid the problems of data transcription and therefore to increase the accuracy of the input. Name several methods of automated data collection and identify the ways in which each contributes to the goals of data accuracy and completeness.

10-20. Why is the area of forms control given so much attention in computer output? After all, what does a company really have to lose if a blank sheet of output or two is missing?

10-21. Discuss the methods of safeguarding the

physical assets of the computer center. What extra costs would you anticipate when these controls are used?

10-22. Explain the concept of the grandfather-father-son method of file control. Whom would *you* trust with the grandfather file?

10-23. A computer programmer had a grudge against his company. To get even, he coded a special routine in the mortgage loan program that erased a small, random number of accounts on the tape file every time the program was run. The company did not detect the routine until almost all of its records had been erased. Discuss what controls might have protected this company from its own programmer.

10-24. An accountant working for a medium-size distributor set up several dummy companies and began directing the computer to write checks to them for fictitious merchandise. He was apprehended only when several of the company executives began to wonder how he could afford a ski vacation in the Alps every year. What might have prevented this?

10-25. The controls for the MSB Company's payroll example given in the chapter supplement (see pp. 376-379) outline a set of procedures to ensure accuracy and completeness in the data-gathering, data processing, and check-distribution functions of this application. It is possible that several additional controls besides those mentioned in the payroll discussion might have occurred to you for possible implementation within this application. Suggest several such controls that would assist the accountant in this application.

Problems

10-26. Identify one or more application controls that would guard against each of the following errors or problems. For each control you identify, also explain *how* the control would protect against each error or problem.

a. Leslie Thomas, a secretary at the university, indicated that she had worked 40 hours on her regular time card. The university paid her for 400 hours worked that week.

b. The aging analysis indicated that the Grab and Run Electronics account was so far in arrears that the credit manager decided to cut off any further credit sales to the company until it cleared up its account. Yet, the following week, the manager noted that

three new sales had been made to that company— all on credit.

c. The Small Company employed Mr. Fineus Eyeshade to perform all its accounts receivable data processing. Mr. Eyeshade's 25 years with the company and his unassuming appearance helped him conceal the fact that he was lapping accounts receivable in order to cover his gambling losses at the racetrack.

d. The Blue Mountain Utility Company was having difficulty with its customer payments. The payment amounts were entered directly onto a terminal and the transaction file thus created was used to update the customer master file. Among the problems encountered with this system was the application of customer payments to the wrong accounts and the creation of multiple customer master file records for the same account.

e. The Landsford brothers had lived in Center County all their lives. Ben worked for the local mill in the accounts payable department, Tom owned the local hardware store. The sheriff couldn't believe that the brothers had created several dummy companies that sold fictitious merchandise to the mill. Ben had the mill pay for this merchandise in its usual fashion and he wrote off the missing goods as "damaged inventory."

10-27. Identify one or more controls that would guard against each of the following errors.

a. A bank deposit transaction was accidentally coded with a withdrawal code.

b. The key-entry operator keyed in the purchase order number as a nine-digit number instead of an eight-digit number.

c. The date of a customer payment was keyed 1909 instead of 1990.

d. A company employee was issued a check in the amount of $-135.65 because he had not worked a certain week but most of his payroll deductions were automatic each week.

e. The patient filled out her medical insurance number as 123465 instead of 123456.

f. An applicant for the company stock option plan filled out her employee number as 84-7634-21. The first two digits are a department code. There is no department 84.

g. A new key operator did not know which input line on the terminal was for the "purchase order number" and which input line on the terminal was for "customer account number."

h. A high school student was able to log onto the

telephone company's computer as soon as he learned what telephone number to call.

i. The accounts receivable department sent 87 checks to the computer center for processing. No one realized that one check was dropped along the way and that the computer therefore processed only 86 checks.

j. The information documenting sales orders was often incomplete. Sales representatives frequently used plain sheets of paper to write up their orders.

10-28. Identify one or more application controls that would guard against each of the following problems.

a. The company computer developed a processing malfunction: it thought that 4 plus 6 was 11.

b. Due to a power surge, a data bit was dropped in the transmission of file records from a disk drive to the CPU.

c. In a computer program, the programmer divided the total wage budget of each department by the number of employees in the department to compute an average wage. The data base administrator had been assigned his own department of size 1 and he had just quit. The computer divided by zero.

d. A newly written computer program incorrectly computed the number of deductions for each payroll employee. The systems analyst wanted to review the program's logic.

e. A programmer accidentally erased the computer's operating system when she used too much computer memory for an accounting program.

f. The company accounts receivable file was accidentally used as a scratch tape.

g. The supervisor of the production department was accidentally given a complete copy of the company's payroll report, showing the salaries of all the corporation's executives.

h. After approving the company's budget, the executive committee members threw the computer-printed copies in the boardroom wastepaper basket. An enterprising janitor retrieved these copies later and sold them to a rival company for a considerable sum of money.

i. The local river overflowed and the corporate computer center, which was located in the basement, where it would be out of the way of regular employees, was flooded.

10-29. Compute check digits for the following account numbers using the method described in the chapter.

a. 123456   d. 821652
b. 826431   e. 356211
c. 545323   f. 352253

10-30. A check-digit system uses only every other digit in a nine-digit account number to guard against data errors. The sum of these values is added and then the digits in the sum are added continuously until a single number remains to serve as the check digit. Thus, for the account number 123456789, just the values, 2, 4, 6, and 8 are used. Their sum is 20 and the sum of these digits is $2 + 0 = 2$. Hence, 2 becomes the check digit for this account number. Using this method, compute the check digits for each of the following account numbers.

a. 375621883   d. 443216820
b. 537662115   e. 956821654
c. 872216535   f. 631862477

10-31. A check-digit system uses the odd numbers beginning with 3 to compute a check digit for a four-digit account number as follows. The low-order digit is multiplied by 3, the next lowest order digit is multiplied by 5, the next lowest order digit is multiplied by 7, and the high-order digit is multiplied by 9. These multiples are then summed and the low-order digit of the sum is used as the check digit. Thus, for the account number 1234, the multiples are $4 \times 3 = 12$, $3 \times 5 = 15$, $2 \times 7 = 14$, and $1 \times 9 = 9$. The sum of these multiples is $12 + 15 + 14 + 9 = 50$, and the check digit is therefore 0. Compute check digits for the following account numbers using this system.

a. 4569   d. 6951
b. 3827   e. 1219
c. 4342   f. 9995

10-32. The most common check-digit system in use today is the somewhat complicated modulus-11 check-digit system, which, for technical reasons, has been shown to be superior to similar systems using a different modulus from 11. The system works as follows.

1. Assign weights to each number. The low-order number is given a weight of 2, the next-low-order number is given a weight of 3, and so forth.
2. Multiply each digit in the number by its weight.
3. Add the products computed in step 2 to obtain a single number.
4. Divide the value found in step 3 by 11.
5. Examine the remainder. If the remainder is 0, the check digit is also 0. If the remainder is not 0,

subtract the remainder from 11 to obtain the check digit. A check digit of 10 is usually written as "x."

Example: For account number 123456, for each digit, reading from left to right, the weights are, respectively, 7, 6, 5, 4, 3, and 2. The product of these digits times their respective weights is $1 \times 7 = 7$, $2 \times 6 = 12$, $3 \times 5 = 15$, $4 \times 4 = 16$, $5 \times 3 = 15$, $6 \times 2 = 12$. The sum of these products is 77. When this number is divided by 11, the remainder is 0 and thus the check digit is 0. The new account number is therefore 1234560.

For each of the following numbers, perform a similar computation.

a. 254667   c. 334886
b. 765895   d. 965334

10-33. The Blatz Furniture Company uses an online data input system for processing its sales invoice data, salesperson data, inventory control data, and purchase order data. Representative data for each of these applications are shown in the following table. Identify spe-

cific editing tests that might be used to ensure the accuracy and completeness of the information in each data set.

10-34. In June 1979, United Airlines made its customers a very unusual offer. Every person taking a United Airlines flight in the month of June would be issued a half-price coupon that entitled the bearer to a 50% reduction in the full-fare price of any flight taken between July 1, 1979, and December 15, 1979. The purpose of the promotion was to lure travelers back to United Airlines flights after the company had suffered from a devastating strike. An interesting feature of the coupons was that there were very few restrictions on their use. For example, a traveler could take a $90 flight on one of the company's short trips, yet apply the half-fare discount to a second, transcontinental flight from, say, New York to Los Angeles. Further, the ticket itself was not encoded with the name of the passenger. Thus, in effect, such coupons were transferable.

As illustrated in Figure 10-11, each coupon was stamped with a seven-digit accounting number that was also coded on a perforated stub portion of the

Application	Field Name	Field Length	Example
Invoicing	Customer number	6	123456
	Customer name	23	Al's Department Store
	Salesperson number	3	477
	Invoice number	6	123456
	Item catalog number	10	9578572355
	Quantity sold	8	13
	Unit price	7	10.50
	Total price	12	136.50
Salesperson activity	Salesperson number	3	477
	Salesperson name	20	Kathryn Wilson
	Store department number	8	10314201
	Week's sales volume	12	1043.75
	Regular hours worked	5	39.75
	Overtime hours worked	4	0.75
Inventory control	Inventory item number	10	9578572355
	Item description	15	Desk lamp
	Unit cost	7	8.50
	Number of units dispersed this week	4	14
	Number of units added to inventory	4	20
Purchasing	Vendor catalog number	12	059689584996
	Item description	18	Desk pad
	Vendor number	10	8276110438
	Number of units ordered	7	45
	Price per unit	7	8.75
	Total cost of purchase	14	313.75

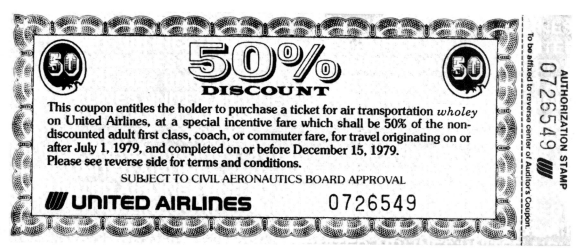

FIGURE 10-11 A United Airlines flight coupon.

ticket. This stub was torn from the ticket coupon at the time of use and affixed to the accounting copy of the passenger's airline ticket. Thus, the affixed stub portion of the coupon indicated that the 50% discount had been applied to the price of the passenger's ticket. As with other airlines, all accounting copies of the United Airlines tickets are collected at the company's national accounting headquarters for processing purposes.

Requirements

1. What strengths and weaknesses do you perceive in the United Airlines discount scheme?
2. For each weakness you mentioned in Question 1, also identify a means of avoiding it.

10-35. The Kim Boal Company uses a computerized accounts receivable system. Information required to update the company's online master file is first recorded on source documents. Information for five representative transactions are illustrated in Figure 10-12. A careful inspection of this data, however, will reveal a number of potential errors.

Requirements

1. Identify as many errors as you can.
2. For each error, identify a control that might have been used to catch it.
3. Using the data in the table, compute at least one

Account Number	Trans- action Code[a]	Credit Sale or Cash Receipt Amount	Discount Allowed (Percent)[b]	Discount Allowed (Dollars)	Net Amount
53162	2	$52.00	(blank)	$1.04	$50.96
53175	1	250000	02	5000	245000
53781	2	2 0095	−2	00000	20095
53192	2	45000	20	9000	360000
53198	3	41.0.00	02	820	40180

[a] 1 = credit sale, 2 = cash receipt

[b] Assume all sales terms are x/10, n/30, where x is the percent in the column.

FIGURE 10-12 Representative accounts receivable transactions for the Kim Boal Company.

Member Number	Billing Date	Plane Code[a]	Hours Logged[b]	Total Charge
172	101580	C	5.40	$81.00
195	101780	C	0250	005000
L51	103280	P	320	005760
048	110308	E	0400	080000
391	110580	C	015–	002250

[a] C = Cessna, P = Piper, E = Commanche.

[b] Expressed to nearest hundredth hour, decimal point omitted.

FIGURE 10-13   Data entries for the Alpine Flight Club.

example of each of the following: financial control total, hash total, and record count.

10-36. The Alpine Flight Club is an organization of amateur pilots with 182 members. The club owns three airplanes: a Cessna, a Piper, and a Comanche, which it rents out for $15, $18, and $20 per hour, respectively, to club members. The club performs its billing with the aid of a microcomputer-based accounting system. The data for a few representative entries are shown in Figure 10-13. (a) Identify the errors in each data set (row of the table). (b) For each error, suggest an editing control that would detect it. (c) Using the data, compute at least one example of each of the following: financial control total, hash total, and record count.

10-37. Figure 10-14 illustrates a representative master file record utilized by the Sterling National Bank to process its customers' checking accounts. Also shown is a representative file segment control record. A separate such segment control record is used for every branch of the bank. This record is the last record of each file segment.

Account numbers consist of a two-digit branch number followed by a six-digit account number. The bank has recently installed an Automatic Loan Approval (ALA) feature in which certain customers are permitted to overdraw their accounts. Thus, for approved accounts (ALA flag = 1 in the master file record), the account balance can be negative.

Identification numbers in the segment-control record contain the two-digit branch number, followed by 999999. The account balance field in the control record is the sum of all positive account balances for the corresponding branch accounts. The loan balance field is the sum of all negative account balances for the corresponding branch accounts.

MASTER RECORD

Account Number	Name	Address	Phone Number	Account Balance	Savings Account Ref. No.	ALA Flag
						1 = yes
						0 = no

SEGMENT-CONTROL RECORD

Control Record Identifier Field	Branch Name	Number of Accounts this Segment	Account Balance Total	Loan Balance Total

FIGURE 10-14   Master file record layout and segment control record layout for the Sterling National Bank.

The checking account master file is processed with customer transactions for such customer activities as writing checks, making deposits, and changing home addresses. Besides updating the account balances, the processing routine performs certain processing-control functions:

1. Checking account number field check: the account number should have exactly eight numerical digits, as described earlier. No alphabetic or other special symbols are permitted. In addition, the latter six digits of each account number should be 100,000 or larger.
2. Phone number field check: this field should contain a positive, 10-digit numerical number.
3. Checking account balance field check: only numerical information should be found here. In addition, the field can only be negative if the ALA flag is on (i.e., is set to 1).
4. Savings account reference number field check: this field can be blank if the customer does not have a savings account with the bank. If the field is not blank, it must contain a nine-digit numerical value.
5. ALA flag field test: this field can only be 0 or 1.
6. Segment identification number field test: this field should pass the same tests as the account number in step 1.
7. Control total check: the number of records for each branch should equal the "number of accounts" stored in the associated segment-control record. The sum of the positive account balances for the accounts of each branch should equal the "account balance total" in the associated segment-control record. The sum of the negative account balances for the accounts of each branch should equal the "loan balance total" in the associated segment-control record.
8. Trailer record processing: the trailer record contains grand-total fields similar to those of the segment-control records. At the completion of all processing, the same tests as in 7 should be performed for the entire file.

Prepare a microflowchart for a computer program to perform this editing and testing. If errors in any of the fields of an account record are detected, the program should print out the information contained in the entire record, along with an error message indicating the type of problem encountered. Cross-footing errors detected by step 7 should be communicated via a printed output message indicating the branch and the nature of the problem. A similar attack should be made for problems encountered when processing the trailer record in step 8.

CASE ANALYSES

10-38. The Lottery*

During the past few years some states have implemented lottery systems as an alternative to raising or levying new taxes. The results from these lotteries have run the gamut from very disappointing to very good. However, it appears that in states where the computer was utilized extensively in the lottery system, the results have been generally good. One of the most important advantages of the computerized system is that the administrator of the lottery can implement extensive control procedures to minimize fraud and deception.

You are a systems analyst employed by a state that has decided to implement a lottery. Your assignment is to analyze the controls in the lottery system considered most successful to date. Figure 10-15 is a ticket that was purchased from a lottery office. The only additional facts that you have at this time are that this ticket was printed on a central computer and manually distributed to the sales outlets.

Based on this information only, prepare a report describing the possible controls in the lottery systems operations.

*Used with the permission of John G. Burch, Jr., and Felix R. Strater, Jr., *Information Systems: Theory and Practice* (New York: Wiley, 1979).

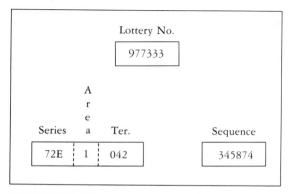

FIGURE 10-15 A state lottery ticket.

10-39. *Airpower Industries*

Airpower Industries, a manufacturer of hand-pump pellet guns, is a company that was started 20 years ago by John Stewart, the company's current president. Airpower Industries has relatively few competitors and its sales have increased consistently each year. Last year, sales exceeded $12 million and a computer system was installed by a national business machine firm to assist the company with its paperwork.

Last month, John Stewart decided to request a review of data processing control procedures by a well-known CPA firm, Bruce Wilson and Sons. Douglas Shafter, the controller of Airpower Industries, was called to assist the CPA firm with its review. Douglas Shafter was a loyal employee of the company and had been promoted through the ranks as the firm had grown and prospered. He had no formal computer education but was responsible for the operating practices of the company's newly created EDP system.

Bruce Wilson and Sons assigned its computer specialist, Phillip Marris, to manage the review. During his first meeting with Douglas Shafter, Mr. Marris requested a tour of the facilities. Mr. Shafter thereupon led the way to the computer center, which was located on the ground floor of the company office building in the offices of the company personnel department.

In the computer room, the company programmer and systems analyst were testing programs and going over the results. In response to an inquiry about developmental responsibilities. Mr. Marris was informed that all programs were tested by the programmer and systems analyst. Based upon their review, these two employees gave the programs final approval when they were sure everything was in order. A similar procedure was followed for program modifications. As Mr. Shafter and Mr. Marris toured the center, Mr. Shafter pointed with pride to the new computer, which was prominently displayed near the personnel department's interviewing rooms. Mr. Shafter pointed out to Mr. Marris that the computer was considered one of the company's most innovative developments. Because almost every employee in the company had to conduct some business with the company personnel office at one time or another, Mr. Shafter explained that the computer placement maximized its visibility and was thought to be a real employee motivator.

Mr. Shafter also showed Mr. Marris the computer tape files and program library. Both the tape files and programs were stored on open shelves in the middle of the computer room. Mr. Shafter explained that such a location was convenient to both operators and programmers and eliminated such problems as the need for the programmer to ask anyone else for a particular program if modifications were required. In fact, Mr. Shafter went on to explain, this turned out to be very important because the company programmer had just bought a new house and was putting in a lot of overtime on nights and weekends to help pay for it.

When Mr. Marris expressed concern about the possibility of a lost tape file. Mr. Shafter began to chuckle. The company had already thought of that, he explained. Backup copies of the tapes, along with the transaction tapes needed to recreate current files, were stored with the current copies to guard against that possibility, he said. Thus, even if the original copy of the tape were lost, he noted, there would still be the backups.

Computer cards, work tapes, and most of the forms used within the data processing center (such as purchase orders, payroll checks, and storeroom transfer documents) were stored next to the tape and program library shelves. Phillip Marris noticed that the computer operator was able to halt the computer during the regular processing of accounts receivable. When he asked about the company's insurance program, Douglas Shafter replied that all raw materials for production and the manufacturing equipment were adequately covered, but because the computer hardware was leased, it therefore did not require insurance coverage. Furthermore, when Marris asked Shafter about fidelity bonds, Shafter was not aware of what they were. When asked about backup facilities in emergency procedures. Shafter said that the maintenance lease of the national business machine company had provided excellent service and was very responsive to the company's needs.

Question

What preventive controls would you recommend to Airpower Industries if you were the CPA reviewing this company's operating procedures?

10-40. *Olympia Manufacturing Company*

In connection with her examination of the financial statements of the Olympia Manufacturing Company, Laura Lannan, CPA, is reviewing procedures for accu-

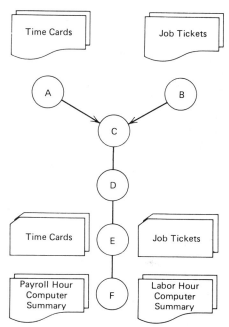

FIGURE 10-16 A system flowchart for the Olympia Manufacturing Company.

Step	Possible Errors or Discrepancies	Control Procedures

(AICPA Adapted)

10-41. Simmons Corporation

Simmons Corporation is a multilocation retailing concern with stores and warehouses throughout the United States. The company is in the process of designing a new, integrated, computer-based information system. In conjunction with the design of the new system, the management of the company is reviewing the data processing security to determine what new control features should be incorporated. Two areas of specific concern are (1) confidentiality of company and customer records and (2) safekeeping of computer equipment, files, and EDP facilities.

The new information system will be employed to process all company records, which include sales, purchase, financial, budget, customer, creditor, and personnel information. The stores and warehouses will be linked to the main computer at corporate headquarters by a system of remote terminals. This will permit data to be communicated directly to corporate headquarters or to any other location from each location within the terminal network.

At the present time certain reports have restricted distribution because not all levels of management need to receive them or because they contain confidential information. The introduction of remote terminals in the new system may provide access to this restricted data by unauthorized personnel. Simmons top management is concerned that confidential information may become accessible and be used improperly.

The company also is concerned with potential physical threats to the system, such as sabotage, fire damage, water damage, power failure, or magnetic radiation. Should any of these events occur in the present system and cause a computer shutdown, adequate backup records are available so that the company could reconstruct necessary information at a reasonable cost on a timely basis. However, with the new system, a computer shutdown would severely limit company activities until the system could become operational again.

mulating direct labor-hours. She learns that all production is by job order and that all employees are paid hourly wages, with time-and-a-half for overtime.

Olympia's direct labor-hour input process for payroll and job-cost determination is summarized in the flowchart of Figure 10-16. Steps A and C are performed in timekeeping, step B in the factory operating departments, step D in payroll audit and control, step E in data preparation (keypunch), and step F in computer operations.

Questions

1. Redraw the diagram, using familiar document flow-charting symbols.
2. For each input processing step, cite possible errors or discrepancies that might arise and identify the corresponding control procedure that should be in effect for each error or discrepancy. Use the following table organization.

Questions

1. Identify and briefly explain the problems Simmons Corporation could experience with respect to the confidentiality of information and records in the new system.
2. Recommend measures Simmons Corporation could incorporate into the new system that would ensure the confidentiality of information and records in the new system.
3. What safeguards can Simmons Corporation develop to provide physical security for its (a) computer equipment, (b) files, and (c) EDP facilities?

(CMA Adapted)

10-42. VBR Company

VBR Company has recently installed a new computer system that has online, real-time capability. Cathode ray tube (CRT) terminals are used for data entry and inquiry. A new cash receipts and accounts receivable file maintenance system has been designed and implemented to use with this new equipment. All programs have been written and tested, and the new system is being run in parallel with the old system. After two weeks of parallel operation, no differences have been observed between the two systems other than keypunch errors on the old system.

Al Brand, data processing manager, is enthusiastic about the new equipment and system. He reveals that the system was designed, coded, compiled, debugged, and tested by programmers utilizing an online CRT terminal installed specifically for around-the-clock use by the programming staff; he claimed that this access to the computer reduced programming elapsed time by one-third. All files, including accounts receivable, are online at all times as the firm moves toward a full data base mode. All programs, new and old, are available at all times for recall into memory for scheduled operating use or for program maintenance. Program documentation and actual tests confirm that data entry edits in the new system include all conventional data error and validity checks appropriate to the system.

Inquiries have confirmed that the new system conforms precisely to the document flowcharts, a portion of which is shown in Figure 10-17. A turnaround copy of the invoice is used as a remittance advice (R/A) by 99% of the customers; if the R/A is missing, the cashier applies the payment to a selected invoice. Sales terms are net 60 days, but payment patterns are sporadic.

Statements are not mailed to customers. Late payments are commonplace and are not vigorously pursued. VBR does not have a bad debt problem because bad debt losses average only 0.5% of sales.

Before authorizing the termination of the old system, Cal Darden, controller, has requested a review of the internal control features that have been designed for the new system. Security against unauthorized access and fraudulent actions, assurance of the integrity of the files, and protection of the firm's assets should be provided by the internal controls.

Questions

A. Describe how fraud by lapping of accounts receivable could be committed in the new system and discuss how it could be prevented.
B. Based on the description of VBR Company's new system and the document flowchart that has been presented:

1. Describe any other defects that exist in the system.
2. Suggest how each other defect you identified could be corrected.

(CMA Adapted)

10-43. OBrien Corporation

OBrien Corporation is a medium-sized, privately owned industrial instrument manufacturer supplying precision equipment manufacturers in the midwest. The corporation is ten years old and operates a centralized accounting and information system. The administrative offices are located in a downtown building while the production, shipping, and receiving departments are housed in a renovated warehouse a few blocks away. The shipping and receiving areas share one end of the warehouse.

OBrien Corporation has grown rapidly. Sales have increased by 25 percent each year for the last three years, and the company is now shipping approximately $80,000 of its products each week. James Fox, OBrien's controller, purchased and installed a computer last year to process the payroll and inventory. Fox plans to fully integrate the accounting information system within the next five years.

The Marketing Department consists of four salespersons. Upon obtaining an order, usually over the telephone, a salesperson manually prepares a pre-

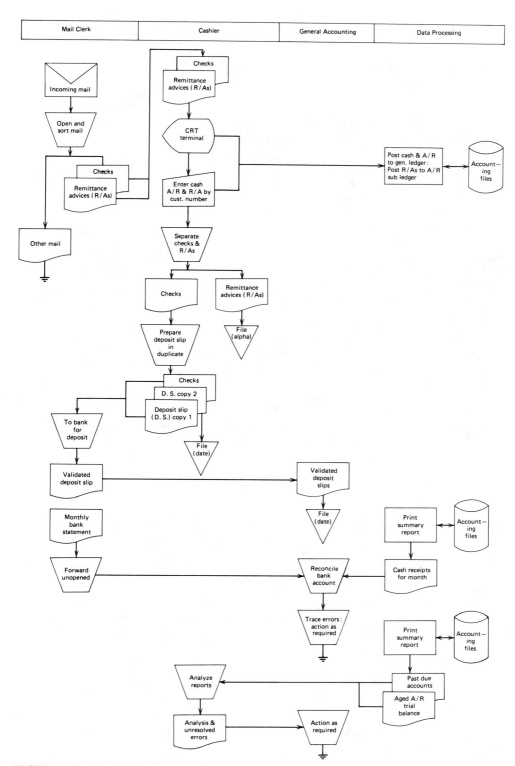

| Mail Clerk | Cashier | General Accounting | Data Processing |

FIGURE 10-17 VBR Company—Document Flowchart.

numbered, two-part sales order. One copy of the order is filed by date and the second copy is sent to the Shipping Department. All sales are on credit, f.o.b. destination. Because of the recent increase in sales, the four salespersons have not had time to check credit histories. As a result, 15 percent of credit sales are either late collections or uncollectible.

The Shipping Department receives the sales orders and packages the goods from the warehouse, noting any items that are out of stock. The terminal in the Shipping Department is used to update the perpetual inventory records of each item as it is removed from the shelf. The packages are placed near the loading dock door in alphabetical order by customer name. The sales order is signed by a shipping clerk indicating that the order is filled and ready to send. The sales order is forwarded to the Billing Department where a two-part sales invoice is prepared. The sales invoice is only prepared upon receipt of the sales order from the Shipping Department so that the customer is billed just for the items that were sent, not for back orders. Billing sends the customer's copy of the invoice back to Shipping. The customer's copy of the invoice serves as a billing copy, and Shipping inserts it into a special envelope on the package in order to save postage. The carrier of the customer's choice is then contacted to pick up the goods. In the past, goods were shipped within two working days of the receipt of the customer's order; however, shipping dates now average six working days after receipt of the order. One reason is that there are two new shipping clerks who are still undergoing training. Because the two shipping clerks have fallen behind, the two clerks in the Receiving Department, who are experienced, have been assisting the shipping clerks.

The Receiving Department is located adjacent to the shipping dock, and merchandise is received daily by many different carriers. The clerks share the computer terminal with the Shipping Department. The date, vendor, and number of items received are entered upon receipt in order to keep the perpetual inventory records current.

Hard copy of the changes in inventory (additions and shipments) is printed once a month. The Receiving Supervisor makes sure the additions are reasonable and forwards the print-out to the Shipping Supervisor who is responsible for checking the reasonableness of the deductions from inventory (shipments). The inventory print-out is stored in the Shipping Department by date. A complete inventory list is only printed once a year when the physical inventory is taken.

The flowchart in Figure 10-18 presents the document flows employed by OBrien Corporation.

Questions

OBrien Corporation's marketing, shipping, billing, and receiving information system has some weaknesses. For each weakness in the system:

1. Identify each weakness and describe the potential problem(s) caused by each weakness.
2. Recommend controls or changes in the system to correct each weakness.

Use the following format in preparing your answer.

Weaknesses and Potential Problem(s)	Recommendation(s) to Correct Weaknesses

10-44. Ajax Inc.

Ajax Inc., an audit client, recently installed a new EDP system to process more efficiently the shipping, billing, and accounts receivable records. During interim work, an assistant completed the review of the accounting system and the internal accounting controls. The assistant determined the following information concerning the new EDP system and the processing and control of shipping notices and customer invoices.

Each major computerized function, i.e., shipping, billing, accounts receivable, etc., is permanently assigned to a specific computer operator who is responsible for making program changes, running the program, and reconciling the computer log. Responsibility for the custody and control over the magnetic tapes and system documentation is randomly rotated among the computer operators on a monthly basis to prevent any one person from having access to the tapes and documentation at all times. Each computer programmer and computer operator has access to the computer room via a magnetic card and a digital code that is different for each card. The systems analyst and the supervisor of the computer operators do not have access to the computer room.

The EDP system documentation consists of the following items: program listing, error listing, logs, and record layout. To increase efficiency, batch totals and processing controls are omitted from the system.

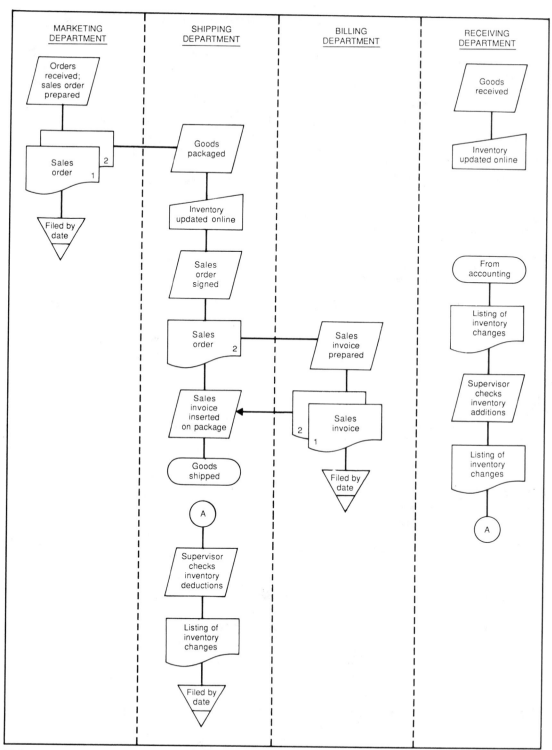

FIGURE 10-18 Flowchart for the OBrien Corporation.

375

Ajax ships its products directly from two warehouses, which forward shipping notices to general accounting. There, the billing clerk enters the price of the item and accounts for the numerical sequence of the shipping notices. The billing clerk also prepares daily adding machine tapes of the units shipped and the sales amount. Shipping notices and adding machine tapes are forwarded to the computer department for processing. The computer output consists of:

- A three-copy invoice that is forwarded to the billing clerk, and
- A daily sales register showing the aggregate totals of units shipped and sales amounts that the computer operator compares to the adding machine tapes.
- The billing clerk mails two copies of each invoice to the customer and retains the third copy in an open invoice file that serves as a detail accounts receivable record.

Question

Describe one specific recommendation for correcting each weakness in internal accounting controls in the new EDP system and for correcting each weakness or inefficiency in the procedures for processing and controlling shipping notices and customer invoices.

(AICPA Adapted)

CHAPTER 10 SUPPLEMENT

An Example of Controls: The MSB Company Payroll

Chapter 9 has emphasized manual controls for accounting information systems, whereas this chapter has stressed automated controls for accounting information systems. This distinction was largely for organizational convenience and is not meant to suggest that a company should use only one type or another. Both manual and automated controls should be implemented wherever the benefits of either type are expected to outweigh their costs.

One common accounting application in which both manual and automated controls are integrated in a single processing system is in the preparation of a company's payroll. Therefore, to illustrate the implementation of the many different types of controls into one operational system, we illustrate an example of a computerized payroll for the MSB Company. The system flowchart for the data processing is illustrated as Figure 10-19, and will now be described briefly.

At a certain production facility of the MSB Company, employees are paid weekly. Overall responsibility for the payroll has been given to the director of personnel, whose office is in charge of maintaining the payroll file information for the production facility. The payroll file itself is a master file stored on magnetic disk. Each record contains basic information about one employee, including employee name, address, social security number, department code, deduction codes, pay rate, and so forth. Changes to this file are initiated by employees in the personnel department, using remote terminals located within the personnel office.

At the end of each week, employee time cards are collected. The information on the time card includes employee name, social security number, department code, number of regular hours worked, and number of overtime hours worked. The time cards are batched by production department and then forwarded to the EDP subsystem for input to the payroll processing routines. The output from these routines includes (1) payroll checks, (2) a summary report of payroll checks listed by check number, (3) a summary report of payroll checks listed by department, and (4) an updated master file (containing new year-to-date information).

One of the chief concerns in the processing of the payroll is the accuracy of the payroll master file. Preprinted job application forms are used by the production facility to ensure completeness in the information used to create employee records, for example. When an individual applies for a job, this application form is filled out first and left with the subsystem manager conducting the job interview. Both the signature of the subsystem manager and the signature of the director of personnel are required on the form before a payroll master file record can be created for a

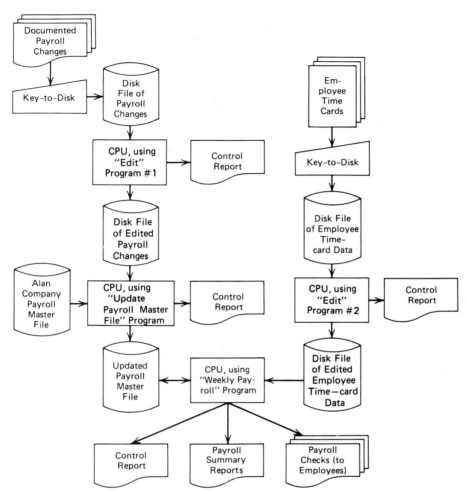

FIGURE 10-19   System flowchart for the computerized processing of the MSB Company payroll.

new hire. This controls the potential creation of a fictitious employee on the master file. Similarly, when changes to the master file involve pay rate increases or changes in certain categories of deductions, the signatures of both a personnel department employee and the director of personnel are required.

To control the payroll processing still further, the personnel director will maintain a manual control total of the number of company employees eligible to receive paychecks and the total dollar amount of approved pay raises. Each time the company payroll is prepared, the computer

will print out these control totals on a separate line of the summary report. The personnel director can then compare the control-total figures maintained in the personnel office with those on the report. Any discrepancies should be investigated immediately by the director. Thus, if the personnel director's control total of employees eligible to receive paychecks was 2504, and the computer printout indicated that 2505 paychecks had actually been processed, it would appear that one paycheck too many had been prepared!

The managers of each operating department within the MSB Company facility also play a role in payroll control. To guard against unauthorized overtime work, for example, the company requires the signature of a manager on all time cards indicating overtime hours. Also, when employees in a specific department turn in their time cards, the total hours of regular work and the total hours of all overtime work are computed. These figures are double-checked for accuracy and then handwritten on a special slip of paper that is affixed to the set of time cards sent to the computer center for data processing.

At the computer center, the time-card data are keyed into the computer for eventual processing and the control slips are forwarded to the personnel office. Using these slips, the personnel director prepares a master list of control totals for each department at the production facility. When the computer processes the time-card data, these figures will be recomputed and printed on the output report listing employee payroll checks by department. The personnel director is given a copy of this report as soon as it is prepared, and then compares the control totals of the report with the control totals prepared manually by each work department. Discrepancies attributable, for example, to unauthorized overtime hours can then be investigated.

The MSB Company employees responsible for accumulating and processing the payroll data should not also distribute employee paychecks. Depending on company preference, the company employees delegated this responsibility should come from the accounting subsystem, the internal audit staff, or perhaps some other organizational area. If the individuals in charge of payroll distribution physically maintain possession of all paychecks until they are handed to *individual employees,* it is very difficult for any other employee of the company to cash an unauthorized paycheck. Those employees that should be excluded from payroll distribution include the subsystem managers who accumulate the hours worked by their employees and EDP personnel such as programmers and machine operators involved in processing the payroll data.

A common deception practiced by dishonest managers working with uncontrolled payroll systems is to submit earnings data for a fictitious employee ostensibly working in that manager's department. Thus, when an extra paycheck is subsequently processed for this employee and returned in a batch of paychecks to the manager for the *manager* to distribute, the paycheck could simply be pocketed and later cashed. With the previously described payroll system, such a deception would not be possible. As long as paychecks were distributed to *individuals* instead of simply left on the manager's desk, it would be difficult for a fictitious employee to be given a paycheck. Further, as long as the payroll master file was accurate, it would be impossible to process a paycheck for an "extra" employee. This is because there would be no record for the employee and therefore no authorization for payment. Thus, with good computer controls, the no-master-record-found condition, which would result for the fictitious employee when the payroll program was run, would be indicated on a separate page of each of the output reports from the payroll processing run. Such a condition would then trigger an investigation.

Another effective payroll control for those companies with a large number of employees is to maintain a separate checking account for payroll disbursements. If paychecks were issued from the MSB Company's general checking account (i.e., the account used to pay such items as credit purchases of equipment and supplies), errors or irregularities in the payroll area would be more difficult to resolve because payroll disbursements become mixed with other disbursements. Thus, the MSB Company uses an *imprest payroll system*, in which dollars required for the payroll are transferred to a separate payroll account on a cash-needed basis. For the present example, therefore, the cash required for the payroll would be transferred to the payroll checking account shortly before the Alan Company's production employees are due to receive their paychecks. Clearly, such a system limits the amount of cash involved at any one time within the payroll function, and thereby reduces the opportunity for anyone to embezzle funds from the payroll checking account. In addition, it might be added, the imprest system frees up monetary funds that might otherwise stand idle and unproductive if left in the payroll account from month to month.

Another aspect of the MSB Company payroll system involves the control of the payroll output reports. To make sure that each report is complete, the pages of each report are prenumbered sequentially and also computer-numbered as part of the report processing. Copies of each payroll report are maintained at the computer center until each authorized user visits the center to receive his or her copy. At the time a report is taken, the user signs a report-distribution logbook maintained by the computer center. In this log, the name of the report, the report's preprinted page numbers, the name of the employee picking up the report, and the employee's identification number are recorded. Should problems arise at a later time regarding the distribution or whereabouts of a given copy of a report, this log is used.

A final consideration involving the MSB Company payroll processing is control over the physical check forms themselves. These forms are kept in a locked storage room of the computer facility, and a special forms log is maintained by the EDP manager. When a computer operator is about to run the payroll programs, the numbers preprinted on the check forms are recorded in this log by the manager. The total number of forms used is then compared with the personnel director's control total of eligible payroll employees to verify the proper number. Should forms be destroyed during the actual course of data processing, a careful accounting of these forms is made, and the EDP manager's verification signature on a special EDP form is filed for accounting purposes.

As checks are processed, the computer prints a number on each check, thus providing a further forms control. Preprinted check numbers and computer-generated check numbers that do not match would be cause for investigation.

Once the checks are prepared, they are forwarded to the facility's treasurer's office for signature. Here, the checks can be further scrutinized for accuracy and completeness. Again for accountability, the check number sequence is recorded at this point so that the numbers can be compared with the control information of the EDP manager's forms log. Finally, with the payroll checks duly signed and completed, they may be distributed to the MSB Company employees.

11 Accounting Information Systems and Computer Crime

Among the important questions that you should be able to answer after reading this chapter are:

1. Why is it difficult to define *computer crime?*
2. Why is there an absence of good data on computer crime?
3. Is computer crime on the *upswing* or on the *downswing?*
4. How was the Equity Funding fraud committed? Was it a computer crime?
5. What characteristics of an individual might be recognized at the time of initial hire that might indicate criminal intelligence?

INTRODUCTION

In 1966, a programmer working for a bank had an overdrawn bank account. Fortunately, or perhaps unfortunately, it was the same bank. He meticulously programmed his IBM 1401 computer to ignore his $300 overdraft, intending to replace the money three days later. But he did such a good job of hiding his "loan" that, four months later, he had increased this amount to over $350. He was caught when the computer broke down, thus earning him the dubious honor of becoming the world's first known computer criminal.

This chapter is about computer crime, frauds, and other irregularities that have occurred in the past, and that, in many instances, can still occur in the future. The connection between computers, computer crime, and accounting information systems is both straightforward and important. Computers tend to concentrate the asset-bearing information of an organization into a compact, but highly vulnerable, format. An accounting information system exploits this format for efficiency in data gathering, data processing, data storage, and data dissemination. The cost-effectiveness of such an accounting system begins to diminish, however, if it is unprotected and abused. Thus, an understanding of computer crime and its deterrents is an important control for accounting information systems.

For the purposes of discussion, this chapter is divided into three sections. In the first section, we take a closer look at computer crime and review what facts are presently available about the incidence of computer abuse now on record.

In the second section, we examine six specific examples of computer crime. With the exception of the Equity Funding case, which has been included in the discussion principally because of its enormity, each of these cases has been selected as a model representing a class, or category, of computer abuse. Accompanying each case is a small analysis section that examines why the computer abuse was not detected through normal processing controls, and indicates what controls might have been installed to thwart the crime. Because you are already familiar with many accounting controls from the last two chapters, you might want to read the case descriptions first and then decide for yourself what might have been done before turning to the analysis sections.

Finally, in the third section of this chapter, we conclude with a profile of the computer criminal. In this section, we examine those characteristics of individuals involved in computer crime that seem to reappear in computer-abuse reports and make some observations about what can be done to avoid computer abuse in the future.

COMPUTER CRIME— AN OVERVIEW

Computer crime has become a hot topic in the field of computerized data processing, and even such prestigious publications as *Fortune* magazine, *Business Week*, and the *Wall Street Journal* have devoted space to general discussions of computer abuse. Public interest has also inspired expanded reporting of computer crimes in local newspapers, radio, and television. Because computers and the information systems that use them

are still highly technical, however, mass-media coverage has been limited in scope and details. Thus, the most informative reports of computer abuses may still be found in computer trade journals, of which **Computerworld** has been an especially important source.

The number of in-depth surveys of computer abuse conducted to date has been surprisingly small. This is partially attributable to the relatively small proportion of computer crime that ever gets detected, and the even smaller proportion that ultimately gets reported in sufficient detail to permit accurate classification and evaluation. Most of the analysis that follows is based on the studies of Parker,[1] Allen,[2] Seidler, Andrews, and Epstein,[3] BloomBecker,[4] and DeWitt.[5]

Computer Crime—What Is It?

A definition of computer crime is elusive. In some circumstances, the use of a computer to deceive for personal gain is clearly an example of what might commonly be termed a **computer crime.** Thus, when a police chief was charged with altering his own driving record through an online computer terminal, there is good reason to call this a computer crime. However, many so-called computer crimes would probably be more accurately classified as other types of crimes. Consider the following cases.

1. A programmer changed a dividends-payment program to reduce the dividends of eight stockholders and issue a check to a fictitious person in the total amount of $56,000.
2. A company charged a computer-equipment vendor with fraudulently representing the capacity and capability of a computer system. It charged that the full system was never delivered and did not have adequate software.
3. In a fit of resentment, a keyboard operator shattered a CRT screen with her high-heeled shoe at Orly Airport in France.
4. A credit bureau sent notices to those individuals listed as bad risks in its files. For a fee, the bureau would withhold the damaging credit

information and keep it from being put into a larger computer-based credit system.
5. A computer-dating service was sued because referrals for dates were so few and inappropriate. The new owner of the dating bureau said that no computer was used at that time, although the use of a computer was advertised.

The first case, which involved dividend payments, could just as easily be called embezzlement—the computer was just a means toward this end. The second, a computer-equipment case, concerns misrepresentation; the item involved in the transaction could just as easily have been a toaster. In the third case, a CRT screen, and not a computer, was damaged. In the fourth case, the attempt to sell credit information was a straightforward attempt to threaten individuals' credit reputations. Perhaps a better description for such a crime is extortion. Finally, in the last case, the use of a computer to match blind dates was guaranteed where none, in fact, was used. It is questionable to call this a computer crime.

A strict definition of what constitutes a particular type of crime must come from the law. As illustrated in Figure 11-1, most of the individual states have passed some type of computer crime legislation, and many states have also revised their earlier codes. Note in Figure 11-1 that most of these laws have provisions that (1) define terms, many of which vary from state to state; (2) declare some acts to be misdemeanors—that is, minor crimes; and (3) declare some acts to be felonies—that is, major crimes.

Not stated in the figure is the fact that most states also require some type of willful intent for convictions. Thus, words like *maliciously, intentionally,* and *recklessly* are often used and their presence must be established for successful prosecution. This may seem difficult. However, according to the **National Center for Computer Crime Data** (NCCCD—a collector of computer crime information), 77% of computer crime cases brought to court end in guilty pleas and another 8% result in cases in which the defendant is found guilty by trial.

[1]See Donn B. Parker, *Computer Abuse Assessment,* a monograph available from Stanford Research Institute, Menlo Park, Calif. 94025, SRI Project 5068; and Donn B. Parker, *Crime by Computer* (New York: Scribner's 1976). Copyright © 1976 by Donn B. Parker. Used by permission of Charles Scribner's Sons.

[2]See Brandt Allen, "The Biggest Computer Frauds; Lessons for CPAs." *The Journal of Accountancy,* May 1977, pp. 52–62.

[3]See Lee J. Seidler, Frederick Andrews, and Marc J. Epstein. *The Equity Funding Papers, The Anatomy of a Fraud* (New York: Wiley, © 1977).

[4]See Jay BloomBecker (ed.), *Computer Crime, Computer Security, Computer Ethics—The First Annual Statistical Report of the National Center for Computer Crime Data (Los Angeles: National Center for Computer Crime, 1986).*

[5]See Phillip Elmer DeWitt, "Invasion of the Data Snatchers," *Time,* September 26, 1988, pp. 62–67.

	Year Law First Enacted	Years Law Revised	Law Defines Most Terms	Acts Forbidden				Misdemeanor Provision?	Felony Provision?	Maximum Prison Term (Years)
				Any Type of Access or Use	Alter, Damage, or Destroy Hardware or Software	Alter, Take, or Disclose Data	Disrupt Services			
AL	1985		✓	✓	✓	✓	✓	✓	✓	—
AK	1978	1982, 84	✓	✓	no	✓	no	✓	✓	—
AR	1987		✓	✓	✓	✓	✓	✓	✓	3
AZ	1978	1978, 80, 81, 82, 83	✓	✓	✓	no	no	no	✓	—
CA	1979	1981, 83, 84, 85	✓	✓	✓	no	no	✓	✓	3
CO	1979	1983, 85	✓	✓	✓	no	no	✓	✓	—
CT	1984		✓	✓	✓	✓	✓	✓	✓	—
DE	1982	1984	✓	✓	✓	✓	✓	✓	✓	—
FL	1978		✓	✓	✓	no	✓	✓	✓	—
GA	1981	1982	✓	✓	✓	✓	no	no	✓	15
HI	1984		✓	✓	✓	✓	no	✓	✓	—
ID	1984		✓	✓	✓	no	no	✓	✓	—
IL	1979	1984	✓	✓	✓	no	no	✓	✓	—
IN	1986		✓	✓	✓	✓	✓	✓	✓	4
IA	1984		✓	✓	✓	no	no	✓	✓	—
KS	1985		✓	✓	✓	no	no	✓	✓	—
KY	1984		✓	✓	no	no	no	✓	✓	—
LA	1984		✓	✓	✓	✓	no	✓	✓	5
ME	1976		no	no	no	✓	no	no	no	—
MD	1984		✓	✓	no	✓	no	✓	no	3
MA	1983		✓	no	no	✓	no	no	no	—
MI	1980		✓	✓	✓	no	no	✓	✓	—
MN	1982		✓	✓	✓	no	no	✓	✓	10
MS	1985		✓	✓	✓	✓	no	✓	✓	5
MO	1982	1983	✓	✓	✓	✓	✓	✓	✓	—
MT	1981		✓	✓	✓	no	no	✓	✓	10
NE	1985		✓	✓	✓	✓	✓	✓	✓	—
NV	1983		✓	✓	✓	✓	✓	✓	✓	6
NH	1985		✓	✓	✓	✓	✓	✓	✓	—
NJ	1984		✓	✓	✓	✓	no	✓	✓	—
NM	1979		✓	✓	✓	no	no	✓	✓	—
NC	1980	1981	✓	✓	✓	✓	no	✓	✓	—
ND	1983		✓	✓	✓	no	no	no	✓	—
NY	1986		✓	✓	✓	✓	no	✓	✓	4
OH	1981	1982	✓	✓	✓	no	no	no	no	—
OK	1984		✓	✓	✓	no	no	✓	✓	10
OR	1985		✓	✓	✓	✓	no	✓	✓	—
PA	1984		✓	✓	✓	no	✓	✓	✓	—
RI	1979	1983	✓	✓	✓	✓	no	no	✓	5
SC	1984		✓	✓	✓	✓	✓	no	✓	10
SD	1982	1984	✓	✓	✓	✓	no	✓	✓	10
TN	1983		✓	✓	✓	✓	no	no	✓	—
TX	1985		✓	✓	✓	✓	no	✓	✓	—
UT	1979		✓	✓	✓	no	no	✓	✓	—
VA	1984	1985	✓	no	✓	✓	✓	✓	✓	—
VT	none		—	—	—	—	—	—	—	—
WA	1975	1983, 84	no	✓	✓	no	no	✓	✓	—
WV	none		—	—	—	—	—	—	—	—
WI	1982	1983, 84	✓	✓	✓	✓	no	✓	✓	—
WY	1983	1985	✓	✓	✓	✓	✓	✓	✓	10

Source: Jay BloomBecker (ed.), *Computer Crime, Computer Security, Computer Ethics* (Los Angeles: National Center for Computer Crime Data, 1986).

FIGURE 11-1 State computer crime laws.

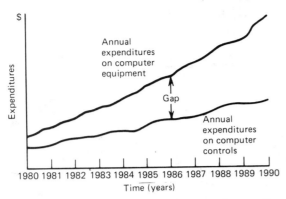

FIGURE 11-2 The gap between annual expenditures on computer equipment and computer controls is widening, thereby increasing exposure to computer abuse.

A definition of computer crime is important because it affects how the statistics on such crimes are tallied. For example, the largest computer crime on record—the Equity Funding case—involved the loss of $200 million if only direct company losses are counted, and over $2 billion if indirect losses to other companies and investor losses in common stock and bonds are counted. Either way, these losses are so large that including them as computer-crime losses severely affects the statistics on such activities. The question, however, is whether we should count the Equity Funding case in our sample of known computer abuse. We shall look more closely at this case later in this chapter.

In reviewing the methods and practices of computer criminals we find that many are common deceptions that have been tried many times before. For the selected cases studied by Brandt[6], for example, over half of them involved a simple transfer of funds through a set of accounts, with the dollars ultimately winding up in the hands of the perpetrators. In terms of methodology, therefore, one computer expert has described computer crimes simply as "old wine in new bottles." The technology may be random access and hexa-

decimal but the scheme itself should be as familiar to the auditor as debits and credits."[7]

One of the few types of automated activities that might satisfy the purist as a computer crime involves the theft of computer time or computer programs. In such instances, both the computer resource itself and the means by which it is obtained usually require an intimate knowledge of computers and computing methodology. The following cases might fall under this category.

1. European news media reported that a 15-year-old London schoolboy compromised a commercial time-sharing system by obtaining and using operating system program listings to discover privileged user access codes and was able to take over the time-sharing system.
2. The owner of a software-leasing company convinced programmers to take copies of programs from their employers and sell them to the software-leasing company, which then marketed the software as it own.
3. A Denver programmer short-circuited his computer 56 times in a misguided attempt to shut down the computer. By the time the programmer was caught, the company had spent half a million dollars attempting to find a hardware failure.
4. An unknown person gained access to a computer-terminal room by asking the custodian to open the door for him. He picked the locks of the telephones and terminals to gain unauthorized use of time-sharing services.
5. Two computer and peripheral-equipment manufacturers engaged in charges and countercharges of unfair competition and industrial espionage, including wiretapping and destruction of products and facilities.

Although these cases would appear to qualify as computer crimes, there is still some basis for doubt. Where students are involved in "bugging" the computer center at universities, for example, the crime often has taken on the appearance of a prank. Thus, "challenge," more than "personal

[6]Brandt Allen, "The Biggest Computer Frauds: Lessons for CPAs," *The Journal of Accountancy*, May 1977.

[7]*Ibid.*, p. 60.

gain," is the primary motive. Similarly, in case 3, the real problem appeared to be an unstable individual much more than a theft of real property for personal gain. The conclusion is therefore rather disappointing—a clear definition of computer crime is lacking.

Computer Crime—We Don't Have Many Statistics

The statistics on computer crime are notable for their absence. Since the first commercial computer (1952), for example, there have been less than 2000 documented cases of such crime. The likelihood that this figure includes the total number of crimes committed in more than three decades is remote. The fact that there are presently over 200,000 computers and 2.5 million EDP-related employees in the United States adds to this unlikelihood.

The absence of good data on computer crime becomes even more remarkable when average losses are calculated. Even when excluding the Equity Funding case, the average loss from known computer crime is $650,000, as compared with only $19,000 in average losses resulting from other types of white-collar crime. Thus, if the perpetrator can get away with it, computer crime pays—and pays big!

An explanation for the absence of complete information on computer crime includes several factors. One possible cause is the large proportion of computer crime committed in private companies that are handled as an internal matter and thus, never reported. A second explanation is that the definition of computer crime is of sufficient ambiguity to forestall an accurate listing. For example, when several thousand employees of one federal government agency were asked to enumerate all the computer crimes that had been detected during the last year, there was only one positive reply. However, when the survey was redistributed to these same employees and asked about deceptions in data or information that eventually would have been computer processed, or, in fact, had been computer

processed already, there were thousands of responses.

The most obvious explanation for the lack of good computer-crime data, however, is that most computer crime is not discovered! Thus, the cases of verified computer crime now known are believed to be just the tip of the iceberg. Because the majority of computer criminals are caught by chance, accident, or just luck, rather than through internal computer controls, this is really no surprise. Nonetheless, it leaves us wondering what the clever computer criminals are doing if we catch only the unlucky ones!

For these reasons, we can only consider the presently known cases of computer crime a sample, rather than a population, of modern computer abuse. Although it is possible to derive descriptive statistics from such data, care must be exercised in extrapolating results because there is good reason to believe that the sample is biased by the type of crime likely to be reported, by the problem of estimating losses, and by the influence of civil cases in which both actual and punitive (punishment) damages are awarded in the courts.

Having noted these difficulties, we must also state that the historical record of computer crime provides a fascinating study in modern criminology. The positions of the perpetrators, the number of accomplices involved in a particular incident, and the methodology of the crimes themselves have attracted the attention and study of several specialists in the area. Some tentative conclusions about computer crime are presented in the following paragraphs.

The Growth of Computer Crime

There are at least four reasons to believe that computer crime is growing. For one thing, the number of computers in the United States has more than doubled in the last five years and the amount of computer *power* has grown exponentially. As our reliance on computers continues to grow, so does the potential for computer abuse. For another, the number of microcomputers in the United States has increased from less than 2 million in 1980 to more than 30 million in 1990. This also increases the potential for computer abuse since micros are often used as personal computers and micro users are often not aware of, or as conscientious about, controls. Third, we observe that more people are becoming knowledgeable about computers and work with them—again increasing general exposure to computer abuse.

A final reason for believing that computer crime is growing comes from comparing annual computer expenditures with annual spending on computer controls. As reflected in Figure 11-2, annual spending on *computers* has grown at an accelerated rate. In contrast, there is ample evidence that annual spending on *computer controls* has, at best, grown linearly. The reason that specific dollar amounts for expenditures are not provided in Figure 11-2 is due to the fact that the exact annual amounts are not known in the two categories. The widening gap between annual expenditures in these two categories suggests an increasing vulnerability to computer abuse— and therefore the likelihood of more computer crime.

It is better to talk about the *potential* for computer abuse than about *known* computer abuse because what we don't know about computer crime is probably much greater than what we do know. Said Donn Parker about computer crime statistics: "We don't produce these anymore because so many people quote them as though they are representative of all computer crime. . . . The data are based only on cases we have time and fortune to find."

Conclusions

The most fundamental conclusion we can draw from computer crime is that we know very little about it. The fact that the number of reported cases of computer crime has increased substantially tempts us to conclude that computer crime is on the rise. However, it is not clear whether this is indeed true or merely the result of better

reporting. It would also appear that computer crimes involve large sums of money. Again, whether the averages calculated from our samples of known computer crimes accurately reflect the overall magnitude is speculative.

An understanding of computer crime is perhaps best gained by studying selected abuses that have occurred in the past. Thus, in the next section of this chapter, we take a closer look at six specific cases of computer crimes with the hope of learning from the experiences of others.

SIX REPRESENTATIVE COMPUTER CRIMES

As one reads the fascinating accounts of different computer crimes, a pattern of classifications begins to emerge. One type of crime clearly involves vandalism, another the falsification of the input data, and yet a third the unauthorized use of output documents. In this section, we discuss six computer crimes that are fairly representative of certain classes of computer fraud *as we know it today.*

The Round-Off Trick

Perhaps one of the most commonly discussed examples of computer fraud is the manipulation of the round-off error that occurs when fractions of a cent are involved in computer computations. Normally, a computer program is instructed to follow the rounding convention you learned as a child in grammar school: round down if the fraction is below .5; round up if it is .5 or greater. Thus, if the interest calculations for two bank accounts were $2.534 and $7.787, the first account would be credited with a total interest of $2.53 and the second with a total interest of $7.79.

The **accumulation error** from this rounding is the sum of the actual payments subtracted from the (more accurate) computed payments, or

$$
\begin{array}{rl}
\ \$10.321 & (= \$2.534 + \$7.787) \\
-\ \underline{10.32} & (=\ \ 2.53\ \ +\ \ 7.79\ \ ) \\
=\ \ \ \ .001
\end{array}
$$

In general, the accumulated error will be very small since the round-ups will offset the round-downs, leaving an expected value for the accumulated error of zero. A bank can maintain a slush fund of a few dollars in a special account to absorb, or pay out, an accumulation error that results from any particular processing run of its regular accounts.

A programmer performs the **round-off trick** by ignoring this rounding convention, always rounding down, *and crediting his or her own account with the accumulation error*. Note that for the two accounts above, this error is not $0.001, but $0.011 because the programmer receives four-tenths of a penny from the first account ($=$2.534 - 2.53), plus seven-tenths of a penny from the second account ($=$7.787 - 7.78). With this system, the programmer will take, on average, a half-cent per account. Thus, the total amount of money that can be stolen with this scheme depends on the number of accounts in the company files and how often these files are updated. A programmer working for a bank with 100,000 accounts, for example, could be expected to generate an accumulation error of $500 *per run*—not bad for a few minutes work of programming! If the bank were to compute interest quarterly, the total theft would be $2000 per year. If the programmer were lucky enough to work for a savings and loan that compounded interest daily—a common practice today—the yearly net would be approximately $182,500 ($=.005 \times 100,000 \times 365$)!

Analysis

The round-off trick is a classic example of the "magic" involved in computer crime. The total interest paid by the bank or savings and loan to each of its customers will differ from the correct amount by at most one penny, an amount hardly noticeable to most people today. Moreover, for approximately half of the customers, the interest amount for any given payment period will be exactly correct because a round-off in the downward direction would follow proper convention.

The "magic" part of the round-off trick occurs in the distribution of the accumulation error. This amount will be credited to the account of the dishonest programmer. In effect, therefore, the programmer collects the odd "round-up" pennies that should by rights be credited to the individual accounts that generated them.

The round-off trick can also be used by programmers working for organizations other than banks or savings and loan institutions. Any company that is responsible for periodic interest payments is a likely target of this scheme. Banks, however, are particularly vulnerable inasmuch as there is a high concentration of wealth, the data processing is performed often, and almost all banks today use computerized methods to service their accounts. Variations of the rounding trick include the embezzlement of interest only on inactive accounts, manipulations of pension-fund interest, and the transient theft of large sums of money just long enough to credit another account with interest payments.

Partial safeguards for the control of manipulations involving interest payments include the following.

1. Require authorization for program changes. Once a computer program has been written and approved for use, any subsequent changes in that program should require authorization from the programmer's supervisor. A programmer should not have the authority to make program changes unilaterally, and authorized changes should be scrutinized wherever possible. Use of "canned programs" to perform routine data processing also helps because such programs are often maintained by an independent vendor and, in any event, can always be checked against an original copy to ensure their integrity.

2. Separate related organizational functions. A programmer should not be permitted to perform the functions of an operator. Thus, for a programmer to write a fictitious program and execute it when such a control was in force would require the collusion of two or more

people. Of course, separation of duties cannot ensure processing integrity, but it is a useful control nonetheless because collusion requires twice as much dishonesty as when the programmer and computer operator are the same person.

3. Perform complete audits of personnel accounts. With limited resources, auditors rarely scrutinize every account in an accounting information system. However, although a random sample of customer accounts may be sufficient for some purposes, a 100% sample of the accounts of employees may be performed if desired. Most bank auditors do this as a matter of course. Also, whenever possible, the audit should be performed on a surprise basis in order to observe data processing during a typical operation cycle.

4. Audit the data processing results. A random sample of accounts should be taken and the data processing results from the computer run(s) should be compared against manually prepared results. The computer program(s) can also be audited using methods described in the following chapter.

5. Know your employees. Employees who are in financial trouble, not challenged by their jobs, or unhappy are those most likely to manipulate programs to their own advantage.

6. Perform statistical tests of round-off error. In this case, the proper test would be a "runs test." During normal processing, a random mix of round-ups and round-downs could be expected, just as a random mix of heads and tails would be expected when tossing a fair coin. The runs test looks at the number of successive round-ups and round-downs that occur sequentially. An excessive number of runs in either direction would signal the need for closer observation. Alternately, the computer program could simply count the number of round-ups. The expected value is half the total number of accounts processed.

Authors' note. Although the penny round-off trick is an interesting example of fraudulent data

processing using a computer, there is no documentary evidence that such a crime has even been committed. It *is* possible that such a crime was committed and never formally reported. In any event, we have chosen to include this case as an easily understood example of a *type* of fraud that can be perpetrated by altering the programming code of an accounting information system computer program.

The Equity Funding Case

The **Equity Funding case** has become the landmark case of computer crime. The fraud itself was uncovered in April 1973, although various illegal activities had been going on for years prior to this date. The total sum of the losses resulting from these activities was enormous. As noted earlier, minimal direct losses to the company have been fixed at approximately $200 million, although figures as high as $2 billion have been quoted if such indirect losses as legal expenses and common stock price declines are included in the total.

Ironically, there is substantial question whether or not the Equity Funding case is a computer crime. On the one hand we have the Bankruptcy Report of Mr. Robert M. Leoffler, the trustee, which stated:

> Least of all was this a modern "computer" fraud. . . . While the computer may have generated a paper "screen" for some aspects of the fraud, in fact the role it played was no bigger and more complicated than that played by the company's adding machines.[8]

On the other hand, we have the statement of Gleeson Payne, the California state insurance commissioner.

> This massive fraud was peculiarly a crime of the computer. The computer was the key to the fraud. I would certainly call it a computer fraud.

---

[8]See Donn B. Parker, *Crime by Computer* (New York: Scribner's, 1976), pp. 118–174; or Seidler et al., *The Equity Funding Papers* (New York: Wiley, 1977), pp. 126–154.

Under the old, hard copy methods of keeping insurance records you . . . couldn't build up bogus records in this kind of volume or in this kind of time. The insurance industry assumed computers were always accurate; computer fraud wasn't expected. Equity was the most advanced in use of computers. Few file cabinets or physical records were found. The computer was the key to the fraud. Auditors have computer programs, but Equity had a secret code which made the computer reveal only real insurance policies. We had a situation in which technology surprised and surpassed our examination system. We do not have a program to audit computers, nor do departments in other states. It is something that must be developed. Our examiners are not equipped to check out a computer run and find out if it is authentic.[9]

The facts pertinent to our study of Equity Funding begin in 1959 when the Equity Funding Corporation of America was formed for the purpose of selling insurance, mutual funds, and special funding programs (described later) that combined features of both mutual fund and insurance investments. From the start, the major emphasis in the company was an aggressive sales program and the acquisition of other, similar companies—principally through the exchange of common stock. Equity Funding placed a very strong emphasis on company growth. Thus, the price of EFCA's shares of common stock became very important because higher stock prices placed the company's management in a better position to make favorable deals through acquisitions and mergers. The higher the company's earnings, the more favorably investors viewed the company, and therefore the higher the stock price on the open (stock) market.

Much of the company's hopes for sustained internal growth rested on its sales of the aforementioned funding programs. These programs worked as follows. A participant signed up for a 10-year program. The individual purchased shares of selected mutual funds that were then pledged as collateral for a loan from Equity Fund-

ing Corporation. The money from this loan was applied to the purchase of term life insurance. After the 10-year period, the term insurance expired and the participant could either renew the program or "cash out." To cash out, the participant either paid off the loan from EFCA directly with cash or simply sold off a sufficient number of mutual fund shares to cover the insurance costs.

The objective of the funding programs was to take advantage of expected appreciation of the mutual fund shares of stock while maintaining bona fide life insurance. In this sense, the investor was "to have his cake and eat it too!" Ideally, the appreciation in the mutual fund shares would be high enough to cover (1) interest on the loan made against these shares, (2) the management fees charged against the various transactions involved, and (3) even the term insurance costs. Thus, the investor got "free insurance" and had the potential to make substantial capital gains if the price of the mutual fund shares soared high enough.

The funding programs were of considerable advantage to Equity Funding as well. Although Equity Funding's marketing scheme was not new, the plan had great appeal to investors during the early years when it was marketed and initial sales were high. In addition, the company received commissions on both the mutual fund and life insurance activities of the business. Thus, an investor who bought into a funding program generated a double sale for Equity Funding.

The key to the success of the funding programs was a rising stock market. To the disappointment of the management of EFCA, however, the stock market failed to increase appreciably over the last few years of the first program. The company compounded the problem by writing funding programs without careful attention to their profitability. An overemphasis on sales and an underemphasis on administration detail caused earnings to suffer and this, in turn, threatened the acquisition program of the company.

To bolster profits, EFCA management turned to recording commissions on nonexistent loans

[9]Seidler, et al., p. 119.

taken out against fictitious mutual fund programs. This first phase of the fraud, identified as the *inflated earnings phase,* went on until 1967 and is said to have generated over $85 million in bogus earnings. The problem with the system, in addition to the work required to cover up the fraud, was that it necessitated the generation of fictitious funding programs. Each dollar in commission supposedly had been generated from an individual participant in the program. As years went by, it became increasingly difficult to account for these nonexistent programs.

The inflated earnings phase of the EFCA scandal did not involve a computer. The accounting entries perpetuating the hoax were all performed manually, and little effort was made to provide underlying documentation. As the company's cash needs continued to grow, however, EFCA management turned to a second, *foreign phase* of fraud. Within this phase, the company set up a series of offshore subsidiaries whose primary purpose appears to have been nothing more than to act as bogus assets for the parent organization. Through a series of complicated transactions, EFCA's accountants played a complex shell game with these subsidiaries, in which assets were double, triple, and even quadruple counted by cleverly transferring them back and forth between the subsidiary companies. At times, EFCA management even went so far as to record the transference of funds from one company to another without recording offsetting amounts to other accounts.

When even these efforts proved to be insufficient, the company turned to a third, *insurance phase* of its fraud. In concept, the scheme was simplicity itself. The company merely sold some of its own fictitious insurance policies from its phase-one activities to other insurance companies! In order to sell nothing for something, however, the company resorted to the perfectly legal practice of *coinsurance*. Under this arrangement, the issuing, or primary, insurance company sells a block of insurance policies to a second company, called a *coinsurer*. The primary company maintains physical control of the actual

policies (fortunately for EFCA) and continues to perform the routine data processing. The coinsurer rarely even sees its policies and is often simply sent a letter identifying the serial numbers of the policyholders. However, the coinsurer commonly would pay 180 to 190% of the first-year premiums for its role in the coinsurance agreement.

The practice of coinsurance is well known. It represents a sale to the primary company, which may need cash for other purposes, and an investment to the purchasing company, which may have extra cash and be interested in buying insurance policies from other companies. In the case of Equity Funding and its insurance subsidiary, Equity Funding Life Insurance Company (EFLIC), however, the practice proved to be its downfall. The reason becomes clear when the mechanics of the agreement are understood. EFLIC collected sums equal to 180 or 190% of the first year's insurance premiums on the "policies" it had sold its coinsurers. EFLIC, however, was required to forward to these coinsurers the insurance premiums paid by the policyholders. Thus, in the first year of a given sale, the company had to give back nearly $1 for every $2 of its coinsurance business. In subsequent years, as for the first year, EFLIC was expected to forward policy premiums to its coinsurance partners. Because the policies were fictitious in the first place, *there were no premiums!* Thus, the only way the company could stay ahead of the game was to sell yet more bogus policies to coinsurance buyers. This practice had a pyramiding effect, and by 1972 the company had incurred $1.7 million in losses associated with its bogus coinsurance transactions. By this time, however, the company was in too deep to quit and the fraud fed upon itself. By April 1973, when the fraud was discovered, nearly two-thirds of the company's 97,000 insurance policies—over 64,000 of them—were phonies!

Analysis

The obvious question that comes to mind when reading about the Equity Funding case is, "How did the company ever manage to hide over 64,000 fictitious insurance policies from its auditors?" The answer is that all of the company's insurance policies were maintained on magnetic tape files, and little documentation of any kind was maintained. As noted in the state insurance commissioner's report, bogus policies were systematically assigned special policy numbers, and the computer programs used to process the insurance files were simply instructed to ignore these bogus policies.

Occasionally, of course, coinsurance companies would ask for information concerning their policies. Sometimes, Equity Funding would supply the requestor with a list of random digits designed to look like account numbers. Most of the time, however, this was not necessary because the perpetrators at EFLIC had been clever enough to program an occasional death of a fictitious policyholder to avoid arousing suspicion. When coinsurers asked for a printout of the names and addresses of their policyholders, selected personnel at EFLIC would use a special program to generate the fictitious accounts and randomly use the names of conspirators and friends over and over until the required number of policyholders had been printed.

External auditors for the company were similarly duped. In the early years, the auditors were treated lavishly during their visits and were often entertained in the plush executive suites of the company's fabulous Century City office building in downtown Los Angeles. When the auditors requested the EFCA people to provide them with a sample of insurance policies for checking purposes, the EDP personnel of course made sure that all of the policy numbers in the "random sample" were legitimate policyholders. When the auditors chose their own sample of policyholders for auditing purposes and asked to see hard-copy documents (e.g., insurance policy application forms), however, the auditors were told that those particular documents were being used by another department and would be provided the next morning. The company management team would then stay up at all-night "fraud parties," handwriting the requested hard-copy documentation.

How long Equity Funding could have continued its hoax is speculative. Certainly, the company had been able to play its hand well beyond the time that an effectively performed audit could have detected the situation as fraud. Thus, it is not surprising to learn that the Equity Funding fraud was not discovered by an audit at all, but rather by a tip from a former EFLIC employee named Ronald Secrist. Secrist's employment had been terminated on March 15, 1973, in an effort to cut payroll costs. On March 7, 1973, just prior to his departure and in retaliation, he telephoned the New York State Insurance Department and revealed what he knew. Examiners from their Illinois Insurance Department (which shared regulatory responsibility for EFLIC with California) were notified and shortly thereafter descended on Equity Funding. In a meticulous audit, and acting with the information supplied by Secrist, the hoax was discovered.

An additional question that might be raised in connection with the fraud is, "How could that many employees at Equity Funding be dishonest?" One answer is that not everyone at the company appears to have been "in" on the fraud. The EDP department maintained two computers: an IBM 360 (later upgraded to an IBM 370), which did most of the routine data processing, and a smaller IBM System/3, which was used principally by EFLIC's actuarial group. Controls within the EDP department were extremely lax. For example, the company maintained an open library, and almost all of the company's master files were set on open racks, available for anyone to borrow, use, and, as it turned out, alter. Similarly, the machine room was run as an **open shop**, in which any of the employees working for any one of Equity's 100 companies could walk into the machine room at any time to run their own programs on the computer.

EDP requests to tighten up on controls were routinely ignored by top management. Moreover, the actuarial group at the company made frequent use of the insurance policy master tapes and, as time went on, began to insert fictitious policy records in the master tape. EDP personnel were told that such records were for "simulation purposes" and they were instructed to ignore these records in legitimate processing runs. At other times, the EDP personnel themselves were requested to insert new policies in the master file. Frank Hyman, manager of the MIS system, reported that, in a typical input run, he often saw that as many as 600 new policies were specially coded because they had been sold at a group rate to a union or some other special organization and required special identification. Only later, when the true use of these records came to light, did many of the programmers and EDP managers with the company realize what had happened.

The TRW Company Credit Data Case

There is a tendency to view the typical computer crime as a situation in which a perpetrator compromises the computer system in order to gain access to a company's physical assets, especially the cash in the company's bank account or the company's inventories stored in the warehouse. A major class of computer crime, however, merely involves illegal access to the valuable information stored within the computer system.

Valuable-information computer crime is well known. In some cases, the information involved is simply a company's computer programs because such software (1) is proprietary (i.e., owned by an independent developer and leased to users), (2) may give the firm a competitive advantage in its industry, and (3) is often worth more than the company's hardware in terms of development and replacement costs. Thus, several cases of corporate computer espionage involving the theft, or attempted theft, of key programs have been reported in the literature. Because of the difficulty of collecting proof of such espionage when remote terminals are involved, there is every indication that a substantial number of additional cases have gone unreported.

In other situations, the valuable information involved in computer crime has been a company's processing files—information that would be of little value to an outsider but that is vital to the normal functioning of the company that owns the files. In 1977, for example, one disgruntled EDP employee working for a Netherlands company decided to exploit this fact in retaliation for the organization's failure to promote him. In January of that year, Rodney Cox "kidnapped" both his company's financial tape and disk files and their backup copies—a total of 594 tapes and 48 disks—and held them for over $500,000 ransom. (He was eventually caught by Scotland Yard investigators when his accomplice attempted to pick up the money).

In the **TRW Credit Data case,** the valuable information was computerized credit data. TRW is the largest credit-rating company in the United States. In 1976, when the fraud was discovered, the company was collecting and disseminating credit information on approximately 50 million individuals. To handle its processing, the company used two IBM 370/158 computers, one IBM 370/155 computer, 380 Datapoint terminals, 2000 teleprinters, and 100 Raytheon CRT terminals. Clients of the company included banks, retail stores, and such credit-conscious concerns as Diner's Club, American Express, MasterCard, VISA, Sears, Roebuck and Co., and several leasing establishments.

TRW advised its clients of bad credit risks on the basis of information maintained on its data files. Clearly, however, this file information could be changed. The fraud began when six company employees, including a key TRW clerk in the consumer-relations department, realized this fact and decided that they could sell "good" credit ratings for cash to individuals with bad credit ratings logged in their computer records. The names and addresses of the bad credit risks were already on file; it merely remained to contact these individuals and inform them of a newfound method of altering their records. Accordingly, individuals with bad credit ratings were approached by the TRW employees and offered a "clean bill of health" in return for a management fee.

Those people who decided to buy paid TRW employees "under the table," and the clerk in the consumer-relations department then input whatever false information was required to reverse the buyer's bad credit rating. In some cases, this required the deletion of unfavorable information already stored in the individual's credit record; in other cases, it required the addition of favorable information. Fees for such services varied from a few hundred dollars to $1500 per individual. Ironically, the TRW clerk who ultimately input the false information to the computer system received only $50 for each altered record. However, the losses resulting from these activities were not so inconsequential. Independent estimates have placed this figure at close to $1 million.

The principal victims of the fraud were TRW's clients, who acted on credit information that ultimately turned out to be fraudulent. Exactly how many file records were actually altered is difficult to say. Lawyers for the prosecution had documented 16 known cases, but there was reason to believe the number was in excess of 100. Paradoxically, the prosecution had difficulty in acquiring testimonies because the buyers as well as the TRW sellers were technically in violation of the law by conspiring to falsify credit-rating information.

Officials at TRW played down the whole case as a local matter that involved the Federal Trade Commission (FTC) only because of the type of crime involved. A TRW spokesperson stated, for example, that "this is a nonpublic investigation and we believe it should remain nonpublic as it was intended to be. To us, it's not unusual to have the FTC conducting this type of investigation. It is chartered to enforce the Fair Credit Reporting Act, and it's just doing business as normal as far as we are concerned."

Reports concerning outside tampering with TRW's files continue to come in—for example, in 1984 and 1986. These episodes along with the fact that a serious abuse of TRW's file information has occurred already give us pause to wonder: "How safe is our credit information, especially in the hands of a private and, to a large extent, unregulated profit-seeking company?"

Analysis

There are two key issues here: (1) the propriety of the input information used in updating a specific accounting information system, and (2) the protection afforded both consumer and user in the accuracy and use of credit information gathered by a private company. With regard to the first point, it is clear that the fraud was successful only because the perpetrators were able to enter false information into the computer system. This observation once again points to the importance of controls, for example, the presence of hard-copy validation of credit changes to safeguard the accuracy and completeness of file information. In light of what had already been discovered, the statement of the TRW spokesperson about the FTC's investigation carries a note of irony:

> We don't believe the investigation is going to lead to any significant results. As far as we're concerned, we're in full compliance with the law. Our measures and our standards have been the highest in the industry. . . . We've always gone beyond the letter of the law in operating policies and procedures.[10]

The opinion of the prosecuting attorney contrasts sharply with this statement. He suggested that the entire operation did "not take a great deal of intelligence" and only proved that there are weaknesses in any system. Thus, one is led to the conclusion that "the highest standards in the industry" were insufficient to thwart an "unintelligent" fraud. One thing is certain. At the time that the fraud was perpetrated, the security measures of the company were inadequate to control the crime. In fact, as is true of so many cases of computer crime, the six employees involved in

[10]Molly Upton and E. Drake Lundell, Jr., "Six Charged with Altering TRW Credit Data Files as FBI Breaks L.A. Ring," *Computerworld,* Vol. X, No. 37 (September 13, 1976), p. 4.

the case were caught only by chance: an individual approached with an offer to buy a good credit rating for $600 became angry and called the FBI. Later, the TRW clerk in the consumer relations department decided to turn state's evidence.

The second point involving the protection of the consumer and user of credit information encompasses a much larger issue. In 1970, Congress passed the **Fair Credit Reporting Act,** which requires that an individual be informed why he or she is denied credit.[11] The consumer also has the right to contest the information maintained by the credit-rating company, although there is clearly a vast difference between the right to *challenge* and the right to *change* credit information. TRW reported that since the Fair Credit Reporting Act had gone into effect, consumer inquiries had increased a hundredfold, and that at the time the fraud was detected, approximately 200,000 consumers annually were complaining about their credit ratings. The fact that, by TRW's own admission, fully one-third of these inquiries resulted in a file change or update is unsettling. Moreover, it is not known how much more information collected by TRW is inaccurate but simply not being challenged because either the inaccuracy is not communicated to the individual involved or the consumer does not know he or she has recourse through the law.

Roswell Stephens and the Union Dime Savings Bank Case

Banks have been obvious targets of computer fraud and embezzlement because they are large holders of liquid assets, and also because the banking industry was one of the first to automate its operations. At present, the American banking system processes over 30 billion checks each year, and the cost to clear these checks is in excess of $10 billion. As noted in Chapter 18,

banks depend heavily on the industry's standard MICR code and automated check-processing equipment to keep processing costs low. The potential for computer crime within the banking industry's electronic environment is high and this potential, together with other banking industry factors mentioned earlier in the chapter, have conspired to yield a rich and growing literature of computer abuse in the banking world.

One of the most famous cases of computer bank fraud involved **Roswell Stephens,** a bank supervisor working for the **Union Dime Savings Bank** in New York City. Heavyset, balding, and the father of two daughters, Roswell was well liked and was earning a respectable salary in the job which he had held for 9 years. But at 41 years of age, and unbeknownst to all but his bookies, Roswell had a serious gambling problem that was financially destroying him. Thus, after trying to moonlight as a taxi driver at night and finding himself shot at twice, he decided to pursue a safer activity and steal from his bank.

The keys to Stephens' embezzlement were his unique position as a new-teller trainer, his vast experience in the banking profession, his intimate knowledge of his bank's operating procedures, and his ability to override account information in his bank's computer system simply by inputting "corrective" data through his personal terminal. Stephens could blame obvious discrepancies in customer statements on his new trainees and cover up his other embezzlements because of his position. For example, Roswell would take several thousand dollars from his cash drawer and enter a fictitious withdrawal transaction from a customer account into the computer system to justify the cash reduction. At the end of the quarter, both the depositor's balance and the depositor's interest would be incorrect. The depositor would be mailed a statement from the bank. If the depositor failed to complain, Roswell did nothing. If the depositor did complain, Roswell would blame the problem on an error committed by one of his trainees, pretend to find the discrepancy, and enter a correction, which did little more than steal from

[11]See Consumer Credit Protection Act, Section 601, Title 6 of Public Law 91-508, "Federal Deposit Insurance Act," October 26, 1970.

another account through his supervisor's terminal.

Stephens also used a number of other tricks to steal from his bank and support his gambling habit. For example, he would take a valid deposit from a customer, properly credit the customer's account, and then later reverse the transaction and withdraw most, if not all, of the deposit through his terminal for his own use. He would also embezzle from the bank by failing to deposit the money customers wished to invest in long-term certificates of deposit. In this latter situation, Stephens would prepare the necessary paperwork for the customer, and the customer would believe that all the necessary steps had been taken to make the deposit. But all this was just for appearance. Stephens would prepare no input for the computer about the transaction, and thus the bank would have no record of the deposit. Stephens would then have two years (at a minimum) to return the money.

Perhaps one of the most interesting ways in which Stephens stole from his bank was through the manipulation of new savings accounts. When a customer wished to open a new passbook account, Stephens would secretly take two new passbooks from the bank vault. The customer would be given the first of these passbooks, with all the prerequisite information clearly showing. But Stephens would carefully enter the transaction under the account number of the second passbook, which he kept for himself. The new deposit would therefore be entered under a different account number than that assigned the customer. Later, at his leisure, Stephens could withdraw all the money from the second account, destroy the corresponding passbook, and eliminate almost all traces of the switch. Stephens was able to get away with this particular fraud for quite a while because the bank did not appear to keep records of the passbooks stored in its vaults.

Banks perform numerous tests, counts, and audits to ensure processing accuracy and control financial resources, but Stephens, with his superior knowledge of the banking profession in general and his intimate knowledge of the con-

trols of his own bank in particular, was able to avoid every one of them. One of the controls of special importance involved the crediting of interest. Because Stephens had withdrawn a great deal of money from selected accounts, the principal balances, and therefore the interest computations, would not match the amounts expected by the bank or anticipated by the bank's customers.

Stephens used several methods to solve his problem. Under one method, for example, he would use his terminal to transfer funds from certain accounts to others to create the appearance of an interest payment when, in fact, the transfer actually involved principal balances. In another method, he would enter interest payments through his terminal, later reversing these transactions after the desired effect had been accomplished. Finally, for those instances in which customers would bring their passbooks into the bank, Stephens would manually enter a fictitious interest payment to the passbook in a hand that shook so much the bank's customers began to fear for the man's health. Of course, the manual entry had absolutely no relationship to the customer's computer-controlled balance, which was unaffected.

The last, particularly effective, ploy that Stephens used to avoid interest-computation scrutiny was to exploit the fact that at the Union Dime Savings Bank, interest payments for passbook accounts were computed on the last day of each quarter of the year, whereas time-deposit account interest was computed two days *after* the last day of the quarter. Stephens would bring the passbook accounts up to their appropriate levels in time for the interest computations, and then, in the two-day lag period, quickly transfer funds from the passbook accounts to the time-deposit accounts in time to receive the proper interest on these latter accounts. In effect, therefore, Stephens was shifting funds through accounts rapidly enough to make his bank pay double interest on the same dollars. In reality, those dollars were long gone at the racetrack!

Stephens was also able to avoid the scrutiny of

the auditors. Normally, the bank auditors always gave him advance notice of their arrival and much of his embezzlement could therefore be covered up in time to avoid detection. He claims that he could almost predict what the auditors were going to do at each moment. In addition, small discrepancies could easily be blamed on the mistakes of inexperienced tellers who were training under Stephens' supervision. In one fascinating close call, however, an auditor was about to discover a $20,000 shortage in one of Stephens' two cash boxes. Through a stroke of good luck and what had to be a very dexterous sleight of hand, however, Stephens removed the $20,000 that had already been counted from the first cash box, and placed it in the second cash box just in time for the auditor to count it again!

The thing that Stephens could not avoid was discovery through audit confirmation. In such instances, the auditing team selects a random sample of depositors and mails letters of inquiry to the customers requesting a confirmation of their account balances. Because the total number of accounts Stephens was manipulating was relatively small (approximately 50 at any one time), Stephens was lucky enough to avoid detection during the 3½ years that he practiced his deception.

Analysis

Given the background of the foregoing computer cases, it should come as no surprise to learn that Stephens was not caught through banking controls. Rather, his luck ran out when the police raided his bookie and discovered that a bank teller was placing weekly bets of $30,000! The Union Dime Savings bank was alerted and a full-scale inquiry was secretly put into effect. Putting "two and two together" and using a massive audit, the bank came up $1.4 million short!

As the largest known bank fraud of its time, the Roswell Stephens—Union Dime Savings Bank case has attracted considerable attention. Learning from the incident, the banking industry in general has installed tighter controls, which will undoubtedly go far to prevent a repetition of the crimes so successfully executed by Roswell Stephens. (At least this is true for the Union Dime Saving Bank.)

Perhaps the easiest control the Union Dime Savings Bank failed to enforce was the **two-week vacation rule.** The kinds of activities in which Stephens was engaged required almost constant attention. It is therefore very unlikely that the crime would have gone undetected during his two-week absence when another bank employee would have performed Stephens' job functions. Luckily for Stephens, however, the required vacation rule was never enforced at the Dime and he was able to concentrate on his customer account manipulations undisturbed.

A major area that the bank failed to pursue adequately was the unusually large number of discrepancies that appeared in customer account balances at Stephens's branch bank. A comparison of trainee errors at this bank with the average number of mistakes at other bank branches surely would have revealed an unusual situation worthy of further investigation. When even routine teller activity would disclose discrepancies in passbook entries as compared with the computer listings, grounds for suspicion are clear. Such discrepancies should have been reported to special investigatory authorities (such as the bank's internal auditors). Requiring that any substantial account balance correction be made with the approval of two responsible individuals, instead of concentrating such authority in the hands of only a single hard-pressed supervisor, would be an added control. A similar statement regarding joint supervision might be made when accounts are opened and also when they are closed, especially for those accounts involving substantial amounts of money. Random checks of account closings, for example, using a confirmation letter, would have been beneficial. Some banks also mail a "welcome-aboard" letter to new depositors, which thanks the customer for his or her patronage and, incidentally, verifies the depositor's account balance. Special letters of inquiry can also be made when suspicious correction transactions are observed in the processing flow.

Lax audit procedures must also be mentioned as a possible reason why Stephens' embezzlement went undetected for so long. The surprise audit is a most effective method of detecting fraud and, perhaps, serves as a deterrent.

Procedure is also important. The auditors were careless when counting Stephens' two cash boxes, enabling him to conceal a $20,000 cash shortage. The auditors should have taken control of both cash boxes simultaneously prior to beginning their count. This procedure would have prevented Stephens from transferring $20,000 from the first cash box to the second after the first box had been counted. Moreover, the bank audit should be thorough and uncompromising, and the validity of all transactions examined should be proven with hard-copy evidence of legitimacy. Close scrutiny of unusual activity in dormant accounts, less-than-active accounts, and time-deposit accounts is especially important because these types of accounts are common targets for computer crime. The advantage of larger samples for audit confirmation is also clear.

The question of whether computers can be programmed to detect computer crime arises at this point and raises an interesting issue. As noted in the previous chapter, a computer can easily be programmed to test for valid and consistent data and also to perform certain cross-checking and cross-footing activities to ensure processing accuracy. In the present case, however, the input data easily passed all of these tests because the perpetrator was clever enough to construct "good" transaction data initially. A computer can still serve as an aid to fraud control, however, if it is programmed to perform analyses of funds-transfer transactions, activity-reversal transactions, and other special correction transactions. A pattern of increasing activity in these types of transactions may signal possible problems, and thereby prompt management to take a closer

look at probable causes. Thus, the management-by-exception principle may be utilized in such situations.

Illegal Access and the Milwaukee 414s

The term **hacking** describes the process of gaining illegal entry to computer files from remote locations. Many young microcomputer users "hack" for fun, competing to see who can break into the most prestigious computer file. In July of 1983, the FBI discovered the "414 Club"—a group of teenage hackers in Milwaukee whose telephone area code was 414.

While there was no evidence of intent to commit sabotage or destroy vital file information, it is believed that the members broke into 60 different business and government computers, including those at the Los Alamos National Laboratory in New Mexico, the Security Pacific National Bank in Los Angeles, and the Sloan-Kettering Memorial Cancer Center in New York.

One of the most important aspects of this case was the apparent ease with which the individuals involved gained unauthorized access to sensitive information stored on the files of public time-sharing services. This was unfortunate because some of the victim organizations had purposely used such public networks to facilitate communications among bona fide users. In this case, the objective backfired.

This episode is also important because it triggered new interest in passing federal legislation to outlaw hacker activities and to provide stiff penalties for perpetrators. Partly in response to this episode, the U.S. congress passed our first federal computer crime law in 1986. Among other things, this law makes it a federal offense to access computer files for unauthorized purposes.

A final issue regarding this case was the media treatment. Some authorities complained that the news coverage treated the Milwaukee 414 students more as creative wizards than apprehended wrongdoers. Their worry was that news coverage of this type loses sight both of the unethical nature of the activities and the costs such activities cause their victims. In such cases, authorities fear that the resultant notoriety may actually encourage, rather then discourage, offenders.

Analysis

Hacking continues to be a widespread problem—especially in education. For example, despite both federal and state laws that specifically identify "unauthorized access" as a punishable offense, young students are often caught compromising, or attempting to compromise, their school's computer systems. Thus, the system-design objective of providing easy access to bonafide users conflicts with the security objective of denying system access to hackers.

One potential remedy for hacking is user education. Potential hackers should be taught about the ethics of computer use and made aware of the inconveniences, time, and costs incurred by victim organizations when even innocent hacking requires extensive investigations. At least in the case of the Milwaukee 414s, it is likely that the students may have behaved more responsibly if they had been more aware of the amount of trouble their activities ultimately caused.

Although better state and federal laws may also help deter computer hacking, the most effective deterrents are preventive measures rather than the threat of punishment or prosecution. One safeguard is the strict use and control of passwords. As noted in Chapter 10, these passwords should be randomized digits rather than complete, recognizable words, and these passwords should also be changed regularly. Users must also be educated about protecting their own passwords—for example, discouraged from giving them to others or taping them to their CRT screens or desk corners. Finally, new passwords should be communicated through external channels—not through the computer system itself.

Two additional security measures are lock-out systems and dial-back systems. **Lock out systems** disconnect telephone users after three unsuccessful password tries. They thus stop a hacker from successfully dialing into a computer system, and then using a microcomputer to generate as many combinations of password digits as required to guess a legitimate one. Similarly, **dial-back systems** first disconnect all users, but redial legitimate ones after looking up their passwords in lists of bonafide user codes. Dial-back systems may be even more effective than lock-out systems since only authorized users already recognized by the system will be reconnected.

Some hackers have gained access to high-level files and other sensitive information by successfully upgrading their security levels once they are "in" a system. This procedure enables these individuals to elevate their own system status to that of "privileged user," and therefore arms them with the priority level required to access a system's most sensitive data. These activities are thwarted by developing and using system programming routines that test for or deny such "bootstrapping," and that also immediately identify such attempts as possible security violations.

The Pakistani Virus

A computer virus is a small, destructive processing routine that a computer user accidentally introduces into his or her system—for example, while copying a computer program from a floppy to a hard disk. These virus routines often lie dormant in the computer system, only becoming "active" or executable when the software is copied and run on nonlicensed machines. Once operative, however, they "infect" a system by displaying unwanted messages onscreen, halting data processing, erasing computer files, altering operating system commands, or otherwise disrupting computer operations. The analogy to a biological virus is a good one since both types of viruses tend to "hide," can reproduce themselves, are often parasites, and are harmful to their hosts.

The **Pakistani virus** is a case in point. During late 1986 and 1987, this small program infected all microcomputers into which it was introduced, eventually halting all processing capabilities and displaying error messages. The virus was eventually traced to two brothers—Amjad Farooq Alvi and Basit Farooq Alvi—who operated the small Brain Computer Services store in Lahore, Pakistan. Angry that computer users were illegally copying the store's legitimate software, the brothers inserted a small virus program on many of their store's software diskettes. Like other viruses, this one could both replicate itself and destroy data files when run. This particular virus also left a message in a special file directing the discoverer to call Lahore for costly corrections. Through repeated copying, the virus pyramided itself and infected over 100,000 floppy disks.

The brothers stated that anti-American sentiment and resentment over illegal copying were two primary motives for creating the Pakistani virus, but other motives include personal anger or the challenge of accomplishing something universally disruptive. The Alvi brothers claim they stopped distributing contaminated software in late 1987, after they were satisfied that they had made their point to software pirates. To the thousands of unsuspecting users whose systems were disrupted, the point had been made only too well.

Analysis

The Pakistani virus is one of many computer routines or "bugs" that have been written primarily to disrupt legitimate computer activities. Many of them have been written by local authors—not foreigners. In 1988, an estimated 250,000 computers—from the smallest micro computer to the largest mainframe—were infected by this, or similar, contagious programs. The costs of such infections can be small—for example, just the inconvenience of reformatting a disk and reloading a few programs. But these costs can also be quite large—for example, the expenses incurred by a company whose 40-year old programmer

infected its computer system with a virus that deleted more than 168,000 sales records.

The idea of infecting a computer system with a high-priority program that takes control and disrupts functions is not new. It was first discussed in a 1949 paper by John Von Neumann, studied at length at AT&T's Bell Labs starting in 1959, dramatized in the 1983 movie "War Games," and even publicly discussed in a May, 1984, landmark article in *Scientific American*. What distinguishes computer viruses from the "Core Wars" concept that preceded them is that the initial thinking only considered a runaway program in a stand-alone device. Remedying the core-war problem was therefore relatively simple: merely shut down the computer and reload backup programs. In the case of Pakistani Virus and similar viruses, the infection is capable of spreading to many systems because the computer code replicates itself in any new computer system.

Computer viruses can be thwarted in a number of ways. One possible protection is to acquire an "anti-virus program" that either protects a computer system from harm, identifies existing programs that are already infected, or "cleanses" a sick computer system after infection has occurred. Generally speaking, however, these programs provide less than optimal protection since new, more powerful viruses have been written that can avoid known protection/detection schemes. Even worse: some anti-virus programs themselves contain virus routines.

For microcomputer users, better safeguards are to: (1) buy shrink-wrapped software from reputable sources, (2) avoid illegal software copying, and (3) maintain complete backup files in the event you must rebuild your system from scratch. Additional safeguards include: (1) load your operating system only from your own, write-protected DOS disk, (2) be wary of public domain software or software obtained from public bulletin boards, (3) carefully label all floppy disks and create printed copies of their contents (which you check regularly for changes), and (4) note any unusual activity in your system that does not seem warranted by your commands.

The best *organizational safeguards* against microcomputer viruses include (1) educating employees about viruses, and (2) making sure that each employee practices prevention and detection techniques. Additional safety precautions include policies that (1) discourage the free exchange of computer disks or network programs among employees, (2) require uncompromised passwords of all network users, (3) disallow nonsystem personnel to load new programs on networks, and (4) use virus-detecting filters on all remote lines. Finally, in larger commercial systems, the importance of a disaster recovery plan that has both been approved and tested is critical.

A PROFILE OF THE COMPUTER CRIMINAL

There is a school of thought on accounting controls that holds that an accounting information system is only as effective as the people who use it. Under such a theory, understanding the criminal mind is just as important in thwarting computer crime as the "mechanical" computer controls that help deter unauthorized use of accounting information. To prevent given types of crimes, criminologists often look for common characteristics in individuals who have committed certain illegal acts. This helps detect patterns of action or behavior that identify the potential problem individual before a crime occurs. A set of such characteristics is called a *profile*. Of course, it is not always possible to construct a profile for a given type of crime. In the case of computer crime, however, there appears to be a remarkable number of similarities among the individuals who have been caught using a computer illegally. A few of these characteristic features of the computer criminal are now examined briefly.

Superior Background

Figure 11-3 provides the occupations of a selected set of computer crime defendants. The impression that computer programmers are the most likely type of employee to commit a computer crime conflicts with earlier studies by Parker and others that have identified data entry personnel and students as the most likely computer abusers. For example, an AICPA study found that over 70% of bank crime was committed by persons in lower levels of computer

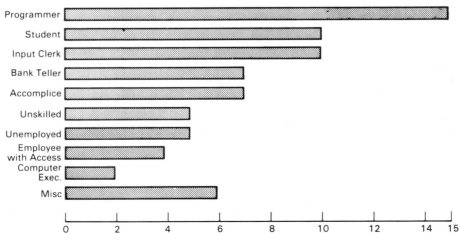

FIGURE 11-3   Occupations of computer crime defendants. (NCCCD Computer Crime Census, 1986.)

operations and expertise and that over 40% were attributed to clerical personnel.[12]

According to Donn Parker, the best way to identify the potential perpetrator is on the basis of the unique skills, knowledge, and experience possessed by those engaged in computer technology.[13] Computer criminals tend to be bright, talented, qualified individuals with good intellects and superior educational backgrounds. Ironically, it is usually these very qualifications that enable such individuals to acquire jobs as data processing employees in the first place. It is obvious, however, that a data processing employee must be smart enough not only to understand the company computer system but also to recognize its limitations if he or she is going to be able to commit a crime. Thus, high intelligence and a superior educational background would have to be considered important characteristics of the computer criminal.

A second fact of possible relevance in the identification of potential computer abusers is that most computer criminals are males under 30 years of age. In a study performed by the NCCCD, for example, over 70% of computer crime defendants were under 30. Since a number of computer crime cases involve students, there is undoubtedly some bias in any computation of an average age of the computer criminal. However, the fact that data processing as we know it today is less than 40 years old and that the special skills required of today's data processing personnel have only recently been taught in colleges and universities may help to explain the youthfulness of the computer-oriented perpetrator. The fact that young people are often in greater need of money and are often more willing to take a risk may contribute to these reasons.

Morals

The tenet that "a thief has no morals" does not seem to hold in the area of computer crime. Most computer criminals consider themselves to be relatively honest people who simply use a computer to take what other employees steal from a filing cabinet. Many perpetrators actually view themselves as long-term borrowers rather than thieves, and several have exercised great care to avoid harming individuals when performing their illegal activities. Alternatively, the belief that computer theft involves an impersonal company or system that can afford a loss, rather than another individual, is often expressed by computer criminals when apprehended.

The element of challenge in beating the system is often presented as a rationale for computer abuse. Said one writer, "The challenge of defrauding the computer and avoiding detection is often irresistible."[14] Such an attitude tends to remove the "crime" stigma from illegal computer activities, and casts computer abuse more in the role of game-playing than a violation of moral conduct. Such an attitude, for example, would probably explain a vast proportion of the student abuse of computer time at colleges and universities. A number of commercial cases of computer abuse also seem to be best explained by this thinking process.

The fact that certain illegal practices are common in the data processing industry has also been used as a rationale for computer abuse. Thus, tampering with an important bank-processing program might be in technical violation of the law, yet such tampering occurs quite frequently in order to meet computer-implementation deadlines imposed by management. Alternatively, at the civil trail of Fred Darm, who stole a computer program from the computer memory of a rival firm through the use of a remote terminal, the point was made that it was common practice for the programmers of rival firms to "snoop" each other's data files in order to obtain competitive information. Thus, when Darm was apprehended for his offense, not only was he surprised, he was quite offended!

---

[12]Gordon Mathews, "Computer-Related Crime Tied to Low-Expertise Employees," *American Banker,* March 3, 1983, p. 2.
[13]Parker, *Crime by Computer,* p. 45.

[14]Adrian R. Norman, *Computer Insecurity* (New York: Chapman and Hall, 1983), p. 18.

A final rationale for computer abuse may be the impersonality of the crime itself. The perpetrator almost never deals with another individual, just the computer system. This often gives the thief anonymity, plus the dubious satisfaction that he or she is not stealing from an individual. Most computer criminals have been quite emphatic on this point. One bank embezzler who was apprehended after stealing thousands of dollars from inactive bank accounts explained that he never took more than $20,000 from any one account because the accounts (at that time) were only insured up to $20,000. Other embezzlers have argued that they were only doing on a larger scale what the inventory clerks and stock people were doing in the warehouse, that is, helping themselves to corporate assets as a fringe benefit of their jobs.

The overwhelming conclusion drawn from considerations of morality in computer criminals is that average perpetrators tend to be ordinary in their beliefs but unlucky in their positions. Thus, the real distinguishing feature of the criminals is that they find themselves in the unfortunate situation of believing that the assets controlled by the computer are within their grasp and available, at least temporarily, for their own use.

Noncriminal Background

The question of criminal background in computer abuse becomes important because of the fear that such abuse may be linked to organized crime. In studies conducted to date, however, very little connection has been shown, although an absence of proof does not necessarily imply an absence of organized crime in the computer field. Obtaining proof is difficult. In one case, for example, a computer perpetrator agreed to turn state's evidence to implicate his underworld brethren but was gunned down on a street in New York before he could testify.

According to the experts, almost all computer criminals are amateur, first-time offenders rather than professional criminals. Few individuals who have been caught stealing with the aid of a computer have been proud of their activities or considered their embezzlement to be their principal work. Thus, very few of the individuals apprehended for suspicion of computer crimes have a previous criminal record. In a study of 374 cases of computer crime committed prior to 1976, for example, only one case involved an exconvict.[15] At the time this book went to press, the only additional case with which the authors are familiar involving previously convicted criminals concerned prisoners at Leavenworth Penitentiary in Kansas. In this fascinating crime, the prisoners learned how to file fraudulent, but acceptable, claims on their federal income tax returns (which even prisoners have to file), thus enabling them to obtain huge bogus refunds. One prisoner was finally caught with a government check for $20,000. (Back to making license plates!)

The identification of the computer criminal as a first-time offender has important implications for EDP control. Screening individuals on the basis of an existing criminal record is insufficient, for example, to avoid computer crime. The stability of the applicant may offer clues as to future behavior, however. The historical record suggests that employee disgruntlement is sometimes present in the environment of the computer criminal. Causes vary, but the fact remains that an unhappy employee is a very dangerous threat to a vulnerable accounting information system.

Environment

The computer criminal must have an opportunity to commit his or her crime. Thus, we conclude with a telling description of the environment

---

[15]Parker, *Computer Abuse Assessment.*

most likely to offer the computer embezzler the ideal circumstances for computer abuse.

> The most vulnerable EDP operation is the one which performs financial processing and produces negotiable instruments. Employee and management relations are poor, with a high degree of employee disgruntlement. There is a significant lack of separation of tasks requiring a great amount of trust and responsibility. In other words, employees are given wide-ranging responsibilities with minimal checking or observation of their activities. Employees are unsupervised when they are working in the EDP facilities outside normal hours. This weakness is supported by a number of cases that occurred at night or on weekends when employees, especially programmers, were given access to computers for program development work. The computer application programs lack controls to detect anomalous activities and events. The programs are difficult to test and provide few opportunities for the development of audit trails, the means by which transactions can be traced from the end product back to source data. Finally, there is little or no accounting of use of the computer system. Programmers, computer operators, or any employees can use computer services without any direct accountability. Actual experience shows that any EDP organizations which have some significant combinations of these weaknesses are particularly vulnerable to computer abuse.[16]

SUMMARY

In this chapter, we have focused our attention on computer crime and its relationship to accounting information systems. For the purpose of discussion, the chapter has been divided into three sections: (1) an overview of what is known about computer crime, (2) a brief description of six representative cases of accounting/computer

crimes, and (3) a general profile of the computer criminal.

The most fundamental conclusion is that we know very little about computer crime. Less than 2000 cases have been reported, but there is very good reason to believe that many more cases go unreported and, even worse, undetected. Because most computer criminals are caught by luck, chance, or accident, rather than by controls, our sample of known cases is not random. From our limited information about computer fraud, however, we have drawn two tentative conclusions. The first is that computer crime appears to be growing. The second is that computer crime involves large sums of money, usually much more than comparable white-collar crime.

A large number of computerized accounting information systems are vulnerable to computer crime and abuse because they directly or indirectly control valuable assets. In the second section of the chapter, we reviewed six cases: (1) the round-off trick, (2) the Equity Funding case, (3) the TRW Credit Data case, (4) the Union Dime Savings Bank case, (5) the Milwaukee 414s case, and (6) the Pakistani Virus case. These cases were chosen for review because of their notoriety or because they represent a type or class of computer crime. The analyses that followed each case suggested safeguards that might have prevented or detected that particular problem. It should be noted that these safeguards may not be effective in settings different from those described in this chapter.

The last section of the chapter attempted to construct a profile of the computer criminal. Internal controls have not thwarted major computer crimes and prior recognition of the computer criminal may prove a better safeguard. We observed that the typical computer criminal is bright, young, typically male, and in possession of a good education. Most computer criminals view themselves as moral and, in fact, most of them are first-time offenders. There is little evidence to support the claim that computer criminals are involved in organized crime.

[16]Parker, *Crime by Computer,* p. 40.

Key Terms You Should Know

accumulation error	Milwaukee 414s
computer crime	National Center for Computer Crime Data (NCCCD)
computer criminal profile	open shop
computer fraud and embezzlement	Pakistani virus
computer virus	Roswell Stephens
dial-back system	round-off trick
Equity Funding case	two-week vacation rule
Fair Credit Reporting Act	TRW Credit Data case
hacking	Union Dime Savings Bank case
lock-out system	valuable-information computer crime

Discussion Questions

Unless otherwise stated, all names and incidents in these questions are fictitious.

11-1. Why is a definition of computer crime elusive? Would you be willing to call computer crime a white-collar crime? Why or why not?

11-2. Give some examples of computer crime drawn from this chapter, your outside reading, or, perhaps your own experience. What characteristics do your examples have in common?

11-3. Known cases of computer crime have been described as just "the tip of the iceberg." Would you consider this description accurate? Why or why not?

11-4. A historical fact not widely known is that in 1856, the manager of the U.S. Patent Office quit his job because he thought that everything that could possibly be invented had already been invented. Would you consider computer crime a "new invention" or is there nothing in "modern" computer crime that would have prevented the manager from quitting?

11-5. Most computer crime is not reported. Give as many reasons as you can why much of this crime is purposely downplayed. Do you consider these reasons valid? Discuss several arguments favorable to the reporting of all computer crime.

11-6. Rosemarie Lux was an external auditor for Bill Sandmeyer and Associates, a small, independent CPA firm. She had just finished her audit of the Tracy Company and had found that one of the company's employees had been embezzling from the company's inventory accounts by manipulating inventory records stored on the company's computer system. Discuss what professional reasons would prevent her from making a statement to the press.

11-7. Denny Jacobs, a one-time computer expert and presently the town drunk, had been thrown in the city slammer to "dry out." In one of his more lucid moments, he turned to his fellow drinking partner and cell mate and said "You know, mate, I've just realized that computer controls are really for friends—the crooks are going to get around them anyway." Do you agree? Why or why not?

11-8. According to recent statistics, the odds of a white-collar criminal being convicted of a crime in the courts when caught are 33 to 1. If this is true, why do you suppose that some experts continue to claim that computer crime does pay?

11-9. Why have most computer experts suggested that computer abuse is growing despite the fact that so little is known about it?

11-10. Banks have been frequent targets of embezzlers and criminal perpetrators because, by definition, banks are large holders of liquid assets. Inasmuch as a good number of bank swindle cases have involved nothing more complicated than the switch of a deposit slip, why are many of these swindle cases reported as computer crime? Would you say that many of these crimes would be better reported as other types of crimes? Discuss.

11-11. There is an old saying that "it takes a thief to catch a thief." How accurate would you say this observation is when applied to the area of computer crime?

11-12. In 1973, the president of the United States imposed a wage and price freeze in this country in order to stabilize the economy and curb inflation. To implement the program, a special Wage and Price Control Board was set up with powers to make exceptions and with a supervisory staff to identify violations. After administering the freeze for a few months, William Simon, the chief executive of the Control Board, stated:

"I used to think that 95 percent of the American people are 100 percent honest. I have come to find out that 100 percent of the American people are 95 percent honest." What implications does this observation have for computer crime?

11-13. The Citizen's Capitalist Bank uses a computerized data processing system to maintain both its checking accounts and its savings accounts. During the last year, there have been a number of complaints from customers that their balances have been in error. Mr. Carl Doyle, the EDP bank manager, has always treated these customers very courteously, and has personally seen to it that the problems have been rectified quickly, sometimes by putting in extra hours after normal quitting time to make the necessary changes. This extra effort has been so helpful to the bank that this year, the bank's top management has made plans to award Mr. Doyle with the Employee-of-the-Year Award. Comment.

11-14. Explain the round-off trick. What type of position would an individual have to occupy within a company to successfully perform it? What controls would you recommend to avoid dishonest rounding in a computer?

11-15. Outline the details of the Equity Funding case. What is meant by the "inflated earnings phase," the "foreign phase," and the "insurance phase" of the fraud? What would you say was the most fundamental problem that permitted the fraud to go undetected for so long?

11-16. Explain why there is controversy over whether or not the Equity Funding case was a computer fraud. What is your opinion on the matter?

11-17. What is meant by the term *open shop* at the computer center? Why is an open shop a hazard? What can be done to minimize the dangers of this practice? Why do you suppose business firms or other organizations ever allow an open shop in view of the problems such a policy entails?

11-18. What is meant by the term *valuable-information computer crime?* In what way(s) does a grandfather-father-son file system guard against the perpetration of this type of computer abuse? In what way(s) does it fail to guard against such abuse?

11-19. Steven Brown was a computer specialist working for a management consultant firm, and his friend Dennis Coleman held a similar job with the local police department. One day, while the two men were having lunch, Dennis said, "You know, Steve, I wish more of you folks would step forward when you

uncover a computer fraud—it would sure make my job a lot easier. One of the best ways to control crime is to convince the criminal he can't get away with it. Putting the spotlight on some of these penny-ante computer crooks would probably keep a lot of others from trying their hand at it. Companies that keep these things hush-hush are not doing anyone any favors and, in addition, actually are in technical violation of the law for not reporting it." Comment.

11-20. Identify the key manipulations that enabled Roswell Stephens to steal from the Union Dime Savings Bank. Enumerate as many controls as you can that would have prevented Stephens from getting away with his actions. Would you imagine that such controls are active at your bank? Discuss.

11-21. The TRW Company Credit Data case involves two issues: (1) the propriety of computer-based information and (2) the protection afforded the consumer in the use of credit information. Identify each of these issues more fully and explain your own position on these matters. Do you feel, for example, that a company has the right to collect, store, and disseminate information about your purchasing activity without your permission?

11-22. What enabled the employees at TRW to get away with their crime? What controls might have prevented the crime from occurring?

11-23. The TRW case has been identified as an unusual case because the information stored on the company's computer files, rather than any liquid assets, was the major target of the perpetrators. From your reading of this and the previous chapter, plus your outside readings, discuss other cases that appear to fall into this category of computer crime.

11-24. In an early portion of this chapter, it was suggested that some experts feel that computer crime is just a "new twist on an old rope." Would you agree or disagree? What bearing does the definition of computer crime have on this issue?

11-25. In a recent news bulletin, it was announced that the FBI has organized a special section of its force to investigate crimes related to the use of computers. What advantages are there in training the employees of a federal agency to investigate the computer crime of a local company? In what way is federal jurisdiction justified? What special skills would you like to see these FBI investigators possess that a keypunch operator or computer operator would not be likely to have?

11-26. With regard to Question 11-25, envision the following (imaginary) conversation between Mr. Warren Gulko, the FBI computer division supervisor, and his staff. "Ladies and gentlemen, I am proud to be the supervisor of such an elite and well-trained staff. With your skills I have every confidence that we shall not only catch more computer thieves, but that we shall also prevent more computer crimes." Comment in light of the historical record.

11-27. Describe the case of the Milwaukee 414s. In your opinion, was this really a computer crime? For example, was there "criminal intent?" Defend your answers.

11-28. What is "hacking?" Why do people "hack?" How would you say the growth of microcomputer use has contributed to hacking? What can be done to prevent hacking?

11-29. What is a computer virus? Is it really a biological entity? Is it an infection? Is it contagious? Explain each of your answers in detail.

11-30. Describe the Pakistani Virus case. Would you describe this as a computer crime? Why or why not? What can be done to thwart viruses such as the one in this case?

11-31. There once was a man from Ann Arbor,
who decided to outsmart his computer.
He faked a transaction,
and much to his satisfaction,
he wound up, in the end, quite richer.
Comment. (Not about the quality of the poetry!)

11-32. Discuss the motivations for computer crime. Is all computer crime ultimately for financial gain? Explain.

11-33. Rodney Smallskull was apprehended for grand larceny shortly after he poured gasoline over his company's central processing unit, igniting both the machine and his trouser leg with a single match. After being taken into custody, Rodney was assigned legal counsel, who advised him to plead innocent by reason of temporary insanity. In your opinion, how sound was this advice? (*Hint:* If you wanted to harm a computer center, what would *you* do?)

11-34. In the past several years, there have been several incidents of CPA firms failing to detect major computer crimes committed by the firms' audit clients. Do you feel that these failures normally are caused by the incompetency of the external auditors or the cleverness of the individuals who commit the computer crimes? Discuss.

11-35. What are the lessons to be learned from computer crime, if any? From what you have read in this chapter, would you say that there is such a thing as a "secure" computer system? Discuss.

Problems

11-36. Zollinger National Bank has 8429 savings accounts, and credits interest to these accounts on a daily basis. Deborah Knowlton, one of the bank's assistant programmers, has often considered the use of a round-off scam to augment her own savings account balance. Assuming that she could get away with it, how much could she expect to accumulate in her account at the end of a year with such a scheme? Assume daily processing.

11-37. In many companies, there is a great volume of transactions affecting their "accounts receivable" asset account and this account has a large dollar balance. Try to think of an example whereby a computer crime could be committed successfully on a company's accounts receivable. (Assume that the company's accounts receivable subsidiary ledger is maintained on magnetic tape storage media.) Outline in detail the steps to be taken in order to commit a fraud. What internal controls could be established within the company that likely would have prevented the computer crime you have described

11-38. A computer crime case not documented in this textbook was the electronic funds transfer scandal perpetrated by Mark Rifkin at a bank in Los Angeles. Using outside source materials, obtain information about this case and prepare an analysis similar to those for the cases presented in this chapter. In your analysis, you should address the following questions: (1) Was this a computer crime? (2) How was the crime committed? (3) What safeguards might have prevented this crime? (4) How was the crime discovered?

11-39. (Library Research) Newspapers and such journals as *DATAMATION* and *Computerworld* are prime sources of computer crime articles. Find a description of a computer crime not already discussed in this chapter and prepare an analysis similar to the cases presented.

11-40. Match each term on the left with a corresponding term on the right.

NCCCD
accumulation error
Equity Funding Case
open shop
TRW Case
Fair Credit Reporting Act
Union Dime Savings Bank
Milwaukee 414s
lock-out system
dial-back system
computer virus
modal occupation of computer crime defendants

redials users entering legitimate passwords
inflated earnings phase
a noncontrolled computer-room environment
Roswell Stephens
hacking
computer programmer
the round-off trick
an infectious computer routine
National Center for Computer Crime Data
valuable information computer crime
enables individuals to access credit information
three strikes and you're out

CASE ANALYSES

11-41. *The Case of the Purloined Computer*

Below is a true account of a computer that was stolen from its company. The story is taken from the March 1979 issue of *The Printout* (p. 10).

On January 2, Dave Dumas, vice-president of Appliance Parts Company, Inc., came to work at 8 : 30 A.M. and discovered that his computer system had been stolen from its second-floor home during the New Year's holiday. The system, which had been installed for about two years, had become a critical part of his business because it was an online system with many terminals located in different parts of his company.

Missing were the main computer, a disk drive, four video display terminals, the system and applications software disk pack, and all of the operating manuals.

After notifying the police, Dumas called Euclid Lee, the local representative for Triad Systems Corporation. Euclid immediately packed his demonstration system into the back of his station wagon and arrived at the offices of Appliance Parts Co. in time to see the police still conducting their investigation. After receiving police clearance to set up a replacement system, Euclid and his crew installed a fully operational system

in place of the one stolen. Fortunately, Dumas had been operating his data-processing activity according to generally accepted security practices for disaster protection and had a complete set of current files backed up at an off-site location. The combination of management foresight and vendor response enabled APC to come back online by 11 : 30 that morning.

The stolen computer had been insured against everything—except theft. No one thought it likely that it would be dismantled and purloined from its rather difficult location on the second floor. Euclid called Bill Stevens, president of Triad Systems Corporation, and explained the problem. Stevens decided to replace the original system for APC at one-half Triad's cost. A new system was shipped from California on Wednesday evening of that same week and by Friday was in full operation. Total down time for the Appliance Parts Company, Inc. online system: four hours!

Questions

1. Is this an example of a computer crime? Why or why not?
2. Discuss the controls that might have thwarted this crime. Why do you suppose such controls were not in place?
3. The report is presented here in its entirety. Is such a report sufficient for aggregating good statistics on computer crime? Why or why not?

11-42. *Charles Lasher and Associates*

Of all the programmers working for Charles Lasher and Associates, Ray Williams was probably the most competent and, at the same time, the least motivated. His father, Ray Williams, Sr., had sent Ray Jr. to the best private schools in the area, and had even managed to pay for Ray's four-year education at Branard College— a considerable expense and one that was more than he could afford. Thus, when his father got Ray a job at Charles Lasher and Associates through an old friend of the family, Ray felt obligated to take it and try to do well.

The problem was that Ray did not like the work or the work environment. Charles Lasher and Associates was a management consulting firm with branches in several East Coast cities, and several of the company's clients required analysis work on their various computer files. The Lasher Company's customer representatives, who were not well versed in computer programming, constantly promised jobs to these clients without allowing enough time for the company's programming staff to complete them. On several occasions, in fact, the entire EDP staff of the company was told to cancel all their plans for the coming weekend because an important client needed some work done immediately and the staff was expected to get the job done "no matter what!" At other times, however, the work would slack off and there would be virtually nothing to do. Usually, nonbusy periods would occur during the summer months when the temperatures rose to the high 80s and the air conditioners decided to stop functioning. At these times, the staff would swelter in the inner, windowless offices assigned to the EDP department, drink coffee, and tell stale jokes that they all had heard from each other "about a million times."

Some of the work that Ray did for the company involved the extraction of selected information from client master files. A common task would be to take a master file containing 10,000 to 20,000 accounts receivable records and print out the name and address of those retail accounts that matched a specific customer profile. Thus, for example, a client might ask to have the computer print out the accounts of customers who simultaneously had income levels of at least so much, lived in certain zip code areas, had at least so many children, and had credit ratings of a certain level or higher.

For Ray, the programming aspects of this work were easy, and most of the job actually involved acquiring the detailed specifications of the computer file used in the extraction process and determining what format the client desired for the final report. From this information, Ray could easily scan the client's master file and direct the computer to print out the required information.

Ray knew that the computer files with which he worked contained sensitive data, but at first he simply did what was asked of him. As time went on, however, Ray became curious why the types of information he was extracting from the files were of interest to the clients, and he began to ask questions. His boss told him that these clients "liked to keep Ray busy," but somehow Ray didn't think that was the answer. The "moment of truth" actually came from a chance remark of an insurance client, Bob Tomlinson. Tomlinson had brought a tape reel of subscribers to *Business Month* magazine and asked for a profile printout as described earlier. Bob let slip, however, that his company was planning to use the information as leads for its insurance business. In effect, each name on the file matching the prescribed customer profile was a potential buyer of insurance, and Tomlinson's insurance company planned on contacting each of these customers by mail in hopes of selling them one or more policies. This information struck Ray like a bolt of lightning. "So that's why they want these fool reports," he thought!

At the time that Ray found out about the insurance mailing, he was in a particularly foul mood. He had worked all weekend on another project and he felt that he was being treated unfairly. The fact that he was on salary and thus received no overtime for his troubles especially rankled him. But the news about the insurance mailing started him thinking. There were other insurance companies around. Perhaps they, too, would be interested in the list he had prepared for Tomlinson's company. . . .

In the spring and summer, Ray played softball in a league that included younger guys from around the local neighborhood. One of them was Carl Weeks. Carl worked for Indemnity Life and Casualty Company, a rival company of Bob Tomlinson's company, and Ray was pretty sure that Carl would be interested in acquiring a copy of the hot leads in the report Ray had just prepared for Tomlinson's company. Thus, at the softball game the following Saturday, Ray casually mentioned to Carl that such a list "could be provided for a price." Carl jumped at the chance and it was agreed that, for $1000, Ray would deliver such a list the following weekend.

For Ray, printing out the list was a simple matter. On Monday morning, he walked into the computer room and told the computer operator that he needed "one more run" on the Tomlinson Company's *Business Month* file. The computer operator, who was a friendly chap, said, "Sure, Ray—no problem. In fact, I'm a little hung over from a party last night so if you don't mind, here's the tape file; run it yourself while I go get some more coffee."

Ray ran the program and, with the good fortune of the "disappearing computer operator," had no trouble in disposing of all traces of the extra program run. The next weekend, Ray delivered the "extra" computer list to Carl. Carl, in turn, handed over $1000 to Ray in small bills, and then both men retired to the local tavern—ostensibly to celebrate their 15-to-3 loss to their rival softball team. Ray treated.

During the next few months, Ray had a number of similar opportunities. In one instance, for example, an auditor wanted the computer to prepare a list of names and addresses drawn from a computer file for audit-confirmation purposes. For a fee, Ray "fixed" the program so that only those people known to have active, valid accounts were chosen for audit confirmation, thus assuring the auditor of a trouble-free audit-confirmation job. In another instance, Ray got his hands on the Chadwick Department Store accounts receivable file and had the computer print out a list of retail customers who were behind in their payments. He sold this list to a collection agency hungry for business. Using the information obtained from the listing, the agency was able to convince the Chadwick Store's management that it could do a very efficient job performing its collecting business, and thus landed a "fat" account. In yet a third instance, Ray copied over an entire file belonging to *Woods and Streams* magazine. He then sold copies of this subscription file to rival magazines. In one notable gambit, Ray actually stole the subscription list of a second rival magazine and sold this back to the subscriptions manager of *Woods and Streams*. Neither manager knew that, through Ray, each was "ripping off" the other!

It wasn't until almost a year had gone by that things began to get a little sticky for Ray. Bob Tomlinson had returned to Ray's office several times complaining that the leads acquired from the *Business Month* file "weren't panning out," and that he couldn't understand it. He said the industry was competitive and that most of the insurance customer leads, he was discovering, seemed to have just bought new insurance policies from other companies—especially Indemnity Life and Casualty Company. Bob wondered if Ray knew anything about that.

Questions

1. Why is Ray's work environment conducive to computer crime?

2. Does Ray fit the profile of a computer criminal? Defend your answer.

3. What controls appear to be missing at Charles Lasher and Associates that enable Ray to get away with the things he's been doing? Briefly identify each weakness at the company, and recommend one or more controls that might be used to eliminate this weakness.

4. Bob Tomlinson suspects something. What steps might be taken to confirm the suspicion that there is a security leak at the Lasher Company? What evidence might be collected, assuming it was available? (*Note:* For this last question, you may assume that desirable security controls not discussed in the case have, in fact, been installed at Charles Lasher and Associates.)

11-43. The Department of Taxation

The Department of Taxation of one state is developing a new computer system for processing state income tax returns of individuals and corporations. The new system features direct data input and inquiry capabilities. Identification of taxpayers is provided by using the social security number of individuals and federal identification number for corporations. The new system should be fully implemented in time for the next tax season.

The new system will serve three primary purposes:

• Data will be input into the system directly from tax returns through CRT terminals located at the central headquarters of the Department of Taxation.

- The returns will be processed using the main computer facilities at central headquarters. The processing includes
    1. Verification of mathematical accuracy.
    2. Auditing the reasonableness of deductions, tax due, and so forth, through the use of edit routines; these routines also include a comparison of the current year's data with prior years' data.
    3. Identification of returns that should be considered for audit by revenues agents of the department.
    4. Issuing refund checks to taxpayers.
- Inquiry service will be provided taxpayers on request through the assistance of Tax Department personnel at five regional offices. A total of 50 CRT terminals will be placed at the regional offices. A taxpayer will be allowed to determine the status of his or her return or get information from the last three years' returns by calling or visiting one of the department's regional offices.

The state commissioner of taxation is concerned about data security during input and processing over and above protection against natural hazards such as fire or floods. This includes protection against the loss or damage of data during data input or processing, or the improper input or processing of data. In addition, the tax commissioner and the state attorney general have discussed the general problem of data confidentiality that may arise from the nature and operation of the new system. Both individuals want to have all potential problems identified before the system is fully developed and implemented so that the proper controls can be incorporated into the new system.

Questions

1. Describe the potential confidentiality problems that could arise in each of the following three areas of processing and recommend the corrective action(s) to solve the problem.
    a. Data input.
    b. Processing of returns.
    c. Data inquiry.
2. The State Tax Commission wants to incorporate controls to provide data security against the loss, damage, or improper input or use of data during data input and processing. Identify the potential problems (outside of natural hazards such as fire or floods) for which the Department of Taxation

should develop controls, and recommend the possible controls for each problem identified.

(CMA Adapted)

11-44. Imtex Corporation

Imtex Corporation is a multinational company with approximately 100 subsidiaries and divisions, referred to as reporting units. Each reporting unit operates autonomously and maintains its own accounting information system. Each month, the reporting units prepare the basic financial statements and other key financial data on prescribed forms. These statements and related data are either mailed or telexed to corporate headquarters in New York City for entry into the corporate data base. Top and middle management at corporate headquarters utilize the data base to plan and direct corporate operations and objectives.

Under the current system, the statements and data are to be received at corporate headquarters by the twelfth working day following the end of the month. The reports are logged, batched, and taken to the Data Processing Department for coding and entry into the data base. Approximately 15 percent of the reporting units are delinquent in submitting their data, and three to four days are required to receive all of the data. After the data are loaded into the system, data verification programs are run to check footings, cross statement consistency, and dollar range limits. Any errors in the data are traced and corrected, and reporting units are notified of all errors by form letters.

Imtex Corporation has decided to upgrade its computer communication network. The new system would allow data to be received on a more timely basis at corporate headquarters and provide numerous benefits to each of the reporting units.

The Systems Department at corporate headquarters is responsible for the overall design and implementation of the new system. The Systems Department will utilize current computer communications technology by installing smart computer terminals at all reporting units. These terminals will provide two-way computer communications, and also serve as microcomputers that can utilize spreadsheet and other applications software. As part of the initial use of the system, the data collection for the corporate data base would be performed by using these terminals.

The financial statements and other financial data currently mailed or telexed would be entered by terminals. The required forms would initially be transmitted (downloaded) from the headquarters computer to the terminals of each reporting unit and stored permanently on disk. Data would be entered on the forms appearing on the reporting unit's terminal and stored under a separate file for transmission after the data are checked.

The data edit program would also be downloaded to the reporting units so the data could be verified at the unit location. All corrections would be made before transmitting the data to headquarters. The data would be stored on disk in proper format to maintain a unit file. Data would either be transmitted to corporate headquarters immediately or retrieved by the computer at corporate headquarters as needed. Therefore, data arriving at corporate headquarters would be free from errors and ready to be used in reports.

Charles Edwards, Imtex's Controller, is very pleased with the prospects of the new system. He believes data will be received from the reporting units two to three days faster, and that the accuracy of the data will be much improved. However, Edwards is concerned about data security and integrity during the transmission of data between the reporting units and corporate headquarters. He has scheduled a meeting with key personnel from the Systems Department to discuss these concerns.

Questions

Imtex could experience data security and integrity problems when transmitting data between the reporting units and corporate headquarters.

1. Identify and explain the data security and integrity problems that could occur.
2. For each problem identified, identify and explain a control procedure that could be employed to minimize or eliminate the problem.

(CMA Adapted)

11-45. Aidbart Company

Aidbart Company has recently installed a new online, data base computer system. CRT units are located throughout the company with at least one CRT unit located in each department. James Lanta, Vice-President of Finance, has overall responsibility for the company's management information system, but he relies heavily on Ivan West, Director of MIS, for technical assistance and direction.

Lanta was one of the primary supporters of the new system because he knew it would provide labor savings. However, he is concerned about security of the new system. Lanta was walking through the Purchasing Department recently when he observed an Aidbart buyer using a CRT unit to inquire about the current price for a specific part used by Aidbart. The new system enabled the buyer to have the data regarding the part brought up on the screen as well as each Aidbart product that used the part and the total manufacturing cost of the products using the part. The buyer told Lanta that, in addition to inquiring about the part, he could also change the cost of parts.

Lanta scheduled a meeting with West to review his concerns regarding the new system. Lanta stated, "Ivan, I am concerned about the type and amount of data that can be accessed through the CRTs. How can we protect ourselves against unauthorized access to data in our computer file? Also, what happens if we have a natural disaster such as a fire, a passive threat such as a power outage, or some active threat resulting in malicious damage—could we continue to operate? We need to show management that we are on top of these things. Would you please outline the procedures we now have, or need to have, to protect ourselves."

West responded by saying, "Jim, there are areas of vulnerability in the design and implementation of any EDP system. Some of these are more prevalent in online systems such as ours—especially with respect to privacy, integrity, and confidentiality of data. The four major points of vulnerability with which we should be concerned are the hardware, the software, the people, and the network."

Questions

1. For each of the four major points of vulnerability identified by Ivan West above:
   a. give one potential threat to the system, and
   b. identify action to be taken to protect the system from that threat.
2. Ivan West knows that he must develop a contingency plan for Aidbart Company's new system in order to be prepared for a natural disaster, passive threat, or active threat to the system.
   a. Discuss why Aidbart should have a contingency plan.
   b. Outline and briefly describe the major components of a contingency plan that could be implemented in the case of a natural disaster, passive threat, or active threat to the system.

(CMA Adapted)

12

Auditing Computerized Accounting Information Systems

Among the important questions that you should be able to answer after reading this chapter are:

1. What are the differences between internal auditing and external auditing?
2. Under what circumstances could an audit be considered successful even if no system weaknesses or embezzlements were uncovered?
3. How might an auditor use a computer utility program to assist in auditing the contents of a computer file?
4. What is the difference between "around-the-computer" auditing and "through-the-computer" auditing?
5. What are the techniques involved in auditing "with the computer"?

Case Analyses
Linder Company
Wholesale Cosmetics
Mark Tick, Auditor Extraordinaire
Vane Corporation
Ristan Enterprises
Tenney Corporation

Supplement: The Use of a Generalized Auditing Package

References and Recommended Readings for Part Three

INTRODUCTION

Chapters 9 and 10 stressed the importance of internal controls in the efficient operation of an accounting information system. To make sure that these controls are functioning properly, and to make sure that additional controls are not needed, the typical business organization performs examinations, or *audits,* of the system as a means of measuring the accounting system's effectiveness. Auditing is usually taught in one or more separate courses within the typical accounting curriculum and a single chapter of a book is not sufficient to cover the spectrum of topics involved in a complete audit of an organi-

zation. Thus this chapter will be merely introductory and, because of the complex nature of the auditing function, limited to areas of immediate consequence to accounting information systems.

To narrow the discussion still further, we have chosen to focus primarily on the audit of computerized accounting systems because this area is central to our textbook and is also likely to complement, rather than repeat, the coverage of an auditing course. An accountant who specializes in auditing computerized accounting information systems is called an *electronic data processing auditor,* or **EDP auditor.** This chapter is about the work that such a person performs.

THE AUDIT FUNCTION

This discussion begins with some introductory comments about the nature of auditing, including a discussion that emphasizes the distinction between internal and external auditing, a discussion of the major purposes of the audit, and a discussion of the importance of the audit trail in laying the foundation for the investigative auditor. These comments in turn provide a context for the more detailed material concerning the methodologies to be used when auditing *around* the computer, auditing *through* the computer, and auditing *with* the computer.

Internal Versus External Auditing

Conventionally, we distinguish between two types of audits: the **internal audit** and the **external audit.** As the names imply, an internal audit is typically performed by the accounting employees of the company itself, whereas an external audit is normally conducted by an accountant (or team of accountants) working for an independent CPA firm. The fact that an audit may be performed "internally" is somewhat misleading to the uninformed because it conjures images of self-regulation—like the basketball team that hires its own referees. In actuality, internal au-

diting positions are staff positions reporting to top management. Whereas an audit might be internal to a company, it is invariably *external* to the corporate department or division being audited. Thus, the objectivity and professionalism required for the auditing function is preserved.

Although similar in their need for objectivity, internal and external audits are quite different in their operational goals. The internal audit is concerned primarily with employee adherence to company policies and procedures—for example, the use of an official form when preparing payroll vouchers or completing purchase orders. On the other hand, the external audit's chief function is to give an opinion whether the financial statements of a firm are fairly presented—for example, to make sure that generally accepted accounting principles have been used to determine the balance sheet value of the company's unsold inventories.

Although the primary goals of external and internal audits differ somewhat, they are complementary within the context of accounting information systems. For example, the data processing controls examined by the internal auditor observing managerial procedures are in part designed to increase the accuracy of the external financial reports of interest to the external auditor. Similarly, the use of an acceptable method of inventory valuation such as FIFO or LIFO, as required by the external auditor, is likely to be an important corporate policy falling under the domain of the internal auditor.

Most of the discussion that follows regarding the audit of computerized accounting information systems is applicable to both internal and external auditors. Therefore, except where specific reference is made to one or the other, the term *auditor* is used broadly to encompass both types.

What an EDP Audit Is Supposed to Do

EDP (electronic data processing) auditing may be defined as the "process of collecting and evaluating evidence to determine whether a computer system safeguards assets, maintains data integrity, achieves organizational goals effectively, and consumes resources efficiently."[1] Thus, traditional audit objectives are still present in EDP auditing. These include **attest objectives** such as the safeguarding of assets and data integrity, and **management objectives** such as operational effectiveness and efficiency.

As illustrated in Figure 12-1, the EDP audit function encompasses all of the components of a computer-based accounting information system: people, procedures, hardware, software, and data bases. These components are viewed as a system of interacting elements that auditors examine for the purposes outlined above.

It is also important to understand what an audit is *not*. Some individuals believe, for example, that an audit is primarily punitive—that is, punishment for discovered or suspected wrongdoing. Employees undergoing either internal or external audits for the first time are consequently nervous and uncertain, even to the point of making mistakes in front of auditors that they have never made before. In one notable case, for example, a new computer operator became so

[1] Ron Webber, *EDP Auditing—Conceptual Foundations and Practice* (New York: McGraw-Hill, 1982), p. 7.

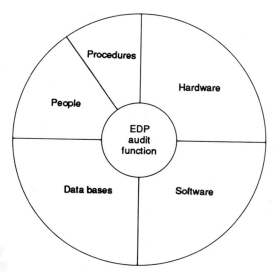

FIGURE 12-1   The five components of a computer-based accounting information system examined in an EDP audit.

flustered when he was informed that the auditors had arrived and were watching him that he mounted the wrong tape on a tape drive and erased two-thirds of the company's accounts receivable records.

Audits are not intended to punish anyone, and certainly are not performed for the purpose of intimidation. In the case of the internal audit, for example, the principal goal is to verify that the company's established policies and procedures are in effect, and that they are sufficient to ensure effective operating performance. Thus, the easiest and most efficient way for employees to satisfy an internal audit is to provide simple evidence that their jobs are being performed according to company specifications.

Auditing has often been likened to detective work in police investigations. Although this analogy implies professional skill, meticulous attention to details, and perhaps thoroughness, it also has the unfortunate implication that the primary goal is to catch a crook. This is *not* the major purpose of either the internal or external auditor. Of course, it *is* true that many audits have uncovered fraud, but this is typically a byproduct of the investigation rather than an objective in itself. However, such activities as embezzlement or theft are sometimes discovered in the course of an audit, for clearly such activities must violate company policy and, in covering up the fact that assets have been stolen, result in an overstatement of the true worth of the company. The distinction between what auditors are *assigned* to do, however, and what they ultimately find, is important and should be kept in mind when audit tasks are being studied.

For these reasons, most modern auditors consider themselves accounting consultants in a position to assist managers in their planning and controlling functions rather than "police workers" in search of criminals. In this sense, the auditor is someone interested in verifying the present strengths, safeguards, and controls of the organization's accounting information system, and only as a consequence of the auditor's position, someone who is able to discover potential or existing weaknesses requiring further managerial consideration. For example, an internal auditor might discover that the addition of a simple edit test in a computer program would enable the company to detect a certain type of erroneous transaction in the processing cycle, or, alternatively, an external auditor might suggest (from experience) that a costly control presently used in a client company could be eliminated with little risk. Thus, an auditor and a company are on the same side, despite the arm's-length relationship that must be maintained to ensure objectivity in the review process.

Planned Versus Surprise Audits

For the most part, accounting audits must be **planned audits** because of the need to coordinate visits to the various accounting activity sites of the company, the need to schedule managerial assistance in providing pertinent documents, and the need for computer time to review important computer files and data processing programs. However, both internal and external audits can be performed either on a planned or surprise basis.

As the name suggests, a **surprise audit** is an unscheduled investigation of system activity in which the auditors completely take over the operations of the systems and check the integrity and accuracy of the current data processing. In his famous book, *The Money Changers,* Arthur Hailey describes such a surprise audit at the "First Mercantile American Bank," a fictitious commercial bank with branches scattered throughout a large metropolitan urban area.

> . . . An essential part of the audit function was to descend irregularly and without warning on any of the bank's branches. Elaborate precautions were taken to preserve secrecy and any audit staff member who violated it was in serious trouble. Few did, even inadvertently.
>
> For today's maneuver, the score of auditors involved had assembled an hour ago in a salon of a downtown hotel, though even that destination had not been revealed until the latest possible moment. There they were briefed, duties allocated, then inconspicuously, in twos and threes, they had walked toward the main downtown branch of FMA. Until the last few crucial minutes they loitered in lobbies of nearby buildings, strolled casually, or browsed store windows. Then, traditionally, the most junior member of the group had rapped on the bank door to demand admission. As soon as it was gained, the others, like an assembling regiment, fell in behind him. Now, within the bank, audit team members were at every key position.[2]

The element of surprise in an audit serves a dual role. On the one hand, it gives the auditors a chance to examine the organization's processing during what is hoped to be a typical processing cycle. Thus, there is good reason to expect the data to be fairly representative of daily input and therefore to give the auditors a good idea of organization procedures in present use. On the other hand, the element of surprise serves to

[2] Arthur Hailey, *The Money Changers* (Garden City, N.Y.: Doubleday, 1975), pp. 86–87.

limit severely the amount of time the embezzler must have to cover a fraud. This aspect is crucial to catching systematic processing frauds, as Hailey explains.

> A convicted bank embezzler of the 1970s, who successfully concealed his massive defalcations for some twenty years, observed while eventually en route to prison, "The auditors used to come in and do nothing but shoot the breeze for forty minutes. Give me half of that time and I can cover up anything."
>
> The audit department of First Mercantile American, and other large North American banks, took no such chance. Not even five minutes passed after the surprise of the auditors' arrival until they were all in preassigned positions, observing everything.
>
> Resigned, regular staff members of the branch went on to complete their day's work, then to assist the auditors as needed. Once started, the process would continue through the following week and part of the next. But the most critical portion of the examination would take place within the next few hours.[3]

In the computer room, the auditor's approach is similar to that described by Hailey for other portions of the bank. The operations of the computer center are closely observed by the auditing staff and the input, processing, and output of the computer run(s) are carefully examined. If need be, the contents of computer programs or files can be "dumped" onto printer pages and checked against authorized versions to make sure they agree with the documentation.

The Importance of a Good Audit Trail

As we have now observed in several earlier chapters, a good **audit trail** means that a manager or any other employee is able to follow the path of the organization's accounting transactions from their initial source documents to their final dis-

position on a report. The audit trail is probably one of the most important controls in the accounting information system because it enables management to know what is happening as transactions wind their way through the various phases of manual and computerized data processing. As a result, management is in a position to detect and correct any errors and irregularities occurring during the course of normal accounting activity.

A good audit trail is also important when it comes time to *audit* an accounting information system. Like the concerned manager, the auditor must be able to trace the flow of accounting transactions as these transactions pass through the accounting information system in order to test data processing accuracy as well as to verify the controls used to safeguard the integrity of the data. Without a good audit trail, the auditor's job is virtually impossible to perform. If the audit trail is obscured, the auditor is similarly left "in the dark."

The introduction of a computer into a company's system often causes audit-trail problems. Transaction processing under the company's manual system is visible to the human eye, making the audit trail relatively easy to follow. When a company's data processing activities are handled by the computer, however, accounting transactions are processed internally by computer hardware and are not visible. The audit trail thus becomes more difficult to follow.

When a real-time accounting information system is used to process data from remote terminals, the audit trail has the potential to be even more difficult to follow. The reasons for this are twofold. First, the physical location of the source document data and of the computer that processes these data may be separated by hundreds or even thousands of miles. Thus, discrepancies that appear on a summary listing of processing maintained at the computer center cannot be traced immediately to the source documents that relate to the processed data. In effect, the audit trail has "leaped" a great dis-

[3] Ibid., p. 87.

tance. The auditor following an audit trail, therefore, must also leap this distance in order to follow the processing logic and information flow involved. To permit the auditor to perform this tracing task successfully, clear identification of transactions and record updating must be available to make the audit path continuous and easy to follow.

The second audit trail problem related to real-time accounting information systems is the lack of a regular schedule for processing specific types of accounting transactions. In order for a manager to trace a particular business transaction through the computer system, it is necessary to know when that transaction was processed. For example, if a company's sales manager desired information about a sales transaction that took place during the third week of February, and the company used a weekly batch-processing computer system, the manager could trace the transaction in question by looking at the data processing for sales occurring in that week. If the company utilized a real-time system, however, the sales manager's tracing of the audit trail for the required sales transaction could be more difficult. Assuming the manager knew which terminal location was used to process the sales transaction, the determination of which particular day of the week this transaction was processed could still be extremely hard, obviously causing audit trail problems.

A popular control used in many organizations' real-time processing systems is the **internal transaction log** maintained by the operating system of the computer. Each time a transaction is processed from remote terminal input, or perhaps each time a terminal requests processing time from the CPU, it is possible to log detailed information about the user or the processing request on magnetic disk or tape. Periodically (perhaps daily), the contents of the internal transaction log can be printed out, thereby providing a report that is human readable. This *hard-copy* printout, containing detailed information about each terminal's input transactions, establishes an audit trail of processed transactions. The sales

manager in the previous example could therefore have obtained the transaction log hard-copy printout of the specific terminal in question for the third week of February.

AUDITING AROUND THE COMPUTER

When computers were first used for accounting data processing functions, the typical auditor knew very little about automated data processing. The basic auditing approach, therefore, was to follow the audit trail up to the point at which accounting data entered the computer and pick it up again when the data reappeared in processed form as computer output. This is called **auditing around the computer.** Historically, the auditor paid little attention to the accounting controls that were, or were not, used in the CPU itself because it was assumed that the presence of accurate output verified proper processing operations. Thus, as long as the output from the accounting information system was valid and could be traced back to the input from which it was generated, the auditor was satisfied with the data processing portion of the accounting information system.

To illustrate around-the-computer auditing, consider the simplified payroll processing for a company in Figure 12-2. Payroll data are input to the computer based on time cards punched by employees as they report for work, leave work, take time off for lunch, and so forth. These data are then processed once a week in a batch. A master file of employee records, containing such information as social security number, name, year-to-date tax withholdings, and so forth, is also used in the processing. Output from the processing run includes the company's payroll checks, an updated master file, and a payroll register indicating what payroll disbursements have been authorized as a result of the computer processing. Conceptually, therefore, the payroll data processing consists of a set of inputs, processing programs that update one or more computer

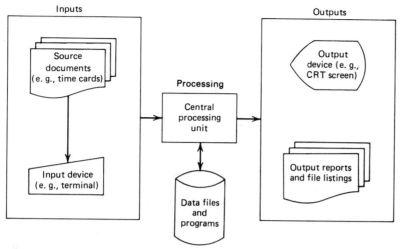

FIGURE 12-2 When auditing around the computer, the auditor concentrates on inputs (*left box*) and outputs (*right box*), not on data processing performed by the CPU.

files, and a set of outputs as illustrated in the figure.

The auditor begins with the verification of the source documents—in this case, the employee time cards—to check for accuracy and authenticity. Next, the auditor would follow these time cards to the input phase and verify that they are properly transcribed. The auditor would then literally walk around the computer to the output and verify that the payroll checks have been prepared properly. Thus, around-the-computer auditing involves an investigation of the large boxes in Figure 12-2. A correct match of the output with the manual calculations performed from the input would thus serve as the audit test. Finally, for completeness, a printout of the payroll master file before and after the processing run takes place would also have to be made to permit the auditor to verify that this file has been updated properly.

When performing a payroll audit, a question naturally arises as to how many employees should be screened when checking the computer processing. Because cash disbursements are involved in preparing payroll checks, a verification of the complete set of time cards and input files involved in the processing run would be desirable. Where the payroll checks for thousands of employees are involved in a single processing run, however, this task would probably be too time-consuming to perform manually, and only a subset of employees (say, from randomly selected departments) would be chosen for the audit.

The advantages of around-the-computer auditing include the following: (1) it is relatively straightforward, (2) it can be performed with minimum, if any, disturbance of the company records, (3) it can be performed with live (as opposed to artificial) data, (4) it can be performed completely with the company's existing computer equipment, (5) it requires little skill or training in computers of the auditor, and (6) it requires little assistance from the accounting or EDP staff. For these reasons, such auditing is also relatively inexpensive to perform.

The chief disadvantage of around-the-computer auditing is that it does not test enough. In testing controls, the exceptions, not the normal transactions of a typical processing run, are of interest to the auditor, and these are basically overlooked in around-the-computer auditing practice. Consider again the payroll example of Figure 12-2. How will the processing run treat a "nonexistent" employee, especially an employee who has been fired but whose computer payroll record has not yet been removed from the master file? What happens if an "old" employee's time card data from week 1 is processed again in week 2's computer run? Will the employee be paid double? What happens if there are two employees with the same name or, by mistake, the same social security number?

As you can see, around-the-computer auditing ignores the processing controls designed to test these cases, and therefore has the potential to reveal only those system weaknesses that can be detected under normal processing conditions. In this sense, around-the-computer auditing is actually a *feedback control* rather than a *preventive control*. Therefore, at best, it can be used only to audit the accounting information system "after the fact." It cannot identify problems before they occur.

A further problem with around-the-computer auditing is that it makes no use of the computer itself, the most powerful tool for processing data, so that audit tests are limited to the manual resources of the auditor. This means, in particular, that auditing cannot be performed in volume. The result is that only a fraction of the transactions involved in a typical computerized processing environment are likely to be scrutinized when around-the-computer auditing is being performed, and these transactions are likely to be perfectly valid, but uninteresting, situations. Thus, we need further tests to investigate the questions of exceptions and completeness, and this requires *through-the-computer auditing*.

AUDITING THROUGH THE COMPUTER

When **auditing through the computer,** an auditor follows the audit trail as it proceeds within the internal-computer-operations phase of automated data processing. Unlike around-the-computer auditing, therefore, through-the-computer auditing attempts to verify the processing controls involved in the accounting information system programs as well as ensure that accurate data processing is performed in the normal course of accounting activity.

Although through-the-computer auditing would, for completeness, also include tests of computer hardware, it is usually assumed that the central processing unit, peripheral tape and disk drives, and other interfacing equipment are functioning properly. This leaves the auditor the principal task of verifying processing and control logic as opposed to computer accuracy. The four primary methods of through-the-computer auditing are (1) the preparation of a special set of test transactions, called *test data,* (2) the validation of computer programs themselves through a variety of specialized auditing techniques to ensure that authorized versions of the accounting programs are, in fact, being used for data processing purposes, (3) the use of an *integrated test facility,* or ITF, and (4) use of embedded audit modules. Each of these four methods is discussed at greater length in the following paragraphs.

Test Data

It is the auditor's responsibility to develop a set of transactions that tests, as completely as possible, the range of exception situations that might challenge the computer processing of the accounting data under normal processing conditions. Conventionally, this is called **test data.** Possible exception situations for our payroll application in Figure 12-2, for example, include (1) out-of-sequence conditions, (2) no-master-file-record-found conditions, (3) invalid employee number, (4) processing wrong input, (5) invalid dates, pay rates, or deduction codes, (6) processing wrong files, (7) use of alphabetic data where numeric data are required, or vice versa, and (8) invalid field relationships, such as a pay-rate amount and a pay-rate code. Of course, these are just examples for our payroll illustration; additional test conditions would be developed on a program-by-program basis as audit needs dictate. In more sophisticated accounting information systems, for example, it is common to find that an initial set of transaction data will serve as the input to more than one processing routine. This makes the development of suitable test data that much more difficult inasmuch as the set of exceptions must be expanded to include the possibilities involved for all programs using the input data. The point, however, is that as many different exception situations as possible should be built into the test data in order to provide a thorough audit test.

Once the auditor has assembled appropriate sample data (usually transactions of some type), they are arranged into test sequence in preparation for computerized data processing. To complete the audit test, the auditor will compare the results obtained from processing test data with a predetermined set of answers developed by the auditor on an **audit work sheet.** If the processing results and the work sheet results are not in agreement, further investigation must be made to determine the reasons. It should be pointed out that discrepancies found in an audit test are not always attributable to deficient data processing or the lack of good accounting controls. The use of nonstandard procedures, the introduction of spurious data, the possibility of machine malfunction, or the presence of other random irregularities that might take place during the processing tests are also possible causes of unanticipated results. As far as possible, therefore, the auditor must guard against these situations during audit operations.

Auditing Computer Programs

A clever programmer can thwart the use of test data by substituting a legitimate, but unused, program for a dishonest one when an auditor asks for the processing routine(s) required for the audit. Although there is no 100% foolproof way of validating a program, there are four tests that

may be used to assist in this task: (1) tests of program authorization, (2) control-total tests of the program itself, (3) surprise audits of the program when it is in actual use, and (4) surprise use of an authorized program when data processing is scheduled.

Test of Program Authorization

At a typical computer center, the EDP manager is required to make the final approval of all computer programs used in the normal course of the organization's data processing. Of course, the EDP manager may choose to delegate this responsibility to subordinate managers and this delegation of responsibility is almost always exercised when minor changes to existing programs are to be made. Regardless of how major or minor a program change might be, however, it is the auditor's responsiblity to ensure that proper authorization procedures have been formulated and that the organization's employees observe these procedures in the normal course of processing accounting data.

The place to start a **test of program authorization** is with the documentation found at the EDP subsystem. An efficient organization usually will have internal forms that authorize a change to an existing program or the development of one or more new programs. Included on these *program authorization forms* should be the names of the individual(s) responsible for the work and the signature of the supervisor responsible for approving the final programs. Similarly, there should be forms that indicate that the work has been completed and a signature authorizing the use of the program(s) for present data processing. These authorizing signatures affix responsibility for the data processing routines and ensure accountability when problems arise. We call this a **responsibility system of computer program development and maintenance.**

Figure 12-3 illustrates a complete responsibility system of computer program development and maintenance in flowchart form. The auditor's role in reviewing this system would include:

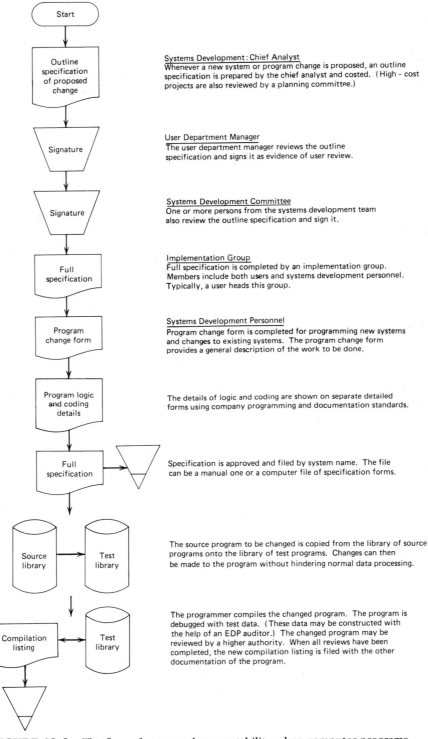

Systems Development: Chief Analyst
Whenever a new system or program change is proposed, an outline specification is prepared by the chief analyst and costed. (High-cost projects are also reviewed by a planning committee.)

User Department Manager
The user department manager reviews the outline specification and signs it as evidence of user review.

Systems Development Committee
One or more persons from the systems development team also review the outline specification and sign it.

Implementation Group
Full specification is completed by an implementation group. Members include both users and systems development personnel. Typically, a user heads this group.

Systems Development Personnel
Program change form is completed for programming new systems and changes to existing systems. The program change form provides a general description of the work to be done.

The details of logic and coding are shown on separate detailed forms using company programming and documentation standards.

Specification is approved and filed by system name. The file can be a manual one or a computer file of specification forms.

The source program to be changed is copied from the library of source programs onto the library of test programs. Changes can then be made to the program without hindering normal data processing.

The programmer compiles the changed program. The program is debugged with test data. (These data may be constructed with the help of an EDP auditor.) The changed program may be reviewed by a higher authority. When all reviews have been completed, the new compilation listing is filed with the other documentation of the program.

FIGURE 12-3 The flow of personnel accountability when computer programs are changed or altered.

422

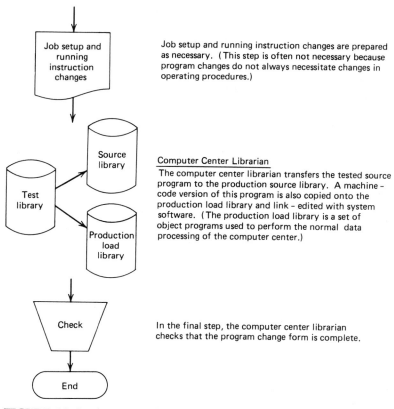

Job setup and running instruction changes are prepared as necessary. (This step is often not necessary because program changes do not always necessitate changes in operating procedures.)

Computer Center Librarian
The computer center librarian transfers the tested source program to the production source library. A machine-code version of this program is also copied onto the production load library and link-edited with system software. (The production load library is a set of object programs used to perform the normal data processing of the computer center.)

In the final step, the computer center librarian checks that the program change form is complete.

FIGURE 12-3   (Continued)

1. A check to see that all program changes were documented on the proper change-request forms.
2. A check to see that program change requests are properly costed and that high-cost projects are properly reviewed by the proper planning committee.
3. A check to see that both computer development personnel and users sign the outline specification form, thereby establishing authorization for the programming work.
4. A cross-check of program changes against the programs in the production load library (where currently used programs are stored).
5. A check to see that documentation matches the production version of a computer program.
6. A check of librarian functions, especially a review of the paperwork involved with the documentation of program change requests.

The chief purpose of a responsibility system at the computer center is not to affix blame in the event of program failures but to ensure accountability and adequate supervisory controls in the critical area of data processing. It is a well-known fact that individuals are more careful and meticulous when they are responsible for a given piece of work. As a result, tighter control over both the development of new programs and changes to existing programs is achieved and better computer software may thus be anticipated. In this sense, responsibility programming is an important preventive control that should be observed carefully in the course of an EDP audit.

Control-Total Tests

A **Trojan horse computer program** is a program with a hidden, intentional error created by a programmer for private gain. Usually, a Trojan horse program is difficult to detect because the typical commercial accounting computer program is thousands of instructions in length and the very few unauthorized instructions that might cause difficulties in the computer program may be hidden anywhere in the programming code. Moreover, a smart programmer will not change the source language code of an authorized program for illicit purposes; the programmer will use the human-unreadable machine language code for this task.

To guard against unauthorized program tampering, especially at the machine-language level, it is possible to perform certain **control-total tests of program authenticity.** The most common is a test of length. To perform this test, the auditor obtains the latest version of a program to be verified and counts the number of bytes or words of computer memory required to store the program in machine language when it resides in the central processing unit of the computer. This length count is then compared with a security table of length counts of all valid accounting programs at the computer center. Program lengths that do not match these control totals are subjected to further scrutiny.

A length count is an excellent test of program security because it is difficult for a computer programmer to alter a computer program in such a way that the tampered-program length comes out the same as the valid-program length. A similar control-total test would be a check-sum comparison of the total number of source-language instructions in the program. For technical reasons, however, this test is not as efficient as the length test. Yet a third test is to treat the machine-language instructions of the program as binary numbers that are added to compute a hash total. In all these tests, the computed control total is compared with a table of security values to test the validity of the program.

Surprise Audits

As the name implies, this test involves the examination of a set of accounting computer programs on a surprise basis. Here, the auditor will appear unannounced at the time that specific processing runs are scheduled and request duplicate copies of the computer programs just after they have been used to perform their required data processing tasks. Usually, these programs will be copied onto a spare magnetic tape reel that the auditor brings for this purpose. Once the complete set of programs has been copied, the auditor can compare the "in-use" programs with "authorized" versions that were acquired previously for checking purposes. This test, by the way, need not be performed at the computer center, but can be performed elsewhere and later if desired.

It might also be noted that manually checking computer programs against their source listings is a very arduous, time-consuming process because thousands of instructions are involved in the coding. Consequently, many auditors use special computerized comparison programs for this purpose. In effect, comparison programs are special computer programs that use source-language accounting programs as input data. The comparison program will compare the surprised program (in use at the computer center at the time the surprise audit takes place) with the authorized program on a line-by-line (instruction-by-instruction) basis. Unmatched instructions in either program are identified on a discrepancy report and form the basis of further inquiry.

Surprise Use

Here, the auditor visits the computer center unannounced and requests that previously attained authorized programs be used to perform the required data processing. If this request is denied, the reasons for the denial are carefully documented and investigated. If the request is honored, the auditor will then perform the specific accounting tasks required using the alternative programs. Unusual conditions that occur during the processing runs should be carefully scrutinized.

The surprise use of a set of authorized computer programs guards against unwarranted program changes and the use of unwarranted computer files or data input. For example, the authorized program will not be able to access a dummy file as might be used by an illegitimate program because the file-identification instructions of the authorized program will not match those of the bogus tape or disk file. Similarly, if illegitimate data are being processed in a tampered computer program, the authorized version of the program with proper data-testing controls may be able to identify these data on an exception basis. If desired, the auditor can also run a test set of special transactions on the "in-use" program at the time the surprise visit is conducted.

Integrated Test Facility (ITF)

The purpose of an **integrated test facility** is to audit an accounting information system in an operational setting. It works as follows. A set of fictitious accounts is created by the auditor and appropriate master records are placed on the computer files of the accounting information system. For example, a number of fictitious credit customers might be created and appropriate accounts receivable master records would be placed on the company's accounts receivable computer files. From the standpoint of the auditor, of course, the information contained on these records is for test purposes only. To most of the employees of the company, however, these records represent bona fide customers entitled to purchase company merchandise inventory or services on credit.

To use the integrated test facility, the auditor will introduce artificial transactions into the data processing stream of the accounting information system and have the company routinely handle the business involved. In a truly integrated test facility, this may mean actually shipping merchandise (not ordered by anyone) to designated addresses, or billing customers for services not rendered. Because of the amount of work involved, however, it may be necessary to have the ordered merchandise intercepted at the shipping department and the billing transactions reversed at the managerial level.

The auditor's task is to examine the results of the transactions and to determine how well the accounting information system under examination performs the tasks required of it. The auditor does this by examining printouts of the computer file records and data processing runs used to update them and by comparing the information on these reports with anticipated results. Discrepancies between actual results and anticipated results form the basis of further inquiry.

The greatest advantage of an integrated test facility is that it enables the auditor to examine both the manual steps and the computerized steps that are used by a company as it processes business transactions. For example, in testing an accounts receivable processing application, the auditor will be able to ascertain (1) how quickly a new customer can order merchandise on credit, (2) how credit sales are approved and processed, (3) how the company reacts to credit customers who exceed their credit limits, (4) how the company bills its customers for merchandise, (5) how sales returns and allowances are handled, and (6) how the company handles delinquent accounts. The examination of many different aspects of an accounting application is what is meant by *integrated* in the term *integrated test facility*.

The greatest drawback of the integrated test facility is that it introduces artificial transactions in the data processing stream. For the sake of accuracy in the company's financial statements, however, these transactions must be reversed. There are two principal ways of accomplishing this. With a **filtering system,** the artificial test transactions are identified when they are input for processing, and are separated out of the transaction stream for special treatment. Often, this is accomplished by having all audit transactions occur for an artifical entry in the accounts structure—for example, a fictitious department with department code number 99. The test transactions (with code 99) are used to update the appropriate accounting records of the company, but are filtered out of the data processing flow as far as further business activities are concerned.

A filtering system is relatively straightforward, although it may require a substantive amount of coordinative work between the auditor, the EDP subsystem, and accounting subsystem for implementation. This method is also undesirable because it may defeat the integrative nature of the test facility and therefore fail to perform important validation functions.

An alternative to the filter approach is to *manually reverse test transactions* at the very end of the accounting cycle. For example, in the accounts receivable illustration, this would mean manually reversing the company's final sales figures in the general ledger by the amount of artificial sales generated during the course of the company's audit testing. To the extent that such a procedure requires accountants to alter directly the financial information output by an accounting information system, such an approach may be objectionable to management. The increasing use of online systems and the fact that such systems are often used by many individuals at dispersed locations also makes this approach difficult. However, because it enables the auditor to test the accounting information system, it is considered the more desirable method.[4]

Embedded Audit Modules

A fourth approach to auditing through the computer is use of **embedded audit modules** or audit subsystems to capture audit related data. With this approach, the application program incorporates subroutines for audit purposes. For

example, an application program for a payroll would include a code that causes transactions meeting prespecified criteria to be written to a file called the **system control audit review file (SCARF).** For payroll applications, these could be payroll transactions for employees to be paid for more than a predetermined number of hours worked. Another example would be to have transactions that violate a certain control, such as unauthorized attempts to access high security files, to be recorded and written onto the SCARF. The auditor can then review the contents of the SCARF and determine whether or not the exceptions captured are appropriate or in fact are indicative of real control violations.

An advantage of embedded audit modules is that they provide for continuous auditing of application processing. The auditor must be involved in the development of these programs initially, but once implemented, the system can capture information that will be valuable to the auditor on an ongoing basis. Of course, use of this approach means that auditors must have a thorough knowledge and understanding of systems and programming logic.

Advantages and Disadvantages of Auditing Through the Computer

The chief advantage of through-the-computer auditing techniques over around-the-computer auditing techniques is that the former enables the auditor to test for computer controls and exceptions in addition to testing the basic capacity of the computer programs to process normal accounting data. This advantage, in turn, enables the auditor to become more closely involved with the data processing under scrutiny. As a result, the auditor has the potential to offer a company valuable insights in areas of weakness or areas that could be improved at minimal cost.

Clearly, through-the-computer auditing is a more thorough test of accounting data processing than around-the-computer auditing, and therefore enables auditors to examine ac-

---

[4] See, for example, John Burch, Jr., and Joseph L. Sardinas, Jr., *Computer Control and Audit: A Total Systems Approach* (New York: Wiley, 1978), pp. 431–441.

counting information systems more effectively. This in turn enables external auditors to provide better services to their clients or internal auditors to provide better services to their company.

Through-the-computer auditing also has disadvantages. Perhaps the most apparent is that it is much more demanding of EDP and accounting resources. For example, special computer time must be set aside for auditing runs with test data, and EDP subsystem staff must be assigned to the auditor in order to provide computer documentation, library files of computer programs, work tapes, and so forth. Where data processing is performed on a tight schedule, this requirement of additional resources is often difficult to satisfy.

Through-the-computer auditing demands more technical skills of the auditor. For example, it is difficult to imagine an auditor designing test data without some knowledge of automated accounting practices and procedures. (The fact that many practitioners lack these skills perhaps explains the high demand for computer-trained EDP auditors in today's job market.)

Although through-the-computer auditing is likely to be more thorough in evaluating the strengths and weaknesses of a given accounting information system, it must also be remembered that, at best, through-the-computer auditing is only a limited test of a complete accounting information system. Manually prepared test data are a particular issue here because they may not examine every data processing possibility, and thus some processing weaknesses may go undetected. An effort to improve audit techniques in this area is the **automatic generation of test data,** which enables the auditor to examine all possible program logic paths.[5] A number of commercial products are now available for this purpose.

EVALUATING THE EFFECTIVENESS OF CONTROLS

One of the most important responsibilities of the auditor is to probe an accounting information system for system weaknesses and report such weaknesses to management. For external auditors, this reporting is mandatory. *Statement on Auditing Standards No. 20,* which sets forth standards on Required Communication of Material Weaknesses in Internal Accounting Control, states, for example:

> . . . the independent auditor should communicate to senior management and to the board of directors or its audit committee (or the equivalent level of authority, such as a board of trustees) any material weaknesses that come to his attention during the course of his examination of the financial statements if such weaknesses have not been corrected before they come to his attention. Preferably, the auditor's findings should be communicated in a written report to reduce the possibility of misunderstanding. If the auditor's findings are communicated orally, he should document the communication by appropriate notations in his audit working papers.[6]

Although there is no similar legal requirement binding internal auditors to report system weaknesses to management, such a requirement is implicit in their positions within their companies. Thus, both internal and external auditors should present their findings to responsible organizational staff, and the auditors should accomplish this reporting on a timely basis.

Accounting textbooks have tended to emphasize the detection and correction of system weaknesses rather than system strengths. In a sense, this is logical because system deficiencies are almost always costly if they are not corrected,

---

[5] See, for example, Cori A. Clarke, "A System to Generate Test Data and Symbolically Execute Programs," *IEEE Transactions on Software Engineering* (September 1976), pp. 215–222.

[6] "Required Communication of Material Weaknesses in Internal Accounting Control," *Codification of Statements on Auditing Standards* (New York: American Institute of Certified Public Accountants, 1985), AU Section 323.08.

whereas system strengths can only contribute positively toward the efficient operation of accounting functions. However, the myth prevails that an accounting information system cannot have too many controls. It is important that this myth be dispelled. As we have noted during the last few chapters, specific system controls should be implemented only if their anticipated benefits exceed their anticipated costs.

One method by which an auditor can evaluate the desirability of controls for a particular aspect of accounting data processing is through a **hazard-and-loss analysis.** A table constructed in the course of this analysis is provided in Figure 12-4. Basically, the idea is to estimate the expected losses that might reasonably be anticipated if a given hazard or disaster were to occur, and to compare these expected losses with the cost of providing one or more controls to safeguard against the hazard. For those areas in which protection costs are less than anticipated losses, the auditor recommends that preventive controls be implemented. For those areas in which the costs of protection are greater than anticipated losses, the conclusion is that the risk is not high enough to warrant the expenditure for preventive controls and the auditor recommends that the specific controls not be installed.

To understand how expected losses are computed, examine Figure 12-4 in detail. The first column of the table identifies a particular type of hazard, the second column identifies the probability that this hazard will occur, and the third and fourth columns state low and high dollar estimates of losses resulting from the hazard (as provided by appropriate organizational management). Multiplying these low and high estimates of losses by the probability of such losses (column 2) provides the expected dollar losses of columns 5 and 6. Thus, for example, the table states that the probability of equipment malfunction is .05, that a low estimate of the losses involved in such a difficulty would be $100,000, that a high estimate of losses involved would be $250,000, and that the range of expected costs of

these losses would therefore be between $5000 and $12,500.

The seventh column of the table provides estimates of the costs of providing preventive controls that guard against a particular type of accounting difficulty. These values would either be provided by management or estimated by the auditor. Once the expected losses and the hazard-control costs have been ascertained, a decision regarding whether or not to install preventive controls for a particular difficulty can be made on a hazard-by-hazard basis. For those hazards whose control costs are less than the low expected loss (column 5), the benefits of the control exceed their costs and the controls should be maintained (or installed.) This is the case in the example of equipment malfunction, in which the total estimated costs of guarding against such an occurrence are $1000 but anticipated losses are at least $5000. In effect, $1000 worth of controls are "buying" (guarding against) at least $5000 worth of anticipated losses (or $5000 worth of benefits). Therefore, these controls should be installed.

Where the estimated costs of control exceed the high estimate of expected losses, the opposite conclusion would be reached and the controls should not be implemented. Thus, for example, in the case of power brownouts and failures, the control or safeguard (e.g., the maintenance of a standby generator) is too costly ($6000 compared with the high expected loss of $5000) and not worth its benefits. The control, therefore, should not be implemented.

The most difficult decision is when the estimated cost of controlling a particular hazard falls within the range of expected losses. In this instance, the costs of protection would be too great if losses were small, but well worth their costs if losses were high. In these situations, it is the auditor's responsibility to report such findings to management and not to make a recommendation. The decision must be made by management.

A hazard-and-loss analysis is not easy to pre-

Hazard (1)	Probability that Hazard Will Occur (level of exposure) (2)	Losses		Expected Losses		Estimated Hazard Control Costs (7)
		Low Estimate (3)	High Estimate (4)	Low (5)	High (6)	
Malfunctions and Human Errors						
Equipment	.05	$100,000	$ 250,000	$ 5,000	$ 12,500	$1,000
Software bugs	.10	10,000	100,000	1,000	10,000	2,000
Programmer error	.70	1,000	20,000	700	14,000	8,500
Computer operator error	.60	1,000	10,000	600	6,000	4,350
Maintenance	.90	1,000	10,000	900	9,000	2,550
User error	.90	1,000	15,000	900	13,500	500
General personnel	.50	1,000	20,000	500	10,000	1,000
Fraud						
Embezzlement	.05	10,000	100,000	500	5,000	250
Confiscation of files	.10	10,000	100,000	1,000	10,000	250
Wire tapping	.05	10,000	100,000	500	5,000	100
Program changes	.20	5,000	25,000	1,000	5,000	5,000
Power and Communications Failures						
Power brownouts and failures	.50	1,000	10,000	500	5,000	6,000
Power surges	.30	1,000	50,000	300	15,000	7,500
Electrical line failure	.70	1,000	20,000	700	4,000	1,000
Fire and Natural Disasters						
Fire	.07	100,000	250,000	7,000	17,500	1,250
Sabotage	.20	20,000	60,000	4,000	12,000	2,500
Earthquake	.01	500,000	3,000,000	5,000	30,000	2,750
Flood	.10	500,000	3,000,000	50,000	300,000	3,000
Lightning	.01	10,000	1,000,000	100	10,000	260

FIGURE 12-4   A hazard-and-loss analysis.

pare. Neither the costs of implementing specific accounting controls nor the losses that might occur in the absence of such controls are always identifiable. Furthermore, because the statistical probabilities required to compute expected losses are not given quantities but must be estimated subjectively, they are unsettling for decision making. A third problem is that certain occurrences may result in multiple losses—a set of circumstances at best only indirectly handled by the hazard-and-loss table. Finally, the entire analysis is somewhat questionable to the extent that it uses expected losses, computed as probabilities times anticipated losses, rather than full losses, for comparative purposes. For all these reasons, a hazard-and-loss analysis is not a definitive means of evaluating the desirability of specific internal controls. Rather, it is better considered one of the many tools that the auditor may wish to apply in this evaluation process.

AUDITING WITH THE COMPUTER

In addition to auditing *through* the computer in order to verify processing accuracy and the presence of adequate processing controls, auditors can use the computer to assist them in various other auditing tasks. Where an accounting information system has been automated, in fact, **auditing with the computer** is virtually mandatory because the accounting data are stored on computer media and manual access is impossible. However, there are many other positive reasons beyond the need to access computerized accounting data for using a computer in performing audit functions.

One of the most important reasons for auditing with the computer is that computer-based accounting information systems are rapidly increasing in sophistication. Soon, the *only* effective way to audit such systems will be with a computer. Figure 12-5 illustrates the increasing complexity of advancing computer technology. If auditing techniques are to keep up with this evolutionary process, the computer *must* be used as an auditing tool.

Another important reason why an accountant should audit with the computer is to save time. An early example of the use of a computer to assist in performing an audit is provided by Kenneth Cadematori.[7] His assignment was to audit a computerized payroll system, which included (1) verification of wage rates, (2) the checking of

[7] Kenneth Cadematori, "Computer Auditing," *New York CPA* (June 1959), p. 433.

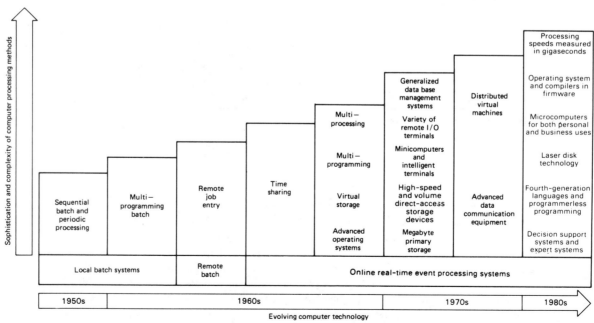

FIGURE 12-5 The evolution of computer technology has also increased the complexity of computer-based accounting information systems.

income tax and social security deductions, and (3) the validation of the accuracy of the payroll files with respect to employees who had left, new employees, and changes in pay rates. There were approximately 25,000 employees, whose payroll records were stored on three magnetic tape files. Cadematori estimated that it would have taken over 5000 hours to audit the payroll system manually. Instead, he spent approximately 300 hours to develop a computer program that accomplished the same thing. This program took only 2 hours to execute on the computer and, once written, was available for years of subsequent auditing use.

With prewritten auditing software (discussed later), this same task today would have taken little development time and much less computer execution time. The important point is the savings in time that results from the use of a computer to audit a computer-based accounting information system.

In discussing auditing with the computer (also called *computer-assisted audit techniques*), the American Institute of Certified Public Accountants defines audit software as follows:

Audit software consists of computer programs used by the auditor, as part of his auditing procedures, to process data of audit significance from the entity's accounting system. It may consist of package programs, purpose-written programs, and utility programs. Regardless of the source of the programs, the auditor should substantiate their validity for audit purposes prior to use.

- *Package programs* are generalized computer programs (also called *generalized auditing packages*) designed to perform data processing functions which include reading computer files, selecting information, performing calculations, creating data files, and printing reports in a format specified by the auditor.
- *Purpose-written programs* are computer programs designed to perform audit tasks in specific circumstances. These programs may

be prepared by the auditor, by the entity, or by an outside programmer engaged by the auditor. In some cases, existing entity programs may be used by the auditor in their original or in a modified state because it may be more efficient than developing independent programs.

- *Utility programs* are used by the entity to perform common data processing functions, such as sorting, creating, and printing files. These programs are generally not designed for audit purposes and, therefore, may not contain such features as automatic record counts or control totals.[8]

Auditing *with* the computer usually focuses on the verification of accounting data stored on computer files. Functional tasks along these lines are described in the following sections.

File Printouts

An auditor can print, or sequentially display on a CRT screen, the entire contents of a file with the use of a computer. Inasmuch as the amount of data stored on the typical computer file is likely to be voluminous, it usually makes sense for the auditor to print out the contents of a file on a selective basis. For example, when examining an inventory file, an auditor would probably not wish to see the file records for each inventory item. Instead, the auditor might examine only those records for inventory items whose purchase-cost field (indicating the per-unit cost of the item) exceeded a specified amount.

File Verification

An auditor can verify the contents of a file by performing such functions as testing for (1) internal consistency, (2) arithmetic accuracy, (3) cross-footing, (4) computing subtotals, (5)

[8] "Computer-Assisted Audit Techniques," *Codification of Statements on Auditing Standards* (New York: American Institute of Certified Public Accountants, 1985), AU Section 8016.05.

making record counts, and (6) searching for discrepancies. In *testing for internal consistency,* for example, an auditor can make sure that computer records are in proper, ascending order, compare redundant data fields of a single record (e.g., a product code and a product description in an inventory-file record) to make sure that the fields are in agreement, or compare record key numbers to make sure that they correspond to appropriate file-segment numbers. In *checking for arithmetic accuracy,* an auditor can have the computer reperform any arithmetic computations that were initially made when the record was created—for example, the extension of sales-ticket information within a sales file—to check for the accuracy and completeness of file data.

Cross footing requires that a set of figures be added twice, each time using a different classification of the data. For example, with a computer file containing information about the sales performance of marketing personnel, the sum of a month's sales by all sales representatives should equal the sum of the month's sales by regions. Where cross-footing is not successful, the auditor is obliged to report the discrepancy to management and, where the discrepancy is material in dollar amount, ascertain causes.

Computing subtotals and *making record counts* have been discussed at length in Chapter 10 and therefore need not be discussed again. This leaves *discrepancy reporting.* Here, the auditor looks for file records that appear to be exceptions to normal conditions, and requests the computer to print out such records on an individual basis. This type of auditing is an excellent example of the *management-by-exception principle* discussed in Chapter 2. Because the discrepancy report focuses attention only on those items that have failed a specific validity test, it is a very efficient auditing tool.

Most of the audit verification functions just described could be used by the auditor as a basis for preparing a **discrepancy report.** Some additional examples would include the detection of outdated records on a "current" transactions file,

the listing of accounts receivable records for customers whose balances exceeded specified credit limits, and the listing of payroll records for employees whose gross pay exceeded predetermined pay levels. In each case, the auditor would be concentrating only on those items that fell outside a predetermined range of "normal" values. The discovery of exceptional records does not mean that such records are necessarily in error. Rather, such discoveries simply form the *basis* of further inquiry because they are in some way unusual, and therefore reasonable targets for auditing scrutiny.

File Profiles

Another name for this use of the computer might be **data-reduction techniques** because the objective of preparing **file profiles** is to categorize the accounting data of a computer file into one or more classifications, or data "strata," for the purpose of reviewing the file's contents. An example is the preparation of an aging analysis of accounts receivable. Here, the strata categories are (1) the amount of accounts receivable not yet past due, (2) the amount of accounts receivable 1–30 days past due, (3) the amount of accounts receivable 31–60 days past due, and so on. Similar profiling of an inventory file, for example, might be used to identify which inventory items require the greatest use of the company's cash asset, which suppliers provide the bulk of the company's production supplies, which of the company's manufacturing divisions make the greatest use of certain types of raw materials, and which suppliers offer cash discounts of greatest advantage to the company.

In addition to one-dimensional data profiles, in which the contents of a computer file are sorted according to only one categorizing criterion, two-dimensional profiles are also possible. For example, a computer file of the Alan Company's sporting goods sales could be categorized by both product type and sales region, as shown in Figure 12-6. (For illustrative purposes, only a few of the company's products are included in

Alan Company Sales Profile: Product by Region

Month of June 1991

Product	Sales Region					Totals
	Northeast	Southeast	Midwest	Northwest	Southwest	
Baseball gloves	$ 6,431	$ 4,322	$ 3,652	$ 2,587	$ 3,451	$20,443
Baseballs	2,561	7,575	5,431	3,443	2,666	21,676
Golf bags	482	952	2,544	1,295	3,498	8,771
Basketballs	1,382	3,451	6,431	8,436	3,222	22,922
Footballs	4,631	3,321	974	2,139	1,389	12,454
Tennis balls	829	119	1,630	2,884	2,145	7,607
Totals	$16,316	$19,740	$20,662	$20,784	$16,371	$93,873

FIGURE 12-6   A two-dimensional profile of sales data for the Alan Company.

the figure.) A report of this type might be of great value to the vice-president of marketing because it would indicate those regional areas in which certain product sales were the strongest and, perhaps even more important, also indicate those regions in which certain product sales were weakest.

An auditor could also make good use of a report of this type. For example, where sales of a particular product were not being reported for a certain marketing region, the two-dimensional report would make this system deficiency obvious because the appropriate table element would be missing.

One especially notable case of profiling known to the authors was performed by an ironworks manufacturing company that supplied construction materials to local contractors. An audit of the company's business sales over a two-year period revealed the startling fact that 90% of the company's sales volume was concentrated in the hands of only 10 customers! Said one manager of the company, "We knew these guys were important, but none of us had any idea they were *that* important!" As a result of this discovery, the company streamlined its customer-support operations to make sure that these "top 10" clients got first-class service.

Statistical Sampling

Rarely is it manually possible or cost-effective for an auditor to examine 100% of the records stored on a computer file. Thus, where magnetic tape or disk files are involved, an auditor may also use a computer to select a statistically determined subset of the computer records for auditing purposes. The size of the sample varies according to the needs of the auditor and is determined through a variety of statistical methods.[9]

Systematic Sampling

Perhaps the most straightforward sampling procedure is the **systematic sampling** of every nth record on the computer file (e.g., every tenth accounts receivable record within the accounts receivable subsidiary ledger file). Where sequential files are involved, the systematic selection process is easy to program and the sample is relatively unbiased. (However, care must be taken that the file does not have a systematic storage feature that would defeat this systematic-

[9] For a nonmathematical treatment of sampling that conforms to *Statement on Auditing Standards No. 9,* see Carl Warren et al., "How to Implement Nonstatistical Sampling Under SAS No. 9," *Journal of Accountancy* (January 1982) pp. 62–72.

selection purpose.) Where a computer file has been arranged in segments—for example, where customer checking account data for multiple branches of a bank are stored in separate segments of a file—this sampling technique also automatically ensures that the number of elements drawn from each file segment is proportional to the size of the file segment.

Selective Sampling

Because the exceptions are sometimes of special interest to the auditor, audit sampling is often performed on a more discriminatory basis. **Selective sampling** enables the auditor to specify data conditions that automatically trigger the selection of special records for confirmation purposes. For example, an auditor will usually want to review the large, inactive accounts of a bank because these accounts are especially vulnerable to unauthorized manipulation. Other conditions under which selective sampling might wisely be used include those general ledger accounts having large or unusual balances, those computer records appearing to have unusual activity, those employee payroll records with an unusual amount of overtime, or those inventory records reflecting unusually high or low inventory turnover rates.

Discovery Sampling

A final relatively uncommon form of selective sampling is called **discovery sampling.** Here, the auditor looks for at least one example of a particular type of error—for instance, the creation of a fictitious accounts payable invoice or a fictitious payroll record. Discovery sampling is difficult to perform unless the auditor knows precisely what is required when searching the computer file. For this reason, and also because neither internal nor external auditors are concerned primarily with the detection of fraud when performing their normal audit functions, discovery sampling will only be implemented when special circumstances warrant it.

Confirmation Auditing

With **confirmation auditing,** the auditor verifies computer-file information by drawing a sample of file records and using some type of feedback investigation. If the auditor is primarily concerned with the monetary information of the computer records (as, for example, in the confirmation of the dollar balances of the computerized accounts receivable subsidiary ledger), this type of confirmation auditing is termed **estimation sampling for variables.** When nonmonetary information is the primary focus (e.g., in verifying that inventory receipts are correctly recorded), this type of confirmation auditing is termed **estimation sampling for attributes.**

The most common form of confirmation sampling is **positive confirmation,** in which a selected sample of accounts (e.g., credit-sales customers) are mailed polite letters of inquiry and asked to verify their account-balance information as shown in the letter. A return envelope is customarily enclosed for the convenience of the respondents. Usually it is possible to use a standard preprinted letter. The only computer-generated information to be added is the customer's name and address and, of course, the file-record information to be confirmed—for example, the customer's account-balance information available directly from the computer file(s) being audited.

With positive confirmation techniques, it is necessary to keep a list of which respondents reply to the confirmation letter and which do not. The maintenance of a separate computer file is convenient for this purpose because (1) the file can be created by the computer at the same time the initial sample is drawn, (2) the credit customers responding to the confirmation letter can automatically be "checked off" the list of accounts in the file if a machine-readable turnaround document is provided in the original letter of inquiry, (3) a second, follow-up letter of inquiry can be computer-generated in a manner akin to the first letter for those credit customers who have not responded by a specified date, and (4) the automated handling of the confirmation sample permits the auditor to examine a larger portion of the original computer file than could be achieved manually.

Negative confirmation is also possible. Here, credit customers are also sent a letter of inquiry but are asked to respond only if a discrepancy in their account-balance information is noted. The negative-confirmation approach is typically used for auditing receivable accounts with relatively small dollar balances. Because negative confirmation is based on our now familiar management-by-exception principle, it is often more efficient than a positive-confirmation approach: valuable auditor time, EDP staff time, and management time are devoted entirely to those accounts requiring investigation. Negative confirmation is also less expensive to perform because only the costs of the return mail for the discrepancies are incurred. Finally, with negative confirmation, it is not necessary to maintain a computer file as it was for the positive-confirmation process.

The biggest problem with negative confirmations is that an auditor cannot distinguish between those credit customers whose balances are correct and therefore do not respond, and those customers whose balances are incorrect but do not respond. Where the confirmation mailing is large enough or where there is a strong incentive for the "discrepancy account" to respond (e.g., a credit-sales customer discovers an unfavorable error or the customer is offered a reward for reporting the error), the negative confirmation may be quite satisfactory.

Beyond positive and negative confirmation sampling, there is also **physical confirmation,** which requires the auditor to verify account information using some physical process. Where inventory records are involved, for example, the auditor confirms the inventory account balances by actually visiting the warehouse site and counting the number of units of specific inventory items. In one famous case, auditors were required to examine the holding vats of a vegetable-oil company in order to verify this (liquid) asset of the company. The auditors climbed to the tops of huge holding vats, observed that they were full, and filed a positive report. They never realized that almost all the vats had fake bottoms and that the tanks contained less than 3 feet of oil.

Computer Utility Programs

Utility programs are computer programs that are usually supplied by computer manufacturers or software companies to perform common data-transfer and reorganization tasks. Auditors can use utility programs to perform the following tasks.

1. Printing or displaying the contents of data files or programs on a variety of output devices in order to examine their contents.
2. Copying files or programs or parts of files or programs for review work.
3. Merging computer files together—for example, combining two employee files into a single sequentially ordered file to see if there are corresponding employee records in each.
4. Sorting file records into a desirable arrangement using one or more record keys.
5. Preparing directory lists of files or programs that present such items as name, file type, recording mode, file format, creation date, change date, and program version.

Figure 12-7 illustrates the use of an interactive sort program that an auditor might use to examine a computer file of accounts receivable records. The left side of the screen contains requests for information required by the program to perform the desired sorting task. The auditor answers these requests by providing the information on the right side of the screen. Note that to provide these answers, the auditor must be able to identify the names of the record fields in the file under study. This information is obtained from the manual documentation about the file.

Once the auditor has input the information indicated to the display screen, the utility pro-

```
SORT REQUESTS                USER'S RESPONSE

ENTER FILE NAME:             ACTREC
ENTER FILE PASSWORD:         ABCD1234
FIRST DATA FIELD OF SORT:    BALANCE-AGE
SEQUENCE:                    DESCENDING
SECOND DATA FIELD OF SORT:   NONE
OUTPUT DEVICE:               PRINTER
FIELDS TO BE PRINTED:        ACCTNO, BALANCE, CUST-NAME, CUST-ADD,
                               BALANCE-AGE


SPECIFICATIONS CORRECT?      YES
  (YES OR NO)


PROGRAM WORKING . . .


SORT COMPLETED
OUTPUT IN PRINTER QUEUE
```

FIGURE 12-7 The display screen an auditor might see when using an interactive utility program to sort the computer records of an accounts receivable file.

gram asks the auditor if the input file specifications are correct. The auditor can correct any mistakes in the input information by typing "NO" and subsequently inputting alternative data. If the auditor types "YES," as indicated in Figure 12-7, the utility program will execute the sorting task specified and provide the output as a printed report.

Utility programs are quite helpful to an auditor. Since they are prewritten computer programs, they spare the auditor the task of developing the same programs from scratch. Utility programs can be used to examine an entire computer file. Thus, they enable the auditor to examine and reexamine computer records with a minimum of manual effort. A third advantage of utility programs is that they typically require very few instructions to operate. As a result, the auditor needs to know very little computer programming to use the program for the auditing tasks at hand. Finally, most utility programs require very little knowledge about the computer systems on which they run. Thus, an auditor need not be familiar with a specific computer system to use

the typical utility program available on it for auditing purposes.

Utility programs suffer disadvantages as audit tools. For one thing, they require some computer understanding on the part of the auditor. For another, their capabilities are limited to simple file-manipulation tasks—they usually cannot perform the detailed field examinations often required in the audit of computer file records. Finally, they are not generally effective in auditing random-access files, which must instead be read first by a special access program.

Computer Audit Packages

The need to audit accounting files with the aid of the computer has inspired the development of **generalized auditing packages.** These are prewritten computer programs that enable the auditor to review computer files without continually rewriting processing programs. Almost all large CPA firms have at least one such audit package, and additional packages can be acquired from various software suppliers.

Most generalized auditing packages are basically file-manipulation programs written in a high-level programming language such as COBOL. Some representative examples, together with selected operating characteristics, are identified in Figure 12-8. All of these audit packages are capable of performing basic data-manipulating tasks such as statistical sampling, mathematical computations, cross-footing, categorizing, summarizing, comparing fields, matching fields in separate file records, merging two files together, sorting records, and printing reports. In each package, the user can specify the input/output media used in the process (e.g., tape or disk). Audit packages can be used with sequential files and random-access files. However, not all auditing packages are currently able to handle the complexities of data base management systems.

Generalized audit packages are more alike than they are different. Primarily, the differences fall into three areas: (1) what computer hardware the software programs will run on, (2) the number of reports that can be generated in one pass through the computer file being audited, and (3) the number of data fields of a single computer file record that can be accessed and manipulated for auditing purposes. Of these differences, hardware requirements are probably the least re-strictive. This is because it is usually possible to reformat a tape or disk file so that the file can be processed on the hardware available to the auditor. Reformatting a file increases the time and difficulty of the audit, however.

The number of reports that can be generated, per pass, from a given file is important in terms of resource efficiency. The greater the number of reports that can be generated from a computer file in a single pass, the less computer time and other resources are required for the audit. There are only so many reports an auditor is likely to want from any given file, however, and thus, even the capability of producing two or three reports is often sufficient for auditing purposes.

The last difference, the number of data fields per record that the audit program can extract and manipulate, is probably the most crucial. Certain types of analysis require the use of many fields of data. If the data fields are not available because of this field limitation, the analysis cannot be performed. In commercial accounting applications, a typical computer record on an important master file is likely to have hundreds of data fields. Thus, the larger the number of fields that an audit program can access per record, the more data processing that can be performed in a single pass of the computer file.

Name	CPA Firm	Type of Hardware Required	Number of Output File Requests/Run	Number of Extractable Data Fields/Run
AUDITAPE	Deloitte, Haskins & Sells	IBM, Honeywell, Univac	—	12
AUDITPAK II	Coopers & Lybrand	IBM	9	No limit
AUDITRONICS 32	Ernst & Whinney	IBM, Honeywell (with conversions)	98	100
STRATA	Touche, Ross & Co.	IBM, Honeywell, Burroughs	20	99
SYSTEM 2190	Peat, Marwick, Mitchell & Co.	IBM, Honeywell, Burroughs	5	50

FIGURE 12-8 Names and selected operating characteristics of six generalized auditing packages.

MICROCOMPUTERS AND AUDITING

Microcomputers As Audit Tools

It is impossible to conclude our review of computer-based auditing techniques without also discussing the role of microcomputers as audit tools. This role has become so important that many auditors automatically use microcomputers in audit engagements and most CPA firms now have them in quantity. Space does not permit a complete listing of the many uses of micros in audit work. Here, we shall concentrate on five major uses: (1) spreadsheet applications, (2) computation and documentation, (3) direct auditing, (4) managing audit engagements, and (5) word-processing applications.

One important use of microcomputers is in running electronic spreadsheets. As noted in Chapter 3, almost anything that can be done on a manual worksheet can also be done faster, neater, and more accurately on an electronic spreadsheet. Typical uses of electronic spreadsheets for auditing purposes include (1) creating trial balances, (2) verifying depreciation schedules, (3) authenticating interest and lease calculations, and (4) performing budgeting reconciliations (for government accounting). Indirectly, these applications also assist auditors in such functions as making accounting consolidations and preparing summary financial statements.

A second important auditing use of microcomputers is as computation and documentation aids. Micros with prewritten computer software assist auditors by (1) computing optimal sampling sizes based on the client's individual population (i.e., file) parameters, (2) identifying several accounts that should appear as single items on financial statements, (3) comparing current-period financial data with the data of a previous period in order to identify those discrepancies that may warrant closer audit scrutiny, (4) computing financial ratios (e.g., current ra-tios), and (5) creating computer-generated document flowcharts.

A third use of microcomputers is for direct auditing purposes. For example, an auditor can use a microcomputer as an intelligent terminal to interact with application programs much like any remote user. Here, however, the auditor uses a micro to audit *through* the computer using the techniques discussed previously in the chapter. At least one software-development company has also recently announced a microcomputer-based expert system that uses artificial intelligence for evaluating the effectiveness of internal controls. Another typical auditing technique is for the auditor to *download* (i.e., transfer) file data directly to a microcomputer and then use a data base management program to audit with the computer (as discussed earlier). This latter approach avoids the formalities of auditors requesting the use of specific files from EDP personnel as well as the need for mainframe or minicomputer time.

A fourth auditor use of microcomputers is for controlling audit engagements themselves. For example, a number of software companies now sell programs that (1) prepare checklists of audit tasks that have been tailored to client needs, (2) track the hours of staff time used during an audit engagement, and (3) compute master budgets for audit engagements based on auditor inputs.

A final use of microcomputers in auditing is for running word processing software. As is true of other professions, the output of an auditor's work must be documented in written reports that are often reviewed by several auditor levels and sometimes require extensive revisions before being finalized. Word processing software enables auditors to draft working versions of their reports quickly, revise them as necessary, check documents for spelling and certain other types of errors, format them in pleasing styles, and, finally, print professional final reports. Many auditors now use integrated word processing software that enables them to use the capabilities of data base management software, electronic spreadsheets, and graphics software as well as word processing capabilities at the same time.

Auditing Electronic Spreadsheets

The value of electronic spreadsheets in an accounting information system was discussed in Chapter 3. The increase in the popularity of these tools introduces some new problems for auditors in terms of control over spreadsheet errors. It has been estimated that approximately one out of every three business spreadsheets contains an error of some type.[10] While errors may also be present in manual worksheets, the magnitude of an error is greatly increased by the power of electronic spreadsheets since a change to one value in the spreadsheet can change many dependent cells, footings, and cross-footings. In one well-known case, a manager of a Florida construction company inserted a line for $254,000 of costs, not noticing that the inserted line was outside the range to be summed for total cost. This mistake caused the company to underbid a job by that amount.

Since spreadsheet errors are likely to be pervasive and costly, special audit techniques should be used to guard against them. One thing that can be done by the developer of the spreadsheet is to visually inspect the spreadsheet, checking for anything that doesn't make sense. Auditors can also perform this function. They may choose to inspect graphs as well as spreadsheets since abnormalities are often more apparent in a graphical format. The auditor will also examine models used in the spreadsheet to see if they are logically consistent.

Increasing recognition of the importance of guarding against spreadsheet errors has prompted some software vendors to develop special **spreadsheet audit software.** This audit software may be included as part of the spreadsheet program itself (error checking routines) or sold as a separate program. The follow-

ing examples of spreadsheet audit software and the functions they perform illustrate their value in detecting spreadsheet errors.

1. The *Spreadsheet Auditor* from Computer Associates has the ability to highlight those cells that help create a designated cell's value or cells that use the designated cell's value in subsequent computations.
2. *Cambridge Spreadsheet Analyst* by Turner-Hall Publishing Company uses an assortment of edit tests to check a spreadsheet for internal data consistency.
3. Lotus Development Corporation's *HAL* shows where formulas are in a spreadsheet and how ranges are used in the formulas.
4. *Save Our Software* by Goldata Computer Services can be used for saving spreadsheets at timed intervals in order to avoid damage from loss of data.

This special audit software is useful in detecting many types of errors but is not foolproof. Regular audit techniques that test transactions are also necessary. It should be noted that in order to accomplish audit tasks for electronic spreadsheets, it is vital that all spreadsheets be well documented to provide an audit trail.

SUMMARY

This chapter has discussed the general topic of auditing from the viewpoint of a computerized accounting information system. Although both the internal and external auditor are concerned with the accounting information system, there are important differences in the goals of internal and external auditing. The external auditor's chief concern is that the financial statements of the company are fairly presented, whereas the internal auditor verifies adherence to company policies and procedures.

One important goal in the audit of an accounting information system is to evaluate its controls and to make recommendations where changes seem appropriate. Thus, the intent is not

---

[10] Steve Ditlea, ''Spreadsheets Can Be Hazardous To Your Health,'' *Personal Computing* (January 1987), p. 60.

to catch crooks. In the sense that both planned and surprise audits are feedback controls, however, the detection of fraud, should it exist and be material, is a natural by-product of the auditor's investigative responsibilities. It was also noted that a good audit trail is an absolute necessity in the audit process. Because computerized accounting tends to obscure this audit trail, the auditor must make sure that input transactions are traceable throughout the processing cycles. This is especially problematic where real-time data processing accounting systems are in use because remote input obscures the origin of some transactions and updating in place on magnetic disk files changes the status of the file records.

There are three approaches to auditing a computerized accounting information system: (1) auditing *around* the computer, (2) auditing *through* the computer, and (3) auditing *with* the computer. Today, and in most cases, auditing *around* the computer is the least viable investigative approach; the auditor must audit *through* the computer and *with* the computer to do a thorough job. The four primary methods of auditing *through* the computer involve (1) the use of specially prepared test data, (2) the validation of the computer-processing programs themselves to ensure the accuracy and integrity of the data processing logic, (3) the use of an integrated test facility, and (4) use of embedded audit modules. The test data examines both the processing capabilities of the accounting information system and the controls that safeguard these capabilities. The procedures involved in the validation of the computer-processing programs include (1) tests of program authorization, (2) control-total tests, (3) surprise audits of programs while they are in use, and (4) surprise substitution of auditor-controlled programs for those in use at the computer center. An integrated test facility enables the auditor to create fictitious accounts and audit an accounting information system on an operational basis. Finally, embedded audit modules allow auditors to capture and test audit data on a continuous basis.

An auditor may also be asked to evaluate the effectiveness of controls either already installed within the accounting information system or contemplated for the system when design changes are about to be made. A useful device for this evaluation process is a hazard-and-loss analysis report. For each set of potential hazards, the estimated costs of associated controls are weighed against the expected benefits from these controls. Although the computation of a single benefit figure is possible for each set of controls, this chapter has suggested the alternative computation of a *range* of benefit values, based on the likelihood of various hazards causing harm to the normal functioning of the accounting information system. We noted that the computation of such a range of benefits makes the ensuing analysis a little more complicated. On the other hand, such an approach is probably more realistic in terms of calculating the true "exposure" of the acounting information system to the various problems that might occur. The problems of multiple failings of control systems greatly complicates this analysis.

When an accountant audits *with* the computer, the computer is used as a tool to assist in the various audit processes. The computer can prepare printouts or displays of magnetic tape and disk files, verify the information on a file and report discrepancies on an exceptions basis, prepare statistical profiles of accounting data (e.g., an aging analysis of accounts receivable), assist in the preparation of confirmation letters to credit customers, and take any number of statistical samples for investigative purposes.

Many auditors are now using microcomputers as audit tools. This chapter discussed five major uses of microcomputers for auditing purposes: (1) spreadsheet applications, (2) computation and documentation applications, (3) direct auditing tasks, (4) managing audit engagements, and (5) word processing applications. Since microcomputers are very versatile, portable, and powerful computers, these applications are just representative of the many uses of microcomputers in auditing settings. However, outputs from microcomputers may need special audit attention. This chapter looked at auditing electronic spreadsheets as an example.

Many CPA firms make use of generalized audit packages. These are prewritten computer programs that perform various auditing tasks and therefore assist auditors in their examination work. Generalized audit packages typically require little computer programming skill by the auditor. An example of the use of one such package, STRATA, is provided in the supplement of this chapter.

Key Terms Your Should Know

attest objectives
auditing around the computer
auditing through the computer
auditing with the computer
audit trail
audit work sheet
automatic generation of test data
confirmation auditing
control-total tests of program authenticity
data-reduction techniques
discovery sampling
discrepancy report
EDP auditor
embedded audit modules
estimation sampling for attributes
estimation sampling for variables
external audit
file profile
filtering system (integrated test facility)
generalized auditing package

hazard-and-loss analysis
integrated test facility (ITF)
internal audit
internal transaction log
management objectives (in an audit)
negative confirmation
physical confirmation '
planned audit
positive confirmation
responsibility system of computer program
    development and maintenance
selective sampling
spreadsheet audit software
surprise audit
system control audit review file (SCARF)
systematic sampling
test data
test of program authorization
Trojan horse computer program

Discussion Questions

12-1. Distinguish between the roles of an internal auditor and an external auditor. Cite at least two examples of auditing procedures that might reasonably be expected of the internal auditor but not the external auditor. Which type of auditor would you rather be? Why?

12-2. "Inasmuch as the internal auditor works for the same company he or she audits, the question of objectivity is a moot point—no sane person is going to blow the whistle on his or her own people." Discuss.

12-3. Bob Hogan worked as an administrative assistant for Janet Cornelius Publishers. Part of Bob's responsibilities included the supervision of the petty cash fund. When the disbursements from the fund failed to match the voucher receipts for the third straight week, Bob's boss called him into her office,

told him that his work was "unsatisfactory," and informed him that a full external audit would be required of his department because of his negligence in handling the petty cash fund. Discuss this situation in light of the chapter materials.

12-4. In the text, it was stated that "auditing is like police investigations." In what ways would this analogy make sense? In what ways would this analogy not make sense?

12-5. Discuss some of the advantages of the surprise audit as opposed to a planned audit. What disadvantages are involved in the surprise audit?

12-6. Linda Carr Cosmetics distributes a full line of cosmetics for women, including facial makeup, eyeliners, beauty and skin creams, and so forth. Phil Morena was the company's treasurer. One evening, after consuming an excessive number of Manhattans at his favorite bar, Phil stated to an accountant friend,

"You know, ole buddy, you accounting people don't fool anybody. We have both announced and surprise audits at the company, but the only "surprise" in the surprise audit is how long the auditors will take to finish up. Last year when the auditors 'burst' through the door, for example, we even had baked a cake with their names on it. We went right to coffee instead of wasting time in our accounting office. The whole thing is just a big waste of time." Comment.

12-7. Why is a good audit trail important to both the internal and external auditor? How is the audit trail followed in a real-time processing environment?

12-8. Chia and Corter Enterprises manufactured "antique" furniture, which it then sold to distributors on both coasts. The inventory-control system kept track of raw materials on a real-time basis. Thus, the inventory records for such items as sheets of stock plywood and hardware were updated on a magnetic disk as issuances and receipts took place. Once a week, the contents of the inventory file were printed out to provide management with current information on the status of the major inventory items. The issuances and receipts slips for the previous week were then destroyed. Because the company had little room for excess paper and because the primary emphasis was on manufacturing and not on paperwork, it had been the practice to empty the week's issuances and receipts slips from the "inventory-activity" hopper once this report had been reviewed by management. Comment from the standpoint of the internal auditor and also from the standpoint of the external auditor.

12-9. Distinguish among the following terms, *auditing around the computer, auditing through the computer,* and *auditing with the computer.* Which is least effective in performing the audit of an accounting information system? Justify your answer, providing specific examples of an accounting application of your choice.

12-10. Describe the use of test data when auditing through the computer. Cite some examples of exception conditions that test data might discover in auditing an accounts receivable accounting information system.

12-11. Why is the assembly of test data more difficult when accounting data are accumulated for a "job stream" of computer programs? Provide an example.

12-12. Describe four methods by which an auditor might audit the computer programs of an accounting information system. Which method do you think would be the easiest to use? Which is the hardest? If you could use but one of the four methods described, which would you choose? Why?

12-13. The Hillside Company is an auditing firm whose auditors are notorious for conducting "merciless" surprise audits. The company's president, Mr. Jackson Suyderhoud, in fact, often bragged about the severity of his firm's scrutiny and the fact that none of the firm's surprise audits lasted less than a month. Said Mr. Suyderhoud, "Hillside prides itself on a thorough, complete job for its clients. If there is any fraud left undetected in a company we audit on a surprise basis, I'll eat it!" Comment.

12-14. Through-the-computer auditing has several advantages over around-the-computer auditing, but it also has some disadvantages. What are some of these disadvantages? For each disadvantage discussed, suggest a method of solving the problem, or at least lessening it, without abandoning the through-the-computer approach.

12-15. How does an auditor evaluate the internal controls of an automated accounting information system? How is the element of uncertainty handled in the audit examination?

12-16. Mr. Robert Sproule was the one and only internal auditor of a medium-size communications firm. The company used a computer for most of its accounting applications, and recently, several new software packages had been implemented to handle the increased volume of the company's business. To evaluate the packages' control capabilities, Mr. Sproule had performed a cost benefit study and found that many of the controls were potentially useful but not clearly cost-effective. The problem, therefore, was what to say in his report. After pondering this question for some time, he decided to recommend almost all the controls on the idea that a company was "better to be safe than sorry." Comment.

12-17. Mr. Joseph Taylor was the head of the accounting department at Pomona Graphics, Inc., a company that specialized in lettering, artwork, and other graphics-design work used in commercial business. Joe was familiar with computer audit techniques but felt a little uncomfortable about the distinction between auditing through the computer and auditing with the computer. Are there any differences? Explain.

12-18. The Pan Pacific Computer Company purchases independent computer components, which it then uses to manufacture custom-made computer hardware. Since it deals with a number of vendors, it has computerized the accounting procedures for its accounts payables. Describe how an auditor might use an integrated test facility to audit the accounting application.

12-19. Why do we say that use of embedded audit modules provides "continuous" auditing? What is contained in a SCARF?

12-20. How can the auditor verify the contents of a computer file? Describe as many tests as you can. Would the tests for a master file of accounts receivable be the same as the tests for the year-to-date transactions file in this same application? (You might wish to review the detailed discussion of this accounting application in Chapter 8.

12-21. What is a "profile," as might be generated from an accounting information file? What uses are made of these profiles? Provide an example of a profile that might be generated for each of the following accounting applications: (a) accounts receivable file, (b) accounts payable file, (c) sales file, (d) purchase order file, (e) employee payroll file, and (f) inventory file.

12-22. Discuss the advantages and the disadvantages of the statistical sampling techniques discussed in the chapter. What roles do confirmation techniques play in auditing? Are there any circumstances in which an auditor would choose *not* to confirm the contents of a computer file in one of the sampling techniques you mentioned?

12-23. What is a generalized auditing package? What makes it "general"? Why are there so many of them?

12-24. John Wells was an auditor working for the independent auditing firm of Pat Gilbert and Associates. John's training at the local college of business had been thorough and he loved his job because it gave him an opportunity to use his extensive computer skills in his chosen auditing profession. On one particular job, John was asked to verify the contents of several large computer files. "No problem," he said. "I can write a set of computer programs which can get the job done in a few weeks." His boss replied, "Why not use the auditing firm's SCAN program—it should do almost all the verification work for us. John replied that he liked to program and could write as many tests as necessary to get all the verification work done. Comment.

12-25. Describe three ways spreadsheet audit software can detect errors in electronic spreadsheets.

Problems

12-26. David Cuttler, Inc., specializes in the distribution of computer programs for automotive-parts stores. For its accounts payable operations, the company's vendor purchase invoice data are recorded on OCR cards as illustrated in the following diagram.

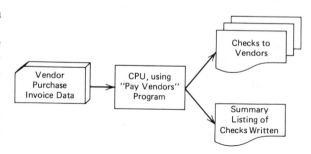

These cards are used to produce checks that are mailed to the vendors. Describe the steps an auditor might take in performing an around-the-computer audit of this accounts payable accounting application. What potential weaknesses in this processing system might not be detected by such around-the-computer auditing practice? What additional tests in a through-the-computer audit might be used to identify the system weaknesses you have outlined in your answer?

12-27. A CPA accumulates various kinds of evidence with which to base an opinion on the fairness of financial statements under examination. Among this evidence are the confirmations from third parties and written representations from the client.

Requirements

a. What is an audit confirmation?

b. What characteristics should an audit confirmation possess if a CPA is to consider it as valid evidence?

c. Distinguish between a positive confirmation and a negative confirmation in the auditor's examination of accounts receivable.

d. In confirming an audit client's accounts receivable, what characteristics should be present in the accounts if the CPA is to use negative confirmations?

e. List the information a CPA should solicit in a standard bank confirmation inquiry sent to an audit client's bank.

(AICPA Adapted)

12-28. The Foy Company recently had an outside consulting firm perform an audit of its data processing department. One of the consultants identified some hazards and their probability of occurrence. Estimates of the potential losses and estimated hazard control costs are also given in Figure 12-9.

| Hazard | Probability That Hazard Will Occur | Losses | | Estimated Hazard Control Costs |
		Low Estimate	High Estimate	
Equipment failure	.08	$ 50,000	$150,000	$2,000
Software failure	.10	4,000	18,000	1,400
Vandalism	.65	1,000	15,000	8,000
Embezzlement	.05	3,000	9,000	1,000
Brownout	.40	850	2,000	250
Power surge	.40	850	2,000	300
Flood	.15	250,000	500,000	2,500
Fire	.10	150,000	300,000	4,000

FIGURE 12-9   A hazard-and-loss table for the Foy Company.

a. Using this information, develop a hazard-and-loss analysis for the Foy Company.

b. If you were the EDP manager responsible for the Foy Company's data processing system, which hazard controls would you implement and why?

12-29. Bogle Billboards is an outdoor advertising company that maintains several hundred billboards and side-of-building advertising displays in and around Center City. The company recently computerized its accounting operations and one of its computer files is called BOARD1. This file describes all of its poster billboards. The data fields in the typical computer record for this file are listed below, along with character information.

Field	Type	Size (in characters)
Bilboard number (used as record key)	Numeric	4
Location (description)	Alphabetic	50
Direction board faces (e.g., NW)	Alphabetic	2
Illumination ("no" or code for type of lighting)	Alphabetic	2
Zone of town (commercial, residential)	Numeric	1
Exposure value (how many people drive by it per day)	Numeric	4
Date last scraped	Numeric	6
Data available	Numeric	6
Presently reserved for future? (Y or N)	Alphabetic	1

The file is arranged in ascending sequence by billboard number.

Inasmuch as outdoor advertising is the Bogle Company's primary business, information concerning its billboards is very important in determining the net worth of the company. Describe what an auditor might do to audit the BOARD1 file in order to verify the information contained on it. Be as thorough as possible.

12-30. The Gary Corporation is the publisher of *Computerweek Magazine,* a popular trade publication for microcomputer users. The company maintains subscriber information on a computer file. A typical computer record is illustrated in Figure 12-10. Numbers in the record format represent the number of characters in each field of the record.

From time to time, the Gary Corporation prepares copies of this file, which it sells to other companies interested in soliciting business from *Computerweek* readers. Thus, the file is itself an asset to the Gary Corporation. As an auditor, describe what tests you would perform to verify the information on this file. Be as thorough as possible.

12-31. Presented in Figure 12-11 is an order form used for Automated Information Systems, Inc., to sell its computer package called ASKIT. According to the information on this form

a. What is ASKIT?

b. What accounting tasks might such a programming system perform for a typical business organization?

c. Interpret the "operating characteristics" indicated in item A of the form.

d. Why would a user require cards as offered in item B instead of a magentic tape as offered in item A?

e. Would the typical commercial company use this

Last Name	First Name(s)								
Subscriber Name 30		Street Address and City 30	State 2	Zip Code 5	Date Subscription Expires 6	Type Code (1 = Business, 2 = Personal) 1	Number of Renewals 2	Blank 40

FIGURE 12-10   The record layout of the subscriber file of the Gary Corporation.

form as an invoice as suggested in the form? Why or why not?

CASE ANALYSES

12-32. *Linder Company*

Linder Company is completing the implementation of its new computerized inventory control and purchase order system. Linder's controller wants the controls incorporated into the programs of the new system to be reviewed and evaluated. This is to ensure that all necessary computer controls are included and functioning properly. He respects and has confidence in the EDP department's work and evaluation procedures, but he would like a separate appraisal of the control procedures by the internal audit department. Such a review should reveal any weaknesses or omissions in control procedures and lead to their immediate correction before the system becomes operational.

The internal audit department carefully reviews the input, processing, and output controls when evaluating a new system. When assessing the processing controls incorporated into the programs of new systems applications, the internal auditors regularly employ the technique commonly referred to as "auditing through the computer."

Questions

1. Identify the types of controls that should be incorporated into the computer programs of the new system.
2. Explain how the existence of the computer controls and their proper functioning are verified using auditing-through-the-computer techniques.

(CMA Adapted)

12-33. *Wholesale Cosmetics*

An auditor is conducting an examination of the financial statements of Wholesale Cosmetics, a distributor with an inventory consisting of thousands of individual items. The distributor keeps its inventory in its own distribution center and in two public warehouses. An inventory computer file is maintained on a computer disk and at the end of each business day the file is updated. Each record of the inventory file contains the following data.

- Item number.
- Location of item.
- Description of item.
- Quantity on hand.
- Cost per item.
- Date of last purchase.
- Date of last sale.
- Quantity sold during year.

The auditor is planning to observe the distributor's physical count of inventories as of a given date. The auditor will have available a computer tape of the data on the inventory file on the date of the physical count and a general-purpose computer software package.

Questions

The auditor is planning to perform basic inventory auditing procedures. Identify the basic inventory auditing procedures and describe how the use of the general-purpose software package and the tape of the inventory-file data might be helpful to the auditor in performing such auditing procedures.

AUTOMATED INFORMATION SYSTEMS, INC.
P. O. BOX 875
HANDSON, PENNSYLVANIA 19040

INVOICE-ORDER FORM FOR ASKIT

"AUTOMATED SEQUENTIAL COMPUTER TO INQUIRE TERMINALS"

AUTHOR: Dr. Johnathan Streffler
VERSION: x1.2 (September, 1991)

This program enables the user to test the contents of any magnetic tape or disk file. The program will indicate the status of a particular master file record, prepare frequency distributions of selected data according to preselected data fields, prepare cross-tabulations for aging analysis or salesperson reports, and perform simple linear regressions. Additional support, including error corrections and telephone conversations, is available at two levels to suit processing and support needs (see below, items C and D). Just fill in the form below.

CHECK ITEMS DESIRED BELOW

ITEM	DESCRIPTION	CHARGES
A	Basic programs in source language on magnetic tape, including sample data deck. The tape is a 9-track tape prepared on an IBM 370/168 with the following operating characteristics: DSB-DATA, RECFM = FB, LRECL = 80, BLKSIZE = 12960, DENSITY = 1600 bpi. (University rate: $1500; Nonuniversity rate: $3000)	$_____
B	Card deck instead of above magnetic tape. (University rate: $1550; Nonuniversity rate: $3050)	_____
C	Service level (1) for user support. Includes notice of errors, modifications, contributed changes to the program for users, and one year's membership in USER GROUP. (Yearly cost: $25)	_____
D	Service level (2) for user support. Includes all support identified in (C) above, plus 5 hours telephone service to answer specific questions and advise user clients on use of system. (Yearly cost: $200)	_____
	TOTAL AMOUNT	$_____

Your name: _____

Company name: _____

(Payment must accompany order)

Company address: _____

City/State/Zip Code: _____

SAVE: RETAIN THIS INVOICE FOR YOUR RECORDS. SEND US A COPY WITH TOTAL AMOUNT REMITTED. ORDERS OUTSIDE THE UNITED STATES AND CANADA MUST INCLUDE $15 ADDITIONAL FOR POSTAGE AND HANDLING.

FIGURE 12-11   An order form used by Automated Information Systems, Inc.

Organize your answer as follows:

Basic inventory auditing procedure	How general-purpose computer software package and tape of the inventory-file data might be helpful
1. *Observe the physical count, making and recording test counts where applicable*	1. *Determine which items are to be counted by selecting a random sample of a representative number of items from the inventory file as of the date of the physical count.*
	(AICPA Adapted)

12-34. Mark Tick, Auditor Extraordinaire*

The following paragraphs describe an audit of the computer center of the Jim Harmon Company, as performed by Mark Tick, Auditor Extraordinaire.

Driving up to headquarters, Mark could sense he was close to his destination, probably because of the neon sign on the roof indicating that the division's data center was located in the basement of the main building on the river side, which was four inches below flood level.

Mark donned his dark glasses, adjusted his CIA-emblazoned belt buckle, checked his supply of red and blue dual-pointed pencils, and, approaching the receptionist, asked for the data center manager. Without questioning Mark's identity or reason for being there, she informed him that the manager was away from the data center for a few minutes and told him to wait in the computer room.

"We have all our visitors wait here. They seem to be infatuated with the twinkling little lights on the console," she crooned.

"What's a console?" asked Mark.

* Adapted from Paul D. Johnson, "Mark Tick's Data Center Audit," *EDPACS* (June 1974), pp. 16–17. Copyright © 1974. Automation Training Center, Inc., Reston, VA. Reprinted with permission.

"It's the thing next to the 10-gallon gas-fired coffee urn," was her reply.

Mark walked toward the data center, down a hallway crowded with employees on their way to the cafeteria. On both sides of the hall he noticed, without interest, open racks of magnetic tapes labeled neatly with such titles as "Accounts Receivable Master File," "YTD Payroll Master," "Stockholder Records," "General Ledger Summary," etc. He paused for a moment to watch a pickup game of ring toss, noting that the lunch crowd had obtained the rings from the sides of magnetic tape reels.

"Ingenious people," he thought, "finding use for those worthless little rings."

As Mark walked through the keypunch room, he noticed employees drifting into the room and dumping loose source documents into a box labeled "Input." The keypunch operators were taking out handfuls of the documents for punching. Mark, ever alert, recognized that documents were selected in conformity with the generally accepted "Random LIFO" method.

Entering the computer room, Mark waved to the sole occupant, a machine operator who was hastily punching up cards and inserting them in a deck labeled "Payroll Source Code."

"Obviously, a valuable employee," mused Mark. "It's good to see someone putting forth some extra effort."

Mark poured a cup of coffee, and, as he started to count the petty cash, placed it on top of the 4-foot high stack of dust-covered disk packs. He wondered if the small amount of coffee he spilled would stain the floor as it drained through the disks. Noticing that the hot cup was causing the plastic top of the disk to bend a bit, he pulled a few cards from a deck labeled "Daily Sales Update," which was lying on the console, to use for a coaster.

Mark noticed that the mechine operator, having run the unnumbered payroll checks through the check signer, was separating the carbons from the checks. The fourth copy of the checks passed neatly into the fiberboard wastebasket as the machine hummed smoothly, giving the operator a chance to have a smoke and discuss with two mailboys who had just entered how much the various vice-presidents were being paid. Mark was impressed with the operator's concern for neatness, displayed by his having run the console log sheets through the shredder as soon as he finished the payroll run. Mark drew an appreciative smile from the operator as he quipped, "Nobody could make anything out of the gobbledy-gook the typewriter just printed, so better to destroy it than get buried under it."

Mark saw a box in the corner labeled "To Disaster File" and inquired, "What's this for?"

The operator explained that the maintenance department's foreman allowed the data center to store copies of important programs in the bottom of his locker.

"What type of programs?" asked Mark.

"Well, as far as I know, the only program over there is the one which causes the printer to use millions of little x's to form a nude girl saying "Merry Christmas!" was the reply.

Mark glanced at the bulletin board and immediately got an indication as to how well organized the data center manager was and that he was nobody's fool. The three signs that impressed him the most read:

- "Fairness is our motto. All input is processed on a first-come, first-served basis."
- "This is a data processing operation, not a delivery service. All output for the current week will be placed on the big table in the cafeteria before 4 p.m. each Friday. Help yourself."
- "To expedite processing and cut down on unnecessary paper shuffling, all documents rejected by the computer because of out-of-balance controls or invalid data will be immediately corrected and reentered by the machine operators."

The data center manager came in and introduced himself to Mark. He apologized for being away so long. He explained that he had had a hard time finding a garden hose long enough to reach into the data center through a hole in the plywood partition separating it from the adjacent boiler room.

"Good idea," Mark said approvingly. "A lot cheaper than buying fire extinguishers for the data center."

"Well, how does the place look?" the manager asked, perspiring slightly in the 90-degree heat.

"Great!" said Mark. "There will be only one item in my report. There is the serious matter of the 47-cent unexplained shortage in your $5 petty cash fund. Now, as soon as you buy me lunch, I can be off on my next adventure."

Question

Write a critique of this audit, indicating what company procedures and auditing procedures could stand improvement, and also indicating what you would recommend to correct the identified weaknesses.

12-35. Vane Corporation

The Vane Corporation is a manufacturing concern that has been in business for the past 18 years. During this period, the company has grown from a very small family-owned operation to a medium-size manufacturing concern with several departments. Despite this growth, a substantial number of the procedures employed by Vane Corp. have been in effect since the business was started. Just recently, Vane Corp. computerized its payroll function.

The payroll function operates in the following manner. Each worker picks up a weekly time card on Monday morning and writes in his or her name and identification number. These blank cards are kept near the factory entrance. The workers write on the time card the time of their daily arrival and departure. On the following Monday the factory supervisors collect the completed time cards for the previous week and send them to data processing.

In data processing, the time cards are used to prepare the weekly time file. This file is processed with the master payroll file which is maintained on magnetic tape according to worker identification number. The checks are written by the computer on the regular checking account and imprinted with the treasurer's signature. After the payroll file is updated and the checks are prepared, the checks are sent to the factory supervisors who distribute them to the workers or hold them for the workers to pick up later if they are absent.

The supervisors notify data processing of new employees and terminations. Any changes in hourly pay rate or any other changes affecting payroll are usually communicated to data processing by the supervisors.

The workers also complete a job time ticket for each individual job they work on each day. The job time tickets are collected daily and sent to cost accounting where they are used to prepare a cost distribution analysis.

Further analysis of the payroll function reveals the following.

1. A worker's gross wages never exceed $300 per week.
2. Raises never exceed $0.55 per hour for the factory workers.
3. No more than 20 hours of overtime is allowed each week.
4. The factory employs 150 workers in 10 departments.

The payroll function has not been operating smoothly for some time, but even more problems have surfaced since the payroll was computerized. The supervisors have indicated that they would like a weekly report indicating worker tardiness, absenteeism, and idle time, so they can determine the amount of productive time lost and the reason for the lost time. The following errors and inconsistencies have been encountered the past few pay periods.

1. A worker's paycheck was not processed properly because he had transposed two numbers in his indentification number when he filled out his time card.
2. A worker was issued a check for $1,531.80 when it should have been $153.81.
3. One worker's paycheck was not written, and this error was not detected until the paychecks for that department were distributed by the supervisor.
4. Part of the master payroll file was destroyed when the tape reel was inadvertently mounted on the wrong tape drive and used as a scratch tape. Data processing attempted to reestablish the destroyed portion from original source documents and other records.
5. One worker received a paycheck for an amount considerably larger than he should have. Further investigation revealed that 84 had been recorded instead of 48 hours worked.
6. Several records on the master payroll file were skipped and not included on the updated master payroll file. This was not detected for several pay periods.
7. In processing nonroutine changes, a computer operator included a pay rate increase for one of his friends in the factory. This was discovered by chance by another employee.

Question

Identify the control weaknesses in the payroll procedure and in the computer processing as it is now conducted by the Vane Corp. Recommend the changes necessary to correct the system. Arrange your answer in the following columnar format.

Weaknesses	Recommendations
	(AICPA Adapted)

12-36. *Ristan Enterprises*

Ristan Enterprises manufactures and sells colored plastic bottles. Ristan's financial and manufacturing control systems are completely automated.

Christine Field, Director of Internal Audit, is responsible for coordinating all of the operational and financial audits conducted by Ristan's Internal Audit Department. She has been reading and has observed how external auditors use computers in their audits. She believes that Ristan should acquire computer audit software to assist in the financial audits that her department conducts. For instance, a generalized computer audit program would assist in basic audit work such as data retrieval of computer files for review. It would also extract samples, conduct other tests, and generate balances, all of which would be printed out so that conventional audit investigation techniques could be used. She also could use an integrated test facility (ITF) which uses, monitors, and controls dummy test data. This data would be processed with the regular data. The ITF and the test data would check the existence and adequacy of program data entry controls and processing controls.

She has also read of computer-assisted audit software. While this software primarily is used to generate lead schedules, it is also useful in preparing analytical reviews, adjusting entries, and financial statements. However, for her department's basic function, she cannot identify applications that are not performed by the other two types of software.

Field intends to prepare a proposal recommending that Ristan acquire generalized computer audit software and an ITF.

Questions

1. Without regard to any specific computer audit software, identify the advantages and disadvantages to the internal auditor of using computer audit software to assist with audits.
2. Describe the steps to be followed by the internal auditor to use:
   a. generalized computer audit software.
   b. an integrated test facility, incorporating the use of dummy test data.
3. Would a computer-assisted audit software package provide any benefits to an internal audit department? Explain your answer.

(CMA Adapted)

12-37. Tenney Corporation

You are reviewing audit work papers containing a narrative description of the Tenney Corporation's factory payroll system. A portion of that narrative is as follows:

Factory employees punch time-clock cards each day when entering or leaving the shop. At the end of each week the time-keeping department collects the time cards and prepares duplicate batch-control slips by department showing total hours and number of employees. The time cards and original batch-control slips are sent to the payroll accounting section. The second copies of the batch-control slips are filed by date.

In the payroll accounting section, payroll transaction cards are key-punched from the information on the time cards, and a batch total card for each batch is keypunched from the batch-control slip. The time cards and batch-control slips are then filed by batch for possible reference. The payroll transaction cards and batch total card are sent to data processing where they are sorted by employee number within batch. Each batch is edited by a computer program, which checks the validity of employee number against a master employee tape file and the total hours and number of employees against the batch total card. A detail printout by batch and employee number is produced, which indicates batches that do not balance and invalid employee numbers. This printout is returned to payroll accounting to resolve all differences.

In searching for documentation you found a flowchart of the payroll system which included all appropriate symbols (American National Standards Institute, Inc.) but was only partially labeled. The portion of this flowchart described by the preceding narrative appears on page 451.

Questions

1. Number your answer 1 through 17. Next to the corresponding number of your answer, supply the appropriate labeling (document name, process description, or file order) applicable to each numbered symbol on the flowchart.
2. Flowcharts are one of the aids an auditor may use to determine and evaluate a client's internal control system. List advantages of using flowcharts in this context.

(ATCPA adapted)

CHAPTER 12 SUPPLEMENT

The Use of a Generalized Auditing Package

The use of a popular generalized audit package—STRATA (Touche Ross)—is illustrated in Figures 12-12, 12-13, and 12-14. First, the auditor must plan the flow of data processing. This is done with a logic flowchart as illustrated in Figure 12-12, which shows the computation of the age of accounts receivable transactions.

The auditor must next specify the data fields in each computer record to be accessed. This specification includes each field's location within the computer record, size, format, decimal place, and work name to be used when performing auditing computations and printing output information. Using STRATA, the auditor performs this task by using the *Data Field Selection* form illustrated in Figure 12-13.

Finally, the auditor indicates the calculations and other operations to be performed on the data fields—for example, subtracting cost from sales price to calculate gross profit. This is done using the *Calculate-Stratify* form illustrated in Figure 12-14. This form enables the auditor to indicate what calculations should be performed, and in what order. The resulting output is then used by the auditor to perform the desired audit task.

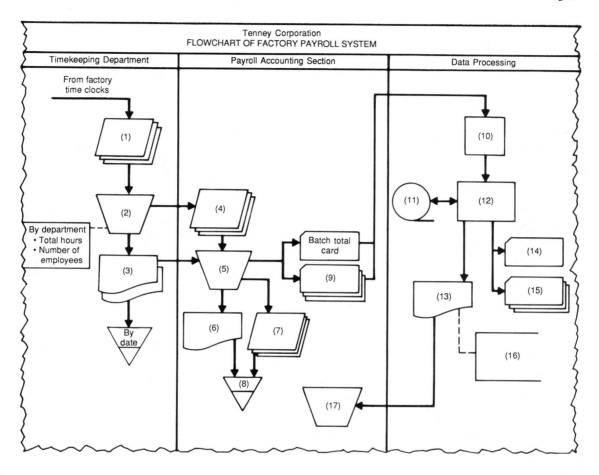

Tenney Corporation
FLOWCHART OF FACTORY PAYROLL SYSTEM

Timekeeping Department	Payroll Accounting Section	Data Processing

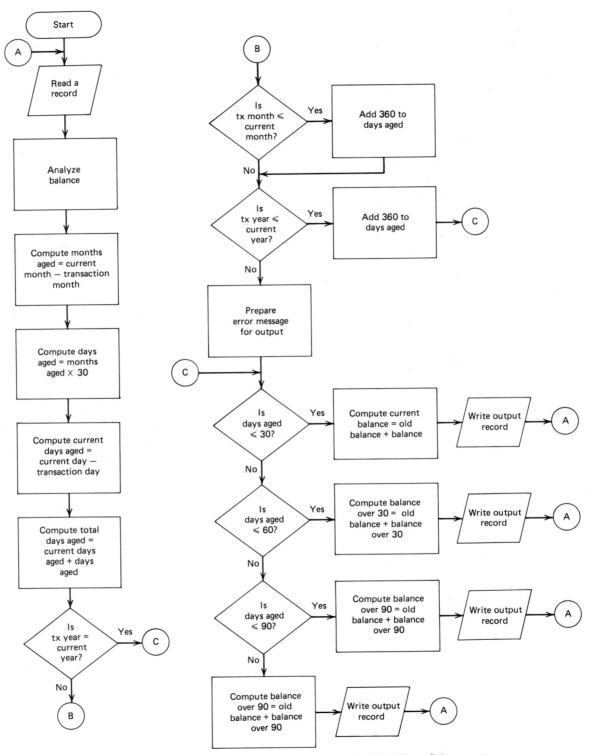

FIGURE 12-12 A program flowchart for use in implementing the STRATA auditing program.

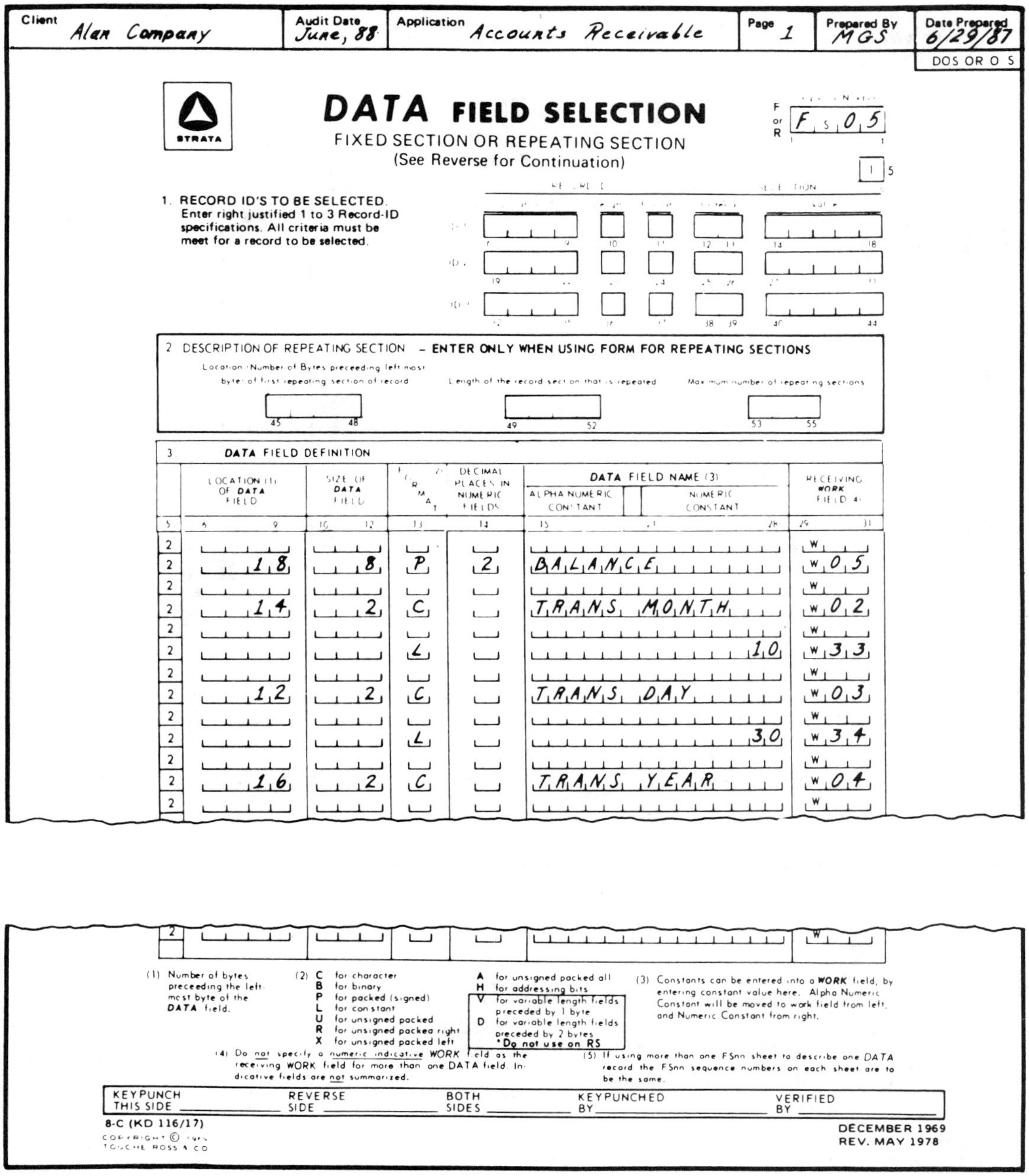

Client: *Alan Company* | Audit Date: *June, 88* | Application: *Accounts Receivable* | Page: *1* | Prepared By: *MGS* | Date Prepared: *6/29/87*

DOS OR O S

STRATA

DATA FIELD SELECTION

FIXED SECTION OR REPEATING SECTION
(See Reverse for Continuation)

F or R: *F S 0 5*

1. RECORD ID'S TO BE SELECTED. Enter right justified 1 to 3 Record-ID specifications. All criteria must be meet for a record to be selected.

2. DESCRIPTION OF REPEATING SECTION – ENTER ONLY WHEN USING FORM FOR REPEATING SECTIONS

Location (Number of Bytes preceeding left most byte of first repeating section of record) | Length of the record section that is repeated | Maximum number of repeating sections

3. DATA FIELD DEFINITION

Card	Location (1) of DATA Field	Size of DATA Field	Format (2)	Decimal Places in Numeric Fields	DATA Field Name (3): Alpha Numeric Constant / Numeric Constant	Receiving WORK Field (4)
2						W
2	18	8	P	2	BALANCE	W05
2						W
2	14	2	C		TRANS MONTH	W02
2						W
2			L		10	W33
2						W
2	12	2	C		TRANS DAY	W03
2						W
2			L		30	W34
2						W
2	16	2	C		TRANS YEAR	W04
2						W
2						W

(1) Number of bytes preceeding the left-most byte of the DATA field.

(2) C for character; B for binary; P for packed (signed); L for constant; U for unsigned packed; R for unsigned packed right; X for unsigned packed left; A for unsigned packed all; H for addressing bits; V for variable length fields preceded by 1 byte; D for variable length fields preceded by 2 bytes. *Do not use on RS

(3) Constants can be entered into a WORK field, by entering constant value here. Alpha Numeric Constant will be moved to work field from left, and Numeric Constant from right.

(4) Do not specify a numeric indicative WORK field as the receiving WORK field for more than one DATA field. Indicative fields are not summarized.

(5) If using more than one FSnn sheet to describe one DATA record the FSnn sequence numbers on each sheet are to be the same.

KEYPUNCH THIS SIDE ____ REVERSE SIDE ____ BOTH SIDES ____ KEYPUNCHED BY ____ VERIFIED BY ____

8-C (KD 116/17)
COPYRIGHT © 19?? TOUCHE ROSS & CO

DECEMBER 1969
REV. MAY 1978

FIGURE 12-13 An example of the STRATA Data Field Selection Form. This form, which is part of a generalized audit package, is used to specify the data fields in each file record to be accessed and the calculation variables (receiving work fields) to be used in the audit calculations.

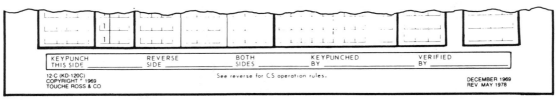

FIGURE 12-14 The STRATA Calculate-Stratify form used to indicate what calculations should be performed with the file data.

REFERENCES AND RECOMMENDED READINGS FOR PART THREE

Allen, Brandt. "The Biggest Computer Frauds: Lessons for CPA's." *The Journal of Accountancy* 143 (May 1977), pp. 52–63.

American Accounting Association. "Report of the Committee on Concepts and Standards-Internal Planning and Control." In *Committee Reports: Supplement to Vol. XLIX of The Accounting Review.* Sarasota, FL: 1974, pp. 79–94.

American Institute of Certified Public Accountants. *Audit Approaches for a Computerized Inventory.* New York: AICPA, 1980.

American Institute of Certified Public Accountants. *Computer Assisted Audit Techniques.* New York: AICPA, 1979.

American Institute of Certified Public Accountants. *Considerations in Electronic Funds Transfer Systems.* New York: AICPA, 1978.

American Institute of Certified Public Accountants. *Codification of Statements on Auditing Standards, Numbers 1 to 49.* New York: AICPA, 1985.

Arens, Alvin A., and Loebbecke, James K. *Auditing: An Integrated Approach,* 2nd ed. Englewood Cliffs, NJ: Prentice-Hall, 1984.

Arthur Andersen and Company. *A Guide for Studying and Evaluating Internal Accounting Controls.* Chicago: 1978.

Atkins, William. "Jesse James at the Terminal." *Harvard Business Review* 63 (July–August 1985), pp. 31–37.

Auditing Standards Committee, American Institute of Certified Public Accountants. *The Effects of EDP on the Auditor's Study and Evaluation of Internal Control.* Statement on Auditing Standards No. 3, New York: AICPA, 1974.

Baab, John G., Paroby, Stephen, M., and Marquard, William H. "A Three-Dimensional Look at Computer Fraud." *Financial Executive* 52 (October 1984), pp. 21–28.

Baird, Byrin N., and Michenzi, Alfred R. "Impact of the Foreign Corrupt Practices Act." *The Internal Auditor* 40 (June 1983), pp. 20–22.

Banks, Ira D. "Internal Control of On-Line and Real Time Computer Systems." *Management Accounting* 58 (June 1977), pp. 28–30.

Bequai, August. *How to Prevent Computer Crime.* New York: Wiley, 1983.

BloomBecker, Jay (Ed.). "Computer Crime, Computer Security, Computer Ethics." National Center for Computer Crime Data, First Annual Statistical Report (Los Angeles: National Center for Computer Crime Data, 1986).

BloomBecker, Jay Buck. "New Federal Law Bolsters Computer Security Efforts." *Computerworld* 20 (October 27, 1986), pp. 53–66.

BloomBecker, Jay Buck. "Computer Security—For the People." *Computer Society* 14 (Fall 1985), pp. 12–15.

Borthick, Faye A. "Audit Implications of Information Systems." *The CPA Journal* 56 (April 1986), pp. 40–46.

Briner, R. "Database Security." *Management Accounting* 62 (October 1981), pp. 10–11.

Burch, John G., and Sardinas, J. *Computer Control and Audit: A Total Systems Approach.* New York: Wiley, 1978.

Buss, M. D. J., and Salerno, L. M. "Common Sense and Computer Security." *Harvard Business Review* 62 (March–April 1984), pp. 112–121.

Campitelli, Vincent A. "Is Your Computer a Soft Touch?" *Financial Executive* 52 (February 1984), pp. 10–14.

Carlow, Alan, and Johnson, Bart. "Overcoming the Mystique in EDP Auditing." *Management Accounting* 66 (August 1984), pp. 30–37.

Cash, James, I., Jr., Bailey, Andrew D., Jr., and Whinston, Andrew B. "A Survey of Technques for Auditing EDP-Based Accounting Information Systems." *The Accounting Review* 52 (October 1977), pp. 813–832.

Cerullo, Michael. "Application Controls for Computer-Based Systems." *Cost and Management* 56 (June 1982), pp. 18–23.

Cerullo, Michael, and Shelton, F. A. "Analyzing the Cost Effectiveness of Computer Controls and Security." *The Internal Auditor* 38 (October 1981), pp. 30–37.

Chalmers, Leslie S. "Computer Viruses, the Security Act, and Integrity Security." *Journal of Accounting & EDP* 4 (Fall 1988), pp. 60–62.

Chester, Jeffrey A. "Corporate US Security Up for Grabs?" *Infosystems* 35 (January 1988), pp. 24–25.

Chrysler, Earl. "Impact of Computer Crime on EDP Audits." *Journal of Systems Management* 38 (November 1987). pp. 33–42.

Chrysler, Earl and Keller, Donald E. "Preventing Computer Fraud." *Management Accounting* 68 (April 1988), pp. 28–33.

Cirtin, Arnold. "Controls for Data Base Systems." *The Internal Auditor* (June 1982), pp. 33–35.

Clowes, Kenneth W. *EDP Auditing.* Toronto: Holt, Rinehart and Winston of Canada, Ltd, 1988.

Collier, Paul, Dixon, Rob, and Marston, Claire. "Computer Fraud: Interim Research Findings." *Management Accounting (UK)* 66 (October 1988), pp. 24–25.

Compton, Ted R. "A Cost-Effective Internal Control System—Management's Dilemma." *Journal of Systems Management* 36 (May 1985), pp. 21–25.

Davis, Gordon B., Adams, Donald L., and Schaller, Carol A. *Auditing and EDP,* 2nd ed. New York: AICPA, 1983.

Davis, Gordon G., and Weber, Ron. "The Audit and Changing Information Systems." *The Internal Auditor* 40 (August 1983), pp. 34–38.

Davis, Keagle W., and Perry, William E. *Auditing Computer Applications.* New York: Wiley, 1982.

EDP Auditors Association, Inc. *Control Objectives*. Hanover Park, IL: EDPAA, 1975.

Farmer, Dale F. "Confessions of an EDP Auditor." *Datamation* 29 (July 1983), pp. 193–198.

Fazzolari, Salvatore D. "How Harsco Integrates Financial Auditing." *Management Accounting* 69, (January 1988), pp. 28–30.

Fialka, John J. "Study Sheds Light on Vulnerability of Computers to Electronic Spying." *The Wall Street Journal.* October 18, 1985, p. 31E.

Forcht, Karen A. "The Special Considerations of Computer Security in the Microcomputer Environment." *Computer Crime Digest* 5 (January 1987), pp. 1–5.

Garsombke, H. Perrin, and Cerullo, Michael, "Auditing Advanced Computerized Systems in the Future." *The EDP Auditor* 2 (1984), pp. 1–11.

Goldner, Gary. "EDP Auditing with a Small Staff." *Journal of Accounting and EDP* 2 (Winter 1987), pp. 36–42.

Gurlwy, Katy. "Auditors Wield Growing Clout." *Computerworld* 22 (August 1, 1988), p. 59.

Holly, Charles L., and Miller, Fredrick. "Auditing the On-Line Real-Time Computer System." *Journal of Systems Management* 34 (January 1983), pp. 14–19.

Holly, Charles L., and Reynolds, Keith. "Audit Concerns in an On-Line Distributed Computer Network." *Journal of Systems Management* 35 (June 1984), pp. 32–36.

Honan, Patrick. "Data Security." *Personal Computing* 11 (January 1987), pp. 101–107.

Hooper, Paul, and Page, John. "Internal Control Problems in Computer Systems." *Journal of Systems Management* 33 (December 1982), pp. 22–27.

Jancura, Elise G., and Boos, Robert V. *Establishing Controls and Auditing the Computerized Accounting System*. New York: Van Nostrand Reinhold, 1981.

Johnson, Jeffrey A. and Needle, Sheldon. "Automated Work Papers: A New Audit Tool." *Journal of Accountancy* 160 (August 1985), pp. 123–135.

Johnson, R. E. "Logical and Physical Data Protection." *Infosystems* 35 (March 1988), p. 26.

Johnson, R. E. "The People in the Black Hats." *Infosystems* 34 (September), p. 35.

Johnson, R. E. "Protection on the PC." *Infosystems* 32 (June 1985), pp. 92–94.

Joyce, Edward J. "Software Viruses: PC-Health Enemy Number One." *Datamation* 34 (October 15, 1988), pp. 27–30.

Juris, Robbin. "EDP Auditing Lessens Risk Exposure." *Computer Decisions* 18 (July 15, 1986), pp. 36–42.

Karabin, Stephen. "Cardinal Sins of the PC Environment." *Internal Auditing* 4 (Fall 1988), pp. 78–80.

Kneer, Dan C., and Lampe, James C. "Distributed Data Processing: Internal Control Issues and Safeguards." *EDPACS* 10 (June 1983), pp. 1–14.

Kochar, Ips. "On-Line Security Strategies for Inter-Connected Computer Systems." *Journal of Systems Management* 35 (November 1984), pp. 32–35.

Lampe, James C., and Kneer, Dan C. "Audit Implications of Distributed Data Processing." *The EDP Auditor* 3 (1984), pp. 39–50.

Lee, Mary M. "The Challenge of EDP Auditing," *Management Accounting* 68 (March 1988), pp. 52–53.

LeGore, Laurence B. "Smoothing Data Base Recovery." *Datamation* 25 (January 1979), pp. 177–180.

Leong, Clara J. "Procedures and Controls For Micro-Based Accounting Systems." *Journal of Accountancy* 158 (January 1986), pp. 110–113.

Li, David H. "Preventive Controls and Detective Controls in a Computer Environment." *The EDP Auditor,* (Spring 1983), pp. 21–28.

Lobel, Jerome, "Planning a Secure System." *Journal of Systems Management* 27 (July 1976), pp. 14–19.

Loebbecke, James K., Mullarkey, John F., and Zuber, George R. "Auditing in a Computer Environment." *Journal of Accountancy* 155 (January 1983), pp. 68–78.

Mair, William, C., Wood, Donald R., and Davis, Keagle W. *Computer Control & Audit*. Altamonte Springs, FL: Institute of Internal Auditors, 1978.

Martin, James, *Security, Accuracy, and Privacy in Computer Systems*. Englewood Cliffs, NJ: Prentice-Hall 1973.

Mastromano, Frank M. "The Changing Nature of the EDP Audit." *Management Accounting* 62 (July 1980), pp. 27–30.

Moscove, Stephen A. "Is Computer Fraud a Fact of Business Life?" *The National Public Accountant* 23, 8 (August 1987), pp. 16–22.

Moscove, Stephen A. "Legal Theories on Programmer Liability." *Journal of Systems Management* 36 (June 1985), pp. 20–28.

Moskowitz, Robert, "Spreadsheets' Quiet Horror." *Computerworld* 21 (May 4, 1987), pp. 35–40.

Moulton, Rolf T. "Network Security." *Datamation* 29 (July 1983), pp. 121–124.

Nadel, Robert B. "Computer Auditing—Has Its Time Come?" *The CPA Journal* 57 (March 1987), pp. 24–29.

Norman, Adrian R. D. *Computer Insecurity.* New York: Chapman and Hall, 1983.

O'Donoghue, Joseph. "The 1986 Mercy College Report on Computer Crime in the Forbes 500 Corporations." Mercy College Internal Report.

Paroby, Stephen M. and Barrett, William J. "Preventing Computer Fraud—A Message for Management" *The CPA Journal* 57 (November 1987), pp. 36–49.

Pleier, Joseph R. "Computer-Assisted Auditing" *The Internal Auditor* 11 (1984), pp. 13–20.

Porter, W. Thomas, and Perry, William E. *EDP Controls and Auditing,* 4th ed., Boston: Kent, 1985.

Pound, G. D. "A Review of EDP Auditing." *Accounting and Business Research* (Spring 1978), pp. 52–60.

Render, Barry, Coffinberger, Richard, Gardner, Ella P., Ruth, Stephen R., and Samuels, Linda. "Perspectives on Computer Ethics and Crime." *Business* (January–March 1986), pp. 30–36.

Ried, Gordon L. "Decentralizing Data Security." *Datamation* (December 1, 1984), pp. 147–148.

Rothstein, Philip J. "Up and Running: How to Ensure Disaster Recovery." *Datamation* 34 (October 15, 1988), pp. 86–96.

Simkin, Mark. "How to Validate Spreadsheets." *Journal of Accountancy* 164 (December 1987), pp. 130–138.

Simkin, Mark. "Nevada's Computer Crime Law." *Nevada Review of Business and Economics* (Spring 1984), pp. 6–9.

Simkin, Mark. "Is Computer Crime Important?" *Journal of Systems Management* 33 (May 1982), pp. 34–38.

Simkin, Mark. "Computer Crime: Lessons and Direc-

tion." *The CPA Journal* 51 (December 1981), pp. 10–14.

Smith, Frank S., III. "Encryption: What It Is and What It Can Do." *Journal of Accounting & EDP* 4 (Fall 1988), pp. 24–32.

Snyders, Jan. "The Fire Behind the Smoke." *Infosystems* 34 (April 1987), pp. 44–48.

Sorkin, Horton Lee, Harvey, Barron, and Hicks, Margaret. "Four Vital Control Areas in Complex EDP Environments." *Internal Auditing* 4 (Fall 1988), pp. 26–33.

Spencer, Cheryl. "Weeding Out Worksheet Errors." *Personal Computing* 10 (November 1986), pp. 160–162.

Strehlo, Christine. "The Well Protected Network." *Personal Computing* 12 (January 1988), pp. 135–141.

Watne, Donald A., and Turney, Peter B. *Auditing EDP Systems.* Englewood Cliffs, NJ: Prentice-Hall, 1984.

Watt, Pat. "The Power—and Pitfalls—of Electronic Spreadsheets." *Government Finance Review* 1 (August 1985), pp. 32–33.

Weber, Ron. "Audit Trail System Support in Advanced Computer-Based Accounting Systems." *The Accounting Review* 57 (April 1982), pp. 311–325.

Weber, Ron. *EDP Auditing: Conceptual Foundations and Practice.* New York: McGraw-Hill, 1982.

Weiss, Ira R. "Auditability of Software: A Survey of Techniques and Costs." *The EDP Auditor* 1 (Spring 1983), pp. 29–44.

Wilkinson, Joseph W. "Evaluating Controls in Advanced Computer Systems." *The Internal Auditor* 35 (October 1978), pp. 53–59.

Wilson, Glenn T. "Computer Systems and Fraud Prevention." *Journal of Systems Management* 35 (September, 1984), pp. 36–39.

Wolfe, Christopher, ed. "Virus Protection for Microcomputer Systems." *Journal of Accountancy* 166 (December 1988), pp. 123–126.

Wood, Charles C. "Countering Unauthorized Systems Accesses." *Journal of Systems Management* 35 (April 1984), pp. 26–28.

Zimmerman, Joel S. "PC Security: So What's New?" *Datamation* 31 (November 1, 1985), pp. 86–92.

PART FOUR

Systems Studies for Effective Accounting Information Systems

Accounting information is often required by an organization's management when making business decisions. For this information to be readily available, an accurate and responsive accounting information system must exist within the organization. Up to this point, the text has stressed the accounting information system's contributions to an efficient and effective business information system. Part One discussed the accounting information system's vital role in managerial planning and controlling activities, Part Two examined the accounting information system's relevant role in collecting, recording, and storing financial-oriented data needed for managerial decision making, and Part Three analyzed the accounting information system's important role relating to internal control systems. Part Four will tie together many of the previous chapters' materials by examining in considerable depth the work involved when performing a **systems study,** the purpose of which is to develop efficient and effective information systems within organizations.

A systems study is often performed because of problems in a company's present information system, which result in a lack of good decision-making information for management. These problems are frequently the direct or indirect result of weaknesses in the flow of accounting information through the system. Consequently, accountants normally participate in performing a systems study to help an organization solve its problems associated with inefficient information flows to management for its decision making. Part Four will thus examine the activities that are essential when performing a systems study of a company's information systems problems,

459

stressing accountants' functions in systems study work. Much of the discussion assumes that accountants are working for a consulting firm and they are participating in systems studies of companies' information systems problems. Furthermore, the emphasis will be on a systems study to convert an organization's manual accounting information system to a computerized system.

The first two steps in a systems study, called **planning** and **analysis,** will be discussed in Chapter 13. From analysis, strengths and weaknesses in a company's present system are identified. The analysis work leads to the **design** of changes into the company's system so that previously identified weaknesses can be eliminated. The design of changes into a system will be examined in Chapter 14. Once design changes have been planned, these changes must be incorporated into the company's system. The subject of **implementing** systems revisions and then operating the newly implemented system is the topic of Chapter 15. This chapter also discusses the work involved in analyzing the effectiveness of a newly implemented business information system (i.e., **follow-up studies**) and then making additional systems modifications, if necessary.

13 Systems Study: Planning and Analysis

Among the important questions that you should be able to answer after reading this chapter are:

1. What is a *management consulting team* and what is a *steering committee?*
2. What role should auditors play in a systems study?
3. What are the procedures and techniques used to survey an existing information system and analyze the survey results?
4. Is it necessary to understand and consider human behavior in systems study work?
5. Because managerial employees should already be familiar with their company's strong and weak points, isn't it a waste of time and money to have a consultant perform a systems survey of the company's strengths and weaknesses?

INTRODUCTION

One common cause of an organization's operating problems is a breakdown in its accounting information system. This breakdown is the result of such things as delays in communicating financial information to specific managers who need the information for decision making, or certain managers never receiving the types of financial information feedback necessary for effective decision making. Obviously, business problems can result from factors other than the failure of the accounting information system (e.g., negative attitudes by employees toward their work environment, caused by boring jobs or the lack of responsibility). However, because a large majority of an organization's business decisions are based on accounting information, the failure of an accounting information system to provide relevant and timely managerial information typically will lead to inefficient organizational activities, thereby causing problems for the company.

Because many business problems result from a company's lack of effective decision-making information being provided by the accounting information system, accountants (especially managerial accountants) are actively involved in helping organizations solve their current information systems problems. It is important, therefore, for today's accountants to have a thorough understanding of how to perform a systems study of an organization's information problems so that they can make positive recommendations to solve these problems.

A systems study is broken down into phases that constitute a system development life cycle. There are four such phases: Planning, analysis, design,

and implementation and follow-up. This chapter discusses the planning and analysis phases of a systems study. Chapter 14 will examine the systems study design phase, and Chapter 15 will discuss the remaining phase, implementation and follow-up. After studying these three chapters, you should have a good understanding of how to perform a systems study of an organization's information systems problems.

Because this text has emphasized the computer's role in accounting information systems, the discussion in Chapters 14 and 15 will focus on the conversion of a company's manual data processing system to a computerized data processing system. Naturally, not all systems studies will involve such a conversion. For example, a company may already have a batch processing computer system. The company's management may hire a consulting firm to perform a systems study that analyzes the feasibility of converting to an online, real-time system for processing its accounting data. However, concentrating on the conceptual and procedural aspects of a major conversion from a manual to a computerized data processing system in Chapters 14 and 15 provides a much broader coverage of the systems study process.

It should also be noted that the four phases discussed may be accomplished differently in small versus large organizations and that some approaches to system development organize the systems study phases differently. For example, while this book stresses the use of management consultants and steering committees, in small organizations the entire systems study may be performed by outsiders. Alternatively, some large organizations have sufficient expertise "in-house" to perform their own systems study without the help of outside consultants.

THE SYSTEM DEVELOPMENT LIFE CYCLE

As discussed in Chapter 1, a systems study involves four major steps (or phases). These are:

1. *Planning* for the company's information systems function. This involves organizing the systems study team, hiring consultants, and strategic planning for information systems study.

2. The *analysis* of a company's current operating system to determine information needs and the system's strong and weak points.

3. The *design* of changes into the company's current system so that the system's weak points

462

can be eliminated (or at least minimized) and the strong points maintained.

4. The *implementation* and *follow-up* of the newly designed system. Implementation includes acquisition of resources for the new system, as well as initial operation. Follow-up is an ongoing process to determine whether previous weaknesses (or problems) have been eliminated and whether or not any new problems have arisen.

These four steps encompass the system development life cycle (SDLC) of a business information system. As Figure 13-1 illustrates, this life cycle reflects the time span during which a company's system is operating on a daily basis and is subsequently revised as a result of some problem (or problems). Each time a newly revised system takes over the company's daily operating activities, a new life cycle begins.

The dashed arrows in Figure 13-1 emphasize the fact that follow-up of an ongoing system should be a continuous process. Periodically (e.g., every three months, six months, annually, etc., as determined by management), the system should be evaluated to ascertain whether it is still operating efficiently. The continued efficiency of the system means that no further revisions are necessary. Thus, the same system continues its daily functioning. (The route from the follow-up studies solid arrow back to the system operation on a daily basis is taken.) However, if the follow-up studies indicate that the previous systems problems have recurred or new problems exist, or both, the route is from the follow-up studies dashed arrow to the recognition of systems problems part of the figure. The complete systems study steps are then repeated.

Each of the four major phases of a systems study will be discussed separately in this and the next two chapters. However, it should be emphasized that in actual practice there is a certain amount of overlap between these four phases. For example, although management consultants and the systems steering committee (management) are currently involved in isolating specific systems weaknesses (the analysis phase), they may simultaneously be considering possible system changes (the design phase) that will eliminate these weaknesses. Therefore, the subsequent discussion of a systems study will use the same approach; that is, while analyzing a specific systems study step, comments may also be included regarding one or more of the other systems study steps.

SYSTEMS PLANNING

In performing systems studies for organizations to develop new systems, the following negative results associated with the systems development process may occur.[1]

- Systems are developed that do not meet users' needs.
- Systems are developed that are not flexible enough to meet the business needs for which they were designed.
- The development process significantly overruns what seemed like a reasonable budget.
- The development process significantly overruns its development schedule.

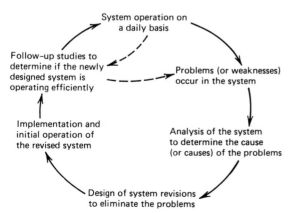

FIGURE 13-1 Life cycle of a business information system.

[1] Ian A. Gilhooley, "A Methodology for Productive Systems Development," *Journal of Information Systems Management* 3, 1 (Winter 1986), p. 36.

- Systems are developed without proper management approval.
- Systems are developed that are difficult and costly to maintain.

Hopefully, these potential negative results can be eliminated by the use of the systems approach in a systems study.

The **systems approach** to planning a systems study for analyzing a company's current problems and making change recommendations to help solve the problems encompasses two major aspects: (1) approaching a specific organizational problem (or problems) from a broad point of view and (2) utilizing a consulting team and steering committee for performing a systems study of an organization's problems. These aspects are part of the planning process in a systems study and each will be discussed briefly in this section of the chapter. It should be noted that systems planning is not limited to these aspects, however. Planning is a pervasive process that continues throughout all phases of the systems study.

Broad Viewpoint in a Systems Study

When management hires consultants to help solve a specific problem, the consultants should take into consideration what effects their recommendations will have on the organization's total system environment. This environment includes all the specific subsystems within the organization as well as the external environment outside of the organization's boundaries.

For example, assume that the actual time required to manufacture basketballs within the Alan Company's production subsystem is continually exceeding the standard time. As a result of these production delays, the Alan Company's customers are not receiving their basketball purchases on schedule as promised by the company's sales staff. To help solve this problem, the Alan Company's management hires the Reliable Professional Consulting Firm to analyze the

problem and to make recommendations for improving the basketball production process. As an accounting consultant, you are assigned the task of reviewing the standard cost accounting system for manufacturing basketballs (i.e., reviewing the raw materials standard, the direct labor standard, and the manufacturing overhead standard). Based on this review, you feel that the major cause of basketball production delays is the inefficient performance by those direct laborers involved in the basketball manufacturing process. This inefficiency was hidden by the loose time standards originally established for basketball production. Even with these loose time standards, the direct laborers' actual hours for production are still exceeding standard hours. Therefore, you recommend to the Alan Company's management that employees of higher skill level (who naturally earn higher wages) be used in manufacturing basketballs and that a stricter production time standard be adopted.

Impressed with these observations, the management of the Alan Company incorporates your suggestions into its basketball production operations. The company soon discovers that with higher-skilled employees manufacturing the basketballs, however, the actual cost per basketball increases considerably. This happens because the increase in efficiency of the higher-skilled workers is not enough to offset their higher wages. The increase in cost causes management to increase the basketball selling price. Because competitors have not increased their basketball selling prices, the Alan Company's sales drop steadily, causing a decline in the company's total gross margin (excess of sales revenue over cost of goods sold) on basketballs sold.

This example illustrates what can occur when a consultant tackles an organization's systems problem from a narrow point of view. Your recommendation as a management consultant to upgrade the skill level requirement of those employees who manufacture basketballs was based on only the positive effects within the Alan Company's production subsystem. If, however, you had approached the company's basketball production problem from a broad point of view, you would have considered as well the possible implications of your recommendation on the company's total systems environment. You would have studied the prices of basketballs charged by the Alan Company's competitors (an external environmental factor) and attempted to ascertain how the sales of the Alan Company's marketing subsystem (an internal environmental factor) might change as a result of higher priced basketballs.

From this analysis, you would have learned that the competitive nature of the basketball sales market does not make it feasible for the Alan Company to increase the selling price of basketballs without harming the company's market position. Therefore, rather than recommending higher-skilled employees to manufacture basketballs, you might have recommended that the present basketball manufacturing employees be provided additional on-the-job training to increase their production capabilities. Alternatively, you might determine that a compensation plan which rewards higher productivity is appropriate.

In general, when a change is made in one aspect of a company's system, the change will likely affect other parts of the system. Unless the consultants realize this fact and take into consideration what effect a specific recommendation will have on the total system, their systems study work may be unproductive. Thus, management consultants (and management) should always have a total systems viewpoint (or broad viewpoint) when helping a company solve a problem. Otherwise, they may solve the specific problem but in the process create new problems.

Consulting Team in a Systems Study

The *consulting team* follows from the importance of a broad viewpoint when performing a systems study. Because a management consultant normally has specialized training in one particular discipline (e.g., accounting or marketing),

the consultant is not expected to be an expert in all phases of a company's operations. However, when approaching a systems problem broadly by analyzing the consequences of a specific recommendation on other operating areas of a client company, knowledge of several disciplines is essential. Therefore, most consulting firms [including the management advisory services (MAS) departments or information systems consulting departments of CPA firms] hire employees with many different educational backgrounds to work as management consultants on specific jobs for clients. These individual employees will possess specialized knowledge in such areas as accounting, management, marketing, electronic data processing, psychology (to analyze organizational behavior problems), and engineering (to analyze complex organizational production systems). They may also possess specialized knowledge pertinent to a particular industry, such as banking, retailing, insurance, or manufacturing.

Depending on the expertise required for a specific systems study, the consulting firm sends a team of experts to a company to help solve the company's systems problems. Just as an efficiently operated system requires coordination and communication among its subsystems, this team of consultants must coordinate the systems study work and must also have good communications among its members in order to perform efficiently for the client company. In the previous discussion of the Alan Company's basketball production problem, for example, the accountant performing the analysis of the company's standard cost accounting system would probably not be qualified to perform the market analysis study of future expected basketball demand as a result of increasing the per-unit selling price. Rather, a marketing specialist on the consulting team would undertake this market study. The marketing specialist would communicate his or her findings to the accountant. These input data from the marketing expert could then be used by the accountant in reaching a decision about revisions, if any, within the basketball production process.

It should be emphasized, however, that in a systems study for a small business (e.g., revising the accounting information system for a lawyer who operates a small law office), a consulting team of experts would normally be unnecessary. A knowledgeable accountant from the consulting firm should be able to handle this systems study job alone. On the other hand, a consulting job performed for a major corporation with several divisions would likely require a team of specialized consultants to analyze the corporation's information system and make recommendations regarding this organization's complex structure.

The Steering Committee in a Systems Study

The team of outside consultants must interface with company management in a way that promotes communication between the two groups. To provide this interface, management generally chooses a steering committee to work with the outside consultants in accomplishing the systems study. This steering committee should be organized on a permanent basis, to be continuously involved in systems planning and follow-up activities. Ideally, the committee consists of members of top management, such as the controller, the vice-president of finance, functional vice-presidents, the top-level information systems manager (information systems vice-president or chief information officer), and an auditor. Top management commitment and involvement in the systems study is vital to the ultimate success of the system.

Either the external or internal auditor, or both, should be included on the steering committee. The inclusion of auditors in the systems development process ensures that the system will include adequate controls and also that it will be "auditable." Activities of auditors in the systems development process include assuring the adequacy of:

- General controls prescribed in the system design
- Application of controls prescribed in the system design
- Compliance with prescribed general controls
- Compliance with prescribed application controls
- Efficient allocation of resources
- Use of resources in conformity to policy
- System meets stated objectives (effectiveness)
- Provision for adequate documentation
- Auditability of files/databases/records
- Availability of backup files[2]

Making sure that sufficient internal controls are included in the new system is particularly important because it usually costs much more to add controls after the system is implemented. Evaluation of controls in a present system will be discussed later in this chapter.

The steering committee will serve several purposes. First, simply having such a committee requires management to focus on the subject of information systems development. It is a demonstration of *top management commitment* to improving information systems and the recognition of information as a valuable resource. Secondly, the presence of a steering committee ensures that management will be involved with the consultants so that the newly designed system will be one that the company wants and needs, not just the system that the outside consultants think the company wants and needs. The steering committee members will be involved in all phases of systems development. They are particularly involved in the planning phase and are usually responsible for hiring the outside consultants. They are conferred with during the other phases and their ideas should be obtained on systems analysis reports, systems designs, and the implementation plan.

[2] Kent T. Fields, "Assignment of Audit Responsibility in Computer Systems Development Projects," *Journal of Information Systems* 2, 2 (Spring 1988), p. 53.

SYSTEMS ANALYSIS

The systems analysis phase of a company's information system life cycle begins following the recognition of some problems (or weaknesses) in the company's current system (see Figure 13-1). At that point, the company's top management (the steering committee) or board of directors decides to hire a consulting firm to help solve its systems problems. The basic purpose of systems analysis is to enable the consultants to familiarize themselves thoroughly with a company's current operating system so that they can eventually make recommendations for improving the system. Figure 13-2 shows the logical procedures that would be followed by the consultants when performing their systems analysis work. Each of these procedures associated with systems analysis will now be discussed.

Define the Problem (or Problems)

Before management consultants are able to make any valid recommendations to improve a company's information system, the consultants first must make sure they have identified the "real" problem (or problems) of the current system. In the process of hiring consultants to perform a systems study, the company's management (the steering committee) will normally tell the con-

sultants what it believes the systems problems are. The consultants, however, should not accept management's comments without doing some preliminary investigation of their own to make sure that management's impressions of the actual problems are correct. In fact, the major factor that may be compounding a company's current information systems problems is management's failure to distinguish the company's real problems from the symptoms of these problems. (When people are so close to a situation, it is easy for them to lose sight of what is actually happening.) For example, the Alan Company's management may be blaming production supervisors for the manufacturing inefficiencies occurring within their departments. However, the real problem is the slowness of the company's information system to provide timely production control reports to these supervisors. By receiving quicker "after-the-fact" performance reports, the supervisors could have taken immediate action to correct the manufacturing inefficiencies before they became too serious. Thus, the production supervisors' operating performances are only a symptom of the problem.

In order for the consultants to define the systems problems of a company, they must first understand the goals of the company's system. It is likely that the company's current problems are caused by certain aspects of the present system failing to accomplish its original planned systems goals. Thus, the consultants must adequately define the goals of the company's system and then, through subsequent systems analysis, ascertain which goals are being achieved under the present system and which are not. It is also important for the consultants to find out *why* some goals aren't being accomplished.

For the purposes of this discussion, a company's systems goals can be examined at three levels: (1) general systems goals, (2) top management systems goals, and (3) operating management systems goals. Each of these three goal categories is now briefly analyzed.

SYSTEMS ANALYSIS PROCEDURES

Define the Problem (or Problems)
in the Present System
↓
Systems Survey to Acquire Sufficient Information
Relating to Present Systems Problem (or Problems)
↓
Suggest Possible Solutions to Solve
the Systems Problem (or Problems)

FIGURE 13-2   Systems analysis procedures.

General Systems Goals

It is possible to identify broad principles of good systems design that should contribute to an effectively operated business information system. Included among these general systems goals are:

1. **Cost awareness.** When designing a system's internal control structure, its report structure, its use of manual and automated data processing techniques, and so on, the benefits associated with a specific system component should, at a minimum, equal the component's costs.

2. **Relevant output.** The information provided by the system should be accurate, be communicated to management on a timely basis, and be useful for management's decision-making functions. If output information is to be relevant, the methods used for data gathering (i.e., accumulating the input information) must be reliable. Thus, when the input data for reports are incorrect, the processed output reports are not relevant for management decision making.

3. **Simplified structure.** If a system's design is so complex that most company employees become frustrated with its structure, the system's potential usefulness may be lost. To obtain the most benefits from an information system, its structure must be as simple as possible so that organizational employees will understand the system's data processing and reporting capabilities and be able to use these capabilities when needed.

4. **Flexible structure.** The system should be able to accommodate the changing information needs of management, and should have backup procedures that permit information processing to continue if a breakdown occurs in the automated data processing equipment. (For instance, if a company's central processing unit is malfunctioning, alternative manual or automated procedures should be available that will permit data processing to continue until the computer hardware is operating again.) The system should not only be capable of processing decision-making information to

management but should also be able to interact with the company's customers to answer their inquiries. (For example, some credit customers of a retail organization may telephone to ask questions about their account balances.)

These general goals are applicable to most organizations' information systems. Each contributes positively to an efficiently operated business information system. It is important that the management consultants ascertain whether these goals are incorporated into their client company's information system design. The inability of the information system to achieve one or more of these general systems goals may be the cause of the company's present problems.

Top Management Systems Goals

Chapter 2 emphasized that top management is responsible for its organization's long-range planning functions. Top management develops broad, nonoperational goals (e.g., achieving a satisfactory level of net income and manufacturing high-quality inventory items) to guide the operations of the entire organization. As discussed in Chapter 3, individual organizational components will submit long-range program proposals which a company's budget committee evaluates for possible implementation into the system. Ongoing programs should be reviewed periodically by the budget committee (which includes top management personnel) and decisions made regarding their renewal.

Since the planning and controlling functions of top management affect the entire organization, it is often difficult to specify the types of decision-making information needed by these top-level managers. Furthermore, much of the information required by top management is for long-range planning and controlling activities and is not available within the organization's internal information system. In carrying out long-range planning, top management must have a good deal of external environmental data (including report data on such things as the company's long-range market potential, the future economic outlook for the country and how this will affect the company, and the future effects on company sales from the introduction of new products by competitors) which are not generated internally by the organization's accounting information system. On the other hand, information required by a production supervisor (an operating manager) regarding the efficiency of manufacturing activities can be generated internally from the company's standard cost accounting system.

Even though it is often difficult to pinpoint the specific information needs of top management, this task is not impossible. The accountant, in the role of budget coordinator, can provide top management executives with long-range planning data to enable them to make effective strategic decisions for the future. Through periodic performance reports (the control function), top management is provided feedback about the effective execution of its long-range plans. Top management must also be informed about the short-range operating performance of the organization's subsystems. After each subsystem's short-range budget has been developed, the accountant is responsible for providing top management with summary information about the individual subsystems' budgetary projections compared with their actual operating results.

Because of the large variety of planning and controlling information required by top management (both internally and externally generated data), it is possible that a company's systems problems can be caused (at least partially) by the system's failure to satisfy top management's information needs. It is therefore essential for the consultants to understand thoroughly the information needs of top management and then ascertain whether these needs are being satisfied by the company's current information system. This will be discussed further in the systems survey section of this chapter.

Operating Management Systems Goals

Compared with top management's systems goals, the information needs of operating management (those managers working within specific organizational subsystems) are normally much easier to ascertain. The decision-making activities of operating managers typically relate to well-defined and narrower organizational areas than those of top management. Also, the majority of operating management's decisions are for the current business year (in contrast to top management's long-range decision making). Most of the information required for operating managers' decisions can be generated internally as a by-product of processing a company's accounting data (in contrast to top management's need for a large amount of external data that are not internally generated by the accounting information system).

All these factors make it easier for management consultants to determine each operating manager's specific information needs and ascertain whether those needs are being met by the present information system. For example, in order to analyze a manufacturing department's operating efficiency, the department's production manager needs timely responsibility accounting reports comparing the actual raw materials and actual direct labor costs with the predetermined standard costs of these two manufacturing cost items. As a further example, in order to analyze the sales results of specific product lines as well as the performance of the sales staff, a marketing manager requires timely sales reports comparing each salesperson's actual product-line sales with his or her budgeted product-line sales. The discussion of prior chapters indicated that these types of reports required by the production manager and the marketing manager could be processed by a company's EDP subsystem on a management-by-exception basis.

When analyzing the systems goals of operating management and deciding whether its information needs are being satisfied, the consultants may find that the client company's accountants are overemphasizing the communication of monetary data to the operating managers. In fact, the accountants' preoccupation with reporting monetary data is sometimes cited as a major criticism of an accounting information system. Because many subsystem managers are likely to make decisions based on nonmonetary data (e.g., number of units produced per shift, pounds of raw materials required per unit, etc.), the accountants perform a disservice by reporting only monetary data to these managers. Most organizations, especially those having a computerized data processing system, maintain within their information systems both monetary and nonmonetary accounting data. When the accountants draw upon these data to prepare a computerized report for a subsystem manager, however, the report will often include only monetary information. The subsystem manager (i.e., the report recipient) might better understand the report information and thereby make more effective decisions if the report included nonmonetary, qualitative, or annotated information.

Systems Survey

Systems Survey Objectives

There are several objectives of a systems survey. These are primarily associated with obtaining a complete understanding of the present operational information system. One such objective is to understand the current system in terms of its *strengths* and *weaknesses*. The strengths will indicate which components of the old system to keep, whereas the weaknesses will suggest areas for improvement with a new system.

Understanding Management Information Needs

The systems survey also has as its objective to gain an understanding of **management information needs.** This is a particularly difficult task. It is not sufficient to just ask managers what information they want or need. In that event, they may request too much information and perhaps omit requests for the most critical information. A better approach is to ask managers what deci-

sions they make and determine what information is required for each decision. These decisions will require different kinds of information depending on the management systems goals discussed in the previous section of this chapter.

Understand the Human Element

Another important objective of the systems survey is to understand the **human element** in the current information system and to gain the *cooperation* of the people involved. Many people dislike any changes that affect their present job responsibilities. Because the appearance of management consultants on the work scene usually implies changes in a company's system, employees often develop negative attitudes toward these "outside" consultants. Unless the consultants deal directly with this potential human relations problem at the beginning of the systems study, it is very likely that any recommendations incorporated into the client company's system will not be effective. In essence, employees are the crucial elements in determining the effectiveness of a newly implemented system. Since company employees will be directly involved in the daily operations of the new system, the best-designed system "on paper" is likely to fail when implemented if the system does not have wide user support.

Ideally, top management, operating management, and nonmanagerial workers should all participate in the systems study. For example, creating a steering committee with top management representation ensures this group's participation. It is extremely important for top management to have a positive attitude about the valuable services the consultants can provide to its organization. If top management personnel resent "outsiders" coming into their organization and suggesting changes, the likelihood of a successful systems study will be slim. If lower-level employees observe top management's resentment toward the consultants, chances are these employees will quickly lose interest in the consultants' endeavors. A major task faced by the consultants during the systems survey is to gain the active cooperation of the operating managers and the nonmanagerial employees (including inventory clerks, bookkeepers, accountants, secretaries, and salespersons). Employees' uncertainty about the systems survey activities often creates hostility in those persons who may have the greatest potential to aid in the survey work. If the systems study involves a major overhaul of the company's present system, many employees may become fearful of losing their jobs. (This fear is often the result of rumors among employees regarding job cutbacks.)

To avoid these types of problems, the consultants (as well as top management) should communicate openly with the company's operating managers and nonmanagerial employees from the inception of the systems study and throughout all phases of the systems work. Before beginning the systems survey, the consultants should have formal meetings with all the operating managers of the various subsystems in order to explain the scope and purpose of the systems study and the advantages that contemplated changes will offer to each operating manager. For example, if the systems study involves the conversion from a manual to an automated data processing structure, the consultants should explain to the operating managers how the new system will alleviate a large part of their routine and boring functions, thereby providing them with opportunities for more challenging work. In addition, the consultants should encourage the operating managers to (1) voice their opinions about any weaknesses they perceive in the present system and (2) provide suggestions for eliminating these weaknesses.

If the purpose of the current systems study is to analyze the feasibility of computerizing the company's manual information system, there is a strong possibility that displacement of employees will occur. Rather than avoiding this issue, the consultants should openly admit the likelihood of a work-force reduction when the automated system is implemented. In most conversions from a manual to a computerized system, however, there is an opportunity for many employees to be assigned to different jobs within the new system. Assuming that the company's top management supports the retention of as many current employees as possible, the consultants should stress this fact to the operating managers. The company's personnel subsystem can offer training programs to enable displaced employees to perform alternative jobs within the automated system (e.g., a training program that trains a typist to become a terminal operator in an on-line computerized system). Management should provide displaced employees with severance pay and possibly letters of recommendation for available jobs in other organizations.

Enlist Management Participation and Cooperation

In a systems study for a large organization, it would be quite time-consuming for the consultants to communicate personally all the preceding information to the many nonmanagerial employees. Therefore, the consultants and the steering committee should encourage individual operating managers to communicate the systems study information to their subordinates. The operating managers can schedule meetings with their workers to provide this information and also answer any questions about the systems study. At these meetings, nonmanagerial employees should be encouraged to cooperate with the consultants and make suggestions concerning any revisions they feel would improve the company's information system. Operating managers should stress to their workers the opportunities that the new system will provide for both improving the employees' skill levels and promoting them to higher level jobs.

If a human-relations approach is followed by the management consultants, the entire systems study should progress smoothly. When organizational employees are well informed about the purpose, scope, and contemplated outcome from the systems study, they should have a rational perspective about the consultants' important job in revising their company's information system.

Systems Survey Data Gathering

A **systems survey** requires the consultants to gather facts and data about the existing system. There are several ways of gathering these data. Four of them are (1) review of documentation, (2) observation, (3) questionnaires, and (4) interviews.

Review of Documentation

The review of documentation in the systems survey is an important first step in understanding the present system. Two general categories of documentation should be examined in this process. One category is documentation about the existing information system. If the system is a manual one, this documentation may be scanty. But if the system is already automated in some form, there should be some documents such as program and system descriptions, data flow diagrams, and systems and program flowcharts (see Chapter 8). The other category of documentation is descriptive data about the organization. This includes organization charts, company policies and procedures, the chart of accounts, and job descriptions.

Observation

Observation is another method which can be used to survey the existing system. Observation involves "looking at" the system in operation. In a manual system, this primarily involves watching the employees as they carry out their various functions and duties. In an automated system, this includes observing computer operations. The consultants will be looking to answer certain questions as they observe the system in operation. Some of these questions are:

- Does the system operate in a way corresponding to the systems documentation?
- Are job functions performed in a manner consistent with job descriptions?
- Does the system deliver information to users in a timely manner for decision making?
- What is the general atmosphere or morale of workers as they perform tasks related to the information system?

- Is the computerized system often "down"?
- Do employees seem to be generally busy or is their work-load very cyclical?

Some of these questions can be answered by observation alone, while others will have to be answered as the survey data are analyzed.

Questionnaires

One relatively efficient way to gather data from a large number of people is by using a **questionnaire.** Questionnaires can be directed at any group of workers in the organization, from clerical personnel to top management. Questions can be phrased as either open-end or closed-end. Open-end questions allow respondents to provide feedback in an unstructured manner. These can be very effective since the answers are not necessarily limited to preconceived categories of responses. A problem, however, is that these types of responses are difficult to categorize and analyze. Closed-end questions, on the other hand, include categories of responses. The question may be answered with a "yes" or "no" response, an indication of preference or importance, or a ranking of suggested alternatives. The types of answers can be subjected to statistical analysis (e.g., determination of the mean response) and thus are more efficient when a large survey population is involved. An example of each type of question is illustrated in Figure 13-3.

Interviews

Questionnaires have the advantage over interviews of protecting the confidentiality of respondents. Therefore, when data are needed about sensitive issues (e.g., extent of satisfaction or dissatisfaction with the current information system), a questionnaire may be preferable. Interviews, however, may be used effectively to gather facts in more depth. For example, the interviewer may note a respondent's discomfort or vagueness about certain issues in the interview process. The interviewer can then follow-up certain questions with others designed to uncover more detail. Interviews are also an effective way of determin-

Example of an Open-end Question on a Systems Survey Questionnaire:

> Please explain why you are either satisfied or dissatisfied with the current general ledger system?

Example of a Closed-end Question on a Systems Survey Questionnaire:

> Please indicate your level of satisfaction with the current general ledger system by checking the appropriate response below:

> ____ Very Satisfied
> ____ Somewhat Satisfied
> ____ Neither Satisfied nor Dissatisfied
> ____ Somewhat Dissatisfied
> ____ Very Dissatisfied

FIGURE 13-3   Sample questions on a systems survey questionnaire.

ing management information needs. As was previously stated, asking managers what information they need or want is not sufficient. The interview process can be used to help managers identify what decisions they make. These decisions can then be categorized according to such attributes as *frequency of decision, structure* (decision structures are discussed thoroughly in Chapter 16), or the *nature of variables involved.* Once the decisions are determined and categorized, the interviewer (consultant) can work with the managers to determine what information would be most useful in the decision process.

Systems Survey Data Analysis

Once all facts and data regarding the existing business information system have been gathered, they must be analyzed. This analysis may involve simply compiling all the data, it may involve quantitative analysis (e.g., calculation of means and variances), or it may consist of developing systems flowcharts. Two special techniques for analyzing data about job functions are (1) work measurement techniques and (2) work distribution analysis. Each will be discussed separately.

Work Measurement Techniques

For those job functions that are highly repetitive (such as typing and working on the assembly line of a production plant), the consultants may decide to use **work measurement techniques** to evaluate the efficiency of the employees performing these jobs. One technique is to analyze a specific job in terms of throughput for various activities. For example, the number of invoices prepared for payment per week by an accounts payable clerk can be tallied. Another popular work measurement technique available is based on **average throughput** (i.e., the amount of useful work that can be performed within a specific period of time with respect to a particular task). With this technique, the average output results from many individuals working together during a typical business day are used as the criterion for evaluating efficient employee performance. The average throughput approach avoids the difficulty of evaluating a specific employee's individual operating performance.

An alternative work measurement technique (in fact, one of the first techniques ever used for evaluating job performance) is called **time-and-motion study.** Under this approach, a repetitive-type job is first broken down into the specific tasks required to complete it. Then, specific employees' operating performances in completing these job tasks are secretly timed with a stop watch. The time-and-motion study technique is subject to many problems and is thus seldom used today. For instance, a major problem involves the selection of specific employees whose operating performances will be observed. Furthermore, if employees are aware that their job functions are being observed, the performance results will likely be misleading because the employees will not be working under normal conditions (i.e., without timing their every move).

Work measurement techniques can be a valuable data analysis tool for consultants in companies already having standard cost accounting systems, as well as in those companies planning to implement standards into their cost systems. In the former case, the consultants can utilize average throughput procedures as a means of evaluating the reasonableness of their client's existent labor time standards for repetitious job functions. These observations may lead the consultants to conclude that the company's preset standards are inaccurate. For the latter situation, the consultants' objective in using average throughput procedures is to enable them to derive the specific labor time standards that will be incorporated into their client's newly designed standard cost accounting system.

In a consulting job regarding the possible expansion of a company's production capacity (by purchasing additional manufacturing equipment, hiring additional production workers, etc.) to meet increased sales demand, the average throughput technique can also be an effective analysis tool. The results from this work measurement approach might reveal, for instance, that production output within the company's present plant facility is low because of inefficient performance by the team of manufacturing employees. Therefore, the consultants could recommend that, as an alternative to plant expansion, the current production workers be given the necessary training to make them more efficient. The improved worker efficiency should cause sufficient production output increases in the existent plant facility to nullify the need for expansion.

Work Distribution Analysis

An analysis technique that is similar to work measurement techniques is a **work distribution analysis.** This type of analysis focuses on a particular employee's job function. The job function is analyzed in terms of the amount of time spent on each particular task in the job description. An example of a work distribution analysis for payroll clerks is presented in Figure 13-4. The work distribution analysis can be used to determine how much time is consumed for each task. Those tasks which are the most time consuming, and yet repetitive in nature, may benefit most from automation in the new system.

Other Data Analysis Tools

Other valuable tools for analyzing a company's information reporting system are **systems flowcharts** and **data flow diagrams.** A special type of systems flowchart, the **document flowchart,** may be used to analyze control points. Data flow diagrams can be used to describe the flows of data in a transaction processing application. The subjects of flowcharting and data flow diagrams were discussed in Chapter 6. Using a document flowchart in identifying a company's control points was illustrated in Chapter 9.

Document flowcharts can make a valuable contribution to the consultants' systems survey. An organization's systems problems are often

	Hours Spent By		
	Clerk 1	Clerk 2	Clerk 3
Tasks			
Updating employee payroll records	3.0	3.8	2.7
Preparing paychecks	27.4	13.4	18.7
Preparing payroll register	5.0	18.2	12.3
Preparing tax reports	4.6	3.2	0
Preparing withholding reports	0	0	5.3
Other	0	1.4	1.0
Total hours per week	40.0	40.0	40.0

FIGURE 13-4 Work distribution analysis for payroll clerks.

caused by inadequate communications to those employees involved in decision making. On the other hand, the organization's systems problems may result from too much irrelevant document data being communicated to specific employees. The document flowchart provides the consultants with a logical picture of how the communication flow currently takes place within a specific organizational area. By understanding the types of feedback data required by various employees to execute their assigned organizational functions effectively, the consultants can thoroughly analyze their previously prepared document flowcharts and determine if these employees' information needs are being satisfied.

If the client company's information communication network reveals weaknesses, the consultants can suggest positive systems revisions that will eliminate these weaknesses. Furthermore, as previously discussed, the document flowchart may reveal some inefficiencies in the client company's data processing methods. The consultants' suggestions for revising their client company's data processing methods can increase significantly the operating effectiveness of the information system.

The Internal Control Structure

The importance of good internal control within an organization's system has been emphasized in Part Three of this text. Chapter 9 distinguished between **preventive controls** (designed to safeguard a company's assets and to check the accuracy and reliability of its accounting data) and **feedback controls** (designed to encourage organizational operating efficiency so that management's prescribed policies and goals are achieved). The use of **feedforward control systems** in some companies to supplement their feedback control systems was also examined in Chapter 9. Because weaknesses in an organization's internal control structure can cause major systems problems, the management consultants (in conjunction with one or more auditors) will normally spend considerable time reviewing

their client's internal control system. The following discussion illustrates how consultants would gather systems survey information about the strengths and weaknesses of a company's preventive controls and feedback controls.

Systems Survey of Preventive Controls

A questionnaire is commonly used by consultants in reviewing their client company's preventive control system (Figure 13-5). It contains a detailed list of questions regarding the preventive controls within each organizational subsystem. These questions are usually closed-end questions and are normally stated in such a manner that "yes" answers indicate the existence of the controls within the company's system and "no" answers indicate an absence of these controls. Because the same internal control questionnaire is typically used on all consulting jobs, some of the specific questions may not apply to an individual company's system characteristics. Therefore, the consultants also include a column on the questionnaire for answering "not applicable." Finally, space is normally provided for the consultants' "comments" regarding an internal control question. For example, if further investigation of a specific internal control area is desired at a later time, the consultant can make a note of this in the "comments" column.

Figure 13-5 illustrates portions of an internal control questionnaire that might be used by a management consulting team and the auditor in reviewing the preventive controls within a company's individual subsystems. In order that students can look at a "real-world" internal control questionnaire, an example of a control environment questionnaire prepared by a management consultant (this might also be prepared by an auditor) is shown in the supplement at the end of this chapter. The purpose of a control environment questionnaire is discussed in the supplement.

The detailed work required to answer the items on an internal control questionnaire will make the consultants quite knowledgeable of their client's information system. For those ques-

Questions	Answers			Date & Name[a]	Comments
	Yes	No	Not Applicable		
Subsystem: *Accounting*					
1. Is fidelity bond coverage provided for those employees handling liquid-type assets?					
2. Is there separation of duties between the cash-handling function and the record-keeping function relating to cash?					
3. Is a voucher system with prenumbered checks used for cash-disbursement transactions?					
Subsystem: *Production*					
1. Is there separation of duties between the inventory-handling function and the record-keeping function relating to inventory?					
2. Is the inventory storage room accessible only to properly authorized employees?					
3. Are periodic physical counts made of the inventory on hand and then reconciled to the inventory records?					
Subsystem: *Marketing*					
1. Are periodic analyses prepared showing each salesperson's product-line sales by territories and by contribution margins?					
2. Is a periodic accounts receivable aging analysis prepared as a means of evaluating credit customers' outstanding balances?					
3. Is proper authorization required by a designated employee (or employees) to write off a customer's account balance as a bad debt?					
Subsystem: *Electronic Data Processing*					
1. Are the job functions of systems analyst, programmer, and operator adequately separated?					
2. Do adequate input controls exist to detect any errors in transferring source document data to computer storage media?					
3. Is each computer run well documented?					
Subsystem: *Personnel*					
1. Are training programs offered to increase the operating efficiency of employees?					
2. Do equitable company-wide policies exist for salary and promotion rewards to subsystems' employees?					
3. Is there separation of duties in the payroll preparation and distribution processes?					

[a] In addition to including the date (or dates) on which a specific internal control question was investigated and subsequently answered, the particular consultant who performed the investigative work should include his or her initials next to the date. This initialing process thus recognizes the consultant's responsibility for examining the specific internal control area.

FIGURE 13-5   Portions of an internal control questionnaire.

tions answered "no," the consultants should determine what negative effects, if any, might result within the client's information system from the absence of the particular controls. After further investigation, the consultants may conclude that major improvements could be made in the company's information system by implementing one or more of these previously nonexistent preventive controls.

Because preventive control systems within a company's accounting and EDP subsystems have been covered extensively in Part 3, the following analysis will briefly examine some of the important preventive controls within a company's production, marketing, and personnel subsystems. (Our intention is not to explore these subsystems in depth, but rather to discuss a few applicable preventive controls.)

1. Production Subsystem. One of the important decisions that must be made in the production area is whether to use a **perpetual inventory system** (in which inventory records are updated each time a transaction occurs that affects the inventory balances), a **periodic inventory system** (in which inventory records are typically updated only at specific time intervals prior to preparing financial statements), or a combination of these two systems. For control purposes, a perpetual system is considered superior because it provides day-to-day information about the status of a company's various inventory balances. As a result of having current inventory data, management is able to plan its company's optimal on-hand inventory balances more efficiently. Some companies use periodic systems because they are less costly to operate than perpetual systems.

If consultants are hired to help a company design its inventory control system, these consultants should perform a cost/benefit analysis as a basis for recommending the best inventory system to meet the company's informational needs. For a company selling high-volume inventory items of small unit cost (e.g., pencils, construction nails, and paper clips), a periodic rather than a perpetual system is often used because the operating costs of updating the inventory accounts each time one of these items is sold (as required by a perpetual system) may exceed the perpetual system's benefits. On the other hand, a company that sells new automobiles (i.e., inventory items with a high unit cost) would probably favor a perpetual system because the volume of transactions is usually low, and the benefits to management from having daily account balance information regarding these large unit cost items would likely exceed the perpetual system's oper-

ating costs. Finally, a discount store selling both large unit cost items (e.g., television sets, furniture, and stereos) and small unit cost items (e.g., aspirins, books, and underwear) might use a perpetual system for the high unit cost items and a periodic system for the low unit cost items. Innovations in technology, as well as lower prices for hardware and software, may make perpetual systems more beneficial for low value inventory items than they were in the past. The consultant may discover that a company could benefit from a perpetual system which was impractical several years ago.

2. Marketing Subsystem. Because an organization's marketing subsystem is usually the major revenue-generating area, serious information systems problems involving the marketing function can adversely affect the organization's profitability. When attempting to plan its optimal sales mix of product lines for the coming budget year, the company's marketing managers should consider both volume and unit contribution margin factors.

For example, suppose the Safe and Sturdy Car Company manufactures and sells three automobile models (the xy compact, the ty compact, and the zz deluxe) to dealers throughout the country. The company's annual budget of sales is based on the anticipated volume sales of these three models. In comparing the 1991 profit performance with 1990, top management is confused by the fact that even though both sales volume and sales revenue were higher in 1991 than in 1990, net operating income actually declined during 1991. The management consultants who were hired to investigate this income decline problem revised the company's sales performance reports by incorporating contribution margin data into the reporting system. Figure 13-6 illustrates the performance report for one of the car company's East Coast sales representatives, "Honest" John Turner, for the year ended December 31, 1991, under both the original and revised reporting structure.

The sales results of the company's other sales-

The Safe and Sturdy Car Company
Sales Performance Report of John Turner
For the Year Ended December 31, 1991

Original Reporting Structure

Car Model	Unit Sales			Sales Revenue		
	Actual	Budget	Per Unit Selling Price to Dealers	Total Actual Revenue	Total Budgeted Revenue	Variance— Favorable (Unfavorable)
xy compact	500	450	$2500	$1,250,000	$1,125,000	$125,000
ty compact	300	280	2800	840,000	784,000	56,000
zz deluxe	120	180	2600	312,000	468,000	(156,000)
TOTALS	920	910		$2,402,000	$2,377,000	$ 25,000

Revised Reporting Structure

Car Model	Unit Sales			Contribution Margin (CM)		
	Actual	Budget	Per Unit CM	Total Actual CM	Total Budgeted CM	Variance— Favorable (Unfavorable)
xy compact	500	450	$ 400	$200,000	$180,000	$20,000
ty compact	300	280	500	150,000	140,000	10,000
zz deluxe	120	180	1000	120,000	180,000	(60,000)
TOTALS	920	910		$470,000	$500,000	($30,000)

FIGURE 13-6   A sales report.

people were similar to John Turner's. For the most part, each salesperson's actual unit sales of car models xy compact and ty compact exceeded his or her budget projection, whereas the actual unit sales of car model zz deluxe were below the budget projection. As shown under the heading "Original Reporting Structure" in Figure 13-6, John Turner's actual total unit sales and actual total sales revenue generated during 1991 exceeded his budget figures. This same favorable performance also existed when the 1991 operating activities of all the sales staff were combined.

The major cause of the company's net operating income decline during 1991 is revealed by the consultants' "Revised Reporting Structure" shown in Figure 13-6. As was true for John Turner as well as the other salespersons, the actual unit sales of the car model with the greatest contribution margin per unit (model zz deluxe) were

considerably below the budget projections. On the other hand, the company's 1990 actual unit sales of model zz deluxe were considerably higher than the 1991 sales of this model. (The 1990 sales data are not provided here.) Because those product items with the largest contribution margin per unit make the largest "contribution" toward covering a company's fixed costs and providing a net operating income, the Safe and Sturdy Car Company's sales volume decline in model zz deluxe automobiles appears to be the major cause of the 1991 net operating income decline.

This example demonstrates the valuable service that consultants can provide as a result of reviewing their client company's information reporting structure. On the surface, the Safe and Sturdy Car Company's sales performance looked good in 1991 because both actual sales volume .and actual sales revenue exceeded the 1991 budget as well as the 1990 sales volume and sales revenue actual results. The company's critical variable, contribution margin per car sold, however, was completely excluded from its original reporting structure. The revised reporting system suggested by the consultants emphasized contribution margin data, thereby providing the company's management with relevant information explaining the critical factor causing the 1991 decline in net operating income.

An important preventive control for the marketing subsystem's credit sales activities is to require proper authorization from a designated marketing employee (or employees) before a customer's account balance can be written off as a bad debt. To help safeguard a company's asset resources from improper use, the consultants should ascertain whether or not this preventive control is present. For example, without this control procedure, a customer payment for $100 could be "pocketed" by the company's accountant, followed by his or her recording of the journal entry below.

Allowance for uncollectibles	100	
Accounts receivable		100

This entry gives the customer full credit for payment. Rather than debiting the "cash" account for the customer's payment, however, the embezzlement procedure of the accountant is covered up by giving the impression that the customer's balance was never collected; thus, the debit to the "allowance" for uncollectibles" account.

The accountant's fraudulent activity probably could have been prevented by requiring the credit and collection department manager's formal approval for all bad debt write-offs. This control procedure would have hindered the accountant's embezzlement of the $100 cash receipt because the debit portion of the preceding journal entry could not have been recorded without approval from the credit and collection department manager. The consultants' recommendation to require formal approval for all uncollectible account write-offs can thus increase the efficiency of their client company's data processing system.

3. Personnel Subsystem. In some companies, frequent errors and irregularities occur in their personnel subsystems' payroll preparation and distribution processes. Errors and irregularities occur more often in large organizations in which hundreds or thousands of employees receive weekly paychecks. This is due to the massive volume of data processing activities required to prepare each week's payroll, which increases the opportunities for both human processing errors and fraud. Examples of payroll fraud by employees of companies include such things as maintaining fictitious names on the payroll, padding the number of hours worked by specific employees, and giving unauthorized salary increases to specific employees.

Because of the increased risk of both human and intentional errors in the payroll area, the management consultants will often review the preventive control structure surrounding their client's payroll functions. In the processing of payroll transactions, it is quite common to find the payroll being prepared with the assistance of a computer. Because Chapter 10 discussed some of the relevant controls for computerized payroll systems, there is no need to reiterate these controls here. The most important factor in the systems survey regarding payroll functions is that an adequate review of payroll controls be made by the management consultants and the auditor. Any control weaknesses detected during the survey of a company's payroll system should be noted for further investigation. Change recommendations to improve the control structure for payroll activities should contribute to increased efficiency within the company's information system.

Systems Survey of Feedback Controls

It was emphasized in Chapter 9 that timely performance reports under a responsibility accounting system are the principal means by which most organizations achieve feedback control. These performance reports are designed to measure the operating efficiency of various preventive controls within a company. Hopefully, any inefficiencies disclosed by the performance reports would be eliminated by managerial corrective action. For example, within the Alan Company, a timely performance report disclosing significant unfavorable variations between a manufacturing supervisor's standard and actual controllable production costs (controllable costs are the responsibility of the supervisor) will enable immediate managerial action to eliminate or at least reduce these inefficiencies.

If a company's feedback reporting structure is to achieve its control objective, each specific report must be communicated to the manager(s) with decision-making authority and responsibility for the subject matter contained in the report. For instance, a report analyzing the causes of direct labor variances in the Alan Company's production plant would be of little use to a marketing manager. Because both the content and the communication network of an organization's reports can significantly affect the efficient performance of its information system, the management consultants normally spend considerable time in systems survey work analyzing their client company's report structure. Document flowcharts can be particularly useful for this task.

Report on Systems Analysis

The final procedure in systems analysis is to communicate the consultants' systems survey work in a **systems analysis report.** This report signifies the end of the analysis phase. It should be presented to management personnel so that they can consider the findings and have a basis for evaluating the types of solutions the consultants recommend to solve the current system's problems.

As shown in Figure 13-1, the analysis phase of a systems study is immediately followed by the design phase (discussed in the next chapter). This latter consulting work involves the preparation of detailed systems change proposals that should solve the client company's current problems. Normally, before consultants begin the detailed time-consuming and technical job of designing systems changes, they will report on possible solution approaches to their client. Be-

cause these suggestions are presented to the client before beginning any in-depth design work, this systems study procedure is considered part of the consultants' systems analysis function. It may be referred to as a preliminary design phase since these suggestions often represent "conceptual" designs.

For example, after the consultants have completed systems planning and analysis (specifically, defining their client's systems problems and performing the systems survey), they may conclude that the company's major systems problems are caused by the failure of its manual data processing methods to provide timely managerial decision-making information. Before the consultants *jump into* the detailed work of designing various possible computerized systems to solve the company's current problems, however, they would first discuss their conclusions and suggestions for changes with the client's management, represented by the steering committee. These discussions may take place in a formal meeting in which the consultants present their findings and suggestions in a systems analysis report.

It is possible that the client company's management will not favor implementing a computerized system into its organization. This negative attitude may be the result of such things as the excessive costs associated with computerization or bias against change, particularly when it involves increased automation. If management's arguments against a computerized system appear to be irrational (e.g., fear of computers due to a lack of understanding), the consultants should attempt to change these negative attitudes by sound, logical arguments. However, because the consultants are outsiders and the company's management has, within reasonable limits, the prerogative to do whatever it wants, the consultants' suggestions may be rejected. If this should happen, the steering committee may ask the consultants to perform additional systems analysis work to provide *better* revision suggestions. (Or top management could politely ask the consultants to discontinue any further systems study work!)

The point of this example is that management consultants should not begin their detailed systems design work until they get approval from their client. Positive client reaction to the consultants' recommendations will justify the next major systems study phase, the detailed design of specific changes that should eliminate the weaknesses in the current system. Chapter 14 will examine the consultants' approach to designing changes in their client's information system.

SUMMARY

Modern management consultants should utilize a *systems approach* when performing a systems study. Under this approach, the consultants view their client company's information systems problems broadly by considering the positive or negative effects that will likely occur in all organizational areas as a result of a specific systems change recommendation. To utilize the systems approach effectively, a team of management consultants having different specialized knowledge are often involved in performing a system's study.

The first major phase of a systems study is the systems planning phase. During this phase, top management recognizes that there are problems with the current information system and begins strategic planning for a new system. This includes organizing a steering committee and hiring management consultants. Systems planning, once started, is an ongoing process which overlaps with the other systems study phases.

The second phase of a systems study is systems analysis. In this phase, the consultants become thoroughly familiar with their client's current operating system so that they can identify the system's strengths and weaknesses. By the time the systems study has been completed, the consultants should be able to introduce systems changes that eliminate the weaknesses and maintain the strengths of their client's information system. The initial procedure in performing systems analysis is to define the present problem (or

problems) in the client company's current information system. A company's systems problems are often caused by the system's failure to achieve its intended goals. Therefore, when attempting to ascertain what the problems are, the consultants should define the three levels of their client's systems goals: (1) general systems goals, (2) top management systems goals, and (3) operating management systems goals.

After defining these goals, the next important procedure in systems analysis, called the systems survey, begins. In their survey work, the consultants perform a detailed investigation of the client's present information system to enable them to determine which of the levels of systems goals are not being accomplished. During this investigation, consultants will review all records and documents related to the existing system and observe the system in operation. They will also use questionnaires and interviews to develop an understanding of the system. Upon discovering specific systems weaknesses, the consultants should be able to recommend changes that eliminate these weak points in their client's information system. Because an organization's employees often resent outside consultants, the management consultants should be aware of this potential human-relations problem and attempt to deal positively with the employees' negative attitudes. A company's systems problems may be caused by inefficient job performances by employees. Therefore, as part of the systems survey work, the consultants might use a work measurement technique or a work distribution analysis to evaluate the operating efficiency of employees in performing repetitive jobs.

When gathering the systems survey information, consultants normally will spend considerable time examining their client's preventive control system and feedback control system. A popular tool for analyzing the preventive controls is a questionnaire. By answering a series of preventive control questions about each organizational subsystem, the consultants are able to identify specific control weaknesses in their client's current system. Recommendations can subsequently be made for eliminating these weaknesses. Document flowcharts are often used in analyzing a client's feedback controls.

Before beginning the intensive systems design work to eliminate weaknesses in an information system, the consultants should communicate to the client company's steering committee their possible solutions(s) to the systems problems. If top management has a positive reaction, the consultants can then proceed into the design phase of their systems study.

Key Terms You Should Know

average throughput
broad viewpoint in systems study
consulting team
cost awareness
cost/benefit analysis
data flow diagrams
document
document flowchart
feedback controls
feedforward control systems
flexible structure
general systems goals
human element
internal control questionnaire
management information needs
observation
operating management systems goals
periodic inventory system

perpetual inventory system
preventive controls
questionnaire
relevant output
review of documentation
simplistic structure
steering committee
systems analysis
systems analysis report
systems approach
systems flowcharts
system strengths and weaknesses
systems survey
time-and-motion study
top management systems goals
total systems viewpoint in systems study
work distribution analysis
work measurement techniques

Discussion Questions

13-1. The Clean Free Diaper Company has been in business 50 years without completing a single "life cycle" of its information system. Is this situation good or bad? Explain.

13-2. Discuss the major differences, if any, between the planning phase, analysis phase, and design phase of a systems study.

13-3. You have recently graduated from college and passed the CPA examination. You are interested in working as a management consultant and therefore accept a position in the management advisory services department of Koote, Katch, and Kramer (a major public accounting firm). Upon being assigned your first systems study job, you are told by the chief consultant that the "systems approach" will be used in performing the necessary work on the client company's information system. Discuss in detail what the chief consultant means when he or she uses the term *systems approach*. Do you feel that this approach will increase or decrease your opportunities for creative thinking when performing the systems study? Explain.

13-4. Assume that you are one of the partners of a major consulting firm and are responsible for hiring an additional consultant to work in your firm. You feel that this new employee's educational specialty (such as accounting, marketing, personnel, or mathematics) is not too important because the consulting firm already has professional employees with a wide variety of educational backgrounds. You believe, however, that the new employee should have other qualifications. List the *four* most important traits that you would want this newly hired consultant to possess. (*Note:* Trait 1 should be the most important employee characteristic, trait 2 the second most important characteristic, etc.) For each of these listed traits, indicate why you think the specific trait is important.

13-5. When beginning the analysis phase of a systems study, why is it important to first define the existing problem(s) in the client company's information system?

13-6. "For consultants to define the problem(s) that currently exists in their client company's information system, they must first define the goals of the client's system." Do you agree or disagree with this statement? Discuss.

13-7. Three levels of a client company's systems goals that the management consultants should understand are general systems goals, top management systems goals, and operating management systems goals. If you had to select one of these categories of systems goals as the most important to the effective operation of an organization's information system, which one would you choose? Explain the reasons for your choice.

13-8. The Clayton Gordon Delight Company manufactures and distributes low-priced bottled wines to retailers. You are hired as a management consultant to help this company solve some of its present systems problems. Describe the types of decision-making information that probably would be needed by the company's

a. Supervisor of the production plant.
b. Top management.
c. Marketing manager.

13-9. An organization's accounting information system should be able to communicate relevant decision-making information to both top management and operating management. For which of these two managerial groups is the accountant's communication tasks normally easier? Why?

13-10. At lunch yesterday, Don Wilson was telling his friend Manny Koral about the valuable changes that were introduced into his company's system five months ago by the Zebra Consulting Firm. Don indicated that, as a result of these systems changes, his company's net operating income has increased threefold. Manny was so impressed with Don's comments that when he returned to his office after lunch, he immediately called the Zebra Consulting Firm. Manny indicated to the firm's chief consultant that he had heard about the successful consulting work in Don Wilson's company, and that he would therefore like to have the same changes incorporated into his company's system. Do you agree with Manny's reasoning? Explain.

13-11. In most consulting jobs, why wouldn't it be desirable to eliminate *completely* a client's present information system and replace this system with a new one?

13-12. Do you think it is feasible for a consultant to use a work measurement technique such as *average throughput* to evaluate the operating efficiency of a company's top management personnel? Explain.

13-13. At the annual awards banquet of the Society for Consenting Consultants, the guest speaker was Arnold A. Arnstein. Mr. Arnstein has been a practicing management consultant for the past 40 years. In concluding his three-hour speech, Arnstein made the following comments.

To be an efficient and effective management consultant in today's sophisticated business world, you must let your client know from the beginning who is the *boss*—which is obviously *you!* Don't waste your time listening to suggestions from the client company's employees. It will only delay the completion of the consulting job. After all, if the client's employees were that bright in the first place, the company would not have requested your services. Should the company's management initially dislike your systems change recommendations, don't worry. As soon as your systems revisions are implemented, management will probably love you for making such valuable contributions to its organization's operating efficiency. Good luck and just remember—the business world could not survive without us consultants!

As a novice management consultant attending the awards banquet, how would you react to Arnold A. Arnstein's closing observations? Explain thoroughly.

13-14. This chapter emphasized that the three major groups of company personnel (top management, operating management, and nonmanagerial workers) should participate in a management consultant's systems study. Discuss the type of role that each of these three groups normally would play. If you could have only *one* of these three company personnel groups actively involved in your systems study work (while the other two groups were completely unaware of what was happening), which group would you choose? Why?

13-15. George Beemster, management consultant, is currently performing a systems survey of the Louisville Sales Corporation, which recently installed an off-line electronic computer. The following comments have been extracted from Mr. Beemster's notes on computer operations and the processing and control of shipping notices and customer invoices.

- To minimize inconvenience, Louisville converted immediately (without documenting the changes) its existing data processing system, which utilized tabulating equipment. The computer company supervised the conversion and has provided training to all computer department employees (except keypunch operators) in systems design, operations, and programming.

- Each computer run is assigned to a specific employee, who is responsible for making program changes, running the program, and answering questions. This procedure has the advantage of eliminating the need for records of computer operations because each employee is responsible for his or her own computer runs.

- At least one computer department employee remains in the computer room during office hours, and only computer department employees have keys to the computer room.

- System documentation consists of those materials furnished by the computer company—a set of record formats and program listings. These and the tape library are kept in a corner of the computer department.

- Company products are shipped directly from public warehouses, which forward shipping notices to general accounting. There a billing clerk enters the price of the item and accounts for the numerical sequence of shipping notices from each warehouse. The billing clerk also prepares daily adding machine tapes ("control tapes") of the units shipped and the unit prices.

- Shipping notices and control tapes are forwarded to the computer department for keypunching and processing. Extensions are made on the computer. Output consists of invoices (in six copies) and a daily sales register. The daily sales register shows the aggregate totals of units shipped and unit prices, which the computer operator compares with the control tapes.

- All copies of the invoice are returned to the billing clerk. The clerk mails three copies to the customer, forwards one copy to the warehouse, maintains one copy in a numerical file, and retains one copy in an open invoice file that serves as a detailed accounts receivable record.

Requirement

Describe weaknesses in internal control over information and data flows and the procedures for processing shipping notices and customer invoices, and recommend improvements in these controls and processing procedures. Organize your answers as follows.

Weakness	Recommended Improvement

(AICPA Adapted)

13-16. As part of their systems survey work, the management consultants normally give considerable attention to the client company's "human element" area. What is meant by the "human element" area and why is it important to the consultants?

13-17. Try to think of several advantages and disadvantages of management consultants' use of a yes/no-type questionnaire in analyzing a client company's preventive control system. For each item listed, indicate your reasons for including it as either an advantage or a disadvantage.

13-18. A portion of an internal control questionnaire was provided in this chapter (see Figure 13-5). It illustrated a few examples of specific questions that management consultants might investigate when performing their systems survey of a client company's preventive controls. Try to think of some additional questions in each of the five subsystem areas (accounting, production, marketing, electronic data processing, and personnel) that you would expect to find on the consultants' questionnaire. (*Note:* Make any reasonable assumptions you wish about the type of company for which a systems study is being performed.)

13-19. Percy McBridge is one of the three partners of a management consulting firm called Brains Unlimited. The firm's motto is "Your Problem, Our Solution." Percy's consulting firm has recently been hired by the Quick Clothing Store to perform a systems study regarding the store's inventory system. In his first meeting with the clothing store's top management personnel, Percy learned the following facts about the store's business operations.

The Quick Clothing Store sells all types of medium-priced women's apparel (such as dresses, blouses, shoes, and nightgowns). The store utilizes a periodic system for inventory record-keeping purposes. At least twice a month, some of the salespeople will visually inspect the inventory on hand to determine which inventory items, if any, require reordering. On each December 31 (the end of the store's accounting period), a complete physical count is made of the inventory and reconciled to the inventory accounting records. At the close of the previous calendar year, the comparison of the physical count with the accounting records indicated some major shortages of inventory. For example, the store's records disclosed that 350 pairs of women's dress shoes, model TS66, were in stock as of December 31. However, the physical count by the store's salespeople revealed only 295 pairs of these shoes.

Because of last year's excessive inventory shortages, the Quick Clothing Store wants Percy McBridge's consulting firm to determine the causes of these shortages and also suggest some possible changes in its inventory system that will eliminate any future inventory discrepancies.

Requirements

Assume that you are Percy McBridge, ace consultant of Brains Unlimited. With the available information provided about the Quick Clothing Store's inventory system, attempt to answer the following questions.

1. Before formally beginning your systems survey work, top management asks your opinion regarding the possible causes of its clothing store's inventory shortages. What response would you give to management at this stage of the systems study?
2. What specific questions would you want to be answered during your systems survey of the clothing store's inventory activities? How would you go about acquiring answers to these questions?

13-20. The treasurer of the Rockhill Company, a corporation that employs approximately 500 workers, recently made the following comments.

I am so happy that our company has finally acquired a computer to handle the payroll-processing activities. Under our previous manual system for payroll preparation, I was always worried about the possibility of either accidental human errors or fraudulent acts occurring in payroll. Now, with our computerized payroll system, I no longer have sleepless nights. The computer's sophisticated processing capabilities eliminate the likelihood of either errors or irregularities in our company's weekly payroll.

Do you agree or disagree with these observations by the Rockhill Company's treasurer? Explain.

13-21. As pointed out in this chapter, document flowcharting is often used by management consultants when performing a systems survey of their client company's feedback controls. Could consultants also utilize a document flowcharting approach in their systems survey of the client's preventive controls? Discuss.

13-22. Who should be on a steering committee for a systems study?

13-23. Discuss the role of the internal and external auditors in the systems development process. Why do you think they are important to this process?

13-24. What are the objectives of a systems survey? Which of these objectives do you feel is most important? Why?

13-25. As shown in Figure 13-2, the final procedure in systems analysis is the consultants' suggestion of possible solutions to solve the client company's systems problem(s). Because the consultants are actually recommending changes in the design of their client's present system structure, wouldn't it be more logical to include this final systems analysis procedure as part of the systems design phase of a consulting job? Explain.

13-26. During the beginning stages of a systems study, it is extremely important that the consultants define the information needs of their client company's management. Why?

13-27. Business organizations are required to modify or replace a portion of all of their financial information systems in order to keep pace with their growth and to take advantage of improved information technology. The process involved in modifying or replacing an information system, especially if computer equipment is involved, requires a substantial commitment of time and resources. When an organization undertakes a change in its information system, a series of steps or phases is taken. The steps or phases included in a systems study are as follows.

- Survey of the existing system.
- Analysis of information collected in the survey and development of recommendations for corrective action.
- Design of a new or modified system.
- Equipment study and acquisition.
- Implementation of a new or modified system.

These steps or phases tend to overlap rather than being separate and distinct. In addition, the effort required in each step or phase varies from one systems study job to another depending on such factors as extent of the changes or the need for different equipment.

Requirements

A. Explain the purpose and reasons for surveying an organization's existing system during a systems study.
B. Identify and explain the general activities and techniques that are commonly used during the systems survey and analysis of information phases of a systems study conducted for a financial information system.
C. The systems survey and analysis of information phases of a financial information systems study are often carried out by a project team composed of a systems analyst, a management accountant, and other persons in the company who would be knowledgeable and helpful in the systems study. What would be the role of the management accountant in these phases of a financial information systems study?

(CMA Adapted)

13-28. You are the management consultant for the Alaska Branch of Far Distributing Company. This branch has substantial annual sales that are billed and collected locally. As a part of your systems survey work, you find that the procedures for handling cash receipts are as follows.

Cash collections on over-the-counter sales and C.O.D. sales are received from the customer or delivery service by the cashier. Upon receipt of cash, the cashier stamps the sales ticket "paid" and files a copy for future reference. The only record of C.O.D. sales is a copy of the sales ticket, which is given to the cashier to hold until the cash is received from the delivery service.

Mail is opened by the secretary to the credit manager, and remittances are given to the credit manager for review. The credit manager then places the remittances in a tray on the cashier's desk. At the daily deposit cutoff time, the cashier delivers the checks and cash on hand to the assistant credit manager, who prepares remittance lists and makes up the bank deposit, which he also takes to the bank. The assistant credit manager also posts remittances to the accounts receivable ledger cards and verifies the cash discounts allowable.

You also ascertain that the credit manager obtains approval from the executive office of Far Distributing Company, located in Chicago, to write off uncollectible accounts and that he has retained in his custody (as of the end of the fiscal year) some remittances that were received on various days during last month.

Requirements

A. Describe the irregularities that might occur under the procedures now in effect for handling cash collections and remittances.
B. Give procedures that you would recommend to strengthen internal control over cash collections and remittances.

(AICPA Adapted)

Problems

13-29. Charting, Inc. has hired your consulting firm to perform a systems study. As part of the survey work, you determine that the company processes its sales and cash receipts documents in the following manner.

1. *Payment on account.* The mail is opened each morning by a mail clerk in the sales department. The mail clerk prepares a remittance advice (showing customer and amount paid) if one is not received. The checks and remittance advices are then forwarded to the sales department supervisor, who reviews each check and forwards the checks and remittance advices to the accounting department supervisor.

   The accounting department supervisor, who also functions as credit manager in approving new credit and all credit limits, reviews all checks for payments on past due accounts and then forwards the checks and remittance advices to the accounts receivable clerk, who arranges the advices in alphabetical order. The remittance advices are posted directly to the accounts receivable ledger cards. The checks are endorsed by stamp and totaled. The total is posted to the cash receipts journal. The remittance advices are filed chronologically.

After receiving the cash from the previous day's cash sales, the accounts receivable clerk prepares the daily deposit slip in triplicate. The third copy of the deposit slip is filed by date and the second copy and the original accompany the bank deposit.

2. *Sales.* Sales clerks prepare sales invoices in triplicate. The original and second copy are presented to the cashier. The third copy is retained by the sales clerk in the sales book. When the sale is for cash, the customer pays the sales clerk who presents the money to the cashier with the invoice copies.

A credit sale is approved by the cashier from an approved credit list after the sales clerk prepared the three-part invoice. After receiving the cash or approving the invoice, the cashier validates the original copy of the sales invoice and gives it to the customer. At the end of each day the cashier summarizes the sales and cash received and forwards the cash and the second copy of the sales invoices to the accounts receivable clerk.

The accounts receivable clerk balances the cash received with cash sales invoices and prepares a daily sales summary. The credit sales invoices are posted to the accounts receivable ledger and all invoices are then sent to the inventory control clerk in the sales department for posting to the inventory control cards. After posting, the inventory control clerk files all invoices numerically. The accounts receivable clerk posts the daily sales summary to the cash receipts journal and sales journal and files the sales summaries by date.

The cash from cash sales is combined with the cash received on account to comprise the daily bank deposit.

3. *Bank deposit.* The bank validates the deposit slip and returns the second copy to the accounting department, where it is filed by date by the accounts receivable clerk.

Monthly bank statements are reconciled promptly by the accounting department supervisor and filed by date.

Requirement

You recognize that there are weaknesses in the existing system and believe that a flowchart of information and document flows would be beneficial in evaluating this client's internal control system. Complete the document flowchart in Figure 13-7 for sales and cash receipts of Charting, Inc., by labeling the appropriate symbols and indicating information flows. The flowchart is complete as to symbols and document flows.

(AICPA Adapted)

13-30. Long, CPA, has been engaged to examine and report on the financial statements of Maylou Corporation. During the review phase of the study of Maylou's system of internal accounting control over purchases, Long was given the document flowchart for purchases shown in Figure 13-8.

Requirements

A. Identify the procedures relating to purchase requisitions and purchase orders that Long would expect to find if Maylou's system of internal accounting control over purchases is effective. For example, purchase orders are prepared only after giving proper consideration to the time to order and the quantity to order. **Do not comment on the effectiveness of the flow of documents as presented in the flowchart or on separation of duties.**

B. What are the factors to consider in determining

1. The time to order?
2. The quantity to order?

(AICPA Adapted)

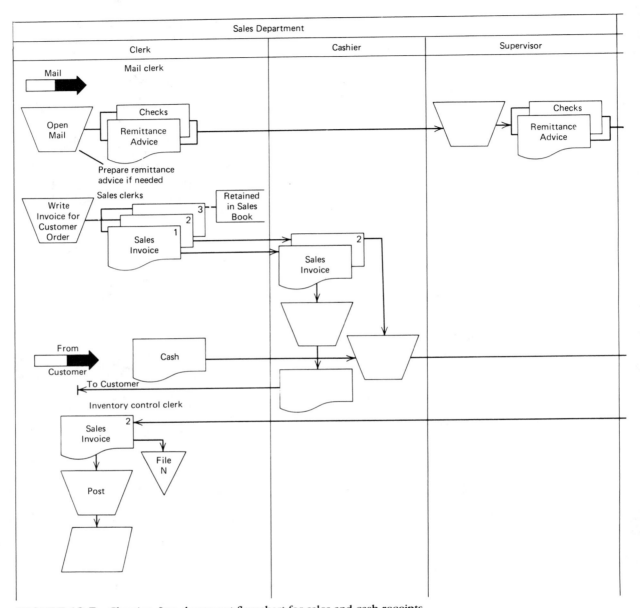

FIGURE 13-7 Charting, Inc. document flowchart for sales and cash receipts.

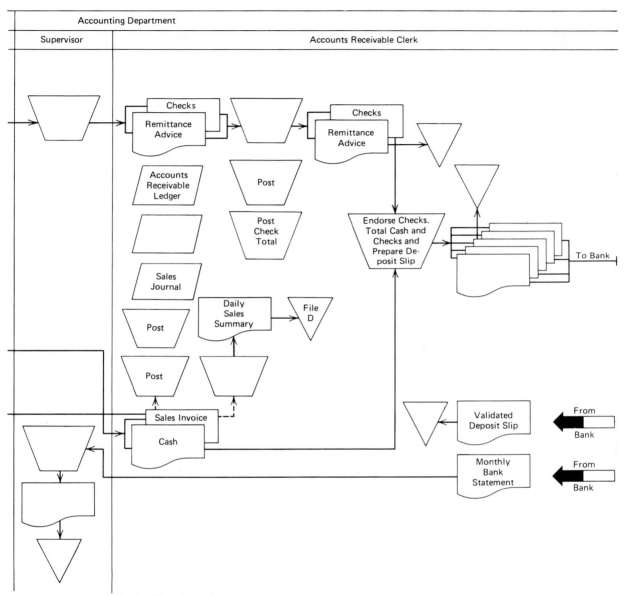

FIGURE 13-7 (Continued)

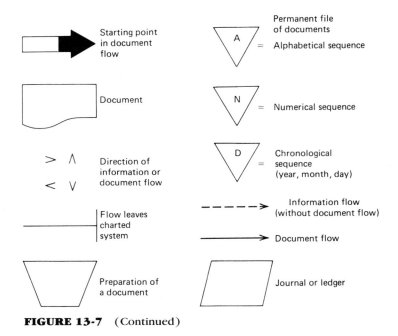

FIGURE 13-7   (Continued)

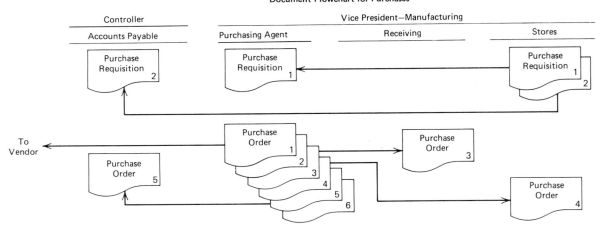

FIGURE 13-8   Document flowchart for purchases of the Maylou Corporation.

CASE ANALYSES

13-31. *Wright Company*

Wright Company employs a computer-based data processing system for maintaining all company records. The present system was developed in stages over the past five years and has been fully operational for the last 24 months.

When the system was being designed, all department heads were asked to specify the types of information and reports they would need for planning and controlling operations. The systems department attempted to meet the specifications of each department head. Company management specified that certain other reports be prepared for department heads. During the five years of systems development and operation, there have been several changes in the department head positions due to attrition and promotions. The new department heads often made requests for additional reports according to their specifications. The systems department complied with all of these requests. Reports were discontinued only on request by a department head, and then only if it was not a standard report required by top management. As a result, few reports were discontinued. Consequently, the data processing system was generating a large quantity of reports each reporting period.

Company management became concerned about the quantity of report information that was being produced by the system. The internal audit department was asked to evaluate the effectiveness of the reports generated by the system. The audit staff determined early in the study that more information was being generated by the data processing system than could be used effectively. They noted the following reactions to this information overload.

1. Many department heads would not act on certain reports during periods of peak activity. The department heads would let these reports accumulate with the hope of catching up during subsequent lulls.
2. Some department heads had so many reports they did not act at all on the information or they made incorrect decisions because of misuse of the information.
3. Frequently actions required by the nature of the report data were not taken until the department heads were reminded by others who needed the

decisions. These department heads did not appear to have developed a priority system for acting on the information produced by the data processing system.
4. Department heads often would develop the information they needed from alternative, independent sources, rather than use the reports generated by the data processing system. This was often easier than trying to search among the reports for the needed data.

Questions

1. Indicate whether each of the foregoing four reactions contributes positively or negatively toward the Wright Company's operating effectiveness. Explain your answer for every one of the four reactions.
2. For each reaction that you indicated as negative, recommend alternative procedures the Wright Company could employ to eliminate this negative contribution to operating effectiveness.

(CMA Adapted)

13-32. *Wooster Company*

Wooster Company is a beauty and barber supplies and equipment distributorship servicing a five-state area. Management generally has been pleased with the overall operations of the company to date. However, the present purchasing system has evolved through practice rather than having been formally designed. Consequently, it is inadequate and needs to be redesigned.

A description of the present purchasing system is as follows. Whenever the quantity of an item is low, the inventory supervisor phones the purchasing department with the item description and quantity to be ordered. A purchase order is prepared in duplicate in the purchasing department. The original is sent to the vendor, and the copy is filed in numerical order in the purchasing department. When the shipment arrives, the inventory supervisor sees that each item received is checked off on the packing slip that accompanies the shipment. The packing slip is then forwarded to the accounts payable department. When the invoice arrives, the packing slip is compared with the invoice in the accounts payable department. Once any differences between the packing slip and the invoice are reconciled, a check is drawn for the appropriate amount and is mailed to the vendor with a copy of the invoice. The packing slip is attached to the invoice and filed alphabetically in the paid invoice file.

Questions

Wooster Company intends to redesign its purchasing system from the point in time when an item needs to be ordered until payment is made. The system should be designed to ensure that all of the proper controls are incorporated into the system.

1. Identify the internally and externally generated documents that would be required to satisfy the minimum requirements of a basic system and indicate the number of copies of each document that would be needed.
2. Explain how all of these documents should interrelate and flow among Wooster's various departments including the final destination or file for each copy.

(CMA Adapted)

13-33. XLB Company

Harold Seymour is a management accountant with XLB Company. He is serving on a project team that is responsible for recommending a new regional sales distribution system. Although the project team has approved the draft for the final report of the project team that is to be submitted to top management, Seymour is not pleased with the approved report.

Jim Bier of the marketing department was appointed the leader of the team because he had experience with sales distribution systems. Seymour was assigned to the team for his expertise in budgets and cost analysis and because of his involvement in a similar project with a previous employer.

The project team worked well together identifying the positive and negative factors of the various alternatives. These factors were considered as the proposed regional distribution system was molded and designed. Seymour used his prior experience to explain the impact some of the negative factors could have on the volume and cost estimates for the proposed system.

The draft of the final report was composed by Bier. Seymour agrees with the proposed system and the overall conclusions of the report, but he does not believe the report is complete. Bier strongly favored the proposed system even though he had not developed the basic design. Bier's strong positive attitude for the proposed system is reflected throughout the report. The sales volume, costs, and cost savings estimates are very optimistic. The major negative factors and their impact have been discussed in the meetings but are not mentioned in the report or in the supporting financial data. Seymour knows from his previous experience that some of the negative factors could easily occur and could have a significant influence on the estimated financial benefits of the system to the company.

In other words, Seymour believes that the final report lacks a proper balance. He argued that the potential negative factors and their financial impact should be identified and discussed in the report for top management. The project team as a whole did not think the report needed to be revised because the system as designed was good and the final conclusions would be the same.

Questions

1. Does Harold Seymour have a responsibility to the XLB Company management to communicate his belief that the report lacks a proper balance because it does not identify the major negative factors and does not discuss their financial impact? Explain.
2. Without prejudice to your answer to Question 1, assume Harold Seymour decides that the negative factors need to be disclosed.
   a. What alternative actions are available to Seymour?
   b. Which one would you recommend?
   c. Why would you recommend that course of action?

(CMA Adapted)

13-34. ConSport Corporation

ConSport Corporation is a regional wholesaler of sporting goods. The document flowchart shown in Figure 13-9 and the following description present ConSport's cash distribution system.

1. The accounts payable department approves for payment all invoices (1) for the purchase of inventory. Invoices are matched with the purchase requisitions (PR), purchase orders (PO), and receiving reports (RR). The accounts payable clerks focus on vendor name and skim the documents when they are combined.
2. When all the documents for an invoice are assembled, a two-copy disbursement voucher (DV) is prepared and the transaction is recorded in the voucher register (VR). The disbursement voucher

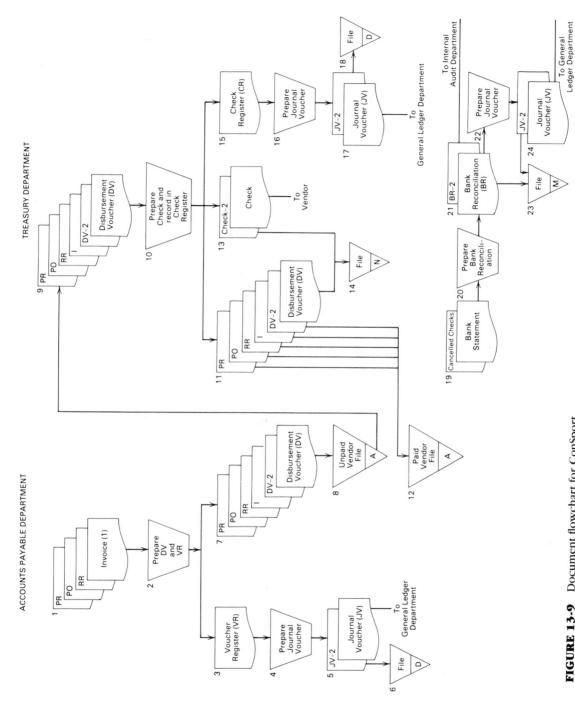

ACCOUNTS PAYABLE DEPARTMENT

TREASURY DEPARTMENT

To Internal Audit Department

To General Ledger Department

FIGURE 13-9 Document flowchart for ConSport.

493

and supporting documents are then filed alphabetically by vendor.

3. A two-copy journal voucher (JV) that summarizes each day's entries in the voucher register is prepared daily. The first copy is sent to the general ledger department, and the second copy is filed in the accounts payable department by date.

4. The vendor file is searched daily for the disbursement vouchers of invoices that are due to be paid. Both copies of disbursement vouchers that are due to be paid are sent to the treasury department along with the supporting documents. The cashier prepares a check for each vendor, signs the check, and records it in the check register (CR). Copy 1 of the disbursement voucher is attached to the check copy and filed in check-number order in the treasury department. Copy 2 and the supporting documents are returned to the accounts payable department and filed alphabetically by vendor.

5. A two-copy journal voucher that summarizes each day's checks is prepared. Copy 1 is sent to the general ledger department and Copy 2 is filed in the treasury department by date.

6. The cashier receives the monthly bank statement with canceled checks and prepares the bank reconciliation (BR). If an adjustment is required as a consequence of the bank reconciliation, a two-copy journal voucher is prepared. Copy 1 is sent to the general ledger department. Copy 2 is attached to Copy 1 of the bank reconciliation and filed by month in the treasury department. Copy 2 of the bank reconciliation is sent to the internal audit department.

Questions

ConSport Corporation's cash-disbursement system has some weaknesses. Review the cash-disbursement system and for each weakness in the system:

1. Identify where the weakness exists by using the reference number in the document flowchart that appears to the left of each symbol.
2. Describe the nature of the weakness.
3. Make a recommendation on how to correct the weakness.

Use the following format in preparing your answer.

Reference Number	Nature of Weakness	Recommendation to Correct Weakness

(CMA Adapted)

13-35. Rose Publishing Company

Rose Publishing Company devotes the bulk of its work to the development of high school and college texts. The printing division has several production departments and employs 400 persons, of which 95% are hourly rated production workers. Production workers may work on several projects in one day. They are paid weekly based on total hours worked.

A manual time card system is used to collect data on time worked. Each employee punches in and our when entering or leaving the plant. The timekeeping department audits the time cards daily and prepares input sheets for the computerized functions of the payroll system.

Currently, a daily report of the previous day's clockcard information by department is sent to each departmental supervisor in the printing division for verification and approval. Any changes are made directly on the report, signed by the supervisor, and returned to the timekeeping department. The altered report serves as the input authorization for changes to the system. Because of the volume and frequency of reports, this report changing procedure is the most expensive process in the system.

Timekeeping submits the corrected hourly data to general accounting and cost accounting for further processing. General accounting maintains the payroll system that determines weekly payroll, prepares weekly checks, summarizes data for monthly, quarterly, and annual reports, and generates W-2 forms. A weekly and monthly payroll distribution report is prepared by the cost accounting department that shows the labor costs by department.

Competition in college textbook publishing has increased steadily in the last three years. While Rose has maintained its sales volume, profits have declined. Direct labor cost is believed to be the basic cause of this decline in profits, but insufficient detail on labor utilization is available to pinpoint the suspected inefficiencies. Chuck Hutchins, a systems consultant, was engaged to analyze the current system and to make recommendations for improving data-collection and processing procedures. Excerpts from the report that Hutchins prepared are reproduced in Figure 13-10.

Questions

1. Compared with the traditional clockcard system, what are the advantages and disadvantages of the recommended system of electronically recording the entry to and exit from the plant?
2. Identify the items to be included in the individual employee's master file.
3. The TALC system allows the employee's departmental supervisor and the personnel department to examine the data contained in an individual employee's master file.

   a. Discuss the extent of the information each should be allowed to examine.
   b. Describe the safeguards that may be installed to prevent unauthorized access to the data.

4. The recommended system allows both the departmental supervisors and the project managers to obtain current labor distribution data on a limited basis. The limitations mentioned can lead to a conflict between a departmental supervisor and a project manager.

   a. Discuss the reasons for the specified limitations.
   b. Recommend a solution for the possible conflict that could arise if a departmental supervisor and a project manager do not agree.

13-36. Medford Bank and Trust

Linda Fry is the supervisor for the bookkeeping department of Medford Bank and Trust. The department processes 10,000 to 15,000 checks and related items daily. Six clerical employees perform this work under Fry's direct supervision.

The sequence of events in preparing canceled checks for processing by the bookkeeping department is as follows.

• Checks are processed through the proof department, where the dollar amount is microencoded onto the check and a record of the transaction is input to the computer records.

. . . An integrated Time and Attendance Labor Cost (TALC) system should be developed. Features of this system would include direct data entry; labor cost distribution by project as well as department; online access to time and attendance data for verification, correction, and update; and creation and maintenance of individual employee work history files for long-term analysis.

. . . The TALC system should incorporate uniquely encoded employee badges that would be used to electronically record entry to and exit from the plant directly into the data system.

. . . Labor cost records should be maintained at the employee level, showing the time worked in the department by project. Thus, labor cost can be fully analyzed. Responsibility for correct and timely entry must reside with the departmental supervisors and must be verified by project managers on a daily basis because projects involve several departments.

. . . Online terminals should be available in each department for direct data entry. Access to the system will be limited to authorized users through a coded entry (password) system. Departmental supervisors will be allowed to inspect, correct, verify, and update only time and attendance information for employees in their respective departments. Project managers may access information recorded for their projects only and exceptions to such data must be certified outside the system and entered by the affected supervisor.

. . . Appropriate data should be maintained at the employee level to allow verification of employee personnel files and individual work history by department and project. Access to employee master file data should be limited to the personnel department. Work-history data will be made available for analysis only at the project or departmental level, and only to departmental supervisors and project managers for whom an employee works.

FIGURE 13-10 Excerpts from Hutchins' report.

- Computer printouts for the daily check-processing activities are printed overnight. The printout, along with the cancelled checks, arrives at the bookkeeping department at the beginning of each workday.

Specific operations within the bookkeeping department include the following.

- A sample of payor signatures on the checks is verified for authenticity.
- All checks over $500 are examined for an endorsement.
- All check errors are identified and appropriate special handling provisions are completed.
- All stop-payment checks are identified and reversed out of the computer records.
- Insufficient-fund checks are identified and reversed out of the computer records. The check is returned to the endorser and appropriate charges are made to the customer's account.
- Questions from customers and creditors concerning check verification, account balance, and collected balance are answered via telephone conversations.

Medford's top management believes in exercising tight control and authority over all departments. The nature of the banking business and the need for strong internal control procedures underlie the philosophy put forth by the executives. While top management encourages the interchange of ideas, the communication process essentially follows a top-down structure.

To facilitate control and performance within the bookkeeping department, authority and decision making reside with Fry. She assigns duties and responsibilities to the clerical workers and carefully reviews the performance of her employees. Fry believes she has the employees' respect and feels she can recognize internal conflict and discontent.

Top management perceives that employees hired for the bookkeeping department tend to be unskilled and may lack ambition. However, several employees have shown a willingness to learn a new skill and are amenable to training programs. The employees function best when there are specific guidelines and directions for a particular job and when the lines of authority are clear. The jobs, however, tend to be somewhat dull and repetitive over time and provide little opportunity for incentive or personal satisfaction.

In spite of the nature of the work and the skill levels of the employees, productivity in the bookkeeping department is good and has been improving. The employees get along and work well with each other. They have retained their current positions from one to three years and are efficient at their specific job functions. However, the employees generally regard the work as an unpleasant task, and the repetitiveness of the work has led to morale and motivation problems.

Questions

1. a. Identify the management style that appears to be followed in the bookkeeping department.
   b. What factors presented in this situation support your selection of this management style?
   c. Explain whether this style can be a means of promoting effective work flow and improving productivity.

2. Identify circumstances that may have led to the morale and motivation problems of the bookkeeping department employees.

3. Recommend changes Linda Fry may wish to implement in the bookkeeping department to improve employee morale and motivation while at the same time maintaining the desired standards of performance and productivity.

(CMA Adapted)

CHAPTER 13 SUPPLEMENT

Example of a Control Environment Questionnaire

In the performance of a systems survey of a company's preventive controls, the management consulting team may complete a **control environment questionnaire.** This type of questionnaire will be useful in identifying and documenting practices that contribute to an effective control environment. The sections typically included on the control environment questionnaire cover ownership influences, organization and personnel practices, monitoring procedures (including financial reporting, budgets, and reconciliations), and internal audit activities.

Presented in this supplement is an example of a control environment questionnaire prepared by Steve Morris (management consultant for Southern California Consulting Firm) as part of his consulting firm's systems survey work being performed for Wilson Powertronics, Inc. (*Note:* There may be some specific items contained in the control environment questionnaire that you do not completely understand. Because

this questionnaire is for illustrative purposes only, you should not be concerned if you are unable to understand every single item included in it. The designation "N/A" that appears at various places within our questionnaire illustration stands for "Not Applicable.")

Control Environment Questionnaire

Company _____ **Wilson Powertronics, Inc.** _____

Subsidiary or Division _____

Prepared or Updated by	Date	Approved by	Date
Steve Morris	7-17-91	R. D. Hunt	7-31-91
		M. Grimm	8-2-91

This questionnaire should assist in assessing the overall effectiveness of the control environment. It focuses on ownership influences, organization and personnel practices, monitoring procedures (including financial reporting, budgets, and reconciliations), and internal audit activities. A "No" response does not necessarily indicate a deficiency in the control environment. Rather, the combined effect of the various factors should be considered in arriving at an overall assessment.

	Yes	No
I. OWNERSHIP INFLUENCES		

A. Concentration of Ownership.
In a separate memorandum, describe the concentration of ownership, including approximate number of shareholders, any significant shareholders, whether shares are actively traded, and extent of management's ownership interest.*

B. Board of Directors
In a separate memorandum, describe the makeup of the board of directors, including number of directors, affiliations of outside directors, relationship of each director to the organization, and number of years as a director.*

C. Is there an audit committee? (**Company plans to form one**)   _____ X

How many members serve on the committee? _____ N/A _____

How many are outside directors? _____ N/A _____

How often does the committee meet? _____ N/A _____

Are minutes of meetings prepared and retained?   N/A _____

D. Duties of the Board and its Committees
Excerpt from articles of incorporation and bylaws a description of the duties assigned and performed by the board of directors, its audit committee, and any other committees of the board. Include description of any specific authorizations retained by the board or its committees.

Comment on ownership influences

Ownership is spread among many small shareholders except for Jenks, CEO, who owns 5%. No undue pressures to achieve particular results. Present lack of audit committee is not considered a problem, because there are three outside directors— they appear to have an independent influence on the Board.

	Yes	No
II. ORGANIZATION AND PERSONNEL PRACTICES		

Organization
A. Does documentation include up-to-date:

Corporate structure chart?   X _____

Personnel organization chart?   X _____

* Memorandum is not necessary to obtain a general understanding of this questionnaire and is therefore omitted from this example.

	Yes	No
Obtain copies. If none, prepare charts for systems survey. (**In systems study file**)		
B. Do the charts clearly reflect areas of responsibility and lines of reporting and communication?	X	
C. Are there formal position descriptions for administrative and financial personnel?	X	
Do they clearly set out duties and responsibilities?	X	

Comment on organization practices:

Organization provides for separation of related functions. No discernible gaps or overlaps in assignment of responsibility. Company always has been effectively supervised by upper management; good monitoring of overall activities.

Personnel

	Yes	No
D. Does the recruitment and selection process for new employees in the administrative and financial areas require investigation of background and references?	X	
E. Are personnel policies and employee benefits documented and communicated to employees?	X	
F. Is there a formal conflict of interest policy or code of conduct in effect? Obtain copies.		X
Does it require periodic declarations by officers, directors, and key employees?	N/A	
Are there established procedures by which employees may confidentially report violations of the company's code of conduct or other standards?	N/A	
In a separate memorandum, describe the system used to monitor compliance with the conflict of interest policy and/or code of conduct.	See Item F below	
G. Are employees who handle cash, securities, and other valuable assets bonded?	X	
H. Do related employees, if any, have job assignments that minimize opportunities for collusion?	X	
I. Is rotation of duties enforced by mandatory vacations?	X	
J. Is job performance periodically evaluated and reviewed with each employee?	X	
K. Are there training programs for administrative and financial personnel?	X	

In a separate memorandum, describe the training programs.　　See Item K below

Comment on personnel practices:

Company has effective policies and procedures for hiring, evaluation, compensation, promotion, etc. The company puts emphasis on recruiting and employing college graduates.

(Item F.) Client is drafting a conflict of interest policy and code of conduct, which will be reviewed by our consulting firm prior to being implemented, probably 4th quarter 1991.

(Item K.) Marketing Training Program—Newly recruited salespeople get four weeks intensive training. This is a significant element in control over the level of sales returns.

III. MONITORING PROCEDURES

	Yes	No

Financial Reporting

	Yes	No
A. Are financial statements submitted at regular intervals to operating management?	X	
To the board of directors?	X	
To the audit committee?	N/A	
Are they accompanied by analytical comments?	X	
Do they show comparisons with:		
Prior periods?	X	
Budgets?	X	
Forecasts?	X	

B. Operating Analyses

In a separate schedule, list the principal operating analyses used. Describe contents and indicate frequency of preparation. Samples may be attached in lieu of schedule.　　See Item B below

	Yes	No
C. Are the same accounting and closing practices followed at interim dates as at year-end?	X	
D. Is prior review and approval by a responsible official required for financial information for public distribution (e.g., press releases, filings with regulatory bodies, and shareholders' reports)?	X	

E. Does documentation include up-to-date:

	Yes	No
Accounting policies and procedures?	X	
Chart of accounts describing nature of each account?	X	

Obtain copies.

F. Are all general journal entries other than standard entries required to be authorized by a responsible official not involved with the organization of entries?   X

Are the entries supported by explanation and/or documentation?   X

G. In a separate memorandum, summarize the qualifications of the key employees responsible for preparation and issuance of financial statements. Include for each employee his or her name, job responsibilities, background, and number of years in present position.*

H. Is access to accounting and financial records restricted to authorized pesonnel?   X

Comment on financial reporting practices:

Financial reports are sufficiently detailed to permit identification of significant operating and financial changes. Treasurer-Controller, Executive V.P., and President meet with operating managers quarterly to review results to date and current forecasts.

(Item B.) Monthly agings of receivables, and sales and earnings breakdowns by division are submitted to Treasurer-Controller and Executive V.P.

Budgets

	Yes	No
I. Is there a budgetary system?	X	
Do budgeting procedures cover all divisions and departments?	X	
Do budgets and forecasts cover:		
Revenues?	X	
Costs and expenses?	X	
Capital expenditures?	X	
Cash flow?	X	
Are budgets and forecasts submitted to management on an established timetable?	X	

* Memorandum is not necessary to obtain a general understanding of this questionnaire and is therefore omitted from this example.

	Yes	No
Are forecasts updated on a regular basis during the year?	X	
Are budget variances reported and analyzed?	X	

Comment on budget practices:

Budget preparation is on a detail item basis (i.e., specific items and expense amounts) and management meets quarterly to review and analyze status vs. plan. Responsibility for achieving forecasts and adhering to budgets parallels plan of organization. Budgets have been effective for evaluating performance, helping ensure that transactions are executed in accordance with management's authorization, and enforcing accountability at all levels. Budget consciousness pervades the company.

Reconciliations

These questions should be considered when evaluating the specific control objectives referenced parenthetically (see "Note to Students" below).

	Yes	No	Frequency	Performed By
J. Are the following assets reconciled with accounting records:				
Cash (F-1, F-4)?	X		Monthly	E. Hampton
Inventory (P-2, P-6, P-7, P-8)?	X		*	M. Reynolds
Property, plant, and equipment (P-12, P-13, P-14)?		X		
Investments (F-8, F-11)?	X		Monthly	M. Reynolds
K. Are detail and control accounts kept in balance as to:				
Accounts receivable (S-5, F-2)?	X		Monthly	D. Stevens
Notes receivable (S-5, F-2)?	N/A			
Inventory (P-7, P-8)?	N/A			
Property, plant, and equipment (P-12, F-4)?	X		At least annually	B. Dillon

* Cycle counts throughout year; annual physical count at 10/31.

Note to Students: Wilson Powertronics, Inc., has developed control objectives that its accounting information system should achieve in order to provide reasonable assurance that the financial information is accurate and complete and that the assets are safeguarded. We have omitted these control objectives from our example since they are not relevant to obtaining a general understanding of this questionnaire.

	Yes	No	Frequency	Performed By
Investments (F-8)?	X		Monthly	M. Reynolds
Accounts payable (A-2, P-2, P-12, F-4)?	X		Monthly	D. Patterson
Debt (F-4, F-5)?	X		Monthly	M. Reynolds
Capital stock (F-6)?	X		Quarterly	M. Reynolds

L. Are changes between beginning and ending balances accounted for as to:

	Yes	No	Frequency	Performed By
Property, plant, and equipment (P-11, P-12, P-13, P-14)?	X		At least annually	M. Reynolds
Allowances for depreciation (P-13, P-15)?	X		At least annually	M. Reynolds
Long-term debt (F-4, F-5)?	X		At least annually	M. Reynolds
Deferred income taxes (A-7)?	X		At least annually	M. Reynolds
Capital stock (F-6)?	X		At least annually	M. Reynolds

Comment on reconciliation practices:

Reconciliations are effective for identifying and reporting errors, differences, and deviations from expected results. Duties are segregated as to physical custody of assets and related reconciliations. Discrepancies are reported to appropriate personnel. Emphasis on timely resolution of any out-of-balance conditions.

IV. INTERNAL AUDIT ACTIVITIES

A. Is the scope of internal audit activities planned in advance with:

	Yes	No
		See Note below
Senior management?	N/A	
Board of directors or audit committee?	N/A	
Independent auditors?	N/A	

B. Are the results of the internal audit activities reported to:

	Yes	No
Senior management?	N/A	.

	Yes	No
Board of directors or audit committee?	N/A	_____
Independent auditors?	N/A	_____

C. Do internal auditors have direct access to senior management and the board of directors or audit committee?   N/A _____

D. Do internal auditors prepare and follow written audit programs?   N/A _____

E. Do internal audit working papers include systems documentation?   N/A _____

F. Are internal audit reports prepared and issued on a timely basis for all assignments?   N/A _____

Are the reports issued to appropriate executives?   N/A _____

Are responses to recommendations documented?   N/A _____

Is implementation of internal audit recommendations monitored?   N/A _____

G. Are there training programs for internal auditors?   N/A _____

In the memorandum discussed below in I, describe the training programs (e.g., training to review computer systems), including any established continuing education requirements.

H. Are any internal auditors or members of their families related to other employees? (Describe in the memorandum in I.)   N/A _____

I. In a separate memorandum, describe the normal duties of the internal auditors (including extent of financial audits and operational audits) and an evaluation of their competence and objectivity. Consider responses in questions A through H and the following:

Size and organization of the staff (including ratio of supervisors to staff)

Prior experience of staff members

Number of CPAs and CIAs

Extent of supervision of less experienced staff

Specificity of audit programs

Administrative reporting responsibility

Scope restrictions

Perceptions of internal audit management and operating and financial managers as to their influence on audit assignments, procedures, and reports.

Note: The Internal Auditor, Mr. White, has twelve years of experience in public accounting and private industry and is a CPA. However, since his employment in 1990, he has been working on special projects for the President and, thus, has performed no significant internal auditing procedures. His work has had no effect on our systems study.

14

Systems Study: Systems Design

Among the important questions that you should be able to answer after reading this chapter are:

1. What is a feasibility evaluation and why is its performance such an important aspect of the management consultants' systems study work?
2. How is a cost/benefit analysis performed for a proposed computer system?
3. What are some specific benefits that normally result when a company converts from a manual to a computerized accounting information system?
4. How do management consultants prepare a detailed systems design?
5. What is a systems specifications report, what information does it contain, and who gets it?
6. How is a service bureau different from a time-sharing organization?

INTRODUCTION

The "life cycle" of a business information system was illustrated in the previous chapter (see Figure 13-1). The existence of problems within a company's current system often leads its top management to hire an outside consulting firm to help solve the problems. Of the four major phases of a systems study (planning, analysis, design, implementation, and follow-up), only the planning and analysis phases were discussed in Chapter 13. This chapter will continue the discussion by examining the design phase.

The final procedure in systems analysis is the submission of a final report containing management consultants' suggestions of possible solutions to the company's information systems problem. If the client's top management reacts positively toward these suggestions, the consultants can then begin the next major systems study phase, called **systems design.** In the subsequent discussion of systems design, the assumption will be made that the consultants' systems analysis work revealed weaknesses in their client company's present manual data processing methods. For discussion purposes we shall assume, in particular, that the growth in size and complexity of the client's business has led to

inability of a manual data processing system to provide timely informational reports to both top management and operating management for decision making. Therefore, the consultants have suggested that the company consider the possibility of converting to a computerized data processing system. The steering committee's reaction to this suggestion was quite favorable and as a result, the systems study design phase commences.

Prior to preparing a detailed design for an information system, it is necessary to conduct a feasibility evaluation of the general system plan. This is critical because if, for example, an online real-time system could not be implemented in a particular organization due to operational constraints, a different type of system must be designed. Once a general system plan or design is determined to be feasible, work can begin on the detailed design. This involves specifying outputs, processing steps, and inputs for the new system. The detailed design is part of the systems specifications report sent to vendors. Detailed design techniques and the process of preparing the systems specifications report are described in this chapter. This chapter also discusses the final procedure in systems design, the submission of the systems specifications report to hardware and software vendors.

SYSTEMS DESIGN

The systems design work for acquiring a computerized data processing system involves four major activities or procedures. These procedures are shown in logical sequence in Figure 14-1. The feasibility evaluation is, in effect, a specialized type of system survey whereby the consultants attempt to determine whether or not it is practical for their client company to convert its present noncomputerized data processing system to a computerized one. Alternatively, if a company already has an automated system (such as a batch processing computerized system), the feasibility evaluation might involve the study of converting this system to an online, real-time configuration.

The systems specifications report for hardware and software supplier evaluation includes detailed, written descriptions of the specific design of the proposed computerized system. This calls for detailed design of system outputs, processing steps, and inputs. The consultants may use one or more structured techniques in preparing this design. They may also decide that prototyping (explained below) is an appropriate approach for developing of some system applications.

The systems specifications report is submitted to hardware and software suppliers (such as IBM, Honeywell, and Unisys) for their review. These suppliers (or vendors) will subsequently submit hardware and software proposals to the company. A company may be in the market to acquire

Systems Design Procedures

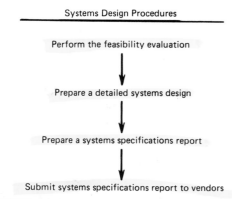

Perform the feasibility evaluation

↓

Prepare a detailed systems design

↓

Prepare a systems specifications report

↓

Submit systems specifications report to vendors

FIGURE 14-1 Systems design procedures.

a completely new computerized system, or they may just be interested in acquiring a single piece of hardware or one or more software programs if their objective is to improve an existing system rather than replace it. They may also decide to acquire computer services, rather than processing data on their own computer system. The types of vendors to whom the systems specification report may be sent are discussed later in this chapter. We will begin with a description of the first phase of systems design, the feasibility evaluation.

The Feasibility Evaluation

After obtaining a positive response from the client company's top management regarding the conversion of its current manual data processing system to a computerized data processing system, the consultant must begin a detailed feasibility evaluation of different possible computerized systems. The alternatives to be evaluated might include (1) a batch processing system, (2) an online, real-time processing system, and (3) a combination of these two systems (e.g., a major airline might use an online, real-time system for flight reservations and a batch processing system for accounting applications such as accounts receivable, payroll, and accounts payable). For each computerized system under consideration, four feasibility areas must be examined by the consulting team: (1) techni-

cal feasibility, (2) operational feasibility, (3) schedule feasibility, and (4) economic feasibility. Because the accountants on the consulting team normally are responsible for the economic feasibility evaluation work, the following discussion of these four feasibility areas will emphasize the economic evaluation activities.

Technical Feasibility

This phase of the feasibility evaluation typically is performed by the computer experts on the management consulting team because a thorough understanding of computer hardware and software is essential. The consultants may have developed a preliminary hardware configuration for an envisioned computerized system that would meet their client's information processing needs. Before further steps can be taken to implement this system, however, the consultants must analyze the technological state of the computer industry as well as the technological expertise that currently exists within the client company. Obviously, a suggested computer system would be impractical if the specific hardware and software requirements indicated in the initial design proposal could not be supplied by any of the computer manufacturers. In addition, the consultants must determine whether the technological skills needed by employees to handle this proposed system either currently exist in their client's operating structure or can be acquired in the near future. (This evaluation of technological skills overlap into the operational feasibility investigation.) If a specific computerized system is too sophisticated for a company's employees, it is likely that the system's implementation and subsequent day-to-day operation will be unsuccessful.

Operational Feasibility

This area of the feasibility evaluation attempts to ascertain how the newly proposed system will affect the client company's existing operational environment. A company's operational environment includes current personnel and the many functional activities performed by these employees. The consultants must analyze the capabilities of the client's personnel to perform the specific functions required by the newly proposed system. If additional employees with specialized training are necessary to operate the system when it is implemented, the consultants should disclose this fact to their client. The need for any training programs to update the skill levels of current personnel should also be considered.

In effect, the operational feasibility analysis is also a human-relations study because it is strongly oriented toward *people problems* that are likely to occur in the new system. (For this reason, personnel management specialists on the consulting team often participate in the operational feasibility evaluation.) By considering possible human-relations problems in advance, they should be avoided. As discussed in Chapter 13, people often have a negative attitude toward change. Because a proposal to convert a company's manual data processing system to a computerized system will cause many changes in employees' organizational duties, the client company's human resources (i.e., its personnel) must be directly considered before the automated system is implemented. Hopefully, if the client's personnel are kept well informed about such things as the need for the systems change, how the new system will affect their organizational functions, and so forth, any resistance by employees to the systems revisions can be minimized. Also, the employees should be encouraged to make suggestions regarding changes in the system that they feel are necessary. Unless the human element of a systems change is considered, the best-designed system "on paper" will often be a failure when it is implemented.

Recently, for example, a computerized inventory system was installed in a company's large warehouse. After a three-week operational period, top management discovered that there were more processing errors in the new system than there had been in the old manual system. These processing error problems persisted for months. Finally, the company hired a management consultant to perform a systems study. The

consultant quickly found the difficulty. The company's system was so mechanized that employees had very little to do but punch buttons. These employees were purposely sabotaging the system out of boredom! Since a company's personnel must carry out the day-to-day operations required in a system, their positive motivation is an essential prerequisite to the successful functioning of systems revisions.

Schedule Feasibility

If the initially designed systems changes are approved by the client company's top management, the consultants must estimate how long it will take for a new system to become operative. Because a major conversion from a manual to a computerized data processing system could take several years to implement, the client's management should be given an estimate of the time required to make the system operational. The company's top management may visualize a time interval of approximately six months until the revised system is implemented. Upon learning that the conversion will take several years, top management may decide to reject the systems design proposal for a simpler alternative that can be implemented in a shorter time (e.g., a batch processing computerized system rather than an online computerized data base system).

When performing the schedule feasibility analysis, the consultants often utilize a PERT (Program Evaluation and Review Technique) network diagram to help them coordinate the many activities necessary to implement the newly designed system. When a systems implementation involves the conversion from a manual to a computerized data processing system, the computer experts on the management consulting team normally will have a major role in the schedule feasibility work. A PERT network diagram for planning and controlling a systems implementation will be illustrated in Chapter 15.

Economic Feasibility

As discussed in Chapter 3, on budgetary accounting information systems, a program proposal for a major capital expenditure should not be approved for implementation until a cost/benefit analysis has been performed. All programs' cost/benefit analyses submitted to the budget committee for review and subsequent acceptance or rejection are ranked according to their **excess present value indexes.** Based on the number of dollars budgeted for long-range programs, those program proposals with the highest rankings are accepted. Because the consultants' proposal to computerize their client's present manual data processing system involves a major long-term asset investment, the consulting team's accountants should perform a cost/benefit analysis of this proposal. The program proposal's excess present value index will be ranked with other program proposals' indexes. The budget committee of the client company can then decide whether to accept or reject the consultants' program proposal. (Of course, the results must also be positive from the other three feasibility areas before top management will accept the consultants' proposal.)

To illustrate the calculations required in a cost/benefit analysis for the conversion of a company's manual information system to a computerized batch processing information system, assume that the consultants estimate a four-year useful life for the computerized system proposal. Further assume that the client's opportunity cost is estimated to be 10%. Figure 14-2 reflects the cost/benefit analysis performed by the consulting team's accountants on a proposed medium-size computer system for their client.

It should be kept in mind that the consultants might develop a preliminary design of other types of computer systems (e.g., an online, real-time data base system) in addition to the batch processing proposal discussed here. For each alternative system proposed, a cost/benefit analysis similar to the one in Figure 14-2 would be prepared.

As discussed in Chapter 3, the benefits from a program proposal often are quite difficult to quantify monetarily. Normally, when attempting to project these benefits, a large degree of sub-

jectivity is necessary. Thus, the seven benefit categories listed in Figure 14-2 reflect the accountants' subjective estimates of the monetary advantages from the batch processing computerized system proposal. Furthermore, because the details of this proposal have not yet been discussed with a hardware and software supplier (which is part of the third major activity in systems design), the costs included in Figure 14-2 are also based on the accountants' subjective estimates. We will now briefly examine the specific cash benefits and the specific cash costs of the batch processing system proposal.

Cash Benefits

The first benefit listed in Figure 14-2 is the savings from reduced employee clerical costs. The computerized system will handle a large number of processing functions (such as the accounting cycle data processing steps, the preparation of sales analyses, and the preparation of production reports) previously performed manually by organizational employees. Therefore, many of the manual clerical jobs that exist under the present data processing system (such as accounts receivable bookkeeper and payroll clerk) will be eliminated if the computerized system is implemented. Also, under a manual data processing system, clerical employees often have to work overtime in order to get reports prepared on schedule. As a result of computerization, most of the previous overtime pay to clerical workers should be eliminated.

Benefits 2, 3, and 4 relate to more productive use of the company's working capital resources (i.e., the current assets). A computerized inventory system will enable the company to control better its merchandise inventory activities. Under the present manual inventory system, management reports on quantity balances of specific inventory items may have been prepared infrequently, causing management to be unaware of the updated inventory quantities on hand. This situation may have resulted in too large a physical-quantity balance for some inventory items (with excessive dollars invested in these items rather

		Years			
	1[a]	2	3	4	5
Cash Benefits					
1. Reduction in employee clerical costs		$ 950,000	$ 970,000	$ 990,000	$1,300,000
2. Additional return due to reduction in average annual inventory balance *plus* reduction in lost sales caused by stockouts		350,000	360,000	370,000	400,000
3. Additional return due to reduction in average annual accounts receivable balance and average annual cash balance		27,000	46,000	65,000	84,000
4. Reduction in bad debt write-offs		3,000	4,000	5,000	6,000
5. Better customer services		700,000	750,000	900,000	900,000
6. Better market planning		600,000	625,000	670,000	770,000
7. More efficient management control		900,000	950,000	900,000	1,050,000
Total Benefits		$3,530,000	$3,705,000	$3,900,000	$4,510,000
Cash Costs					
1. Computer hardware and software	$ 600,000	$ 900,000	$ 900,000	$ 900,000	$ 900,000
2. Environment	520,000	9,000	10,000	11,000	12,000
3. Physical installation	90,000				
4. Training	100,000	8,000	8,000	8,500	8,500
5. Programming	240,000	100,000	85,000	85,000	75,000
6. Conversion	1,400,000				
7. Operation		1,180,000	1,500,000	1,500,000	1,600,000
8. Additional systems study work	350,000	20,000	5,000	5,000	5,000
Total Costs	$3,300,000	$2,217,000	$2,508,000	$2,509,500	$2,600,500
Excess of Annual Cash Benefits Over Annual Cash Costs	—	$1,313,000	$1,197,000	$1,390,500	$1,909,500
× present value factors at a 10 percent opportunity cost (see the present value table in Figure B-1 of Appendix B)		× .826	× .751	× .683	× .621
Present Value of Annual Cash Benefits Over Annual Cash Costs		$1,084,538	$ 898,947	$ 949,712	$1,185,800

[handwritten margin note:] hard to quantify these costs →

EXCESS PRESENT VALUE INDEX
= Total Net Cash Flow Present Value/Total Asset Investment Present Value
= ($1,084,538 + $898,947 + $949,712 + $1,185,800)/$3,300,000
= 1.248, or 124.8%

[a] It is assumed that a full year is required to implement this system. Therefore, no benefits occur during the first year. Also, this illustration assumes that because the computer center is not operative until the second year, all the first-year cash costs ($3,300,000) reflect the present value of the total asset investment required for the computer system. The 4-year estimated useful life of this information system actually begins in year 2 when the computer center becomes operative.

FIGURE 14-2   Cost/benefit analysis of computerized system proposal.

than in more productive investments) and too small a physical-quantity balance for other inventory items (thereby increasing the possibility of stockouts and the resultant lost sales; in a production process, a stockout of specific raw materials could cause a stoppage of the entire manufacturing activities). Through timely computer printouts (on an exception basis) of those inventory items that should be replenished, optimal inventory balances should be maintained. Ordinarily, these timely feedback inventory reports will enable a company to reduce its average annual total investment in inventory as well as reduce the incidence of stockouts.

A possible reason for a large accounts receivable asset balance is the slowness of a company's manual system in preparing and mailing billing statements to customers. (Most credit customers will not pay their account balances until they receive billing statements.) By batching credit-sales data and preparing customers' statements on the computer, the company's billing function can be performed faster than with a manual system. Consequently, an individual customer would receive a billing statement much sooner after the credit sales transactions, and the company would thus receive the cash payment much faster. A shorter turnaround time (from credit sale to cash collection) would cause the company's average annual accounts receivable balance to decline. The company can then use this cash collection money much sooner for an income-generating investment rather than have the money tied up in the accounts receivable asset (where a productive return is not being earned, except for the possible carrying charges billed to credit customers).

With the use of a computer, a company is usually able to do a better job of forecasting its future needs for cash. Prior to a computerized system, the company's inability to forecast accurately its future cash requirements may have caused the company's financial managers to attempt to avoid the risk of a cash shortage by maintaining a larger-than-necessary cash balance. Because cash is a fairly unproductive asset

(e.g., you can invest your cash in a savings account and earn an annual return of only approximately 6 or 7%), computerized forecasting of future cash receipts and future cash disbursements should provide the company with a more accurate picture of the optimal cash balance that should be maintained. The cash in excess of this optimal balance can then be invested in productive income-generating activities (e.g., purchasing stocks or bonds of another corporation—the return from these investments should be considerably higher than the interest paid on a bank savings account). The computerized forecasting system will thus enable the company to reduce its average annual cash balance.

A computerized data processing system enables the credit and collection department managers to receive more timely reports on credit customers' past-due account balances. The accounts receivable aging analyses will provide essential information to these credit managers so that they can observe the slowness or promptness of specific customers' cash payments. If, for example, the credit managers felt that the number of accounts over 90 days past due was becoming too large, they could take steps to tighten their company's credit-granting policies. This action should lead to a reduction in the company's bad debt write-offs. Also, by receiving prompt computer printouts of those customers' accounts that are past due, the credit managers can take immediate action to attempt to collect these account balances. If information regarding customers' past-due account balances is slow in reaching the credit managers (as can occur in a manual data processing system), the delinquent customers may be more difficult to locate. They may, for example, have moved to another city without leaving any forwarding addresses. As a result, the company's bad debt write-offs are likely to increase.

Computerization of a company's data processing system should help in providing better services to customers (benefit 5 in Figure 14-2). Among these services would be such things as the company's ability to process customers' orders in a fast and efficient manner, to respond promptly to customers' questions regarding the present status of their account balances, and to provide customers with more accurate projections of when the manufacturing work on their purchased production items will be completed. If a company is involved in a highly competitive business, these customer services should be especially helpful in increasing sales.

As pointed out in Chapter 3, a computer can greatly aid a company's market planning (benefit 6 in Figure 14-2). By using mathematical sales-forecasting models (such as multivariate forecasting), the company is able to develop more accurate short- and long-range sales demand projections, thereby contributing to effective budgetary planning. Simulation techniques can also be employed to enable the company's management to generate various possible sales forecasts under differing assumptions regarding changes in key variables. For example, if the Alan Company's budget committee anticipated a significant rise in inflation during the coming year, different expected effects on sporting goods sales from this inflation variable could be incorporated into the company's computer analyses of possible sales projections. Mathematical forecasting models and simulation techniques are difficult, if not impossible, to use without a computer.

Benefit number 7 (more efficient management control) encompasses all aspects of a company's operational activities. As emphasized throughout this book, the computer's ability to provide timely feedback performance reports on subsystems' actual operations compared with their budgets will enable management to take quicker action to correct areas of significant budget deviations. These faster after-the-fact performance reports should contribute to increased operating efficiency within all phases of the company's system.

Cash Costs

It is assumed in Figure 14-2 that the company will lease rather than purchase its required hardware

and software. The consultants' estimate that this annual fixed-lease cost will be $900,000 (cost item 1). We are also assuming in Figure 14-2 that this $900,000 annual lease cost will not be incurred in its entirety during year 1. Since year 1 is the period of implementation, the computer hardware and software will not be acquired until several months into the implementation work (thus making the lease cost less than $900,000 for year 1). Most lease agreements with computer suppliers are for a period of at least three years. Lease payments are normally made monthly and the lease covers all maintenance work necessary on the computer system. A major advantage of leasing versus purchasing the computer hardware and software system is the increased flexibility provided the company. At the end of the lease period, the company can cancel the contract for the use of a specific computer system if its data processing needs have changed. Company management may decide to switch to a more efficient computer system offered by the same or another supplier. Many leasing contracts provide a clause that enables the user, if so desired, to purchase the hardware and software system at a later date. This purchase price is often stated within the lease contract and normally is below the original retail price of the system, thereby giving the user an allowance for prior lease payments.

Cost item 2 of Figure 14-2 (environment costs) includes all monetary expenditures in initially preparing the company's premises for the computer installation as well as additional site preparation costs that may be necessary during the life of the computer system. As can be seen in Figure 14-2, the first-year costs associated with site preparation are by far the largest ($520,000), and these costs significantly decline in years 2 through 5. A company often establishes its computer center as a separate subsystem apart from the accounting subsystem. Therefore, a specific area within the company's building structure would have to be found for locating the EDP subsystem. (If no current space is available, it might be necessary for the company to construct a new building to house the computer.) Some of the environmental costs associated with a computer installation include offices and conference rooms for computer personnel, air conditioning of the computer center (to ensure more efficient functioning of the computer equipment), electric outlets for providing the proper power voltage requirements to operate the computer equipment, and furniture and fixtures needed in the computer center. The building location in which the computer system is housed should be protected from electrical interference, dust, and any other environmental factors that would deter the system's efficient functioning. For effective internal control, adequate safeguards should exist to prevent unauthorized employees from entering the computer center and using the equipment.

Physical installation costs (item 3 in Figure 14-2) include the expenditures for transporting the computer equipment to the company's premises (even when acquiring a small computer system, for example, the freight costs for transporting this system can be considerable) as well as using cranes or other special equipment to carry the hardware to its specific organizational location, such as the fourteenth floor of the company's building. Training (cost item 4) is usually high during the first year of computer implementation but declines significantly in subsequent years (as illustrated in Figure 14-2). Training includes all the costs in preparing the company's present employees as well as newly hired employees to operate the computer system efficiently. The necessary training sessions may be provided to the user company's employees "at no charge" by the hardware and software supplier. If the supplier does not offer training, however, the company will have to incur the costs of sending its employees to outside training programs.

The fifth cost item shown in Figure 14-2 includes all the costs associated with writing specific computer programs to perform a company's data processing activities, testing the correctness (or logic) of these programs before they are im-

plemented into the system, and making revisions to old programs based on later design changes in systems operations. One method of testing a company's programs prior to implementation is through simulation. For example, the mathematical logic of an accounts receivable processing program could be ascertained by creating a fictitious customer with a $300 balance owed the company. If a $50 credit sale to this customer is then assumed, the program will be run with the preceding data to determine whether the computer printout indicates a $350 updated account balance for the customer. Companies are often able to reduce their programming costs by leasing or purchasing from the computer suppliers' prewritten, "canned" programs (called **proprietary software**) for various data processing functions. However, these canned program packages may be costly and, in many cases, a number of modifications are required in the prewritten programs to meet the specific data processing needs of an organization's system.

The cost of converting a company's current data processing system to the new one (cost item 6 in Figure 14-2) depends on the magnitude of changes involved. For example, if some minor modifications were made in the Alan Company's present batch processing system, the conversion costs would likely be minimal. However, a conversion from a manual to a computerized system will entail large dollar expenditures to make the new system operative. Among these costs will be monetary expenditures: (1) to transfer a company's financial data from its present storage media to computerized storage media (e.g., transferring the accounts receivable subsidiary ledger data to magnetic tape files), (2) to establish good internal controls for the new computerized system, and (3) to test the operations of the new system before it replaces the old system (discussed in Chapter 15 under the implementation phase of a systems study). Thus, the conversion costs associated with a new system are basically setup-type costs, which are incurred only in the first year of a new system to enable this system to take over a company's data processing functions.

The next cost category shown in Figure 14-2 (7, operation) reflects the expenditures necessary to enable the new computerized system to operate on a day-to-day basis once it is implemented. These costs include (1) the salaries of employees working in the EDP subsystem (such as systems analysts, programmers, data-entry operators, security officers, and tape librarians), (2) the necessary supplies needed in the EDP subsystem (such as magnetic disks, magnetic tapes, and printer paper), (3) the monthly electricity bill, and (4) the insurance coverage premiums for fire and vandalism.

If the current system proposal is eventually approved for implementation by the company's top management, additional systems study work will be required by the consultants. The cost of this additional work is reflected as cost item 8 in Figure 14-2. The further work performed by the consultants includes preparing a "systems specifications report" for use in discussions with various hardware and software suppliers regarding specific computer systems to meet their client's needs, supervising the implementation of the new computer system (discussed in Chapter 15), and performing periodic follow-up tests of the new system's effectiveness after it becomes operative (also discussed in Chapter 15).

Concluding Comments on the Feasibility Evaluation

To enable the consultants to proceed into the next major activity of systems design, the preparation of a detailed systems design, all four feasibility areas (technical, operational, schedule, and economic) must be "feasible" (i.e., capable of being accomplished based on the client company's specific systems goals). Furthermore, top management must have positive reactions regarding each of the feasibility evaluations. For example, if top management personnel (as well as their budget committee) believe that the estimated excess present value index of 124.8% for the proposed computer system (see Figure 14-2) is far too low in comparison with the company's

other long-range programs, no further consideration of this computer system proposal may be warranted. To permit the consultants to provide their client company with a *total* feasibility evaluation analysis, all four feasibility areas must be considered simultaneously. If one or more of these areas cannot be accomplished or if top management and various budget committee members have negative feelings about any of the four feasibility evaluations, the consultants' design proposal is not *totally feasible*. Top management personnel may then ask the consultants to develop an alternative design proposal that would be suitable for their company.

Our assumption here is that the batch processing computer system proposal of the consultants does "pass" the feasibility evaluation stage of the systems design work. We will therefore begin discussing the second major activity of systems design.

Prepare Detailed Systems Design

The next step in the systems design phase of the systems study is the preparation of a detailed systems design. In designing a business information system, the consultants begin with the outputs of the system. This means that the reports are designed first. The consultants then determine the processing steps and inputs that will be necessary to provide the desired reports. This section of the chapter discusses each part of this detailed design and describes some techniques that are useful in the design process.

Designing System Outputs

The consultants will use the data gathered about management decisions in the systems survey to decide what kinds of reports are needed and to design layouts for those reports. These reports may be classified according to which functional area will be requesting the reports (e.g., marketing, personnel, accounting, or manufacturing). The reports might also be classified based on how frequently they are to be produced (e.g., daily, weekly, monthly, or annually). Perhaps the report is not needed on a regular basis, but the system should be able to provide it on demand (a **demand report**) or when triggered by a certain condition being met (an **exception report**). For example, an accounts receivable report on a specific customer's payment history might be issued on demand or it might automatically be generated by the system when a customer owes the company in excess of a specified amount.

Once the number and types of reports are specified, the consultant should begin designing the reports. This includes determining what information should appear on the report and also the format for that information. Although most reports will contain information in a tabular format, such as the report picture in Figure 14-3, some reports may be improved with graphs or charts. A report showing actual sales versus budgeted and prior period sales, for example, might be more informative in a graphic format.

Process Design

The next step in detailed systems design is to determine processing procedures that produce the desired reports. This involves deciding which application programs are necessary, and what processing would be performed by each program. There are several tools available to the systems design consultant in preparing struc-

The XYZ Company Sales Report			
	Sales Dollars (in thousands)		
	April 1990		
SALESPERSON	**Actual**	**Budgeted**	**April 1989**
A. McDermott	$22.6	$19.3	$18.7
T. Domzal	$36.4	$37.0	$34.6
A. Riley	$23.7	$28.2	$25.6
T. Grow	$42.4	$31.9	$28.8
TOTAL	$125.1	$116.4	$107.7

FIGURE 14-3 A tabular report.

tured designs for processing applications. A few of these will be discussed here.

HIPO Charts

HIPO charts represent a structured design technique that was developed by IBM. HIPO stands for hierarchy plus input, processing, and output. Basically, the system application is represented in a hierarchical structure, with each successive lower level of the hierarchy providing detail about the one above. The hierarchical chart for a particular processing application is depicted in a Visual Table of Contents (VTOC). A hierarchical chart for an accounts payable application is pictured in Figure 14-4. Each block in the chart is

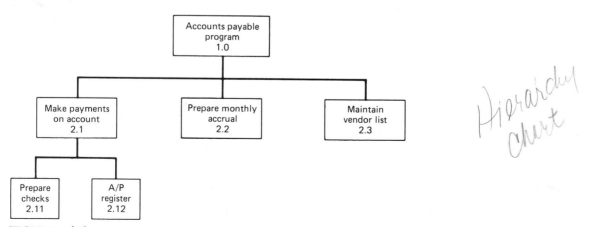

FIGURE 14-4 Visual table of contents in a HIPO chart.

Inputs 2.11	Processing 2.11	Outputs 2.11

Invoices
Receiving Reports
Purchase Orders
Shipping Notices
	Test to see if data
	   on invoice matches
	   receiving report
	Test to see if data
	   on purchase order
	   matches receiving
	   report
	Check invoices and
	   shipping notices for
	   delivery terms and
	   dates shipped
	Check payment dates
		Checks
		Check
		   Register
		Updated
		   Payment
		   History
		Discrepancy
		   Reports

FIGURE 14-5   The input-processing-output portion of a HIPO chart.

numbered. The number references the input-processing-output detail for each module in the HIPO chart. For example, module 2.11 is the preparation of accounts payable checks. The input-processing-output detail designates what inputs are necessary for this application (invoices, receiving reports, purchase orders, etc.), the processing tasks (matching documents and checking payment dates), and the outputs (checks, an update of payment history, and a discrepancy report). The input-processing-output detail for an accounts payable application is illustrated in Figure 14-5. By preparing HIPO charts for all applications in the system, computer programming is facilitated.

Warnier-Orr Diagrams

Another type of structured design technique is the **Warnier-Orr diagram.** This technique also uses hierarchies to structure a particular processing application. Instead of flowing top-down, however, as in HIPO charts, the hierarchy is structured from left to right. A Warnier-Orr diagram for an accounts payable application is shown in Figure 14-6. Warnier-Orr diagrams are useful in that they employ a hierarchical, structured approach to computer program design. However, these diagrams do not specific inputs and outputs as clearly as HIPO charts and so their use may be limited.

FIGURE 14-6   A Warnier-Orr diagram for preparing checks on accounts payable

Prototyping

Another tool that is useful in systems design and development is prototyping. Basically, a prototype is a model. A prototype of an information systems application is a software model. Instead of spending a lot of time on systems analysis and specification of inputs, processing, and outputs, a systems designer who uses prototyping will concentrate on building a working model of the system quickly, addressing the basic processing functions, and then modifying the system as it is tested and used.

The steps in prototyping are as follows. First, the users and systems designers meet to talk about the basic needs of the user and systems requirements. The designers then develop a basic working prototype to satisfy those requirements. This process may take only a few days or several weeks. The users and designers will then work together, either solving sample problems or problems in a real work environment. The system will be revised, enhanced, and tested over and over until it satisfies all of the users' needs.

Prototyping can be used effectively for many types of applications. Powerful fourth generation software languages serve as tools for building these systems. Inexpensive hardware with heavy-duty processing power and large memory capabilities also allows systems applications to be prototyped.

Prototyping has several advantages. For one thing, it sets the system "up and running" quickly, at least providing basic functions. It also encourages communication between the users and the systems designers, since both are involved in modifying and testing the system. An especially important advantage is that if systems specifications are not accurate or inclusive, deficiencies in the system can be resolved later. Many information systems in the past have been carefully designed and implemented, only to be scrapped because user needs were not satisfied. Prototyping avoids this problem by allowing users and designers to change the system as it is used.

Other Design Tools

There are various other tools that can be used to design the processing procedures and their appropriate sequence in a business information system. These include **data flow diagrams** and **flowcharts.** These were discussed in Chapter 6. They are mentioned here to emphasize that their use is for not only documentation of an existing system, but also for planning and designing a future system.

Computers are frequently used in the systems design process. Some design tools are now available in microcomputer software packages. One type of microcomputer software for systems design is the **computer-aided software engineering (CASE) tool.** This software allows systems designers to create data flow diagrams and a data dictionary interactively on the microcomputer. These diagrams and the dictionary are used to develop structured specifications for the system. CASE tools are one example of the changing nature of systems design.

Designing System Inputs

Once outputs and processing procedures have been specified, the consultant can begin to think about what data needs to be collected and input to the new system. At this point the consultant is likely to have determined whether data will be contained in a **data base** or whether **files** will be used. Advantages and disadvantages of each of these as well as a discussion of alternative file and data base structures are included in Chapter 7. Regardless of whether data will be maintained in files or a comprehensive data base, each data element must be identified in the systems design. Descriptions of the data are also necessary (e.g., alphanumeric versus numeric, maximum number of characters, etc.). These descriptions are often stored in a separate file called a **data dictionary.** Once the input data are identified and described, the source documents can be designed. Specifications for design inputs, processing, and outputs will be included in the systems specifications report, to be discussed now.

Preparation of a Systems Specifications Report

This activity of the consultants' systems design work builds on the detailed systems design. The **systems specifications report** is a type of **request for proposal (RFP)**, in essence asking vendors to submit a bid proposal for an information system. The specifications report is prepared by the consultants and it contains detailed information about the systems design proposal. It may be that the consultants have prepared more than one detailed systems design, since more than one design may meet the feasibility specifications. For example, a detailed design might have been prepared for both a batch processing proposal and an online, real-time proposal.

The systems specifications report containing information on each design proposal is the focal point for discussions between the consultants and the hardware and software suppliers (also called vendors). Before vendors such as IBM or Honeywell can submit a specific hardware and software package proposal to the consultants' client, they must first be provided with detailed descriptions of the company's information processing needs. Normally, the consultants will want to receive hardware and software proposals from several computer suppliers. This will permit the consultants and their client's management to evaluate the pros and cons of each vendor's offerings, with the objective of selecting the proposal that best meets the company's information needs.

The systems design work of preparing a systems specifications report builds on the detailed systems design and data from the feasibility evaluation. This systems design activity is, in actuality, a continuation of the detailed design and feasibility evaluation processes. When the consultants were performing their feasibility survey work, they did not analyze in detail the specifications of each proposed computer system design. This detailed work was unnecessary because the purpose of the feasibility evaluation was to ascertain whether or not one or more types of com-

puterized data processing systems appeared *totally feasible* for the client company. Once this determination was made and assuming that it appeared to be *totally feasible* for incorporating some type of computerized information system into the client's organization, the detailed design work on each system proposal could then be performed. The results of the design work are included in the systems specifications report and are provided to computer suppliers so that they will know the specific requirements of the organization's system. This detailed information will enable the computer suppliers to recommend specific hardware and software systems.

Among the information contained in a systems specifications report is the following.

1. Historical background information about the company's operating activities. Included here would be facts about the types of products manufactured and sold by the company, the financial condition of the company, the type of building structure occupied by the company, the company's current data processing methods, the peak volume of data processing activities, and the types of equipment currently being used in the company's data processing system. This information familiarizes the computer hardware and software suppliers with the company's operational environment so that they can make computer systems recommendations.

2. Detailed information about the problems in the company's current data processing system. By understanding the present systems problems, the hardware and software suppliers should have a better idea of what type of specific computer application will eliminate the company's system weaknesses. The consultants may also include information about how soon they would like to receive the suppliers' recommendations (e.g., two months from the date their report is provided to the computer suppliers), and the approximate date that the final decision will be made by their client regarding which supplier's hardware and software system will be purchased (or leased).

3. Detailed descriptions of the consultants' systems design proposals. For every design proposal, information should be included about such things as the input and the output of specific computer runs, the types of master files needed (or data base) and the approximate volume of each file, the frequency of updating each master file, the format of each output report, the approximate length of each output report, the types of information included in each report and how often the various reports will be prepared, the organizational managers to whom every report will be distributed, and the company's available space for locating the computer center. This detailed information about each of the consultants' systems proposals should provide the hardware and software suppliers with adequate data for making suggestions concerning specific computer systems to handle the company's requirements.

4. An indication of what the consultants expect the hardware and software suppliers to include in their proposals to the company. This section of the systems specifications report, in effect, tells the computer suppliers how detailed they should make these proposals. The company's consultants might request information regarding the following: the speed and size of the central processing unit needed, the type and quantity of input and output hardware units as well as the speed capabilities of these devices, the specific programming language that would be best for the company's system, the availability of compiler programs, the availability of prewritten canned programs that could be used for specific processing activities, the training sessions offered by the suppliers to teach the company's employees the operating details of the new system, the help provided by the suppliers in implementing and testing the new system, the maintenance services available from the suppliers should the hardware have mechanical failures, and the suppliers' provisions for backup data processing facilities while the hardware is being repaired. The consultants would likely want the hardware and software suppliers to indicate the costs of their computer systems recommendations under both purchase and lease arrangements.

5. A time schedule for implementing the new system. This final section of the report will request the hardware and software suppliers to estimate the number of weeks, months, or years that will be necessary to implement their recommended computer systems into the company.

To demonstrate the types of information contained in a systems specifications report, Figure 14-7 illustrates a systems flowchart reflecting the design of a company's new computerized system for processing fixed-asset acquisitions (other than *land,* which is not subject to depreciation) and for recognizing depreciation on these fixed assets. (Explanations will follow.)

The Accounts Payable Detail File (created from another computer run) contains information about all credit purchases during the period such as inventory, office supplies, and fixed assets. By using the Fixed Assets Extraction program, those credit purchases of fixed assets during the period are reflected on a *fixed assets new purchases on credit report.* Both the Fixed Assets Extraction program (which extracts those credit purchases of fixed assets from the accounts payable detail file) and the Add Cash Purchases program (which processes the few, if any, fixed assets purchased for cash) are used to create the New Property File. This file contains information describing all new acquisitions of fixed assets. By then using the New Property program with the data from the new property file, a *new property report* and *equipment identification labels* are prepared. A separate identification label is processed by the computer for each piece of new equipment. The identification label for every new item of equipment can be attached to the equipment to enable specific identification and control of the fixed asset resource.

The Property Depreciation program and the data from the New Property File and the Property Master File (which contains all fixed asset records other than *land*) are then used to prepare

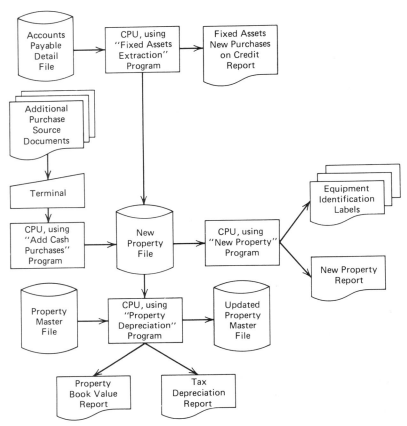

FIGURE 14-7 Systems flowchart for fixed-asset acquisitions and depreciation on fixed assets.

the Updated Property Master File, the *property book value report* (reflecting the cost *minus* accumulated depreciation on each fixed asset), and the *tax depreciation report*. Because a company may have different depreciation amounts for tax purposes compared with book purposes, the data included in the tax depreciation report will be used as input when the company prepares its tax returns for the government.

In addition to the systems flowchart shown in Figure 14-7 being prepared for the systems specifications report, a detailed description of the various files and their contents would also be provided in the specifications report. To illustrate, Figure 14-8 lists some common data that would likely be included for each fixed asset resource within a company's Property Master File.

1. Purchase cost of fixed asset.
2. Purchase date of fixed asset.
3. Vendor data (name, address, etc.).
4. Depreciation method selected.
5. Estimated salvage value of fixed asset.
6. Estimated useful life of fixed asset.
7. Insurable value of fixed asset.
8. Book value of fixed asset.
9. Identification number of fixed asset.
10. Description of fixed asset.
11. Classification of fixed asset (e.g., factory equipment, office furniture, etc.).
12. Organizational location of fixed asset.
13. Maintenance schedule for fixed asset.

FIGURE 14-8 Illustration of common data included within property master file.

Items 1 through 3 in Figure 14-8 would be obtained from the Accounts Payable Detail File. The data indicated in items 4 through 6 are required to compute each fixed asset's periodic depreciation. Upon determining a fixed asset's depreciation, the asset's *book value* can then be updated (item 8). Items 9 through 13 are largely for control purposes. For example, data regarding the maintenance schedule on production equipment (item 13) are important to ensure that the equipment is properly cared for and thus operates efficiently whenever it is used. Without regular maintenance, the equipment's useful life of service would likely be decreased.

To enable students to examine a *real-world* systems specifications report, an example of one is provided in the supplement at the end of this chapter. Our example is based on a certified public accountant (CPA) who currently operates his small accounting practice with a manual data processing system. Because his accounting practice has been growing recently, the CPA feels that a computer may be a useful tool to aid his growth in business clients. A systems specifications report for computer vendors is therefore prepared.

Submitting Systems Specifications Report to Computer Vendors

Upon finalizing the systems specifications report, the consultants must decide which hardware and software suppliers should receive it so that they can submit proposals for computer services. Since there are many types of hardware and software vendors, as well as vendors who offer particular kinds of services, this section of the chapter will discuss the different kinds of vendors to whom a systems specifications report might be submitted.

Hardware Vendors

The major hardware computer vendors include Control Data Corporation, Digital Equipment Corporation, Honeywell, IBM, Prime, Unisys, and Wang. These vendors offer not only central

processing units of all sizes, but also peripheral equipment and software. There are many options available to a company interested in acquiring additional hardware. Besides the simple purchase of computer equipment, the company may rent, lease, or rent with an option to buy. Computer leasing companies may offer hardware for lease at a lower rate than hardware manufacturers. The tradeoff is that they require a longer lease period and the company is locked into the lease. Because there are tradeoffs, as well as significantly different tax factors associated with the decision to lease or buy, the decision can become quite complicated.

While our systems study discussion has focused on the acquisition of a complete new computer system, a company may also approach hardware acquisition from the standpoint of **systems improvements.** At times, this systems improvement will require little more than the acquisition of an extra terminal or tape drive. However, there are other occasions when management considers such a large expansion of its data processing activities that a more radical approach than the simple acquisition of additional peripheral equipment seems necessary.

Single-Item Hardware Acquisition

Given the fact that a tape drive or disk drive can cost almost $1000 a month to lease, it is clear that peripheral machinery is not inexpensive. Thus, although such a dollar amount would not represent a very large proportion of the operating budget of a typical commercial computer installation (a rough rule of thumb for a company is an operating budget for the electronic data processing subsystem of 1% of the company's retail business), it is certainly large enough to warrant a careful analysis of needs before making an acquisition decision.

The reasons why an EDP center might wish to expand its inventory of processing equipment are many and varied. An extra tape drive, for example, might permit the purchase of a more efficient sorting program, which, in turn, might significantly reduce the processing time required for an accounts receivable application. Similarly, the acquisition of an additional disk drive might permit the company to switch to a more productive operating system, enabling a larger number of terminals to use the computer simultaneously for such applications as an inventory-control system. Finally, because almost all central processing units are **I/O bound** (i.e., input/output bound, meaning that they can compute faster than their peripherals can read or write), it is common to find computer center personnel shopping for an extra disk drive or printer in order to increase the productive utilization of the computer center's CPU.

At times, the justification for the acquisition of additional hardware is clear and the acquisition decision is thus primarily contingent on the budget of the computer center. At other times, however, the reasons for further hardware expenditures are not so obvious, and a careful analysis of the utilization of existing hardware may be in order. A convenient way to monitor the use of a company's computer equipment is with a **run log of equipment utilization,** as illustrated in Figure 14-9. This log can be updated manually by the computer operator or, if necessary, reconstructed from the system console log of the central processor. Note that the primary function of the equipment utilization log is simply to keep track of what computer equipment is being used when. An entire day's use of all the machinery of the computer center may be recorded on a single page, or possibly a few pages.

It should be mentioned that some operating systems come with optional built-in **hardware-monitor modules.** These modules automatically keep a record of what peripheral equipment is being used each second the central processor is in operation. Printouts showing equipment utilization, number of input/output operations, and even the number of parity errors as well as automatic tape-cleaning operations can be obtained. In larger computer centers supporting time-sharing operations (discussed shortly) and more than 20 disk drives, the manual maintenance of an equipment run log is virtually impos-

sible. In these circumstances, the hardware monitor of the operating system is the only effective means for the computer center to accurately log equipment utilization.

There is an interesting story about an EDP manager who switched jobs from one computer installation to another. When he first arrived at his new location, his subordinates submitted a request for the acquisition of an additional tape drive. Before agreeing to the subordinates' wishes, the new manager had his computer operators maintain an equipment run log for a month in order to determine the utilization of the existing equipment. The tabulations revealed not only that the additional tape drive was unnecessary, but that two existing tape drives could be returned to the manufacturer and still fulfill the computer center's data processing needs completely!

Once the decision to obtain a new piece of data processing equipment has been made as part of systems study, the next decision concerns the make and model of equipment to acquire. In the past, there has been a strong tendency for computer processing centers to exhibit a **one-vendor syndrome** when it comes to hardware purchases; that is, to buy or lease additional equipment from the manufacturer of the installation's existing hardware. At one time, this often made sense because the computer equipment of different manufacturers were rarely compatible with each other and complicated interfacing made "mixing" peripheral equipment too costly.

Today, however, this interface reservation would no longer seem to be a problem. There are many vendors of reliable hardware that are "plug-to-plug" (i.e., electronically) compatible with, for example, IBM, Honeywell, or Control Data Corporation equipment. Thus, it is usually wise for the user company (or the management consultants performing the systems study work) to examine carefully what is available on the open market and make the decision regarding new data processing equipment on the basis of such factors as needs, costs, and availability of equipment maintenance.

RUN LOG

ALAN COMPANY
125 King Street
Honolulu, Hawaii 96822

Operator __Susan Chandler_____ Employee I.D. No. __532-65-2133_____

Date(s) __January 21, 1991_____

Time (hour)	Tape Drives				Disk Drives					Optical Character/ Reader		Printer		
AM	1	2	3	4	1	2	3	4	5	1	2	1	2	3
00:00–00:15	√	√			√					√		√	√	
00:15–00:30	√	√	√	√	√	√	√			√		√	√	√
00:30–00:45	√	√			√	√			√		√	√	√	√
00:45–01:00			√		√			√		√		√	√	
01:00–01:15		√		√		√	√			√	√	√		
. . . .														
23:45–24:00														
Total Times														

FIGURE 14-9 A run log of equipment utilization. Check marks indicate use during the time period.

The Second Computer

A systems study may reveal that a company needs to acquire a second central processor and additional input/output equipment to enable the computer center to share an additional data processing burden between two units. The acquisition of an additional CPU often makes sense when an organization is seriously contemplating large processing expansions that are expected to overload the existing system. The University of California at Berkeley, for example, successfully used two interlocking Control Data Corporation CPUs for years: One unit performed data processing computations, whereas the other handled the many remote terminal requests and input/output tasks required by the university's information system network.

There is a strong used-computer market in which to shop for second-hand equipment. Some of this equipment can be very cost-effective to a computer installation that does not require highly sophisticated technology to accomplish its data processing goals. Like any other piece of used equipment, of course, an older CPU is likely to need more repairs and will therefore involve a more costly maintenance contract. Nonetheless, if the acquisition price is low enough and processing feasibility for the equipment's use appears likely, the older CPU may be a good option.

Dedicated Computer Systems

A **dedicated computer system** is a computer system that is used for one primary data processing function. For example, a bank will sometimes use a dedicated computer as an inquiry system for customers wanting to know their account balances. The bank will delegate other data processing functions to a different computer system that is more appropriate for batched (as opposed to online) data processing tasks. Similarly, a university may obtain a computer for faculty research use (highly computational), delegating student processing and administrative processing needs to another computer system. Dedicated computer systems are often smaller than large, general-purpose computer systems, with their uses more limited and their tasks constrained to one type of data processing function. As a result, the total cost of dedicated computer systems may be less than the marginal cost of upgrading a medium-size computer system to a larger computer system. In some instances, it makes sense for a company to acquire an additional small computer system rather than attempt to upgrade its existing facilities.

An especially convenient type of dedicated computer system is the so-called **turn-key computer system.** This type of system comes complete with both hardware and compatible software, specifically developed for a particular set of processing tasks, and is thus an independent processing entity. The convenience of acquiring such a computer system results from the avoidance of any coordination efforts with existing hardware equipment or software packages. Therefore, the purchaser is ready to begin data processing as soon as the equipment is installed. In this sense, the new computer system is analogous to a new car that has been readied for use—the purchaser simply "turns the key" and starts out. Most minicomputer systems are essentially turn-key systems.

The acquisition of a dedicated computer system offers several advantages. One is the previously mentioned cost factor. Another advantage is that its acquisition has the potential to cause minimal disruption of normal data processing—the new computer system can be acquired, tested, and implemented independently. This avoids the risk of "contaminating" a company's day-to-day processing of "live" accounting transactions. Finally, the acquisition of a dedicated system may yield valuable insights into the processing tasks involved in an accounting application. In the course of evaluating the merits of a dedicated computer system for processing inventory transactions, for example, a manufacturing company in Hawaii discovered that its old, card-handling system created a lag of almost three weeks from the time that the initial inventory data was prepared to when the inventory records were finally updated in a master file. The acquisition of a dedicated computer system to process inventory transactions on a real-time basis enabled the manufacturing company to update its inventory balances immediately when inventory transactions took place.

Dedicated computer systems also have their drawbacks. These computer systems tend to be more limited in what they can do, constrained in how much peripheral equipment can be added to the CPU mainframe, and restricted in the kinds of programming languages and other software support that can be used in the data processing environment. Another consideration is the fact that dedicated hardware is flexible but the software often is not. Thus, for example, the software written for an inventory-processing system to run on a small computer is usually inefficient when run on a larger computer system. (The acquisition of inflexible programming support is definitely not recommended, although it sometimes proves a necessary evil.) A final negative factor is the observation that, by definition, dedicated systems provide little opportunity for interfacing with other accounting information systems software. Thus, for example, if a company's inventory-processing software package were to be run in a dedicated environment, there would be limited opportunity for this inventory accounting application to interface with the general ledger system run on the company's main computer system. In addition, the inventory information stored on the files of the dedicated system may not be available for use in a generalized accounting information system database. The consultants will take both the positive and negative aspects of dedicated computers into consideration during their systems study.

Software Vendors

Our previous discussions on systems study have pointed out the importance of good software to perform the processing tasks required by an accounting information system. Often, in fact, it is the presence or absence of good software application programs that proves to be the crucial factor in the selection of one hardware manufacturer's equipment over another. Thus, for example, one computer manufacturer may have superior hardware in terms of processing capability but still lose sales to the manufacturer of "weaker" equipment with better-developed software.

The acquisition, development, and maintenance of computer programs for firms' accounting information systems are a continuing process in almost all active EDP centers. In the United States, for example, it is estimated that over 1% of our gross national product—over $10 billion—is spent on software each year. In addition, surveys of software users reveal that the software budget of the typical user of a computer system is rising by 20% every year.

Usually, a company will begin with a comparatively "bare bones" system, adapting it to the company's processing needs and acquiring additional software support as time and resources permit. Because typical EDP centers of companies have at least as much money invested in software support as they do in hardware, it is clear that software acquisition involves important resource decisions. In this section, we analyze factors important to these decisions.

For the purposes of discussion, it is convenient to group all computer-program software into three major categories: (1) operating systems, (2) utility programs, and (3) application programs. Of these three categories, the first has traditionally been the exclusive domain of the hardware manufacturers. This is because the hardware manufacturer usually develops systems software in parallel with hardware, and therefore has time to work on improved versions of its operating systems before such software actually reaches the market. Thus, generally speaking, very few companies develop their own operating systems. In recent years, however, both the hardware manufacturers and the users of EDP systems themselves have sometimes modified acquired operating system programs in order to accommodate special idiosyncrasies of a particular computer center. One of the most common modifications, for example, is to revise the operating system to cause a third- (or fourth-) generation operating system to "emulate," which means to simulate the behavior of a second- (or third-) generation system in order to permit companies with "old" software to run their programs on newer, more efficient equipment. Thus, emulation eases the transition to higher generation equipment.

The biggest market in software products, however, lies in utility and application programs (categories 2 and 3 of computer-program software mentioned previously). In these two areas of programs, hardware manufacturers, software-development houses, and even individual user companies of EDP systems have been able to develop good software products. Thus, in the last few years, the supplier market for software products has been growing and becoming increasingly more competitive. As a result, it is now possible to purchase (or lease), for instance, a sorting program or an accounts payable program from a large number of vendors.

From the perspective of the individual EDP center, the basic software decision is whether to lease or purchase an already developed proprietary software package from an independent vendor or to develop a particular software system "in-house" (i.e., by the user company itself). The software-acquisition decision is a classic case of the make-or-buy decision especially in the area of application programs. All other things being equal, of course, the choice is simple: acquire the most effective system (based on its expected costs compared to its expected benefits) whether this means an in-house development job or an external acquisition. Because all other things rarely are equal, however, it is necessary to look further into the factors that weigh heavily in the decision-making process regarding software acquisition. Management consultants, as part of their systems design work on a company's computerized system, would become involved in the decision-making process regarding the acquisition of software from an independent vendor (i.e., acquiring proprietary software) or the in-house development of software. We will now examine the proprietary software and the in-house development of software areas.

Advantages of Acquiring Software from an Independent Vendor

The advantages of acquiring proprietary software include (1) low risk, (2) lower cost, (3) shorter implementation time, (4) standardization, (5) internal control, and, of course, (6) avoidance of an in-house effort.

Low risk refers to the likelihood of the company that sells the software going out of business. At one time, most software vendors depended on program software sales not only for their revenues, but also for their very existence. Many of these software companies were small and had limited, easily outdated products. Consequently, the software vendors often went bankrupt, thereby making recourse to their assistance extremely risky in the event of software problems. In certain instances, an absence of documentation for some of this software and a buyer's fear that the software company would not stand behind its product added to these risks. As a result, EDP users were very hesitant to purchase programming packages from independent software vendors, even though the software was often of superior quality. Thus, earlier EDP users looked to the big hardware manufacturers in the belief that at least the hardware companies would be around to service products when trouble developed. Ironically, history has revealed that such confidence in the "big" hardware manufacturers has often been misplaced. For example, GE, RCA, and Xerox corporations each spent millions of dollars to develop, manufacture, and promote their own computer equipment, only to pull out of the computer market several years later when anticipated profits failed to materialize. Companies that were then utilizing these corporations' equipment were faced with limited future hardware and software support.

Today, it would appear that many of the aforementioned fears no longer apply. Most experts in the computer field recognize the software-development field as a legitimate, thriving industry in its own right. Recent surveys indicate that program packages developed by independent software houses are often preferred, in terms of quality, to packages developed by hardware manufacturers (also called hardware and software suppliers). Many hundreds of such independent software houses are operating profitably today.

Lower cost refers to the purchase price of the proprietary software in comparison with an in-house development effort to write and document the same set of programs. A commonly quoted ratio is a purchase-cost amount of one-fifth the developmental cost. Thus, as a general rule of thumb, it will cost a company five times more to write its own software package than to buy a comparable software package on the open market. It would stand to reason that purchase costs would be cheaper than development costs since the software vendor is able to spread the development costs over more users, thereby enabling a lower cost per package. Because many user companies require FORTRAN or COBOL compilers, sorting routines, and elementary statistical packages, these items tend to be fairly inexpensive to acquire. On the other hand, highly specialized inventory-control packages or integrated accounting routines—for example, routines that simultaneously process a company's credit-sales transactions, update the accounts receivable subsidiary ledger and the inventory file, as well as compute the cost of merchandise sold relating to the sales transactions—tend to be more expensive to acquire.

Lower cost also means that the software vendor's price is a "known-in-advance" charge to the user. Sometimes, this is a one-time fee (i.e., the purchase cost), but more often it is a monthly rental agreement cost or a lease contract cost for a specified duration. Usually, the rental agreement or the lease contract includes a limited "maintenance contract." The maintenance contract guarantees a restricted amount of modification work to be performed by the vendor on the software system to correct errors detected during the course of the software's use. The contract also usually guarantees continued maintenance for a specified period beyond the date the system was obtained. It should be noted, however, that there is nothing necessarily standard about such maintenance contracts. Rather, the buyer and seller are free to negotiate the terms of their contract.

Shorter implementation time refers to the fact that most of the software vendor's programs have been pretested and that the documentation is already available prior to purchase. Thus, implementation problems are usually limited to compatibility constraints with the user company's present hardware and software system. This does not mean that any new computer software package written for a company's existing equipment is ready for use "off the shelf," but rather that the

software vendor is likely to have anticipated the user's needs and that the package may be expected to perform according to the specifications outlined by the vendor.

Standardization indicates that the programs are usually written in conformance with "standard" programming procedures and that adequate documentation will be available for the user company to (1) understand the individual programs comprising the package and (2) make modifications as necessary. Standardization normally suggests a certain degree of conformance of the programming package with existing vendor software perhaps already in use by the potential buyer. For example, a company might start out with a simple general ledger accounting package developed by an independent vendor for a particular IBM computer system. Later, it might be advantageous for the company to purchase a specific inventory-processing package from this same vendor because the new package could also run on the IBM computer system already in use and could be expected to interface easily with the existing accounting programs.

Standardization also assures the user company that the processing effort—for example, preparing the payroll—will always be performed the same way regardless of the location of the processing system. This means both uniform accounting procedures and consistent output listings will occur. For companies with multiple EDP centers scattered across the country, this type of standardization is sometimes invaluable.

We have discussed the importance of *internal control* in Chapters 9 through 12. Programs that handle sensitive data must be secured from unauthorized use. This security is especially important in time-sharing and remote-terminal environments. Similarly, programs that process financial data must be free of both accidental and intentional errors. Because such security features are required by a variety of potential data processing users, the purchased packages are likely to contain many of these important security features as a matter of course.

Avoidance of an in-house effort has been

listed as a separate category because of several factors. As noted previously, in-house development is usually more costly than the acquisition of software from an independent vendor, and this, in itself, may be sufficient to motivate the user company toward the purchase or lease option. Furthermore, the purchase or lease of software may be the only option if the programming expertise required for the in-house development job is not available in a company or the company's EDP budget cannot be expanded to permit acquisition of additional developmental staff. Another consideration is the fact that in-house developmental projects are notoriously overoptimistic about what can be done with the time and resources allotted the programming effort. In one project, for example, all the software for a planned two-year systems-development job familiar to the authors had not been completed by the fifth year of effort, even with the addition of two extra systems analysts! This situation is not unusual in the history of systems software development.

Advantages of In-House Development of Software

The merits of acquiring proprietary software are considerable, but the acquisition of proprietary software also has drawbacks. The disadvantages of acquiring proprietary software are basically the advantages of in-house software development. Among the advantages of in-house software development are (1) "custom" work, (2) cost and the avoidance of proprietary software revisions in order to conform to a company's specific data processing needs, (3) assurance of system compatibility, (4) minimization of start-up and training costs at implementation time, and (5) higher EDP employee morale.

Perhaps the most important advantage of the in-house developmental effort is that it is a "custom job." For certain specialized applications, of course, the in-house programming effort may be the only choice available. But even if this were not the case, the in-house option still has the advantage of providing the user just what

processing is desired in just the proper amounts. Thus, the user does not pay for unnecessary frills or options and, of course, the user company is also free to design whatever unique features are needed in its organization. Moreover, since the effort is performed in-house, changes and additions are also likely to be easier to make because the programming expertise required for such alterations already resides within the user company's EDP staff. Maintenance becomes easier for the same reason. Finally, because the user's EDP staff is familiar with the system, training and implementation can be performed in parallel with the developmental effort. Thus, staffing requirements for the new system can be forecast in advance, suggestions from employees within the system can be incorporated into the system while it is still under development, weaknesses in the new system can be corrected more easily, and so forth.

In the previous discussion regarding the acquisition of software from an independent vendor, lower cost was considered to be one of the advantages. However, in specific situations, the cost of an in-house effort may still prove to be cheaper in the long run. For example, rarely can an accounting package be acquired by a company from a software vendor, "thrown" on the company's computer, and run directly "off the shelf." Rather, revisions must typically be made to make the package programs conform to company standards, file structures, input/output equipment configurations, and so forth. Therefore, additional cash resources beyond the initial purchase expenditure must be included in the cost calculations for a given package acquisition. The logical conclusion is: it *can* cost more to purchase and make extensive modifications to a proprietary software programming package than to develop the same software system in-house.

Because proprietary software is written for the mass market, there is no assurance that any particular package will be compatible with a user company's other application programs. The in-house effort ensures system compatibility. Thus, such considerations as successful data-file interface (to ensure that the system can use the company's existing files in their present form) and hardware limitations (e.g., CPU and input/output capacities) are not a problem with in-house development because the software programs are designed with these constraints in mind. Proprietary software, on the other hand, may not have this compatibility.

System compatibility must also include a volume dimension. For example, it usually does not make sense for a company to acquire an externally prepared accounts receivable program written for a large data processing user with 50,000 accounts if the intended application presently processes one-tenth the volume of customer accounts. Of course, room for expansion is important in any data processing system, and the company is wise to plan for a reasonable increase in processing volume as projections of future data flows might warrant. However, processing programs for large-scale users are rarely cost-effective for the small-scale data processor. The programs for large-scale users normally necessitate peripheral hardware and software that the small-scale users would find too expensive to acquire.

The area of start-up costs and training costs associated with new software is important regardless of whether the software is developed in-house or acquired from an independent vendor. There is little doubt that such costs will be incurred no matter which new software system (i.e., proprietary or in-house) is implemented. The real question is not under which option such costs can be avoided but rather which of the two options is more cost-effective. For reasons already mentioned (such as compatibility), it would appear that the in-house development may have a "start-up" and "training" advantage over proprietary software. For example, there is much to be said for the convenience of having immediate access to the programmers and systems analysts who designed the software system as well as being able to rely on dedicated company personnel to provide instructional support and guidance during the initial implementation

and subsequent operation of the new software system.

Our last advantage of in-house development is higher EDP employee morale. For a particular EDP installation, of course, it is possible that the present staff of programmers are so busy that they would welcome the acquisition of proprietary software and thereby avoid the additional responsibility of a new software system development. However, this is not always the case. Avoiding the in-house effort is sometimes considered a management "vote of no confidence" and in isolated cases may actually bring about a reduction in the size of the existing programming staff. Moreover, there is the "not-invented-here" syndrome—an attitude held by many programmers and systems analysts that only an in-house effort will truly serve the processing needs of a company's installation(s). This attitude undoubtedly has inspired some programmers to call proprietary software "out-house" programming. In any event, however, it is clear that the decision to pursue a software-developmental effort in-house is a vote of confidence for the company's existing team of programmers and systems analysts. Morale is positively affected, and this consideration in and of itself may sometimes tilt the decision toward the in-house development of software.

Acquisition of Computer Services

We should mention that because a company acquiring its first computerized data processing system normally will not have trained computer personnel, it may decide to negotiate with an independent organization called a **facilities-management services organization.** These organizations will manage a company's data processing facilities on a contract basis. The company will typically own or lease its computer hardware and will pay a monthly fee to the facilities-management services organization for providing trained computer personnel to handle its data processing activities. Banks and insurance companies, for example, are common users of facilities-management services.

By contracting with a facilities-management services organization for data processing work, a company is thereby freed from the daily operation of its computer center. For the novice company with little or no knowledge of the technical aspects of computers, facilities-management services organizations can also provide assistance in acquiring computer hardware and software, modernizing computer installations, and determining efficient operating policies and procedures. A user of facilities-management services is relieved of such personnel activities as recruiting and training the new employees needed for its computer center. Perhaps the greatest disadvantage of using facilities-management services organizations is that control of valuable information is turned over to outsiders (i.e., employees of the facilities-management services organization). These outsiders may not be sensitive to the importance of accuracy and security in their daily data processing tasks.

Let us assume for a moment that none of the hardware and software vendors' proposals were satisfactory to a company's steering committee. The principal reason for management's negative reactions to each proposal was cost. When the consultants compared the anticipated cash benefits and cash costs of various computer design proposals, the excess present value indexes were favorable for several possible computer configurations. Therefore, the hardware and software supplier evaluation stage of the consultants' systems design work began. When each vendor's detailed systems proposal was eventually presented to top management, however, the specific costs of the individual proposals were considerably higher than anticipated. At this point, the company's steering committee may do one of three things: (1) request additional systems proposals from other hardware and software suppliers, (2) abandon the idea of converting to a computerized data processing system, or (3) investigate the acquisition of computerized data processing services from an outside organization.

The two major types of organizations that provide computerized data processing services to other companies (called user companies) are **service bureaus** and **time-sharing organizations.** It is common for small companies that do not have the volume of transactions to justify acquiring their own computer systems, but yet desire the benefits of computerized data processing, to use either a service bureau or a time-sharing organization to process their financial data. However, even medium-sized and large companies often find it advantageous to use the services offered by these data processing organizations. A user company's data processing costs can be significantly reduced by sharing the computer facilities of service bureaus and time-sharing organizations with other users, rather than leasing or purchasing its own computer system.

A service bureau often provides users with batch processing of their financial data. The bureau's fee normally is based on the time required to process a company's batch of data. Some service bureaus require the user to physically transport its source document input data to the service bureau and subsequently pick up the processed output data. Other service bureaus have regular pickup and delivery service (included in the price). For example, an organization may hire a service bureau to process its semi-monthly payroll. Prior to the actual payday (perhaps one or two days), the organization will send its payroll information (employee time cards, any hourly wage rate changes, etc.) to the service bureau. The service bureau will have previously prepared a master file (such as a magnetic tape file) containing relevant payroll information about the organization's employees. The output from the payroll processing run will be a payroll register and the paychecks.

As this example demonstrates, the organization obtains the benefits from computerized processing of its accounting data without incurring the major costs of purchasing or leasing its own computer system. There are, however, certain disadvantages in using a service bureau rather than one's own computer system. The principal disadvantage is the data-security problem. The user company must send its important source documents to the outside service bureau organization and run the risk that some of these source documents may get lost in transit, be misplaced by the service bureau's employees, or be fraudulently manipulated. Consequently, before hiring a service bureau to handle its data processing functions, the user company should inquire about the service bureau's security features. The user can also establish some of its own controls to detect any loss of source documents either in transit or on the service bureau's premises (e.g., hash totals and record counts). Another disadvantage of having a service bureau process a company's financial data is possible delays in receiving the output information. Due to the back-log of work required on other users' financial data, the service bureau may be unable to process a company's financial transactions in as short a time as the company desires.

Whereas a service bureau offers batch processing of financial data, **time-sharing organizations** provide user companies with online capabilities. Thus, each user company has an online input device (such as a remote keyboard terminal) which is directly connected to the time-sharing organization's central processing unit. This online capability permits real-time processing of a company's financial transactions. Rather than physically transporting its source documents to the service bureau for processing, the user company inputs data directly to the time-sharing organization's CPU. In many accounting applications processed through a time-sharing organization, the user also requests immediate output reports (e.g., a report on updated inventory balances).

The online, real-time data processing capability offered by time-sharing organizations tends to be more costly than the batch processing methods of service bureaus. If a company desires fast feedback report information for management decision making, however, time-sharing is likely to be better than a service bureau. Also, if a company has sporadic processing needs that require a lot of computing power, a time-sharing organization may be cost-effective. The monthly cost of

a time-sharing organization's services includes a fixed cost for the terminal equipment facilities and a variable cost for the communication time (in processing data) between the terminal and the central processing unit. An additional variable cost is for the quantity of file storage used.

Some time-sharing organizations offer their users access to a centralized data base of financial information. For example, a retail store that allows customers to use store credit cards for purchasing merchandise can obtain immediate credit-rating information about individual customers from a time-sharing organization's data base file of credit reference information. This feedback enables the store to evaluate the advisability of granting credit cards to specific customers.

From a security point of view, a company using a time-sharing organization's services should establish controls that prevent unauthorized employees from entering transactions (which could be fictitious transactions to commit a fraudulent act) on its data terminal. Chapter 10 emphasized that password codes can be utilized in an online system. The code numbers should be known only to the specific organizational employees who are responsible for data input. As a further means of preventing unauthorized employees from learning the code numbers, many companies change their codes periodically (e.g., weekly or monthly).

SUMMARY

This chapter has continued the discussion of the systems study started in Chapter 13 by analyzing the design phase of a systems study. The beginning of the chapter assumed that a company's top management personnel were in favor of converting their present data processing system from a manual to a computerized system. Therefore, the consultants began the phase of their systems study called design.

The first major activity in systems design is the feasibility evaluation concerning the acquisition of a computerized data processing system. Four types of feasibility are investigated by consultants: (1) technical feasibility, (2) operational feasibility, (3) schedule feasibility, and (4) economic feasibility. The accountants on the management consulting team are involved principally in the economic feasibility evaluation. Here, a cost/benefit analysis is performed on each preliminary design proposal for computerizing a company's manual system. A proposed computer system will be worth further consideration only if the findings from all four feasibility evaluations are positive.

The second major step in systems design is the preparation of a detailed systems design. This design is based on the systems analysis work and the results of the feasibility evaluation. The consultants begin by designing system outputs (i.e., specifying the types and content of reports). Designing the processing for an information system means providing an overview of the processing steps that will be included in computer programs. Input design includes design of source documents for the data elements that will be stored and processed in either a data base or file-based structure. Several design tools such as HIPO Charts, Warnier-Orr diagrams, prototyping, data flow diagrams, and flowcharts may be used for planning and designing the inputs, processing steps, and outputs for a new system.

The third stage of systems design is to prepare a systems specifications report for hardware and software supplier evaluation. This report contains detailed information about each design proposal that satisfies the feasibility requirements. This includes background information about the company, detailed information about the company's current data processing system and its problems, detailed specifications of outputs, processing and inputs for each detailed systems design proposal, an indication of what the vendors should include in their proposals, and a time schedule for systems implementation.

The specifications report is sent to various computer suppliers to use as the basis for their submission of specific hardware and software proposals to the company in the final stage of systems design. The vendors may be asked to provide a complete new computerized information system, or just specific hardware or software. Hardware required to improve a current data processing system may consist of a second computer, a dedicated computer, or peripheral equipment. The types of software that might be needed are operating systems, utility programs, application programs, or all three of these. An alternative to acquiring hardware and software is for the company to use computerized data processing services from an outside organization. The two major types of organizations that perform computerized data processing work for other companies are service bureaus (which offer principally batch processing services) and time-sharing organizations (which offer online data processing services). By using either of these organizations, a company is able to obtain computerized processing of its financial data without incurring the major costs involved in purchasing or leasing its own hardware and software system.

Key Terms You Should Know

canned programs
cash benefits
cash costs
computer-aided software engineering (CASE) tool
cost/benefit analysis
data base
data dictionary
data flow diagrams
dedicated computer system

demand report
economic feasibility
exception report
excess present value index
facilities-management services organization
feasibility evaluation
files
flowcharts
hardware and software suppliers

hardware-monitor modules
HIPO charts
I/O bound
one-vendor syndrome
operational feasibility
proprietary software
prototyping
request for proposal (RFP)
run log of equipment utilization

schedule feasibility
service bureaus
systems design
systems improvements
systems specifications report
technical feasibility
time-sharing organizations
turn-key computer system
Warnier-Orr diagram

Discussion Questions

14-1. Why does the detailed systems design work begin with the design of system outputs?

14-2. Name some of the reports that might be outputs from an inventory control system. What is the nature of these reports (i.e., are they issued on a regular basis, on demand, or when triggered by a predesignated event)?

14-3. Why would the use of special design tools, such as HIPO charts and Warnier-Orr diagrams, be necessary in designing the processing steps for a particular computerized application?

14-4. What are some advantages of prototyping? How is it different from traditional systems development?

14-5. If you were designing a completely new integrated accounting information system for a medium-size retailer, would you use prototyping at all? Why or why not?

14-6. One of the benefits that normally results from computerizing a company's previous manual data processing system is a reduction in the company's average annual accounts receivable balance. How is this reduction usually accomplished, and why is the accounts receivable reduction considered beneficial to a company?

14-7. As discussed in this chapter, simulation techniques can be used to test a company's computer programs before the programs are implemented into the company's system. A simulation technique for testing the mathematical logic of a company's accounts-receivable processing program was illustrated in this chapter. Try to think of several additional simulation techniques that might be employed to test a company's computer programs for processing other types of accounting transactions.

14-8. Why does the design phase of a systems study follow the analysis phase?

14-9. What is the purpose of the feasibility evaluation activity of systems design work? Should this activity precede or follow the preparation of a systems specifications report for hardware and software supplier evaluation? Explain.

14-10. As part of their systems design work, management consultants should examine four feasibility areas. Discuss the reason (or reasons) for evaluating each of these feasibility areas.

14-11. Discuss some of the annual cash benefits and annual cash costs that a company would normally have from converting its manual data processing system to a computerized batch processing system.

14-12. "In order for the consultants to begin the work of preparing a systems specifications report for hardware and software supplier evaluation, their design proposal must be totally feasible." Discuss the meaning of this statement.

14-13. Howard Berry, management consultant for the International Consulting Organization, has just completed a feasibility evaluation regarding the conversion of his client company's batch processing computerized system to an online, real-time system. The results from his technical, operational, and schedule feasibility evaluations were all positive. However, the economic feasibility evaluation outcome was quite negative. In your opinion, what course of action should now be taken by Howard Berry?

14-14. What is the purpose of a "systems specifications report"? In what ways, if any, does the data included in this report differ from the data accumulated by the consultants during their feasibility evaluation work?

14-15. Henry Heron is the owner of a minor league baseball team. His team has completed 60 games of its 140-game schedule. Henry is currently worried about two major problems: (1) the low attendance at home games and (2) the strong possibility that many of his cashiers working at the ticket windows are pocketing portions of each game's cash receipts. To help solve these problems, Henry has hired an outside consultant, Ozzie Seaver. Regarding the low-attendance problem, Ozzie is told by the baseball team's traveling secretary that many promotional activities have been tried in an effort to draw fans to the home games. Most of these promotions, however, turned out to be financial disasters. For example, at one of last week's games, every paying customer was given a baseball autographed by the team. Even though a large crowd came to the ball park for this promotional event, the cost per baseball (approximately $2.50) exceeded the average ticket price paid by each customer (approximately $2.25) attending that night's game. Regarding the problem with the cashiers, the only suggestion that has been made by the baseball team's management is to fire all the present cashiers and hire a completely new crew.

Assuming that you are Ozzie Seaver, what are some possible suggestions that you could offer to solve the baseball team's two systems problems?

14-16. In each of the following hypothetical cases, indicate a method of data processing that you would recommend and the reasons why. State both the advantages and shortcomings of your recommended methods.[1]

Case 1: A small supply company that handles 300 different inventory items and processes most orders by mail. On the average 30 orders are processed daily. This company has 40 employees.

Case 2: A medium-size medical clinic that has on its staff 25 physicians, 15 technicians, 46 nurses, and 30 administrative and clerical personnel. On the average, the clinic handles 450 patients per day who either pay for their treatment through an insurance program (government or private) or have a charge account. Thus, few patients pay cash.

Case 3: A large, nationwide supply company that has in its warehouses from 20,000 to 30,000 different inventory items. Ninety percent of its orders are placed by telephone where most of the customers wish to know if the items requested are on hand for immediate delivery. Most customers will not accept backorders. The company employs 4000 people.

Case 4: A large motel organization has 300 motels scattered across the nation.

Case 5: A large manufacturing company has 16 plants and 175 warehouses throughout the country. In addition to general administrative data processing requirements (the company employs 26,000 people and has 40,000 customers), the company implements many management science techniques such as PERT, linear programming, forecasting, inventory control, and so forth.

14-17. The data contained within a systems specifications report include "detailed information about the problem (or problems) in a company's current data processing system." Why is it necessary to include this type of information in the systems specifications report that a consultant prepares for a client company?

14-18. Distinguish between a service bureau and a time-sharing organization. Under what circumstances might a specific company elect to utilize the facilities offered by a service bureau or a time-sharing organization?

14-19. Discuss some of the relevant factors that should be considered by a company's consultants and top management personnel when they are comparing proposals from various hardware and software suppliers for converting the company's manual data processing system to a batch processing computerized system. (*Note:* For each named factor, make sure to indicate why it is important to the decision-making process of selecting a specific hardware and software supplier's computer system.)

14-20. What factors should be considered in the decision to lease a tape or disk drive from a computer hardware manufacturer? What reasons might the EDP manager have for seeking to acquire yet additional hardware equipment?

14-21. A company can either purchase or lease its hardware and software system from a computer vendor. If you were a management consultant for an organization that was acquiring its first computerized system, what are some of the important factors that you should consider when recommending to the company's management either the purchasing or the leasing of the automated system?

14-22. Ed Meld, employed by the AAZ Consulting Firm, was asked by his friend Burt Bones (the general manager and majority stockholder of the Pacific Worldwinds, a professional football team) to design an

---

[1] Used with permission of John G. Burch, Jr. and Felix R. Strater, Jr., *Information Systems: Theory and Practice* (New York: Wiley, 1986).

online, real-time computer system for "the more efficient operation of the football franchise." Ed was quite confused because he could not think of any possible uses for an online, real-time system within the operational activities of a football team (or any other type of athletic team). Assume that you are also employed at the AAZ Consulting Firm. Provide several suggestions to Ed concerning specific areas of athletic teams' (football teams, baseball teams, etc.) information systems where an online, real-time computer configuration might be beneficial to managerial decision making.

14-23. Sandown Power and Light Company (SP&L Co.) is an electric utility in the southwest United States. The demand for electricity is quite seasonal in the area served by SP&L Co. because of the heavy use of air conditioning during the summer months. Currently, customers are billed monthly for the amount of electricity consumed during the previous month. The rates charged by SP&L Co. for the consumption of electricity are the same for all volume levels.

SP&L Co.'s assistant to the financial vice-president has suggested that the company adopt an equal monthly billing system. Under this plan, a customer's total annual electrical needs would be estimated for the coming year from past experience; the customer would be billed on the first of each month for one-twelfth of the estimated annual amount. At the end of the billing year the customer would be billed for the amount of electricity consumed in excess of the annual estimate or receive reimbursement for the underusage. Consequently, the customer would receive a bill for the same amount each month and then either an additional bill or reimbursement, depending on his or her actual usage of electricity, at the end of the twelfth month. SP&L Co.'s rate structure for electricity consumption will not change with the new billing system.

The billing cycle would begin in November and end with October. The annual "settlement" would occur at the end of October.

Requirements

A. Discuss the advantages and disadvantages of an equal monthly billing system for Sandown Power and Light Company. Include in your discussion the effect(s) of this billing system on SP&L's cash flow, accounts receivable balances, and profitability.
B. If you were a residential customer of SP&L Co. and had been offered a choice between the new equal

monthly billing system and the current billing system, what would be the important factors that you would consider before reaching a decision as to which system to select?

(CMA Adapted)

14-24. Rockland Company is a large printing firm with about 500 outstanding customer accounts at any one time.

The credit and collections department of the sales division is responsible for granting credit, which includes evaluating the credit worthiness of new customers and reviewing the credit status of current customers. This department is also responsible for any follow-up calls to customers who may be slow or delinquent in paying their accounts. The recording of sales and subsequent payments on account and maintenance of subsidiary account records are among the responsibilities of the company's accounting department.

Periodically, the amount of the allowance account to be deducted from the "Accounts Receivable" on the balance sheet should be reviewed to be sure that it does reflect a reasonable estimate of the amount of the uncollectible accounts included in the accounts receivable balance. A careful and comprehensive review of this allowance account would seem to require input from both the credit and collections and accounting departments.

The balance of the "Allowance for Uncollectible Accounts Receivable" account appearing in Rockland Company's financial statements is the result of the following.

1. The current-year provision for uncollectible accounts, calculated by applying a percentage to the amount of credit sales.
2. The actual customer accounts determined to be uncollectible and written off.
3. The allowance account balance at the beginning of the year.

Requirements

Present the program you would recommend to review the adequacy of the "Allowance for Uncollectible Accounts Receivable" account. In your recommended program, identify the information and analyses that could best be provided by

1. The accounting department.
2. The credit and collections department.

(CMA Adapted)

14-25. There are significantly different income tax treatments associated with lease versus purchase plans for hardware and software resource acquisitions. Drawing from your previous courses in accounting, identify the important tax advantages and disadvantages that would be expected with each option.

14-26. Tom Henry, the planning vice-president of Elaine Dolgin's Dress Company, had just been presented an expenditure proposal from his EDP manager, Lee Tracy. As the vice-president began to read the report, he realized that his right-hand person was suggesting that the company purchase a second computer system for its data processing. Throwing the report down on his desk, he roared to his secretary: "Get that woman in here! Buying another computer system is the last thing this company needs!" What possible justification could Lee Tracy have had for acquiring a second computer system if the company already had one?

14-27. Charles Sterling Portwood III was the well-respected head of the Pan Pacific Engineering Company. The company had flowered from a proprietorship organization in 1980 to a partnership organization (with three partners) in 1988. There are 20 full-time employees working for Pan Pacific Engineering Company. The company had recently acquired a small business computer to perform some of its data processing functions, and Lance O'Neal, a company employee, had been put in charge of acquiring a payroll software package. After a week's searching, Lance reported to his boss, "Charles, I think I've found just the right thing for us. This payroll system will run on anything from a small computer up to a million-dollar central processor and handle the payroll for up to 10,000 employees. If we buy it tonight, I can probably have it running tomorrow in time for the end-of-the-month payroll." Comment.

Problems

14-28. The wing commander of a tactical fighter wing has requested the implementation of a formal information system to assist him in evaluating the quality of aircrew members. Although there are many factors related to determining an individual's quality level, it has been recommended that one source of objective data is from the testing process administered by the Standardization/Evaluation Section in the fighter wing. Each flight crew member is tested periodically either by an instrument check or by a tactical/proficiency check to detect violations of standardized operating procedures or errors in judgment. The result of a test is either pass or fail and discrepancies such as single-engine landing, dangerous pass, incorrect holding pattern, and so forth are noted where applicable. A general feeling exists in the Standardization/Evaluation Section that if these reports were prepared and distributed in a timely fashion, the wing commander could take swift corrective action to prevent a hazardous practice or critical weakness from occurring. Further analysis indicates that such a report can be prepared daily, five days a week throughout the year, at a cost of $14.10 per report. This time period for reporting is judged acceptable by the Standardization/Evaluation Section.

Although there are many benefits anticipated from implementing such a system in terms of preventing the loss of aircrew members' lives and the loss of aircraft property, as well as increasing the effectiveness of the fighter wing, the wing commander has requested that all new information systems be initially justified on pure economic grounds before other considerations are evaluated. As the management consultant assigned to this project, you have decided to take the approach that the proposed system will help reduce the rate of major accidents from 2 to 1.5% (as similar systems have done elsewhere to economically justify their implementation). From your investigation, you have

Cost of Major Accident

Certain Costs	
Aircraft	$1,600,000
Accident investigation	6,000
Property damage (impact point)	2,000
Total	$1,608,000
Possible Costs (both crew members are lost)	
Invested training in crew members	
2 @ $25,000	$ 50,000
Survivors benefits and mortuary costs	
2 @ $50,000	100,000
Total	$150,000
Probability of crew loss is .25	

gathered the following statistics concerning major accidents.

Requirement

Can the proposed system be economically justified using this approach? Explain. Identify other economic factors not considered in the problem.[2]

14-29. (Library Research) To attract clients, service bureaus often advertise in such publications as *Datamation, Computerworld,* and the *Journal of Systems Management.* Local newspapers and more technical trade publications are also likely sources of such advertisements. Find three advertisements by service bureaus and compare them. What special services appear to be emphasized in each advertisement? What kinds of features offered by these service bureaus would motivate customers to choose one service bureau over another?

CASE ANALYSES

14-30. Milok Company

Vincent Maloy, Director of Special Projects and Analysis for Milok Company, is responsible for preparing corporate financial analyses and projections monthly and for reviewing and presenting to upper management the financial impacts of proposed strategies. Data for these financial analyses and projections are obtained from reports developed by Milok's Systems Department and generated from its mainframe computer. Additional data are obtained through terminals via a data inquiry system. Reports and charts for presentations are then prepared by hand and typed. Maloy has tried to have final presentations generated by the computer but has not always been successful.

The Systems Department has developed a package utilizing a terminal emulator to link a microcomputer to the mainframe computer. This allows the microcomputer to become part of the current data inquiry system and enables data to be downloaded to the microcomputer's disk. The data are in a format that allows printing or further manipulation and analyses using commercial software packages (e.g., spreadsheet analysis). The Special Projects and Analysis Department has been chosen to be the first users of this new computer terminal system.

Maloy questioned whether the new system could

[2] Used with permission of John G. Burch, Jr. and Felix R. Strater, Jr., *Information Systems: Theory and Practice* (New York: Wiley, 1986).

do more for his department than implementing the program modification requests that he has submitted to the Systems Department. He also believed that his people would have to become programmers.

Lisa Brandt, a supervisor in Maloy's department, has decided to prepare a briefing for Maloy on the benefits of integrating microcomputers with the mainframe computer. She has used the terminal inquiry system extensively and has learned to use spreadsheet software to prepare special analyses, sometimes with multiple alternatives. She also tried the new package while it was being tested.

Questions

1. Identify five enhancements to current information and reporting that Milok Company should be able to realize by integrating microcomputers with the company's mainframe computer.
2. Explain how the utilization of computer resources would be altered as a result of integrating microcomputers with the company's mainframe computer.
3. Discuss what security of the data is gained or lost by integrating microcomputers with the company's mainframe computer.

(CMA Adapted)

14-31. Polynesian Textile Company

Background

The Polynesian Textile Company, located in Hawaii, started business in 1954. Initially, the company was primarily a family operation. However, during the 1950s and 1960s business had been good and the company expanded rapidly. The firm finally incorporated in 1970.

Although the Polynesian Textile Company had grown in size, the products and services it provides in 1991 are basically the same as those offered in 1954. The Polynesian Textile Company manufactures Hawaiian fabrics in its three production plants. The fabric is sold to various local outlets (e.g., ready-to-wear "muumuu" and "aloha shirt" manufacturers and retail department stores).

Organizational Structure

There are two major functional divisions in the organization—the production and marketing/sales depart-

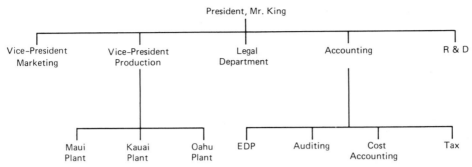

FIGURE 14-10   Organization chart.

ments. The production and marketing/sales functions are supported by several administrative departments: accounting, research and development, legal staff, and public relations. The organization chart is depicted in Figure 14-10.

Computer Acquisition

On the advice of the firm's controller, Mr. Bob Shade, Polynesian Textile acquired and implemented a computer system in 1970. Bob Shade convinced the president, Mr. King, that a computer could facilitate the processing of routine and clerical activities. Because the computer was to be used primarily in accounting/financial applications, the controller was given primary jurisdiction over the operation of the computerized system.

Mr. King was pleased with Bob Shade's work with the computer system. Ever since the computer's installation, Polynesian Textile has experienced a reduction in its operating costs.

Even though most of the company's data processing activities are handled by the computer, the computer center still is not operating at full capacity. At the present time, the computer time is allocated as follows.

1. Accounting applications	65%
2. Research and development	7%
3. Production	5%
4. Marketing	6%
5. Idle time	17%

Bob Shade, as well as Mr. King, is anxious to increase the use of the computer to full capacity. Both men have noticed recently that the cost savings generated by the computer center are slowing down. They believe that by decreasing the amount of idle com-

puter time, the company can increase its rate of return from the computer investment. Therefore, Shade and King are looking for computer applications that would facilitate efficient and effective operations within the entire organization.

Increasing Nonfinancial Applications

Mr. King recently attended a conference on computer applications for business organizations. At this conference, nonfinancial applications of the computer were discussed. Excited about the conference discussions, Mr. King wants to decrease the idle capacity time of his company's computer system by utilizing the computer for nonfinancial applications.

Mr. King discussed some of the ideas presented at the conference with Bob Shade. The next week the following memorandum was sent to all of King's managers.

TO: All Managerial Employees
FROM: Mr. King, President
RE: Utilization of Computer Facilities

Did you realize that our computer facilities and computer staff can help you with planning and controlling your divisional operations? Computer applications in nonfinancial areas are feasible and can be profitable for the whole organization.

If you have an operational area which could be facilitated by the computer, please do not hesitate to talk to our controller, Bob Shade. He will be able to explain the capabilities of our computer system. Moreover, he can help you develop programs for your particular project.

I am encouraging all of you to think of ways in which the computer facilities can be useful to your department.

Conversation Between Mr. King and Bob Shade

Six months after the memorandum was distributed, Mr. King and Bob Shade had the following conversation.

Mr. King: I don't understand it. Following the initial installation of the computer, we experienced significant reductions in our processing and operating costs. Yet, by expanding the computer applications to nonfinancial areas, we have not yet experienced comparable cost savings.

Mr. Shade: My department has tried to give the nonfinancial user departments as much help in developing programs and suggesting potential applications as possible. In fact, I have designated a staff member to help these operating departments. His job is solely to facilitate coordination between the accounting department and the other user departments.

Mr. King: Well, according to the conference speakers, we should be reaping benefits equal to or exceeding those experienced from computerizing our financial applications. Something must be wrong!

The Investigation

Mr. King hired an outside consultant, John Dole, to investigate the situation and to make change recommendations.

After reviewing the standard computer procedures and departmental policies with the controller and EDP manager, the consultant talked to some of the organization's personnel. Presented next are excerpts of his conversations with the production manager and the marketing manager.

Conversation Between Mr. Dole and Mr. Cooke (production manager)

Mr. Dole: How useful do you think computer applications are for your department?

Mr. Cooke: I really haven't given it much thought. Mr. King was talking to me about using the computer for inventory control, but I just don't have the time right now to explore all the possible computer applica-

tions. All I know is that the accounting department sends me a lot of reports. . . . more than I know what to do with. My time is limited. Therefore, I only glance at a portion of what accounting sends me. What do I need another set of reports for? Furthermore, I have indicated to Bob Shade that I would like to receive production reports expressed in quantities rather than in dollar figures. He said that he would see what could be done, but nothing has happened so far. If he can't accommodate me in this one small request, how could he be of much help in designing programs outside of the accounting area?

Conversation Between Mr. Dole and Mr. Bishop (marketing manager)

Mr. Dole: What do you think about increasing your department's use of computer applications.

Mr. Bishop: I can see great possibilities for increased computer applications for my department. Especially in the area of decision making, the computer could help us in a function such as sales forecasting.

Unfortunately, the accounting department often vetoes our proposed applications. If our projects are not rejected, they are usually given a low priority rating. The reasons for denial are many. The major argument given by the accounting department for rejecting our project proposals is that these projects will not provide a direct economic benefit to the company.

I think our controller is too wrapped up with efficiency. In the long run, the company will suffer if Shade continues limiting the types of applications processed by the computer.

Recommendations

After talking to these various people, the consultant felt that he could provide several recommendations to Mr. King for solving the existing problem(s).

Questions

1. Assuming that you are the consultant, John Dole, define the problem(s) that exist in Polynesian Tex-

tile Company. What do you feel are the causes of the problem(s)?

2. As John Dole, what would you recommend to solve the company's problem(s)?

14-32. *Kenbart Company*

Kenbart Company decided increased emphasis had to be placed on profit planning and the analysis of results compared to its plans. A new computerized profit planning system has been implemented to help in this objective.

The company employs contribution margin reporting for internal reporting purposes and applies the concept of flexible budgeting for estimating variable costs. The following terms are used by Kenbart's executive management when reviewing and analyzing actual results and the profit plan.

- **Original Plan**—Profit plan approved and adopted by management for the year.
- **Revised Plan**—Original plan modified as a consequence of action taken during the year (usually quarterly) by executive management.
- **Flexed Revised Plan**—The most current plan (i.e., either original plan or revised plan, if one has been

prepared) adjusted for changes in volume and variable expense rates.

- **YTD Actual Results**—The actual results of operations for the year.
- **Current Outlook**—The summation of the actual year-to-date results of operations plus the flexed revised plan for the remaining months of the year.

Executive management meets monthly to review the actual results compared with the profit plan. Any assumptions or major changes in the profit plan usually are incorporated on a quarterly basis once the first quarter is completed.

An outline of the basic Profit Plan Report, which was designed by the data processing department, is reproduced below. This report is prepared at the end of each month. In addition, this report is generated whenever executive management initiates a change or modification in its plans. Consequently, many different versions of a company profit plan exist, which makes analysis difficult and confusing.

Several members of executive management have voiced the disapproval of the Profit Plan Report because the plan column is not well defined and varies in meaning from one report to another. Furthermore, no current-outlook column is included in the report. Therefore, the accounting department has been asked

Kenbart Company
Profit Plan Report
Month, Year

	Month				Year-to-Date			
			Over/ (Under)				Over/ (Under)	
	Actual	Plan	$	%	Actual	Plan	$	%
Sales								
Variable Manufacturing Costs								
Raw materials								
Direct labor								
Variable overhead								
Total variable manufacturing costs								
Manufacturing Margin								
Variable selling expenses								
Contribution Margin								
Fixed Costs								
Manufacturing								
Sales								
General administration								
Income Before Taxes								
Income taxes								
Net Income								

to work with the data processing department in modifying the report so that users can understand better the information being conveyed and the reference points for comparison of results.

Questions

1. What advantages are there to Kenbart Company from having its profit plan system computerized?
2. Redesign the layout of the Profit Plan Report so that it will be more useful to Kenbart's executive management in its task of reviewing results and planning operations. Explain the reason for each modification you make in the report.
3. What types of data would Kenbart Company be required to capture in its computer-based files in order to generate the plans and results which executive management reviews and analyzes?

(CMA Adapted)

14-33. *Hilberg Corporation*

Hilberg Corporation was a leader and dominant in its industry from 1949 to 1977. Since 1977, its share of the market has decreased and several of its competitors have become significant factors in the industry. A management review of the situation led to the conclusion that product lines were satisfactory, product quality was still high, and manufacturing costs and sales prices were among the best in the industry. However, the company had been slow to adopt computer technology for internal record keeping and analysis. Consequently, management was not provided with timely and accurate information that would allow it to respond promptly to competitive situations. Also, the company has been unable to provide customers with timely information on available product quantities and delivery dates.

To rectify this situation, Hilberg entered into a crash program to obtain appropriate computer hardware, systems, and managerial personnel trained in the use of computers. Top management considers the program to be successful because the decline in market share has stopped and the sales department reports improved levels of customer satisfaction.

Although the crash program has been successful in bringing Hilberg into the computer age, it has created serious personnel problems among the older middle managers. A number of new management positions were created, and young people trained in computer technology were hired to fill them. Many of the middle managers who have been with the company over 20

years and were instrumental in its success during the first 25 years of its existence feel passed over. They see no real future with the company. To a considerable extent they blame top management because it was late in adopting computer technology. Furthermore, management had not been willing to provide educational reimbursement for what had been called in the early 1970s "a pie in the sky technology."

Top management, concerned because many of these middle managers are loyal employees and have contributed to the company's success, appointed an ad hoc committee to address the problem. The committee developed the following three proposals for consideration by Hilberg's Board of Directors.

Proposal 1

The company shall provide, and all middle-management employees without computer skills will be expected to attend, on-site training programs intended to upgrade their skills in electronic data processing procedures and computer-assisted management techniques. Consideration for advancement will include evaluation of each manager's ability to use the computer effectively.

Proposal 2

The company shall implement a tuition refund and release time program. Middle-management personnel would be encouraged to attend postsecondary-level courses to upgrade their skills in electronic data processing procedures and computer-assisted management techniques.

Proposal 3

Any middle manager who has attained the age of 55 years and who has credited service with the company of at least 25 years shall be eligible for an early retirement program that will provide the employee with a monthly pension equal to 50% of the employee's average monthly compensation for the final 5 years with Hilberg.

Questions

1. Discuss how effective each of the three proposals is in addressing the needs of the older middle managers of Hilberg Corporation.
2. Exclusive of cost considerations, discuss the advantages and disadvantages to Hilberg Corporation of each of the three proposals.
3. Assume Hilberg Corporation adopts Proposal 2. What responsibility, if any, does a middle manager

have to take advantage of this educational opportunity offered by Hilberg? Explain your answer.

(CMA Adapted)

14-34. *Framar National Bank*

Clyde Davids, chairman of the board of directors of Framar National Bank, announced the appointment of Jon Frank as the bank's new president. Frank was a senior officer of a large metropolitan bank before his appointment as president. At the same time Davids revealed a major reorganization of the bank. This resulted in restructuring duties and some changes in officers and officer titles.

The reorganization was not a surprise to the employees because a board subcommittee had studied this issue for over a year. However, the extent of the realignment and reassignments were not expected.

Figure 14-11 presents the organizational structure of Framar National Bank prior to the reorganization. Figure 14-12 presents the new organizational structure. The major changes in the organizational structure were made to improve bank operations and to give bank executives titles similar to their colleagues in other banks. A summary of these changes is as follows.

- Clyde Davids, who has been president and chairman of the board, will continue as chairman of the board only. His duties are unchanged by the reorganization. As president, he had not involved himself in the day-to-day operations of the bank.
- The president will now function as the chief operating officer of the bank. In the past these duties had been carried out by the executive vice-president. In effect, the title of executive vice-president has been changed to president.
- The board has expanded from one senior vice-president to four. Formerly, 13 departments headed by vice-presidents reported to the one senior vice-president. These departments now will be distributed among the four senior vice-presidents. No more than five departments will report to a senior vice-president. The distribution of the 13 departments, as shown in Figure 14-12, is likely to undergo some slight changes as the reorganization is fully implemented.
- The bank audit department, which previously reported to the executive vice-president, will now report directly to the board. The audit department vice-president, who is in the same employee classification as the other 13 vice-presidents, reports to

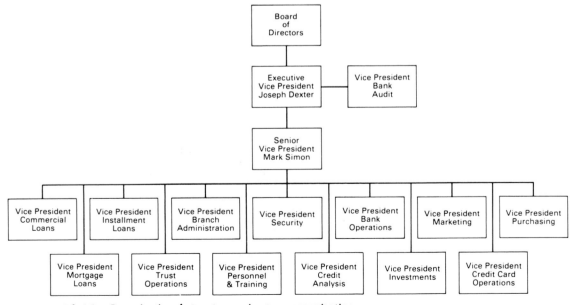

FIGURE 14-11 Organizational structure prior to reorganization.

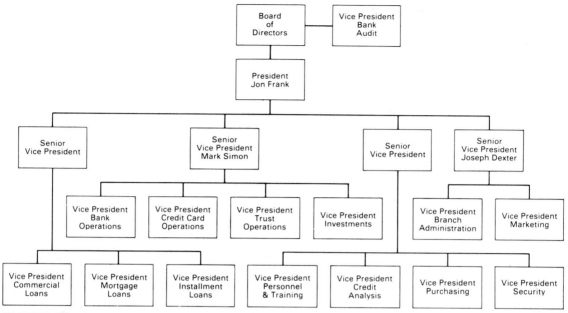

FIGURE 14-12   New organizational structure.

the board because this department is responsible for auditing all other departments.

The changes in the organizational structure were accompanied by some personnel reassignments. A summary of the important changes is as follows.

- Jon Frank will be chief operating officer replacing Joseph Dexter, who was the executive vice-president.
- Joseph Dexter was asked to become senior vice-president for branch administration and marketing.
- Mark Simon, who previously was the only senior vice-president and who worked closely with Joseph Dexter, was asked to become senior vice-president over several departments.
- The two remaining senior vice-presidents have not been selected yet. The new president plans to fill the positions as soon as possible and will consider both current employees and outside candidates.

Framar National Bank has expanded greatly in the 15 years since Joseph Dexter became executive vice-president. The fact that bank deposits have tripled and

the number of branches have expanded from 4 to 15 is due primarily to Dexter's expertise and leadership in marketing and branch banking. The trust department was also established during Dexter's tenure. The bank is financially sound and has had a good earnings record under his leadership.

While the bank has been successful and Dexter has done a good job, the board of directors believes the bank is entering a new development phase. The period of rapid growth and expansion is over and the bank must now devote its efforts to consolidating its position in the market and improving service and cost control. The board believes that Dexter is not as well suited to lead the bank in this new phase. However, the board wishes to retain Dexter's expertise in branch administration and marketing and has offered him the senior vice-presidency over these departments. Dexter has not informed the board whether he will accept this position.

The board subcommittee had interviewed the vice-presidents regarding the activities and responsibilities of their departments. However, proposed structural changes had not been presented to the vice-presidents for their opinions. Because the reorganization activity had continued for over a year and no "hard" facts were available, a number of rumors had circulated throughout the bank. As a consequence, there was a great deal of confusion and employee morale was low.

The vice-presidents are surprised by the replacement of Dexter and most of them are skeptical about the new organizational structure. They all agree some changes had to be made, but they are not supportive of the way they were developed and implemented. In addition, some of the groupings are not as logical as they could be. For instance, the credit card operation and credit analysis are more closely related with the loan departments. The trust and investment departments would be better grouped together, as would bank operations, personnel and training, and security. However, the branch administration and marketing departments are grouped logically in the opinion of the vice-presidents.

Questions

1. Explain why a reorganization from one to four senior vice-presidents probably was needed by Framar National Bank.
2. The methods employed by the board of directors to reorganize Framar National Bank caused behavioral problems among the bank employees. Explain:
   a. Why this occurred.
   b. What steps the board could have taken to eliminate, or at least minimize, any behavioral problems among the upper levels of the organization.
3. If Joseph Dexter continues with Framar National Bank as a senior vice-president, discuss the behavioral issues confronting:

   a. Joseph Dexter.
   b. The other vice-presidents.

(CMA Adapted)

CHAPTER 14 SUPPLEMENT

Example of a Systems Specifications Report

Roland Numbers is a CPA and partner of the accounting firm ABC Accountants. His firm currently uses a manual data processing system for all of the record-keeping activities (such as billing clients for audit work performed). Due to the recent growth in business, Roland is of the opinion that a computerized data processing system may be needed by his accounting firm. Therefore, he has hired the Efficient Systems Consulting Firm to perform a systems study to determine whether ABC Accountants should automate its data processing system.

The systems specifications report that follows was prepared by the consulting firm for XYZ Vendor Company. The report would also be sent to other hardware and software suppliers besides XYZ Vendor Company. Presented here is a copy of the cover letter sent to XYZ Vendor Company by Efficient Systems Consulting Firm. Following this letter, the complete systems specifications report is provided. (*Note:* There may be some specific items contained in the systems specifications report that you do not completely understand. Since this report is for illustrative purposes only, you should not be concerned if you are unable to understand every single item included in the report.)

Letterhead

XYZ VENDOR COMPANY   June 30, 1991
1234 Vendor Street
Vendor City, California

Gentlemen:

ABC Accountants (ABC) is now soliciting bids for a computer system as specified in the enclosed Systems Specifications Report (SSR).

Multiple proposals may be submitted by each vendor. Vendors should provide schematics for each of the proposed configurations. For multiple proposals, please provide secondary responses to questions only where the answers differ from the primary responses.

While systems specifications represent those features considered required, vendors are invited to take exception as described in the section entitled "Proposal Guidelines." It is important that vendors clearly justify any exceptions taken in terms of costs and benefits to ABC. This provision is intended to provide vendors with greater flexibility in responding to this SSR.

We believe that our SSR approach will simplify the bidding process while providing ABC with a consistent base of required information. Responses to the questions in the SSR, together with related cost data supporting documentation, will be used to make the final selection.

It is the objective of this SSR to solicit as many meaningful proposals as possible in order to give ABC a range of alternatives from which to choose. To facilitate this objective, we will be pleased to work with your organization in answering any questions concerning the requirements of ABC as outlined in this SSR. Vendor proposals must be submitted on or before August 15, 1991 (Proposal Due Date). Further information regarding these key dates and the appropriate vendor actions is provided under general information. All questions should be directed to my attention as representative of Efficient Systems Consulting
Firm.

We appreciate your consideration and assistance in this matter. We are looking forward to the receipt of your proposal and to the development of a closer relationship in the near future.

                                        Very truly yours,

                                        Efficient Systems Consulting Firm

                                        _____
                                        By Stephen A. Moscove
                                        Partner

Enclosures:
  Request for Proposal
  Vendor Questionnaire (2)

Systems Specifications Report		June 30, 1991

Table of Contents

* Not illustrated in SSR but follows the identical format.

ii

Systems Specifications Report June 30, 1991

Section I
General Information

1. Intent of SSR

The intent of this SSR is to establish the specifications for a data-processing system for ABC Accountants (ABC). The specifications contained herein are intended to provide vendors with sufficient information to enable them to prepare an acceptable response to this SSR.

2. Vendor Inquiries

All inquiries to this SSR should be submitted in writing to:
Stephen A. Moscove
Efficient Systems Consulting Firm
8970 Consultants Avenue
Consulting City, California
(213) 555-7515
Inquires should make reference to specific section numbers of the SSR and, where appropriate, paragraph numbers. A vendor's questions and answers to these questions will be communicated to all vendors.

3. SSR Addenda

In the event that modifications, clarifications, or additions to the SSR become necessary, all vendors will be notified and receive, in writing, addenda to the SSR.

4. Important Dates

The following dates are significant in terms of this SSR:

SSR issue date	June 30, 1991
Intent to bid date	July 15, 1991
Proposal submission date	August 15, 1991
Vendor selection date	September 15, 1991
Desired hardware installation date	October 15, 1991
Desired conversion date	November 15, 1991

5. Acceptance of Vendor Proposals

ABC reserves the right to accept or reject any or all bids, to take exception to these SSR specifications, or to waive any formalities. Vendors may be excluded from further consideration for failure to fully comply with the specifications of this SSR.

6. Vendor Selection

ABC reserves the right to make an award based solely on the proposals or to negotiate further with one or more vendors. The vendor selected for the award will be chosen on the basis of greatest benefit to ABC, not necessarily on the basis of lowest price.

iii

Systems Specifications Report   June 30, 1991

7. Guidelines for Proposal Evaluation

Vendor proposals will be evaluated using a comprehensive set of criteria. A partial list of these criteria is presented below:

- Does the vendor properly understand the problem?
- Are system software checklists completed?
- Are vendor capabilities stated in the proposal?
- Is vendor approach stated in the proposal?
- Are the system requirements addressed in the proposal?
- Are vendor participation and responsibility clearly defined?
- Are customer participation and responsibility clearly defined?
- Availability of high-quality service and maintenance?
- Are one-time implementation fees, start-up costs, and time estimates clearly stated?
- Are estimated monthly recurring fees clearly defined?
- Is requested vendor information complete?
- Is requested proposal information complete?
- Is requested system information complete?
- Can the vendor meet the time constraints and proposed schedule?

8. Notification of Vendor Selection

All vendors who submit proposals in response to this SSR will be notified of the results of the selection process.

9. Financial Statements

Vendors may be requested to submit financial statements prior to final selection. These may be optionally included in the proposal.

10. Proposal Preparation Costs

All costs incurred in the preparation and presentation of the proposal shall be wholly absorbed by the vendor. All supporting documentation and manuals submitted with this proposal will become the property of ABC unless otherwise requested by the vendor at the time of submission of the proposal.

11. Confidential Materials

Any material submitted by any vendor that is to be considered as confidential in nature must be clearly marked as such.

12. Contractual Obligations

The selected vendor shall be considered as the prime contractor and shall assume total responsibility for installation and maintenance of all hardware and software in the vendor's proposal. Furthermore, the proposal contents of the selected bid shall be considered as contractual obligations. Failure to meet obligations may result in the cancellation of any contracts.

Systems Specifications Report June 30, 1991

13. Contract Negotiation

ABC reserves the right to negotiate a contract with the selected vendor. This contract may include methods of procurement, (1) purchase, (2) lease/purchase, and/or (3) lease in any combination, and may, at the discretion of ABC, include a third-party financial institution or contract negotiation team.

14. Intent to Bid

Vendors intending to submit proposals should respond in writing no later than the intent to bid date.

15. Withdrawal Notification

Vendors who receive this SSR and do not wish to bid should reply with a letter of "No bid" no later than the intent to bid date. Vendors who wish to withdraw from the bidding are requested to submit a letter of withdrawal.

16. Demonstrations and Benchmarks

ABC reserves the right to require any vendor to demonstrate and/or benchmark any hardware or software in the vendor's proposal. After the initial evaluation of vendor proposals, vendors can anticipate that demonstration will be requested.

17. Terminology Unique to Our Industry

The terms "work in process" and "unbilled work in process" represent hours worked and chargeable to a client, together with any out-of-pocket expenses, for which the client has not yet been billed. The term "inventory" represents both "unbilled work in process" and "accounts receivable."

Systems Specifications Report   June 30, 1991

Section II
Proposal Guidelines

1. Proposal Format

To obtain vendor information in a form which ensures that the evaluation criteria can be systematically applied, vendors are requested to submit their proposal in the following general format:

Letter of transmittal: Each proposal shall include a letter of transmittal that bears the signature of an authorized representative of the vendor and that also includes the names of individuals authorized to negotiate with ABC, as well as the names of vendor-appointed sales representatives.

Vendor questionnaire: The vendor questionnaire is an integral part of the SSR. Extra copies have been included to assist vendors in preparing their proposal. The vendor should present all information in a concise manner, neatly arranged, typed, and in terms understandable to a non-EDP-oriented reader.

Vendor attachments: Attachments include vendor standard contracts, lists of users of similar processing systems, vendor financial statements, and other materials.

2. Number of Copies

Vendors should prepare two (2) copies of their proposal.

3. Multiple Proposals

Vendors who wish to submit multiple proposals for various models of hardware or versions of software are invited to do so. It is requested that the vendor select one proposed system as the "primary" system and supply complete information for this system. Secondary proposals need only include information that differs from the primary proposal. Secondary proposals should follow the same format as the primary proposal.

4. Exceptions to the SSR

It is anticipated that vendors may find instances where their hardware or software does not function in a manner consistent with the specifications of this SSR. In such cases, it is permissible to take exception to the SSR. All that is required is that exceptions be clearly identified and that written explanations for the exceptions should include the scope of the exceptions, their ramifications, and a description of the advantages to be gained by ABC.

5. Supporting Materials

Each specification section of the SSR includes a series of questions to be used as an aid in making a selection. All questions, unless specifically instructed to do otherwise, should be answered in terms of the system quoted for the primary proposal. The answers to each question should be documented, wherever possible, by stating title and page number of the supporting documentation. For multiple proposals, provide secondary answers to these questions only where the answers differ from the primary proposal.

6. Vendor Terminology

Vendors should make every attempt to use terminology in their proposals that is consistent with that of ABC. Comparable terminology may be substituted where appropriate if the vendor provides clear and concise definitions.

Systems Specifications Report   June 30, 1991

7. Documentation

As part of each bid, the vendor shall include the cost of two sets of all available hardware and system software manuals in each category, copies of the Table of Contents of each, and individual prices for single items.

8. Vendor Contracts

Vendors should submit, as part of their proposals, a copy of their standard contracts. If appropriate, both hardware and software contracts should be included. Standard addenda to these contracts should also be included for evaluation but need not be filled in.

Section III
System Requirements

1. Present Systems

ABC's present accounting and information systems are as follows:

System	Present processing	Computerize in-house
Revenue:		
Time accounting*	Manual	Yes
Billing	Manual	Yes
Accounts receivable	Manual	Yes
Payroll	Manual	No
Accounts payable	Manual	Yes
Fixed assets	Manual	No
General ledger	Service bureau	Yes
Word processing	Manual	Yes
Client bookkeeping	Manual	Yes
Income tax:		
Planning	Manual	Yes
Return preparation	Manual	Yes

The remaining portions of this section set forth our present volumes as well as our volume estimates three years into the future. Our accounting and information needs have been identified and draft report layouts are also included.

---

* Described on first page of Section VI (see page xxxvii).

Systems Specifications Report

June 30, 1991

2. Input Volumes

Input Volume Summary

| System | Record Length | Monthly No. of Input Characters | | | |
| | | Present | | Three Years | |
		Average	Peak	Average	Peak
Revenue:					
Time accounting	XXX	XXX,XXX	XXX,XXX	XXX,XXX	XXX,XXX
Billing	XXX	XXX,XXX	XXX,XXX	XXX,XXX	XXX,XXX
Cash receipts	XXX	XXX,XXX	XXX,XXX	XXX,XXX	XXX,XXX
Cash disbursements	XXX	XXX,XXX	XXX,XXX	XXX,XXX	XXX,XXX
Client bookkeeping	X,XXX	XXX,XXX	XXX,XXX	XXX,XXX	XXX,XXX
General ledger	XXX	XXX,XXX	XXX,XXX	XXX,XXX	XXX,XXX
Total accounting		XXX,XXX	XXX,XXX	XXX,XXX	XXX,XXX
Word processing	na		Varies		
Income tax:					
Planning	XXX	XX,XXX	XXX,XXX	XX,XXX	XXX,XXX
Returns	X,XXX	XXX,XXX	XXX,XXX	XXX,XXX	XXX,XXX

Systems Specifications Report   June 30, 1991

3. File Requirements

   a. Summary

Files Volume Summary

System	File description	Masterfiles Peak month characters Present (in thousands)	Three years (in thousands)	File description	Transaction files Annual number of characters Present (in thousands)	Three years (in thousands)
Revenue:						
Time accounting	Work in process	XX,XXX	XX,XXX	Time sheets	XXX	XXX
	Billing rate	X	X			
Billing	Accounts			Billings	XXX	XXX
Cash receipts	receivable	X,XXX	X,XXX	Receipts	XX	XX
	Client address	XX	XX			
Client bookkeeping	Clients	XX,XXX	XXX,XXX	Client trans.	XXX	X,XXX
Accounts payable	Accounts payable	X,XXX	X,XXX	Purchases	XX	XX
				Distribution	XXX	XXX
				Disbursements	XX	XX
General ledger	Chart of accounts	XX	XX			
	GL balances	X,XXX	X,XXX	GL distribution	XXX	XXX
Word processing	Letters	XXX	XXX			
	Labels	XXX	XXX			
Income tax:						
Planning	Projections	XXX	XXX			
Returns	Returns	XX,XXX	XXX,XXX	Tax input	XXX	XXX
Target companies	Targets	X,XXX	X,XXX			
Totals		XXX,XXX	XXX,XXX		X,XXX	XX,XXX

x

Systems Specifications Report June 30, 1991

b. Details

Time Accounting Files

Field description	Field length	
	Work-in-process master file	Transaction file
Client name	XX	XX
Client number	XX	XX
Employee name	XX	XX
Employee number	XX	XX
Employee billing rate	XX	XX
Timesheet period	XX	XX
Service code	XX	XX
Employee hours	XX	XX
Out-of-pocket expenses	XX	XX
Total record length	XXX	XXX
Master file volumes	*Present*	*Three years*
Total record length	XXX	XXX
Peak active clients	XXX	XXX
Product	XX,XXX	XX,XXX
Peak time sheet line items	XXX	XXX
Product	X,XXX,XXX	X,XXX,XXX
Number of months open items in unbilled work in process	X	X
Maximum file size	XX,XXX,XXX	XX,XXX,XXX
Transaction file volumes	*Present*	*Three years*
Total record length	XXX	XXX
Average line items per month	XXX	XXX
Average monthly volume	XX,XXX	XX,XXX
Annualize	12	12
Annual file size	XXX,XXX	XXX,XXX

Note: Details of other files are not illustrated but would be included here.

Systems Specifications Report   June 30, 1991

4. Output Requirements

a. Volume summary

Output Volume Summary by System*

Report Title	Freq	Printer Location	Number of Lines per Period	
			Present	Three Years
Revenue:		Accounting		
Unbilled work in process				
Chargeable time analysis	S		XX	XXX
Chargeable hours by client	A		X,XXX	X,XXX
Client details	M		XX,XXX	XX,XXX
Aging by client	M		XXX	XXX
Control report	S		XX	XX
Billing				
Invoices	M		X,XXX	X,XXX
Journal	M		XXX	XXX
Realization reports				
Service code				
Current month	M		XXX	XXX
Year to date	M		X,XXX	X,XXX
Alpha by client				
Current month	M		XXX	XXX
Year to date	M		XXX	XXX
Revenue forecast	A		XXX	XXX
Budget comparison	M		XX	XX
Accounts receivable				
Client details	M		X,XXX	X,XXX
Aging	M		XXX	XXX
Cash receipts journal	M		XXX	XXX
Control report	M		X	X
Cash balance control	D		X	X
Accounts payable:		Accounting		
Purchase journal	M		XXX	XXX
Distribution journal	M		XXX	XXX
Cash requirements	W		XXX	XXX
Vendor open invoices	M		XXX	XXX
Checks	M		XXX	XXX
General ledger:		Accounting		
Chart of accounts	R		XXX	XXX
GL entries	M		XXX	XXX
Financial statements	M		XXX	XXX
Trial balance	M		XXX	XXX

xii

Systems Specifications Report   June 30, 1991

Word processing:	D	Secretary	X,XXX	X,XXX
Income tax:				
Projections	D	Tax depart-ment	XXX	XXX
Tax returns	D	Accounting	X,XXX	X,XXX
Client bookkeeping:	M	Accounting	X,XXX	XX,XXX

* Frequency legend: D—Daily, W—Weekly, S—Semimonthly, M—Monthly, Q—Quarterly, A—Annual, R—Request.

Output Volume Summary by Printer Location

	Printer Location							
	Accounting		Tax department		Secretary		Total	
	Present	Three Years	Present	Three Years	Present	Three Years	Present	Three Years
Frequency	*(In thousands of lines)*							
Daily	XX	XX	X	XX	XX	XX	XX	XXX
Weekly	X	X						X
Bimonthly	X	X						X
Monthly	XX	XXX					XX	XXX
Quarterly								
Annual	XX	XX					XX	XX
Request	X	X					X	X
Totals	XX	XXX	X	XX	XX	XX	XX	XXX

Systems Specifications Report   June 30, 1991

   b. Report layouts

Billing Realization Report: Client Sequence

	Frequency—monthly				*Number of lines—peak month*				
	Current month				*Present: XX Three years: XX*				
	Year to date				*Present: XX Three years: XX*				
			Standard					*Billed*	
	Hours	*Rate*	*$*	*Exp*	*Total*	*Total*	*Exp*	*Fees*	*Rate*	*%*
	(1)	*(2)*	*(3)*	*(4)*	*(5)*	*(6)*	*(7)*	*(8)*	*(9)*	*(10)*
Client									*(8/2)*	*(6/5)*
A	XX	XX.XX	XXXX	XX	XXXX	XXXX	XX	XXXX	XX.XX	XX
B	XX	XX.XX	XXXX	XX	XXXX	XXXX	XX	XXXX	XX.XX	XX
Totals	XXX	XX.XX	XXXXX	XXX	XXXXX	XXXXX	XXX	XXXX	XX.XX	XX

Note: Other report layouts are not illustrated but would be included here.

Systems Specifications Report June 30, 1991

Section IV
Vendor General Questionnaire

1. Vendor Background

a. Attach a brief narrative regarding your business history.

b. How long have you actively participated in the data-processing industry?

Comments

_____ Less than 2 years _____

_____ 2 to 5 years _____

_____ Over 5 years _____

c. As to our industry, provide the following information:

Number of years you have actively participated in our industry. _____

Percentage of your total revenues derived from our industry. _____

Number of your employees committed to our industry. _____

d. How many data-processing systems have you installed to date?

	This year	In total
None	_____	_____
1 to 10	_____	_____
Over 10	_____	_____

e. Will you commit to a full implementation schedule?

	Yes	No
Site preparation	_____	_____
Equipment delivery	_____	_____
Equipment installation	_____	_____
User training	_____	_____

Systems Specifications Report   June 30, 1991

 f. What is your yearly gross sales volume?

  Hardware   _____

  Software   _____

  Combination   _____

   Total   _____

 g. Indicate contractural agreements that would be applicable if your proposal is ultimately accepted by us. Attach sample copies.

  _____   Hardware purchase

  _____   Hardware maintenance

  _____   Systems software purchase

  _____   Systems software license

  _____   Systems software maintenance

  _____   _____

  _____   _____

 h. List references of installed users:

Name	Title	Telephone	City
_____	_____	_____	_____
_____	_____	_____	_____
_____	_____	_____	_____
_____	_____	_____	_____

2. Vendor User Groups

If a user group does not exist, leave this section blank.

How long has the group been in existence? _____

State annual membership fee, if any. _____

If there is a national users group, complete the following:

 Name of chairman _____

 Address _____

 City, state, zip code _____

Systems Specifications Report June 30, 1991

    Telephone number (_____) _____

    Number of currently active members _____

    How many meetings does the group hold per year? _____

If there is an active local chapter, complete the following:

    Chairman _____

    Address _____

    City, state, zip code _____

    Telephone number (_____) _____

3. Vendor-Supplied Training

  a. Describe the extent and type of free training included in your fee proposal.

_____

_____

_____

_____

_____

  b. Describe all pertinent vendor-supplied training courses. For each course, include the following information:

Cost of course
Location
Duration
Frequency of offering
Prerequisites
General description

_____

_____

_____

_____

_____

_____

_____

Systems Specifications Report   June 30, 1991

4. Vendor Bid Summary

a. System costs:

Hardware cost (see hardware section for detail) $ _____

System software cost (see system software section for detail) $ _____

Application software cost (details below) $ _____

Application subsystem	Monthly maintenance	Base price	Enhancements	Total
_____	_____	_____	_____	_____
_____	_____	_____	_____	_____
_____	_____	_____	_____	_____
_____	_____	_____	_____	_____
_____	_____	_____	_____	_____
_____	_____	_____	_____	_____
_____	_____	_____	_____	_____
_____	_____	_____	_____	_____

Total application software cost $ _____

Shipping $ _____

Site preparation (estimated: air, power, floor, etc.) $ _____

Installation costs (estimated) $ _____

Conversion costs (estimated) $ _____

User training costs $ _____

Travel costs $ _____

Documentation $ _____

Other costs, if any (describe):

_____ $ _____

_____ $ _____

Total system cost $ _____

Systems Specifications Report June 30, 1991

  b. Monthly recurring costs:

	Usage	Maintenance
Hardware under leasing arrangements (describe)	$ _____	$ _____
System software	$ _____	$ _____
Application software	$ _____	$ _____
Representative monthly cost	$ _____	$ _____

  c. Maintenance and support:

	Hourly cost	Proposed cost
Hardware maintenance	_____	_____
Operating system maintenance	_____	_____
Training	_____	_____
Application maintenance	_____	_____
Programming	_____	_____
Systems analysis	_____	_____

  d. Quotation period:

  Period through which proposal bid is fixed _____

  Authorized negotiator _____

5. System Implementation Schedule

  a. Hardware installed and operational within _____ days of contract acceptance.

  b. Application system operational as follows:

Applications system	Days from contract acceptance
_____	_____
_____	_____
_____	_____
_____	_____
_____	_____

  c. Complete documentation available within _____ days.

xix

Systems Specifications Report   June 30, 1991

    d. User training to be completed within:

       System operations   _____ days

       Application software   _____ days

    e. Attach representative implementation plan based on vendor's experience and ABC's constraints set forth in this SSR, showing development, testing, conversion, training, and implementation milestones by application.

xx

Systems Specifications Report June 30, 1991

Section V
Vendor Hardware and System Software Questionnaire

1. Hardware

a. Hardware equipment list

List all equipment and system hardware components (i.e., CPU, peripherals, cables, etc.) included in the proposed hardware configuration. The first page or pages should be the components recommended for initial installation. Additional components recommended for future upgrades should be listed on separate, properly labeled pages. Continue on additional pages as needed.

System component	Model, Part	Description	Purchase	Price Monthly maint.	Rental
————	————	————	————	————	————
————	————	————	————	————	————
————	————	————	————	————	————
————	————	————	————	————	————
————	————	————	————	————	————
————	————	————	————	————	————
————	————	————	————	————	————
————	————		————	————	————
		Totals	————	————	————
		Sales tax	————		
		Grand total	————		

b. Describe the expertise required for our personnel to operate the proposed initial hardware configuration.

_____

_____

_____

_____

Systems Specifications Report   June 30, 1991

c. Overall capacity

The maximum capacity of the proposed hardware and upgrade capabilities are:

	Proposed	Next largest	Largest
Model			
Main memory			
Disk storage:			
Fixed:			
Number of drives			
Capacity per drive			
Removable:			
Number of drives			
Capacity per drive			
Printers:			
Number			
Speed			
Terminals, number			
Tape drives, number			

Elaborate on required software conversion activities and costs (CPU and software conversion) to accomplish upgrade.

_____

_____

_____

_____

_____

_____

d. Central processing unit

Manufacturer _____ Model No. _____

Date of first delivery _____

Mean time between failures _____

xxii

Systems Specifications Report   June 30, 1991

Recommended memory _____

Maximum memory available for this model _____

Type of memory _____

Memory expansion increments _____

Word length _____

Maximum partition size _____

Cycle time _____

Maximum memory needed by operating system _____

	Yes	No
Power fail, auto restart	_____	_____
Real-time clock	_____	_____
Automatic program load	_____	_____
Battery backup	_____	_____

Describe any other features available. _____

_____

_____

_____

_____

e. Disk and tape devices

	Types of drives proposed					
	Disk			*Tape*		
	Hard disk					
	Fixed	*Removable*	*Floppy*	*Cartridge*	*Reel*	*Cassette*
Number of drives	_____	_____	_____	_____	_____	_____
Manufacturer	_____	_____	_____	_____	_____	_____
Model number	_____	_____	_____	_____	_____	_____
Date of first delivery	_____	_____	_____	_____	_____	_____
Mean time between failures	_____	_____	_____	_____	_____	_____

xxiii

Systems Specifications Report   June 30, 1991

Capacity _____ _____ _____ _____ _____ _____

Maximum number available _____ _____ _____ _____ _____ _____

Average access time _____ _____ _____

Data transfer rate _____ _____ _____ _____ _____ _____

Describe other features _____

_____

Is backup processing accomplished by using system utilities? Yes _____ No _____
Describe recommended approach for backup processing.

_____

_____

Amount of time required to copy entire disk units to disk or tape depending on backup approach recommended above.

_____

_____

f. Printers

	Type (dot matrix, etc.)			
	Printer 1	Printer 2	Printer 3	Printer 4
Manufacturer	___	___	___	___
Model number	___	___	___	___
Date of first delivery	___	___	___	___
Mean time between failure	___	___	___	___
Number recommended	___	___	___	___
Maximum number available with central processor proposed	___	___	___	___
Data transfer rate	___	___	___	___
Rated speed worst case	___	___	___	___

Systems Specifications Report June 30, 1991

Describe character sets.

_____

_____

_____

Describe other features and options.

_____

_____

_____

Describe other printers available (model number, rated speed, cost).

_____

_____

_____

g. Remote devices

Manufacturer _____

Model number _____

Date of first delivery _____

Mean time between failures _____

Number recommended _____

Maximum number available with central processor proposed _____

Terminal type (serial, editing, intelligent) _____

Data transfer rate _____

Describe how terminals are set up with controllers. _____

_____

Maximum distance from CPU direct wired without signal regenerator.

_____

Maximum distance from CPU direct wired with signal regenerator.

_____

Systems Specifications Report   June 30, 1991

Briefly describe approach for user programming/control of terminals (special programming language, etc., required).

_____

_____

Display characteristics: Characters/line _____

    Lines/page _____   Special symbols _____

Describe capabilities of printer attached to terminal, if available. _____

Terminal characteristics	Yes	No
Keyboard detachable	_____	_____
Cursor positioning up and down	_____	_____
Cursor positioning left and right	_____	_____
Cursor blinking	_____	_____
Character, field blinking	_____	_____
Variable brightness/intensity	_____	_____
Partial screen transmit	_____	_____
Character repeat	_____	_____
Audible alarm	_____	_____
Full screen transmit	_____	_____

Use this area to elaborate on any of your responses to questions in this section.

_____

_____

_____

h. Installation

Do you provide physical planning services? Yes _____ No _____

If yes, describe services and costs. _____

_____

_____

_____

xxvi

Systems Specifications Report   June 30, 1991

Indicate services included as part of installation:

Physical planning   _____

Facility preparation   _____

Machine checkout   _____

System generation   _____

Other (describe)   _____

_____

Environmental requirements for equipment in computer location:

Square feet required   _____

Temperature range   _____

Humidity range   _____

Power   _____

Raised floor   _____

Air conditioning   _____

Separate power line   _____

List all hardware components to be installed in the computer location and power required for each:

Device	*Power*
_____	_____
_____	_____
_____	_____

When are the machine and software considered installed and when do applicable financial charges begin?

_____

For all devices proposed for installation outside the computer location, fully describe any special environmental requirements.

Device	*Power*	*Humidity*	*Temperature*
_____	_____	_____	_____
_____	_____	_____	_____
_____	_____	_____	_____

xxvii

Systems Specifications Report June 30, 1991

i. Warranties

Indicate which portions of the proposed configuration are warranted and date warranty commenses.

	Check	*Length of time*	*Indicate date warranty commences (shipment, receipt, acceptance, etc.)*
CPU	_____	_____	_____
Memory	_____	_____	_____
Tape drives	_____	_____	_____
Disk drives	_____	_____	_____
CRT terminals	_____	_____	_____
System interfaces	_____	_____	_____
Printers	_____	_____	_____
_____	_____	_____	_____
_____	_____	_____	_____

j. Maintenance

Primary service location for servicing ABC:

Name _____

Street address _____

City, state, zip code _____

Telephone _____

Distance from ABC _____

Number of field engineers at the above location. _____

Number of similar systems currently serviced there. _____

Address of secondary service location. _____

Will you guarantee that hardware maintenance will be available for any equipment proposed for a five-year period?

Yes _____ No _____

Guaranteed service call response time. _____

Systems Specifications Report June 30, 1991

Will all spare components be inventoried at the primary service location? Describe procedures.

_____

_____

_____

Location of alternate parts supply. _____

Average response time for field engineers to arrive:

On weekdays _____ On weekends _____

Average time to correct a problem (mean time to repair).

_____

_____

Describe preventive maintenance policy and procedures.

_____

_____

When the manufacturer (or vendor) initiates an engineering change for a component of the proposed configuration, will the system be modified free of charge?

Yes _____ No _____

If no, describe associated costs.

_____

_____

Describe any extra maintenance services/costs not included in the proposed maintenance contract.

_____

_____

_____

Describe provisions for rebates on rental charges and maintenance costs for extended periods of downtime.

_____

_____

_____

Systems Specifications Report   June 30, 1991

Describe provisions for penalty payments from vendor to customer for extended periods of downtime.

_____

_____

_____

Does the proposed maintenance contract include extra charges for:

	Yes	No
Weekends	_____	_____
Nights	_____	_____
Travel	_____	_____
Cases when trouble isn't found	_____	_____
User errors	_____	_____
Operator errors	_____	_____
Vendor holidays	_____	_____

If yes as to any of the above, explain extra charges.

_____

_____

_____

_____

_____

_____

_____

_____

_____

2. Systems Software

a. System software summary

Specifically list all system software included as part of the proposed configuration including the following types of software: operating systems (OS), assemblers (AS), compilers (CO), interpreters

Systems Specifications Report June 30, 1991

(IN), text editors (TE), word processors (WP), data-base management systems (DB), report generators (RG), and file utilities (FU) (sort/merge, copy, delete, etc.).

Description (name, version, and release date)	Type	Price			Number Installed
		Purchase	Monthly Maintenance	Monthly Lease	
————	————	————	————	————	————
————	————	————	————	————	————
————	————	————	————	————	————
————	————	————	————	————	————
————	————	————	————	————	————
————	————	————	————	————	————
————	————	————	————	————	————
————	————	————	————	————	————
————	————	————	————	————	————
————	————	————	————	————	————
————	————	————	————	————	————
————	————	————	————	————	————
————	————	————	————	————	————
————	————	————	————	————	————

b. Operating system
Indicate those features listed below that will be provided as part of the proposed operating system software:

	Yes	No	Comments
Multiprogramming	————	————	————————
Multitasking	————	————	————————
Task scheduling	————	————	————————
Priority assignment	————	————	————————
Memory mapping	————	————	————————
Spooling	————	————	————————

xxxi

Systems Specifications Report   June 30, 1991

	Yes	No	Comments
Job accounting	―――	――	――――――――
User accounting	―――	――	――――――――
Password accounting	―――	――	――――――――
Record level lock	―――	――	――――――――
Library management	―――	――	――――――――
Device diagnostics	―――	――	――――――――
Console log	―――	――	――――――――
Automatic file allocation	―――	――	――――――――
Multilevel interrupt	―――	――	――――――――
―――――――――	―――	――	――――――――
―――――――――	―――	――	――――――――
―――――――――	―――	――	――――――――
―――――――――	―――	――	――――――――
―――――――――	―――	――	――――――――
―――――――――	―――	――	――――――――

Is operating system memory allocation made on the basis of:

	Yes	No	Comments
Fixed partitions?	―――	――	――――――――
Dynamic contiguous allocation?	―――	――	――――――――
Dynamic noncontiguous allocation?	―――	――	――――――――
Other ―――――	―――	――	――――――――

How many batch or background programs may be concurrently executing? ―――――――

How many foreground programs may be concurrently executing? ―――――――

May a user dynamically create and delete disk files? Yes ――― No ―――

xxxii

Systems Specifications Report   June 30, 1991

c. **Programming languages**

   Indicate languages available on the proposed configuration:

	Interpretive	Pseudocompiled	Compiled
Assembly			
ALGOL			
APL			
BASIC			
COBOL			
FORTRAN			
PASCAL			
PL1			
RPG			

d. **Utilities**

   Which of the following features is supported by the proposed system in an online, terminal-oriented mode?

	Yes	No	
Source code preparation, editing			
Compilation or assembly			
File cataloging			
Program execution			

   If a stand-alone sort utility is available, how long will it take to sort 5000 records that are 80 characters long using a 10-character sort key?

   _____

   _____

e. **Support software**

   If any of the following features are available, briefly describe capabilities, limitations and system resource requirements, etc.

Systems Specifications Report   June 30, 1991

Report generator/writer

_____

_____

Query language

_____

_____

Data base management

_____

_____

Print spoolers

_____

_____

Screen formatters

_____

_____

f. Installation

Describe extent of services included as part of the installation:

Systems software testing

_____

_____

Data conversion

_____

_____

Applications systems testing

_____

_____

Systems Specifications Report June 30, 1991

Parallel running

_____

_____

Operator training

_____

_____

User training

_____

_____

g. Warranties

How long is the software warrantied?

Systems software _____ days   Application software _____ days

When do the terms of the software warranties begin (shipment, receipt, installation, acceptance, other)?

Systems software _____   Application software _____

What medium is used to deliver the systems software? _____

How many complete sets of supporting technical systems software documentation will be provided free? _____

h. Maintenance

Is a hardware maintenance contract a prerequisite for systems software maintenance?

Yes _____   No _____

Describe the types or levels of systems software maintenance available, specify location of service (on site or off site), and indicate contractual response times:

_____

_____

What are the standard and optional services provided under the system software maintenance contract and the related costs?

_____

_____

Systems Specifications Report June 30, 1991

What must ABC do to receive a new version or release of a system software product to which it is licensed?

_____

_____

For how many months will the proposed system be covered by a system software maintenance contract after a new version or release is available if ABC decides not to upgrade?

_____

What is the fastest way for ABC to obtain assistance in the event of a system software-related failure or a failure whose cause is unclear?

_____

_____

Other vendor comments:

_____

_____

_____

_____

Systems Specifications Report   June 30, 1991

SECTION VI
VENDOR APPLICATIONS QUESTIONNAIRE

System requirements, including volumes and required reports, are included in Section III of the SSR. This section uses the following general format:

1. For each application a narrative overview of processing is provided together with a brief description of system interrelationships.

2. Vendors are required to respond as to whether the required reports will be provided. In this regard, the report layouts in Section III are not the only way to present the information. Vendors may deviate from the requested format provided that all the required information is presented. Vendor responses should be in accordance with the response codes shown below.

3. Vendors are requested to respond as to whether the indicated features will be provided. Vendor responses should be in accordance with the response codes shown below.

Response Codes

Code	Meaning	Description
S	Standard	Requirement provided as a standard part of the package
E	Enhancement	Requirement will be met by an enhancement to the package without additional charge
R	Report writer	User can satisfy this requirement by using the capabilities of the report writer provided with the package
C	Custom	Requirement will be met by customizing the package; the additional charge is included in the fee proposal
A	Alternative	A suitable alternative is being presented and is explained
U	Unavailable	Requirement will not be provided at any cost

Revenue System

1. Narrative overview

Time accounting: Time sheets reflecting hours worked for specific clients and cash disbursements (for out-of-pocket expenses) are the primary source for updating work in process. Standard hourly rates will be maintained by the system. The system will calculate standard time charges to clients and update work in process for both standard time charges and out-of-pocket expenses. Work in process will be automatically relieved by billings.

Billing: Computer-generated work in process listings by client will be manually notated ("turnaround document") and are the primary source for relieving work in process, generating invoices and the monthly billing journal, and updating accounts receivable.

Accounts receivable: Manual and computer-generated billings together with cash receipts are the primary source for updating accounts receivable.

xxxvii

Systems Specifications Report   June 30, 1991

2. Reports

Report Title	Frequency	Response	Comments
Unbilled work in process:			
Chargeable time analysis	Semimonthly	_____	_____
Chargeable hours by client	Annual	_____	_____
Aging by client	Monthly	_____	_____
Control report	Monthly	_____	_____
Billing:			
Invoices	Monthly	_____	_____
Journal	Monthly	_____	_____
Realization reports:			
Service code:			
Current month	Monthly	_____	_____
Year to date	Monthly	_____	_____
Alpha by client:			
Current month	Monthly	_____	_____
Year to date	Monthly	_____	_____
Revenue forecast	Annual	_____	_____
Budget comparison	Monthly	_____	_____
Accounts receivable:			
Client details	Monthly	_____	_____
Aging by client	Monthly	_____	_____
Cash receipts journal	Monthly	_____	_____
Changes control report	Monthly	_____	_____
Cash balance control	Daily	_____	_____

3. Features

Feature	Response	Comments
Ability to handle user-defined service codes	_____	_____
Ability to handle narrative comments re time charges	_____	_____

Systems Specifications Report   June 30, 1991

Feature	Response	Comments
Ability to handle advance billings (retainers, monthly billings, etc.)		
Ability to produce file maintenance reports, including hash totals		
Ability to generate general ledger entries		
Ability to produce work-in-process listings by client to facilitate the billing process		
Ability to partially relieve hours or expenses		
Ability to apply advance billings to specific items in work in process		
Ability to relieve work in process for manual billings		
Ability to forecast billings, by client and service code, based on historical information using "what if" techniques		
Ability to handle adjustments (billings, write-offs, etc.)		
Ability to apply cash to specific invoices		
Online inquiry capability		
Ability to age by invoice		
Open-item technique versus balance forward		

15

Systems Study: Implementation and Follow-up

*Among the important questions that you
should be able to answer after reading this
chapter are:*

1. How should vendor proposals be evaluated
   and how are final selections of hardware and
   software made?
2. What is a point-scoring system?
3. How can a PERT network analysis aid management consultants in planning and controlling the implementation of their client company's new information system?
4. Of what importance is a PERT "critical path"
   to the successful implementation of a company's new accounting information system?
5. What is a parallel systems conversion?
6. Is a systems study ever finished?

INTRODUCTION

As discussed in Chapter 13, the existence of a systems problem(s) starts the *life-cycle* of a company's information system (see Figure 13-1). In an effort to solve its information systems problem(s), the company's management will often hire outside consultants to perform a systems study. The first major phase of the consultants' systems study work (examined in Chapter 13) is **planning.** After planning and organizing, the next phase, **systems analysis,** begins. Through their analysis, the consultants will identify the strengths and weaknesses of the client company's present information system. By isolating the system's weaknesses, the consultants can recommend systems revisions that should correct these inefficiencies. The discussion of Chapter 13 concluded that major systems problems detected by the consultants were the result of the client company's manual data processing system's failure to provide timely managerial decision-making information. Therefore, the consultants suggested that their client acquire a computer system.

Based on the systems analysis findings, the consultants then began the third major systems study phase, the **systems design** phase (discussed in Chapter 14). In their design work, the consultants examine the feasibility of replacing their client's present data processing system with a computerized system. They next prepare a detailed systems design that is used to prepare a systems specifications report. This report is submitted to hardware and software vendors. Each vendor will subsequently develop specific computer proposals for the company's system (or a component of that system).

When the vendors respond to the systems specifications report, the consultants must make vendor selections. This selection process starts the next phase of systems study, the systems implementation phase. Once selections of vendors have been made, the system is implemented. After implementation, **follow-up** work is necessary to determine whether the system is functioning as planned. Follow-up is an ongoing process in systems study and can be linked back to systems planning as the "life cycle" continues. In this way, the systems development life cycle is a complete circle. The implication of this circular process is that the development of an accounting information system is never complete.

This chapter discusses the work required to implement and initially operate a company's computerized batch processing system. The consultants' follow-up analysis on a newly implemented system is also examined briefly. Thus, by the conclusion of this chapter, the entire life cycle of an accounting information system will have been discussed.

SYSTEMS IMPLEMENTATION

Systems implementation includes selecting vendors, computer hardware, and computer software. It also includes the actual installation of computer resources and the initial operation of the complete system. These topics are discussed, in turn, in the paragraphs that follow.

Vendor Selection

Upon receipt of the hardware and software suppliers' proposals, the difficult task begins of selecting the particular vendor's proposal (if any) that best meets the client company's data processing needs. This decision is normally made by both the consultants and their client's top management (represented by the steering committee). Each computer vendor submitting a proposal will likely send a representative to the company to discuss its proposed computer system with the consultants and the steering committee. The consultants should act as advisors to management when evaluating the individual proposals because the company's top management has final responsibility for deciding which hardware and software supplier's computer system will be acquired. After evaluating all the proposals, management may decide to acquire its computer system from more than one vendor.

For instance, the decision may be to lease the central processing unit as well as the peripheral input-output equipment from one vendor but to lease or buy the software from another vendor. Evaluation of software packages purchased separately will be discussed later in the chapter. The following discussion describes vendor selection when the entire system (or a major portion of the system) is to be acquired from one vendor.

Selecting a Specific Computer System

The computer specialists on the management consulting team will have the major responsibility for advising the client company about the pros and cons of each vendor's systems proposal. Often, the final decision on which vendor's system to choose is quite difficult because the differences among the proposals may be minimal. Some of the key factors that should be considered when comparing each hardware and software supplier's proposal are as follows.

1. The **performance capability** of each proposed system in relation to the system's cost. It is imperative that a vendor's hardware and software system be capable of processing the company's data within the time schedules desired by management. Otherwise, delays in providing needed output reports will occur once the computer system is operational. There are many measures of performance including speed, response time, number of users supported, and system testing. The hardware and software operating efficiency of the various proposals may be tested by using what is called a **benchmark problem.** Under this approach, a data processing task that the company's computer system will eventually have to perform is selected (e.g., weekly batch processing of inventory transactions). Then, with the approval of each computer vendor, some representative transactions of the data processing task (e.g., purchase transactions that increase the inventory balance and sales transactions that decrease the inventory balance) are processed by every supplier's proposed hardware and soft-

ware system. This processing can be performed at the various supplier's own premises or even on other companies' computers (assuming the systems are identical with the ones being proposed). After this data processing task is performed on the suppliers' proposed hardware and software systems, comparisons can be made of each system's operating efficiency. The accountants on the consulting team will be concerned principally with analyzing the costs of every vendor's proposed system in relation to the system's performance. Concerning the cost factors, the accountants should analyze the monetary differences between purchasing and leasing each vendor's computer system. If the company's top management elects to purchase its computer system, the accountants should then advise management on a realistic depreciation program for the newly acquired system.

2. The **modularity** of each proposed system. This refers to the ease with which a proposed computer system can be altered at a later date. For example, the company may initially choose a less expensive, slower central processing unit. Good modularity would enable the company to easily add components to its CPU at some future time in order to handle changing data processing requirements. The company might subsequently want to increase the CPU's size by adding more primary storage or to increase the input-output peripheral equipment. Also, good modularity would enable the company to substitute a disk unit for a tape unit with minimum computer programming changes.

3. The **compatibility** of each proposed system to the company's current data processing system. This is especially important if the company already has an automated data processing system and wants to "upgrade" its system; for example, a company may decide to add an additional CPU to its present computer system. If both the old CPU and the newly acquired CPU can function together effectively and handle the same input data without major program rewrites, good compatibility exists between these two central

processing units. As can be seen, compatibility is closely related to modularity.

4. The **reputation** of the computer vendor as well as the vendor's ability to **support** the implementation and subsequent operation of the system. Obviously, the hardware and software supplier whose system is chosen should have a good reputation in the business community. (It's like buying an unknown-brand television set; the initial cost may be smaller than for a familiar-brand model, but the later headaches and expenses may be greater when breakdowns occur!) The vendor's support includes such things as training programs to familiarize the company's employees with the unique operating characteristics of the new system, help in implementing and testing the new system, contracts for maintenance on the new system, and providing backup systems for temporarily processing the company's data if the new system fails to operate. Almost all computer vendors charge for these services. In computer terminology, the word **bundling** refers to the amount of software support provided by computer vendors without additional fees. For example, a computer vendor who provides all software support services to a company free of charge is considered to be **completely bundled.** On the other hand, if the vendor charges the company a fee for each software service it provides, then the hardware and software supplier is **totally unbundled.** Finally, if some vendor software support services are provided without charge and others at a charge, the hardware and software supplier is considered to be **semi-bundled.**

After each vendor has presented its systems proposal to the consultants and their client's management, the specific proposal that best meets the company's data processing needs should be selected. As mentioned previously, this decision is the responsibility of the company's top management. It is quite likely, however, that the consultants' recommendations will be given considerable weight in the decision making process.

Selecting Software Packages

If management decides to purchase software separately from hardware, a further decision must be made regarding a choice of software supplier. Actually, the company may decide to write its own software. The advantages of in-house software development versus acquiring software from an independent software vendor were discussed in Chapter 14. Here, we will consider only how to select an independent software supplier. The number of independent software vendors that offer reliable products has grown over the years, thereby expanding the software for application and utility programs.

A richer variety of software has led to more difficult decision making from the standpoint of the user company because there are more packages to evaluate. Cost, of course, continues to be an important constraint in the final decision, but cost, in turn, is dependent on a myriad of other factors that affect the implementation and ultimate operating performance of the software system under study. Among such other factors are (1) reliability, (2) compatibility, (3) security, (4) flexibility, (5) training, and (6) maintenance. Because we have already discussed these factors in this and previous chapters, we will not dwell on them here. Of greater importance from the standpoint of the user company is how to tell whether a given software package meets minimal levels of performance in, for example, each of the foregoing six factors when the potential purchaser or lessee has never used the package before.

At a minimum, a company interested in acquiring software for its computer system can ask for a detailed prospectus of the vendor's products. Experts in the computer field suggest that the potential user prepare a checklist of needs and performance requirements in advance (i.e., systems specifications) so that several competitive products can be evaluated with uniform criteria. Thus, for instance, an organization with three disk drives which is presently in the market for an accounts receivable package would probably eliminate from further consideration those proprietary software packages that require four or more disk drives.

For situations in which two or more software packages are able to meet minimal performance specifications, a further evaluation using a **point-scoring system** can be made to determine the best choice. A typical approach would be to allocate 100 points among those factors considered critical for the particular software application under study, assigning more points to the factors considered most important by the user company. For example, a company considering the acquisition of a payroll accounting package might use a scheme awarding (at most) 25 points to "reliability," 20 points to "compatibility," 10 points to "security," 20 points to "flexibility," 10 points to "training," and 15 points to "maintenance." The company would then proceed to rate the independent software vendor candidates with this scoring system, choosing the vendor's accounting package with the highest aggregate score. Cost can also be included as an evaluation factor if competing products don't cost the same.

To illustrate the point-scoring system (see Figure 15-1) for the evaluation of accounting information system software, suppose that the Alan Company has decided to acquire a new accounts payable computer software package. The management consultants would interview members of the accounting department, the purchasing department, the inventory department, and even the receiving department to ascertain which characteristics in an accounts payable software package these departments consider most important. These characteristics are listed on the left margin of Figure 15-1.

For simplicity, assume that two proprietary software packages have been identified that appear to satisfy the requirements of the users interviewed in the company's initial survey. (The identification of more than two packages would not change the analysis appreciably, however.) One of these packages is marketed by Vendor A and the other by Vendor B. Both packages can be leased for about the same cost; thus, cost is not an issue. Therefore, in evaluating these packages, the management consultants (with the approval

Characteristics for Decision	Possible Points	Vendor A	Vendor B
I. Ease of Use	40		
(a) Operations	8	8	7
(b) Administration interface	8	5	4
(c) Customer service	8	2	6
(d) Response time	8	8	3
(e) Amount of input required per transaction	8	8	2
II. Ease of Conversion	30		
(a) Adherence to company reporting	10	10	7
(b) Business services	10	6	6
(c) Interface with existing general ledger package	10	8	0
III. Vendor Support	30		
(a) Back-up in case of loss or disaster	6	6	5
(b) Programming assistance for changes	6	6	6
(c) Training	6	5	0
(d) Software upgrade support	6	3	3
(e) Miscellaneous support	6	2	4
Totals		77	53

FIGURE 15-1　Illustration of the point-scoring system for the Alan Company's evaluation of two independent vendors' accounts payable computer software packages.

of management) have decided on three major decision criteria: (1) ease of use, (2) ease of conversion (to the Alan Company's existing accounting information system), and (3) vendor support. On the basis of their earlier survey of the user departments, the consultants have further decided to weight ease of use 40 points, ease of conversion 30 points, and vendor support 30 points. Weights for subcategories (such as "adherence to company reporting" within the general category of ease of conversion) are determined on an equal-weight basis (although this does not have to be the case). Thus, for example, with three subcategories under ease of conversion, each subcategory is weighted as one-third the total weight of the general (ease of conversion) category— in this case, 10 points apiece.

These weights are maximum values that can be assigned to each subcategory element identified in the evaluation. The actual number of points to be awarded each vendor package for a given subcategory will depend on the software package's individual merit. For example, a software package whose output report formats would have to be completely revised to make the reports compatible with the informational needs of the user company would probably be given an actual score of zero for the "adherence to company reporting" subcategory. On the other hand, a package whose formats for reports were already perfectly acceptable to management would likely be awarded the highest possible score (10 points) for the same subcategory.

Figure 15-1 illustrates a set of possible ratings for our hypothetical point-scoring system illustration. After all of these points have been awarded, the scores are summed to obtain a final score for each software vendor. In this case, Vendor A's final score of 77 turns out to be considerably higher than Vendor B's final score of 53. Thus, in this case, the Alan Company should acquire Vendor A's computer software package. If both vendors' scores were low, the company might reject both packages. In this instance, the company would probably search further for suitable accounting software or reconsider developing the software in-house.

The recommendations that result from such point-scoring system evaluations are sometimes surprising even to the participants themselves. For example, one EDP manager reported that he had been placed in charge of acquiring an accounts receivable software package for his medium-size company and that he had narrowed the choice to two possibilities: a large hardware manufacturer's (the XYZ Company) software package and an alternative package developed by a small, but reputable, independent vendor. The EDP manager knew that it would be a simple matter to gain budgetary approval for the hardware manufacturer's software product inasmuch as XYZ's position in the data processing field was well known to the manager's superiors and the executive staff of the company trusted XYZ products. Management's unfamiliarity with the products of the alternative software vendor would make managerial approval of the alternative product more difficult. Thus, at first glance, the XYZ Company choice seemed obvious.

As a conscientious worker, however, the EDP manager decided to perform an objective evaluation. He therefore quizzed the potential users of the new software package to determine their data processing needs. The manager then created weights for a point-scoring system evaluation and directed his staff to rate the two packages according to the criteria developed in his survey. To everyone's surprise, the independent vendor's product won by a wide margin! The independent vendor's software package turned out to have twice as many desirable features as XYZ's software and was also cheaper to acquire. The EDP manager used the point-scoring system evaluation results in his report to top management to justify the software acquisition from the independent vendor, and he acquired the independent vendor's software to everyone's satisfaction.

Not all software acquisitions have happy endings. Some software products look good on paper but turn out to be *dogs* when placed in actual use. Thus, the real test of proprietary software lies in hands-on experience with the product under study. Acquiring such experience without risks is difficult but not impossible. Some software vendors are willing to let potential users try their products free, or at nominal cost, for a 30-, 60-, or even 90-day trial period. Usually, the company testing the software product will run its old programs and the new programs in parallel so that unforeseen problems with the new system will not affect the company's normal operations. Some software vendors will even make their own computer equipment available to the potential user company for testing purposes to avoid tying up the potential user's equipment, to render assistance to the new user, and of course, to make sure the potential user is aware of all the advantages of the vendor's software products. Experience with a software product is one of the most efficient ways of evaluating software. Thus, when acquiring software packages for accounting information systems, testing before buying is a good idea.

Implementation and Initial Operation

This step in the systems study is often called the "action" phase because the recommended changes from the prior analysis and design work are now put into operation. To implement efficiently and effectively the necessary changes into an organization's system, the consultants must do considerable planning and controlling. A systems implementation ordinarily involves the performance of several specific activities to convert a company's present system to the newly designed one. These activities must be performed in a logical sequence. Thus, some activities must be completed before others can commence. Certain activities can be implemented simultaneously (or in "parallel"). Unless the consultants plan the systems implementation project logically, the project's coordination may suffer and the completion of the implementation may be unreasonably prolonged.

As specific activities are being performed, the consultants can provide feedback reports to management that compare the actual implementation time with the estimated implementation time.

These control reports enable both the consultants and the company's management to be aware of any delays in implementing specific activities (the actual time exceeding the original estimate) and what effect, if any, the delays may have on the entire implementation process. For example, if a specific implementation activity is behind schedule, the consultants may allocate additional human resources to the activity to speed it up. Or, if another activity is proceeding ahead of schedule, the resources working on this activity may be reduced.

Because of the importance of good planning and controlling when implementing systems changes, many consultants utilize a PERT (Program Evaluation and Review Technique) network for scheduling the sequence of activities that must be performed in the implementation phase of a systems study. Using PERT, a diagram reflecting the logical sequence of systems implementation activities is prepared. The time required for implementing each activity is estimated and included in the **PERT network diagram.** When introducing some minor revisions into a company's present system (e.g., changing the formats of certain computerized feedback reports within the Alan Company) or implementing a new system into a *small* company, the consultants typically will not use a PERT network diagram for guiding the implementation activities because the number of required activities will be minimal. For a major systems conversion involving a large number of implementation activities, however, a PERT network diagram can be a valuable tool for planning and controlling the consultants' systems implementation work.

The time required to implement the various activities in a systems change is based on reasonable estimates for each activity. Because the future involves uncertainty, there is always the risk that the actual time required to implement a specific activity will vary from the estimated time. Because of this uncertainty regarding the actual time interval for implementing specific systems conversion activities, statistical probabilities can be incorporated into the PERT network analysis.

Quantitative analysis example 2 in Appendix A illustrates the use of statistical probability theory in a PERT network diagram. To emphasize the systems implementation process (and deemphasize the mathematics), the following discussion of a PERT network's use in planning and controlling the revision of a company's current system will ignore statistical probabilities in estimating the completion time for implementing a new system.

In our discussion of PERT, the reader should keep in mind that the drawing of a PERT network diagram is only a *tool* to aid consultants in their systems implementation work. The heart of systems implementation is the performance of the specific activities required to implement systems revisions successfully. We will discuss PERT before beginning a detailed examination of the activities required to implement systems changes. However, in actual practice, the development of a PERT network diagram and the determination of the detailed work that must be performed to implement each activity in a systems change are executed "hand in hand." After all, how can you develop a logical sequence of systems implementation activities without knowing the detailed work required for each activity?

PERT Network Diagram for Systems Implementation

From the systems design discussion of Chapter 14, it should be remembered that the consultants and their client company's top management reached a decision to convert the company's manual data processing system to a batch processing computerized system. Figure 15-2 describes the various activities, the consultants' estimates of the time required to implement each activity, and the predecessor activities (i.e., those activities, if any, that must be completed before a specific activity can commence) for converting the client's present information system to a medium-size, computerized batch processing system. Based on the data in Figure 15-2, a PERT network diagram of the systems implementation process is then prepared, as illustrated in Figure 15-3.

The arrows on the PERT network diagram designate the activities required to implement the computer system. (In this PERT network diagram, the length of each arrow has no relationship to the estimated completion time for an activity.) Conventionally, these arrows flow from left to right. The circles (called **nodes**) with numbers inside represent events. The events signal either

Systems Implementation Activities

Activity	Estimated Time (in weeks)	Predecessor Activities	Description of Activity[a]
A	19	None	Prepare the physical site location for the delivery of the computer system.
B	14	None	Determine the necessary functional changes in the system.
C	2	B	Select and assign personnel.
D	6	C	Train personnel.
E	1	A	Acquire and install the computer equipment.
F	7	B	Establish controls and standards.
G	6	E, F	Convert data files to computer storage media.
H	6	E, F	Acquire computer programs.
I	5	H	Test computer programs.
J	26	D, G, I	Test new system's operational capabilities by parallel conversion and eliminate old system.

[a] Each of these activities will be discussed later in the chapter.

FIGURE 15-2 Systems implementation activities.

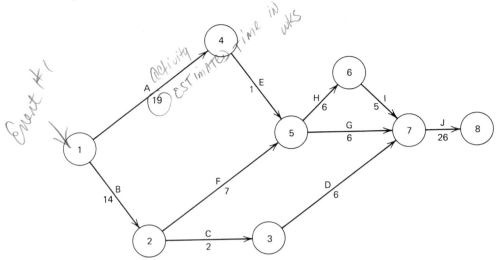

Event #1 *Activity* *ESTIMATED time in wks*

FIGURE 15-3   PERT network diagram of systems implementation process.

the start or the completion of specific activities and do not absorb any time. Event 1 is the beginning of the implementation process. Since neither activity A nor activity B requires any predecessor activities (see Figure 15-2), both can begin simultaneously at node 1. Since activity B is expected to be implemented before activity A (14 weeks for activity B compared with 19 weeks for activity A), the completion of activity B is reflected as event 2 in Figure 15-3. Once node 2 is reached, activities C and F can begin. Node 3 indicates the completion of activities C and B, requiring an estimated 16 weeks (from Figure 15-3, 14 weeks for activity B + 2 weeks for activity C). Activity A's completion, estimated to require 19 weeks, is designated as the fourth event in the implementation process. Node 5, the completion of activities B and F as well as activities A and E, will be reached in an estimated 21 weeks. Since both of these routes must be completed to reach node 5, and route B,F (14 weeks + 7 weeks = 21 weeks) is estimated to require more time than route A,E (19 weeks + 1 week = 20 weeks), the former's route time of 21 weeks is the earliest possible time that node 5 can be reached. Because the approach used in computing the estimated number of weeks to reach each of the remaining network events is the same as that

discussed above, no further computations will be illustrated here. (For your information, however, node 6 will be reached in an estimated 27 weeks, node 7 in an estimated 32 weeks, and node 8 in an estimated 58 weeks.)

From the viewpoint of successfully meeting the systems implementation schedule (starting at event 1 and finishing at event 8 in Figure 15-3), the consultants must monitor closely that sequence of activities that is expected to require the longest period of time through the network. In order to determine the network's most time-consuming sequence of activities, each path's estimated time duration from event 1 to the completion of event 8 is computed, as follows.

A−E−H−I−J = 57 weeks *[noted in about class]*
(19 + 1 + 6 + 5 + 26)

A−E−G−J   = 52 weeks (19 + 1 + 6 + 26)

B−F−H−I−J = 58 weeks   *CRITICAL PATH*
(14 + 7 + 6 + 5 + 26)

B−F−G−J   = 53 weeks (14 + 7 + 6 + 26)

B−C−D−J   = 48 weeks (14 + 2 + 6 + 26)

The most time-consuming network path is thus B−F−H−I−J (requiring an estimated 58 weeks), and this network path is called the **critical path.**

If any delay in BFHIJ activity, then whole project will be delayed

The word *critical* is used for each activity within this longest path through the network because any delays in implementing a critical-path activity will delay the entire implementation project. Thus, it is extremely important that the consultants as well as their client company's top management closely monitor the performance of each critical-path activity so that delays in implementing these activities can be avoided. For the noncritical activities (i.e., those not on the critical path), some time delays can occur in their implementation without a delay in implementing the entire system. Thus, management does not have to monitor these noncritical-path activities as closely as the critical-path activities.

The term **slack time** is used to indicate the amount of delay time that can occur in non-critical-path activities and still not delay the estimated completion time (58 weeks in our example) of the entire systems implementation project. Obviously, the greater the slack time for a noncritical activity, the less closely that activity has to be monitored. Because no delays in critical-path activities can occur without a time delay in completing the project, the slack time for any critical-path activity is always *zero*.

To illustrate the computation of the slack time for a noncritical-path activity, assume that top management wanted to know how much delay could occur in completing activity G (an estimated time of 6 weeks in Figure 15-2) without causing the systems implementation project to extend beyond 58 weeks (the critical-path time estimate). When determining the slack time of a noncritical-path activity, you must compute the activity's earliest and latest possible completion times. The difference between the two represents the activity's slack time. From Figure 15-3, the earliest possible completion time for activity G is 27 weeks (activity B + activity F + activity G = 14 + 7 + 6). The latest possible completion time for activity G is determined by taking the project's total estimated implementation time (which is the critical-path time) and subtracting from this figure the estimated times required for all activities performed after activity G. Thus, the

latest time for completing activity G is 32 weeks [58 weeks estimated for implementing the entire project *minus* 26 weeks estimated for implementing activity J (the only activity performed after activity G)]. In other words, because activity J requires 26 weeks, the maximum number of weeks into the project for implementing activity G without causing the entire project to take longer than 58 weeks is 32 weeks (32 weeks + 26 weeks for activity J = 58 weeks). If, for example, it took 39 weeks to complete activity G and thus be at event 7, then the earliest possible completion time for the entire implementation project would be 65 weeks (39 weeks + 26 weeks for activity J). This 65-week implementation period would result in a 7-week delay from the original critical-path estimate of 58 weeks. The slack time for activity G is therefore 5 weeks (32 weeks for the latest possible completion time *minus* 27 weeks for the earliest possible completion time).

This discussion has attempted to analyze briefly the valuable information that can be obtained by using a PERT network diagram for planning and controlling a systems implementation project. In order to develop the PERT network diagram, the consultants have to *plan* the logical sequence of activities that must be performed to implement their systems changes successfully. By closely monitoring the actual implementation time required compared with the estimated time for each critical-path activity and also being aware of the slack time permitted for noncritical-path activities, the PERT network diagram is also a useful *control* mechanism for consultants and their client's top management during the actual systems installation process.

The PERT network diagram of Figure 15-3 had only one critical path. It should be noted, however, that it is possible to have more than one critical path of activities; for example, the total estimated times for completing the two longest routes through the PERT network diagram may be identical, resulting in two critical paths. Also, if the actual completion times for various implementation activities should vary significantly from their estimated completion times, it is possible for the critical path itself to change at some point during the implementation process.

Gantt Charts

Another tool that may be used for scheduling the various activities in implementing the system is the **Gantt chart.** Gantt charts are useful for tracking as well as scheduling projects since actual progress can be indicated directly on the chart and contrasted with the planned progress. A Gantt chart that shows the implementation activities in our example, as well as planned and actual schedules for completion, is shown in Figure 15-4. Gantt charts are very straightforward and easy to understand. Note, though, that a disadvantage of the Gantt chart versus PERT network diagrams is that the Gantt chart does not indicate the relationships between the activities. Instead, the gantt chart treats each task as though it is independent of others. For this reason, Gantt charts are probably better suited to less complex projects, where relatively few interrelationships between activities exist. For simpler projects they are an excellent control tool since they do a better job than PERT at showing in simple terms a comparison of *expected* to *actual*.

We will now examine each of the activities required to convert the company's manual data processing system to a computerized batch processing system.

Activity A: Prepare the Physical Site

When introducing a computerized data processing system into an organization, the work required to prepare the physical site location for

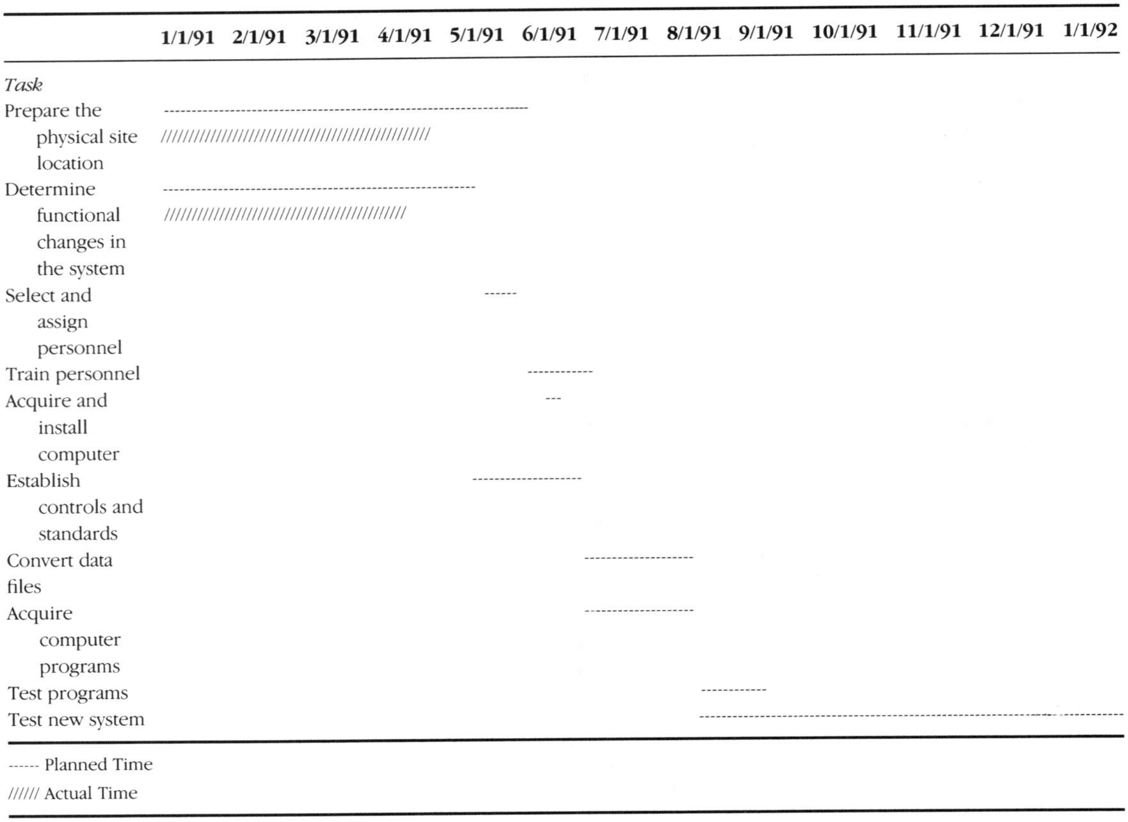

Task	1/1/91	2/1/91	3/1/91	4/1/91	5/1/91	6/1/91	7/1/91	8/1/91	9/1/91	10/1/91	11/1/91	12/1/91	1/1/92
Prepare the physical site location	Planned ------------------------------ Actual ////////////////												
Determine functional changes in the system	Planned ------------------------ Actual ////////////////												
Select and assign personnel					------								
Train personnel						------------							
Acquire and install computer						---							
Establish controls and standards					------------------								
Convert data files							------------------						
Acquire computer programs							------------------						
Test programs								------------					
Test new system								--					

------ Planned Time

////// Actual Time

FIGURE 15-4 Gantt chart for systems implementation activities.

the subsequent delivery of the computer system can be quite time-consuming (estimated to take 19 weeks in Figure 15-2). The consulting team's accountants will be especially concerned about the incremental costs (i.e., those costs that will increase as a result of a specific activity) associated with physical site preparation. If the company already has available building space for the computer center and this space is neither being used currently nor anticipated to be used in the future for any other organizational activities, then the incremental cost of utilizing the physical space is zero. However, the building area designated for the computer center may be occupied or plans may exist for its future use in other organizational functions. In this case, the incremental cost of using the specific space area for the computer center is the opportunity cost of being unable to use the area for the other intended purposes.

The company may even decide to construct additional building space to house the new computer center. The costs of performing this construction work would be classified as incremental costs. Additional incremental costs that are normally required in preparing the physical site location include the costs for air conditioning, for electrical outlets, for a library to store data files and computer programs, and for furniture and fixtures. The number of entrances and exits to the computer room should be minimized to prevent the entry of unauthorized employees.

Activity B: Determine the Functional Changes

Included in this implementation activity is the consultants' analysis of job function changes caused by the computerized system and their analysis of the types of data that will be processed and reported by the new computerized system.

The automated system likely will eliminate certain jobs that existed under the old manual system (such as accounts receivable bookkeeping for preparing the monthly customer billing statements) and will also create new jobs (such as computer programming). The manner of performing the work tasks may change even for those job functions that are not eliminated. For example, under the Alan Company's old manual system, the inventory bookkeeper maintained a handwritten subsidiary ledger disclosing the balances of each inventory item. This ledger was updated monthly by the bookkeeper from the various sales invoices, purchase invoices, and receiving reports. With the Alan Company's batch processing computer system, however, the inventory bookkeeper will review for accuracy the copies of the invoices for sales and purchases as well as the inventory receiving reports, then send them to the EDP center, where the data from these source documents (such as the code numbers and quantities of inventory items sold and purchased) are transferred to a computer storage medium (such as magnetic tape) and processed to update the various inventory account balances.

The types of transactions—for example, inventory, cash, and accounts receivable transactions—that will be processed by the computer center and the manner in which the transaction data will be stored must be analyzed by the consulting team's accountants. For instance, a decision may have been made initially to record and store a company's inventory transaction data on magnetic tape according to inventory code numbers. A weekly transaction tape of inventory activities (sales and purchases) would be prepared and processed with the master inventory tape file in order to update the inventory balances and print out purchase orders for those inventory items reaching their reorder points. For control purposes, a grandfather-father-son system of tape files may be maintained. After further discussions with the hardware and software vendor, however, the consulting team's accountants may decide to have the inventory transaction data recorded and stored on magnetic disk.

The format of the output reports from the inventory processing functions must also be ascertained. This requires an analysis of both the specific information to be included on output reports and those employees who will receive copies of these reports. To determine which employees should receive output reports and the data that should be included on the reports, the accountants on the consulting team must be familiar with the employees' organizational functions and the decision-making information they require to perform their functions. A specific report should not be distributed to employees unless they need the information from the report to execute their duties effectively. For example, the raw materials inventory report distributed to the Alan Company's purchasing agent (who is responsible for placing orders for additional sporting goods raw material inventory items) may be prepared on an exception basis, disclosing only those inventory tiems requiring reorder. On the other hand, the Alan Company's basketball production manager's output report may include information about the current balances of every basketball manufacturing raw material inventory item. If, for instance, a major production order of basketballs is scheduled in four weeks, this detailed inventory report will enable the production manager to ascertain whether an adequate supply of specific types of raw materials needed for basketball manufacturing is currently available for processing the future order. If sufficient balances of certain raw materials are not on hand, the basketball production manager can then request the purchasing agent to order these specific items immediately.

Activity C: Select and Assign Personnel

After determining the necessary functional changes required in the new computer system (activity B), the consultants will be able to write job descriptions for the various employees' work activities under the revised system. Based on these job descriptions, the personnel subsystem of the consultants' client company will be responsible for selecting the necessary employees and assigning them to specific job functions. Ultimately, people are responsible for the day-to-day efficiency and effectiveness of a business information system. Moreover, people must ultimately make use of the valuable information that the system generates. Thus, *personnel* comprise a

key resource that affects the success or failure of an organization's information system.

When converting from a manual to a computerized data processing system, false rumors often circulate among employees about the jobs that will be eliminated, thus lowering morale. To prevent this motivational problem, the consultants and their client's management should communicate openly with the employees regarding the creation of new jobs and the elimination of present jobs. Those employees whose jobs are either eliminated or materially altered as a result of the revised system should be given an opportunity to apply for the newly created jobs. As discussed under activity D, employees can often be trained to perform the new job duties required by the revised system. Individuals are needed for a myriad of positions in the accounting and EDP areas ranging from data entry operators and data coders to programmers, budget analysts, controllers, cost accountants, systems analysts, and data processing managers. Some of the job titles associated with data entry are key-to-tape operator, key-to-disk operator, and supervisor of data entry operators. An individual who was previously employed as a typist in the manual accounting system may be retrained to fill some of these data entry jobs in the new computerized system. Retraining of employees has become very common in industry during the past few years as more and more companies automate or replace their systems.

The highly technical job functions (e.g., computer programming and systems analysis) that must be performed in the new system may be impossible to fill with the company's present employees. Consequently, the personnel subsystem will seek qualified individuals from outside the organization. The hardware and software vendor can often aid the company in locating personnel with the specialized knowledge needed to perform computer-related job functions.

From the standpoint of an organization seeking to hire additional personnel support for its computerized accounting information system, the most important qualifications are almost always experience and technical competence. For example, computer operators and data entry personnel are expected to know the functions of specific pieces of equipment. An organization's job-specification descriptions usually pinpoint how many years of experience with what hardware and software is desired of personnel. Although the number of years of experience required of a job applicant is a somewhat arbitrary figure, there can be little doubt but that experience is crucial in the hiring of personnel. Similarly, with regard to technological expertise, knowledge of specific programming languages is critical when hiring programmers, and sometimes familiarity with specific types of software such as utility programs, data bases, or operating systems is also required.

Most companies use general aptitude tests and specialized data processing tests to screen applicants for data processing jobs. In the United States, for example, the Computer Programmer Aptitude Battery (CPAB) and the Programmer Aptitude Test (PAT) have been used extensively to measure data processing abilities. Included in such tests are (1) exercises in recognizing letter sequences, (2) exercises in manipulating algebraic terms, (3) tasks requiring rapid approximations to numerical calculations, (4) exercises in flowcharting, (5) exercises requiring the individual to draw inferences from stated facts, and (6) general tests of reasoning, analytical skills, and verbal expression. Several of the larger companies in the United States have their own specialized examinations as well.

For jobs in accounting, those applicants who have passed the CPA (Certified Public Accountants) examination or the CMA (Certificate in Management Accounting) examination (in Canada, the Charter Accountant examination is given), or both, would likely be good candidates for accounting-oriented positions. In addition to these "technical" tests, many companies use standardized psychological tests to augment the review profile of prospective employees. Testing can also be used today to screen new employees in other ways. For example, although controver-

sial, drug testing and lie detector tests are sometimes used as personnel hiring practices.

An alternative to hiring additional staff to perform certain data processing tasks is to contract the work out to another firm—an option that some companies have found attractive. Hiring parttime or temporary help has also proven quite beneficial to companies with substantial seasonal fluctuations in data processing volume, enabling organizations to obtain needed assistance during *rush times* but avoid expensive payrolls during "lulls."

There are some disadvantages to work contracting. Security problems are one disadvantage. The need to specify precisely what is required from the outside contractor is a second disadvantage. Because contract work is not cheap, its cost is a third possible disadvantage. In short, the decision to contract data processing tasks *outside* has both pros and cons. Hard and fast guidelines are difficult to establish; rather, it is necessary to examine each individual company's data processing needs on a case-by-case basis.

The employees who will be terminated by the company should receive ample notice to enable them to secure other jobs before their employment ends. Because the entire implementation process normally takes many months to complete, providing terminated employees with ample notices of their job displacements should not be difficult. If possible, these employees should be given some time off with pay (perhaps a few days or even a week) to look for other positions while still working for the company. The company's top management may also consider early retirement for employees who qualify for it.

Activity D: Train Personnel

Both the consultants and the employee representatives from the computer vendor will normally participate in training the company's personnel to operate the newly designed computerized system efficiently. Seminars should be provided for many of the company's employees to make them aware of the various advantages offered by the new computer system. Specific procedural training should be given to those employees whose job functions are altered as a result of the systems revisions. This training can take place in either a classroom environment or the actual on-the-job environment. When using classroom procedures, simulation is a popular learning technique. Through simulation, the employees learn operational functions by performing their new duties on artificially created data that are representative of the actual data with which they will eventually work.

Training will also be required for those newly hired employees already possessing specialized knowledge of computer systems. The training sessions will be designed to teach the EDP subsystem's computer specialists the most effective ways of utilizing the automated system within their company's operating environment. Even if the computer equipment has not yet been installed on the company's premises (activity E), the hardware and software supplier's personnel can provide this training within their own building facility.

Before the employees are taught specific job functions, they should be given an overview of how their jobs fit into the entire company structure. This knowledge will give each employee a good understanding of his or her contribution to the company's goals. As a result, the employees should have a better grasp of the meaning and significance of specific functions, thus motivating them to perform their job duties successfully.

Activity E: Acquire and Install Computer Equipment

After preparing the physical site location for the new computer system (activity A), the hardware equipment must be acquired from the computer vendor. This equipment includes the central processing unit, the input and output devices, and the secondary storage devices. The hardware and software vendor's employees normally will have the major responsiblity for installing the computer equipment into the company's system. Computer specialists on the management con-

sulting team as well as client company employees may also participate in the computer system installation.

Activity F: Establish Controls and Standards

Upon determining the functional changes for the new system (activity B), necessary controls and standards must be established. The accountants on the consulting team should have a major role in this systems implementation activity. It is important to note that although the establishment of controls and standards is treated as a separate activity in this chapter and is not performed until the functional changes in activity B have been determined, the process of thinking about the controls and standards that are needed for the new system should actually begin as part of activity B.

Chapter 9 emphasized that an effective internal control system should safeguard an organization's asset resources and should encourage operating efficiency so that management's prescribed policies are achieved. A company's assets are safeguarded through such preventive controls as a good audit trail and the separation of related organizational functions.

As discussed further in Chapter 9, the introduction of a computer into an organization's system often causes difficulty in following the audit trail of accounting transactions. The consulting team's accountants should make sure there is adequate documentation to describe the operating features of the new system. Good documentation contributes to an effective audit trail. Based on an analysis of the anticipated costs compared with the anticipated benefits of specific controls, many computerized controls should be incorporated into the revised system. The newly implemented system will cause changes in some of the employees' job duties, as was emphasized previously. As old job functions are eliminated and new ones created, the accountants on the consulting team should strive for good separation of related organizational functions when company personnel are assigned to specific job duties under the revised system. For these new job functions (such as computer programming), standards of performance for the employees should be established.

Operational efficiency is evaluated through feedback controls such as a responsibility accounting system and timely performance reports. The responsibility accounting structure should be revised based on the operating changes introduced into the company's system. A major function of timely performance reports is to aid in evaluating the efficiency of employees in meeting job standards. Because the new system will cause a change in job duties and performance standards for many of the employees, the accountants must redesign their client company's performance reporting system so that it continues to measure employees' operating efficiency fairly.

Activity G: Convert Data Files

Under the company's old manual system, its data files of accounting information were maintained on traditional storage media. For example, the information about each general ledger account was recorded manually in a bound book containing preprinted ledger paper, a different page being used for each account. Separate ledger books were also used for the accounts receivable and accounts payable subsidiary ledger information. Data regarding the balances of individual inventory items (both raw materials for production and finished goods) were kept in an inventory subsidiary ledger.

Each of these data files must now be converted to computer storage media. Because the company is implementing a batch processing system, a storage medium such as magnetic tape would be used. Any revised standards (established in activity F) affecting a data file should be incorporated into the file at the time of conversion. For example, the computerized processing of the company's cost accounting production reports will cause a change in the dollar amount of allocated standard overhead charged to work-in-process and finished goods inventories. Under the previous manual system, the standard over-

head charged to production included an allocated share of the salaries of cost accountants (who prepared the production reports manually). Because production reports will now be prepared by the computer rather than by the company's cost accountants, a new standard overhead amount relating to report preparation must be determined. This standard will then be incorporated into the inventory production master file.

When converting the manual data files to computer storage media, care must be taken to ensure that no errors occur during the conversion process. For example, when the accounts receivable subsidiary ledger book is converted to a magnetic tape master file, it is important that each customer's correct account number be transferred to the tape file. Because the newly established computer file will serve as the basis for all future credit-sales processing activity, the need for complete accuracy is imperative when creating this file. As a means of detecting the transfer of inaccurate customers' account numbers to the new computer master file, a hash total of these account numbers can be accumulated from the subsidiary ledger book. At the completion of the conversion to magnetic tape, a hash total of customers' account numbers computed from this new master tape file can be compared with the originally determined hash total from the subsidiary ledger book. These two hash totals should be identical. Any discrepancies between them must be investigated. Many of the additional controls discussed in Chapter 10 (e.g., editing checks, control totals, and field checks) can also be used advantageously when establishing computer files for accounting applications.

If the company desires a high degree of integration among its various master files of accounting information, it must somehow coordinate the accounting data contained within these files in a meaningful way. One approach (as discussed in Chapter 7) is to develop an integrated data base of accounting data in which the data required by various users would all be consolidated in the company's data base files. An alternative approach would be to coordinate the master files through a **supervisory index file.** The index file would contain the storage addresses of the various master files and link these master files together. Thus, when managers require different types of accounting information (such as inventory and sales information) for specific decision-making endeavors, they can obtain the needed information simultaneously from the several master files through the use of the supervisory index file.

During processing runs to update the company's master files for accounting activities, transaction files are normally used to update the master files. When updating these master files, there is always the risk of errors that cause master file data to be destroyed (e.g., writing over a portion of a magnetic tape master file). To provide security against the destruction of master file data, backup files containing the master file information are typically maintained. For example, as discussed previously, the grandfather-father-son system of backup file information might be used.

Activity H: Acquire Computer Programs

For each of the processing functions to be handled by the company's computerized system, programs msut be available in such computer languages as COBOL, FORTRAN, or BASIC. Compiler programs (acquired from the hardware and software supplier) will then be used to convert the programs into machine language.

In the past few years, hardware and software vendors have made great strides in developing software packages for use by companies when performing their computerized data processing functions. These software packages can be purchased or leased by companies, and the packages include prewritten *canned programs* for handling such accounting applications as inventory processing and accounts receivable processing. As mentioned in Chapter 14, canned programs that are leased or purchased from computer suppliers are called proprietary software. Because proprietary software packages are written for the

mass market and each company's specific data processing needs will be somewhat different, a proprietary software package normally requires various modifications before it can be used within a company's system.

Due to the current popularity of hardware and software vendors' proprietary software packages among companies implementing a new computer system or modifying a present system, we will assume in this chapter that the company implementing a new batch processing system will lease prewritten programs from a computer vendor. It should be noted, however, that if a company did elect to develop from *scratch* its own computer programs (called **in-house development**), this activity in the systems implementation process would likely be performed prior to activity E (acquire and install computer equipment). The development of computer programs is very time-consuming and often requires many months to perform. Therefore, the company probably would not want to acquire and install its expensive computer equipment only to remain idle for months until the computer programs were developed.

The process of obtaining and making modifications to a hardware and software vendor's proprietary software package will often take considerably less time (estimated at six weeks in Figure 15-2) than developing computer programs from scratch. Thus, we will assume that the computer equipment was acquired and installed (activity E) as well as the controls and standards of the new system being established (activity F) prior to acquiring the proprietary software.

When making modifications to a hardware and software supplier's prewritten canned programs, it is important for a company to have its controls and standards already established. For example, one of the important considerations by accountants on the consulting team when initially establishing their client company's feedback controls is the types of information that should be included in performance reports to specific managers. Having made this determination in activity F, the prewritten computer canned programs can then be modified (normally with help from the hardware and software vendor's staff of computer experts) to enable the managers to obtain their needed decision-making information. As another example, when the credit managers' information needs for effective decision making were being evaluated, the consulting team's accountants determined that the weekly feedback aging analysis report (prepared on an exception basis) for these managers should include only information about those credit customers' account balances that are more than 60 days past due. In modifying the proprietary software program that processes the company's weekly accounts receivable aging analysis report, this information concerning the content of the credit managers' exception report must be known.

Activity I: Test Computer Programs

After the computer programs have been acquired (activity H), the logic of all modified canned programs must be adequately tested before these programs can be used in the day-to-day processing functions of the company. This testing activity on the computer programs is called **debugging** because the objective is to eliminate the errors (or "bugs") in the modified programs. Simulation is quite useful for testing the logic of a company's computer programs. The hardware and software vendor's staff of computer experts normally will aid the consultants in testing these computer programs.

Failure to test adequately the newly acquired canned computer programs that have been modified could lead to disastrous consequences. Assuming that programming errors go undetected and the programs are used to process the company's actual operating data, the output information on reports from the specific processing runs would be incorrect. The subsequent use of these incorrect output reports for management decision making, and so forth, would obviously be detrimental to the company's present and future business success!

Activity J: Test New System and Eliminate Old System

At this stage, all the prior systems implementation activities have been completed and the new system should be ready to take over the company's processing functions. As yet, however, the new system has not passed the *final test* of being able to process correctly the company's *real-world* operating data. Therefore, rather than immediately eliminate the old system by replacing it with the newly designed system (the **direct conversion** method, discussed later), many companies take a gradual approach to implementing their new systems.

A popular operational testing method for introducing a new system into a company's day-to-day processing activities is called **parallel conversion.** Using this method, both the old system and the new system operate simultaneously (or *in parallel*) for a certain period of time. Thus, all of the company's processing activities are handled independently by both systems. The resultant outputs from each system are then compared and any differences reconciled. Assuming that the old system's processing accuracy is already well established from prior years of company use, those output discrepancies between the old and new systems will likely be attributable to errors in the latter system. The causes of these errors can be investigated and revisions made in the final design of the new system.

The time necessary for parallel conversion (assumed to be 26 weeks in Figure 15-2) depends on the number of processing discrepancies detected and the time required to make revisions in the new system. In addition to testing for processing discrepancies under the parallel conversion method, the implemented controls of the new system (established in activity F) should also be observed and tested to make sure they are functioning as originally planned. For example, if a "check-digit" control (discussed in Chapter 10) for inventory account numbers was implemented into the computer system, the consultants should evaluate the effectiveness of this control by reviewing the handling of those incorrectly coded inventory account numbers detected by the "check-digit" control.

When the consultants are satisfied with the operational functioning of the new system, this system completely replaces the old system in handling the company's data processing activities. A major advantage of parallel conversion is that the company's data processing activities are protected from a possible failure in the new system. Because the old system remains in operation during the parallel conversion period, it will continue to process the company's data correctly even if processing errors occur within the new system.

The obvious disadvantage of the parallel conversion method is the cost factor. Because each accounting transaction is processed by both the old system and the new system throughout the parallel conversion period, company facilities and personnel must be available to handle the dual processing work. This dual processing often leads to considerable overtime work.

The opposite of a parallel conversion is called a **direct conversion.** Under this conversion method, the old system is immediately discontinued when the new system is implemented, and the new system "sinks or swims." Direct conversion is thus a relatively inexpensive systems implementation approach. The direct conversion method might be employed under any of the following circumstances: (1) the old system has so many weaknesses that a parallel conversion would serve no useful purpose, (2) the revisions to be implemented into the company's system are either very minor or simple—which would undoubtedly not be true when converting from a manual to a computerized data processing system, or (3) the new systems design differs drastically from that of the old system, thereby making comparisons between the two systems meaningless.

One additional systems implementation method is called **modular conversion** (or the **pilot conversion** approach). With this method, a specific data processing activity (e.g., batch

processing of all inventory transactions) is broken down into smaller units, called modules. The implementation of the new data processing activity is then executed "piecemeal" for the specific units associated with the activity.

To illustrate the modular conversion method, assume that a company has five separate divisions that purchase and sell inventory. Using modular conversion, each of these divisions' inventory transactions would be treated as a specific unit (or module). A new batch processing computerized inventory system would be implemented for one of the five divisions. After satisfactorily testing the inventory system's operation in this division, the batch processing system could be implemented for the second division. Successful results in the second division would lead to the system's implementation for the third division, and so on. The major advantage of modular conversion is that specific problems discovered in a new system can be corrected before further implementation occurs. A possible drawback of using modular conversion is the long time period normally required to complete the entire implementation process.

Regardless of which conversion method is used, activity J's work results in the disappearance of the old system and the emergence of the new system to handle the company's data processing functions. After completing activity J, some management consultants might feel that their systems study work is finished. However, they would be wrong! The final aspect of a systems study, called **follow-up,** is discussed in the next section.

SYSTEMS FOLLOW-UP

As emphasized in Chapter 13, a company's information system should contribute toward three levels of goals: (1) general systems goals such as a simplistic structure and a flexible structure, (2) top management systems goals, and (3) operating management systems goals. When goals are not being achieved in one or more of these three levels within the company's current operational system, problems (or weaknesses) normally occur in the system. Management consultants may then be hired to help solve the problems by performing a systems study for their client company.

The consultants' initially implemented system should be designed to eliminate the problems of the old system. As the new system operates on a day-to-day basis, however, the company's original systems problems may recur or new problems may surface. Therefore, after the initially implemented system has been in operation for a few months, representatives from the management consulting firm should return to their client company's premises to evaluate the new system's effectiveness in contributing toward the three levels of goals.

The follow-up analysis work by the consultants on the implemented batch processing computerized system discussed in this chapter might include the following activities: (1) talk with top management personnel and operating management personnel about their satisfaction with the output reports (both the content and the timeliness of these reports) received from the computer center, (2) evaluate the controls of the system to ascertain whether they are functioning properly, (3) observe some of the employees' work performances to ascertain whether the employees are executing their assigned job functions correctly, and (4) evaluate whether data preparation functions as well as computer processing functions are being performed efficiently, and also determine if output schedules for reports (both internal and external reports) under the new computer system are being met.

As Figure 13-1 illustrated, the follow-up studies can lead in one of two directions in the life cycle of a company's information system. If the consultants are satisfied as a result of their follow-up work that the initially implemented system has eliminated the company's previous information systems problems, no further revisions are required. Thus, the new system continues processing the company's daily transactions. On the other hand, if the consultants' follow-up analysis reveals that problems still exist in the newly implemented system, the systems study steps (analysis, design, implementation and initial operation, and follow-up studies) must be repeated in an attempt to solve these problems. Hopefully, the resultant revisions will eliminate the problems within the system, thereby contributing toward the achievement of the company's general systems goals, top management systems goals, and operating management systems goals.

The dashed arrow in Figure 13-1 from the system operation on a daily basis to the follow-up studies indicates that the follow-up phase of a systems study should continue throughout the life of a company's system. Even though an information system is currently satisfying the company's needs, this may not be the case at some future time. For example, because of increased competition or new governmental regulations, the information needs of top management personnel may change. To satisfy top management's new information requirements, the company's system will have to be modified.

As indicated in Chapter 13, the consultants should periodically return to their client's company (e.g., every six months) to ascertain whether the current information system is still satisfying the organization's needs. These periodic reviews will normally lead to few, if any, revisions in the company's data processing system. However, the follow-up work and resultant modifications to a computerized information system can become quite involved.

AIS at Work—Automating the Disaster Accounting System at the American Red Cross

The American Red Cross's systems development projects are part of its Corporate Management Information System (CMIS) long-range planning. In 1986, preliminary studies indicated that the manual Disaster Accounting System was a prime candidate for automation, the objective being to improve the efficiency while reducing the cost of processing disaster relief payments. The Disaster Accounting System is used primarily for making payments to vendors who supply disaster victims with goods and services.

When a major disaster occurs, the Red Cross sends a team, called the Disaster Field Operations Staff, to the site. Victims are interviewed by case workers who determine which relief services should be provided such as goods to replace or reconstruct damaged items lost in the tragedy. The Disaster Field Operations Staff issues a disbursing order to the victim (similar to a purchase order) and the victim in turn presents this order to a local vendor when acquiring goods. Vendors then process the disbursing orders and send them to the national office of the American Red Cross. There they are processed as payment requests by the Disaster Accounting System. Travel and maintenance reimbursement requests of the Field Operations Staff are also processed by the System in addition to direct relief reimbursements. The Disaster Accounting System also processes relief reimbursement requests of local Red Cross chapters, supplying them with payments for goods or services on receipt of Disaster Vouchers, which detail vendor payments made on behalf of victims at the local chapter level. Reports on payments and other activities are periodically provided by the Disaster Accounting System to the Disaster Operations Administration and many other departments within the Red Cross.

Once the decision had been made to proceed with possible automation of Disaster Accounting, a systems development project team was formed consisting of analysts from CMIS and accountants from Disaster Accounting. Led by Harun Murray, an Accounting Division manager, the team adopted a phased approach to systems development. First, the system requirements were defined using structured systems analysis. The information flows were specified and the activities were defined in terms of discreet processes. The resulting data flow diagrams, process descriptions, and data dictionary became the physical model of the system before any changes were proposed. A computer-aided software engineering (CASE) tool was used, which allowed the team to continually refine the highly complex model of the system. A CASE tool has interactive graphics for diagrams coupled with a data dictionary in the background. The physical model created using the CASE tool defined how the manual system worked. A logical model was then created defining what the system did without considering "how" processes were accomplished. New requirements were then added to this logical model and this completed the system requirements definition phase.

The next phase dealt with system design alternatives. First, each of the processes were reviewed and a decision was made whether to include them within the automation boundary. Then, two vendor software packages were evaluated, one of them being an integrated fund accounting system. Since many of the processes of the Disaster Accounting System were contained in this standard software, a decision was made to utilize the general ledger and accounts payable modules of this vendor package. Not all of the system requirements were met and modifications would be necessary. The project team realized that if the standard package were modified to fit the system requirements, subsequent updates and enhancements to the vendor's standard software would not be easily available to a custom version. With this in mind, the vendor and the project team worked out a plan whereby a custom "front end" documents data base would be written by the vendor based on the unmet system requirements. This would allow the custom automated accounting information system to interface with the vendor's standard software and minimize problems of implementing future upgrades.

The third phase consisted of detailed specifications of screens and reports, and defining standard operating procedures for interfacing with the automated system. Once these specifications were complete, the vendor proceeded with internal program design and programming and, as each module was completed and delivered, the project team proceeded with unit testing and system testing according to a test plan. As of this writing, this system development life cycle continues as the project team completes its testing and prepares for conversion and implementation of the automated Disaster Accounting System.

SUMMARY

Following the decision to acquire a specific computer system, the implementation phase of the systems study begins. Before the actual activities involved in getting the system operating can take place, the hardware and software vendors must be selected. Several considerations that must be taken into account in making that selection are (1) performance capability, (2) modularity, (3) compatibility of the proposed new system, and (4) reputation of the vendor, including the vendor's ability to support the new system.

Because there are so many activities involved in implementing and initially operating the new system, a useful tool often employed by consultants for planning and controlling the systems implementation project is PERT. By preparing a PERT network diagram that reflects the logical sequence of conversion activities and the time estimates for performing these activities, the implementation of a new system should proceed in an efficient manner. To avoid delays when implementing the new system, the sequence of conversion activities requiring the most time (called the critical path activities) should be closely monitored by both the consultants and their client's top management. Gantt charts may also prove useful in planning and controlling the systems implementation project, although they are somewhat limited since they do not consider the interrelationships among activities.

Many different tasks are involved in implementing and initially operating a computerized information system where a manual system existed previously. First, the physical site must be prepared for delivery of the new computer hardware. At the same time, the consultants must determine what functional changes are necessary. Following this step, the selection and assignment of personnel begins. This is particularly important, as the human element is crucial to the success of the new system. Personnel who will be working with the new system must next be trained. The remaining activities are to acquire and install the new computer, establish controls and standards, convert the data files to computerized storage media, acquire and test the computer programs, and finally, test the new system.

Once the new system is operational, some follow-up activity should take place. The objective of this systems study work is to evaluate whether or not the newly implemented system has solved the company's previous information systems problems and is therefore meeting the information needs of the organization's management. After the new system has been functioning for a few months, the consultants will evaluate the system's effectiveness in accomplishing its intended purpose(s). If the revised system has failed to solve previous systems problems or possibly caused new problems, further changes are required. The consultants will then repeat their systems study steps in order to make the necessary revisions. Follow-up reviews by the consultants should be performed periodically throughout the system's life to determine if further changes are necessary.

Key Terms You Should Know

benchmark problem	parallel conversion
bundled hardware and software	performance capability
compatibility	PERT network diagram
completely bundled	pilot conversion
critical path	point-scoring system
debugging	reputation
direct conversion	semibundled
follow-up	slack time
Gantt chart	support
in-house development	supervisory index file
modular conversion	systems analysis
modularity	systems implementation
nodes	totally unbundled

Discussion Questions

15-1. The following terms were analyzed in this chapter: the benchmark problem, the modularity capability, and the compatibility of a system. Discuss the importance of each when a company is trying to decide which hardware and software vendor's computer system to acquire.

15-2. Discuss the importance of cost in the software acquisition process. Why is cost often considered only one of the many factors in the decision analysis?

15-3. Describe the point-scoring system of evaluating computer software. Could such a system also be used when evaluating computer hardware? What drawbacks can you foresee in the use of such an evaluation mechanism?

15-4. Discuss the use of psychological, general aptitude, drug, lie-detector, and specialized data processing tests in screening programmer and systems analyst job applicants. What are the advantages and disadvantages of using such tests? Would you call such tests discriminatory? Why or why not?

15-5. Discuss the advantages and disadvantages of using PERT networks versus Gantt charts for planning and controlling the activities involved in implementing an information system.

15-6. In the text, it was stated that an alternative to hiring additional staff was to contract the work out. Would you imagine that contracting would always be possible? What jobs would you say are better performed in-house and which jobs would you say are better performed on a contract basis?

15-7. When a company acquires a computerized data processing system for the first time, what are some of the incremental costs the company normally incurs during the preparation of the physical site?

15-8. Tommy Solton has just finished the implementation of an online, real-time system for his client, the Archy Bald Company. Tommy works as a management consultant in the firm called Consultants for Success. At a cocktail party the other night, Tommy was bragging to one of his friends about how efficient he was in performing the systems study work for the Archy Bald Company. Tommy's comments were as follows.

The company's president, Archy B. Bald, was very frustrated with the slowness of reports coming from his organization's manual data processing system. About three days before I was contacted by Bald, I read an advertisement in a trade journal about IBM's new 1991-model online, real-time computer system. Therefore, as soon as I arrived at the Archy Bald Company to discuss my potential systems job, I immediately showed this advertisement to Mr. Bald. He was so excited that he immediately hired me to supervise the implementation of the online system. The next day I contacted the IBM people and a short time thereafter, the new computer system was delivered and implemented into the company. Before the company's employees knew what had happened, their old and outdated manual system had been replaced by this superior computerized system. Bald was so pleased with my speed in implementing the new system that he paid me an extra $500 over the fee I charged his company. I deserved this extra money, of course, because Bald's new accounting information system should function so efficiently that he will never need to call me back for further work.

What are your reactions to Tommy Solton's comments?

15-9. Jordan Finance Company opened four personal loan offices in neighboring cities on January 2, 1991. Small cash loans are made to borrowers who repay the principal with interest in monthly installments over a period not exceeding two years. Ralph Jordan, president of the company, uses one of the offices as a central office and visits the other offices periodically for supervision and internal auditing purposes.

Mr. Jordan is concerned about the honesty of his employees. He came to your office in December 1991 and stated, "I want to engage you to install a system to prohibit employees from embezzling cash." He also stated, "Until I went into business for myself I worked for a nationwide loan company with 500 offices and I'm familiar with that company's system of accounting and internal control. I want to describe that system so you can install it for me because it will absolutely prevent fraud."

Requirements

A. How would you advise Mr. Jordan about his request that you install the large company's system of accounting and internal control for his firm? Discuss.
B. How would you respond to the suggestion that the new system would prevent embezzlement? Discuss.

(AICPA Adapted)

15-10. Curtis Company operates in a five-county industrial area. The company employs a manual system for all its record keeping except payroll; the payroll is processed by a local service bureau. Other applications have not been computerized because they could not be cost-justified previously.

The company's sales have grown at an increasing rate over the past five years. With this substantial growth rate, a computer-based system seemed more practical. Consequently, Curtis Company managers engaged the management consulting department of their public accounting firm to conduct a feasibility study for converting their record-keeping system to a computer-

based system. The accounting firm reported that a computer-based system would improve the company's record-keeping system and still provide material cost savings.

Therefore, Curtis Company decided to develop a computer-based system for its records. Curtis hired a person with experience in systems development as manager of systems and data processing. His responsibilities are to oversee the entire systems operation with special emphasis on the development of the new system.

Requirement

Describe the major steps that should be undertaken to develop and implement Curtis Company's new computer-based system

(CMA Adapted)

15-11. The following statement was made in this chapter: "The follow-up phase of a systems study should continue throughout the life of a company's system." What is the meaning of the preceding statement? Do you agree or disagree with this statement? Why?

15-12. The Len Hoss Consulting Firm is currently in the process of completing the systems implementation activities for converting the Samuel Company's data processing system to an online computerized system. The major reason for eliminating the manual system was its slowness in providing needed reports to Samuel Company managers. Because of unexpected delays in performing specific implementation activities, the Len Hoss Consulting Firm's chief consultant, Stanly Dungfield, is concerned about meeting the scheduled implementation completion date. The only remaining implementation activity to perform is the testing of the new computer system by parallel conversion and the subsequent elimination of the old manual system. Stanly's assistant, Katie Fignery, has suggested that the original estimated date for completing the new system's implementation still could be met if direct conversion rather than parallel conversion were used.

Assuming that you are Stanly Dungfield, how would you react to Katie Fignery's suggestion? Discuss.

15-13. Al Hedge recently graduated from college and is working as a management consultant for the Diamond Consulting Firm. Al's first major consulting assignment involved a systems study to convert the Bogie Company's manual system for processing accounts receivable and inventory transactions to batch processing computerized methods. Upon performing the analysis and design phases of the systems work, Al and his consulting team were ready to implement the newly designed system. Markus Williams, the chief consultant supervising the Bogie Company's systems work, assigned Al the job of preparing a PERT network diagram for the systems implementation activities. Because Al is unfamiliar with PERT networks, he has asked Percy Sneed (who has been with the Diamond Consulting Firm for five years) to advise him regarding the preparation of a PERT network diagram.

Assuming that you are Percy Sneed, first explain to Al Hedge the advantages, if any, of using a PERT network diagram in systems implementation. Second, describe for Al Hedge the procedures that should be used to prepare the PERT network diagram for implementing the necessary changes into the Bogie Company's system.

15-14. When converting a company's manual data processing system to a computerized system, two of the implementation activities required are (1) to establish controls and standards and (2) to convert data files to computer storage media. What is the rationale for performing implementation activity 1 before activity 2?

15-15. One of the important implementation activities that must be performed when converting a company's manual system to a computerized system is "determining the necessary functional changes in the system." Describe some of the functional changes in a company's system that would likely be necessary when management consultants perform this systems implementation activity. (*Note:* Because you are not provided with detailed information about an actual systems change, your discussion will have to be in general terms. Feel free, however, to make any reasonable assumptions about an imaginary company that is currently undergoing functional changes.)

15-16. What is the purpose of the follow-up analysis of a systems study? Describe some of the specific activities that management consultants would perform in their follow-up work.

15-17. *For each of the three situations* identify the problem, discuss the issues, and recommend the action to be taken by the named employees—Don Kline, John Wood, and Tim Spencer.

1. The Majina Plant of Reed Manufacturing Co. produces automative components and accessories. Recently Don Kline has been assigned to the accounting department at the Majina Plant. Kline spent a great deal of time reviewing the plant's operations, operating procedures, and reporting practices in order to become familiar with the plant's activities.

During this review period, Kline discovered an inconsistency in the reporting of production and finished goods inventory to corporate headquarters. The normal rejection rate on components manufactured at the Majina Plant was 5%. The production reports indicate that Majina's experience during periods of normal production activity was much better than this rate. Yet when reporting to corporate headquarters, Majina reported spoiled units at above 5% rather than the lesser quantity of actual units spoiled.

Further analysis disclosed that the units representing the difference between the actual and reported defective rates were stockpiled in the plant warehouse for future disposition. The plant would release these units whenever they were needed. These "extra" units proved convenient especially when the plant was asked to operate at a higher than normal production rate or when there was an unexpected order to be filled. Under such circumstances extra demands were placed on Majina manufacturing facilities. This usually resulted in a larger than normal defective rate. The "stockpiled" units could then be released to offset the large spoilage rate.

By the end of the year Majina's inventory and production records were in agreement with the actual activities. Don Kline was concerned about the reporting discrepancies that occurred throughout the year.

2. Olson Company is a small manufacturer of jewelry. Although most of Olson's jewelry is sold directly to retailers, its fine jewelry is sold on a consignment basis to jewelry stores.

Olson Company's jewelry was well known for its excellent quality. The company's operations have been profitable in the past. Recently, the company has expanded its operations and, as a result, has experienced some cash flow problems. In October 1992, Olson Company applied to the Merchants Union Bank for a loan to finance the acquisition of raw materials to be used in making jewelry. The bank was familiar with the company and its operations. As part of its normal procedure, the bank required Olson Company to submit its audited financial statements for the past year (1991) and unaudited statements for the nine-month period ending September 30, 1992.

John Wood, manager of the accounting department, was on vacation when the nine-month financial statements were prepared and submitted with the loan application. Upon Wood's return the company treasurer asked him to review the financial statements and pending loan application. During this review Wood noted that the revenues appeared disproportionately large and the inventory of finished goods unusually small. After further checking he discovered that the sales reflected revenue from jewelry still out on consignment at the end of September. The error resulted in a material overstatement of income. By the date when the loan is expected to be approved, however, a large part of the consigned goods probably will be sold.

3. Daton Community Hospital is a 140-bed hospital serving a community of 75,000 people. The hospital employs bookkeeping machines to maintain its accounts receivable and other related accounting records. The hospital administrator believes the hospital's volume is great enough to justify the use of computerized record keeping. However, he does not think the hospital should acquire its own computer system at this time.

A member of the accounting department who had some systems experience was assigned the responsibility of surveying the service bureaus in the area. After considerable study he recommended that the hospital should seriously consider Compudat, Inc. The administrator confirmed that Compudat was a growing and well-respected service bureau by checking with business organizations that were using or had used Compudat's services. Preliminary arrangements were made with Compudat to begin designing a system for Daton Community Hospital, and the accountant who made the recommendation was named project manager.

Tim Spencer, a member of the administrator's staff, was given the responsibility of monitoring the progress of the conversion to computerized billing. At a meeting between Spencer and the project manager, the project manager reported that the work was progressing as planned. The project manager further commented, "Compudat's work is very professional and progressing on schedule. I'm not surprised because my cousin Max, who owns Compudat, is well qualified in systems and computer operations. He has been able to put together an excellent staff in a short period of time. I'm so convinced of his ability that I provided him with 25% of his capital needs in the form of a long-term loan."

Tim Spencer asked the project manager if the administrator was aware of his family ties with Compudat, Inc. The project manager stated that he did not know because the topic had never been discussed in their conversations. Spencer has heard from others that the work is progressing smoothly on the new system.

(CMA Adapted)

15-18. Appliance City (a discount store selling all types of home appliances such as toasters, ovens, etc.) has recently acquired a computer system for handling its customer billings, its inventory records, and other accounting functions. The following notice appeared on the employee bulletin board.

TO: Appliance City Bookkeeping Department Employees
FROM: Monroe Cycle, President
REGARDING: Job Termination

It is my sad duty to inform each of you that by the end of this workweek, your services as employees will no longer be needed at Appliance City. Our new computer system for processing accounting transactions eliminates the functional duties which you have been performing for the company. I am aware of the loyal services performed by many of you to help foster Appliance City's sales growth. However, modern computer technology cannot be given a back seat in our company's future growth plans. I hope that each one of you will feel free to drop by the store any time and say hello.

Requirements

A. Comment on the technique used by Appliance City's president to notify the bookkeeping department's employees of their termination. If you disagree with the president's method of notifying his terminated employees, what would you do differently?

B. Discuss some possible alternative steps that might have been taken by Appliance City's president instead of terminating all the bookkeeping department employees. (*Note:* In answering this part of the question, make any reasonable assumptions regarding Appliance City's system.)

15-19. Three different methods for implementing a new system into an organization were analyzed in this chapter: modular conversion, parallel conversion, and direct conversion. Discuss the advantages and the disadvantages of using each of these three systems implementation methods.

15-20. A new batch processing computer system is currently being implemented into the Monarch Company. Bob See, president of the Monarch Company, is concerned about the fact that many of the implementation activities are requiring more time to complete than originally estimated by the company's consultants. To hasten the implementation process, See has asked the consultants to postpone the establishment of systems controls and standards until after the new computer system is operative. Assume that you are one of the consultants participating in the implementation of the Monarch Company's computerized system. How would you react to the request made by Bob See? Explain.

15-21. When implementing an online, real-time computer system to replace a company's previous manual data processing system, one of the important implementation activities is to convert the data files. Why is this implementation activity necessary? Give several specific illustrations of how accounting data files would be converted. (*Note:* Make any assumptions that you feel are necessary regarding the operational characteristics of the company for which the computerized system is being implemented.)

15-22. In your opinion, which of these major systems study phases (analysis, design, implementation and initial operation, and follow-up) would you consider the most difficult to perform? Why?

15-23. When converting a company's manual data processing system to a computerized system, two of the required implementation activities are (1) to establish controls and standards and (2) to acquire computer programs. What is the rationale for performing implementation activity 1 before activity 2?

Problems

15-24. The Dryfus Company specializes in large construction projects. The company management regularly employs the Program Evaluation and Review Technique (PERT) in planning and controlling its construction projects. The following schedule of separable activities and their expected completion times have

been developed for an office building that is to be constructed by Dryfus Company.

	Activity Description	Predecessor Activity	Expected Activity Completion Time (in Weeks)
a.	Excavation	—	2
b.	Foundation	a	3
c.	Underground utilities	a	7
d.	Rough plumbing	b	4
e.	Framing	b	5
f.	Roofing	e	3
g.	Electrical work	f	3
h.	Interior walls	d,g	4
i.	Finish plumbing	h	2
j.	Exterior finishing	f	6
k.	Landscaping	c,i,j	2

Requirement

Identify the critical path for this project and determine the expected project completion time in weeks.

(CMA Adapted)

15-25. Edward Jones is responsible for finding a suitable building and establishing a new convenience grocery store for Thrift-Mart, Inc. Jones enumerated the specific activities that had to be performed and the estimated time to complete each activity. In addition, he prepared the PERT network diagram of Figure 15-5 to aid in the coordination of the activities. The activities to locate a building and establish a new store are listed in the following table.

Thrift-Mart, Inc.

Activity Number	Description of Activity	Estimated Time Required (in Weeks)
1-2	Find building	4
2-3	Negotiate rental terms	2
3-4	Draft lease	4
2-5	Prepare store plans	4
5-6	Select and order fixtures	1
6-4	Delivery of fixtures	6
4-8	Install fixtures	3
5-7	Hire staff	5
7-8	Train staff	4
8-9	Receive inventory	2
9-10	Stock shelves	1

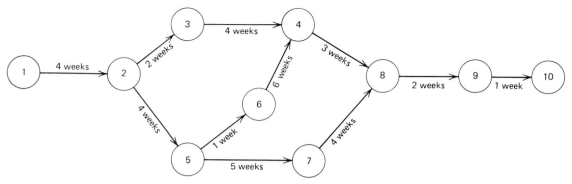

FIGURE 15-5 PERT network diagram for Thrift-Mart, Inc.

Requirements

A. Identify the critical path for finding and establishing the new convenience store.

B. Edward Jones would like to finish the store two weeks earlier than indicated by the schedule, and as a result, he is considering several alternatives. One such alternative is to persuade the fixture manufacturer to deliver the fixtures in four weeks rather than six. Should Jones arrange for the manufacturer to deliver the fixtures in four weeks if the sole advantage of this schedule change is to open the store two weeks early? Justify your answer.

C. A project such as the one illustrated by the PERT network diagram for the new conveience store cannot be implemented unless the required resources are available at the required dates. What additional information does Jones need to administer the proposed project properly?

(CMA Adapted)

15-26. Whitson Company has just ordered a new computer for its financial information system. The present computer is fully utilized and no longer adequate for all of the financial applications Whitson would like to implement. The present financial system applications must all be modified before they can be run on the new computer. Additionally, new applications that Whitson would like to have developed and implemented have been identified and ranked according to priority.

Sally Rose, manager of data processing, is responsible for implementing the new computer system. Rose listed the specific activities that had to be completed and determined the estimated time to complete each activity. In addition, she prepared a PERT network diagram to aid in the coordination of the activities.

Figure 15-6 is an activity list and Figure 15-7 is a PERT network diagram.

Requirements

A. Determine the number of weeks that will be required to implement fully Whitson Company's financial information system (i.e., both existing and new applications) on its new computer and identify the activities that are critical in completing the project.

B. The term *slack time* is often used in conjunction with network analysis.
   1. Explain what is meant by *slack time*.
   2. Identify an activity that has slack time and indicate the amount of slack time available for that activity.

C. Whitson Company's top management would like to reduce the time necessary to begin operation of the entire system.
   1. Which activities should Sally Rose attempt to reduce in order to implement the system sooner? Explain your answer.
   2. Discuss how Sally Rose might proceed to reduce the time of these activities.

D. The general accounting manager would like the existing financial information system applications to be modified and operational in 22 weeks.
   1. Determine the number of weeks that will be required to modify the existing financial information system applications and make them operational.

(CMA Adapted)

15-27. Crespi Construction Company uses critical-path analysis in scheduling its projects. The following

Activity	Description of Activity	Expected Time Required to Complete (in Weeks)
AB	Wait for delivery of computer from manufacturer	8
BC	Install computer	2
CH	General test of computer	2
AD	Complete an evaluation of work-force requirements	2
DE	Hire additional programmers and operators	2
AG	Design modifications to existing applications	3
GH	Program modifications to existing applications	4
HI	Test modified applications on new computer	2
IJ	Revise existing applications as needed	2
JN	Revise and update documentation for existing applications as modified	2
JK	Run existing applications in parallel on new and old computers	2
KP	Implement existing applications as modified on the new computer	1
AE	Design new applications	8
GE	Design interface between existing and new applications	3
EF	Program new applications	6
FI	Test new applications on new computer	2
IL	Revise new applications as needed	3
LM	Conduct second test of new applications on new computer	2
MN	Prepare documentation for the new applications	3
NP	Implement new applications on the new computer	2

FIGURE 15-6   Activities of the Whitson Company for installing a new computer system.

list of activities and the network diagram, presented in Figure 15-8, were prepared by Crespi for the Cherry Hill Apartment project prior to the start of work on the project.

The Cherry Hill Apartment project is now in progress. An interim progress report indicates that the city

water and sewage lines, rough plumbing, and wiring are all one-half complete and the exterior siding and painting have not yet begun.

Crespi will soon begin work on a building for the Echelon Savings Bank. Work on the building was started by another construction firm that has gone out

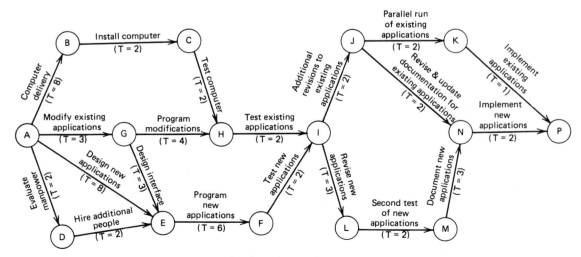

FIGURE 15-7   PERT network diagram for the Whitson Company.

Activity	Description of Activity	Estimated Time Required (in Weeks)
A	Site selection and land purchase	6
B	Survey	1
C	Excavation	3
D	Foundation	4
E	City water and sewage lines	8
F	Rough plumbing	8
G	Framing and roofing	6
H	Wiring	4
I	Interior walls	3
J	Plumbing fixtures	3
K	Exterior siding and painting	9
L	Landscaping	2

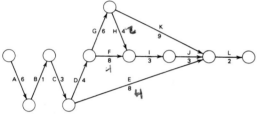

FIGURE 15-8 List of activities and network diagram for the Cherry Hill Apartment project.

Activity	Description of Activity	Predecessor Activity	Estimated Time Required (in Weeks)
A	Obtain on-site work permit	—	1
B	Repair damage done by vandals	A	4
C	Inspect construction materials left on site	A	1
D	Order and receive additional construction materials	C	2
E	Apply for waiver to add new materials	C	1
F	Obtain waiver to add new materials	E	1
G	Perform electrical work	B,D,F	4
H	Complete interior partitions	G	2

FIGURE 15-9 Schedule of activities and related expected completion times for the Echelon Savings Bank project.

of business. Crespi has agreed to complete the project. Crespi's schedule of activities and related expected completion times for the Echelon Savings Bank project are presented in Figure 15-9.

Requirements

A. Define what is meant by *the critical path for a project*.
B. Refer to the list of activities and the network diagram prepared for the Cherry Hill Apartment project prior to the start of the project.
   1. Identify the critical path by letters and determine the expected time in weeks for the project.
   2. Identify an activity that has slack time for this project and indicate the amount of slack time available for that activity.
C. Using the interim progress report for the Cherry Hill Apartment project, identify the critical path by letters and determine the expected number of weeks for the remainder of the project.
D. Refer to Crespi's schedule of activities and ex-
pected completion times for the work to be completed on the Echelon Savings Bank project.
   1. Identify the critical path by letters and determine the expected time in weeks for the project.
   2. Explain the effect on the critical path and expected time for the project if Crespi were not required to apply and obtain the waiver to add new materials.

(CMA Adapted)

CASE ANALYSES

15-28. Wenrock's Use of Delmo's Computer System

Delmo Inc. is a wholesale distributor of automotive parts that serves customers in the states east of the Mississippi River. The company has grown during the last 25 years from a small regional distributorship to its present size.

The states are divided into eight separate territories in order to service Delmo customers adequately. Delmo salespersons regularly call on current and prospective customers in each of the territories. Delmo customers are of four general types.

1. Automotive parts stores.
2. Hardware stores with an automotive parts section.
3. Independent garage owners.
4. Buying groups for garages and filling stations.

Because Delmo Inc. must stock such a large variety and quantity of automotive parts to accommodate its customers, the company acquired its own computer system very early and implemented an inventory control system first. Other applications such as cash receipts and disbursements, sales analysis, accounts receivable, payroll, and accounts payable have since been added.

Delmo's inventory control system is comprised of an integrated purchase ordering and perpetual inventory system. Each item of inventory is identified by an inventory code number; the code number identifies both the product line and the item itself. When the quantity-on-hand for an item falls below the specified stock level, a purchase order is automatically generated by the computer. The purchase order is sent to the vendor after approval by the purchasing manager. All receipts, issues, and returns are entered into the computer daily. A printout for all inventory items within product lines showing receipts, issues, and current balance is prepared weekly. However, current status for a particular item carried in the inventory can be obtained daily if desired.

Sales orders are filled within 48 hours of receipt. Sales invoices are prepared by the computer the same day that the merchandise is shipped. At the end of each month, several reports are produced that summarize the monthly sales. The current month's sales and year-to-date sales by product line, territory, and customer class are compared with the same figures from the previous year. In addition, reports showing only the monthly figures for product line within territory and customer class within territory are prepared. In all cases the reports provide summarized data; that is, detailed data such as sales by individual customers or product are not listed. Terms of 2/10, net 30 are standard for all of Delmo's customers.

Customers' accounts receivable are updated daily for sales, sales returns and allowances, and payments on account. Monthly statements are computer prepared and mailed following completion of entries for the last day of the month. Each Friday a schedule is prepared showing the total amount of accounts receivable outstanding by age—current accounts (0–30 days), slightly past-due accounts (31–90 days), and long overdue accounts (over 90 days).

Delmo Inc. recently acquired Wenrock Company, a wholesale distributor of tools and light equipment. In addition to servicing the same type of customers as Delmo, Wenrock sells to equipment rental shops. Wenrock's sales region is not as extensive as Delmo's, but the Delmo management has encouraged Wenrock to expand the distribution of its product to all of Delmo's sales territories.

Wenrock Company uses a computer service bureau to aid in its accounting functions. For example, certain inventory activities are recorded by the service bureau. Each item carried by Wenrock is assigned a product code number that identifies the product and the product line. Data regarding shipments received from manufacturers, shipments to customers (sales), and any other physical inventory changes are delivered to the service bureau daily, and the service bureau updates Wenrock's inventory records. A weekly inventory listing showing beginning balance, receipts, issues, and ending balance for each item in the inventory is provided to Wenrock on Monday morning.

Wenrock furnishes the service bureau with information about each sale of merchandise to a customer. The service bureau prepares a five-part invoice and records the sales in its records. This processing is done at night, and all copies of each invoice are delivered to Wenrock the next morning. At the end of the month, the service bureau provides Wenrock with a sales report classified by product line showing the sales in units and dollars for each item sold. Wenrock's sales terms are 2/10, net 30.

The accounts receivable function still is handled by Wenrock's bookkeeper. Two copies of the invoice are mailed to the customer. Two of the remaining copies are filed—one numerically and the other alphabetically by customer. The alphabetic file represents the accounts receivable file. When a customer's payment is received, the invoice is marked "paid" and placed in a paid invoice file in alphabetic order. The bookkeeper mails monthly statements according to the following schedule.

10th of the month	A–G
20th of the month	H–O
30th of the month	P–Z

The final copy of the invoice is included with the merchandise when it is shipped.

Wenrock has continued to use its present accounting system and supplies Delmo management with monthly financial information developed from this system. However, Delmo management is anxious to have Wenrock use its computer and its information system because this will reduce accounting and computer costs, make the financial reports of Wenrock more useful to Delmo management, and provide Wenrock personnel with better information to manage the company.

At the time Delmo acquired Wenrock, it also hired a new marketing manager with experience in both product areas. The new manager wants Wenrock to organize its sales force using the same territorial distribution as Delmo to facilitate the management of the two sales forces.

The new manager also believes that more useful sales information should be provided to individual salespersons and to the marketing department. Although the monthly sales reports currently prepared provide adequate summary data, the manager would like additional details to aid the sales personnel.

The acquisition of Wenrock Company and expansion of its sales to a larger geographic area have created a cash strain on Delmo Inc., particularly in the short run. Consequently, cash management has become much more important than in prior years. A weekly report that presents a reliable estimate of daily cash receipts is needed. The treasurer heard that a local company had improved its cash-forecasting system by studying the timing of customers' payments on account to see if a discernible payment pattern existed. The payment pattern became the model that was applied to outstanding invoices to estimate the daily cash receipts for the next week. The treasurer thinks that this is a good approach and wonders if it can be done at Delmo.

Questions

1. Identify and briefly describe the additional data Wenrock Company must collect and furnish in order to use the Delmo data processing system. Also, identify the data, if any, currently accumulated by Wenrock that no longer will be needed because of the conversion to the Delmo system.

2. Using only the data currently available from the Delmo data processing system, what additional reports could be prepared that would be useful to the marketing manager and the individual salesperson? Briefly explain how each report would be useful to the sales personnel.

3. If Delmo Inc. were to use a cash-forecasting system similar to the one suggested by the treasurer, describe:
   a. The data currently available in the system that would be used in preparing such a forecast.
   b. The additional data that must be generated.
   c. The modifications, if any, that would be required in the Delmo data processing system.

(CMA Adapted)

15-29. *Westside Electric Company*

The production manager, chief accountant, marketing manager, and president of Westside Electric Company are discussing the feasibility and the desirability of changing their batch processing system to an online, real-time system. Westside Electric is a medium-size firm that manufactures small electrical equipment. Its business is centered in Los Angeles.

Presented here is an excerpt from their conversation.

President: After reading this article in the *Harvard Business Review* on the benefits of a real-time system, I think we should seriously consider changing our present system to an online, real-time system. Our operations are large enough so that we probably could benefit from a simple real-time system. I was thinking of a three-terminal arrangement . . . something like this.

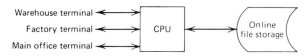

Marketing Manager: You know, a real-time system could give us a tremendous competitive advantage. Under this automated design, a perpetual inventory system could easily be implemented. Then, with each order placed, the inventory files could be immediately updated. My sales staff would be able to know at any point in time how much stock we have available for sale.

Chief Accountant: If the general ledger and accounts receivable subsidiary ledger are also online, the accounts within these two ledgers could be updated at the time orders are placed. This will facilitate invoice processing. Moreover, the billing and collection process will probably be faster.

Production Manager: Not only that, but if the information from invoices could be transmitted through a data terminal to our warehouse, we could speed up delivery to the customers. A faster turnover would certainly be beneficial to the whole organization.

President: The *Harvard Business Review* article also indicated that with an online system, you are able to immediately test the outcomes of various decision alternatives. This can help us with our planning process. . . . I can see that the real-time system will be extremely beneficial to us. Shall I call in the IBM people to see what kind of package they can give us?

Chief Accountant: But, wait a minute! Installing a real-time computer system is a big undertaking. I understand that the costs associated with the hardware and software of a real-time system as well as the operating costs are far more than with our present batch processing system.

Marketing Manager: You accountants are always worried about costs. Surely, in the long run, the benefits from the real-time system will exceed any of the associated costs. After all, many of the larger firms already have installed real-time systems. I haven't heard anything negative about their automated systems.

Chief Accountant: But it's more than the cost aspect that I'm worried about. What about the control of the system? For example, how am I to monitor the use of the terminals? How can my internal auditing staff

make sure that only authorized personnel have access to the terminals? You know that if someone inputs incorrect data accidentally or intentionally, our files will be contaminated. With so many input points, it will be difficult, if not impossible, to track down errors. Under batch processing, we have control over the computer hardware, so the unauthorized personnel problem is minimal. Furthermore, because similar transactions are processed at one time, we can easily pinpoint any mistakes in the input data.

Production Manager: I think you're exaggerating the security aspect of a real-time system. Granted there must be security precautions, but let's not go overboard.

Chief Accountant: Well, let me tell you, if incorrect data are input and you make decisions using the invalid data, your effectiveness as a manager will be significantly reduced. The real-time system can make a major contribution to our operations, but until this security and data reliability aspect can be controlled, I don't think we should implement such a system.

President: There's more controversy to this proposal than I anticipated. Let me think about what all of you have said. If you have any more input, I want to hear from you.

Questions

1. Assuming that the president is still strongly in favor of implementing an online, real-time system, what would be his next step?
2. One of the management accountant's major functions is to maintain good internal control within his or her organization. Are the chief accountant's concerns about security and data reliability warranted? Why or why not? Are there ways to overcome security and data reliability problems? Discuss.

15-30. *Audio Visual Corporation*

Audio Visual Corporation manufactures and sells visual display equipment. The company is headquartered near Boston. The majority of sales are made through seven geographical sales offices located in Los

Angeles, Seattle, Minneapolis, Cleveland, Dallas, Boston, and Atlanta. Each sales office has a warehouse located nearby to carry an inventory of new equipment and replacement parts. The remainder of the sales are made through manufacturer's representatives.

Audio Visual's manufacturing operations are conducted in a single plant that is highly departmentalized. In addition to the assembly department, there are several departments responsible for various components used in the visual display equipment. The plant also has maintenance, engineering, scheduling, and cost accounting departments.

Early in 1990, management decided that its management information system (MIS) needed upgrading. As a result, the company ordered an advanced computer in 1990, and it was installed in July 1991. The main processing equipment is still located at corporate headquarters, and each of the seven sales offices is connected with the main processing unit by remote terminals.

The integration of the new computer into Audio Visual Corporation's information system was carried out by the MIS staff. The MIS manager and the four systems analysts who had the major responsibility for the integration were hired by the company in the spring of 1991. The department's other employees— programmers, machine operators, and keypunch operators—have been with the company for several years.

During its early years, Audio Visual had a centralized decision-making organization. Top management formulated all plans and directed all operations. As the company expanded, some of the decision making was decentralized although the information processing was still highly centralized. Departments had to coordinate their plans with the corporate office, but they had more freedom in developing their sales programs. However, as the company expanded, information problems developed. As a consequence, the MIS department was given the responsibility to improve the company's information processing system when the new equipment was installed.

The MIS analysts reviewed the information system in existence prior to the acquisition of the new computer and identified weaknesses. They then redesigned old applications and designed new applications in developing the new system to overcome the weaknesses. During the 18 months since the acquisition of the new equipment, the following applications have been redesigned or developed and are now opera-

tional: payroll, production scheduling, financial statement preparation, customer billing, raw material usage in production, and finished goods inventory by warehouse. The operating departments of Audio Visual affected by the systems changes were rarely consulted or contacted until the system was operational and the new reports were distributed to the operating departments.

The president of Audio Visual is very pleased with the work of the MIS department. During a recent conversation with an individual who was interested in Audio Visual's new system, the president stated, "The MIS people are doing a good job and I have full confidence in their work. I touch base with the MIS people frequently, and they have encountered no difficulties in doing their work. We paid a lot of money for the new equipment and the MIS people certainly cost enough, but the combination of the new equipment and new MIS staff should solve all of our problems."

Recently, two additional conversations regarding the computer and information system have taken place. One was between Jerry Adams, plant manager, and Bill Taylor, the MIS manager; the other was between Adams and Terry Williams, the new personnel manager.

Taylor—Adams Conversation

Adams: Bill, you're trying to run my plant for me. I'm supposed to be the manager, yet you keep interfering. I wish you would mind your own business.

Taylor: You've got a job to do but so does my department. As we analyzed the information needed for production scheduling and by top management, we saw where improvements could be made in the work flow. Now that the system is operational, you can't reroute work and change procedures because that would destroy the value of the information we're processing. And while I'm on that subject, it's getting to the point where we can't trust the information we're getting from production. The mark sense cards we receive from production contain a lot of errors.

Adams: I'm responsible for the efficient operation of production. Quite frankly, I think I'm the best judge of production efficiency. The system you installed has reduced my work force and increased the work load of the remaining employees, but I don't see that this has improved anything. In fact, it might explain the high error rate in the cards.

Taylor: This new computer costs a lot of money and I'm trying to be sure that the company gets its money's worth.

Adams—Williams Conversation

Adams: My best production assistant, the one I'm grooming to be a supervisor when the next opening occurs, came to me today and said he was thinking of quitting. When I asked him why, he said he didn't enjoy the work anymore. He's not the only one who is unhappy. The supervisors and department heads no longer have a voice in establishing production schedules. This new computer system has taken away the contribution we used to make to company planning and direction. We seem to be going way back to the days when top management made all the decisions. I have more production problems now than I used to. I think it boils down to a lack of interest on the part of my management team. I know the problem is within my area but I thought you might be able to help me.

Williams: I have no recommendations for you now, but I've had similar complaints from purchasing and shipping. I think we should get your concerns on the agenda for our next plant management meeting.

Questions

1. Apparently the development of and transition to the new computer-based system has created problems among the personnel of Audio Visual Corporation. Identify and briefly discuss the apparent causes of these problems.
2. How could the company have avoided the problems? What steps should be taken to avoid such problems in the future?

(CMA Adapted)

15-31. *Peabock Company*

Peabock Company is a wholesaler of softgoods. The inventory is composed of approximately 3500 different items. The company employs a computerized batch processing system to maintain its perpetual inventory records. The system is run each weekend so that the inventory reports are available on Monday morning for management use. The system has been functioning satisfactorily for the past 15 months, providing the company with accurate records and timely reports.

The preparation of purchase orders has been automatic as a part of the inventory system to ensure that the company will maintain enough inventory to meet customer demand. When an item of inventory falls below a predetermined level, a record of the inventory item is written. The record is used in conjunction with the vendor file to prepare the purchase orders.

Exception reports are prepared during the update of the inventory and the preparation of the purchase orders. These reports disclose any errors or exceptions identified during the processing. In addition, the system provides for management approval of all purchase orders exceeding a specified amount. Any exceptions or items requiring management approval are handled by supplemental runs on Monday morning and are combined with the weekend results.

Figure 15-10 reflects a system flowchart of Peabock Company's inventory and purchase order procedure.

Questions

1. The illustrated system flowchart of Peabock Company's inventory and purchase order system was prepared before the system was fully operational. Several steps that are important to the successful operations of the system were inadvertently omitted from the chart. Now that the system is operating effectively, management wants the system documentation complete and would like the flowchart corrected. Describe the steps that have been omitted and indicate where the omissions have occurred. **The flowchart does not need to be redrawn.**
2. In order for Peabock's inventory/purchase order system to function properly, control procedures would be included in the system. Describe the type of control procedures Peabock Company would use in its system to ensure proper functioning and indi-

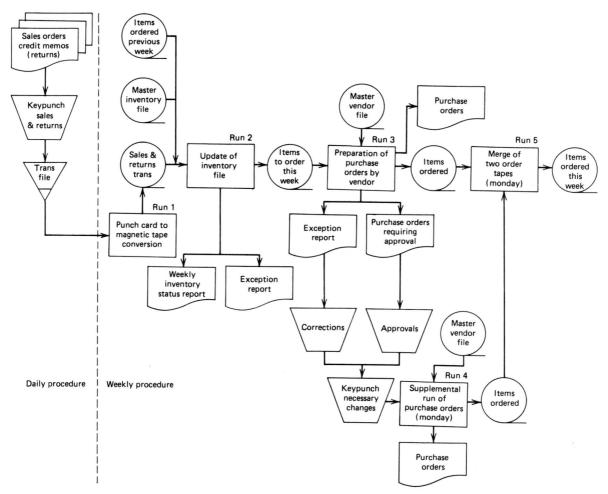

FIGURE 15-10 A system flowchart of the inventory and purchase order system of the Peabock Company.

cate where these procedures would be placed in the system.

(CMA Adapted)

15-32. B&B Company

The B&B Company manufactures and sells chemicals for agricultural and industrial use. The company has grown significantly over the last 10 years but has made few changes in its information-gathering and -report-

ing system. Some of the managers have expressed concern that the system is essentially the same as it was when the firm was only half its present size. Others believe that much of the information from the system is not relevant and that more appropriate and timely information should be available.

Dora Hepple, chief accountant, has observed that the actual monthly cost data for most production processes are compared with the actual costs of the same processes for the previous year. Any variance not explained by price changes requires an explanation by the individual in charge of the cost center. She believes that this information is inadequate for good cost control.

George Vector, one of the production supervisors, contends that the system is adequate because it allows for explanation of discrepancies. The current year's costs seldom vary from the previous year's costs (as adjusted for price changes). This indicates that costs are under control.

Vern Hopp, general manager of the Fine Chemical Division, is upset with the current system. He has to request the same information each month regarding recurring operations. This is a problem that he believes should be addressed.

Walter Metts, president, has appointed a committee to review the system. The charge to this "System Review Task Force" is to determine if the information needs of the internal management of the firm are being met by the existing system. Specific modifications in the existing system or implementation of a new system will be considered only if management's needs are not being met. William Afton, assistant to the president, has been put in charge of the task force.

Shortly after the committee was appointed, Afton overheard one of the cost accountants say, "I've been doing it this way for 15 years, and now Afton and his committee will try to eliminate my job." Another person replied, "That's the way it looks. John and Brownie in general accounting also think that their positions are going to be eliminated or at least changed significantly." Over the next few days, Afton overheard a middle-management person talking about the task force, saying, "That's all this company thinks about— maximizing its profits—not the employees." He also overheard a production manager in the mixing department say that he believed the system was in need of revision because the most meaningful information he received came from Brad Cummings, a salesperson. He stated, "After they have the monthly sales meeting, Brad stops by the office and indicates what the sales plans and targets are for the next few months. This sure helps me in planning my mixing schedules."

Afton is aware that two problems of paramount importance to be addressed by his System Review Task Force are (1) to determine management's information needs for cost control and decision-making purposes and (2) to meet the behavioral needs of the company and its employees.

Questions

1. Discuss the behavioral implications of having an accounting information system that does not appear to meet the needs of management.
2. Identify and explain the specific problems B&B Company appears to have with regard to the perception of B&B's employees concerning:
   a. The accounting information system.
   b. The firm.
3. Assume that the initial review of the System Review Task Force indicates that a new accounting information system should be designed and implemented.
   a. Identify specific behavioral factors that B&B's management should address in the design and implementation of a new system.
   b. For each behavioral factor identified, discuss how B&B's management can address the behavioral factor.

(CMA Adapted)

15-33. *Caltron Inc.*

Caltron Inc. produces computer-controlled components for a wide variety of military hardware. As a defense contractor, the company is often under severe time and scheduling constraints. The development of a new component, Vector-12, is no exception; the project has the potential for future contracts that could generate substantial revenue if development and testing can be accomplished in the allotted time.

The planning of the Vector-12 project has been assigned to Norm Robertson. This is Robertson's first assignment as a Project Director for Caltron, and he is eager to demonstrate his capabilities.

This project, like many of Caltron's projects, cuts across departments. Therefore, scheduling and coordination among departments is crucial. Caltron's management has long been an advocate of the Program Evaluation and Review Technique (PERT). Therefore, Robertson prepared the PERT diagram for the Vector-12 project that is presented below.

The circles with letters inside correspond to the completion of a significant activity while the arrows connecting the circles correspond to an activity. The numbers by the activity arrows represent the expected time in weeks required to complete each activity. The responsibility for the critical path, Start-B-C-F-I-J-Finish, is shared by two departments, Electro-

Mechanical Engineering (EME) and Fabrication (FAB). Resource Appropriation and Processing (RAP) is responsible for Start-A-D-G-J.

Robertson developed the PERT diagram with minimal input from the department directors affected. He did review the preliminary diagrams with the Directors of EME and FAB. Robertson was unable to contact the Director of RAP, Shiela Neill, and Robertson neglected to talk with Neill when she returned to the office. The Directors of EME and FAB offered suggestions to Robertson on how to revise the diagrams in terms of ordering activities and time estimates. They also indicated how Neill's activities would coordinate with their activities. However, none of the directors reviewed the final PERT diagram that is shown below.

As the Vector-12 project entered its fourth week, Robertson requested progress reports from the department directors. Neill told Robertson that activity A-D would take 10-12 weeks. When Robertson asked Neill to explain the delay, Neill replied, "I could have told you there would be a problem, but you never asked for my input. The time for activity A-D is understated as is, and I cannot even start until activity B-E is completed by FAB."

Questions

1. Discuss the advantages and disadvantages of network analysis as a means of organizing and coordinating projects.
2. Identify the specific reason that would cause Norm Robertson to be concerned about the delay in activity A-D.
3. Critique the way Norm Robertson developed the PERT diagram for the Vector-12 project.
4. Discuss the behavioral problems that could arise within Caltron Inc. as a consequence of the planning of the Vector-12 project.

(CMA Adapted)

REFERENCES AND RECOMMENDED READINGS FOR PART FOUR

Ahituv, Niv, Neumann, Seev, and Hadass, Michael. "A Flexible Approach to Information Systems Development." *MIS Quarterly* 8 (June 1984), pp. 69–78.

American Institute of Certified Public Accountants. *Guidelines for Development and Implementation of Computer-Based Application Systems.* Management Advisory Services Guideline Series Number 4. New York: AICPA, 1978.

Ang, James, and Chua, Jess. "Corporate Models That Failed." *Managerial Planning* 29 (September–October 1980), pp. 34–38.

Appleton, Daniel S. "Data-Driven Prototyping." *Datamation* 29 (November 1983), pp. 259–268.

Bailey, James E., and Pearson, Sammy W. "Development of a Tool for Measuring and Analyzing Computer User Satisfaction." *Management Science* 8 (May 1983), pp. 530–545.

Bartholomew, John J. "Implementing a Change in the

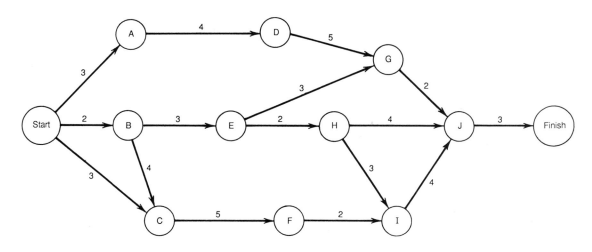

Accounting MIS of a Bank." *Cost and Management* 55 (March–April 1981), pp. 14–20.

Beard, Larry H. "Planning a Management Information System: Some Caveats and Contemplations." *Financial Executive* 45 (May 1977), pp. 34–39.

Benjamin, Robert I. *Control of the Information System Development Cycle.* New York: Wiley, 1971.

Bernheim, Richard C. "The Right Way to Design a Cost Accounting System." *Management Accounting* 65 (September 1983), pp. 63–67.

Biggs, Charles L., Birks, Evan G., and Atkins, William. *Managing the System Development Process.* Englewood Cliffs, NJ: Touche Ross & Co. and Prentice-Hall, 1980.

Blaustein, Eric B. "Planning for the Introduction of New Software." *Journal of Systems Management* 39 (September 1988), pp. 6–10.

Bler, Germain. "A Decision Oriented Information System." *Journal of Systems Management* 23 (October 1972), pp. 36–39.

Boulding, Kenneth E. "General Systems Theory—The Skeleton of Science." *Management Systems,* 2nd ed., Peter P. Schoderbek, ed. New York: John Wiley & Sons, 1971.

Bowman, Brent, Davis, Gordon B., and Wetherbe, James C., "Three Stage Model of MIS Planning." *Information and Management* 6 (February 1983), pp. 11–25.

Bryan, Marvin. "Diary of an Accounting System Upgrade." *Personal Computing* 12 (July 1988), pp. 100–108.

Burch, John. "Information Systems Building Block." *Journal of Systems Management* 37 (March 1986), pp. 7–11.

Buss, Martin D. J. "How to Rank Computer Projects." *Harvard Business Review* 61 (January–February 1983), pp. 118–125.

Buss, Martin, D. J., and Herman, Elaine. "Packaged Software: Purchase or Perish." *Financial Executive* 51 (January 1983), pp. 26–33.

Camillus, C., and Lederer, Albert L. "Corporate Strategy and the Design of Computerized Information Systems." *Sloan Management Review* 27 (1985), pp. 35–42.

Carey, Jane M., and McLeod, Raymond. "Use of System Development Methodology and Tools." *Journal of Systems Management* 39 (March 1988), pp. 30–35.

Carlyle, Ralph Emmett. "Managing IS at Multinationals." *Datamation* 34 (March 1, 1988), pp. 54–66.

Carroll, Archie B. "Behavioral Aspects of Developing Computer Based Information Systems." *Business Horizons* 25 (January–February 1982), pp. 42–51.

Cerullo, Michael J. "Designing Accounting Information Systems." *Management Accounting* 67 (June 1985), pp. 37–42.

Cerullo, Michael J. "MIS: What Can Go Wrong?" *Management Accounting* 60 (April 1979), pp. 43–48.

Chervany, Norman I., and Dickson, Gary W. "Economic Evaluation Management Information Systems: An Analytical Framework." *Decision Sciences* 1 (July–August 1970), pp. 296–308.

Chubb, Timothy D. "Why Computer Systems Conversions Are Tricky." *Management Accounting* 65 (September 1983), pp. 36–41.

Churchman, C. West. *The Systems Approach.* New York: Dell, 1968.

Clark, David M. "Guidelines for Software Package Selection." *Journal of Accounting & EDP* 3 (Spring 1987), pp. 18–26.

Collard, Albert F. "Sharpening Interviewing Skills." *Journal of Systems Management* 26 (December 1975), pp. 6–10.

Collins, Frank. "The VCurve: A Road Map for Avoiding People Problems in Systems Changes." *Journal of Systems Management* 34 (February 1983), pp. 31–35.

Cushing, Barry E., and Romney, Marshall B. *Accounting Information Systems and Business Organizations* 4th ed. Reading, MA: Addison-Wesley Publishing Co., Inc., 1987.

Dougar, J. Daniel, and Knapp, Robert W. (Eds.) *Systems Analysis Techniques.* New York: John Wiley & Sons, 1974.

Davis, William S. *Systems Analysis and Design: A Structured Approach.* Reading, MA: Addison-Wesley, 1983.

Dewhirst, John F. "Framework for the Analysis of Management Accounting Information Systems." *Cost and Management* 46 (November–December 1972), pp. 28–35.

Dickson, G. W., and Simmons, John K. "The Behavioral Side of MIS: Some Aspects of the 'People' Problem." *Business Horizons* 12 (August 1970), pp. 59–71.

Dight, Janet. "Training + Technology = Profits." *Datamation* 30 (April 1, 1984), pp. 161–166.

Doll, William J. "Avenues for Top Management Involvement in Successful MIS Development." *MIS Quarterly* 9 (March 1985), pp. 17–35.

Doll, William, and Ahmed, Mesbah U. "Managing User Expectations." *Journal of Systems Management* 34 (June 1983), pp. 6–11.

Drury, D. H. "An Evaluation of Data Processing Steering Committees." *MIS Quarterly* 8 (December 1984), pp. 257–265.

Egyhazy, Csaba J. "Technical Software Development Tools." *Journal of Systems Management* 36 (January 1985), pp. 8–13.

El-Badawi, Mohamed H. "A Computerized Corporate Financial Model." *Cost and Management* 58 (March–April 1984), pp. 22–27.

Er, Meng C. "Prototyping, Participative and Phenomenological Approaches to Information Systems Development." *Journal of Systems Management* 38 (August 1987), pp. 12–15.

Faerber, Leroy G., and Ratliff, Richard L. "People Problems Behind MIS Failures." *Financial Executive* 48 (April 1980), pp. 18–25.

Fields, Kent T. "Asignment of Audit Responsibility in Computer System Development Projects." *Journal of Information Systems* 2 (Spring 1988), pp. 51–57.

Forman, Fred L., and Hess, Milton S. "Form Precedes Function." *Computerworld* 22 (September 5, 1988), pp. 65–70.

Foss, W. B. "Guidelines for Computer Selection." *Journal of Systems Management* 28 (March 1976), pp. 36–39.

Framel, John E. "Managing Information as an Asset." *Management Accountant* 70 (July 1988), pp. 27–31.

Friend, David. "Graphics for Managers: The Distributed Approach." *Datamation* 38 (July 1982), pp. 76–96.

Gane, Chris, and Sarson, Trish. *Structured Systems Analysis: Tools and Techniques.* Englewood Cliffs, NJ: Prentice Hall, 1979.

Gibson, Michael L. "A Guide to Selecting CASE Tools." *Datamation* 34 (July 1, 1988), pp. 65–66.

Giovinazzo, Vincent J. "Designing Focused Information Systems." *Management Accounting* 71 (November 1984), pp. 34–40.

Gore, Marvin, and Stubbe, John W. *Elements of Systems Analysis.* Dubuque, IO: William C. Brown, 1988.

Green, Gary I., and Wilcox, Earl A. "Find the Right Software Through Specifications." *Management Accounting* 64 (January 1982), pp. 43–49.

Gremillion, Lee L., and Pyburn, Philip. "Breaking the Systems Development Bottleneck." *Harvard Business Review* 41 (March April 1983), pp. 130–137.

Gremillion, Lee L., and Pyburn, Philip. *Computers and Information Systems in Business: An Introduction.* New York: McGraw-Hill Book Company, 1988.

Guimaraes, Tor, and Praxton, William E. "Impact of Financial Analysis Methods on Project Selection." *Journal of Systems Management* 35 (February 1984), pp. 18–22.

Hamilton, Scott, and Chervany, Norman L. "Evaluating Information System Effectiveness—Part I: Comparing Evaluation Approaches." *MIS Quarterly* 5 (September 1981), pp. 55–67.

Hammer, William E. "Systems Design in a Data Base Environment." *Journal of Systems Management* 33 (November 1982), pp. 24–29.

Helms, Glenn L., and Weiss, Ira R. "Auditor Involvement in the Systems Devlopment Life Cycle." *The Internal Auditor* 40 (December 1983), pp. 41–44.

Highsmith, Jim. "Structured Systems Planning." *MIS Quarterly* 5 (September 1981), pp. 35–54.

Honan, Patrick. "Powerful Platforms for Productivity." *Personal Computing* 12 (October 1988), pp. 33–34.

Hughes, G. David. "Computerized Sales Management." *Harvard Business Review* 61 (March–April 1983), pp. 102–112.

Hurtado, Corydon D. "EDP Effectiveness Evaluation." *Journal of Systems Management* 29 (January 1978), pp. 18–21.

Huser, Karen Grigalawski. "From Silence to Action." *Infosystems* 34 (March 1987), pp. 52–53.

Isaacs, P. Brian. "Warnier-Orr Diagrams in Applying Structured Concepts." *Journal of Systems Management* 34 (October 1982), pp. 28–32.

Ives, Blake, and Olson, Margrethe H. "User Involvement and MIS Success: A Review of Research." *Management Science* 30 (May 1984), pp. 586–603.

Kaplan, Ronald E. "Automation of an Accounting Firm-A Case History." *The CPA Journal* 57 (December 1987), pp. 123–129.

Keim, Robert T., and Janaro, Ralph. "Cost/Benefit Analysis of MIS." *Journal of Systems Management* 34 (September 1982), pp. 20–25.

King, William R. "Integrating Computerized Planning Systems into the Organization." *Managerial Planning* 32 (July–August 1983), pp. 10–13.

King, William R., and Epstein, Barry J. "Assessing Information System Value: An Experimental Study." *Decision Sciences* 14 (January 1983), pp. 34–45.

Kleim, Ralph L. "Selecting the Right Structured Analysis Software Package." *Journal of Systems Management* 39 (August 1988), pp. 11–13.

Kleim, Richard. "Computer-Based Financial Modeling." *Journal of Systems Management* 33 (May 1982), pp. 6–13.

Kneer, Dan, "Systems Procedures and Controls." *Journal of Systems Management* 34 (September 1983), pp. 28–33.

Kolle, Michael, "Going Outside for MIS Implementation." *Information and Management* (October 1983), pp. 261–268.

Ladd, Eldon. "How to Evaluate Financial Software." *Management Accounting* 46 (January 1985), pp. 39–43.

Lammert, Thomas B., and Ehrsam, Robert. "The Human Element: The Real Challenge in Modernizing Cost Systems." *Management Accounting* 68 (July 1987), pp. 32–38.

Lay, Peter M. Q. "Beware of the Cost/Benefit Model for IS Project Evaluation." *Journal of Systems Management* 36, 6 (June 1985), pp. 30–35.

Leavitt, Don. "Integrated Software Tools for Today." *Datamation* 33 (July 1, 1987), pp. 48–54.

Lees, John D., and Lees, Donna D. "Realities of Small Business Information System Implementation." *Journal of Systems Management* 38 (January 1987), pp. 6–13.

Lehman, John A., Vogel, Doug, and Dickson, Gary. "Business Graphics Trends." *Datamation* 40 (November 15, 1984), pp. 119–122.

Lin, W. Thomas, Sardinha, J. Carlos, and El-Badawi, Mohamed H. "An On-Line Interactive Corporate Financial Model." *Cost and Management* 54 (July–August 1980), pp. 28–33.

Lustman, Francois. "Project Mangement in a Small Organization." *Journal of Systems Management* 34 (December 1983), pp. 15–21.

Markus, M. Lynne, and Pfeffer, Jeffery. "Power and the Design and Implementation of Accounting and Control Systems." *Accounting, Organizations and Society* 8, 2/3 (1983), pp. 205–218.

Martin, Merle P., and Fuerst, William. "Communications Frameworks or Systems Design." *Journal of Systems Management* 35 (March 1984), pp. 18–25.

Mathusz, Donald V. "The Value of Information Concept Applied to Data Systems." *Omega* 5,5 (1977), pp. 593–604.

McFarlan, F. Warren. "Portfolio Approach to Information Systems." *Harvard Business Review* 59 (September–October 1981), pp. 142–150.

McFarlan, F. Warren. "Problems in Planning the Information System." *Harvard Business Review* 49 (March–April 1971), pp. 75–88.

McLeod, Raymond Jr., and Jones, Jack William. "A Framework for Office Automation." *MIS Quarterly* 11 (March 1987), pp. 87–106.

Melone, N. Paule, and Wharton, T. J. "Strategies for MIS Project Selection." *Journal of Systems Management* 35 (February 1984), pp. 26–33.

Mendes, Kathleen S. "Structured Ssytems Analysis: A Technique to Define Business Requirements." *Sloan Management Review* 21 (Summer 1980), pp. 51–63.

Mendus, Sharon Lee. "Computer Systems Development: Why Not Let Auditors Help?" *Journal of Systems Management* 37 (May 1986), pp. 36–40.

Methodios, Yannis. "Design of Data Entry Screens." *Journal of Systems Management* 33 (September 1982), pp. 29–31.

Meyers, Kenneth D. "Total Project Planning." *Datamation* 30 (April 1, 1982), pp. 143–148.

Mingione, Al. "Search for Excellence Within a Systems Development Project." *Journal of Systems Management* 37 (March 1986), pp. 31–34.

Mosard, Gil. "Problem Definition: Tasks and Techniques." *Journal of Systems Management* 34 (June 1983), pp. 16–21.

Moscove, Stephen A. "The Changing Role of the Accountant." *The National Public Accountant* 26 (September 1981), pp. 10–18.

Moscove, Stephen A. "The Changing Role of the Accountant-Part II." *The National Public Accountant* 26 (October 1981), pp. 24–30.

Multinovich, J. S., and Vlahovich, Vladimir. "A Strategy for a Successful MIS/DSS Implementation." *Journal of Systems Management* 35 (August 1984), pp. 8–15.

Murry, John P. "How an Information Center Improved Productivity." *Management Accounting* 65 (March 1984), pp. 38–44.

Myers, Edith. "Here Come the Super Service Bureaus." *Datamation* 30 (October 15, 1984), pp. 110–118.

Naumann, Justus D., and Jenkins, A. Milton. "Prototyping: The New Paradigm for Systems Development." *MIS Quarterly* 6 (September 1984), pp. 29–44.

Newman, Michael. "User Involvement-Does it Exist, Is It Enough?" *Journal of Systems Management* 35 (May 1984), pp. 34–37.

Nitterhouse, Denise and Silhan, Peter A. "Formatting Accounting Outputs for Improved Usability" *Journal of Systems Management* 38 (May 1987), pp. 6–11.

Nokansson, Nils C. I. "Change and the Systems Person." *Journal of Systems Management* 38 (May 1987), pp. 30–35.

Nolan, Richard L. "Managing the Crises in Data Processing." *Harvard Business Review* 57 (March–April 1979), pp. 115–126.

Nolan, Richard L. "Managing Information Systems by Committee." *Harvard Business Review* 60 (July–August 1982), pp. 72–79.

Nolan, Richard L. *Managing the Data Resource,* 2nd ed. New York: West, 1982.

Notowidegdo, M. H., "Information Systems: Weapons to Gain the Comeptitive Edge." *Financial Executive* 52 (February 1984), pp. 20–25.

Pappas, Richard A., and Remer, Donald S. "Status of Corporate Planning Models." *Management Planning* 32 (March-April 1984), pp. 4–16.

Porter, W. Thomas, and Perry, William E. *EDP Controls and Auditing,* 4th ed. Boston: Kent, 1984.

Potter, Doug. "Long Range Systems Planning." *Datamation* 33 (May 15, 1987), pp. 113–116.

Rajarman, M. K. "Structured Techniques for Software Development." *Journal of Systems Management* 34 (March 1983), pp. 36–38.

Robey, Daniel, and Markus, M. Lynne. "Rituals in Information System Design." *MIS Quarterly* 8 (March 1984), pp. 5–16.

Robinson, Leonard A., Davis, James R., and Alderman, C. Wayne. *Accounting Information Systems: A Cycle Approach.* New York: Harper & Row, 1982.

Rochfield, A., and Tardieu, H. "MERISE: An Information System Design and Development Methodology." *Information and Management* 6 (June 1983), pp. 143–155.

Rockart, John F. "Chief Executives Define Their Own Data Needs." *Harvard Business Review* 57 (March–April 1979), pp. 81–93.

Roy, S. Paul, and Cheung, Joseph K. "Early Warning Systems: A Management Tool for Your Company." *Managerial Planning* 33 (March–April 1985), pp. 16–21.

Rudkin, Ralph Il, and Shere, Kenneth D. "Structured Decomposition Diagram: A New Technique for System Analysis." *Datamation* 25 (October 1979), pp. 130–146.

Ryckman, H. O. "Requirement Definition Techniques." *Journal of Information Management* 8 (Summer 1987), pp. 17–21.

Schmaltz, Joseph H. "A Management Approach to a Strategic Financial Planning System." *Sloan Management Review* 21 (Winter 1980), pp. 3–13.

Sethi, Narendra K. "MIS and the Planning Process." *Managerial Planning* 32 (November–December 1983), pp. 46–51.

Shah, Arvind D. "Data Administration: It's Crucial." *Datamation* 30 (January 1984), pp. 187–192.

Shiflett, Arnold D. "How We Automated Our Accounting Department." *Management Accounting* 64 (June 1983), pp. 34–38.

Simkin, Mark G. *Computer Information Systems for Business.* Dubuque, Iowa: William C. Brown, 1987.

Sinclair, Stuart W. "The Three Domains of Information Systems Planning." *Journal of Information Systems Management* 3 (Spring 1986), pp. 8–16.

Snyders, Jan. "The CASE of the Artful Dodgers." *Infosystems* 35 (March 1988), pp. 28–32.

Squires, James W., IV. "A Perfect Fit: Minicomputers and Medium-Sized Companies." *Management Accounting* 66 (July 1984), pp. 42–48.

Stevens, Robert I., and Bieber, Walter J. "Work Measurement Techniques." *Journal of Systems Management* 28 (February 1977), pp. 15–27.

Stivers, Bonnie P., and Beard, Larry H. "Information Systems: Getting Back to Basics" *Journal of Systems Management* 38 (March 1987), pp. 35–40.

Sumner, Mary, and Sitek, Mary. "Are Structured Methods for Systems Analysis and Design Being Used?" *Journal of Systems Management* 37 (June 1986), pp. 18–23.

Synnott, William R., and Gruber, William H. "The Care and Feeding of Users." *Datamation* 28 (March 1982), pp. 191–204.

Teagan, Mark, and Young, Liz. "The Dynamics of Prototyping." *Computerworld* 22 (August 8, 1988), pp. 53–55.

Taruth, Eileen. "Research-oriented Perspective on Information Management." *Journal of Systems Management* 35 (July 1984), pp. 12–17.

Treleven, Carl. "Documenting the Financial Planning Model—An Overlooked Problem." *Managerial Planning* 31 (March–April 1983), pp. 18–25.

Tsichritzis, D. C., and Lochovsky, F. H. "Designing the Data Base." *Datamation* 24 (August 1978), pp. 147–151.

Vaid-Raizada, Vishist, K. "Incorporation of Intangibles in Computer Selection Decisions." *Journal of Systems Management* 34 (November 1983), pp. 30–36.

Vanecek, Michael. "Computer System Acquisition Planning." *Journal of Systems Management* 35 (May 1984), pp. 8–13.

Venkatakrishnan, V. "The Information Cycle." *Datamation* 29 (September 1983), pp. 175–180.

Wahi, Pran N., Popp, Kenneth A., and Stier, Susan M. "Applications Systems Planning at Weyerhaeuser." *Journal of Systems Management* 34 (March 1983), pp. 12–21.

Weisman, Randy. "Six Steps to AI-Based Functional Prototyping." *Datamation* 33 (August 1, 1987), pp. 71–72.

Wetherbe, James C. *Systems Analysis for Computer-Based Information Systems.* New York: West, 1979.

"Why Software Prototyping Works." *Datamation* 33 (Aug. 15, 1987), pp. 97–103.

Wilkinson, Joseph W. *Accounting and Information Systems* 2nd ed. New York: John Wiley and Sons, 1986.

Willoughby, T. C. "Project Selection Top Priority for MIS Executives." *Journal of Systems Management* 34 (Dec. 1983), pp. 9–11.

Withington, Frederic G. "The Golden Age of Packaged Software." *Datamation* 26 (December 1980), pp. 313–314.

Woolcock, P. H. "A Structured Approach to Systems Development." *Management Accounting (UK)* 65 (February 1987), pp. 32–35.

Wysong, Earl M., Jr. "Using the Internal Auditor for System Design Projects." *Journal of Systems Management* 34 (July 1983), pp. 28–33.

Zawacki, Robert A. "Performance Standards, Goals and Objectives for DP Personnel." *Journal of Systems Management* 35 (January 1984), pp. 12–15.

Zenker, David M. "The PC as Prototype Problem-Solver." *Management Accounting* 68 (May 1987), pp. 30–33.

Zmud, Robert W. "Design Alternatives for Organizing Information Systems Activities." *MIS Quarterly* 8 (June 1984), pp. 79–93.

PART FIVE

Special Topics Related to Accounting Information Systems

The focus of earlier chapters in this book was primarily on transaction processing systems for large business organizations. While transaction processing (or data processing) is the most prevalent form of processing in an accounting information system, new systems are processing information and knowledge in addition to data and transactions. Chapter 16 describes these "higher level" processing systems in some detail.

In addition to information and knowledge processing, Part Five addresses three specific types of organizations that have not been discussed in prior chapters. These are small business organizations, service organizations, and not-for-profit organizations. There may be overlap between these three types of organizations, both with each other and with larger systems. However, each has some unique features affecting their accounting information system. Chapter 17 discusses accounting information systems for small business organizations, and Chapter 18 examines accounting information systems for service and not-for-profit organizations.

Advances in technology, as well as lower costs for computer hardware and software, have made more complex types of processing systems such as decision support and expert systems feasible (described in Chapter 16). In addition, many small companies are now able to afford computerized systems of their own for processing accounting data. Thus, in discussing the small business firm in Chapter 17, we will look at some of the various types of computer systems (such as microcomputers and minicomputers) that can satisfy the data processing needs of small

627

businesses. Also, because of the tremendous growth in the use of microcomputers by organizations, a supplement to Chapter 17 has been included that examines strategies for effective microcomputer management. In Chapter 18's discussion of service organizations and not-for-profit organizations, we will analyze some of the unique operating characteristics of these organizations. This chapter also mentions several of the budgetary attributes associated with these types of organizations.

16

Operational, Decision Support, and Expert Systems

Among the important questions that you should be able to answer after reading this chapter are:

1. What are the different levels of processing in an accounting information system?
2. What are operational support systems and how can they be used to generate accounting information?
3. What are the characteristics and components of a decision support system? What are some accounting applications for these computerized systems?
4. Can computers think? How can the science of artificial intelligence help accounting?
5. What are the characteristics and components of an expert system? How can accountants use expert systems and expert system shells?

INTRODUCTION

Earlier chapters of this book have mostly discussed accounting examples of *transaction processing systems*. However, advances in computer hardware technology and software design have enabled accounting systems to evolve from systems that primarily process transaction data to systems that process information and impart knowledge. In this chapter, we look at higher levels of processing systems—particularly, decision support systems and expert systems. An overview of why we need so many different types of computer systems is provided in the first section of the chapter.

Operational support systems are used by managers and accountants to support the operational activities of their organizations. Three examples of such systems are real-time systems, interactive systems, and communications-based systems. Each of these is described in the second part of the chapter.

Operational systems work well for accomplishing and controlling many of the daily tasks of an organization, but are often incapable of helping managers plan or forecast. The purpose of a *decision support system* is to improve the efficiency and effectiveness of managerial decisions in these areas. Decision support systems are discussed in the third section of the chapter.

The highest level of processing is *knowledge processing*—the type of processing that uses artificial intelligence. The aspect of artificial intelligence that appears to hold the most promise for accounting information systems is *expert systems*. These are systems that can use reasoning techniques, learn, help train decision makers, and even make decisions. Some of these systems are already in accounting practice, and it is expected that there will be a large increase in the use of accounting expert systems in the future. Expert systems are discussed in the fourth and final section of the chapter.

WHY SO MANY TYPES OF PROCESSING SYSTEMS?

One of the earliest applications of computerized processing was *transaction data processing*. This involved processing data in volume, and usually also required computers to perform simple, repetitive tasks—for example, computing the net pay for employees in payroll applications. This type of data processing worked well for automating some of the straightforward tasks required of early accounting systems. But these systems did not lend themselves to preparing the summary reports, custom-designed reports, and data analyses required for upper level management decisions. The information required was different, and the data processing involved required more sophisticated systems.

Strategic, Tactical, and Operational Decision Making

To understand how informational needs differ in an organization, it is useful to review the different types of decision-making that take place in one. Typically, an organization can be divided into three levels (Figure 16-1), each of which tends to make different types of decisions: (1) strategic decisions, (2) tactical decisions, and (3) operational decisions. Let us look at each of these types of decisions in a little more detail.

Strategic Decisions

As noted in Chapter 3, top managers make **strategic decisions.** These are decisions involving long-range planning horizons and commitments of large amounts of resources. An example

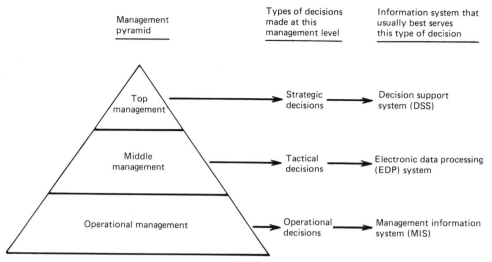

FIGURE 16-1 columns:

Management pyramid | Types of decisions made at this management level | Information system that usually best serves this type of decision

Top management → Strategic decisions → Decision support system (DSS)

Middle management → Tactical decisions → Electronic data processing (EDP) system

Operational management → Operational decisions → Management information system (MIS)

FIGURE 16-1 The informational needs of management often differ according to the managerial level of the decision makers. Usually, different types of information systems best fulfill these different needs. *Source:* Simkin, *Introduction to CIS for Business,* (Dubuque, Iowa: William C. Brown, 1987).

of a strategic decision would be where to build a new plant.

Tactical Decisions

Once strategic decisions have been made, they must be translated into specific actions. **Tactical decisions** involve translating a company's long-range plans into specific plans and activities. Examples of questions involving tactical planning are: (1) What should the schedule of production be for the current month? (2) What specific steps should be implemented to improve production efficiency next month? (3) Should product Z be manufactured internally or purchased from an outside supplier? and (4) How should the working capital needs of the next quarter be met? The tactical planning decisions of a firm normally involve decision-making situations that are more routine and cover a shorter time period than long-range planning problems. Tactical decisions are also narrower in scope and require less judgment than long-range planning decisions.

Operational Decisions

After strategic decisions have been made, they must be operationalized into specific, meaningful tasks. In a typical application, this means establishing standards based on previous tactical plans, evaluating operating performances, and making the necessary decisions required to correct inefficient operating performances. These are **operational decisions.** Some examples of questions that the operational control process attempts to answer are: (1) What changes should be made in the production system to reduce the usage of raw material B? (2) How can the low labor productivity in the manufacturing operations be improved? (3) Which employees, if any, should be retrained to handle different job tasks in the newly designed computerized accounting information system? and (4) What changes are necessary to finish a production job on schedule?

Operational control and tactical planning both deal with short-range organizational problems that are fairly routine and highly structured. These two functions differ, however, in that they relate to different phases of a company's overall planning and controlling activities. Decisions made in the tactical planning area are usually concerned with future courses of action. In contrast, operational decisions are concerned with correcting ongoing operating activities or modifying existing courses of action. In most cases, operational decisions involve shorter time spans than tactical decisions.

Three Levels of Processing Systems

The different levels of decision-making just described are often satisfied with different levels of processing systems. Figure 16-2 identifies three of these. The first, or lowest, level is often called **transaction processing** because it typically involves converting transaction data into useful information. Most of the earliest accounting information systems were transaction processing systems, and several examples of these systems have been described in earlier chapters of this book. Given their level of detail, transaction processing systems seem to best help managers with operational decisions.

The second or middle level of processing is information processing. This involves processing nonroutine data for management planning and control. An example of an information system that can be used for these purposes is a decision support system—basically, a computerized system that helps users make more effective decisions. These systems are especially used by managers making tactical decisions, although both strategic and operational managers can also use such systems effectively.

The highest level of processing is knowledge processing. Knowledge processing is possible today due to recent advancements in software and hardware technology. For example, the availability of such specialized computer languages as LISP and PROLOG has contributed significantly to the viability of computerized knowledge processing. These systems are especially useful to those individuals making strategic or specialized decisions. Many of these are expert systems.

OPERATIONAL SUPPORT SYSTEMS

Even at the lowest (operational) level, employees need computer systems that provide detailed information in a timely fashion. **Operational support systems** are computer systems that emerged in the later 1960s for short-range planning and control. These systems help lower-level managers promote efficiency in "operational" tasks, such as tasks that focus on technical functions rather than managerial performance.

Three examples of operational support systems are: (1) real-time systems, (2) interactive systems, and (3) communications-based systems. Some accounting information systems are examples of exactly one of these systems, while others are combinations of all three. Let us look at each type in a little greater detail.

Real-time Systems

Real-time systems are systems that process data as soon as they are entered into a computer. Thus, real-time systems receive data about processes or operations, perform the necessary data analysis (or analyses), and respond in time to allow users to control them. Typical features of real-time accounting applications include:

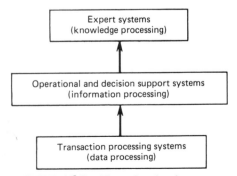

FIGURE 16-2   Three levels of support systems.

1. Online input and processing so that the information stored within the computer system is current,
2. Use of direct-access files so that data stored within the computer system can be retrieved directly and immediately from online storage, and
3. Time-sharing so that different users can obtain information simultaneously from the computer system.

Some real-time systems are activated by built-in mechanisms such as the temperature-control systems in production applications. An accounting example might be a credit-verification system that automatically compares customers' current credit statuses against personal credit limits. When a credit-sales order is entered into a computer, the customer's order is rejected if a particular customer exceeds his or her credit limit. In contrast, some real-time systems are activated by human input. An accounting example is a savings and loan application, in which customer deposits are immediately added to account balances.

Interactive Systems

Interactive systems are real-time systems that allow users to converse or **dialogue** with a computer. This enables users to answer processing questions or to provide additional data or instructions. In a typical setting, first the user inputs data or a command. Then the computer processes this data or executes the command. The user then observes the results and either exits the system or provides more input. This is an important improvement over a simple real-time system in that users can respond to computer processing and therefore better direct computer operations. With timely information, managers are able to make decisions that contribute to the efficiency and effectiveness of their organization.

An important characteristic of many interactive systems is the availability of menus such as the Assist menu of dBASE IV or the command menus of LOTUS 1-2-3. Such menus contain processing choices, thus enabling users to pick the task they require from a list of possibilities. These menus also make interactive systems easy to learn (i.e., make them "user friendly") as well as easy to use.

Not all interactive systems are "menu-driven." A common alternative is a **command-driven system,** which typically requires users to learn lists of package-specific commands. An example would be the commands of a DOS operating system. These systems are usually harder to learn and use.

Communications-Based Systems

A large organization that has several plants, warehouses, and sales offices scattered throughout the country may decide to use a computer network that electronically links its several facilities to each other. These systems are called **communications-based systems.** The functions of a communications-based system are to receive inquiries or transaction data from individuals at remote locations, to transmit the received inputs to a central location for processing by the computer, and to retransmit the processed information back to the remote locations for decision-making purposes.

A communications-based system gives the managers in a branch office access to the same data bases, computing power, or programs that they would have if they were physically located in the home office. Thus, a communications-based system can contribute to timely and integrated information communications in an organization. For example, in a communications-based credit-verification system (as discussed in the previous section), a credit-sales order at a company's branch office would be entered from the branch terminal and transmitted to the company's home office. The customer placing the order is automatically credit-checked by the computer system at the home office. If the computer system rejects the order because the customer has exceeded his or her credit limit, this information is immediately transmitted to the branch office.

Communications-based systems also work well in local offices. For example, many firms find it desirable to link their microcomputers together in **local area networks,** thereby enabling several people to share computer files (such as accounting data bases), equipment (such as printers or hard disks), and software (such as accounting software). These systems also enable several users to input data to the same central file—perhaps even from different types of microcomputers. This is an important advantage for small businesses who require several users to input accounting data to the system.

DECISION SUPPORT SYSTEMS

The concept of **decision support systems (DSSs)** evolved in the 1960s from studies of decision-making in organizations. These studies noted that managers required more flexible systems that could respond to less-well-defined questions. Advances in hardware technology, interactive computing design, and developments in programming and software engineering contributed to this evolution.

Examples of Decision Support Systems

Perhaps the best way to understand decision support systems is to study examples. Below are several illustrations of decision support systems used in accounting applications.

A Portfolio Analysis System

At one time, a bank's account managers analyzed portfolios manually—a time-consuming task with a high potential for clerical error. An online portfolio analysis system developed for the department now enables managers to inspect both personal portfolios or groups of portfolios in different ways—for example, to measure income or growth performance over time, to evaluate

risk, or to examine the composition of a portfolio by type of industry. The large amount of data required for this analysis was already in the bank's computer system, but was not readily available or usable prior to this DSS. More importantly, these managers are now better able to analyze client portfolios, advise them about holdings, and recommend changes if warranted. In other words, these managers can make better decisions with the help of the system.

A Financial Planning System

A company required its finance committee to make decisions on how to allocate funds to investment areas and therefore minimize idle cash. The committee was required to project both future income from the company's business and future rates of return from various investment sources. Since these projections are difficult and may change drastically from quarter to quarter, the company developed a source-and-application-of-funds DSS to help it plan. The committee members input various projections of sales levels by product line, plus assumptions concerning returns on various investment instruments. The model is then run over and over, seeking optimal investment allocations over a two-year horizon and helping the committee reach investment decisions.

An Insurance Renewal System

Car drivers seeking to renew their insurance must be re-evaluated by company officials on such matters as age, driving record, new state laws, and many additional factors that may or may not affect their renewal rates. When this was done manually, rate calculations were often inaccurate or inconsistent. A new DSS implemented by the insurance company now calculates these values automatically based on standard assumptions. Underwriters simply prepare input specifications, which they alter if the model assumptions do not apply for any particular renewal case. The system relieves the underwriters of the clerical burdens of their jobs, and enables them to concentrate on their jobs' decision making.

A Budget Variance Analysis System

A financial institution relies heavily on its budgeting system for controlling costs and evaluating managerial performance. It now uses a computerized DSS to generate monthly variance reports for division comptrollers. The system allows these comptrollers to graph, view, analyze, and annotate budget variances, as well as create additional one- and five-year budget projections using the line-item forecasting tools provided in the system. The system thus helps the comptrollers create and control budgets for the cost-center managers reporting to them.

An Audit-Staff Scheduling System

An important problem in large audit offices is deciding how to assign staff members to auditing engagements in an effective manner. A DSS developed for one such company relies on an integer programming model to recommend auditing assignments. This model considers client requirements, audit difficulty, auditor expertise, and corporate policies. It also allows audit schedulers to make, test, modify, and update assignments as required. The DSS is considered an important planning tool since audit-staff morale and employee turnover are heavily affected by these auditing assignments.

Characteristics of Decision Support Systems

Although the foregoing applications are very different, they possess several characteristics that are fairly consistent with most other decision support systems. These characteristics help to distinguish DSSs from operational support systems, other types of management information systems, or expert systems. Some of these are as follows:

Decision Support—not Decision-Making

One characteristic of DSSs is that they generally *support* management decision making, but do not make choices themselves. Although they are most heavily used for tactical decisions, they can also be used by operational managers (e.g., to solve scheduling problems) or by top managers (e.g., to decide whether or not to drop a product line). The decision should be better using a DSS. The important thing is that, while the system supports the decision, it is the user who ultimately makes the final choice.

Unstructured Problems and Nonroutine Data

A second characteristic of DSSs is that they are aimed at relatively **unstructured problems**— i.e., problems with no clear solution procedures and therefore problems in which some managerial judgment is necessary. Thus, in contrast to transaction processing systems, decision support systems typically use nonroutine data as input. This type of data is not easily gathered, may not be available inside the organization, and may even have to be estimated.

Flexibility

Decision support systems are rarely developed for one-time use, but are usually used to solve a particular type of problem on a regular basis. Thus, another attribute of decision support systems is that they are sufficiently *flexible and adaptive* for ongoing use. Flexibility and adaptability are traits they share with expert systems which are discussed later in this chapter.

What-If?

Since managers must plan for *future* activities, they rely heavily upon assumptions of future interest rates, supply prices, consumer demand, and similar variables. But what if these assumptions are wrong? A key characteristic of many decision support systems is that they allow users to ask "what if" questions, and to examine the results of these questions. For instance, a manager may build an electronic spreadsheet model that attempts to forecast future departmental budgets. The manager cannot know in advance how inflation rates might affect his or her projection figures, but the manager can examine the consequences of alternate assumptions by changing the parameters (in this case, growth rates) affected by these rates. Decision support systems are useful in supporting this type of analysis.

Ease of Use

Finally, decision support systems may be characterized by their relatively "friendly" interactive computer mode. Since they are used primarily by managers and other decision makers who are nonprogrammers, they must be easy to use. The availability of nonprocedural modeling languages, such as those discussed below, facilitates communication between the user and the system.

Components of Decision Support Systems

Identifying the *characteristics* of decision support systems is useful for distinguishing these systems from others. Identifying the *components* of such systems is helpful for understanding how these systems work. A decision support system has four basic components: the user, the modeling or planning language, the data base, and the model base (Figure 16-3).

The User

The user of a decision support system is usually a manager with an unstructured or semistructured problem to solve. The manager may be at any level of authority in the organization—either staff or line personnel. The user does not need a computer background to use a decision support system for problem solving. The most important knowledge is a thorough understanding of the problem and the variables to be considered in finding a solution.

One or More Data Bases

DSS users typically interact with one or more data bases. These data bases typically contain

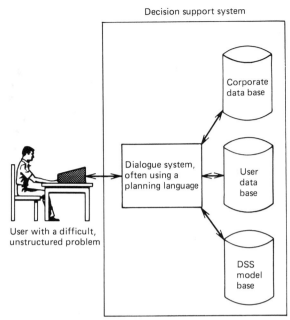

FIGURE 16-3   The components of a decision support system. *Source:* Simkin, *Introduction to Computer Information Systems* (Dubuque, Iowa: William C. Brown, 1987).

both routine and nonroutine data from both internal and external sources. The data from external sources are data about the operating environment surrounding the organization. These might include data about economic conditions, market demand for the organizations' goods or services, and industry competition.

Additional data bases may be constructed by DSS users themselves. Some of this data may come from internal sources and are typically generated by the organization in the normal course of operations—for example, data from the financial and managerial accounting systems. Data from other subsystems such as marketing, production, and personnel may also be captured in this data base. Finally, additional data bases may be required to store the results of alternate user assumptions, simulation trials, or other experiments.

A *Planning Language*

One reason why DSS users do not need extensive education in computer programming is because communication within the DSS is performed with a special modeling or planning language. Often, these languages are nonprocedural, meaning that they allow the user to concentrate on *what* should be accomplished rather than *how* the computer should perform each step.

Two types of planning languages often used in decision support systems are: (1) general-purpose planning languages, and (2) special-purpose planning languages. **General-purpose planning languages** allow users to perform a wide variety of tasks—for example, retrieve various data from a data base or execute statistical routines. The languages in most electronic spreadsheets are good examples of general planning languages in that they enable users to tackle a broad range of budgeting, forecasting, and other worksheet-oriented problems. Additional examples of general-purpose planning languages are CUFFS, EMPIRE, EXPRESS, FOCUS, IFPS, and SIMPLAN.

Special-purpose planning languages tend to be more limited in what they can do, but usually do certain jobs better than the general purpose languages. Examples include DYNAMO, GASP, GPSS, and SIMSCRIPT. Some of the statistical languages such as BMD, SAS, and Minitab are additional examples.

A *Model Base*

A planning language also allows users to maintain a dialogue with the **model base.** The model base is called the "brain" of the decision support system, since it performs data manipulation and computations with the data and information provided to it by the user and the data base. There are many types of model bases, but most of them perform some types of mathematical functions—regression, time series analysis, linear programming, econometrics, or financial computations.

The analysis provided by the routines in the model base is the key to supporting the user's decision. The model base may dictate the type of data included in the data base and/or the data input by the user. Even where the sophistication of the quantitative analysis is fairly low, a decision support system that requires users to concentrate on certain kinds of data in making a decision can be helpful in improving the effectiveness of the decision itself.

EXPERT SYSTEMS

Successes with decision support systems have led system designers to ask whether or not computers can be programmed to think. This is an important question since a "yes" means that computers can actually be programmed to become their own experts, as opposed to only helping humans reach conclusions.

Artificial Intelligence

The branch of computer science that concerns itself with computer "thinking," is called **artificial intelligence (AI).** The concept is not new; it was discussed as early as 1956 at a conference in Dartmouth College. The conference was organized by scientists to consider the question of whether or not machines can think—a question still argued today.

One proof that computers can be as intelligent as humans is a **Turing test.** This test was devised by Alan Turing, a mathematician who is often called the "father of artificial intelligence." It is described in Figure 16-4.

As the study of artificial intelligence has grown, many AI research centers have begun in universities, government, and private industry. As one might expect, the Department of Defense is particularly interested in AI research. For example, the Defense Advanced Research Projects Agency (DARPA) was organized in 1958 to finance research in high technology areas, and has contributed significantly to advance the science of artificial intelligence.

To conduct the test, an individual interrogator is placed in a room with a computer terminal. The terminal is connected by computer to two other terminals in a separate room, attended by a male and a female. In the first step of the test, the interrogator asks questions of the male and female via the computer link. The male and female must answer the questions, but one of them must tell the truth and the other must not. The object is for the interrogator to determine which person responding is the male and which is the female. A record is kept of how many times an interrogator is able to correctly identify the male versus female.

The second step in a Turing test involves substituting a computer for one of the people. The object for the interrogator is then to determine which respondent is human and which is the computer. The human is obligated to answer all questions truthfully; the computer's objective is to fool the interrogator. The final step in the Turing test is to compare the results of performance in the first and second steps. The computer is considered capable of thought if the interrogator was fooled as frequently in the first step as in the second.

A simple, revised Turing test has evolved in which only the second step of the original test is conducted. Whenever the computer fools the interrogator into believing it is human, the computer is considered by some to be intelligent. The test has limitations, of course, and because of these, many people still do not believe that computers can really think or reason.

FIGURE 16-4   How a Turing Test works.

Private businesses now also perform extensive AI research. Explorations include robotics, vision and speech recognition, natural language processing, neural networks, and expert systems. Robotics is the study and application of robot technology. Unlike simple robots, which are mechanical, electronic robots can be programmed. This makes the robot better able to perform manual tasks in place of humans (e.g., because the robots don't tire), more adaptable to changing conditions (e.g., welding different sized cars), and more useful in environments which would be uncomfortable or unfit for humans (e.g., transferring radioactive fuel rods in nuclear power plants).

Vision and speech recognition systems enable a computer (within limits) to "see" and "hear" like humans. **Natural language processing** allows computers to both produce and understand a natural human language such as English. Finally, **neural networks** enable computers to develop feedback mechanisms, and therefore to learn from their mistakes like humans.

At present, the technology that appears to hold the greatest promise for businesses and accounting applications is **expert systems.** These are software packages that use facts, knowledge, and reasoning techniques to solve problems that typically require human expert abilities.

The first expert system was introduced at the previously mentioned Dartmouth College meeting in 1956. The system, called *Logic Theorist,* was developed to generate proofs for mathematical theorems. In one case, the program was able to generate a proof that had been overlooked by experts. Despite this early beginning, expert-system development was slow until the late 1970s and 1980s. The lack of (1) software tools for developing these systems, (2) fast computers on which to run them, and (3) experience with using them made the task of developing these systems formidable and costs prohibitive.

Expert systems can be used in many different application areas. An early, and well-known, system is a medical system called MYCIN. This system was developed in the 1970s to diagnose certain types of bacterial infections. A recent article in an accounting journal identified several applications of systems which have been or are currently being developed to:

- Identify faulty lines in telephone networks.
- Find failures in diesel locomotives.

- Configure the components of computer systems.
- Screen the underwriting of insurance policies.
- Diagnose failures of oil well drill bits.
- Control the operating system of large computers.
- Find bugs in an electronic funds transfer network.[1]

Breakthroughs in various hardware, software, and building technologies have put these systems within practical reach for commercial development. Figure 16-5 lists additional expert systems that have been developed, or are currently under development, for accounting problems.

Characteristics of Expert Systems

Just as there are certain characteristics which distinguish decision support systems from other types of systems, there are several distinct characteristics of expert systems. These are outlined in the paragraphs that follow.

Make Expert Decisions

The goal of an expert system is to make expert decisions. This does not mean that experts are no

[1] Borthick, A. Faye and West, Owen D., "Expert Systems—A New Tool for the Professional," *Accounting Horizons* (March 1987), pp. 9–16.

longer necessary if an expert system is in place, but rather that the system actually recommends a specific course of action. Of course, the recommendation may be treated as a second opinion if the system is used as a consultant. Alternatively, the system may be used to make decisions when human experts are unavailable.

Trace Logic

Most operational and decision support systems follow a path of logic to solve a problem, but generally these systems cannot retrace this path when asked. In contrast, most expert systems must be able to retrace the logic they followed to reach a conclusion, and usually are also required to communicate this to users on display screens or printed output. Thus, at any given point during a session, a user is able to input the answer to a question, ask the system why it is asking the question, and (especially at the end) ask how a conclusion was reached (Figure 16-6).

Part of this logic-tracing requirement is necessary for error-checking purposes when the system is first designed. However, the ability of these software programs to explain why certain questions are asked of the user, and how decisions are reached, also makes them particularly valuable for training purposes. Finally, users appear to become more comfortable and more trusting of the system if they can challenge it

Program	Application	Developer
ANSWERS	Financial data analysis and analytical review	Financial Audit Systems
AUDITOR	Assess allowance for bad debts	C. Dungan
		University of Illinois
EDP AUDITOR	Audits advanced EDP systems	J. V. Hansen and W. F. Messier, Jr.
		University of Florida
EXPERTAX	Tax planning	Coopers & Lybrand
TAXADVISOR	Estate planning	R. Michaelson
		University of Illinois
TICOM	Evaluation of internal controls	A. D. Bailey, Jr. and G. Duke
		University of Minnesota
		A. B. Whinston and M. Gagle
		Purdue University

FIGURE 16-5 Expert systems for accounting applications.

```
  ┌─────────────────────────────────────────┐   ┌─────────────────────────────────────────┐
  │         CAR REPAIR EXPERT SYSTEM         │   │         CAR REPAIR EXPERT SYSTEM         │
  │                                          │   │                                          │
  │  QUESTION:  CAN YOU INDICATE THE         │   │  QUESTION:  CAN YOU INDICATE             │
  │             GENERAL PROBLEM AREA?        │   │             THE ELECTRICAL PROBLEM?      │
  │                                          │   │                                          │
  │      1   DRIVETRAIN PROBLEM              │   │      1   STARTING THE ENGINE             │
  │      2   ELECTRICAL PROBLEM              │   │      2   LIGHT(S) DON'T WORK             │
  │      3   FUEL PROBLEM                    │   │      3   BATTERY DOESN'T CHARGE          │
  │      4   SUSPENSION PROBLEM              │   │      4   NO POWER TO AUXILIARY DEVICES   │
  │      5   EXHAUST PROBLEM                 │   │      5   FUSE PROBLEMS                   │
  │      U   UNKNOWN                         │   │      U   UNKNOWN                         │
  │      H   HELP                            │   │      H   HELP                            │
  │      W   WHY DO YOU ASK?                 │   │      W   WHY DO YOU ASK?                 │
  │      X   EXIT                            │   │      X   EXIT                            │
  │                                          │   │                                          │
  │  YOUR ENTRY?  2                          │   │  YOUR ENTRY?  4                          │
  └─────────────────────────────────────────┘   └─────────────────────────────────────────┘
```

FIGURE 16-6 An example of how an expert system is used to solve a problem—in this case, diagnose what is wrong with a car. In the first screen, the user indicates the general area of concern. In the second screen, more specific areas are identified. The process continues in this fashion, with the program asking questions and the user providing answers (including "do not know"), until the system is able to provide a tentative diagnosis or indicate what further information is required.

when desired, and ask the system to defend its reasoning.

Reasoning by Inference

Expert systems are also characterized by their use of reasoning or *inference techniques,* as opposed to the use of more-straightforward algorithms and computations. This characteristic allows these systems to simulate an expert's thinking in solving problems.

The way in which inferential reasoning works is often explained by analogy to the game of chess. In chess, the number of possible moves is almost infinite. The human player does not consider all possible moves on every turn, but instead uses *heuristics* (rules of thumb) to eliminate options that don't make sense. Expert systems are programmed similarly. This is accomplished in basically one of two ways; (1) with if-then rules, or (2) with semantic networks.

With if-then rules, the computer is programmed to test input data for key factors. An example of this approach is as follows:

If a particular account represents an economic resource that the firm possesses, *then* it is an asset.

If an asset account can become liquid in one year or less, *then* it is a current asset.

If accounts receivable is an economic resource that the firm possesses, and it can become liquid in one year or less, *then* it is a current asset.

These if-then rules are called **production rules.** They are widely used in expert systems for representing heuristics or other reasoning.

Another way to capture heuristics or reasoning in software systems is to use **semantic networks.** A semantic network is a group of facts, connected with other facts through word links that represent relationships. Semantic networks work well at representing knowledge and reasoning when an application contains complex interrelationships among facts. The following is a simplified example of how a semantic network could be used:

All current assets represent economic resources that the firm possesses which can become liquid in one year or less; accounts receivable are current assets; therefore, accounts receivable represent economic resources that the firm possesses which can become liquid in one year or less.

Ability to Learn

Expert systems are not only *flexible* and *adaptive* enough to be used on a regular basis, they are also capable of *learning*. Unlike decision support systems, expert judgment is built into the system—not input each time by the user. This means that the system must be capable of easy modification. It should also be able to learn as new information is introduced. For example, if an expert system were developed to act as an automobile mechanic, the system would consider the "symptoms" of a malfunctioning car and determine what was wrong with it.

Suppose, however, that it misdiagnoses the problem (not unlike human auto mechanics). The user should be able to let the system know of its mistake. The system should then be able to use that information about its mistake to modify itself so that it would not make that particular error again. In this way, an expert system can be said to "learn."

Certainty Factors

The data input into most operational systems (and some decision support systems) are known with certainty and therefore treated as constants. In contrast, many expert systems allow users to assign **certainty factors** to data—for example, "Pays-on-time cf .25" (meaning the user is 25 percent certain that an account always pays on time). Similarly, many expert systems also *output* results with certainty factors attached to answers—e.g., "Won't pay debt (cf .60); Will pay debt (cf .40)." These answers can be unsettling to those wanting definitive answers to difficult questions. But these answers also reflect the fact that even human experts cannot always be sure about their conclusions—especially when provided with ambiguous data.

Components of Expert Systems

As illustrated in Figure 16-7, there are five major components in an expert system. These are: (1) the people who interact with an expert sys-

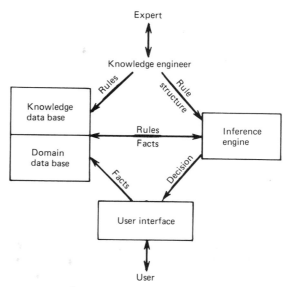

FIGURE 16-7 Components of an expert system.

tem, (2) the domain data base, (3) the knowledge data base, (4) the inference engine, and (5) the user interface. Each of these is described briefly below.

People

The people associated with an expert system are the user, the expert, and the knowledge engineer. As stated earlier, the *user* is the person who communicates with the system in order to solve a problem. The user provides facts to the domain data base and receives conclusions from the system's inference engine via the user interface. Typically, the system allows the user to ask questions and infer facts. The user may question "why" a particular input is requested or "how" an inference was made.

The *expert* is the person or persons upon whose knowledge and experience the system is based. An effective expert system must capture the knowledge or rules that an expert uses in making decisions. This is the most difficult task in developing these systems. Many times, experts cannot tell you how they make decisions—only that they were acting on "hunches" or "gut instinct" gained through experience.

It is the **knowledge engineer's** job to capture these instincts or hunches in the form of decision rules. A knowledge engineer might be said to "mine" the knowledge of experts and use it to build an expert system. Sometimes this process calls for much more creativity than simply asking questions of the expert(s). One such knowledge engineering process is explained later in this chapter in the description of an expert system at work.

Domain Data Base

The **domain data base** contains all of the facts about a particular domain or subject. This set of data is often similar to a company's data base. For example, if the expert system is an auditing system, the domain data base might contain information about a company's financial status—e.g., a chart of accounts, trial balance, and various other financial statement data or information. These facts are the domain data base for the system.

Knowledge Data Base

The **knowledge data base** contains procedural knowledge or rules that dictate which actions to follow. When a knowledge data base contains such rules, the expert system is said to be a production type of system. The rules which might be included in a knowledge data base for an auditing system might be based on Statements of Auditing Standards. The system may also have some *meta rules*—i.e., "rules about rules"—which direct the order of application of the rules. In some expert systems, the domain and knowledge data base are combined into one data base and are together referred to as the knowledge data base.

Inference Engine

Both the domain data base and the knowledge data base interact with the **inference engine** to determine when to apply rules and the order in which they apply. Thus, the inference engine is said to "drive" the expert system. It does this by using the information and knowledge contained in the data bases to infer new knowledge or reach conclusions. This is accomplished through either forward chaining or backward chaining.

Using **forward chaining,** the inference engine works through the rules, decides when to apply them, and executes the appropriate ones until a solution is reached. Again, a good analogy would be the decisions in a chess game. The end is not known, but specific rules of thumb can be applied if the circumstances appear to warrant them.

In contrast, **backward chaining** starts with the solution, and works backward through the rules and facts to determine whether or not they support the solution. Thus, the process of backward chaining may be likened to solving a maze puzzle. It is often easier to start from the back, and then work your way forward to the "start."

The decision to use forward chaining versus backward chaining in the design of an expert system depends upon the type of problem to be solved by the system. For example, backward chaining may be more appropriate for diagnostic systems, such as our automobile repair example. After the diagnosis is made, the inference engine works backward through the rules in the knowledge data base to see if it is correct.

Expert System Shells

At one time, most expert systems were written with special AI programming languages such as LISP, INTERLISP, and PROLOG. Using these languages to build a system from scratch requires special expertise and is very time consuming. An **expert system shell** is an inference engine that is packaged and sold separately from a domain and knowledge base. The shell can be used as a development tool in building several different types of expert systems. This is very important if such systems are developed for commercial purposes since development costs might otherwise be prohibitive. Many available shells can also be

---

TEXAS INSTRUMENTS PERSONAL CONSULTANT™

THIS IS A SAMPLE DOCUMENT ONLY.

The name of the client is as follows: Ron

The amount of money for you to invest in a money-market fund is as follows: 8000

My recommendation is as follows:

Since your *risk profile* seems to indicate that you can accommodate a low degree of risk in your investment strategy, invest in a money-market fund that buys only U.S. Treasury bills and other direct obligations of the U.S. government and paper from agencies such as the Federal National Mortgage Association.
A comparison of current yields may be found in the Money Market Funds column of the Wall Street Journal. (70%)

FIGURE 16-8 Example of a consultation with Personal Consultant.

used by nonexperts and can greatly facilitate the development process.

Examples of expert system shells that can be used on microcomputers are EXPERT-EASE (Human Edge Software), Personal Consultant (Texas Instruments), and VPEXPERT (Paperback Software). These packages are general-purpose software tools that can be adapted to a wide variety of problems. The user adds the expert knowledge in the form of if-then production rules. The pre-programmed inference engine searches through the rules and applies them appropriately until a conclusion is reached. Figure 16-8 is an example of an exchange between a user and the Personal Consultant shell. The availability of shells such as this should increase the use of expert systems in accounting in the next decade.

SUMMARY

This chapter has identified three different levels of processing and has explained how each affects accounting information systems. The lowest level of processing is data or transaction processing. This type of processing is representative of many accounting information systems, such as simple payroll processing applications.

The second level of processing is system support system processing. Two types of systems at this level are operational support systems and decision support systems. Operational support systems assist managers in short-range planning and control decisions. Operational support systems may be real-time systems, interactive systems, and/or communications-based systems.

Decision support systems were developed to improve the efficiency and effectiveness of a manager's decision-making process. Decision support systems have several distinguishing characteristics. These include (1) support for decision making, (2) a focus on relatively unstructured decisions, (3) flexibility, (4) what-if capabilities, and (5) ease of use. The components of a decision support system are the user, one or more data bases, a planning language, and a model base.

The highest level of processing is knowledge processing. Knowledge processing is an aspect of artificial intelligence. The science of artificial intelligence has many implications for computerized systems—particularly expert systems. Expert system characteristics are the ability to make expert decisions, the ability to trace logic, the use of inference techniques for reasoning, and the ability to learn. The components of an expert system are people, the domain data base, the knowledge data base and, the inference engine.

Several expert systems have been developed recently by accounting firms and accounting researchers. These can be used to improve the AIS environment by training less-experienced personnel and freeing experts to apply their experience and knowledge to problems which are non-recurring or those which cannot be solved by other types of computerized accounting information systems.

AIS at Work—An Expert System

ExperTax is an expert system developed in 1986 by the public accounting firm of Coopers & Lybrand. This software system was initially designed to help auditors evaluate their client's tax accrual, as well as provide a review of tax compliance and planning. The accrual process is necessary to reconcile differences between income tax expense and taxes payable. These differences arise since certain tax rules and rates are applicable for financial reporting versus others for reporting income on the tax return. Prior to the development of ExperTax, senior auditors would evaluate their client's tax accruals using a checklist. The checklist consisted of a series of questions that the auditor and client answered with "yes" or "no" responses. The checklist was over 70 pages long and took several hours to complete. Because certain responses might indicate that some questions could be skipped or that other questions were particularly relevant, it was necessary for the auditor to have a good understanding of tax law and accounting principles to use the checklist most effectively. This meant that an audit manager or experienced auditor was needed to complete the checklist or at least review it. The process of completing the checklist was a difficult and tedious one.

Initially, ExperTax was an automated version of the accrual checklist, which runs on a personal computer. It uses forward chaining and has more than three thousand production rules. It is superior to the checklist in several ways, however. First, the experience and expertise of more than 40 tax and audit experts is incorporated in the software. This expertise and experience was "mined" or acquired from the experts by knowledge engineers. It was used to develop interactive software that has the ability to assimilate a combination of responses to questions asked and "search" for the next set of appropriate questions. In this way, the program identifies those issues that should be addressed by the client and auditor and asks the questions pertinent to those issues. This has the advantage of efficiency because instead of progressing through the checklist sequentially, irrelevant questions can be skipped. It also means that the expert system is able to identify issues that should be considered in tax planning. Finally, the program ensures consistency and a high level of quality every time the accrual process takes place. This is because the expert knowledge is used to make decisions about which issues are important; the checklist does not rely on an individual auditor to make those decisions. This feature allows relatively inexperienced staff accountants to work through the program with the client, thus providing a higher level of service.

Since its introduction in 1986, the program has been modified two or three times each year so that it is current with new tax law and accounting principles. When the program was initially developed, the process of acquiring or modifying knowledge was quite complex. At one point, it was done by having tax experts guide a junior accountant through a sample accrual process, while cameras recorded the interaction. There were many sessions with experts and program developers. The knowledge engineers then used the output from the sessions to design the program. Now, modifications to the program are made using two experts at a time working with the knowledge engineer to write rules in an interactive mode. This is accomplished with a knowledge base maintenance system.

A valuable feature of ExperTax is its ability to assist in training auditors in the intricacies of the U.S. tax law. The program user (auditor) can ask the system "why" a particular question is asked by pressing a function key. The software will provide an explanation. This allows the auditor to "learn" from the system.

Although several expert systems have been developed in recent years, not many of them have proved to be as productive in practical application as ExperTax. Its success has led to new supplements to ExperTax for specific industries. Since special tax rules apply in industries such as insurance, health care, and oil and gas, special programs that incorporate those rules are necessary. Building future programs that are derivatives of ExperTax will be much easier since Coopers & Lybrand developed an expert system shell, QShell, to facilitate the process. As to the question, "Can computers think?", ExperTax provides an answer of sorts. When the program is searching for issues based on a set of question responses, a corner of the monitor screen flashes the word "thinking" on and off.

Key Terms You Should Know

artificial intelligence (AI)
backward chaining
certainty factors
command-driven system
communications-based systems
decision support systems (DSSs)
dialogue
domain data base
expert systems
expert system shell
flexible and adaptive
forward chaining
general-purpose planning languages
inference engine
interactive systems
knowledge data base
knowledge engineer
learning
local area networks

model base
natural language processing
neural networks
nonprocedural
operational decisions
operational support systems
parameters
planning language
production rules
real-time systems
semantic networks
special-purpose planning languages
speech recognition systems
strategic decisions
tactical decisions
transaction processing
Turing test
unstructured problems
vision and speech recognition systems

Discussion Questions

16-1. What advances in technology have fueled the evolution of computer processing? Describe these advances in terms of software, hardware, and the processing environment.

16-2. How can data or transaction processing be characterized? What are some of the transaction processing systems which have been discussed so far in this text?

16-3. What types of management decisions are supported by operational support systems? Are these types of decisions different from those supported by decision support systems? In what ways?

16-4. Name three examples of operational support systems and describe their features. How do they differ from one another?

16-5. What are the characteristics of decision support systems? Are any of these characteristics similar to those of other processing systems? How so?

16-6. Name some accounting decisions which might be improved by the use of a decision support system. What are the special characteristics of these decisions which make them amenable to decision support?

16-7. Several examples of decision support systems are described in the chapter. Can you think of some others?

16-8. What kinds of models might be used in a decision support system model base?

16-9. What kind of data would be included in a decision support system data base?

16-10. What are some of the types of artificial intelligence? Name some possible applications for each of these.

16-11. Do you believe that computers can think? Why or why not?

16-12. Is the Turing test a good determinant of the thinking ability of a computer? Can you think of some other tests which might prove or disprove that a computer can reason? Explain.

16-13. What are production rules? How are they used to accomplish reasoning?

16-14. Construct some production rules using If-Then statements for an accounting problem such as the decision about whether or not a lease should be capitalized. Do you see how Generally Accepted Accounting Principles might be represented by such rules?

16-15. Which employees tend to use expert systems? What are the responsibilities of each? How do they make the system work? What kinds of data or information is provided by each of these people to the system?

16-16. What is the difference between a domain data base and a knowledge data base?

16-17. How does the inference engine "drive" the expert system?

16-18. Explain the difference between forward and backward chaining.

16-19. Explain how expert system development tools can facilitate the building of expert systems.

16-20. What is an expert system shell? Why is it called a "shell?"

16-21. What are the goals or objectives of decision support versus expert systems? Explain how you think each of these kinds of systems might be used in a practical sense in an AIS environment.

16-22. If you were a knowledge engineer, how would you gain an understanding of the thought processes of an expert? In other words, how might you "mine" knowledge regarding experience and expertise from an expert?

16-23. Refer to Figure 16-5. What are some application areas for expert systems in accounting that are not shown here?

Problems

16-24. (Library Research) From such publications as *Management Accounting, The Journal of Accountancy, The CPA Journal,* or other sources, obtain an article which describes an operational support system, a decision support system, or an expert system in detail. Does the article describe the system in terms of some of the characteristics mentioned in this chapter?

16-25. For each of the following accounting application areas, indicate whether they are best served by a data processing system, an operational support system, a decision support system, or an expert system.

a. Check processing in accounts payable.
b. Individual income tax return preparation.
c. Determining the estimated amount of allowance for uncollectible accounts.
d. Calculating reorder points for parts inventory.

e. Determining the best tax planning strategy for a partnership.
f. Making a capital budgeting decision regarding investment in plant and equipment.
g. Fixed asset management and depreciation calculations.
h. Determining audit scope based on preliminary internal control system evaluation and compliance tests.
i. Projecting future sales based on economic forecasts and market predictions.

16-26. Expert systems are developed to make expert decisions. They are programmed with the experience and knowledge of an expert. Do you think there is a risk that an expert system could replace accountants and auditors? Why or why not?

16-27. Boris Baker owns and operates a small local chain of Bulgarian restaurants. He currently uses an integrated accounting package for processing general ledger, accounts receivable, accounts payable, and inventory transactions. He uses a data processing service for his payroll processing. Boris is wondering if he could use a decision support or expert system in his business.

Requirements

A. Advise Boris as to whether or not he should buy some decision support system software or an expert system shell.
B. Suggest what kinds of decisions a decision support system could be used for in a local restaurant chain.
C. What are some characteristics of a business you would look for in determining whether decision support or expert system software is useful?

16-28. Choose an accounting statement issued by the Financial Accounting Standards Board or Accounting Principles Board which would lend itself well to automation as an expert system. List several production files, in the form of if-then statements, which would automate the application of that particular accounting principle.

16-29. The following is a math problem with missing digits. Each letter represents a digit. Try to find which letter represents which digit. In solving the problem, think about the reasoning process you use. How would a computer solve this problem? How do you think your reasoning process could be captured in if-then production rules in an expert system?

$$\times \begin{array}{r} AR \\ 9T \\ \hline A0T \\ 2NF \\ \hline AKFT \end{array}$$

(Hint: A *must be equal to either 2 or 3.)*

CASE ANALYSES

16-30. *The Crawford Company*

After extensive analysis of several integrated accounting software packages, Peggy Joyce, the controller of the Crawford Company, had eliminated all but three as being unsatisfactory but was still unsure about which package to select for her business. The cost and hardware requirements for each product were approximately equal. Package A seemed to have the best Payroll and General Ledger systems, but its Accounts Receivable module was very weak. Package B handled Accounts Receivable well, but all other modules were only marginally adequate. Finally, Package C's strength was its Accounts Receivable and General Ledger modules, but it was particularly poor in the areas of Accounts Payable and Payroll due to weaknesses in its internal control features. In order to select a software package among these three, Peggy decided to use *Expert Choice,* a decision support system available from Decision Support Software of McLean Virginia.

Expert Choice is an interactive program that can be run on personal and small business computers. It has been used by managers and other decision-makers to support many different types of decisions in areas such as transportation, politics, and business. To analyze problems with *Expert Choice,* the user forms a problem into a hierarchical structure. The problem hierarchy will have at least three levels. The top of the hierarchy defines the problem's goal, the second level will consist of criteria to be considered relative to that goal, and the bottom level consists of alternative solutions to the problem.

Figure 16-19 is a printout from *Expert Choice* of the hierarchy Peggy Joyce constructed to solve her prob-

lem. The top of the hierarchy is the goal, which in this case is the selection of the best software package. The second level contains the various modules in the integrated packages. These are the factors to be considered in selecting the best software. The lowest level of the hierarchy consists of the three alternative packages being considered. At first the relative weights or rankings of each factor and each alternative are equal. To prioritize the factors and alternatives, the user (Peggy Joyce) will interact with the computer to evaluate each criterion (the accounting information system modules). For example, the relative importance of the Accounts Receivable module versus the Accounts Payable system is indicated by Peggy. This illustrates an important feature of a decision support system: The user ultimately does the evaluation and makes the decision—the decision support system is simply a tool to assist the decision-maker. *Expert Choice* is valuable in that it helps a decision-maker to consider all the variables for the decision in an optimal and logical fashion. Once all of the judgments are input by the user, *Expert Choice* activates its model base to rank the factors.

The final step in using *Expert Choice* to help Peggy select the best integrated accounting package for her firm is to indicate the relative strength of each alternative package in handling each of the relevant accounting modules. For example, we know that Package A has the best Payroll subsystem, Package B handles Payroll adequately, and Package C's Payroll module is poor. Peggy will indicate this, again in an interactive mode with the computer. *Expert Choice* then uses all of the decision maker's inputs to indicate a ranking of the alternatives. Figures 16-10 to 16-13 are some of the printouts generated by the software which show the results of this analysis.

Required:

1. What do you see as the advantage of using *Expert Choice* to solve this problem? Are there any disadvantages?

2. How do you think a decision support system such as *Expert Choice* could be used to help accountants make other decisions in their work? What types of decisions would lend themselves to this type of analysis?

3. Why is *Expert Choice* a decision support system rather than an expert system?

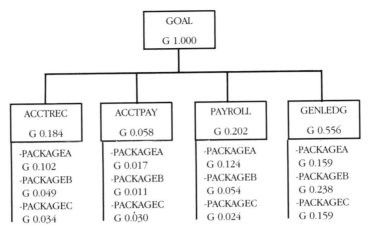

ACCTPAY   — ACCOUNTS PAYABLE MODULE
ACCTREC   — ACCOUNTS RECEIVABLE MODULE
GENLEDG — GENERAL LEDGER MODULE
PACKAGEA — SOFTWARE PACKAGE A
PACKAGEB — SOFTWARE PACKAGE B
PACKAGEC — SOFTWARE PACKAGE C
PAYROLL   — PAYROLL MODULE

G   — GLOBAL PRIORITY: PRIORITY RELATIVE TO GOAL

FIGURE 16-9   The hierarchy of data printed by Expert Choice, a decision support software package, for a software—selection decision.

Select Best Software Package

Synthesis of Leaf Nodes with respect to GOAL

OVERALL INCONSISTENCY INDEX = 0.06

PACKAGEA 0.402
PACKAGEB 0.352
PACKAGEC 0.246

1.000

PACKAGEA—SOFTWARE PACKAGE A
PACKAGEB—SOFTWARE PACKAGE B
PACKAGEC—SOFTWARE PACKAGE C

FIGURE 16-10   The user should select the alternative with the largest value—in this case, software package A.

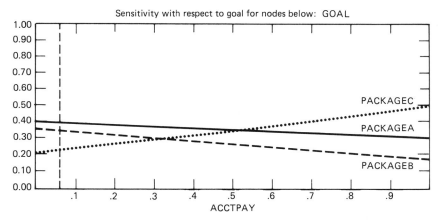

FIGURE 16-11 How the rankings of the three packages vary if the accounts payable component varies from a weight of 0 to a weight of 1. The current weight (.058 from Figure 16-9) is shown by the vertical dotted line.

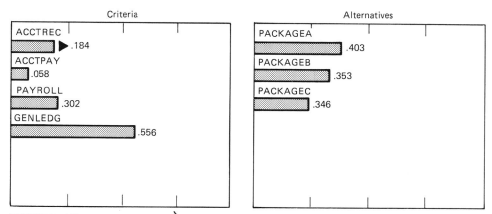

FIGURE 16-12 A bar chart of the criteria weights from Figure 16-9, and the final choice rankings from Figure 16-10. Discrepancies are due to rounding.

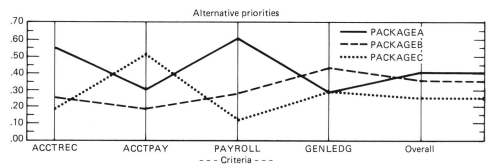

FIGURE 16-13 This figure shows how each software package would fare if only one criterion—for example, accounts receivable—were used for the evaluation.

16-31. *An Accounting Expert System*

Figure 16-5 in this chapter provided some examples of real-world expert systems for accounting applications. Identify another accounting application for which an expert system would be appropriate. For this application, determine what would be included in the domain data base, the knowledge data base, and the inference engine. Explain how the knowledge engineer would gather specific information for this program.

17

Accounting Information Systems for Small Businesses

Among the important questions that you should be able to answer after reading this chapter are:

1. What is meant by the term *small* in small business?
2. What are the informational needs of the small business and how do these needs differ from those of the larger organization?
3. What are the major drawbacks of no formal accounting system in a small business?
4. What type of computer hardware and software is available for the small business that wants to computerize some of its accounting applications?
5. How should the small business choose the computer hardware and software for an automated accounting information system? Are there other alternatives available to the small business besides the purchase or lease of expensive computer products?

INTRODUCTION

The informational needs of the small business may differ from those of a larger organization. As a result, it is necessary to design specialized accounting information systems to meet these needs. Design considerations, special factors involved in implementation and maintenance, and the availability of computer hardware and software as alternatives to manual systems all play a role. These are the subjects of this chapter.

To begin, it is important to make clear what is meant by *small business*. The definition is provided by the Small Business Administration of the federal government and depends on the type of work involved. In manufacturing, the classification is based on the number of employees within a certain type of industry. Thus, apparel and textile companies are regarded as "small" if they have no more than 250 employees, whereas for producers of aircraft and ammunition, the number is 1500 employees.

In the service industries, the criterion is dollar volume of sales: a maximum of $7.5 million for department stores and groceries, $6.5 million for auto dealers, $2 million for most other retailers, $9.5 million for general contractors, and $9.5 million for most wholesalers. Thus, *small business* does not necessarily imply "tiny business."

As we have defined them, there are over 9 million small businesses in the United States. This represents 95% of all businesses, over 50% of the entire national payroll, and about 30% of the gross national product.

Small companies tend to be more flexible than larger companies in the ways they do business, but they are also more vulnerable to unfavorable turns in the economy. Although it is tempting to joke that the major needs of a small business are money, money, and more money, the fact remains that small businesses often find themselves in financial binds. Business failures, which are disproportionately high in small businesses, are an important element in the total business turnover (liquidations, takeovers, mergers, etc.) within the economy.

One of the primary causes of small business failures is a simple lack of accounting information of one kind or another. Examples include an inability to forecast cash needs, incomplete information regarding the balances of individual merchandise inventory items, inadequate communication between the small business and its suppliers, and a weak audit trail of transactions. In some instances, the necessary accounting data are being collected, but at too slow a pace to be of much use.

In the sections of the chapter that follow, therefore, we examine the informational needs of small businesses and those accounting methods and machines particularly designed to meet small business needs in an efficient, cost-effective manner. A supplement at the end of this chapter discusses the use of microcomputers in small business. The supplement looks at strategies for effective microcomputer management.

DESIGN CONSIDERATIONS

The owners of small businesses are prone to look on accounting as a time-consuming nuisance or, at best, an inconvenience. They may feel that only large companies need a formal accounting information system. Because of this misconception, many owners attempt to remain in operation without any specific system of accounting, or with a system inadequate for their organizations' needs.

It is true that many small businesses do not need elaborate financial reporting systems because they have a low volume of accounting transactions as compared with larger organizations, and they need not devote a large amount of resources to record-keeping operations. However, these businesses still need a functional accounting system that provides timely information to internal decision makers and to external parties such as stockholders, creditors, government tax agencies, and various governmental regulatory agencies such as the Securities and Exchange Commission.

When designing an accounting information system for a small business, the following characteristics of small businesses should be considered in the design of an effective accounting information system.

1. **Simplicity.** Small businesses tend to be less complicated. Thus, the accounting information system designed for them should be simple and straightforward.
2. **Lack of Specialized Accounting Personnel.** In the very smallest organizations, the owner is often also the accountant. In most small businesses, however, there tends to be a concentration of accounting responsibilities in a small staff. As a result, accounting expertise may be limited, the number of financial reports prepared may be small, and the separation of related organizational responsibilities may be difficult to achieve. The design of an affective accounting information system must deal with these limitations.
3. **Closely Held Ownership.** Family ownership or a very limited number of stockholders may eliminate the need for lengthy financial reports. Owner familiarity with the daily operations of the company may also limit the amount of detail required in financial statements.
4. **Lack of Working Capital.** The entrepreneurial small business is often described as "long on ideas, short on money." Without much working capital, the need for a cost-effective accounting information system becomes that much more important.
5. **Lack of Financial Skills.** Unless the small business itself is an accounting firm, it is likely that the managers of the company have technical, marketing, or artistic backgrounds rather than accounting backgrounds. Thus, these managers may be uninterested in the accounting system of the organization or unskilled in using a good one effectively.
6. **Informal Organizational Structure.** The small size of the business will usually foster communication among employees and therefore limit the number of formal reports required. A lack of rules and policies may also result in only loosely defined accounting procedures and controls. An informal managerial style may not need a sophisticated accounting system, but the absence of consistent accounting practice will usually work against good managerial decision making.
7. **Lack of Integrated Accounting Applications.** The maintenance of a manual accounting system or the computerization of accounting applications one at a time usually results in a nonintegrated financial system. As a result, financial reporting may be piecemeal and extra work will be required to prepare important financial reports.
8. **Lack of Computer Expertise.** The officers of a small business must concentrate on daily operations, leaving little time or inclination to keep up with computer technology. The lack of in-house computer expertise usually leads to a dependence on outside vendors for computer hardware and software. As a result, the small business may purchase equipment or software that does not fully meet informational needs or, alternatively, purchase computer resources in excess of data processing requirements.

These design considerations make clear the special nature of small businesses and the specialized needs that such businesses must meet when designing effective accounting information systems. The following paragraphs describe several types of accounting information systems that might meet these needs.

MANUAL ACCOUNTING SYSTEMS FOR SMALL BUSINESS

The small business that utilizes a manual accounting system will likely have either no formal accounting system or a double-entry accounting system.

No Formal Accounting System

Some small businesses really have no organized method of recording data—that is, they have no formal accounting system. Under these circumstances, there is usually a single bank checking account into which all business income is deposited and out of which all bills and salaries are paid. Usually, the business with no formal accounting system temporarily employs an outside accountant to perform what bookkeeping or tax-preparing tasks are required, and this person is forced to rely on minimal documentation.

A characteristic of no-system accounting is the absence of any journals or ledgers with which to systemically record financial transactions. This is called a **ledgerless accounting system.** Using a ledgerless accounting system, the small business relies on such items as payment receipts, check stubs, and cash register tapes to provide accounting data.

The chief advantage of the ledgerless accounting system is its simplicity. The fact that no accounting skills are required is another advantage. Minimal cost might be a third advantage, although the lack of an accounting system may prove expensive in the long run.

The chief drawbacks of a ledgerless system are (1) minimal accounting documentation, (2) no double-entry recording of transactions with which to ensure recording accuracy and completeness, (3) an absence of accounting controls, (4) no accurate way with which to measure company performance or net worth, (5) great difficulty in detecting or recovering from lost documents, and (6) no audit trail by which to trace the processing of accounting documents. In the opinion of the authors, an absence of systematic procedures with which to record and aggregate accounting transactions is both inefficient and irresponsible.

Double-Entry Accounting Systems

With a **double-entry accounting system,** each accounting transaction is recorded in a jour-

nal (or journals, when specialized journals such as sales journals and cash receipts journals are used). Each accounting transaction is then posted to the appropriate general ledger account (and possibly subsidiary ledger accounts) affected by the transaction. Inasmuch as double-entry accounting systems are studied extensively in introductory accounting courses, they will not be examined further in this chapter. However, a unique type of manual accounting system that might be worthy of special attention is the **matrix accounting system** presented in Appendix C of this text.

The establishment of a double-entry accounting system offers a number of advantages to a small business. A few of these advantages are:

1. An effective double-entry accounting system enables the small business to accumulate financial data in an orderly manner. The systematic use of accounting source documents is itself an improvement over no accounting system.

2. A double-entry accounting system enables the small business to create conventional financial reports. These reports can then be used by (a) internal managers to aid decision making and (b) external creditors and investors.

3. An effective double-entry accounting system establishes an audit trail. As a result, the accountant can trace financial transactions through the information system of a small business.

4. The establishment of a double-entry accounting system provides the small business with a feedback control mechanism. This is the internal check function discussed in Chapter 9. Since the total debits must equal the total credits from all recorded business transactions, any recording errors should be detected through the preparation of such reports as a trial balance. Thus, the trial balance becomes an important feedback control within the double-entry accounting system of a small business.

COMPUTERIZED ACCOUNTING INFORMATION SYSTEMS

Today, even the smallest business can usually benefit from some kind of electronic data processing device when performing its accounting functions. The following sections describe several types of computer systems that a small business might consider.

Microcomputers

Over the last few years, the market for microcomputers has been growing in excess of 40% per year. Much of this market is attributable to small businesses that are now able to afford computerized systems for the first time.

The technology of the microcomputer has been changing so rapidly that it is difficult to write anything that will not be outdated within a year. For the purposes of discussion, however, it is convenient at this time to classify microcomputers into three types: (1) lap-top microcomputers, (2) personal microcomputers, and (3) business microcomputers.

Laptop Microcomputers

A laptop microcomputer is characterized by its size—it is small enough to literally fit in the user's lap. Laptop microcomputers are portable and can be stored in a briefcase. This is an advantage for users who need to take their computers to the field. For example, a busy executive can use a laptop computer on an airplane to prepare for meetings at his or her destination. Journalists can use laptops at the site of their story to word-process and transmit the story back home (most laptops have an internal modem). Auditors can use laptops to analyze financial statements while working at their client's offices.

Laptop computers have come a long way in terms of their processing power and other capabilities. Early laptops had the advantage of being portable but were limited in terms of memory, display, and availability of software. New laptops have expanded memory with high-speed hard disks, easier to read displays, and much of the same software that is available on full size microcomputers. For example, the Compaq SLT/286 laptop computer has an 80286 processor, a 40 megabyte hard disk, and yet it measures only 13.5 inches wide by 8.5 inches deep and 4 inches thick. This computer can run for over five hours on a battery pack and a spare can be inserted if necessary. As for software, the Compaq SLT/286 can run about anything, including graphics packages and OS/2 software. The Compaq represents the high end of the laptop market, both in size (14 pounds versus 4 for some) and a relatively expensive price tag. Innovations in this class of computer are expected to continue and sizes and prices will most likely keep decreasing and capability increasing in the next few years.

Personal Microcomputers

The **personal microcomputer** gets its name from the fact that it is usually designed and marketed for the use of one person. However, both small and large business managers can make good use of personal microcomputers to process business data, prepare budgets, simulate future business conditions, type memos, and communicate with other managers via electronic mail. Most of these business applications are critically dependent on microcomputer software, which is either **bundled** (i.e., included in the price of the computer hardware at the time of sale) or must be purchased separately at additional cost. Microcomputer software is discussed in detail later in this chapter.

The typical personal microcomputer includes 640k of memory, a full-size keyboard with user-programmable keys, one or more floppy disk drives, an optional hard disk drive, several expansion slots, and an optional modem. Printers and monitors are extra. Figure 17-1 provides an example. Most modern *16- or 32-bit microcomputers* enable their users to expand memory size to over 1 megabyte of computer storage.

FIGURE 17-1   An example of a desktop microcomputer—and IBM personal computer. The IBM PC was one of the first 16-bit personal microcomputers developed.

Some portable microcomputers come with built-in CRT screens called monitors with which to view computer data. Other micros require the addition of an external screen device such as a household TV or a separately purchased monitor. The screen displays of the personal microcomputers are often in color and some have the capability to draw high-resolution pictures called **computer graphics.** As illustrated in Figure 17-2, graphics capabilities enable the user to draw bar graphs, pie charts, and other pictorial displays that aid the user in presenting ideas to business customers and clients. Graphics displays are also useful in providing visual depictions of financial data for internal business uses.

Personal microcomputers usually come as desktop models, meaning that they can sit comfortably on a corner of a desk. The square footage of desk space occupied is sometimes called the **footprint** of the microcomputer. Where office space is at a premium, the small space occupied by a personal microcomputer is important.

Business Microcomputers

The typical small business will probably be most interested in acquiring a **business microcomputer** to process its accounting data. Sometimes, the business microcomputer is an enhanced personal microcomputer that has been configured with additional internal memory, additional

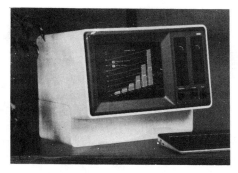

FIGURE 17-2   An example of computer graphics used to present financial data in an interesting and informative manner.

floppy disk drives, a **letter-quality** (i.e., high-quality) **printer,** a hard-disk drive for large files of data or sets of programs, and accounting application software. At other times, however, a business microcomputer is a machine that has been designed specifically for business data processing. Figure 17-3 provides an example.

A business microcomputer can usually be programmed in a number of high-level programming languages such as BASIC, COBOL, FORTRAN, or PASCAL. Since business data processing is often dependent on master files and transaction files, the business microcomputer is usually configured with a large amount of file space either in the form of multiple, large-capacity floppy disk drives or a hard (multimega byte) disk. Since output reports are also vital to business data processing, the business microcomputer is typically connected to one or more high-quality printers.

More than any other type of data processing, business data processing is typically performed with **canned computer software.** Thus, the business microcomputer is usually a machine for which a variety of accounting programs are available and immediately implementable on the microcomputer.

Both small and large businesses that purchase microcomputers may want their machines linked together. In such instances, each microcomputer can act as either a stand-alone processor or a communications terminal in a **computer network.** For example, local area networks enable users to transfer files, computer programs, reports, and personal messages to one another.

Microcomputer Software

There is a vast array of computer software available for microcomputers, and much of it is de-

FIGURE 17-3   An example of a microcomputer system specifically designed for a small business.

signed for the benefit or amusement of the individual. Here, we limit our discussion to software of potential interest to the small business.

There are five major accounting applications typically available on microcomputers.

1. General ledger.
2. Accounts receivable.
3. Accounts payable.
4. Inventory control.
5. Payroll.

It is difficult to imagine any business microcomputer that does not have the software to perform *at least* these five major accounting functions and most business microcomputers have available software that goes well beyond these basic accounting needs. It is also important to note that much of the best software for business microcomputers is supplied by independent vendors and software companies that specialize in developing computer programs for microcomputer business applications.

A number of additional software packages may be of interest to the small business. These include the following.

Microcomputer Operating Systems

A microcomputer **operating system** is a set of supervisory/control programs under which application software is run. The operating system of a microcomputer is therefore much like the operating system of the larger computer discussed in Chapter 4. Like most other application software, accounting software for microcomputers must be run under an operating system of some type. At the time this book was written, the most popular operating system for 16-bit microcomputers was *MS/DOS* (MicroSoft Disk Operating System).

Electronic Spreadsheet Software

An **electronic spreadsheet** enables the user to develop columns and rows of numbers on a video screen. The resulting grid of entries can be used for planning purposes—for example, the preparation of a budget or the development of a detailed forecast. One advantage of the electronic spreadsheet over the manually prepared grid is the user's ability to define complex formulas that are computed automatically when the appropriate data are provided and to change data values as requirements dictate. These and other advantages of electronic spreadsheets were discussed extensively in Chapter 3.

Word Processing

Word-processing software permits the user to create and edit documents such as memos, letters, and other written reports on a video screen instead of a typewriter. The computer files created by this software are simply records containing words instead of financial figures. Most word processors can also assist the user in formatting text, changing the design of output reports, and paginating the final copy. Space does not permit a full discussion of all the processing capabilities of modern word processors, but such software is clearly desirable to both small businesses with limited secretarial support and to business managers from an organization of any size who must prepare documents.

Spellers

A **speller** is a computerized dictionary of English words and a software program that checks the words from a text file (i.e., a computerized document) against this dictionary. The speller goes through the words of the user's text one by one, looking up each word. The speller catches misspellings and other "typos" because these mistaken words are not in the dictionary. Some dictionaries are specially created for certain applications (e.g., medical or legal applications) and therefore have technical terms not likely to be found in regular dictionaries. Most spelling systems will also permit the user to add new words to their dictionaries if desired. Speller software is typically sold in conjunction with word-processing software, although word-processing software and spelling software are typically separate software packages.

Data Base Management Systems

Data base management systems permit the microcomputer user to create his or her own files with individually designed record formats. As a result, the user is not dependent on the file design specifications of the canned software packages but can create business files for custom uses. For the most part, the data base management systems designed for the microcomputer are not nearly as powerful or flexible as those available for mainframe computers. On the other hand, the current popularity of this type of software reflects the large number of uses for microcomputer-based data-management systems.

The major growth in the use of microcomputers by companies has made it more difficult for the managements of these companies to exercise control over their firms' data processing functions. Therefore, to provide a more in-depth examination of microcomputer systems, the supplement at the end of this chapter discusses strategies for effective microcomputer management.

Minicomputers

A **minicomputer** is a computer that is larger than a microcomputer and smaller than a full-size, mainframe computer. Figure 17-4 provides an example. The typical minicomputer costs between $10,000 and $100,000. The distinction between the most expensive microcomputer (i.e., the **high** end of the microcomputer scale) and the least expensive minicomputer (i.e., the *low* end of the minicomputer scale) is blurry.

Some individuals have found it useful to distinguish between *minicomputers* and **small business computers.** Where a computer manufacturer has chosen to develop a system of computer hardware and software suited to the general needs of the small business, this distinction is meaningless. In such instances, the small business computer *is* a minicomputer. However, many larger organizations have found other uses for minicomputers, especially as dedicated machines. In these latter instances, the distinction between a minicomputer and a small business computer may make sense.

FIGURE 17-4 An example of a minicomputer that a small business might use to meet its data processing needs.

Minicomputers use at least 2 bytes for each computer word in their memories and most use 4 bytes for this purpose. As a result, the addressable memory of the typical minicomputer can be expanded to well over 10 megabytes of primary storage. Thus, the capabilities of many minicomputers equal those of larger systems, and often it is only *price* that distinguishes minicomputers from larger types of central processing units.

A minicomputer often best serves the needs of small businesses that want to provide multiuser access to the same computer files—a common requirement of accounting applications. A minicomputer can also support a large number of peripheral devices, including high-speed printers, full-fledged tape drives, and specialized types of communication equipment. Thus, in contrast to the microcomputer, many minicomputers are full-fledged business machines capable of performing all of the data processing functions of a business.

Software

The lack of programming expertise in the typical small business means that the manufacturers of small business machines must anticipate the informational needs of small business management and provide for these needs in software support. In the area of accounting, this had led to the development of integrated accounting systems that may be purchased by the small business and used for typical accounting applications. The accounting programs are integrated in the sense that several programs are likely to use the same set of disk or tape files and are likely to have standardized input and output formatting. Consistent, easily understood programming documentation may also be expected.

Figures 17-5 and 17-6 illustrate reports from a typical small business system that were processed on a Burroughs B80 small business computer. Figure 17-5 illustrates two reports that would be used for inventory control. Note that the Buyer's Guide will answer such fundamental questions as: (1) Do we have to place an order?

(2) How many widgets do we currently have on hand? (3) When did we last receive a shipment? (4) Which vendor usually supplies this item? (5) How many of these items have we ordered to date? Similarly, the Potential Excess Stock on Hand Report can answer such questions as: (1) Where is there excess inventory? (2) How much excess money do we have tied up in extra inventory stock? (3) How many periods can we go before a new order would be required? (4) Are our reorder points or safety stock values poorly determined? (5) Is the lead time realistic?

Figure 17-6 illustrates two potential reports for an accounts payable application. Questions that can be answered by the Cash Requirements Report include: (1) How much money is currently due? (2) How much money is due in the future? (3) Are there any invoices overdue? (4) How much discount should be taken? (5) How much discount will be lost? (6) Should payment be made in foreign currency? (7) Should only partial payment be made? (8) Which companies must we pay first, and for which companies can we delay payment? Similarly, for the Periodic Liabilities Forecast we can answer a number of questions, but by now you get the idea.

Inasmuch as the typical small business has limited computer expertise, it is often at a distinct disadvantage when shopping for computer software. Usually, the shopping objective is clear: to find accounting packages that will meet the small business's individual needs. In so doing, however, the small business must strike a delicate balance between room for growth on the one hand and needless, costly sophistication on the other. The following sources of accounting software may enable the small business to begin its search for the right system.

Minicomputer Manufacturers

This is usually the first place to look for business software, as many computer manufacturers develop customized accounting software for their equipment in parallel with the development of their computer hardware. Most of the CPU manu-

ABC COMPANY

BUYER'S GUIDE

PRD CAT STOCK NUMBER DESCRIPTION-REFERENCE	VNDR NO	STD ORD QTY / RE-ORDER PT	STOCK AVAILABLE / ON ORDER	BALANCES ON HAND / SAFTY STK	UNIT AVG CST / UNIT RPL CST	CURRENT ISS PER TO DTE / YEAR TO DTE	PREVIOUS ISS PER TO DTE / YEAR TO DTE	DATE LAST ISSUE / RECEIPT	LEAD TIME DAYS
004 12415710 SCREWDRIVER 6"	2141678	250 / 500	755	755 / 100	1.185 / 1.193	703 / 1,203	479 / 1,090	02 25 8- / 02 10 8-	015
004 12415730 SCREWDRIVER 8"	2141678	250 / 500 **	383 / 500	983 / 500	1.3152 / 1.32	613 / 1,251	534 / 906	02 13 8- / 01 28 8-	015
004 12415740 SCREWDRIVER 10"	2141678	250 / 500 **	450	450 / 200	1.47 / 1.5215	345 / 612	476 / 820	02 27 8- / 02 20 8-	015
004 12415750 SCREWDRIVER 12"	2141678	250 / 500 **	315	315 / 200	1.6554 / 1.6554	282 / 571	321 / 530	02 26 8- / 02 26 8-	021

ABC COMPANY

POTENTIAL EXCESS STOCK ON 03 01 8-

PRD STOCK NUMBER CAT DESCRIPTION-REFERENCE	NET ISSUES THIS YEAR CURRENT PER / YEAR TO DATE	ISSUES LAST YEAR CURRENT PER / YEAR TO DATE	QUANTITY ON HAND ON ORDER	NO OF PRDS ISS ON HND PER YR TO DATE	THEORETICAL MAX QTY OH / STANDARD ORDER QTY	POTENTIAL QUANTITY CURRENT PER / YEAR TO DATE	EXCESS VALUE CURRENT PER / YEAR TO DATE	LEAD TIME DAYS
004 12415710 SCREWDRIVER 6"	703 / 1,203	479 / 1,090	755	1.1 / 1.3	350 / 250	405 / 253	480 / 300	015
004 12416101 PLIERS 6"	12 / 31	8 / 41	75	6.3 / 4.8	40 / 20	35 / 49	111 / 156	021
004 12447401 PLIERS 8"	423 / 792	520 / 1,025	1,295	3.1 / 3.3	600 / 200	695 / 712	2,853 / 2,923	021
004 12447601 PLIERS 10"	363 / 699	203 / 509	801	2.2 / 2.3	200 / 100	601 / 637	2,545 / 2,698	021

TOTAL PRODUCT CATEGORY 004   5,989 / 6,077

GRAND TOTALS   78,436 / 105,295

FIGURE 17-5 Two inventory control reports for a small business system. (Forms courtesy of Burroughs Corporation.)

ABC COMPANY — ACCOUNTS PAYABLE CASH REQUIREMENTS

DATE 03 20 8-   PAGE 3

TRANS CTRL NO	PC INVOICE NUMBER	INVOICE DATE	INVOICE DUE DATE	GROSS AMOUNT	DISCOUNT ALLOWABLE	NET AMOUNT DUE CURRENT 03 20 8-	FUTURE 03 31 8-
2000030 RICHARDSON DIVISION							
214	A534567	03 15 8-	03 25 8-***	500.00	10.00	490.00	
			TOTAL VENDOR	500.00	10.00	490.00	.00
2900680 URBAN OFFICE SUPPLIES							
176	60139	02 18 8-	03 18 8-***	300.00	.00	300.00 *	
			TOTAL VENDOR	300.00		*	.00
4000618 ROBERTS METALS							
198	A06194	03 05 8-	03 15 8-***	325.00	6.50 *	325.00	
230	A06896	03 19 8-	03 29 8-	400.00	8.00	392.00	
			TOTAL VENDOR	725.00	8.00	717.00	.00
8000618 KUROSAKA ELECTRONICS ***							
217 1	30619-1	03 10 8-	04 10 8-	166.67	.00		166.67
217 2	30619-2	03 10 8-	05 10 8-	166.67	.00		166.67
217 3	30619-3	03 10 8-	06 10 8-	166.66	.00		166.66
				500.00	.00		500.00

* DISCOUNT TO BE LOST   * PAST DUE

ABC COMPANY — ACCOUNTS PAYABLE PERIODIC LIABILITIES FORECAST

DATE 03 19 8-   PAGE 3

TRANS CTRL NO	CHECK NO	TRN ST	INVOICE NUMBER	---0--- 03 10	---1--- 03 20	---2--- 03 31	---3--- 04 11	---4--- 04 22	---5--- 05 03	---6--- 05 14	---7--- 05 25	---8--- 06 05	---9--- 06 16
4000618 ROBERTS METALS				***	***								
198		INVOIC	A06194	325.00									
230		INVOIC	A06896		400.00								
			VENDOR TOTALS	325.00	400.00								
8000618 KUROSAKA ELECTRONICS						***							
217 1		INVOIC	30619-1			166.67							
217 2		INVOIC	30619-2						166.67				
217 3		INVOIC	30619-3									166.66	
			VENDOR TOTALS			166.67			166.67			166.66	
			GRAND TOTALS	3,750.00	2,800.00	1,300.00	700.00	816.67	800.00	375.00	666.66	425.00	

FIGURE 17-6 Two accounts payable reports for a small business system. (Forms courtesy of Burroughs Corporation.)

663

facturers will have general-purpose accounting software available for their machines.

Software Houses

Software houses are independent companies that develop proprietary software for either sale or lease. These companies often specialize in the development of computer software for a specific industry or specific types of computer systems. Software houses are an especially good source for accounting software that has been customized to a particular type of business—for example, an auto parts distributor or a fast-food restaurant chain.

Software Brokers

A **software broker** is an individual who specializes in matching a client's software require-ments with available software packages. These individuals are valuable to the small business facing the unfamiliar chores of assessing com-puter needs and doing its own shopping for a computer system.

Software Listings

There are several "encyclopedias" of computer software that the individual small business may purchase. Although the listings in these pub-lications may be sketchy, they may also provide a useful lead to desired computer packages.

Advertisements in Computer Periodicals

There are over 200 computer trade publications, and the vast majority of these carry adver-tisements for computer software. Three exam-ples of advertisements for minicomputer ac-counting software are provided in Figure 17-7.

FIGURE 17-7   Advertisements for accounting software developed specially for minicomputers.

SELECTION CRITERIA FOR SMALL BUSINESS

The first step in the design or selection of an accounting system for a small business is the same as for a large organization: a survey and assessment of informational needs. The formation of a **computer-evaluation committee** is a good approach for accomplishing this task. For the small business, the computer-evaluation committee may consist of just one individual, or it may consist of many individuals representing the various interests of the company. For example, each of the following individuals could make a major contribution to the computer-selection process.

1. Representatives from the user group(s) requiring data processing services.
2. Technical experts, such as data processing planners and systems personnel, to prepare requests for computer vendor proposals.
3. Accounting personnel to prepare cost/benefit analyses of various proposals and to evaluate procurement alternatives.
4. Legal representatives to protect the rights of the company in contracts with vendors and to seek legal remedies in the event of default by vendors.
5. EDP auditors to ensure the presence of adequate accounting controls.

The committee's first job is to analyze the company's actual data processing needs. To determine the size of the computer system required, the committee must ascertain if the company is meeting its present data processing objectives and also attempt to project the company's future data processing needs. The committee must also be able to communicate its company's data processing needs through a systems specifications report (discussed in Chapter 14). This report is submitted to hardware and software vendors and forms a basis for vendors' subsequent computer proposals. It is called a **request for proposal (RFP).**

A small business may have a difficult time in executing these procedures. Among the special problems that tend to arise in the small business are:

1. In-house computer expertise may be lacking.
2. The small business may not be able to assess its own data processing needs very well.
3. Management may not wish to use much employee time shopping for a computerized system.
4. The company's geographical location may limit access to a large number of hardware and software vendors.
5. Top management may be too busy or too disinterested to prioritize accounting and information processing needs.
6. The individuals who do the investigation may do so informally and unsystematically.
7. No formal *RFP* may be prepared and sent to vendors.

Following are eight key ideas that may be useful to a small business in its search for an effective computerized accounting system.

Assess Requirements

The small business should prepare a "shopping list" of data processing requirements before it starts looking for an accounting system. This list of requirements should be developed by the new system's *users*—perhaps with input from top management and with the help of a management consultant. Budget constraints should be only one of the many criteria on the list.

Software Drives Hardware

What is most required of an accounting system is the ability to generate useful information, usually in the form of output reports—not an expensive electronic device. The vast majority of the accounting requirements of a small business will therefore be met with accounting *software,* and only indirectly with computer hardware. Choosing accounting software is a difficult task, as there are many factors to consider. There is no single *best* package that will fit all small business accounting needs, but rather different packages have distinct advantages and disadvantages for a particular business. For example, one software package may have a very strong accounts receivable function, including the ability to handle a large number of customers. The same package might, however, not compare favorably with others in its chart of accounts structure. The trick is to find the *best* package for your particular business.

In choosing accounting software, be careful not to let vendor claims sway you. Check other sources of information to learn about software features. Your CPA or management consultant is one source. Another source are the many journals that periodically evaluate accounting software. *PC Magazine, PC World,* and *Personal Computing* all provide evaluations of accounting software, enumerating the features of different packages. There are also some guides available to accounting software. Examples of guides offered by Computer Training Services[1] are: *Guide to Accounting Software for Microcomputers, Guide to Accounting Software for the Construction Industry,* and *Guide to Small Business Bookkeeping Software.* In addition to these guides, Computer Training Services offers a software package that can be used to help a company select the software best for them based on their particular needs (*The Requirements Analyst*). This software is used by many microcomputer consultants to help select optimal software for small business clients.

Allow for Growth

It is natural for a small business to outgrow any particular accounting system *in time.* However,

[1] Computer Training Services, 5900 Tudor Lane, Rockville, Maryland 20852, (301) 468-4800.

allowance for growth should be made so that this does not happen too quickly. The small business should consider the following:

1. The number of master file records it will want to store on each of its files.
2. The daily volume of accounting transactions in each of its major accounting applications.
3. The number of potential real-time users of its computer.
4. The level of interaction among its different accounting applications.
5. The number of new software packages likely to be added in the future.

Select Systems with Good Controls

There is no guarantee that any particular accounting software package will include good controls. The small business must look for these. Examples of such controls include:

1. Clear user manuals and training guides.
2. Good editing tests to guard against the system's acceptance of inaccurate or incomplete data.
3. Good input, processing, and output controls as discussed in Chapter 10.
4. Clear audit trails.
5. Controls that enable the user to "back out of " error transactions.
6. Ability to assist users with such "user friendly" aids as instruction guides, menu-driven options, and hands-on training sessions.
7. Controls that support computer security, such as the preparation of backup files and the implementation of recovery procedures.

Plan Ahead

An all-too-common practice is to buy a computer without adequate preparation for its arrival. Space must be reserved, electrical fittings must be prepared, environmental factors such as air conditioning, ventilation, and proximity to furnace or water hazards must be considered, and computer security must be planned. Maintenance contracts must be secured, and a continuing source of supplies for such items as ribbons, paper, and preprinted forms must be located. Users must be trained. All of these matters require advanced planning.

Consider Alternatives Before Buying

No law says a small business *must* own a computer. The small business should also consider the use of a time-sharing organization or a service bureau as an alternative means of processing all, or part, of its accounting data.

Use Management Consultants

In the legal profession, it is said that a lawyer who represents himself in a court of law has a fool for a client. Some people say there is an analogy for the small business that shops for its own equipment. Unless a small business employs individuals who are professionally knowledgeable about computer systems and the wide range of accounting software that can be implemented on them, it will usually pay for the small business to hire a management consultant. An excellent source for such a consultant would be the **management advisory services (MAS)** department of a public accounting firm. A knowledgeable consultant should be able to assist the small business in acquiring and implementing an accounting system, and perhaps other types of computer software, that are suited to the company's needs. In the long run, the likelihood is great that the cost of a good consultant will be more than offset by the cost *savings* from the implementation of good professional advice.

Have Realistic Expectations

Computers do not walk on water. They cannot resolve disputes between managers, they cannot convert bad data into useful information, and they cannot magically increase profits. If the users of an accounting system know ahead of time what they can reasonably expect from a newly acquired accounting system, they will not be disappointed when the system is finally implemented.

Not all businesses need to be computerized. Often companies that experience rapid growth see computerization as a necessary step. This may or may not be the case. Careful analysis of realistic benefits and costs should be made before going ahead.

Alan Liebert, who has spent a career designing cost-effective computer systems, emphasizes the care that is necessary when acquiring a computer system. For the company that has decided to computerize, Liebert has the following advice.

1. Don't be in a hurry to spend money.
2. Carefully select the best computer and peripheral equipment for your needs.
3. Look at the financial implications of your selection.
4. Don't try new applications purely for sex appeal—cost justify them.[2]

Knowledge and experience in data processing are essential to ensure effective selection, installation, and use of data processing equipment. Because such an acquisition usually requires a substantial dollar investment, management involvement is a "must" for effective utilization of computer equipment. This involvement should start with detailed studies of a company's data processing alternatives and should continue long after a computer system choice is made.

---

[2] Alan Liebert, "Reducing the Cost of Computing," *Data Processing* (November–December 1973), p. 390.

AIS at Work—A Small Business Accounting Information System

Behrens and Robson is a CPA firm with two offices, one in Falls Church, Virginia and the other in Richmond, Virginia. The firm has annual revenue approaching $500,000 and employs 10 or more professionals and para-professionals. Behrens and Robson conducts a wide variety of consulting services for small businesses. These consulting services include audit, tax, and business prospectus for clients. The firm uses microcomputers in their business, mostly by the accountants in conducting their work for clients. One microcomputer is used by the office manager and assists with office and account management.

The following is a description of Behrens and Robson's microcomputer based accounting information system. The office manager uses several software programs to manage the firm's business. The company purchased much of the software that handles services from tax planning to loan amortization. The management software assists with salaries, taxes, ratios, inventory—the operations include all of the usual business and personnel management phases. Some modules include general ledger, accounts receivable, accounts payable, spreadsheets, fixed assets, check writing, proprietary tax preparation, and so on. The general ledger module contains a chart of accounts and typical financial accounting functions.

The office manager inputs journal entries for daily transactions on a periodic basis and generates trial balances, an income statement, and a balance sheet for each month's operations. Both branch offices can operate independently, but if one office gets a heavy load or emergency projects, the other branch is able to help relieve the crisis.

The time and billing modules are used to track billable work by each accountant. All clients know how their charges occurred. Each employee has a time sheet on which they record hours or fractions of hours worked for individual clients. Data recorded on the time sheet includes client name, client number, time, and a description of the type of work (e.g., tax, audit, write-up). Time spent on client work is called billable hours. Time spent on other tasks, such as obtaining new clients, administrative activities, vacation time, and sick time is also recorded on the time sheet. The office manager inputs the data to the time and billing program from the time sheets on a monthly basis. Each month, the program generates a printed report of client billings based on time worked multiplied by hourly rates for each employee. The report includes a running balance of previous billings, less payments received.

This program also generates statements that are sent to clients after being reviewed by one of the firm's two partners. Another report indicates the specific components completed by each employee. This includes:

The number of billable versus nonbillable hours.

Specifics of all client's accounts (as a legal backup).

An aged accounts receivable.

A third module includes an accounts payable subsystem. As a service firm, the company has limited vendors. A master list is maintained for regular vendors, with a special vendor name, "miscellaneous vendor," used for one-time payments. Typical monthly payments include rent, utilities, office supplies, and all of the other operational expenses. After inputing each of the expenses, the office manager inputs invoices weekly and indicates their due dates. The computer generates a pre-check register or cash requirements report each week to direct payment of bills. A check register is generated next that shows amounts paid to each vendor. Since the software is integrated, transactions such as vendor payments are linked to the general ledger module to update accounts.

Many small businesses elect to use service bureaus to process payroll. Behrens and Robson handles this function in-house. Service bureaus can assist in keeping tax ratios and salary changes up to date, but current checkwriting software is convenient to change as well. Behrens and Robson's payroll is less complex than other businesses and this is the reason they use their in-house microcomputer and payroll software to generate checks and payroll reports. The small number of employees, all of whom are salaried, makes this cost-effective. Paychecks and reports required for tax reporting are all generated by the microcomputer with the special payroll software.

SUMMARY

There are several characteristics that make an accounting system for a small business unique. Requirements for streamlined systems, a lack of specialized accounting or financial skills, closely held ownership, a lack of working capital, an informal managerial style, a lack of integrated accounting applications, and a lack of computer expertise may make the design of an effective accounting information system difficult for a small business.

For any particular small business concern, a manual accounting system may be superior to a computerized one. In such instances, however, a matrix accounting system or a double-entry accounting system would be superior to a ledgerless accounting system.

It is difficult to imagine even the smallest business that would not benefit from some type of computerized data processing. Small, personal microcomputers might be used for limited accounting tasks, although these devices are better considered personal managerial tools than commercial data processing alternatives. The most favorable choices are business microcomputers and minicomputers, both of which can be acquired with such accounting application software as accounts receivable, accounts payable, general ledger, inventory control, and payroll. Additional software that may prove desirable to the small business includes operating systems, electronic spreadsheets, word processors, speller, and data base management systems. All of these software packages are typically available for both microcomputers and minicomputers.

A small business should use care when selecting computer hardware and software. A computer evaluation committee should be formed to survey needs and help in the assessment process. Other considerations that might help the small business in the selection process are (1) to remember that software drives hardware, (2) to allow for growth, (3) to select systems with good controls (4) to plan ahead, (5) to consider alternatives to buying equipment, (6) to use management consultants, and (7) to have realistic expectations.

Following the discussion questions, problems, and case-analyses sections of this chapter, a supplement is provided that analyzes strategies for effective microcomputer management.

Key Terms You Should Know

bundled software	letter-quality printer
business microcomputer	management advisory services (MAS) of a CPA firm
canned computer software	matrix accounting system
computer evaluation committee	minicomputer
computer graphics	monitor
computer network	operating system of a computer
data base management system (for microcomputers)	personal microcomputer
dedicated minicomputer	request for proposal (RFP)
double-entry accounting system	small business computer
electronic spreadsheet software	software broker
footprint of a microcomputer	software house
lap top microcomputer	speller (microcomputer software)
ledgerless accounting system	word processing

Discussion Questions

17-1. How small is "small business"? Would the million-dollar-a-year manufacturing company be included on a list of small businesses?

17-2. What are the characteristics of a small business that uniquely influence the selection of an accounting system? Would you say that any of these characteristics would also apply to larger business organizations or nonbusiness organizations? Discuss.

17-3. What is a ledgerless accounting system? What advantages does such a system enjoy? What disadvantages does such a system suffer? If you were the owner of a small business, would you implement such a system in your company? Why or why not?

17-4. What advantages does a double-entry accounting system have over a ledgerless accounting system? Use your accounting background to provide an in-depth answer.

17-5. What is a matrix accounting system? What advantage(s), if any, might a matrix accounting system offer a small business as compared with a conventional manual system? Hint: see Appendix C.

17-6. Describe the differences between a programmable calculator and a lap top microcomputer. Given the choice, which type of device would you prefer to have and why?

17-7. What are the differences, if any, between a personal microcomputer and a business microcomputer? Why is a business microcomputer usually better suited to the data processing needs of a small business?

17-8. A type of microcomputer not discussed in the text is the portable microcomputer. Among these types of machines are devices manufactured by Compaq. There are others. From your outside knowledge of these devices, discuss what uses a small business might make of them. Would you prefer them to, say, a business microcomputer? Why or why not?

17-9. Provide a brief description of each of the following types of software available on microcomputers.

a. operating system
b. electronic spreadsheet
c. word processor
d. speller
e. data base management system

How would a small business use each of these software packages in its daily operations?

17-10. Below are a set of terms normally associated with microcomputers. Some of these terms were discussed in this chapter and others in Chapter 4. Define each term.

a. bundled software
b. monitor
c. ROM
d. RAM
e. graphics
f. 16-bit word
g. footprint
h. letter-quality printer
i. network

17-11. Describe how an electronic spreadsheet would be used to prepare a forecast of profits for a company. What advantages does the electronic spreadsheet have over the manual spreadsheet?

17-12. As discussed in this chapter, what is the difference between a microcomputer and a minicomputer? How do these computers relate to small business computers?

17-13. What are some of the sources for accounting software for a small business? Of the sources you have mentioned, which would you consider the most promising and why?

17-14. In an advertisement, you read about an interesting microcomputer called the Star I. It has 64k of memory, 2 floppy disk drives, and comes bundled with electronic spreadsheet software, data base management software, and word processing software. How would you classify such a device and how useful would you say such a device was as a small business computer?

17-15. What are the advantages and disadvantages of acquiring a minicomputer from the standpoint of the small business? Why would a business buy or lease a minicomputer when it could also buy several microcomputers for the same money?

17-16. Explain the difficulties in classifying computers as microcomputers, minicomputers, and small business computers. Would you prefer to keep the meaning of these three terms distinct or would you prefer to call all "nonlarge" computers "minicomputers"? Justify your answer.

17-17. How important is computer software to the small business? Why don't most small businesses write their own computer programs?

17-18. In the text, it was noted that many accounting information systems using small business computers were "integrated." What does this term mean, and why would integration concern the small business?

17-19. Examine the Accounts Payable Periodic Liabilities Report illustrated in Figure 17-6. Discuss as many uses as you can for such a report. Which personnel within a small company would need the information contained in this report?

17-20. Describe the process by which a small business might decide to purchase a particular computer. How does this process differ from the process used in acquiring the computer hardware for a large company's informational system?

17-21. What are the factors that influence the "computerization" of the small business? What are the pitfalls to avoid?

Problems

17-22. Describe the differences between a programmable calculator, a microcomputer, and a minicomputer. Which type of computer system might best be used by (a) a real estate broker, (b) a small CPA firm, (c) an engineer working on a small problem, (d) a student, and (e) a minor league baseball team.

17-23. Ma and Pa Smallfield have worked all their lives in their own grocery store, which is located in a small town near Kent, Ohio. Outside of Sally Peterson, the checkout girl, and an occasional part-time stock boy or two, the Smallfields are the only employees. Recently, Pa Smallfield was approached by a computer salesman from nearby Smokeville. The salesman was hoping to get Ma and Pa interested in leasing a small minicomputer to help keep their records. Not wishing to push the Smallfields into a hasty decision, the salesman left some literature and promised to return a week later. The couple pondered over pictures of the newfangled device and debated the issue.

Ma Smallfield, ever the more open-minded of the two, liked the idea very much. "It's just what we need," she said, "to help us with the paperwork."

"Fiddlesticks," replied Pa. "We've gotten along just fine without one of those Rube Goldbergs for the last 30 years, and I see no reason to start now. Do you realize that if we go ahead and get one of those 'misty-computers', or whatever those things are, we probably wouldn't need Sam Peterson, your cousin's brother-in-law, to do the books. I'd sure hate to fire Sam. Sam's wife has been laid up in the hospital, you know, and they need the money. Besides, I kinda like havin' Sam come around once a month and play checkers after he's through with the books. I vote no."

Analyze this problem in detail and make a recommendation.

17-24. Refer to Figure 17-5. Design a computer file record that would enable a computer program to print out the reports illustrated in the figure. The order in which you list the data fields is not as important as the completeness of your list. What additional fields would be desirable in the computer record?

17-25. Refer to Figure 17-6. Design a computer file record that would enable a computer program to print out the reports illustrated in the figure. The order in which you list the data fields is not as important as the completeness of your list. What additional fields would be desirable in the computer record?

17-26. (Library Research) From such publications as *Datamation, Computerworld,* or some other source, obtain copies of an advertisement for a programmable calculator, an advertisement for a microcomputer, and an advertisement for a minicomputer. What features appear to distinguish one machine from the other? What types of accounting functions could be performed on the smallest machine as well as on each of the two larger machines?

17-27*. Alex Road operates a part-time plumbing business a few hours each week. His business is called the Clean Sewer Company. Because of the small volume of transactions, Mr. Road uses a matrix accounting system to accumulate his company's monetary data for monthly financial statements. The Clean Sewer Company's June 1, 1991 post-closing trial balance is shown below.

Cash	$ 700	
Accounts receivable	300	
Plumbing equipment	800	
Accumulated depreciation— plumbing equipment		$ 500
Accounts payable		200
Alex Road, capital		1100
	$1800	$1800

The company's June 1991 accounting transactions are as follows.

June 1	Paid the June store rent, $300.
June 5	Provided plumbing services to a customer and received $600 cash.

* Instructor's note: This problem should only be assigned if the matrix accounting system of Appendix C is covered.

June 10　Paid $75 of the accounts payable liabilities.

June 17　Provided plumbing services to a customer and billed him $200.

June 23　Collected $100 from an accounts receivable customer.

June 30　Paid the June utilities bill on the store, $75.

June 30　Paid the part-time employee his monthly salary, $250 (ignore social security taxes and other deductions).

June 30　Recognized the monthly depreciation on the plumbing equipment, $25.

Requirements

Perform the following accounting functions for the Clean Sewer Company:

A. Utilizing a matrix system, record the Clean Sewer Company's June 1991 accounting transactions within its matrix.

B. Using the data from the Clean Sewer Company's completed June matrix, prepare the company's June 1991 financial statements (i.e., its income statement and its balance sheet).

17-28. As the manager of West End Publishers, you have been asked to forecast an operating budget for the next five years. Listed below are a set of expenditure categories and the assumptions you have made about their growth patterns during the next five-year period.

Expenditure Category	Assumption	Current Level
Salaries—professional	Grow at a rate of 7½% per year	$200,000
Salaries—clerical	Grow at a rate of 9% per year	50,000
Travel	Grow at a rate of 5% per year	25,000
Office supplies	No growth	5,000
Utilities	Grow at a rate of 15% per year	2,000
New equipment	Decline at a rate of 5% per year	8,500
Xeroxing, duplicating	No growth	2,500
Miscellaneous	Grow at a rate of 8% per year	3,000

Requirements

A. Manually prepare a forecast for the years 1990, 1991, 1992, and 1993 based on these data.

B. Describe how such a problem might be implemented on an electronic spreadsheet.

C. Using a microcomputer and spreadsheet software, perform this problem electronically. Forecast for the years 1990 through 1995.

D. Alter each current value by +$5000 and −$5000 (except utilities, xeroxing and duplicating, and miscellaneous). Perform your work again.

CASE ANALYSES

17-29. Ward's Farm

Ward's Farm is a 3000-acre grain farm located in White County, near Carmi, Illinois. Paul Ward, the owner, has been farming since 1971. He initially purchased 325 acres and has made the following land purchases since then: 300 acres in 1975, 150 acres in 1978, 1000 acres in 1979, 900 acres in 1984, and 325 acres in 1988. The cost of farmland has inflated over the years so that, although Mr. Ward has a total investment of $919,000, the land is currently valued at $2,950,000.

The farm is separated into 48 different fields averaging over 60 acres per field. Several larger fields exceed 100 acres, whereas others run 10 to 12 acres. The farm also covers several types of terrain and has several types of soil. Some of the land is high and hilly, some of the land is low and claylike, and the rest is humus-rich prairie soil. Fertilizer mixes are determined by type of soil and type of grain to be planted. Mr. Ward now determines mix by his experienced "rules of thumb."

The equipment used on the farm consists of nine tractors (farm type), three combines with assorted grain heads, four tandem-axle grain bed trucks, one tractor-trailer, three pickup trucks, and numerous discs, plows, wagons, and assorted tractor and hand tools. Additionally, the farm has three equipment storage barns, an equipment maintenance shed, and a 165,000-bushel grain elevator/drier. The equipment and buildings have an estimated worth of $625,000.

Mr. Ward employs five full-time farmhands, a mechanic, a bookkeeper, and has contracted part-time accounting/tax assistance with a local CPA firm in Carmi. All employees are salaried. The farmhands are paid $15,000 a year, as is the bookkeeper. The mechanic is paid $15,000 annually and the CPA contract costs are $8250 a year.

In 1988, the farm produced 25,300 bushels of wheat, 68,800 bushels of soybeans, and 119,000 bushels of yellow corn. The gross income was $681,321, with Mr. Ward's net income after taxes being $57,500.

Ray Ward, Mr. Ward's son, has just returned from college. He knows that the farm is profitable, but feels that proper work scheduling and implementation of proper internal controls could increase profitability and reduce his father's work load even more. He also knows that his father still thinks of the farm as a small business that requires only a knowledge of farming for proper management. There are no controls over parts inventory, no schedules for preventive maintenance, and no scientific application of crop rotation or crop food principles.

Questions

1. Some people still think of farming as small, family-run operations, but the average farm today exceeds 200 acres. Large corporate farms seem to be the development of the future. With this in mind, what are some data-processing areas where the capability of the computer could assist farm owners in their accounting functions?
2. Given the limited information in this case, recommend a cost-effective approach to computerizing some of the accounting functions suggested.

17-30. *Papakolea Country Club*

Papakolea Country Club is a small golf facility that has grown from a nine-hole golf course at its inception in 1938 to its present 18-hole status. Other facilities include a paddle tennis court, shuffleboard, lawn sports, and a modest clubhouse with a small bar and snack shop. The pro shop is operated by the golf professional. All other facilities are under the control of the club manager, who is guided by a board of directors.

The membership is made up of 350 regular members and 150 social members. The club is located in a suburban environment. The membership is primarily made up of "self-made" small business entrepreneurs who do not have a great deal of sophistication in the planning and control techniques of a business concern.

Management personnel of the club have been very basic in their approach, choosing to "fly by the seat of their pants." Salary levels in the management area have not justified or attracted high-level management personnel. In addition, the directors, elected from the club membership, serve two-year terms. This fact and normal membership attrition give very little continuity to the board.

Existing operating departments are (1) golf, which has subfunctions of golf course operations, carts, pro shop, and lockers, and (2) the snack bar and liquor bar. Staff functions of administration, promotions, and maintenance are also an integral part of the club operation. Revenues and expenses attributable to these two operating departments vary according to season and the degree of activity generated by the current board of directors in the way of tournaments, social functions, and the like. The largest source of revenues is from initiation fees and monthly dues.

The current practice with regard to accounting records is for the manger and the office assistant to accumulate monthly documents and forward them to a small bookkeeping service, which subsequently furnishes an income statement and balance sheet to the club manager and board of directors. These financial statements are received by the twentieth of the month following the previous month's operations. The statements are hard to interpret and provide no comparative basis for analysis. Because of the lack of information and the lack of timeliness provided by the financial reports, it is difficult for the club to define objectives for future operations, measure the efficiency of operations, and generally plan and control the club's financial matters.

You have been hired by the club as an independent consultant. A review of the existing state of affairs has revealed the facts just disclosed. As an initial means to alleviate the club's problems, you are thinking of implementing an operational budget with resultant performance reports.

Questions

1. Design a basic format for the operational budget.
2. As a tool to assist in implementing the budget system, enumerate the ways in which the budgetary system will assist the club management, board of directors, and membership.
3. As a consultant you have been queried on the appropriateness of installing a computer system to help the club in its accounting functions. Discuss

the pros and cons of computerizing the club's accounting information system.

17-31. Minicomputer Considerations for a Small Business

Minicomputers are small, programmable digital computers. The term *microcomputer* is used to describe a computer of even smaller dimensions, but the distinction between minicomputers and microcomputers has become blurred because of the advancements in modern technology. Consequently, we will use minicomputer to refer to both types of computer systems.

A typical minicomputer system consists of a central processing unit, input device(s), output device(s), memory, and software. Minicomputers are being used extensively in business as small but complete data-processing systems. Although minicomputers are used in businesses of all sizes, the greatest area of applications has been in small business.

Questions

1. Identify and discuss the advantages and limitations generally associated with minicomputer systems.
2. Identify and explain the factors a business should consider before it decides to use a minicomputer.
3. Discuss the internal accounting control considerations to be reviewed by a company using a minicomputer system.

(CMA adapted)

17-32. Major Dan Cooper*

An inheritance of $700,000 and a $2,000 monthly pension had enabled Major Dan Cooper to take an early retirement from a military career as an electronics engineer. One day, when lining up to rent video cassettes, Dan and his wife noted that the store was always crowded and that most of the time their selection was not available due to the limited number of copies carried by the store. Dan's wife suggested that video cassettes should be rented from vending machines, somewhat like the good old juke box. Dan found this idea so interesting that he spent the next year de-

---

* Adapted, with permission from Canadian Institute of Chartered Accountants Examination, 1987, The Canadian Institute of Chartered Accountants, Toronto, Canada. Changes to the original questions and/or suggested approaches to answering are the sole responsibility of the authors and have not been reviewed or endorsed by the CICA.

signing and developing a Video Cassette Renting Machine (VCRM).

Dan arranged with the manager of a nearby shopping center to install his VCRM for a six-month test period. He paid $1,000 per month to rent the space. During this period, he ironed out the technical problems. He is satisfied that the VCRM not only works perfectly but is also well received by customers. In mid-September 1987, he approaches you, CA (Chartered Accountant), to get advice before proceeding any further, and in the course of discussion he gives you the following information.

Dan has approached a manufacturer to produce and install the VCRMs and has gathered financial data you may find useful (Exhibit I). He is confident that this data is representative of the prospective revenue and costs of the project, although they may be slightly optimistic. Dan and his wife still have a 12%-yield certificate of deposit for $250,000 which they can invest, if needed; five friends of theirs are prepared to invest $50,000 each. Another friend of Dan's, who is an investment dealer, told him that a bank would probably finance at least 80% of the cassette inventory. The dealer also said that Dan can arrange to obtain venture capital from a limited number of private investors if more funds are required or if Dan wants to limit his investment to what he already has provided to develop the VCRM.

The VCRM is a self-contained unit, occupying about six square yards, which can be placed at a suitable location in a shopping mall and attached to electrical and telephone outlets. A customer inserts a special magnetic membership card to activate the microcomputer selection system, which reads the card number and validates it against a list of approved numbers.

The selection system employs two user-friendly menus. The first menu displays available categories on a touch-sensitive screen. When the customer touches the desired selection displayed on the screen, the system automatically displays the second menu—pages listing the titles available. A single touch of the screen gives access to the previous or to the next page. When the customer has made a choice, the customer touches the screen where the title appears. The system then displays a brief description of the movie and waits for a response: Reject or Accept.

In the "Accept" box is touched, an invoice is prepared and a transaction number is stored on a magnetic strip on the cassette. The magnetic strip also contains a serial number unique to each cassette. The

EXHIBIT 1   Financial Data Prepared by Major Dan Cooper

Costs incurred on project date:

Out-of-pocket development costs	$335,000
Out-of-pocket market testing costs	25,500
Dan's salary for 18 months	70,000
	$430,500

The manufacturer has given a quotation to produce and install 50 VCRMs for a total cost of $925,000 that would be payable as follows: $200,000 on October 1, 1987; $450,000 on January 3, 1988, on the delivery of 25 VCRMs; and the balance on March 31, 1988, on delivery of the remaining 25 VCRMs. The test unit is in storage. It would be given to the manufacturer for helping in the production design and would not be reused.

The test generated $1000 in revenue per week on average, within two months of installation. This level of inflow stayed fairly constant over the remaining four months of the test period.

The weekly inflow for the final four months of the test period breaks down on average as follows:

Rentals	$ 620
Memberships	200
Sales	180
	$1,000

The business will be conducted in the same manner as it was during the test period, but on a larger scale. Of all the shopping malls approached, 20 are receptive to renting out space for $1,100 per month plus 5% of the gross revenue.

To obtain the magnetic membership card, the customer will pay a $50 initial fee, of which $20 will be refunded on the return of the card. A credit check will be made on each new member.

Customers who fail to return a video cassette within one week will be billed $30 for it as a sale but will not be charged any rental fee. It is estimated that cassettes will have to be replaced every 24 months, at an average cost of $20 each. An average number of 500 cassettes will be required for each location. Cassettes considered sold will be replaced immediately.

One person will service 3 to 4 VCRMs and will receive an average salary of $24,000 a year and a travel allowance of 10% of the gross salary. One part-time supervisor for the central computer will be hired and paid $20,000 per year.

Electricity and telephone costs are expected to be $1200 per year per location and will be billed for each location on a consolidated bill by each utility company.

It is estimated that costs and expenses for insurance, replacement parts, membership cards, advertisements, business taxes, and so forth, will amount to approximately $3000 per year per location.

Exhibit II   Sketch of Management System by Major Can Cooper

The management system will be controlled from Dan's house by the central computer that will communicate with each VCRM's microcomputer by telephone.

After business closing each day, the central computer will automatically contact each VCRM to update its file of valid membership card numbers. It will also extract a listing of the day's rentals and sales, detailing validated membership card numbers, the cassette serial numbers, and the time and date of each transaction, together with the VCRM's identification number.

The central computer will then use the data from the VCRMs to update its accounts receivable and inventory files.

Once a month, statements for each customer will be printed out from the information stored in the central computer and will be mailed by the supervisor.

The entries in the inventory files will be analyzed weekly by the central computer to create usage statistics and to produce a purchase order to the cassette supplier.

At the end of each month, monthly financial statements will be prepared, along with inventory lists, usage statistics, and a list of cassettes ordered from the supplier.

The central-computer supervisor will deposit the day's mail collections and will ensure that the central computer is operating properly. The supervisor will also be expected to resolve any major programming problems encountered in the central computer and the microcomputers.

---

invoice is released from the VCRM, together with the cassette selected. The list of available cassettes is then updated in the VCRM microcomputer. It also stores the transaction data and periodically transfers the information by telephone to the central computer.

To return a cassette, the customer deposits it in a return slot. The transaction number and the serial number are read from the magnetic strip on the cassette and stored for transmission to the central computer.

A daily service call is necessary to check and rewind all returned cassettes before they are replaced in their inventory location and to report damaged cassettes. The list of available cassettes is again updated.

Dan's goal is to minimize both his time and his payroll costs through electronic automation. He does not want to become a slave to his business, as he plans to spend several months a year sailing in the Caribbean. He has sketched out a management system to control his business (Exhibit II).

Dan is satisfied as a result of the testing that the system can be controlled from his central computer and that the manufacturer he has selected will be able to produce an initial order of 50 VCRMs made to his specifications. Each VCRM will be put into operation within a few days of delivery and will be installed within 40 miles of his house.

Dan concludes by saying: "I'll need an auditor to keep an eye on the business and to advise me from time to time, but right now I want to get started with the business. Please look at the information I have given you, and we'll meet next week to discuss it."

Questions

1. Use a spreadsheet to evaluate the system proposed by Major Cooper.
2. Evaluate the management system proposed.
3. Do you think Dan is ready to begin business?

(Institute of Chartered Accountants adapted)

CHAPTER 17 SUPPLEMENT

Strategies for Effective Microcomputer Management

Microcomputer hardware and software systems technology has advanced to the point where no organization can ignore the potential application of these systems in its business. The hardware is more powerful, portable, and affordable. Software is more reliable, sophisticated, and integrated as well as easier to use. Users of microcomputer systems are becoming more sophisticated and less dependent on central computing services. They are discovering that such applications as word processing, data-base management, and business graphics are accessible and adaptable to their needs. In addition, vendors are introducing such new applications as electronic mail and providing integrated services that enhance data transfer as well as internal and external communication.

Critical Areas Affected by Microcomputers

With each of the advances in the microcomputer systems, however, organizations are exposed to greater data abuses. Management is especially challenged by computing systems that, by their very nature, defy central control. We will now describe the impact of microcomputers on various critical areas of companies.

Security

Unlike mainframes, microcomputers are usually not physically controlled; they are, by design, accessible to many users. Diskettes, documentation, peripherals, expansion circuit boards, and even the microcomputer itself are highly transportable and easily stolen. Unauthorized users can copy, manipulate, or destroy diskettes without leaving an audit trail and can steal data diskettes containing confidential information, leaving no record of a security breach and thereby exposing the organization to business and legal liabilities. The unauthorized copying of program diskettes violates license agreements and thus subjects the organization to litigation. Finally, microcomputers can be used to gain unauthorized access to mainframes and minicomputers.

Data Integrity

Microcomputers that do not communicate with other computers must receive information from manually entered data contained on source documents such as sales invoices. Data-entry errors are therefore common, and erroneous record keeping as well as software differences increase the probability that the data in the microcomputer will differ from the data on the source documents. Because printed computer reports are often regarded as more authoritative than reports generated by other means, management may not question the discrepancy, which could seriously affect the accuracy of their decisions.

Incompatibilities

Microcomputer systems comprise numerous components, including hardware, operating systems, application software, programming languages, and data-communication capabilities. When any of these components are incompatible with other microcomputers in the organization, the sharing of data and applications becomes difficult or impossible. Such incompatibility can also render employees' microcomputer experiences useless when they are transferred to new positions.

Data Recoverability

Data can be lost or damaged as a result of data-entry errors, software errors, mechanical failures, or such environmental hazards as fire and magnetic interference. Without backup provisions, data reconstruction is difficult. Although accounting professionals have learned, and now practice, data backup, many microcomputer users are unacquainted with the dangers of system failures.

Application Controls and Audit Trails

Most microcomputer users purchase software for their computer applications. Although there are many advantages to purchased software, it allows the user to implement only those security controls that the vendor provides. The vendor, of course, cannot meet the individual control needs of each customer. For example, providing an audit trail requires more RAM space than the minimum configuration. The vendor therefore may not provide the audit trail because this feature reduces memory available for other tasks. Even for inhouse software development applications, hardware and operating system limitations act as constraints on the controls and audit trails that can be implemented. Without such application controls as edit tests and check digits, specific accounting software application packages (such as a payroll application package) may not be reliable or auditable.

Acquisition and Use

Inexperienced users are unacquainted with systems development techniques, which can identify their requirements before they acquire hardware and software. Because these users are often unable to evaluate technical features, they are more susceptible than MIS professionals to vendor sales pressure. In addition, it is often difficult to thoroughly test the hardware and software before purchase. In fact, most software cannot be returned after the packaging seal is broken. Similarly, microcomputer users are often unfamiliar with proper techniques for using hardware and software and thus cannot properly evaluate the advantages of such controls as documentation and preventive maintenance.

Costs

Before acquiring mainframes and minicomputers, most organizations performed a formal cost/benefit analysis. Because microcomputers are relatively inexpensive, however, many users easily justify their acquisitions without any formal review. Some users acquire microcomputers because it is the popular thing to do, bypassing formal qualification procedures by classifying the new equipment as a miscellaneous office expense. Microcomputers obtained in this way are usually underutilized or used for nonproductive purposes (e.g., games). Although the unit cost per computer is low, the total investment made by an organization to acquire microcomputers can be substantial.

Establishing Controls

An organization should establish a task force of users, MIS personnel, and auditors to plan the control of microcomputer acquisition and use. Employees in areas such as purchasing and finance should also be consulted, and task force recommendations should be consistent with organizational policy.

Planning Approaches

The task force can follow one of two planning approaches. In the first approach, a risk analysis should be performed to identify all potential control problems, calculate their probabilities of occurring, and estimate their cost. Controls that reduce the probability of the problems occurring or mitigate their consequences should be identified. The projected benefits of these controls should be weighed against implementation and maintenance costs.

The objective of the second approach is to implement and maintain a reasonable level of control without unduly restricting microcomputer users. This level of control is reached by implementing cost-effective controls formulated through surveys, interviews, and brainstorming sessions. The second approach is based on the recognition that although individual controls are insufficient to control the acquisition and use of microcomputers, controls are effective as an integrated unit.

The first approach should be considered when particular potential control problems need special attention. For example, an insurance company gave each of its agencies a microcomputer to process essential information. Such controls as reconciling the data contained on source documents to the data entered into the microcomputers and educating the agents to use the computer properly were therefore critical and accorded highest control priority. The second approach can be used for organizations planning for general microcomputer applications.

Survey

The task force must first survey existing computing facilities to determine user experience as well as hardware and software constraints. Case studies of past computer implementations are particularly informative. If microcomputers are not currently used in the organization, simulation testing of microcomputer systems should be implemented. The costs and benefits from these tests should be evaluated before microcomputers are introduced on a large scale.

Responsibilities

A control plan must specify the responsibilities of every group contributing to the plan. We will now describe the responsibilities of each group involved in the acquisition and use of microcomputers.

Task Force

The task force should develop the control plan, including policies and standards, and make recommendations to senior management. The task force must designate personnel to maintain recommended controls and a microcomputer coordinator whose full-time responsibility is to oversee the control plan's execution. Task force members should recognize that a control plan changes with technological developments and user requirements.

Senior Management

Senior (i.e., top) management must approve the control plan and ensure that the resources necessary to implement and maintain the plan are available. The plan cannot succeed unless senior management gives its commitment and support.

MIS

The MIS department or an independent microcomputer staff should provide microcomputer users with such technical services as installation, consulting, and training. The MIS staff should also monitor adherence to predetermined policies and standards as well as perform such administrative activities as evaluating microcomputer acquisition requests.

One MIS employee should support users as a microcomputer coordinator or information center manager. This person may also evaluate all acquisition requests for microcomputers.

Auditor

The auditor (internal or external auditor, depending on the particular organization) should regularly review the control plan, including policies and procedures, while application controls are developed or maintained. The auditor should also periodically test the controls to ensure that the planned controls are enforced and effective.

Recommended Controls

Controls can typically be implemented so that they apply to all microcomputers and associated applications, or they can be implemented for isolated applications. The following sections address general controls.

Support Approaches

Adequate MIS support in acquiring, implementing, and using microcomputer systems can provide control in many critical areas. The MIS department can provide support in one or more of the following tasks.

Recommending Hardware and Software

The microcomputer user is faced with thousands of hardware and software options, many of which are incompatible with each other or with systems already in an organization. Selection from a list of approved hardware and software should therefore be required or at least, recommended. This list should include market evaluations as well as products that are currently working well in the organization. The user should be able to select quality products that are consistent with the rest of the organization; marginally acceptable products should be identified as such on the list. Microcomputer users should be able to select unapproved products only after submitting written justification for their acquisition. The list of approved products should reflect the changing needs of the organization and technological advances.

Training and Consulting

Training and consulting services for recommended products are an attractive incentive for users to choose from the approved list; they are also a tool for promoting optimum microcomputer use. This support can range from one consultant who answers occasional microcomputer-user questions to a full-time group that helps users acquire products and formally trains them in productive uses of the new equipment. Support consultants can also help develop specific accounting applications (such as a perpetual inventory system application).

Large-scale training and consulting services should include refresher courses and a help hot-line as well as initial training. Computer-based training and experienced microcomputer users working as instructors enhance the quality of an organization's training program.

The level of training and consulting needed depends on such factors as microcomputer-user experience, the specific application's sophistication, and the resources of the organization. Although most organizations hesitate to create a large support staff at the beginning of the project, some training and consulting must be provided to guide microcomputer purchases and lend other basic support.

Newsletters

A newsletter addressing general microcomputing concerns as well as security and control problems should be published regularly for all microcomputer users. The microcomputer coordinator can edit the newsletter, but the users should submit the articles. The newsletter should present case studies, disseminate general news and product announcements, offer product reviews, and recommend further reading.

Security and control articles do not create policy, but they develop security awareness and inform users of proper control practices. For example, a corporate policy requiring diskette backup copies would be explained in a newsletter article. When users understand policy rationale, they are more likely to adhere to its dictates.

User Groups

User groups complement the newsletters. Users should meet regularly to exchange information and make recommendations for improving support, products, and policies. Community user groups are helpful, but they attract a diverse audience and may not fulfill the specific needs of an organization. Internal user groups are therefore preferred.

Information Exchange Network

The microcomputer coordinator should maintain a catalogue of all significant applications and products in his or her organization. Microcomputer users should refer to this catalogue and consult with other users and application authors because shared applications and experience reduces duplicated effort and costly mistakes.

Purchasing and Maintenance

Large organizations can usually negotiate significant hardware, software, and maintenance discounts with their purchasing power. The microcomputer coordinator should be responsible for negotiating these discounts with appropriate assistance from other departments (e.g., law, purchasing, or finance) for contracts, purchase orders, and leasing arrangements.

Extended purchasing services include acquiring products on loan for extended demonstration purposes. A company store, or information center, should be established in large organizations to allow microcomputer users to learn more about alternative products without being pressured by salespersons. Organizations that are completely committed to microcomputer standardization can acquire all their systems in one major purchase.

Value-Added Services

Specific tools can be developed or acquired to improve the value of hardware and software products. For example, an interface that allows data from a mainframe application to be down-loaded and reformatted into microcomputer applications for further processing is valuable to users who manually enter data. If the interface is supported only for certain products, microcomputer users will have a strong incentive to follow the recommendations of the microcomputer coordinator.

Staffing Considerations

Although the microcomputer support staff needs technical expertise to evaluate hardware and software products properly, communications skills are even more important. The staff needs patience and compassion to help new microcomputer users. Those users who have demonstrated microcomputer expertise are good candidates for the support staff. A teaching or consulting background is also helpful.

Policies and Procedures

The aforementioned controls address acquiring and using microcomputers without consideration being given to formal policies and procedures. Nevertheless, an organization must have sufficient controls to ensure that its assets are safe and its applications are auditable. Although formal policies and procedures are needed to ensure this, they must not be unduly restrictive. We will now discuss some recommended policies and procedures for an organization's microcomputer system.

Valid Applications

Some applications are inappropriate for the microcomputer. For larger organizations, financial applications that require extensive controls and audit trails should be run on their mainframes or minicomputers. In addition, data base systems for data shared among multiple departments may not belong on a microcomputer.

A strong policy states that all proposed user applications must be reviewed and approved. A slightly less stringent, but more practical, policy requires this review process for only significant financial applications and for applications that cross departmental boundaries.

The reviewer (usually from the MIS department) ensures that business needs are established and a cost/benefit analysis is performed before any products are acquired. The reviewer helps determine whether a microcomputer-based application is appropriate for satisfying the specific business needs.

Standard Products

A list of approved and required products ensures a reasonable degree of compatibility. For example, to facilitate the transfer and integration of information, an organization should establish a standard data communications protocol. Other products that can be standardized include hardware, operating systems, programming languages, and applications software.

Separation of Related Organizational Functions

Although the traditional control of separating related organizational duties in order to ensure that errors are detected and improper activities are deterred applies to microcomputers, the separation of related duties is not possible when a microcomputer user also acts as a programmer and operator. In this case, supervisory reviews and periodic audits can be compensating controls. As in traditional MIS operations, a backup should be designated to support the applications if the primary user is not available. But, for sensitive applications, separation of critical duties is mandatory.

Physical Environment

Some of the physical controls associated with mainframe and minicomputers may not be applicable to microcomputers. The following policies, however, should be considered.

* Microcomputers should be in an area that has limited traffic and can be secured during off hours.
* Inventory records should be maintained of all hardware (including peripherals and expansion boards), software diskettes, and documentation. These records should be periodically compared with a physical inventory.
* Microcomputers should have surge protectors, antistatic protection, and approved electrical service.

* Smoking, drinking, and eating should not be permitted near a microcomputer.
* Cleaning and general housekeeping should be performed on a regular basis.
* Data diskettes should be stored away from extreme temperatures, humidity, dust, magnets, CRT terminals, telephones, and radios. They should be labeled with a felt-tip pen, kept in their protective jackets when not in use, and stored in an upright position.

Data Security

Because it is so easy to copy and remove diskettes, measures should be taken to protect data from unauthorized users. Prohibiting the home use of company microcomputers may help, but an increasing number of users have computers at home. Data security becomes an even greater concern when a home microcomputer can communicate with a host (i.e., company) computer, in which case data can be manipulated or destroyed or copied from the host onto a diskette. The following measures can prevent unauthorized data access.

* Data diskettes should be kept in a secure location.
* Sensitive data on disks should be protected by password requirements or encrypted.
* The host computer should have a security system that allows access only by authorized microcomputer users.
* After access is granted to the host computer, a microcomputer user should be permitted access only to specific files and for limited functions (e.g., for inquiry or downloading).
* The host computer should log all system accesses, and violations should be investigated.

Authorized users, however, must be trusted with their data unless an organization is willing to search them physically for diskettes.

Backup and Recovery

Cost-effective controls should be established to prevent the loss or damage of hardware, software, and data. If disaster does strike, a recovery plan should be in place to reduce the consequences of the disaster. The recovery plan should specify the following.

* Diskettes should be write-protected when they are not being updated.
* Diskettes and disks should be backed up after each

update. The backups should be stored in a secure location away from the microcomputer.

- A backup microcomputer with an equivalent configuration should be available if the primary microcomputer cannot be used.

In addition, a maintenance agreement and insurance coverage should be considered.

Documentation

Those microcomputer applications that are used frequently should be documented. Documentation is especially useful when the microcomputer user changes jobs. Documentation standards should be established, although the amount of documentation should vary based on the complexity of the application. Documentation should include:

- Clear labeling of all data diskettes and documentation.
- A brief narrative of the application, including functions performed and major data elements used.
- A listing of the source code.
- Vendor-supplied documentation.
- Such information as application author, software product used, and file names.

Software Integrity

Software applications should have adequate controls and audit trails. The extent of the controls depends on the type of application and potential exposures. In addition, all applications should have controls to ensure that the software is working as planned. These software integrity controls include ensuring that the most current vendor software is used and that extensive testing is performed on software applications prior to their actual utilization in processing an organization's data.

Miscellaneous

Other controls that should be considered include:

- Proprietary software should not be copied except for archival purposes or to use a hard disk.
- Warranty cards should be completed.
- Microcomputers should not be used for nonbusiness purposes.

Why You Need a Control Plan

An organization using microcomputers must prepare a control plan for the acquisition and use of microcomputers. The control plan should assign responsibilities, determine how microcomputer users will be supported, and establish policies and procedures. Periodic audits should be performed to ensure that the control plan is working as anticipated. Finally, the control plan should be continually updated to keep it current with changing technologies and organizational objectives. The checklist shown in Figure 17-8 provides the basis of a thorough program that can ensure that an organization's microcomputer investment is well protected.

	Yes	No	NA*	Comments
Responsibilities				
Is there a microcomputer coordinator?				
Are users responsible for controls?				
Support				
Does microcomputer support include:				
• Recommending hardware and software?				
• Training and consulting?				
• Information exchange network?				
• Purchasing and maintenance assistance?				
Microcomputer Applications				
Are valid microcomputer applications defined?				
Are proposed applications reviewed?				
Is a systems development life cycle used for larger applications?				
Standard Products				
Are there standards for:				
• Communications protocol?				
• Hardware?				
• Operating systems?				
• Programming languages?				
• Applications software?				
Are the standards being followed?				
Separation of Related Organizational Functions				
For sensitive applications, have critical duties been separated?				
Where separation of duties is inadequate, do compensating controls exist?				
Physical Environment				
Is the microcomputer in an area that has limited traffic and is secured during off-hours?				
Is an inventory of all hardware, software, and documentation maintained?				
Are the inventory records periodically compared with a physical inventory?				
Does the microcomputer have antistatic protection and approved electrical service?				
Are smoking, drinking, and eating prohibited near the computer?				
Is preventive maintenance performed?				
Are data diskettes:				
• Stored away from extreme temperatures, humidity, magnets, CRT terminals, telephones, and radios?				
• Labeled with a felt-tip pen?				
• Handled carefully (no touching, folding, bending, or stapling)?				
• Stored in protective jackets in an upright position?				

* Not Applicable

FIGURE 17-8   Controlling microcomputer checklist.

	Yes	No	NA*	Comments

Data Security

Are data diskettes kept in a secure location?
Is sensitive data on disks password-protected or encrypted?
Does the host computer allow access by only authorized
    microcomputer users?
Is microcomputer access permitted for only specific files? Are
    levels of authority (e.g., inquiry, update, downloading or
    uploading) restricted appropriately
Does the host computer log all system accesses?
Are all security violations investigated?

Backup and Recovery

Are write-protection labels in place for all backup diskettes?
Does each diskette and disk have a backup?
Are backups as current as the working copies?
Are backups stored in a secure location away from the
    microcomputer?
Is a backup microcomputer with an equivalent configuration
    available?
Is a maintenance agreement used?
Is insurance coverage in force?

Documentation

Is there adequate documentation for each application?
Does the documentation include:

- Clear labeling of all data diskettes and documentation?
- Brief application narrative including functions performed and
  major data elements?
- Source code listing?
- Vendor-supplied documentation?
- Such information as application author, software product used,
  and file names?
- Training manuals?
- A hot line number?

Software Integrity

Is the most current vendor software used?
Are applications tested before they are used?
Are application controls and audit trails adequate?

Miscellaneous

Is the copying of proprietary software prohibited except for
    archival purposes or to facilitate use on a hard disk?
Are warranty cards completed promptly?
Are the microcomputers used for only business purposes except
    when proper approval is given?

* Not Applicable

FIGURE 17-8   (Continued)

18

Accounting Information Systems for Service and Not-for-Profit Organizations

Among the important questions that you should be able to answer after reading this chapter are:

1. What are some common accounting information systems problems in a service organization such as a law firm or a medical clinic?
2. Why doesn't a service organization such as a consulting firm have a "merchandise inventory" asset on its balance sheet?
3. Why are the budgetary planning and controlling systems in service organizations typically less effective than the budgetary systems in nonservice organizations?
4. Why is effective budgetary planning and controlling more important in a not-for-profit organization such as a state university than in a profit-oriented organization?
5. Would a hospital be classified as a service organization, a not-for-profit organization, or a combination of both types of organizations?

INTRODUCTION

Up to this point, little attention has been given to either service organizations (such as law firms, CPA firms, consulting firms, medical clinics, banks, and restaurants) or not-for-profit organizations (such state universities, the military, and the police). A service organization normally provides "intangible services" rather than "tangible goods" to its customers and is a profit-oriented organization. Since a not-for-profit organization (sometimes called a **nonprofit** organization) also typically provides "intangible services" to its customers, the not-for-profit organization is a type of service organization. However, by defi-nition, not-for-profit organizations are not profit-oriented. These organizations' successes are evaluated based on their contributions to the public welfare.

This chapter will analyze some of the major oper-ating aspects of both service organizations and not-for-profit organizations. Since many college graduates will be employed by one of these types of organizations, an entire chapter covering them is essential. Primary attention will be devoted to discussing those accounting information systems characteristics that are unique to the service and the not-for-profit organizations. Also provided are some practical examples of the use of com-puters in service and not-for-profit organizations.

SERVICE ORGANIZATIONS

The term **service organization** encompasses a wide variety of business establishments that pro-vide services to customers. Included within the service organization classification of business en-tities are restaurants, hotels, barber and beauty shops, law firms, CPA firms, transportation firms, medical clinics, consulting firms, banks, motion picture and television studios, and athletic orga-nizations such as professional baseball or foot-ball teams.

Unique Characteristics of Service Organizations

Compared with organizations that provide tangi-ble goods (such as an automobile manufacturer) to their customers, service organizations have several unique operating characteristics. The dis-tinguishing characteristics of most service orga-nizations include (1) the absence of an inventory of saleable merchandise, (2) the importance of professional employees, (3) the difficulty in mea-suring the quantity and quality of output, and (4) the smallness of size. Each of these four char-acteristics will now be discussed.

Absence of Merchandise Inventory

This characteristic can greatly affect the revenue-earning activities of a service organization. A manufacturer of tangible goods (such as the Alan Company, which manufactures sporting goods) builds up an inventory of merchandise for both current and future sales. This inventory serves as a buffer against future possible sales fluctuations. For example, if the Alan Company expects next month's basketball sales to exceed the basketball manufacturing capacity of the plant, the company can increase the current month's basketball pro-duction. Alternatively, if the Alan Company loses some sporting goods sales this month as a result of poor marketing efforts, perhaps these sales can be made up in subsequent months (for in-stance, through more efficient marketing pro-grams).

Most service organizations cannot manufac-ture an inventory of merchandise for present and future sales. The so-called inventory that a service organization sells in its revenue-earning endeav-ors consists of the *services* that the organization's employees provide to customers. These services cannot be accumulated in an inventory. There-fore, any failure today to earn revenues from services cannot directly be made up tomorrow or next month. The revenue lost from not providing the services today has a high probability of never being earned. For example, on a Saturday night, the Fine Taste Restaurant may have to turn away some customers because all the available table space has been reserved. These customers will likely make reservations at another restaurant, causing the Fine Taste Restaurant to lose forever the revenues that could have been earned from them that evening. Of course, the customers turned away on Saturday night may make reservations at the Fine Taste Restaurant for Sunday night or next weekend. The point, however, is that a service organization such as a restaurant is unable to stockpile an inventory to meet fluctuations in sales demand. The Fine Taste Restaurant may have 75% of its dining tables unoccupied on Monday night, whereas the demand for dining tables on Saturday night may exceed the supply. Ideally, the restaurant's management could plan an inventory buildup of customer dining services Monday night and then sell these services Saturday night. Obviously, this type of inventory buildup would be impossible.

Importance of Professional Employees

In many service organizations, the most important "asset resources" are the specialized skills of their personnel. True, skilled employees are also important to the efficient operation of a nonservice organization such as a manufacturing firm. But for a large number of service organizations, the *only* product offered is the professional talents (an *intangible* product) of their human resources. For example, a law firm could not function properly without trained lawyers. Similarly, how could a professional football team operate without the talents of its athletes?

Measurement of Quantity and Quality of Output

In a manufacturing firm such as the Alan Company, the organization's accountants can develop both quantity and quality standards for the manufactured inventory items. If the actual physical

quantity of manufactured sporting goods within a specified time period varies significantly from the predetermined standard production quantity, management-by-exception reports can be prepared to disclose these variations. Furthermore, as the Alan Company's tangible sporting goods inventory items come off the assembly line, quality control experts can inspect the merchandise for defective items. Thus, any defective merchandise can be discovered before it is sold to customers.

Quantity and quality standards of output are difficult, if not impossible, to develop in most service organizations because a tangible output product does not exist. A further problem when attempting to establish output quantity standards in a service organization is the fact that much of the work performed is nonrepetitive, thereby making it extremely difficult to develop a standard quantity of output for a specified period of work time. In an eight-hour workday, for example, a lawyer may talk to four clients with four completely different problems. (One of the clients may be facing a murder charge, whereas another client is filing for a divorce!) The lawyer may consult with each of these clients for approximately two hours. However, the number of hours spent with a client is no indication of the quantity of actual services provided to the client since the services (the legal advice) are an intangible product. Because each client's problems are unique, any attempt to establish a quantity standard of legal services per hour would be very difficult. Furthermore, because no tangible product (whose quality level can be physically inspected) results from the lawyer's services, any attempt to establish a quality standard of output would be highly subjective. For example, the client facing a murder charge may receive a 20- to 30-year prison sentence. The lawyer may feel that he or she performed a "brilliant" defense because the client could have received a life sentence. The client, on the other hand, may be quite dissatisfied with the lawyer's work because this client expected to receive only a 10-year sentence. The debate concerning the quality of the lawyer's performance could continue indefinitely without being resolved.

The difficulty of establishing a quality standard of performance for professional workers (whether an accountant, a lawyer, an engineer, or a doctor) and then determining whether or not this standard has been met is probably the major factor in the number of negligence suits filed against professionals. If, for example, a doctor performs heart surgery on a patient and the patient subsequently dies, the deceased person's family may sue the doctor for negligence. Because of the difficulty involved in assessing the quality of care provided to this deceased patient, the matter of negligence is often a subjective issue.

Smallness of Size

This characteristic does not apply to all service organizations. (For example, some CPA firms have 500 or more partners and offices in over 100 cities.) However, many service organizations are relatively small business firms that operate from a single office. Service organizations' smallness enables such companies' top management personnel to exercise close control over day-to-day operating activities rather than having to delegate this control function to lower-level managers (as in large organizations).

From a cost/benefit standpoint, the limited daily volume of financial transactions that occur in most small service organizations would not justify these companies' having large and expensive computerized data processing systems. However, because of the stiff competition that often exists among several service firms in the same geographical location (e.g., it is common to find 100 or more small restaurants within a city's boundaries) and the resultant need for timely information that contributes to more efficient and effective decision making, many service organizations utilize some form of automated data processing. A restaurant, for example, may contract with a service bureau to process its monthly sales transactions, its inventory transactions for food supplies, and its accounts payable data. It is also quite common for small service organizations to acquire their own microcomputer or minicomputer systems. These systems are inexpensive and can be used very effectively for many accounting data processing functions of the small service firm. For instance, it is important for a restaurant to have timely data about the current balances of the many inventory food items in stock so that a specific inventory item can be reordered when its balance gets too low. Otherwise, the firm may run out of a needed item (such as hamburger meat) before it can be replenished. As a consequence, the restaurant would be unable to fill customers' requests, possibly causing these customers to take their business to the restaurant across the street. To obtain timely inventory data and avoid such problems, the restaurant might purchase a microcomputer to maintain current food inventory information rather than continue to utilize its manual inventory record-keeping system. The restaurant could also use its microcomputer system for other accounting applications such as general ledger, payroll and accounts payable. The use of microcomputers in service organizations will be discussed further in a later section of this chapter.

In the past several years, various types of minicomputer systems have been developed to meet the specific data processing needs of small service organizations. For example, a minicomputer system called the *dental management computer system* has been designed by Praxis, Ltd. for use by dentists who have their own small medical firms to service patients. This computer system includes 12-inch cathode ray tube (CRT) video display terminals, a high-speed printer, a 70-megabyte dual hard disk storage unit, a central processing unit, and dental software packages. The dental management computer system is capable of performing seven major data processing functions: personal communication, appointment book, patient records maintenance, accounts receivable, disbursements, general ledger, and payroll. Figure 18-1 reflects a schematic diagram of the specific data processing activities that the minicomputer system can perform within each of these seven functions. (The diagram also indicates the types of "maintenance and utilities" functions that the system is able to execute.)

As another example of the use of minicomputer systems by service organizations, MCAUTO Health Services, a major divisional company of McDonnell Douglas Corporation, has developed what it calls a *mini-based hospital system (MHS)*. This system enables hospitals to process on a timely basis both internal and external reports. The MHS automates all important accounting functions of hospitals and provides them with immediate access to both patient and accounting information. The minicomputer system allows a hospital to start with only one terminal and expand up to 48. The hospital's computer can grow from a 32,000-byte memory system to a 512,000 byte memory system and from 20 million characters up to 514 million characters of disk storage without buying a new processor or rewriting applications software. Printers are available for the system at 150, 300, or 600 lines per minute as well as 165 characters per second. The mini-based hospital system permits multiple CRT terminal operators easily to update and retrieve information stored in online data files. Reports can be printed at the same time data are being entered into a terminal. Figure 18-2 presents a schematic diagram of the mini-based hospital system.

The *patient accounting subsystem* of MHS performs functions that provide hospital management with information to manage patient accounts, control revenue, bill patients and insurance companies, and monitor accounts receivable. Some examples of reports that are processed for this subsystem are as follows.

Patient Account Management. Daily operating summary and accounts receivable summary aging analysis.

Patient and Insurance Billing. Patient final bill, patient detail bill, and Medicare claim forms.

Accounts Receivable. Statement of accounts, aged trial balance, delinquent account list, and summary of incurred charges.

Revenue Control. Detail revenue report, revenue analysis by area as well as by errors and exceptions, and late-charge register.

The *general accounting subsystem* of MHS includes the general ledger, responsibility reporting, accounts payable, and payroll and personnel functions. Following are a few examples of reports that are processed for the general accounting subsystem.

Responsibility Reporting. Responsibility reports with statistical analysis as well as significant variance reports.

General Ledger. Detailed income statement, detailed balance sheet, and department budget reports.

Accounts Payable. Alphabetic vendor list, detailed cash requirements, daily cash disbursements, check register, and detailed expense distribution.

Payroll and Personnel. Current payroll register, payroll analysis, labor distribution register, abnormal hours report, and employee birthday list.

Having analyzed several of the operating characteristics found in most service organizations, we will now discuss some specific budgetary planning and controlling attributes that are common to many of these organizations.

Budgetary Attributes of Service Organizations

Most service organizations' budgetary planning and controlling systems are not as effective as the budgetary systems of those business firms that manufacture and sell tangible goods. Among the principal reasons for service organizations often having ineffective budget planning and controlling systems are (1) the smaller investment in

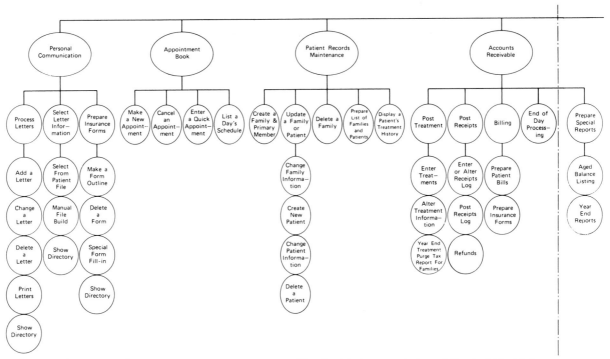

FIGURE 18-1 Dental management computer system. (Used with the permission of Praxis, Ltd., Alpine, Utah.)

long-term tangible assets, (2) the difficulty in defining operational goals, and (3) the difficulty in evaluating performance. Each of these three reasons is now examined in greater detail.

Smaller Investment in Long-Term Tangible Assets

As discussed in Chapter 3, most long-range budgetary planning decisions involve the evaluation of alternative program proposals, each of which requires a major dollar investment in long-term assets (e.g., a new building or new machinery). Because of the large cost involved in acquiring long-term tangible assets such as a building or additional machinery and the difficulty of reversing the acquisition decision once it is made, many organizations will perform rather sophisticated long-range budgetary planning prior to

committing themselves to long-term asset investments. For each major long-term asset investment under consideration, an organization should, for example, compare the present value of the total expected net cash flows from the asset's use with the present value of the total expected cash investment necessary to acquire the asset (i.e., employ the "excess present value index" method discussed in Chapter 3). Then, those investment alternatives having the largest expected excess present value indexes are selected for implementation.

For the typical service organization, however, the principal assets in both the long run and in the short run are people rather than things. (There are exceptions, of course, such as a hotel with its major dollar investment in a building facility.) As a result, the only long-range budgetary planning commonly performed in many

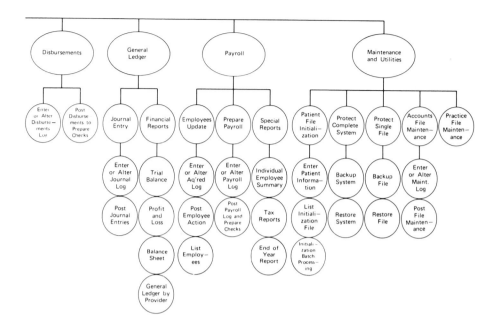

FIGURE 18-1   (Continued)

service organizations (such as those law firms, CPA firms, restaurants, and athletic organizations that lease rather than purchase their building facilities) are forecasts of long-range employee staffing needs. However, even when projecting long-range staffing needs, most service organizations do not use formal quantitative methods (such as the "excess present value index" method) in the budgetary planning of their future labor requirements. Rather, a service organization's top management will often hire additional personnel based on highly subjective judgments about the firm's current and future staffing needs. One major reason for this subjective and normally less effective budgetary approach in service organizations is the difficulty of quantifying the anticipated benefits from hiring additional staff. On the other hand, a manufacturing firm considering the acquisition of new pro-

duction equipment can attempt to measure the benefits from this equipment (although not easily measured) by analyzing the additional tangible goods that the equipment will be able to manufacture and then estimating the additional revenue that will be earned from selling the goods produced.

A second major reason for less effective long-range budgetary planning methods in service organizations is the result of the increased flexibility of these organizations in reversing a previous long-range budget decision. For example, if a CPA firm hires two additional staff members and subsequently (say, a year later) the two employees' services are no longer needed, the CPA firm's top management can terminate their employment without great difficulty and cost to the firm. However, if a manufacturing organization acquires additional machinery costing $500,000

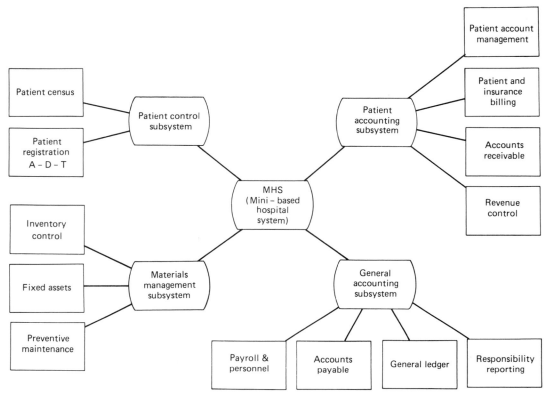

FIGURE 18-2   Mini-based hospital system. (Used with the permission of McDonnell Douglas Corporation, Hazelwood, Missouri.)

and a year later realizes that this equipment is unnecessary, the difficulty and cost of reversing the previous decision could be detrimental to the success of the organization's operations.

Difficulty in Defining Operational Goals

As has been emphasized previously in our text, the development of a budgetary system requires that an organization's long-range nonoperational multiplicity of goals first be established. Then, based on these nonoperational goals (such as achieving a satisfactory level of net income, achieving a high quality of manufactured inventory items, etc.), the organization develops its short-range and long-range operational budgets. For business firms that manufacture and sell tangible goods and normally have a major investment in long-term tangible assets, the budgeted

level of net income performance can be based on a satisfactory "return-on-assets employed" (i.e., net income ÷ total assets). However, for a service organization, the quantity of tangible assets required to earn a satisfactory net income is often minimal. Rather, the major resource that contributes to many service organizations' income-earning capabilities is the *skills* of their professional staff (e.g., the accountants in a CPA firm and the doctors in a medical firm). Because it is difficult, if not impossible, to quantify monetarily the skills of a service organization's professional staff, the determination of a satisfactory "return-on-assets employed" operational goal monetary measure for budgetary planning is unattainable. Without a monetarily determined asset base from which a satisfactory level of net income performance can be planned, budget forecasting of the service organization's acceptable future net income level is extremely difficult.

In its budgetary planning, a manufacturing firm can establish a "quality level" operational goal for its inventory and then plan the production process (e.g., purchase the proper quality of raw materials to be used in the manufacturing activities) so that this preestablished quality level can be achieved. As discussed earlier, the products sold by most service organizations are of an intangible rather than a tangible nature (such as the systems change recommendations provided to a client by a consulting firm). Therefore, any efforts by a service organization to develop preestablished operational quality goals for its intangible products involve considerable subjectivity.

Another factor that makes defining operational goals quite difficult (especially in professional service organizations such as law firms, CPA firms, and medical clinics) is the motivation of the professional staff. A professional often has motivational goals that point in two conflicting directions: (1) goals that contribute to the operational success of the business firm where he or she works and (2) goals that contribute to the professional's recognition by colleagues. The former goals are positively related to the goals of the professional worker's organization, whereas the professional worker's latter goals may be inconsistent with the goals of the organization. For example, during a doctor's normal eight-hour workday in a medical clinic, approximately six of these hours may be devoted to patient care and the other two to the doctor's personal research. The six hours during which the doctor is working with patients contribute directly to the medical clinic's profit goal because the doctor's services earn revenue for the clinic. However, the direct contribution that the doctor makes to the medical clinic's goals during the two hours devoted to research may be questionable. If the research work enables the doctor to publish several articles in professional medical journals, this doctor will receive positive recognition from colleagues. But during the two-hour daily research

period, the doctor is not directly involved in earning any clinic revenues, which otherwise could be earned if the medical doctor were seeing patients. Thus, the work time that is spent on research would actually be inconsistent with the medical clinic's profit goal. (Of course, if the doctor becomes well known from the research, more patients may start coming to the medical clinic, thereby causing the clinic's net income to increase significantly!) When a service organization attempts to establish operational goals as the basis for budgetary planning, it becomes very difficult to forecast what positive effects might accrue to the organization as a result of the employees' professional recognition goals.

Difficulty in Evaluating Performance

Chapters 2 and 3 discussed the importance of timely performance reports disclosing significant variations between budget projections and actual results. The information from these control reports enables a company's management to investigate any significant budget variations and institute corrective action.

The difficulty in evaluating a service organization's operating performance arises from the previously discussed reason (i.e., the difficulty in defining operational goals) for these types of organizations having less effective budgetary systems. It is a vicious circle with no escaping! In order to develop an effective budgetary planning system, a business firm first must clarify its operational goals. If an organization is unable to define its operational goals formally (as is true in many service organizations), the process of preparing financial budgets becomes extremely difficult. Without reliable budget data available to compare with actual operating data, any attempt to evaluate the efficiency of the firm's operational performance is a difficult undertaking. Even in specific situations where a fairly reliable budget projection can be made for a service organization's operating activities, the evaluation of the organization's subsequent performance is usually still quite difficult.

For example, a consulting firm's top management may be able to estimate that approximately 350 hours will be necessary to perform a systems study for its client company. Based on this estimate, the consulting firm's budget planners can develop financial forecasts of the expected costs and revenues from performing the consulting job. When the systems study work is finished, the budget projections can be compared with the actual results. However, these comparisons do not reveal the true efficiency or inefficiency of the consulting firm's services to its client. The consulting firm did not provide the client company any "tangible product" whose quality could be examined. Rather, an "intangible product" (the systems change recommendations) resulted from the consulting firm's work. Since there are often so many variables beyond the consulting firm's control that determine the effectiveness of its client company's new system (such as the competency of the client's employees and the financial stability of the client company), any attempt to evaluate the efficiency or inefficiency of the consultants' systems change recommendations will be very subjective. Furthermore, the newly designed system may have to operate for several years before an evaluation can be made of the system's effectiveness in contributing to the client company's goals.

Computers in Service Organizations

This section of the chapter provides some practical examples of how computers are being used today in a few types of service organizations, with an emphasis on microcomputers and their use in service firms. In the past several years, many service organizations have integrated microcomputers into their information systems. A previous section of this chapter has illustrated minicomputer systems for dentists and for hospitals. The specific types of service organizations that will be examined here are railroads, banks, and a restaurant.

Computers and Railroads

When a freight train passes by, the first thing you see is a powerful locomotive chugging away, pulling the train. Locomotives are extremely expensive items; thus, railroad organizations spend millions of dollars each year buying and repairing them. Microcomputers are now helping railroads improve their management functions such as cost planning. In Washington, D.C., at the Association of American Railroads (AAR) (a trade group that supports commercial freight railroads) analysts have developed a spreadsheet model to aid railroads in their cost planning activities.

This customized spreadsheet model uses Lotus 1-2-3 or Symphony on an IBM PC/XT. The model can be used by any member railroad to plan for expenditures when replacing or repairing worn-out locomotives. With appropriate formulas programmed into the model, any railroad can quickly discern the financial picture in managing its locomotive fleet, or can experiment with different financial scenarios. In the past, railroads were forced to figure costs with pencil and paper. Because that took a great amount of time, analysts could consider only a very few spending plans. Now that planning can be done on a microcomputer, budget planners have many more viable alternatives to consider, which makes managing budgets a much smoother process.

A specific example of a railroad that today uses microcomputers is the Canadian Pacific Railroad, which has been in operation since 1885. Although Canadian Pacific is an old railroad, it has entered the computer age. At first, Canadian Pacific did this with large mainframe computers and terminals. Today the railroad is also using small but very powerful microcomputers. These micros are transforming the way work is being done at Canadian Pacific Railroad.

One of the most dazzling feats microcomputers perform for the railroad is to help with the dispatching of trains. Dispatchers manage the movements and clearances of trains over hundreds of miles of track. Following complex safety rules, they must keep trains from colliding or running onto a section of track under repair. In the past, the dispatching function was performed with a handwritten log. Now the job is handled by an IBM PC and a program that "knows" all the rules. This program has the potential to save lives as well as millions of dollars through the elimination of jobs.

Jack Rutko, a dispatcher in Canadian Pacific Railroad's Saskatoon, Saskatchewan station, uses the program every day. "The computer to us is the best thing since sliced bread," Rutko says. On the microcomputer screen, commercial freight trains moving into or out of the 720 miles of track he dispatches are shown as color-coded bars. Each time he issues a dispatch, Rutko keys in the information, and the colored bars advance on-screen, so he can see at a glance which sections of track are busy and where each train is currently located.

Like air traffic controllers, dispatchers work under a great deal of pressure and try to picture mentally what the traffic situation is at all times. "Now with the computer and a color monitor, the picture is always there right in front of you," Rutko says. The microcomputer is also much speedier. "The computer saves us time, and it relieves a lot of pressure," Rutko says.

Perhaps most important, all the rules are programmed in, "So there's less chance for us to make a mistake," states Rutko. In the past, human errors were probable when the handwritten system was used. "I could have two trains go head on, or two trains tail-end each other," Rutko says. Since the microcomputer program has been in use, there have been fewer dispatching mistakes.

Overall, this single microcomputer program has made Canadian Pacific Railroad a much more efficient and effective company. "Let's put it this way," Rutko says. "The Canadian National Railroad, which is our competition, wishes it had this program."

Computers and Banks

Banks were among the first institutions to use **data communications systems.** A data com-munications system transmits data from one location (called the source) to another location (called the receiver). To illustrate, a remote terminal transmits data to a centralized computer for processing. The data to be transmitted, referred to as the *message,* are entered into the sending terminal and stored. When the terminal is ready to transmit the data, a communications interface device, such as a modem, converts the input data to signals that can be transmitted over a communications channel (for example, a telephone line). At the message's destination another communications interface device converts the data back into internal computer code and forwards the message to the receiving computer. When the receiving unit sends a message back to the source to verify that the message is received, the data communications process is reversed. Communications software controls the system and manages all communications tasks.

In a banking system, many customer functions are performed at teller windows and at automated teller machines (ATMs). A major function at a bank is checking a customer's account to determine whether the account balance is large enough for a withdrawal being made by the waiting customer. In addition, deposits and withdrawals may be posted to customer accounts through the system. Hardware requirements of a bank's data communications system include a data terminal for each teller window, ATMs at various locations, and online file storage to maintain a record of every customer's account.

A bank's data communications system makes an up-to-date record of each customer's account available to every teller and ATM, even those tellers and ATMs located at a considerable distance from the main bank. These data communications systems enable banks to provide faster and more convenient service to their customers, and, at the same time, allow banks to reduce the number of tellers required to wait on customers.

Many banks have expanded their computer applications into additional areas, such as mortgages, consumer loans, commercial loans, and credit files. In recent years the concept of one large data communications system to handle all banking transactions has emerged. For example, retail merchants can be tied into the banking network through point-of-sale terminals and microcomputers. A sales transaction of a retail merchant can be immediately charged to the customer's bank account and simultaneously credited to the merchant's account. As another example, individuals, using microcomputers and modems, can access their bank's system and pay all their bills electronically. This approach to paying bills has become known as **electronic funds transfer** (EFT). Deposit of paychecks directly to the bank accounts of employees by their employers can also be done electronically under an electronic funds transfer system.

The ATM provides bank customers with banking services twenty-four hours each day. All customers have to do is find an ATM, insert their specially coded plastic bankcard, and punch in a PIN (personal identification number). The PIN is a confidential code known only to the bank's customer and the computer. Using the bank's data communications network, the ATM checks the PIN to see if it matches the account number on the bankcard. If a match occurs, the user can withdraw or deposit funds. With the proper ATM and data communications links, the user can also purchase a variety of other items, such as airline tickets and theater tickets.

Computers and a Restaurant

When you think of hamburgers and fries, you probably think of McDonald's. However, Burger King runs a close second. In its endeavors to increase sales, Burger King is peddling hamburgers from mobile vans, called the Burger King Express, which are wheeled to baseball parks, colleges, and military bases. Burger King also has more than 900 company-owned restaurants. In addition, there are many more Burger King restaurants operated by franchisers.

The managing of these far-flung restaurants is a demanding job that requires assistance by microcomputers. Large mainframes at corporate headquarters in Miami hold extensive data bases containing information about each Burger King restaurant in the country. However, day-to-day management of the restaurants is handled by a number of regional offices, all equipped with microcomputers.

In his job as regional accounting manager in the Detroit office, Scott Phillips makes extensive use of the corporate data base on his micro. By communicating with the Miami mainframe via modem, he can find out what he needs to know—from a restaurant's identification number and address to the name of its franchisee, sales volume, and contract information. Phillips needs this information to make sales projections, to establish sales trends based on sales histories, and to find out when certain lease contracts will expire so he can budget for new ones.

Phillips depends continuously on the micro and the data base. "The computer is on from eight in the morning until six at night," he says. "It's an extension of my right hand." If Phillips wants to further examine any information from the mainframe, he downloads the data to a file for his micro, using programs such as Condor or dBASE III. "I can download any time at my convenience and get current information due to the mainframe data base being constantly updated," he says. For example, Phillips can download information on restaurant openings, sort it by date, and find out what restaurants opened in the last ten years. Information regarding when a restaurant opened is needed to calculate its average monthly sales volume.

The kind of sorting needed by Phillips cannot be done by dialing up the mainframe. It can be performed only by manipulating data on a micro. "The micro allows for better reporting, because we can sort and track, versus doing individual queries on the corporate data base," Phillips says.

Concluding Comments on Service Organizations

Accounting information systems face a major challenge due to the unique characteristics of service organizations. The main reason for this challenge is that most service organizations provide their customers with intangible products in which quantity and quality standards are difficult to measure. The measurement problems associated with service organizations are partly the result of the historical development of cost accounting systems. The cost accounting field was originally developed to aid manufacturing companies in accumulating the costs of their work-in-process and finished goods inventories for financial statement reporting. Methods of establishing standards and of reporting variances from standard performance were designed for manufacturing companies' tangible inventory items.

Only in recent years have accountants started to look at some of the measurement problems in service organizations and to recognzie the need for more effective accounting systems (e.g., cost accounting systems) in these types of business firms whose principal assets are often the skills of employees. Some accountants have attempted to measure the value of a service organization's human resource asset. In those service organizations where the employees' professional skills are the major "products" sold, a monetarily measured human resource asset would be equivalent to a manufacturing firm's monetarily measured merchandise inventory asset. As mentioned in the previous section of this chapter, computers (especially microcomputers) have been integrated into many service organizations' information systems.

Having completed the discussion of service organizations, we now turn our attention to not-for-profit organizations and some of the major operating aspects associated with these types of organizations.

NOT-FOR-PROFIT ORGANIZATIONS

The various types of organizations we have discussed throughout the book were assumed to have the earning of a satisfactory net income as one of their goals. A **not-for-profit organization,** on the other hand (e.g., a governmental organization such as a public hospital, a state university, a police department, a church, or a fire department), exists primarily to provide services for the protection and betterment of society and does not have a profit goal.

In the previous analysis of service organizations we discussed several unique characteristics that typically distinguish a service organization from an organization that sells tangible goods. This same type of approach will again be used in examining not-for-profit organizations. Thus, we will now look at some of the specific characteristics that distinguish a not-for-profit organization from a profit-oriented business firm.

Unique Characteristics of Not-for-Profit Organizations

The distinguishing characteristics of most not-for-profit organizations include (1) a service organization usually staffed by professional employees, (2) a lack of a profit measure, (3) a smaller role of the market mechanism, and (4) a political emphasis. Each of these four characteristics will now be examined.

Service Organization Usually Staffed by Professional Employees

Many not-for-profit organizations are similar to service organizations in that (1) the not-for-profit organizations also provide their customers intangible services rather than tangible goods, and (2) the professional skills of the not-for-profit organizations' employees are the most important asset resources. For example, the major asset of relevance to a state university is the knowledge of the faculty. In addition, the principal product offered by a state unviersity is an intangible service, "education." Whereas a state or city publicly financed educational institution (financed through taxpayers' income tax payments, etc.) is a not-for-profit type of organization, a privately operated school is profit-oriented and would thus be classified as a service organization. Similarly, a publicly financed hospital or medical clinic is a not-for-profit organization, but a privately operated hospital or medical clinic has a profit goal and is therefore considered a service organization.

Since the provision of intangible services to customers and the importance of professional employees exist both in service and not-for-profit organizations, many of the previously discussed characteristics of service organizations also apply to not-for-profit organizations. Most not-for-profit organizations are unable to accumulate an inventory of merchandise for current and future sales, and these types of organizations often have difficulty measuring the quantity and quality of their output. For example, a church cannot build up an inventory of religious inspirational motivation to offer its members, and it is normally quite difficult to measure the quantity and quality of the output from the church. Earlier in this chapter we discussed the systems problems resulting from a service organization not being able to accumulate an inventory of saleable merchandise and from the difficulty in measuring the quantity and quality of output. These same systems problems can also occur in a not-for-profit organization.

Lack of a Profit Measure

As emphasized in Chapter 3, on budgetary accounting information systems, a profit-oriented business organization is able to measure both its inputs (costs or expenses) and its outputs (revenues) monetarily. The organization's operating effectiveness can then be evaluated based on the extent to which its outputs exceed its inputs (a "net income"). For most not-for-profit organizations, however, inputs can be measured monetarily but outputs are difficult, if not impossible, to quantify in monetary terms. Without a monetary measure of both the inputs and the outputs from a specific organizational activity, a profit measure for evaluating the activity's effectiveness cannot be obtained. True, a not-for-profit organization, by definition, does not have a profit goal.

However, in order to survive and continue its principal goal of providing useful services to society, one of a not-for-profit organization's goals should be a "break-even" operating performance level (i.e., that level of performance where the input expenses exactly equal the output revenues).

The inability to measure the output performance monetarily makes it very difficult to evaluate several proposed courses of action that a not-for-profit organization might pursue. Consider the case of a city government that is attempting to evaluate two program alternatives for possible implementation: (1) expand the police department by hiring five additional law-enforcement officers or (2) expand the fire department by hiring five additional fire fighters. Ideally, a cost/benefit type of analysis should be performed on each alternative program proposal so that the alternative with the greatest benefits in relation to costs can be selected. Approximate costs can be reasonably estimated for the two preceding alternatives. The costs of the individual programs will include such things as the anticipated annual salaries and fringe benefits provided to the law-enforcement officers under the one program and the fire fighters under the other program. However, any attempt to measure monetarily the anticipated benefits (or *outputs*) from each program alternative would be extremely difficult. After all, how can one place a monetary measure on the value of protecting a citizen's life and personal property as a result of hiring additional law-enforcement officers or measure monetarily the value of protecting a citizen's life and personal property as a result of hiring additional fire fighters? Because of the difficulties encountered by many not-for-profit organizations when attempting to determine the monetary benefits from program proposals, highly subjective means are often used in selecting specific programs for implementation.

Smaller Role of the Market Mechanism

The typical profit-oriented business firm operates in a highly competitive market environment and must continually evaluate consumer's demands for goods and services. Profit-oriented organizations must also be highly concerned about cost efficiency so that they can sell their products or services at a competitive price and earn a profit on their various revenue-producing activities.

On the other hand, many not-for-profit organizations are only slightly, if at all, affected by competition, and they typically need not be as concerned about consumers' demands for specific goods and services as profit-oriented firms. For example, a publicly financed university usually will offer educational programs to the residents of its state at a substantially smaller cost than either a private university or a publicly financed university in another state (because the residents would have to pay the higher out-of-state tuition if they elected to attend another state's university). Due to the rising costs of education and the limited number of dollars many families have for sending their children to college, a publicly financed university normally will have little, if any, competition regarding the educational opportunities offered in its state. This lack of competition from other educational institutions often causes a publicly financed university to give minimal attention to its consumers' (i.e., the students') demands. Courses within various curricula may be designed for faculty members' subject interests rather than for students' requests for topic coverage. Because of lack of competition, the school attracts adequate student "consumers" even though little or no attention is given to the students' curricula demands.

The continued survival of a not-for-profit organization is not dependent on earning an income. As a result, some not-for-profit organizations are unconcerned about cost efficiency and they have weak feedback control systems for evaluating the effectiveness of operational performance. A major reason for a lack of effective feedback controls in some governmental organizations, for example, is that the *owners* of these not-for-profit organizations are actually the taxpayers. Because taxpayers are a diverse group of people who do not directly evaluate the day-to-day operating performance of a governmental organization, inefficiencies that occur within a particular governmental organization may go unnoticed by the taxpayers.

The market competition encountered by a profit-oriented organization and the desire to increase periodic net income performance ordinarily causes the organization to institute promotional activities that attract more customers, thereby resulting in more sales revenue. However, many not-for-profit organizations, whose annual operating budgets are fixed by appropriations (such as in governmental organizations), must sometimes turn customers away. Because of their fixed annual budget appropriations, many publicly financed universities, for example, place a quota on the number of students admitted each year. Consequently, some potential student "customers" are refused admission.

Political Emphasis

Politics has a major impact on the operational environment of many not-for-profit organizations (especially governmental organizations). In governmental agencies (whether a city, state, or federal agency) where the "top management" personnel are elected by the voters, executives are often selected for reasons other than their managerial abilities. The reasons may range from the political candidates' pleasing personalities to their financial standing. A negative consequence may be that once the individuals are elected to office, their lack of managerial skills can lead to inefficiencies.

Another negative aspect of governmental organizations' operating activities is that these institutions must function within the framework of specific statutes enacted by legislators. As a result, a not-for-profit governmental organization often has less flexibility than a profit-oriented organization. Once statutes are established that control the types of operating activities a governmental organization can perform, it is normally very difficult and time-consuming to change these statutes.

Budgetary Attributes of Not-for-Profit Organizations

The following analysis of not-for-profit organization's budgetary systems will center on the two principal forms of budgeting performed in these types of organizations: (1) long-range budgeting for time intervals beyond the coming one-year period and (2) short-range budgeting for the coming one-year period.

Long-Range Budgeting

The use of cost/benefit analysis with zero-based budget reviews (discussed in Chapter 3) is a popular technique for evaluating long-range budgetary programs of profit-oriented organizations. Through this cost/benefit analysis technique, a profit-oriented organization's limited asset resources can be allocated to the most productive program proposals. Not-for-profit organizations also have limited asset resources for implementing long-range budget program proposals. Furthermore, they should strive to utilize these resources in ways that will contribute most effectively to the protection and betterment of society. As a result, many not-for-profit organizations (especially governmental organizations) also employ formal long-range budgetary techniques such as cost/benefit analyses in evaluating program proposals for subsequent implementation. In fact, the federal government started formal use of the cost/benefit analysis technique with zero-based budget reviews many years before profit-oriented organizations were using this long-range budgetary technique. The term **planning-programming-budgeting system (PPBS)** was coined to designate the federal government's cost/benefit analysis approach to long-range budgeting.

As previously discussed, a not-for-profit organizatin's long-range program proposals should be directed toward the protection and betterment of society. Thus, when performing a cost/benefit analysis of a specific program proposal, the anticipated costs and benefits to society must be quantified monetarily. In most cases, however, a monetary determination of society's benefits from a long-range program is very difficult to make. For example, a department of the federal government may be proposing a program to subsidize automobile manufacturers for the costs of installing safety devices on cars. This program's principal benefits would result from the reduced number of automobile accident deaths. Therefore, in performing a cost/benefit analysis of the automobile safety program proposal, the value of saving a human life in an automobile accident must be monetarily quantified. Obviously, the quantification in monetary terms of a person's life would be extremely difficult, thereby making the decision regarding the proposed safety program quite difficult.

Short-Range Budgeting

The establishment of a good short-range budgetary planning and controlling system is normally more important in a not-for-profit organization than in a profit-oriented organization. The reason for the added importance of good short-range budgetary planning and controlling in not-for-profit organizations is the result of the fixed, rather than flexible, nature of most not-for-profit organizations' 12-month budgets. In a profit-oriented organization, flexibility is normally built into its budgetary system. Thus, as the budget year unfolds and management determines that some budgetary costs were underestimated, the profit-oriented organization can revise its budget projections and allocate more dollars to specific expenditures.

However, in a not-for-profit organization, budgetary revisions are difficult, if not impossible, to implement once the budget year begins. For example, in a governmental organization such a publicly financed state university, the educational institution's annual operating budgets are approved by the state legislators and the governor. If subsequent operations under the approved budgets reveal that actual costs will be higher than anticipated in specific areas of the university, additional budgetary appropriations normally will be impossible to obtain. Because these additional appropriations would require legislative action and the state legislators would not be in session (legislative sessions for budget approval typically are held only once a year), the university would have to live with its original budgets. Thus, in those not-for-profit organizations subject to **fixed** (also called **static**) budgets, good short-range planning is necessary to obtain accurate budget projections for the coming year. Hopefully, effective budgetary planning will avoid such a situation in which the state university's budgeted costs were inadequate to meet actual operating needs. Of course, effective budgetary control is also an essential element that contributes to a not-for-profit organization's actual operating costs being within the original budget appropriations. In the budgetary control area, a computerized data processing system can play a valuable role. Through timely computerized reports that disclose operational areas where a not-for-profit organization's actual costs exceed original budget appropriations, management can immediately investigate and initiate corrective action before these actual expenditures get too far out of hand.

A further difficulty often encountered in not-for-profit organization's budgetary systems is the absence of a monetary measure of output accomplishments. For example, a city police department does not bill citizens when law-enforcement officers investigate burglaries at their homes. (Of course, citizens pay indirectly for the police services through taxes!) Traditional budgeting typically centers on the planning of both inputs (costs or expenses) and outputs (revenues) in monetary terms. Since monetary output measures may not exist in certain not-for-profit organizations, alternative quantitative output measures will therefore be needed. A common nonmonetary output performance measure used in some not-for-profit organizations' short-range budget systems is a **process measure** (i.e., a measure relating to a specific "activity" performed by an organization's employees). For

instance, within a police department's short-range budget system, one possible process measure could be the number of traffic tickets issued per month by each law-enforcement officer. At month's end, traffic citations actually issued by a law-enforcement officer could be compared with his or her budgeted number of traffic citations to be issued. It should be kept in mind, however, that a specific officer is not necessarily inefficient merely because the actual issued traffic tickets are below the budgeted number in any one month. It may be that people are just driving more carefully!

Computers in Not-for-Profit Organizations

The analysis of service organizations discussed how computers (especially microcomputers) are playing important roles in these organizations' information systems. Computers (both mainframes and micros) are also being used extensively within many not-for-profit organizations' information systems.

For example, in an article written by Clyde Jeffcoat (the Army's senior civilian accountant), he describes changes that are taking place in the accounting information systems of the military. As Jeffcoat states regarding the Army's accounting information systems,

> Technology has necessitated change. We—like much of American industry—have found ourselves in need of modernized systems to meet the increased information demands of management and, in our case, Congress. In fact, the Department of Defense receives some 700,000 inquiries from Congress annually, many of which require information from our accounting systems.[1]

Since the early 1980s, the Army has been involved in changing from numerous, separate accounting systems toward its end goal of a single

[1] Clyde E. Jeffcoat, Jr. "A Different Beat for Army Accountants," *New Accountant,* Volume 4, Number 6, February 1989, pp. 8–9.

integrated computerized accounting system. This system will use a standard government general ledger and basic internal controls for accountability and accuracy. The system will also provide an all-inclusive source of financial management information, regardless of the need or requester. Concerning the Army Accounting System, Jeffcoat describes this system as follows:

> When fully designed and implemented, the Army Accounting System will consist of eight subsystems each of which supports a specific subfunction, such as: civil works, material, field-level retail stock funds, pay for soldiers, pay for civilians, pay for retired soldiers, headquarters-level accounting, and field-level general funds accounting. The data in this system will need to be entered only once and then transferred to appropriate accounts or other parts of the system.[2]

Much of the work has already been completed in designing and implementing the computerized Army Accounting System. Among the positive changes that have been introduced into the integrated computerized accounting system of the Army are:

1. Eliminating the need for 180 personnel by implementing (a) a computerized military pay system in which data are input only once and then these data pass from system to system, and (b) a pay inquiry system.
2. Utilizing labor-saving microcomputer systems for travel disbursements and accounts payable.

The above brief discussion of the military's concern for a more effective accounting information system that integrates the computer into the system was for illustrative purposes only. The important point that we are attempting to make is that most not-for-profit organizations, just like profit-oriented business firms, want to have effective accounting information systems. The development and operation of an effective accounting information system in this day and age, whether in a not-for-profit or a profit-oriented

firm, typically require the integration of some form of computerization into the firm's system.

Concluding Comments on Not-for-Profit Organizations

The major challenge that accounting information systems face regarding not-for-profit organizations is the difficulty in evaluating their operating performances. Because we are all taxpayers who provide financial support for many not-for-profit organizations, we are entitled to receive informational reports that disclose whether or not our tax dollars are being used efficiently and effectively.

The lack of profit measures in not-for-profit organizations makes it difficult for accounting information systems to report on the operational effectiveness of these organizations. Conventional accounting information systems are designed to measure organizational performance by comparing monetary inputs with monetary outputs. But, in many not-for-profit organizations, monetary output measures do not exist. As a result, these organizations' accountants must develop alternative nonmonetary measures (such as a **process measure**) of output performance, and the alternative measures often are inferior to monetary performance indicators. The inferiority of nonmonetary output measures is due to the fact that the evaluation of a not-for-profit organization's operational activities cannot be performed with a common measuring unit. That is, because a not-for-profit organization's inputs are measured in dollars, ideally the organization's outputs should also be measured in dollars. This would enable a realistic evaluation of performance because the output accomplishments could be related to the input efforts with an identical measuring unit—dollars. However, since many not-for-profit organizations' output accomplishments are measured on a nonmonetary basis, whereas their input efforts are measured on a monetary basis, any attempt to evaluate the organizations' operating performances using these two dissimilar measuring bases can be quite difficult.

[2] *Ibid.,* p. 10.

SUMMARY

Several important operating aspects of service organizations (e.g., restaurants, law firms, consulting firms, and CPA firms) and not-for-profit organizations (e.g., governmental organizations) were analyzed in this chapter. The discussion of service and not-for-profit organizations centered on several of the accounting information systems problems that occur because of their unique characteristics. As pointed out in the chapter, many service organizations and not-for-profit organizations have integrated computers into their information systems in order to make their systems more effective in providing information to users.

Service organizations' employees are often professionally trained individuals who provide "intangible services" to the organizations' customers. As a result of most service organizations selling intangible products (such as legal advice from a law firm or systems revision advice from a consulting firm) rather than tangible goods, these organizations are unable to build up an inventory of their products for current and future sales. In addition, the intangible nature of many service organizations' revenue-producing output makes it quite difficult to develop predetermined quantity and quality standards for this output. Regarding budgetary planning and controlling, several reasons were discussed as to why service organizations normally have less effective budget systems than organizations that manufacture and sell tangible goods. Included among these reasons were the minimal long-term tangible asset investments required by most service organizations (making sophisticated long-range budget techniques unnecessary) and the difficulty in defining the operational goals of many service organizations, an essential first step in establishing effective budgetary accounting information systems.

Not-for-profit organizations have several characteristics that are similar to service organizations. Most not-for-profit organizations, for example, also offer their customers intangible services and hire professionally trained employees. On the other hand, a service organization has a profit goal, and a not-for-profit organization, by definition, does not (other than achieving a "break-even" performance level). In many not-for-profit organizations, monetary quantification is feasible for their inputs but not their outputs. The unavailability of monetary output measures often makes it difficult to establish effective budget systems within a not-for-profit organization. In the area of long-range budgeting, for example, not-for-profit organizations often utilize cost/benefit analyses to evaluate program proposals. To evaluate each proposal effectively, however, both the costs and the benefits must be subject to monetary quantification. For many program proposals of a not-for-profit organization, only the cost inputs can be monetarily quantified. Because the benefit outputs are typically difficult, if not impossible, to quantify in monetary terms, the decision-making process regarding which programs to accept can be perplexing. Upon approval, not-for-profit organizations' short-range budgets are normally fixed rather than being subject to later change. Therefore, good short-range budgetary planning is important so that reasonably accurate annual budget projections can be prepared initially. Monetary measures of output performance for short-range budgetary planning and controlling often are nonexistent in a not-for-profit organization. As an alternative to a monetary measure, a nonmonetary indicator such as a *process measure* may have to be used.

Key Terms You Should Know

break-even operating performance level	dental management computer system
cost/benefit analysis	electronic funds transfer
data communications systems	fixed budgets

flexibility in budgetary system
inputs
intangible services
long-range budgeting
market mechanism
microcomputer systems
mini-based hospital system
minicomputer systems
motivational goals of professional employees
not-for-profit organization

outputs
planning-programming-budgeting system
political emphasis in not-for-profit organizations
process measure
quality standards
quantity standards
return-on-assets employed
service organization
short-range budgeting
static budgets

Discussion Questions

18-1. Four unique characteristics of service organizations were discussed in this chapter. Of these four characteristics, which one do you feel causes the greatest problem for a service organization's accounting information system? Explain.

18-2. Why isn't it possible for a service organization such as a law firm to have a "merchandise inventory" asset? What effect (or effects) does the absence of a "merchandise inventory" asset have on a service organization's revenue earning activities?

18-3. Why is it very difficult to establish quantity and quality standards in most service organizations? If you were an accountant given the responsibility for establishing quantity and quality standards for the food served in an exclusive restaurant, which one of these two types of standards do you feel would be more difficult to determine? Why?

18-4. Jack Butcher is a well-recognized heart surgeon who has been employed at the Healthy House Medical Clinic for the past 10 years. During a recent luncheon, Doctor Jack (as he is called by his friends) made the following comments to his wife.

> Here I am a successful surgeon and currently facing a $100,000 malpractice suit from one of my patients. I talked to our clinic's accountants this morning and they indicated that very little information from the accounting system could help my court defense. A major revision of our accounting information system is definitely needed, and fast, so that when other clinic doctors are facing court action from patients at some future time, these doctors will be able to call on our accountants for help!

Do you agree or disagree with Doctor Jack's comment regarding the clinic's accounting information system? Discuss.

18-5. The Spicy Pizza Parlor has been in operation for the past six months. The restaurant currently uses a manual system for processing such accounting transactions as the weekly payroll for its 10 employees, the monthly payments to creditors for the purchase of ingredients used in cooking pizzas, the acquisition of additional food ingredients when the balances of specific ingredients get too low, and the payment of the monthly rent and utilities bill. The Spicy Pizza Parlor's owner, Don Bartenfelder, feels that business is so good that a computer should be acquired for processing the restaurant's accounting transactions. The pizza parlor's monthly sales have been gradually increasing during each of the six months the business has been functioning (e.g., last month's sales were $7000—a $500 sales increase over the previous month). Don believes that the improved information that could be provided by a computerized data processing system would cause the future operating performance of his restaurant to increase considerably.

Assume that you are a consultant hired by Don Bartenfelder to help him plan the necessary changes in the restaurant's current accounting information system. With the limited information provided here about the restaurant's operations, indicate the procedures you would use in evaluating the pizza parlor's data processing needs. (*Note:* You can make any reasonable assumptions necessary concerning the restaurant's operating activities.) What type of data processing system (a manual system, a purchased or leased online, real-time computerized system from a hardware and software vendor, etc.) would probably be best suited to handle the restaurant's financial transactions? Discuss.

18-6. The following idea was expressed in this chapter: "For the typical service organization, the principal assets in both the long-run and in the short-run are people rather than tangible assets." Discuss the implications of this statement to a service organization's budgetary planning and controlling system.

18-7. Bill Hunt, a partner in the law firm of Hunt, Jacobs, and Bogle, made the following statement during a recent luncheon speech he gave to the Busy Budgeters of America.

> Our law firm recognizes the important role that good budgetary planning and controlling plays in an organization's operational success. All of the partners in our firm participate in developing detailed annual operating budgets. However, when it comes to long-range budgeting, very little, if any, financial projecting is performed. I think the reasons for our lack of attention to long-range budgeting are obvious to all of you.

What do you believe are the obvious reasons for the lack of attention that Bill Hunt's law firm gives to long-range budgeting?

18-8. Discuss some of the factors that typically make it more difficult to define the operational goals of a service organization. How, if at all, does the difficulty in defining a service organization's operational goals affect the organization's budgetary planning and controlling system?

18-9. A major goal common to all universities is the provision of quality education. To help achieve this goal, a university should include in its budgetary planning system adequate provisions for faculty salaries, classroom teaching aids such as overhead projectors and video tape machines, and so forth. What do you think would be the employment goals of faculty members working at a university? For each one of the goals you mentioned, indicate (and give reasons) why you feel the specific goal would contribute positively or negatively to the university's goal of a high-quality student education.

18-10. Do the types of workers employed in an organization (e.g., assembly-line workers in a manufacturing plant compared with accountants in a consulting firm) affect the organization's budgetary planning and controlling activities? Discuss.

18-11. The town of Commuter Park operates a private parking lot near the railroad station for the benefit of town residents. The guard on duty issues annual prenumbered parking stickers to residents who submit an application form and show evidence of residency. The sticker is affixed to the auto and allows the resident to park anywhere in the lot for 12 hours if four quarters are placed in the parking meter. Applications are maintained in the guard office at the lot. The guard checks to see that only residents are using the lot and that no resident has parked without paying the required meter fee.

Once a week the guard on duty, who has a master key for all meters, takes the coins from the meters and places them in a locked steel box. The guard delivers the box to the town storage building, where it is opened, and the coins are counted manually by a storage department clerk who records the total cash counted on a weekly cash report. This report is sent to the town accounting department. The storage department clerk puts the cash in a safe and on the following day the cash is picked up by the town's treasurer, who manually recounts the cash, prepares the bank deposit slip, and delivers the deposit to the bank. The deposit slip, authenticated by the bank teller, is sent to the accounting department, where it is filed with the weekly cash report.

Requirement

Describe weaknesses in the existing system and recommend one or more improvements for each of the weaknesses to strengthen the internal control over the parking lot cash receipts.

Organize your answers as follows.

Weakness	Recommended Improvement(s)

(AICPA Adapted)

18-12. Two major types of not-for-profit organizations are a publicly financed university and a publicly financed hospital. For each of these organizational types, discuss some data processing functions for which (1) an online, real-time computerized system would likely be most beneficial and (2) a batch computerized system would likely be most beneficial.

18-13. Discuss some of the major operating characteristics that are similar and dissimilar in a service organization such as a consulting firm and in a not-for-profit organization such as a police department.

18-14. Would a college be classified as a service organization, a not-for-profit organization, or a combination of both? Explain.

18-15. It was emphasized in this chapter that most not-for-profit organizations lack a profit measure. What effect (or effects), if any, does this lack of a profit measure have on a not-for-profit organization's short- and long-range budgetary planning and controlling system?

18-16. From the viewpoint of society, do you feel that the lack of market competition that many not-for-profit organizations enjoy is good or bad? Explain with a few examples of specific not-for-profit organizations and their positive or negative effects on society.

18-17. The operational environment of a city government unit such as the police department is influenced by politics. Try to think of some positive and negative effects that may occur within the police department's system because of the political impact on the department's operational environment.

18-18. The following statement was made in this chapter: "The establishment of a good short-range budgetary planning and controlling system is normally more important in a not-for-profit organization than in a profit-oriented organization." Do you agree or disagree with this statement? Explain.

18-19. Why might a not-for-profit organization use a process measure in its short-range budgetary system? For each of the following not-for-profit organizations, suggest possible process measures that might be used in its short-range budgetary system: (a) a city fire department, (b) a publicly financed state university, (c) a publicly financed state museum, and (d) a cancer research institute.

18-20. Why is long-range budgetary planning usually more difficult to perform in a not-for-profit organization than in a profit-oriented organization?

18-21. Joan Moward, the mayor of Green Grass City, has convinced the city council that a new pollution control department is necessary to preserve the town's clean environment. The city's budget committee is currently meeting to discuss the pollution control department's short- and long-range budgetary system. Assuming that you are a member of Green Grass City's budget committee, discuss some of the difficulties that the committee might face in its budgetary planning and controlling activities associated with the pollution control department's short- and long-range budget system. (*Note:* Make any reasonable assumptions you feel are necessary regarding the specific functions that the newly established pollution control department will perform.)

18-22. The board of trustees of a local church has asked you to review its accounting procedures. As a part of this review, you have prepared the following comments relating to the collections made at weekly services and the record keeping for members' pledges and contributions.

The church's board of trustees has delegated responsibility for financial management and audit of the financial records to the finance committee. This group prepares the annual budget and approves major disbursements but is not involved in collections or record keeping. No audit has been considered necessary in recent years because the same trusted employee has kept church records and served as financial secretary for 15 years.

The collection at the weekly service is taken by a team of ushers. The head usher counts the collection in the church office following each service. He then places the collection and a notation of the amount counted in the church safe. Next morning the financial secretary opens the safe and recounts the collection. He withholds about $100 to meet cash expenditures during the coming week and deposits the remainder of the collection intact. In order to facilitate the deposit, members who contribute by check are asked to draw their checks to "cash."

At their request, a few members are furnished prenumbered and predated envelopes in which to insert their weekly contributions. The head usher removes the cash from the envelopes so that it can be counted with the loose cash included in the collection. He immediately discards the envelopes. No record is maintained of issuance or return of the envelopes, and the envelope system is not encouraged.

Each member is asked to prepare a contribution pledge card annually. The pledge is regarded as a moral commitment by the member to contribute a stated weekly amount. Based on the amounts shown on the pledge cards, the financial secretary furnishes a letter to requesting members to support the tax deductibility of their contributions.

Requirement

Describe the weaknesses and recommend improvements in procedures for:

a. Collections made at weekly services.

b. Record keeping for members' pledges and contributions.

Organize your answers as follows.

Weakness	Recommended Improvement(s)

(AICPA Adapted)

Problems

18-23.   Each month the department heads of the National Association of Trade Stores receive a financial report of the performance of their departments for the previous month. The report is generally distributed around the 16th or 17th of the month. Although the association is a not-for-profit trade and educational association, it does attempt to generate revenues from a variety of activities to supplement the members' dues. The association has several income-producing departments: research, education, publications, and promotion consulting services. As a general rule, each department is expected to be self-supporting, and the department head is responsible for both the generation of revenue and the control of costs for the department.

As an example of the monthly department report, the March 1991 report of the education department is presented in Table 18-1 with the comment of the accounting department.

The annual revenue target, which becomes the revenue budget, is established by the executive director and the association's board of directors. The annual and monthly expense budgets are then developed at the beginning of the year by the department heads for all costs except rent, utilities, janitorial services, equipment depreciation, and allocated general administration. The amounts for these cost items are supplied by the accounting department. The monthly budget figures for revenues are also determined by the department heads at the beginning of the year. The monthly budget amounts for revenues and expenses are not revised during the year.

For example, the following changes in operations have taken place but the monthly budgets have not been revised: (1) a new, home-study course was introduced in February, one month earlier than scheduled;

(2) a number of the week-long courses were postponed in February and March and rescheduled for April and May; and (3) the related promotion effort—heavy direct-mail advertising in the two months prior to a course offering—was likewise rescheduled.

Requirements

Identify and briefly discuss the good and bad features of the monthly information communication report presented for the education department in terms of:

A. Its form and appearance in presenting the operating performance of the education department.
B. Its content in providing useful information to the department head for managing the education department.

Include in your discussion the changes you would recommend to improve the report as a communication device.

(CMA Adapted)

18-24.   The Argon County Hospital is located in the county seat. Argon County is a well-known summer resort area. Its population doubles during the vacation months (May–August), and hospital activity more than doubles during these months. The hospital is organized into several departments. Although it is relatively small, its pleasant surroundings have attracted a well-trained and competent medical staff.

An administrator was hired a year ago to improve the business activities of the hospital. Among the new ideas he has introduced is responsibility accounting. This program was announced along with quarterly cost reports supplied to department heads. Previously, cost data were presented to department heads infrequently. Excerpts from the announcement and the report received by the laundry supervisor (see Table 18-2) follow.

> The hospital has adopted a responsibility accounting system. From now on you will receive quarterly reports comparing the costs of operating your department with budgeted costs. The reports will highlight the differences (variations) so you can zero in on the departures from budgeted costs. (This is called *management by exception.*) Responsibility accounting means you are accountable for keeping the costs in your department within the budget. The variations from the budget will help

Table 18.1
National Association of Trade Stores
Education Department
Report for the Month of March 1991

	Budget			Actual			Variance			Variance as Percentage of Budget	
	Person Days or Units	$	%	Person Days or Units	$	%	Person Days or Units	$	Person Days or Units	%	
Revenue											
Week-long courses	1500	$225,000	71.4%	1250	$187,500	66.4%	(250)	$(37,500)	(16.6)%	(16.6)%	
One-day seminars	50	15,000	4.8	17	5,100	1.8	(33)	(9,900)	(66.0)	(66.0)	
Home-study courses	1000	75,000	23.8	1100	89,700	31.8	100	14,700	10.0	19.6	
		$315,000	100.0%		$282,300	100.0%		$(32,700)		(10.4)%	
Expenses											
Salaries		$174,000	55.2%		$167,000	59.1%		$ 7,000		4.0%	
Course material		35,500	11.3		34,670	12.3		830		2.3	
Supplies, telegraph, and telephone		4,000	1.3		4,200	1.5		(200)		(5.0)	
Rent, utilities, and janitorial services		7,000	2.2		7,000	2.5		—		—	
Equipment depreciation		700	.2		700	.2		—		—	
Allocated general administration		5,000	1.6		5,000	1.8		—		—	
Temporary office help		5,000	1.6		3,750	1.3		1,250		25.0	
Contract employees		15,000	4.8		18,500	6.6		(3,500)		(23.3)	
Travel		12,000	3.8		11,500	4.1		500		4.2	
Dues and meetings		500	.2		500	.2		—		—	
Promotion and postage		32,000	10.1		36,500	12.9		(4,500)		(14.1)	
Total expenses		$290,700	92.3%		$289,320	102.5%		$ 1,380		0.5%	
Contribution to the Association		$ 24,300	7.7%		$ (7,020)	(2.5)%		$(31,320)		(128.9)%	

Comment: The department did not make its budget this month. There was a major shortfall in the week-long course revenues. Although salaries were lower than budget, this saving was entirely consumed by overexpenditure in contract employees and promotion. Further effort is needed to increase revenues and to hold down expenses.

you identify what costs are out of line, and the size of the variations will indicate which ones are the most important. Your first such report accompanies this announcement.

The annual budget for 1991 was constructed by the new administrator. Quarterly budgets were computed as one-fourth of the annual budget. The administrator compiled the budget from analysis of the prior three years' costs. The analysis showed that all costs increased each year, with more rapid increases between the second and third year. He considered establishing the budget at an average of the prior three years' costs, hoping that the installation of the system would reduce

Table 18-2
Argon County Hospital
Performance Report—Laundry Department
July—September 1991

	Budget	Actual	(Over) Under Budget	Percentage (Over) Under Budget
Patient-days	9,500	11,900	(2,400)	(25)
Pounds of laundry processed	125,000	156,000	(31,000)	(25)
Costs				
Laundry labor	$ 9,000	$12,500	$(3,500)	(39)
Supplies	1,100	1,875	(775)	(70)
Water and water heating and softening	1,700	2,500	(800)	(47)
Maintenance	1,400	2,200	(800)	(57)
Supervisor's salary	3,150	3,750	(600)	(19)
Allocated administration costs	4,000	5,000	(1,000)	(25)
Equipment depreciation	1,200	1,250	(50)	(4)
	$21,550	$29,075	$(7,525)	(35)

Administrator's comments: Costs are significantly above budget for the quarter. Particular attention needs to be paid to labor, supplies, and maintenance.

costs to this level. However, in view of the rapidly increasing prices, he finally chose 1990 costs *less* 3% for the 1991 budget. The activity level measured by patient-days and pounds of laundry processed was set at 1990 volume, which was approximately equal to the volume of each of the past three years.

Requirements

A. Comment on the method used to construct the budget.
B. What information should be communicated by variations from budgets?
C. Recast the budget to reflect responsibility accounting, assuming the following.
  1. Laundry labor, supplies, water and water heating and softening, and maintenance are variable costs. The remaining costs are fixed.
  2. Actual prices are expected to be approximately 20% above the levels in the budget prepared by the hospital administrator.

(CMA Adapted)

CASE ANALYSES

18-25. *Conflict at Boyd College*

College Publications (CP) was established in 1972 by the president of Boyd College to advance the quality and effectiveness of the college's graphic commu-

nications. CP provides professional editing, designing, and planning services to all academic and administrative units requesting help in the publication of catalogues, brochures, booklets, posters, and other forms of printed material. CP is under the vice-president for public affairs, employs a professional staff of 20, and has an annual operating budget of $500,000.

To encourage the use of CP's services, the costs of operating CP have not been allocated or charged to units requesting services. Instead, these operating costs are included in central administration overhead. However, to maintain as much uniformity as possible in the content and design of the college's publications, all items submitted to CP for publication are reviewed and approved by CP. Thus, CP can reject or require the complete revision of a unit's publication. The number of copies for each publication is determined jointly by CP and the unit requesting service.

During the last two years, Boyd College has experienced considerable financial pressure. Inflation has increased operating costs, a downturn in the stock market has reduced endowment income, and various governmental agencies have cut back on research support. During the spring of 1991, the president of the college established a number of task forces to review various aspects of the college's operations. These task forces collectively concluded that there was a need to emphasize and promote fiscal responsibility among administrative and academic units. Consequently, the task force on publications recommended the use of a charge-back system in which user units pay for services requested from CP.

In the fall of 1991, the president issued a memorandum requiring the use of a charge-back system for the services of CP. The memorandum stated that the purpose of the new system was "to put control and responsibility for publication expenditures where the benefits were received and to make academic and administrative units more aware of the publication costs they were incurring." The memorandum suggested that the costs of operating CP be charged back to user units on the basis of actual hours used in servicing their publication needs.

The academic and administrative units that purchased publication services through CP were generally pleased with the president's memorandum, even though they had some reservations about how the charge-back rate would be calculated. They had not been happy about having to obtain CP's approval in purchasing publication services. Their major complaint had been that CP imposed excessively high standards that resulted in overly expensive publications.

The director of CP was very upset about the president's memorandum. He believed that the charge-back system was a political maneuver by the president to get the task force pressures off his back. He believed that the task force had paid too much attention to publication costs and that the new system would reduce the effectiveness of CP to the college as a whole. He also was upset that the president took unilateral action in establishing the new system. He believed that it was a big jump from the memorandum to the installation of the new system and he was concerned about whether the new system would achieve the desired results.

Questions

1. What are the likely motivational and operational effects of the new system on:
   a. Academic and administrative units requesting and using the services of CP?
   b. College Publications?
   c. Boyd College?

2. Evaluate the president's method for instituting an organizational change with respect to College Publications.

(CMA Adapted)

18-26. City System*

The purpose of a city is to provide public services desired or demanded by its citizens. These services or functions, of which there are many, include such things as (1) protection of the citizens from those who break the law, (2) provision of water and sanitary services, and (3) provision for the transportation of people and goods. The total of these functions can be broadly grouped into four sectors: (1) public safety, (2) human-resource development, (3) public finance, and (4) physical and economical development.

Present Conditions

In cities, as in any large complex organization, there is a multiplicity of requirements for the same information. Too frequently, however, these requirements are satisfied by each user independently collecting and storing data for himself. The tax assessor, the fire department, and the building inspector, for example, all require similar information about buildings, including such things as (1) address, (2) dimensions, (3) construction type, (4) number of access ways, etc. Frequently, in many cities, there are a vast number of people whose job it is to "massage" data, putting it into a form useful for managerial decisions ranging from "what are my budget requirements for next year" to "which of the traffic signals should have preventive maintenance performed."

There is a preponderance of the latter type of inquiry which, in many instances, requires routine decisions but which, at the same time, occupies so much of a manager's time. By way of examples, such decisions include (1) designation of which properties in the city should be reappraised, (2) scheduling vehicles and equipment for preventive maintenance, and (3) preparation of lists of those people who should be sent notifications of their failure to pay tickets.

Requirements for Proposed Municipal Information System

1. Furnish information to top management, operating management, and other users necessary to carry out the day-to-day activities.

---

* Used with the permission of John G. Burch, Jr., and Felix R. Strater, Jr., *Information Systems: Theory and Practice* (New York: Wiley, 1986).

2. Provide a means to interface the system with outside organizations or special districts including (a) independent school boards, (b) water districts, (c) citizen or civic organizations, and (d) economic development districts. In addition, the system must also be responsive to the many reporting demands of the Federal Government.

Questions

Assume that you are a systems analyst for a consulting firm. Answer the following questions.

1. Conceptualize, in broad terms, the kind of municipal information system you propose. Draw any schematics and write all narratives that you feel are necessary in communicating your systems design. Be as specific as you can, but bear in mind that this design is introductory in nature.
2. Prepare, in addition to your conceptual systems design, a complete report on some of the benefits that you envision will accrue to the city should the mayor and others commission you for the development and implementation of the information system. Be specific.
3. Prepare a list of questions that you intend to ask the mayor and divisional heads in your meeting with them.
4. Enumerate the advantages as well as the disadvantages of your proposed system.

18-27. Employee Productivity Cases

Improved productivity is considered an important way to reduce or control expenditures during periods of inflation. Productivity improvement can be obtained in a variety of ways, including additional capital investment and more effective employee performance. The three cases presented here focus on attempts to increase employee productivity without added capital investment.

Case 1

The customer complaints department is in charge of receiving, investigating, and responding to customer claims of poor service. The volume of paperwork is very large and is growing because each complaint requires the processing of several forms and letters. A large staff is required for handling this processing.

There is a wide span of control, with 15 to 20 staff members reporting to each supervisor. The number of complaints processed per worker has shown a noticeable decline in recent months.

The department manager recommends that supervisors require increased performance. They should do this by setting performance objectives, making their presence more obvious, monitoring breaks and lunch hours, and seeing to it that talking among staff members is strictly curtailed. The supervisors should also make the staff aware that failure to achieve performance objectives will result in a negative evaluation of their performance.

Case 2

A department of an insurance company in charge of processing medical-related claims has had its budget reduced even though the number of claims has been increasing. This reduction comes after very small annual appropriation increases in prior years. Given the recent rate of inflation, the actual resources available to do the work have decreased.

Top management recently has specified that certain claims be processed within 48 hours of receipt, a requirement that leads to special handling of such claims. Consequently, the budget reduction causes the processing of other claims to be delayed even more. The department manager complains that the budget cuts and the priority treatments of certain claims will reduce the department's overall productivity.

This manager recommends that top management allow all managers to participate more actively in the budget development and budget adjustments during the budget year. Further, once the general objectives for a department are established, the department manager should be allowed to set the priorities for the work to be accomplished.

Case 3

Investigative auditors within a welfare agency are responsible for detecting cases of welfare fraud. Because of the latest recession, the number of welfare fraud cases was expected to be significantly higher than in recent history. However, the number of cases discovered has not increased significantly. This may be because investigators are becoming discouraged by the lack of follow-up action taken on their findings. Cases are backed up in legal processing. Even when the individuals are found guilty, the penalties are often very light. The investigators wonder if all their time and effort to uncover the fraudulent claims are justified.

The manager of the investigative audit department has recommended an annual performance incentive program for the investigators that is related only to the number of cases of fraud detected. The annual performance evaluation report would be filed in each investigator's personnel record and each investigator's annual salary adjustment would be based primarily on the number of fraud cases detected. Currently, evaluations relate to the number of cases closed with convictions.

Question

For each of the three cases presented, discuss whether or not the proposal of the department manager will improve productivity within the department. Explain, in detail, the reasons for your conclusion in each case.
(CMA Adapted)

18-28. *Division of Social Services*

Scott Weidner, the controller in the Division of Social Services for the state, recognizes the importance of the budgetary process for planning, control, and motivation purposes. He believes that a properly implemented participative budgeting process for planning purposes and a management-by-exception reporting procedure based upon the participative budget will motivate his subordinates to improve productivity within their particular departments. Based on this philosophy, Weidner has implemented the following budget procedures.

* An appropriation target figure is given to each department manager. This amount is the maximum funding that each department can expect to receive in the next fiscal year.
* Department managers develop their individual budgets within the following spending constraints as directed by the controller's staff.

  1. Expenditure requests cannot exceed the appropriation target.
  2. All fixed expenditures should be included in the budget. Fixed expenditures would include such items as contracts and salaries at current levels.
  3. All government projects directed by higher au-

thority should be included in the budget in their entirety.
* The controller's staff consolidates the departmental budget requests from the various departments into one budget that is to be submitted for the entire division.
* Upon final budget approval by the legislature, the controller's staff allocates the appropriation to the various departments on instructions from the division manager. However, a specified percentage of each department's appropriation is held back in anticipation of potential budget cuts and special funding needs. The amount and use of this contingency fund is left to the discretion of the division manager.
* Each department is allowed to adjust its budget when necessary to operate within the reduced appropriation level. However, as stated in the original directive, specific projects authorized by higher authority must remain intact.
* The final budget is used as the basis of control for a management-by-exception form of reporting. Excessive expenditures by account for each department are highlighted on a monthly basis. Department managers are expected to account for all expenditures over budget. Fiscal responsibility is an important factor in the overall performance evaluation of department managers.

Weidner believes his policy of allowing the department managers to participate in the budget process and then holding them accountable for their performance is essential, especially during these times of limited resources. He further believes the department managers will be motivated positively to increase the efficiency and effectiveness of their departments because they have provided input into the initial budgetary process and are required to justify any unfavorable performances.

Questions

1. Explain the operational and behavioral benefits that generally are attributed to a participative budgeting process.
2. Identify deficiencies in Scott Weidner's participative budgetary policy for planning and performance evaluation purposes. For each deficiency identified, recommend how the deficiency can be corrected. Use the following format in preparing your response.

Deficiencies	Recommendations

(CMA Adapted)

18-29. *Paradise Hotel*

Company Background

The Paradise Hotel is an independent, medium-size hotel catering to the middle-class market. Because the hotel lacks the prestigious image of a national chain hotel, it is necessary to depend on satisfied customers to return on their future trips and to tell their friends about the hotel. Mr. Williams, the general manager of the hotel, claims that Paradise Hotel has a consistent above-average occupancy rate compared with other independent hotels because all employees are trained to provide good service and the management spends so much effort in follow-up work such as sending thank-you letters and promotional materials to previous guests.

Being confident of the capability of a very experienced front-desk staff, the general manager has become increasingly concerned over the front-desk staff's complaints regarding the difficulty in organizing their work. There are two front-desk clerks in the day shift, two clerks in the swing shift, and one clerk in the "graveyard" shift. The responsibilities of front-desk clerks include reservations, check-in and check-out procedures, cashiering, switchboard operation, providing information for hotel guests, safekeeping keys and valuables for hotel guests, and various other chores when guests seek service or help from the front desk.

Front-Desk Operational Problems

Several problems plagued the front-desk operations. One such problem involved the housekeeping operations. At the close of each shift, the housekeeping department would send a list of checked-out rooms that were cleaned by the maids. The clerk responsible would then update the room inventory sheet so that the next shift would start with complete inventory information. However, the front-desk clerks had no idea what rooms were cleaned *during* the shift.

A second problem concerned the restaurant, gift shop, and laundry department. The supervisors of these operations would forward signed guest bills to the front office twice during a shift listing the different charges to the hotel guests. There were cases when a guest checked out before the front-desk clerk received the billing information that would list the charges for services. In such cases, the hotel would have to send a bill to the guest's residence. It turned out that few people who received such bills bothered to send any payment or response. The uncollected sales plus extra clerical and mailing costs involved in the collection process amounted to an average of $64,000 per year, or approximately 1.5% of total hotel revenues.

In view of these problems, Mr. Williams ordered a change in operations two months ago. These changes required the maids to call the front office every half-hour to inform the front office of rooms cleaned, and required the different departments (such as food service) to call the front office as soon as a charge to a hotel guest was made. Since the change, the front-desk staff has been complaining that they are kept so busy manually posting the room inventory sheet and the hotel guests' accounts that they cannot perform their other tasks.

Paradise Hotel has recently automated its accounting operations by installing an IBM computer system. The new accounting system works extremely satisfactorily in preparing the hotel payroll and in preparing the hotel's financial statements. Mr. Williams suspects that the front-office operations could also be improved through computerization. He contacted Mr. Parks, the systems analyst who had designed the computerized accounting system for Paradise Hotel, and Mr. Parks agreed to do a systems study of the front-office operations.

Mr. Parks spent two weeks observing the front-desk clerks performing their tasks. He noted that as a customer comes in and asks for a room with certain facilities, the front-desk clerk checks the room inventory sheet to see whether such a room is available. If it is not, the clerk suggests an alternate room listed on the room inventory sheet as available. If the alternate room is satisfactory, the customer completes a registration card that requires information on name, address, number of persons in the room, hotel room number, room rate, check-in date, and check-out date. (See Exhibit 1.) The customer is given the room key and the check-in procedure is completed. The front-desk clerk then prepares a guest ledger card for the customer

```
                        PARADISE   HOTEL

                    REGISTRATION    CARD




                                              Date _____


        Name _____

        Street & No. _____

        City _____  State _____


    ┌──────────┬──────────┬──────────┬─────────────────┬──────────────┬──────────────┐
    │ Room     │ Rate     │ Arrived  │ No. in Party    │ Departed     │ Remark       │
    │          │          │          │                 │              │              │
    │          │          │          │                 │              │              │
    └──────────┴──────────┴──────────┴─────────────────┴──────────────┴──────────────┘

        ██PH██
                                                      _____
                                                       Room Clerk Initial
```

EXHIBIT 1

who has just checked in. The purpose of the guest ledger card is to record all the charge transactions pertaining to the guest's account. Every time a front-desk clerk receives a call from a revenue-producing department informing him or her of a charge incurred by a guest, the clerk takes the guest's ledger card out from the card file and records the amount on the ledger card. (See Exhibit 2.) Charges are also entered in the cash register in the front office. The tape from the cash register is transferred to the accounting department at the end of a day for auditing and account posting. Because a guest may decide to leave at any moment, the hotel guests' accounts must be complete, accurate, and up-to-the-minute. The front-desk clerk is also responsible for entering on the Front Desk Cash Sheet all transactions that occurred. (See Exhibit 3.) At the end of their shift, the clerks rule off their sections of the cash sheet, summarize their own transactions, and count their cash on hand. When a guest checks out, the front-desk clerk totals the amount on the guest ledger card and collects the balance due from the

guest. The check-out date is entered on the guest registration card, which is then transferred from the active file in the front office to the history file in the sales department.

The Recommended System

After his two-week study, Mr. Parks concluded that efficient information flow and efficient transaction-recording procedures were the most important requirements of a good front-office system. He recommended that the hotel install a terminal at the front desk and a computerized data processing system to handle the paperwork. This system is now described.

After a guest fills out the registration card, the clerk inputs the data through a terminal, thereby establishing a new computer record. All records are arranged and stored according to room numbers. No ledger cards are prepared because all business transactions between the guest and the hotel are keyed in through computer terminals located at the hotel's restaurant, gift shop, and laundry. At the end of a shift, the com-

```
                    PARADISE HOTEL

                  GUEST LEDGER CARD


  Name _____  Room No. _____


        Date of Arrival _____        Room Rate per Day $ _____
        Date of Departure _____        No. Guests _____
```

Date	Brought Forward			TOTAL
Rooms				
Meals				
Beverages				
Local Phone				
L.D. Phone				
Laundry				
Miscellaneous				
Cash Adv.				
Telegrams				
Transfer				
Total Chgs. Today				
Previous Balance				
TOTAL				
Less Cash				
Balance Due				

EXHIBIT 2

puter calculates the total amount of cash receipts and disbursements and the cash balance so that the clerks can reconcile their on-hand cash to the computer records. At the end of the day, the computer calculates the total sales, total accounts receivable, total cash receipts, and total cash disbursements, and automatically updates the various hotel guest accounts within the accounting information system. When a guest checks out, the computer calculates the total balance due from the guest after the clerk has keyed in the room number and depressed the "Total" key on the terminal. When a clerk depresses a "Paid-in-Full" key, the computer prints out a receipt for the guest and the record is removed from the file. The registration card is then transferred to the history file in the sales department.

The computer also stores all room inventory information, which is available to the front-desk clerk through the terminal. When a clerk receives information from the housekeeping department on the rooms cleaned, he or she inputs the information through the front-desk terminal instead of the room inventory sheet.

Mr. Parks estimates that the system will cost $22,000 to install, including training costs. Maintenance will be

Room No.	Name	Room Charge	Food and Beverages	Phone	Long Distance	Laundry	Gift Shop	Cash	Miscellaneous		Paid Out	
									Item	$	Item	$

PH — FRONT DESK CASH SHEET — Date _____

EXHIBIT 3

under $5000 per year. The system is expected to be adequate for the present volume of business at Paradise Hotel and for all foreseeable future volumes of business.

Questions

1. Prepare a document flowchart for the computerized front-desk operations of the Paradise Hotel.
2. Using any format you like, document how the check-in process, the room-inventory process, the check-out process, and the front-desk recording of hotel guests' transactions would function under the computerized version of the front-desk operations.
3. Discuss how the proposed computerized system would solve some of the problems of the front desk at Paradise Hotel.
4. When reviewing Mr. Parks' recommendations, Mr. Williams noted that it would be useful to save the information about check-out guests in a guest history file. Evaluate this suggestion. What uses might such a file serve?
5. Including the guest history file, describe the computer files required for Paradise Hotel's accounting information system. For each file, indicate how the file would be organized, how long it would be retained, and how it would be updated. Also, for each file, indicate what specific information would be stored in a typical file record.

18-30. Middleton University

Middleton University is a state supported, tax-exempt institution. The university has decided to replace the computer that is being used for Middleton's financial and administrative applications. The current computer is over eight years old and can no longer serve the university's needs adequately.

Donald Abel, Vice-President of Finance, prepared the analysis of the proposed computer that was submitted to Middleton's Board of Regents. The analysis indicated that a new computer would provide the university with annual cost savings of $400,000, excluding the computer's maintenance and insurance. The proposed computer would cost $1,000,000 and have an economic life of five years. The vendor has assured Abel that the computer could be sold for $100,000 after five years. The annual maintenance and insurance costs are estimated to be $50,000.

Abel and the Board of Regents are convinced that the proposed computer is justified. The new computer will provide substantial cost savings. Furthermore, it will meet the university's needs and provide other benefits that cannot be quantified. How to finance the computer acquisition is the only decision left to be made on this project.

Abel has narrowed the financing decision down to two alternatives. The first financing alternative available to Abel is to borrow the money from a commercial bank to purchase the computer. Commerce Bank would give Middleton a five-year $1,000,000 loan at an annual interest rate of 15 percent. The bank would require the interest to be paid annually at the end of each year with the principal amount due at maturity.

The second financing alternative Abel is considering is a proposal from DataBit, a computer leasing company. DataBit would lease the proposed computer to Middleton under a five-year operating lease arrangement. The lease arrangement calls for rental payments at the beginning of each year starting with $340,000 at the beginning of the first year and decreasing by $40,000 in each of the subsequent four years.

Regardless of its decision to borrow or lease, Middleton would be responsible for paying the maintenance and insurance on the new computer. Abel believes that the university's opportunity investment rate is 20 percent, and the current risk free interest rate is 12 percent.

Both Commerce Bank and DataBit are subject to a 40 percent income tax rate. In addition, DataBit can claim the 10 percent investment tax credit on the computer it leases to Middleton University.

Discount tables for several different interest rates are given below.

Present Value of $1.00 Received at the End of Period

Period	9%	12%	15%	20%
1	.92	.89	.87	.83
2	.84	.80	.76	.70
3	.77	.71	.65	.58
4	.71	.64	.57	.48
5	.65	.57	.50	.40

Present Value of an Annuity of $1.00 Received at the End of Each Period

Period	9%	12%	15%	20%
1	.92	.89	.87	.83
2	1.76	1.69	1.63	1.53
3	2.53	2.40	2.28	2.11
4	3.24	3.04	2.85	2.59
5	3.89	3.61	3.35	2.99

Questions

1. Prepare a financial analysis that will show which computer financing arrangement—borrowing from Commerce Bank or leasing from DataBit—will be better for Middleton University.

2. Identify factors other than the cost of financing that Middleton University should consider when making the lease versus borrow decision.

(CMA Adapted)

REFERENCES AND RECOMMENDED READINGS FOR PART FIVE

Ahituv, Niv, and Munro, Malcolm C. "Controlling the Acquisition of a Small Business Computer." *Cost and Management* 57 (March–April 1983), pp. 6–15.

Akers, Michael D., Porter, Grover L, Blocher, Edward J., and Mister, William G. "Expert Systems for Management Accountants." *Management Accounting* 67 (March 1986), pp. 30–34.

EDP Technology Research Subcommittee, American Institute of Certified Public Accountants. *An Introduction to Artificial Intelligence and Expert Systems.* AICPA, 1987.

Alexander, Tom. "Why Computers Can't Outthink the Experts." *Fortune* (August 20, 1984), pp. 108–118.

Alter, Steven. "A Taxonomy of Decision Support Systems." *Management Science* 14 (December 1967), pp. B147–B156.

Adriole, Stephen J. "The Promise of Artificial Intelligence." *Journal of Systems Management* 36 (July 1985), pp. 8–17.

Ardoin, Kathleen. "The Joys of Small Firm Accounting," *New Accountant* 6 (March 1986), pp. 7–12.

Backes, Robert W., and Glowacki, Robert J. "Microcomputers: Successful Management and Control." *Management Accounting* 65 (September 1983), pp. 48–51.

Berliner, Harold I., and Golland, Marvin. "Minicomputer Systems: A Practical Approach to Computer Implementation." *Financial Executive* 48 (November 1980), pp. 24–29.

Bitner, Larry N., and Powell, Judith D. "Expansion Planning for Small Retail Firms." *Journal of Small Business Management* 25 (April 1987), pp. 47–54.

Blankenship, Ronald C., and Schaller, Carol. "The CPA, the Small Company and the Computer." *The Journal of Accountancy* 142 (August 1976), pp. 46–51.

Bonczek, Robert H., Holsapple, Clyde W., and Whinston, Andrew B. "Future Directions for Developing Decision Support Systems." *Decision Sciences* 11 (October 1980), pp. 616–631.

Booker, Jon A., and Kick, Russell C., Jr. "Expert Systems in Accounting: The Next Generation of Computer Technology." *The Journal of Accountancy* 161 (March 1986), pp. 101–103.

Canning, Richard G., and McNurlin, Barbara. "Micros Invade the Business World." *Datamation* 24 (August 1978), pp. 93–95.

Cerullo, Michael J. "Safeguard Your Minicomputer System." *Financial Executive* 51 (July 1983), pp. 30–41.

Colgrove, Dean W. "Dummies Need Not Apply." *Infosystems* 34 (November 1987), pp. 34–39.

Coon, Jennifer I. "Documenting Microcomputer Systems." *EDPACS* 11 (October 1983), pp. 1–8.

Cooper, Michael S. "Micro-Based Business Graphics." *Datamation* 30 (May 1, 1984), pp. 99–105.

Curling, Douglas C., and Hicks, James O., Jr. "Minicomputer Feasibility in the Small Business Environment." *Cost and Management* 53 (March–April 1979), pp. 4–10.

Dascher, Paul E., and Harmon, W. Ken. "The Dark Side of Small Business Computers." *Management Accounting* 65 (May 1984), pp. 62–67.

Data Decisions. "Micros at Big Firms: a Survey." *Datamation* 29 (November 1983), pp. 161–174.

Davis, Michael W. "Anatomy of Decision Support." *Datamation* 40 (June 15, 1984), pp. 201–208.

Decker, Thomas J. "MICROMANIA—Or, How to Spend $8,000 and Create a $75,000 Problem." *Management Accounting* 66 (November 1984), pp. 42–48.

Diebold, John. "Laptops With Storage to Spare." *PC World* 6 (December 1988), pp. 134–145.

Donnelly, Robert M. "Keep Up With Decision Support Systems." *Financial Executive* 51 (August 1983), pp. 44–46.

Doost, Roger K. "Small Business Audit of a Computerized Entity: A Different Challenge for the Auditor." *The CPA Journal* 58 (September 1988), pp. 96–99.

Edwards, Chris. "Developing Microcomputer-Based Business Systems." *Journal of Systems Management* 34 (April 1983), pp. 36–38.

Elliott, Robert K., Rabinovitz, Mark E., and Knight, Sherry D. "Expert Systems for Accountants." *The Journal of Accountancy* 160 (September 1985), pp. 126–134.

Firdman, Henry Eric. "Expert Systems: Are You Already Behind?" *Computerworld* 22 (April 18, 1988), pp. 99–105.

Firdman, Henry Eric. "How Not to Build an Expert System Shell." *Computerworld* 21 (February 16, 1987), pp. 57–61.

Flores, Ivan, and Terry, Christopher. *Microcomputer Systems.* New York: Van Nostrand Reinhold, 1982.

Franz, Robert. "Adapting Microcomputers to Wall Street." *Byte* 7 (October 1982), pp. 80–92.

Freeland, James R. "Can a Personal Computer Really Help You?" *Business Horizons* 26 (January–February 1983), pp. 56–63.

Ghandforoush, Parviv. "Model for Minicomputer Selection." *Journal of Systems Management* 33 (June 1982), pp. 11–13.

Gordon, William Larry, and Key, Jeffrey R. "Artificial Intelligence in Support of Small Business Information Needs." *Journal of Systems Management* 38 (January 1987), pp. 24–29.

Hansen, James V., and Messier, William F., Jr. "Expert Systems for Decision Support in EDP Auditing." *International Journal of Computer and Information Sciences* 11 (October 1982), pp. 357–378.

Harmon, Paul. "Smart Buys In Artificial Intelligence." *Datamation* 33 (August 1, 1987), pp. 63–66.

Harris, Larry R. "When Bigger AI isn't better." *Computerworld* 22 (October 31, 1988), pp. 79–83.

Helmi, Medhat A. "Integrating the Microcomputer into Accounting Education-Approaches and Pitfalls." *Issues in Accounting Education* (Spring 1986), pp. 102–111.

Himrod, Bruce W. "Microcomputers for Small Business." *The Journal of Accountancy* 145 (December 1979), pp. 44–50.

Hocking, Ralph T., and Hocking, Joan M. "The Evolution of Decision Systems." *MSU Business Topics* 24 (Summer 1976), pp. 55–59.

Hoffman, Robin Bacon. "AICPA Computer Survey." *The Journal of Accountancy* 166 (September 1988), pp. 146–150.

Houdeshel, George, and Watson, Hugh J. "The Management Information and Decision Support (MIDS) System at Lockheed, Georgia." *MIS Quarterly* 11 (June 1987), pp. 127–140.

Hughes, G. David. "Computerized Sales Management." *Harvard Business Review* 61 (March–April 1983), pp. 102–112.

Jefferson, Clyde E., Jr. "A Different Beat for Army Accountants." *New Accountant* 4 (February 1989), pp. 8–12.

Johnson, Bart. "Why Your Company Needs Three Accounting Systems." *Management Accounting* 66 (September 1984), pp. 39–46.

Jordan, Mary Lou. "Executive Information Systems Make Life Easy for the Lucky Few." *Computerworld* 22 (February 29, 1988), pp. 51–57.

Kahn, Beverly R., and Garceau, Linda R. "Controlling the Microcomputer Environment." *Journal of Systems Management* 35 (May 1984), pp. 14–19.

Kaplan, S. Jerrold, and Ferris, David. "Natural Language in the DP World." *Datamation* 38 (August 1982), pp. 114–120.

Keen, Peter G., and Wagner, Jerry. "DSS: An Executive Mind-Support System." *Datamation* 35 (November 1979), pp. 117–122.

Kerr, Susan. "Users, Vendors Team on Expert Systems." *Datamation* 33 (September 1, 1987), pp. 18–20.

Khadem, R., and Schultzki, A. "Planning and Forecasting Using a Corporate Model." *Managerial Planning* 31 (January–February 1983), pp. 37–43.

King, Martin J. "Microcomputers—The Central Support Approach." *EDPACS* 11 (December 1983), pp. 1–4.

Kliem, Ralph I. "Disaster Prevention and Recovery for Microcomputers." *Journal of Systems Management* 35 (March 1984), pp. 28–29.

Knorr, Eric. "Laptops of Luxury." *PC World* 6 (November 1988), pp. 94–95.

Landry, Richard, and Koessel, Karl. "Is Smaller Better?" *PC World* 6 (November 1988), pp. 98–100.

Leitch, Robert A., Dillon, Gadis J., and McKinley, Sue H. "International Control Weaknesses in Small Businesses." *The Journal of Accountancy* 147 (December 1981), pp. 97–101.

Lin, Engming. "Expert Systems for Business Applications: Potentials and Limitations." *Journal of Systems Management* 37 (July 1986), pp. 18–21.

MacNichols, Charles, and Clark, Thomas. *Microcomputer-Based Information and Decision Support Systems for Small Businesses.* Reston, VA: Reston Publishing, 1983.

Mahmood, M. A. "Choosing Computer Services for Small Businesses." *Journal of Systems Management* 33 (July 1982), pp. 22–24.

Mansfield, Mark D. "Plugging the DP Gap: Small Computers for Big Business." *Management Accounting* 65 (September 1983), pp. 58–62.

Martin, James R. "An Interactive Computer Time-Sharing Application for a Small Manufacturing Firm." *Cost and Management* 53 (September–October 1979), pp. 34–43.

Martins, Gary R. "The Overselling of Expert Systems." *Datamation* 30 (November 1984), pp. 76–80.

Martorelli, William P. "PC-Based Expert Systems Arrive." *Datamation* 34 (April 1, 1988), pp. 56–66.

McCarty, L. Thorne. "Reflections on TAXMAN: An Experiment in Artificial Intelligence and Legal Reasoning." *Harvard Law Review* 90 (March 1977), pp. 837–893.

McCosh, Andrew M., and Scott Morton, Michael S. *Management Decision Support Systems.* London: Macmillan, 1978.

McKee, Thomas E. "Does Your Practice Have a Place for an Expert System?" *The CPA Journal* 58 (January 1988), pp. 114–120.

McKee, Thomas E. "Expert Systems: The Final Frontier?" *The CPA Journal* 56 (July 1986), pp. 42–46.

McLean, Ephraim R. "Computer-Based Planning Models Come of Age." *Harvard Business Review* 58 (July–August 1980), pp. 46–58.

McNurlin, Barbara Canning, ed. "Trends in Artificial Intelligence." *I/S Analyzer* 26 (February 1988), pp. 1–14.

Michaelsen, Robert, and Michie, Donald. "Expert Systems in Business." *Datamation* 29 (November 1983), pp. 240–246.

Michaelsen, Robert, and Michie, Donald. "Prudent Expert Systems Applications Can Provide a Competitive Weapon." *Data Management* 24 (July 1986), pp. 30–34.

Mishkoff, Henry C. *Understanding Artificial Intelligence.* Indiana: Howard W. Sams & Co., 1985.

Moad, Jeff. "Building a Bridge to Expert Systems." *Datamation* 33 (January 1, 1987), pp. 17–19.

Mosard, Gil. "Problem Definition: Tasks and Techniques." *Journal of Systems Management* 34 (June 1983), pp. 16–21.

Moscove, Stephen A. *Accounting Fundamentals for*

Non-Accountants. Reston, VA: Reston Publishing, 1984.

Moscove, Stephen A. "The Changing Role of the Accountant." *The National Public Accountant* 26 (September 1981), pp. 10–18.

Moscove, Stephen A. "The Changing Role of the Accountant-Part II." *The National Public Accountant* 26 (October 1981), pp. 24–30.

Nadel, Robert B. "What Is Artificial Intelligence?" *The CPA Journal* 56 (June 1986), pp. 93–95.

National Society of Public Accountants. *Portfolio of Accounting Systems for Small and Medium-sized Businesses.* Englewood Cliffs, NJ: Prentice-Hall, 1986.

Nauman, Seev, and Hadass, Michael. "DSS and Strategic Decisions." *California Management Review* 22 (Spring 1980), pp. 77–84.

Oxman, Steven W. "Expert Systems Represent Ultimate Goal of Strategic Decision Making." *Data Management* 23 (April 1985), pp. 36–38.

Papageorgiou, John C. "Decision Making in the Year 2000." *Interfaces* 13 (April 1983), pp. 77–86.

Partow-Navid, Parviz. "Misuse and Disuse of DSS Models." *Journal of Systems Management* 38 (April 1987), pp. 38–42.

Pieptea, Dan R., and Anderson, Evan. "Price and Value of Decision Support Systems." *MIS Quarterly* (December 1987), pp. 515–530.

Person, Stanley. "A Microcomputer in a Small CPA Firm." *The CPA Journal* 54 (March 1984), pp. 20–25.

Petersen, Perry. "Branch Office Microcomputing." *Datamation* 30 (November 15, 1984), pp. 104–109.

Pollack, Andrew. "Setbacks for Artificial Intelligence." *The New York Times* (March 4, 1988), pp. D1–D5.

Rector, Robert L. "Decision Support Systems—Strategic Planning Tool." *Managerial Planning* 31 (May–June 1983), pp. 36–40.

Remus, William, and Kottleman, Jeffery E. "Semi-Structured Recurring Decisions: An Experimental Study of Decision-Making Models and Some Suggestions for DSS." *MIS Quarterly* 11 (June 1987), pp. 233–244.

Rockart, John R., and Treacy, Michael, E. "The CEO Goes On-Line." *Harvard Business Review* 60 (January–February 1982), pp. 82–88.

Rohm, Wendy Goldman. "A Remote Promise." *Infosystems* 33 (September 1986), pp. 52–56.

Rose, Twan A. "Microcomputers for Financial Consulting." *Management Accounting* 65 (February 1984), pp. 42–45.

Ryan, Jody L. "Expert Systems in the Future: The Redistribution of Power." *Journal of Systems Management* 39 (April 1988), pp. 18–21.

St. Clair, Linda. "Security for Small Computer Systems." *EDPACS* 11 (November 1983), pp. 1–10.

Schwartz, Donald A. "Microcomputers Take Aim on Small Business Clients." *The Journal of Accountancy* 145 (December 1979), pp. 57–62.

Seilheimer, Steven D. "Current State of Decision Support System and Expert System Technology." *Journal of Systems Management* 39 (August 1988), pp. 14–20.

Shim, Jae K., and Rice, Jeffrey S. "Expert Systems Applications to Managerial Accounting." *Journal of Systems Management* 39 (June 1988), pp. 6–13.

Shurkin, Joel N. "Expert Systems: The Practical Face of Artificial Intelligence." *Technology Review* 10 (November–December 1983), pp. 72–78.

Shuster, Harvey L., and Warner, Paul D. "Micros for Small Business: The Time is Now." *Management Accounting* 65 (July 1984), pp. 45–48.

Smith, Murphy L., and Bain, Craig E. "Computer Graphics for Today's Accountant." *The CPA Journal* 57 (February 1987), pp. 18–34.

Snyder, Paul Stewart, and Frailie, Donald L. "Microcomputers: The Next Generation." *The Journal of Accountancy* 166 (August 1988), pp. 110–117.

Snyders, Jan. "Unraveling Artificial Intelligence." *Infosystems* 34 (July 1987), p. 48.

Soucie, Ralph. "Accounting Tools of the Trades." *PC World* 6 (November 1988), pp. 236–241.

Sprague, Ralph H. "A Framework for the Development of Decision Support Systems." *MIS Quarterly* 4 (December 1980), pp. 1–26.

Sprague, Ralph H., and Carlson, Eric D. *Building Effective Decision Support Systems.* Englewood Cliffs, NJ: Prentice-Hall, 1982.

Sprague, Ralph H., and Watson, Hugh J. "Bit by Bit: Toward Decision Support Systems." *California Management Review* 22 (Fall 1979), pp. 60–67.

Squires, James W., IV. "A Perfect Fit: Minicomputers and Medium-Sized Companies." *Management Accounting* 65 (July 1984), pp. 42–49.

Stoner, Greg. "Expert Systems: Jargon or Challenge?" *Accountancy* (February 1985), pp. 142–145.

Sullivan, William G., and Reeve, James M. "Xventure: Expert Systems to the Rescue." *Management Accountant* 70 (October 1988), pp. 51–58.

Sussman, Philip N. "Evaluating Decision Support Software." *Datamation* 30 (October 15, 1984), pp. 171–172.

Tannenbaum, Michael D. "How to Save Money Buying New Computers." *The CPA Journal* 58 (May 1988), pp. 101–103.

Todd, Peter, and Benbasat, Izak. "Process Tracing Methods in Decision Support Systems Research: Exploring the Black Box." *MIS Quarterly* 11 (December 1987), pp. 493–514.

Venditto, Gus. "Compaq SLT/286: For Super Power Users Only." *PC Magazine* 7 (December 13, 1988), pp. 273–289.

Wagner, G. R. "Decision Support Systems": Computerized Mind Support for Executive Problems." *Managerial Planning* 29 (September–October 1981), pp. 17–33.

Walsh, Myles E. "Will the Real IBM Personal Computer Please Stand Up?" *Journal of Systems Management* 35 (November 1984), pp. 8–18.

Watkins, Paul R. "Perceived Information Structure Implications for Decision Support Systems Design." *Decision Sciences* 13 (January 1982), pp. 38–59.

Wentz, Davie J. "How We Match Costs and Revenues in a Service Business." *Management Accounting* 66 (October 1985), pp. 36–42.

Wilkinson, Joseph W. *Accounting and Information Systems* 2nd ed. New York: John Wiley & Sons, 1986.

Wood, Donald R. "The Personal Computer: How It Can Increase Management Productivity." *Financial Executive* 52 (February 1984), pp. 15–19.

Wynne, Robert C., and Frotman, Alan. "Microcomputer: Helping Make Practice Perfect." *The Journal of Accountancy* 147 (December 1981), pp. 34–39.

PART SIX | Comprehensive Cases

Accounting information systems within a computerized environment have been stressed throughout this book. Real-world cases are effective tools to help students better understand the dynamic areas of accounting information systems and illustrate actual problems that have occurred in companies' systems.

Short cases have been provided within most of our book's eighteen chapters. As a means of emphasizing the practical application of many of the concepts stressed in the text, this section will present five comprehensive cases that require extensive analysis. There is no one correct solution to any case. Rather, the cases are designed to stimulate class discussions that will bring forth creative ideas.

The five comprehensive cases are completely independent of each other. Thus, one or more of them can be excluded if so desired. Presented here is a brief description of the five cases.

CASE 1
Vancouver Recreational Products

This case concerns a company that is having problems with its present data processing system. An extensive systems study job is performed to determine whether or not a computerized system should be implemented into the company.

CASE 2
Aqua Spray

This case deals with the recommendation of changes in a company's accounting information system for processing inventory and sales transactions as well as suggesting recommendations for maintaining control over inventory activities. In addition, evaluation is required of data processing equipment alternatives to handle the company's inventory and sales transactions.

CASE 3
Laub Group, Incorporated

This case concerns a company that is currently using a service bureau to process its accounting information. An evaluation is required of (1) the company's accounting information system in meeting management's decision-making needs and (2) the company's control procedures associated with accounts receivable and accounts payable. In addition, whether the company should purchase or lease its own computer and the types of procedures and controls that should be incorporated into a computerized accounting information system must be considered.

CASE 4
State Consumer Reporting Bureau

This case involves the data processing requirements of a collection agency. A team of management consultants has proposed a computerized accounting information system to replace the organization's manual system. Questions remain regarding what kinds of information the collection agency should maintain in its data base as well as the advantages and disadvantages of the proposed computerized system.

CASE 5
Autoticket Inc.

This case is about a Canadian company that provides a computerized ticket-selling service. The company has contracted with an accountant to provide a special report describing its computerized system. This includes an assessment of strengths and weaknesses of the system.

CASE 1

Vancouver Recreational Products*

Company Background

Vancouver Recreational Products (V.R.P.), a privately owned company, has the exclusive distributorship for motorized recreation vehicles across Canada. The company name has been associated with motorized recreation sales for some 60 years, with the different retail outlets operating as separate companies.

The partners, Tom Jones and Henry Leeds, operate the business out of Vancouver, although 70% of the volume sales (100 dealers across Canada) is in the eastern provinces. Their warehouse for vehicle parts distribution is located in Toronto and employs 18 people. The Vancouver headquarters has a staff of 12. In addition to the partners, most of the general responsibility is in the hands of Malcolm Redford, the office manager.

Annual sales for the company during 1988 were approximately $9 million. Replacement parts sales generally accounted for 10–15% of total sales. Vehicle sales for 1988 were around 2000 units, with the largest volume occurring during the summer months. Vehicle inventory on hand at any one time might be 800 units, stored in warehouses at four centers (i.e., Toronto,

* This case was prepared by Associate Professor Albert S. Dexter and Moira E. Barnett, Arthur Andersen & Company, as the basis for class discussion.

    Copyright © 1978, The University of British Columbia Case materials of the Faculty of Commerce and Business Administration of the University of British Columbia are for the purpose of classroom discussion. They do not attempt to illustrate examples of effective or ineffective handling of administrative practices. The materials presented here were provided by a firm that wishes to remain anonymous; thus, the names of the company and personnel are disguised. Revised June 1978.

    Distributed by the Intercollegiate Case Clearing House, Soldiers Field, Boston, Mass. 02163. All rights reserved to the contributors. Printed in the USA.

Montreal, Winnipeg, and Vancouver). Replacement parts inventory is approximately 12,000–13,000 units, having a value of between $600,000 and $1,000,000.

The company supplies retailers and also sells directly to 18–25 major buyers of the vehicles, including some provincial police departments and some divisions of the R.C.M.P. (i.e., the Royal Canadian Mounted Police). The police seemed to prefer the large, powerful vehicles. Although some Japanese manufacturers had begun competing lately, Tom felt that this competitive threat was relatively minor, with straying customers eventually returning to purchase V.R.P.'s product once more.

Day-to-day operations of Vancouver Recreational Products were handled by Malcolm Redford or one of the partners. Expertise in the accounting and control areas was obtained from outside the company through the company auditors. No senior management positions existed in the Toronto office, so decisions emanated from Vancouver.

Events Leading to the First System Outline

As early as 1987, Tom Jones saw the need not only for improvements in the accounting and inventory systems, but also for having sufficient planning to make any system changeover as smooth as possible.

Tom spent a great deal of time analyzing and then outlining what he considered to be the problems and the needs of the company in the area of data processing. He realized that automation could well be the answer to various areas of concern but also felt that these decisions could not be made without outside guidance.

The method of handling product inventory was a major contributing factor in the consideration of automating all data processing. Inventory was divided into two main categories—vehicles and parts. All parts were stored in the Toronto warehouse, so all parts activity emanated from there. Regular orders to the factory were placed once a week, with rush orders occurring once or twice a week. An average of 50 dealer inquiries on items took place daily. Dealers sent invoices to the warehouse, or orders were taken over the phone or by Telex (in which case invoices were completed at the warehouse). Parts inventory was controlled by means of a Cardex (index card) system.

Vehicles, by model and color, were warehoused at four locations. Control over the release of vehicles (after payment was received or credit checked) was in the Vancouver or Toronto office. Vehicle inventory control was kept manually in Vancouver and Telexed to Toronto daily. A serial register was maintained of all vehicles in stock. Telex was also used to release vehicles from warehouses, and Telex was needed to advise Vancouver of the serial number of the vehicle that was released.

An NCR bookkeeping machine was used to post accounts receivable, prepare statements, post accounts payable, and update the general ledger accounts. Other systems (warranties and payroll) as well as sales analysis were handled manually. Reports for management (cash flow, parts inventory, budgeting, sales, etc.) were obtainable, but unfortunately not on a timely basis. The monthly reports needed by Tom Jones and Henry Leeds, such as cash flow, budgeting, unit sales, and profitability statements, were produced two or three weeks after month's end. Tom and Henry had no correct idea of how well they were doing on the present orders. Tom felt that if this information were timely and easily accessible, their management decisions would be greatly enhanced.

During 1987, Tom was reevaluating the existing systems as they related to their changing environment. With the geographic diversity of the operation and its rate of growth, the manual record keeping and control systems were not adequate in all cases. It appeared to Tom that with proper monitoring of parts inventory procedures, the inventory value in the short run could be greatly reduced, thus reducing carrying costs. In the long run, inventory turnover could be improved. This type of control would require the hiring of an extra person in Toronto, or finding a way to control more efficiently from the remote head office. It also appeared, however, that the manual inventory system would be unable to handle any increase in volume—largely due to physical limitations of such a method.

Tom was concerned about the cost involved in using the Telex as extensively as the inventory system required and also was worried about the duplication of work and records between the Vancouver and Toronto locations. Tom also felt that the efficiency of manual control over inventory levels of warranty claims was further reduced due to the complexity of both procedures. For example, warranty claims submitted by dealers to the Vancouver office were checked against a warranty registration file and then the dealers were credited. Claims were prepared,

batched, and then sent to the factory. Manual maintenance of the vehicle file and warranty claim file were a
tedious procedure. This system was showing signs of
being unable to handle the increased volume of transactions.

Both Tom and Henry felt that their biggest problem
was the back orders of the parts inventory. The process
was a people-dependent routine, and thus was prone
to error. The error rate at times reached 15–20% of
the file. Staff turnover, because of the routine nature
of the clerical tasks, was also a problem. Tom discussed
the back-order problem with Henry. An order from a
dealer was written on an invoice and transferred to the
card for the Cardex machine; unfilled amounts were
back-ordered; receipts coming in from the factory had
to be matched against back orders by dealers in FIFO
order sequence to produce a packing slip. This
packing-slip process could add a dimension of complexity to any automated system. One packing slip was
produced per dealer rather than one packing slip per
order. It seemed to Tom that if an automated system
could improve parts inventory processing, it should be
given serious consideration.

Tom gave some thought to the problems and needs
of the company in the area of data processing. As one
of the alternatives to solving V.R.P.'s problem was computer usage in some form, Tom attempted to find out
what the industry had to offer. Thus, as early as 1987,
Vancouver Recreational Products was "in the market"
for an automated data processing system. Tom discovered that there was no shortage of computer salespeople; however, glossy photographs of sleek machinery
did not answer the following questions that he was
concerned about.

Does the machine meet the needs of our company?

Is the machine large enough? Too large?

Should the hardware be in Toronto (where the parts
    and accessories were stored) or in Vancouver (lo-
    cation of the head office and the majority of present
    manual systems)?

What price range can be justified on a cost/benefit
    basis?

How can I make sure that the automated system will do
    what I want it to do?

The last question was crucial. Tom had witnessed
small companies "get burned" to some degree in the
purchase of a minicomputer, and could recall stories
of small accounting systems sitting idle on the controller's desk. Although these systems were capable of
handling all the functions of the firm, nobody knew
how! Stories of too much hardware, outdated hardware, or lack of expansion capabilities were numerous, and Tom was sure of one thing: time and money
were best spent in research *prior* to making the critical
choice of an automated system.

Initial System Description
and Requirements

During 1988, Tom spent much time gleaning information from different sources (e.g., computer users, university texts, and computer science graduates). Because the parts inventory system was the area most in
need of attention, Tom contacted the factory's parts
division personnel, and they in turn spoke to their own
systems people. As a result, Tom received literature on
the newly released NCR hardware and software packages. Tom also contacted other vendors. Munroe and
DEC set up demonstrations for Tom at the headquarters in Vancouver, and IBM invited him to a demonstration at their office. In the Munroe situation, however,
after fairly impressive displays of the magnetic strip
card machine's capabilities, it was apparent on questioning that their system could not handle Vancouver
Recreational Products' inventory setup. The Munroe
system was better designed for the smaller accounting
environment. Tom had difficulties in communicating
the problems, as this vendor was quite prepared to
squeeze Vancouver Recreational Products' situation to
fit their available software. Upon Tom's explanation of
the back-order problem, however, Munroe's salesmen
weren't able to show how their company's system
could be applied to solve it. In the DEC case, the
software would be handled by a separate software
house whose experience was largely in scientific applications. Tom felt very uncomfortable with the prospect
of buying a piece of hardware without backup on
business software support. In the IBM situation, Tom
felt somewhat overwhelmed by the presentation and
therefore unable to judge confidently the true capabilities of the system. Upon reflection, Tom viewed the
vendor experience as too time-consuming for the benefits gained. He believed strongly that it took much
more prior preparation than he had done to relate well
to the vendors. Without some considerable preparation he would simply be putting too much faith in the
vendors' statements of what they could do for him.

Tom felt no nearer to being able to make a deci-

EXHIBIT 1 Objectives.

1. Improved control and elimination of duplication
2. Instantly updated inventory
3. A constantly balanced accounts receivable—automatic posting and instantaneous updating
4. Reports for management, both marketing and financial
5. Ability to obtain current status as well as historical information quickly through centralization of files
6. In-house control
7. Reserve capacity
8. The ability to update and add to the system

sion, and he realized that in order to obtain a system that would achieve his company's objectives, the data processing requirements had to be detailed as completely as possible. It was at this point that he compiled a seven-page outline of the company's present system and his expectations for any proposed automated system. The document is summarized and presented in Exhibits 1, 2, and 3. Tom made use of textbooks as well as advice from people in the EDP industry.

Tom's documentation concluded with topics about which the possible vendors should supply details, as shown in Exhibit 4.

Consulting Assistance

For the next few months, other items of importance took precedence over the data processing problems.

Early in 1989, the company's auditors of some 30 years' standing, Smythe, Hunter, Robinson, and MacKay, suggested that Tom make use of the services offered by their management consultants, Smythe, Hunter, and Associates. Recognizing that Vancouver Recreational Products lacked the expertise in the field of electronic data processing, Tom agreed to discuss developments to date with Oliver Carruthers, a management consultant of Smythe, Hunter, and Associates. In March 1989, Oliver was retained by Vancouver Recreational Products to look at the present system and suggest what he felt was needed. Tom forwarded the documentation he had drawn up to Oliver. It was obvious to Oliver that Tom had done a great deal of mental and written preparation regarding the needs of the company. However, Tom made it clear that he would be open to any feasible suggestions that Oliver put forward.

Oliver visited V.R.P. in order to do an initial evaluation of the situation. After a two-week study of the operation from the Vancouver end, Oliver wrote to

EXHIBIT 2 **Applications and volume.**

Billing and Accounts Receivable

Volumes:	**1.** 1000 invoices per month
	400 Vancouver
	600 Toronto
	2. 5 lines per invoice
	3. 100 customer accounts
Applications:	**1.** Customer invoicing
	(a) Parts
	(b) Vehicle
	2. Customer statement preparation
	3. Cash receipts and adjustments
	4. Aging analysis

Inventory Control

Volumes:	**1.** 18,000 item parts inventory
	—active 12,000
	(a) 10-digit numbers;
	i.e., 43506-62 P.A.
	2. 20-item unit inventory (vehicle)
	(a) 12 models
	(b) 5 colors

Accounts Payable

Volumes:	**1.** 165 supplier accounts
	2. 500 supplier invoices per month
	3. 250 checks per month
Applications:	**1.** Check writing
	2. Vendor record updating
	3. Accounts distribution
	4. Vendor analysis

General Ledger

Volumes:	**1.** 14 salaried employees paid biweekly
	—Vancouver
	1 hourly employee paid biweekly
	—Vancouver
	2. 12 salaried employees paid biweekly
	—Toronto
	1 hourly employee paid biweekly
	—Toronto
Applications:	**1.** Payroll check writing
	2. Payroll register
	3. Statutory reporting

Sales Analysis

Volumes:	**1.** Dealers
	2. Item unit inventory
Applications:	**1.** Sales by dealer—unit dollars
	2. Sales by unit
	3. Sales by parts dollar
	4. Sales by dealer to consumer
	5. Warranty by model
	6. Warranty by dealer

EXHIBIT 3   Overview of desired system.

Sales orders generated at the dealer level could be entered through a sales order system to produce a packing list that is sent to the warehouse for filling. Quantities in the inventory are reserved, and back orders would be established at the time the order is entered.

Outstanding order lists and back-order lists by part number and dealer should be produced upon demand.

When these orders are shipped, a copy of the packing list is returned from the warehouse and these orders are marked for invoicing in the system.

The invoicing system would handle prebilling situations as well as credit memos.

Output by Destination

Invoices	—Customer
Invoice Journal	—Accounting
Customer List	—Sales/Accounting
Sales Data	—Sales Analysis Module
Shipped Items	—Inventory Module
Receivable Outstanding	—Accounts Receivable Module

1. Accounts receivable to accept manual input.
2. As cash received on account is posted, it should also be posted to the general ledger system.
3. Monthly customer statements and an aging analysis are produced.
4. A dealer volume report by area should be produced.
5. A purchasing module would provide the method of producing purchase orders and keeping track of stocks on order and received. It would also be used to make entries to accounts payable and the general ledger. A list of purchase orders would be able to be run when necessary.

Note: Within the systems overview, Tom included more detail on input methods and output requirements such as reports, statements, and checks.

Tom in March 1989, formalizing some of their discussions and giving some preliminary conclusions. Parts of the letter have been reproduced in Appendix 1 at the end of this case.

Because of V.R.P.'s geographic locations, it appeared that an in-house system would offer greater flexibility, control, and accessbility than a service bureau. Oliver felt that the "purchase price for the hardware and programs" would be in the $65,000–$100,000 range. He outlined potential areas of savings, largely for Telex, telephone, and inventory carrying charges. Details of cost savings are given in the excerpts from the letter in Appendix 1 of this case.

Oliver had further discussions with Tom in order to obtain a better perspective of Vancouver Recreational Products' operations.

In April 1989, Tom received further correspondence from Oliver confirming the decision that Vancouver Recreational Products would proceed with the next step in the selection of a suitable computer system. Having completed the initial feasibility study, Oli-

ver was convinced of the need for, and cost justification of, an automated system. He suggested vendors who marketed the size system that would suit Vancouver Recreational Products' needs. Tom now took the opportunity to see demonstrations of some other companies' existing systems that both paralleled their own and had an inventory system of even greater complexity than theirs. Tom felt the experience of seeing other, similar users of equipment was very worthwhile in his learning process.

Oliver's services for the initial investigation, culminating in the findings outlined in his March letter, had cost V.R.P. $800. In the April correspondence, Oliver estimated that his assistance in preparing a "request for Proposal" and helping select a vendor "would not exceed $4500." This step in the process would necessitate Oliver becoming more conversant with present clerical procedures and accounting methods. To do this he would need to spend time with people both in Toronto and Vancouver.

Further, should Tom require Oliver's involvement

Exhibit 4 Some areas for questioning vendors.

1. *Disk Storage Requirements*
   Customer Master File
   Dealer Master File
   Inventory Master File
   Invoice File
   Sales Detail File
   Sales Summary File
   Accounts Receivable File
   Vendor Master File
   Accounts Payable File
   General Ledger Transactions File
   Financial Statement Table File
   Payroll Master File
   System Software
2. *Harware Recommended and Pricing*
3. *Monthly Lease (Purchase Option?)*
4. *Anticipated Line Cost*
   Assuming Toronto Hookup in Future
   Assuming Discount Mailing or Shipping
5. *Maintenance*
   Warranty—Parts and Labor
   Monthly and Yearly Rate
   Parts, Labor, Calls, and Preventive Maintenance
6. *Environment Requirements*
7. *Application Software*
   Required Software Costs
   Optional Modules
   Software Backup and Support
8. *Discount Package Price List*
9. *Future Expansion Options*
10. *Education*
11. *Language—Program Language Options*

during the implementation phase of the proceedings, the charge would likely be another $4500. In both cases Oliver stated, "If it appears that the charges are going to go higher, I will discuss it with you in advance."

Tom realized he now had to assess the work Oliver had done, decide on his continuing involvement, and decide just how far this involvement should go. Oliver had certainly brought some organization into the decision process. In Tom's opinion, Oliver had assisted him without overwhelming him. Tom felt the $800 had been well spent but was unsure regarding further commitment.

Tom pondered the present situation. Oliver had made contact with five suppliers he felt worthy of consideration, had arranged some demonstrations of hardware and software for Tom, and had presented Tom with some detail on what price range and charac-

teristics he should look for in a system. Now Tom faced the decision of whether to let Oliver proceed; and, if so, whether he was prepared to spend $4500, $9000, or perhaps even more on the project; or whether to take over himself once again, armed with newfound knowledge and awareness.

Appendix 1

Excerpts from Oliver's letter to Tom dated March 25, 1989.

This letter will serve to confirm our various discussions and also to report on my progress over the past two weeks.

Previously, we have agreed on the following points.

a. A computer system of some size or sort is required for at least the inventory control problem provided that it can be justified on the combined basis of increased control and reduced investment in inventory.
b. The computer, because of management location and control considerations, must be located in the Vancouver area instead of Toronto.
c. We should attempt to purchase or lease a complete package of hardware, software, programming, and hardware maintenance from a single supplier, and it would be preferable if the supplier was represented in both Toronto and Vancouver.
d. Although the factory's system division is anxious to cooperate in any way, we do not want to go so far as becoming a part of their system.

I have talked to four potential suppliers so far in general terms only and have reached the following conclusions.

a. The configuration involves a small CPU with disk storage, a printer, and a CRT terminal in Vancouver, and a remote CRT and printer in Toronto.
b. The purchase price for the hardware and programs will be in the $65,000 to $100,000 range, with hardware maintenance about $200 to $400 per month.
c. The competition between suppliers at this level of computer is fairly intense and there should not be any problem negotiating a fair price.

Some possible areas of cost savings are shown below. The true savings cannot be measured until after the computer system is installed, but one can see the potential.

a. Telephone and Telex—Of the $28,000 per year, about $5600 is related to inventory and invoicing problems. We should be able to cut that by at least 60% for a cost reduction of $3360 per year.

b. Inventory carrying charges—At last year-end, inventory value was $950,000. At a 10% rate, carrying charges equal $95,000. If that were cut by 1/3, the potential yearly savings would be about $31,600.

c. Staff savings—At present, 5 to 6 people are working full-time on inventory bookkeeping, invoicing, etc. With 6 people at $12,000 including fringe benefits gives a $72,000 annual cost. It may be possible to reduce that to as low as 3 people. Savings could therefore be $36,000 annually.

d. Inventory storage space reduction.

In addition to the equipment costs, the communication between Vancouver and Toronto must also be considered. I have done some preliminary investigation and found that a "Data-route" hookup to Toronto for 14 hrs./day, 7 days a week, costs $876/month (which can be partly offset by the reduced telephone and Telex costs shown above).

I will be arranging a demonstration for you of at least two suppliers' hardware and standard inventory packages to give you some idea of what is available in the marketplace. We can then decide what the next step is and whether I will have to go to Toronto to look at the warehouse operation.

Discussion Topics

1. Thoroughly describe the circumstances that led Vancouver Recreational Products to consider the need for changing its current data processing procedures.

2. Evaluate the systems study work performed by Tom Jones. This evaluation should include an analysis of Exhibits 1, 2, 3, and 4.

3. Assuming that you are Tom Jones, what decision would you make regarding the continued involvement of Oliver Carruthers in V.R.P.'s systems study work? Thoroughly explain your reasoning.

4. Based on the available information provided in this case about Vancouver Recreational Products, attempt to design a data processing system that would fit the needs of the company. (*Note:* Make any reasonable assumptions about the company's operations that you consider necessary.)

CASE 2

Aqua Spray*

Company Background

Aqua Spray, a Milwaukee-based firm, was founded in 1970 by Andrew and June Digrovani. The sole product at this time, an underground sprinkler system, was marketed from a store at 1728 North Mayfair Road. The product line was gradually expanded to include in-ground and aboveground swimming pools, pool tables, game tables, and artificial Christmas trees. In 1982, the company purchased a store at 9900 West Capital Drive in Milwaukee, where it moved its entire operation. In 1987, Aqua Spray rented a facility at 1300 South 108th St. in West Allis. In 1988, an additional outlet was acquired at 6112 South 27th St. in Greenfield. All administrative functions are centralized at the Capital Drive store.

Since 1970, gross sales have been increasing an average of 10% a year, with total sales for the fiscal year ended March 1988 of approximately $1,800,000. The corporation is considering expanding to other outlets if market conditions permit.

Aqua Spray functions primarily in the capacity of a retailer and contractor. However, it sells chemicals for swimming pools on both a retail and wholesale basis. The firm experiences a very seasonal business due to the nature of its products. To illustrate this, sales items have been divided by product group, sales period, and percentage of total sales as shown on the next page.

Aqua Spray's current operations center on its president and founder, Mr. Andrew Digrovani (see Exhibit 1). Mr. Digrovani is responsible for purchase authorizations, pricing policy, advertising, personnel, and finance (including the function of treasurer). June Digrovani, the corporation vice-president, and Mr. William Frankle, the corporation expediter and setup man, are primarily responsible for the corporation's inground pool division. All the work is subcontracted through Swimming Pool Services. The board of directors is composed of Andrew and June Digrovani.

* This case study was prepared by Professor Kailas J. Rao for class discussion rather than to illustrate effective or ineffective handling of inventory and sales systems. Copyright © 1977 by Kailas J. Rao. Presented at a Case Workshop and distributed by the intercollegiate Case Clearing House, Soldiers Field, Boston, Mass. 02163. All rights reserved to the contributors. Printed in the U.S.A.

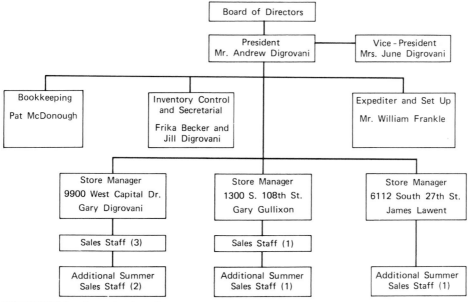

EXHIBIT 1   Organization chart.

The three store managers meet frequently with the president and are responsible for store setup, personnel control, and sales. Payments to store managers are on a salary plus commission basis. Salespersons receive only a commission. They are allowed to draw a stated amount of their commission against a drawing account. The entire sales staff, with the exception of the store managers, are part-time, with additional help being hired during the summer.

The firm is currently experiencing competition from Allied Pools, American Pool Table Company, M & M Sporting Goods, and Pool Park.

Systems Description and Problem Definition

The sales processing system of Aqua Spray (see Exhibit 2) begins with the preparation of a sales invoice by the salesman upon receipt of a customer order. Two types of sales invoices are in use. One is a three-part invoice used for small ticket items. The other, a four-part invoice, is only used for large items which must be shipped.

The last copy of either invoice is given to the customer as a receipt. In the case of the four-part invoice, the third copy is filed at the store of sale pending shipping of the merchandise when it becomes the bill of lading. The first and second copy are sent to bookkeeping and inventory control at the Capital Drive store on a daily basis. In inventory control the quantity of sales (as well as purchases) of aboveground swimming pools are recorded by model in inventory

Product Group	Sales Period	Percent of Sales
1. Underground sprinkler systems	April through September	5
2. Swimming pools		
(a) Aboveground	February through September	25
(b) Inground	January through June	25
3. Pool tables, air hockey, football, ping-pong, and accessories	All year	30
4. Christmas trees	October through December	10
5. Chemicals	May through September	5

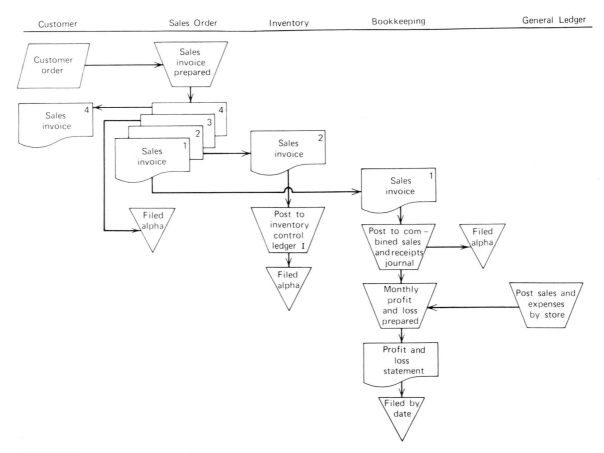

Customer   Sales Order   Inventory   Bookkeeping   General Ledger

EXHIBIT 2 Sales processing flowchart.

control ledger I. The firm plans to expand this to include pool tables as well. This ledger is set up in the following manner. It contains five columns for each model of aboveground swimming pool. These columns are date, order number (the number stamped on each prenumbered purchase order and sales invoice), received (purchases), delivered (sales), and a running balance. In this way a perpetual count can be maintained on aboveground swimming pools in inventory. The invoices are then filed alphabetically.

In bookkeeping, pat McDonough, a former public accountant, posts sales by store and product classification. The sales invoices are then filed alphabetically and act as the accounts receivable subsidiary ledger. All large receivables are financed through a local finance company.

Expenses are likewise segregated by store and

classification in a cash disbursements journal. Sales and expenses are then posted by store on a monthly basis to the general ledger. From the general ledger a monthly statement of profit and loss is prepared for each store. This statement contains the following revenue and expense classifications: aboveground pools, inground pools, sprinklers, sprinkler service, pool tables, Christmas trees, greenhouses, spas, miscellaneous, cost of goods sold, rent, heat, utilities, truck and auto, insurance, salaries, commissions, taxes (including payroll), dues and subscriptions, personal property tax, interest, maintenance, travel and entertainment, bad debts, cash over and short, and unclassified. Other revenue items such as interest and investment income are then added in to reach the bottom-line figure. Cost of goods sold is based on an estimated percentage of sales, currently 67%. To simplify the making of entries, the firm employs a chart of accounts.

In the purchasing system (see Exhibit 3) a three-part purchase order is prepared by the inventory clerk upon authorization by the president. At this time an entry is made in inventory control ledger II by the inventory clerk who records the quantities and prices of items ordered. This ledger contains both retail prices and quantities of *all* inventory items broken down by product type. This ledger has four headings

for each product. These are on hand, on order, received, and sold. The on-hand figures are arrived at through a bimonthly physical inventory count. The quantities sold are determined by subtracting the latest physical inventory from the total of on-hand and received merchandise. Figures from the sales invoices are not used in determining sales for the two-month period (for purposes of this ledger) between physical counts.

Part one of the purchase order is then mailed to the

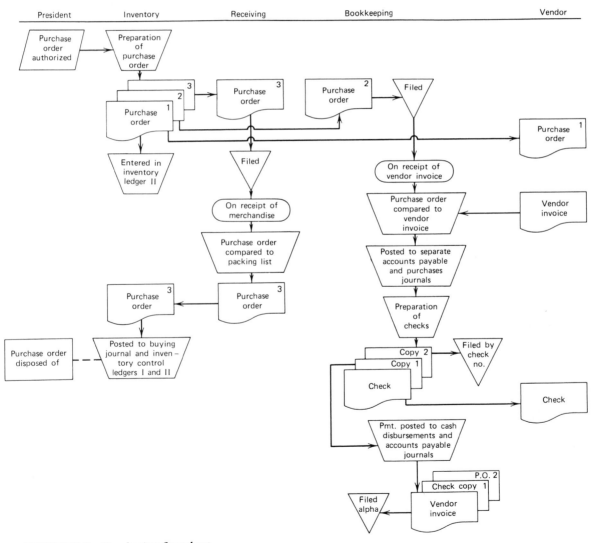

EXHIBIT 3 Purchasing flowchart.

vendor. Part two is sent to bookkeeping, where it is filed pending receipt of the vendor invoice. Part three is sent to receiving, where it is filed pending receipt of the merchandise. Although the firm has no specific receiving department, each store manager is responsible for merchandise deliveries to his or her respective store. Merchandise is currently sent by vendors to both the Capital and 108th St. stores as well as the corporation warehouse.

The vendor invoice is mailed directly to bookkeeping. At this time it is compared to the purchase order. If both documents agree, the totals are posted to separate accounts payable and purchases journals. These invoices are recorded alphabetically by vendor and include the invoice number. Accounts payable are aged weekly so that no purchase discounts are lost.

Checks are now prepared, each with two copies. The check itself is mailed to the vendor. Copy one of the check is used to post payments to the accounts payable and cash disbursements journals. The check number is also entered in both journals. Copy one is then attached to the purchase order and vendor invoice and filed alphabetically by vendor. Copy two of the check is filed by check number pending receipt of the monthly bank statement for reconciliation purposes.

When merchandise is received by the firm, the store manager compares the purchase order to the packing list and the merchandise. If the documents are in agreement with the shipment, the purchase order is forwarded to inventory control, where the purchase quantities are posted to inventory control ledgers I and II as well as a special buying journal maintained by the inventory clerk to assist in planning future purchases. The purchase order is then disposed of.

The present inventory control system is repetitive and poorly coordinated with sales processing. With the exception of aboveground swimming pools, the current system can provide only a rough figure on inventory shrinkage. The firm is currently unable to determine what quantities are on hand at a given store on a given date, except through a physical count. For this reason, even if an accurate shrinkage figure could be determined, it could not be determined which sales outlets are responsible. This information is desirable for purposes of store manager evaluation. The president also desires a more detailed breakdown of sales by individual stores.

Discussion Topics

1. Thoroughly describe the weaknesses that exist in Aqua Spray's present system for processing sales (Exhibit 2) and for processing inventory purchases (Exhibit 3).
2. Recommend design modifications for Aqua Spray's current sales processing and inventory purchasing systems in order to coordinate these two systems. (*Note:* To reflect clearly your design modifications, it would be quite useful to draw flowcharts of your recommended sales processing and inventory purchasing systems.)
3. The accounting procedures for processing sales transactions and inventory purchase transactions are presently performed manually by Aqua Spray's bookkeeping function. Based on the limited information available about the company's sales and inventory purchase transactions, recommend some possible data processing hardware and software systems that might be preferable to Aqua Spray's current manual system. For each suggested data processing system, indicate both the positive and the negative aspects of your suggestion.

CASE 3

Laub Group, Incorporated*

Company Background

Laub Group, Incorporated is a relatively small insurance agency that matches its private and commercial customers' desired coverage with the insurance policies offered by various companies. The initial capital contribution of $3,349 grew to $55,646 in 1985 and has since remained constant. Losses from 1980 to 1985 increased until they reached $93,936 in 1985 (retained deficit of $330,610), but profits were made in the last two years. (See Exhibit 1 for profit/loss and revenue trends.) Total assets held by the company in 1988 equaled $1,427,223, of which $897,649 were current.

In 1938, Mr. Rudolf A. Laub formed the Rudolf A. Laub Agency at 825 North Jefferson Street, Milwaukee,

* This case was prepared by Professor Kailas J. Rao as a basis for class discussion rather than to illustrate either effective or ineffective handling of administrative problems. Copyright © 1977 by Kailas J. Rao. Presented at a Case Workshop and distributed by the intercollegiate Case Clearing House, Soldiers Field, Boston, Mass. 02163. All rights reserved to the contributors. Printed in the U.S.A.

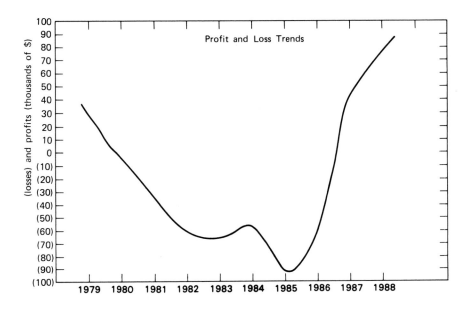

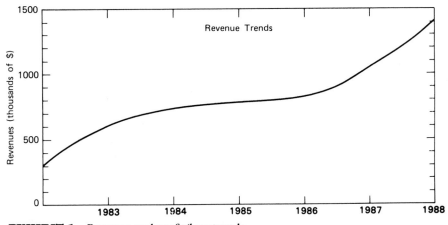

EXHIBIT 1 Revenue and profit/loss trends.

Wisconsin. The agency moved to the Wells Building of Milwaukee in 1947, and continued to operate as a sole proprietorship until its incorporation as the Rudolf A. Laub Agency, Inc., on February 1, 1976. After Rudolf Laub passed away in early March of 1979, his son, Raymond, purchased the business from his father's estate executors, assumed the duties and responsibilities of president, and changed the company's name to Laub Agency, Incorporated. Mr. Raymond Laub subse-

quently expanded both the amount and kinds of insurance written to include underwriting property, liability and crime protection, employee benefit and bonding coverage for commercial accounts, plus auto, home, and health protection for individuals.

Growth of the company was accomplished by the acquisition of various Milwaukee insurance concerns in 1981 and other similar organizations throughout Wisconsin thereafter. At this time, Mr. Laub again al-

EXHIBIT 2 Companies Laub Group, Incorporated represents.

Aetna Insurance	Hartford Steam Boiler
Aetna Life and Casualty	Home
American States	INA Insurance
Atlantic Companies	Kemper Group
Chubb and Son	Maryland American General
Connecticut General	New Hampshire
Connecticut Mutual Life	Northwestern National
Continental Assurance	Ohio Casualty
Continental Insurance	Reliance Companies
CNA Insurance	Safeco
Fidelity and Deposit	St. Paul
Fireman's Fund American	Time Insurance
General Casualty	Tower
Great American	U.S. Fidelity and Guaranty
Hartford Group	Zurich American

tered the name of his firm to Laub Group, Inc., to reflect the consolidation with the following insurance agencies: Warner Insurance Agency (Milwaukee—3/4/81); and Jensen and Phillips Agency, Inc. (Janesville—1/22/81). Presently, Laub Group also has major subsidiaries in Wausau (acquired on 2/19/88), Madison (2/1/85), and Racine and Appleton (both acquired on 6/1/88). Laub Group, Inc. now represents 30 independent insurance companies (see Exhibit 2 for a complete list). On January 1, 1989, Laub Group, Incorporated's Milwaukee office at 324 E. Wisconsin Avenue assumed control over all subsidiary and branch cash payments and receipts. Also, coordination of all consolidated operations became the responsibility of the home office executives.

Of the 61 company employees, 23 are subsidiary sales and office staff, and four part-time employees perform similar services for the branches.

The majority of workers are stationed in the Milwaukee home office, since most of the agency's customers are located in this area. They are supervised by an executive staff consisting of the president, executive vice-president, senior vice-president, and the administrative vice-president.

The home office is composed of three distinct operating divisions. Customers are solicited by the producers, who determine the individual's or group's insurance needs and suitable coverage. The office staff then submits all insurance applications to one of the 30 companies they represent for policy approval. Once a client has been accepted, an invoice is prepared by the producer and sent to the accounting department,

where the transaction is properly processed and recorded. (See Organizational Chart, Exhibit 3.)

Our analysis is mainly concerned with the accounting department, which consists of four employees and is managed by Mr. Wayne Seidens. Mr. Seidens, who was recently appointed to his position as accounting manager, is responsible for the preparation of all financial reports, cash flow statements, daily bank balance summaries, the branch payroll, and is also responsible for the collection of premiums on overdue accounts. To assist him in these functions, Mrs. Virginia Van Buskirk and her staff prepare invoices, type checks, file reports, post cash and accounts receivable entries, etc. Mrs. Van Buskirk personally reconciles all bank balances and updates the accounts receivable journal for the consolidated entity.

Detailed Description of the Problem

All of Laub Group, Inc.'s monthly reports are compiled by Agency Records Control, Inc. (ARC) in Texas. Any information that should be included in these periodic reports must be submitted to ARC by Laub on the first working day of the following month. This requirement forces subsidiaries and branches to close their books several days before the end of the month to allow for delivery to Milwaukee. Any relevant transactions that occur after closing must be posted manually to be reflected in the financial summaries. Currently, these adjustments are not made. With this lack of proper cutoff, the monthly statements produced by the software package do not accurately represent Laub Group, Inc.'s financial position and may not be a reliable source of information for decision making.

The insurance agency's accounting information system inputs consist of invoices, a cash-received sheet, check copies, and a journal entry form to record general items. Most data are generated through the invoices, including the customer's name, the customer's identification number, the salesperson, the insurance company's respective commissions and numbers, the type of policy, the premiums due, and the month the invoice was entered into the system.

The invoice consists of an original and three copies. The original is mailed to the customer, and two copies are filed manually in the bookkeeping and accounts receivable aging file. The remaining copy is sent to ARC. Once received by ARC, the invoice initiates the process of updating the subsidiary, branch, or home office's respective account, the Z-ledger (a general summary of all transactions), and the 3500 account. The 3500

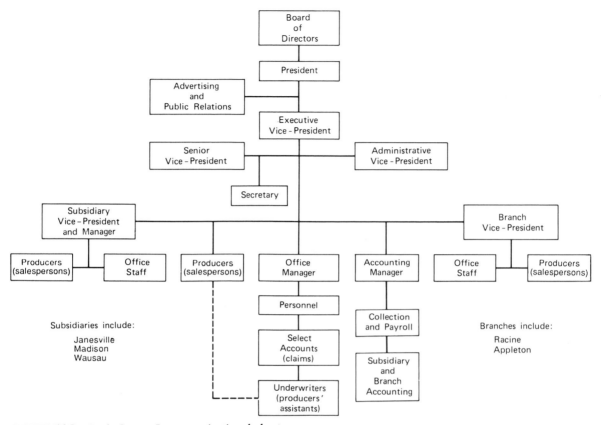

EXHIBIT 3 Laub Group, Inc. organizational chart.

account is used to consolidate and control all of Laub's cash payments and receipts. This information, along with data submitted through the cash received forms, journal entry forms, new account lists, and checks, is coordinated into various summaries, ledgers, and statements. These reports are then mailed to Laub Group, Inc., where they are reviewed by management and subsequently filed in the accounting department. (See Exhibit 4 for a diagram of this accounting information system's inputs and outputs.)

Few errors occur when ARC processes the insurance agency's financial data; however, the sales staff occasionally makes mistakes while filling out invoices. Any errors that may arise in the preparation of an invoice cannot be corrected once it is received by ARC. When discovered, the error may be rectified only by submitting an adjustments sheet containing the proper entry with the following month's inputs. Often, errors

cannot be discovered until the processed reports are returned from Texas 7 to 10 days after the month's end. This time lag between sending data and receiving the various reports, coupled with the delay in correcting errors subsequently detected, reduces the processed reports' usefulness.

The current accounting information system does not provide an accurate aging of accounts receivable. Customer account balances are now separated by ARC according to the invoices' entry dates. Premiums are due on or before the policy's effective date with a 30-day grace period. Considering that an invoice may be entered well in advance of the date policy coverage becomes effective, the accounts receivable analysis cannot be used to determine which customers are actually behind in their payments.

Another inconsistency exists between the reports that Laub Group, Inc. desires and those sent by ARC.

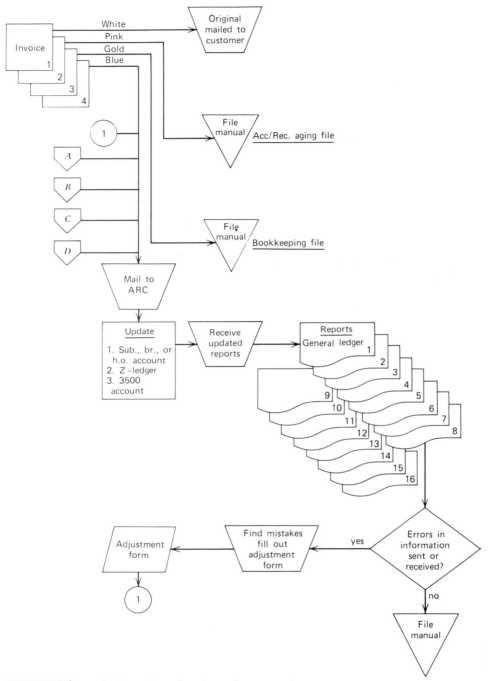

EXHIBIT 4 Laub Group, Inc. flowchart of inputs and outputs.

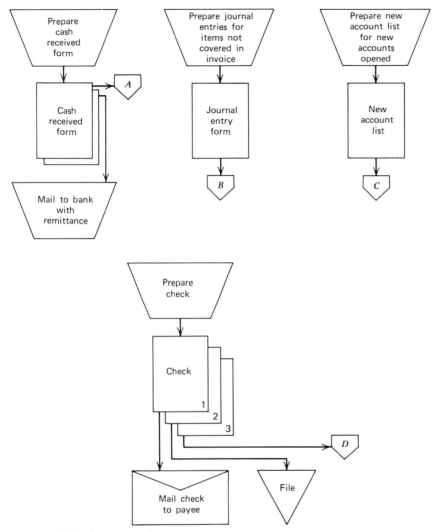

EXHIBIT 4 (Continued)

Along with the monthly report data, ARC also prepares quarterly and year-end statements. However, many of these statements are rarely used by management, and are usually discarded or added to the growing volume of filed data. The agency also desires additional reports not currently produced by the computer, such as a profit and loss statement with budget comparisons, a breakdown of salespersons' expenses, and a statement of cash flows.

Discussion Topics

1. Indicate the strengths and weaknesses that you feel exist in Laub Group, Incorporated's present accounting information system. (These strengths and weaknesses should encompass both specific accounting procedures and internal controls.) Regarding each strength and weakness mentioned, discuss your reason(s) for considering it as such.

2. Raymond Laub would like his company to examine

the possibility of purchasing or leasing its own computer rather than having Agency Records Control, Inc. continue to process the company's accounting data. Describe in detail the systems study work that should be performed by Laub Group, Incorporated in order to reach a decision regarding the purchase or lease of a computer.

3. Based on the systems study work referred to in Discussion Topic 2, assume that Laub Group, Incorporated has decided to acquire its own computer. Making any assumptions you consider reasonable, describe in detail the processing procedures and the controls for handling accounts receivable and accounts payable activities on the company's new computer system. (For example, if you think that customer cash payment transactions should be batched semimonthly for computer processing, then describe the types of hardware and software that should exist, the specific procedures for batching the transaction data, the types of controls to maintain, the specific format of output reports, etc.)

CASE 4

State Consumer Reporting Bureau*

On June 1, 1988, Mr. Robert Markson, president of the State Consumer Reporting Bureau, retained two consultants to assist him in developing methods for handling State's information processing needs. In their initial session with Mr. Markson, the following information was presented which the consultants felt was particularly relevant.

Company Background

Founded in December 1964 by Mr. Robert Markson, State Consumer Reporting Bureau is a customer collection agency. Various retail stores in Metropolitan Boston give them delinquent accounts receivable. Through a combination of collection letters, telephone follow-ups, and, in a few extreme cases, personal visits,

* Copyright © 1976 by the President and Fellows of Harvard College. Reproduced by permission. This case was prepared by F. Warren McFarlan under the supervision of John Dearden.

the company's collection department attempts to collect the overdue amounts. In about 50% of the cases they are successful. The other 50% are either dropped (if the amounts involved are less than $100) or are turned over to the attorneys in the legal department, who file suit against the customer and legally press the matter to a conclusion. The company is paid a fixed percentage on every dollar collected. This percentage increases if legal action must be taken on an account. Currently, the company is trying to collect on approximately 4000 accounts. New delinquent customers' accounts are received at a rate of 500 a month. The firm employs two attorneys, six collectors, and three secretaries, in addition to Mr. Markson.

Company System for Collection Action

When new delinquent accounts arrive at State Consumer, a collection card is prepared by a secretary. This is given to Mr. Irwin Gannich, the company's attorney. Considering such things as the amount due, the store where the sale was made, the elapsed time since the last payment on the account, and previous collection action taken by the store, he decides if immediate collection action is necessary or whether the collection department should be given the account.

If the account is sent to the collection department, the collection card is given to a secretary, who automatically mails the delinquent account the first of the company's four collection letters. Designed to frighten the customer into paying, these letters are printed up by a local printing company. The secretary takes the letter and types the following information in the proper places.

1. The customer's name and address.
2. The store where he or she incurred the bill.
3. The amount of the bill.

The secretary types up an envelope for the letter, mails it, and makes note of the type of letter mailed to the customer and its date on the collection card. The collection card is then routed to one of the six collectors in the collection department.

In general, each collector is responsible for a certain section of the alphabet. Cards of customers whose last names begin with the letters A–E would be given to collector #1, etc. For certain stores, however, continuity of approach makes it desirable that the same collector handle all accounts for this store. Thus, collector #1 is responsible for customers whose last names begin with Letters A–E plus all accounts of the Central Garden Florist Shop.

Upon receiving a collection card, a collector takes no action on it for five days. At the end of this period, if no payment is received, he or she telephones the customer. At the collector's discretion, he or she may also order the mailing of the second, third, and fourth collection letters. A record of all telephone conversations, letters mailed, promises made, and payments given is kept on the collection card. Mr. Markson, in speaking of the collection card, noted:

> This record of information is our collection department's most important tool. They use the customer's past performance as a guide in effective bargaining. When a customer knows you are acquainted with his past activities, he takes you more seriously. Past addresses too may give clues on people who move to another location, leaving no forwarding address. Take away their history record and collection effectiveness is reduced by 60%. Any information processing system must be designed around the preservation of this information for the collector.

Many of the cards are completely covered with notations and have a second card stapled to them. These collection cards are filed alphabetically in a box on the collector's desk. If after 45 days the customer shows complete inaction, the collector automatically turns the card over to the legal department. Similarly, if the collector feels payments are dragging too slowly, he or she refers the account to the legal department.

In talking about the collectors, Mr. Markson said:

> . . . the role of the collector at State is similar to that of a blue-collar assembly worker. They are the company's primary revenue producer, and it is their effectiveness that keeps us in business. It is similar to a detective game and they view it as a contest between themselves and the customer.

Company System for Customer Payments

The collector negotiates a payback agreement with the customer. In some cases the customer will make a lump-sum payment. The majority of the time, however, an installment payback scheme is worked out, sometimes stretching over six or more months.

The collections may be received in three different ways.

1. The customer comes to State's office and makes a payment. He or she is given a receipt and the money is placed in an envelope with the customer's name on it.

2. The customer mails a payment to State (about a third of these payments are cash). The envelope is checked to make sure the customer's name is on the outside.

3. The customer sends a payment to the store where the purchase was made. Within six days after the payment the store sends a notice to State Consumer, giving the customer's name, amount of payment, and date it was made. This notice is placed in an envelope with the customer's name on the outside.

Each day the envelopes are taken to the collection room and a secretary gathers the necessary collection cards. The secretary first posts the amount and date of payment on them. Then, the secretary lists each customer's name, date, and amount of payment on a yellow collection sheet (separate ones for each store) for payments made to State and on blue collection sheets (separate ones for each store) for payments made to the store. The secretary then returns the collection cards to the collection room and files them in the individual collector's box.

The collection sheets are filed away until the end of the month. They are then gathered and each store is mailed a copy of its collections, together with a summary stating how much it collected and how much State collected. This information is used to calculate State's commission.

The legal collections are handled separately from those of the collection department, and separate, more complete statements are sent by the legal department to the stores. Presently the company has two attorneys. They divide the legal business between themselves and initiate a series of letters and telephone calls that culminates in the customer being brought into court if he or she takes no payment action.

When payments are received at State, the secretary can, in most cases, quickly sort the legal payments from the collection department payments. This is because State supplies return mail envelopes to the customers, which are stamped legal if it is an account in legal. About 20% of the legal mail is not identified as such and is sent to the collection department. If the collection card is not found there, the envelope is forwarded to legal.

Information Processing Requirements

Mr. Markson then made the following remarks, which seemed particularly relevant to the two consultants.

> I am not worried about our ability to operate efficiently at the current level of operations. Our current performance from both a cost and efficiency viewpoint is satisfactory. What concerns me is our internal capacity for handling growth. If I thought we could handle it, within six months we would be receiving new customer accounts at the rate of 5000 per month. Organizing and expanding the collection staff is not a major problem. Neither do finances pose a real threat. What is worrying me is the fear of drowning ourselves in a flood of paperwork so that we could neither service the accounts nor produce timely statements for the stores. This could do lasting harm to the firm's prospects. Before we get this additional business, we must be set up to handle it.

Mr. Markson then introduced the two consultants to Miss Duncan, the office manager. During the course of the morning she made the following comments.

> The present system seems to work all right. The only real bottleneck is finding out where a customer's card is. When we get a telephone call, I don't always know whether the card is in the collection room, legal, or with the man on the road. . . . Yes, we have our man out collecting all the time. Every Monday I give him 50 collection cards. I mark them down so if someone calls, I won't spend all day trying to find a card that isn't in the office. Mr. Markson is sold on the idea of automation, so it is coming. It is only a matter of time. I'll do my best . . . a lot of people don't care for the idea. They have been in the collection business for 30 years and have never seen anything like it.

Recommendations

The two management consultants hired by the company have studied the problem carefully and have recommended an automated, magnetic tape system utilizing three major files: (1) a claims file of accounts sent to State for collection, (2) a client master file, and (3) a history file of the company's accounts. The claims file and client file records are illustrated in Exhibit 1.

Claims file master records, containing information about the customers, the client stores involved, and the credit sales involved, are each followed by detail (payment) records representing customers' activities to pay their debts. The client file master records simply contain name and address information of those client stores sending collection accounts to the company, plus a cycle (i.e., review) date. The history file records (not shown) would serve to replace the collection cards of the company. As such, this file would contain the same kind of information as was originally entered by hand on the collection card previously described.

The proposed system would perform the collections operations of the State Consumer Reporting Bureau in four (or more) processing routines as follows.

1. In processing Run No. 1, new account claims would be keyed to floppy disks, edited, and added to the claims file. At the same time, initial letters of inquiry would be sent to customers requesting payments. Finally, in this run, a summary report would be prepared for management review, copies of which would be forwarded to the individual company collection agents.

2. In processing Run No. 2, payment information (also initially keyed on disks) would be added to the claims file as detail records. Updating the account balance information in the claims file would also be performed. Follow-up letters would be sent to those new customers who had yet to make payments on their accounts. A summary report would be prepared and distributed in similar fashion to Run No. 1.

3. Processing Run No. 3 would use the claims file to prepare billing statements for clients. Summary information for each of State's clients would be prepared indicating the total amount of collections received, the total amount due State, the total amount due the client, and so forth. This processing run would also purge the claims file of bills paid off by the customers, and transfer certain summary information to the company's history file.

4. Processing Run No. 4 would prepare an aging analysis of pending claims for each client of the company.

Discussion Topics

1. Prepare a systems flowchart for each of the four separate processing routines described. How often should each of these processing routines be performed? Explain.

Claims File Master Record

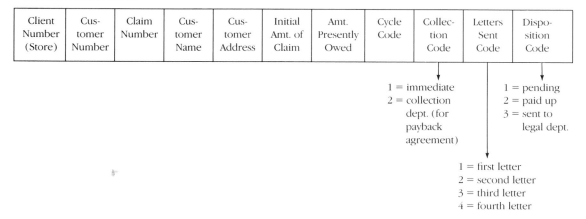

Client Number (Store)	Cus-tomer Number	Claim Number	Cus-tomer Name	Cus-tomer Address	Initial Amt. of Claim	Amt. Presently Owed	Cycle Code	Collec-tion Code	Letters Sent Code	Dispo-sition Code

Collection Code:
1 = immediate
2 = collection dept. (for payback agreement)

Letters Sent Code:
1 = first letter
2 = second letter
3 = third letter
4 = fourth letter

Disposition Code:
1 = pending
2 = paid up
3 = sent to legal dept.

Claims File Detail (Payment) Record

Client Number (Store)	Claim Number	Cus-tomer Number	Amount of Payment	Date of Payment	Pay-ment Code

Payment Code:
1 = payment to State
2 = payment to client store

Client File Master Record

Client Number (Store)	Client Name	Address	Cycle Date

EXHIBIT 1

2. Design the record layout of the company's history file records.
3. What additional information might be added to the fields in the claims file master records? What information might be dropped?
4. What additional types of management information might be obtained from the four processing routines that were not available heretofore but that might now be generated with the proposed collections system?
5. Describe the advantages to State Consumer Reporting Bureau of the proposed automated system over the existing manual system. What disadvantages does the new system create for State?

CASE 5

*Autoticket Inc.**

Autoticket Inc. is a computerized ticket-selling service in a large Canadian city. It has 50 outlets in highly accessible locations, which sell tickets for sports, entertainment, and theatrical events. The operation is only nine months old and is still going through a number of start-up problems. You have been ap-

* Adapted with permission from Canadian Institute of Chartered Accountants 1986 examination, The Canadian Institute of Chartered Accountants, Toronto, Canada. Changes to the original questions and/or suggested approaches to answering are the sole responsibility of the authors.

proached by Autoticket's general manager, who has heard that chartered accountants (the Canadian equivalent of the certified public accountant) can provide special reports on descriptions of systems used by service organizations such as Autoticket. He engages you to write such a report and provides you with the following information.

The owners of Autoticket are three local sports organizations and an entertainment promoter. Although Autoticket is independent of its owners' operations, it was set up primarily to enhance the profitability of their operations. Autoticket is expected to do this by increasing ticket sales because the sales locations and services are convenient for the public and events are promoted across the city through the outlets. In addition, cost savings are anticipated for the processing of season-ticket sales (these costs are expected to fall by 50%) and for the provision of accurate, reliable and up-to-the-minute data on ticket sales. A feasibility study indicated that Autoticket has a profit potential of $500,000 annually on an initial investment of $2.5 million.

In addition to the owners, other organizations that sponsor events use Autoticket to sell their tickets. All participating organizations pay commissions for the processing of season- and single-ticket sales. Autoticket collects a customer service fee between $0.25 to $2.00 per ticket. As a convenience to the public, Autoticket permits limited returns and resales.

Very recently, Autoticket has been negotiating with Domenico Corso, a rock concert promoter, to become an owner and/or user of the system. The promoter has strong doubts about becoming associated with the system because of bad publicity and, as he freely admits, because he does not "trust" computers. The general manager believes that a special report on the description of Autoticket's ticket-selling system would help overcome Corso's distrust of computers. He would like to give a copy of the report to the existing owners and sponsors. He also wants to know of any improvements that could be made to the system.

Autoticket's staff consists of a general manager, a controller, a sales manager, and nine clerical, technical, and computer operations personnel. Ticket-selling locations are staffed by part-time employees who work on a commission basis.

Each selling location consists of a booth with a telephone, a visual display terminal (VDT), a modem, and a special ticket-printer capable of handling up to 18 rolls of tickets at once. Booths are staffed only during peak selling hours. The ticket-sellers also handle lottery ticket sales entirely on their own account and keep all related commissions. This lottery ticket selling arrangement was necessary to induce ticket-sellers to staff the booths.

The computer is a modern "super-microcomputer" with 500 million bytes of disk storage and a two-million-byte CPU. It can handle 96 online terminals. One high-speed and several low-speed printers are located in the main office.

The software for ticket sales was acquired from a specialty software house in the United States. This software is currently being used in over 30 major cities in Canada and the United States and has been favorably reviewed by a well-known computer consultant.

Details of Ticket Selling System

Ticket-sellers can view current events available in the system on the VDT. They can query seat availability for an event by seat, row, or section number; or they can simply ask for the "best available" seats. If a customer decides to purchase one or more tickets, the section, row, and seat number(s) must be keyed in. If, however, the "best available" option is selected, the seller simply keys in the number of seats being purchased. The printer then produces the necessary ticket(s) from the appropriate ticket roll.

The computer system automatically computes the total owing, including the service fee and any miscellaneous charges such as amusement tax. The seller then collects the necessary amount from the customer, in cash or via a credit card. Standard procedures call for sellers to make daily deposits using the night-deposit facilities of nearby banks. These deposits are transferred to Autoticket's account the next day.

The head office technical staff refill and change ticket rolls in selling locations and repair the equipment, as required. They also maintain records of ticket numbers on rolls installed and removed from selling locations. Their most important function, however, is to train the part-time ticket-sellers. There is a high turnover of part-time employees.

The system contains a permanent record (created by head office clerical staff) of the seating layout of each facility used for events. This record is called a "facilities profile," and it is used to create an "event profile" for each current event in the system.

When an event profile is created, the computer head office operator must input seat prices by section, row, and/or individual seat. Service fees and any miscellaneous charges must also be specified at this time. The operator may also reserve seats, exclude certain seats, and create special discount prices for groups such as senior citizens. The operator prepares event profiles in accordance with a printed copy of the facility profile on which the sales manager has defined all of the prices, available seats and other data for specific events.

Reports From the System and Their Use

1. Report on current events—used by the controller to verify the accuracy of event profiles.
2. Daily report of ticket sales, service charges, commissions owing to ticket-sellers, etc., by selling location—used by the clerical staff to reconcile and analyze deposits.
3. Daily report of ticket sales by event—used by the clerical staff to determine the amounts to be remitted to event organizers.
4. Daily sales report by event—sent to organizers daily to show total sales to date.
5. Daily report on ticket number sequences sold—used by clerical staff to help account for all sold and unsold tickets.
6. Weekly report of event sales—used by head office management and organizers to assess profitability of events.
7. Weekly report of deposits—used by head office management to identify problem ticket-selling locations.
8. Monthly summary report—used by head office management and owners to assess Autoticket's activities.

Problems with the Ticket System

1. Ticket-sellers constantly include lottery money with event sales deposits; as a result head office staff are having problems balancing deposits to computer reports. Ticket-sellers usually realize their error and then withhold funds, a day or two later, from their event sales deposits. That further complicates the head office reconciliation process.
2. Ticket-printers frequently become jammed. The printers are quite delicate and are often roughly treated by ticket-sellers. Several have been broken by ticket-sellers trying to fix a jamming problem. Autoticket has received many complaints from the public about this problem.

3. Ticket-sellers often do not show up at their booths at scheduled times. The people willing to take on this type of part-time job do not appear to be very reliable. Over 25 sellers have already been dismissed for persistent lateness or absenteeism.
4. Ticket-sellers do not always make deposits daily. Instead, they take deposits home with them and make the deposits the next time they are on duty, which is sometimes several days later. This delay also complicates the head office deposit/sales reconciliation process.
5. More than 20 robberies have been reported by ticket-sellers, but in only two cases has anyone been arrested. Management is not convinced that all of the reported robberies are genuine. Losses, which are uninsurable, have amounted to over $20,000.
6. Event profiles are sometimes incorrect because special requirements for particular performances (e.g., first five rows cannot be sold) have not been recorded. Thus, tickets have been sold for seats which were actually not available.
7. The owners and organizations sponsoring events have been complaining about not being paid on time and about payments differing from computer reports of ticket sales. These problems arise from the difficulties in reconciling deposits and sales reports.
8. Ticket-seller turnover is causing high error rates in seat sales. Some customers have been sold the wrong seats and discover the error only when they get to the event. Others notice the incorrect seat numbers as they are handed the tickets, but the ticket-sellers frequently do not know how to cancel ticket sales and reissue new tickets.

Head Office Activities

The head office clerical staff spend a great deal of time reconciling ticket sales and bank deposits. As mentioned earlier, there are several significant complications in the reconciliation process. They also perform reconciliations of sold and unsold ticket numbers.

The computer software includes a multiprogramming operating system. All application software was provided to Autoticket in object (i.e., machine language) code. The password system allows senior technical personnel to override all system restrictions. Ticket-sellers have the most restricted access privileges. Head office clerical staff can sell tickets and call for various file displays to assist them in their reconciliations. Head office management can access all files and make corrections.

Season ticket sales are processed only at the head office. The season ticket system requires that all events in a "season" be specified before the start of season ticket sales. Once event profiles for the season have been defined, season ticket orders can be processed. Purchasers are required to pay for their tickets at the time of purchase. Head office clerical staff then prepare deposits and record the sales in the system.

Season tickets are produced on one of the special ticket-printers and then mailed to purchasers. All deposits and season-tickets produced by the system are reconciled by a clerk independent of the deposit and recording function. The system also produces a variety of reports on season ticket sales for management and organizers of season events. No serious problems have been encountered with the season ticket sales processed to date.

The computer also processes the general ledger and accounts payable systems, which are completely independent of the ticket system. These are not large systems: only about 100 checks a month are processed, and the general ledger consists of only 50 accounts. There have been no processing problems with these systems.

The general manager and controller both review much of the input to these systems and review all output. They are satisfied that their review would either prevent or detect any significant errors. The computer systems produce complete, printed audit trails of all processing operations.

The general manager and sales manager work extensively with event organizers to promote the use of the computerized ticket-selling system. Some organizers have been reluctant to use the system because of publicity about some of the problems, but use has begun to increase significantly. Commission revenues for Autoticket are projected to exceed the original estimate of $3 million for the first year of operations. Total ticket sales are expected to exceed $35 million.

Discussion Topics

1. Describe the information you would include in the special report provided to Corso, as well as to the owners and sponsors. Remember that the purpose of the report is to convince Corso to become an owner and/or user of the system.

2. Based on the information supplied, give a preliminary evaluation of system control weaknesses, together with appropriate recommendations. Also provide a preliminary evaluation of system strengths.

Appendixes

A | Quantitative Analysis Examples

EXAMPLE 1: LINEAR PROGRAMMING

Problem Situation

Two products of particular importance to the Alan Company are baseballs and golf balls. Both products are packaged in boxes of one dozen balls each, and both are manufactured by the company in conformance with professional specifications. Demand for these two products has been strong and the company can sell as much as it can produce per year. Management has made long-range plans to expand its manufacturing capabilities. For the present, however, the Alan Company must try to meet its sales requirements with present production facilities. Two production areas of particular importance are the winding machines, which manufacture the cores for both baseballs and golf balls, and the inspection stations, where inspectors must examine finished products. Each winding machine can make either three dozen baseball cores or nine dozen golf ball cores per hour. Each inspector can examine either eight dozen finished baseballs or four dozen finished golf balls per hour. Accountants from the accounting subsystem have provided the following cost figures and selling prices for each dozen baseballs and each dozen golf balls.

	Baseballs	Golf Balls
Direct variable costs	$3.20	$2.75
Allocated fixed costs	1.60	1.30
Selling price	6.80	6.45

Problem Requirement

Using linear programming, determine how many dozen baseballs and golf balls the Alan Company should manufacture per hour to make optimum use of its valuable winding-machine time and inspection time.

Problem Solution

Step 1: Define the Decision Variables

In this problem, we wish to decide how many dozen baseballs and golf balls to produce per hour. Thus, let

x = the number of baseballs to produce/hour (in dozens)
y = the number of golf balls to produce/hour (in dozens)

Step 2: Define the Alan Company's Objective Function

The Alan Company's objective is to make the most effective use of its resources associated with production. The company can do this by deciding the most desirable number of baseballs and golf balls to produce per hour. The more profitable the mix of baseballs and golf balls the company produces and sells, of course, the more efficient its utilization of resources. For this problem, therefore, the company should try to maximize the contribution margin, M, of its two products, or

Maximize $M = \$3.60x + \$3.70y$

The contribution margin of each product is computed as the difference between the selling price of each product and its variable cost. The contribution margin for baseballs, therefore, is $3.60 minus $3.20, or $3.60. The contribution margin for golf balls is $6.45 minus $2.75, or $3.70. Allocated fixed costs for both products are ignored. This is because fixed costs do not vary with the level of production volume and are thus irrelevant to the production mix decision.

Step 3: Define the Linear Programming Problem's Constraints

For the purposes of formulation, it is perhaps easiest to convert baseball production and golf ball production into fractions of an hour per dozen. The winding machine can wind either three dozen baseballs or nine dozen golf balls per hour. Thus, it will take the winding machine 1/3 hour to wind one dozen baseballs and 1/9 hour to wind one dozen golf balls. Similarly, it takes an inspector 1 hour to inspect either eight dozen baseballs of four dozen golf balls. Therefore, an inspector will take 1/8 hour to inspect one dozen baseballs and 1/4 hour to inspect one dozen golf balls.

With these conversions made, it is now a straightforward matter to formulate the mathematical production constraints. We have defined the variable x to be the number of baseballs to produce per hour (in dozens) and the variable y to be the number of golf balls to produce per hour (in dozens). Thus, the constraint

$$\frac{1}{3}x + \frac{1}{9}y \le 1 \text{ (winding constraint)}$$

says that the amount of time it takes the winding

machine to produce one dozen baseballs (1/3 hour) times the number of baseballs produced (x) plus the amount of time it takes the winding machine to produce one dozen golf balls (1/9 hour) times the number of golf balls produced (y) must be less than or equal to the amount of time allotted, or 1 hour. We use 1 hour because we wish to know how many dozen baseballs and golf balls to produce for each unit of time. We shall return to this point after we have solved this problem.

We can formulate a constraint for inspection time in a fashion similar to the winding constraint. It will take an inspector 1/8 hour to inspect a dozen baseballs and 1/4 hour to inspect a dozen golf balls. Thus, the constraint

$$\frac{1}{8}x + \frac{1}{4}y \le 1 \text{ (inspection constraint)}$$

states that the time spent inspecting baseballs (1/8x) plus the time spent inspecting golf balls (1/4y) must be less than or equal to the total time allotted, or 1 hour.

We are almost finished. A final set of constraints that are somewhat intuitive, although not explicitly stated in the problem, are the *non-negativity conditions*: $x \ge 0$, $y \ge 0$. The constraint $x \ge 0$ states that we shall produce either a positive number of baseballs or nothing: we cannot produce a negative number of baseballs. Similarly, the constraint $y \ge 0$ states that we shall produce either a positive number of golf balls or nothing.

We have now completed our formulation. Summarizing, we have

Maximize $M = \$3.60x + \$3.70y$

Subject to

$$\frac{1}{3}x + \frac{1}{9}y \le 1 \text{ (winding constraint)}$$

$$\frac{1}{8}x + \frac{1}{4}y \le 1 \text{ (inspection constraint)}$$

$x \ge 0 \quad y \ge 0$ (nonnegativity conditions)

Step 4: Graph the Constraints

Linear programming problems involving three or more variables are solved with algebraic techniques (such as the *simplex method*) that are beyond the scope of this book. Linear programming problems of only two variables such as the Alan Company's production problem may be solved with simple graphs. Thus, here, we can use a two-dimensional grid to help us determine the optimal number of baseballs and golf balls to produce for the Alan Company.

First, let us consider the nonnegativity conditions, $x \geq 0$ and $y \geq 0$. These conditions restrict the linear programming problem to the upper right-hand quadrant of a graph, as illustrated in Figure A-1. Thus, we need not worry about the other three quadrants, because in each of these quadrants at least one of the two variables is negative.

Next, let us consider the winding constraint. This constraint is the inequality, $1/3x + 1/9y \leq 1$. To plot an inequality like this, first consider this constraint in the equality form, $1/3x + 1/9y = 1$.

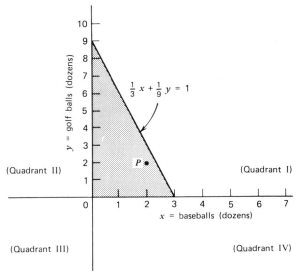

FIGURE A-1 The set of points (x,y) that satisfies the Alan Company's winding constraint: $1/3x + 1/9y \leq 1$.

This is easy to plot. For example, if $x = 0$, then $y = 9$. Alternatively, if $y = 0$, then $x = 3$. We now have two points with which to determine a straight line; that is, the point ($x = 0$, $y = 9$) and the point ($x = 3$, $y = 0$). Connecting these two points, we have the line segment $1/3x + 1/9y = 1$. This line has been plotted in Figure A-1 as shown.

The winding constraint is not an equality but an inequality. As a result, all the points *below* the line segment $1/3x + 1/9y = 1$ will also satisfy the constraint. For example, the point ($x = 2, y = 2$), or point P in the figure, will also satisfy the constraint because $1/3(2) + 1/9(2)$ equals $8/9$, which is also less than 1. Thus, we observe that an inequality constraint determines an entire area of points, each of which will satisfy the constraint $1/3x + 1/9y \leq 1$. This area has been shaded in Figure A-1.

Points that satisfy the constraints of a linear programming problem are said to be *feasible points,* or *feasible solutions,* to a linear programming problem. If the Alan Company had only this one winding constraint, then the area shaded in Figure A-1 would be the set of feasible solutions to the linear programming problem.

The Alan Company, however, has two production constraints. Thus, it remains for us to consider the inspection constraint $1/8x + 1/4y \leq 1$. This is handled in exactly the same way as the winding constraint and thus need not be detailed here. However, in Figure A-2, we have plotted both the winding constraint and the inspection constraint.

The set of points that simultaneously satisfies both constraints in Figure A-2 has been shaded. This area is called the *feasible region*. Note that only points within the feasible region satisfy both constraints. Points such as point Q or point R in Figure A-2 will only satisfy one of the constraints and are therefore not feasible (i.e., *infeasible*). Clearly, if an optimal solution exists to our linear programming problem, we shall find it in this feasible region.

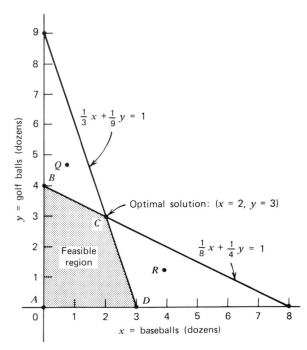

FIGURE A-2 The feasible region and optimal solution for the Alan Company's production problem.

Step 5: Determine an Optimal Solution

The feasible region area contains an infinite number of points. But, if an optimal solution to a linear programming problem exists, we know that it will lie in this area. How can we narrow down the possibilities?

The answer to our question lies in the fact that optimal solutions to linear programming problems always are found at the corners of the boundaries of the feasible region. Referring to Figure A-2, we note that there are four such *corner points* for the problem at hand. They have been labeled point A ($x = 0$, $y = 0$), point B($x = 0, y = 4$), point C($x = 2, y = 3$), and point D($x = 3, y = 0$). The coordinates of point C were determined by solving the two simultaneous equations

$$\frac{1}{3}x + \frac{1}{9}y \quad \text{and} \quad \frac{1}{8}x + \frac{1}{4}y = 1$$

(i.e., the constraint equations expressed as equalities). These four corner points are also called *extreme points*. By theorem, if an optimal solution exists to a linear programming problem, at least one corner point or extreme point will be optimum.

Since we have only four corner points for this linear programming problem, it is a simple matter to test all four points to find the optimum. The analysis is shown in the following table.

Point	$x =$	$y =$	Objective Function Value: $\$3.60x + \$3.70y =$
A	0	0	$ 0.00
B	0	4	14.80
C	2	3	18.30 ←
D	3	0	10.80

We are trying to maximize the value of the objective function. Therefore, we choose as the optimal solution point $C(x = 2, y = 3)$ because this point maximizes the contribution margin of the objective function at $18.30 per hour. The values of $x = 2$ and $y = 3$ mean that the Alan Company should produce two dozen baseballs per hour and three dozen golf balls per hour. In so doing, the company will maximize its contribution margin on these two products and thus make optimal use of its winding-machine time and its inspection time.

This completes our analysis of the Alan Company's production problem. In reviewing the results, four items should be stressed. The first item is that, for this particular linear programming problem, the optimal solution occurred at point C, which happened to be the corner point or extreme point farthest from the origin. This was coincidence. In other linear programming problems, an alternative point, such as point B, point D, or even point A, may be optimal. You cannot tell from the geometry of the problem which corner point will be optimum. Rather, you must test each point in the linear programming problem's objective function to determine the optimum corner point.

The second item involves the fact that our solution came out to nice whole numbers: $x = 2$ and $y = 3$. This does not always happen. Solutions to linear programming problems often come out in decimals or fractions of units. Thus, a linear programming problem's optimal solution is not wrong if it results in partial units. However, when this happens, the question arises: Can you round? The answer depends on the particular linear programming problem under study. Sometimes, rounding will be all right. At other times, especially when rounding up, the results will turn out to violate the constraints or result in suboptimal solutions. Linear programming problems that are required to yield solutions in whole numbers are called *integer programming problems*. This subject is studied at length in advanced operations research courses but is beyond the scope of our analysis here.

The third item involves the fact that our present solution requires the Alan Company to split winding-machine time and inspection time between two products each hour. In real-life situations, of course, it would be unlikely that the Alan Company would divide each hour of its winding-machine time into time spent winding baseballs and time spent winding golf balls. Such a policy would be disruptive and therefore inefficient. However, our optimal solution to the linear programming problem formulated here is still valid because it tells us the *relative* number of baseballs and golf balls to make on the winding machine as well as to inspect at the company's inspection station. As long as the Alan Company makes baseballs and golf balls in the ratio 2:3 (i.e., two dozen baseballs for every three dozen golf balls), the company will still use its resources in the most efficient manner. How this production is ultimately performed is immaterial.

Our last item concerns the resource constraints. In the preceding formulation, it was implicitly assumed that winding-machine time and inspection time were valuable but not severely limited in amount. This assumption enabled us to consider a typical hour of production time as the basic unit of measurement for our productive

resources. If the *total* amount of winding-machine time and the *total* amount of inspection time had been limited, however, an alternative linear programming formulation would have been necessary to express these facts. In this latter situation, the winding-machine constraint would have stated that the amount of time used on the winding machine must be less than or equal to the total winding-machine time available, not 1 hour. A similar formulation would have been made for the inspection constraint. We did not assume limits on the total amount of winding-machine time or inspection time available, and thus proceeded with the type of analysis performed in this problem example.

EXAMPLE 2: PERT WITH STATISTICAL PROBABILITIES

Problem Situation

John Beltcher, management consultant, is preparing to begin the implementation phase of a systems study that his consulting firm is performing for the Big Red Company. There are six activities (A through F) that must be performed to carry out the necessary revisions in Big Red Company's system. Regarding these six implementation activities, John has estimated three possible completion times (i.e., a pessimistic time estimate, a most-likely time estimate, and an optimistic time estimate) for implementing each activity. Figure A-3 shows John's implementation time estimates as well as any predecessor activities for each of the six activities.

Problem Requirements

The Big Red Company's top management is concerned about how many weeks it will take John Beltcher's consulting firm to implement the systems revisions. Also, Big Red's management is worried about the cost to the company of having

Activity	A	B	C	D	E	F
Pessimistic time estimate	24	19	8	30	15	17
Most-likely time estimate	12	10	5	12	9	14
Optimistic time estimate	6	7	2	12	3	11
Predecessor activities	None	None	A	B	C,D	E

FIGURE A-3 Pessimistic, most likely, and optimistic estimates of completion times for six activities of a systems implementation (all numbers in weeks).

its various asset resources working on the systems implementation and therefore not working on regular company operating functions. The top management executives of Big Red Company have approached John Beltcher with two questions: (1) Assuming that Big Red Company's management would like the systems revisions to be implemented within the next 52 weeks, what is the probability of completing the systems implementation activities in 52 weeks or less? (2) Assuming that the estimated cost to the Big Red Company of having its asset resources working on the systems implementation is $1500 per week, and further assuming that the company's top management does not want the total cost of asset resources employed in the systems work to exceed $69,000, what is the probabilty that the total asset resources cost associated with the systems implementation activities will be $69,000 or less?

Problem Solution

Since three time estimates are given for implementing each of the six activities (see Figure A-3), the first step is to compute a weighted average for each activity. The following formula is commonly used to determine the expected time required to implement activities when three different time estimates are given for each activity: Activity completion time = $(a + 4m + b)/6$, where a is the optimistic time estimate, b is the pessimistic time estimate, and m is the most-likely time estimate. The most-likely time estimate is closer to what the actual implementation time is estimated to be; therefore, it is given a weight of 4 in the formula, whereas the optimistic and pessimistic time estimates are each given a weight of 1 (the coefficients of a and b in the formula are 1). Using the preceding formula, the weighted average for the completion time of each activity would be:

Activity	A	B	C	D	E	F
Expected completion time (in weeks)	13	11	5	15	9	14

For example, to compute the weighted average for activity A, we have

$$\frac{[a + 4m + b]}{6} = \frac{[6 + 4(12) + 24]}{6} = \frac{78}{6} = 13$$

To confirm these values, compute the expected completion times for each of the remaining activities B through F to see if your answers agree with the foregoing values.

Once the expected completion time for each activity has been determined, a PERT network with these figures can be drawn in a diagram. Such a network diagram for the present example is illustrated in Figure A-4. Note that the "predecessor activities," as set forth in Figure A-3, must also be used to determine the sequence of activities in the diagram. Following PERT convention, the lines or "arcs" drawn in Figure A-4 represent activities, and the circles or "nodes" of Figure A-4 represent events—that is, the completion of one activity or the commencement of a new activity.

To estimate the completion time of the entire project, it is necessary to examine the various paths through the network. The shortest completion time of the entire project is determined

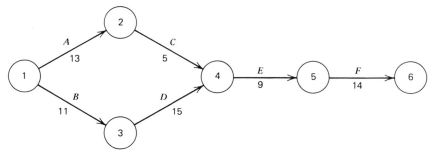

FIGURE A-4 A PERT network diagram.

by the longest path through the network. This longest path is termed the *critical path* because delays in the completion of those activities on the *critical path* will delay the completion time of the project as a whole. For the problem at hand, an examination of the PERT network diagram reveals that the *critical path* is B−D−E−F, a total of 49 weeks (= 11 + 15 + 9 + 14).

Because the activity time estimates on the PERT network diagram are weighted averages, there is a possibility that the actual time required to implement each activity will vary from the expected (i.e., average) implementation time. In statistics, the term *standard deviation* is used to measure relative dispersion (or amount of variation) from an arithmetic average (or mean). Thus, for each of the six implementation activities, a standard deviation can be computed using the formula

$$\text{Standard deviation of an activity} = \frac{(b - a)}{6}$$

where b is the pessimistic time estimate and a is the optimistic time estimate. Employing this formula, the standard deviations for activities A through F would be:

Activity	A	B	C	D	E	F
Standard deviation	3	2	1	3	2	1

Because the estimated project completion time (the critical path of 49 weeks) was com-

puted with the use of weighted-average times, there is a possibility that the actual project completion time will vary from the expected completion time. Consequently, it is now necessary to determine the standard deviation of the total project completion time from the 49-week weighted-average project completion time. This can be done using the following formula.

Standard deviation of project =

$$\sqrt{\begin{array}{l}\text{Summation of the squares}\\\text{of all critical path}\\\text{activities' standard}\\\text{deviations}\end{array}}$$

The standard deviation of the completion time of the Big Red Company's systems implementation project would thus be

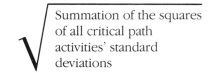

$$\sqrt{2^2 + 3^2 + 2^2 + 1^2} = \sqrt{18} = 4.24$$

activity activity activity activity
  B   D   E   F

To answer the first question asked by Big Red Company's top management concerning the probability of completing the systems implementation activities in 52 weeks or less, we must compute the number of standard deviations of our *given time* (52 weeks) from our *expected time* (49 weeks—the critical-path time estimate), and then associate the result with a probability value. In statistics, the term *z-score* is used to reflect the number of standard deviations of a given time from an expected time and is determined from the following formula.

$$z = \frac{(\text{given time} - \text{expected time})}{\text{standard deviation of project}}$$

The z-score for Big Red Company's systems implementation project would thus be computed as follows.

$$z = \frac{(52 \text{ weeks} - 49 \text{ weeks})}{4.24 \text{ (computed above)}} = .7$$

The .7 z-score must now be converted to a probability. This is accomplished by using a statistical table that reflects areas under a normal bell-shaped curve. A table of probabilities associated with z-score values under the normal curve is shown in Figure A-5.

From Figure A-5, it can be seen that a z-score of .7 gives a probability factor of .75804. Thus, John Beltcher's consulting firm is now able to tell Big Red Company's top management that there is a 76% probability (rounded off) that the systems implementation project will be finished in 52 weeks or less.

To answer the second question asked by Big Red Company's top management regarding the probability that the total asset resources cost associated with the systems implementation activities will be $69,000 or less, we must first compute the number of weeks of systems implementation work that will result in an asset resources cost of $69,000. Since *problem requirement 2* assumes a per-week cost of $1500, the total number of systems implementation weeks required to incur a $69,000 asset resources cost is therefore 46 ($69,000 *divided by* $1500). In our formula for computing a z-score, the 46 becomes the *given time* and the z-score is computed as

$$z = \frac{(46 \text{ weeks} - 49 \text{ weeks})}{4.24} = -.7$$

Looking up the value of $-.7$ in Figure A-5, we obtain a probability factor of .24196. Thus, John Beltcher's consulting firm is now able to tell Big Red Company's top management that there is a 24% probability (rounded off) that the total asset resources cost associated with the systems implementation project will be $69,000 or less.

z [a]	P [b]	z [a]	P [b]	z [a]	P [b]	z [a]	P [b]
-3.0	.00135	-1.4	.08076	0.2	.57926	1.8	.96407
-2.9	.00187	-1.3	.09680	0.3	.61791	1.9	.97128
-2.8	.00256	-1.2	.11507	0.4	.65542	2.0	.97725
-2.7	.00347	-1.1	.13567	0.5	.69146	2.1	.98214
-2.6	.00466	-1.0	.15866	0.6	.72575	2.2	.98610
-2.5	.00621	-0.9	.18406	0.7	.75804	2.3	.98928
-2.4	.00820	-0.8	.21186	0.8	.78814	2.4	.99180
-2.3	.01072	-0.7	.24196	0.9	.81594	2.5	.99379
-2.2	.01390	-0.6	.27425	1.0	.84134	2.6	.99534
-2.1	.01786	-0.5	.30854	1.1	.86433	2.7	.99653
-2.0	.02275	-0.4	.34458	1.2	.88493	2.8	.99744
-1.9	.02872	-0.3	.38209	1.3	.90320	2.9	.99813
-1.8	.03593	-0.2	.42074	1.4	.91924	3.0	.99865
-1.7	.04457	-0.1	.46017	1.5	.93319		
-1.6	.05480	0.0	.50000	1.6	.94520		
-1.5	.06681	0.1	.53983	1.7	.95543		

[a] z is the number of standard deviations from the mean.

[b] P is the probability that the actual value of the variable will be z or less.

FIGURE A-5 Areas under the normal curve.

B

Present Value Tables and Illustrations of Present Value Computational Analysis

PRESENT VALUE COMPUTATIONAL EXAMPLES

To illustrate the computation of present value, suppose you wanted to invest just enough money in the bank (which pays 6% annual interest) at the beginning of the year to enable you to withdraw $1 (after interest) at year's end. How much money must you therefore invest? To solve this problem, let X be the (unknown) investment amount and r be the annual interest rate (which is based on the compounding of interest). The following computation is made.

$$\text{Investment} + \text{interest} = \$X + \$X(r)$$
$$= \$X(1 + r)$$

$$\$1 = \$X(1 + .06)$$
$$\$1 = \$X(1.06), \text{ or}$$

$$\$X = \frac{\$1}{(1.06)} = \underline{\$.943}$$

Thus, you should invest roughly 94 cents in the bank at the beginning of the year to permit you to withdraw $1 at the end of the year. The present value of $1 received 1 year hence (using a 6% interest rate) is therefore $.943.

A similar analysis can be made if you wanted to find the investment amount that would enable you to withdraw $1 two years hence. Again, let X be the unknown investment amount and r the annual interest rate (which is still assumed to be 6%). You already know that the total amount of the investment plus interest at the end of one year would be $\$X(1 + r)$. The total amount of investment plus interest at the end of the second year would therefore be this amount again multiplied by $(1 + r)$, or $\$X(1 + r)^2$. Thus, to solve for the investment amount required at the beginning of the first year, you have

$$\$1 = \$X(1 + r)^2$$
$$\$1 = \$X(1.06)^2, \text{ or}$$

$$\$X = \frac{\$1}{(1.06)^2} = \underline{\$.890}$$

Therefore, if you were to invest 89 cents in the bank (which pays 6% annual interest) at the beginning of year 1, then by the end of the second year, you would have accumulated sufficient interest on this investment to enable you to withdraw a total of $1. The present value of $1 received two years hence (using a 6% interest rate) is thus $.89.

From the previous two examples, it should be clear that the computation of a present value is dependent on (1) the rate of interest r and (2) the number of years between making the investment and ultimate repayment. For a one-year investment, the present value of $1 was computed from the term $\$1/(1 + r)^1$, and for a two-year investment, the present value of $1 was computed from the term $\$1/(1 + r)^2$. Similarly, the present value of $1 in a three-year investment would be computed from the term $\$1/(1 + r)^3$, in a four-year investment, from the term $\$1/(1 + r)^4$, and in an n-year investment, from the term $\$1/(1 + r)^n$.

Years	5%	6%	8%	10%	12%	14%	15%	16%	18%	20%	22%	24%	25%
1	0.952	0.943	0.926	0.909	0.893	0.877	0.870	0.862	0.847	0.833	0.820	0.806	0.800
2	0.907	0.890	0.857	0.826	0.797	0.769	0.756	0.743	0.718	0.694	0.672	0.650	0.640
3	0.864	0.840	0.794	0.751	0.712	0.675	0.658	0.641	0.609	0.579	0.551	0.524	0.512
4	0.823	0.792	0.735	0.683	0.636	0.592	0.572	0.552	0.516	0.482	0.451	0.423	0.410
5	0.784	0.747	0.681	0.621	0.567	0.519	0.497	0.476	0.437	0.402	0.370	0.341	0.328
6	0.746	0.705	0.630	0.564	0.507	0.456	0.432	0.410	0.370	0.335	0.303	0.275	0.262
7	0.711	0.665	0.583	0.513	0.452	0.400	0.376	0.354	0.314	0.279	0.249	0.222	0.210
8	0.677	0.627	0.540	0.467	0.404	0.351	0.327	0.305	0.266	0.233	0.204	0.179	0.168
9	0.645	0.592	0.500	0.424	0.361	0.308	0.284	0.263	0.225	0.194	0.167	0.144	0.134
10	0.614	0.558	0.463	0.386	0.322	0.270	0.247	0.227	0.191	0.162	0.137	0.116	0.107
11	0.585	0.527	0.429	0.350	0.287	0.237	0.215	0.195	0.162	0.135	0.112	0.094	0.086
12	0.557	0.497	0.397	0.319	0.257	0.208	0.187	0.168	0.137	0.112	0.092	0.076	0.069
13	0.530	0.469	0.368	0.290	0.229	0.182	0.163	0.145	0.116	0.093	0.075	0.061	0.055
14	0.505	0.442	0.340	0.263	0.205	0.160	0.141	0.125	0.099	0.078	0.062	0.049	0.044
15	0.481	0.417	0.315	0.239	0.183	0.140	0.123	0.108	0.084	0.065	0.051	0.040	0.035
16	0.458	0.394	0.292	0.218	0.163	0.123	0.107	0.093	0.071	0.054	0.042	0.032	0.028
17	0.436	0.371	0.270	0.198	0.146	0.108	0.093	0.080	0.060	0.045	0.034	0.026	0.023
18	0.416	0.350	0.250	0.180	0.130	0.095	0.081	0.069	0.051	0.038	0.028	0.021	0.018
19	0.396	0.331	0.232	0.164	0.116	0.083	0.070	0.060	0.043	0.031	0.023	0.017	0.014
20	0.377	0.312	0.215	0.149	0.104	0.073	0.061	0.051	0.037	0.026	0.019	0.014	0.012

FIGURE B-1   The present value of $1.

These values are easily computed, but because it is inefficient to recompute them every time you wish to solve a new problem, a convenient table of such values, called *discount factors,* may be found in Figure B-1 of this appendix for various interest rates and various years of investment. Note that we have already derived two entries in the figure's table—the first two numbers under the 6% column: .943 and .890. Note also that the numbers under each column *diminish* as you go down the column. This reflects the fact that the longer you must wait for the repayment of an investment at any interest rate, the less that investment return (of $1) is worth to you today.

A slightly different problem often found in investment analysis is the computation of the present value of a uniform series of payments (called an *annuity*) spread out over a number of years. For example, suppose you wished to invest enough money in the bank (paying 6% annual interest) to enable you to withdraw $1 at the end of the first year and a second dollar at the end of the second year. How much money would you have to invest in the bank at the beginning of the first year?

Actually, this problem has already been almost solved by you. You know that at 6% annual interest, the present value of $1 paid a year hence is $.943 and the present value of $1 paid two years hence is $.890. Therefore, the present value of this uniform series of dollar payments received at the end of two consecutive years must be the sum of these, or $1.833 ($.943 + $.890). You would thus have to invest approximately $1.83 in the bank at the beginning of the first year. Similarly, if you wanted to compute the present value of a uniform series of dollar payments over three consecutive years at 6% annual compound inter-

Years (N)	5%	6%	8%	10%	12%	14%	15%	16%	18%	20%	22%	24%	25%
1	0.952	0.943	0.926	0.909	0.893	0.877	0.870	0.862	0.847	0.833	0.820	0.806	0.800
2	1.859	1.833	1.783	1.736	1.690	1.647	1.626	1.605	1.566	1.528	1.492	1.457	1.440
3	2.723	2.673	2.577	2.487	2.402	2.322	2.283	2.246	2.174	2.106	2.042	1.981	1.952
4	3.546	3.465	3.312	3.169	3.037	2.914	2.855	2.798	2.690	2.589	2.494	2.404	2.362
5	4.330	4.212	3.993	3.791	3.605	3.433	3.352	3.274	3.127	2.991	2.864	2.745	2.689
6	5.076	4.917	4.623	4.355	4.111	3.889	3.784	3.685	3.498	3.326	3.167	3.020	2.951
7	5.786	5.582	5.206	4.868	4.564	4.288	4.160	4.039	3.812	3.605	3.416	3.242	3.161
8	6.463	6.210	5.747	5.335	4.968	4.639	4.487	4.344	4.078	3.837	3.619	3.421	3.329
9	7.108	6.802	6.247	5.759	5.328	4.946	4.772	4.607	4.303	4.031	3.786	3.566	3.463
10	7.722	7.360	6.710	6.145	5.650	5.216	5.019	4.833	4.494	4.192	3.923	3.682	3.571
11	8.306	7.887	7.139	6.495	5.937	5.453	5.234	5.029	4.656	4.327	4.035	3.776	3.656
12	8.863	8.384	7.536	6.814	6.194	5.660	5.421	5.197	4.793	4.439	4.127	3.851	3.725
13	9.394	8.853	7.904	7.103	6.424	5.842	5.583	5.342	4.910	4.533	4.203	3.912	3.780
14	9.899	9.295	8.244	7.367	6.628	6.002	5.724	5.468	5.008	4.611	4.265	3.962	3.824
15	10.380	9.712	8.559	7.606	6.811	6.142	5.847	5.575	5.092	4.675	4.315	4.001	3.859
16	10.838	10.106	8.851	7.824	6.974	6.265	5.954	5.669	5.162	4.730	4.357	4.033	3.887
17	11.274	10.477	9.122	8.022	7.120	6.373	6.047	5.749	5.222	4.775	4.391	4.059	3.910
18	11.690	10.828	9.372	8.201	7.250	6.467	6.128	5.818	5.273	4.812	4.419	4.080	3.928
19	12.085	11.158	9.604	8.365	7.366	6.550	6.198	5.877	5.316	4.844	4.442	4.097	3.942
20	12.462	11.470	9.818	8.514	7.469	6.623	6.259	5.929	5.353	4.870	4.460	4.110	3.954

FIGURE B-2   The present value of $1 received annually for N years.

est, you would add the discount factors from Figure B-1 for years 1, 2, and 3, obtaining a present value of $2.673 ($.943 + $.890 + $.840).

Because the computation of the present value of a uniform series of annual dollar payments is as mechanical as the computation of a single payment, it is convenient to create another table similar to Figure B-1. This is accomplished in Figure B-2. Thus, for example, at 6% annual interest, the first present value number in the table of Figure B-2 is the same $.943 as in Figure B-1, but the present value for two years is our previously computed $1.833 and the present value for three years is our previously computed $2.673. At different annual interest rates, other present values

of uniform $1 payments are easily found in similar fashion.

Although these present value tables are based on $1 payments, it is quite easy to use the $1 discount factors when dealing with problems involving payments of any dollar magnitude. Once you know the $1 discount factor, it is a simple matter of multiplying this discount factor by the specific dollar magnitude involved. For example, if the bank pays 8% annual interest and you wanted to withdraw $1000 at the end of one year, you would have to invest $926 ($.926 from Figure B-1 × $1000) in the bank at the beginning of the year.

C

Matrix Accounting Information Systems*

A small business could save time and effort in recording and classifying its financial transactions by using a *matrix accounting system* to replace the conventional journals and ledgers. An example of a small company's matrix accounting system is presented here.

Assume that the Mike Por Company is a small proprietorship organization that sells office supplies. Its December 31, 1990 post-closing trial balance is shown in Figure C-1. (Small numbers have been used intentionally in this example to simplify the presentation.)

The Por Company uses a perpetual inventory system. Its January transactions are:

1. Sold merchandise on account at a $350 retail price. Cost of this merchandise to the Por Company, $140.
2. Paid the January store rent, $75.
3. Paid the January salary to part-time employee, $100.
4. Received $50 in payment of an accounts receivable.
5. Paid $200 of the accounts payable liabilities.

Based on the December 31, 1990 post-closing trial balance and the above transactions, the matrix in Figure C-2 is prepared. (Explanations will follow.)

The matrix columns are for recording debits, and the rows are for recording credits. Since a debit or credit may occur in each account, all of the accounts are listed in both columns and rows. The same debit and credit rules for increasing and decreasing accounts are used with a matrix

Cash	$ 500	
Accounts receivable	400	
Merchandise inventory	2800	
Accounts payable		$1400
Mike Por, capital		2300
	$3700	$3700

FIGURE C-1 Mike Por Company post-closing trial balance, December 31, 1990.

accounting system: (1) asset and expense account increases are recorded in columns (debits) and decreases in rows (credits), and (2) liability, owner's equity, and revenue account increases are recorded in rows (credits) and decreases in columns (debits).

Each rectangular box within the matrix is called a *cell*. For discussion purposes, these cells are numbered. Based on the Por Company's post-closing trial balance (see Figure C-1), the January 1 account balances are entered in their proper cells. Since the asset accounts have debit balances, the cash, accounts receivable, and merchandise inventory balances are recorded in column cells 1, 2, and 3, respectively. The liability and owner's equity accounts reflect credit balances and are therefore recorded in row cells 48 and 60, respectively.

* This discussion is taken from Stephen A. Moscove, *Accounting Fundamentals for Non-Accountants* (Reston, Va.: Reston Publishing Company, 1984).

Rows for Credits / **Columns for Debits**

FIGURE C-2 January matrix for the Mike Por Company.

	January 1, 1991 Account Balances	Cash	Accounts receivable	Merchandise inventory	Accounts payable	Mike Por, capital	Sales	Cost of merchandise sold	Salaries expense	Rent expense	Row Totals	January 31, 1991 Account Balances
		Assets (Increases)			**Liabilities (Decreases)**	**Owner's Equity (Decreases)**	**Revenues (Decreases) and Expenses (Increases)**					
January 1, 1991 Account Balances →		(1) 500	(2) 400	(3) 2800	(4)	(5)	(6)	(7)	(8)	(9)	(10)	(11)
Assets (Decreases) — Cash	(12)	(13)	(14)	(15)	(16) (5)200	(17)	(18)	(19)	(20) (3)100	(21) (2)75	(22) 375	(23) —
Accounts receivable	(24)	(25) (4)50	(26)	(27)	(28)	(29)	(30)	(31)	(32)	(33)	(34) 50	(35) —
Merchandise inventory	(36)	(37)	(38)	(39)	(40)	(41)	(42)	(43) (1)140	(44)	(45)	(46) 140	(47) —
Liabilities (Increases) — Accounts payable	(48) 1400	(49)	(50)	(51)	(52)	(53)	(54)	(55)	(56)	(57)	(58) 1400	(59) 1200
Owner's Equity (Increases) — Mike Por, capital	(60) 2300	(61)	(62)	(63)	(64)	(65)	(66)	(67)	(68)	(69)	(70) 2300	(71) 2300
Revenues (Increases) and Expenses (Decreases) — Sales	(72)	(73)	(74) (1)350	(75)	(76)	(77)	(78)	(79)	(80)	(81)	(82) 350	(83) 350
Cost of merchandise sold	(84)	(85)	(86)	(87)	(88)	(89)	(90)	(91)	(92)	(93)	(94) —	(95) —
Salaries expense	(96)	(97)	(98)	(99)	(100)	(101)	(102)	(103)	(104)	(105)	(106) —	(107) —
Rent expense	(108)	(109)	(110)	(111)	(112)	(113)	(114)	(115)	(116)	(117)	(118) —	(119) —
Column Totals	(120)	(121) 550	(122) 750	(123) 2800	(124) 200	(125) —	(126) —	(127) 140	(128) 100	(129) 75	(130) 4615	(131) —
January 31, 1991 Account Balances	(132)	(133) 175	(134) 700	(135) 2660	(136) —	(137) —	(138) —	(139) 140	(140) 100	(141) 75	(142) —	(143) 3850

FIGURE C-2 January matrix for the Mike Por Company.

Transaction 1

In journal form, this transaction would have been recorded as

Accounts receivable	350	
Sales		350
Cost of merchandise sold	140	
Merchandise inventory		140

Cell number 74 reflects the first entry. This cell is in the accounts receivable debit column and sales credit row. Since the Por Company uses a perpetual inventory system, the second entry is also required. It is recorded in matrix cell number 43 (the cost of merchandise sold debit column and merchandise inventory credit row).

Transaction 2

In journal form, this transaction would have been recorded as

Rent expense	75	
Cash		75

Cell number 21 represents this entry (the rent expense debit column and cash credit row).

Transaction 3

In journal form, this transaction would have been recorded as

Salaries expense	100	
Cash		100

This salary payment is recorded in cell number 20 (the salaries expense debit column and cash credit row).

Transaction 4

In journal form, this transaction would have been recorded as

Cash	50	
Accounts receivable		50

Matrix cell 25 reflects this entry (the cash debit column and accounts receivable credit row).

Transaction 5

In journal form, this transaction would have been recorded as

Accounts payable	200	
Cash		200

This liability payment is recorded in cell number 16 (the accounts payable debit column and cash credit row).

FIGURE C-3 January transactions of the Mike Por Company.

After these account balances have been recognized, the January transactions are then recorded in the matrix cells. Each transaction is illustrated in Figure C-3. (If adjusting entries are required at the end of an accounting period, they are recorded within the proper matrix cells in the same manner as the journal entries described in Figure C-3.)

When a conventional accounting system with journals and ledgers is used, the recorded journal entries are posted to general ledger accounts in order that each account balance can be determined. A matrix accounting system does not require all this work. Rather, an account balance is computed by adding the "column" and "row" monetary items for the account and then sub-tracting the smaller total from the larger one to determine its balance (see Figure C-2). For example, the cash column total is $550 (cell number 121) and its row total is $375 (cell number 22). The cash account therefore has a January 31 debit balance of $175 ($550 − $375). This is shown in cell number 133. The same process is followed to determine each account balance. Since matrix columns reflect debits, the monetary balances of the asset and expense accounts (having debit balances) appear in columns. The matrix rows represent credits. Thus, the dollar balances of the liability, owner's equity, and revenue accounts (having credit balances) are reported in rows. For example, the $1200 accounts payable liability balance is shown in matrix cell number 59 [$1400

MIKE POR COMPANY
Income Statement
For the Month Ended January 31, 1991

Revenues		
Retail price of merchandise sold		$350 (cell 83)
Less: *Operating Expenses*		
Cost of merchandise sold	$140 (cell 139)	
Salaries expense	100 (cell 140)	
Rent expense	75 (cell 141)	
Total operating expenses		315
Net income		$ 35

FIGURE C-4   Mike Por Company income statement.

row total (cell number 58) *less* $200 column total (cell number 124)].

The $4615 in cell number 130 is a "check figure" showing that the total of the column items (the debits) equals the total of the row items (the credits). Before preparing financial statements, a company should determine that its accounts with debit balances equal the accounts with credit balances. To accomplish this, a "trial balance" is prepared. Under the matrix accounting system, a separate trial balance is unnecessary since the equality of debit and credit account balances can

be ascertained directly from the matrix. Cell number 143 on the Por Company's matrix reflects its trial balance results. The January 31 *debit* account balances from the "column" financial items (asset and expense accounts) are added. Their total is $3850. Then the January 31 *credit* account balances from the "row" financial items (liability, owner's equity, and revenue accounts) are added. Since this total is also $3850, the Por Company's trial balance is finished.

The financial statements can now be prepared. Based on the account balances disclosed in the

MIKE POR COMPANY
Balance Sheet
January 31, 1991

ASSETS		LIABILITIES & OWNER'S EQUITY		
Current assets		Current liabilities		
Cash	$ 175 (cell 133)	Accounts payable		$1200 (cell 59)
Accounts		Owner's equity		
receivable	700 (cell 134)	Mike Por,		
Merchandise		capital, Jan. 1	$2300 (cell 71)	
inventory	2660 (cell 135)	*Plus:* Net In-		
		come for Jan.	35	
		Mike Por,		
		capital, Jan. 31		2335
		Total liabilities and		
Total assets	$3535	owner's equity		$3535

FIGURE C-5   Mike Por Company balance sheet.

Por Company's January matrix, its month-end income statement and balance sheet are prepared in Figures C-4 and C-5. The matrix cell number of each financial item is shown in parentheses.

The Por Company's February accounting transactions are recorded on a new matrix in the same manner as the January transactions. The January 31 asset and liability account balances are reported as the February 1 balances on this matrix. With a system of journals and ledgers, the revenue and expense account balances would have been closed into the owner's equity account at the end of January. Since journal entries are not utilized under a matrix system, the Por Company's January net income is added to the Mike Por capital account. The resulting $2335 (see the owner's equity section of Figure C-5) is then reflected as the February 1 balance of the Mike Por capital account on the February matrix. Each revenue and expense account would have a zero balance to begin this new accounting period.

A matrix system is practical only for those organizations having a low volume of financial transactions. This system eliminates the need for journals and ledgers and may therefore be useful to small businesses. It should be noted that electronic spreadsheets (discussed in Chapter 3) could be used quite effectively for companies' matrix accounting information systems.

Index